colon (*say* <u>koh</u>-luhn)

noun a punctuation mark (:)
used to separate the main part of a
sentence from an explanation, or a list
of examples, as in *I want you to bring the
following things: a pencil, a rubber, and a
piece of paper.*

notes on punctuation

You use a **colon** to show that you are going to
explain, or give examples of, whatever you have
just written. For instance:
> *The kennels cared for a number of breeds of
> dog: terriers, spaniels, corgis, labradors
> and German shepherds.*

In informal writing, a dash could have been
used in the above example instead of a colon.
Look up **dash**.

Colons can be used before quoting someone's
speech:
> *The teacher said: 'Sit down in that
> chair!'*

Instead of a colon, you can use a comma here,
or you can leave out the punctuation altogether.
Look up **quotation mark**.

computer geek

noun a person who spends too much time
with computers

definition of
the headword

cooee (*say* <u>koo</u>-ee)

noun a long, loud call used to signal someone,
especially when you are in the bush

Word history: from an Aboriginal language of
New South Wales called Dharug. See the map
of Australian Aboriginal languages at the end
of this book.

Word history —
where the word
comes from

core

noun the inner or middle part, especially
of fruit

Word building: **core** *verb* to remove the core

core/corps Don't confuse **core** with **corps**. A
corps is a unit of soldiers.

explanation of
words often
confused

corgi (*say* <u>kaw</u>-gee)

noun a dog with short legs and a thick body

Word building: The plural is **corgis**.

MACQUARIE
PRIMARY
DICTIONARY

MACQUARIE
PRIMARY
DICTIONARY
AUSTRALIA'S NATIONAL DICTIONARY

General Editor
Alison Moore

www.jaconline.com.au

First published 2010 by
John Wiley & Sons Australia, Ltd
42 McDougall Street, Milton, Qld 4064

Typeset in 9/10 pt Monotype News Plantin

© Macquarie Dictionary Publishers Pty Ltd

National Library of Australia
Cataloguing-in-publication data

Title:	Macquarie primary dictionary / Susan Butler, executive editor; Alison Moore, general editor.
ISBN:	978 1 74246 072 7 (pbk.)
Target Audience:	Upper primary school students.
Subjects:	English language — Dictionaries, Juvenile. English language — Australia — Dictionaries, Juvenile.
Other Authors/ Contributors:	Butler, Susan. Moore, Alison
Dewey Number:	423

Editorial staff

General editor	Alison Moore		
Editorial staff	Ann Atkinson	Kris Burnet	Laura Davies
	Maree Frakes	Lyn Jones	Margaret McPhee
	Victoria Morgan	Susanne Read	
Computer systems	Andrew Doyle		
Editor, Macquarie Dictionary	Susan Butler		

Cover adapted from a design by Natalie Bowra

Cover images: © Andrew Chin (kookaburra), © Robyn Mackenzie (gum leaves). Both 2010, used
under licence from Shutterstock

Internal design: © pakowacz (keyboard), 2010 used under licence from Shutterstock.com

Illustrated by Glenn Lumsden, Stephen Francis and the Wiley Art Studio

MACQUARIE
DICTIONARY
AT

THE UNIVERSITY OF
SYDNEY

Typeset in India by Aptara

Printed in China by
Shenzhen Donnelley Printing Co., Ltd.

10 9 8 7 6 5 4 3 2

John Wiley & Sons Australia, Ltd, places great
value on the environment and is actively involved
in efforts to preserve it. The paper used in the
production of this dictionary was supplied by mills
that source their raw materials from sustainably
managed forests.

Contents

How to use the dictionary

The *Macquarie Primary Dictionary* is easy to use. Information about a word is arranged so that the spelling and pronunciation come first, followed by the meaning of the word and other information about it. The next few pages explain a dictionary entry in detail. By reading this, you will be able to find your way around the *Macquarie Primary Dictionary* and make the most of all the valuable information it contains.

How to find the word

It is easy to find words in the *Macquarie Primary Dictionary*. The words are listed in alphabetical order. The word that you are looking up is called the **headword**. If you know the correct spelling of the headword, then you will find it quickly. Otherwise, you may have to find it by following the letters that you are sure about and then checking a few words until you find the word you want.

If you still can't find the word, then maybe it has a tricky spelling. The English language is famous for these difficult spellings. The word might begin with a letter that you don't sound when you say the word, or a letter that is said in a different way to normal. When this happens, you should look at the table called *Helpful hints for the spelling of tricky words* in the pages at the end of the dictionary.

Headwords that are spelt in the same way, but have different meanings because their history is different, are entered separately and have small numbers after them to show this difference, such as **bat**[1] and **bat**[2].

How to say the word

It is sometimes difficult to work out how to say a word. In these cases, a **pronunciation guide** is given in brackets after the headword. There are three different methods for doing this: using 'say ...', 'sounds like ...', or rhymes with ...'. For example:

> **rendezvous**   (*say* <u>ron</u>-day-vooh)
>
> **doubt**   (*rhymes with* out)
>
> **thyme**   (*sounds like* time)

In the pronunciation guide you will see that the word has been separated into parts. These parts are called syllables. If you are not sure how to say a word, saying it syllable by syllable (part by part) will help.

If a word has more than one syllable, the part that is said more loudly or with more force than the others is underlined. This syllable is called the stressed syllable. Here is an example showing how stress can change the meaning of a word:

produce (*say* pruh-<u>dyoohs</u>)
verb **1** to bring into being: *This soil produces good crops.* **2** to pull out and present: *The magician produced a rabbit from a hat.* **3** to assemble the cast for and generally organise and control: *to produce a play*
noun (*say* <u>proj</u>-oohs) **4** things that are grown: *Farmers take their produce to market.*
Word building: **producer** *noun* **production** *noun*

For more information on how to say a word, see the *Pronunciation key* on page xi.

The part of speech

After the headword or pronunciation guide is the **part-of-speech label**. This will be *verb* (for words that tell you what someone or something does or feels, like *give*); *noun* (for words that name something, like *kangaroo*); *adjective* (for words that describe nouns, like *happy*); *adverb* (for words that add meaning to verbs, adjectives, or other adverbs, like *quickly*); *preposition* (for words that are placed before nouns to show their relation to other words in the sentence, like *through*); *interjection* (for exclamations that might interrupt a conversation or speech, like *shush*); *pronoun* (for words that stand for other nouns, like *we*, *she* or *who*); *conjunction* (for words that join parts of a sentence, like *because*).

Sometimes phrases are listed under a headword (such as **answer back**, in the entry for **answer**), and these have the label *phrase*.

Entries for word parts that can be put in front of words to change their meaning, like *centi-*, have the label *prefix*.

The meaning of the word

After each part-of-speech label there is an explanation of what the word means. This is the **definition**.

Some words have more than one meaning. These meanings can be similar to each other or very different. When they are similar, each meaning is numbered and listed under the same headword. They are ranked according to the most commonly used meaning of the word.

The following example shows the definitions of *bill*. You can see that the most commonly used meaning of *bill* is 'a written statement telling you how much you owe for something' which is listed before other meanings such as 'a poster or advertisement on display', or 'a plan for a new law to be presented to Parliament'.

bill[1]
noun **1** a written statement telling you how much money you owe for something **2** a poster or advertisement on display **3** a plan for a new law to be presented to Parliament
Word building: **bill** *verb*

When the meanings of a word are different because their history is different, they are listed separately and each is marked with a small number. For example, there is another meaning of *bill* that is very different to the meanings shown above. Because these meanings are so different, they are listed separately in the dictionary.

bill[1]
noun **1** a written statement telling you how much money you owe for something **2** a poster or advertisement on display **3** a plan for a new law to be presented to Parliament

Word building: **bill** *verb*

bill[2]
noun a bird's beak

Many definitions also contain an **example phrase or sentence** that shows how the word is used in context. These appear immediately after the definition. When two examples are given, they are separated by a slanting line.

sombre   (*say* som-buh)
adjective gloomily dark or dull: *the sombre interior of the deserted castle | sombre clothes*

A **secondary headword** is a phrase containing the headword, but with a special meaning. It appears in **bold** letters, followed by a definition.

bat[1]
noun **1** the stick used to hit the ball in games like cricket and softball
phrase **2 off your own bat,** on your own, without help or advice

Word building: **bat** *verb* (**batted, batting**) **batter** *noun*

Sometimes a word or one of its meanings is not suited to formal situations. The label *Informal* is used to indicate this.

Extra information about the word

Some entries include a **Word use** section at the end that gives extra information about the word. This can be information on a word that means nearly the same, but is more usual; a word that means the opposite; an alternative spelling; a suitable comparison; or general information about how the word is usually used. Here are some examples:

altercation
Word use: The more usual word is **argument**.

amateur   (*say* am-uh-tuh)
Word use: The opposite of this is **professional**.

verandah

Word use: Another spelling is **veranda**.

matador

Word use: Compare this with **picador**.

utility

Word use: Definition 3 is also called a **ute** in informal language.

personal computer

Word use: The short form of this is **PC**.

Words related to the headword

At the end of some entries there is a **Word building** section that gives words that are related to the headword, as well as different verb forms, plurals, and different forms of adjectives and adverbs, when they are not formed in the usual way. Sometimes short definitions or example phrases are also included. Here are some examples:

reflect

Word building: **reflection** *noun*
reflective *adjective*   **reflector** *noun*

run

Word building: Other verb forms are **I ran, I have run, I am running**.

battery

Word building: The plural is **batteries**.

battle

Word building: **embattled** *adjective* caught in a battle   **battle** *verb*   **battler** *noun*

referee

Word building: **referee** *verb* (**refereed, refereeing**): *to referee a football game*

The origin of the word

The **Word history** section tells you where the word has come from. Many of the words in English come from other languages or sometimes from people's names.

alligator

Word history: from a Latin word meaning 'lizard'

gorgeous

Word history: from a French word meaning 'fashionable' or 'colourful'

kangaroo

Word history: from an Aboriginal language of Queensland called Guugu Yimidhirr. See the map of Australian Aboriginal languages at the end of this book.

braille

Word history: named after its inventor, Louis *Braille*, 1809 to 1852

Confusing words

It is easy to confuse words that sound the same. The *Macquarie Primary Dictionary* contains a special shaded section at the end of certain entries warning against possible mix-ups. This extra information serves as an aid to spelling and a help to understanding the differences of meaning between words that sound the same. For example:

buoy

buoy/boy Don't confuse **buoy** with **boy**, which is a male child.

Words that could be used instead of the headword

There is evidence that certain words are used more often than other words with similar meanings in students' writing. Other words could easily be used in their place in order to capture a more precise meaning, to vary and to extend your vocabulary, or at least to present options in your writing that you may not have thought about. Many definitions in the *Macquarie Primary Dictionary* are followed by suggestions of words you might want to use in your writing as an alternative to the headword. For example:

mad

adjective **1** insane or mentally unbalanced: *Do you think he is mad?*
Other words: **crazy, demented, deranged**
2 *Informal* angry: *I am mad because you teased me.*
Other words: **annoyed, cross, furious**
3 wild or excited: *I have a mad urge to travel.*
Other words: **crazy, impulsive**

Word building: **madden** *verb* to make mad or angry   **madly** *adverb*   **madness** *noun*

Pronunciation key

When a word is hard to say, a pronunciation guide is given in brackets after the headword. The following key will help you to understand the pronunciation guides.

Vowels

a sounds
a as in 'pat'
ah as in 'part'
ay as in 'bay'

e sounds
e as in 'pet'
ee as in 'feet'
air as in 'pair'

i sounds
i as in 'pit'
uy as in 'buy'
ear as in 'hear'

o sounds
o as in 'pot'
oh as in 'boat'
aw as in 'paw'
ow as in 'how'
oy as in 'boy'

u sounds
u as in 'but'
oo as in 'book'
ooh as in 'boot'

er sounds
er as in 'pert'
uh as in 'fatter'

Consonants

th as in '**th**in'
dh as in '**th**en'
sh as in '**sh**ow'
zh as in 'mea**s**ure'

ch as in '**ch**ase'
j as in '**j**ug'
g as in '**g**ame'
ng as in 'si**ng**'

Emphasis

Stress the part of the word which is underlined.

Look at the 'How to use the dictionary' section on page vi for more help.

Aa

a

indefinite article You use the indefinite article before nouns: **1** to mean one member of a class of things, but not a particular one: *Gina is a teenager.* | *She was holding a surfboard.* **2** to mean one of something: *He bought a kilogram of prawns.* | *They drove for a hundred kilometres.* **3** to mean each or every one of something: *We need to walk the dog twice a day.*

Word use: Another form is **an**, used when the following word begins with a vowel sound (usually words starting with *a*, *e*, *i*, *o* or *u*).

abacus (*say* <u>ab</u>-uh-kuhs)

noun a frame with rods through it which hold beads used for counting

Word building: The plural is **abaci**.

abalone (*say* ab-uh-<u>loh</u>-nee)

noun a type of shellfish that is good to eat

Word building: The plural is **abalone**.

abandon¹

verb **1** to leave and not mean to come back: *We had to abandon our car and walk the rest of the way.* **2** to give up: *Don't abandon hope.* | *If it keeps raining, then we'll have to abandon the softball match.*

Word building: **abandonment** *noun*

abandon²

noun freedom from worry or care: *When the war was over people danced with abandon.*

abattoir (*say* <u>ab</u>-uh-twah)

noun a building or place where animals are killed for food: *The abattoir has closed down.*

Word use: The plural form **abattoirs** is often used.

abbey

noun a building or group of buildings where monks or nuns live

Other words: **convent, monastery**

Word building: **abbess** *noun* a nun in charge of a convent **abbot** *noun* a monk in charge of a monastery

abbreviate

verb to make shorter by leaving out some letters: *We abbreviate 'Mister' to 'Mr'.*

Word building: **abbreviation** *noun*

abdicate

verb to give up a position, especially the throne: *King Edward VIII abdicated in 1936.*

Word building: **abdication** *noun*

abdomen (*say* <u>ab</u>-duh-muhn)

noun **1** the main part of the body that contains the stomach and other organs **2** the last section of the body of an insect or spider

Word building: **abdominal** *adjective*

abduct

verb to kidnap or carry away by force

Word building: **abduction** *noun* **abductor** *noun*

abhor (*say* uhb-<u>haw</u>)

verb to think of with disgust: *I abhor cruelty to animals.*

Word use: The more usual word is **hate**.
Word building: Other forms are **I abhorred, I have abhorred, I am abhorring.** | **abhorrent** *adjective* hateful **abhorrence** *noun* loathing **abhorrently** *adverb*

abide

verb **1** to put up with: *I can't abide rude people.* **2** *Old-fashioned* to stay: *Abide with me.*

phrase **3 abide by, a** to accept or act according to: *to abide by the rules* **b** to stand by: *to abide by a friend* **c** to await or accept the consequences of: *to abide by the decision*

Word use: For definition 1, the more usual word is **bear**.
Word building: Other verb forms are **I abode** or **abided, I have abode** or **abided, I am abiding**. | **abiding** *adjective*

ability

noun **1** the power to do or act: *The baby has the ability to crawl now.*
Other words: **capability, capacity**
2 skill: *She has great ability in music.*
Other words: **competence, proficiency, talent**

Word building: The plural is **abilities**.

ablaze

adjective **1** on fire **2** shining brightly: *The house was ablaze with lights.*

able

adjective **1** having enough power, skill, or time: *Are you able to come to the party?*
2 skilled: *an able pianist*

Word building: **ably** *adverb*

abnormal

adjective unusual: *The heat is abnormal for this time of the year.*

Word use: The opposite of this is **normal**.
Word building: **abnormality** *noun* (**abnormalities**) **abnormally** *adverb*

abode

noun **1** *Old-fashioned* the place where you live
verb **2** the past form of the verb **abide**

abolish

verb to put an end to: *to abolish slavery*
Word building: **abolition** *noun*

abominable

adjective hateful or disgusting: *Slavery was an abominable practice.*

Word building: **abominate** *verb* **abomination** *noun* **abominably** *adverb*

aboriginal

adjective **1** having to do with the earliest inhabitants of a country **2 Aboriginal**, having to do with Australian Aborigines

aborigine

(*say* ab-uh-<u>rij</u>-uh-nee)
noun a person belonging to the original group of people living in a country

Word history: from a Latin word meaning 'from the beginning'

Aborigine

(*say* ab-uh-<u>rij</u>-uh-nee)
noun a person descended from the people who have lived in Australia from earliest known times

Word use: Many people prefer to use the word **Aboriginal** for this.

abortion

noun the removal of a baby from its mother's womb before it has grown enough to live on its own

Word building: **abort** *verb* **abortionist** *noun*

abound

verb **1** to exist in great numbers: *Fish abound in this river.*
phrase **2 abound with**, to be filled with: *This river abounds with fish.*

Word building: **abounding** *adjective*

about

preposition **1** concerning or having to do with: *a book about pirates*
2 close to: *a person about your age*
3 in various directions around: *to wander about the place*
adverb **4** near: *about 100 kilometres* | *about half an hour* **5** nearly or almost: *I'm about ready.* **6** nearby: *He's somewhere about.*
phrase **7 about to,** going to do something very soon: *about to leave*

above

adverb **1** in or to a higher place: *the sky above*
preposition **2** higher than: *flying above the clouds* | *the class above mine*
phrase **3 above all**, most important of all

Word use: The opposite of this is **below**.

abrasion

noun a wound or sore that is caused by a scrape: *an abrasion on the knee*

abrasive

adjective used for rubbing or grinding: *an abrasive powder for kitchen cleaning*

Word building: **abrasive** *noun*

abreast

adverb **1** side by side: *They walked four abreast along the lane.* **2** keeping up with or not behind the latest developments: *I try to keep abreast of the latest fashions.* | *They are abreast with the latest developments in AIDS research.*

Word use: Definition 2 is followed by *of* or *with*.

abridged

adjective a shortened version of a story, with parts left out: *An abridged version of my story is being printed in the school magazine.*

Word building: **abridge** *verb* **abridgement** *noun*

abroad

adverb out of your own country: *to go abroad*

abrupt

adjective **1** sudden or without warning: *an abrupt end to a story* **2** (of a response, remark, and so on) rudely short: *She made an abrupt remark before storming out of the classroom.*
Other words: **brusque, curt, gruff, short, terse**

Word building: **abruptly** *adverb* **abruptness** *noun*
Word history: from a Latin word meaning 'broken off'

abscess *(say ab-ses)*

noun an infected swelling in part of the body: *I have an abscess under my tooth and it's killing me!*

abscissa *(say ab-sis-uh)*

noun the horizontal distance on a graph

abscond

verb to run away secretly: *The treasurer absconded with the funds.*

Word building: **absconder** *noun*

abseil *(rhymes with fail)*

verb to lower yourself down a cliff, using ropes

absent

adjective **1** away or not present: *Lei is absent from school today.* **2** missing or not found: *Giuseppe's usual smile was absent from his face.*

Word building: **absentee** *noun* someone who is away **absence** *noun* **absent** *verb* **absenteeism** *noun* **absently** *adverb*

absentee vote

noun the vote of somebody who is not in the area where they normally vote on the day elections are held

absent-minded

adjective forgetful or vague

Word building: **absent-mindedly** *adverb*

absolute

adjective complete or perfect: *I told the absolute truth.*

Word building: **absolutely** *adverb*

absorb

verb to soak up or drink in: *This sponge will absorb the spilt milk.* | *The student absorbed all the facts.*

Word building: **absorbing** *adjective* very interesting: *an absorbing book* **absorbent** *adjective* **absorption** *noun*

abstain

verb to keep yourself from doing something: *I wish people would abstain from smoking.*

Word use: Compare this with **refrain**.
Word building: **abstention** *noun* an act of abstaining **abstinence** *noun* the habit of abstaining **abstinent** *adjective*

abstract

adjective **1** having to do with ideas rather than things: *My composition was about horses, but Jill wrote an abstract one about love.* **2** hard to understand: *abstract arguments*

Word use: The opposite of this is **concrete**.
Word building: **abstraction** *noun* **abstractly** *adverb*

abstracted

adjective lost in thought: *My father has an abstracted look on his face.*
Other words: **preoccupied**

abstract noun

noun a word which refers to something that our five senses (touch, sight, hearing, smell, and taste) can't pick up: *'Fear', 'love', 'size', and 'beauty' are all abstract nouns.*

Word use: The opposite of this is **concrete noun**.

abstruse

adjective hard to understand: *abstruse answers*

Word building: **abstrusely** *adverb*
abstruseness *noun*
Word history: from a Latin word meaning 'concealed'

absurd

adjective **1** foolish or without common sense: *an absurd question*
Other words: **bizarre, ludicrous, preposterous, ridiculous, silly**
2 very funny: *an absurd clown*
Other words: **comical, hilarious**

Word building: **absurdity** *noun*
absurdly *adverb*

abundant

adjective plentiful or more than enough: *The canteen has an abundant supply of sausage rolls.*

Word building: **abundance** *noun*
abundantly *adverb*

abuse (*rhymes with* shoes)

verb **1** to speak nastily to **2** to use wrongly: *Don't abuse my trust in you.*
noun (*rhymes with* goose) **3** insults or hurtful language **4** wrong use **5** use of something in an extreme amount: *drug abuse / alcohol abuse*

Word building: **abusive** *adjective* **abusively** *adverb* **abusiveness** *noun*

abysmal

adjective so bad that it could not be worse: *an abysmal exam result*
Word building: **abysmally** *adverb*

abyss (*rhymes with* kiss)

noun a hole or space that is too deep to measure

Word history: from a Greek word meaning 'without a bottom'

acacia (*say* uh-**kay**-shuh)

noun a small tree that grows in warm areas of the world, and has small, ball-shaped yellow flowers

Word use: It is also called **wattle**.

academic

adjective **1** belonging to a college or university: *academic studies* **2** full of theory instead of common sense: *an academic argument*

Word building: **academic** *noun*
academically *adverb*

academy

noun a school or society for learning

Word building: The plural is **academies**.

accede (*say* uhk-**seed**)

verb to agree or consent: *I accede to your wishes.*

accelerate (*say* uhk-**sel**-uh-rayt)

verb to move faster or speed up

Word building: **acceleration** *noun*

accelerator (*say* uhk-**sel**-uh-ray-tuh)

noun a pedal in a car, which the driver presses to make the car go faster

accent (*say* **ak**-sent)

noun **1** your own way of speaking: *I have an Australian accent.* **2** a stress or stronger tone given to part of a word or a musical note, to make it different from the rest **3** a mark showing a stress or emphasis

Word building: **accent** *verb* **accentual** *adjective*

accentuate (*say* uhk-**sen**-chooh-ayt)

verb to give importance to: *The brown eye shadow accentuates your eyes.*

Word building: **accentuation** *noun*

accept (*say* uhk-**sept**)

verb to take or receive willingly: *I accept your invitation.*

Word building: **acceptable** *adjective*
acceptance *noun* **accepted** *adjective*

accept/except Don't confuse **accept** with **except**, which means 'excluding or leaving out': *Everyone understood the joke except me.*

access (*say* **ak**-ses)

noun **1** the right to visit or approach: *Our school principal makes sure that we have access to her.* **2** a way of getting to: *This street gives easy access to the highway.*
verb **3** to get into: *You can access the classroom through this door.* **4** to find in a computer: *to access information*

Word building: **accessible** *adjective*
accessibility *noun*

accessory (*say* uhk-**ses**-uh-ree)

noun **1** something added but not necessary: *My red handbag is an accessory that matches my red dress.* **2** someone who helps carry out a crime: *The person who hid the thief was charged with being an accessory to the crime.*

Word building: The plural is **accessories**.

accident   (say <u>ak</u>-suh-duhnt)
noun **1** an unwanted or unlucky happening: *We had a bad accident in our car.* **2** something that happens by chance: *We met them by accident.*

Word building: **accidental** *adjective*: *an accidental meeting*   **accidentally** *adverb*

acclaim
verb to praise with sounds of approval: *The singer was acclaimed with shouts and clapping.*

Word use: The more usual word is **applaud**.
Word building: **acclamation** *noun*

acclimatise
verb to get used to new conditions: *He acclimatised slowly to living in the bush.*

Word use: The more usual word is **adjust**. | Another spelling is **acclimatize**.
Word building: **acclimatisation** *noun*

accommodate
verb **1** to have space for: *This motel accommodates 200 people.* **2** to change or adapt: *to accommodate themselves to a new plan*

accommodation
noun somewhere you stay while away from your home, such as a hotel or motel: *Have you booked accommodation for our holiday?*

accompany
verb **1** to go or be with: *to accompany a friend* **2** to play or sing with: *My mother accompanies me on the piano while I play the violin.*

Word building: Other forms are **I accompanied, I have accompanied, I am accompanying**. | **accompaniment** *noun* a part written to play with a tune

accomplice   (say uh-<u>kum</u>-pluhs)
noun someone who shares in a crime: *The robber's accomplice watched out for the police.*

accomplish   (say uh-<u>kum</u>-plish)
verb to carry out successfully
Other words: **complete, do, finish, perform**

Word building: **accomplished** *adjective* highly skilled: *an accomplished violinist*   **accomplishment** *noun*

accord
noun agreement or harmony: *The brothers are in accord with each other.*

Word building: **accordance** *noun*   **accordant** *adjective*   **according** *adverb*   **accordingly** *adverb*

accordance   (say uh-<u>kaw</u>-duhns)
noun agreement: *Everything the builders did was in accordance with the plans.*

accordion
noun a musical instrument that is squeezed to produce sound, and which you play using buttons or keys

Word building: **accordionist** *noun* an accordion player

accost
verb to come up and speak to, usually in an unpleasant way: *The bully accosted me in the playground today.*

Word history: from a Latin word meaning 'put side by side'

account
noun **1** a sum of money in a bank or building society which you can add to or take away from **2** a record of money paid out and received by a person or business **3** a list of particular happenings: *I'll give you an account of my day at school.* **4** importance or value: *things of no account* **5** judgement or consideration: *I will take that into account.*
phrase **6 account for,** to explain: *That accounts for his disappearance.*

accountant
noun someone whose job is to examine and record all the money that is earned and spent in a business

Word building: **accountancy** *noun* the work of an accountant   **accounting** *noun*

accumulate
verb to collect or pile up: *I accumulated a large collection of stamps.* | *Don't let papers accumulate on your desk.*

Word building: **accumulation** *noun*   **accumulator** *noun*   **accumulative** *adjective*

accurate
adjective correct or exact: *an accurate copy*
Other words: **precise, true**

Word building: **accuracy** *noun*   **accurately** *adverb*

accuse

verb to blame openly for doing something wrong: *I accused my friend of cheating.*

Word building: **accused** *noun* someone charged with a crime: *The judge let the accused go free.* **accusation** *noun* **accusatory** *adjective* **accuser** *noun*

accustomed

adjective **1** usual: *The library opened at the accustomed time.*

phrase **2 accustomed to,** in the habit of: *She is accustomed to working hard.*

Word building: **accustom** *verb*: *to accustom yourself to the heat*

ace

noun **1** a playing card with a single spot: *the ace of spades* **2** a serve in tennis which the other player cannot touch with their racquet **3** an expert: *an ace at dancing | a flying ace from World War I*
adjective Informal **4** excellent: *an ace party*

acetylene   (*say* uh-<u>set</u>-uh-leen)

noun a gas which, when combined with oxygen, burns with a very hot flame and is used in welding

Word use: Acetylene is used in an **oxyacetylene torch.**

ache   (*rhymes with* cake)

noun a dull continuous pain: *a stomach ache*

Word building: **ache** *verb*: *My leg is aching.*

achieve

verb to gain or bring about by effort: *to achieve an ambition*

Word building: **achievement** *noun* **achiever** *noun*

acid

noun **1** a chemical substance which can eat away metals
adjective **2** sour: *Lemons have an acid taste. | an acid remark*

Word building: **acidic** *adjective* **acidity** *noun*

acknowledge

verb **1** to admit to be real or true: *He acknowledged that he was to blame.* **2** to show that you have received: *to acknowledge a signal | to acknowledge an invitation*

Word building: **acknowledgement** *noun*

acne   (*say* <u>ak</u>-nee)

noun a rash with a lot of pimples, especially on your face

acorn

noun a nut with a cup-shaped bottom part, which grows on an oak tree

acoustics   (*say* uh-<u>kooh</u>-stiks)

noun **1** the science or study of sound **2** the properties of a building which affect the quality of the sounds produced in it: *The concert hall has good acoustics.*

Word building: **acoustic** *adjective* **acoustically** *adverb*

acquaintance

noun **1** knowledge: *acquaintance with the facts* **2** a person you know: *He is an acquaintance, but I wouldn't call him a friend.*

acquainted

verb **1** familiar with, or informed about: *The police officer talked to the witnesses so she could become acquainted with the details of the crime.*

phrase **2 get acquainted,** to get to know someone: *Let's leave those two to get acquainted.*

Word building: **acquaint** *verb*

acquire

verb to get or obtain: *She has acquired a new bike.*

Word building: **acquisitive** *adjective* eager to collect things **acquisition** *noun*

acquit

verb **1** to declare innocent: *They were acquitted by the jury.*

phrase **2 acquit yourself,** perform: *She acquitted herself well in the exam.*

Word use: The opposite of definition 1 is **convict.**
Word building: Other verb forms are **I acquitted, I have acquitted, I am acquitting. | acquittal** *noun*

acre   (*rhymes with* baker)

noun a large area of land in the imperial system, that is equal to almost half a hectare

Word building: **acreage** (*say* <u>ay</u>-kuh-rij) *noun*: *They keep their horse on some acreage outside the city.*

acrid

adjective having a bitter or unpleasant taste or smell
Other words: **harsh, pungent**

acrobat

noun someone who performs daring gymnastic tricks: *The acrobat at the circus walked the tightrope.*

Word building: **acrobatic** *adjective*
acrobatics *noun*
Word history: from a Greek word meaning 'walking on tiptoe'

acronym   (*say* ak-ruh-nim)

noun a word made from the first letters of other words: *'ANZAC' is an acronym from 'Australian and New Zealand Army Corps'.*

across

preposition **1** from one side to the other side of: *The log fell across the creek.* **2** on the other side of: *I live across town.* **3** from one side to another: *Let's rollerblade across!*

acrostic   (*say* uh-kros-tik)

noun a series of words or lines, often of a poem, in which the first or last letters form a word, a phrase, the alphabet, or anything like this

acrylic   (*say* uh-kril-ik)

noun **1** a synthetic material used for clothing **2 acrylics**, a paint made from synthetic material: *At school we used acrylics for the poster.*

Word building: **acrylic** *adjective*

act

noun **1** something done or performed: *an act of bravery* **2** a law or order: *an act of Parliament* **3** one of the main divisions of a stage play: *A ghost appeared in the third act of the play.* **4** a single performance in a concert: *a singing act*
verb **5** to do something: *He acted quickly when danger was near.* **6** to do someone's duties when they are unable to: *The deputy acted as principal while she was away.* **7** to play the part of: *to act Peter Pan in the school play* **8** to behave as: *to act the fool*

Word building: **acting** *noun*   **actor** *noun*
actress *noun*

action

noun **1** an act or deed: *a brave action* **2** the state of being active: *The nurses went into action when the ambulance arrived.* **3** a way of moving: *the action of a horse*

activate

verb to make active or set in motion: *He activated the machine by pulling a lever.*

Word building: **activation** *noun*

active

adjective **1** taking part or doing things: *Ashanta is active on the committee.* **2** continuously busy: *Con leads an active life.* **3** able to move quickly: *an active puppy* **4** having to do with a verb which has the doer of the action as its subject, as 'punished' in *His father punished him.*

Word use: Compare definition 4 with **passive**.

activist

noun someone who works very hard for something they believe in: *Juan's uncle was an activist in the peace movement.*

activity

noun a thing you do, often energetically: *The main activity for the day was swimming.*

Word building: The plural is **activities**.

actor

noun someone who acts the part of a character in a play: *The actor who played the killer was frightening.*

actress

noun a woman who acts in a play

Word building: The plural is **actresses**.

actual

adjective real or existing
Other words: **authentic, factual, genuine, tangible**
Word building: **actually** *adverb*

acumen   (*say* ak-yuh-muhn)

noun good judgement: *Your business acumen will help you to make money.*

acupuncture   (*say* ak-yuh-punk-chuh)

noun a Chinese type of medicine which treats illness or pain by sticking needles into certain parts of the body

Word building: **acupuncturist** *noun*

acute

adjective **1** very sudden and severe: *an acute attack of asthma* **2** clever: *an acute remark* **3** having less than 90°: *an acute angle*

Word building: **acutely** *adverb*   **acuteness** *noun*
Word history: from a Latin word meaning 'sharpened'

AD

short for *anno domini,* Latin words meaning 'in the year of our Lord': *Humans first walked on the moon in AD 1969.*

Word use: Our calendar dates events from the year of Christ's birth; years after this are called **AD** and years before this are **BC**. The abbreviation **CE** (as in *1792 CE*) is sometimes used instead of **AD** if the speaker or writer wants to avoid the reference to Christ. It stands for *(of the) Common Era.*

adage   *(say* ad-ij)

noun a wise saying: *'More haste less speed' is a common adage.*

adagio   *(say* uh-dah-zhee-oh)

adverb played or sung slowly and calmly

Word use: This is an instruction in music.

adamant   *(say* ad-uh-muhnt)

adjective staying firm in what you decide: *She was adamant that she would not go.*

Word use: The more usual word is **determined.**

adapt

verb **1** to change or adjust: *We adapted the design of our model aeroplane so that it flew better.*
Other words: **alter, amend, modify, vary**
phrase **2 adapt to,** become used to: *She found it hard to adapt to a new school.*

Word building: **adaptor** *noun* an extra part which changes a machine or tool to a different use   **adaptability** *noun*   **adaptable** *adjective*

adaptation

noun **1** an adjustment of some kind: *an adaptation of a piece of music for three guitars instead of one* **2** in biology, the change that happens to an organism so that it can continue to live if the environment changes

add

verb **1** to join so as to increase: *to add another bead to the necklace* **2** to find the sum of: *to add up all the numbers*
Other words: **count, tally, total**
phrase **3 add to,** to increase or make bigger: *to add to my surprise*
Other words: **heighten**

added value

noun something added to a product that makes it more attractive or valuable for people to buy: *They have increased the price of these cleaning products because of the added value provided by the 'environmentally friendly' labelling.*

adder

noun a small venomous snake

addict   *(say* ad-ikt)

noun someone who can't do without something, especially drugs: *a coffee addict*

Word building: **addiction** *noun*   **addicted** *adjective*   **addictive** *adjective*
Word history: from a Latin word meaning 'devoted'

addition

noun **1** something added which increases the size or number of things: *A new bathroom is the latest addition to our house.* **2** the act of adding numbers together

Word building: **additional** *adjective* **additionally** *adverb*

additive

noun something which is added, especially a chemical added to food to keep it fresh

address

noun **1** the details of the place where you live **2** a formal speech: *to give an address at a meeting* **3** the special series of numbers and letters that you key in to a computer to get to a particular website or when you are sending email to someone
verb **4** to write the receiver's name, street and town on: *I addressed the letter wrongly.* **5** to speak to: *The politician addressed the meeting.* **6** to deal with: *These are the issues you should address in your essay.*

Word building: The plural form of the noun is **addresses.**

adenoids

plural noun the mass of soft growths at the back of the nose which sometimes block it and have to be removed

adept

adjective skilful: *She was adept at ball games.*

Word building: **adeptness** *noun*

adequate

adjective suitable or enough: *That light jacket isn't adequate for this cold weather.*

Word building: **adequacy** *noun*   **adequately** *adverb*

adhere

verb to stick firmly: *The grass seeds adhered to our socks. | They adhered strictly to the rules.*

Word building: **adherent** *noun* someone who follows or supports a person or idea **adherence** *noun*

adhesive
noun a substance which sticks things together

Word building: **adhesive** *adjective* sticky **adhesion** *noun*

adjacent (*say* uh-<u>jay</u>-suhnt)
adjective lying near or close: *Our block of land was adjacent to the railway line.*

adjective
noun a word which describes a noun, such as 'tall' in *a tall building*

Word building: **adjectival** *adjective* **adjectivally** *adverb*

adjourn (*say* uh-<u>jern</u>)
verb **1** to put off: *We will adjourn the meeting till tomorrow.* **2** to move: *Shall we adjourn to the living room?*

Word building: **adjournment** *noun*

adjudicate (*say* uh-<u>jooh</u>-duh-kayt)
verb to act as judge: *The principal adjudicated in our debate.*

Word building: **adjudication** *noun* **adjudicator** *noun*

adjust
verb to cause to fit or work properly: *I adjusted my belt. | I adjusted the tuning on the TV.*

Word building: **adjustable** *adjective* **adjustment** *noun*

administer
verb **1** to run or have charge of: *A solicitor administered the inheritance.* **2** to give: *The vet administered a big dose of medicine to the sick horse.*

Word use: Another form of this word is **administrate**.

administration
noun the people that run a business or government: *If you don't like the rules, complain to the administration.*

Word building: **administrative** *adjective* **administrator** *noun*

admiral
noun the highest ranking officer in the navy

Word building: **admiralty** *noun* the office or duty of an admiral

admire
verb to think very highly of

Other words: **appreciate, esteem, respect**

Word building: **admirable** *adjective* excellent **admirably** *adverb* **admiration** *noun* **admirer** *noun*

admission
noun **1** the process of entering a place: *Her admission into hospital took longer than she expected.* **2** the price paid to enter a place, such as a theatre, movie or sportsground **3** confession of a crime or mistake: *She made an admission of guilt.*

admit
verb **1** to let in: *Only admit one car at a time.*
Other words: **allow**
2 to agree to the truth of: *I admitted my guilt.*
Other words: **acknowledge, concede, confess**

Word use: For definition 2 you usually only admit something bad.
Word building: Other forms are **I admitted, I have admitted, I am admitting.** | **admittance** *noun*: *We were worried that there would be no admittance after the performance had started.*

admonish
verb to warn or caution: *We admonished the boys not to be noisy.*

Word building: **admonition** *noun* **admonitory** *adjective*

adolescence (*say* ad-uh-<u>les</u>-uhns)
noun the time between being a child and being grown-up

Word building: **adolescent** *noun* a teenager **adolescent** *adjective*

adopt
verb to take as your own: *They adopted the baby.*

Word use: Compare this with **foster**.
Word building: **adoptive** *adjective* related by adoption **adoption** *noun*

adore
verb to feel very strong love for: *The children adored their puppy.*

Word building: **adorable** *adjective* **adoring** *adjective* **adoration** *noun*

adorn
verb to make more beautiful or pleasant: *Flowers adorned the altar of the church.*
Other words: **decorate, embellish**

Word building: **adorningly** *adverb* **adornment** *noun*

adrenaline (*say* uh-<u>dren</u>-uh-luhn)
noun a chemical which your body sends into your blood when you are feeling anxious or stressed, or when you are involved in strenuous activity. It makes your heart beat faster and it increases your blood pressure and the amount of sugar in your blood.

Word use: Another spelling is **adrenalin**. | This word is related to the word **adrenal** which is based on the Latin word for the kidneys; the **adrenal glands**, which make adrenaline, are found near the top of the kidneys.

adult
adjective **1** grown-up or mature: *This film is only suitable for an adult audience.*
noun **2** someone who is fully grown
Word building: **adulthood** *noun*

adulterate
verb to spoil by adding something inferior: *to adulterate food*
Word building: **adulteration** *noun*

adultery
noun a sexual relationship in which at least one of the two people is married to someone else
Word building: **adulterer** *noun* **adulterous** *adjective*

advance
verb **1** to move or bring forwards: *She advanced to the front of the room.*
Other words: **continue, proceed, progress**
2 to improve or develop: *The new students are advancing rapidly in learning English.*
Other words: **progress**
noun **3** progress or movement forwards
Other words: **advancement, progression**
4 a loan: *an advance of $10*
phrase **5 in advance, a** in front or before: *in advance of other pupils* **b** ahead of time: *They paid the rent in advance.*
Other words: **early**
Word building: **advanced** *adjective* **advancement** *noun*

advantage
noun something that puts you ahead of others: *Having strong arms is an advantage when you are swimming.*
Other words: **asset, benefit, boon, help, plus**
Word building: **advantageous** *adjective* **advantageously** *adverb*

adventure
noun an exciting experience

Other words: **escapade, exploit**
Word building: **adventurer** *noun* **adventurous** *adjective* **adventurously** *adverb*

adverb
noun a word which tells you something extra about a verb, adjective or another adverb, such as *beautifully* in *to sing beautifully*, *almost* in *almost ready*, and *very* in *very slowly*
Word building: **adverbial** *adjective*

adversary (*say* <u>ad</u>-vuhs-ree)
noun someone you compete against or fight with
Word use: The more usual word is **opponent**.
Word building: The plural is **adversaries**. | **adverse** *adjective* hostile **adversity** *noun* misfortune

advertise (*say* <u>ad</u>-vuh-tuyz)
verb to praise or draw attention to, especially in order to sell: *We advertised our car in the newspapers.*
Word building: **advertiser** *noun* **advertising** *noun*

advertisement (*say* uhd-<u>vert</u>-uhs-muhnt)
noun a notice telling you about an event that is coming, or about something lost or for sale

advice (*say* uhd-<u>vuys</u>)
noun an opinion someone gives you to help you decide what to do: *George gave me advice about the best way to fix my bike.*
Other words: **counsel, guidance**

advisable
adjective sensible: *It's advisable not to take the steep, dangerous track.*
Word building: **advisability** *noun*

advise (*say* uhd-<u>vuyz</u>)
verb to tell what you think should be done: *We advised that they not go to the desert in summer.*
Other words: **counsel, recommend, suggest**
Word building: **adviser, advisor** *noun*

advisory
adjective giving advice or being able to give advice: *an advisory committee*

advocate (*say* <u>ad</u>-vuh-kuht)
noun **1** someone who speaks in favour of a person or cause: *the criminal's advocate* | *an advocate of peace*

verb (*say* <u>ad</u>-vuh-kayt) **2** to speak in favour of: *We advocate peace rather than war.*

Word use: For definition 1, the more usual word is **supporter**; for definition 2, **support**.

aeon (*say* <u>ee</u>-on)
noun a long period of time: *aeons ago when dinosaurs lived*

Word use: Another spelling is **eon**.
Word history: from a Greek word meaning 'a lifetime' or 'an age'

aerial
noun **1** a wire or rod that you put up to receive radio or television signals
adjective **2** living in or reaching into the air: *The plant has aerial roots.*

aero-
prefix a word part meaning **1** air: *aerobics* **2** gas: *aerosol* **3** aeroplane: *aerodrome*

aerobics
plural noun exercises done to music to improve your fitness

aerodrome
noun a landing field for aeroplanes which is smaller than an airport but which has hangars and other buildings

aeronautics
noun the science of flight

Word building: **aeronautical** *adjective*
Word history: from a Latin word meaning 'sailing in the air'

aeroplane
noun a winged machine which is driven through the air by its propellers or jet engines

aerosol (*say* <u>air</u>-ruh-sol)
noun a container for keeping liquids, such as paint or household cleaner, under pressure so that you can spray them

aesthetics (*say* uhs-<u>thet</u>-iks)
noun the study of beauty, especially in art

Word use: Another spelling is **esthetics**.
Word building: **aesthete** *noun* **aesthetic** *adjective*

affable
adjective friendly and approachable: *The affable old woman told the children stories of her travels.*

Word building: **affability** *noun* **affably** *adverb*

affair
noun **1** an event or matter: *Tell us about the whole affair.* **2** a sexual relationship between two people

affect[1]
verb to cause a change in: *Your sad story affected our mood. | The heat affected the milk and turned it bad.*

Word building: **affected** *adjective* moved or touched: *I am always very affected when I hear beautiful music.*

affect/effect Don't confuse **affect** with **effect**. They are rather alike in meaning but **affect** is usually a verb and **effect** is usually a noun.
Warm weather affects me and makes me sleepy. The effect of the warm weather is to make me sleepy.
Note that **effect** *can* be a verb meaning 'to make happen': *to effect a change in the program*

affect[2]
verb to pretend or make a show of: *He affected not to know what we were talking about, though we knew he really did.*
Other words: **feign**

Word building: **affected** *adjective* artificial: *The actress's voice was very affected.*

affectation
noun an exaggerated sort of behaviour: *We thought that the new student's American accent was an affectation.*

affection
noun warm feelings of love

Word building: **affectionate** *adjective* **affectionately** *adverb*

affiliate
verb to join or become connected: *Our business will affiliate with a larger company.*

Word building: **affiliate** *noun* **affiliation** *noun*
Word history: from a Latin word meaning 'adopt as a son'

affinity
noun a natural liking or sense of closeness: *Patrick felt an affinity for the boy his own age.*

Word building: The plural is **affinities**.

affirm
verb to declare definitely: *The minister affirmed her support for the poor.*

Word building: **affirmation** *noun* agreement

affirmative

adjective agreeing: *an affirmative reply*

Word use: The opposite is **negative**.
Word building: **affirmatively** *adverb*

afflict

verb to trouble greatly or cause pain: *He was afflicted with sickness.*

Word building: **affliction** *noun*

affluent   (*say* af-looh-uhnt)

adjective wealthy or rich: *an affluent country*

Word building: **affluence** *noun*

afford

verb to have enough money to pay for: *They couldn't afford a new car.*

affront

noun something that hurts your pride or your feelings: *Zhong's rudeness was an affront to the visitors.*

Word use: The more usual word is **insult**.
Word building: **affronted** *adjective* offended   **affront** *verb*

afraid

adjective **1** frightened or feeling fear
Other words: **fearful, petrified, scared, terrified**
2 feeling sorry or regretful: *I'm afraid I can't come.*

afresh

adverb again: *After each interruption she started the book afresh.*

aft   (*rhymes with* raft)

adverb at or towards the back of a ship: *Thomas went aft to his cabin.*

Word use: The opposite of this is **fore**.

after   (*say* ahf-tuh)

preposition **1** at a time later than: *You can watch television after you do your homework.* **2** behind: *You were after me in the tuckshop line, that's why you missed out on the yummy cake.*

aftermath

noun conditions which follow a disaster: *the aftermath of the fire*

afternoon

noun the time from midday till evening

after-school care

noun a place where you can go in the afternoon when school finishes, where people look after you until you go home

afterwards

adverb later: *We'll have lunch first, and afterwards we'll go for a swim.*

Word use: Another form of this word is **afterward**.

again   (*say* a-gen)

adverb another time or once more

against   (*say* a-genst)

preposition **1** on or next to: *Don't lean against the wall.* **2** in the opposite direction to: *The skateboard goes slower when you're riding against the wind.*

agate   (*rhymes with* maggot)

noun a type of hard stone which is often marked with stripes or swirls of colour

age

noun **1** the length of time that someone or something has existed: *Yan is thirteen years of age.* **2** a period of historical time: *the Middle Ages* **3** a stage of human life: *old age*
verb **4** to grow old or look older: *Our grandmother has aged since her illness.*

Word building: Other verb forms are **I aged, I have aged, I am ageing** or **aging**. | **aged** *adjective* very old

agency   (*say* ay-juhn-see)

noun an organisation which helps or acts for people: *You can go to an employment agency if you need help finding a job.*

Word building: The plural is **agencies**.

agenda   (*say* uh-jen-duh)

noun the list or plan of what has to be done or talked about, especially at a meeting: *There were three items for discussion on the agenda.*

agent   (*say* ay-juhnt)

noun **1** someone who acts or organises things for you: *a travel agent* **2** something used for a special purpose: *a cleaning agent* **3** a secret agent; spy

aggravate   (*say* ag-ruh-vayt)

verb **1** to make worse: *Tiredness aggravated Michiko's bad temper.* **2** to annoy: *Don't aggravate the teacher by shuffling your feet.*

Word building: **aggravation** *noun*

aggregate   (*say* ag-ruh-guht)

noun the total or sum of single things: *the aggregate of all your marks in the test*

Word building: **aggregation** *noun*   **aggregately** *adverb*   **aggregative** *adjective*

aggressive

adjective likely to attack: *an aggressive guard dog*

Other words: **belligerent, hostile**

Word building: **aggression** *noun* **aggressively** *adverb* **aggressiveness** *noun* **aggressor** *noun*

aggrieved

adjective feeling hurt or wronged: *I was aggrieved that no-one asked me to join the party.*

aghast   (*rhymes with* mast)

adjective shocked and frightened: *They were aghast at the unexpected result of their plan.*

agile   (*say* <u>aj</u>-uyl)

adjective lively and active: *an agile gymnast*

Word building: **agilely** *adverb* **agility** *noun*

agitate

verb **1** to shake about: *to agitate the water* **2** to upset or disturb: *The bad news agitated her so much she had to go home.* **3** to try to get public support: *to agitate for a change of government*

Word building: **agitatedly** *adverb* **agitation** *noun* **agitator** *noun*

agnostic   (*say* ag-<u>nos</u>-tik)

noun someone who believes that you can't know anything about God

Word use: Compare this with **atheist**.
Word building: **agnostic** *adjective* **agnosticism** *noun*

ago

adverb past: *many years ago*

agog

adjective excited and eager: *Santa's sleigh arrived and the children were all agog.*

Word history: from French words meaning 'in a merry mood'

agony

noun great pain or suffering
Other words: **anguish, distress, torment**

Word building: The plural is **agonies**. | **agonise** *verb*

agrarian   (*say* uh-<u>grair</u>-ree-uhn)

adjective having to do with the land or farming: *an agrarian way of life*

agree

verb **1** to say yes: *I agreed to share my toffees.*
Other words: **assent, consent**
2 to have the same opinion: *I think that we should leave now and I hope that you agree.*
Other words: **concur**
3 to arrange: *We agreed to meet after lunch.*
Other words: **organise, plan**
phrase **4 agree with, a** to suit: *The food doesn't agree with me.* **b** to think like

agreeable

adjective **1** pleasant or likeable: *agreeable weather* **2** willing to agree: *We will go now if you are agreeable.*

Word building: **agreeableness** *noun* **agreeably** *adverb*

agreement

noun **1** the same way of thinking: *John and I are in agreement about that film.*
2 arrangement: *They came to an agreement about sharing the bike.*
Other words: **deal, pact, settlement, understanding**

agriculture

noun farming: *Much of Australia's wealth comes from agriculture.*

Word building: **agricultural** *adjective* **agriculturalist** *noun* **agriculturally** *adverb*

ahead

adverb before or in front: *Jonah is ahead of me in the queue | There's a sharp curve in the road ahead.*

aid

noun **1** help or support
Other words: **assistance**
phrase **2 first aid**, emergency help to someone

Word building: **aid** *verb*

AIDS   (*say* aydz)

noun a disease caused by a virus called HIV which breaks down the body's natural defences, causing very bad infections, skin tumours and death

Word history: an acronym made by joining the first letters of *acquired immune deficiency syndrome*

ailing

adjective not well, or sickly: *an ailing child*

Word building: **ailment** *noun* an illness **ail** *verb*

aim

verb **1** to direct or point: *It was mean to aim that question at me | You must aim a gun carefully before firing.*
Other words: **level**
2 to try very hard: *We aim to succeed.*
Other words: **intend, mean, plan, seek**
noun **3** a purpose or target: *Our aim was to win the race.*
Other words: **ambition, aspiration, goal, intention, object**
phrase **4 take aim,** to point a weapon
Word building: **aimless** *adjective* without purpose **aimlessly** *adverb*

air

noun **1** the mixture of gases which surrounds the earth and which we breathe **2** appearance: *She has an air of success.* **3** a tune or melody
verb **4** to let air into: *Open the window to air the room.* **5** to make known to people: *The meeting was a chance for her to air her views.*
Word building: **airing** *noun: to give clothes an airing* **airless** *adjective* stuffy

air/heir Don't confuse **air** with **heir**, which is a person who inherits something.

air conditioner

noun a machine that makes a place cooler

aircraft

noun any machine that can fly, such as an aeroplane or helicopter

airfare

noun the price of a flight on a commercial aircraft: *They decided to go by train because the airfare was too dear.*

air force

noun the part of a country's armed forces which uses planes for attack and defence

airline

noun a company which provides a regular plane service for passengers and goods
Word building: **airliner** *noun* a large passenger aircraft

airport

noun a large area where planes land and take off, usually with buildings for staff, passengers and planes

air pressure

noun **1** the pressure caused by the weight of the atmosphere at a particular place on the earth **2** the pressure of air in something, usually inside a tyre
Word use: Other names for definition 1 are **atmospheric pressure** and **barometric pressure.** | You measure the pressure in definition 1 with a barometer.

airtight

adjective tightly closed so that air can't get in or out: *an airtight jar*

airtime

noun the amount of time taken up by a presenter or a program or a topic on radio or television: *The entrepreneur spent thousands of dollars buying airtime to advertise the show.*

airy

adjective **1** having air moving through it: *an airy room* **2** careless or light-hearted: *He went off with an airy wave of his hand.*
Word building: Other forms are **airier, airiest.** | **airily** *adverb* **airiness** *noun*

aisle　(*rhymes with* pile)

noun a clear path as between seats in a church or hall, a train, bus or aeroplane, or between shelves in a supermarket, and so on

ajar

adverb partly open: *Leave the door ajar.*

akimbo

adverb with your hands on your hips and your elbows pointing out: *to stand with arms akimbo*

akin

adjective related or alike: *Emus are akin to ostriches.*

alacrity　(*say* uh-lak-ruh-tee)

noun cheerful willingness: *Abeke went to do the messages with alacrity.*

alarm

noun **1** a warning sound or signal **2** sudden fear caused by discovering that you're in danger: *The smoke filled me with alarm.*
verb **3** to frighten: *The sudden crash alarmed me.*
Word building: **alarming** *adjective* **alarmist** *noun*
Word history: from Italian words meaning 'to arms'

albatross
noun a very large seabird that can fly long distances

Word building: The plural is **albatrosses**.

albino   (*say* al-<u>bee</u>-noh)
noun a human or an animal with pale skin, white hair and pink eyes

Word building: The plural is **albinos**. | **albino** *adjective*

album
noun **1** a book with blank pages used for keeping things like photographs and stamps **2** a recording on which there is a collection of songs or pieces

alcohol
noun a colourless liquid which is found in some drinks and which makes you drunk if you have too much

alcoholic
noun someone who continually drinks too much alcohol

Word building: **alcoholic** *adjective*

alcoholism
noun a disease caused by drinking too much alcohol for a long time

alcove
noun a small space or recess set off the main part, especially in a room

alderman
noun someone elected to a local council: *I complained to the alderman about the holes in the footpaths.*

Word building: The plural is **aldermen**.

ale
noun beer not flavoured with hops

alert
adjective watchful and quick to react: *The guard was alert and noticed the robbers creeping around the back of the building.*
Other words: **attentive, observant, vigilant**

Word building: **alert** *verb*   **alertness** *noun*

alga   (*say* <u>al</u>-guh)
noun singular of **algae**

algae   (*say* <u>al</u>-jee)
plural noun seaweed or weed growing in ponds or streams

Word building: The singular form is **alga**.

algebra
noun the branch of maths which uses letters to stand for numbers

Word building: **algebraic** *adjective* **algebraically** *adverb*

algorism
noun a sum in arithmetic

algorithm
noun a step-by-step method for doing a sum

alias   (*say* <u>ay</u>-lee-uhs)
noun **1** a false name: *The criminal is said to be living under an alias in South America.*
adverb **2** also called: *Superman, alias Clark Kent*

Word building: The plural form of the noun is **aliases**.
Word history: from a Latin word meaning 'at another time or place'

alibi   (*say* <u>al</u>-uh-buy)
noun a defence by someone that they were somewhere else when a crime was committed

alien   (*say* <u>ay</u>-lee-uhn)
noun **1** someone who is not a citizen of the country in which they are living **2** a foreigner: *aliens from outer space*

Word building: **alien** *adjective*
Word history: from a Latin word meaning 'belonging to another'

alienate
verb to make unfriendly: *You'll alienate all your friends if you keep being rude to them.*

Word building: **alienation** *noun*

alight¹
verb **1** to get down: *to alight from a horse* | *to alight from a train* **2** to settle or stay after coming down: *a bird alights on a branch*

Word building: Other forms are **I alighted, I have alighted, I am alighting**.

alight²
adjective burning or lighted up: *The fire is alight at last.*

align   (*rhymes with* fine)
verb to bring into line: *to align the pictures on the wall*

Word building: **alignment** *noun*

alike

adverb **1** in the same manner: *She treats all pupils alike.*
adjective **2** similar: *Their clothes are alike.*

alimentary canal   (*say* al-uh-ment-ree kuh-<u>nal</u>)

noun the passage in an animal's body which extends from the mouth to the anus and which is used for digesting food

Word use: Another name for this is **alimentary tract.**

alive

adjective living, not dead: *Are your grandparents still alive? | Even though I haven't been watering it, my rose bush is still alive.*

alkali   (*say* <u>al</u>-kuh-luy)

noun a chemical that reduces the effect of acid

Word building: **alkaline** *adjective*
Word history: from an Arabic word for the ashes of certain beach plants

all

adjective **1** the whole of something: *I must confess: I've eaten all the cake.*
2 every one of something: *I've arranged all my CDs in alphabetical order.*

allay   (*say* uh-<u>lay</u>)

verb to make less: *to allay suspicion | to allay the pain*

Word use: The more usual word is **relieve.**

allege   (*say* uh-<u>lej</u>)

verb to declare without proof: *Kim alleged that Mei broke the window.*

Word building: **allegation** *noun*   **allegedly** *adverb*

allegiance   (*say* uh-<u>lee</u>-juhns)

noun loyalty or faithfulness: *They swore allegiance to the queen.*

allegory   (*say* <u>al</u>-uh-gree)

noun a story which seems simple but has an extra underlying meaning

Word building: The plural is **allegories.** | **allegorical** *adjective*

allegro

adverb played or sung at a fast speed
Word use: This is an instruction in music.

allergy   (*say* <u>al</u>-uh-jee)

noun an unusual sensitivity to things that are normally harmless, like pollen, dust and certain foods: *I sneezed in the pet shop because of my allergy to cats.*

Word building: The plural is **allergies.** | **allergen** *noun* something which causes an allergic reaction   **allergic** *adjective*

alleviate   (*say* uh-<u>lee</u>-vee-ayt)

verb to make easier to bear: *The aspirin has alleviated the pain.*

Word use: The more usual word is **ease.**
Word building: **alleviation** *noun*

alley

noun **1** a narrow lane between buildings **2** a long narrow enclosure with a smooth wooden floor for games like tenpin bowling

Word building: The plural is **alleys.**

alliance   (*say* uh-<u>luy</u>-uhns)

noun an agreement to work together: *Australia has a military alliance with the United States. | The local people are in alliance to prevent the building of a freeway.*

alligator

noun an animal like a crocodile, but with a broader snout, found mainly in America
Word history: from a Latin word meaning 'lizard'

alliteration

noun the repeated use of the same letter or sound to start two or more words in a group, as in 'Around the rugged rocks the ragged rascal ran'
Word building: **alliterative** *adjective*

allocate

verb to set apart for a special purpose: *to allocate some of your pocket money for sweets*
Word building: **allocation** *noun*

allot

verb **1** to hand out or distribute: *to allot equal shares* **2** to set apart: *to allot money for the new park*
Word building: Other forms are **I allotted, I have allotted, I am allotting.** | **allotment** *noun*

allow

verb **1** to give permission to or for: *Will your parents allow you to come?*
Other words: **authorise, let, permit**
2 to set aside: *to allow space for a margin*
Word building: **allowed** *adjective* permitted

allowance

noun **1** money given for a special purpose: *a travelling allowance*
phrase **2 make allowance(s) for**, to take into account: *Please make allowances for my broken arm.*

alloy

noun a metal made by mixing different metals together: *Bronze is an alloy of copper and tin.*

all right

adjective **1** safe: *I'm all right now.*
2 adequate or good enough to accept: *Your answer is all right, but it could have been more interesting.*
adverb **3** correctly or to an acceptable standard: *Zoe did her homework all right.*
Word use: Another spelling is **alright**.

allude

verb to refer casually: *She alluded to my late arrival.*

Word building: **allusion** *noun* passing mention of something   **allusive** *adjective*
allusively *adverb*
Word history: from a Latin word meaning 'play with'

allure

noun temptation or attraction: *the allure of the toy shop*
Word building: **allure** *verb*   **alluring** *adjective*

alluvial

adjective made of sand or mud which has been washed down by a river: *alluvial soil*

ally   (*say* <u>al</u>-uy)

noun **1** a country which has signed an agreement to help another country: *an ally in times of war* **2** a friend or supporter
Other words: **helper, partner**
verb (*say* uh-<u>luy</u>) **3** to join together to help one another
Other words: **combine, unite**

Word building: The plural form of the noun is **allies**. | Other verb forms are **they allied, they have allied, they are allying**. | **alliance** *noun*

almanac   (*say* <u>awl</u>-muh-nak)

noun a calendar which gives information about the sun, moon, tides, weather or other special information
Word use: An old-fashioned spelling is **almanack**.

almighty

adjective **1** very powerful: *an almighty king*
2 very great: *to be in almighty trouble*

almond   (*say* <u>ah</u>-muhnd)

noun an oval-shaped, cream-coloured nut with a sweet taste

almost

adverb nearly: *It's almost time for dinner!*

alms   (*sounds like* arms)

plural noun money and other gifts given to poor people
Other words: **aid, donations, charity**

alone

adjective **1** by yourself: *He was alone in the house all night.*
Other words: **isolated, solitary**
2 only: *She alone knows the real story.*
Other words: **exclusively**

Word building: **alone** *adverb*   **aloneness** *noun*

along

preposition **1** from one end to the other: *We walked along the beach.*
adverb **2** with someone: *Do you want to come along?*

aloof   (*rhymes with* roof)

adjective **1** withdrawn and proud: *She seems aloof and unfriendly, but she's really only shy.*
adverb **2** at a distance apart: *to stand aloof from the crowd*

aloud

adverb **1** in a normal speaking voice: *to read aloud* **2** loudly: *to cry aloud with pain*

alp

noun **1** a high mountain **2 alps**, a high mountain range, usually covered with snow, such as the Australian Alps or the Swiss Alps
Word building: **alpine** *adjective* having to do with a cold mountainous place: *alpine flowers*

alphabet

noun all the letters of a language arranged in their usual order

Word building: **alphabetical** *adjective*
alphabetically *adverb*   **alphabetisation** *noun*   **alphabetise** *verb*
Word history: from Greek words for the letters 'A' and 'B'

already

adverb sooner then expected: *Have you finished your homework already?*

alright

adjective **1** safe: *I'm alright now.*
2 adequate or good enough to accept: *Your answer is alright, but it could have been more interesting.*
adverb **3** correctly or to an acceptable standard: *Zoe did her homework alright.*

Word use: Another spelling is **all right**.

Alsatian   *(say* al-<u>say</u>-shuhn)

noun a large, strong, wolf-like dog, often trained as a guard dog and used by the police

Word use: Another name is **German shepherd**.

also

adverb too, as well or in addition: *There will also be cake as well as biscuits.*

altar

noun a table which is used for religious ceremonies in a church or temple

alter

verb to change: *Your appearance alters as you grow up. | My brother has altered his hairstyle again.*
Other words: **amend, modify, transform, vary**

Word building: **alteration** *noun*

altercation

noun an angry disagreement or dispute

Word use: The more usual word is **argument**.

alternate   *(say* <u>awl</u>-tuh-nayt)

verb **1** to follow one another in turn: *Day and night alternate with each other.*
adjective *(say* awl-<u>ter</u>-nuht)
2 every second one of a series: *They visit their grandmother on alternate weekends.*

alternative   *(say* awl-<u>ter</u>-nuh-tiv)

noun **1** one of two or more choices: *to provide orange juice as an alternative to milk | a list of alternatives*
adjective **2** giving a choice between one thing and another: *the alternative route to Brisbane*

alternative energy

noun energy to make machines work that comes from sources that will not run out as oil will do but will continue to exist, such as the sun, wind, the tides, and so on

alternative medicine

noun treatment for sickness and injury often based on traditional natural remedies, which are outside what is offered by mainstream medicine: *She practised a form of alternative medicine and said I should stop eating all dairy foods.*

although   *(say* awl-<u>dhoh</u>)

conjunction even though: *I'm still tired although I had an early night.*

altimeter   *(say* <u>al</u>-tuh-meet-uh)

noun the instrument in a plane which measures altitude or height

altitude

noun height above sea level: *to fly at a high altitude*

alto   *(say* <u>al</u>-toh)

noun **1** the range of musical notes which can be sung by a female singer with a low voice: *Megan sings alto in the choir.*
2 a woman with a low singing voice
3 an instrument of a range between soprano and tenor

Word use: Another word is **contralto**. | The **alto** range is higher than **bass**, **baritone** and **tenor** but lower than **soprano**.
Word building: **alto** *adjective*: *Tran plays the alto saxophone.*
Word history: from a Latin word for 'high'

altogether

adverb **1** completely or totally: *to be altogether correct* **2** in total: *That costs $10 altogether.* **3** on the whole: *Altogether, I'm glad its over.*

aluminium   *(say* al-yuh-<u>min</u>-ee-uhm)

noun a lightweight silver-grey metal which is used to make drink cans and cooking utensils and can be rolled into thin sheets of silver foil

always

adverb **1** all the time: *She is always here.*
2 every time: *She always wears purple lipstick.*

a.m.

short for *ante meridiem*, Latin words meaning 'before noon': *I get up at 6 a.m.*

amalgamate   *(say* uh-<u>mal</u>-guh-mayt)

verb to mix together or combine: *to amalgamate two classes | The classes amalgamated when the teacher was away.*

Word building: **amalgamation** *noun*

amateur (*say* am-uh-tuh)
noun **1** an athlete who does not earn money from playing sport **2** someone who does something for enjoyment and not to earn money from it **3** someone who does a job unskilfully: *This fence must have been built by an amateur.*
Word use: The opposite of this is **professional.**
Word building: **amateurish** *adjective*   **amateur** *adjective*
Word history: from a Latin word for 'lover'

amaze
verb to surprise and astonish: *Domingo's friends were amazed when he won the race.*
Other words: **astound, dumbfound, shock, stun**
Word building: **amazement** *noun*   **amazing** *adjective*

amazon (*say* am-uh-zuhn)
noun a tall powerful woman
Word building: **amazonian** *adjective*

ambassador
noun **1** the chief official who is sent by a government to represent it in a foreign country **2** someone, such as a famous singer or sports star, who brings credit to their own country while visiting another

amber
noun **1** a hard yellow-brown substance which can be polished as a gem stone **2** the yellowish-brown colour used as the warning light of a traffic signal

ambergris (*say* am-buh-grees)
noun a waxy substance taken from the intestines of the sperm whale, used in making perfume
Word history: from French words meaning 'grey amber'

ambi-
prefix a word part meaning 'both' or 'on both sides': *ambidextrous*
Word history: from Latin

ambidextrous
adjective able to use both hands equally well
Word building: **ambidexterity** *noun*

ambiguous (*say* am-big-yooh-uhs)
adjective with more than one meaning: *to give an ambiguous reply*

Word building: **ambiguity** *noun* (**ambiguities**)   **ambiguously** *adverb*

ambition
noun **1** strong desire for something in the future, especially money or fame: *to be poor but filled with ambition* **2** the object that is desired: *My ambition is to win the race.*
Word building: **ambitious** *adjective* **ambitiously** *adverb*

ambivalent (*say* am-biv-uh-luhnt)
adjective having opposite and conflicting feelings towards someone or something: *Although I enjoy parties I am ambivalent about going to one without my best friend.*
Word building: **ambivalence** *noun* **ambivalently** *adverb*

amble
verb to walk at a relaxed or comfortable pace
Word building: **ambling** *adjective*

ambulance
noun a vehicle which is specially equipped to carry sick or injured people and which is driven by experts in first aid

ambush
verb **1** to attack after lying in wait in a hidden place
noun **2** a sudden attack from a hidden place

amenable
adjective agreeable and cooperative: *amenable to the idea of a picnic*
Word building: **amenably** *adverb*

amend
verb **1** to alter: *to amend a law* **2** to improve or correct: *to amend bad behaviour*
Word building: **amendment** *noun*

amends
singular or plural noun in the phrase **make amends**, to make up for wrong or injury done: *to make amends for hurting someone*

amenity
noun anything which makes a place more comfortable and pleasant: *a motel with such amenities as hot showers, laundry, swimming pool and restaurant*
Word building: The plural is **amenities.**

amethyst   (*say* <u>am</u>-uh-thuhst)

noun a purple-coloured precious stone

Word history: from a Greek word meaning 'without drunkenness' (from the belief that the stone prevented intoxication)

amiable   (*say* <u>aym</u>-ee-uh-buhl)

adjective friendly and good-natured: *an amiable conversation*

Word building: **amiability** *noun*   **amiably** *adverb*

ammonia

noun a strong-smelling gas, often dissolved in water to make a liquid which may be used for cleaning

ammunition

noun powder or bullets used in firing guns or other weapons

amnesia

noun loss of memory: *He suffered from amnesia after he hit his head in the accident.*

amnesty

noun a pardon given to everyone, usually for crimes against a government

amoeba   (*say* uh-<u>mee</u>-buh)

noun a one-celled animal which can only be seen with a microscope

Word building: The plural is **amoebae** (*say* uh-<u>mee</u>-bee) or **amoebas**. | **amoebic** *adjective* Word history: from a Greek word meaning 'change'

among

preposition surrounded by: *Can you find the lemon among the oranges?*

amorous

adjective feeling or showing love, especially of a sexual kind: *an amorous person | an amorous smile*

Word building: **amorously** *adverb* **amorousness** *noun*

amount

noun **1** quantity or extent: *Is there a large or small amount of food left?* **2** total of two or more things: *What is the amount of the bill?* *phrase* **3 amount to**, to add up to or be equal to: *The cost of my Christmas shopping amounted to $20. | My dad's advice didn't amount to much in the end.*

ampere   (*say* am-pair)

noun a unit of measurement of an electric current

Word use: The symbol for ampere is **A**.

ampersand

noun the sign '&' which is used to mean 'and' as in *Cobb & Co.*

amphi-

prefix a word part meaning **1** of both kinds: *amphibian* **2** around: *amphitheatre*

Word history: from Greek

amphibian

noun an animal that begins life in the water and lives on land as an adult, such as a frog

Word building: **amphibious** *adjective* able to live or move both on land and in water

amphitheatre

noun a round building with an open area in the centre and rows of seats rising around it: *The ancient Romans watched plays in amphitheatres.*

ample

adjective **1** more than enough in size or amount: *There was ample space for us all to fit in.*
Other words: **abundant, copious, plentiful**
2 large or well filled out: *She has an ample figure.*

Word building: **ampleness** *noun* **amply** *adverb*

amplify

verb **1** to make louder: *The microphone will amplify my speech.* **2** to enlarge or expand by adding details: *Please amplify your story so that I can understand what happened.*

Word building: Other forms are **I amplified, I have amplified, I am amplifying.** | **amplification** *noun*

amputate

verb to cut off in a medical operation: *The doctor amputated his injured leg.*

Word building: **amputee** *noun* someone who has had a limb amputated **amputation** *noun*

amuse

verb **1** to entertain so that the time passes pleasantly: *The games amused the children for hours.*
Other words: **interest, occupy**
2 to make laugh or smile: *Your jokes amused them.*

Word building: **amusedly** *adverb* **amusingly** *adverb*

amusement

noun **1** the feeling of being amused
2 something which amuses, such as a
concert or a merry-go-round

an

indefinite article another form of the article
a, used when the following word begins
with a vowel sound (usually words starting
with *a, e, i, o* or *u*): *I just had an idea! |
What an unusual creature.*

anaemia   (*say* uh-<u>neem</u>-ee-uh)

noun a lack of red blood cells or red
colouring in the blood, making someone
look pale and weak

Word use: Another spelling is **anemia**.
Word building: **anaemic** *adjective* pale and
sickly

anaesthetic   (*say* an-uhs-<u>thet</u>-ik)

noun a drug that makes you unable to feel
pain: *He was given an anaesthetic before the
operation.*

Word use: Another spelling is **anesthetic**.
Word building: **anaesthetise** *verb* to make
unable to feel pain   **anaesthetist** *noun* the
doctor who gives an anaesthetic   **anaesthesia**
noun

anagram

noun a word made by changing the order
of the letters in another word: *'Caned' is an
anagram of 'dance'.*

analgesic   (*say* an-uhl-<u>jee</u>-zik)

noun a medicine that removes or lessens
pain

Word building: **analgesia** *noun* the inability
to feel pain   **analgesic** *adjective* causing the
removal of pain

analog

adjective showing measurement by use of a
display or pointer that keeps on changing,
such as the needle on a car speedometer: *an
analog watch*

Word use: Compare this with definition 2 of
digital.

analogy

noun a likeness between two or more
things which makes you compare them:
*Teachers sometimes draw an analogy between
the heart and a pump.*

Word building: The plural is **analogies**. |
analogous *adjective* similar   **analogously**
adverb

analyse

verb **1** to examine in detail in order to find
out the meaning: *to analyse behaviour | to
analyse a story* **2** to separate into parts: *The
scientist analysed the strange liquid.*

Word building: **analyst** *noun*   **analytical**
adjective   **analytically** *adverb*

analysis   (*say* uh-<u>nal</u>-uh-suhs)

noun **1** the act of analysing
2 separation into parts

Word use: Compare definition 2 with
synthesis.

Anangu   (*say* uh-<u>nang</u>-gooh)

noun an Aboriginal person from Central
Australia

anarchy   (*say* <u>an</u>-uh-kee)

noun **1** a society where there is no
government or law **2** any situation where
there is no control or rules: *There was
anarchy in the classroom when the teacher was
not there.*

Word building: **anarchism** *noun*   **anarchist**
noun
Word history: from a Greek word meaning
'lack of a ruler'

anatomy

noun **1** the structure of an animal or plant:
*Bones are an important part of the human
anatomy.* **2** the study or science of the
structure of animals and plants

Word building: **anatomical** *adjective*
anatomist *noun*

ancestor

noun someone related to you who lived
long ago: *What country did your ancestors
come from?*

Word use: The study of who your ancestors
were is called **genealogy**.
Word building: **ancestral** *adjective*   **ancestrally**
adverb   **ancestry** *noun*

anchor   (*rhymes with* banker)

noun a heavy object chained to a boat and
dropped into the water to stop it from
floating away

Word building: **anchor** *verb*   **anchorage** *noun*

anchovy   (*say* <u>an</u>-chuh-vee)

noun a small fish with a very salty taste,
often made into a paste for eating

Word building: The plural is **anchovies**.

ancient   (*say* <u>ayn</u>-shuhnt)

adjective **1** happening or living long ago: *ancient history*; *the ancient Romans* **2** very old: *an ancient man* | *an ancient book*

and

conjunction **1** with, as well as: *pens and pencils* **2** as a result: *Study hard and you will get a good mark in your test.* **3** afterwards: *Brush your teeth and go to bed.*

Word use: This word is used for connecting words, phrases or clauses.

andante   (*say* an-<u>dan</u>-tay)

adverb played or sung fairly slowly and evenly

Word use: This is an instruction in music.
Word history: from an Italian word meaning 'walking'

anecdote   (*say* <u>an</u>-uhk-doht)

noun a short story that tells about a funny or interesting person or event: *I can tell you a lot of anecdotes about our holiday.*

Word building: **anecdotal** *adjective*

anemone   (*say* uh-<u>nem</u>-uh-nee)

noun **1** a small flower, usually red, blue or white **2** an animal that lives in the sea and catches food with its tentacles

Word use: Another name for definition 2 is **sea anemone**.
Word history: from a Greek word meaning 'windflower'

angel   (*say* <u>ayn</u>-juhl)

noun **1** in Judaism, Christianity and Islam, one of God's messengers or attendants, usually pictured to look like humans with wings **2** someone who is very kind, good or beautiful

Word building: **angelic** *adjective*   **angelically** *adverb*

---

angel/angle Don't confuse **angel** with **angle**, which is the point where two lines or surfaces meet. We pronounce it ang-*guhl*.

---

anger

noun **1** a strong feeling of annoyance caused by thinking that something wrong has been done to you
verb **2** to make angry: *Your rudeness angered me.*

angle¹

noun **1** the pointed shape made when two straight lines or surfaces meet each other: *The streets met at a sharp angle.* **2** point of view: *a new angle on the problem*
verb **3** to bend, move or place at an angle: *Consuelo angled the ball away from the fielder.* **4** to put a bias or slant on: *The barrister angled the question to suit the argument.*

angle²

verb to fish with a hook and line

Word building: **angler** *noun*

angry

adjective feeling or showing anger: *an angry person* | *an angry look*
Other words: **annoyed, cranky, cross, fuming, furious, incensed, irate, livid, mad**

Word use: You are angry *with* or *at* a person, but you are angry *about* or *at* a thing or something that has happened.
Word building: Other forms are **angrier, angriest.** | **angrily** *adverb*

anguish

noun very great pain, sorrow or worry: *The parents suffered anguish over their daughter's disappearance.*

Word building: **anguish** *verb*

angular

adjective having a pointed or sharp shape like an angle: *The model's face had angular features.*

Word building: **angularity** *noun*

animal

noun **1** a living thing that is not a plant and can feel and move about **2** any animal except a human being: *Many people keep animals as pets.* **3** someone who is rough and badly-behaved

animate   (*say* <u>an</u>-uh-mayt)

verb **1** to make lively and energetic: *The thought of going to the beach animated the whole class.* **2** to make move as if alive: *to animate cartoons*
adjective (*say* <u>an</u>-uh-muht)
3 alive: *animate creatures*

Word building: **animated** *adjective*   **animation** *noun*

animation   (*say* an-uh-<u>may</u>-shuhn)
noun **1** the art of creating films with drawings of funny characters that appear to move and act like humans or animals: *He is great at drawing and wants to do animation when he grows up.*
2 liveliness: *The whole class was full of animation at the prospect of going to the beach.*

animosity
noun a strong feeling of dislike or unfriendliness: *She looked at her enemy with animosity.*

aniseed
noun a strong-smelling seed which is used in cooking and medicines

ankle
noun the part of the body which joins the foot to the leg

anklet
noun an ornament worn around the ankle

annals   (*say* <u>an</u>-uhlz)
plural noun historical records that are kept year by year
Word building: **annalist** *noun*

annex
verb to obtain and join to what is already owned: *The farmer annexed the neighbouring land.*
Word building: **annexation** *noun*

annexe
noun a building added on to a larger building

annihilate   (*say* uh-<u>nuy</u>-uh-layt)
verb to destroy or defeat completely: *They annihilated the enemy's army.*
Word building: **annihilation** *noun*

anniversary
noun a yearly celebration of something which took place in an earlier year: *our fifth wedding anniversary*
Word building: The plural is **anniversaries**.

announce
verb to tell or make known in public: *Felicity announced that she was leaving school.*
Other words: **declare**
Word building: **announcement** *noun*

announcer
noun someone on radio or television who talks about or introduces a program

annoy
verb to irritate or make cranky: *Very loud music annoys me.*
Other words: **aggravate, bother, irk**
Word building: **annoyance** *noun*

annual
adjective **1** happening once a year: *Our school sports day is an annual event.*
noun **2** a plant that lives for one season or year
3 a book or magazine published once a year
Word building: **annually** *adverb*

anoint
verb to put ointment or oil on: *The priest anointed the dying man.*
Word building: **anointment** *noun*

anonymous   (*say* uh-<u>non</u>-uh-muhs)
adjective having no name given: *The book was written by an anonymous author.*
Word building: **anonymity** *noun* **anonymously** *adverb*

anorexia   (*say* ana-<u>rek</u>-see-uh)
noun **1** a lack or loss of appetite for food **2** an illness in which the person has an obsessive desire to lose weight by refusing to eat
Word use: Definition 2 is a short way of saying **anorexia nervosa**.
Word building: **anorexic** *adjective*

another
pronoun **1** one more: *Can I please have another piece of cake?*
adjective **2** a different: *I am going to try another program today.*

answer
noun **1** a reply or response **2** a solution to a problem
Other words: **remedy**
verb **3** to respond or reply: *She answered with a nod.* **4** to reply to: *Hurry up and answer the question.*
phrase **5 answer back**, to make a rude or cheeky reply

answerable
adjective **1** responsible: *I am answerable for my child's safety.* **2** able to be solved or answered

answering machine

noun a machine connected to the telephone that records messages which can be played back afterwards

ant

noun a small insect that usually lives in a large family group or community called a colony

antagonise (*say* an-tag-uh-nuyz)

verb to make angry or make an enemy of: *The bully antagonised the children by spoiling their game.*

Word use: Another spelling is **antagonize**.
Word building: **antagonist** *noun* an enemy or opponent **antagonism** *noun* **antagonistic** *adjective*

antarctic (*say* ant-ahk-tik)

adjective **1** having to do with the area near the South Pole
noun **2 the Antarctic,** the area near the South Pole

Word use: Another name for definition 2 is **Antarctica**.
Word history: from a Greek word meaning 'opposite the north'

ante-

prefix a word part meaning 'before in space or time': *antecedent*

Word history: from Latin

anteater

noun an animal with a long sticky tongue that feeds on ants or termites

Word use: Different varieties are called **echidnas** or **numbats**.

antecedent (*say* ant-uh-seed-uhnt)

noun anything that goes before another

antelope

noun a slightly-built and swift animal which has horns, chews its cud and is related to cattle, sheep and goats

antenna

noun **1** a sense organ or feeler found on the head of insects or crabs **2** a radio or television aerial

Word building: The plural is **antennae** for definition 1, and **antennas** for definition 2.

anthem

noun **1** a ceremonial song for an organisation or country: *'Advance Australia Fair' is Australia's national anthem.*
2 a hymn

anthology

noun a collection of poems, plays or short stories by various authors or from various books

Word building: The plural is **anthologies**. | **anthologist** *noun*
Word history: from a Greek word meaning 'a gathering of flowers'

anthropogenic

(*say* an-thruh-puh-jen-ik)
adjective caused by human beings: *anthropogenic climate change*

anthropology

noun the scientific study of the beginnings and growth of humankind

Word building: **anthropologist** *noun*

anti-

prefix a word part meaning **1** against: *antibiotic* **2** opposed to: *anticlockwise*

Word use: Another spelling is **ant-**.
Word history: from Greek

antibiotic

noun a drug capable of killing bacteria and other germs

Word building: **antibiotic** *adjective*

anticipate

verb **1** to know or realise in advance what is going to happen or what to expect: *to anticipate the disaster* | *to anticipate the excitement of Christmas* **2** to think of or mention before the proper time: *To anticipate your objection, I think you're being too cautious.*

Word building: **anticipation** *noun* **anticipatory** *adjective*

anticlimax

noun a disappointing, or less exciting than expected, ending or result: *The ending of the movie was such an anticlimax.*

Word building: **anticlimactic** *adjective*

anticlockwise

adjective going round in the opposite direction to the hands on a clock face

Word use: The opposite of this is **clockwise**.

antics

plural noun odd or silly behaviour

antidote

noun something to stop the bad effects caused by a disease or a poison: *The doctor gave Hiroko the antidote for the spider bite.*

antipathy   (*say* an-<u>tip</u>-uh-thee)
noun a feeling of strong dislike: *The dog
had a strong antipathy to strangers.*

Word building: **antipathetic** *adjective*

antipodes   (*say* an-<u>tip</u>-uh-deez)
plural noun **1** places directly opposite
each other on the earth **2 the Antipodes,**
Australia as the antipodes of Britain

Word building: **antipodean** *adjective*

antiquated   (*say* <u>an</u>-tuh-kway-tuhd)
adjective old-fashioned or out of date: *an
antiquated textbook*

Word building: **antiquary** *noun* an expert on
ancient things   **antiquarian** *adjective*

antique   (*say* an-<u>teek</u>)
noun an object of art or piece of furniture
which was made long ago: *I collect antiques.*

Word building: **antique** *adjective* dating from
earlier times
Word history: from a Latin word meaning 'old'

antiquity   (*say* an-<u>tik</u>-wuh-tee)
noun **1** ancient times or the early stages
of history **2** great age: *a family of great
antiquity*

Word building: The plural is **antiquities**.

antiseptic
noun a chemical used to kill germs that
produce disease

Word building: **antiseptic** *adjective*

antithesis   (*say* an-<u>tith</u>-uh-suhs)
noun **1** the direct opposite: *Andrew was
the antithesis of a good student.* **2** a contrast
between two opposites: *the antithesis
between light and dark*

Word building: The plural is **antitheses**.

antivenene   (*say* an-tee-vuh-<u>neen</u>)
noun an injection to fight the venom from
a spider or snake bite

antler
noun a long, hard, branch-like horn on
the head of a male deer and other similar
animals

antonym   (*say* <u>ant</u>-uh-nim)
noun a word which has an opposite
meaning to another word: *'Fast' is the
antonym of 'slow'.*

anus
noun the opening in someone's bottom
where waste material from the bowel
comes out

Word building: **anal** *adjective*

anvil
noun a heavy iron block with a smooth
surface on which hot metals are hammered
and shaped before they go cold and hard

anxiety   (*say* ang-<u>zuy</u>-uh-tee)
noun **1** worry or uneasy feelings: *A parent
feels anxiety if their child becomes lost.*
2 eagerness: *My anxiety to do well made me
try harder.*

Word building: The plural is **anxieties**.

anxious   (*say* <u>ang</u>-shuhs)
adjective **1** full of anxiety or worry: *I was
very anxious about my sick dog.*
Other words: **concerned, distressed,
nervous, troubled**
2 eager: *I was anxious to please my parents.*
Other words: **desperate, keen**

Word building: **anxiously** *adverb*

any   (*say* <u>en</u>-ee)
adjective one or some: *Have you got any
lollies in your packet?*

anyhow
adverb **1** anyway, in any case: *I forgot my
swimming costume, but I don't want to go
swimming anyhow.* **2** carelessly: *She tossed
her books in her bag anyhow.*

anyone
pronoun any person: *Is anyone home?*

Word use: Another word for this is **anybody**.

anything
pronoun any thing at all, or any kind of
thing: *Is there anything in that drawer? | We
like all types of food, so bring anything you
like.*

anyway
adverb anyhow, in any case: *It's about
to rain, but I'm going to go for a swim
anyway.*

anywhere
adverb in, at or to any place: *We can go
anywhere you like on our holiday.*

Anzac

noun **1** the name given to a member of the Australian and New Zealand Army Corps during World War I: *The Anzacs fought their first battle at Gallipoli.* **2** a soldier from Australia or New Zealand

adjective **3** relating to Anzacs, Anzac Day, or the events at Gallipoli in World War I: *the Anzac spirit*

Word history: an acronym made by joining the first letters of the words *Australian and New Zealand Army Corps*

Anzac biscuit

noun a biscuit made from flour, oats, coconut, and a sweet syrup

aorta   (*say* ay-<u>aw</u>-tuh)

noun the main artery carrying blood from the left side of the heart to nearly all parts of the body

Word building: **aortic** *adjective*

apart

adverb **1** to pieces: *He took the calculator apart to see how it worked.* **2** separated or not together: *You must keep these animals apart.*

Word building: **apart** *adjective*

apartheid   (*say* uh-<u>paht</u>-hayt)

noun a policy of the separation of races in a country according to their differences in colour: *In a country which has a policy of apartheid, white people do not mix with black people.*

apartment

noun **1** a single room or set of rooms, among others in a building **2** a home unit

apathy   (*say* <u>ap</u>-uh-thee)

noun no feeling for, or interest in things other people find interesting or exciting: *Ameenah was sunk in apathy after her father's death.*

Word building: **apathetic** *adjective* **apathetically** *adverb*

ape

noun **1** a large monkey without a tail verb **2** to imitate or copy: *The child aped the strange way the clown was walking.*

aperture   (*say* <u>ap</u>-uh-chuh)

noun a hole, crack or other opening, especially the opening in a camera that limits the amount of light it lets in

apex

noun the peak, summit or highest point: *Every mountain has an apex.*

Word building: The plural is **apexes** or **apices**.

aphid   (*say* <u>ay</u>-fuhd)

noun a small insect which sucks the sap from plants

Word use: It is also called **aphis**.
Word building: The plural is **aphides**.

apiary

noun a place where beehives are kept

Word building: The plural is **apiaries**. | **apiarist** *noun*

aplomb   (*say* uh-<u>plom</u>)

noun the ability to handle difficult or unusual situations: *Our school captain introduced the guest speaker with aplomb.*

apocalypse   (*say* uh-<u>pok</u>-uh-lips)

noun the discovery or revealing of some great event, such as the end of the world

Word building: **apocalyptic** *adjective*

apologise

verb to say you are sorry: *She apologised for being late.*

Word use: Another spelling is **apologize**.
Word building: **apologetic** *adjective* full of regret   **apology** *noun* (**apologies**)

apostle   (*say* uh-<u>pos</u>-uhl)

noun someone who strongly supports a new idea: *an apostle of change in education*

Word building: **apostolic** *adjective* having to do with an apostle, or with the pope
Word history: from a Greek word meaning 'someone sent away'

apostrophe   (*say* uh-<u>pos</u>-truh-fee)

noun **1** a punctuation mark (') used to show that a letter has been left out, as in *They're here.* **2** a sign (') used with *s* to show that something is owned, as in *Tom's pencil case* and *the lions' manes*

There are two reasons why you use **apostrophes:**

(i) to show that something has been left out of a word: *they've gone*

(ii) to show ownership: *Juanita's skateboard*

(i) You use an apostrophe to show that you have left a letter (or sometimes more than one letter) out of a word or phrase:

it's	it is
she'll	she will
I've	I have
all's well	all is well
John'll	John will (or shall)
might've	might have

These are called <u>contractions</u>. They are quite common in speech, but usually avoided in formal writing.

(ii) You use an apostrophe when you want to show that something belongs to a person or thing.

(a) When a word is <u>singular</u>, whether it already ends in an <u>s</u> or not, you add an apostrophe and then an <u>s</u> at the end of the word:

The bike's wheel came loose.
Here is Chris's computer game.

(b) When a word is <u>plural</u>, if it already ends in an <u>s</u>, you simply add an apostrophe at the end of the word, not an <u>s</u> as well:

All the girls' fathers came to the meeting.

(c) When a word is plural but does not end in an <u>s</u>, you add an apostrophe and then an <u>s</u> as well:

The children's playground was unsafe.

Note that apostrophes are often not used in the titles of institutions, organisations and so on:

Girls High School
Secondary Teachers College

These days apostrophes are often left out of <u>plural</u> words in expressions of time:

five weeks time
two months holiday

However the apostrophe should be there if the time word is <u>singular</u>:

a week's time
one month's holiday

Its and it's
A tricky point to remember is that *it's* is short for *it is*, whereas *its* (without an apostrophe) shows ownership.

The dog wagged its tail.
It's raining cats and dogs.

One way of remembering this is to remind yourself that *its* is a pronoun like *her* and *his*, and they don't have apostrophes for ownership.

Beware!
Never use an apostrophe with ordinary plural words. For example, you wouldn't write *Banana's for sale.* But when letters are used as words, we use apostrophes to avoid confusion and to make the text easier to read:

Dot the i's and cross the t's.

app
noun a short form of **applications program**

appal
verb to make very fearful: *The thought of nuclear war appals me.*

Word building: Other forms are **it appalled, it has appalled, it is appalling.**
Word history: from a French word meaning 'become or make pale'

apparatus   *(say* ap-uh-<u>rah</u>-tuhs*)*
noun a collection of tools or machines used for a particular purpose: *the apparatus used by firefighters*
Other words: **equipment, gear**

Word building: The plural is **apparatus** or **apparatuses.**

apparel
noun your outer clothing
Word use: The more usual word is **clothes.**

apparent
adjective **1** able to be seen or understood: *My spelling error was apparent when I checked in the dictionary.* **2** seeming, not necessarily real: *the apparent motion of the sun*
Word use: The more usual word for definition 1 is **obvious.**
Word building: **apparently** *adverb*

apparition
noun something that appears in an unusual way: *A ghostly apparition in the empty house frightened me.*
Other words: **ghost, phantom, spectre, spirit**

appeal
noun **1** a call or request for something needed: *The school made an appeal for money for a new library.*
Other words: **entreaty, plea**
2 the ability to attract or interest: *Sport has an appeal for most people.*
Other words: **allure, attraction, charm, draw, fascination, pull**
verb **3** to make an appeal: *They appealed for help.*
Other words: **ask, plead**
Word building: **appealing** *adjective*

appear
verb **1** to come into sight: *The sun appeared over the horizon.* **2** to seem or have a certain look: *The chairperson appears to be sick.*
Word building: **appearance** *noun*

appease

verb **1** to make peaceful, quiet or happy: *He appeased the angry customer.*
2 to satisfy: *to appease hunger*

Word building: **appeasement** *noun*

appendicitis   (*say* uh-pen-duh-<u>suy</u>-tuhs)

noun a painful inflammation of the appendix

appendix

noun **1** a section added to the main part of a book to give extra information **2** a small tube-like piece of flesh joined to the bowel in the right side of the abdomen

Word building: The plural is **appendixes** or **appendices**.

appetising

adjective looking or smelling good to eat: *the appetising smell of roast lamb*

Word use: Another spelling is **appetizing**.
Word building: **appetiser** *noun* food or drink that makes you feel like eating more

appetite

noun **1** the wish for food or drink: *Exercise gives you a good appetite.* **2** an interest in something or a desire for something: *She has an endless appetite for reading mystery stories.*

applaud

verb to praise or express approval, especially by clapping your hands or calling out: *The audience applauded the actors in the play.*

Word building: **applause** *noun*

apple

noun a crisp round fruit with thin red or green skin

applet

noun a small computer program which can be transferred over the internet to a person's own computer, and which then runs on the person's computer instead of on the server

appliance

noun a tool which has a motor worked by electricity: *My mother has some useful kitchen appliances.*

applicable   (*say* uh-<u>plik</u>-uh-buhl)

adjective suitable or able to be used: *a rule only applicable to children*

Word building: **applicability** *noun*   **applicably** *adverb*

applicant

noun someone who applies for something: *an applicant for a job*
Other words: **candidate, contender**

application

noun **1** a request: *to make an application for a job* **2** something put or laid on: *an application of paint* **3** the quality of being useful for a particular purpose: *a tool with many applications* **4** hard work or close attention: *The teacher praised them for their application to their studies.*

applications program

noun a computer program written to perform a special task

Word use: A shortened form of this is **app**.

apply   (*rhymes with* fly)

verb **1** to put yourself forward to be considered for a job, an award, a place at a university, and so on **2** to put on: *to apply make-up* **3** to put to use: *to apply rules*

Word building: Other forms are **I applied, I have applied, I am applying.** | **applied** *adjective* put to practical use: *applied science*   **applier** *noun*

appoint

verb to choose for special duties: *The principal appointed the school captain.*
Other words: **commission, name, select**

Word building: **appointee** *noun*

appointment

noun **1** the arrangement of a special time: *an appointment to see the dentist* **2** the placing of someone in a special position: *the appointment of a new school captain* **3** the job or special position to which someone is appointed

appraise

verb to judge the value of: *The judges appraised the paintings in the competition.*

Word use: The more usual word is **assess**.
Word building: **appraisal** *noun*

appreciable   (*say* uh-<u>preesh</u>-uhb-uhl)

adjective **1** able to be seen or noticed: *There has been an appreciable increase in the number of people who do not smoke.*
2 fairly large: *We have travelled an appreciable distance.*

Word building: **appreciably** *adverb*

appreciate

verb **1** to think highly of: *I appreciate your help.*
Other words: **prize, value**
2 to understand or be aware of: *I don't think you appreciate the danger of going ahead with your plan.*
Word building: **appreciation** *noun* **appreciative** *adjective*

apprehend

verb to take into keeping: *The police apprehended the thieves.*
Word use: The more usual word is **catch**.

apprehension

noun fear that something bad might happen: *I went to the principal filled with apprehension.*
Word building: **apprehensive** *adjective*

apprentice

noun someone who is learning a trade
Word building: **apprenticeship** *noun*

approach

verb **1** to come near to: *to approach your house* **2** to come to with a request or an idea: *I approached the principal for permission to leave early.*

approachable

adjective friendly and easy to talk to: *My teacher is very approachable.*

appropriate (*say* uh-proh-pree-uht)

adjective **1** suitable for a particular use: *appropriate clothes for wet weather*
verb (*say* uh-proh-pree-ayt) **2** to take for your own use: *She appropriated Sheng's desk.*
Word building: **appropriately** *adverb* **appropriateness** *noun* **appropriation** *noun*

approval

noun agreement or permission: *The teacher needed the principal's approval before sending the class home.*

approve

verb **1** to agree to: *My father approved my plan.*
phrase **2 approve of**, to consider good or satisfactory: *to approve of your attitude*

approximate

adjective nearly right: *Tell me the approximate number of children in the class.*
Word building: **approximately** *adverb* **approximation** *noun*

apricot

noun a small, round, yellow fruit with soft juicy flesh and one large seed inside

April (*say* ayp-ruhl)

noun the fourth month of the year, with 30 days
Word use: The abbreviation is **Ap** or **Apr**.

apron

noun a piece of clothing worn in front to protect the clothes underneath it
Word history: from a Latin word meaning 'napkin' or 'cloth'

apt

adjective **1** likely or inclined: *The baby is apt to cry when his mother leaves the room.*
2 suitable or appropriate: *an apt remark*
3 quick to learn: *an apt pupil*
Word building: **aptly** *adverb* **aptness** *noun*

aptitude

noun the ability to learn quickly: *an aptitude for music*

aqualung

noun a cylinder of air strapped to the back of a diver, with a tube that takes air to the mouth or nose

aquamarine

noun a greenish-blue stone used in jewellery
Word history: from Latin words meaning 'sea water'

aquarium (*say* uh-kwair-ree-uhm)

noun a glass tank in which fish and water plants are kept
Word building: The plural is **aquariums** or **aquaria**.

aquatic (*say* uh-kwot-ik)

adjective **1** living or growing in water
2 done in or on water: *aquatic sports*

aqueduct (*say* ak-wuh-dukt)

noun a bridge built for carrying a water pipe or channel across a valley

aquiline

adjective curved or hooked like an eagle's beak: *an aquiline nose*

arable
adjective suitable for growing crops: *arable land*

Word history: from a Latin word meaning 'that can be ploughed'

arbitrary
adjective based on your own feelings and ideas rather than on rules or reasons: *an arbitrary decision*

Word building: **arbitrarily** *adverb* **arbitrariness** *noun*

arbitration
noun the settling of a disagreement by someone chosen to do so

Word building: **arbitrate** *verb* **arbitrator** *noun*

arboreal   (*say* ah-<u>baw</u>-ree-uhl)
adjective having to do with, or living in trees: *Monkeys are arboreal animals.*

arbour
noun a shady place formed by trees and shrubs

Word use: Another spelling is **arbor**.

arc
noun a curved line

Word history: from a Latin word meaning a 'bow'

arc/ark Don't confuse **arc** with **ark**, which is a large boat like the one that Noah and the animals lived in during the Flood, as the story is told in the Bible.

arcade
noun a covered passage with shops on either side

arch
noun **1** a curved structure which helps support a bridge or building or forms the top of a doorway
verb **2** to curve or make into a curved shape: *A horse arches its neck.*

Word building: Other verb forms are **it arched, it has arched, it is arching**. | The plural form of the noun is **arches**.

archaeology   (*say* ah-kee-<u>ol</u>-uh-jee)
noun the study of the people and customs of ancient times made by digging up and describing the remains of buried cities, tombs, and so on

Word use: Another spelling is **archeology**.
Word building: **archaeologist** *noun* **archaeological** *adjective*

archaic   (*say* ah-<u>kay</u>-ik)
adjective so old-fashioned that it is not used any more: *an archaic word*

Word building: **archaism** *noun*

archangel   (*say* <u>ahk</u>-ayn-juhl)
noun one of the chief angels

archbishop
noun a head bishop

archer
noun someone who shoots with a bow and arrows

Word building: **archery** *noun*

archipelago   (*say* ah-kuh-<u>pel</u>-uh-goh)
noun **1** a large body of water with many islands **2** a group of islands in a sea

Word building: The plural is **archipelagos** or **archipelagoes**.
Word history: from an Italian word meaning 'the chief sea'

architect   (*say* <u>ah</u>-kuh-tekt)
noun someone whose job is to plan new buildings and make sure they are built correctly

Word history: from a Greek word meaning 'the chief builder'

architecture
noun the art or science of drawing up plans for buildings

Word building: **architectural** *adjective*

architrave   (*say* <u>ah</u>-kuh-trayv)
noun the frame around a doorway or window

archives   (*say* <u>ah</u>-kuyvz)
plural noun a collection of historical documents about a family, business or country: *The archives are kept in the library.*

Word building: **archival** *adjective* **archivist** *noun*

arctic
adjective **1** having to do with the area near the North Pole **2** very cold
noun **3 the Arctic**, the area near the North Pole

Word history: from a Greek word meaning 'of the bear' (constellation of stars) or 'northern'

ardent
adjective enthusiastic or full of feeling: *an ardent admirer of poetry | ardent promises of lasting love*

Word building: **ardency** *noun* **ardently** *adverb*

ardour (*rhymes with* harder)

noun **1** a very strong feeling: *the ardour of love for your country* **2** eagerness or enthusiasm: *Rain does not dampen our ardour for bushwalking.*

Word use: Another spelling is **ardor**.

arduous

adjective needing a lot of hard work: *Climbing mountains is an arduous sport.*
Other words: **difficult, exhausting, laborious, strenuous, taxing, tiring**

area

noun **1** a particular part: *a suburban area | a quiet area*
Other words: **precinct, quarter, section, zone**
2 the size of a flat or curved surface: *The area of this hall is 100 square metres.*

arena

noun an enclosed space for sports events

Word history: from a Latin word meaning 'sand' or 'sandy place'

arguable

adjective **1** able to be proved by argument: *He put forward an arguable case for having classroom monitors.* **2** doubtful

Word building: **arguably** *adverb*

argue

verb to quarrel or disagree: *Ashur argued with Hanna about which film to see.*
Other words: **bicker, dispute, feud, fight, squabble, wrangle**

Word building: Other forms are **I argued, I have argued, I am arguing.**

argument

noun **1** a quarrel or disagreement **2** a reason: *a good argument for doing exercises*

argumentative

adjective liking to argue or quarrelsome: *an argumentative person*

aria (*say* ah-ree-uh)

noun a song sung by one person in an opera

arid

adjective dry and hot: *an arid desert*
Word building: **aridity** *noun*

arise

verb **1** to appear or come into being: *The question of new school colours may arise.* **2** to rise or move upwards: *They told us to arise and follow them.*

Word building: Other forms are **I arose, I have arisen, I am arising.**

aristocracy (*say* a-ruh-stok-ruh-see)

noun the people of highest rank, usually by birth
Other words: **nobility**

aristocrat (*say* a-ruh-stuh-krat)

noun someone who belongs to the nobility of a country, such as a duchess or an earl

Word building: **aristocratic** *adjective* **aristocratically** *adverb*

arithmetic

noun calculation with numbers

Word building: **arithmetical** *adjective* **arithmetician** *noun*

ark

noun the large covered boat like the one built by Noah to escape from the Flood, as the story is told in the Bible

ark/arc Don't confuse **ark** with **arc**, which is a curve.

arm[1]

noun **1** the part of your body from shoulder to hand **2** the part of a chair on which your arm rests

arm[2]

verb to supply weapons to

Word building: **armed** *adjective*: *the armed forces*

armada (*say* ah-mah-duh)

noun a large number of warships

armadillo (*say* ah-muh-dil-oh)

noun a South American burrowing animal with a covering of bony plates

Word building: The plural is **armadillos**.

armament

noun the weapons on an aeroplane or warship

armistice (*say* ahm-uh-stuhs)

noun an agreement between countries at war to stop fighting and talk about peace
Other words: **truce**

armour

noun **1** metal or leather covering that knights used to wear when fighting **2** the protective plates on army tanks and naval ships

Word use: Another spelling is **armor**.
Word building: **armoured** *adjective*: *an armoured car*

armoury

noun a place for storing weapons

Word use: Another spelling is **armory**.
Word building: The plural is **armouries**.

armpit

noun the hollow part under your arm at the shoulder

arms

plural noun weapons: *The soldiers were given arms to fight with.*

army

noun **1** the part of a country's armed forces which is trained to fight on land **2** a large number: *An army of workers cleaned up after the fire.*

Word building: The plural is **armies**.

army reserve

noun a part of the army which is not used all the time but available when there is a special need: *The army reserve was brought in to help with the bushfires.*

aroma

noun a pleasant smell: *the aroma of coffee*
Other words: **bouquet, fragrance, perfume, scent**

Word building: **aromatic** *adjective*
Word history: from a Greek word meaning 'spice' or 'sweet herb'

around

adverb **1** in a circle on every side of: *We stood around the tree.* **2** here and there: *to drive around* **3** in a circular movement: *The hands of the clock went slowly around.* *preposition* **4** surrounding: *She wore a scarf around her neck.* **5** on the other side of: *the shop around the corner* **6** about, approximately: *Let's meet around lunchtime.*

arouse

verb **1** to bring into being: *to arouse doubts* **2** to wake from sleep

Word building: **arousal** *noun*

arpeggio (say ah-pej-ee-oh)

noun a musical chord played by sounding its notes one after the other

Word building: The plural is **arpeggios**.
Word history: from an Italian word meaning 'play on the harp'

arrange

verb **1** to put in order: *to arrange books alphabetically on a shelf*
Other words: **array, group, organise, place, position**
2 to plan: *to arrange a party*
Other words: **organise, prepare**

Word building: **arrangement** *noun*

array

verb **1** to put into position: *The soldiers were arrayed for battle.*
noun **2** a group of things on show: *an excellent array of children's art*

arrest

verb **1** to take prisoner: *The policeman arrested the thief.* **2** to stop: *The bags of sand arrested the flood waters.*
noun **3** capture by police: *under arrest*

arrive

verb **1** to reach the end of a journey **2** to come: *The moment has arrived.* | *She arrived just before the end.*

Word building: **arrival** *noun*
Word history: from a Latin word meaning 'come to shore'

arrogant (say a-ruh-guhnt)

adjective showing that you think you are very important

Word building: **arrogance** *noun* **arrogantly** *adverb*

arrow

noun **1** a thin, pointed piece of wood shot from a bow **2** a sign used to point the way to go

arrowroot

noun a white floury substance used in cooking

arsenal

noun a store of weapons and ammunition

arsenic

noun a poisonous chemical substance

arson

noun the deliberate burning of a building or other valuable property

Word building: **arsonist** *noun*

art

noun **1** the production and expression of what is beautiful, especially by painting, drawing or sculpture **2** the beautiful things people make: *Our city has a building where works of art are kept.* **3** a skill: *There is an art in making good furniture.*

artefact   (*say* ah-tuh-fakt)

noun a useful thing made by someone

Word use: Another spelling is **artifact**.

artery

noun a blood vessel which takes blood from the heart to other parts of the body

Word building: The plural is **arteries**. | **arterial** *adjective*

artesian bore   (*say* ah-tee-zhuhn baw)

noun a well sunk through a layer of rock holding water, in which pressure keeps the water rising to the surface and pumping is not needed

Word use: Another name is **artesian well**.

arthritis   (*say* ah-thruy-tuhs)

noun a disease that causes swelling and pain in the joints of the body

Word building: **arthritic** *adjective*

artichoke

noun a thick round flower which grows on a thistle-like plant and is used as a vegetable

article

noun **1** a particular thing: *an article of clothing*
Other words: **item, object, piece**
2 a piece of writing about a particular subject in a newspaper or magazine
Other words: **column, item, story**
3 a word, such as *a, an* and *the*, which comes before a noun to show if it relates to one particular person or thing

articulate   (*say* ah-tik-yuh-layt)

verb **1** to speak clearly: *He articulated every word so that everyone could hear.*
adjective (*say* ah-tik-yuh-luht) **2** able to put your ideas clearly into words

Word building: **articulately** *adverb* **articulation** *noun*

articulated

adjective connected by joints, either ones that can move or ones that cannot: *an articulated truck*

artificial

adjective made by human beings: *artificial flowers*
Other words: **imitation, manufactured, synthetic**

Word use: The opposite of this is **natural**.
Word building: **artificiality** *noun* **artificially** *adverb*

artillery

noun **1** large guns on wheels **2** the part of an army that uses these guns

artisan

noun a skilled worker who makes things

artist

noun **1** someone who creates beautiful things, such as a painter or sculptor **2** a performer or entertainer

Word building: **artistic** *noun* able to create beautiful things **artistically** *adverb* **artistry** *noun*

arvo

noun *Informal* a short form of **afternoon**

as

adverb **1** to the same degree or amount: *as good as gold*
conjunction **2** though: *Funny as it was, the movie was far too long.* **3** while: *As the sun came up, the birds began to sing.* **4** because or since: *I'll get something for dinner, as I'm going to the shops anyway.*

asbestos

noun a grey substance which is mined, and was once used to make fireproof materials

ascend

verb to climb or go upwards: *I ascended the ladder.* | *Smoke ascended from the chimney.*

Word use: The opposite is **descend**.
Word building: **ascent** *noun* **ascension** *noun* an upward movement. Christ's rising from earth to heaven is called the **Ascension**.

ascertain   (*say* as-uh-tayn)

verb to find out or determine: *to ascertain the truth*

Word building: **ascertainable** *adjective* **ascertainment** *noun*

ascetic (*say* uh-<u>set</u>-ik)
noun someone who, for religious reasons, lives simply without many of the usual comforts of life

Word building: **ascetically** *adverb* **asceticism** *noun*
Word history: from a Greek word meaning 'monk' or 'hermit'

ash¹
noun **1** the powder left after something has been burnt: *cigarette ash | hot ash*
2 ashes, what is left after a human body has been cremated

Word use: Definition 1 is often plural as in *The ashes are in the fireplace.*
Word building: **ashy** *adjective* (**ashier, ashiest**)

ash²
noun a tree from which we get a valuable hard timber

ashamed
adjective **1** feeling shame or sorrow: *After I hit the dog I felt ashamed.* **2** unwilling because you're afraid of being laughed at: *ashamed to put your hand up*

Word building: **ashamedly** *adverb*

aside
adverb **1** on or to one side: *to turn aside*
noun **2** words spoken quietly so that only some people present can hear: *'Curses! Foiled again', said the villain in an aside to the audience.*

ask
verb **1** to inquire about: *I will ask the way.*
2 to put a question to: *The teacher asked me for the name of the national capital.*
3 to invite: *I will ask her to the party.*

askance (*say* uh-<u>skans</u>)
adverb showing distrust: *He looked askance at my offer.*

askew (*rhymes with* few)
adverb out of position: *He knocked my hat askew.*
Other words: **awry**

asleep
adverb **1** in or into a state of sleep: *I fell asleep.*
adjective **2** sleeping: *He is asleep.*
3 numb: *My foot is asleep.*

asp
noun a small venomous snake found in Egypt

asparagus
noun a plant with long green shoots, used as a vegetable

aspect
noun **1** the way a thing appears: *the burnt aspect of the land after the bushfire | to think about every aspect of a problem*
2 the direction a building faces: *a northern aspect*

Asperger's syndrome
(*say* <u>as</u>-per-guhz sin-drohm, <u>as</u>-per-juhz, as-<u>per</u>-guhz, as-<u>per</u>-juhz)
noun a condition that causes people not to understand how to relate to people around them, affecting their behaviour in different ways

asperity
noun roughness or harshness of manner: *He spoke me with some asperity in his voice.*

aspersion
noun a harmful remark: *He cast aspersions on my character.*

asphalt (*say* <u>ash</u>-felt)
noun a black sticky substance like tar, mixed with crushed rock and used for making roads

aspic
noun a jelly used to set fish, meat or vegetables in a mould

aspire
verb to aim eagerly: *to aspire to be school captain*
Word building: **aspirant** *noun*   **aspiration** *noun*

aspirin
noun a drug used to stop pain

ass
noun a long-eared animal in the same family as the horse

Word use: Another word for this animal is **donkey**.
Word building: The plural is **asses**.

assassin (*say* uh-<u>sas</u>-uhn)
noun someone who murders a well-known person such as a politician

Word building: **assassinate** *verb* **assassination** *noun*

assault
noun an attack: *to make an assault on the fort*
Word building: **assault** *verb*

assemble

verb **1** to bring or put together: *to assemble a machine* **2** to come together: *We assembled in the playground.*

assembly

noun **1** a number of people gathered together for a special purpose
2 the putting together of something that is in parts: *a factory for the assembly of motor cars*

Word building: The plural is **assemblies**.

assent

verb to agree: *to assent to her suggestion*

Word building: **assent** *noun*

assert

verb to state or declare strongly: *to assert your innocence*

Word building: **assertion** *noun* a strong positive statement **assertiveness** *noun* the quality of expressing yourself strongly **assertive** *adjective*

assertion   (*say* uh-<u>ser</u>-shuhn)

noun a statement which someone makes very definitely or positively: *He seemed very sure of his assertion that eating too much orange peel could kill you.*

assess

verb to work out the value of: *to assess your work*

Word building: **assessment** *noun* **assessor** *noun*

asset

noun **1** something you own: *A house is a valuable asset.* **2** anything of value: *Good health is an asset.*

assign   (*rhymes with* fine)

verb to give or allocate (a job or a role): *My new teacher is going to assign some special duties to each student in the class.*

assignment

noun a particular task: *Our assignment was to write a composition.*

assimilate

verb to take in and make part of yourself: *I assimilated the information.*

Word building: **assimilation** *noun*

assist

verb to help: *She assisted me with my homework.*

Word building: **assistant** *noun* **assistance** *noun*

associate   (*say* uh-<u>soh</u>-see-ayt)

verb **1** to connect in your mind: *I associate the beach with holidays.* **2** to spend time with or to work with: *I associate with people who enjoy the same hobbies.*
noun (*say* uh-<u>soh</u>-see-uht) **3** a partner or someone who shares your interests: *She is my associate in business.*

association

noun **1** a group of people interested in the same thing: *an association of stamp collectors* **2** the connection of ideas in your mind: *the association of sleep with bed*

assonance

noun the repetition of the same vowel sound in words close together, as in 'fly high'

Word building: **assonant** *adjective*

assortment

noun a collection of things of various kinds: *an assortment of lollies*

Word building: **assorted** *adjective*

assume

verb **1** to believe without proof: *Don't assume that he'll come — ask him!* **2** to agree to carry out: *to assume the duties of school captain*

Word building: **assumption** *noun*

assurance

noun **1** a promise or guarantee: *to give an assurance of continuing support* **2** confidence or faith in your own ability: *to do something with assurance*

assure

verb **1** to tell with certainty: *He assured us he would come.* **2** to make sure or certain: *Hard work assures success.*

asterisk   (*say* <u>as</u>-tuh-risk)

noun a star shape (*) used in printing or writing to show something has been written at the bottom of a page

Word history: from a Greek word meaning 'star'

astern

adverb behind or at the back of

Word use: This word is only used of ships or boats.

asteroid

noun one of the hundreds of tiny planets lying between Mars and Jupiter

Word history: from a Greek word meaning 'like a star'

asthma   (*say* <u>as</u>-muh)

noun a breathing disorder which causes wheezing, coughing and a feeling of tightness in the chest

Word building: **asthmatic** *noun*   **asthmatic** *adjective*

astonish

verb to amaze or surprise greatly
Other words: **astound, dumbfound, stagger, stun**

Word building: **astonishment** *noun* **astonishing** *adjective*

astound

verb to amaze or surprise: *When I looked through the telescope, I was astounded at what I saw.*

Word building: **astounding** *adjective*

astray

adverb away from the proper path: *to go astray*

astride

adverb with the legs on either side of: *He stood astride the low fence.*

astringent   (*say* uh-<u>strin</u>-juhnt)

noun **1** a liquid put on the skin to tighten it and cause it to tingle
adjective **2** tightening and refreshing the skin: *an astringent lotion* **3** harsh or bitter: *astringent remarks about their behaviour*
Word building: **astringency** *noun*

astrology

noun the study of the possible effects of the stars and planets on our lives

Word building: **astrologer** *noun*   **astrological** *adjective*

astrology/astronomy Don't confuse **astrology** with **astronomy**, which is the scientific study of the sun, moon, stars and planets.

astronaut

noun someone specially trained to travel in a spaceship

Word building: **astronautics** *noun* the science of flight in space

astronomical

adjective **1** having to do with astronomy **2** very large: *The patient got an astronomical bill from the hospital.*

astronomy

noun the scientific study of the sun, moon, stars and planets

Word building: **astronomer** *noun*

astronomy/astrology Don't confuse **astronomy** with **astrology**, which is the study of the possible effects of the stars and planets on our lives.

astute

adjective having clear and quick understanding: *an astute business executive*
Other words: **discerning, perceptive, sharp, shrewd, wise**
Word building: **astuteness** *noun*

asunder

adverb *Old-fashioned* in or into pieces: *to tear asunder*

asylum   (*say* uh-<u>suy</u>-luhm)

noun **1** protection or safety: *political asylum in another country* **2** a shelter that offers safety or care

at

preposition a word used to show place, time and so on: *at school | at 11 o'clock | at home*

atheist   (*say* <u>ay</u>-thee-uhst)

noun someone who believes that there is no God or gods
Word use: Compare this with **agnostic**.
Word building: **atheism** *noun*   **atheistic** *adjective*

athlete   (*say* <u>ath</u>-leet)

noun someone who trains in sports such as running, jumping, or throwing
Word building: **athletic** *adjective*   **athletics** *noun*

atlas

noun a book of maps

ATM

noun a short form of **automatic teller machine**

atmosphere

noun **1** the air that surrounds the earth
2 a feeling or mood: *an unpleasant atmosphere in the room after a quarrel*
Word building: **atmospheric** *adjective*

atoll

noun a coral island with a salt water lake in the middle

atom

noun the smallest part that an element can be divided into and still keep its special qualities or take part in a chemical reaction
Word history: from a Greek word meaning 'not able to be divided'

atomic

adjective **1** having to do with atoms **2** driven by atomic energy: *an atomic submarine* **3** using atomic weapons: *atomic warfare*

atomic bomb

noun a bomb which explodes with great force because of the energy released from the splitting of atoms

atomic energy

noun the energy or power which is obtained by causing changes within atoms
Word use: Another word for this is **nuclear energy**.

atonal   (*say* ay-<u>tohn</u>-uhl)

adjective not in any musical key: *The composer wrote a piece of atonal music for the school orchestra.*

atone

verb to make up or show you are sorry: *I atoned for my laziness by helping with the housework.*
Word building: **atonement** *noun*

atrium

noun either of the two upper cavities of the heart in which blood collects
Word use: Compare this with **ventricle**.

atrocious   (*say* uh-<u>troh</u>-shuhs)

adjective **1** terribly wicked or cruel: *an atrocious crime* **2** very bad or lacking in taste: *atrocious taste in clothes*
Word building: **atrociousness** *noun*

atrocity   (*say* uh-<u>tros</u>-uh-tee)

noun a terribly wicked or cruel act
Word building: The plural is **atrocities**.

atrophy   (*say* <u>at</u>-ruh-fee)

verb to lose strength or size: *Muscles atrophy if they aren't used.*
Word building: Other forms are **it atrophied, it has atrophied, it is atrophying**.

attach

verb **1** to fasten or join: *Attach the label to the suitcase.*
phrase **2 be attached to,** to like or love: *She is very attached to her old suitcase.*

attack

verb **1** to begin to use force or weapons: *The army attacked at dawn.*
Other words: **strike**
2 to use force or weapons against: *to attack the enemy*
Other words: **hit, strike**
3 to go to work on strongly: *to attack a difficult task*
Other words: **tackle**
Word building: **attack** *noun*

attain

verb to reach or achieve by trying hard: *He attained a high pass in English.*
Word building: **attainable** *adjective* **attainment** *noun*

attempt

verb **1** to try: *to attempt to swim*
Other words: **endeavour, seek**
2 to try to do: *to attempt a course of study*
noun **3** an effort or try: *I said I would make an attempt to climb the mountain.*
Other words: **bid, endeavour**

attend

verb **1** to be present at **2** to look after: *The nurse attended the patient.* **3** to pay attention or take notice: *to attend to your teacher*
Word building: **attendance** *noun*

attendant

noun someone who helps or looks after someone else: *a cloakroom attendant*

attention

noun **1** the act of fixing your mind on something: *This job needs all your attention.* **2** a position in which you stand straight and still: *The soldiers stood at attention.*
phrase **3 pay attention,** to concentrate: *Please pay attention.*
Word building: **attentive** *adjective* observant or paying attention

attic

noun a room or a space directly under the roof of a building: *We store junk in the attic.*

attire

verb to dress, particularly for a special occasion: *to attire yourself in your best clothes*

Word building: **attire** *noun*

attitude

noun **1** a way of holding your body: *He stood in a threatening attitude.* **2** the way you think or behave: *Ben has a helpful attitude to small children.*

attorney (*say* uh-<u>ter</u>-nee)

noun a person, usually a solicitor, appointed by someone to do business for them

Word building: The plural is **attorneys**.

attract

verb to pull or draw: *A magnet attracts steel pins.* | *His smile attracts people.*

Word building: **attraction** *noun*

attractive

adjective **1** pleasing: *an attractive idea*
Other words: **agreeable, alluring, appealing, enticing, inviting, tempting**
2 pleasing to look at: *an attractive person*
Other words: **beautiful, gorgeous, handsome, pretty**

attribute (*say* uh-<u>trib</u>-yooht)

verb **1** to think of as belonging or due: *The crop failure may be attributed to the drought.*
noun (*say* <u>at</u>-ruh-byooht) **2** something thought of as belonging: *Wisdom is one of her attributes.*

Word building: **attribution** *noun* **attributive** *adjective*

atypical (*say* ay-<u>tip</u>-ik-uhl)

adjective not typical, or different from usual: *Huang's grumpiness is atypical of his usual pleasant nature.*

auburn

adjective reddish-brown: *auburn hair*

auction

noun **1** a public sale at which things are sold to the person who offers the most money
verb **2** to sell by auction: *They decided to auction the cottage.*

Word building: **auctioneer** *noun* someone whose job is to sell things by auction

audacious

adjective bold or daring: *an audacious reply | an audacious attempt on Mount Everest*

Word building: **audacity** *noun*

audible

adjective able to be heard: *Your voice was barely audible over the noise of the stereo.*

Word building: **audibility** *noun*

audience

noun **1** a group of people listening or watching **2** an interview with someone important: *an audience with the Queen*

audit

noun an inspection and checking of business accounts, usually once a year

Word building: **audit** *verb* **auditor** *noun*

audition

noun **1** a test given to see how suitable an actor or performer is for a particular job: *Elsa is having an audition for a part in the new play.*
verb **2** to test by giving an audition to: *The band leader auditioned two new trumpet players.* **3** to give a trial performance: *They auditioned for the choir.*

Word use: An audition for a part in a film is called a **film test**.
Word history: from a Latin word meaning 'a hearing'

auditorium

noun a hall or other large space for meetings or concerts

auditory

adjective having to do with hearing or the ears: *an auditory signal*

augment

verb to make larger: *My uncle works at night to augment his income.*

Word building: **augmentation** *noun*

august (*say* aw-<u>gust</u>)

adjective causing you to feel awe and respect: *the august atmosphere of Canberra's War Memorial*

August (*say* <u>aw</u>-guhst)

noun the eighth month of the year, with 31 days

Word use: The abbreviation is **Aug.**
Word history: named after the first Roman emperor, *Augustus* Caesar

aunt
noun **1** the sister of your father or mother **2** your uncle's wife

aura
noun a special character or atmosphere: *The garden has an aura of peace.*

aural
adjective having to do with hearing or listening: *The first part of the music exam was an aural test.*

aural/oral Don't confuse **aural** with **oral**, which has to do with the mouth. An **oral** exam is one in which you speak your answers. **Oral** rhymes with *moral*.

auricle
noun another word for **atrium**

aurora   (*say* uh-<u>raw</u>-ruh)
noun a natural display of moving lights in the sky

auspices   (*say* <u>aw</u>-spuhs-es)
noun the help and encouragement that a person or group provides: *There was a match set up between the visiting team and ours under the auspices of the local football club.*

auspicious
adjective favourable or showing signs of success: *an auspicious occasion*

Aussie   (*say* <u>oz</u>-ee)
noun Informal an Australian
Word building: **Aussie** *adjective*

Aussie Sports
noun sports with slightly changed rules making it easier for all children to play

austere   (*say* ost-<u>ear</u>)
adjective **1** severely simple: *The nuns live in austere surroundings.* **2** stern or grim: *The doctor had an austere manner.*
Word building: **austerity** *noun*

Australian Rules
plural noun a type of football played by two teams of 18 players each. It was first played in Australia.

Word use: Other names for this are **Australian National Football, Australian Football** and **Aussie Rules.**

authentic
adjective genuine or real: *an authentic diamond*
Word building: **authenticate** *verb* to prove to be genuine   **authenticity** *noun*

author
noun **1** someone who writes a book, article or poem **2** the creator of anything: *Wellington was the author of Napoleon's downfall.*
Word building: **authorship** *noun*

authorise
verb **1** to give legal power to: *He authorised the deputy to decide the question.* **2** to approve officially: *The grant for the new library has been authorised.*
Word use: Another spelling is **authorize.**
Word building: **authorisation** *noun*

authoritarian
adjective acting without considering people's freedom: *an authoritarian government*
Word building: **authoritarianism** *noun*

authority
noun **1** the right to decide or judge: *The courts have authority over people who come before them.* **2** a right that gives power: *The police have authority to control traffic.* **3** a reliable source of information: *She is an authority on gardening.*
Word building: The plural is **authorities.** | **authoritative** *adjective* having or giving authority

autistic
adjective suffering from an illness of the mind in which you live in your own imagination and are not very aware of other people
Word building: **autism** *noun*

auto-
prefix a word part meaning 'self': *autobiography*
Word history: This prefix comes from Greek.

autobiography
noun your own life story written by yourself
Word building: The plural is **autobiographies.** | **autobiographical** *adjective*

autocracy   (*say* aw-<u>tok</u>-ruh-see)

noun **1** unlimited rule by one person over others **2** a country ruled by someone with unlimited power

Word building: The plural is **autocracies**. | **autocrat** *noun*   **autocratic** *adjective*

autograph

noun someone's own handwriting, especially their signature

Word building: **autograph** *verb*

automatic

adjective **1** working or going by itself: *an automatic washing machine* **2** like a machine: *Their reaction to the bell was automatic.*

noun **3** a car with a gear change that works by itself

Word building: **automatically** *adverb*

automatic teller machine

noun a machine that you get money from by using a coded plastic card and a PIN

Word use: The short form of this is **ATM**.

automation   (*say* aw-tuh-<u>may</u>-shuhn)

noun the use of machines instead of people to do jobs in factories

automaton   (*say* aw-<u>tom</u>-uh-tuhn)

noun a robot or someone who acts like a robot

Word building: The plural is **automata**.

automobile

noun an American word for **car**

autonomous   (*say* aw-<u>ton</u>-uh-muhs)

adjective self-governing: *an autonomous nation*

Other words: **independent**

autopsy

noun the examination of a dead body to discover the cause of death

Word use: It can also be called a **post-mortem**.
Word building: The plural is **autopsies**.
Word history: from a Greek word meaning 'seeing with your own eyes'

autumn

noun the season of the year following summer, when the leaves from some trees change colour and fall

Word building: **autumnal** *adjective*

auxiliary

adjective **1** aiding or helping: *an auxiliary text* **2** kept in case it is needed or in reserve: *an auxiliary engine*

Word building: **auxiliary** *noun* (**auxiliaries**)

auxiliary verb

noun a 'helper' verb that goes with a main verb to show things like person and tense. Common auxiliary verbs include those that come from *be* and *have*, as in 'I *am* eating', 'they *were* eating' and 'I *had* eaten'.

available

adjective ready, or able to be used: *There are three tennis courts available.* | *Hamidi is available to help.*

Word building: **availability** *noun*

avalanche

noun a large mass of snow sliding or falling suddenly down a mountain slope

avarice   (*say* <u>av</u>-uh-ruhs)

noun greediness for money

Word building: **avaricious** *adjective*

avenge

verb to get revenge for: *'I will avenge my father's murder!' cried the knight as he drew his sword.*

Word building: **avenger** *noun*

avenue

noun a street or road, especially one lined with trees

average

noun **1** the result of dividing the sum of two or more quantities by the number of quantities: *The average of 1, 2 and 3 is 2.* **2** an ordinary amount, kind, quality or rate: *Her ability is well above the average.*

verb **3** to do or have an average: *to average twelve kilometres a week on your bike* | *to average four meals a day*

averse

adjective opposed or not willing: *averse to work*

aversion

noun **1** a strong dislike: *I have an aversion to spinach.* **2** a person or thing disliked: *Smoking is my pet aversion.*

avert

verb **1** to turn away: *I averted my eyes so that they couldn't see my tears.*
2 to prevent: *to avert danger*

avian flu

noun a type of influenza virus which normally passes between birds but which can sometimes be transferred to humans

Word use: Another word for this is **avian influenza** or **bird flu**.

aviary

noun a large cage or enclosure where birds are kept

Word building: The plural is **aviaries**.
Word history: from the Latin word for 'bird'

aviation

noun the science or act of flying in a plane: *Amy Johnson was a pioneer of aviation.*

Word building: **aviator** *noun* pilot

avid

adjective keen or eager: *an avid swimmer*

Word building: **avidity** *noun*   **avidly** *adverb*

avocado

noun a green pear-shaped fruit used in salads

Word building: The plural is **avocados**.

avoid

verb to keep away from: *to avoid danger*
Other words: **evade**

Word building: **avoidable** *adjective*
avoidance *noun*
Word history: from a French word meaning 'empty out'

await

verb **1** to wait for: *I await your commands.*
2 to be ready for: *Supper awaits you.*

awake

verb **1** to wake up: *When I awoke the sun was shining.* **2** to excite or stir up: *to awake our interest*

Word building: Other forms are **I awoke, I have awoken, I am awaking.**

awaken

verb to wake up or alert: *A kookaburra awakened the campers. | Dieter awakened them to their danger.*

awakening

noun **1** a waking up from sleep
2 a renewing of interest: *an awakening among the people in the cause of peace*

award

verb **1** to give for merit or achievement: *to award prizes*
noun **2** something won by merit or achievement: *an award for bravery*
3 a ruling about wages and conditions of work given by an industrial court: *the metal industry award*

aware

adjective having a feeling or knowledge: *I was aware of a stealthy step behind me.*

Word building: **awareness** *noun*

away

adverb **1** somewhere else: *Go away!*
2 not near: *to stand away from the window*
3 from your possession: *I'm giving some of my CDs away.* **4** at once: *right away*
adjective **5** absent: *She's away from school today.* **6** distant: *ten kilometres away*

awe

noun a feeling of great respect mixed with fear: *The convicts were in awe of the overseer's whip.*

Word building: **awe** *verb*

awe/oar/or/ore Don't confuse **awe** with the other three words that sound the same.
You use an **oar** for rowing a boat.
You use **or** to connect alternative words, phrases or clauses:
I don't know which colour to choose — red, yellow or green.
Ore is a rock or mineral which is mined for the metal it contains.

awesome

adjective **1** filling you with feelings of respect and fear: *an awesome height above the valley* **2** *Informal* very good or wonderful: *an awesome party*

awful

adjective very bad or unpleasant: *an awful mess*
Other words: **abominable, abysmal, atrocious, dreadful, horrible, shocking, terrible**

awfully

adverb **1** very badly: *He sings awfully — perhaps he could turn the pages instead.*
2 extremely: *It was an awfully long way — I thought I would die!*

awkward

adjective **1** clumsy: *an awkward person who is always bumping into things*
Other words: **gawky, uncoordinated, ungainly**
2 inconvenient: *an awkward room to furnish | an awkward time*
Other words: **difficult, tricky, troublesome**

Word building: **awkwardness** *noun*

awning

noun a covering to give shelter from the weather: *a shop awning*

awry   (*rhymes with* fly)

adverb **1** turned to one side: *to wear your hat awry | to look awry* **2** wrong or amiss: *Our plans went awry.*

Word use: Sometimes for definition 1 you can use the word **askew**.

axe

noun **1** a tool with a blade for chopping
verb **2** *Informal* to discontinue (a project, TV program, a job, and so on)
phrase **3 have an axe to grind**, to have private or selfish reasons for doing things **4 the axe**, *Informal* **a** a cutting down or reduction of spending **b** the sack or dismissal from a job

Word building: Other verb forms are **I axed, I have axed, I am axing.**

axiom

noun something that is obviously true

Word building: **axiomatic** *adjective*

axis

noun **1** an imaginary line which something revolves around: *The earth rotates on its axis once every 24 hours.* **2** a central line that divides something exactly in half: *an axis of symmetry*

Word building: The plural is **axes** (*say* <u>ak</u>-seez).

axle

noun the rod in the middle of a wheel on which the wheel turns

axolotl   (*say* aks-uh-<u>lot</u>-l)

noun an amphibian with a long tail and short legs, found in Mexican lakes: *We kept our axolotl in the tank with our goldfish.*

ayatollah   (*say* uy-uh-<u>tol</u>-uh)

noun the name given to a Muslim religious leader in Iran

azalea   (*say* uh-<u>zayl</u>-yuh)

noun a shrub with attractive flowers that bloom in spring

azure   (*say* <u>ay</u>-zhuh)

adjective pale blue or sky-blue

Bb

babble

verb to speak quickly and unclearly: *The shy boy babbled his answer.*

Word building: **babble** *noun*   **babbler** *noun*

baboon

noun a large monkey with a mouth like a dog and a short tail, found in Africa and Arabia

Word history: from a French word meaning 'stupid person'

baby

noun **1** a very young child or animal
adjective **2** like or suitable for a baby: *a baby face | baby clothes*
verb **3** to treat like a baby: *to baby the child*

Word building: The plural form of the noun is **babies**. | Other verb forms are **I babied, I have babied, I am babying**. | **babyish** *adjective*

babysit

verb to look after (a child) while the parents are out: *I'm going to babysit my little brother tonight.*

Word building: Other forms are **I babysat, I have babysat, I am babysitting**. | **babysitter** *noun*   **babysitting** *noun*

bachelor

noun a man who isn't married

back

noun **1** the part of something that is farthest from the front: *the back of the room*
2 the rear part of your body, from your neck to the bottom of your spine
3 a defending player in football and other games

verb **4** to reverse: *Dad backed the car into the garage.* **5** to support: *They backed their local team.* **6** to bet on: *to back a horse*
adverb **7** at or to the rear: *to step back*
8 in reply or in return: *to write back | to pay back* **9** in or towards an earlier time or place: *to go back to your home*

Word building: **backer** *noun* someone who gives money to support a business, film, play, and so on   **back** *adjective*

backbone

noun **1** the spine of your body or the similar set of bones in some animals
2 courage to stand up for what you believe

backfire

verb **1** to make a loud explosive sound because petrol was burnt too early: *The car's engine backfired.*
2 to have a very different effect from what you intended: *Our plan backfired.*

Word building: **backfire** *noun*

backgammon

noun a board game in which two people take turns to move pieces after throwing dice

background

noun **1** the back part of a view or scene: *in the background of the picture* **2** the events and conditions that lead up to and explain something: *the background of today's disaster* **3** your social position, experience and education
phrase **4 in the background**, out of sight, or not noticed

backing

noun **1** support of any kind, such as a piece of material placed behind another to strengthen it or money made available to help a project **2** musical background for a singer

backlog

noun a piling up of things that need to be done or looked at: *There is a backlog of letters to be answered.*

backpack

noun a strong bag carried on the back, with straps that go over the shoulders

backpacker

noun a person who travels from one place to another with everything they need, like clothes, some food, and so on, carried in a backpack: *We picked up two backpackers and gave them a lift to the next town.*

backslash

noun a short diagonal line (\) either printed or on a computer screen: *To organise your files, put a backslash between 'My documents' and your name, and then another one before 'Very Important Files'.*

backstroke

noun a stroke in swimming in which you lie on your back and move your arms backwards in turn

back-to-back

adjective **1** consecutive or happening one after the other: *The concert was back-to-back musical items from the kindergarten kids — the parents loved it.*
adverb **2** consecutively or one after the other: *They played three games back-to-back.*

backup

noun **1** support or help: *We will give your plan a lot of backup.* **2** something kept in reserve, to be used when it is needed: *We will keep the extra food as a backup in case we run out.* **3** a second copy of a computer file, disk, or tape, to be used if the original becomes damaged, lost, or destroyed

Word use: Another spelling is **back-up**.
Word building: **back up** *verb* to make a copy as a backup   **backup** *adjective*

backward

adjective **1** turned or moving towards the back: *a backward look | a backward step* **2** behind the others in growth, or ability to learn: *a backward reader*

Word building: **backward** *adverb*   **backwards** *adjective*   **backwards** *adverb*

backwater

noun **1** a pool of still, stale water that is joined to a river but not reached by its current **2** a place where nothing seems to happen

backyard

noun the enclosed area behind a house

Word building: **backyard** *adjective*

bacon

noun the salted meat from the back and sides of a pig

bacteria

plural noun microscopic living bodies that can cause disease and decay

Word building: The singular form is **bacterium**. | **bacterial** *adjective*
Word history: from a Greek word meaning 'a little stick'

bad

adjective **1** not good in behaviour: *I was in trouble because I had been bad in class.*
Other words: **badly-behaved, disobedient, mischievous, naughty**
2 serious or severe: *a bad accident | a bad mistake*
Other words: **damaging, harmful, nasty**
3 sick or unhealthy: *I was sick but I'm not bad now.* **4** rotten or decayed: *bad meat*
Other words: **off, spoiled, tainted**

Word use: **Worse** and **worst** describe greater degrees of badness.
Word building: **badness** *noun*   **badly** *adverb*

badge

noun a disc or label that you wear on your clothes to show people what you're a member or supporter of

badger

noun **1** a burrowing mammal found in Europe and America, which has a white mark on its head
verb **2** to pester or annoy: *My little brother always badgers our parents with questions.*

badminton

noun a game in which two or four players use racquets to hit a feathered shuttlecock over a high net

Word history: named after *Badminton*, a village in England, where the game was first played

baffle

verb to confuse or puzzle: *The unusual question baffled me.*

Word building: **bafflement** *noun*   **baffling** *adjective*   **bafflingly** *adverb*

bag

noun **1** a container for holding or carrying things: *a bag of cement | a shopping bag* **2 bags,** *Informal* plenty or a lot: *She's got bags of money.*

Word building: **bag** *verb* (**bagged, bagging**)

bagel   (*say* bay-guhl)

noun a small hard roll, in the shape of a ring and made of dough

Word history: from Yiddish

baggage

noun the suitcases and boxes which belong to a traveller: *I left my baggage with a porter.* Other words: **luggage**

bagpipes

plural noun a musical instrument you play by blowing into a bag with pipes attached

bail¹

noun money which must be paid so that someone who is charged with a crime can go free until they are tried in court

Word building: **bail** *verb*

bail²

noun one of the two small pieces of wood that rest on top of cricket stumps

bail³

verb another spelling for **bale²**

bail/bale Don't confuse **bail** with **bale**, which refers to a large bundle of goods, such as *a bale of wool*.
The word may be spelt **bale** or **bail** when it is used with *out* to mean either 'to remove water from a boat with a bucket', or 'to jump from a plane with a parachute'.

bait

noun **1** food used on a hook, or in a trap, to catch fish or animals **2** food with poison in it, used to kill or drug animals *verb* **3** to use bait **4** to tease in order to upset or annoy

bake

verb **1** to cook in an oven **2** to make hard by heating: *to bake pots in a kiln*

baker

noun someone whose job is to bake bread and cakes

Word building: **bakery** *noun* the place where bread and cakes are baked

baker's dozen

noun thirteen

baklava   (*say* buh-klah-vuh, bak-luh-vuh)

noun a cake made from thin pastry, nuts and honey, first made in Greece, Turkey, and so on

balaclava   (*say* bal-uh-klah-vuh)

noun a knitted cap that pulls down over your head and under your chin: *Your grey balaclava looks like a helmet.*

Word history: named after *Balaclava*, a seaport on the Black Sea, where soldiers first wore these caps in the Crimean War which lasted from 1853 to 1856

balance

verb **1** to make or keep steady: *I can't balance on my new rollerblades. | Can you balance a stick on your nose?* **2** to be equal, especially in weight: *The package I have added balances the one taken away.* *noun* **3** steadiness: *balance of judgement | I can't keep my balance.* **4** the difference between the total of the money paid into, and the money taken out of, an account **5** an instrument for weighing, often a swaying bar with containers hanging at the ends
Other words: **scales**

balanced

adjective **1** having weight evenly spread: *The seesaw was perfectly balanced and then Wang got off without telling anybody first!* **2** fair and not biased: *The judge gave a balanced review of everyone in the competition.*

balance of nature

noun the balanced way in which plants and animals feed on one another, where there is no danger of extinction to any species

balcony

noun **1** an upstairs verandah that often has a roof and railings **2** the highest floor of seats in a theatre

Word building: The plural is **balconies**.

bald

adjective **1** without hair: *a bald head*
2 plain and to the point: *a bald statement*

Word building: **balding** *adjective*   **baldness**
noun

bale¹

noun a large amount of goods to be stored
or transported, such as wool, hay or straw,
tied up tightly with cords or wire

bale²

verb **1** to empty a boat with a bucket or
can: *They baled furiously after each wave hit
them.*
phrase **2 bale out**, to jump from a plane
with a parachute: *When the engine failed he
baled out.*

bale/bail Don't confuse **bale** with **bail**.
The word **bail** in its legal sense is the money
left with a court to ensure that the accused
person comes back for trial. To **bail** someone
out means 'to help someone get out of trouble'.
Bail in its cricketing sense is part of a wicket.
The word may be spelt **bale** or **bail** when it
is used (often with 'out') to mean 'to remove
water from a boat with a bucket', or (always
with 'out') 'to jump from a plane with a
parachute'.

baleful

adjective full of hate: *The bull watched us
with a baleful expression before charging.*

Word building: **balefully** *adverb*   **balefulness**
noun

ball¹

noun **1** a round or egg-shaped thing which
you can bounce, or which you can kick,
catch or hit in games **2** something which
is shaped like a ball: *a ball of string | a ball
of wool*

ball²

noun a very grand or formal dance: *My
parents wore their best evening clothes to the ball.*

ball/bawl Don't confuse **ball** with **bawl**. When
people **bawl** they cry noisily.

ballad

noun a simple poem with short verses, which
tells a story and is often turned into a song

ballast

noun heavy material carried by a ship to
keep it steady, or by a balloon to control its
height

ballerina   (*say* bal-uh-<u>ree</u>-nuh)

noun a female ballet dancer

ballet   (*say* <u>bal</u>-ay)

noun a formal sort of dancing, performed
by a group, who act out a story, using
graceful and controlled movements

Word history: from an Italian word meaning
'little ball'

ballistics

noun the study of the movement of
missiles, bullets, or other objects fired from
a gun

Word building: **ballistic** *adjective*

balloon

noun **1** a small rubber bag which is filled
with air or gas and used as a toy
2 a large bag filled with hot air or other
light gas, which may have a basket for
passengers and can rise and float in the air
verb **3** to swell out: *The sail ballooned in the
wind.*

Word building: **balloonist** *noun* someone who
travels by balloon
Word history: from an Italian word meaning
'ball'

ballot

noun **1** a ticket or paper you must fill in to
record your vote: *They counted our ballots to
see who had won the election.* **2** a secret way
of voting

Word use: Another word for definition 2 is
secret ballot.
Word building: **ballot** *verb* (**balloted, balloting**)

ballpoint pen

noun a pen whose point is a small ball
which rolls around

Word use: Another name is **ballpoint.**

balm   (*rhymes with* farm)

noun **1** a sweet-smelling ointment or
oil which heals or makes something less
painful **2** something soothing: *The good
news was balm to the anxious parents.*

balmy

adjective fine or pleasant: *In the balmy
spring weather they were often outdoors.*

Word building: Other forms are **balmier,
balmiest.**

balsa   (*say* <u>bawl</u>-suh)

noun the very light wood of the balsa tree,
often used in crafts

balsam (*say* <u>bawl</u>-suhm)
noun **1** a sweet-smelling gum that comes from some trees **2** a kind of garden plant with red, pink or white flowers

balustrade (*say* <u>bal</u>-uh-strayd)
noun a rail with a row of short pillars holding it up, usually part of a balcony or staircase

Word building: **baluster** *noun* one of the short pillars in the row

bamboo
noun a woody, tree-like plant whose hollow stem is used for building and making light furniture

bamboozle
verb to confuse or deceive: *He bamboozled them with conjuring tricks.*
Other words: **baffle, bewilder**

ban
verb to bar or forbid: *Yoyos were banned from the classroom.*

Word building: Other forms are **I banned, I have banned, I am banning**.

banal (*say* buh-<u>nahl</u>)
adjective ordinary and unoriginal: *The TV film was so banal that we turned it off.*

Word building: **banality** *noun*

banana
noun a long curved fruit with a yellow skin

band[1]
noun **1** a group of people acting together: *a band of outlaws* **2** a group of musicians: *a rock band | a brass band*

Word building: **band** *verb* to join in a group

band[2]
noun **1** a strip of material for tying, binding or decorating: *a hat band | a rubber band* **2** a narrow strip that contrasts with its surroundings: *a band of red paint*
Other words: **stripe**

Word building: **banded** *adjective* striped

bandage
noun a strip of cotton or elastic material used to bind up a wound

Word building: **bandage** *verb*

bandaid
noun a cover that you stick over an abrasion or sore to protect it

bandana (*say* ban-<u>dan</u>-uh)
noun a bright scarf: *The horse trainer wore a red bandana around his neck.*

Word use: Another spelling is **bandanna**.
Word history: from a Hindustani word for a form of dyeing in which the cloth is tied to stop some parts from receiving the dye

bandicoot
noun a rat-like Australian marsupial which feeds at night on insects, worms and plant roots. Some species are vulnerable or endangered. See the table at the end of this book.

Word history: from a Telugu word (a language spoken in south-eastern India) for the pig-rat of India and Sri Lanka

bandit
noun an armed robber

bandy
verb **1** to exchange: *The rivals bandied insults, then punches.*
adjective **2** having legs bending outwards at the knees: *The old jockey has bandy legs from so much riding.* **3 bandy-legged**, having crooked legs

Word building: Other verb forms are **I bandied, I have bandied, I am bandying**.

bane
noun someone or something that ruins or destroys: *She says that having to sit in traffic jams on the way to work is the bane of her life.*

Word building: **baneful** *adjective* **banefully** *adverb* **banefulness** *noun*

bang
noun **1** a sudden loud noise: *There was a bang as the two cars collided.*
Other words: **boom, crash, thud**
verb **2** to hit or shut noisily: *They banged the cymbals together.*
Other words: **bash, beat, pound**

bangle
noun a band worn as an ornament round your wrist or ankle

banish
verb to send away as a punishment: *The disloyal army general was banished from his country forever.*
Other words: **evict, exile, expel**

Word building: **banishment** *noun*

banister

noun the rail that runs along a stairway: *She slid down the banister.*

Word use: Another spelling is **bannister**.

banjo

noun a musical instrument with a round body which you play by plucking or strumming its strings

Word building: The plural is **banjos**. | **banjoist** *noun*

bank¹

noun **1** a pile or mass: *a bank of earth | a huge cloud bank* **2** the land beside a river or stream
verb **3** to make into a pile or mass: *to bank up the snow* **4** to tip or slope sideways: *The aeroplane banked steeply, then straightened out.*

bank²

noun **1** a place where you can keep your money and take it out again when you wish
verb **2** to place in a bank
phrase **3 bank on**, to rely on: *I'm banking on you to help.* **4 bank up**, to gather or accumulate: *The line of cars banked up.*

bankbook

noun a book given by a savings bank to customers as a record of how much money they have

Word use: Another word for this is **passbook**.

bankrupt

adjective **1** unable to pay money you owe to other people: *He became bankrupt when his business failed.*
noun **2** someone who is unable to pay their debts

Word building: **bankrupt** *verb* to make bankrupt **bankruptcy** *noun*

banksia

noun an Australian shrub or tree with leathery, notched leaves and tiny yellow flowers massed together in spikes

Word history: named after the naturalist Joseph *Banks*

banner

noun a flag which sometimes has a message or slogan on it: *The marchers carried a big banner which said 'Peace'.*

banquet

noun a large formal dinner for many guests: *At the jubilee banquet there was good food but too many speeches.*
Other words: **feast**

Word building: **banquet** *verb* (**banqueted**, **banqueting**)

bantam

noun a small breed of domestic fowl

Word history: named after *Bantam*, a village in western Java, where these fowls are said to have come from

banter

noun playful teasing: *Their banter never led to a fight.*

Word building: **banter** *verb*

baptism

noun a Christian ceremony in which someone is sprinkled with, or put under, water to show that they are accepted as a member of the church
Other words: **christening**

Word building: **baptise** *verb* **baptismal** *adjective*

bar

noun **1** a long plank or piece of metal or other hard material, often used as a barrier: *the top bar of the fence*
Other words: **rail, slat**
2 the counter in a hotel where drinks are served **3 a** one of the upright lines drawn across the stave in written music, to separate the groups of beats **b** the part between two of these lines
verb **4** to stop or prevent: *Guards barred them from entering.*
Other words: **ban, forbid, prevent, prohibit**

Word use: Another word for definition 3a is **bar-line**.
Word building: Other verb forms are **I barred, I have barred, I am barring**.

barb

noun **1** the sharp point that sticks out backwards on a fish hook, head of an arrow or fence wire **2** a hurtful remark

Word building: **barbed** *adjective*: *barbed wire*

barbarian   (*say* bah-<u>bair</u>-ree-uhn)

noun someone with bad manners and not much education

Word building: **barbarian** *adjective*: *The invading barbarian tribes destroyed the town's statues.*   **barbarism** *noun*   **barbarity** *noun*
Word history: first used by the ancient Greeks and Romans to describe a person belonging to an uncivilised country

barbaric   (*say* bah-<u>ba</u>-rik)
adjective wild, savage or cruel: *barbaric acts of torture*

Word building: **barbarous** *adjective* crude or rough in manners or style   **barbarically** *adverb*   **barbarously** *adverb*

barbecue
noun **1** a fireplace or metal frame for cooking meat over an open fire
2 an outdoor meal or party where the food is cooked on a barbecue

Word use: Other spellings are **barbeque** and **bar-b-q**, but many people say these shouldn't be used in your best writing. | Short forms of this are **barbie** and **barby**.
Word building: **barbecue** *verb*

barber
noun someone whose job is to cut men's hair and to shave or trim their beards

barbiturate   (*say* bah-<u>bit</u>-chuh-ruht)
noun a drug used to ease pain or to calm and soothe someone, and which people can get addicted to

bar code
noun a printed code with a series of vertical bars that identify all goods being sold in a shop, which a computerised cash register can scan

Word building: **bar coding** *noun*

bard
noun *Old-fashioned* a poet or singer
Word building: **bardic** *adjective*

bare
adjective **1** uncovered or naked: *bare walls* / *bare knees*
Other words: **exposed**
2 plain or simple: *the bare truth*
Other words: **basic**

Word building: **barely** *adverb* just, or no more than   **bareness** *noun*

bare/bear Don't confuse **bare** with **bear**, which is a large furry mammal. It can also mean 'to carry or support something':
I can't bear your weight any longer.

barely
adverb only just: *There's barely enough food to make dinner.*

bargain
noun **1** something bought cheaply: *The shoes were a bargain at half price.*
Other words: **good buy, good deal**
2 an agreement or arrangement to buy or sell something
Other words: **bond, contract, deal**

Word building: **bargain** *verb* to argue for a better price   **bargainer** *noun*

barge
noun **1** a flat-bottomed boat that carries cargo
verb **2** to make way by pushing or shoving: *He barged through the crowd.*

barista   (*say* buh-<u>ris</u>-tuh)
noun a person skilled in making espresso coffee in a cafe or restaurant

baritone
noun **1** the range of musical notes which can be sung by a male singer with a fairly deep voice: *I sing baritone in the choir.*
2 a man with a fairly deep singing voice

Word use: **Baritone** range is higher than a **bass** but lower than **soprano, alto** and **tenor**.
Word building: **baritone** *adjective*

barium   (*say* <u>bair</u>-ree-uhm)
noun a substance which shows up on X-ray when it is swallowed

bark[1]
verb to make the noise of a dog
Word building: **bark** *noun*

bark[2]
noun **1** the outer covering of a tree
verb **2** to scrape or graze: *I barked my elbow on the edge of the table.*

barley
noun a grain used as food, and in making beer and whisky

bar mitzvah   (*say* bah <u>mits</u>-vuh)
noun the Jewish ceremony and feast held when a boy reaches his thirteenth birthday and is old enough to take on religious responsibilities as an adult member of the Jewish community

Word history: from a Hebrew word meaning 'son of the commandment'

barn
noun a shed to store hay or shelter animals

barnacle
noun a shellfish which clings to the bottoms of ships and other underwater objects

barometer
noun an instrument that measures air pressure, used to help work out what height you're at and what changes in the weather can be expected: *The barometer is falling, which means we shall have bad weather.*

Word use: When you use a barometer to see what height you're at it is called an **altimeter**.
Word building: **barometric** *adjective*

baron
noun a nobleman: *The baron left his castle to fight for the king.*

Word building: **baroness** *noun* **baronial** *adjective*

barrack
verb to shout encouragement: *We barracked for our favourite team.*

Word building: **barracker** *noun*

barracks
plural noun the buildings where soldiers live

barrage   (*say* ba-rahzh)
noun an overwhelming attack, especially of gunfire: *a barrage of questions | a barrage of bullets*

Word building: **barrage** *verb*

barramundi   (*say* ba-ruh-mun-dee)
noun a large silver-grey coloured fish, which is good to eat

Word history: This word comes from an Aboriginal language of Queensland.

barrel
noun **1** a large container made of vertical strips of wood held together with iron hoops **2** the metal tube of a gun

barren
adjective unable to produce children or crops: *a barren woman | barren land*

barrette   (*say* buh-ret)
noun a metal or plastic clasp for holding the hair in position, usually made of two pieces joined with a hinge

barricade
noun a barrier or wall, especially one built in a hurry: *a barricade to stop traffic | The street-fighters hid behind a barricade of rubble.*

Word building: **barricade** *verb* to block or defend with a barricade

barrier
noun anything which bars or blocks the way: *a road barrier | a trade barrier*
Other words: **obstruction**

barrister   (*say* ba-ruh-stuh)
noun a lawyer whose main work is in the higher courts, where important cases are heard

barrow
noun **1** a street seller's cart
2 a wheelbarrow

barter
verb to trade by swapping food and other goods instead of using money

base¹
noun **1** the bottom part of anything, which gives support: *the base of a statue*
2 the centre of operations: *Report back to base when you finish your mission.*
3 the starting point for a counting system in maths, such as ten in the decimal system
4 one of the four fixed positions on a baseball or softball field to which the players try to run

Word building: **base** *verb* rest or fix: *to base an argument on facts*

base²
adjective Old-fashioned mean or selfish: *a base trick*

Word building: **basely** *adverb* **baseness** *noun*

baseball
noun **1** a game played by two teams with a long thin bat and a hard ball, on a field with four bases around which the batter must pass to score a run **2** the ball used in this game

basement
noun a room or area of a building below the ground floor

bash
verb **1** to hit hard or wildly: *I bashed the ball.*
noun **2** Informal a try or attempt: *Give it a bash.*

bashful

adjective very modest or shy: *She felt bashful about making a speech.*

Word building: **bashfully** *adverb*   **bashfulness** *noun*

basic

adjective main or most important: *The basic ingredient for toffee is sugar.*

Other words: **essential, fundamental, key, primary, vital**

Word building: **basically** *adverb*

basil

noun a herb used in cooking and salads

Word history: from a Greek word meaning 'royal'

basin

noun **1** a sink or container that holds water for washing **2** a bowl for mixing or cooking **3** an area of water surrounded by land: *a river basin* **4** land drained by a river

basis

noun **1** a foundation or support that forms the base of something: *The basis of the story was an incident that really took place.* **2** the main part or ingredient

Word building: The plural is **bases** (*say* <u>bay</u>-seez).

bask   (*rhymes with* ask)

verb to lie in or enjoy warmth: *to bask in the sun*

basket

noun a woven container for storing or carrying: *a clothes basket | a shopping basket*

basketball

noun **1** a ball game played by two teams of five people who try to score points by shooting a ball through a hoop or basket at the top of the other team's goal post **2** the ball used in this game

bass   (*sounds like* base)

noun **1** the range of musical notes which can be sung by a male singer with a deep voice: *Mario sings bass in the choir.* **2** a man with a deep singing voice

Word use: **Bass** range is lower than a **soprano, alto, tenor** and **baritone**.
Word building: **bass** *adjective*

basset

noun a long-bodied dog with short legs and long ears, used for hunting foxes and badgers

Word use: It is also called a **basset hound**.

bassinette

noun the basket in which a very young baby sleeps

Word use: Another spelling is **bassinet**.

bassoon   (*say* buh-<u>soohn</u>)

noun a bass woodwind instrument

Word building: **bassoonist** *noun*

bastard

noun **1** someone whose parents were not married when he or she was born **2** *Informal* an unpleasant or bad-tempered person, usually male **3** *Informal* an unpleasant thing

Word use: Definitions 2 and 3 are not polite and using them might offend people.

bastion   (*say* <u>bas</u>-tee-uhn)

noun **1** a fortified place **2** a strong supporter: *He is a bastion of the old way of life.*

Word history: from an Italian word meaning 'build'

bat[1]

noun **1** the stick used to hit the ball in games like cricket and softball
phrase **2 off your own bat**, on your own, without help or advice

Word building: **bat** *verb* (**batted, batting**) **batter** *noun*

bat[2]

noun a mouse-like winged mammal which is active at night

batch

noun a number of things made at the same time or grouped together: *a batch of biscuits | this year's batch of students*

Word building: The plural is **batches**.

bath

noun **1** a container for washing yourself in, which is large enough for you to sit or lie in **2** the water used in the bath

Word building: **bath** *verb*: *to bath the baby*

bathe

verb **1** to wash clean: *Bathe your sore eye in salty water.* **2** to swim: *We bathed in the creek.*

Word building: **bather** *noun* swimmer   **bathers** *plural noun* a swimsuit

bathroom

noun a room fitted with a bath or a shower (or both), and sometimes with a toilet and basin

batik

noun **1** a way of dyeing cloth in which the parts not to be coloured are covered with wax **2** cloth dyed in this way

Word history: from a Malay word meaning 'painted'

bat mitzvah   (*say* baht <u>mits</u>-vuh)

noun the Jewish ceremony and feast held when a girl turns twelve, and becomes an adult member of the Jewish community

Word history: from a Hebrew word meaning 'daughter of the commandment'

baton

noun **1** a thin stick used by the conductor of an orchestra to beat time **2** a short stick, especially one handed by one runner to the next in a relay race

battalion

noun an army unit of three or more smaller groups of soldiers known as companies

batten

noun a light strip of wood, used to strengthen or support something

batter¹

verb to beat or hit hard or often: *to batter on the door*

Word building: **battery** *noun* the act of beating   **battering** *noun*

batter²

noun a mixture of flour, eggs and milk or water beaten together for use in cooking

battery

noun **1** a group of electric cells connected together to make or store electricity: *a torch battery | a car battery* **2** a group of guns or machines to be used together **3** a large number of cages in which chickens and other animals are kept

Word building: The plural is **batteries**.

battle

noun **1** a large-scale or serious fight between armed forces: *Many soldiers were injured in the battle.*

Other words: **clash, combat, conflict, war**
2 any serious or intense fight: *a battle to save the old building*
Other words: **campaign, struggle**

Word building: **embattled** *adjective* caught in a battle   **battle** *verb*   **battler** *noun*

battlement

noun a wall with openings for shooting through: *The archers shot their arrows from the battlement.*

battleship

noun a heavily armed warship

bauble   (*say* <u>baw</u>-buhl)

noun a cheap bright ornament: *to hang baubles on the Christmas tree*

Word history: from a Latin word meaning 'pretty'

baulk   (*rhymes with* fork)

verb to stop and refuse to do something: *The horse baulked at the jump. | to baulk at making a speech*

bauxite   (*say* <u>bawk</u>-suyt)

noun the rock that you crush to get aluminium

bawdy

adjective containing rough talk and jokes about sex: *a bawdy story*

Word use: Other forms are **bawdier, bawdiest**.
Word building: **bawdily** *adverb*   **bawdiness** *noun*

bawl

verb **1** to cry noisily: *He bawled when the ball hit him.* **2** to shout out loudly: *to bawl from across the playground*
phrase **3 bawl out**, to scold harshly: *to bawl someone out for lying*

Word building: **bawl** *noun*

bawl/ball Don't confuse **bawl** with **ball**, which is a round object, or a formal dance.

bay¹

noun a sheltered part of a sea or lake, formed by a curve in its shore

bay²

verb **1** to howl like a dog: *to bay at the moon*
noun **2** the deep long bark of a hunting dog
phrase **3 at bay**, **a** forced to stand and face an enemy: *The kangaroo stood at bay.*

b away or at a distance: *I kept my sad thoughts at bay by working hard.*

bay³

noun a space, section or area: *a bomb bay | a parking bay*

bay⁴

adjective reddish-brown: *a bay horse*

bayonet

noun a blade for stabbing which can be joined to the end of a rifle

Word building: **bayonet** *verb* (**bayoneted, bayoneting**) to stab with a bayonet
Word history: named after *Bayonne* in France, where these weapons were first made

bazaar (*say* buh-<u>zah</u>)

noun **1** a market with stalls selling many different kinds of goods **2** a sale to raise money for charity

BC

short for 'before Christ': *Julius Caesar invaded Britain in 55 BC.*

Word use: Our calendar dates events from the year of Christ's birth; years before this are called **BC** and years after this are **AD**. The abbreviation **BCE** (as in *55 BCE*) is sometimes used if the speaker or writer wants to avoid the reference to Christ. It stands for *Before* (*the*) *Common Era.*

be

verb **1** You can use **be** if you are describing someone or something, or saying where they are, when something happens, and so on: *She is beautiful. | I am tired. | The children were very noisy. | The dog is under the bed. | The wedding was last Saturday.* **2** You can use **be** to say that someone or something is the same as another thing: *She is a doctor. | Tomorrow is Tuesday.* **3** Be is used as an auxiliary or 'helping' verb with another verb: *He is running. | The house was destroyed.*

Word building: Other forms are **I am**; **you, we, they are**; **he, she, it is**; **I, you, he, she, it was**; **you, we, they were**; **I have been**; **I am being.**

beach

noun **1** the sandy or pebbly land at the edge of a sea, lake or river
verb **2** to drive or pull onto the beach from the water: *We beached the boat when we reached the shore.*

Word building: The plural form of the noun is **beaches**.

beach/beech Don't confuse **beach** with **beech**, which is a kind of tree.

beacon

noun a signal which shows the way or warns of danger: *We lit a fire on the hill to serve as a beacon for the fishermen.*

bead

noun **1** a small ball with a hole through the middle, which can be threaded on a string **2** a drop of liquid: *beads of sweat* **3 beads,** a necklace

Word building: **beady** *adjective* (**beadier, beadiest**): *beady little eyes*

beagle

noun a small hunting dog with short legs and long ears

beak

noun the hard, horny part of a bird's mouth
Other words: **bill**
Word building: **beaked** *adjective*

beaker

noun **1** a large cup or mug **2** a glass container with a pouring lip shaped like a beak, used in laboratories

beam

noun **1** a long strong piece of wood, concrete or metal often used as a support: *beams supporting the floor | a balancing beam for gymnastics* **2** the widest part of a ship: *ten metres across the beam* **3** a ray of light: *the beam of a search light | a beam of sun*
verb **4** to send out rays of light **5** to smile happily: *She beamed when she heard the good news.*
phrase **6 off beam,** *Informal* wrong: *The answer was completely off beam.*

bean

noun **1** a plant with smooth seeds growing in a long pod **2** the seed or pod of a bean plant which can be eaten fresh or dried
phrase **3 full of beans,** *Informal* full of energy: *The children are full of beans now the holidays have started.* **4 spill the beans,** *Informal* to let out a secret

bean/been Don't confuse **bean** with **been**, which is the past participle of the verb **be**:
I have been sick.
Have you been waiting long?

beanbag

noun **1** a large cushion that you can sit on, filled with pellets **2** a small cloth bag filled with beans and thrown in catching games

bear¹

verb **1** to hold up or carry: *a branch strong enough to bear your weight*
Other words: **support, sustain, uphold, withstand**
2 to put up with or tolerate: *I can't bear pain. | I can't bear people who tell tales.*
Other words: **abide, endure, stand**
3 to produce or give birth to: *This tree bears oranges. | She bore three children.* **4** to have or show: *The sisters bear no resemblance to each other. | to bear signs of damage*
phrase **5 bear out,** to prove right: *The facts bear me out.* **6 bear up,** to keep cheerful in times of trouble

Word use: The word **born** as in *She was born in 1980* also comes from this verb.
Word building: Other verb forms are
I bore, I have borne, I am bearing. |
bearer *noun* someone who brings or carries something: *the bearer of good news* **bearable** *adjective* **bearably** *adverb*

bear²

noun a large heavy mammal with short rough fur and a very short tail

bear/bare Don't confuse **bear** with **bare**. Someone is **bare** when they are naked.

beard

noun **1** the hair that grows on a man's chin and face **2** a beardlike tuft, such as that on a goat's jaw, below a bird's beak and growing on wheat
verb **3** to challenge or oppose daringly: *Tomorrow, I'm going to beard her on this issue.*
Word building: **bearded** *adjective*

bearing

noun **1** the way you stand or behave: *a woman of proud bearing*
Other words: **carriage, demeanour, deportment**
2 a supporting part of a machine
phrase **3 bearing on,** connection or relevance to: *This information has no bearing on the problem.* **4 bearings,** direction or position: *We lost our bearings in the dark.*

beast

noun **1** a four-footed animal **2** a rough, cruel person, especially someone you dislike
Word building: **beastly** *adjective* horrible or nasty **beastliness** *noun*

beat

verb **1** to hit again and again: *to beat a drum | to beat someone severely | The rain beat on the window.* **2** to make any movement over and over again: *My heart beat loudly. | A bird was beating its wings.* **3** to stir thoroughly: *to beat cream* **4** to defeat: *She beat him in the race.*
noun **5** a sound made over and over again: *the beat of a drum* **6** regular rhythm in music: *The conductor kept the beat while the orchestra played.* **7** a path or route which someone usually takes: *A policeman walks a beat.*
phrase **8 beat it,** *Informal* to leave: *We'd better beat it before someone comes.*
9 beat up, to attack and hurt: *The criminal gang beat him up.*
Word building: Other verb forms are **I beat, I have beaten, I am beating.** | **beating** *noun*: *to give someone a beating* **beater** *noun*

beat/beet Don't confuse **beat** with **beet**, which is a kind of vegetable.

beaut

adjective *Informal* very good and enjoyable: *a beaut party*

beautician

noun someone who works in a beauty salon

beautiful

adjective pleasing and enjoyable to look at, touch, smell, taste or hear: *beautiful music | a beautiful painting*
Other words: **exquisite, gorgeous, lovely**
Word building: **beautifully** *adverb*

beauty

noun **1** the quality of being beautiful: *a garden famous for its beauty* **2** a beautiful person or thing: *My new bike is a beauty.* **3** advantage: *The beauty of this machine is that it runs on batteries.*
Word building: The plural is **beauties.** | **beauteous** *adjective* **beautify** *verb* (**beautified, beautifying**)

beaver
noun a brown furry animal of North America, with sharp teeth, webbed back feet and a wide flat tail, which builds dams in streams

because
conjunction for the reason that: *I can't go to school today because I am sick.*

beckon
verb to signal by waving your hand, or nodding your head: *He beckoned them to follow.*

become
verb **1** to come or grow to be: *to become hungry* **2** to suit or look good on: *That dress becomes you.*
phrase **3 become of,** happen to: *What will become of me?*

Word building: Other verb forms are **I became, I have become, I am becoming.**

becoming
adjective **1** proper or suitable: *behaviour which is becoming to a ten year old* **2** flattering or making you look attractive: *a becoming dress*

Word building: **becomingly** *adverb*

bed
noun **1** a place to sleep, especially a piece of furniture with a mattress, pillow and covers **2** a plot of earth in a garden: *a flower bed* **3** the ground under a sea or river: *a river bed* **4** a base or foundation **5** a layer of rock

Word building: **bedding** *noun* the things you make your bed with, especially sheets and blankets or doonas

bedlam
noun a scene of great noise and confusion: *There was bedlam in the room when the teacher was away.*

bedouin (*say* bed-ooh-uhn)
noun a wandering Arab who lives in the deserts of North Africa or the Middle East

Word use: Another spelling is **Bedouin.**

bedraggled (*say* buh-drag-uhld)
adjective wet, dirty and hanging limply: *long bedraggled hair*

bedridden
adjective forced to stay in bed: *I was bedridden with the flu.*

bedrock
noun **1** the solid, unbroken rock under the top layers of soil **2** the bottom level of anything: *The team's spirits hit bedrock when they lost another match.*

bedroom
noun a room in a home with a bed or beds for sleeping in

bee[1]
noun a stinging insect with four wings, which collects nectar and pollen from flowers to make into honey

Word use: The place where bees live is called a **beehive** or **hive,** and a group of bees together is called a **swarm.**

bee[2]
noun **1** a small group of people gathered together for some type of work: *a sewing bee* **2** a contest: *a spelling bee*

beech
noun a tree with smooth grey bark and triangular nuts, whose hard wood is useful for making furniture

Word building: The plural is **beeches.**

beech/beach Don't confuse **beech** with **beach,** which is the sandy or pebbly shore of a river, sea or lake.

beef
noun the meat from a cow or bull: *roast beef for dinner*

Word building: **beefy** *adjective* (**beefier, beefiest**) solid and with plenty of muscles

beeline
noun a direct line, like the course bees take when returning to the hive: *The children made a beeline for the food.*

beer
noun an alcoholic drink made from malt and flavoured with hops

beet
noun a plant with a root that is good to eat and from which sugar can be made

beet/beat Don't confuse **beet** with **beat,** which is a regular rhythm, such as a heartbeat or the beat of music. It is also a verb with many meanings:
Beat the eggs.
This yacht can beat them in the race.
The cruel man beat his horse.

beetle

noun a large insect with two pairs of wings, one of which is hard and protects the delicate flying wings underneath

Word history: from an Old English word meaning 'biter'

beetroot

noun the red root of the beet plant which is eaten as a vegetable

befall

verb to happen to: *Whatever befalls us, we will be together.*

Word building: Other forms are **it befell, it has befallen.**

befit

verb to be suitable or appropriate for: *Your clothes do not befit the occasion.*

before

preposition **1** at a time earlier than: *You must have your bath before you go to bed.* **2** in front of: *You were before me in the tuckshop line and you got the yummy cake.*

beforehand

adverb in advance: *We can buy tickets beforehand.*

before-school care

noun a place where you can go in the mornings, where people look after you before school starts

befriend

verb to aid or be friendly towards: *to befriend a stray kitten*

befuddled

adjective confused or muddled: *We felt befuddled by so many people talking at once.*

beg

verb to ask humbly: *I beg you to forgive me.* | *to beg for money to buy food*
Other words: **beseech, implore**

Word building: Other forms are **I begged, I have begged, I am begging.**

beggar

noun **1** someone who lives by begging **2** *Informal* someone you feel sorry for: *You poor beggar.*

Word building: **beggarly** *adjective* very poor   **beggar** *verb*

begin

verb to start or commence: *Please begin work now.* | *How did the trouble begin?*

Word building: Other forms are **I began, I have begun, I am beginning.** | **beginning** *noun* the time or place when something begins

beginner

noun someone who is just learning something

begrudge

verb **1** to envy: *They begrudge you your talent.* **2** to be unwilling to give: *We begrudged paying for bad service.*

beguile   (*say* buh-**guyl**)

verb to charm or enchant: *The children were beguiled by the witch's magic.*

Word building: **beguiling** *adjective* charming

behalf

phrase **on behalf of,** on the side of or for: *to speak on behalf of my friend*

behave

verb **1** to act: *to behave like a child*
phrase **2 behave yourself,** to act properly or in an acceptable way: *to behave yourself in school*

Word building: **behaviour** *noun* the way you behave

behead

verb to cut off the head of: *They beheaded many people during the French Revolution.*

behind

preposition **1** at the back of: *We keep the broom behind the kitchen door.* **2** later than; after: *Our project is behind schedule.*

beige   (*say* bayzh)

adjective very light brown

being

noun **1** something which lives: *beings from outer space* | *a human being* **2** existence or life: *to come into being*

belated

adjective late: *I forgot her birthday so I sent a belated birthday card.*

Word use: This word is never used of people, only of things.
Word building: **belatedly** *adverb*   **belatedness** *noun*

belch

verb **1** to pass wind noisily from your stomach through your mouth: *Fizzy drink makes me belch.* **2** to throw out violently: *The volcano belched out lava.*
noun **3** the rumbling noise you make when belching

Word building: The plural form of the noun is **belches.**

belfry   (*say* <u>bel</u>-free)

noun a tower with a bell hanging in it: *the belfry of the local church*

Word building: The plural is **belfries.**

belief

noun **1** something that you believe and accept as true: *It is my belief that children should enjoy school.* **2** trust or faith: *children's belief in their parents*

believe

verb **1** to trust or have confidence in: *I can't believe that story.* **2** to think: *I believe they will be late.*
phrase **3 believe in,** to accept as real or true: *Do you believe in fairies?*
4 make believe, to pretend: *Let's make believe we're creatures from outer space.*

Word building: **believer** *noun* someone who believes, especially in a god or goddess   **believable** *adjective*   **believably** *adverb*

belittle

verb to make seem unimportant: *She hurt their feelings when she belittled their work.*

bell

noun **1** a hollow metal cup with a clapper hanging inside which can hit the side of the cup and make a ringing sound
2 the ringing sound of a bell **3** something which makes the sound of a bell

bellbird

noun a small bird that has a clear ringing call like the sound of a bell and lives in bushy areas along the east coast of Australia

belligerent   (*say* buh-<u>lij</u>-uh-ruhnt)

adjective **1** angry and aggressive: *We were surprised by the new student's belligerent behaviour.* **2** involved in a war: *a belligerent country*

Word building: **belligerence** *noun*
belligerently *adverb*

bellow   (*rhymes with* yellow)

verb to roar or cry loudly: *to bellow an answer* | *The bull bellowed with anger.*

Word building: **bellow** *noun*   **bellowing** *noun*

bellows

plural noun an instrument for pumping air: *We pumped the bellows to make the fire burn brightly.*

belly

noun **1** the front part of the body containing the stomach and intestines: *to hit someone in the belly* **2** the inside of anything: *the belly of a ship*

Word building: The plural is **bellies.**

belong

verb **1** to be owned by someone: *This pen must belong to you, because mine is still in my bag.* **2** to be part of: *I belong to a swimming club.* **3** to be in the right place: *Does this book belong on the top shelf?*

belongings

plural noun things that you own: *Our belongings are stored in a warehouse.*
Other words: **possessions**

beloved   (*say* buh-<u>luv</u>-uhd, -<u>luvd</u>)

adjective **1** much loved: *a beloved friend*
noun **2** someone you love very much: *to kiss your beloved*

below

adverb **1** beneath: *to grow below the sea* | *to live in the flat below*
preposition **2** lower than: *below the knee* | *below the usual cost*

Word use: The opposite of this is **above.**

belt

noun **1** a strip of strong material, often worn around your waist or hips
2 a large strip of land where a particular thing is grown: *the wheat belt* | *a belt of trees*
verb **3** to fasten with a belt **4** to beat or hit very hard: *She belted the rug to get rid of the dust.*
phrase **5 belt out,** *Informal* to sing very loudly **6 belt up,** *Informal*
a to be quiet: *Why don't you belt up?*
b to fasten a safety belt

Word building: **belting** *noun* a beating

bemused   (*say* buh-<u>myoohzd</u>)
adjective **1** muddled or confused **2** lost in thought: *a bemused look on the child's face*

bench
noun **1** a seat long enough for several people: *a park bench* **2** a strong work table: *a carpenter's bench* **3** a seat for members of parliament or judges in court: *the opposition benches | The prisoner stood before the bench.*
Word building: The plural is **benches**.

bend
verb **1** to turn or curve in a particular direction: *to bend a piece of wire | The road bends to the left.* **2** to stoop: *to bend over to pick up something*
noun **3** a curve or change in direction: *a bend in the road*
phrase **4 bend over backwards,** to try as hard as you can: *I bent over backwards to get you a ticket to the concert.*
Word building: Other verb forms are **I bent, I have bent, I am bending.**

bene-
prefix a word part meaning 'well': *benediction*
Word history: from Latin

beneath
adverb **1** in a lower place than: *The treasure is hidden somewhere beneath the sand.*
preposition **2** under: *The skin beneath the bandage was badly scarred.*

benediction   (*say* ben-uh-<u>dik</u>-shuhn)
noun the blessing at the end of a church service

benefactor
noun someone who gives help or money to those who need it
Word building: **beneficence** *noun*   **beneficent** *adjective*

beneficial
adjective helpful: *beneficial advice | the beneficial effect of a good night's sleep*
Word building: **beneficially** *adverb*

beneficiary   (*say* ben-uh-<u>fish</u>-uh-ree)
noun someone who receives assistance, especially money left in a will
Word building: The plural is **beneficiaries**.

benefit
noun **1** anything that is good for you: *the benefits of education* **2** a concert to raise money for charity
verb **3** to be good for: *A holiday will benefit you greatly.*
Word building: Other verb forms are **I benefited** or **benefitted, I have benefited** or **benefitted, I am benefiting** or **benefitting.**

benevolent
adjective wanting to help other people: *The Red Cross is a benevolent organisation.*
Word building: **benevolence** *noun* **benevolently** *adverb*

benign   (*rhymes with* mine)
adjective **1** kind and gentle: *a benign smile* **2** not harmful to the body: *The lump taken out of my neck by the doctor was benign.*
Word use: The opposite of this is **malignant**.
Word building: **benignity** *noun* **benignly** *adverb*

bent
adjective **1** crooked or curved: *a bent pipe* Other words: **bowed, twisted**
noun **2** a liking or preference: *a bent for painting*
phrase **3 bent on,** determined or set on: *bent on playing football*

bequeath
verb to hand down or pass on to someone who comes after you: *to bequeath money in a will*
Word building: **bequest** *noun* money left by someone in a will

bereaved
adjective sad because of someone's death: *The bereaved husband wept at his wife's funeral.*
Word building: **bereavement** *noun* the loss of someone dear to you **bereave** *verb*

beret   (*say* <u>be</u>-ray)
noun a soft round cap
Word history: from a Latin word meaning 'cloak'

berry
noun a small fruit, often brightly coloured
Word building: The plural is **berries**.

berry/bury Don't confuse **berry** with **bury**, which means 'to put something in the ground and cover it with earth'.

berserk (say buh-<u>zerk</u>)

adjective uncontrollably crazy and wild: *The dogs went berserk when they were untied.*

berth

noun **1** a place to sleep on a boat or train: *Our cabin has four berths.* **2** a place where a ship can tie up
verb **3** to tie up at a dock: *The ship berthed at 7 o'clock.*

berth/birth Don't confuse **berth** with **birth**, which is the beginning of a life.

beseech

verb to ask anxiously: *Help me, I beseech you!*

Word use: The more usual word is **beg**.
Word building: Other forms are **I besought** or **beseeched, I have besought** or **beseeched, I am beseeching.**

beside

preposition next to: *If I sit beside you, then we can read the book together.*

besides

preposition **1** as well as: *Is anyone coming besides you? | Besides being a boiling hot day, it was also very humid.* **2** other than: *Is there anything to eat besides cereal?*
adverb **3** as well as what has already been said: *Besides, I have too much homework to do.*

besiege

verb **1** to crowd round and surround: *The enemy troops besieged the town for three weeks.* **2** to set upon or attack: *The speaker was besieged with questions.*

besotted

adjective filled with foolish love: *She is absolutely besotted with cats.*

best

adjective **1** finest or highest quality **2** favourite: *my best friend*
adverb **3** most successfully: *She swims best.* **4** most: *I like that one best.*
noun **5** your nicest clothes: *to put on your best for the party*

Word use: For other forms of the adverb see **well**.

best man

noun the chief attendant or helper of the bridegroom at a wedding

bestow (*rhymes with* show)

verb to give as a gift or reward: *The queen bestowed a medal on the soldier for bravery.*

Word building: **bestowal** *noun*

bet

noun **1** a promise that you will give money or something like that to someone who differs from you, if that person is right and you are wrong: *Ann made a bet that she was taller than Yuki.* **2** the money or thing that you promised: *I lost my bet.*
verb **3** to risk as part of a bet: *I bet you fifty cents I can jump this fence.*
4 to make a bet

Word building: Other verb forms are **I bet** or **betted, I have bet** or **betted, I am betting.**

betray

verb **1** to be unfaithful or disloyal to: *The spy betrayed her country by selling important secrets to the enemy.*
Other words: **doublecross**
2 to show or reveal: *Your face betrayed your anger. | to betray a secret*
Other words: **expose**

Word building: **betrayal** *noun*　**betrayer** *noun*

betrothed (*rhymes with* clothed)

adjective engaged to be married

Word building: **betrothal** *noun*　**betrothed** *noun*　**betroth** *verb*

better

adjective **1** of higher quality, or of more value: *This furniture is made of better wood than that.* **2** larger, or greater: *It took us the better part of our lives to build this house.* **3** improved in health: *I hope you are feeling better today.*
adverb **4** in an improved or more suitable manner: *I behaved better today.*
verb **5** to improve: *I bettered my score in the first round by two points.*

bettong (say <u>bet</u>-ong)

noun a very small kangaroo that looks like a small wallaby with a short nose. It is endangered. See the table at the end of this book

Word use: Another word for this is **squeaker**.
Word history: from an Aboriginal language of New South Wales called Dharug. See the map of Australian Aboriginal languages at the end of this book.

between

preposition **1** within the space, time or amount that separates two or more things: *a park between the river and the road | to arrive between 3 o'clock and 4 o'clock | a difference between prices* **2** joining: *a bridge between the two islands* **3** concerning or involving: *an agreement between the Chinese and Australian governments | This argument is between Rashid and me — you stay out!* **4** by sharing an effort or action: *We'll work it out between us.*

beverage

noun a drink of any kind

beware

verb to be careful: *If you go in, beware of the dog.*

Word use: This verb is usually followed by *of*.

bewilder

verb to confuse or puzzle: *The maze completely bewildered us.*
Other words: **baffle, perplex**

Word building: **bewilderment** *noun*

bewitch

verb **1** to put under a magic spell **2** to charm: *The class choir bewitched the audience with their delightful voices.*

beyond   (*say* bee-<u>yond</u>)

preposition further than: *I bet you that I can throw the ball beyond the fence.*

bi-

prefix a word part meaning **1** two: *bicycle* **2** twice: *bigamy*

Word history: from Latin

biannual

adjective happening twice a year: *a biannual school concert*

Word use: Compare this with **biennial**.
Word building: **biannually** *adverb*

bias   (*say* <u>buy</u>-uhs)

noun **1** a strong opinion which often stops you from seeing the other side of an argument: *His bias towards football was obvious.* **2** a slanting line or direction

Word building: **bias** *verb* (**biased, biasing**) **biased** *adjective*

bib

noun **1** a small cloth tied under a baby's chin to protect its clothes at mealtime

2 the part of an apron or pair of overalls above the waist

Word history: from a Latin word meaning 'drink'

Bible

noun the sacred book of the Christian religion, consisting of the Old and New Testaments

Word building: **biblical** *adjective*
Word history: from a Greek word meaning 'book'

biblio-

prefix a word part meaning 'book': *bibliography*

Word history: from Greek

bibliography   (*say* bib-lee-<u>og</u>-ruh-fee)

noun **1** a list of all the books read or used by a writer when writing a book or essay **2** a list of everything written by a particular writer, or about a particular subject: *a bibliography of Australian wildlife*

Word building: The plural is **bibliographies**. | **bibliographer** *noun* **bibliographic** *adjective* **bibliographical** *adjective*

bicentenary   (*say* buy-suhn-<u>teen</u>-uh-ree)

noun a 200th anniversary: *Australia had its bicentenary in 1988.*

Word building: The plural is **bicentenaries**. | **bicentennial** *adjective*

biceps   (*say* <u>buy</u>-seps)

noun a large muscle at the top of your arm or the back of your thigh that helps you to bend your elbow or knee

Word history: from a Latin word meaning 'two-headed', as this muscle is joined at the top in two places

bicker

verb to squabble or argue about little things

bicycle

noun a two-wheeled machine for riding on, which you steer by handlebars and propel by pushing pedals

Word use: The shortened form is **bike** which is more suited to informal language.
Word building: **bicyclist** *noun*

bid

verb **1** to order or command: *The queen bids her people to do as she wishes.* **2** to say or tell: *The teacher bids the class good morning every day.* **3** to offer or make an offer to buy at an auction: *I bid $200 for the table. | He bid for the chair.*

noun **4** the amount offered for something, especially at an auction **5** an attempt to achieve a goal or purpose

Word building: **bidder** *noun* **bidding** *noun*

biennial (*say* buy-<u>en</u>-ee-uhl)

adjective **1** happening every two years **2** living for two years: *Onions and parsnips are biennial plants.*

Word use: Compare this with **biannual**.
Word building: **biennial** *noun* **biennially** *adverb*

bier (*sounds like* beer)

noun a stand on which a dead body, or the coffin holding it, rests before it is buried

bifocals

plural noun a pair of glasses with lenses which have two parts, one for seeing things far away and one for seeing things close to you

Word building: **bifocal** *adjective*

big

adjective **1** large in size or amount: *Uluru is a very big rock.*
Other words: **colossal, enormous, giant, huge, immense, massive**
2 elder: *my big brother*
Other words: **older**
3 having a high rank or status: *Our school planned a special welcome for the big visitor.*
Other words: **eminent, important, prestigious**
4 important: *Your wedding is a big event in your life.*
Other words: **major, momentous, significant**

Word building: Other forms are **bigger, biggest**.

bigamy (*say* <u>big</u>-uh-mee)

noun the crime of marrying someone while you are still married to someone else

Word use: Compare this with **monogamy** and **polygamy**.
Word building: **bigamist** *noun* **bigamous** *adjective*

bight (*sounds like* bite)

noun a bend or curve in the shore of the sea

---

bight/bite/byte Don't confuse **bight** with **bite** or **byte**.
A **bite** is a mouthful of something or a wound made using teeth or something similar.
A **byte** is a unit of information stored in a computer.

---

bigot (*say* <u>big</u>-uht)

noun someone who is convinced that their opinion is right and who gets irritated by people who disagree

Word building: **bigoted** *adjective* **bigotry** *noun*

bike

noun a bicycle or motorcycle

bike rack

noun a structure to which bikes can be locked for safety

bikini (*say* buh-<u>kee</u>-nee)

noun a two-piece swimming costume for women

Word history: named after *Bikini* Atoll in the northern Pacific Ocean, where the United States tested nuclear bombs from 1946 to 1958

bilateral

adjective of or affecting two sides: *The two countries came to a bilateral agreement about trade.*

bilby (*say* <u>bil</u>-bee)

noun a type of bandicoot that is vulnerable. See the table at the end of this book.

Word building: The plural is **bilbies**.
Word history: from an Aboriginal language of New South Wales called Yuwaalaraay. See the map of Australian Aboriginal languages at the end of this book.

bile

noun a bitter yellowish liquid which is produced by the liver and which helps you digest food

bilingual (*say* buy-<u>ling</u>-gwuhl)

adjective able to speak two languages

Word building: **bilingualism** *noun* **bilingually** *adverb*

bilious (*say* <u>bil</u>-yuhs)

adjective **1** having, or caused by, too much bile: *a bilious attack* **2** feeling sick in the stomach

Word building: **biliousness** *noun*

bill[1]

noun **1** a written statement telling you how much money you owe for something **2** a poster or advertisement on display **3** a plan for a new law to be presented to Parliament

Word building: **bill** *verb*

bill[2]

noun a bird's beak

billabong

noun a waterhole which used to be part of a river

Word history: from an Aboriginal language of New South Wales called Wiradjuri. See the map of Australian Aboriginal languages at the end of this book.

billet

noun a place for someone to live for a while: *The soldier was given a billet in the captain's own home.*

Word building: **billet** *verb* (**billeted, billeting**): *We billeted a student from Japan in our home.*

billiards　　(*say* bil-yuhdz)

noun a game played by two or more people on a special table, with hard balls hit by a long stick called a cue

billion

noun **1** a number, one thousand times one million, 1 000 000 000 or 10^9
2 a number, one million times one million, 1 000 000 000 000 or 10^{12}

Word use: Definition 2 is rare nowadays.
Word building: **billion** *adjective* **billionth** *adjective*

billionaire　　(*say* bil-yuh-nair)

noun an extremely rich person whose wealth is worth at least a billion dollars, euros, and so on: *She aimed to become a billionaire by selling exclusive pet accessories.*

billow

noun **1** a large wave: *the billows of the ocean*
verb **2** to swirl or rise like billows: *Smoke billowed from the chimney.*

Word building: **billowy** *adjective*

billy

noun a tin container with a lid, used for boiling water

Word building: The plural is **billies**.

billycart

noun a four-wheeled cart which has a box for a seat and which you steer by ropes attached to its front axle

billy goat

noun a male goat

Word use: The female is a **nanny goat** and the young is a **kid**.

bin

noun a box or container used to store things: *Put the empty packet in the garbage bin.*

binary　　(*say* buy-nuh-ree)

adjective **1** made up of two parts or things
2 using the numbers 0 and 1: *binary code*

bind　　(*rhymes with* find)

verb **1** to tie up or fasten: *The girls bind their hair with ribbons.* **2** to cover or bandage: *I always have to bind my wrist before a hockey game* **3** to fasten with a cover: *to bind a book*
noun **4** a nuisance or a bore: *Doing the dishes is a bind.*

Word building: Other verb forms are **I bound, I have bound, I am binding.** | **binder** *noun*　**binding** *noun*

bindi-eye

noun a small plant with tiny sharp thorns which sometimes in grass

Word use: It is also called a **bindi**.
Word history: from Aboriginal languages of New South Wales called Kamilaroi and Yuwaalaraay. See the map of Australian Aboriginal languages at the end of this book.

binge

noun Informal a period of too much eating, drinking or spending money

bingo

noun a gambling game in which you cross numbers, called in any order, off a card
Word use: Other names for this are **housie-housie** and **lotto**.

binoculars　　(*say* buh-nok-yuhl-uhz)

plural noun double magnifying glasses for both eyes, used for making distant objects seem nearer

Word building: **binocular** *adjective* using two eyes

bio-

prefix a word part meaning 'life' or 'living things': *biology*
Word history: from Greek

biodegradable

adjective able to be broken down by the action of very small living things like bacteria: *Most detergents are biodegradable.*

biodiesel

noun a biodegradable fuel, made from field crop oils, especially from recycled cooking oil

biodiverse　　(*say* buy-oh-duy-vers, buy-oh-duh-vers)

adjective having a variety of examples of plant and animal organisms in an area: *The reef was so biodiverse — full of waving seaweed, small crabs, and masses of different fish.*

biofuel (*say* <u>buy</u>-oh-fyoo-huhl)
noun a fuel that is made from biological material such as vegetable oil or from plants high in sugar content: *The more cars use biofuel, the less we will use up oil from the ground that cannot be replaced.*

biography
noun the story of a person's life, written by someone else

Word use: Compare this with **autobiography**. Word building: The plural is **biographies**. | **biographer** *noun* **biographical** *adjective*

biology
noun the science or study of all living things

Word building: **biological** *adjective* **biologist** *noun*

bionic (*say* buy-<u>on</u>-ik)
adjective having parts of your body replaced by electronic equipment so as to give you superhuman strength

biopsy
noun the removal of a small section of someone's body to check if it is diseased

Word building: The plural is **biopsies**.

birch
noun a tree of cold countries, with slender branches and smooth bark

Word building: The plural is **birches**.

bird
noun **1** a two-legged creature which lays eggs and has wings and feathers **2** *Informal* a person: *He's a funny old bird.*

birth
noun **1** the act of being born **2** any beginning: *the birth of a nation*

birth/berth Don't confuse **birth** with **berth**, which is the bunk or room where a traveller sleeps on a ship or train. It can also be the space for a ship to tie up at a dock.

birthday
noun **1** the day on which someone is born **2** the annual celebration of the day of someone's birth: *It is my eleventh birthday today.*

biscuit (*say* <u>bis</u>-kuht)
noun a small thin cake which has been baked until it is crisp

Word history: from Latin words meaning 'cooked twice'

bisect
verb to cut or divide into two parts or two equal parts

Word building: **bisector** *noun* a line that bisects an angle **bisection** *noun*

bisexual
noun **1** an animal, human or plant which has both male and female sex organs **2** someone who is sexually attracted to both males and females

bishop
noun **1** a church minister of high rank, in charge of a whole district **2** a chess piece which can only move diagonally

Word use: **Episcopal** is a word meaning 'having to do with a bishop'. Word building: **bishopric** *noun* the district the bishop is in charge of

bison (*say* <u>buy</u>-suhn)
noun a large American animal with high shoulders and shaggy hair

Word building: The plural is **bison**.

bistro (*say* <u>bis</u>-troh)
noun a small, casual restaurant or wine bar

Word building: The plural is **bistros**.

bit[1]
noun **1** a metal bar placed in a horse's mouth and attached to the reins, used to help control it **2** the part of some tools which is used for cutting and making holes

bit[2]
noun a small piece or amount of something

bit[3]
noun a single basic unit of information, used in connection with computers

bitch
noun **1** a female dog, fox or wolf **2** *Informal* an unpleasant or bad-tempered person, usually female
verb **3** *Informal* to complain: *He was bitching about the bad weather.*

Word use: For definition 1 the male animal is a **dog**. | The use of this word as in definition 2 will offend people. Word building: The plural form of the noun is **bitches**. | **bitchiness** *noun* **bitchy** *adjective*

bite

verb **1** to grab or cut or take a piece out with your teeth: *He bit the apple.* **2** to hurt or sting: *The mosquitoes are biting tonight.* **3** to take the bait: *The fish were biting well yesterday.*

noun **4** a wound made by biting **5** a snack or small amount of food: *I'll just have a bite to eat at the restaurant.* **6** the act of biting: *The baby had one or two bites of the biscuit.*

Word building: Other verb forms are **I bit, I have bitten, I am biting**.

---

bite/bight/byte Don't confuse **bite** with **bight** or **byte**.
A **bight** is a bay, as in the *Great Australian Bight*.
A **byte** is a unit of information stored by a computer.

---

bitmap

noun a computer image made up of rows and columns of dots stored as bits (**bit³**)

bitter

adjective **1** having a sharp unpleasant taste
Other words: **acidic, astringent, sour, tart**
2 hard to accept or bear: *Tim felt a bitter sorrow when his grandmother died.*
Other words: **sharp, poignant**
3 very cold: *a bitter wind*
Other words: **freezing, harsh, piercing, sharp**

Word building: **bitterly** *adverb* **bitterness** *noun*

bitumen   (*say* bit-chuh-muhn)

noun **1** a sticky black mixture, like tar or asphalt, used to make roads **2** a tarred road: *You must ride your bike on the bitumen, not on the footpath.*

bivouac   (*say* biv-uh-wak)

noun **1** a camp set up for a short time: *The soldiers went on a bivouac in the bush for the weekend.*
verb **2** to camp out: *The cadets bivouacked for a week at the end of each term.*

Word building: Other verb forms are **I bivouacked, I have bivouacked, I am bivouacking**.

bizarre   (*say* buh-zah)

adjective very strange or unusual

blab

verb **1** to talk too much: *My friend blabbed for hours.* **2** to tell or reveal without thinking

Word building: Other forms are **I blabbed, I have blabbed, I am blabbing.** | **blabbermouth** *noun* someone who blabs

black

adjective **1** completely dark, or without colour and brightness: *a black night | a black dress* **2** having dark-coloured skin **3** sad or gloomy: *It was a black day for the children when their dog died.* **4** angry: *He gave me a black look.* **5** evil or wicked: *Murder is a black deed.* **6** without milk or cream: *I have my coffee black.*
noun **7** someone who has dark-coloured skin

Word building: **blacken** *verb*

blackberry

noun a prickly plant which grows in tangled bushes, or its small, sweet, black or purple fruit

Word building: The plural is **blackberries**.

blackboard

noun a smooth dark board that you use for writing or drawing on with chalk

blackcurrant

noun a small black fruit which grows on a garden shrub

blackguard   (*say* blag-ahd)

noun someone who is dishonourable

blackhead

noun a small, black-tipped pimple, usually on your face

black hole

noun a region in outer space from which no light or matter can escape, thought to be the result of a star collapsing under its own gravity

blackmail

noun the act of demanding money from someone by threatening to reveal secrets about them

Word building: **blackmail** *verb* **blackmailer** *noun*

blackout

noun **1** an electrical power failure **2** a loss of memory, consciousness or sight which lasts for a short time

blacksmith

noun someone who makes or repairs things made of iron

bladder

noun **1** a bag of skin inside your body which stores urine until it is passed out **2** any bag that gets bigger if you fill it with air or liquid, like the rubber bag inside a football

blade

noun **1** the flat cutting part of a knife, sword or dagger **2** the leaf of a plant: *a blade of grass* **3** the thin flat part of something, like an oar or a bone **4 blades**, *Informal* rollerblades

blame

noun **1** the responsibility for a mistake: *He shares the blame for the accident.* *verb* **2** to place blame on

Word building: **blameless** *adjective* **blameworthy** *adjective*

blanch

verb **1** to make or become white or pale: *The man blanched with fear.* **2** to put in boiling water for a short time, and then in cold, in order to remove the skins or to kill germs before freezing: *to blanch nuts, vegetables, or fruit*

bland

adjective **1** pleasant or polite but often without real feeling: *a bland smile* **2** smooth and mild: *bland food*

Word building: **blandly** *adverb* **blandness** *noun*

blank

adjective **1** not written or printed on: *a blank piece of paper* **2** showing no understanding or interest: *As I explained it to him, he had a blank look on his face.* *noun* **3** an empty space left for someone to fill in: *Just fill in the blanks on this form please.* **4** a gun cartridge which has powder inside it but no bullet: *The army uses blanks for its practice shooting.*

Word building: **blankly** *adverb* **blankness** *noun*
Word history: from a French word meaning 'white'

blanket

noun **1** a large piece of soft woollen or cotton material, used as a bed covering **2** any layer or covering that hides something: *There was a blanket of snow covering the ground.*

blare   (*rhymes with* hair)

verb to make a loud harsh sound: *The car horns blared.*

Word building: **blare** *noun*: *the blare of traffic*

blasé   (*say* blah-<u>zay</u>)

adjective not caring about and bored by the enjoyments and pleasures of life

Word use: The accent over the 'e' is a clue that this word was originally French.

blaspheme   (*say* blas-<u>feem</u>)

verb to speak without respect about your god or things to do with your god

Word building: **blasphemer** *noun* **blasphemy** *noun* (**blasphemies**) **blasphemous** (*say* <u>blas</u>-fuh-muhs) *adjective*

blast

noun **1** a sudden strong gust of wind or air **2** the shrill sound of a whistle or horn **3** an explosion **4** *Informal* a severe criticism: *They were given a blast for being late.* *verb* **5** to set off explosives **6** *Informal* to criticise: *My parents blasted me for being so naughty.*

blatant   (*say* <u>blay</u>-tuhnt)

adjective very obvious: *a blatant lie*

Word building: **blatancy** *noun* **blatantly** *adverb*
Word history: made up by the English poet Edmund Spenser and based on a Latin word meaning 'babble'

blaze[1]

noun **1** a bright flame or fire **2** a gleam or glow of brightness: *a sudden blaze of sunlight* **3** a bright or sparkling display: *The garden was a blaze of colour.* **4** sudden fury: *a blaze of temper* *verb* **5** to burn brightly: *The fire blazed in the fireplace.* **6** to shine or glow like a flame: *The oval blazed with lights during the match.*

blaze[2]

noun **1** a mark made on a tree to point out a path **2** a white patch on the face of a horse or cow *verb* **3** to mark a path with blazes: *The scouts blazed a trail through the bush.*

blazer

noun a jacket, sometimes with a crest sewn on the pocket

bleach

verb **1** to make white, pale or colourless: *My mother bleached the stains out of my dress.*
noun **2** a chemical used for bleaching

bleak

adjective **1** cold and harsh: *A bleak winter wind was blowing.* **2** empty and dreary: *A prisoner in jail has a bleak life.*

bleary

adjective dimmed from tears or tiredness: *bleary eyes*

Word building: Other forms are **blearier, bleariest.** | **blearily** *adverb* **bleariness** *noun*

bleat

verb **1** to make the cry of a sheep or goat **2** to complain

Word building: **bleat** *noun*

bleed

verb **1** to lose blood **2** to draw or drain blood, liquid or air from: *to bleed the brakes of a car*

Word building: Other forms are **I bled, I have bled, I am bleeding.**

blemish

verb to spoil with a spot or stain
Other words: **damage, mar, stain, taint**

Word building: **blemish** *noun* (**blemishes**)

blend

verb to mix or combine: *He blended the flour and water.* | *The flour and water blended well.*
Word building: **blend** *noun*

blender

noun an electric appliance which chops and mixes food

bless

verb to make sacred: *The bishop blessed the church.*
Other words: **consecrate, sanctify**

Word building: **blessing** *noun* a good thing that has happened to you **blessed** *adjective* **blessedly** *adverb* **blessedness** *noun*

blight

noun **1** a plant disease: *tomato blight* **2** something that damages or destroys
Word building: **blight** *verb*

blind

adjective **1** not able to see **2** unwilling to understand or be fair: *He was blind with anger.*
verb **3** to make unable to see
noun **4** a window cover which keeps out light **5** a cover for hiding the truth

Word building: **blindly** *adverb* **blindness** *noun*

blindfold

verb to cover the eyes of, to prevent from seeing: *The captors blindfolded their victim.*

Word building: **blindfold** *noun* a cover for the eyes

blink

verb to shut and open the eyes quickly and often: *I blinked in the bright sunlight.*
Word building: **blink** *noun*

bliss

noun great happiness
Word building: **blissful** *adjective* **blissfully** *adverb*

blister

noun **1** a small watery swelling on your skin
verb **2** to cause blisters on: *The hot sun blistered my bare shoulders.* **3** to get blisters: *My bare shoulders blistered at the beach.*

Word building: **blistering** *adjective*: *blistering heat* **blistery** *adjective*
Word history: from a French word meaning 'clod' or 'lump'

blithe

adjective happy or cheerful
Word building: **blithely** *adverb*

blitz

noun a sudden attack: *a blitz on a city in wartime* | *a blitz on drivers who drink*
Word building: **blitz** *verb*

blizzard

noun a storm with snow and strong winds

bloat

verb to make bigger or cause to swell, especially with air or water

bloc

noun a group of countries sharing the same political ideas: *the communist bloc*

block

noun **1** a solid piece of hard material: *a child's building block* **2** a piece of land on which a house is built **3** a group of buildings or houses surrounded by streets *verb* **4** to be in the way of: *The accident blocked the traffic.*
Other words: **bar, obstruct**
Word building: **blockage** *noun*

blockade

noun the closing of a port by enemy ships or soldiers to stop supplies going in or out
Other words: **siege**
Word building: **blockade** *verb*

blockbuster

noun **1** a heavy powerful bomb dropped during World War II, especially on fortifications **2** anything large and exciting: *The new James Bond movie is an absolute blockbuster.*

blog

noun a record of items on the internet often about particular subjects that people can comment on, with links to other possibly interesting sites: *Kali set up a blog to get in touch with other people who liked the same bands as she did.*

bloke

noun Informal a man

blond

adjective having light-coloured hair and skin
Word building: **blonde** *noun* a woman with light-coloured hair   **blond** *noun*
Word history: from a Latin word meaning 'yellow'

blood

noun **1** the fluid that flows through the arteries and veins of your body
phrase **2 in cold blood**, calmly and without feeling

bloodbath

noun the cruel killing of a large number of people
Other words: **carnage, massacre, slaughter**

bloodcurdling

adjective very frightening and horrible: *a bloodcurdling tale of evil and murder*

bloodhound

noun a large dog with a good sense of smell, used for hunting animals or finding lost people

bloodshot

adjective showing streaks of blood: *bloodshot eyes*

bloodthirsty

adjective wanting to kill: *The bloodthirsty pirates took no prisoners.*

blood type

noun one of a group of blood types, each differing from each other in how they clot: *They love me at the blood bank because I've got a rare blood type.*

bloody

adjective **1** with blood on it **2** causing loss of life: *a bloody battle* **3** *Informal* very great: *a bloody pest | a bloody miracle*
Word use: The use of this word as in definition 3 might offend people.
Word building: Other forms are **bloodier, bloodiest.**

bloom

verb to produce flowers: *The rose bush blooms in summer.*
Other words: **blossom, bud, flower**
Word building: **bloom** *noun* a flower **blooming** *adjective*

bloomers

plural noun loose underpants
Word history: named after a Mrs Amelia Bloomer, a magazine publisher of New York, who helped make these pants popular in about 1850

blossom

noun **1** the flower of a fruit tree
verb **2** to produce flowers **3** to develop: *He blossomed into a fine athlete.*

blot

noun **1** a spot of ink on paper **2** a stain: *a blot on your reputation*
verb **3** to dry or soak up: *to blot the ink*
phrase **4 blot out**, to take away: *to blot out a bad memory*
Word building: Other verb forms are **I blotted, I have blotted, I am blotting.**

blotch

noun a large unevenly shaped mark
Word use: The plural is **blotches.**
Word building: **blotchy** *adjective*

blouse   (*say* blowz)

noun a loosely fitting shirt usually gathered, or tucked in, at the waist

blow[1]

noun **1** a hard stroke with the hand or something held in it
Other words: **bang, bash, clout, knock, thump**
2 a sudden shock: *a blow to your pride*
Other words: **disappointment, upset**

blow[2]

verb **1** to be in motion: *The winds blow.*
2 to be moved by the wind: *Dust blew down the street.*
Other words: **waft**
3 to produce a current of air, with bellows or your mouth: *Blow on the fire.* **4** to make a noise by blowing into: *Blow the whistle.*
Other words: **sound, toot**
5 to burn out or burst: *The light bulb has blown.* | *The tyre blew.* **6** to put out with a puff of air: *Blow out the candle.*
noun **7** a storm with strong wind
phrase **8 blow up,**
a to force air into: *to blow up a balloon*
Other words: **inflate**
b to destroy with explosives: *to blow up a bridge*
Other words: **explode**

Word building: Other verb forms are **it blew, it has blown, it is blowing.**

blowfly

noun a fly which lays eggs on meat and rubbish

Word building: The plural is **blowflies.**

blubber

noun **1** the fat of a whale or similar sea animal
verb **2** to cry noisily

bludge

verb Informal to avoid doing what you should: *While others worked, he bludged.*

Word building: **bludger** *noun*

bludgeon (say bluj-uhn)

noun a short heavy piece of wood used as a weapon

Word building: **bludgeon** *verb* to hit with a bludgeon

blue

adjective **1** having the colour of a clear sky
2 *Informal* sad and depressed: *I'm feeling blue.*
noun **3** the colour blue **4** *Informal* a mistake
phrase **5 true blue,** loyal

Word building: Other adjective forms are **bluer, bluest.**

---

blue/blew Don't confuse **blue** with **blew,** which is the past tense of **blow:**
The wind blew the blue banners down.

bluebottle

noun **1** a small blue sea animal with long tentacles which can sting you
2 a large blue and green fly

blueprint

noun **1** a copy of a building plan printed in white on blue paper **2** any detailed plan which can be copied at a later time

blues

plural noun **1** *Informal* feelings of sadness: *to have the blues* **2** a style of music, first performed by African-Americans, usually sad in character and slow in tempo

Word history: short for *blue devils*

blue-tongue

noun a large Australian lizard with a broad blue tongue

bluetooth wireless technology

noun radio technology that lets computers and telecommunication devices like mobile phones connect with each other

Word history: from the name of a Viking king, Harald *Bluetooth*, who was successful in uniting Denmark and Norway under one rule

bluff[1]

noun a wide steep cliff

bluff[2]

verb **1** to trick by showing you aren't afraid: *She bluffed her way past the guard, whistling as she went.* **2** to pretend you aren't afraid hoping you will get your own way: *Don't take any notice of him, he's only bluffing.*
noun **3** a pretence of having no fear: *It was a big bluff.*

blunder

noun **1** a silly mistake
Other words: **error, misjudgement, slip**
verb **2** to make a silly mistake
Other words: **err, slip**
3 to move or act clumsily: *I blundered into the cupboard.*
Other words: **lurch, stagger, stumble**

blunt

adjective **1** not sharp: *a blunt knife*
2 plain or direct: *a blunt refusal*
Other words: **forthright, frank,
straightforward**

Word building: **blunt** *verb* **bluntly**
adverb **bluntness** *noun*

blur

verb **1** to make unclear or confused: *Tears
blurred my sight.*
noun **2** something that is unclear or
confused: *We drove so fast the countryside
was a blur.*

Word building: Other verb forms are **it
blurred, it has blurred, it is blurring.** | **blurry**
adjective (**blurrier, blurriest**)

blurb

noun information about a book or a
recording, often printed on its cover

Word history: made up by the American
humorist and illustrator, Gelett Burgess, who
lived from 1866 to 1951

blush

verb to become red in the face when you're
embarrassed or ashamed

Word building: **blush** *noun* (**blushes**)

bluster

verb **1** to speak or act in a noisy or violent
way: *Richard blustered when he was criticised.*
2 to force by blustering: *Estella blustered her
way through.*

Word building: **blustery** *adjective* loud and
violent: *a blustery wind*

BMX bike

noun a strongly-built bicycle, good for
riding in rough areas

Word history: short for *Bicycle Motocross*, with
the *cross* changed to *X* and pronounced as the
letter 'x'

boa constrictor

noun a snake which winds round its victim
to crush and kill it

boar

noun a male pig

Word use: The female is a **sow** and the young
is a **piglet**.

boar/bore/boor Don't confuse **boar** with
bore or **boor**.
A **bore** is either a tedious and uninteresting
person, or a hole made by drilling.
Bore is also the past tense of the verb **bear**.
A **boor** is someone who is rude or
inconsiderate.

board

noun **1** a flat piece of wood, cut into long
thin pieces: *a floor board* **2** a thin flat
piece of wood or other material made
for a special purpose: *a chess board* | *an
ironing-board* | *a noticeboard* **3** a group of
people who are in charge of a business or
organisation: *the board of the club*
verb **4** to get on: *to board a ship or bus*
5 to pay for the use of a room, or for a
room and meals: *I board at the hotel.*

board/bored Don't confuse **board** with
bored, which is to feel no interest in
something.

boarder

noun **1** a pupil who lives at a school
2 someone who pays for meals and a room
to sleep in: *Our neighbour takes in boarders.*

boarder/border Don't confuse **boarder** with
border, which is the edge of something, like
a boundary line separating one country from
another.

boast

verb **1** to speak with too much pride: *Don't
boast so much about your mark in the test.*
Other words: **brag, crow**
noun **2** something which is spoken of with
pride

Word building: **boaster** *noun* **boastful**
adjective **boastfully** *adverb* **boastfulness**
noun

boat

noun **1** a small uncovered vessel for
carrying people or things over water
phrase **2 in the same boat,** in the same
unpleasant situation

Word building: **boating** *noun* travelling in
boats: *Boating is my favourite sport.*

boater

noun a straw hat with a hard flat brim

boat people

plural noun people who escape from South-
East Asian countries in boats

Word use: People who are forced to leave their
own country are **refugees**.

bob¹

noun **1** a short quick movement: *a bob of the head*
verb **2** to make a short quick movement up and down: *The float bobbed in the water.*
phrase **3 bob up,** to come into sight suddenly: *He bobbed up from behind the tree.*

Word building: Other verb forms are **I bobbed, I have bobbed, I am bobbing.**

bob²

noun **1** a short haircut in which the hair is cut in a straight line evenly around the head
verb **2** to cut short: *He bobbed the horse's tail.*

Word building: Other verb forms are **I bobbed, I have bobbed, I am bobbing.**

bobbin

noun a small reel on which thread is wound for use in a sewing machine or in spinning

bodice   (*say* bod-uhs)

noun the part of a woman's dress above the waist

body

noun **1** the whole physical structure of a person or animal **2** the physical part of a person or animal without the head, arms or legs
Other words: **torso, trunk**
3 a dead person or animal
Other words: **cadaver, corpse**
4 the main part: *the body of a car | the body of the speech* **5** a group of people or things: *a body of friends*

Word building: The plural is **bodies.** | **bodily** *adjective*

body art

noun the use of various methods to decorate the human body such as tattooing, painting, piercing, and so on

body image

noun the picture that a person has of how their own body looks: *People with anorexia have a body image of a really fat person even though they might be quite thin.*

bog

noun **1** an area of muddy ground
verb **2** to make or become stuck: *The mud bogged the car. | The car was bogged in the mud.*

Word building: Other verb forms are **it bogged, it has bogged, it is bogging. | boggy** *adjective* (**boggier, boggiest**)

bogey   (*say* boh-gee)

noun **1** a swimming hole **2** a bath or shower
verb **3** to swim or bathe

Word use: Another spelling is **bogie.**
Word history: from an Aboriginal language of New South Wales called Dharug. See the map of Australian Aboriginal languages at the end of this book.

boggle

verb to show fear or surprise

Word building: Other forms are **I boggled, I have boggled, I am boggling.**

bogie   (*say* boh-gee)

noun **1** a small trolley used by workmen on a railway line **2** a set of wheels supporting a railway engine or carriage

bogong

noun a large Australian moth sometimes used as food

Word use: Another spelling is **bugong.**
Word history: from an Aboriginal language of New South Wales and Victoria called Ngarigo. See the map of Australian Aboriginal languages at the end of this book.

bogus   (*say* boh-guhs)

adjective not real or true: *The bogus doctor was arrested by the police.*
Other words: **fake, false, pretend, sham**

bogy   (*say* boh-gee)

noun anything that frightens or worries you

Word building: The plural is **bogies.**

boil¹

verb **1** to cause to become so hot that bubbles form and steam comes off: *I boiled water for tea.* **2** to become as hot as that: *The water boiled.* **3** to hold, or be in, a boiling liquid: *The kettle is boiling. | The peas are boiling.* **4** to cook by boiling: *I boiled the potatoes.*

boil²

noun an infected swollen sore under your skin

boiler

noun **1** a container with a lid used for boiling things **2** a closed container in which steam is produced to drive engines

boilersuit

noun overalls with sleeves, used when doing hard dirty work

boisterous

adjective rough and noisy

Word building: **boisterously** *adverb* **boisterousness** *noun*

bold

adjective **1** without fear **2** having no shame or modesty **3** rude **4** easy to see: *bold handwriting*

Word building: **boldly** *adverb* **boldness** *noun* **embolden** *verb*

bolster   (*say* bohl-stuh)

noun **1** a long round pillow **2** a support: *a bolster to your courage* *verb* **3** to help make strong: *Success will bolster your shattered pride.*

bolt

noun **1** a sliding bar which fastens a door or gate **2** a thick metal pin which holds pieces of wood or metal together *verb* **3** to fasten with a bolt **4** to run away because you are afraid: *They bolted when they saw the police.* **5** to swallow quickly or without chewing: *He had indigestion because he had bolted his food.* *phrase* **6 a bolt of lightning**, a flash in the sky, with thunder

Word use: Another word for definition 3 is **thunderbolt**.

bomb

noun **1** a container filled with an explosive and used as a weapon **2** *Informal* an old car *verb* **3** to attack with bombs

Word building: **bomber** *noun*

bombard

verb **1** to attack with heavy guns or bombs: *The castle was bombarded by the enemy.* **2** to overwhelm with repeated questions, requests, comments, and so on: *The fans bombarded the movie star with questions and compliments.*

bombast

noun words or remarks that sound important but are often not sincere: *The speech was full of bombast.*

Word use: The more usual word is **pompous**. Word building: **bombastic** *adjective* **bombastically** *adverb* Word history: from a Latin word meaning 'silkworm' or 'silk'

bombshell

noun **1** a bomb **2** something which causes surprise and shock

bond

noun **1** something that joins or holds together: *a bond of friendship* **2** a promise or agreement: *to sign a bond to work for the government* *verb* **3** to join or hold together: *to bond with glue*

bondage

noun the state of being controlled by someone or something Other words: **captivity, slavery**

bone

noun **1** one of the separate pieces of hard tissue that form a skeleton: *a hip bone* *verb* **2** to take out the bones of: *to bone a fish* *phrase* **3 have a bone to pick**, to have something to argue about

Word building: **bony** *adjective* (**bonier, boniest**)

bonfire

noun a large outdoor fire

bongo

noun one of a pair of small drums, which you play by beating with your fingers

Word building: The plural is **bongos** or **bongoes**.

bonnet

noun **1** a close-fitting hat, tied under the chin: *a baby's bonnet* **2** any other hood or protective covering, such as the metal cover over the engine of a car

bonsai   (*say* bon-suy)

noun **1** the art of keeping trees and shrubs very small by cutting their roots and branches **2** a tree or shrub grown this way

Word history: from the Japanese word for 'pot' added to the Japanese word meaning 'to plant'

bonus

noun **1** extra money paid to a worker as a reward for good work **2** something that is extra and not expected: *The nurse that looked after me was very thoughtful. The fact that she was funny as well was a bonus.*

bonzer

adjective Informal excellent or pleasing: *a bonzer picnic*

Word use: Another spelling is **bonza**.

boobook

noun a small brownish owl with a white-spotted back and wings, found in Australia and New Zealand

boogie board

noun a small, light and slightly curved board that you take into the surf so that you can lie on it and let the waves take you back to the shore

book

noun **1** a number of pages bound together inside a cover, for writing in or for reading *verb* **2** to reserve or buy early: *They booked seats on the train. | to book theatre tickets* **3** to record or take the name of: *A policeman booked Bem for speeding.*

Word building: **booking** *noun*

bookend

noun a support placed at the end of a row of books to stop them falling over

bookish

adjective eager to read or study: *The athletic girls teased Jane for being bookish.*

bookkeeping

noun the job of keeping records of all the money earned and spent in a business

Word building: **bookkeeper** *noun*

bookmaker

noun someone who takes the bets of other people, especially at a racecourse

Word building: **bookmaking** *noun*

bookmark

noun **1** a strip of paper, cloth, or something similar placed between the pages of a book to mark a place **2** a link to a website that you wish to visit again, which is stored on your computer for easy reference

bookworm

noun someone who loves reading

boom¹

verb **1** to make a deep echoing noise: *Our voices boomed in the cave.* **2** to suddenly do very well: *During the gold rush business was booming.*

Word building: **boom** *noun*

boom²

noun **1** a long pole, used to keep the bottom of a sail straight **2** a movable arm that holds a microphone or floodlight above the actors in a television or film studio

boomer

noun a large male kangaroo

boomerang

noun a curved stick traditionally used as a weapon by Aboriginal people, which sometimes returns when you throw it

Word history: from an Aboriginal language of New South Wales called Dharug. See the map of Australian Aboriginal languages at the end of this book.

boon

noun a help or advantage: *The car is a boon now that I live so far from the city.*

boor   (*say* baw)

noun someone who is rude or inconsiderate

Word building: **boorish** *adjective* **boorishly** *adverb*
Word history: from the Dutch word meaning 'peasant'

boor/bore/boar Don't confuse **boor** with **bore** or **boar**.
A **bore** is either a tedious and uninteresting person, or a hole made by drilling.
Bore is also the past tense of the verb **bear**.
A **boar** is a male pig.

boost

verb to increase: *The teacher's praise boosted the nervous child's confidence.*
Other words: **augment, enhance, expand, strengthen**

Word building: **boost** *noun* an upward push **booster** *noun* something which gives an increase

boot¹

noun **1** a shoe which covers part of the leg **2** a separate space for baggage at the back of a car

boot²

verb to start up a computer by loading its memory system

Word use: You can also use **boot up**.

booth

noun a small closed-in place usually made just big enough for one person: *a telephone booth | a ticket booth*

bootleg

adjective made illegally: *The old man went to jail for making bootleg whisky.*

booty

noun anything taken or won, especially in times of war: *The pirates shared their booty of gold.*

booze

noun Informal alcoholic drink: *They bought some booze for the party.*

Word building: **booze** *verb*: *to booze at the pub*   **boozer** *noun*   **boozy** *adjective*

border

noun **1** the edge or side of anything: *to sew a pattern around the border*
Other words: **fringe, rim**
2 a line at which one country or state ends and another begins
Other words: **boundary, frontier**

Word building: **border** *verb*

border/boarder Don't confuse **border** with **boarder**, which is commonly a student at a boarding school.

borderline

adjective near the edge or boundary: *a borderline pass in the exam*

bore¹

verb **1** to make a round hole: *to bore through wood*
noun **2** a deep hole drilled to reach an underground water supply

bore²

verb to tire or weary: *You bore me with your complaints.*

Word building: **bore** *noun* a dull person   **boredom** *noun*   **bored, boring** *adjective*

bore³

verb a form of **bear¹**

bore/boar/boor Don't confuse **bore** with **boar** or **boor**.
A **boar** is a male pig.
A **boor** is someone who is rude or inconsiderate.

borer

noun an insect that bores into wood
Other words: **termite**

born

verb a form of **bear¹**

boronia   (*say* buh-<u>roh</u>-nee-uh)

noun an Australian shrub with small pink or brown flowers

Word history: named after the Italian botanist, Francesco *Borone*, who lived from 1769 to 1794

borrow

verb **1** to take or get on the understanding that you have to return it: *I borrow three library books every week.* **2** to get from somewhere else and make use of: *English has borrowed words from many languages.*

Word building: **borrower** *noun*

bosom   (*say* <u>booz</u>-uhm)

noun someone's chest or breast, especially a woman's

boss

noun someone who employs and directs people, or controls a business

Word building: **boss** *verb* to order around   **bossy** *adjective* (**bossier, bossiest**) acting like a boss

botany

noun the study of plants

Word building: **botanist** *noun* someone who studies plants   **botanical** *adjective*

botch

verb to spoil or bungle: *He botched the cake by taking it out of the oven too soon.*

Word building: **botch** *noun*

both

adjective the two together: *Both children went to the circus.*

bother

verb **1** to annoy or pester: *The flies bothered them so much they couldn't concentrate.*
2 to worry or confuse: *The maths problem bothered him.*

Word building: **bothersome** *adjective*

bottle

noun a glass container used for holding liquids: *milk bottles*

Word building: **bottle** *verb* to put in a bottle

bottlebrush

noun an Australian plant with red or pink brush-like flowers

bottleneck

noun a place where progress becomes slow, especially the narrow part of a road where traffic cannot flow freely

bottom   (*say* bott-om)

noun **1** the lowest part of anything **2** the round part of the body at the base of your back

bougainvillea   (*say* boh-guhn-vil-ee-uh)

noun a tropical plant with brilliantly coloured leaves, widely grown in parts of Australia

Word history: named after Louis Antoine de *Bougainville*, a French scientist and explorer of the Pacific region, who lived from 1729 to 1811

bough   (*rhymes with* cow)

noun one of the larger main branches of a tree

bough/bow Don't confuse **bough** with **bow**, which is the bending movement you make to indicate respect.
Note that **bow** with this meaning is pronounced to rhyme with *cow*. When **bow** rhymes with *so*, it's a different word, as in *bow and arrow* or *a bow in your hair*.

boulder   (*rhymes with* colder)

noun a large smooth rock

boulevard   (*say* booh-luh-vahd)

noun a wide avenue or city street lined with trees

Word use: Another spelling is **boulevarde**.

bounce

verb **1** to strike against and return: *The ball bounced on the pavement.* **2** to throw against and cause to return: *Maria bounced the ball along the footpath.* **3** *Informal* (of a cheque) to be returned unpaid: *My cheque bounced.*

Word building: **bouncing** *adjective* big, strong and healthy   **bounce**

bound¹

adjective **1** tied up: *The hostage had bound hands and feet.* **2** fastened within a cover: *a nicely bound book* **3** sure: *If you don't put the bike away, it's bound to be stolen.* **4** having a duty, or under an obligation: *Once you've promised you're really bound to help.*

bound²

verb to move with big steps or leaps: *to bound over a fence* | *to bound after a ball*

Word building: **bound** *noun* a leap

boundary

noun **1** a dividing line or limit: *the boundary between states* | *He rode around the farm's boundary.* **2** a hit in cricket which sends the ball beyond the boundary of the field

Word building: The plural is **boundaries**.

bountiful

adjective plentiful or generous: *The rains produced a bountiful harvest.*

Word building: **bountifully** *adverb*

bounty

noun **1** generosity **2** a reward given for a special purpose: *There was a bounty for the killing of wild pigs which were causing damage.*

Word building: The plural is **bounties**.

bouquet   (*say* booh-kay, boh-kay)

noun a bunch of flowers

Word use: The 't' is silent because this came from French.

bout

noun **1** a contest: *a wrestling bout* **2** a period or spell: *a bout of hard work* | *a bout of flu*

boutique   (*say* booh-teek)

noun a small shop, especially one that sells expensive or fashionable clothes

Word use: The pronunciation is unusual because this word came from French.

bovine   (*say* boh-vuyn)

adjective having to do with the family of cud-chewing animals that includes cows, bulls and oxen

bow¹   (*rhymes with* cow)

verb to bend or stoop down: *The cast bowed in response to the loud applause.*

Word building: **bow** *noun*

bow²   (*rhymes with* so)
noun **1** a piece of wood bent by a string stretched between its ends, which is used to shoot arrows **2** a knot, made up of two loops and two ends **3** the special stick used to play stringed instruments like the violin

bow³   (*rhymes with* cow)
noun the front end of a boat

bow/bough Don't confuse **bow** with **bough**, which is a branch of a tree.

bowel
noun the long tube in your body which carries food from the stomach out of the body

Word use: The plural **bowels** is often used. | Another word for this is **intestine**.
Word history: from a Latin word meaning 'sausage'

bower
noun a leafy shelter

bowerbird
noun an Australian bird which makes a bower-like shelter where it keeps special objects and courts its mate

bowl¹
noun **1** a deep round dish used for holding food or liquid **2** something shaped like a bowl: *the bowl of a pipe*

bowl²
verb **1** to throw or roll: *to bowl a hoop along the ground* **2** to throw a cricket ball with a straight arm towards the person batting **3** to get out by bowling: *Shane bowled the opening batsman with his first ball.*

Word building: **bowl** *noun* a heavy weighted ball used in the game of bowls   **bowler** *noun*

bowler¹
noun a hard felt hat with a rounded top and a narrow brim

bowler²
noun **1** the player who bowls the ball in cricket, and other similar games **2** someone who plays bowls or tenpin bowling

bowls
noun a game in which heavy balls are rolled across a lawn

box¹
noun **1** a wooden or cardboard container with a lid **2** a small room or raised stand: *a box at the theatre | a witness box*
phrase **3 the box**, *Informal* a television set
Word building: The plural form of the noun is **boxes**.

box²
verb to hit with your hand or fist
Word building: **boxer** *noun* someone who fights with his fists   **boxing** *noun*

box office
noun the place in a theatre where tickets are sold

boy
noun a male child
Word building: **boyhood** *noun*   **boyish** *adjective*   **boyishly** *adverb*

boy/buoy Don't confuse **boy** with **buoy**, which is a marker which floats on water.

boycott
verb **1** to refuse to go to: *to boycott a meeting* **2** to stop buying or using: *to boycott the new soap powder*
Word history: named after Captain Charles C Boycott, 1832 to 1897, an Irish land agent who was ignored by his tenants when he refused to lower rents in hard times

boyfriend
noun a man or boy with whom someone has a romantic relationship: *We met my cousin's boyfriend.*

bra
noun underwear which supports the breasts
Word history: a shortened form of **brassiere**

brace
noun **1** something which holds parts together or in place **2 braces**, **a** wires placed on your teeth to help straighten them **b** straps worn over your shoulders for holding up your trousers
Word building: **brace** *verb* to steady

bracelet
noun a chain or band worn around your wrist
Word history: from a Latin word meaning 'arm'

bracken

noun a fern which is often found in the wetter parts of Australia

bracket

plural noun one of a pair of signs (either ( ) or [ ]) used to enclose words which interrupt a sentence but add information to it, as in *John (the butcher's son) brought meat for our barbecue.*

brackish

adjective slightly salty: *The cattle wouldn't drink the brackish water.*

brag

verb to boast

Word building: Other forms are **I bragged, I have bragged, I am bragging**. | **braggart** *noun* someone who is always boasting

braid

verb **1** to weave or plait
noun **2** a plait: *She wore her hair in one long braid.* **3** a woven trimming: *The officer's uniform was edged with braid.*

braille   (*rhymes with* rail)

noun a system of printing using raised dots which blind people can read by touch

Word history: named after its inventor, Louis *Braille*, 1809 to 1852

brain

noun **1** the soft greyish mass of nerve cells inside your skull, which controls feeling, thinking and movement **2** understanding or intelligence: *He has a good brain.* **3** a very clever or well-informed person: *She's a real brain.*

Word use: The plural **brains** is often used for definition 2, as in *He has brains.* | **Cerebral** is a word meaning 'having to do with the brain'. Word building: **brainy** *adjective* (**brainier, brainiest**) clever

brainiac

noun *Informal* a very intelligent person: *He wore serious-looking glasses so that he could look more like a brainiac.*

brainstorm

noun a sudden brilliant idea

brainwave

noun a sudden good idea: *I've just had a brainwave about what to buy Mum for Christmas.*
Other words: **inspiration**

braise

verb to fry quickly in a pan, then stew gently in a covered pot

brake

noun something which slows or stops a machine

Word building: **brake** *verb* to slow or stop

brake/break Don't confuse **brake** with **break**.

bramble

noun any thorny bush growing wild

Word building: **brambly** *adjective*

bran

noun the outer shell of wheat or rye, sometimes used in breakfast cereal

branch

noun **1** the limb of a tree or shrub **2** a part or section which divides from the main part: *the branch of a river* **3** part of a large organisation: *the local branch of my bank*
verb **4** to divide or separate
phrase **5 branch out**, to develop in a new direction

Word building: The plural form of the noun is **branches**.

brand

noun **1** the mark or label on something which shows where it comes from or who makes it **2** the particular kind or make of something: *my favourite brand of jam*

Word building: **brand** *verb* to mark with a brand

brandish

verb to shake or wave: *The soldiers brandished their swords.*

brandy

noun a strong alcoholic drink made from wine

Word building: The plural is **brandies**.

brash

adjective bold or over-confident: *The brash youth kept bragging to everyone.*

Word building: **brashly** *adverb*

brass

noun **1** a yellowish metal mixed from copper and zinc **2** the group name for the trumpet and horn family of musical instruments: *The conductor brought in the strings, the woodwinds and then the brass.*

Word building: **brass** *adjective*: *brass instruments* **brassy** *adjective* **braze** *verb* **brazen** *adjective*

brassiere (*say* <u>braz</u>-ee-uh)

noun underwear which supports the breasts

Word use: This is the full form of **bra**.

brat

noun a child: *The little brat put chewing gum in my hair!*

Word use: This word is usually used in an unfriendly way.

bravado (*say* bruh-<u>vah</u>-doh)

noun bravery and confidence which is often pretended: *He was full of bravado until the time came for him to perform.*

brave

adjective full of courage
Other words: **courageous, fearless, hardy, heroic, valiant**

Word building: **brave** *verb* **bravely** *adverb* **bravery** *noun*
Word history: from a Spanish word meaning 'vicious' (first used about bulls)

brawl

noun a noisy quarrel or fight
Word building: **brawl** *verb*

brawn

noun **1** well-developed muscles or muscular strength: *to be all brawn and no brains* **2** cooked meat, pressed in a mould and set in its own jelly, used with salads and in sandwiches

Word building: **brawny** *adjective* (**brawnier, brawniest**) strong and muscly

bray

noun the loud harsh noise a donkey makes
Word building: **bray** *verb*

brazen

adjective **1** made of brass
2 cheeky or rude: *brazen behaviour*

brazier

noun a metal container for holding burning fuel and used for heating or cooking

breach

noun **1** a failure to keep or observe: *a breach of promise* | *a breach of the law*
2 a gap or opening: *a breach in the line of defence*

Word building: The plural is **breaches**. | **breach** *verb*

bread (*say* bred)

noun **1** a food made by baking flour and water, usually with yeast to make it rise: *a loaf of bread*
2 a general word for food: *to earn our daily bread*
3 *Informal* money

breadth

noun the distance from one side to the other
Other words: **width**

breadwinner

noun someone who earns the money to keep a family

break

verb **1** to divide into pieces violently
2 to fail to keep: *to break a promise*
3 to crack a bone of: *to break a leg*
4 to do better than: *to break a record in running* **5** to interrupt: *to break the silence*
6 to make known: *to break the news*
7 to change in tone: *My big brother's voice broke.* **8** to begin racing before the starting signal has been given: *Two swimmers broke.*
noun **9** a gap: *a break in the fence*
10 an attempt to escape: *a break for freedom*
11 a short rest: *They took a break from work.*
phrase **12 break down, a** to collapse **b** to overcome **c** to stop working properly
13 break up, a to separate or finish: *to break up a marriage* **b** to finish a school term for the holidays **c** *Informal* to explode into laughter

Word building: **breakable** *adjective* **breakage** *noun*

---

break/brake Don't confuse **break** with **brake**, which is a device for stopping a wheel going round.

breakdown

noun **1** a collapse or failure: *a nervous breakdown* **2** separation into simple parts: *the breakdown of soil* **3** an analysis: *a breakdown of all our accounts*

breakfast

noun the first meal of the day

Word building: **breakfast** *verb* to have breakfast

breakneck

adjective dangerous: *to drive at a breakneck speed*

breakthrough

noun any important new development which allows for further progress to take place: *a breakthrough in finding a cure for cancer*

bream　(*sounds like* brim)

noun an Australian saltwater fish which is good for eating

breast

noun **1** an old-fashioned word for **chest** **2** one of the two parts of a woman's body that produce milk

breaststroke

noun a way of swimming in which your arms move outwards and back from your chest and your legs kick in a frog-like manner

breath

noun **1** the air taken into your lungs and let out again: *short of breath* **2** an act of breathing once: *Take a deep breath.* **3** a light current: *A breath of air cooled the stuffy room.*

Word building: **breathy** *adjective*　**breathless** *adjective*

breathalyser

noun a machine used to measure the amount of alcohol in someone's breath

breathe

verb **1** to draw in and give out air: *We breathe without thinking.* **2** to speak softly **3** to live or exist: *Everything that breathed was destroyed in the flood.*

Word building: **breather** *noun* a pause for rest

breathtaking

adjective causing excitement or pleasure: *a breathtaking adventure | breathtaking beauty*

breech

noun the barrel of a gun

breeches　(*rhymes with* stitches)

plural noun trousers covering the hips and thighs: *riding breeches*

breed

verb **1** to produce young: *Rats were breeding in the garbage.* **2** to produce, by keeping the parents for the purpose: *He breeds prize bulls.* **3** to cause: *Dirt breeds disease.* *noun* **4** a type or kind: *a breed of sheep*

Word building: Other verb forms are **I bred, I have bred, I am breeding.** | **breeder** *noun* someone who breeds animals

breeding

noun **1** the mating and rearing of animals **2** good manners which are the result of training

breeze

noun a light wind or movement of air

Word building: **breezy** *adjective* (**breezier, breeziest**)　**breezily** *adverb*　**breeziness** *noun*

brethren　(*say* bredh-ruhn)

plural noun Old-fashioned brothers

brevity　(*say* brev-uh-tee)

noun shortness or briefness: *The brevity of the priest's sermon surprised us.*

brew

verb **1** to make or prepare: *Let's brew a pot of tea. | to brew a stronger beer* **2** to cause or bring about: *to brew trouble* **3** to be forming or gathering: *Trouble is brewing.*

Word building: **brewery** *noun* (**breweries**) a place where beer is made　**brew** *noun*　**brewer** *noun*

briar　(*rhymes with* fire)

noun a prickly bush

bribe

noun money or a gift given to someone if they promise to do something they shouldn't for you

Word building: **bribe** *verb*: *He tried to bribe the policeman to let him go.*　**bribery** *noun*

brick

noun **1** a small hard block of baked clay, used for building **2** something shaped like a brick: *a brick of ice-cream*

Word building: **bricklayer** *noun* someone who builds with bricks

bride

noun a woman who is going to be married or who has just been married

Word building: **bridal** *adjective* having to do with a bride or a wedding

bridegroom

noun a man who is going to be married or who has just been married

bridesmaid

noun a woman who helps a bride on her wedding day

bridge¹

noun **1** a structure built over a river, road or railway line, to provide a way of getting from one side to the other **2** a raised platform above the deck of a ship for the captain or other senior officers **3** the upper part of your nose
verb **4** to make a bridge over: *When the government bridged the river, ferries were no longer needed.*

bridge²

noun a card game for two pairs of players

bridle

noun **1** the leather straps, bit and reins fitted around a horse's head and used to control it
verb **2** to put a bridle on **3** to curb or restrain: *Bridle your temper.*

brief

adjective **1** short: *a brief visit | a brief speech*
Other words: **momentary, quick**
noun **2** an outline of information or instructions on a subject, especially for use by a barrister conducting a legal case
Other words: **summary**

Word building: **brevity** *noun*   **briefness** *noun*   **briefly** *adverb*

briefcase

noun a flat rectangular case for carrying books and papers

briefs

plural noun close-fitting underpants without legs

brigade

noun **1** a large group of soldiers **2** a group of people trained for a special purpose: *a fire brigade*

Word building: **brigadier** *noun* an army officer in charge of a brigade

brigalow

noun a type of acacia that grows in Queensland and northern New South Wales, and which has strong heavy wood traditionally used by Aboriginal people for carving

Word history: from an Aboriginal language of New South Wales called Kamilaroi. See the map of Australian Aboriginal languages at the end of this book.

brigand   (*say* brig-uhnd)

noun one of a gang of robbers who live in mountain or forest areas

bright

adjective **1** shining or giving a strong light: *a bright silver coin | a bright lamp*
Other words: **brilliant, dazzling, gleaming, luminous**
2 clever: *a bright pupil*
Other words: **brilliant, intelligent, smart**
3 cheerful and happy: *Sad people need bright company.*

Word building: **brighten** *verb*   **brightly** *adverb*   **brightness** *noun*

brilliant

adjective **1** shining brightly
2 extraordinarily clever: *a brilliant plan | a brilliant pianist*

Word building: **brilliance** *noun*   **brilliantly** *adverb*

brim

noun **1** the top edge or rim of something hollow: *He filled the glass to the brim.*
2 the outer edge of a hat
verb **3** fill or be full to the edge or rim of something hollow

Word building: **brimming** *adjective*
Word history: from an Old English word meaning 'sea'

brindled

adjective grey or brownish-yellow with darker streaks or spots

brine

noun strongly salted water, often used in preserving some foods

Word building: **briny** *adjective*: *the briny sea*

bring

verb **1** to carry: *I will bring the book.*
2 to cause to come: *The drought brought suffering to everyone.*

Word building: Other forms are **I brought, I have brought, I am bringing.**

brink

noun the edge of a steep or dangerous place or time: *the brink of a cliff | on the brink of war*

brisk

adjective fast and lively: *a brisk walk | a brisk breeze*

Word building: **briskly** *adverb*   **briskness** *noun*

bristle

noun **1** a short stiff hair or hairlike material: *pigs' bristles | the bristles of a brush*
verb **2** to raise the bristles: *The dog bristled when it saw the burglar.* **3** to show anger: *He bristled at the idea.*

Word building: **bristly** *adjective*: *a bristly beard*

brittle

adjective likely to break easily: *brittle shells*
Other words: **delicate, fragile**

Word building: **brittleness** *noun*

broach

verb to ask about for the first time: *I broached the subject of buying a dictionary.*

broad

adjective **1** very wide: *a broad river | broad knowledge* **2** widely spread or complete: *broad daylight* **3** not detailed: *the broad outline of the story* **4** having a strong accent: *He speaks broad Australian.*

Word building: **broaden** *verb*   **broadly** *adverb*

broadband

noun access to the internet on a cable that is wide enough to take a number of different amounts of information at the same time: *Broadband is great — we can speak on two phones and have two computers going as well — all on the one phone line!*

broadbased

adjective taking into account a wide range of factors: *To take a broadbased view, you have to think of the loggers as well as the greenies.*

broadbrush

adjective ranging widely and generally without lots of detail: *The teacher gave a broadbrush talk on the history of computers.*

broadcast

verb **1** to send by radio or television: *to broadcast a program* **2** to send radio or television programs: *They are broadcasting now.*

Word building: Other forms are **I broadcast, I have broadcast, I am broadcasting.** | **broadcast** *noun*   **broadcaster** *noun*

broad-minded

adjective able to accept other people's ideas and ways
Other words: **tolerant, unbiased, unprejudiced**

Word building: **broad-mindedly** *adverb* **broad-mindedness** *noun*

broadside

noun the firing of all the guns on one side of a ship

brocade   (*say* bruh-<u>kayd</u>)

noun cloth woven with a raised pattern on it

Word building: **brocaded** *adjective*

broccoli   (*say* <u>brok</u>-uh-lee)

noun a green vegetable similar to a cauliflower

brochure   (*say* <u>broh</u>-shuh)

noun a small book with a paper cover, containing information or advertisements
Other words: **leaflet, pamphlet**

Word history: from a French word meaning 'stitch'

brogue[1]   (*say* brohg)

noun a broad accent, especially an Irish one

brogue[2]   (*say* brohg)

noun a strongly made, comfortable shoe

broke

adjective *Informal* having no money

Word use: This word comes from the verb **break.**

broken

adjective **1** separated into pieces: *a broken plate*
Other words: **cracked, damaged, fragmented, shattered, smashed**
2 not working because of the breaking of one of the parts: *a broken watch | a broken arm*

Other words: **damaged**

3 not kept or obeyed: *a broken promise | broken rules* **4** imperfectly spoken: *He spoke broken English.*

Word use: This word comes from the verb **break**.

broker

noun someone who buys or sells things for someone else: *a stockbroker or wool broker*

Word building: **brokerage** *noun*

brolga

noun a large silvery-grey bird with long legs, which dances

Word use: This used to be better known as **native companion**.
Word history: from an Aboriginal language of New South Wales called Kamilaroi. See the map of Australian Aboriginal languages at the end of this book.

bronchitis   (*say* brong-<u>kuy</u>-tuhs)

noun an illness in which the lining of the air passages in the chest becomes red and sore

brontosaurus   (*say* bron-tuh-<u>saw</u>-ruhs)

noun a giant lizard-like animal that died out millions of years ago

Word use: A brontosaurus is a type of **dinosaur**.
Word history: from a Greek word for 'thunder' added to a Greek word for 'lizard'

bronze

noun **1** a brown-coloured metal mixed from copper and tin
adjective **2** of the colour of bronze

brooch   (*rhymes with* coach)

noun an ornament made to be fastened to your clothes with a pin

Word building: The plural is **brooches**.

brood

noun **1** a number of young animals, especially birds, hatched at the same time
verb **2** to sit on eggs to hatch them
phrase **3 brood on,** to worry about: *Don't brood on your failure.*

Word building: **broody** *adjective*: *a broody hen*

brook   (*rhymes with* book)

noun a small stream

Word use: Australians usually call this a **creek**.

broom

noun a brush with a long handle, used for sweeping

broth

noun a thin soup of fish, meat or vegetables

brothel

noun a house where prostitutes work

brother

noun **1** a male relative who has the same parents as you **2** a fellow worker or colleague: *They are brothers in the fight against crime.* **3** a male member of certain church organisations

Word building: **brotherhood** *noun*   **brotherly** *adjective*

brother-in-law

noun **1** the brother of your husband or your wife **2** the husband of your sister **3** the husband of the sister of your wife or husband

Word building: The plural is **brothers-in-law**.

brow   (*rhymes with* now)

noun **1** the bony ridge over your eye **2** the hair growing on that ridge **3** the edge or top of a steep place: *the brow of a hill*

Word use: Another word for definition 1 is **forehead**. | Another word for definition 2 is **eyebrow**.

browbeat

verb to bully

Word building: Other forms are **they browbeat, they have browbeaten, they are browbeating**.

brown

adjective **1** of the colour of wood, a mixture of red, yellow and black **2** having skin that has been darkened from being in sunlight: *She was very brown after a week at the beach.*

Word building: **brown** *verb* to become or make brown   **brown** *noun*

brownie

noun **1** a thick brown biscuit **2** a junior **guide** (def. 4)

Word use: Definition 2 is sometimes spelt with a capital letter.

browse

verb **1** to feed or graze: *The cattle browsed in the clover.* **2** to glance casually through a book or at the goods in a shop

Word building: **browse** *noun*   **browser** *noun*

browser   (*say* brow-zuh)

noun software set up to search for different sites and topics on the internet

bruise

verb **1** to cause a discoloured mark on the body: *The punch bruised my arm.* **2** to develop such a bruised mark: *I bruise easily.*

Word building: **bruiser** *noun* someone who is strong and tough   **bruise** *noun*

brumby

noun a wild horse living freely in the bush

Word building: The plural is **brumbies**. Word history: perhaps from an Aboriginal language, or perhaps named after Lieutenant *Brumby*, a horse-breeder who let some horses run wild in the early 1800s

brunch

noun a meal in midmorning instead of breakfast and lunch

Word use: This word is called a **blended** or **portmanteau word**. Word building: The plural is **brunches**. Word history: made by joining the first two letters of *br(eakfast)* to the last four letters of *(l)unch*

brunette

noun a female with dark hair

brunt

noun the main shock or force: *to bear the brunt of an attack*

bruschetta   (*say* broos-<u>ket</u>-uh, broo-<u>shet</u>-uh)

adverb grilled slices of bread brushed with olive oil and fresh garlic, and served with various toppings: *Yum! Bruschetta with anchovies and cheese!*

brush[1]

noun **1** an instrument made of hair or bristles set in a handle: *a paint brush | a hair brush* **2** an act of brushing: *Give my coat a brush.* **3** an argument: *I had a brush with him over using my new paints.* *verb* **4** to use a brush on: *Brush your hair every day.* **5** to touch lightly: *She brushed me as she passed.*

phrase **6 brush aside**, to ignore: *The teacher brushed my arguments aside.*

Word building: The plural form of the noun is **brushes**.

brush[2]

noun a thick growth of bushes

brush turkey

noun a large bird found in Eastern Australia, the male of which builds large mounds of leaves to incubate the female's eggs: *They had to chase the brush turkey out of the garden with the hose.*

brusque   (*say* brusk, broosk)

adjective quick to say something and not very polite: *My mum's brusque manner sometimes upsets people.*

Word use: The more usual word is **abrupt**. Word building: **brusquely** *adverb* **brusqueness** *noun*

brussels sprout

noun a green vegetable like a tiny cabbage

brutal

adjective savagely cruel: *a brutal blow*

Word building: **brutality** *noun*   **brutally** *adverb*

brute

noun **1** an animal or beast **2** a cruel person

bubble

noun **1** a small ball of air or gas rising through liquid **2** a small ball of air in a fine coating of liquid: *to blow bubbles*

Word building: **bubble** *verb* to send up bubbles   **bubbly** *adjective*

bubblegum

noun chewing gum which can be blown into bubbles

bubbler

noun a small fountain which sends up a short stream of drinking water

buccaneer

noun a pirate

buck[1]

noun a male deer, rabbit or hare

Word use: The female is a **doe**.

buck[2]

verb **1** to jump with arched back and stiff legs: *The young horse bucked the first time it was saddled.* **2** to throw by bucking: *The horse bucked the rider off.*

bucket

noun a round open container with a flat bottom and a handle

Word building: **bucketful** *noun*

buckle

noun **1** a clasp for fastening a belt or strap **2** a bend or bulge in a sheet of hard material
verb **3** to fasten with a buckle **4** to cause to bend or bulge: *The heat buckled the picture frame.* **5** to bend or bulge: *The heat caused the picture frame to buckle.*

bucktooth

noun a tooth in your upper jaw that sticks out

Word building: The plural is **buckteeth**. | **bucktoothed** *adjective*

bucolic   (*say* byooh-<u>kol</u>-ik)

adjective having to do with farming or the country: *living in bucolic isolation*
Other words: **rural, rustic**

bud

noun **1** a flower or leaf before it has fully opened **2** a small shoot on the stem of a plant which will grow into a leaf or flower

Word building: **bud** *verb* (**budded, budding**) to produce buds

Buddhism   (*say* <u>bood</u>-iz-uhm)

noun a world religion, founded by the teacher Buddha who lived in India about the sixth century BC, which teaches that we can achieve happiness by ridding ourselves of greed and hatred. Followers of Buddhism are called Buddhists, and worship in a temple.

Word building: **Buddhist** *adjective*: *a Buddhist temple*
Word history: named after *Buddha*, a Sanskrit name meaning 'wise' or 'enlightened'

buddy

noun Informal a friend or mate: *my best buddy*

Word building: The plural is **buddies**.

budge

verb to move: *I won't budge until you return.* | *I can't budge that heavy table.*

Word use: This is usually used with the word *not*.

budgerigar   (*say* <u>buj</u>-uh-ree-gah)

noun a small yellow and green parakeet found in inland parts of Australia, but also kept in cages and bred in other colours

Word use: The shortened form is **budgie**.
Word history: from an Aboriginal language of New South Wales called Kamilaroi. See the map of Australian Aboriginal languages at the end of this book.

budget

noun **1** a plan showing what money you will earn and how you will spend it
verb **2** to make such a plan
adjective **3** not costing much: *budget clothes*

Word building: Other verb forms are I **budgeted, I have budgeted, I am budgeting.**

buff

adjective **1** light yellow
noun **2** an expert: *a film buff*

buffalo

noun a kind of ox sometimes used for pulling heavy loads, especially in parts of Asia and Africa

Word building: The plural is **buffaloes** or **buffalos**.

buffer

noun something that softens a blow, especially one of the two springs at each end of a railway carriage to take the shock of a collision

buffet¹   (*say* <u>buf</u>-uht)

verb to strike, shake or knock about: *The big waves buffeted the boat.*

Word building: Other forms are **I buffeted, I have buffeted, I am buffeting.** | **buffet** *noun* a blow or a slap

buffet²   (*say* <u>buf</u>-ay)

noun **1** a table or counter holding food **2** a low cupboard for holding cups and plates
adjective **3** set out on a table from which you serve yourself: *a buffet dinner*

Word use: This word came from French.

buffoon

noun someone who acts the fool

Word building: **buffoonery** *noun*   **buffoonish** *adjective*

bug

Informal

noun **1** any tiny insect **2** an illness caused by an infection **3** something that is going wrong: *There's a bug in my computer program.* **4** a hidden microphone

verb **5** to hide a microphone in: *The spy bugged the room.* **6** to annoy: *Your silliness bugs me.*

Word building: Other verb forms are **I bugged, I have bugged, I am bugging.**

bugbear

noun something that worries or annoys you: *Exams are my bugbear.*

buggy

noun a light carriage with two wheels, pulled by one horse

Word building: The plural is **buggies.**

bugle　(*say* byooh-guhl)

noun a wind instrument, used in the army to sound signals

Word building: **bugler** *noun*

Word history: from a Latin word meaning 'ox'

build

verb **1** to make by joining parts together: *to build a house | to build a model aeroplane*

noun **2** the shape of someone's body: *a heavy build*

phrase **3 build up,** to increase or make stronger

Word building: Other verb forms are **I built, I have built, I am building.** | **builder** *noun*

building

noun something built for people to live or work in, such as a house or office block

bulb

noun **1** the rounded root-like stem of certain plants, such as the onion **2** anything with a shape like that: *an electric light bulb*

Word building: **bulbous** *adjective*

bulge

noun **1** a round part that swells out

Other words: **bump, lump, swelling**

verb **2** to swell outwards

Other words: **balloon, bloat, expand, protrude**

Word building: **bulging** *adjective*

bulk

noun **1** the size of something including its length, width and depth: *a ship's bulk* **2** the main part: *The bulk of the work has been done.*

Word building: **bulky** *adjective* (**bulkier, bulkiest**)　**bulkiness** *noun*

bull

noun **1** a male of the cattle family **2** a male elephant, whale or seal

Word use: The female of definition 1 is a **cow** and the young is a **calf.**

bull ant

noun a large ant which can give a painful bite

Word use: Another name is **bulldog ant.**

bulldog

noun a type of dog with a large head and a small strong body

bulldozer

noun a powerful tractor with a blade in front, used to move trees and rocks and to level land

Word building: **bulldoze** *verb*

bullet

noun a small piece of metal shot from a small gun

bulletin

noun a short written or spoken news report: *the latest bulletin on the floods*

bullfight

noun an entertainment in which a person fights with, and usually kills, a bull

Word building: **bullfighter** *noun*　**bullfighting** *noun*

bullion　(*say* bool-yuhn)

noun bars of gold or silver

bullock

noun a bull that has had its sex organs removed

Other words: **steer**

Word building: **bullocky** *noun* the driver of a bullock team

bullroarer

noun a thin piece of wood on a string, which is whirled in the air to make a roaring noise, traditionally used by Aboriginal people in religious ceremonies

Word use: The Aboriginal name for this is **churinga.**

bullseye
noun **1** the central spot on a target
2 a round hard sweet

bully
noun someone who hurts, frightens or
orders about smaller or weaker people

Word building: The plural is **bullies**. | **bully**
verb (**bullied, bullying**) to behave as a bully
towards

bulrush
noun a kind of tall rush which grows in wet
places, such as on the banks of rivers, and
which is used to make mats, and so on

Word use: Another spelling is **bull-rush**.

bumblebee
noun a large hairy kind of bee

bump
verb **1** to knock against: *I bumped the table*
2 to hit: *I bumped my head on the tree.*
noun **3** a light hit or knock **4** a small raised
area: *a bump on the head | a bump on the
road*
phrase **5 bump into,** to meet by chance
6 bump off, *Informal* to kill

Word building: **bumpy** adjective (**bumpier,
bumpiest**)

bumper bar
noun the bar across the front or back of a
car which protects it in a collision

bumpkin
noun someone who is awkward and clumsy

Word use: This word is insulting.
Word history: from a Dutch word meaning
'little barrel'

bumptious   (*say* <u>bump</u>-shuhs)
adjective showing your importance in a way
that offends people: *They were irritated by
her bumptious manner.*

Word building: **bumptiously** adverb
bumptiousness noun

bun
noun **1** a kind of round bread roll which
can be plain or sweetened
2 hair arranged at the back of your head in
the shape of a bun

bunch
noun a group of things joined or gathered
together: *a bunch of grapes | a bunch of roses*

Word use: The plural is **bunches**.
Word building: **bunch** verb to gather together

bundle
noun **1** a group of things loosely held
together: *a bundle of sticks*
verb **2** to put together loosely: *I bundled the
books into my bag.* **3** to send away quickly: *I
bundled them out of the room.*

bung
noun **1** a stopper for the hole in a wine
cask
verb **2** to close with a bung, or to block
with any obstruction: *The drain is bunged
up.* **3** *Informal* to throw or toss: *Bung it
over here, Bruce!*

bungalow
noun a house with only one storey

bungee jumping   (*say* <u>bun</u>-jee
jump-ing)
noun a sport in which you jump from a
high place to which you are attached by a
long, thick elastic cord around your feet

bungle
verb to do badly: *He bungled the job.*

Word building: **bungle** noun something badly
done   **bungler** noun

bunion   (*rhymes with* onion)
noun a swelling of a joint on the foot,
especially on the big toe

bunk
noun **1** a bed built like a shelf, in a ship's
cabin **2** one of a pair of beds built one
above the other

bunker
noun **1** a fortified shelter, often
underground **2** a sandy hollow on a golf
course

bunkum
noun insincere or foolish talk

bunting
noun brightly coloured cloth used to make
flags for decoration

bunyip
noun an imaginary creature of Aboriginal
legend, said to live in swamps and billabongs

Word history: from an Aboriginal language of
Victoria called Wembawemba. See the map of
Australian Aboriginal languages at the end of
this book.

buoy (*say* boy)

noun **1** a float anchored in the water, which marks channels and hidden rocks
2 a ring used to help people stay afloat

Word use: You can also use **lifebuoy** for definition 2.
Word building: **buoy** *verb*

buoy/boy Don't confuse **buoy** with **boy**, which is a male child.

buoyant (*say* boy-uhnt)

adjective **1** able to float: *This rubber ring will keep you buoyant.* **2** light-hearted and cheerful

Word building: **buoyancy** *noun* **buoyantly** *adverb*

burden

noun **1** a load: *to carry a heavy burden*
2 a difficult job that you don't really want to do: *The children found looking after the animals a burden.*

Word building: **burden** *verb* to load: *I won't burden you with my problems.* **burdensome** *adjective*

bureau (*say* byooh-roh)

noun **1** a writing-desk with drawers
2 a government office where people can get information: *a tourist bureau*

Word use: Definition 2 sometimes has a capital: *the Weather Bureau.*
Word building: The plural is **bureaus** or **bureaux.**

bureaucracy (*say* byooh-rok-ruh-see)

noun **1** unnecessary rules about the way things have to be done in government offices
phrase **2 the bureaucracy**, the people who make these rules

Word building: The plural form of the noun is **bureaucracies.** | **bureaucrat** *noun* a member of the bureaucracy **bureaucratic** *adjective* **bureaucratically** *adverb*

burglary (*say* ber-gluh-ree)

noun the crime of breaking into a building to steal things

Word building: The plural is **burglaries.** | **burglar** *noun* **burgle** *verb*

burgundy

noun **1** a type of wine **2** a rich dark red colour

Word history: from *Burgundy*, the region in south-eastern France where this wine comes from

burial (*say* be-ree-uhl)

noun the act of putting a dead person into a grave: *We all went to the cemetery for our grandfather's burial.*

Word building: **bury** *verb* (**buried, burying**)

burlesque (*say* ber-lesk)

noun a play or a book which makes people laugh by making fun of serious matters

burly

adjective big and solidly built: *a burly fellow*

Word building: Other forms are **burlier, burliest.**

burn

verb **1** to set or be on fire: *to burn the wood* | *The wood is burning.* **2** to give out heat and light: *This sand burns.* | *The lights burn all night.* **3** to turn black or red by heat or fire: *Put on a hat in case your face burns.* | *to burn the toast* **4** to hurt by heat or fire: *to burn your fingers in the flame* **5** to feel strongly: *to burn with anger* **6** to copy (files) onto a compact disc: *Can you burn the family photos onto this disc?*
noun **7** a sore made by something hot: *She had a bad burn from the iron.*
phrase **8 burn off**, to clear land by setting fire to the trees

Word building: Other verb forms are **I burnt** or **burned, I have burnt** or **burned, I am burning.**

burner

noun the part of a stove or lamp where the flame comes out

burning

adjective very interesting and important: *a burning question*

burnish

verb to make bright and shiny by polishing: *to burnish the copper pot*

Word building: **burnished** *adjective*: *Her hair shone like burnished gold.*

burp

verb **1** to noisily pass wind from your stomach through your mouth: *Drinking lemonade makes me burp.* **2** to help to burp, especially by patting on the back: *to burp the baby after its feed*

Word building: **burp** *noun*

burqa (say ber-kuh)

noun a traditional Muslim garment for women, covering the full body with a narrow opening for the eyes

Word use: Another spelling is **burka**.

burr

noun the prickly case around some seeds, such as a chestnut seed

burrow

noun **1** a hole in the ground dug by an animal, to live and shelter in: *The wombat was hiding in its burrow.*
verb **2** to dig a burrow **3** to search with a digging movement: *I burrowed in my school bag for my bus money.*

bursary

noun money given to a student to help pay for school fees, textbooks, uniforms and other expenses

Word building: The plural is **bursaries.** | **bursar** *noun* the person in charge of money at a school or college

burst

verb **1** to split or break open: *The sausages burst when we cooked them.* | *to burst a balloon* **2** to rush suddenly: *The children burst into the room.* **3** to be full or overflowing: *The shopping basket was bursting with goodies.* **4** to express your feelings suddenly: *to burst out laughing*
noun **5** a sudden effort, or action: *a burst of speed* | *a burst of clapping*

Word building: Other verb forms are **I burst, I have burst, I am bursting.**

bury (rhymes with very)

verb **1** to put in the ground and cover with earth: *Dogs bury their bones.* **2** to cover over completely: *Her books were buried under a pile of clothing.*
phrase **3 bury yourself,** to occupy yourself completely so that you don't notice anything else: *to bury yourself in a book*

Word building: Other verb forms are **I buried, I have buried, I am burying.** | **burial** *noun*

bury/berry Don't confuse **bury** with **berry**, which is a small juicy fruit.

bus

noun a long vehicle with many seats, for carrying passengers: *to catch the bus to school*

Word building: The plural is **buses**.
Word history: a shortened form of **omnibus**

bush

noun **1** a plant like a small tree with many branches coming out from the trunk near the ground: *a rose bush* **2** a tree-covered area of land
phrase **3 beat about the bush,** to take a long time coming to the point in a conversation
4 the bush, the Australian country as opposed to the city: *Our cousins live in the bush.*

Word building: The plural form of the noun is **bushes.** | **bushy** *adjective* thick or dense like a bush: *a fox's bushy tail*

bush band

noun a group of musicians who perform Australian folk music, using instruments such as the accordion and guitar

bushcraft

noun knowledge of how to live in and travel through rough bush country

bushed

adjective **1** very tired: *We are bushed after a hard day's work.* **2** lost or confused: *I was completely bushed when I couldn't find the house.*

bushel

noun a unit of measure in the imperial system of large quantities of goods such as grain or fruit

bushfire

noun a fire in the bush or forest

bushman

noun someone who lives in the bush and knows how to survive there

Word building: **bushmanship** *noun*

bushranger

noun someone who hid in the bush and lived by robbing travellers: *Ned Kelly was a famous Australian bushranger.*

Word building: **bushranging** *noun*

bush regeneration

noun the care of areas of bush in which native plants have been destroyed, either by encouraging native bush to regrow or by planting with species that are thought to be part of the original ecology

bushwalking

noun walking through the bush for exercise or pleasure

Word building: **bushwalk** *verb*　**bushwalker** *noun*

bushwhacker

noun Informal someone who lives in the bush

Word use: Another word is **bushie**.

business　(*say* biz-nuhs)

noun **1** the work someone does to earn a living **2** buying and selling goods to make a profit: *to be in business* **3** a matter which someone has a right to know about: *My exam mark is none of your business.*
phrase **4 mean business**, to be serious: *Those guard dogs look as if they mean business.*

Word building: The plural form of the noun is **businesses**. | **businesslike** *adjective* practical and well-organised　**businessman** *noun*　**businesswoman** *noun*

busker

noun a musician who performs in the street hoping to get donations of money from people passing by

Word building: **busk** *verb*

bust[1]

noun **1** a woman's breasts or chest **2** a sculpture of someone's head and shoulders

bust[2]

Informal verb **1** to break or burst: *to bust a balloon*
2 to arrest: *My cousin was busted for selling drugs.*
phrase **3 bust in**, to rush in suddenly
4 bust up, to quarrel and separate: *I have busted up with my partner.*
5 go bust, to lose all your money: *My family's business has gone bust.*

Word building: **busted** *adjective* broken

bustard　(*sounds like* busted)

noun a large heavy bird which can run fast and lives in the grassy plains of Australia and New Guinea

Word history: from a Latin word meaning 'slow bird'

bustle[1]

verb to move or act busily: *She bustled about tidying the house.*

bustle[2]

noun a pad or wire frame worn in the olden days to puff out the back of a woman's skirt

busy

adjective **1** fully occupied: *I can't come now as I am busy.*
Other words: **engaged, unavailable**
2 full of activity: *Saturday morning is a busy time at the shops.*
Other words: **hectic**
3 already in use: *The telephone was busy.*
Other words: **engaged**
verb **4** to make or keep busy: *I shall busy myself tidying up my room.*

Word building: Other adjective forms are **busier, busiest**. | Other verb forms are **I busied, I have busied, I am busying**. | **busily** *adverb*　**busyness** *noun*

busybody

noun somebody who interferes in other people's business

Word building: The plural is **busybodies**.

but

conjunction **1** and in contrast: *Lien likes chocolate ice-cream the best, but my favourite flavour is cookies and cream.*
preposition **2** except or save: *None of us want to go but you.*
adverb **3** despite this: *But this isn't the last you'll hear from me!*

butcher

noun **1** someone who prepares and cuts up meat to sell **2** a cruel and violent murderer
verb **3** to kill violently: *The murderer butchered each victim.* **4** to make a terrible mess of: *That new hairdresser butchered my hair.*

Word building: **butchery** *noun*

butcherbird

noun a black and grey Australian bird which hangs its dead prey on branches

butler

noun the head male servant in a large house

Word history: from a French word meaning 'bottle'

butt[1]

noun **1** the thick blunt end of a weapon or tool: *the butt of a rifle* **2** an end which is not used up: *a cigarette butt*

butt²

noun **1** someone who is a target: *He is always the butt of their jokes.*
2 a wall of earth which stops bullets or arrows fired at targets in front of it

butt³

verb to push with the head or horns: *The goat butted me.*

Word building: **butt** *noun*

butter

noun soft yellow spread made from cream

Word building: **butter** *verb* to spread butter on **buttery** *adjective*

butterfly

noun an insect with large wings which are often brightly coloured

Word building: The plural is **butterflies.**

butterfly stroke

noun a stroke in swimming in which both your arms are lifted together from the water and thrown forward

buttermilk

noun a sour liquid left after butter has been made from cream

butterscotch

noun a kind of toffee or flavouring

buttock

noun either or the two rounded parts of the body at the base of your back

button

noun **1** a small, usually round, object sewn onto clothing to join two parts together
2 anything shaped like a button, such as a small knob you press to ring a bell

Word building: **button** *verb* (**buttoned, buttoning**): *I buttoned my cardigan.*

buttonhole

noun **1** a slit in a garment through which buttons are passed to fasten it
2 a flower worn in a buttonhole on the lapel of a coat

buttress

noun a support for a wall or building

Word building: The plural is **buttresses.** | **buttress** *verb*

buxom   (*say* buks-uhm)

adjective plump and attractive: *She's a buxom lass.*

buy

verb **1** to get by paying money for
2 to accept: *I don't buy that idea.*

Word building: Other forms are **I bought, I have bought, I am buying.** | **buy** *noun* something bought: *a good buy*

> **buy/by/bye** Don't confuse **buy** with **by** or **bye. By** means 'near or close to something': *Your school bag is by the door.*
>
> **By** has other meanings which you should look up. A **bye** in sport is when your team doesn't have to play in a particular round of a contest. **Bye** can also mean 'goodbye'.

buyer

noun **1** someone who buys: *We have a buyer for our old car.* **2** someone whose job is to buy stock for a store: *He is the chief buyer for a supermarket.*

buzz

noun **1** a low, humming sound: *the buzz of bees | a buzz of conversation*
verb **2** to make a buzzing noise
phrase **3 buzz off,** *Informal* to go or leave

Word building: **buzzer** *noun*
Word history: an imitation of the sound that bees make

buzzard

noun any of various birds of prey related to but smaller than eagles

by

preposition **1** near to: *I live by the school.*
2 using as a way: *to come in by the main gate | to travel by train*
adverb **3** near: *I live close by.*
4 past something nearby: *The car sped by.*

by-

prefix a word part meaning **1** secondary: *by-product* **2** out of the way: *byway*
3 near: *bystander*

Word use: Another spelling is **bye-.**

bye¹

noun an occurrence in a sporting competition, when a team or competitor doesn't have to play in a particular round of the contest

bye²

interjection goodbye

by-election

noun an extra election held to fill the seat of a member of parliament who has died or retired

bypass

noun a road built around a town or a busy traffic area

Word building: **bypass** *verb* to use or make a bypass

by-product

noun something produced in addition to the main product: *Asphalt is a by-product of making petrol.*

bystander

noun someone who happens to be present at, but takes no part in, what is occurring

byte

noun a unit of information stored by a computer

byte/bite/bight Don't confuse **byte** with **bite** or **bight**.
A **bite** is a mouthful of something, or a wound made using teeth or something similar.
A **bight** is a bay, as in the *Great Australian Bight*.

byway

noun a road not used very often

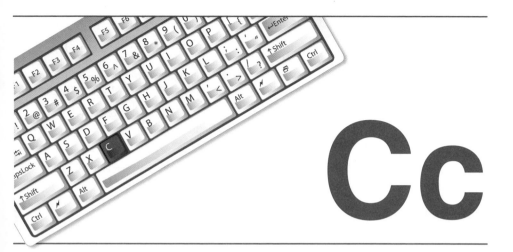

Cc

cab

noun **1** a taxi **2** the covered part of a truck where the driver sits

cabanossi   (*say* kab-uh-<u>nos</u>-ee)

noun a thin beef sausage with seasoning, which you buy already cooked

cabaret   (*say* <u>kab</u>-uh-ray)

noun a musical or comedy show performed at a restaurant or club

cabbage

noun a kind of vegetable with large green leaves

cabbage tree

noun a tall palm with large leaves and with buds that you can eat, found growing along the coast of eastern Australia

Word use: Another name is **cabbage tree palm**. | In the early days of the colony people made wide-brimmed hats from the leaves of this palm.

cabin

noun **1** a small house or hut **2** a room in a ship where passengers sleep **3** the space inside a plane where the crew and passengers sit

cabinet

noun **1** a piece of furniture with shelves and drawers **2** the group of leading people in a government

Word use: Definition 2 is often spelt with a capital letter.

cable

noun **1** thick strong rope, chain or several wires twisted together **2** a bundle of wires that carry electricity **3** *Old-fashioned* a telegram sent to another country

cache   (*sounds like* cash)

noun **1** a hiding place for storing things **2** the things that are hidden in a cache

cackle

verb to laugh or talk with the kind of noisy sound that a hen makes after laying an egg

Word building: **cackle** *noun*

cacophony   (*say* kuh-<u>kof</u>-uh-nee)

noun a loud unmusical sound: *The dogs started a cacophony of barking.*

Word building: **cacophonous** *adjective*

cactus

noun a spiky plant which stores water in its thick skin and grows in hot dry places

Word building: The plural is **cacti** or **cactuses**.

cadaver   (*say* kuh-<u>dav</u>-uh)

noun a dead body, particularly of a human being

Other words: **corpse**

caddie

noun someone who is paid to carry a golfer's playing clubs and find the ball

Word use: Another spelling is **caddy**.

caddy

noun a small box or tin in which tea is kept

Word building: The plural is **caddies**.

cadence (*say* kay-duhns)

noun **1** the rising and falling of sounds, especially in the sound of your voice when reading poetry **2** a group of musical notes or chords which show the end of a section or piece of music

cadet

noun someone who is being trained in a job or an organisation, like the army or a school military group

Word building: **cadetship** *noun*

cafe (*say* kaf-ay)

noun a restaurant where coffee and small meals are served

Word use: The 'e' is pronounced because this comes from the French word *café* which means 'coffee'.

cafeteria

noun a cheap self-service restaurant

Word history: from an American Spanish word for a coffee shop

caffeine (*say* kaf-een)

noun a stimulating drug found in coffee and tea which stops you falling asleep

caftan

noun a long piece of clothing worn over the whole body, with long, wide sleeves, sometimes tied at the waist

Word use: Another spelling is **kaftan**.

cage

noun **1** an enclosure made of wires or bars, in which animals or birds are kept **2** anything that is like a prison

Word building: **cage** *verb*: *The prisoner was caged in his cell.*

cagey

adjective careful not to tell very much: *He became very cagey when the police questioned him.*

Word building: Other forms are **cagier**, **cagiest**. | **cagily** *adverb* **caginess** *noun*

cajole (*say* kuh-johl)

verb to persuade by praising or making promises
Other words: **coax, entice**

Word building: **cajolery** *noun*

cake

noun **1** a sweet food, usually made with butter or margarine, flour, sugar, eggs and a flavouring, which is baked in an oven **2** a small mass of something with a definite shape: *a fish cake* | *a cake of soap*
verb **3** to cover with a thick crust of something: *We cake our hair with powder and pretend that we're ghosts.*

calamari (*say* kal-uh-mah-ree)

noun squid used as food

Word history: from the Italian name for this food

calamity

noun a terrible happening or disaster

Word building: The plural is **calamities**. | **calamitous** *adjective* **calamitously** *adverb*

calcium (*say* kal-see-uhm)

noun a soft silver-white metal that is found in limestone and chalk, and in teeth and bones

calculate

verb **1** to work out using mathematics: *I'll calculate the area of this page.*
Other words: **analyse, compute, gauge, reckon**
2 to work out by thinking about: *Hua calculated that it was worth taking the risk.*
Other words: **assess, estimate, figure, gauge**

Word building: **calculated** *adjective* done deliberately or with careful planning: *a calculated insult* **calculation** *noun*

calculated

adjective deliberate: *The strategy in the second half was a calculated attempt to intimidate the other team.*

calculating

adjective very careful and shrewd: *a calculating look*

calculator

noun a small electronic machine that can be used to do sums

calendar

noun a chart that shows the days and weeks of each month of the year

Word history: from a Latin word meaning 'account book'

calf¹ (*say* kahf)

noun a young cow, whale, elephant or seal

Word building: The plural is **calves**.

calf² (*say* kahf)

noun the back part of your leg, below the knee

Word building: The plural is **calves**.

calibre (*say* kal-uh-buh)

noun **1** the measurement across something round, like a bullet or the barrel of a gun **2** the ability or character of a person: *You can't rely on a person of that calibre.*

Word building: **calibrate** *verb* to measure the calibre of, or to adjust   **calibration** *noun*

calico

noun a rough cotton cloth, usually whitish in colour

Word history: from *Calicut*, a city on the coast of India where this cloth was first made

caliper

noun a metal splint used as a support for an injured leg or arm

Word use: Another spelling is **calliper**.

call

verb **1** to cry out in a loud voice **2** to order to happen: *The principal called a staff meeting.* **3** to read out aloud: *The teacher called the roll.* **4** to shout out to **5** to ask or order to come: *We'd better call a doctor.* **6** to telephone: *Please call me tonight.* **7** to give a name to: *My parents called me Darryl, but my mates call me Dazza.* **8** to give a description to: *Don't call me a cheat.*
noun **9** a shout or cry **10** a short visit **11** a telephone conversation: *a long-distance call*
phrase **12 call at,** to make a short stop at: *Maria called at the shop on her way home.* **13 call for,** to need or be suitable for: *Your success calls for a party.* **14 call off,** to cancel or postpone: *They called off the sports carnival because of rain.* **15 call on,** to make a short visit to: *Why don't we call on Jiro?*

Word building: **caller** *noun*

call centre

noun an office operated by a company to deal with product support and other inquiries from customers: *The call centre for the computer company is based in India.*

calligraphy (*say* kuh-lig-ruh-fee)

noun the art of doing beautiful handwriting

Word building: **calligrapher** *noun* **calligraphic** *adjective*

calling

noun someone's job, profession or trade

callous

adjective showing no concern for another person's feelings: *She gave a callous answer to his call for help.*

Word building: **callousness** *noun*

callus

noun a hard thick part of your skin caused by something rubbing against it: *I've got a callus on my thumb from the handle of my tennis racquet.*

calm

adjective **1** without any rough movements: *a calm sea*
Other words: **quiet, still, tranquil**
2 not windy: *a calm day*
Other words: **quiet, still**
3 not getting excited or upset: *He always stays calm when there is trouble.*
Other words: **collected, composed, poised, unruffled**

Word building: **calm** *verb*: *to calm someone's fears* **calm** *noun* **calmness** *noun* **calmly** *adverb*

calorie

noun a measurement of heat or the energy value of food: *That cake is full of calories.*

Word use: This measurement is now being replaced by **kilojoule**.

camel

noun an animal with a humped back, used to carry people and loads across the desert

cameo (*say* kam-ee-oh)

noun **1** a piece of jewellery made from a stone or shell which has been carved so that the design stands out from its background **2** a small part in a film or play acted by a famous person

camera
noun a machine which takes photographs

camouflage   (*say* kam-uh-flahzh)
noun a kind of disguise, either natural or artificial, that makes something hard to see against its surroundings: *The colour of that insect gives it a good camouflage.*

Word building: **camouflage** *verb*

camp¹
noun **1** a group of tents, caravans or shelters for outdoor living **2** a place for these kinds of shelters
verb **3** to live for a while in a tent: *We camped in the bush during our holidays.*

Word building: **camper** *noun*

camp²
adjective **1** in an exaggerated or amusing style: *The new play is very camp.* | *a camp hairstyle* **2** (of a male) homosexual

campaign   (*say* kam-payn)
noun **1** a series of planned attacks by an army, in a particular area or for a particular purpose: *How many soldiers fought in that campaign?* **2** any planned series of actions with a particular purpose: *They started a campaign to change the school uniform.*

Word building: **campaign** *verb*   **campaigner** *noun*

campervan
noun a motor van with a cabin for the driver at the front and a kitchen, beds, and so on, at the back

Word use: The short form of this is **camper**. | Compare this with **caravan**.

campus
noun the grounds of a university or college

Word history: from a Latin word meaning 'field'

can¹
noun a tin container for food and drink: *a can of oil* | *a can of apples*

Word building: **can** *verb* (**canned**, **canning**) to put in a can   **canned** *adjective*

can²
verb **1** to be able to: *You can lift that box.* **2** to have permission to: *Can I speak to you a moment?*

Word use: This verb is a helping verb, always used with another one in the form **I can** or **I could**. | Some people say you should always use **may** for definition 2, and not **can**.

canal   (*say* kuh-nal)
noun a human-made waterway for ships or barges

canary
noun a small yellow bird that sings sweetly and is often kept as a pet

Word building: The plural is **canaries**.
Word history: named after the *Canary* Islands where these birds were first seen

canasta
noun a card game played by two to six people

cancel
verb **1** to call off: *to cancel a picnic* **2** to cross out by drawing lines through: *He cancelled my name on the list of competitors.*

Word building: Other forms are **I cancelled, I have cancelled, I am cancelling.** | **cancellation** *noun*

cancer
noun the harmful growth of a group of cells in someone's body, which destroys the nearby cells and can spread throughout the whole body, often causing death

Word building: **cancerous** *adjective*

candelabrum   (*say* kan-duh-lah-bruhm)
noun an ornamental holder for a number of candles

Word building: The plural is **candelabra**.

candid
adjective **1** honest and sincere: *He gave a candid answer to the judge's question.* **2** taken without people knowing: *candid photos*

Word building: **candidly** *adverb* **candidness** *noun*

candidate
noun **1** someone sitting for an examination **2** someone who is applying for a job, an award or a place in parliament

Word building: **candidacy** *noun*   **candidature** *noun*
Word history: from a Latin word meaning 'dressed in white', after the white togas that Roman candidates wore when they were standing for office

candle
noun a piece of wax containing a wick which is burnt to give light

candour　(*rhymes with* panda)
noun honesty and sincerity: *He answered with complete candour.*

Word use: Another spelling is **candor**.

candy
noun a sweet made of boiled sugar

Word building: The plural is **candies**. | **candied** *adjective* cooked in sugar　**candy** *verb* (**candied, candying**)

cane
noun **1** the thin woody stem of bamboo, sugar cane and other similar plants
verb **2** to beat with a cane

cane toad
noun a toad brought into Queensland to get rid of cane beetles and which is now a pest

canine　(*say* kay-nuyn)
adjective **1** having to do with dogs
noun **2** any animal belonging to the dog family: *Foxes and wolves are canines.*
3 the pointed tooth on each side of your upper and lower jaws

canister
noun a small container, often made of metal: *a tea canister*

cannabis　(*say* kan-uh-buhs)
noun another name for **marijuana**

cannibal
noun someone who eats human flesh

Word building: **cannibalise** *verb* **cannibalism** *noun*

cannon
noun a large gun on wheels

cannot
verb a form of **can not**

canoe　(*say* kuh-nooh)
noun a light narrow boat that you move by using paddles

Word building: **canoe** *verb* (**canoed, canoeing**)　**canoeist** *noun*

canon[1]
noun **1** a law or rule **2** a set of church laws **3** a piece of music in which the same tune is played or sung by two or more parts overlapping each other

canon[2]
noun a minister connected with a cathedral

canopy　(*say* kan-uh-pee)
noun an ornamental or protective covering: *a bed canopy | a canopy of trees*

Word building: The plural is **canopies**. | **canopied** *adjective*
Word history: from a Greek word meaning 'mosquito net'

can't
verb a short form of **cannot**

cantaloupe
noun a small round melon with orange-coloured flesh

Word use: Another word for this is **rockmelon**.

cantankerous
adjective bad-tempered and quarrelsome: *a cantankerous neighbour*

Word building: **cantankerously** *adverb* **cantankerousness** *noun*

canteen
noun **1** a cafeteria or a counter where food is sold in a factory, office or school
2 a box holding cutlery **3** a small container for carrying drinking water

canter
noun the movement of a horse which is a little slower than a gallop

Word building: **canter** *verb*

cantor
noun a Jewish church leader who sings during the religious service

canvas
noun **1** heavy cotton cloth used for sails, tents and other similar articles **2** a piece of this used for painting on: *an artist's canvas*

canvass
verb to ask for votes or support from: *The candidate canvassed the voters in the electorate.*

Word building: **canvasser** *noun*

canyon
noun a deep valley with steep sides

canyoning
adverb the sport of following a river down a canyon, usually on rafts, and also involving abseiling and rockclimbing

cap

noun **1** a soft close-fitting hat with a peak to shade the face **2** a lid or top **3** a small explosive used in toy guns to make a loud bang
verb **4** to put a cap or top on
5 to improve upon: *I capped my previous record in the high jump.*

Word building: Other verb forms are **I capped, I have capped, I am capping.**

capable

adjective **1** having ability or skill: *He is a capable cook.*
phrase **2 capable of, a** able to: *He is capable of running a kilometre.* **b** likely to do: *He is capable of murder.*

Word building: **capability** *noun*   **capably** *adverb*

capacity

noun **1** quantity or amount which can be held or contained: *This jug's capacity is one litre.* **2** mental ability: *a pupil's capacity to learn a language* **3** the position or standing of someone: *I am arresting you in my capacity as a policeman.*

Word building: The plural is **capacities.**

cape¹

noun a loose cloak which is fastened at your neck and hangs over your shoulders

cape²

noun a piece of land jutting out into the sea

caper

verb to jump or dance about
Word building: **caper** *noun*

capillary   (*say* kuh-pil-uh-ree)

noun one of the smallest blood vessels in your body

Word building: The plural is **capillaries.** | **capillary** *adjective*

capital

noun **1** the main city of a state or country: *Canberra is the capital of Australia.*
2 a large letter: *People's names start with a capital.* **3** the amount of money owned by a business or person **4** any form of wealth used to produce more wealth
adjective **5** chief or main: *a capital city*

Word building: **capitalise** *verb*   **capitalisation** *noun*

capitalism

noun the economic system under which industries are owned privately and not by the government

Word use: Compare this with **communism.**
Word building: **capitalist** *noun*

capital punishment

noun punishment by death

capitulate   (*say* kuh-pit-chuh-layt)

verb to give in or surrender: *The enemy capitulated.*

Word building: **capitulation** *noun*

cappuccino   (*say* kap-uh-chee-noh)

noun coffee with frothy milk added, made with a special machine

Word history: from an Italian word meaning 'hood'

caprice   (*say* kuh-prees)

noun a sudden change of mind without an apparent reason

Word building: **capricious** *adjective* **capriciousness** *noun*

capsicum   (*say* kap-suh-kuhm)

noun a type of pepper plant and its green or red fruit, which is used in salads or to flavour food

Word history: from a Latin word meaning 'box'

capsize

verb to turn over: *The boat capsized.* | *The large waves capsized the boat.*

capsule

noun **1** a small case or covering, like the one that holds a dose of powdered medicine **2** the part of a spaceship which holds the crew or instruments

captain

noun **1** a leader: *captain of the basketball team* **2** someone who commands a group of soldiers **3** someone who is in charge of a ship or aeroplane

Word building: **captaincy** *noun*

caption

noun a heading for a newspaper article or a title for a picture or cartoon

Word building: **caption** *verb*

captivate

verb to charm and delight: *We captivated the audience with our beautiful singing.*

Word building: **captivation** *noun*

captive

noun someone who has been taken prisoner

Word building: **captive** *adjective*   **captivity** *noun*

captive breeding

noun the breeding of wild animals in an enclosure, sometimes to prevent extinction of a species

capture

verb to take by force

Word building: **captor** *noun* someone who captures   **capture** *noun*

car

noun **1** a vehicle with wheels driven by its own engine, for carrying passengers along roads **2** a railway carriage or wagon

Word use: The full name of definition 1 is **motor car**.

carafe   (*say* kuh-<u>rahf</u>)

noun a glass bottle used for serving water, wine or fruit juice at a meal table

caramel

noun **1** a type of sweet, or a colouring or flavouring made from burnt sugar **2** a caramel colour
adjective **3** light brown

carat

noun **1** a unit of weight for measuring gems, equal to 200 milligrams **2** a measure of the purity of gold: *Pure gold is 24 carats.*

caravan

noun **1** a covered van that can be pulled by a car, and in which you can live, especially when you are on holidays **2** a group of people travelling together, especially across a desert

Word use: Compare definition 1 with **campervan**.

caraway

noun a herb with small seeds which are used in cooking

carbine

noun a rifle with a short barrel

carbohydrate

noun a chemical compound, such as sugar or starch, which is present in all living things

carbon

noun a common element found in all living things as well as in such substances as diamonds, graphite and coal

carbon capture

noun the process of removing carbon dioxide from places like power stations, in order to prevent it entering the atmosphere and adding to the greenhouse effect

carbon dioxide

noun a colourless gas which has no smell and does not burn, used in industry as dry ice and in fizzy drinks

carbon footprint

noun the amount of carbon dioxide emissions for which an individual or organisation is responsible: *He thought he'd leave a smaller carbon footprint by showering only once a fortnight.*

carbon monoxide

noun a colourless, poisonous gas which has no smell

carbon paper

noun paper that is coated with carbon, used between sheets of writing or typing paper to make copies

carbon sink

noun a reservoir for holding carbon, such as a natural one like the ocean or a man-made one like a forest planted for that purpose

carbuncle

noun a painful pus-filled swelling, like a large boil

carburettor   (*say* kah-byuh-<u>ret</u>-uh)

noun the part of an engine in which fuel and air are mixed together to form an explosive gas

carcass   (*say* <u>kah</u>-kuhs)

noun the dead body of an animal

Word use: Another spelling is **carcase**.

card

noun **1** a piece of stiff paper or cardboard, usually small and oblong-shaped: *a birthday card | a business card* **2** one of a set of cards used for playing games such as rummy or bridge
phrase **3 on the cards**, likely to happen

cardboard
noun a thick stiff sort of paper

cardi-
prefix a word part meaning 'heart': *cardiac*
Word use: Another spelling is **cardio-**.
Word history: from Greek

cardiac
adjective having to do with the heart: *a cardiac disease*

cardigan
noun a knitted jacket with buttons down the front
Word history: named after the 7th Earl of *Cardigan*, 1797 to 1868

cardinal
adjective **1** chief or of first importance: *a cardinal point to remember*
Other words: **critical, crucial, fundamental, key, major**
noun **2** a high-ranking priest in the Roman Catholic Church

cardinal number
noun a term used in maths for a number such as 1, 2, 3, and so on, which tells you how many things are in a given set but not the order in which they appear
Word use: Compare this with **ordinal number**.

cardiovascular
(*say* kah-dee-oh-<u>vas</u>-kyuh-luh)
adjective having to do with the heart and blood vessels

care
noun **1** worry or anxiety: *The doctor was worn out by care.* **2** thoughtful attention: *Do your work with care.* **3** protection or charge: *under the care of a doctor*
verb **4** to worry: *I care about the future.*
phrase **5 care for, a** to like or love **b** to look after: *We must help care for the sick.* **6 care of**, at the address of: *You can write to him care of his mother.*
Word building: **carefree** *adjective* without care **carer** *noun*

career
noun **1** the job or profession in which you earn your living: *a business career | a career in law*
verb **2** to move rapidly and wildly: *The car's brakes failed and it careered down the hill.*

careful
adjective **1** taking care to avoid risks: *a careful driver* **2** putting time and effort into your work
Word use: Another word for definition 1 is **cautious**. | Another word for definition 2 is **thorough**.
Word building: **carefully** *adverb* **carefulness** *noun*

careless
adjective **1** done without paying enough attention: *careless work* **2** done or said without thinking: *A careless remark can be hurtful.*
Word building: **carelessly** *adverb* **carelessness** *noun*

caress   (*say* kuh-<u>res</u>)
noun an action which shows affection, such as a gentle touch, a hug or a kiss
Word building: **caress** *verb* to touch with affection
Word history: from a Latin word meaning 'dear'

caret   (*say* <u>ka</u>-ruht)
noun a mark (^) you make in writing or printing to show where something has to be added

caretaker
noun someone who looks after a building

cargo
noun the goods carried on a ship, plane, truck, and so on
Word building: The plural is **cargoes**.

caricature   (*say* <u>ka</u>-ri-kuh-choo-uh)
noun a picture or description of someone or something which makes fun of their unusual features
Word building: **caricaturist** *noun* someone who draws caricatures **caricature** *verb*

carillon   (*say* kuh-<u>ril</u>-yuhn)
noun a set of bells hung in a tower and used to play tunes
Word building: **carillonist** *noun* someone who plays these bells

carnage
noun the killing of many people: *the carnage of war*
Other words: **massacre, slaughter**

carnal
adjective having to do with the body

carnation

noun a garden plant with red, pink, or white flowers

carnival

noun **1** a period of time during which sporting events are held: *an athletics carnival | a surfing carnival* **2** a time of processions and public merry-making, usually for a special occasion: *The city is holding a New Year carnival in the main street.*

Other words: **celebration, festival**

carnivore

noun an animal that eats meat: *Cats and dogs are carnivores.*

Word use: Compare this with **herbivore, insectivore** and **omnivore**.
Word building: **carnivorous** *adjective*

carob   (*say* <u>ka</u>-ruhb)

noun a tree which bears a long pod with seeds in a sweet pulp

carol

noun a joyful song, especially a Christmas song or hymn

Word building: **carol** *verb* (**carolled, carolling**)   **caroller** *noun*

carousel   (*say* ka-ruh-<u>sel</u>)

noun **1** a merry-go-round **2** the continuously moving belt from which travellers get their bags at the end of a journey by ship, aeroplane or bus

carp

noun a large freshwater fish often bred in ponds

Word building: The plural is **carp**.

carpenter

noun someone who makes things out of wood and puts up wooden parts of a building

Word building: **carpentry** *noun* woodwork

carpet

noun a thick, woven floor covering

Word building: **carpet** *verb* (**carpeted, carpeting**) to cover with a carpet

car pool

noun an arrangement where a group of people travel together in one car on a regular basis, taking turns to transport the rest of the group each in their own car

carriage

noun **1** one of the passenger-carrying cars on a train **2** a vehicle on wheels for carrying people, pulled by a horse or horses **3** the way you hold your head and body when you walk or stand

Word use: Other words for definition 3 are **bearing** and **deportment**.

carrion

noun the rotting flesh of dead animals

carrot

noun an orange-coloured root vegetable

carry

verb **1** to take from one place to another: *to carry something in your pocket | to carry cargo by ship* **2** to take or bring: *sounds carried by the wind | electricity carried by cables* **3** to walk, stand or behave: *You carry yourself well.*

phrase **4 carry away**, to excite: *I was carried away by the beautiful music.*

5 carry on, a to conduct: *to carry on a business* **b** to continue: *Carry on with what you were doing.* **6 carry out**, to complete: *to carry out a plan*

Word building: Other verb forms are **I carried, I have carried, I am carrying**. | **carrier** *noun* someone or something that carries

cart

noun a small vehicle, sometimes pulled by a horse, used for carrying a load

Word building: **cart** *verb*   **carter** *noun*

cartilage

noun a firm, elastic substance forming part of your bone structure

carton

noun a cardboard box often used for packaging food: *a milk carton | a carton of tinned fish*

cartoon

noun **1** a funny drawing **2** a film made of many slightly different drawings which give the effect of movement when put through a projector

Word building: **cartoonist** *noun*
Word history: from a Latin word meaning 'paper'

cartridge

noun **1** a case which holds the explosive powder, and often also the bullet, for a rifle or other gun **2** a container, as for toner for computer driven printers, or for recording tape for tape recorders, and so on

cartwheel

noun **1** the large wooden wheel of a cart **2** a sideways somersault with legs and arms outstretched

carve

verb **1** to shape by cutting: *He carved a doll from a piece of wood.* **2** to cut up or cut into slices: *to carve a turkey | to carve a leg of lamb*

Word building: **carved** *adjective*   **carver** *noun*   **carving** *noun*

car wash

noun a large machine that washes your car for you automatically

cascade

noun **1** a waterfall over steep rocks *verb* **2** to fall like a cascade: *The ferns cascaded over the cliff.*

case¹

noun **1** an example: *a case of forgetfulness | a case of measles* **2** a list of facts or reasons: *This is our case for a new library.* **3** a charge against someone in a court of law **4** the form of a noun or pronoun which shows its relation to other words in a sentence

Word use: For definition 4 the three cases are **subjective, objective** and **possessive**.

case²

noun **1** a container: *a pencil case | a case of apples* **2** a suitcase: *My case is packed with my holiday clothes.*

casement

noun a hinged window which opens like a door

cash

noun **1** money in notes or coins, rather than cheques: *Have you any cash in your pocket?* **2** money available straight away: *Will you pay cash or charge it?*

Word use: Compare definition 2 with **credit**. Word building: **cash** *verb* to give or get cash for

cashew

noun a small curved nut that you can eat

cashier

noun someone who is in charge of the money in a shop or bank

cashmere

noun fine wool obtained from the Kashmir goats of India, often used to make clothes

casino   (*say* kuh-**see**-noh)

noun a building or large room where gambling games are played

Word building: The plural is **casinos**. Word history: from a Latin word meaning 'cottage'

cask

noun a barrel for holding wine and other liquids

casket

noun a small chest or box

cassata   (*say* kuh-**sah**-tuh)

noun an Italian iced dessert, like gelato, made with chopped nuts or mixed dried fruit, and so on

cassava   (*say* kuh-**sah**-vuh)

noun a family of tropical plants whose roots are used for food

casserole

noun **1** a covered baking dish **2** the food, usually a mixture of meat and vegetables, cooked in it

cassette

noun **1** the plastic container holding the recording tape used in videos and tape recorders *adjective* **2** designed for playing cassettes: *a cassette recorder*

cassette recorder

noun a machine that plays or records cassettes

cassock

noun a long garment worn by members of the clergy

cassowary   (*say* **kas**-uh-wuh-ree)

noun a large three-toed bird found in Australia, New Guinea and nearby islands, which is smaller than an ostrich and cannot fly

Word building: The plural is **cassowaries**.

cast

verb **1** to throw out or fling: *to cast a fishing line | to cast a stone* **2** to cause to fall: *The sun cast a shadow over the field.* **3** to throw off or shed: *A snake casts its old skin.* **4** to select for a play: *They cast Kwame as the villain.* **5** to form in a mould: *The decorative iron railings were cast in 1900.* *noun* **6** all the actors in a play **7** a mould of plaster around a broken limb **8** a permanent squint

Word building: Other verb forms are **I cast, I have cast, I am casting**.

castanets

plural noun a pair of shell-shaped pieces of ivory or wood which you hold in the palm of your hand and strike together in time to music and dancing

Word history: from a Latin word meaning 'chestnut'

castaway

noun someone who has been shipwrecked, especially someone who has escaped from the ship to an island or other lonely place

caste

noun **1** one of the social groups or divisions into which Hindus are born **2** any strictly followed system of social divisions

castigate

verb to criticise or punish severely

Word use: The more usual word is **scold**.
Word building: **castigation** *noun*

castle

noun **1** a large strongly-built fort, used as a home by princes or nobles in the olden days **2** a piece in chess, shaped like a castle

Word use: Another name for definition 2 is **rook**.

castor

noun **1** a small wheel attached to the bottom of a bed or under the legs of some tables and chairs to make them easier to move **2** a bottle with holes in the top, for holding sugar or salt

castor oil

noun a sticky oil pressed from the seeds of a plant and used as a medicine

castrate

verb to remove the testicles from: *to castrate the bull*

Word building: **castration** *noun*

casual

adjective **1** happening by chance: *a casual meeting*
Other words: **accidental, chance, unplanned**
2 without thinking: *a casual remark*
Other words: **careless, offhand, passing, unthinking**
3 informal: *I wear casual clothes on holidays.* **4** employed occasionally: *a casual worker*

Word building: **casual** *noun* a worker employed occasionally   **casually** *adverb*

casualty

noun someone hurt or killed in an accident or war

Word building: The plural is **casualties**.

casuarina   (*say* kazh-yuh-<u>ree</u>-nuh)

noun a type of Australian tree or shrub with leaves which are like the needles of a pine tree and cones with a rather flat top

Word use: Another name is **she-oak**.

cat

noun **1** a small furry animal often kept as a pet **2** a member of the cat family, which includes lions, tigers and other similar animals
Other words: **feline**
3 a spiteful person

Word building: **catty** *adjective* (**cattier, cattiest**) spiteful

catacomb   (*say* <u>kat</u>-uh-kohm, <u>kat</u>-uh-koohm)

noun a series of underground tunnels and caves or rooms, once used as burial places

catalogue   (*say* <u>kat</u>-uh-log)

noun a list, usually in alphabetical order, of names, books or articles on sale or display and some information about them: *a catalogue of artists | a library catalogue | a sales catalogue*

Word building: **catalogue** *verb*   **cataloguer** *noun*

catalyst   (*say* <u>kat</u>-uh-luhst)

noun someone or something that causes a change or a reaction

Word building: **catalyse** *verb*   **catalysis** *noun*   **catalytic** *adjective*

catamaran

noun a boat with two hulls

Word use: The shortened form is **cat**.
Word history: from a Tamil word meaning 'tied tree' or 'wood'

catapult

noun **1** a Y-shaped stick with a length of elastic joined to the prongs, used for shooting stones at things **2** a device for launching planes from the deck of a ship

Word use: Other names for definition 1 are **shanghai, sling** and **slingshot**.
Word building: **catapult** *verb* to throw or be thrown, as if from a catapult

cataract

noun **1** a large waterfall **2** a disease of the eye causing loss of sight

catastrophe   (*say* kuh-<u>tas</u>-truh-fee)

noun a sudden disaster

Word building: **catastrophic** *adjective* **catastrophically** *adverb*

catch

verb **1** to capture, especially after a chase **2** to take in the hands: *to catch a ball* **3** to be in time for: *to catch a bus* **4** to get or contract: *to catch a cold* **5** to surprise or come upon suddenly: *I caught him stealing*.
phrase **6 catch on, a** to become popular **b** to understand **7 catch up**, to reach or become level: *He caught up with the rest of the class.* | *I ran and caught up to the leaders.*

Word building: Other verb forms are **I caught, I have caught, I am catching**. | **catchy** *adjective* easy to remember   **catch** *noun*

catechism   (*say* <u>kat</u>-uh-kiz-uhm)

noun a book of questions and answers meant to help you learn about your religion

Word building: **catechise** *verb*   **catechist** *noun*

category

noun a group or division of people or things

Word building: The plural is **categories**. | **categorical** *adjective* clear and plain, with no doubt   **categorically** *adverb*   **categorise** *verb*

cater

verb to supply food and drink: *My mother is catering for my party*.

Word building: **caterer** *noun* a supplier, especially of food

caterpillar

noun the worm-like grub or larva of a moth or butterfly

caterwaul   (*say* kat-uh-wawl)

verb to cry or howl like quarrelling cats

cathedral

noun the main church in a district which acts as a bishop's headquarters

cattle

noun farm animals such as cows, bulls and oxen: *The cattle are grazing in the far paddock*.

catwalk

noun a long narrow platform on which models walk to display clothes

caucus   (*say* <u>kaw</u>-kuhs)

noun a meeting of the members of parliament belonging to a particular political party

Word history: from a Native American word meaning 'adviser'

cauldron   (*say* <u>kawl</u>-druhn)

noun a large rounded kettle or boiler with a lid and handles

cauliflower

noun a vegetable with a large round head of white flowers

cause

noun **1** someone or something which brings about an effect or result: *My joke was the cause of all the laughter*. **2** something that you believe in: *Peace is a cause worth working for*.
verb **3** to bring about: *to cause trouble*

Word building: **causal** *adjective*   **causally** *adverb*   **causation** *noun*

causeway

noun a raised road or path across low or wet ground

caustic   (*say* <u>kos</u>-tik)

adjective **1** capable of burning or eating away living cells: *caustic soda* **2** critical or sarcastic: *a caustic remark*

Word building: **caustically** *adverb*

cauterise   (*say* <u>kaw</u>-tuh-ruyz)

verb to burn with a hot instrument, especially to kill germs: *to cauterise a wound*

Word use: Another spelling is **cauterize**.
Word building: **cauterisation** *noun*

caution

noun **1** great care when there is danger: *Use caution in crossing city streets.* **2** a warning

Word building: **caution** *verb* to warn **cautionary** *adjective*

cautious

adjective having or showing caution in order to avoid danger or problems: *She is cautious when she is driving and never takes risks. | He is very cautious about spending too much money.*
Other words: **careful, circumspect, prudent, vigilant, wary**

Word building: **cautiously** *adverb*

cavalcade

noun a procession of people on horseback or in horse-drawn carriages

cavalier   (*say* kav-uh-<u>lear</u>)

noun **1** a soldier or knight on horseback
adjective **2** not caring about important things: *Sam has a cavalier attitude towards school work.*

cavalry

noun a group of soldiers on horses

cave

noun **1** a hollow place in a hillside
verb **2** to explore caves **3** to fall or sink: *The ground caved in under their feet.*

cavern   (*say* <u>kav</u>-uhn)

noun a large cave

Word building: **cavernous** *adjective* **cavernously** *adverb*

caviar   (*say* <u>kav</u>-ee-ah)

noun the salted eggs of sturgeon or other large fish

cavity

noun an empty space or hollow: *a cavity in a wall | a cavity in a tooth*

Word building: The plural is **cavities**.

cavort   (*say* kuh-<u>vawt</u>)

verb to dance or jump about

CD

noun a short form of **compact disc**

CD-ROM   (*say* see-dee-<u>rom</u>)

noun a compact disc containing writing, sound, and pictures that can be displayed on a computer

cease

verb to stop: *The noise ceased. | We will cease work now.*
Other words: **conclude, end, finish, terminate**

Word building: **cessation** *noun* a pause or stopping   **ceaseless** *adjective* without stopping   **ceaselessly** *adverb*

ceasefire

noun a suspension of fighting, especially during a war

cedar   (*rhymes with* reader)

noun a type of tree, whose wood is often used to make furniture

cede   (*sounds like* seed)

verb to give away by making a solemn written promise: *to cede land*

ceiling

noun **1** the inside lining that covers the top of a room **2** the top limit that something can reach: *We should put a ceiling on the price of bread.*

> **ceiling/sealing** Don't confuse **ceiling** with **sealing**, which comes from the verb **seal**, to close or fasten tightly:
> *I am sealing the jam jars with wax.*

celebrant   (*say* <u>sel</u>-uh-bruhnt)

noun a special person who leads a ceremony

celebrate

verb **1** to honour with ceremonies and festivities: *Many Australians celebrate New Year's Eve with a display of fireworks.*
Other words: **observe**
2 to perform solemnly: *to celebrate mass* **3** to express your happiness: *When exams are over, we're going to celebrate.*
Other words: **exult, party, rejoice**

Word building: **celebrant** *noun* **celebrated** *adjective* famous **celebration** *noun*

celebrity   (*say* suh-<u>leb</u>-ruh-tee)

noun a famous or well-known person
Other words: **personality, star, VIP**

Word building: The plural is **celebrities**.

celery

noun a vegetable with long green stalks that are good to eat

celestial

adjective having to do with heaven

celibacy   (*say* <u>sel</u>-uh-buh-see)

noun the condition of being unmarried and refraining from sexual intercourse: *Roman Catholic priests live under vows of celibacy.*
Word building: **celibate** *adjective*

cell

noun **1** a small room in a prison or a convent **2** the tiny basic parts of all living matter: *plant cells | blood cells | nerve cells* **3** part of an electric battery

Word building: **cellular** *adjective* having many small holes or cells

cell/sell Don't confuse **cell** with **sell**. To **sell** something is to hand it over to someone in exchange for money.

cellar

noun **1** an underground room **2** a supply of wines

cello   *(say* chel-oh*)*

noun an instrument shaped like a large violin, which has four strings and is held upright on the floor between the knees of the player

Word use: The **cello** sounds lower than the **violin** and **viola** and higher than the **double bass**.
Word building: **cellist** *noun*
Word history: short for **violoncello**

cellulose   *(say* sel-yuh-lohs*)*

noun important material that forms the cell walls of plants and is found in wood, cotton, hemp and paper

Celsius

adjective relating to a scale of temperature in which 0° is the melting point of ice and 100° is the boiling point of water

Word history: named after A *Celsius*, a Swedish astronomer who lived from 1701 to 1744

cement

noun **1** a mixture of clay and limestone, used for making concrete **2** a type of glue

Word building: **cement** *verb*

cemetery

noun a place where people who have died are buried

Word use: Another word is **graveyard**.
Word building: The plural is **cemeteries**.

cenotaph   *(say* sen-uh-tahf*)*

noun a public memorial to those killed in war

censor

noun someone who is specially chosen to decide what books, films or news reports are to be made available to the public

Word building: **censorious** *adjective* critical and fault-finding   **censor** *verb*

censorship

noun the act or practice of censoring

censure   *(say* sen-shuh*)*

verb to find fault with, or condemn: *The manager censured the clerk for being late so often.*

Word building: **censure** *noun*

census

noun an official counting of all the people who live in a place or country

cent

noun a coin worth a hundredth of a dollar

cent/sent/scent Don't confuse **cent** with **sent** or **scent**. **Sent** is the past form of the verb **send**: *My friend sent me this postcard.* A **scent** is the smell of flowers and perfume.

centaur   *(say* sen-taw*)*

noun a creature of Greek legend, said to be half human and half horse

centenary   *(say* sen-teen-uh-ree*)*

noun a 100th anniversary

Word building: The plural is **centenaries**. | **centenarian** *noun* someone who is 100 years old   **centennial** *adjective*

centi-

prefix a word part indicating one hundredth of a given unit: *centimetre*

Word use: Another spelling is **cent-**.
Word history: from Latin

Centigrade

adjective an old-fashioned word for **Celsius**

centimetre

noun a hundredth of a metre

centipede

noun a small insect-like creature with a long thin body and many pairs of legs

centre

noun **1** the middle point of an area: *the centre of a circle* **2** a place for a particular activity: *a shopping centre*
verb **3** to bring or come to a centre: *Try to centre your mind on the job. | Attention centred on the winner.*

Word building: **central** *adjective* **centralise** *verb* **centrally** *adverb*

centrefold

noun the double page in the middle of a magazine, usually having a large photograph for pinning up on a wall

centri-

prefix a word part meaning 'centre': *centrifugal*

Word use: Other spellings are **centr-** and **centro-**.
Word history: from Latin and Greek

centrifugal   (*say* sen-<u>trif</u>-yuh-guhl)

adjective moving outwards from the centre: *centrifugal force*

centurion

noun the leader of one hundred men in the Roman army

century

noun **1** a period of 100 years **2** any group of 100: *He scored a century in the cricket match.*

Word building: The plural is **centuries**.

ceramic   (*say* suh-<u>ram</u>-ik)

adjective **1** made of clay: *a ceramic pot*
noun **2 ceramics**, the craft of making things out of clay: *Ceramics is taught at the art school.* **3** the things made: *We sell ceramics in our craft shop.*

cereal

noun **1** a grain plant, such as wheat, maize or rice **2** a food made from grain, especially a breakfast food

cereal/serial Don't confuse **cereal** with **serial**, which is a story you get one part at a time at regular intervals.

cerebral   (*say* <u>se</u>-ruh-bruhl, suh-<u>ree</u>-bruhl)

adjective having to do with the brain

cerebral palsy   (*say* se-ruh-bruhl <u>pawl</u>-zee)

noun a kind of paralysis caused by injury to your brain, resulting in jerky movements of your arms and legs

ceremony

noun the solemn actions performed on an important occasion: *a wedding ceremony | the opening ceremony for the new school*

Word building: The plural is **ceremonies**. | **ceremonial** *adjective* belonging to or used for a ceremony   **ceremonious** *adjective* elaborately polite: *a ceremonious welcome*

cerise   (*say* suh-<u>rees</u>)

adjective cherry red

certain

adjective **1** confident or having no doubt: *I was certain that I had seen that person before.* **2** sure: *It is certain to happen.* **3** definite or particular, but not named: *a certain person*

Word building: **certainly** *adverb*   **certainty** *noun*

certificate

noun a written paper stating certain facts: *a certificate of health | a birth certificate*

certify

verb to state in writing or declare as fact

Word building: Other forms are **I certified, I have certified, I am certifying**. | **certification** *noun*   **certifier** *noun*

cervix

noun the entrance to the womb

Word building: The plural is **cervixes** or **cervices** (*say* suh-<u>vuy</u>-seez). | **cervical** *adjective*

chador   (*say* <u>chah</u>-duh)

noun a long, dark cloak that covers the whole body, including the face below the eyes, worn by some Muslim women

chafe

verb **1** to wear down or make sore by rubbing: *This saddle chafes my horse.* **2** to become impatient: *She chafed at the delay.*

chaff

noun **1** the husks or dry outer coverings of grain: *to separate the wheat from the chaff* **2** straw cut up small and used for animal feed

chagrin   (*say* <u>shag</u>-ruhn)

noun a feeling of anger and disappointment: *I found to my chagrin that they had already left.*

chain

noun **1** a series of metal rings joined together **2** a series of connected things: *a mountain chain | a chain of events* **3** a number of shops, hotels or theatres that belong to one owner

Word building: **chain** *verb* to fasten with a chain

chainsaw

noun a saw which has teeth on a revolving chain driven by a motor

chair

noun **1** a seat with a back and often with arms
verb **2** to act as a chairperson: *to chair a meeting*

chairperson

noun someone who controls a meeting

Word building: The plural is **chairpersons**. | **chairwoman** *noun* (**chairwomen**) **chairman** *noun* (**chairmen**)

chalet (*say* <u>shal</u>-ay)

noun a mountain cottage, sometimes used as a holiday house

chalk

noun **1** soft white limestone **2** a stick of this for drawing or writing on blackboards

Word building: **chalkiness** *noun* **chalky** *adjective*

challenge

verb **1** to invite to take part or compete in a test of skill or strength: *to challenge someone to fight* **2** to make demands on: *This job will challenge your abilities.*

Word building: **challenge** *noun* **challenger** *noun*

chamber

noun **1** *Old-fashioned* a room, often a private room: *in my lady's chamber* **2 chambers**, rooms of barristers and judges

chamber music

noun music for a small group of players, suitable for playing in a room rather than in a large concert hall

chameleon (*say* kuh-<u>mee</u>-lee-uhn)

noun a lizard that can change its skin colour to blend into its surroundings

Word history: from a Greek word literally meaning 'ground lion'

chamois (*say* <u>sham</u>-ee)

noun a soft cloth for polishing

Word use: Other spellings are **chammy** and **shammy**.

champagne (*say* sham-<u>payn</u>)

noun a bubbly white wine

Word history: from *Champagne*, the region in France where this wine is made

champion

noun **1** someone or something that holds first place in a sport or contest **2** someone who fights for a cause: *She is a champion of women's rights.*

Word building: **championship** *noun*

chance

noun **1** the absence of any known reason for something happening: *They met by chance.* **2** risk: *to take a chance* **3** opportunity: *Now is your chance to tell us.*

chandelier (*say* shan-duh-<u>lear</u>)

noun a branched holder for a number of lights, hanging from the ceiling

change

verb **1** to alter or make different: *You must change your habits.*
Other words: **adjust, amend, modify, transform, vary**
2 to become different: *She has changed since her illness.* **3** to exchange, especially for something else
Other words: **swap, switch, trade**
4 to give or get smaller money for: *to change a $10 note* **5** to change your clothes: *It is time you changed for the party.*
noun **6** something different from before: *a change in the weather* **7** the money you get back when what you've bought costs less than the amount you handed over **8** coins of small value: *I need change for the bus.*

Word building: **changeability** *noun* **changeable** *adjective* **changeably** *adverb* **changeless** *adjective*

channel

noun **1** a passage which water runs through: *a stormwater channel* **2** a passage which ships use to travel between two seas **3** a frequency band for radio or television **4** a way of communicating: *He approached the Minister through the usual channels.*

Word building: **channel** *verb* (**channelled, channelling**)

chant

noun **1** a simple tune, often repeating one note, for church singing **2** words repeated in a sing-song way

Word building: **chant** *verb*

chaos (*say* <u>kay</u>-os)

noun total disorder

Word building: **chaotic** *adjective*   **chaotically** *adverb*

chap
noun Informal a man or boy

chapel
noun a small church or part of a large one

chaperone   (*say* shap-uh-rohn)
verb to accompany in order to ensure respectable behaviour: *The teacher will chaperone the children at the school dance.*

Word use: Another spelling is **chaperon**.
Word building: **chaperone** *noun* an older person who is responsible for younger, less experienced people

chaplain
noun a member of the clergy who works in a school, hospital or the armed forces

Word building: **chaplaincy** *noun* the office or job of a chaplain

chapped
adjective cracked and made rough: *She has chapped hands from the wind.*

chapter
noun one of the main divisions of a book, usually with a number and a title

char
verb **1** to burn to charcoal **2** to scorch or burn slightly

Word building: Other forms are **it charred, it has charred, it is charring.**

character
noun **1** someone in a story or play **2** the special things about you that make you different from someone else **3** an odd or interesting person: *He's quite a character.* **4** honesty, or high moral standards: *a person of character* **5** a mark, letter or other symbol, used in writing and printing

Word building: **characterise** *verb* to be typical of or describe the character of **characterisation** *noun*

characteristic
adjective **1** typical or showing the special qualities: *That boasting is characteristic of her.* *noun* **2** a special feature: *Large loops are a characteristic of your handwriting.*

Word building: **characteristically** *adverb*

charade   (*say* shuh-rahd)
noun **1 charades,** a game in which half the players have to guess a word acted out by the others in a series of short plays **2** any silly pretence which obviously isn't working: *The government should stop this charade, and get on with running the country.*

charcoal
noun partly burnt wood used as a fuel or in sticks for drawing

charge
verb **1** to blame or accuse: *The police charged me with speeding.* **2** to write down as a debt: *Charge it to my account.* **3** to ask as the price: *They charge a dollar each for mangoes.* **4** to supply with electrical energy: *to charge a battery* **5** to attack by rushing violently *noun* **6** an accusation or blame **7** cost or price **8** an amount of explosive to be let off all at once *phrase* **9 in charge,** in control: *Betty is in charge of the tickets.*

Word building: **charger** *noun*

chariot
noun a two-wheeled carriage used in ancient times

Word building: **charioteer** *noun* the driver of a chariot

charisma   (*say* kuh-riz-muh)
noun the power to attract and influence people: *A successful leader should have charisma.*

Word building: **charismatic** *adjective*
Word history: from a Greek word meaning 'gift'

charity
noun **1** the giving of help or money to people who need it **2** an organisation for providing help: *Several charities have put up shelters for the homeless.*

Word building: The plural is **charities.** | **charitable** *adjective* **charitableness** *noun* **charitably** *adverb*

charlatan   (*say* shah-luh-tuhn)
noun someone who claims to have knowledge or skill that they don't really have: *I was treated by a charlatan and now my rash is worse than ever.*
Other words: **quack**

Word history: from an Italian word meaning 'chatter'

charm

noun **1** the power of pleasing and attracting: *The new assistant has a great deal of charm.* **2** a magic spell **3** an ornament or trinket supposed to bring good luck

Word building: **charm** *verb*   **charmer** *noun*   **charming** *adjective*   **charmingly** *adverb*

chart

noun **1** a map, especially of the sea **2** a printed sheet giving information, often as a table or with pictures **3 charts**, an up-to-date list of the best-selling popular recordings

Word building: **chart** *verb*: *to chart unknown seas*

charter

noun **1** a document giving certain legal rights: *The settlers were given a land charter.* *verb* **2** to hire: *They chartered a boat for their holiday.*

chase

verb **1** to follow quickly in order to catch or overtake
Other words: **pursue**
noun **2** a hunt or pursuit **3** a large area of land set aside for plants and animals

chasm   (*say* kaz-uhm)

noun a deep gap or opening in the ground

chassis   (*say* shaz-ee)

noun the frame, wheels and sometimes the machinery of a car or truck, designed to support its body

Word building: The plural is **chassis** (*say* shaz-eez).

chaste

adjective **1** pure and without sexual experience **2** decent and clean: *chaste language*

Word building: **chastity** *noun*: *The knights of old took vows of chastity.*   **chastely** *adverb*

chastise

verb to punish or scold: *Our neighbour chastised me for breaking the window.*

Word building: **chastisement** *noun*

chat

verb to talk in a friendly way: *The sisters chatted about their recent holidays.*

Word building: Other forms are **I chatted, I have chatted, I am chatting.** | **chat** *noun*   **chattily** *adverb*   **chattiness** *noun*   **chatty** *adjective*

chat room

noun an internet venue where people can discuss things by sending messages to each other via the computer

chatter

verb **1** to talk quickly, often without making sense **2** to make a rapid clicking noise: *My teeth were chattering with the cold.*

Word building: **chatterbox** *noun* someone who talks a lot   **chatter** *noun*

chauffeur   (*say* shoh-fuh, shoh-<u>fer</u>)

noun someone whose job is to drive you in your own car: *The chauffeur drives the judge to the court every day.*

Word building: **chaffeur** *verb*

chauvinism   (*say* <u>shoh</u>-vuh-niz-uhm)

noun unthinking support of any cause or group: *male chauvinism*

Word building: **chauvinist** *noun*   **chauvinistic** *adjective*   **chauvinistically** *adverb*

cheap

adjective **1** of a low price: *You can buy cheap fruit at the market.* **2** of poor quality: *Those shirts are made of cheap material.*

Word building: **cheapen** *verb*   **cheaply** *adverb*   **cheapness** *noun*

cheap/cheep Don't confuse **cheap** with **cheep**. Chickens and other small birds **cheep**.

cheat

verb **1** to be dishonest: *to cheat in an exam | to cheat at cards* **2** to take from by tricking: *to cheat someone out of $10*

Word building: **cheat** *noun* someone who cheats   **cheater** *noun*

check

verb **1** to stop or prevent: *The fallen tree across the road checked their progress.* **2** to find out the correctness of: *Please check the names on this list.*
noun **3** something that stops or holds back: *The accident was a check to my career.* **4** a test for correctness **5** a pattern of squares **6** in chess, the position of the king when it is threatened with a direct attack

checkmate

noun in chess, the act of trapping your opponent's king so ending the game
Word building: **checkmate** *verb*

check-up

noun a test to make sure that all is in order, especially your health: *She went to the doctor for her yearly check-up.*

cheddar

noun a fairly hard yellow cheese

Word history: named after *Cheddar*, a town in Somerset in England, famous for its cheese

cheek

noun **1** either side of your face, below your eyes **2** boldness or lack of respect: *He had the cheek to tell me to mind my own business.*

cheeky

adjective impudent or lacking respect: *Your cheeky behaviour annoys me.*
Other words: **disrespectful, impertinent, insolent, pert**

Word building: Other forms are **cheekier, cheekiest**. | **cheekily** *adverb*   **cheekiness** *noun*

cheep

noun a weak, high pitched sound, like that made by chickens or other small birds

Word building: **cheep** *verb*

---

cheep/cheap Don't confuse **cheep** with **cheap** which is an adjective. Something is **cheap** if it is of low price or poor quality.

---

cheer

noun **1** a shout of encouragement or approval
verb **2** to greet with shouts of approval: *They cheered the winner.*
phrase **3** **cheer up**, to make or become happier: *The news of your arrival cheered us up.* | *We cheered up when we heard the news.*

Word building: **cheery** *adjective* (**cheerier, cheeriest**)   **cheerful** *adjective*   **cheerfully** *adverb*   **cheerily** *adverb*

cheer squad

noun a small group of people who cheer a competitor or team, usually a sports team

cheese

noun a food made from milk curds

Word building: **cheesy** *adjective*   **cheesiness** *noun*

cheetah

noun a leopard-like animal that belongs to the cat family and is the fastest animal on earth

chef   (*say* shef)

noun a cook, especially the head cook in a restaurant

chemical

adjective **1** of or about chemistry
noun **2** a substance obtained by or used in chemistry

Word building: **chemically** *adverb*

chemist

noun **1** a scientist who studies and does research in chemistry **2** someone who has studied drugs and medicines and keeps a shop selling them

Word use: Another word for definition 2 is **pharmacist**.

chemistry

noun the science of what substances are made of and the ways they react with each other

cheongsam   (*say* chong-<u>sam</u>)

noun a straight dress, often made of silk and sometimes with a slit skirt, originally worn by Chinese women

cheque   (*say* chek)

noun a written order asking a bank to pay a certain amount of money to a particular person

Word building: **chequebook** *noun* a book of printed forms for cheques

chequered

adjective **1** marked with squares **2** marked by changes in good or bad luck: *a chequered career*

Word building: **chequer** *noun* a pattern of squares

cherish

verb to look after tenderly: *I cherish my pet rabbit called Coz.*

Word history: from a French word meaning 'dear'

cherry

noun **1** a small juicy fruit with a stone in the middle, varying in colour from pink to black
adjective **2** bright red

Word building: The plural form of the noun is **cherries**.

cherub

noun **1** an angel, pictured as a child with wings **2** a child with a chubby face

Word building: The plural is **cherubim** for definition 1, and **cherubs** for definition 2. | **cherubic** *adjective* round and innocent-looking: *a cherubic face*

chess

noun a board game played by two people, each with sixteen pieces, on a chequered board

Word building: **chesspiece** *noun* one of the pieces used in the game

chest

noun **1** the front part of your body from your neck to your waist **2** a box, usually large and strong with a hinged lid

chestnut

noun **1** a European tree or its hard brown nuts
adjective **2** reddish-brown

chew

verb to bite and crush with your teeth

Word building: **chewy** *adjective*

chewing gum

noun a lolly that you only chew and do not swallow

chic   (*say* sheek)

adjective attractive and stylish: *Your new dress is very chic.*

Word history: from a French word, which is why it sounds like this

chick

noun a young chicken or other bird

chicken

noun **1** a hen or rooster, or its meat: *roast chicken for dinner* **2** *Informal* a coward: *He's too much of a chicken to climb that tree.*
phrase **3 chicken out**, *Informal* to back out because you are scared

Word building: **chicken** *adjective* cowardly

chickenpox

noun a disease, common in children, causing fever and itchy blisters

chickpea   (*say* chick-pea)

noun a small, round, yellow vegetable, like a pea

chide

verb to scold or find fault with: *She chided me for not tidying my room.*

Word building: Other forms are **I chided** or **chid, I have chid** or **chidden, I am chiding.** | **chidingly** *adverb*

chief

noun **1** the head person or boss in a group
Other words: **chieftain, elder, head, ruler**
adjective **2** most important or main: *My chief problem is with spelling.*
Other words: **foremost, major, primary, leading**

Word building: **chiefly** *adverb*

chieftain   (*say* cheef-tuhn)

noun the leader of a tribe

chiffon   (*say* shuh-fon)

noun light see-through material made of silk or nylon

chilblain

noun a red swelling on your fingers or toes caused by the cold

child

noun **1** a girl or boy **2** a daughter or son

Word building: The plural is **children.** | **childhood** *noun* the time spent as a child   **childproof** *adjective* made so that children can't use or damage it

childish

adjective **1** silly or stupid: *childish behaviour* **2** of or like a child

Word building: **childishly** *adverb* **childishness** *noun*

chill

noun **1** coldness: *There's a chill in the air.* **2** a cold, shivery feeling, often the first stage of a cold: *Take off your wet clothes before you catch a chill.*
verb **3** to make or become cold

Word building: **chill** *adjective*: *a chill wind* **chilly** *adjective* (**chillier, chilliest**) **chilliness** *noun*

chilli

noun a type of small red or green capsicum which tastes hot and is used in cooking

chime

noun **1** a ringing, musical sound: *the chime of the church bells* **2 chimes**, a set of metal tubes or bells which make musical sounds when rung

Word building: **chime** *verb*
Word history: from a Latin word meaning 'cymbal'

chimney

noun a long tube running from a fireplace to the roof of a building, which draws smoke away from a fire

Word building: The plural is **chimneys**.

chimpanzee

noun a small African ape which is very intelligent and can easily be trained to perform tricks

Word use: The short form of this is **chimp**.

chin

noun the part of your face below your mouth

china (*rhymes with* miner)

noun plates, cups and bowls made from porcelain clay: *We use the best china when guests come for dinner.*

Other words: **crockery**

Word building: **china** *adjective* made of porcelain
Word history: named after the country of *China* where delicate crockery was first made

chink

noun **1** a crack or narrow opening: *There is a chink in the rock that is letting water through.* **2** a flaw in something that makes it easy to attack: *a chink in your armour*

chintz

noun shiny brightly-patterned cotton material, used to make curtains and furniture coverings

Word building: The plural is **chintzes**. | **chintzy** *adjective* shiny and cheap-looking

chip

noun **1** a small piece chopped or split off something larger: *a chip of wood | chocolate chips* **2** a gap where a small piece has broken off: *This plate has a chip in it.* **3** a thin slice of fried potato eaten cold **4** a tiny square which contains electronic circuits, used in a computer, watch or electronic game: *a silicon chip*
verb **5** to cut or break off in small pieces
phrase **6 chip in**, *Informal*
a to contribute money or help: *We all chipped in to buy Sam's birthday present.*
b to interrupt: *It's rude to chip in while others are talking.*

Word use: Another word for definition 3 is **crisp**.
Word building: Other verb forms are **I chipped, I have chipped, I am chipping**.

chipmunk

noun a type of small striped squirrel that lives in the forests of North America and Asia

chiropractor (*say* kuy-ruh-prak-tuh)

noun someone trained to treat back pain and other types of illness by massaging and adjusting the spine

Word building: **chiropractic** *noun* the method of treating disease used by chiropractors

chirp

verb to make a short high sound like a bird or insect

Word use: Another form of the word is **chirrup**.
Word building: **chirp** *noun*

chirpy

adjective lively and cheerful

Word building: Other forms are **chirpier, chirpiest**. | **chirpily** *adverb*

chisel

noun **1** a cutting tool with a sharp end, used to shape wood and stone
verb **2** to cut with or use a chisel
3 *Informal* to cheat or trick: *He chiselled me out of my savings.*

Word building: Other verb forms are **I chiselled, I have chiselled, I am chiselling**. | **chiseller** *noun* a cheat or swindler

chivalry (*say* shiv-uhl-ree)

noun **1** polite behaviour, especially of a man towards a woman **2** the qualities of courtesy and bravery which were valued amongst medieval knights

Word building: **chivalrous** *adjective* **chivalrously** *adverb* **chivalrousness** *noun*

chives

plural noun a small grass-like herb with long thin leaves which tastes like onion and is used in cooking

chlorine (*say* klaw-reen)

noun a poisonous greenish-yellow gas with a strong irritating smell, which is dissolved in water and used to bleach clothes or to disinfect swimming pools

Word building: **chlorinate** *verb* to disinfect with chlorine **chlorination** *noun*

chlorophyll (*say* klo-ruh-fil)

noun the green colouring in leaves and plants, which traps the energy of sunlight and is sometimes used as a dye

chock

noun a block of wood wedged under something to stop it moving: *Put a chock under the door to stop it closing.*

Word building: **chock** *verb*: *to chock open the door*

chocolate

noun **1** a sweet food or drink made from the seeds of a small, tropical American tree *adjective* **2** made with or from chocolate **3** dark brown

Word history: from a Nahuatl word (spoken by the Aztecs and others) meaning 'bitter water'

choice

noun **1** the act of choosing or selecting **2** the thing chosen: *The blue one is my choice.* **3** a number of things from which you can choose: *a wide choice of colours* *adjective* **4** excellent or worthy of being chosen: *a choice apple*

choir (*say* kwuy-uh)

noun an organised group of people who sing together, especially in a church

choke

verb **1** to suffocate or stop breathing: *This tight collar is choking me.* | *He choked on a fishbone.* **2** to clog up or congest: *Mud and leaves are choking the drain.* noun **3** a device used when starting an engine, which controls the amount of air that is mixed with the petrol

Word building: **choker** *noun* a tight necklace or band around the neck

choko

noun a green pear-shaped vegetable with a prickly skin, which grows on a vine

Word building: The plural is **chokos** or **chokoes.**

cholera (*say* kol-uh-ruh)

noun an infectious tropical disease which can kill you

cholesterol (*say* kuh-les-tuh-rol)

noun a substance found in your liver, blood, brain, or in other places, such as the yolk of eggs. It is thought that if a person has too much in their bloodstream they have a greater risk of getting heart disease.

chook

noun *Informal* a chicken

choose

verb **1** to pick out or select: *Choose a number between one and ten.* | *Don't rush me while I'm choosing.* **2** to decide or prefer: *She chose not to go to the party.*
Other words: **elect, opt**

Word building: Other forms are **I chose, I have chosen, I am choosing.** | **choosy** *adjective* hard to please

chop

verb **1** to cut by hitting with quick heavy blows: *to chop wood with an axe* noun **2** a quick cutting stroke **3** a slice of meat with bone in it: *lamb chops* *phrase* **4 get the chop,** *Informal* **a** to be killed **b** to be dismissed from work

Word building: Other verb forms are **I chopped, I have chopped, I am chopping.**

chopper

noun **1** someone or something that chops, especially a butcher's cleaver **2** an informal word for **helicopter**

choppy

adjective forming short broken waves: *a choppy sea*

Word building: Other forms are **choppier, choppiest.**

chopsticks

plural noun a pair of thin smooth sticks, usually made of wood or ivory, used especially in Asia instead of a knife and fork to pick up food

chord (*say* kawd)

noun three or more musical notes played together: *to play chords on a guitar*

chore (*say* chaw)

noun a boring or unpleasant job

choreography (*say* ko-ree-og-ruh-fee)

noun the art of designing ballets and dances

Word building: **choreograph** *verb* **choreographer** *noun*

chorister (*say* ko-ris-tuh)

noun someone who sings in a choir

chortle

verb to chuckle loudly with amusement

Word use: This is called a **blended** or **portmanteau word.**
Word history: made up by Lewis Carroll in *Through the Looking-Glass* in 1871; a blend of **chuckle** and **snort**

chorus (*say* <u>kaw</u>-ruhs)

noun **1** the part of a song that is repeated after each verse
Other words: **refrain**
2 a piece of music for several people to sing together **3** a group of people or a choir singing together

Word building: **choral** *adjective* sung by a choir or chorus **chorus** *verb* to sing or say together

christen (*say* <u>kris</u>-uhn)

verb **1** to give a name to, especially at baptism: *We christened the baby Takeo Shunya.* | *We christened the new boat Mary-Belle.* **2** to use for the first time: *Have you christened your new bike yet?*

Word building: **christening** *noun* the ceremony of baptism

Christianity

noun a world religion which is based on belief in Jesus Christ as the Son of God who lived on earth as a man, died and came back to life on earth before going to heaven. It is also based on Jesus's teachings as written in the New Testament of the Bible, which emphasised kind, good and unselfish behaviour as a response to God's love for the world. Followers of Christianity are called Christians, and worship in a church.

Word building: **Christian** *adjective*: *the Christian faith*
Word history: named after Jesus *Christ*, from a Hebrew name meaning 'anointed'

Christian name

noun your first or given name: *Her Christian names are Isabella Maria and her surname is Sanchez.*

Word use: People who are not Christians prefer to say 'given name' or 'first name'.

Christmas

noun a Christian festival of the birth of Jesus Christ, celebrated on 25 December, when people usually give presents to each other

chromatic

adjective **1** relating to a musical scale that moves by small steps, using all of the twelve semitones **2** having to do with colour

Word building: **chromatically** *adverb*

chrome

noun a hard, shiny, silver-coloured metal used to cover other metals to protect them and to stop rust

Word building: **chrome-plated** *adjective* covered in chrome

chromosome (*say* <u>kroh</u>-muh-sohm)

noun a tiny threadlike body found in the central part of all living cells, which carries the characteristics of the organism: *A human cell has 23 pairs of chromosomes.*

chronic

adjective constant or continuing for a long time: *She has chronic asthma.*

Word building: **chronically** *adverb*

chronicle

noun a record or history of events: *the chronicles of ancient Rome*

Word building: **chronicle** *verb* to record events **chronicler** *noun*

chronological

adjective arranged in order according to when it happened: *I wrote down the most important events in my life in chronological order.*

Word building: **chronology** *noun* an arrangement of past events in order of time **chronologically** *adverb*

chrysalis (*say* <u>kris</u>-uh-luhs)

noun the form that a butterfly or moth takes when changing from a grub to an adult insect, inside a hard-shelled cocoon

Word building: The plural is **chrysalises** or **chrysalids**.

chrysanthemum

(*say* kruh-<u>santh</u>-uh-muhm)
noun a tall plant with big white or brightly coloured flowers, often given as a present on Mother's Day

chubby

adjective plump and round: *a chubby baby*

Word building: Other forms are **chubbier**, **chubbiest**. | **chubbiness** *noun*

chuck *Informal*

verb **1** to throw or fling: *to chuck the ball over the fence* **2** to vomit
phrase **3 chuck it in**, to give up without finishing: *I'm bored with playing football so I'll chuck it in.*

Word building: **chuck** *noun* a toss or throw

chuckle

verb to laugh softly
Other words: **cackle, chortle, giggle**
Word building: **chuckle** *noun*

chunk
noun a thick piece or lump: *a chunk of fresh bread*

Word building: **chunky** *adjective* (**chunkier, chunkiest**) thick or bulky   **chunkiness** *noun*

church
noun **1** a building where Christians gather to worship **2** an organisation of Christians who share the same religious beliefs: *the Catholic Church | the Anglican Church*

Word use: Definition 2 is often spelt with a capital letter.

churinga   (*say* choo-<u>ring</u>-ga)
noun a sacred wooden object important in Aboriginal culture

Word history: from an Aboriginal language of the Northern Territory called Arrernte. See the map of Australian Aboriginal languages at the end of this book.

churn
noun **1** a large metal container for milk **2** a machine for making butter from cream or milk
verb **3** to shake or stir in order to make into butter: *to churn cream* **4** to move about violently: *My stomach churned with nerves before the performance.*

chute   (*sounds like* shoot)
noun a sloping channel or passage for sending or carrying things to a lower level: *a laundry chute*

chutney
noun a spicy jam-like food made from fruit, sugar and vinegar

cicada   (*say* suh-<u>kah</u>-duh)
noun a large flying insect which is found in trees in the summer and which makes a very loud shrill sound in hot weather

cider   (*say* <u>suy</u>-duh)
noun a drink, sometimes containing alcohol, made from apples

Word history: from a Hebrew word meaning 'strong drink'

cigar   (*say* suh-<u>gah</u>)
noun tobacco leaves rolled tightly together for smoking

cigarette
noun a roll of shredded tobacco, for smoking, inside a cylinder of very thin paper

cinder
noun a burnt and blackened piece of wood or coal

cine-
prefix a word part meaning 'motion': *cinema*

Word history: from Greek

cinema
noun a theatre where films are shown

Word use: You can also say **the pictures**.
Word history: a shortened form of *cinematograph*, an old word for a film projector or camera

cinematic   (*say* sin-uh-<u>mat</u>-ik)
adjective having to do with the cinema or film: *the best special effects in cinematic history*

cinnamon   (*say* <u>sin</u>-uh-muhn)
noun a yellowish or reddish-brown spice made from the inner bark of certain trees and used in cooking

cipher   (*say* <u>suy</u>-fuh)
noun secret writing or a code: *The message was sent in cipher so the enemy could not understand it.*

Word use: Another spelling is **cypher**.
Word building: **cipher** *verb* to write in code

circle
noun **1** a perfectly round shape **2** anything that has the shape of a circle or part of a circle: *Sit in a circle to listen to the story.* **3** a group of people who do things together: *a sewing circle* **4** the upper section of seats in a theatre or cinema: *the dress circle*
verb **5** to move around in a circle: *The plane circled the airport. | The plane circled three times before landing.*

Word building: **circular** *adjective* round or shaped like a circle   **circular** *noun* a letter or notice sent to a number of people   **circularity** *noun*   **encircle** *verb*

circuit   (*say* <u>ser</u>-kuht)
noun **1** a circular path or roundabout journey: *The visitors made a circuit of the school.* **2** a circular racing track **3** an arrangement of wires joined so as to carry an electric current: *a closed circuit*

Word building: **circuitous** (*say* suh-<u>kyooh</u>-uh-tuhs) *adjective*: *a circuitous route home*

circulate

verb **1** to move in a circle or circuit: *Blood circulates through your body.* **2** to pass from place to place or person to person: *The news circulated quickly.* | *We circulated a petition.*

circulation

noun **1** continuous circular movement: *the circulation of blood through the body* **2** the number of copies of a newspaper or magazine sent out: *The local paper has a circulation of 20 000.*

circum-

prefix a word part indicating movement all around or on all sides: *circumference*

Word history: from Latin

circumcise

verb to cut away the skin around the end of the penis of: *to circumcise a baby boy*

Word building: **circumcision** *noun*

circumference

noun the distance around something, especially around a circle or circular object: *You can measure the circumference of a tree trunk with a tape measure.*

Other words: **perimeter**

circumnavigate

verb to sail round: *to circumnavigate the earth*

Word building: **circumnavigation** *noun*

circumspect

adjective cautious and watchful

Word building: **circumspection** *noun*

circumstance

noun **1** a condition which influences a person or an event **2 circumstances**, financial position: *They used to be rich, but now their circumstances have changed.*

circus

noun **1** a travelling show with performing animals, clowns, jugglers and acrobats **2** an open area with seats on all sides, used for chariot races and other sports in ancient Rome

Word history: from a Greek word meaning 'ring'

cirrus *(say si-ruhs)*

noun high feathery cloud

cistern *(say sis-tuhn)*

noun a tank for holding water, such as the one above a toilet

citadel

noun a fort or strongly defended place, built to protect or control a city

cite

verb to mention or refer to: *The soldier was cited for bravery in the official dispatch.* | *The teacher cited three examples to explain the meaning of the word.*

Word building: **citation** *noun* a mention

cite/sight/site Don't confuse **cite** with **sight** or **site**.
Your **sight** is your ability to see things. It can also be something worth seeing: *a great sight*.
A **site** is the land where something is built or will soon be built. It is also a short way of saying *website*.

citizen

noun **1** a member of a nation who has certain rights and duties: *All Australian citizens over the age of eighteen must vote in the election.* **2** someone who lives in a particular place: *a citizen of Adelaide*

Word use: Compare definition 1 with **alien**.
Word building: **citizenship** *noun*

citizenship ceremony

noun the special occasion when someone becomes a citizen of a country

citrus

noun a small evergreen tree such as the lemon, orange, lime, grapefruit or mandarin

Word building: **citrus** *adjective*: *citrus fruit*

city

noun **1** a large or important town **2** the people who live in a city: *The whole city turned out to watch the parade.*

Word building: The plural is **cities**.

civic

adjective of or concerning a city or citizens: *The council buildings are in the civic centre.* | *It is your civic duty to put litter in the bins provided.*

civil

adjective **1** having to do with the government: *civil affairs* **2** having to do with citizens or the people: *civil liberties* **3** polite or courteous: *Her way of asking was so civil that we did what she wanted.*

Word building: **civility** *noun*   **civilly** *adverb*

civilian

adjective having to do with ordinary life: *The soldier left the army and entered civilian life as a bus driver.*

Word building: **civilian** *noun*

civilisation

noun the highly developed life of a particular people, including their science, art and writing: *The ancient Greeks brought civilisation to the tribes they ruled. | Chinese civilisation*

Word use: Another spelling is **civilization**.
Word building: **civilise** *verb*

civilised

adjective **1** highly developed: *The Chinese have been a civilised people for thousands of years.* **2** polite and controlled: *They expected him to be angry but he wrote a very civilised letter.*

Word use: Another spelling is **civilized**.

civil war

noun a war between people living in the same country

claim

verb **1** to ask for, as if it's your right: *I will claim my share of the money.* **2** to say definitely: *She claims that her story is true.* *noun* **3** a demand: *The children make too many claims on her.* **4** the right to something: *After all your hard work you have a claim to some holidays.* **5** something claimed, such as a piece of land for mining

Word building: **claimable** *adjective* **claimer** *noun*

clairvoyant   (*say* klair-<u>voy</u>-uhnt)

adjective claiming to be able to see into the future

Word building: **clairvoyance** *noun* **clairvoyant** *noun*

clam

noun a large shellfish whose two shells are hinged and can be tightly closed

clamber

verb to climb up with difficulty: *He clambered onto the roof.*

clammy

adjective cold, damp and sticky

Word building: Other forms are **clammier**, **clammiest**. | **clamminess** *noun*

clamour   (*say* <u>klam</u>-uh)

noun the loud noise of many voices: *an angry clamour*

Word use: Another spelling is **clamor**.
Word building: **clamour** *verb* to make a loud noise or ask noisily   **clamorous** *adjective*

clamp

noun **1** a tool which holds things tightly together
verb **2** to hold tightly: *Vijay clamped his teeth together in anger.* **3** to press down: *The lid was clamped onto the box then locked.*

clan

noun a group of related families who share a common ancestor

Word building: **clannish** *adjective* very close, like the members of a clan

clandestine   (*say* klan-<u>des</u>-tuhn)

adjective secret and unlawful: *The freedom fighters held clandestine meetings away from the town.*

Word building: **clandestinely** *adverb*

clang

verb to ring loudly

Word building: **clangour** *noun* a loud metallic sound   **clangorous** *adjective*

clap

verb **1** to hit your hands together noisily, especially in applause **2** to show approval or enjoyment of, by clapping: *We clapped our favourite actor.*
noun **3** a loud sudden noise: *There was a clap of thunder.* **4** a sign of approval, by clapping: *They've done well — let's give them a clap.*

Word building: Other verb forms are **I clapped, I have clapped, I am clapping.** | **clapper** *noun* something that claps, especially the tongue of a bell

clarify

verb to make clear: *to clarify butter | to clarify the answer to the problem*

Word building: Other forms are **I clarified, I have clarified, I am clarifying.** | **clarification** *noun*

clarinet

noun a musical instrument belonging to the woodwind family which makes a deeper sound than the flute

Word building: **clarinetist** *noun* a clarinet player
Word history: from a French word meaning 'little clarion' (an old-fashioned high trumpet)

clarity

noun clearness: *You could see the fish swimming because of the clarity of the water.* | *The clarity of her arguments convinced us she was right.*

clash

verb **1** to make a loud harsh noise **2** to disagree or differ: *Their opinions clashed.* **3** to happen at the same time: *Their favourite television shows clashed.*

Word building: **clash** *noun*

clasp

noun **1** something which fastens things together **2** a firm hold

Word building: **clasp** *verb* to hold tightly

class

noun **1** a group of people or things which are alike in some way **2** a group of pupils who are taught together **3** someone's place in society, judged by their possessions or their family: *the middle class* **4** the level of comfort in travel: *In the plane's first class, dinner is served.*

Word building: The plural is **classes.** | **class** *verb* to put in a group

classic

adjective **1** of high quality: *That vintage car is a classic model in perfect condition.* **2** typical: *The actress had a classic case of nerves.*
noun **3** someone or something known to be excellent: *'Gone With The Wind' is now considered a film classic.*
4 classics, the writings and language of ancient Greece and Rome

classical music

noun music composed according to traditional European conventions that have existed for a long time, as opposed to newer forms such as jazz, folk, rock or pop music

classified ad

noun a short advertisement in a newspaper, usually advertising a job or something for sale

classify

verb to group according to quality or likeness: *When we had classified the apples the good ones were packed and the bad ones thrown out.*

Word building: Other forms are **I classified, I have classified, I am classifying.** | **classifiable** *adjective* **classification** *noun* **classified** *adjective*

classroom

noun a room in a school where students are taught

clatter

verb to rattle loudly

Word building: **clatter** *noun* disturbance

clause   (*say* klawz)

noun a group of words which contains a subject and a verb, which may be a part of a sentence or a whole sentence, such as *after the boy arrived* and *She heard the news.*

claustrophobia

(*say* klos-truh-<u>foh</u>-bee-uh)
noun the fear of being shut in a small place

Word building: **claustrophobic** *adjective*

claves   (*say* klayvz, <u>klah</u>-vayz)

plural noun a simple musical instrument which consists of two wooden sticks which are hit together

clavichord   (*say* <u>klav</u>-uh-kawd)

noun an early type of piano, whose strings are softly struck with metal blades

claw

noun **1** the sharp curved nail on the foot of an animal or bird **2** the sharp pincers of crabs and lobsters
verb **3** to scratch or seize with nails or claws

clay

noun a dense earth which holds water and is used in making pottery and bricks

Word building: **clayey** *adjective*

clean

adjective **1** without dirt or stains **2** fair: *It was a clean fight.* **3** without a mark: *I started a clean page for the letter.*
Other words: **clear, unmarked**
4 with a smooth edge: *It was a clean cut that would heal easily.*
verb **5** to remove dirt from: *I must clean the bathroom for the visitors.*
Other words: **cleanse**

Word building: **cleaner** *noun* **cleanliness** *noun* **cleanly** *adverb* **cleanness** *noun*

cleanse　(*say* klenz)

verb to make clean or pure: *to cleanse the skin*

Word building: **cleanser** *noun*

clear

adjective **1** light or bright: *It was a clear sunny day.* **2** transparent: *clear glass* **3** easily understood: *The children need clear examples.* **4** without doubt: *a clear win* **5** open or free from obstacles: *a clear road* *verb* **6** to become light or bright: *After a cloudy morning the sky cleared.* **7** to free from blockage: *He cleared the gutters on the roof.* **8** to free from blame: *The jury's verdict cleared her of guilt.* *phrase* **9 clear up**, to make easier to understand: *Can you clear up this point for me?*

Word building: **clear** *adverb*: *to get clear away* **clearly** *adverb* **clearness** *noun*

clearance

noun **1** the space between two things: *The truck had a clearance of ten centimetres under the bridge.* **2** permission to go ahead with something: *They needed a clearance from the council to build their home of mud bricks.*

clearing

noun a piece of cleared land in the middle of bush or forest

clearway

noun a busy street or highway on which cars may park only in case of emergency

cleat

noun a wedge-shaped piece of wood or metal which a climber drives into a steep mountain side to make a support to tread on

cleavage

noun a division or split

cleaver

noun a chopper with a long blade, used by butchers for cutting meat

clef

noun a symbol placed on a line of music that shows the height or pitch of the notes: *treble clef*

Word history: from a Latin word meaning 'key'

cleft

noun a narrow opening or split

clench

verb to close or press tightly: *to clench your teeth in pain* | *to clench your fist in anger*

clergy

noun the priests, ministers, and so on, of a religion

Word building: **clergyman** *noun* someone who belongs to the clergy **clerical** *adjective*: *clerical duties* **cleric** *noun*

clerk　(*rhymes with* bark)

noun someone who works in an office, keeping records and accounts and sorting letters and papers

Word building: **clerical** *adjective* having to do with office workers and clerks

clever

adjective **1** good at thinking quickly Other words: **able, bright, brilliant, capable, intelligent, smart** **2** able or skilful: *My big sister is clever with her hands.* Other words: **adept, handy, talented**

Word building: **cleverly** *adverb* **cleverness** *noun*

cliché　(*say* klee-shay)

noun a saying which has become stale or dull because it has been used too often, such as *as old as the hills*

Word use: There is an accent over the 'e' because this was originally a French word. Word building: **clichéd** *adjective*

click

noun **1** a slight sharp sound *verb* **2** to operate the mouse button to select something on a computer screen: *Click the red button to start the game.*

Word building: **click** *verb* **clicker** *noun*

client

noun a customer, especially of a lawyer or someone in a similar profession

cliff

noun a steep rocky slope

climate

noun the usual weather of a particular place

Word building: **climatic** *adjective* having to do with weather **climatically** *adverb*

climate change

noun a major change in the usual climatic conditions which lasts for a long time, especially a change thought to be caused by global warming

climate refugee

noun someone who escapes for safety, especially to a foreign country, due to catastrophic climate change in their own country

climax

noun the highest or most important and exciting point of anything: *The climax of the show was a fireworks display at night.*

Word building: **climactic** *adjective* **climactically** *adverb*

climb

verb **1** to move or rise upwards: *She climbed the ladder.* | *The aeroplane climbs slowly into the sky.* **2** to slope upwards: *The mountain climbs to a sharp peak.*

Word building: **climb** *noun* **climber** *noun*

clinch

verb **1** to settle once and for all: *The two women clinched the sale by signing the papers.* noun **2** a close hold in boxing, which slows your opponent's punches

Word building: **clincher** *noun*

cling

verb to hold tightly: *The child was clinging to the railing.*

Word building: Other forms are **I clung, I have clung, I am clinging.** | **clingy** *adjective*

clinic

noun a medical centre where you can go to see a doctor or have special treatment, such as an X-ray

Word building: **clinical** *adjective* **clinically** *adverb*

clink

verb to make a light, ringing sound: *The coins clinked in his pocket.*
Other words: **jingle, tinkle**

clip[1]

verb **1** to cut off or shorten with scissors or shears: *The shearer clipped the sheep's wool.* | *Dad clipped the ends of his moustache.* **2** to punch a hole in: *The bus conductor clipped our tickets.* **3** to give a sharp hit: *The bandit clipped the shopkeeper on the jaw.*

noun **4** a trimming: *Please give my hair a clip.* **5** a short section of a film: *The actors saw clips of the film as it was being made.*

Word building: Other verb forms are **I clipped, I have clipped, I am clipping.** | **clipped** *adjective* **clipping** *noun*

clip[2]

noun something which holds things in place: *My bag is open because the clip keeps coming undone.*

Word building: **clip** *verb* to fasten

clipper

noun **1** a cutting tool, especially for your hair or nails **2** a fast sailing ship

Word use: Definition 1 is often plural **clippers.**

clique   (*rhymes with* meek)

noun a small close group of people who keep themselves apart from others

Word building: **cliquey** *adjective* **cliquish** *adjective* **cliquishly** *adverb*
Word history: from a French word meaning 'people hired to applaud in a theatre'

clitoris   (*say* clit-uh-ruhs)

noun the part of a female's genitals at the upper end of the vulva, with which she feels sexual pleasure

cloak

noun **1** a sleeveless coat or cape which does up at your neck
verb **2** to hide or keep hidden: *to cloak your feelings*

clock

noun something which measures and tells you the time

Word building: **clock** *verb* to time

clockwise

adjective going around in the same direction as the hands on a clock face

Word use: The opposite is **anticlockwise.**

clockwork

noun **1** the workings of a clock or a wind-up toy
phrase **2 like clockwork**, smoothly and without interruption: *Our travel plans went like clockwork.*

clod

noun **1** a lump, especially of earth **2** a dull or stupid person

Word building: **cloddish** *adjective* dull or stupid

clog

verb **1** to block or become blocked: *Leaves clogged the gutter.*
noun **2** a heavy wooden shoe

Word building: Other verb forms are **it clogged, it has clogged, it is clogging.**

cloister   (*say* <u>kloy</u>-stuh)

noun **1** a covered path by the side of a building such as a church **2** a place where nuns or priests live quietly, away from the rest of the world

Word building: **cloister** *verb* to seclude or confine, as in a cloister

clone

noun the offspring of a plant or animal which is exactly the same as its parent and has been formed not by the joining of male and female cells but from one of its parent's own cells

Word building: **clone** *verb*
Word history: from a Greek word meaning 'slip' or 'twig'

close   (*say* klohz)

verb **1** to block off: *Heavy snow closed the road.*
Other words: **bar, barricade, obstruct**
2 to shut: *The door closed in the wind. | She closed the window.* **3** to refuse entry to: *Police closed the sportsground.* **4** to end: *After two hours the meeting finally closed. | He closed his show with a song.*
Other words: **conclude, finish**
adjective (*say* klohs) **5** narrow or tight: *The shoes are a close fit.* **6** hard to breathe: *The air in the hot room was too close and someone fainted.*
Other words: **stuffy**
7 near each other: *The children are close in age. | They felt very close after all they had been through.* **8** thorough: *This book needs close study.*
Other words: **careful, detailed, meticulous**

Word building: **close** *noun* conclusion   **close** *adverb*   **closed** *adjective*   **closely** *adverb*   **closeness** *noun*

closet   (*say* <u>kloz</u>-uht)

noun **1** a cupboard or small room where things are stored **2** a toilet

clot

noun **1** a solid lump: *a blood clot*
2 *Informal* a fool
verb **3** to thicken or form into clots: *The blood from his cut began to clot and dry up.*

Word building: Other verb forms are **it clotted, it has clotted, it is clotting.**

cloth

noun a piece of material or fabric: *My shirt is made of linen cloth. | Dad wiped the milk up with a cloth.*

cloth/clothe Don't confuse **cloth** with **clothe.** To **clothe** someone is to give them clothes to wear.

clothe   (*say* klohdh)

verb to provide with clothes: *to clothe the needy children*

Word building: **clothing** *noun*

clothes   (*say* klohdhz)

plural noun the things you wear
Other words: **apparel, attire, clothing, garments, dress**

cloud

noun **1** a white or grey mass of water vapour, ice, smoke or dust that floats in the air **2** anything which looks or acts like a cloud: *a cloud of steam | a cloud of flies*
verb **3** to darken or become darker: *Anger clouded her face. | The mirror clouded with steam.*

Word building: **cloudiness** *noun*   **cloudily** *adverb*   **cloudy** *adjective*

clout

noun **1** a hit with the hand: *I gave the boy a clout on the shoulder.* **2** power or influence: *You need some clout to get a good job like that.*

Word building: **clout** *verb* to hit

clove

noun the dried flower bud of a tropical tree, used as a spice

clover

noun a plant with leaves divided into three parts and a white flower, often used as food for cattle

clown

noun someone in a circus, often dressed up with a white face, a red nose and silly clothes, who makes people laugh
Other words: **buffoon, jester**

Word building: **clown** *verb* to act the fool   **clowning** *noun*   **clownish** *adjective*

club

noun **1** a heavy stick, used as a weapon
2 a stick used to hit the ball in games
like golf **3** a group of people who share
a particular interest or hobby: *We started
a chess club at school.* **4** a place run by a
group, which offers entertainment and
cheap food and drink to those who belong
5 the clover-shaped black sign on some
playing cards
verb **6** to beat with a club
phrase **7 club in**, to join together: *Everyone
in the office clubbed in to buy her a card.*

Word building: Other verb forms are **he
clubbed, he has clubbed, he is clubbing**.

cluck

verb to make the sound a hen makes when
calling its chicks

Word building: **clucky** adjective feeling a strong
desire to have children

clue

noun something which helps to explain a
puzzle or mystery: *a clue in a detective story*

Word building: **clueless** adjective stupid
cluey adjective

clump

noun a group of things growing together,
such as trees or grasses

Word building: **clump** verb

clumsy

adjective **1** awkward in the way you move
about
Other words: **blundering, gawky**
2 without skill: *a clumsy worker*
Other words: **awkward, inept**

Word building: Other forms are **clumsier,
clumsiest**. | **clumsily** adverb   **clumsiness** noun

cluster

noun a number of things growing or
placed close together: *a cluster of grapes | a
cluster of stars*

Word building: **cluster** verb to gather in close
groups

clutch

verb **1** to seize or hold tightly: *The baby
clutched the kitten.*
noun **2** a tight hold **3** part of a
machine which is used in changing
gears **4 clutches,** power: *Now the witch
had Ivan in her clutches.*

phrase **5 clutch at**, to try to seize: *He
clutched at the rope.*

clutter

verb to make untidy: *Papers clutter the
dining room table.*

Word building: **clutter** noun

co-

prefix a word part meaning
1 with: *cohesion* **2** at the same time:
coincidence

Word history: from Latin

coach

noun **1** a closed carriage pulled by horses
2 a tourist bus **3** a railway carriage
4 someone who trains athletes

Word building: **coach** verb to train

coagulate   (*say* koh-<u>ag</u>-yuh-layt)

verb to change from a liquid into a thick
lump, such as a clot

Word building: **coagulation** noun

coal

noun a black or dark brown rock, formed
from the remains of ancient trees, used as
fuel

coalesce   (*say* koh-uh-<u>les</u>)

verb to grow or join together: *The
many small groups coalesced into one
strong party.*

Word building: **coalescence** noun
coalescent adjective

coalition   (*say* koh-uh-<u>lish</u>-uhn)

noun the joining together of two or more
groups, at least for a while: *a coalition of
political parties*

Word building: **coalitionist** noun

coarse   (*say* kaws)

adjective **1** thick or rough: *coarse material |
coarse sand* **2** rude or offensive: *coarse
jokes | coarse language*

Word building: **coarsely** adverb   **coarsen**
verb   **coarseness** noun

coarse/course Don't confuse **coarse** with
course, which is usually a noun and has several
meanings. For example, a **course** is one part of
a meal, as in *the main course.* A **course** is also a
series of lessons.

coast

noun **1** the seashore or the land beside the sea
verb **2** to go downhill in a car or on a bike without using power
Word building: **coastal** *adjective*
Word history: from a Latin word meaning 'rib' or 'side'

coastguard

noun someone whose job is to patrol the coast of a country, helping ships in danger and looking out for smugglers or illegal fishing boats

coat

noun **1** a piece of clothing with sleeves, that you wear over other clothes
2 the fur or wool of an animal
3 a layer: *The house needs a coat of paint.*
Word building: **coat** *verb* to cover

coathanger

noun a curved or triangular piece of wood, plastic, and so on, with a hook attached at the top, for hanging clothes on

coating

noun a covering: *a coating of batter | a coating of flour*

coat of arms

noun the special design, often with a motto, belonging to a noble family or nation: *There is a kangaroo in the Australian coat of arms.*

coax   *(say* kohks)

verb to persuade gently and patiently: *She coaxed the sick child to eat.*
Word building: **coaxer** *noun*   **coaxingly** *adverb*

cob

noun **1** a stocky horse with short legs
2 a male swan **3** the head on which corn seeds grow: *a cob of corn*

cobalt   *(say* koh-bawlt)

noun a silver-white metal which gives a blue colouring to pottery
Word history: from a German word for 'goblin'

cobble

noun a rounded paving stone
Word building: **cobble** *verb* to mend: *to cobble shoes*

cobbler

noun Old-fashioned someone who mends shoes

cobra

noun a venomous snake which can spread out the skin of its neck like a hood

cobweb

noun **1** the fine thread spun by a spider to catch insects **2** something very light or fine
Word building: **cobwebby** *adjective*

cocaine   *(say* koh-kayn)

noun a bitter drug which is made from the leaves of a South American shrub

cock

noun **1** a rooster or male bird **2** the hammer of a gun

cockatiel   *(say* kok-uh-teel)

noun a small parrot with a long tail and a crest on top of its head like a cockatoo

cockatoo

noun a crested parrot

cockeyed   *(say* kok-uyd)

adjective **1** crooked: *Your tie is cockeyed.*
2 foolish or absurd: *a cockeyed plan*
3 having a squinting eye

cockle

noun **1** a shellfish found in Europe, that is good to eat **2 cockles**, deep feelings: *Their kindness warms the cockles of your heart.*

cockpit

noun **1** the front end of a plane where the pilots sit **2** the driver's seat in a racing car

cockroach

noun an insect which lives in the dark warm places where food is stored and comes out at night

cocktail

noun an alcoholic drink made of a spirit mixed with wine, fruit juice, and so on, often chilled and sweetened
Word building: **cocktail** *adjective* small enough to be eaten in your fingers: *cocktail sausages*

cocky[1]

adjective *Informal* too confident or smart: *The new guys on the job are always cocky, until they find out how hard it is.*

Word building: Other forms are **cockier**, **cockiest**. | **cockily** *adverb* **cockiness** *noun*

cocky[2]

noun **1** a cockatoo **2** a farmer, especially of a small farm

Word building: The plural is **cockies**.

cocoa   (*say* <u>koh</u>-koh)

noun **1** the crushed and powdered seeds of a tropical tree **2** a drink made from the brown powder which is also used to make chocolate

coconut

noun the large hard nut of the coconut palm, which is lined with white flesh and contains a clear milk

cocoon   (*say* kuh-<u>koohn</u>)

noun the covering which grubs such as the silkworm spin around themselves before their next stage of growth

Word building: **cocoon** *verb* to cover or protect
Word history: from a French word meaning 'shell'

cod

noun a kind of large fish

coda   (*say* <u>koh</u>-duh)

noun the part which finishes a piece of music

coddle

verb **1** to look after very well: *His father coddled him after he was sick.* **2** to cook in water very slowly: *to coddle eggs*

code

noun **1** a set of rules or laws: *a legal code | a code of honour* **2** a secret language, or a system such as the dots and dashes used in telegraphing messages

Word building: **encode** *verb* to translate into a code   **decode** *verb* to translate from a code

coeducation

noun the joint teaching of boys and girls, in the same school or classroom

Word building: **coeducational** *adjective*

coerce   (*say* koh-<u>ers</u>)

verb to force: *The thief used a gun to coerce the cashier to open the till.*

Word building: **coercion** *noun*   **coercive** *adjective*

coffee

noun **1** a drink made from the roasted and ground beans of a tropical shrub **2** the brown powder you use to make this drink

coffin

noun the wooden box in which a dead body is buried or cremated

cog

noun **1** one of the toothlike bits sticking out of a wheel which connects it with another wheel **2** one of many unimportant people in an organisation

cogitate   (*say* <u>koj</u>-uh-tayt)

verb to think hard

Word building: **cogitation** *noun*   **cogitative** *adjective*

cognac   (*say* <u>kon</u>-yak)

noun a high quality brandy

Word history: from the French town called *Cognac* where this drink was first made

coherent   (*say* koh-<u>hear</u>-ruhnt)

adjective **1** sticking together firmly: *coherent surfaces* **2** agreeing or well thought out: *a coherent argument*

Word use: The opposite of definition 2 is **incoherent**.
Word building: **cohere** *verb*   **coherence** *noun*   **coherently** *adverb*

cohesion   (*say* koh-<u>hee</u>-zhuhn)

noun the state of sticking together or being connected

Word building: **cohesive** *adjective*

coil

verb **1** to wind into loops: *to coil ropes* **2** to form into loops: *The snake coiled itself and struck.*

Word building: **coil** *noun* a loop or spiral

coin

noun **1** a metal piece of money
verb **2** to make coins **3** to invent: *to coin a word*

Word building: **coinage** *noun* metal coins
Word history: from a Latin word meaning 'wedge'

coincide   (*say* koh-uhn-<u>suyd</u>)

verb **1** to happen together by chance **2** to agree: *Our opinions coincide on this point.*

coincidence (*say* koh-<u>in</u>-suh-duhns)

noun the surprising fact of things happening together by chance: *It was just a coincidence that we were on the same ship to Italy.*

Word building: **coincidental** *adjective* **coincidentally** *adverb*

coke

noun a solid fuel made from heating coal

colander (*say* <u>kol</u>-uhn-duh)

noun a bowl with many small holes, which is used in the kitchen for draining off liquid

Word use: Another form of the word is **cullender**.

cold

adjective **1** having a lack of warmth: *It's a cold day.*
Other words: **chilly, cool, freezing, frigid, frosty, icy, wintry**
2 feeling a lack of warmth: *My hands are cold.*
Other words: **freezing, icy**
3 unfriendly: *Our neighbours were cold at first.*
Other words: **aloof, detached, impersonal, indifferent**
noun **4** the absence of heat: *We shivered in the cold of the evening.*
Other words: **coldness, coolness**
5 a viral illness which usually comes with a blocked or a runny nose

Word building: **coldly** *adverb* **coldness** *noun*

cold-blooded

adjective **1** without feelings of pity: *a cold-blooded murder* **2** having a blood temperature which changes as the temperature of the surrounding air or water changes: *Reptiles and fish are cold-blooded animals.*

Word use: The opposite of definition 2 is **warm-blooded**.
Word building: **cold-bloodedly** *adverb* **cold-bloodedness** *noun*

coleslaw

noun a salad made with sliced raw cabbage

colic (*say* <u>kol</u>-ik)

noun a sharp pain in your stomach

Word building: **colicky** *adjective*

collaborate

verb **1** to work together: *They collaborated on the project.* **2** to work together with an enemy inside your own country: *He collaborated with the invaders.*

Word building: **collaboration** *noun* **collaborative** *adjective* **collaborator** *noun*

collage (*say* kuh-<u>lahzh</u>)

noun a picture made from pieces of paper, cloth or other materials, pasted onto paper or board

collapse

verb **1** to fall down or apart suddenly: *The whole building collapsed when the wall gave way.*
Other words: **buckle, crumble, crumple, disintegrate**
2 to fall over suddenly: *The old man collapsed in the street.*
Other words: **faint, slump**
3 to be made so that parts can be folded flat together: *This chair collapses.*

Word building: **collapse** *noun* **collapsible** *adjective*

collar

noun **1** the part of a piece of clothing that is worn around your neck **2** a leather band put around an animal's neck
verb **3** *Informal* to seize by the collar or neck: *The police officer collared the escaping criminal.*

collarbone

noun one of the two thin bones that go from the front of your neck to either shoulder

collate (*say* kuh-<u>layt</u>)

verb to gather together in proper order: *I must collate the pages of my story.*

Word building: **collation** *noun* **collator** *noun*

collateral damage (*say* kuh-lat-uh-ruhl <u>dam</u>-ij)

noun injury or destruction which was not meant to happen, but which sometimes does, as when innocent people are hurt in times of war

colleague (*say* <u>kol</u>-eeg)

noun someone you work with, usually in the same job

collect

verb **1** to gather together or assemble: *Please collect all the rubbish from the floor. | A crowd collected around the smashed car.*
2 to gather and keep examples of: *She collects stamps as a hobby.* **3** to gather money: *We are collecting for the poor.*
4 to call for and take away: *Please collect the parcel at the post office.*

Word building: **collected** *adjective* self-controlled **collectedly** *adverb* **collection** *noun* **collector** *noun*

collective

adjective **1** having to do with a group of people taken as a whole: *It will be done more quickly if we make a collective effort.*
noun **2** a group of people who share what they own and who work together for the good of them all

Word building: **collectively** *adverb*

collective noun

noun a noun that is singular in its form but which stands for a group of individual objects or people: *'Family', 'jury' and 'clergy' are all collective nouns.*

college

noun **1** a place for learning, rather like a university, that you can go to after you finish high school **2** a place within a university where students live **3** a large private school

collide

verb to crash together: *The cars collided.*

Word building: **collision** *noun*

collie

noun a kind of dog with long thick hair and a bushy tail, often used in other countries to guard sheep

colliery

noun a coalmine with all its buildings and equipment

Word building: The plural is **collieries**. | **collier** *noun* a coalminer

colloquial   (*say* kuh-<u>loh</u>-kwee-uhl)

adjective suitable to use in informal language: *'Arvo' is a colloquial way of saying 'afternoon'.*

Word building: **colloquialism** *noun* **colloquially** *adverb*

cologne   (*say* kuh-<u>lohn</u>)

noun a kind of perfume

Word use: Other names are **eau de Cologne** or **Cologne water**.

Word history: named after the German city of *Cologne* where the perfume has been made since 1709

colon   (*say* <u>koh</u>-luhn)

noun a punctuation mark (:) which is used to separate the main part of a sentence from an explanation, or a list of examples, as in *I want you to bring the following things: a pencil, a rubber, and a piece of paper.*

You use a **colon** to show that you are going to explain, or give examples of, whatever you have just written. For instance:
The kennels cared for a number of breeds of dog: terriers, spaniels, corgis, labradors and German shepherds.
In informal writing, a dash could have been used in the above example instead of a colon. Look up **dash**.
Colons can be used before quoting someone's speech:
The teacher said: 'Sit down in that chair!'
Instead of a colon, you can use a comma here, or you can leave out the punctuation altogether. Look up **quotation mark**.

colonel   (*say* <u>ker</u>-nuhl)

noun a senior officer in the army

colonise

verb to start a colony in: *England colonised Australia.*

Word use: Another spelling is **colonize**.
Word building: **colonisation** *noun* **colonist** *noun*

colony   (*say* <u>kol</u>-uh-nee)

noun **1** a group of people who leave their home and form a settlement in a new land ruled by the parent country
2 the land settled in this way: *The early settlements in Australia were colonies of Britain.*
3 a group of animals or plants of the same kind that live close together

Word building: The plural is **colonies**. | **colonial** *noun* someone who lives in a colony **colonial** *adjective*

colossal

adjective very great in size

Word building: **colossally** *adverb*

colour

noun **1** the look that something has which is caused by the way light is reflected by it: *The main colours are red, orange, yellow, green, blue, indigo and violet.* **2** the colour of someone's skin **3** something used to give colour, such as paint or dye **4** details that make something interesting: *That story has a lot of colour.*
verb **5** to put colour on to **6** to go red in the face **7** to influence or change: *His jealousy coloured the way he told the story.*

Word use: Another spelling is **color**.
Word building: **colourful** *adjective*
colourfully *adverb* **colouring** *noun*
colourless *adjective*

colour blindness

noun a fault in someone's eyesight that stops them from being able to tell the difference between some colours, such as red and green

Word use: Another spelling is **color blindness**.
Word building: **colour blind** *adjective*

coloured

adjective **1** having colour **2** belonging to a group of people that do not have white skin

Word use: Another spelling is **colored**.

colt

noun a male horse that is younger than four years old
Word building: **coltish** *adjective*

column (*say* kol-uhm)

noun **1** a long upright support or pillar **2** anything with a similar shape to a column: *a column of smoke* | *The children formed two columns.* **3** an upright row of numbers or of print going down a page **4** a piece of writing on a particular subject that appears regularly in a newspaper or magazine: *I like reading the fashion column.*

Word building: **columnist** *noun* someone who writes a newspaper or magazine column **columnar** *adjective*

coma

noun a very long, deep, unnatural sleep caused by sickness or an injury
Word building: **comatose** *adjective*

comb

noun **1** a piece of plastic or metal with a set of thin pointed teeth, that is used to tidy or hold back hair **2** a comb-shaped part on the head of a hen, rooster or turkey
verb **3** to tidy with a comb **4** to search carefully: *They combed the room for the missing purse.*

combat

verb **1** to fight against: *I must combat my liking for lollies.* | *The army was trained to combat an air attack.*
noun **2** a fight or struggle

Word building: **combatant** *noun* **combatant** *adjective*

combine

verb to mix or join together: *You combine flour and water to make paste.* | *The two schools decided to combine.*

Word building: **combination** *noun*

combustion

noun the process of catching alight or burning

Word building: **combustible** *adjective* able to burn

come

verb **1** to move towards a person or place: *Please come here.* **2** to arrive or happen: *Christmas comes in December.* | *I hope my turn will come soon.* **3** to appear: *The light comes and goes.* **4** to reach or extend: *I want the dress to come below my knees.*
phrase **5 come across,** to meet or find: *I came across this lost dog on my way to the shops.* **6 come from,** to live in or be born into: *I come from Australia.* | *I come from an Italian family.* **7 come over,** to happen to or have an effect on: *What has come over her to make her so quiet?* **8 come to, a** to add up to or equal: *What does the bill come to?* **b** to become conscious again **9 come up with,** to suggest or produce: *Nicole came up with a very good idea.*

Word building: Other verb forms are **I came, I have come, I am coming.**

comedian

noun someone who performs and writes comedy shows

Word building: **comedienne** *noun* a female comedian

comedown

noun a situation where a person suddenly experiences far less success or advantages than they have become used to: *It was a bit of a comedown finishing last, after winning last year.*

comedy

noun **1** a play, film, story or other entertainment that is funny or makes you feel happy **2** any funny event or series of events

Word building: The plural is **comedies**.
Word history: from a Greek word for 'amusement' added to a Greek word for 'singer'

comet

noun an object in space that moves around the sun and has a bright central part surrounded by a misty part that finishes in the shape of a tail

Word history: from a Greek word meaning 'long-haired'

comfort *(say* <u>kum</u>-fuht*)*

verb **1** to cheer or make feel less sad or worried: *Dad comforted my little baby brother by cuddling him.*
Other words: **console, hearten, reassure, soothe**
noun **2** a feeling of being less sad or worried
Other words: **relief**
3 someone or something that comforts: *My mother is a great comfort to me when I feel sad.*
Other words: **consolation, reassurance, relief**
4 pleasant enjoyment with no troubles or needs: *They live a life of comfort.*
Other words: **contentment, ease, luxury, wellbeing**

Word building: **comforter** *noun*   **comforting** *adjective*   **comfortingly** *adverb*

comfortable

adjective **1** giving comfort: *a comfortable chair | a comfortable way of life*
Other words: **cosy, relaxing, restful, snug**
2 feeling comfort in your body or mind: *I am quite comfortable sitting here. | I am comfortable about those problems now.*
Other words: **happy, relaxed**

Word building: **comfortably** *adverb*

comic

adjective **1** having to do with comedy: *Steve Martin is my favourite comic actor.*
2 funny or amusing: *She had a comic look on her face.*
noun **3** a magazine containing a series of drawings that tell a funny story or an adventure story **4** a comic actor or person

comical

adjective funny or amusing: *She put on a comical voice to make us laugh.*

comma

noun a punctuation mark (,) that is used to show small breaks in a sentence

You use a **comma** to separate one item from another within a list:
> *Keiko ran through the final checklist for the party: drinks, food, CDs and the birthday cake.*

You use a comma when you want to separate one section of a sentence from another to make it easier to read:
> *Many of her guests were going first to the beach, then on to the party.*

You may also want to separate one section of a sentence from another, to ensure the reader doesn't misread words from one phrase to the next:
> *All along, the beach was covered in bluebottles.*

Without the comma, this sentence would not work for the reader. It would seem to lack a subject.

Commas sometimes mark off a part of a sentence which adds more information. This may be a <u>phrase</u>, for example:
> *The lifesavers scraped all the bluebottles, <u>large and small</u>, into a hole and covered them with sand.*

Or it may be a <u>clause</u>:
> *This meant that all of Keiko's guests, <u>who were already in their swimming costumes,</u> could race in for a quick swim before the party.*

Note that without the commas in the above example, the meaning of the sentence would be different. It would then mean that only those of Keiko's guests who were already in their swimming costumes could have a swim.

command

verb **1** to order or direct, usually with the right to be obeyed: *The teacher commanded silence. | She commanded us to come immediately.* **2** to be in charge of: *He commanded the army during the battle.*
3 to deserve and get: *Her position commands respect.*
noun **4** an order: *He gave the command to stop.* **5** power to give orders or be in charge: *Who is in command of these soldiers?*

Word building: **commandeer** *verb* to take or seize officially   **commander** *noun*   **commandant** *noun*

commandment

noun a command or order

commando

noun someone who belongs to a small fighting force that is specially trained to make quick attacks inside enemy areas
Word building: The plural is **commandos** or **commandoes**.

commemorate

verb to keep alive or honour the memory of: *This stone commemorates the opening of the school.* | *Anzac Day commemorates the soldiers who fought at Gallipoli.*
Word building: **commemoration** *noun* **commemorative** *adjective*

commence

verb to begin or start: *Commence work now.*
Word building: **commencement** *noun*

commend

verb **1** to suggest as being suitable for trust, a reward, or a job: *He commended his friend as a babysitter.* | *She was commended for a medal after the war.*
Other words: **recommend**
2 to praise: *I commend you for your good work.*
Word building: **commendable** *adjective* deserving praise **commendation** *noun* **commendatory** *adjective*

comment

noun a short note or remark that gives an opinion or explanation
Word building: **comment** *verb*

commentary

noun a series of written or spoken comments: *He is listening to the sports commentary on the radio.*
Word building: The plural is **commentaries**. | **commentate** *verb* **commentator** *noun*

commerce

noun the buying and selling of goods carried on between different countries or between different parts of the same country
Other words: **trade**

commercial   (*say* kuh-<u>mer</u>-shuhl)

adjective **1** having to do with commerce: *Australia established a commercial relationship with China.* **2** likely to be sold in great numbers: *We need products that are commercial.* **3** aimed at making money rather than keeping to standards of high quality: *That is a very commercial film.* **4** relying on money from advertising: *a commercial TV station*
noun **5** an advertisement on radio or television

Word building: **commercialise** *verb* **commercialism** *noun*

commercial artist

noun an artist who makes a living from painting or drawing for advertisements, books, magazines, and so on: *She started out as a commercial artist and then specialised in cartoons.*

commiserate

verb to share someone's sorrow or disappointment: *I commiserated with him when he failed the exam.*
Other words: **sympathise**
Word building: **commiseration** *noun*

commission

noun **1** an order, direction or particular duty, given by someone who is in charge **2** a written paper giving someone a particular duty or rank in the army or navy **3** a group of people who have been given particular official duties: *A commission was set up to investigate traffic accidents.* **4** use or service: *Is your car out of commission today?* **5** a sum of money given to an employee, such as a sales representative, for each successful effort: *He received 10% commission on each car he sold.*
verb **6** to give a duty or task to: *The teacher commissioned me to hand out the books each day.*
Word use: Definition 3 is often spelt with a capital letter, as in *a Royal Commission.*

commissioner

noun **1** someone who is a member of an official commission **2** someone who is in charge of a government department
Word use: Definition 2 is often spelt with a capital letter, as in *the Commissioner for Taxation.*

commit

verb **1** to give into someone's charge or trust: *I am committing these important papers to you.*
2 to put into a particular form in order to keep: *I committed the poem to memory.*
3 to hand over for punishment: *The judge committed the murderer to prison.*
4 to do or perform: *He committed a crime.*
phrase **5 commit yourself**, to bind yourself by making a promise: *Don't commit yourself before you are sure you like the job.*

Word building: Other verb forms are **I committed, I have committed, I am committing.** | **commitment** *noun* **committed** *adjective* **committal** *noun*

committee
noun a group of people selected from a larger group to discuss or make decisions about a particular subject: *A committee was chosen to run the school magazine.*

commodity
noun something useful, especially something that is bought and sold: *This shop has a wide range of stoves, refrigerators and other household commodities.*

Word building: The plural is **commodities.**

commodore
noun **1** a senior captain in the navy **2** the president of a boat club

common
adjective **1** shared by two or more people: *common property* | *common action* **2** general or shared by all: *common knowledge* **3** found or happening often: *a common flower* | *a common event* **4** impolite or vulgar **5** ordinary or not having any special rank: *the common people*

Word building: **commonly** *adverb*

commoner
noun an ordinary person, who is not one of the ruling class in a society

common-law
adjective having to do with a relationship between people that is like a marriage although they have not formally become married

common noun
noun a noun which can be used of any one of a class of things and which does not have a capital letter: *'Susan' is not a common noun, but 'girl' is.*

Word use: Compare this with **proper noun.**

commonplace
adjective ordinary, occurring often: *a commonplace garden pest* | *a commonplace phrase*

common sense
noun the ability to behave sensibly and make sensible decisions

Word use: This can also be written **commonsense.**
Word building: **commonsensical** *adjective*

commonwealth
noun **1** all the people of a country or state **2** **Commonwealth,** a country that is made up of several states, in which there is one government for the whole country as well as a government for each of the states: *the Commonwealth of Australia* **3** a group of people or countries united by a common interest

commotion
noun a wild or noisy disturbance: *There was great commotion in the classroom when the teacher went out.*

communal
adjective shared by several people: *The flats have their own bathrooms but a communal laundry.*

commune[1]   (*say* kuh-<u>myoohn</u>)
verb to talk together so that each person understands the other's thoughts or feelings

Word use: The more usual word is **communicate.**

commune[2]   (*say* <u>kom</u>-yoohn)
noun a group of people who live and work together, following their own rules and beliefs, and sharing their property and possessions
Other words: **collective**

communicate
verb **1** to pass on or make known to someone: *We will communicate the news to her.* **2** to share thoughts or feelings: *They communicate well with each other.*

Word building: **communicative** *adjective* willing or liking to talk or pass on ideas or information **communicator** *noun*

communication
noun **1** the passing on or sharing of thoughts, ideas or information **2** something that is communicated, such as a piece of news **3** **communications,** ways of passing on information, such as by telephone, radio or television

communion
noun the sharing of thoughts, feelings or interests: *I enjoy the communion of my friends.*

communiqué   (*say* kuh-<u>myoohn</u>-uh-kay)
noun an official news report

communism

noun **1** a way of living in which all property is owned equally by all the people in a society **2** a way of organising a country, in which there is only one political party and all trade and business is run by the government

Word use: Compare this with **capitalism**.
Word building: **communist** *noun*

community

noun a large or small group of people who live near each other and share common interests

Word building: The plural is **communities**.

commute

verb **1** to change and make less punishing: *The judge commuted his death sentence to life imprisonment.* **2** to travel regularly between home and work: *I commute by bus.*

Word building: **commuter** *noun* someone who travels a long way to work by public transport
Word history: from a Latin word meaning 'change wholly'

compact (*say* kom-pakt)

adjective **1** fitted or packed closely together
verb (*say* kom-pakt) **2** to join or pack closely together

Word building: **compactly** *adverb*
compactness *noun*

compact disc

noun a disc, about 12 cm across, for storing information which can be read by a laser beam and then sent to a hi-fi system, a computer monitor or a television

Word use: The short form of this is **CD**.

companion

noun **1** someone who goes out with or travels with another: *Are you taking a companion to the party?* **2** someone or something that matches or goes with another: *I wish I could find the companion to this sock.*
Other words: **partner**
Word building: **companionable** *adjective* friendly   **companionship** *noun*

company (*say* kum-puh-nee)

noun **1** a group of people brought together for a purpose, such as to run a business organisation: *a company that makes fridges | a theatrical company* **2** guests: *We've got company tonight.* **3** a group of soldiers forming part of an army

Word building: The plural is **companies**.

comparative

adjective **1** having to do with comparison **2** judged by comparison: *They live in comparative poverty.*
Other words: **relative**
3 having to do with the form of an adjective or adverb which expresses a greater degree: *'Smoother' is the comparative form of 'smooth' and 'more easily' is the comparative form of 'easily'.*

Word use: Compare definition 3 with **superlative**.
Word building: **comparatively** *adverb*: *They are comparatively poor.*

compare

verb **1** to show to be similar: *You can compare the heart to a pump.* **2** to look for the similarities and differences of: *He compared his new bike with Juan's.* **3** to be as good as: *Australian beaches compare with any in the world.*

Word building: **comparable** *adjective*
comparison *noun*

compartment

noun a separate space, room or section: *a compartment in a railway carriage*

compass (*say* kum-puhs)

noun **1** an instrument with a magnetic needle pointing to north which is used to find direction **2** extent or range: *a wide compass of knowledge | the compass of a singer's voice* **3** **compasses**, an instrument for measuring and drawing circles, which has two legs hinged together

Word building: **compass** *verb*
Word history: from a Latin word meaning 'single step'

compassion

noun a feeling of sorrow or pity for someone
Other words: **sympathy**

Word building: **compassionate** *adjective*
compassionately *adverb*

compatible

adjective **1** able to agree or exist side by side: *a compatible married couple | compatible ideas* **2** able to be used together: *The two computers are compatible with each other.*

Word building: **compatibility** *noun*
compatibly *adverb*

compatriot   (*say* kom-<u>pat</u>-ree-uht)
noun someone from your own country: *I met a lot of my compatriots while I was in Greece.*

compel
verb **1** to force to do something: *They can compel you to attend school.*
2 to bring about as if by force: *His angry look compelled an immediate answer.*

Word building: Other forms are **I compelled, I have compelled, I am compelling.** | **compelling** *adjective* holding your attention forcefully

compensate
verb **1** to make up to: *We will compensate you for your expenses.*
Other words: **recompense, repay**
phrase **2 compensate for**, to make up for: *Nothing can compensate for his loss.*

Word building: **compensation** *noun* **compensator** *noun* **compensatory** *adjective*

compere   (*say* <u>kom</u>-pair)
noun someone who introduces the acts in a show

Word building: **compere** *verb*

compete
verb to set yourself against one or more people to gain or win something: *The shops lowered their prices to compete for customers.*

Word building: **competitor** *noun* someone who competes

competent
adjective able or skilful: *He is a competent rider.*

Word building: **competence** *noun* **competency** *noun*

competition
noun **1** a test or situation in which people compete against each other
Other words: **contest**
2 a feeling or act of competing: *There is a lot of competition between the top runners.*
Other words: **rivalry**
3 the people against whom someone competes: *What's the competition like?*

competitive
adjective **1** having to do with or decided by competition: *a competitive exam* **2** liking competition: *a competitive person*

Word building: **competitively** *adverb*

compile
verb to collect and put together into one list, account or book

Word building: **compilation** *noun* **compiler** *noun*

complacent
adjective pleased or satisfied with yourself

Word building: **complacence** *noun* **complacency** *noun* **complacently** *adverb*

complain
verb **1** to express dissatisfaction or find fault: *The hotel guests complained that there was no air conditioning.* **2** to speak loudly about your illnesses, troubles or pains: *She is always complaining.*
Other words: **grizzle, grumble, moan, whine, whinge**

Word building: **complainer** *noun* **complaining** *adjective* **complainingly** *adverb*

complaint
noun **1** an expression of dissatisfaction, blame or pain: *He made a complaint about the poor service in the shop.* **2** a sickness or illness

complement   (*say* <u>kom</u>-pluh-muhnt)
noun **1** something which completes or makes perfect (something else): *The flute was a perfect complement to the sound of the guitar.* **2** the number that is required: *The hockey team now has its full complement of players.*

Word building: **complement** *verb* to complete **complementary** *adjective*

complement/compliment Don't confuse **complement** with **compliment**, which is a word or action expressing praise and admiration.

complementary medicine
noun treatment for disease and injury that is not like the more usual treatments given by doctors and hospitals, but which is sometimes used as well as them, such as hypnosis and acupuncture

complete

adjective **1** having all its parts: *a complete set of coloured pencils*
Other words: **entire, full, whole**
2 finished: *My piano practice is complete.*
Other words: **concluded, done**
3 total or absolute: *Your bedroom is a complete mess.*
Other words: **utter**
verb **4** to finish: *She completed her homework.* **5** to make whole or entire: *to complete a set of tools*
Word building: **completely** *adverb*
completeness *noun* **completion** *noun*

complex

adjective **1** made up of parts connected with each other **2** difficult to understand or explain: *Maths is too complex for me.*
noun **3** a group of buildings or shops: *a shopping complex*
Word building: The plural form of the noun is **complexes.** | **complexity** *noun*

complexion

noun **1** the colour and appearance of your skin, especially of your face **2** aspect or character: *The new evidence puts a different complexion on the murder case.*

compliant   (*say* kuhm-<u>pluy</u>-uhnt)

adjective agreeable or willing to do what is asked or required
Word building: **compliance** *noun*

complicate

verb to make harder to understand or deal with: *Too many directions can complicate a map.*
Word building: **complicated** *adjective*
complication *noun*
Word history: from a Latin word meaning 'folded together'

complicit   (*say* kuhm-<u>plis</u>-uht)

adjective involved in or knowing about something that should not have happened: *He was terrified when he realised he had been complicit in a crime.*

complicity

noun the state of being a partner or taking part in doing something wrong: *complicity in a crime*
Word use: The more usual word is **involvement.**

compliment   (*say* <u>kom</u>-pluh-muhnt)

noun **1** a word or action expressing praise and admiration: *A stranger paid me a compliment about my new jumper.*
verb (*say* <u>kom</u>-pluh-ment) **2** to pay a compliment to

compliment/complement Don't confuse **compliment** with **complement**, which is something which completes or makes perfect something else:
The flute was the perfect complement to the guitar.

complimentary

adjective **1** praising, or expressing a compliment **2** free or without cost: *He gave them complimentary tickets to the show.*

comply

verb to act in agreement with a request, wish, command or rule
Word building: Other forms are **I complied, I have complied, I am complying.**

component

noun a part of a whole: *The picture tube is an important component of a television set.*
Word building: **component** *adjective*: *a component ingredient*

compose

verb **1** to make by putting parts together **2** to make up or form: *Smog is composed of smoke and fog.* **3** to write music or poetry *phrase* **4 compose yourself,** to make your mind and body quiet and calm
Word building: **composed** *adjective*
composedly *adverb* **composer** *noun*

composite   (*say* <u>kom</u>-puh-zuht)

noun something made up of different parts
Word building: **composite** *adjective*: *a composite picture*

composition

noun **1** the putting together of parts to make a whole **2** the way in which parts are combined, or make-up: *What is the composition of smog?* **3** something that has been composed, such as a piece of music **4** a short essay, written as a school exercise

compost

noun a mixture of rotting materials, like old vegetable peelings, leaves and manure, used as a fertiliser for the garden

composure *(say* kuhm-<u>poh</u>-zhuh)
noun calmness of mind, or self-control

compound¹ *(say* <u>kom</u>-pownd)
adjective **1** made up of two or more parts:
'Bedroom' is a compound word.
noun **2** a mixture **3** a chemical substance
made by joining two or more chemicals:
When hydrogen and oxygen are joined together,
they form a compound called water.
verb *(say* kom-<u>pownd</u>) **4** to mix or
combine **5** to add to, or increase

compound² *(say* <u>kom</u>-pownd)
noun a closed-off area with buildings
where people can stay or be kept: *a prison*
compound

compound verb
noun a verb consisting of more than
one word, as *was walking* or *might have*
walked

comprehend
verb **1** to understand the meaning of: *I*
can't comprehend the story. **2** to take in or
include: *The new national park comprehends*
all the old reserves.

Word building: **comprehensive** *adjective*
including a great deal   **comprehendingly**
adverb   **comprehensible** *adjective*
Word history: from a Latin word meaning
'seize'

comprehension
noun **1** the ability to understand or the act
of understanding: *Computers are beyond*
my comprehension. **2** a school exercise in
reading and understanding, usually tested
by a set of short questions

compress *(say* kuhm-<u>pres</u>)
verb **1** to press together, or force into less
space: *Wool is compressed into bales ready for*
transportation.
noun *(say* <u>kom</u>-pres) **2** a soft pad of cloth
applied to an injury and held in place with
a bandage
Word building: **compression** *noun*
compressor *noun*

comprise
verb to include or be composed of: *This*
school comprises an infants section and a
primary section.

compromise *(say* <u>kom</u>-pruh-muyz)
noun **1** the settlement of an argument by
both sides agreeing to give way a bit: *Our*
compromise is to take turns on the bike.
2 something midway between two other
things: *Jogging is a compromise between*
walking and running.
verb **3** to agree to accept less than you
originally wanted: *If you are willing to*
compromise, you can both be happy with the
outcome. **4** to lay open to suspicion or bad
comments from others: *You will compromise*
yourself as class captain if you talk like that.

compulsion
noun the use of force or pressure

compulsory
adjective forced or required: *Attendance at*
school is compulsory for all children.
Word building: **compulsorily** *adverb*
compulsoriness *noun*

compute
verb to calculate or to work out using
maths: *to compute the distance of the moon*
from the earth
Word building: **computation** *noun*

computer
noun an electronic machine which does
mathematical calculations very quickly, and
which stores and gives out information,
according to a set of stored instructions
called a program
Word building: **computerise** *verb*

computer game
noun a game that is played on a computer

computer geek
noun a person who spends too much time
with computers

computerise
verb **1** to put data into a form that can be
processed or stored on a computer: *The*
teacher computerised the exam results.
2 to bring computers into a place, like
an office or a factory, to be used for the
work and processes done there: *We need to*
computerise the warehouse.
Word use: Another spelling is **computerize**.

computer programming
noun the process of writing and
maintaining the set of instructions to a
computer that achieve a particular outcome
in the use of the computer
Word building: **computer programmer** *noun*

computer terminal

noun a machine linked up to a computer and used for receiving or giving information

computing

adjective having to do with computers: *Her computing skills are amazing.*

comrade (*say* <u>kom</u>-rayd, <u>kom</u>-ruhd)

noun a close friend or mate

Word building: **comradeship** noun
Word history: from a Latin word meaning 'chamber' or 'room'

con

noun *Informal* a trick or swindle

Word building: **con** *adjective*: *a con man | a con game*   **con** *verb* (**conned, conning**)
Word history: a shortened form of **confidence trick**

concave

adjective hollow and curved like the inside of a circle: *A saucer is slightly concave.*

Word use: The opposite of this is **convex**.

conceal

verb **1** to hide or keep from sight: *I concealed the knife in my coat pocket.*
2 to keep secret: *She concealed her real reason for coming.*

Word building: **concealment** noun

concede

verb **1** to admit as true or certain: *Everyone concedes that the earth is round.* **2** to allow someone to have or do something: *He conceded us the right to choose our own team.*

Word building: **concession** noun something given or conceded

conceit

noun pride in yourself and your own importance or ability

Word building: **conceited** adjective
conceitedly adverb   **conceitedness** noun

conceive

verb **1** to think of: *to conceive a plan*
2 to become pregnant

Word building: **conceivable** adjective
conceivably adverb

concentrate

verb **1** to focus or direct towards one point: *The photographer concentrated the light on my face.* **2** to direct your attention to one subject: *to concentrate on watching the ball*
3 to make stronger or purer: *Some*

detergents have been concentrated by removing some of the water from them.
noun **4** a substance that has been concentrated

Word building: **concentration** noun

concentration camp

noun a prison camp for prisoners of war or enemies of a country

concentric

adjective having the same centre: *When you drop a stone into water, the ripples form concentric circles.*

concept

noun general idea or understanding of something: *My concept of computer programming is very vague.*

Word building: **conceptualise** verb to form an idea of   **conceptual** adjective
conceptually adverb

conception

noun **1** an idea or thought: *My conception of how the house should look is different to yours.* **2** the beginning of pregnancy, or the act of conceiving a child

concern

verb **1** to be of interest or importance: *This problem concerns us all.* **2** to be anxious or troubled: *I am concerned about your cough.*
noun **3** a matter of interest or importance: *It's no concern of mine.* **4** worry or anxiety: *The teacher's concern for the students' safety was obvious.*

Word building: **concerned** adjective
interested   **concerning** preposition

concert

noun **1** a public musical performance by one or more musicians or other performers
2 agreement in a plan or action: *The children acted in concert to recover the stolen money.*

Word building: **concerted** adjective arranged by agreement

concertina

noun **1** a small musical instrument like an accordion
verb **2** to fold up or collapse like a concertina

Word building: Other verb forms are **it concertinaed, it has concertinaed, it is concertinaing**.

concerto (*say* kuhn-<u>cher</u>-toh,
  kuhn-<u>sher</u>-toh)
noun a piece of music for one or more solo
instruments, such as a piano or violin, and
an orchestra

Word building: The plural is **concertos** or
concerti.

conciliate
verb to make friendly or calm
Other words: **reconcile**
Word building: **conciliation** *noun* the way of
working out arguments, especially between
trade unionists and employers **conciliator**
noun **conciliatory** *adverb*

concise
adjective expressing a lot in a few words: *a
concise account of what happened*

Word building: **concisely** *adverb*
conciseness *noun* **concision** *noun*
Word history: from a Latin word meaning 'cut
up' or 'cut off'

conclude
verb **1** to finish or bring to an end: *After
a short speech, she concluded.* | *The teacher
concluded the lesson with two examples.*
2 to arrange or settle: *The two businessmen
concluded an agreement.*
3 to decide by working out: *After reading
the whole book she concluded the real reason
for the murder.*

Word building: **conclusive** *adjective*
convincing, or decisive **conclusion** *noun*
conclusively *adverb*

concoct
verb **1** to make up or invent: *I concocted a
story to cover up for my absence.*
2 to make up by combining parts, or to
prepare: *I concocted a quick, easy meal.*

Word building: **concoction** *noun*
Word history: from a Latin word meaning
'cooked together' or 'digested'

concrete
noun **1** a mixture of cement, sand, water
and gravel, which hardens as it dries and is
used in building
adjective **2** made of this mixture: *a concrete
floor* **3** real or existing as an actual thing,
not just an idea: *A wedding ring is a concrete
object, but the feeling of love is not.*

Word use: The opposite of definition 3 is
abstract.
Word building: **concrete** *verb*

concrete noun
noun a word which refers to something that
our five senses (touch, sight, hearing, smell
and taste) can pick up: *'Boat', 'sun' and
'dog' are all concrete nouns.*

Word use: The opposite of this is **abstract
noun**.

concubine (*say* <u>kong</u>-kyooh-buyn)
noun a man's second or other wife, in a
country where a man can be married to
more than one woman at a time

concur
verb to agree: *I concur with that decision.*

Word building: Other forms are **I concurred, I
have concurred, I am concurring.** |
concurrent *adjective* occurring together:
concurrent events **concurrence** *noun*
concurrently *adverb*

concussion
noun **1** a shock, or violent shaking caused
by a blow or collision **2** an injury or
jarring of the brain or spine caused by a
blow or fall

Word building: **concuss** *verb*

condemn (*say* kuhn-<u>dem</u>)
verb **1** to express strong disapproval of: *He
condemned the child's bad behaviour.*
2 to judge someone to be guilty or sentence
them to punishment: *The murderer was
condemned to death.* **3** to decide something
is no longer fit for use: *The old building was
condemned by council.*

Word building: **condemnation**
noun **condemnatory** *adjective*

condensation
noun **1** the changing of a gas to a liquid
or solid: *When steam hits something cold,
condensation occurs.* **2** something that has
been condensed: *This book is a condensation
of a much larger novel.*

condense
verb **1** to make thicker or reduce the
volume of: *to condense milk* **2** to change
from a gas to a liquid or solid: *to condense
steam to get water* **3** to say or write
something in fewer words: *Can you
condense your story into just a few pages?*

Word building: **condenser** *noun*

condescend

verb **1** to agree, even though it's below your social level: *The queen condescended to have a meal with her servants.* **2** to act as if you are in a higher social position than others

Word building: **condescending** *adjective* **condescendingly** *adverb* **condescension** *noun*

condition

noun **1** the state of someone or something: *The runner was in top condition before the race.* | *The car was rusty and in very poor condition.* **2** anything that is required before another thing can be done: *Having a licence is a condition of driving a car.* *verb* **3** to put in a fit state: *Long-distance runners condition themselves for their races by training.* **4** to influence or affect: *What we are taught by our parents and teachers conditions the way we live.*

conditional

adjective depending on something else: *They made a conditional agreement to go to the beach only if the weather was good.*

Word building: **conditionality** *noun* **conditionally** *adverb*

condolences

plural noun the expressions of sympathy you make to someone when a relative or friend of theirs has just died: *Please accept my condolences on the death of your husband.*

Word building: **condolence** *noun*: *letters of condolence* **condolatory** *adjective* **condole** *verb* **condolingly** *adverb*

condone

verb to pardon, excuse or overlook: *The teachers will not condone smoking at school.*

conduct (*say* kon-dukt)

noun **1** someone's behaviour or way of acting: *The teacher said that my conduct in class has improved.* *verb* (*say* kuhn-dukt) **2** to behave: *You conducted yourself well today.* **3** to manage or carry on: *The politician conducted a well-planned campaign.* **4** to direct or lead an orchestra or choir **5** to lead: *The mayor conducted us on a tour of the city.* **6** to be a channel for electricity, heat or sound: *The air conducts sound waves to our ears.*

Word building: **conduction** *noun* **conductive** *adjective* **conductivity** *noun*

conductor

noun **1** a guide or a leader **2** someone who collects fares on a tram, train or bus **3** something that easily conducts heat, electricity or sound: *Copper is a good conductor of heat.*

cone

noun **1** a solid shape with a flat round bottom, whose sides meet at the top in a point **2** anything shaped like this: *an ice-cream cone* **3** the cone-like fruit of pine and fir trees

Word building: **conic** *adjective* **conical** *adjective* **conically** *adverb*

confectionery

noun lollies, candies or sweets

Word building: **confection** *noun* **confectioner** *noun*

confederacy

noun a group of people or countries joined together for a common purpose or reason

Word building: The plural is **confederacies**. | **confederate** *noun* an ally or supporter **confederate** *adjective* **confederation** *noun*

confer

verb **1** to give as a gift, favour or honour: *The prime minister conferred a medal for bravery on a girl in our class.* **2** to talk together: *We conferred for some time about the situation.*

Word building: Other forms are **I conferred, I have conferred, I am conferring**.

conference

noun a meeting arranged to discuss something special

confess

verb to admit or own up: *I confess that I broke the cup.* | *The prisoner confessed.*

Word building: **confession** *noun* **confessional** *noun* **confessor** *noun*

confetti

noun small bits of coloured paper, thrown at weddings or carnivals

confide

verb to trust or tell, as a secret: *I confide all my secrets to my best friend.*

Word building: **confidant** *noun* someone you confide in

confidence

noun **1** trust or faith in someone **2** a belief in yourself and what you can do: *She played the tournament with plenty of confidence.* **3** a secret: *Vijay told me his confidences after school.*

confident

adjective having a strong belief or feeling certain: *I am confident that he will arrive soon.*
Other words: **positive, sure**
Word building: **confidently** *adverb*

confidential

adjective **1** secret or not public: *The policeman wrote out a confidential report.* **2** trusted with secrets or private matters: *The director of the company had a confidential secretary.*
Word building: **confidentiality** *noun* **confidentially** *adverb*

confine   (*say* kuhn-<u>fuyn</u>)

verb **1** to restrict or keep within limits: *I confine myself to one chocolate a day.* **2** to shut or keep in: *He was confined to prison for three months.*
Word building: **confinement** *noun*

confirm

verb **1** to make certain or sure: *He confirmed our table booking at the restaurant.* **2** to strengthen or make firm: *What you have told me confirms what I already thought.* **3** to admit as a member of a church in a special ceremony
Word building: **confirmed** *adjective* firmly settled in a habit or condition   **confirmable** *adjective*   **confirmation** *noun*

confiscate

verb to take and keep: *My mum confiscated my comic when I wouldn't do my homework.*
Word building: **confiscation** *noun*
Word history: from a Latin word meaning 'put away in a chest'

conflict   (*say* kuhn-<u>flikt</u>)

verb **1** to disagree or clash: *Our ideas conflict because we are too different.*
noun (*say* <u>kon</u>-flikt) **2** a fight or disagreement: *a conflict between nations*

conflicting

adjective differing or disagreeing: *They had conflicting ideas on how to solve the problem so it was difficult to make a start.*

conform

verb **1** to act according to rules or laws **2** to be like or similar to: *His hairstyle conforms to the latest fashion trend.*
Word building: **conformist** *noun*   **conformity** *noun*

confound

verb to surprise or puzzle: *He confounded the experts by solving the problem.*

confront

verb **1** to meet face to face: *He turned the corner and was confronted by the person he had been trying to avoid.* **2** to face boldly or bravely: *She confronted her problem without hesitation.*
Word building: **confrontation** *noun*

confuse

verb **1** to mix up or puzzle: *The teacher's instructions have confused me.*
Other words: **baffle, bewilder, mystify, perplex**
2 to be unable to tell the difference between: *I always confuse one type of car with another.*
Other words: **mistake, muddle**
Word building: **confused** *adjective*   **confusing** *adjective*   **confusingly** *adverb*   **confusion** *noun*

congeal

verb to thicken or become solid: *Cooking fat or dripping congeals as it cools.*

congenial

adjective pleasant or agreeable: *a more congenial job | congenial friends*
Word building: **congeniality** *noun* **congenially** *adverb*

congenital

adjective existing or being there when you are born: *congenital heart disease*
Word building: **congenitally** *adverb*

congest

verb to fill too much or to become overcrowded: *Cars are congesting the road.*
Word building: **congestion** *noun*

congratulate

verb to praise and show pleasure to: *They congratulated her on her victory.*

Word building: **congratulation** *noun* **congratulatory** *adjective*

congregate

verb to gather together: *The people congregated on the river bank.*

Word building: **congregation** *noun* a group of people gathered together, especially in a church

congress

noun a meeting of people to discuss ideas of interest to them all: *A congress of health workers was held here last week.*
Other words: **conference**

conifer

noun an evergreen tree which grows cones, like the pine or fir

Word building: **coniferous** *adjective*

conjunction

noun **1** a combination or joining together: *the conjunction of two rivers* **2** a word, such as 'and' or 'because', used to join parts of a sentence

conjure   (*say* <u>kun</u>-juh)

verb to do magic tricks

Word building: **conjurer** *noun*

connect

verb **1** to join or unite: *Connect this wire to the end of that rod.* | *These wires should connect somewhere.*
phrase **2 be connected with**, to have to do or be associated with: *Are you connected with the church?*

Word building: **connection** *noun* **connective** *adjective*

connoisseur   (*say* kon-uh-<u>ser</u>)

noun someone who has a special interest or knowledge of a particular subject: *a connoisseur of stained glass* | *a connoisseur of wine*

Word history: from a Latin word meaning 'come to know'

conquer

verb to overcome by force: *The army of the ancient Romans conquered their enemy.*
Other words: **beat, crush, defeat**

Word building: **conqueror** *noun*   **conquest** *noun*

conscience   (*say* <u>kon</u>-shuhns)

noun the ability to see the difference between right and wrong in what you do

conscientious   (*say* kon-shee-<u>en</u>-shuhs)

adjective **1** careful and particular: *a conscientious worker* **2** doing or controlled by what you believe to be right: *a conscientious objector to war*

Word building: **conscientiously** *adverb* **conscientiousness** *noun*

conscious   (*say* <u>kon</u>-shuhs)

adjective **1** aware or having knowledge: *I was not conscious of the bell.* **2** aware of what is happening around you: *The injured pedestrian was still conscious.*

Word building: **consciously** *adverb* **consciousness** *noun*

conscript   (*say* kuhn-<u>skript</u>)

verb **1** to force to join the army, navy or air force
noun (*say* <u>kon</u>-skript) **2** someone who has been conscripted

Word building: **conscription** *noun*

consecrate

verb to declare holy: *The bishop consecrated the new church.*

Word building: **consecration** *noun*

consecutive

adjective following one after another: *The instructions were given in consecutive order.*

Word building: **consecutively** *adverb*

consensus

noun a general agreement

consent

verb **1** to agree: *They consented to go with him.*
noun **2** agreement: *They met by common consent.*

consequence

noun **1** an outcome or result: *This mess is the consequence of your foolishness.* **2** importance or value: *a matter of no consequence*

Word building: **consequent** *adjective* **consequential** *adjective*   **consequently** *adverb*

conservation

noun the protection of nature or of historic buildings, and the careful use of natural things

Word building: **conservationist** *noun*

conservative

adjective **1** careful or moderate: *a conservative opinion | conservative dress* **2** opposed to new ideas and sudden change of any kind: *a conservative political party*

Word building: **conservatism** *noun* **conservative** *noun* **conservatively** *adverb*

conservatorium

noun a school where you can learn music

conservatory

noun a room or building made of glass, where plants are displayed

Word building: The plural is **conservatories.**

conserve *(say* kuhn-<u>serv</u>*)*

verb **1** to keep from being lost or wasted: *to conserve petrol*
noun (say <u>kon</u>-serv*)* **2** a type of jam

consider

verb **1** to think about: *I will consider the problem.* **2** to think or believe: *I consider her to be Australia's best singer.*

considerable

adjective large or important enough to think about

Word building: **considerably** *adverb*

considerate

adjective thoughtful of other people's needs and feelings

Word building: **considerately** *adverb*

consideration

noun **1** careful thought: *I will give the problem my consideration.* **2** something taken, or that should be taken, into account **3** thoughtfulness for others

consist

verb to be made up: *The book consists of two parts.*

consistency

noun **1** agreement or harmony: *There is a consistency about your story which is convincing.* **2** an amount of thickness: *Mix the ingredients until they are the consistency of cream.*

consistent

adjective **1** agreeing: *The message is consistent with what we heard before.* **2** acting or thinking in the same way throughout: *He is always consistent in applying the rules.*

Word building: **consistently** *adverb*

console[1] *(say* kuhn-<u>sohl</u>*)*

verb to comfort or cheer up: *I tried to console my friend whose kitten had been run over.*

Word building: **consolable** *adjective* **consolation** *noun* **consolingly** *adverb*

console[2] *(say* <u>kon</u>-sohl*)*

noun a control panel, especially of a computer

consolidate

verb **1** to make firm or strengthen: *Our team has consolidated its position as the leader in the competition.* **2** to bring together or combine: *The army commander decided to consolidate several units of soldiers into one force.*

Word building: **consolidation** *noun*

consonant

noun **1** a speech sound made by blocking the flow of your breath by the tongue or lips **2** any letter of the alphabet, except *a, e, i, o* or *u*

Word use: Compare this with **vowel.**
Word history: from a Latin word meaning 'sounding together'

consort *(say* <u>kon</u>-sawt*)*

noun the husband of a ruling queen or the wife of a king

conspicuous

adjective noticeable or standing out: *Santa was conspicuous in the red suit.*

conspiracy *(say* kuhn-<u>spi</u>-ruh-see*)*

noun a secret plan decided between a group of people to do something wrong or illegal: *a conspiracy to defraud innocent people*

conspire

verb to plan secretly together: *The men conspired to hijack a plane.*

Word building: **conspiracy** *noun* (**conspiracies**) **conspirator** *noun* **conspiratorial** *adjective*

constable *(say* <u>kun</u>-stuh-buhl*)*

noun a police officer of the lowest rank

Word history: from Latin words meaning 'count of the stable' or 'master of the horse'

constant

adjective **1** going on without stopping: *Her success has been a constant source of pleasure.* **2** faithful: *He has been constant in looking after his mother.*

Word building: **constancy** *noun* **constantly** *adverb*
Word history: from a Latin word meaning 'standing firm'

constellation

noun a group of stars

consternation

noun shock or fear causing you to feel confused: *We were thrown into consternation at the news of the sailor's disappearance.*

constipation

noun the unpleasant condition of not being able to empty your bowels regularly or easily

Word building: **constipate** *verb* **constipated** *adjective*

constituent

noun something that is part of a whole

Word building: **constituency** *noun*

constitute

verb to make up or form: *Lee's absence constitutes only part of the problem.*

constitution

noun **1** the health or condition of your body: *Jim has a strong constitution.* **2** a set of basic rules: *the Australian constitution | the constitution of the rowing club*

Word building: **constitutional** *adjective* **constitutionally** *adverb*

constitutional monarchy

noun a system of government where there is a sovereign, but where the amount of power they have is limited by a constitution, and where power to govern is usually held by a parliament: *Australia is a constitutional monarchy although some people would like it to become a republic.*

constraint

noun **1** something that restricts or controls the way you behave or what you can do at certain times: *There is a constraint on doctors not to advertise for patients.* **2** control or the keeping back of your natural feelings and impulses: *During hard times we don't spend much money and we act with constraint.*

Word building: **constrain** *verb* to compel, or restrain **constrained** *adjective*

constrict

verb to make tighter or narrower: *a drug to constrict the blood vessels*

Word use: The opposite of this is **dilate**.
Word building: **constriction** *noun*

construct

verb to build: *to construct a house | to construct a theory*

Word building: **construction** *noun*

constructive

adjective helpful or useful: *constructive suggestions*

consul

noun an official sent by a government to represent it in a foreign country

Word building: **consular** *adjective* **consulate** *noun* **consulship** *noun*

consult

verb to seek advice from: *to consult a doctor | to consult a dictionary*

Word building: **consultant** *noun* **consultation** *noun*

consume

verb **1** to eat: *to consume a meat pie* **2** to use up or destroy: *They consumed the stock of paper. | The building was consumed by fire.*

consumer

noun someone who uses goods and services: *Advertising aims to make consumers buy more.*

Word use: The opposite of this is **producer**.

consumption

noun **1** eating or using up **2** an old-fashioned word for **tuberculosis**

contact

noun **1** a meeting or touching: *to make contact with someone* **2** the moving part of a switch that completes and breaks an electrical circuit **3** a useful person to meet: *a business contact*

Word building: **contact** *verb*: *to contact an old friend*

contact lenses

plural noun lenses to improve your sight and which fit closely over the iris or coloured part of your eye

contagious

adjective catching or easily spread from one person to another: *Chickenpox is a contagious disease. | Happiness is contagious.*

Word building: **contagion** *noun* **contagiously** *adverb*

contain

verb to have inside itself: *This jug contains milk. | This book contains instructions.*

container

noun **1** anything that contains or can contain **2** a very large crate for carrying goods on ships or trucks

container ship

noun a ship that carries cargo in large containers

contaminate

verb to make dirty or impure: *This meat has been contaminated by flies.*

Word building: **contamination** noun

contemplate

verb to look at or consider thoughtfully: *He contemplated the letter for several minutes. | She is contemplating going to Melbourne.*

Word building: **contemplative** adjective **contemplation** noun

contemporary

adjective **1** existing at the same time: *Francis Greenway was contemporary with Governor Macquarie.* **2** modern or existing now: *The room was decorated in contemporary style.*

Word building: **contemporary** noun (**contemporaries**) **contemporaneous** adjective

contempt

noun the feeling that someone or something is mean and disgraceful: *They felt contempt for the person who had robbed the blind woman.*

Other words: **disdain, disgust, scorn**

contemptible

adjective deserving contempt: *Tripping up the other runner was a contemptible act.*

Word building: **contemptibly** adverb

contemptuous

adjective showing contempt: *She was contemptuous of Sophie's clumsy attempts to dance.*

Word building: **contemptuously** adverb

contend

verb **1** to fight or struggle: *She had to contend with illness.* **2** to say firmly: *He contends that he is only having a look.*

Word building: **contender** noun **contention** noun

content¹ (*say* kon-tent)

noun **1** the information, words and images contained in a text, television program, film, website, and so on
2 the volume, capacity, or amount contained
3 contents, whatever is held or contained: *the contents of the jar | The contents of the textbook are listed at the front.*

content² (*say* kuhn-tent)

adjective **1** pleased or satisfied: *I am content with what I have.*
verb **2** to please or satisfy: *Georgia contented herself with a quick snack.*

Word building: **contentedly** adverb **contentment** noun

contents (*say* kon-tents)

plural noun whatever is inside or contained in: *the contents of a bottle | the contents of a book*

contest (*say* kon-test)

noun **1** a competition
verb (*say* kuhn-test) **2** to struggle for: *They contested the leadership.*

Word building: **contestant** noun

context

noun the surrounding circumstances or words: *It was unfair to take my remarks about my brother out of context.*

continent

noun **1** one of the main landmasses of the world: *Australia is one of the seven continents.* **2 the Continent**, the mainland of Europe, separate from the British Isles

Word building: **continental** adjective
Word history: from a Latin word meaning 'holding together'

continental quilt

noun another name for **doona**

continual

adjective happening often: *I got into trouble for my continual lateness.*

Word building: **continually** adverb

continual/continuous Don't confuse **continual** with **continuous**, which describes something that keeps on going without stopping at all.

continue

verb **1** to keep on: *They continued to walk in the rain.*
Other words: **proceed**
2 to go on after being interrupted: *We will continue the discussion tomorrow.*
Other words: **renew, resume, revive**
3 to go on with: *to continue the search*
Other words: **maintain**
Word building: **continuation** *noun* **continuity** *noun*

continuous

adjective **1** going on without stopping: *The continuous sound of a tap dripping annoys me.* **2** having to do with the form of a verb which shows that something is continuing, such as *am running* in *I am running*
Word building: **continuously** *adverb* **continuousness** *noun*
Word history: from a Latin word meaning 'hanging together'

continuous/continual Don't confuse **continuous** with **continual**, which describes something that happens often but not all the time.

contort

verb to twist out of shape
Word building: **contortion** *noun* **contortionist** *noun*

contour

noun **1** the shape or outline: *the contour of the land* **2** a line on a map joining points of equal height

contra-

prefix a word part meaning 'against', 'opposite', or 'opposing': *contradict*
Word history: from Latin

contraband

noun goods imported or exported illegally

contraception

noun the prevention of pregnancy
Word use: Another name for this is **birth control**.
Word building: **contraceptive** *adjective* **contraceptive** *noun*

contract (*say* kon-trakt)

noun **1** an agreement, especially a legal one: *They signed the contract for building the house.*
verb (*say* kuhn-trakt) **2** to become smaller: *Metal contracts when it is cooled.* **3** to make an agreement
Word building: **contractual** *adjective* belonging to a contract **contraction** *noun*

contradict

verb **1** to deny or say the opposite of: *Whatever I say, you contradict me.* **2** to be the direct opposite of: *This experiment contradicts the results we got before.*
Word building: **contradiction** *noun* **contradictory** *adjective*

contralto

noun **1** the lowest range of musical notes which can be sung by a female singer **2** a woman who sings contralto
Word use: Another word is **alto**. | The **contralto** range is higher than **tenor**, **baritone** or **bass** but lower than **soprano**.

contraption

noun a complicated gadget or piece of machinery: *Deshi has invented a contraption for exercising our pet mice.*
Other words: **apparatus, device, machine, mechanism**

contrary

adjective **1** opposed or different: *My opinion is contrary to yours.*
noun **2** the opposite: *You say he is right, but I can prove the contrary.*
phrase **3 on the contrary,** in opposition to what has been said: *On the contrary, you are wrong.*
Word building: **contrarily** *adverb*

contrast (*say* kuhn-trahst)

verb **1** to compare in order to show differences: *Contrast last year's result with this year's.* **2** to show a difference in comparison: *The red flowers of the grevillea contrast with its green leaves.*
noun (*say* kon-trahst) **3** a marked difference: *a colour contrast | a contrast in attitude*

contribute (*say* kuhn-trib-yooht)

verb **1** to donate or pay a share: *to contribute to a fund* **2** to give to, or write for, a magazine or newspaper: *I have contributed a story to the school magazine.*
Word building: **contribution** *noun* **contributor** *noun* **contributory** *adjective*

contrite (*say* kuhn-truyt)

adjective feeling sorry or sad that you have done something wrong: *I looked so contrite that they had to forgive me.*
Word building: **contritely** *adverb* **contrition** *noun*

contrive

verb to invent or plan cleverly: *He contrived to be absent at the time.*

Word building: **contrivance** *noun*

control

verb **1** to be in charge of or direct: *Miss Bond controls the library.* **2** to adjust as necessary: *This tap controls the flow of water.* **3** to keep in check: *to control your temper*
noun **4** command or check: *Keep your dog under control.*

Word building: Other verb forms are **I control, I have controlled, I am controlling.** | **controllable** *adjective* **controller** *noun*

controversy (*say* <u>kon</u>-truh-ver-see, kuhn-<u>trov</u>-uh-see)

noun an argument or difference of opinion: *The position of the new airport is a matter of controversy.*

Word building: The plural is **controversies.** | **controversial** *adjective*: *a controversial issue*

conundrum (*say* kuh-<u>nun</u>-druhm)

noun a riddle or puzzle

convalesce (*say* kon-vuh-<u>les</u>)

verb to grow stronger after an illness: *He is convalescing at home after a long stay in hospital.*

Word building: **convalescence** *noun* **convalescent** *adjective* **convalescent** *noun*

convection

noun the spreading of heat by the movement of heated air or water

Word building: **convector** *noun*

convene

verb to call or gather together: *to convene a meeting* | *to convene for a quick talk about tactics*

Word building: **convener** *noun*

convenient

adjective suited to your needs: *What would be a convenient time to meet?*
Other words: **appropriate, fitting, suitable**
Word building: **convenience** *noun* **conveniently** *adverb*

convent

noun **1** a group of buildings where nuns live **2** a school run by nuns

convention

noun **1** a large meeting: *A science convention was held at the university.* **2** a rule, often unwritten, which everyone accepts: *There are certain conventions about the use of the tennis courts.*

Word building: **conventional** *adjective* **conventionalism** *noun* **conventionally** *adverb*

converge

verb to join up or meet at a particular place: *The roads converge at the roundabout.* | *The families will converge by the river for a picnic.*

Word building: **convergence** *noun* **convergent** *adjective*

conversation

noun talk among people: *We had an interesting conversation about a new film.*

Word building: **conversational** *adjective* **conversationalist** *noun*

converse¹ (*say* kuhn-<u>vers</u>)

verb to have a talk: *We conversed about music.*

converse² (*say* <u>kon</u>-vers)

adjective **1** turned about or opposite: *to go in a converse direction*
noun **2** the opposite: *He says it is possible but the converse is true.*

Word building: **conversely** *adverb*

convert (*say* kuhn-<u>vert</u>)

verb **1** to change completely: *Cinderella's fairy godmother converted her rags into a ball gown.* **2** to change the belief of: *to convert someone from Christianity to Buddhism*
noun (*say* <u>kon</u>-vert) **3** someone who has changed their religion or other beliefs

Word building: **convertible** *adjective* able to be changed **conversion** *noun*

convex

adjective curved or bulging outwards: *a convex mirror*

Word use: The opposite is **concave.**
Word building: **convexity** *noun*

convey (*say* kuhn-<u>vay</u>)

verb to carry: *The bus conveyed us to town.* | *The card conveyed a message of sympathy.*

Word building: **conveyance** *noun* a car or other vehicle **conveyable** *adjective* **conveyor, conveyer** *noun*
Word history: from a Latin word meaning 'way' or 'journey'

convict   (*say* kuhn-<u>vikt</u>)

verb **1** to find guilty of a crime, especially after a legal trial
noun (*say* <u>kon</u>-vikt) **2** someone who has been found guilty of a crime: *English convicts used to be sent to Australia to serve their sentences.*

conviction

noun **1** the occasion of being found guilty: *As it was my first conviction, I was let off with a warning.* **2** strong belief: *The president spoke with a voice filled with conviction.*

convince

verb to make feel sure, or persuade: *We finally convinced him that he was wrong.*

Word building: **convincing** *adjective* **convincingly** *adverb*

convoy

noun a number of ships or vehicles travelling together, sometimes for protection: *The ocean liner set sail with a convoy of small boats.*

Word building: **convoy** *verb* to travel with as an escort

convulsion

noun a sudden shaking of your body, caused by an illness such as very high fever: *It was when the convulsions started that they suspected he could have malaria.*

cooee   (*say* <u>koo</u>-ee)

noun a long, loud call used to signal someone, especially when you are in the bush

Word history: from an Aboriginal language of New South Wales called Dharug. See the map of Australian Aboriginal languages at the end of this book.

cook

verb **1** to heat until ready for eating
noun **2** someone who cooks or prepares food

Word building: **cookery** *noun* the art of cooking

cookie

noun **1** a sweet biscuit **2** *Informal* a person: *She's a smart cookie.* **3** a small file sent by a website to a computer so that the website will recognise that computer when the user visits that site again

cool

adjective **1** not too cold: *a cool morning*
Other words: **chilly, fresh, nippy**
2 a calm or unexcited: *She remained cool.*
Other words: **collected, composed, poised, unruffled**
b unfriendly: *to be cool towards someone you distrust*
Other words: **aloof, distant, icy**
3 *Informal* attractive or fashionable: *It's not cool to wear those wide trousers.*
Other words: **trendy**
4 *Informal* excellent: *This new computer game is really cool!*
Other words: **brilliant, fabulous, fantastic, great, tremendous**
verb **5** to become or make cool
Other words: **chill**

Word building: **cool** *noun*: *in the cool of the evening* **coolly** *adverb* **coolness** *noun*

coolamon   (*say* <u>kooh</u>-luh-mon)

noun a wooden dish traditionally made and used by Aboriginal people

Word history: from an Aboriginal language of New South Wales called Kamilaroi. See the map of Australian Aboriginal languages at the end of this book.

coolibah   (*say* <u>kooh</u>-luh-bah)

noun a gum tree found in inland Australia which has short twisted branches

Word use: Another spelling is **coolabah**.
Word history: from an Aboriginal language of New South Wales called Yuwaalaraay. See the map of Australian Aboriginal languages at the end of this book.

coop

noun **1** a small cage for hens
phrase **2 coop up**, to keep in a small place: *We were all cooped up in one room.*

cooperate   (*say* koh-<u>op</u>-uh-rayt)

verb **1** to work together: *The two city councils cooperated to build a new pool.* **2** to be helpful: *When we complained about the noise they cooperated by turning down the volume.*

Word building: **cooperative** *adjective* helpful **cooperation** *noun*

coordinate   (*say* koh-<u>awd</u>-uhn-ayt)

verb **1** to combine or put together: *It's hard to coordinate the different things I want to do.* **2** to match or go well together: *The colours of your coat and blouse do not coordinate.* **3** to move together smoothly: *When Brent dances he can't coordinate his feet.*

Word building: **coordinate** *noun* **coordination** *noun* **coordinator** *noun*

cop
Informal
noun **1** a member of the police force
verb **2** to get: *He copped a punch on the nose.*
phrase **3 cop it**, to get into trouble
Word building: Other verb forms are **I copped, I have copped, I am copping.**

cope
verb to manage or get on: *How are you coping in your new job?*

copious   (*say* <u>koh</u>-pee-uss)
adjective more than enough: *a copious supply of milk*
Other words: **abundant, ample, plentiful**

copper
noun **1** a fairly soft reddish-brown metal **2** a large container made of copper for boiling dirty clothes
Word building: **copper** *adjective*

copulate
verb to have sexual intercourse
Word building: **copulation** *noun*

copy
noun **1** something which is made the same as something else: *The secretary took my letter and made two copies.* **2** a single example of the same book or magazine
verb **3** to do or make the same as: *Copy me until you've learned the steps.* | *to copy a set of numbers*
Word building: The plural form of the noun is **copies.** | Other verb forms are **I copied, I have copied, I am copying.** | **copier** *noun* a machine for making photocopies

copyright
noun the legal right you have to protect work that you write or compose, and to control who can copy it

coral
noun the hard colourful shapes formed from the skeletons of small sea animals

cord
noun **1** a strong string, not as thick as rope **2** wire, which is protected by cloth or plastic, used to connect electrical goods to a power point **3** a ribbed material, such as corduroy: *He was wearing a jacket of cord.*
Word use: Another name for definition 2 is **flex.**
Word history: from a Greek word meaning 'gut'

cordial
adjective **1** warmly friendly: *a cordial welcome*
noun **2** a fruit-flavoured syrup that you mix with water to make a drink
Word building: **cordiality** *noun*   **cordially** *adverb*

corduroy
noun a cotton material with a pattern of ridges

core
noun the inner or middle part, especially of fruit
Word building: **core** *verb* to remove the core

core/corps Don't confuse **core** with **corps**. A **corps** is a unit of soldiers.

corella   (*say* kuh-<u>rel</u>-uh)
noun an Australian cockatoo whose plumage is mostly white with small areas of red or pink near or on the head

corgi   (*say* <u>kaw</u>-gee)
noun a dog with short legs and a thick body
Word building: The plural is **corgis.**

coriander   (*say* ko-ree-<u>an</u>-duh)
noun a herb with strong-smelling, seedlike fruit and leaves, used in cooking and medicine

cork
noun **1** the bark of a special kind of tree (the cork oak), used for making stoppers for bottles, floats, mats and so on **2** a piece of cork, or similar material (such as rubber), used as a stopper for a bottle **3** a small float used on a fishing line

corkscrew
noun a sharp metal spiral with a handle, for pulling corks out of bottles

corn¹
noun **1** a grain plant that you eat as a vegetable or grind to make flour
verb **2** to preserve by salting: *to corn beef*

corn²
noun a hard painful lump on your toes or other parts of your feet

corner

noun **1** the place where two straight edges meet: *a street corner | the corner of a room | the corners of a table* **2** a place or region: *The travellers come from all the corners of the earth.*
verb **3** to trap: *The dog cornered the cat in a narrow lane.* **4** to turn a corner, especially at speed: *This car corners well.*

Word building: **corner** *adjective*: *a corner shop*

cornet

noun a wind instrument like the trumpet, but smaller

cornflour

noun the fine flour made from rice or maize which is used in cooking, especially to thicken sauces

coronation

noun the crowning of a king or queen

coroner

noun the official who is in charge of a court inquiry into the cause of sudden or unexplained deaths

coronet

noun a small crown

corporal[1]

adjective physical or having to do with your body: *corporal punishment*

corporal[2]

noun a junior officer in the army or air force

corporation

noun a business or other united group of people: *The children's parents formed a corporation to run their own school.*

corps   (*say* kaw)

noun **1** a unit of soldiers **2** a group of people in the same job: *the press corps*

corps/core Don't confuse **corps** with **core**. A **core** is at the inner or middle part of something, like the **core** of an apple.

corpse

noun a dead body, especially of a human being
Other words: **cadaver**

corpse/corps Don't confuse **corpse** with **corps**, which is pronounced to rhyme with *door* and *refers to a unit of soldiers.*

corpuscle   (*say* <u>kaw</u>-puh-suhl)

noun **1** one of the very small particles in the blood, or certain other parts of the body **2** any very small particle

Word building: **corpuscular** *adjective*

correct

verb **1** to remove or point out the mistakes of
adjective **2** free from mistakes
3 acceptable or proper: *correct behaviour*

Word building: **correction** *noun*   **corrective** *adjective*   **correctly** *adverb*   **correctness** *noun*

correspond

verb **1** to match or be similar: *Those figures almost correspond.* **2** to write letters: *We used to correspond every week.*

Word building: **corresponding** *adjective* **correspondingly** *adverb*

correspondence

noun **1** letters **2** similarity: *Is there any correspondence between the two accounts of what happened?*

correspondent

(*say* ko-ruh-<u>spon</u>-duhnt)
noun **1** someone who writes letters
2 a reporter paid to send in articles and news reports from a distant place

corridor

noun a connecting passage in a building

corroboree   (*say* kuh-<u>rob</u>-uh-ree)

noun an Aboriginal dance ceremony which includes singing and rhythmic music. Many people come together for the ceremony in which the dancers are decorated with clay in traditional designs

Word history: from an Aboriginal language of New South Wales called Dharug. See the map of Australian Aboriginal languages at the end of this book.

corrode   (*say* kuh-<u>rohd</u>)

verb to gradually eat away: *Rust had corroded the old car.*

Word building: **corrosion** *noun*   **corrosive** *adjective*

corrugated   (*say* <u>ko</u>-ruh-gayt-uhd)

adjective ridged or bumpy: *The roof was made of corrugated iron.*

Word building: **corrugate** *verb* to wrinkle **corrugation** *noun*

corrupt

adjective **1** dishonest or able to be bribed
verb **2** to make dishonest, especially by
bribery **3** to change from good to bad: *to
corrupt the language*

Word building: **corruptible** *adjective*
corruption *noun*　**corruptly** *adverb*

corset

noun underwear which gives shape or firm
support to the body

Word building: **corsetry** *noun*

cosmetic

adjective meant to improve the look of
your skin and hair: *the cosmetic effect of
lipstick*

Word building: **cosmetic** *noun* a beauty
aid　**cosmetically** *adverb*

cosmic

adjective having to do with the universe:
cosmic laws

Word building: **cosmically** *adverb*
Word history: from a Greek word meaning 'of
the world'

cosmonaut

noun another name for **astronaut**

cosmopolitan

(*say* koz-muh-<u>pol</u>-uh-tuhn)
adjective **1** having people or customs from
many parts of the world: *a cosmopolitan city*
2 feeling at home in many parts of the
world: *a cosmopolitan outlook*

cosmos　(*say* <u>koz</u>-mos)

noun the universe

cost

noun **1** the price to be paid for something
Other words: **expense, charge, fee, outlay**
2 a loss or expense: *The battle was won at
the cost of many lives.*
Other words: **sacrifice**

Word building: **cost** *verb*: *It cost him his life.*

costly

adjective expensive or costing a great deal
Word building: **costliness** *noun*

costume

noun a set of clothes, especially for
dressing up or for a particular purpose:
The actors had very simple costumes. | *a
swimming costume*

cosy

adjective **1** close and friendly: *There was a
cosy atmosphere in the room.*
Other words: **comfortable, inviting, pleasant,
snug, warm**
noun **2** a knitted cover for keeping a teapot
warm

Word building: The plural form of the noun is
cosies. | **cosily** *adverb*　**cosiness** *noun*

cot

noun a child's bed with raised sides

cottage

noun a small one-storey house

cottage cheese

noun a cheese made from curdled skimmed
milk

cotton

noun **1** a light material made from the soft
white hairs covering the seeds of the cotton
plant **2** a thread used for sewing

cottonwool

noun cotton in a soft and fluffy state used
especially for cleaning your skin and
dressing wounds

couch

noun **1** a seat like an long armchair for two
or more people **2** a padded bed without
sides, often used in a doctor's surgery
verb **3** to put into words: *The message is
couched in very difficult language.*

Word building: The plural form of the noun is
couches.

cough　(*rhymes with* off)

noun the noisy blast of air from your lungs
which you get in some illnesses, or when
something is stuck in your throat

Word building: **cough** *verb*

could　(*say* kood)

verb past tense of **can²**

council

noun **1** a group of people that meets
regularly to discuss or decide certain things
2 the government of a small area such as
a city or its suburbs: *She was elected to the
shire council.*

Word building: **councillor** *noun* a member of
a council

counsel

noun **1** advice **2** a lawyer who is paid to give advice to someone in a court case

Word building: **counsel** *verb* (**counselled, counselling**) to advise   **counsellor** *noun* an adviser, especially a psychologist

count[1]

verb **1** to add up: *He counted the trucks as they passed.* **2** to name the numbers: *She had to count up to ten slowly.* **3** to include: *That makes five of us, counting Johann.* **4** to matter: *What you want doesn't count in prison.* *phrase* **5 count on**, to depend on: *The boss is counting on us being on time.*

Word building: **count** *noun*

count[2]

noun a European noble

Word building: **countess** *noun*
Word history: from a Latin word meaning 'companion'

countenance

noun your face or its expression: *a happy countenance*

counter[1]

noun **1** a long shelf or bar where goods are sold or food is eaten **2** something used for keeping count, especially in a game

counter[2]

adverb **1** in the opposite direction
verb **2** to move against: *He countered their plan with strong arguments.*

Word building: **counter** *adjective* opposed

counterfeit   (*say* kown-tuh-feet)

adjective made to imitate or look like, especially to deceive: *counterfeit money*

Word building: **counterfeit** *noun* an imitation   **counterfeit** *verb*   **counterfeiter** *noun*

counterpart

noun one of two people or things which matches or looks like the other

counterterrorism

(*say* kown-tuh-<u>te</u>-ruh-riz-uhm)
noun actions taken by a government to prevent or control terrorism such as keeping up with information about possible attacks, making sure that places that might be attacked are secure, and so on: *Making the airports around the country secure was the first priority in the counterterrorism being planned by the government.*

country

noun **1** an area of land separated from other areas: *Europe is divided into different countries.* **2** the land where someone is born **3** the undeveloped land beyond the towns and cities

Word building: The plural is **countries**. | **countrified** *adjective* looking like a country area

country and western

noun a type of music that started in the southern part of the United States, consisting mainly of country songs played on guitar or fiddle with somebody singing.

Word use: Another word for this is **country music**.

county

noun a large area within a state, bigger than a shire

Word building: The plural is **counties**.

coup   (*rhymes with* boo)

noun a plan carried out suddenly and successfully: *The generals have been in power since the army coup.*

Word use: The 'p' in **coup** is silent because this is a French word.

couple   (*rhymes with* supple)

noun **1** two people, especially if married: *the couple next door* **2** any two things: *a couple of apples*
verb **3** to join or link together: *The carriages had to be coupled before the train could leave.*

Word building: **coupling** *noun*

couplet   (*say* <u>kup</u>-luht)

noun a pair of lines of poetry which rhyme

coupon   (*say* <u>kooh</u>-pon)

noun **1** a ticket or card which you can exchange for goods or money **2** a form which must be filled in to order goods, or enter a competition

courage   (*say* <u>ku</u>-rij)

noun the strength to do or face something you find frightening: *She needed courage to dive off the top diving board.*
Other words: **bravery, daring, nerve, valour**
Word building: **courageous** *adjective* brave   **courageously** *adverb*

courier   (*say* <u>koo</u>-ree-uh)
noun **1** someone who carries messages or parcels for others **2** someone who looks after a group of tourists and their travel arrangements

Word history: from a Latin word meaning 'run'

course   (*rhymes with* horse)
noun **1** one stage of a meal: *We had chicken and vegetables for the main course.*
2 a series, especially of lessons: *I'm doing a course of exercises.* **3** the ground or water on which a race takes place **4** movement or progress: *the ship's course | in the course of the year*
phrase **5 of course**, certainly: *Of course you can come.*

Word building: **course** *verb* to race

> **course/coarse** Don't confuse **course** with **coarse**, which is an adjective. We call someone **coarse** if their behaviour is rude and offensive. We call material **coarse** if it is thick or rough.

court   (*rhymes with* short)
noun **1** the hard ground where games such as tennis and basketball are played **2** the palace of a king or queen and the people who live or work there **3** the place where legal cases and trials are heard
4 a courtyard or space enclosed by walls
verb **5** to try to win love or favour: *The prince courted the beautiful princess.*

Word building: **courtier** *noun* someone who serves the king or queen at court   **courtly** *adjective*: *courtly manners*   **courtship** *noun*

courteous   (*say* <u>ker</u>-tee-uhs)
adjective well-mannered or polite: *a courteous boy | a courteous reply*
Other words: **civil, gracious**

Word building: **courteously** *adverb*

courtesy   (*say* <u>ker</u>-tuh-see)
noun **1** politeness and good manners **2** permission: *The poems are printed by courtesy of the author.*

court martial
noun a court of officers which tries anyone in the armed forces who breaks the military law

Word building: The plural is **courts martial** or **court martials**. | **court-martial** *verb* (**court-martialled, court-martialling**)

courtroom
noun a room in a court in which a legal trial is held

courtyard
noun an area enclosed by walls or buildings

couscous   (*say* <u>koos</u>-koos)
noun small grains made up mostly of semolina but with some flour and salt added

cousin   (*say* <u>kuz</u>-uhn)
noun a son or daughter of your uncle or aunt

cove
noun a small bay or inlet

covenant
noun a solemn promise: *The covenant between coach and players led to good teamwork.*

cover
verb **1** to hide: *I covered my face with my hands.* **2** to lie over or be spread over: *A quilt covered the bed.* **3** to protect: *to be covered by insurance* **4** to include: *This list covers everything we need.* **5** to be enough to pay for: *Ten dollars should cover expenses.* **6** to get news of: *Three reporters were covering the fire.* **7** to travel over: *We covered a long distance today.*
noun **8** something which covers: *a book cover* **9** shelter: *The rabbit ran for cover into its burrow.*

Word building: **coverage** *noun*: *the TV coverage of the football match*   **covering** *noun*: *a light covering of snow*

covet   (*say* <u>kuv</u>-uht)
verb to want very much to have: *John covets that car of yours.*

Word building: **covetous** *adjective* greedy **covetously** *adverb*   **covetousness** *noun*

cow
noun the female of cattle and of some other large animals, such as the whale

coward
noun someone who acts badly or weakly out of fear

Word building: **cowardice** *noun*   **cowardly** *adverb*

cower

verb to draw away in fear: *The puppy was cowering under a table.*

coxswain   (*say* <u>kok</u>-suhn)

noun the person who steers a boat, especially in rowing

Word use: The short form of this is **cox**.

coy

adjective shy, or pretending to be shy

Word building: **coyly** *adverb*   **coyness** *noun*

coyote   (*say* koy-<u>oh</u>-tee, kuy-<u>oh</u>-tee)

noun a North American wild dog which howls at night

CPR

noun a procedure used to save someone's life if they are not breathing and their heart has stopped beating, by breathing into their mouth, and massaging their chest near the heart

Word history: short for *cardiopulmonary resuscitation*

crab

noun a hard-shelled sea animal with eight legs around a flattish body and a large pair of pincers

crack

verb **1** to split, often with a sharp noise: *The glass jug cracked.* **2** to flick with a loud noise: *The jillaroo cracked her whip.* **3** to give up: *At first he would not confess but finally he cracked.* **4** to break into: *The robbers cracked the safe.* **5** to find the answer to: *to crack a code* **6** to tell: *to crack a joke* *noun* **7** a sudden sharp noise **8** the line of a split: *Cracks appeared but the bowl didn't break.* **9** a hard blow: *He gave himself a crack with the hammer.*

Word building: **crack** *adjective* first-rate **cracked** *adjective*

cracker

noun **1** a thin, crisp, unsweetened biscuit **2** a firework **3** a twisted roll of paper with a surprise inside, which explodes when you pull it

Word use: Another name for definition 3 is **bonbon**.

crackle

verb to make a crunching sound: *The dry leaves crackled underfoot.*

Word building: **crackle** *noun*

cradle

noun **1** a baby's small bed, usually on rockers **2** a frame which supports or protects: *The window cleaners were in a cradle halfway up a building.* **3** a box on rockers used to separate gold dust from sand and dirt *verb* **4** to hold or rock, as if in a cradle

craft

noun **1** skilfulness **2** cunning **3** a job or trade needing special skill with your hands **4** a boat or an aircraft

Word use: For definition 4 the plural is **craft**. Word building: **craft** *verb* to make individually   **craftsman** *noun*   **craftsmanship** *noun*

crafty

adjective clever in a tricky or cunning way

Word building: Other forms are **craftier**, **craftiest**. | **craftily** *adverb*   **craftiness** *noun*

crag

noun a steep rock sticking up from a cliff or mountain

Word building: **craggy** *adjective* (**craggier**, **craggiest**)

cram

verb **1** to stuff tightly: *Asha crammed the papers under her bed.* **2** to fill very full, especially with food

Word building: Other forms are **I crammed, I have crammed, I am cramming**.

cramp

noun **1** a sudden painful tightening of a muscle in your body: *a stomach cramp* *verb* **2** to confine or restrict to a small space: *I feel cramped in this tiny office.*

crane

noun **1** a large bird with long legs, neck and bill, which feeds in shallow water **2** a machine with a long moving arm, which can lift and move heavy weights around *verb* **3** to stretch in order to see: *to crane your neck*

crank

noun **1** a bar for winding or levering: *We could use the crank to jack up the car.* **2** an odd person

cranky

adjective bad-tempered or irritable

Word building: Other forms are **crankier,
crankiest**. | **crankily** *adverb* **crankiness** *noun*

cranny

noun a narrow opening, especially in rock

Word building: The plural is **crannies**.

crash

verb **1** to run into or hit noisily: *The car
crashed into the tree.* **2** to fall and smash:
The aeroplane crashed.
noun **3** the noise of breaking or hitting
4 an accident or collision

Word building: The plural form of the noun is
crashes.

crate

noun a large wooden box

crater

noun **1** the cup-shaped opening at the top
of a volcano **2** a round hole in the ground,
like one made by a meteorite or a bomb

Word history: from the Greek word for a bowl
for mixing wine and water

cravat   (*say* kruh-<u>vat</u>)

noun a man's scarf, loosely tied at the
throat

crave

verb to want desperately: *The thirsty jogger
craved a drink.* | *I crave one favour.*

Word building: **craving** *noun*

crawl

verb **1** to go slowly, especially on hands and
knees **2** to flatter or be nice to someone
to gain an advantage: *He is crawling to the
coach so that he'll be chosen for the team.*
noun **3** a crawling movement **4** another
word for the swimming style known as
freestyle

Word use: You can also use **Australian crawl**
for definiton 4.
Word building: **crawler** *noun*

crayfish

noun a hard-shelled freshwater animal
which looks like a small lobster

Word use: Another name for it is **yabby**.
Word building: The plural is **crayfish** or
crayfishes.

crayon

noun a greasy chalk used for drawing and
colouring

craze

verb **1** to madden: *The wind crazed the
horses.*
noun **2** a short-lived fashion: *a craze for
yoyos*

crazy

adjective **1** mad or insane
Other words: **demented, hysterical**
2 odd or irregular: *crazy paving*
Other words: **absurd, strange, unusual**
Word building: Other forms are **crazier,
craziest**. | **crazily** *adverb* **craziness** *noun*

creak

verb to make a squeaking noise: *The floor
boards creaked.*

Word building: **creaky** *adjective*

creak/creek Don't confuse **creak** with **creek**,
which is a small stream.

cream

noun **1** the rich top of milk **2** anything
which is thick and smooth: *face cream*
3 the top or best part: *Only the cream of
athletes go to the Olympic Games.*
adjective **4** having a yellowish white colour

Word building: **creaminess** *noun* **creamy**
adjective

crease

noun a sharp line or fold, especially in
material or paper

Word building: **crease** *verb* to fold or
wrinkle **creased** *adjective*

create   (*say* kree-<u>ayt</u>)

verb **1** to make or invent
2 to make into: *He was created a knight.*

Word building: **creative** *adjective* good at
making or inventing things **creatively**
adverb **creativity** *noun* **creator** *noun*

creation   (*say* kree-<u>ay</u>-shuhn)

noun **1** something which has been made or
invented **2** the act of creating

creature   (*say* <u>kree</u>-chuh)

noun any living thing: *Noah took two of
every creature onto the ark.*

creche   (*say* kraysh, kresh)

noun a nursery for babies and young
children

Word history: from a German word meaning
'crib'

credit

noun **1** praise or approval: *Give me credit for trying.* **2** trust or belief: *I don't put much credit in their promise to pay.* **3** the amount someone is allowed to spend or borrow: *How much credit do I have?* **4** money paid into an account
verb **5** to believe: *Yumiko was so surprised she couldn't credit what she heard.* **6** to enter on the credit side of an account
phrase **7 on credit**, with agreement to pay later

Word use: Compare definitions 4 and 6 with **debit**. | Compare definition 7 with **cash**. | Someone you owe money to is your **creditor** and someone who owes you money is your **debtor**.
Word building: Other verb forms are **I credited, I have credited, I am crediting**. | **creditable** *adjective* something which brings praise **creditably** *adverb*

credit card

noun a plastic card which is used to make a record of what someone owes when they buy something but don't pay cash

creed

noun a statement of belief

creek

noun a small stream

creek/creak Don't confuse **creek** with **creak**, which is a sharp, rough or squeaking sound. To **creak** is to make this sound.

creep

verb **1** to go very slowly and quietly: *She crept out of the house so as not to wake anyone.* **2** to crawl along the ground
noun **3** *Informal* an unpleasant person: *He's a real creep.*
phrase **4 the creeps**, *Informal* a feeling of fear or disgust

Word building: Other verb forms are **I crept, I have crept, I am creeping**. | **creepy** *adjective* frightening or unpleasant **creepiness** *noun*

creeper

noun a plant which climbs walls or grows along the ground

cremate

verb to burn to ashes: *Before he died, the old man requested that his body be cremated.*

Word building: **crematorium** *noun* the place where bodies are burnt **cremation** *noun*

crepe   (*rhymes with* grape)

noun **1** a light crinkled material made of cotton or silk **2** a finely wrinkled paper **3** a thin pancake

crescendo   (*say* kruh-<u>shen</u>-doh)

adverb gradually increasing in force or loudness

Word use: This is an instruction in music.

crescent   (*say* <u>krez</u>-uhnt)

noun **1** the curved shape of the moon when it is still new **2** anything with a similar shape, especially a curved street

Word use: When definition 2 is the name of a street, you spell it with a capital letter and its abbreviation is **Cres**.

cress

noun a fast-growing herb whose leaves are used in salads

crest

noun **1** the feathers or growth on the top of the heads of some birds **2** the very top of anything: *on the crest of success* **3** part of a coat of arms which is used as a badge: *Their blazer pockets were embroidered with the school crest.*

Word building: **crest** *verb* to reach the top of **crested** *adjective*

crestfallen

adjective disappointed or sad: *He looks quite crestfallen at missing the train.*

crevasse   (*say* kruh-<u>vas</u>)

noun a deep crack in a glacier or river of ice

crevice   (*say* <u>krev</u>-uhs)

noun a crack forming an opening: *a crevice in a rock*

crew

noun a group of people who work together, such as on a ship or aeroplane

Word building: **crew** *verb*: *to crew a boat*

crib

noun **1** a baby's cot **2** a box or rack used to hold food for cattle and horses

cricket[1]

noun a leaping insect, similar to a grasshopper, which makes a loud noise by rubbing its wings on its abdomen

Word history: from a French word that imitates the sound these insects make

cricket²

noun a team game played with ball, bat and wickets

Word building: **cricketer** *noun*
Word history: from a French word meaning 'stick'

crime

noun **1** an act which breaks the law **2** the breaking of laws: *Crime is a serious problem in most cities.*

criminal

adjective having to do with crime: *criminal activities*

Word building: **criminal** *noun* someone who is guilty of a crime   **criminally** *adverb*

crimp

verb to make curly: *to crimp hair*

crimson

adjective deep, purplish-red

Word building: **crimson** *verb* to become crimson, often when you blush   **crimson** *noun*

cringe

verb to bend or bow down in fear
Other words: **cower, quail**

crinkle

verb to wrinkle or crease: *The clown's face crinkled with laughter.*

Word building: **crinkle** *noun*   **crinkly** *adjective*

cripple

noun **1** someone who has lost the use of one or more limbs
verb **2** to damage or make lame

crisis

noun **1** a time of danger or trouble **2** a turning point, especially in the course of an illness

Word building: The plural is **crises** (*say* <u>kruy</u>-seez).

crisp

adjective **1** hard, dry and easily broken: *crisp biscuits*
Other words: **brittle, crunchy**
2 cool, dry and fresh: *crisp air*
Other words: **chilly, nippy**
3 clean and neat: *a crisp uniform*
noun **4** another word for **chip** (def. 3)

Word building: **crispy** *adjective* (**crispier, crispiest**)   **crispness** *noun*

criterion   (*say* kruyt-<u>ear</u>-ree-uhn)

noun a standard or rule for testing something

Word building: The plural is **criteria**.

critic

noun **1** someone who is a judge of quality or excellence: *The newspaper's literary critic praised the author's latest novel.* **2** someone who finds fault

critical

adjective **1** likely to find fault **2** having to do with a crisis: *He kept calm at the critical moment.*

Word use: For definition 2, the more usual word is **crucial**.
Word building: **critically** *adverb*: *critically ill*

critically endangered species

noun a species of plant or animal that faces a very high risk of dying out in the wild very soon

Word use: Compare this with **endangered species** and **vulnerable species**.

criticise   (*say* <u>krit</u>-uh-suyz)

verb to find fault with: *to criticise someone's manners*

Word use: Another spelling is **criticize**.
Word building: **criticism** *noun*

croak

verb to make a low hoarse sound: *The frogs croaked in the pond.*

Word building: **croaky** *adjective*

crockery

noun cups, plates, dishes and similar articles made of china or pottery
Other words: **china**

crocodile

noun a large lizard-like reptile found living in the waters of tropical countries

Word history: from a Greek word meaning 'lizard'

cronyism   (*say* <u>kroh</u>-nee-iz-uhm)

noun giving jobs to people unfairly, based on whether they are friends instead of whether they are suitable for the job: *Giving that plum job to his old mate was pure cronyism and he'll be sorry later — his mate's a fool!*

crook

noun **1** a bent or curved part: *the crook of your elbow* **2** a stick with a bend or curve at one end: *a shepherd's crook* **3** *Informal* a dishonest person
adjective **4** *Informal* sick: *I feel crook.*
5 *Informal* unpleasant: *Scrubbing floors is a crook job.*

Word building: **crook** *verb* to bend or curve: *to crook your finger*

crooked   (*say* krook-uhd)

adjective **1** bent: *a crooked stick* **2** *Informal* dishonest

croon

verb to sing in a soft or sentimental way

Word building: **crooner** *noun*

crop

noun **1** products grown in the ground: *a good wheat crop | a crop of apples* **2** a short whip used by horse riders
verb **3** to cut short: *to crop a horse's tail*
phrase **4 crop up**, to come as a surprise: *a problem cropped up*

Word building: Other verb forms are **I cropped, I have cropped, I am cropping.**

croquet   (*say* kroh-kay)

noun a game played by hitting wooden balls with mallets through metal arches set in a lawn

cross

noun **1** anything in the shape made by two lines going through each other such as '+' or '×' **2** the result of mixing breeds of animals or plants: *My dog is a cross between a terrier and a beagle.*
verb **3** to draw a line across: *to cross a cheque* **4** to form a cross with: *cross your fingers* **5** to pass in the way of: *He crossed my path.* **6** to go from one side of to another: *The bridge crosses the river.*
adjective **7** lying or passing across: *a cross wind* **8** annoyed: *My aunt was cross with me.*
phrase **9 cross out**, to draw a line through

Word building: **crossly** *adverb*   **crossness** *noun*

cross-country

noun a running race which is run across fields, parks and so on and not on a prepared track

cross-examine

verb to question in order to check the truth of something already stated

Word building: **cross-examination** *noun* **cross-examiner** *noun*

crossing

noun **1** a moving across: *The first crossing of the Blue Mountains by whites took place in 1813.* **2** a place where a road, river or railway line can be crossed

crotch

noun a piece or part that forms a fork, such as the human body or a pair of trousers where the two legs join

crotchet   (*say* krot-chuht)

noun a musical note equal to the time of one beat

crotchety

adjective bad-tempered or irritable

crouch

verb to bend your knees and lean forward: *I crouched behind the shrub to hide myself.*

Word building: **crouch** *noun*

croupier   (*say* krooh-pee-uh)

noun someone who takes and pays out the money at a gambling table

crow[1]

noun a black shiny bird with a rough-sounding call

crow[2]

verb **1** to make the sound of a rooster **2** to boast

Word building: Other forms are **it crowed** or (for definition 1) **crew, it has crowed, it is crowing.**

crowbar

noun an iron bar used as a lever or to break hard ground

crowd

noun **1** a large number of people or things gathered closely together
verb **2** to gather in large numbers: *Children crowded around the clown.* **3** to squeeze or push: *They crowded into the room.*

Word building: **crowded** *adjective*

crown
noun **1** an ornament made of gold and jewels worn on the head of a king or queen **2** the top or highest part: *the crown of your head*
verb **3** to put a crown on: *The Archbishop crowned the new queen.* **4** to honour or reward: *Success crowned my efforts.*

crucial   (*say* krooh-shuhl)
adjective of greatest importance: *a crucial decision*

cruciate ligament   (*say* krooh-shee-uht lig-uh-muhnt)
noun one of two bands of tissue connecting the bone above the knee with a bone below the knee and making the knee stable: *He has torn his cruciate ligament and can't play for the rest of the season.*

crucifix   (*say* krooh-suh-fiks)
noun a cross with the figure of Jesus on it, or any cross
Word history: from a Latin word meaning 'fixed to a cross'

crucify   (*say* krooh-suh-fuy)
verb to put to death by nailing to a cross
Word building: **crucifixion** *noun*

crude
adjective **1** in a natural state: *crude oil* **2** rude and not in good taste: *a crude joke* **3** not carefully done: *a crude drawing*
Word building: **crudely** *adverb*   **crudeness** *noun*   **crudity** *noun*

crude oil
noun oil as it is found in nature, usually brown or black, often together with natural gas which forms a cap above it and salty water which collects underneath

cruel
adjective liking or likely to cause pain: *a cruel person* | *a cruel remark*
Other words: **brutal, callous, inhumane, merciless, ruthless, unfeeling**
Word building: **cruelly** *adverb*   **cruelty** *noun*

cruet   (*say* krooh-uht)
noun a set of small containers for salt, pepper and mustard

cruise
verb **1** to sail from place to place: *The battleship cruised in enemy waters.* **2** to travel at a moderate speed
noun **3** a holiday on a ship
Word building: **cruiser** *noun*

cruise ship
noun a large ship on which people take a holiday and sail in a leisurely way from place to place

cruisy   (*say* krooh-zee)
adjective Informal easy to do: *The maths test was cruisy — I think I might have passed.*

crumb
noun **1** a small piece of bread, cake or other dry food
verb **2** to break into crumbs **3** to coat with crumbs: *to crumb steak*

crumble
verb to break into small pieces: *I crumbled the cake.* | *The wall was crumbling with age.*
Word building: **crumbly** *adjective*

crumpet
noun a kind of flat cake, eaten toasted and buttered

crumple
verb **1** to crush into wrinkles: *I crumpled the paper in my hands.* **2** to break down or collapse: *Chandra's face crumpled into tears.* | *The building crumpled after the blast.*

crunch
verb to crush or grind noisily
Word building: **crunchy** *adjective* (**crunchier, crunchiest**) making a crunching sound when eaten

crusade
noun a strong movement of support: *a crusade to save the park*
Word building: **crusade** *verb*   **crusader** *noun*

crush
verb **1** to press together between hard surfaces **2** to break into small pieces: *to crush rocks* **3** to defeat totally: *to crush a rebellion*
noun **4** a strong liking which often doesn't last long: *to have a crush on a film star*

crust
noun **1** the outside surface of bread or a piece of it **2** any hard outer surface
Word building: **crusty** *adjective* (**crustier, crustiest**)

crustacean (*say* krus-<u>tay</u>-shuhn)
noun a type of animal, such as a crab or crayfish, with a hard shell instead of a skeleton, and which usually lives in water

crutch
noun a stick which fits under the arm to help an injured person walk

cry
verb **1** to shed tears
Other words: **bawl, blubber, sob, wail, weep, whimper**
2 to shout: *We cried for help.*
Other words: **bellow, call, scream, shriek, yell**
noun **3** a fit of weeping **4** a shout: *A great cry went up.*
Other words: **howl, roar, scream, shriek, wail, yelp**
Word building: Other verb forms are **I cried, I have cried, I am crying.** | The plural form of the noun is **cries.**

crypt (*say* kript)
noun an underground room under a church, often used as a burial place
Word history: from a Greek word meaning 'hidden'

cryptic (*say* <u>krip</u>-tik)
adjective mysterious, or difficult to understand: *a cryptic message*
Word building: **cryptically** *adverb*

crystal
noun **1** a clear mineral which looks like ice **2** a single grain or piece of this **3** clear sparkling glass
Word building: **crystal** *adjective*: *a crystal bowl*   **crystalline** *adjective*

crystallise
verb **1** to form into crystals **2** to coat with sugar
Word use: Another spelling is **crystallize.**
Word building: **crystallisation** *noun*

cub
noun **1** the young of certain animals such as the lion and bear **2** a junior **scout** (def. 2)
Word use: Definition 2 is sometimes spelt with a capital letter.

cubbyhouse
noun a child's playhouse

cube
noun **1** a solid shape with six equal square sides **2** the result of multiplying a number by itself twice: *The cube of 3 is 3 × 3 × 3, or 27.*
Word building: **cubic** *adjective*

cube root
noun the number which, when multiplied by itself twice, gives the cube: *The cube root of 27 is 3.*

cubicle
noun a partly enclosed small space: *a toilet cubicle*

cuckoo (*say* <u>koo</u>-kooh)
noun a bird which is known for its habit of laying its eggs in the nests of other birds

cucumber
noun a long, thin vegetable which is used in salads

cud
noun food which cattle and some other animals return from their first stomach to chew a second time

cuddle
verb to hug gently
Word building: **cuddle** *noun*   **cuddly** *adjective*

cudgel
noun a short thick stick used as a weapon
Word building: **cudgel** *verb* (**cudgelled, cudgelling**)

cue¹
noun anything said or done as a signal for what follows, especially in a play: *The ringing of a bell was my cue to enter.*
Word building: **cue** *verb* (**cued, cueing**)

---

cue/queue Don't confuse **cue** with **queue**, which is a line of people or cars waiting in turn.

---

cue²
noun a long stick used to hit the ball in billiards and other similar games
Word building: **cue** *verb* (**cued, cueing**)

cuff¹
noun **1** a band or fold at the wrist of a sleeve **2** a part turned up at the end of a trouser leg

cuff²
verb to hit with your open hand

cul-de-sac
noun a short street which is closed at one end

cull
verb to pick out or choose the best from: *to cull ideas or information*

Word building: **cull** *noun*

culminate
verb to reach the highest point: *Our efforts culminated in success.*

Word building: **culmination** *noun*

culottes
plural noun trousers which are cut wide to look like a skirt

culprit
noun someone who has done something wrong: *After he broke the shop window the culprit ran away.*

cult
noun **1** a religion **2** a strong, almost religious devotion to a person or thing: *the cult of jogging*

cultivate
verb **1** to dig the soil for planting and growing: *Our family has cultivated the land here for a hundred years.*
Other words: **till**
2 to grow plants: *Mum is cultivating some native shrubs in our back garden.*
3 to develop or improve: *to cultivate the mind*

Word building: **cultivated** *adjective* **cultivation** *noun* **cultivator** *noun*

culture
noun skills, arts, beliefs and customs passed on from one generation to another: *the culture of Japan*

Word building: **cultural** *adjective*: *cultural achievements*

cumbersome
adjective awkward to handle: *a cumbersome parcel*

cumquat   (*say* <u>kum</u>-kwot)
noun a fruit like a small mandarin but much sourer

Word use: Another spelling is **kumquat**.
Word history: from a Chinese word meaning 'gold orange'

cumulus   (*say* <u>kyooh</u>-myuh-luhs)
noun a cloud, usually white, which is flat at the bottom and has round heaps at the top

Word building: The plural is **cumuli**.

cuneiform   (*say* <u>kyooh</u>-nuh-fawm)
adjective **1** wedge-shaped
noun **2** characters used in writing in ancient Persia and some nearby countries

cunning
noun skill used in a clever plan, or in tricking other people

Word building: **cunning** *adjective* **cunningly** *adverb*

cup
noun **1** a small container with a handle on the side used for drinking **2** an ornamental bowl, usually of silver or gold, given as a prize
verb **3** to form into the shape of a cup: *to cup your hands*

Word building: Other verb forms are **I cupped, I have cupped, I am cupping**.

cupboard   (*say* <u>kub</u>-uhd)
noun a piece of furniture or a built-in space with doors, used for storing things

curate   (*say* <u>kyooh</u>-ruht)
noun a member of the clergy who helps a rector or vicar

Word building: **curacy** *noun* the position of a curate

curator   (*say* kyooh-<u>ray</u>-tuh)
noun someone who looks after a museum, art gallery or similar kind of collection

curb
verb to control or hold back: *Curb your temper.*

Word building: **curb** *noun*

curd
noun a jelly-like substance formed in milk which has been treated with an acid, eaten fresh or used to make cheese

curdle
verb to form into curd: *I curdled the custard by accidentally letting it boil. | The milk curdled on the hot day.*

cure
noun **1** a medicine or treatment which gets rid of an illness or disability
verb **2** to bring back to good health
3 to treat so as to preserve or finish properly: *to cure meat | to cure concrete*

Word building: **curable** *adjective* **curative** *adjective*

curfew

noun an order which says people are not allowed to be out on the streets after a certain time at night

curious

adjective **1** wanting to learn: *to be curious about butterflies*
Other words: **inquiring, inquisitive, interested, questioning**
2 interesting because strange or new: *a curious custom*
Other words: **bizarre, extraordinary, odd, peculiar, unusual, weird**

Word building: **curiosity** *noun* **curiously** *adverb*

curl

noun **1** a small ring of hair **2** a curved or twisted shape: *There were curls of chocolate on the cake.*

Word building: **curl** *verb*: *The vine curled round the tree.* **curly** *adjective* (**curlier, curliest**)

curlew (*say* <u>ker</u>-lyooh)

noun a type of long-legged bird that lives near the shore

currant

noun a small, dried, seedless grape

currant/current Don't confuse **currant** with **current**. A thing is **current** if it belongs to the present. A **current** is also a flow or movement.

currawong

noun a large black-and-white or greyish Australian bird with a large pointed bill and a loud ringing call

Word history: probably from an Aboriginal language of Queensland called Yagara. See the map of Australian Aboriginal languages at the end of this book.

currency

noun money in current use in a country

current

adjective **1** belonging to the present: *current problems*
noun **2** a flow or movement: *a strong current in the river | a current of air from a fan | a current of electricity*

curriculum (*say* kuh-<u>rik</u>-yuh-luhm)

noun a set of courses of study: *the school curriculum*

Word building: The plural is **curriculums** or **curricula**.

curry[1]

noun a spicy sauce or dish of meat and vegetables which tastes hot

Word building: The plural is **curries**. | **curry** *verb* (**curried, currying**) to prepare with this sauce

curry[2]

verb to rub with a brush or comb to clean: *to curry a horse*

Word building: Other forms are **I curried, I have curried, I am currying**.

curse

noun **1** a wish that evil will happen to someone: *to put a curse on someone*
2 a swear word or blasphemy: *to utter a curse*

Word building: **curse** *verb* **cursed** *adjective*

cursive

adjective describing a style of writing or print with the letters joined together

cursor

noun **1** the sliding part of a measuring tool **2** a moving dot, arrow or line on a computer video screen showing you where the next words you key in will appear

curt

adjective rudely brief in speech or manner: *He gave me a curt nod.*

Word building: **curtly** *adverb* **curtness** *noun*

curtail

verb to cut short: *We had to curtail our holiday.*

Word building: **curtailment** *noun*

curtain

noun a piece of material hanging from a rod over a window or across the front of a stage

Word building: **curtain** *verb*

curtsy

noun a respectful bow, usually made by a woman bending her knees with one foot in front of the other

Word building: The plural is **curtsies**. | **curtsy** *verb* (**curtsied, curtsying**)

curve

noun a bending line or shape with no angles: *a curve in a road | the curves of the letter 'S'*

Word building: **curvature** *noun* **curve** *verb* **curvy** *adjective*

cuscus

noun a small furry animal like a possum, which has a long tail and lives in New Guinea and northern Queensland

cushion

noun **1** a soft pad used to sit on, or lean against, especially on a chair
verb **2** to place on a cushion **3** to lessen the force or effect of: *Thick bushes cushioned the fall.*

custard

noun a food made of milk, eggs and sugar and eaten as a dessert

custody

noun **1** keeping or care: *The family jewels are in safe custody at the bank.*
2 imprisonment: *The policeman took the suspect into custody.*
Word building: **custodial** *adjective* **custodian** *noun*

custom

noun **1** habit or usual practice **2 customs**, a tax paid on goods brought into the country

customary

adjective usual or according to custom
Word building: **customarily** *adverb*

custom-built

adjective made in the way you ordered

customer

noun someone who buys goods from other people

cut

verb **1** to make an opening in with something sharp: *to cut your finger* **2** to separate or make shorter with something sharp: *to cut a string* **3** to cross: *One line cut another at right angles.* | *The river rose and cut the road.* **4** to lower: *to cut prices* **5** to be able to cut: *This knife cuts well.*
noun **6** the result of cutting or a piece cut off: *a cut on your leg* | *a cut of meat* **7** a reduction or lowering: *a cut in the price*
phrase **8 cut off**, to stop: *He cut me off before I finished speaking.*
Word building: Other verb forms are **I cut, I have cut, I am cutting.**

cute   (*say* kyooht)

adjective *Informal* very pretty or sweet: *a cute child* | *a cute party dress*
Word building: **cutely** *adverb* **cuteness** *noun*

cuticle

noun the skin around the edges of a finger nail or toe nail

cutlass

noun a short, heavy, slightly curved sword

cutlery

noun the knives, forks and spoons used for eating

cutlet

noun a small cut of meat, usually lamb or veal, that contains a rib

cyanide

noun a very poisonous salt

cyber attack   (*say* suy-buhr uh-tak)

noun an attack on telecommunications or a computer network: *You could cripple the city with a cyber attack because transport would be in chaos.*

cybersecurity

(*say* suy-buh-suh-kyooh-ruh-tee)
noun protection put in place for an information system like a computer or a telecommunications network

cyberspace   (*say* suy-buh-spays)

noun an imaginary place holding all the information that travels between all the world's computer systems: *I guess that lost email is out there somewhere in cyberspace!*

cycle

noun **1** a series of events happening in a regular repeating order: *the cycle of the seasons* **2** a bicycle
Word building: **cycle** *verb* to ride a bicycle **cyclic** *adjective* occurring in cycles **cyclist** *noun*
Word history: from a Greek word meaning 'ring' or 'circle'

cyclone

noun a tropical storm with strong winds
Word building: **cyclonic** *adjective*
Word history: from a Greek word meaning 'moving in a circle'

cygnet   (*say* sig-nuht)

noun a young swan

cylinder

noun **1** a tube-shaped object, either hollow or solid, with perfectly circular ends
2 the part of an engine in which the piston moves

Word building: **cylindrical** *adjective* shaped like a cylinder

cymbal

noun one of a pair of curved brass plates which are struck together to make a sharp, musical, ringing sound

Word building: **cymbalist** *noun*

cynic

noun someone who does not believe in the goodness of people or events and is often scornful of them

Word building: **cynical** *adjective* **cynicism** *noun*

cypress

noun an evergreen cone-bearing tree with dark overlapping leaves

cyst   (*say* sist)

noun a small growth that appears in your body or under your skin, often containing liquid

Word building: **cystic** *adjective*

Dd

dab
> *verb* **1** to put on gently: *Amin dabbed a little cream on his burn.*
> *noun* **2** a small amount: *a dab of lipstick*
> Word building: Other verb forms are **I dabbed, I have dabbed, I am dabbing**.

dabble
> *verb* **1** to splash in water: *to dabble your toes*
> *phrase* **2 dabble in,** to do as a hobby: *to dabble in painting*
> Word building: **dabbler** *noun*

dachshund (*say* <u>daks</u>-uhnd)
> *noun* a small dog with a long body and very short legs
> Word history: from the German words for 'badger' and 'dog'

dad
> *noun* an informal word for **father**

daddy
> *noun* an informal word for **father**

daddy-long-legs
> *noun* a small spider with long, very thin legs
> Word use: The plural form is the same as the singular.

daffodil (*say* <u>daf</u>-uh-dil)
> *noun* a plant which has yellow, bell-shaped flowers in spring

daft (*say* dahft)
> *adjective* foolish or slightly mad
> Word building: **daftly** *adverb* **daftness** *noun*

dagger
> *noun* a weapon with a short pointed blade for stabbing

daily
> *adjective* done or happening every day: *our daily chores*
> Word building: **daily** *adverb*

dainty
> *adjective* small and delicate: *to take dainty steps*
> Word building: Other forms are **daintier, daintiest.** | **daintily** *adverb* **daintiness** *noun*

dairy
> *noun* **1** a cool place where milk and cream are stored and made into butter and cheese **2** the place on a farm where cows are milked
> Word building: The plural is **dairies.** | **dairy** *adjective*: *dairy products*

> **dairy/diary** Don't confuse **dairy** with **diary**, which is a book in which you write what happens each day.

dais (*say* <u>day</u>-uhs)
> *noun* a raised platform at the end of a hall, for a speaker's desk and microphone

daisy
> *noun* a common plant which has white or brightly coloured flowers with many petals surrounding a yellow centre
> Word building: The plural is **daisies.**
> Word history: from an Old English word meaning 'day's eye'

daks

noun Informal pants: *My daks were covered in mud after being on the dirt bike all day.*

Dalai Lama

noun the spiritual and political leader of the Tibetan people

dam¹

noun **1** a lot of water held back by a strong wall built across a river
Other words: **reservoir, weir**
2 the wall itself **3** a waterhole dug out of the ground on a farm

Word building: **dam** *verb* (**dammed, damming**) to hold back: *They dammed the river to provide water for the town.*

dam²

noun a horse's mother

damage   (*say* dam-ij)

verb **1** to harm or injure
Other words: **hurt, mar, spoil**
noun **2** harm or injury **3 damages**, money that a court says you should get to make up for an injury or loss: *The court awarded her damages of a million dollars.*
Other words: **compensation, recompense**

Word building: **damageable** *adjective*

damage control

noun the things that are done to try and control damage that is caused by some disaster, either when it occurs or afterwards: *The fire brigade went straight into damage control.*

dame

noun **1 Dame,** the title used to address a woman of high rank: *Dame of the Order of Australia* **2** *Informal* a woman: *There were no dames at the party.*

Word use: Definition 2 is used mainly in America and may offend people.

damn   (*rhymes with* ham)

verb **1** to wish extreme suffering and misery upon: *You will be damned for your evil deeds.*
interjection **2** an expression of anger or annoyance, as in *'Damn! I've missed the last train.'*

Word use: The use of definition 2 may offend some people.
Word building: **damnation** *noun* everlasting punishment in hell

damned   (*say* damd)

adjective **1** condemned to punishment in hell: *a damned soul* **2** *Informal* very great: *She's a damned nuisance.*
adverb **3** *Informal* very or extremely: *She's damned late.*

Word use: Definitions 2 and 3 are used by some people to express strong feeling.

damp

adjective slightly wet or moist

Word building: **dampen** *verb* to moisten
damp *noun*   **damply** *adverb*   **dampness** *noun*

damper

noun bread made from flour and water mixed to make a dough and baked in the coals of an open fire

dance

noun **1** a series of rhythmical steps, usually performed in time to music **2** a party for dancing: *A new band played at the dance on Saturday.*

Word building: **dance** *verb*: *to dance a waltz*   **dancer** *noun*

dance music

noun a type of modern electronic music written for dancing to

dandelion   (*say* dan-dee-luy-uhn)

noun a wild plant with bright yellow flowers which form light downy balls when they go to seed

Word history: from French words meaning 'lion's tooth' (the leaves look like teeth)

dandruff

noun small white flakes of dead skin from your scalp

danger

noun **1** a possible cause of harm or injury: *A careless driver is a danger on the road.*
Other words: **hazard, menace, peril, risk, threat**
2 a situation in which harm or injury may happen: *When the volcano erupted the people were in great danger.*
Other words: **jeopardy, peril, risk**

Word building: **dangerous** *adjective*: *a dangerous weapon*   **endangered** *adjective* put in danger: *an endangered species*   **dangerously** *adverb*   **dangerousness** *noun*

dangle

verb to hang so as to swing to and fro

dank

adjective unpleasantly damp or moist: *a dank cave*

Word building: **dankly** *adverb*   **dankness** *noun*

dapper

adjective neat and smart

dappled

verb marked with spots or patches: *We dozed in the dappled sunlight under the leafy oak tree.* | *My pony is a dappled grey colour.*

Word building: **dapple** *verb*

dare (*rhymes with* pair)

verb **1** to be bold or courageous enough: *The babysitter was so strict that nobody dared to speak.* **2** to challenge: *I dare you to jump off the roof.*

noun **3** a challenge to do something risky

Word building: Other verb forms are **I dared, I have dared, I am daring.** | **daring** *adjective* bold and adventurous   **daringly** *adverb*

daredevil

noun someone who is very daring or reckless

dark

adjective **1** with very little or no light: *the dark cave*

Other words: **dim, dusky**

2 more like black than white: *a dark colour* **3** angry-looking or gloomy: *He gave us a dark look.*

Other words: **cross, furious**

noun **4** absence of light: *My little brother is afraid of the dark.* **5** night: *Please come home before dark.*

Word building: **darken** *verb* to make or become dark   **darkly** *adverb*   **darkness** *noun*

darkroom

noun a room which is sealed so that no light can get in, used for developing and printing film

darling

noun someone who is loved very much: *Our new baby is a darling.*

Word building: **darling** *adjective*

darn

verb to mend with crossing rows of stitches: *to darn a hole in my socks*

Word building: **darn** *noun* a darned patch in clothing

dart

noun **1** a small metal arrow which is thrown by hand, usually as part of a game or sport

verb **2** to move suddenly or quickly

dash

verb **1** to rush or move quickly: *to dash across the road* **2** to throw or smash violently: *to dash a cup to the floor*

Other words: **cast, fling, hurl, pitch**

3 to spoil or ruin: *to dash someone's hopes*

Other words: **crush, foil, thwart**

noun **4** a sudden or speedy rush: *a dash for the door*

Other words: **race, run, sprint**

5 a small amount: *a dash of salt*

Other words: **bit, dab, drop, pinch, trace**

6 a horizontal line (—) used as punctuation to show a break in a sentence

phrase **7 dash off**, to write or make quickly: *to dash off a letter*

Word building: The plural form of the noun is **dashes.**

Dashes (definition 6) are punctuation marks which are used:

1 to mark off a part of a sentence which may not be necessary, but which explains the topic further or adds interest to it. In this case, dashes work the same way as commas or brackets:

The fashion parade lasted so long — about three hours — that Prince Charles fell asleep.

2 to show an abrupt break or pause in the structure of a sentence:

And suddenly, at the end of the film she — but I won't spoil it for you by telling you the ending.

3 instead of colons at the beginning of an informal list:

He emptied out the contents of his pencil case — a rubber, two pencils, a pencil sharpener and a stapler.

---

dashboard

noun the panel in a car or plane which is in front of the driver's seat and has instruments for measuring things like speed, the distance you have travelled and the temperature of the engine

Word use: A shortened form is **dash**.

dashing

adjective smartly dressed and high-spirited: *a dashing young man*

Word building: **dashingly** *adverb*

data (*say* <u>day</u>-tuh, <u>dah</u>-tuh)

plural noun facts or information: *to gather data for a report on schools in Australia*

Word use: You can use either a singular or plural verb with **data**: *Your data is incorrect* or *Your data are incorrect.*
Word building: The singular form is **datum.**

database

noun a collection of data stored in a computer

date¹

noun **1** the day or year of something happening, or a statement of it in numbers: *What's the date of Easter next year?* | *Today's date is the 29th.* **2** the period of time to which something belongs: *This old coin is valuable because of its early date.* **3** an appointment made for a particular time or someone with whom you have an appointment: *a date with the dentist* | *Do you have a date for the dance on Saturday?* *verb* **4** to mark with a date: *to date a letter* **5** to belong to a particular time: *This vase dates from 50 BC.* **6** to go out with your girlfriend or boyfriend
phrase **7 out of date**, old-fashioned: *The dress I bought last year is already out of date.*

Word building: **dated** *adjective* old-fashioned
Word history: from Latin words meaning 'things given'

date²

noun the small brown fruit that grows on the date palm tree, which tastes very sweet and is often dried for eating

daub (*say* dawb)

verb to cover or coat, especially with something soft or sticky like paint or mud: *to daub a canvas with paint*

Word building: **daub** *noun* sticky clay or mud: *a hut made of wattle and daub*

daughter (*say* <u>daw</u>-tuh)

noun someone's female child: *My parents have two daughters.*

daughter-in-law

noun the wife of your son

Word building: The plural is **daughters-in-law.**

daunt (*say* dawnt)

verb to discourage or make frightened: *We're not daunted by the rain.*

Word building: **daunting** *adjective*
Word history: from a Latin word meaning 'tame' or 'subdue'

dawdle

verb to waste time by being slow: *to dawdle on your way home*

Word building: **dawdler** *noun*

dawn

noun **1** the time of day when it begins to get light
Other words: **sunrise**
2 the beginning of anything: *the dawn of civilisation*
Other words: **outset, start**
verb **3** to begin: *A new day has dawned.*
Other words: **commence, start**
phrase **4 dawn on,** to begin to be understood by: *It finally dawned on her that she needs to practise.*

day

noun **1** the time between sunrise and sunset when the sky is light **2** the 24 hour period between midnight of one day and the following midnight: *There are seven days in a week.* **3** the time when you are actively doing things: *Have you had a good day?* **4** a particular time or period: *There was no television in my grandmother's day.*

Word use: Definition 4 can also be used in the plural form as in *the olden days.*

day care

noun a place where you can go during the day where people look after you: *My little brother isn't old enough to come to school yet, so he goes to day care.*

daydream

verb to dreamily imagine pleasant things: *I often daydream about horses.*

Word building: **daydream** *noun*   **daydreamer** *noun*

daylight saving

noun a system of putting the clock forward by one or more hours during the summer months so as to add more hours of daylight to the time that most people are awake: *6 o'clock in standard time becomes 7 o'clock in daylight saving.*

Word use: Another name is **summertime.**

daze

verb to stun, confuse or bewilder: *dazed by a knock on the head* | *dazed by success*

Word building: **daze** *noun*: *to be in a daze*
dazedly *adverb*

dazzle

verb **1** to make blind by a sudden intense brightness **2** to amaze or surprise: *The children dazzled the audience with their display of gymnastics.*

Word building: **dazzling** *adjective*

de-

prefix a word part meaning 'removal', or expressing the opposite of something positive: *demerit* | *demote*

Word history: from Latin

deacon   (*say* dee-kuhn)

noun someone who assists a priest and has certain duties in the Christian Church

Word building: **deaconess** *noun*

dead

adjective **1** of a person, no longer alive
Other words: **deceased, departed, late**
2 of things, no longer alive or useful: *dead leaves* | *a dead match* **3** numb or unable to feel anything: *to be dead to pain after an anaesthetic*
Other words: **insensitive**
4 very tired or exhausted: *She felt dead after chopping wood all day.* **5** complete or absolute: *dead silence*
Other words: **total, utter**
adverb **6** completely or absolutely: *You're dead right.*
Other words: **entirely, totally, utterly**

deaden

verb to weaken or dull: *Carpet deadens the sound of footsteps.*

deadline

noun the latest time for finishing something: *The deadline for your project is next Friday.*

deadlock

noun the point which people reach in an argument when neither side will give way

deadly

adjective likely to cause death: *a deadly poison*

Word building: Other forms are **deadlier, deadliest.** | **deadliness** *noun*   **deadly** *adverb*

deaf   (*say* def)

adjective **1** not able to hear well
phrase **2 turn a deaf ear**, to refuse to listen

Word building: **deafen** *verb* to make deaf
deafening *adjective*   **deafeningly** *adverb*
deafness *noun*

deal

verb **1** to give out or hand out: *to deal the cards*
Other words: **dispense, distribute**
2 to do business or trade: *to deal with a biscuit company* | *to deal in rare books*
noun **3** quantity or amount: *a great deal of noise* **4** an arrangement or agreement: *We made a deal not to fight any more.*
phrase **5 deal with, a** to be about: *This book deals with Australian explorers.* **b** to take action against: *The police will deal with the culprits who broke the window.* **c** to treat or behave towards: *Our teacher always deals fairly with us.*

Word building: Other verb forms are **I dealt, I have dealt, I am dealing.** | **dealings** *plural noun* business or connections between people

dealer

noun **1** someone who buys and sells things: *a car dealer* **2** the player who gives out the cards in a card game

dean

noun the head priest in charge of a cathedral

Word history: from a Latin word meaning 'chief of ten'

dear

adjective **1** greatly loved: *a dear friend*
Other words: **beloved, cherished, precious**
2 costing a lot
Other words: **costly, expensive**
3 Dear, respected: *Dear Madam or Sir*

Word building: **dear** *noun* someone you love
dearly *adverb*

dear/deer Don't confuse **dear** with **deer**, which is a large grass-eating animal.

death

noun **1** the end of life: *A car accident caused the death of my brother.* **2** the end or destruction of anything: *the death of our hopes of winning a gold medal*
phrase **3 sick to death of**, bored and annoyed with

Word building: **deathly** *adverb* like or as in death: *deathly pale*

debate

noun **1** an organised discussion: *a debate*

in Parliament **2** an organised contest in which two teams of speakers put forward opposite views on a chosen subject

Word building: **debatable** *adjective* open to question or discussion   **debate** *verb* to argue or discuss   **debater** *noun*

debit

noun **1** a record of the money that is taken out of an account, such as your bank account

verb **2** to charge with a debt: *The central computer will debit your account for this purchase.*

Word use: Compare this with **credit** (definitions 4 and 7).

debonair   *(say* deb-uh-<u>nair</u>)

adjective cheerful and with pleasant manners

debris   *(say* <u>deb</u>-ree, duh-<u>bree</u>)

noun the rubbish left when something is broken or destroyed

Word use: The 's' is silent because this word comes from French.

debt   *(rhymes with* met)

noun **1** anything that you owe someone else

phrase **2 bad debt**, a debt that will not be paid: *The shopkeeper was owed $1000 in bad debts.*

Word use: Someone who owes you money is your **debtor** and someone you owe money to is your **creditor**.

Word building: **indebted** *adjective*

deca-

prefix a word part indicating ten times a given unit: *decade / decagon / decahedron*

Word use: Other spellings are **dec-**, **dek-**, or **deka-**.

Word history: from Greek

decade   *(say* <u>dek</u>-ayd)

noun a period of time lasting ten years

Word history: from a Greek word meaning 'a group of ten'

decaffeinated

(say dee-<u>kaf</u>-uh-nayt-uhd)

adjective with the drug caffeine taken out: *decaffeinated coffee*

decagon   *(say* <u>dek</u>-uh-gon)

noun a flat shape with ten straight sides

Word building: **decagonal** *adjective*

decahedron   *(say* dek-uh-<u>heed</u>-ruhn)

noun a solid shape with ten flat faces

Word building: The plural is **decahedrons** or **decahedra**.

decanter   *(say* duh-<u>kan</u>-tuh)

noun a container, often with a spout, for serving wine, water or juice at the table

Word building: **decant** *verb* to pour gently from one container into another

decapitate

verb to cut off the head of

Word building: **decapitation** *noun*

decathlon   *(say* duh-<u>kath</u>-luhn)

noun a contest in which athletes compete for the highest score in ten different events

decay   *(say* duh-<u>kay</u>)

verb to rot or go bad

Other words: **decompose, perish**

Word building: **decay** *noun*

deceased   *(say* duh-<u>seest</u>)

noun dead: *Bob's wife is deceased, so he left his job to stay home and care for the children.*

Word building: **decease** *noun* death: *On the decease of his wife, Bob stayed home with his children.* | **deceased** *noun*: *The will of the deceased was read.*

deceive

verb to trick or mislead: *She deceived us by saying she'd found the money when she'd really stolen it.*

Other words: **dupe, hoodwink, cheat**

Word building: **deceit** *noun*   **deceitful** *adjective*   **deceitfully** *adverb*   **deceitfulness** *noun*

December

noun the twelfth month of the year, with 31 days

Word use: The abbreviation is **Dec**.

Word history: the Latin name for the tenth month of the early Roman year

decent   *(say* <u>dee</u>-suhnt)

adjective **1** respectable or proper: *decent behaviour* **2** reasonable or good enough: *to earn a decent wage* **3** kind and helpful: *It was decent of you to give me a lift home.*

Word building: **decency** *noun*   **decently** *adverb*

deception

noun a trick or something that deceives

Word building: **deceptive** *adjective*
deceptively *adverb*

deci-
prefix a word part indicating one tenth of
a given unit

decibel   (*say* <u>des</u>-uh-bel)
noun a measure of loudness used to
show how much louder one sound is than
another

decide
verb **1** to make up your mind: *I couldn't
work out whether to go or not, but I've decided
now.*
Other words: **choose, determine**
2 to judge or settle: *We will ask the teacher
to decide the argument.*
Other words: **determine, resolve**

decided
adjective **1** definite and obvious: *a decided
difference between my writing and yours*
2 having firmly made up your mind: *I tried
to persuade him but he was quite decided.*
Word building: **decidedly** *adverb* definitely

deciduous   (*say* duh-<u>sid</u>-yooh-uhs)
adjective losing their leaves every year:
*They have a nice mix of deciduous and
evergreen trees in their garden.*
Word use: Compare this with **evergreen**.
Word history: from a Latin word meaning
'falling down'

decimal
adjective **1** based on tenths or on the
number ten: *decimal currency*
noun **2** a decimal fraction or number
Word building: **decimate** *verb* to destroy every
tenth one or a great number: *The soldiers
decimated the enemy in a fierce battle.* |
decimalise *verb*   **decimally** *adverb*

decimal fraction
noun a fraction in which the bottom
number is 10, 100, 1000, 10 000, and
so on, usually written with just the top
number and a dot in front of it, as 0.4
($= \frac{4}{10}$) and 0.126 ($= \frac{126}{1000}$)

decimal number
noun a number consisting of a whole
number and a decimal fraction, separated
by a dot, such as *4.23*

decimal point
noun the dot in a decimal fraction

decipher   (*say* duh-<u>suy</u>-fuh)
verb to solve or find the meaning of: *to
decipher a code*
Word building: **decipherable** *adjective* able to
be understood or read   **indecipherable**
adjective not able to be understood or read

decision
noun **1** the act of making up your mind: *a
difficult decision* **2** an opinion or judgement:
The judge's decision is final. **3** firmness and
certainty in all you think and do: *Georgina
is a woman of decision.*
Word building: **decisive** *adjective*: *a decisive
victory*

deck
noun **1** the floor of a ship or bus
2 an open, raised platform or verandah,
usually made of wood
verb **3** to decorate or dress: *to deck the
Christmas tree with tinsel*
phrase **4 on deck**, on duty or ready for
action
Word history: from a Dutch word meaning
'cover'

declare   (*say* duh-<u>klair</u>)
verb **1** to say firmly: *She declared that she
was innocent.*
Other words: **affirm, assert, state**
2 to announce or make known officially:
The government declared war.
Other words: **proclaim, pronounce**
3 to close a cricket innings before all ten
wickets have fallen
Word building: **declaration** *noun* an
announcement

decline
verb **1** to refuse politely: *to decline an
invitation* | *I asked her to the party but she
declined.* **2** to become worse or less:
His health has declined. | *School attendance
declines in wet weather.*
Word building: **decline** *noun*

decode
verb to translate from code into the
original language or form: *to decode a
message*
Word building: **decoder** *noun*

decompose
verb to rot or break up: *Leaves decomposed
under the forest trees.*
Word building: **decomposition** *noun*

decorate

verb **1** to make bright and pretty by adding something like paint, wallpaper or streamers: *to decorate a room | to decorate the Christmas tree*
Other words: **adorn, embellish**
2 to honour with a medal or badge: *to be decorated for bravery*

Word building: **decor** *noun* the way a room is decorated or furnished | **decoration** *noun* **decorative** *adjective* **decoratively** *adverb* **decorator** *noun*

decorum (*say* duh-<u>kaw</u>-ruhm)

noun proper behaviour, speech or dress: *to act with decorum at school assembly*

Word building: **decorous** *adjective*

decoy (*say* <u>dee</u>-koy)

noun something or someone that tempts or lures, especially into danger or into a trap: *The policewoman was used as a decoy to trap the bag thief.*

Word building: **decoy** *verb*

decrease

verb **1** to make less or lessen gradually: *I have decreased the amount of sugar I take in my tea. | Cinema audiences have decreased.*
Other words: **diminish, lower, reduce**
noun **2** a gradual lessening or reduction: *There has been a decrease in bus services.*
Other words: **cut, decline, drop, fall, reduction**

decree

noun an official order or command: *a government decree*

Word building: **decree** *verb* (**decreed, decreeing**)

decrepit

adjective made weak or broken down by old age: *a decrepit old man | a decrepit car*

Word building: **decrepitly** *adverb* **decrepitude** *noun*
Word history: from a Latin word meaning 'without noise'

dedicate

verb **1** to devote or give up completely: *land dedicated for public use | I'd like to dedicate my life to helping the poor.*
2 to put the name of someone on, as a sign of thanks or respect: *The author dedicated the book to all people striving for justice in Australia.*

Word building: **dedicated** *adjective* **dedication** *noun*

deduce

verb to work out by reasoning: *We deduced that he would be late.*

Word building: **deducible** *adjective* **deductive** *adjective*

deduct

verb to take away: *I'm going to deduct a dollar from your pocket money.*

Word building: **deductible** *adjective*

deduction

noun **1** an amount taken away: *a deduction from my wages* **2** a conclusion or answer worked out from the facts

deed

noun **1** something done: *a good deed*
Other words: **act, exploit, feat**
2 a signed agreement, usually about ownership of land

deep

adjective **1** going far down, in or back: *a deep pool | a deep wound | a deep shelf*
2 being a certain distance down, in or back: *a tank two metres deep* **3** intense or great in amount: *deep sorrow | a deep blue* **4** hard to understand: *This book is too deep for me.* **5** low in pitch: *a deep voice*
Other words: **bass, sonorous**

Word building: **deepen** *verb* **deeply** *adverb* **deepness** *noun* **depth** *noun*

deep-fry

verb to cook food in a pan, using enough fat or oil to completely cover it while it is being cooked

Word building: Other forms are **I deep-fried, I have deep-fried, I am deep-frying.** | **deep-fried** *adjective*

deer

noun a large grass-eating animal, the male of which has branching horns or antlers

Word use: The male is a **buck,** the female is a **doe** and the young is a **fawn.**
Word building: The plural is **deer.**

deer/dear Don't confuse **deer** with **dear,** which means 'greatly loved' or 'costing a lot'.

deface

verb to damage the appearance of: *Someone has defaced the building by spraying paint on it.*

Word building: **defacement** *noun*

de facto

adjective actually existing although not official or legal: *They decided to recognise the de facto government of the rebels.*

Word history: from Latin words meaning 'from the fact'

defame

verb to damage the good name of: *The local newspaper defamed the mayor.*
Other words: **libel, slander**

Word building: **defamation** *noun* **defamatory** *adjective*

defeat

verb **1** to overcome or beat in a battle or contest
Other words: **conquer, crush, overcome**
noun **2** the state of being beaten: *Our defeat on Saturday was the first of the season.*
Other words: **loss**

defect   (*say* <u>dee</u>-fekt)

noun **1** a fault or weakness: *a defect in the glass | a defect of character*
verb (*say* duh-<u>fekt</u>) **2** to leave your country without permission, not intending to return

Word building: **defection** *noun* **defective** *adjective* **defectively** *adverb* **defectiveness** *noun* **defector** *noun*

defence

noun **1** a protection against attack: *A moat was part of the castle's defence.*
Other words: **security, shield**
2 an argument in support of something or in answer to a charge in court: *her defence of Aboriginal land rights | My defence is that I was ill.*
Other words: **explanation, justification**

Word building: **defensible** *adjective* **defensive** *adjective*

defend

verb **1** to protect or keep safe, especially from attack: *to defend a fort | to defend a title*
Other words: **guard, shield**
2 to support by argument: *He defended me against their unfair statements.*

Word building: **defendant** *noun* someone who is charged with a crime in a court of law

defer

verb to put off until another time: *to defer the exam*
Other words: **delay, postpone**

Word building: Other forms are **I deferred, I have deferred, I am deferring.** | **deferment** *noun*

defiance

noun a daring challenge to authority or any opposing force

Word building: **defiant** *adjective* **defiantly** *adverb*

deficient

adjective lacking: *This soup is deficient in flavour.*

Word building: **deficiency** *noun* (**deficiencies**) **deficiently** *adverb*

deficit   (*say* <u>def</u>-uh-suht)

noun an amount of money lacking: *There is a deficit in the accounts.*

defile

verb to make dirty: *Their minds were defiled by reading racist literature.*

define

verb **1** to explain the meaning or nature of: *The easiest words are the hardest to define.*
2 to fix the limits of: *to define a problem*

Word building: **definition** *noun* **definitive** *adjective* **definitively** *adverb*

definite

adjective **1** clearly stated or exact: *a definite request*
Other words: **precise**
2 clear and not allowing any doubt: *It is a definite advantage to be able to run fast.*
Other words: **distinct, obvious**
3 firm in intention: *He was quite definite about where he wanted to go.*
Other words: **certain, sure**

Word building: **definitely** *adverb* **definiteness** *noun*

deflate

verb **1** to let the air out of: *Someone deflated our tyres.* **2** to lower or reduce: *to deflate prices* **3** to make feel less important: *The criticism of our team deflated us.*

Word building: **deflation** *noun*

deflect

verb to turn aside: *The armour deflected the bullet.*

Word building: **deflection** *noun*

defoliate

verb to strip of leaves: *The plague of caterpillars defoliated the trees.*

Word building: **defoliant** *noun* a chemical used to cause the leaves to fall from a tree | **defoliation** *noun*

deforestation

(*say* dee-fo-ruhs-<u>tay</u>-shuhn)
noun the permanent removal of forests or trees from a large area, usually for commercial purposes

deformed

adjective out of shape: *a deformed leg*

Word building: **deformity** *noun* (**deformities**) **deform** *verb* **deformation** *noun*

defrag   (*say* dee-<u>frag</u>)

verb to reorganise a computer disk so that whole files are stored in the same place: *Once we defragged the hard disk, the computer went much faster.*

Word use: This word is a short way of saying **defragment**.

defraud

verb to cheat, especially of money

defrost

verb **1** to remove ice from: *to defrost a refrigerator* **2** to thaw out: *Defrost the chicken before cooking it.*

deft

adjective quick and neat: *deft movements*

Word building: **deftly** *adverb* **deftness** *noun*

defuse

verb **1** to remove the fuse from: *The army expert defused the bomb.* **2** to calm: *to defuse a tense situation*

defy

verb to challenge or resist boldly: *Criminals defy the law.*
Other words: **disobey, flout**

Word building: Other forms are **I defied, I have defied, I am defying**.

degenerate

verb to become bad or worse than before

Word building: **degeneracy** *noun* **degenerate** *adjective* **degenerately** *adverb* **degeneration** *noun*

degrade

verb to lower or make worse in character or nature

Word building: **degradation** *noun*

degree

noun **1** a step or stage: *to advance a degree in difficulty*
Other words: **grade, level**
2 an amount: *She experienced some degree of satisfaction.* **3** a unit of measurement for temperature, angles and latitude or longitude **4** an award given by a university

dehydrate

verb to cause to lose water or other fluids: *to dehydrate vegetables to preserve them | to be dehydrated by the desert sun*

Word building: **dehydration** *noun*

deign   (*rhymes with* rain)

verb to stoop or lower yourself: *The duchess deigned to answer her servant.*

deity   (*say* <u>dee</u>-uh-tee, <u>day</u>-uh-tee)

noun a god or goddess

Word building: The plural is **deities**.

dejected

adjective unhappy or depressed

Word building: **dejectedly** *adverb* **dejection** *noun*

delay

verb **1** to make or be late: *The breakdown delayed us.*
Other words: **detain, hinder, impede**
2 to put off or postpone: *We don't want to delay our visit.*
Other words: **defer, suspend**
noun **3** a hold-up or stoppage: *The delay was due to a signal failure.*

Word history: from a Latin word meaning 'loosen'

delectable

adjective delicious: *delectable food*

Word building: **delectably** *adverb* **delectation** *noun*

delegate   (*say* <u>del</u>-uh-gayt)

verb **1** to give or pass on to someone else: *The manager delegated her authority to her assistant.*
noun (*say* <u>del</u>-uh-guht) **2** a representative or deputy: *There were 50 delegates at the conference.*

Word building: **delegation** *noun*

delete

verb to strike or wipe out: *Delete their names from the list.*

Word building: **deletion** *noun*

deliberate   (*say* duh-<u>lib</u>-uh-ruht)
adjective **1** intentional or carefully
considered
verb (*say* duh-<u>lib</u>-uh-rayt) **2** to consider,
or think carefully
Word building: **deliberation** *noun*

delicacy   (*say* <u>del</u>-uh-kuh-see)
noun **1** fineness: *the delicacy of the lace cloth*
2 a tasty or expensive food: *Caviar is a
delicacy.*
Word building: The plural is **delicacies**.

delicate
adjective **1** finely made or sensitive: *delicate
lace* | *a delicate measuring instrument*
2 easily damaged or weakened: *delicate
china* | *delicate health*
Other words: **fragile**
3 pale or soft: *a delicate shade of blue*
Other words: **gentle, mild, subtle**
Word building: **deliberately** *adverb*
deliberator *noun*

delicatessen   (*say* del-uh-kuh-<u>tes</u>-uhn)
noun Informal a shop which sells a variety
of foods, including cheeses, sausages and
other prepared goods

delicious   (*say* duh-<u>lish</u>-uhs)
adjective very pleasing to smell or taste:
Thanks for a delicious meal.
Other words: **appetising, luscious,
delectable, scrumptious**
Word building: **deliciously** *adverb*
deliciousness *noun*

delight
noun **1** great enjoyment or pleasure: *The
children's faces lit up with delight when they
saw their presents.*
Other words: **glee, happiness, joy**
verb **2** to give great pleasure: *Their singing
delighted everyone.*
Other words: **charm, entrance, please**
3 to have great pleasure: *I delighted in
helping them.*
Word building: **delighted** *adjective*
delightedly *adverb*   **delightful** *adjective*
delightfully *adverb*

delinquent   (*say* duh-<u>ling</u>-kwuhnt)
noun a young person who is in trouble with
the law
Word building: **delinquent** *adjective*: *delinquent
behaviour*   **delinquency** *noun*

delirious   (*say* duh-<u>lear</u>-ree-uhs)
adjective restless, excited and seeing things
that aren't there, as when you have a fever
Word building: **deliriously** *adverb*   **delirium**
noun

deliver
verb **1** to carry and hand over
Other words: **bring, convey, transport**
2 to help at the birth of: *The midwife
delivered the baby.* **3** to cause to move in a
certain direction: *The bowler delivered a fast
ball.* **4** to give or declare: *to deliver a verdict*
5 to save or set free: *The army delivered the
besieged town.*
Other words: **liberate, release, rescue**
Word building: **delivery** *noun*
(**deliveries**)   **deliverance** *noun*

delta
noun the flat rich land at the mouth of a river

delude
verb to trick or mislead: *Alisi and Fetu had
deluded them into thinking that they were
honest.*
Word building: **delusion** *noun* false
belief   **delusive** *adjective*   **delusory** *adjective*

deluge   (*say* <u>del</u>-yoohj)
noun **1** a great flood or downpour
2 anything that pours out like a flood: *a
deluge of words*
Word building: **deluge** *verb*

deluxe   (*say* duh-<u>luks</u>)
adjective of expensive high quality: *a
deluxe hotel with gold taps in the bathrooms*
Word history: from French words meaning 'of
luxury'

delve
verb to search deeply: *The businesswoman
delved into her briefcase for the papers.*

demand
verb **1** to ask for, as if it's your right: *He
demands an apology.*
Other words: **command, order**
2 to need: *This job demands a lot of patience.*
Other words: **require**
noun **3** a request or need: *a demand for
information* | *a big demand for sandals*
Other words: **call, requirement**
4 a question
phrase **5 on demand**, as required
Word building: **demanding** *adjective* requiring
a lot of effort or skill: *a demanding job*

demean

verb to lower in people's opinion: *Don't demean yourself by having tantrums at your age.*

demeanour *(say* duh-<u>meen</u>-uh)

noun the way you behave: *Everyone was upset by Kelly's rude demeanour.*

Word use: Another spelling is **demeanor**.

demented

adjective mad: *For a while she was demented with grief.*

Word building: **dementia** *noun* madness **dementedly** *adverb*

democracy *(say* duh-<u>mok</u>-ruh-see)

noun **1** a way of governing a country, in which you elect people to form a government on your behalf **2** a country with such a government **3** the idea that everyone in a country has equal rights: *Democracy demands that everyone should have the right to vote.*

Word building: **democrat** *noun* someone who supports democracy **democratic** *adjective* **democratically** *adverb*
Word history: from the Greek word for 'people' added to the Greek word for 'rule' or 'authority'

demolish

verb to knock down or destroy: *to demolish an old building | to demolish an argument*

Word building: **demolition** *noun*

demon *(say* <u>dee</u>-muhn)

noun **1** an evil spirit **2** someone who does something with great energy: *She's a demon for tidiness.*

Word building: **demonic** *adjective*

demonstrate

verb to show clearly: *She demonstrated how she felt by bursting into tears.*

Word building: **demonstrable** *adjective* **demonstrably** *adverb* **demonstrator** *noun*

demonstration

noun **1** a march or other act to show support: *There was a big demonstration for land rights.* **2** a public showing in order to advertise: *There is a demonstration of power tools in the hardware store.*

demoralise

verb to destroy the confidence of: *Their jeering demoralised him.*

Word use: Another spelling is **demoralize**.
Word building: **demoralisation** *noun*

demote

verb to lower in importance or rank: *We'll demote you from a captain to an ordinary soldier.*

Word building: **demotion** *noun*

demure

adjective shyly well-behaved: *a demure child*

Word building: **demurely** *adverb*

den

noun **1** an animal's burrow or shelter **2** a quiet room or place separate from other rooms: *Mum is reading in the den.*

denim

noun a heavy cotton material used to make jeans and other clothes

Word history: from French words meaning 'cloth of Nîmes' (a town in France)

denomination

noun a religious group, especially in the Christian church

Word building: **denominational** *adjective*

denominator

noun the number under the line in a fraction which shows how many equal parts it may be divided into: *In the fraction $\frac{3}{4}$, 4 is the denominator.*

Word use: Another word is **divisor**. | Compare this with **numerator**.

denote

verb to mean or show: *A yellow flag on a ship denotes illness on board.*

Word use: The usual word is **mean**.

denounce

verb to speak out against: *He will denounce the traitors.*

Word building: **denunciation** *noun*

dense

adjective **1** closely packed or thick: *a dense crowd | a dense fog*
Other words: **compact, solid**
2 foolish or stupid
Other words: **dumb, obtuse**

Word building: **density** *noun* (**densities**) **densely** *adverb* **denseness** *noun*

dent
noun a small hollow scarring a surface: *The stones made dents on the car.*
Word building: **dent** *verb*

dental
adjective having to do with teeth or dentists

dental floss
noun a soft thin thread used for cleaning between the teeth
Word use: The short form of this is **floss**.

dentist
noun someone who is trained to treat your teeth
Word building: **dentistry** *noun* the work that a dentist does

denture
noun a plate with a false tooth or teeth attached, which fits into your mouth

deny   (*say* duh-**nuy**)
verb **1** to say to be untrue: *Henry denies that he stole the mangoes.* **2** to refuse: *She denied us permission to go.*
Word building: Other forms are **I denied, I have denied, I am denying.** | **denial** *noun*

deodorant   (*say* dee-**oh**-duh-ruhnt)
noun something which prevents or removes bad smells
Word building: **deodorise** *verb*

depart
verb to go away or leave
Word building: **departure** *noun*

department
noun a division in a large organisation such as a government, a college or a store: *The toy department was on the second floor.*
Word building: **departmental** *adjective* **departmentally** *adverb*

department store
noun a very large shop, with many parts to it, where you can buy many different kinds of things

depend
verb **1** to rely: *They depend on us to help them.*
phrase **2 depend on**, to be determined by: *Whether we can afford it depends on how much money we have.*

Word building: **dependability** *noun* **dependable** *adjective* **dependably** *adverb*

dependant
noun someone who relies on or needs the support of another

dependant/dependent Don't confuse the noun **dependant** with the adjective **dependent**. **Dependent** means 'needing support'.

dependent
adjective needing support: *a dependent child*
Word building: **dependence** *noun* **dependency** *noun*

dependent/dependant Don't confuse the adjective **dependent** with the noun **dependant**. A **dependant** is a person who needs the support of someone else.

depict
verb to describe or show in words or pictures: *The artist had depicted a country scene.*
Word building: **depiction** *noun*

deplete
verb to make less: *Don't eat so much or you'll deplete our provisions.*
Word use: The more usual word is **reduce**.
Word building: **depletion** *noun*

deplore
verb to regret or be sorry for: *We deplore the bad condition of the house.*
Word building: **deplorable** *adjective* **deplorably** *adverb*

deport
verb to send out of the country as a punishment: *The government threatened to deport all illegal immigrants.*
Word building: **deportation** *noun* **deportee** *noun*

deportment
noun the way you stand
Other words: **bearing, carriage, posture, stance**

depose
verb to remove from a high position by force: *The general deposed the king.*
Word building: **deposition** *noun*

deposit

verb **1** to put down: *I deposited the heavy box on a chair.* **2** to put away for safekeeping: *I deposited my money in the bank immediately.*
noun **3** an amount given as the first part of a payment, or as a promise to pay
4 money placed in a bank **5** a layer which collects on a surface: *There was a fine deposit of dust on the furniture.*

depot   (*say* <u>dep</u>-oh)

noun **1** a place where goods are stored or unloaded **2** a place where buses, trams or trucks are kept

deprave

verb to make evil in character: *Films showing violence might deprave others.*
Word building: **depraved** *adjective* **depravity** *noun*

depress

verb **1** to make miserable: *Your bad news depressed me.* **2** to press down: *The captain depressed the lever.* **3** to cause to sink lower in level: *to depress the value of their houses*
Word building: **depressed** *adjective* **depression** *noun* **depressive** *adjective* **depressively** *adverb*

deprive

verb to take away or keep from: *to deprive someone of their freedom*
Word building: **deprived** *adjective* lacking **deprivation** *noun*

depth

noun **1** deepness or distance downward **2** strength, especially of colour or feeling: *You can't imagine the depth of my love for her.* **3** **depths**, the deepest part, especially of the sea

deputation

noun people chosen to speak on behalf of the group they belong to
Other words: **delegation**

deputy   (*say* <u>dep</u>-yuh-tee)

noun someone who assists or acts for another person: *The principal's deputy took assembly while the principal was sick.*
Word building: The plural is **deputies**. | **deputise** *verb* **deputy** *adjective*

derail

verb to run off the tracks or rails on which it is travelling: *The train derailed in the bad weather.*
Word building: **derailment** *noun* an accident in which a train comes off its tracks

deranged

adjective wild and uncontrolled in the way you behave, especially because you are crazy or insane: *The deranged man threw all the books on the floor.*
Word building: **derange** *verb* to throw into disorder **derangement** *noun*

derelict   (*say* <u>de</u>-ruh-likt)

adjective **1** empty and run-down: *They found derelict houses in the abandoned mining town.*
noun **2** a poor, homeless and neglected person
Word building: **dereliction** *noun* neglect: *dereliction of duty*
Word history: from a Latin word meaning 'forsaken utterly'

deride

verb to make fun of or mock

derision

noun the act of laughing at or making fun of someone
Word building: **deride** *verb* **derisive** *adjective* **derisively** *adverb*

derive

verb **1** to take or receive from somewhere: *Amy derives her income from two jobs.* **2** to get by working out: *I derived the answer by adding the figures together.*
Word building: **derivation** *noun* origin **derivative** *adjective* coming from something else

dermatitis   (*say* der-muh-<u>tuy</u>-tuhs)

noun dryness and redness of the skin which is itchy or painful

derogatory   (*say* duh-<u>rog</u>-uh-tree)

adjective unfairly critical: *Isabella was upset by derogatory remarks about her family.*

desalination   (*say* dee-sal-uh-<u>nay</u>-shuhn)

noun the process of removing the salts from sea water so that it becomes suitable for drinking water or for use in agriculture

descant (*say* <u>des</u>-kant)
noun a tune played or sung above the main tune

descent (*say* duh-<u>sent</u>)
noun **1** the act of coming or going down: *The old lady's descent of the stairs was very shaky.* **2** the downward slope of a mountain or stairway
Word building: **descendant** *noun* offspring **descend** *verb*

describe
verb to give a picture of someone or something using written or spoken words: *He described what happened after we left.*
Word building: **description** *noun* **descriptive** *adjective*
Word history: from a Latin word meaning 'copy off' or 'sketch off'

deselect
verb to cancel something on the computer that has been selected (like highlighted text) by clicking the mouse on the screen to cancel the selected thing

desert[1] (*say* <u>dez</u>-uht)
noun a sandy or stony place without enough rainfall to grow many plants
Word history: from a Latin word meaning 'abandoned'

desert/dessert Don't confuse **desert** with **dessert**. A **dessert**, pronounced as *duh-<u>zert</u>*, is a sweet dish served at the end of a meal.

desert[2] (*say* duh-<u>zert</u>)
verb to leave or run away without intending to return
Word building: **deserted** *adjective* abandoned, or lonely **deserter** *noun* **desertion** *noun*

desert/dessert Don't confuse **desert** with **dessert**, which sounds the same. A **dessert** is a sweet dish served at the end of a meal.

deserts (*say* duh-<u>zerts</u>)
plural noun something which is deserved, either as a reward or a punishment

deserve
verb to be worthy of
Word building: **deserved** *adjective* **deservedly** *adverb* **deserving** *adjective*

desiccated (*say* <u>des</u>-uh-kay-tuhd)
adjective dried or dried out: *desiccated coconut*

design (*say* duh-<u>zuyn</u>)
verb **1** to draw plans for: *An architect designed the house.*
Other words: **devise, plan**
2 to invent: *She's designed a new type of motor.*
noun **3** a sketch or plan: *Here is my design for a new rabbit hutch.*
Other words: **blueprint, drawing**
4 an ornamental design or pattern: *There is a design of roses on the plates.*
Other words: **motif**
Word building: **designer** *noun*

designated driver
noun a person at a social event where there will be alcohol, who agrees to drink very little or not at all and be responsible for driving other people home safely

desirable
adjective good or beautiful enough to be wanted: *It's a desirable property in the best part of town.*
Word building: **desirably** *adverb*

desire
verb **1** to want very much **2** to ask for: *The queen desired the musician's presence at the palace.*
noun **3** need or craving: *We had a strong desire to laugh in class. | I have a desire for chocolate.* **4** request: *Tell us your desires and we shall try to grant them.*
Word building: **desirous** *adjective*

desist (*say* duh-<u>zist</u>)
verb to stop doing something: *The neighbours asked her not to hit the ball against their wall and she desisted.*

desk
noun **1** a writing table, often with drawers or small spaces for papers **2** the place, usually at the front of an office or hotel, where information is given: *Ask at the desk if there is a room vacant.*

desktop
noun the background image displayed on a computer screen, representing a work space similar to the surface of a desk and with symbols representing programs, documents, and so on

desolate

adjective **1** lonely and without people: *The streets are desolate at 3 a.m.* **2** sad and hopeless: *They felt desolate after losing all their possessions.*

Word building: **desolate** *verb*   **desolately** *adverb*   **desolation** *noun*

despair

noun a feeling of hopelessness: *We were filled with despair when the train left without us.*

Word building: **despair** *verb* to lose or give up hope

desperate

adjective **1** ready to run any risk: *a desperate criminal* **2** tried as a last attempt: *a desperate plan* **3** very bad or dangerous: *a desperate illness*

Word building: **desperately** *adverb* **desperation** *noun*

despise

verb to look down on, especially with hate or scorn: *We despise them for all the bad things that they've done.*
Other words: **abhor, detest, loathe**

Word building: **despicable** *adjective* deserving scorn

despite

preposition in spite of or not prevented by: *Despite the early hour, the children were all dressed and ready to go.*

despondent

adjective depressed or down-hearted: *They look so despondent after losing their game.*

Word building: **despondency** *noun* **despondently** *adverb*

despot

noun a cruel and unjust ruler

Word building: **despotic** *adjective* **despotically** *adverb*   **despotism** *noun*
Word history: from a Greek word meaning 'master'

dessert   (*say* duh-<u>zert</u>)

noun the fruit or sweets eaten at the end of a meal

dessert/desert Don't confuse **dessert** with **desert**, which, when it is pronounced the same, means to leave without intending to return, or when it is pronounced as <u>dez</u>-*uht* is a sandy place without enough rainfall to grow plants.

destination

noun the place you're travelling to, or to which something is sent

destined   (*say* <u>des</u>-tuhnd)

adjective meant by fate: *We were destined to meet.*

destiny   (*say* <u>des</u>-tuh-nee)

noun fate, or something that had to happen: *To die doing the thing she loved was her destiny.*

Word building: The plural is **destinies**. | **destine** *verb*

destitute

adjective without money or the means of getting any: *The parents died leaving the children destitute.*

Word building: **destitution** *noun*

destroy

verb **1** to wreck completely: *Bombs destroyed the city.*
Other words: **annihilate, demolish, devastate, obliterate, pulverise, ruin**
2 to kill: *The dog was destroyed.* | *You have destroyed my affection for you.*

Word building: **destroyer** *noun*   **destruction** *noun*   **destructive** *adjective*

detach

verb to separate or unfasten: *You detach the top copy and keep it.*

Word building: **detached** *adjective* unconcerned and aloof   **detachable** *adjective*
Word history: from a French word meaning 'nail'

detachment

noun **1** the ability to stand aside and not let your judgement be affected by your feelings **2** a force of soldiers or naval ships set aside for a special task

detail

noun **1** one of the single or small parts which go to make up a whole: *the details of a story* **2** fine delicate work: *There is a lot of detail in your drawings.*
verb **3** to report fully: *Michiko was asked to detail her plans.*

detain

verb **1** to delay or hold up: *I won't detain you much longer.* **2** to keep under control or in prison

Word building: **detainee** *noun*   **detention** *noun*

detect

verb to discover or notice: *to detect someone stealing*

Word building: **detectable** *adjective* noticeable   **detection** *noun*

detective

noun a police officer who is trained to discover who committed a crime

Word building: **detective** *adjective*

deter   (*say* duh-<u>ter</u>)

verb to prevent or stop from doing

Word building: Other forms are **I deterred, I have deterred, I am deterring.** | **deterrent** *noun*

detergent

noun powder or liquid used for cleaning

Word building: **detergent** *adjective*

deteriorate   (*say* duh-<u>tear</u>-ree-uh-rayt)

verb to become worse: *Our grandfather's health deteriorated as he grew older.*

Word building: **deterioration** *noun*

determination

noun firmness of purpose: *a determination to win*

determine

verb to settle on or decide: *I have determined my future course of study.*

Word building: **determined** *adjective* firm in purpose: *a determined effort*

detest

verb to hate or loathe

Word building: **detestable** *adjective* **detestation** *noun*

detonate

verb to explode or cause to explode

Word building: **detonation** *noun* **detonator** *noun*

detour

noun **1** a different way round, used when a road is closed
verb **2** to go by way of a detour

detract

phrase **detract from,** to take away some of, or reduce the value of: *Lying will detract from your good name.*

Word building: **detraction** *noun* **detractor** *noun*

deuce   (*say* dyoohs)

noun **1** a playing card with two spots: *the deuce of hearts* **2** a stage in a game of tennis when both players have a score of 40

devalue

verb to lower the worth or value of: *to devalue someone's efforts* | *to devalue the Australian dollar*

Word building: **devaluation** *noun*

devastate

verb to turn into a wasteland: *The fire devastated a large area of bush.*

Word building: **devastation** *noun*

develop

verb **1** to make or grow larger: *Exercise develops the muscles.* | *Muscles develop with exercise.* **2** to advance or expand: *Your mind will develop with age.* **3** to bring into being: *The gardener developed a new type of rose.* **4** to treat with chemicals so as to bring out the picture: *to develop a photograph*

Word building: **developed** *adjective* **developer** *noun* **developing** *adjective* **development** *noun*

deviate

verb to swerve or turn aside: *The rocket deviated from its planned course.* | *to deviate from normal behaviour*

Word building: **deviant** *noun* **deviate** *noun* **deviation** *noun*

device

noun something designed to do a particular task: *an electronic device for turning on the television*
Other words: **appliance, tool, utensil**

Word building: **devise** *verb*

devil

noun **1** a wicked person **2 the Devil,** Satan, the chief spirit of evil

Word building: **devilish** *adjective* **devilishly** *adverb* **devilment** *noun* **devilry** *noun*

devious

adjective tricky or deceitful: *My devious ways made a lot of enemies.*

Word building: **deviously** *adverb* **deviousness** *noun*

devise

verb to think out, form, or invent: *to devise a plan*

devoid

phrase **devoid of**, free from or without: *The street was devoid of shade.*

devote

verb to set apart for a particular purpose: *to devote an hour to a hobby*

Word building: **devoted** *adjective*: *a devoted parent* **devotion** *noun*: *devotion to duty* **devotee** *noun*

devour

verb to eat hungrily

devout

adjective sincerely religious

Word building: **devoutly** *adverb* **devoutness** *noun*

dew

noun small drops of water that form during the night on any cool surfaces out of doors

Word building: **dewy** *adjective* (**dewier, dewiest**)

dew/due Don't confuse **dew** with **due**. Your **due** is what is deserved or owed to you:
When the goodies are handed out you will get your due.
Due also means 'expected to arrive':
The maths assignment is due on Friday.

dexterity

noun skill or cleverness, especially in using your hands

Word building: **dexterous** *adjective*

dhal (*say* dahl)

noun an Indian food made from cooked lentils, herbs and spices

diabetes (*say* duy-uh-<u>bee</u>-teez)

noun a disease in which your body finds it difficult to use sugar and passes it out in your urine

Word building: **diabetic** *noun* **diabetic** *adjective*

diabolic

adjective **1** devilish or wicked
Other words: **fiendish, satanic**
2 very difficult or unpleasant

Word use: You can also use **diabolical**.

diabolo (*say* dee-<u>ab</u>-uh-loh)

noun a game in which you balance a spinning top on a piece of string that is connected to two sticks, one held in each hand

diagnosis

noun the working out of what disease a patient has

Word building: The plural is **diagnoses** (*say* duy-uhg-<u>noh</u>-seez). | **diagnostician** *noun* an expert in making diagnoses **diagnose** *verb* **diagnostic** *adjective*

diagonal

adjective a sloping line joining opposite angles of a rectangle or square

Word building: **diagonally** *adverb*

diagram

noun a drawing which explains how something works or is laid out: *a diagram of the engine | a diagram of a racecourse*

Word building: **diagrammatic** *adjective* **diagrammatically** *adverb*

dial

noun **1** the face of a clock, radio or measuring instrument: *a speedometer dial* **2** a circular disc or knob, marked with measurements or other divisions, which you turn to change the setting of something

Word building: **dial** *verb* (**dialled, dialling**): *to dial a telephone number*
Word history: from a Latin word meaning 'day'

dialect

noun a variety of a language spoken in a particular area or by a particular group of people

dialogue

noun a conversation between two or more people, especially in a play or story

diameter (*say* duy-<u>am</u>-uh-tuh)

noun **1** the straight line which goes through the centre of a circle from one side to the other **2** the length of such a line

Word building: **diametric** *adjective* **diametrically** *adverb*

diamond

noun **1** a very hard precious stone which is clear and sparkling like glass **2** the red four-sided shape on some playing cards

diaphragm (*say* <u>duy</u>-uh-fram)

noun **1** the sheet of muscle inside your body between your chest and abdomen **2** a thin sheet or membrane, especially in a telephone or microphone

diarrhoea (*say* duy-uh-<u>ree</u>-uh)
noun an illness in which you have stomach pains, and watery waste matter passes frequently from your bowel

diary
noun a book in which you write down daily events or thoughts
Word building: The plural is **diaries**. | **diarist** *noun* someone who keeps a diary

diary/dairy Don't confuse **diary** with **dairy**. A **dairy** farm is one where cows are milked.

dibbler
noun a small mouse with spots that lives in Western Australia. It is almost extinct. See the table at the end of this book.
Word history: from an Aboriginal language of Western Australia called Nyungar. See the map of Australian Aboriginal languages at the end of this book.

dice
plural noun **1** small cubes marked on each side with a different number of spots, from one to six, used in games **2** any small cubes
verb **3** to cut into small cubes: *to dice carrots*
Word building: The singular form of the noun is **die**.

dictate
verb **1** to say or read aloud for somebody else to write down: *The manager dictated a letter to the secretary.* **2** to give orders
Word building: **dictation** *noun*

dictator
noun someone who has total power, especially in governing a country
Word building: **dictatorial** *adjective* **dictatorially** *adverb* **dictatorship** *noun*

dictionary
noun a book with an alphabetical list of words, their meanings and pronunciations
Word building: The plural is **dictionaries**. Word history: from a Latin word meaning 'word'

didjeridu (*say* dij-uh-ree-<u>dooh</u>)
noun a pipe-shaped, Aboriginal wind instrument made of wood
Word use: Another spelling is **didgeridoo**. Word history: from an imitation of the sound it makes

die[1]
verb **1** to stop living
phrase **2 die down**, to pass or fade slowly away: *The wind died down.* **3 die out**, to become extinct or no longer live on earth
Word building: Other verb forms are **I died, I have died, I am dying.**

die/dye Don't confuse **die** with **dye**. To **dye** something is to colour it with a **dye** or colouring agent:
I'm sick of my brown hair.
I'm going to dye it black.

die[2]
noun **1** a tool for cutting, stamping or shaping coins or other metal objects **2** the singular form of **dice**
Word building: The plural for definition 1 is **dies**.

diesel engine (*say* <u>dee</u>-zuhl en-juhn)
noun an engine which burns heavy oil, not petrol, with air inside one of its working cylinders

diesel oil
noun a type of fuel for vehicles such as trucks

diet
noun **1** the food you usually eat: *Your diet affects your health.* **2** a particular selection of foods: *a slimming diet | a low-fat diet*
verb **3** to choose what you eat in order to lose weight or improve your health
Word building: Other verb forms are **I dieted, I have dieted, I am dieting.** | **dietician** *noun* someone trained to give advice about the food you eat **dietary** *adjective* **dieter** *noun*

differ
verb **1** to be unlike or not the same **2** to disagree

difference
noun **1** a way of being unlike: *The difference between my sister and me is in our height.* **2** a disagreement or quarrel **3** the amount by which two things differ: *The difference between 6 and 1 is 5.*
Word building: **different** *adjective* **differentiate** *verb* **differently** *adverb*

difficult
adjective hard to do or understand: *a difficult maths problem*
Other words: **complex, tough, tricky**
Word building: **difficulty** *noun* (**difficulties**)

diffident

adjective not confident or sure of yourself: *He is diffident about speaking in public.*

Word use: The more usual word is **shy**.
Word building: **diffidence** *noun*   **diffidently** *adverb*

diffuse   (say duh-<u>fyoohz</u>)

verb **1** to pour out or spread over: *The poisonous gas from the cylinder diffused into the surrounding air.*
adjective (say duh-<u>fyoohs</u>) **2** scattered or spread out thinly **3** using too many words: *a diffuse speech*

Word building: **diffusion** *noun*

dig

verb **1** to break up or turn over with a spade: *to dig the soil* **2** to make by digging: *to dig a tunnel | to dig a garden* **3** to push or poke: *She dug me in the ribs.*

Word building: Other forms are **I dug, I have dug, I am digging.** | **dig** *noun*

digest

verb **1** to break down in your stomach and intestines for use by your body: *to digest food* **2** to think over and take in mentally: *to digest information*

Word building: **digestible** *adjective*   **digestion** *noun*   **digestive** *adjective*

digger

noun **1** a miner: *a digger on the goldfields* **2** an Australian soldier, especially one from World War I

diggings

plural noun a place where miners dig

digit

noun **1** any of the numerals from 0 to 9 **2** a finger or toe

digital

adjective **1** having fingers or toes **2** using digits or numbers but no pointers: *a digital clock* **3** working by storing and using information in a similar way to a computer: *a digital camera | a digital radio*

Word use: Compare definition 2 with **analogue**.

digital camera

noun a camera which stores pictures as digital files which can then be transferred onto a computer

dignitary

noun someone who is in a high position in government or a church

Word building: The plural is **dignitaries**.

dignity

noun **1** nobleness of mind or manner: *She acted with great dignity despite the rudeness of the others.* **2** a high rank or noble position

digress

verb to wander away from the main subject when writing or speaking

Word building: **digression** *noun*   **digressive** *adjective*

dilapidated

adjective shabby and in need of repair: *a dilapidated house*

Word building: **dilapidation** *noun*

dilate

verb to make or become wider or larger: *The drops dilated the pupils of my eyes. | The pupils of her eyes dilated.*

Word use: The opposite is **constrict**.
Word building: **dilatation** *noun*   **dilation** *noun*   **dilator** *noun*

dilemma

noun a situation in which you have to choose between two alternatives: *Her dilemma was that going to the pictures meant missing Justine's party.*

diligent

adjective paying careful and unceasing attention: *a diligent scholar*

Word use: The more usual word is **hardworking**.
Word building: **diligence** *noun*   **diligently** *adverb*

dill[1]

noun a plant bearing a seedlike fruit used in medicine and cooking

dill[2]

noun Informal a fool

dillybag

noun **1** a small bag used for carrying food or your belongings **2** a bag of twisted grass or fibre traditionally used by Aboriginal people

Word history: The word *dilly* comes from an Aboriginal language of Queensland called Yagara and the English word *bag* is added to it.

dilute
verb to make thinner or weaker by adding water: *to dilute disinfectant*

Word building: **dilution** *noun*
Word history: from a Latin word meaning 'washed to pieces' or 'dissolved'

dim
adjective **1** not bright: *a dim light | a dim room* **2** not clear to the mind: *a dim idea*

Word building: **dim** *verb* (**dimmed, dimming**): *to dim the lights of a room* | **dimmer** *noun*: *a light dimmer* **dimly** *adverb* **dimness** *noun*

dimension
noun size measured in a particular direction

diminish
verb to make or become smaller

diminuendo   (*say* duh-min-yooh-<u>en</u>-doh)
adverb gradually reducing in force or loudness

Word use: An instruction in music.

diminutive
adjective **1** very small
noun **2** a word which tells you something is small: *'Booklet' is the diminutive of 'book'.*

dimple
noun a small hollow in your cheek

Word building: **dimple** *verb*

din
noun loud noise that goes on and on

dine
verb to have dinner

Word building: **diner** *noun*

dinghy   (*say* <u>ding</u>-gee)
noun a small rowing boat, especially one that belongs to a launch or ship

Word building: The plural is **dinghies**.

dingo
noun an Australian wild dog which is brownish-yellow, has pointed ears and a bushy tail and makes a yelping noise

Word building: The plural is **dingoes** or **dingos**.
Word history: from an Aboriginal language of New South Wales called Dharug. See the map of Australian Aboriginal languages at the end of this book.

dingy   (*say* <u>din</u>-jee)
adjective having a dull dirty colour and looking shabby: *a dingy room*

Word building: Other forms are **dingier, dingiest**. | **dinginess** *noun*

dinkum
adjective *Informal* honest and sincere: *a dinkum friend*

Word use: Another word is **dinky-di**.
Word building: **dinkum** *adverb* truly

dinner
noun **1** the main meal of the day, usually eaten about noon or in the evening **2** a formal meal in honour of someone or something

dinner suit
noun a man's suit for going to a very formal occasion, usually a black dinner jacket and matching trousers: *He doesn't look too bad in a dinner suit.*

dinosaur   (*say* <u>duyn</u>-uh-saw)
noun any of a number of very large lizard-like animals which died out millions of years ago

Word history: from a Latin word meaning 'terrible lizard'

diocese   (*say* <u>duy</u>-uh-suhs)
noun the district, and the people who live in it, under the care of a bishop

Word building: **diocesan** *adjective*

diorama   (*say* duy-uh-<u>rahm</u>-uh)
noun a miniature scene using coloured backgrounds and models and sometimes lights

dip
verb **1** to put into a liquid for a short time: *I dipped my hand in the river.* | *to dip the sheep in disinfectant to kill insects* **2** to slope down
noun **3** a soft tasty mixture that you dip biscuits into **4** a downward slope or hollow: *a dip in the road* **5** a short swim

Word building: Other verb forms are **I dipped, I have dipped, I am dipping**. | **dipper** *noun*

diphtheria   (*say* dif-<u>thear</u>-ree-uh)
noun a serious infectious disease affecting your throat which makes it hard to breathe and which causes a high fever

diphthong   (*say* <u>dif</u>-thong)
noun a speech sound made by the tongue gliding from one vowel to another in the same syllable, such as *ei* in *vein*

diploma (*say* duh-<u>ploh</u>-muh)

noun an official paper proving that you are qualified in a particular field of study: *a diploma in librarianship*

Word building: **diplomate** *noun* a holder of a diploma

diplomacy (*say* duh-<u>ploh</u>-muh-see)

noun skill in managing relations between nations or people and keeping them friendly

Word building: **diplomat** *noun* **diplomatic** *adjective*

dire

adjective **1** very serious or bad: *Their mistake had dire results.*
phrase **2 in dire straits,** in a very difficult or dangerous situation: *They realised they were in dire straits when it became dark and they were still lost.*

direct

verb **1** to show or tell the way: *I directed the lost motorist to the police station.*
2 to give orders to
adjective **3** going in a straight line or by the shortest way: *a direct route* **4** quoting the exact words said: *direct speech*

Word building: **directly** *adverb* immediately **directness** *noun* **director** *noun*

direction

noun **1** the line towards a certain point or area: *a northerly direction* | *We went in the direction of the sea.* **2 directions,** guidance or instructions: *We got here quickly following your directions.*

Word building: **directional** *adjective*

directory

noun a book containing an alphabetical list of names and addresses, maps or other types of information: *a telephone directory* | *a street directory*

Word building: The plural is **directories.**

dirt

noun **1** loose earth or soil: *He fell in the dirt.* **2** anything that is not clean: *I can't get the dirt out of your jumper.*

Word building: **dirt** *adjective*: *a dirt road*

dirt bike

noun a motorcycle for riding on rough tracks and performing jumps rather than for using on a conventional road

Word use: Another name is **trail bike.**

dirty

adjective **1** covered with dirt
Other words: **filthy, grimy, grotty, grubby, soiled**
2 unfair or mean: *a dirty fight*

Word building: Other forms are **dirtier, dirtiest.** | **dirtily** *adverb* **dirtiness** *noun*

dis-

prefix a word part meaning 'apart', 'away', or expressing the opposite: *discount* | *disagree*

Word history: from Latin

disability

noun a lack of strength or power in part of your body which makes it hard for you to do some things: *Roderick's short leg was a disability which he struggled to overcome.*

Word building: The plural is **disabilities.**

disabled

adjective having been made unable or unfit: *Disabled soldiers receive a pension.*
Other words: **incapacitated**

Word building: **disable** *verb*

disadvantage

noun something that makes what you do more difficult: *Lack of education is a disadvantage.*

Word building: **disadvantage** *verb* **disadvantageous** *adjective*

disagree

verb **1** to differ or fail to agree: *The two reports of the disaster disagree on the number of casualties.* **2** to quarrel

Word building: **disagreement** *noun*

disagreeable

adjective **1** not to your liking: *a disagreeable task* **2** unpleasant or unfriendly in manner: *a disagreeable person*

Word building: **disagreeableness** *noun* **disagreeably** *adverb*

disappear

verb **1** to go out of sight: *He disappeared around the corner.*
Other words: **vanish**
2 to cease to exist: *We argued about why the dinosaurs disappeared.*
Other words: **expire, perish**

Word building: **disappearance** *noun*

disappoint

verb to fail to satisfy the hopes of: *I disappointed my friends when I lost the race.*

Word building: **disappointment** *noun*

disapprove

verb to have a bad opinion: *My father disapproves of my plan to be an actor.*

Word building: **disapproval** *noun*
disapproving *adjective* **disapprovingly** *adverb*

disarm

verb **1** to take weapons from **2** to take away anger from: *Your smile disarmed me.* **3** to reduce the size of your armed forces and weapon supplies: *Both sides agreed to disarm.*

Word building: **disarmament** *noun* **disarming** *adjective* **disarmingly** *adverb*

disarray

verb to put out of order: *The wind disarrayed her hair.*

Word building: **disarray** *noun*: *Her clothes were in a state of disarray.*

disaster (*say* duh-<u>zah</u>-stuh)

noun any sudden terrible happening which causes great suffering and damage
Other words: **calamity, catastrophe, tragedy**

Word building: **disastrous** *adjective*
Word history: from an Italian word meaning 'not having a (lucky) star'

disbelieve

verb to refuse to believe

Word building: **disbelief** *noun*

disc

noun **1** any thin, flat, circular object **2** *look up* **disk** **3** a gramophone record

discard

verb to throw away: *to discard old clothes | to discard an ace in a card game*

Word building: **discard** *noun*

discern

verb **1** to recognise, or understand clearly: *I can easily discern your handwriting.* **2** to recognise as different: *to discern good from bad*

Word use: For definition 1, the more usual word is **see**; for definition 2, **tell**.
Word building: **discernible** *adjective*
discernibly *adverb* **discerning** *adjective*
discerningly *adverb* **discernment** *noun*

discharge

verb **1** to unload: *The ship discharged its cargo.* **2** to fire: *He discharged the gun at the intruder. | The gun discharged.* **3** to give out or off: *The pipe discharged water and steam. | The chimney discharged smoke.* **4** to dismiss from a job **5** to fulfil or pay: *I discharged all my debts.*

Word building: **discharge** *noun*

disciple (*say* duh-<u>suy</u>-puhl)

noun **1** any follower of Christ, particularly one of the first twelve **2** a follower of any set of ideas or of the person who puts them forward: *a disciple of the peace movement*

Word building: **discipleship** *noun*

discipline (*say* <u>dis</u>-uh-pluhn)

noun **1** training given to teach good conduct or behaviour: *Schools hope their discipline will make us good citizens.* **2** orderliness resulting from this training: *Our teacher keeps good discipline in the class room.* **3** punishment
verb **4** to train or control **5** to punish

Word building: **disciplinarian** *noun* someone who believes in strict discipline | **disciplined, disciplinary** *adjective*

disclose

verb to allow to be seen or known: *I disclosed my secret.*
Other words: **divulge, expose, reveal**

Word building: **disclosure** *noun*

disco

noun a place or club in which people dance to recorded music

Word use: The full word is **discotheque**.
Word building: The plural is **discos**. | **disco** *adjective*: *disco music*

discolour

verb **1** to change the colour of: *The spilt coffee discoloured the cloth.* **2** to change colour or fade: *The carpet discoloured with age.*

Word use: Another spelling is **discolor**.
Word building: **discolouration** *noun*

discomfort

noun **1** lack of comfort or pleasure: *Much to my discomfort, I was asked to recite a poem.* **2** pain or uneasiness: *The accident caused me a lot of discomfort.*

disconcert   (*say* dis-kuhn-<u>sert</u>)

verb to cause feelings of embarrassment or distress: *Her accusation disconcerted me.*

Word building: **disconcerted** *adjective* **disconcerting** *adjective* **disconcertingly** *adverb*

discontinue

verb to stop doing or making something: *to discontinue playing loud music | The publishing company decided to discontinue the Sunday magazine.*

Word building: **discontinuation** *noun*

discord

noun **1** lack of agreement: *discord between the two friends* **2** a combination of musical notes which is unpleasant to listen to

Word building: **discordance** *noun* **discordant** *adjective*

discotheque   (*say* <u>dis</u>-kuh-tek)

noun look up **disco**

Word use: Another spelling is **discothèque**, because it was originally a French word.

discount

verb **1** to take an amount off the set price: *They discounted everything in the store by half.* **2** to disregard or take no notice of: *to discount someone's explanation*

Word building: **discount** *noun*: *a discount of $10*

discourage

verb **1** to cause to lose courage: *Their defeat discouraged the team.* **2** to try to prevent: *He will discourage her attempts at hang-gliding.*

Word building: **discouragement** *noun* **discouraging** *adjective* **discouragingly** *adverb*

discover

verb to find or find out, especially for the first time: *I discovered a shorter way home. | He discovered he could run very fast.*
Other words: **ascertain, learn, perceive, realise**

Word building: **discoverer** *noun* **discovery** *noun*

discredit

verb **1** to lower other people's opinion of: *His rudeness discredited him and his family.* **2** to show to be unworthy of belief: *The new discovery discredited the old ideas.*

Word building: **discredit** *noun* **discreditably** *adverb*

discreet

adjective **1** careful to avoid upsetting people: *discreet behaviour* **2** showing ability to keep secrets: *You can confide in a discreet friend.*

Word building: **discreetly** *adverb* **discreetness** *noun*
Word history: from a Latin word meaning 'separated'

discrepancy   (*say* dis-<u>krep</u>-uhn-see)

noun a difference or an unlikeness: *There is a discrepancy between their two stories.*

Word building: The plural is **discrepancies**.

discrete

adjective separate or distinct from other things: *The course was divided into six discrete units.*

discretion   (*say* dis-<u>kresh</u>-uhn)

noun **1** the ability to be discreet: *I can rely on her discretion.* **2** the ability or right to do what should be done: *Use your own discretion.*

Word building: **discretionary** *adjective*

discriminate

verb **1** to be able to tell a difference: *A music lover can discriminate between good and bad playing.*
phrase **2 discriminate against,** to treat unfairly: *We should not discriminate against people because of the colour of their skin.*

Word building: **discriminating** *adjective* having good judgement **discriminatory** *adjective*: *discriminatory laws* **discrimination** *noun*

discus   (*say* <u>dis</u>-kuhs)

noun a circular plate for throwing in athletic contests

Word building: The plural is **discuses** or **disci**.

discuss

verb to talk over

Word history: from a Latin word meaning 'struck apart'

discussion   (*say* di-<u>skush</u>-on)

noun **1** a conversation between people, usually about something important: *I could see a discussion coming up between my mother and me.* **2** a piece of writing which gives more than one opinion on something. See the 'Types of writing and speaking' table at the end of this book.

disdain
verb **1** to look down on with scorn
noun **2** a feeling of dislike for anything thought of as unworthy
Word building: **disdainful** *adjective* **disdainfully** *adverb*

disease
noun a sickness which can affect a part or all of any living thing: *a skin disease | a bone disease | a plant disease*
Word building: **diseased** *adjective*: *a diseased kidney*

disembark
verb to leave a ship or plane
Word building: **disembarkation** *noun*

disfigure
verb to spoil the appearance or beauty of: *Vandals disfigured the monument with paint. | Scars disfigured the criminal's face.*
Word building: **disfigurement** *noun*

disgrace
noun **1** shame or dishonour **2** a cause of shame: *Unsportsmanlike behaviour is a disgrace to the team*
phrase **3 in disgrace**, looked at with disapproval: *Kerry is in disgrace because he lied to the teacher.*
Word building: **disgrace** *verb* **disgraceful** *adjective* **disgracefully** *adverb*

disgruntled
adjective annoyed and sulky: *He was very disgruntled when he lost the election.*
Word building: **disgruntle** *verb* **disgruntlement** *noun*

disguise
verb to change the appearance of: *The detectives dyed their hair and wore sunglasses to disguise themselves.*
Word building: **disguise** *noun*

disgust
verb **1** to cause complete dislike in: *Cruelty disgusts me.*
Other words: **repel, repulse, revolt**
noun **2** strong dislike
Other words: **abhorrence, aversion, hatred, repugnance, repulsion**
Word building: **disgustedly** *adverb* **disgusting** *adjective* **disgustingly** *adverb*

dish
noun **1** an open and rather shallow container for serving food **2** a particular kind of food prepared for eating: *a meat and vegetable dish*
Word building: The plural is **dishes**. | **dish** *verb*

dishevelled   (*say* dish-<u>ev</u>-uhld)
adjective untidy or in disorder: *a dishevelled appearance | Her hair was dishevelled.*

dishonest
adjective **1** likely to lie, cheat or steal: *a dishonest person* **2** showing a lack of honesty: *a dishonest action*
Word building: **dishonestly** *adverb* **dishonesty** *noun*

dishonour   (*say* dis-<u>on</u>-uh)
noun **1** a lack of respect: *Your actions show dishonour to your school.* **2** shame or disgrace: *Your actions brought dishonour on our family.*
Word use: Another spelling is **dishonor**.
Word building: **dishonour** *verb* **dishonourable** *adjective* **dishonourably** *adverb*

dishwasher
noun a machine that washes dishes automatically

disinfectant
noun any chemical substance which kills germs
Word building: **disinfect** *verb*

disintegrate
verb to break up into small parts: *The building disintegrated when the bomb exploded.*
Word building: **disintegration** *noun*

disinterested
adjective not directly involved: *It is wise to get a disinterested outsider to settle an argument.*
Other words: **impartial**

disinterested/uninterested Don't confuse **disinterested** with **uninterested**, which means 'not interested'.

disjointed
adjective not fitting together: *a disjointed account of an adventure*
Word building: **disjointedly** *adverb* **disjointedness** *noun*

disk

noun a thin, flat object used in computers for storing data

Word use: Another spelling is **disc**.

disk drive

noun a machine that allows data to be read from or recorded onto a disk

dislike

verb to not like

Word building: **dislike** *noun*: *I have taken a strong dislike to him.*

dislocate

verb **1** to put out of place: *I dislocated my shoulder when I fell.* **2** to throw into disorder: *The accident dislocated traffic.*

Word building: **dislocation** *noun*

dismal   (*say* <u>diz</u>-muhl)

adjective feeling or causing deep sadness: *I was dismal about my failure.* | *dismal news*
Other words: **depressed, gloomy, miserable**

Word building: **dismally** *adverb*

dismantle

verb to take apart: *We dismantled our tent.*

Word building: **dismantlement** *noun*

dismay

verb to fill with disappointment or fear

Word building: **dismay** *noun*

dismiss

verb **1** to order or allow to leave: *The director dismissed the dishonest employee.* | *to dismiss the class* **2** to declare to be out in cricket: *The umpire dismissed the batsman.*

Word building: **dismissal** *noun*   **dismissive** *adjective*

disobedient

adjective refusing to obey: *a disobedient child*

Word building: **disobedience** *noun*

disobey

verb to refuse to obey: *to disobey an order* | *to disobey your parents*

disorder

noun **1** confusion or lack of order: *The disorder in my room took hours to clean up.* **2** violence and noise in public: *There was disorder in the streets.*

Word building: **disorder** *verb*   **disordered** *adjective*   **disorderly** *adjective*

disorganised

adjective in confusion or disorder: *You have such a disorganised mind it takes you ages to finish a job.* | *a disorganised procession*

Word use: Another spelling is **disorganized**.
Word building: **disorganisation** *noun* **disorganise** *verb*

dispatch

verb **1** to send off: *to dispatch a telegram* | *to dispatch a messenger* **2** to put to death or kill

Word use: Another spelling is **despatch**.
Word building: **dispatch** *noun*
Word history: from a French word meaning 'set free'

dispel

verb to drive off or scatter: *He dispelled my fears.*

Word building: Other forms are **I dispelled, I have dispelled, I am dispelling**.

dispensary

noun the part of a chemist's shop or hospital where medicines are made up and given out

Word building: The plural is **dispensaries**.

dispense

verb **1** to deal out: *The courts dispense justice.* **2** to make up from a prescription and give out: *Any pharmacy will dispense that medicine for you.*
phrase **3 dispense with, a** to do without **b** to get rid of

Word building: **dispensable** *adjective* able to be done without   **dispensation** *noun*   **dispenser** *noun*

disperse

verb **1** to scatter around: *The wind dispersed the leaves on the ground.* **2** to separate and move in different directions: *The crowd dispersed.*

Word building: **dispersal** *noun*   **dispersion** *noun*

displace

verb **1** to put out of the usual place: *War often displaces families.* **2** to take the place of: *Weeds displaced the flowers in the old garden.*

Word building: **displacement** *noun*

display

verb to show or exhibit: *Robin's face displayed anger.* | *He displayed his prize roses.*

Word building: **display** *noun*

displease

verb to annoy or cause to be unhappy or angry: *My bad behaviour displeased my parents.*

Word building: **displeasing** *adjective* **displeasingly** *adverb* **displeasure** *noun*

dispose

verb **1** to influence or make willing: *The sunny weather disposed her to go to the beach.* *phrase* **2 dispose of**, to get rid of: *I disposed of my old books.*

Word building: **disposable** *adjective* **disposal** *noun* **disposed** *adjective*

disposition

noun **1** your personality or particular character: *a happy disposition* **2** arrangement in an order: *the disposition of troops*

dispute

verb **1** to argue loud and long **2** to argue about or against: *to dispute what to do | to dispute a claim*

Word building: **disputable** *adjective* open to argument   **disputation** *noun* discussion   **dispute** *noun* an argument

disqualify

verb **1** to prevent or make unsuitable: *My aunt's income will disqualify her from getting a pension.* **2** to declare unable to compete because a rule has been broken

Word building: Other forms are **I disqualified, I have disqualified, I am disqualifying.** | **disqualification** *noun*

disregard

verb **1** to pay no attention to **2** to treat as unnecessary or unworthy of respect

disrespect

noun rudeness or lack of respect

Word building: **disrespectful** *adjective* **disrespectfully** *adverb*

disrupt

verb to interrupt or throw into disorder: *The demonstrators disrupted the meeting.*

Word building: **disruption** *noun*   **disruptive** *adjective*

dissect

verb to cut apart for close examination: *We dissect plants in biology class.*

Word building: **dissector** *noun*   **dissection** *noun*

dissent

verb to disagree or differ: *I dissent from their view of the matter.*

Word building: **dissension** *noun* a difference of opinion which is often violent   **dissenter** *noun*   **dissenting** *adjective*

dissident

noun someone who has a different opinion or belief, especially about a particular political system

Word building: **dissident** *adjective*

dissipate

verb **1** to scatter or disappear in different directions: *The smoke dissipated in the wind.* **2** to scatter or use wastefully: *My cousin dissipated our money by gambling.*

Word building: **dissipation** *noun*

dissociate   (*say* di-<u>soh</u>-see-ayt)

verb to separate: *She deliberately dissociated herself from the people who were into bullying.*

dissolute   (*say* <u>dis</u>-uh-looht)

adjective having a wasteful and immoral way of life

Word building: **dissolutely** *adverb* **dissoluteness** *noun*

dissolve

verb **1** to mix or become mixed: *I dissolved the sugar in the water. | Salt dissolves in water.* **2** to bring to an end: *The Queen dissolved Parliament. | The court dissolved the partnership.*

Word building: **dissolution** *noun*

dissonance

noun **1** sound that is harsh and unpleasant **2** a combination of musical notes that doesn't sound pleasant

Word building: **dissonant** *adjective* **dissonantly** *adverb*

distance

noun **1** the length of a space: *the distance between Adelaide and Perth* **2** a part far away: *The distance was hidden in mist.*

distant

adjective far off: *a distant town | the distant future*

Word building: **distantly** *adverb*

distaste

noun a dislike: *I have a distaste for people who boast.*

Word building: **distasteful** *adjective* **distastefully** *adverb*   **distastefulness** *noun*

distemper

noun a disease in young dogs which is easily spread

distend

verb to swell or stretch: *Their stomachs distended from over-eating.*

Word building: **distension** noun **distensible** adjective

distil

verb **1** to make pure by heating to a gas and then turning the gas back into a liquid **2** to separate by doing this: *to distil kerosene from petroleum*

Word building: Other forms are **I distilled, I have distilled, I am distilling.** | **distilled** adjective: *distilled water* **distillation** noun **distillery** noun
Word history: from a Latin word meaning 'drip down'

distinct

adjective **1** separate or different: *They were in distinct groups.* | *The new uniform is quite distinct from the old one.* **2** clear and unmistakable: *a distinct difference*

Word building: **distinctly** adverb **distinction** noun **distinctness** noun

distinguish

verb **1** to mark off as different: *A leopard's spots distinguish it from a tiger.* **2** to recognise a difference: *I can distinguish between the twins by their heights.* **3** to make well-known: *My sister distinguished herself as an athlete.*

Word building: **distinguished** adjective famous

distort

verb **1** to twist out of shape: *Pain distorted her face.* **2** to change and make incorrect: *to distort the truth*

Word building: **distorted** adjective **distortion** noun

distract

verb **1** to draw away the attention of: *The noise outside the room distracted the class.* **2** to trouble or disturb: *Worry distracted her to the point of illness.*

Word building: **distracted** adjective nervous and troubled **distractedly** adverb **distraction** noun

distress

noun **1** great pain, worry or sorrow **2** danger or difficulty: *The lifesaver went to the surfer in distress.*

Word building: **distress** verb **distressed** adjective **distressful** adjective **distressing** adjective
Word history: from a Latin word meaning 'drawn tight'

distribute

verb **1** to give or share out: *She distributed gifts to the children.* **2** to scatter or spread: *Distribute the manure evenly over the garden.*

Word building: **distribution** noun **distributor** noun

district

noun **1** a particular area, region or neighbourhood: *What district do you live in?* **2** an area marked out for some official purpose: *a postal district*

disturb

verb **1** to interrupt the quiet, rest or peace of **2** to move or unsettle: *The wind disturbed the smooth surface of the lake.*

Word building: **disturbing** adjective worrying **disturbance** noun **disturbingly** adverb

disuse   (say dis-yoohs)

noun a stopping of use: *The stables fell into disuse when the horse was sold.*

Word building: **disused** adjective

ditch

noun **1** a long narrow hollow dug in the earth, used as a drain or channel for carrying water to dry land
verb **2** *Informal* to get rid of

Word building: The plural form of the noun is **ditches.**

dither

verb *Informal* to be nervous and confused: *They dithered over what to do next.*

Word building: **dither** noun

ditto marks

plural noun two small marks (") used in writing or printing to show that what is above is repeated

ditzy

adjective *Informal* rather stupid: *That was such a ditzy thing to say in front of the teacher!*

divan (*say* duh-<u>van</u>)
noun a low bed or couch without a back or arms

dive
verb **1** to jump, especially headfirst into water **2** to go down suddenly: *The aeroplane dived.*
Word building: **dive** *noun* **diver** *noun* **diving** *adjective*

diverge
verb to branch off: *The road diverged to the left.*
Word building: **divergence** *noun* **divergent** *adjective*

diverse
adjective of many different kinds or forms
Word building: **diversely** *adverb* **diversify** *verb* **diversity** *noun*

divert
verb **1** to turn aside from a path or course: *Police diverted the traffic.* **2** to draw off: *I'll divert their attention from you.*
Word building: **diversion** *noun*

divide
verb **1** to split up or separate into parts **2** to share out: *I divided the books among the children.* **3** to separate into equal parts, using maths: *to divide 69 by 3*
Word building: **divisible** *adjective* **divisive** *adjective* creating division or discord

dividend
noun **1** the number which is divided by another number: *In the sum 16 ÷ 4, 16 is the dividend.* **2** your share of some money which is being given out, especially from the profits of a business
Word use: Compare definition 1 with **divisor**.

divine
adjective **1** having to do with a god **2** *Informal* wonderful or excellent: *Isn't the weather divine?*
verb **3** to discover by instinct, magic or guessing: *The fortune-teller used a crystal ball to divine the future.*
Word building: **diviner** *noun*: *A water diviner uses a rod to find underground water.* | **divination** *noun* **divinely** *adverb*

divining rod
noun a forked stick which is said to tremble when a diviner holds it over a place where there is water or metal underground

divinity
noun **1** a god or divine being **2** the study of religion: *a student of divinity*
Other words: **theology**
Word building: The plural is **divinities**.

division
noun **1** the act of dividing one number by another number in maths **2** a separation or distribution: *division of the class into four teams* **3** a section or group: *an army division* | *He plays football in the under-twelve division.*
Word building: **divisional** *adjective*

divisor (*say* duh-<u>vuy</u>-zuh)
noun a number by which you divide another number: *In the sum 16 ÷ 4, 4 is the divisor.*
Word use: Compare this with **dividend**.

divorce
noun the ending of a marriage by a court of law
Word building: **divorcee** *noun* someone who is divorced **divorce** *verb*

divulge
verb to tell: *I'll tell you a secret if you promise not to divulge it.*
Word use: The more usual word is **reveal**.
Word building: **divulgence** *noun*
Word history: from a Latin word meaning 'make common'

dizzy
adjective **1** having the feeling that you are spinning around: *Don't all talk at once — you make me dizzy.*
Other words: **faint, giddy, wobbly**
2 causing this feeling: *She climbed to a dizzy height.*
Word building: Other forms are **dizzier, dizziest**. | **dizziness** *noun* **dizzily** *adverb*
Word history: from an Old English word meaning 'foolish'

DNA
noun a chemical substance in the cells of living things that passes genetic characteristics, like eye colour and height, from parents to offspring
Word history: short for *deoxyribonucleic acid*

do

verb **1** to perform or carry out: *to do your homework* **2** to be the cause of: *to do harm* **3** to deal with: *to do the dishes* **4** to travel: *We did 30 kilometres today.* **5** to serve or be all right for: *This room will do us.*
noun **6** *Informal* a party: *We are having a do next week.*
phrase **7 make do**, to manage with what you've got

Word building: Other verb forms are **I do, he, she, it does, I did, I have done, I am doing.**

dob   *Informal*

phrase **1 dob in**, to name or suggest, especially for an unpleasant job: *We dobbed James in for cleaning up the playground.*
2 dob on, to report or tell on, especially for doing something wrong: *He dobbed on them for breaking the window.*

Word use: You can also use **dob in** for definition 2.
Word building: Other forms are **I dobbed, I have dobbed, I am dobbing.**

docile   *(say* <u>doh</u>-suyl)

adjective quiet and easily handled: *a docile horse*

Word building: **docility** *noun* **docilely** *adverb*

dock[1]

noun **1** a wharf or pier where a ship ties up when it's in port **2** the part of a large building where trucks can enter to load or unload goods
verb **3** to come or bring into a dock for loading or repair: *The ship docks at 3 o'clock today.* **4** to join together while in orbit: *The spaceships docked successfully.*

dock[2]

verb to cut off or take away a part of: *to dock a dog's tail* | *They docked my wages because I came to work late.*

dock[3]

noun the part of a courtroom where the person on trial is put

docket

noun **1** a ticket or label on a package stating what is inside **2** a receipt, like one from a cash register, proving that you have paid for goods

doctor

noun **1** someone who has learned about diseases and is allowed by law to look after sick people and give them medicine **2** someone who has received the highest degree given by a university: *After many years of research he was made a Doctor of Philosophy.*

Word history: from a Latin word meaning 'teacher'

doctrine   *(say* <u>dok</u>-truhn)

noun something that is believed or taught: *a religious doctrine*

Word building: **doctrinal** *(say* dok-<u>truy</u>-nuhl) *adjective* **doctrinally** *adverb*

document   *(say* <u>dok</u>-yuh-muhnt)

noun **1** a paper giving information or evidence: *Keep an important document like your birth certificate in a safe place.*
2 a file produced by a computer, especially one made by word-processing software
verb (say <u>dok</u>-yooh-ment) **3** to support or back up with documents: *You must document your case well if you hope to convince the judge.*

Word building: **documentation** *noun* the documents provided to support a case

documentary   *(say* dok-yooh-<u>men</u>-tree)

noun a film or radio program about a real event or someone's everyday life

Word building: The plural is **documentaries.**

dodge

verb **1** to duck or move aside quickly, so as to avoid something: *He dodged the ball just in time.* | *She dodged when she saw the ball coming towards her.*
noun **2** a dishonest trick

Word building: **dodgy** *adjective* awkward or tricky **dodger** *noun*

doe

noun the female of animals such as a deer, rabbit or kangaroo

Word use: The male is usually called a **buck.**

doe/dough Don't confuse **doe** with **dough. Dough** is a mixture of flour and water or milk which is baked to make bread or pastry. It is also an informal word for money.

doff

verb to remove or take off: *to doff your hat*
Word use: The opposite is **don.**

dog

noun **1** a four-legged mammal which eats meat and may live in the wild, like a dingo or wolf, or may be kept as a pet or a working dog, like a poodle or a kelpie
2 the male of this type of animal
verb **3** to pursue or follow closely: *Bad luck dogged Jack all his life.*

Word use: The female is a **bitch**.
Word building: Other verb forms are **I dogged, I have dogged, I am dogging.** | **dogged** (*say* dog-uhd) *adjective* determined not to give in
doggedly (*say* dog-uhd-lee) *adverb*

dogmatic

adjective saying what you think very forcefully and expecting others to accept it as true

Word building: **dogma** *noun* a belief or principle which many people hold to be true: *religious dogma* **dogmatism** *noun* **dogmatist** *noun* **dogmatically** *adverb*

doily

noun a small fancy mat that can be put under a cake on a plate or under a vase of flowers

Word building: The plural is **doilies**.
Word history: named after a 17th century draper of London

dole

verb **1** to give in small amounts: *to dole out the soup*
phrase **2 the dole**, money paid by the government to help people who are out of work

doleful

adjective very sad: *a puppy with doleful eyes*
Word building: **dolefully** *adverb* **dolefulness** *noun*

doll

noun **1** a child's toy which is made to look like a person
phrase **2 doll up**, to dress in your best clothes

Word use: Children often use **dolly** for definition 1.
Word history: from *Doll* and *Dolly*, short forms of the woman's name *Dorothy*

dollar

noun a unit of money, either a coin or a banknote, which is equal to 100 cents and is used in Australia, America and some other countries

Word use: The symbol for the dollar is $.

dolphin

noun an intelligent, playful sea mammal with a long sharp nose

Word use: Another word for some types of dolphin is **porpoise**.

domain (*say* duh-mayn)

noun **1** a territory or realm that is owned or controlled: *The land between the mountains and the sea is in the king's domain.*
2 an area of interest or knowledge: *Geology is not my domain.*

domain name

noun the name of an internet site that gives the name of the organisation, followed by the type of organisation and (except for the United States) the country of origin

dome

noun a roof shaped like the top half of a hollow sphere or ball: *The dome of the cathedral stands out from all the other buildings.*

Word building: **domed** *adjective*

domestic (*say* duh-mes-tik)

adjective **1** having to do with the home or family: *Cooking, cleaning and washing are domestic tasks.* **2** tame or living with people: *Dogs and cats are domestic animals.* **3** for or from your own country: *Some of the wheat is for domestic use and the rest will be sold overseas.*

Word building: **domestic** *noun* a servant paid to do housework | **domestically** *adverb* **domesticate** *verb* **domesticity** *noun*

dominate

verb **1** to rule over or control **2** to tower above or overshadow: *The huge gum tree dominates the park.*

Word building: **dominant** *adjective* most important or influential **dominance** *noun* **domination** *noun*

domineering

adjective bossy and overbearing
Word building: **domineer** *verb* **domineeringly** *adverb*

dominion (*say* duh-min-yuhn)

noun **1** power to rule or govern: *Australia has dominion over these islands.* **2** the land ruled by one person or government: *Britain and all her dominions*

domino

noun a flat piece of wood or plastic marked with a number of dots used to play a game

Word building: The plural is **dominoes**.

don

verb to put on: *to don clothing*

Word use: The opposite is **doff**.
Word building: Other forms are **I donned, I have donned, I am donning**.

donate

verb to give as a gift: *to donate books to the school library*

Word building: **donation** *noun* a gift, usually of money

doner kebab

(*say* <u>doh</u>-nuh kuh-bab, <u>don</u>-uh kuh-bab)
noun slices of spicy meat cut from a vertical spit and served rolled up with salad in a piece of flat bread

Word use: A shortened form is **kebab**.
Word history: from the Turkish words for 'turning' and 'roast meat'

donkey

noun **1** a long-eared mammal, related to a horse **2** someone who is stupid or stubborn

Word use: Another word is **ass**. | The male is a **jackass**, the female is a **jennet** and the young is a **foal**.

donor

noun someone who gives or donates something: *The blood bank is calling for blood donors.*

doodle

verb to draw or scribble while you are thinking about something else

Word building: **doodle** *noun*　**doodler** *noun*

doom

noun **1** a dreadful outcome, fate or death: *The ship struck an iceberg and all the passengers went to their doom.*
verb **2** to force or condemn to unhappiness or ruin: *The accident doomed him to life in a wheelchair.*

Word building: **doomed** *adjective*

doona

noun a large bag filled with feathers or other material and used as a quilt on a bed

Word use: Another name is **continental quilt**.

door

noun **1** a large piece of wood which can be moved to open or close the entrance to a house, room or cupboard **2** the entrance to a room or house **3** a house or building: *He lives two doors down the street.*

Word use: Definition 2 is also called **doorway**.

dope　*Informal*

noun **1** a stupid person **2** an illegal drug **3** the actual facts or information: *Give me the dope on that new computer.*

Word building: **dope** *verb*　**dopey** *adjective*
Word history: from a Dutch word meaning 'a dipping' or 'sauce'

dormant

adjective not active, as if asleep or resting: *Some animals lie dormant during winter.* | *This volcano has been dormant for two hundred years.*

Word building: **dormancy** *noun*

dormitory

noun a big room with many beds, especially in a boarding school or hostel

Word building: The plural is **dormitories**.

dose

noun **1** the amount of medicine taken at one time **2** an amount of something unpleasant: *a dose of the flu*

Word building: **dosage** *noun*　**dose** *verb*

dossier　(*say* <u>dos</u>-ee-uh)

noun a bundle of documents containing information about a person or subject: *The police kept a dossier on the bank robber.*
Other words: **file**

dot

noun **1** a small spot or a speck: *We watched the plane until it was just a dot in the sky.*
phrase **2 on the dot**, *Informal* exactly on time

Word building: **dotted** *adjective*

dotcom

noun **1** a company trading over the internet or involved in the information technology industry
adjective **2** having to do with a dotcom

dote

phrase **dote on**, to love so much that you appear to be silly: *She dotes on horses and talks about them all the time.*

Word building: **doting** *adjective*: *doting parents* **dotingly** *adverb*

dot painting

noun a style of Aboriginal art in which ochre or some other colouring is used in a series of dots to build up a picture

dotty

adjective Informal mad or crazy

Word building: Other forms are **dottier**, **dottiest**.

double

adjective **1** twice as big, heavy or strong: *a double helping of mashed potato | a double bed* **2** with two parts: *a double ice-cream | a word with a double meaning*
noun **3** anything that is doubled: *Four is the double of two.* **4** someone who looks almost the same as someone else: *You look so much like my sister you could be her double.*
verb **5** to make or become twice as much: *You double four to get eight. | The bread doubled in size.* **6** to bend or fold in two: *She doubled up with laughter. | to double the handkerchiefs neatly for ironing* **7** to serve or be used in two ways: *The swimming pool doubles as a skating rink in winter.* **8** to carry on a bike or horse: *She doubled me home from school.*
phrase **9 double back**, to turn back the way you came **10 on the double**, very quickly: *Get in here on the double.*

double bass

noun the largest instrument of the violin family, which has a very deep sound

doublecross

verb Informal to betray or deceive by promising one thing and doing another

Word building: **doublecross** *noun*

double take

noun a surprised second look at something, caused by the realisation that what you have just seen is unusual in some way: *He glanced quickly out the window, then did a double take as he realised that there was an elephant in the garden.*

doubt   (*rhymes with* out)

verb **1** to be uncertain or unsure: *I doubt that you will get there on time.*
noun **2** a feeling of uncertainty or suspicion: *There is some doubt about your honesty.*

Word building: **doubtful** *adjective* uncertain **doubtfully** *adverb* **doubtfulness** *noun*

dough   (*rhymes with* slow)

noun **1** a mixture of flour and water or milk which is baked to make bread or pastry **2** *Informal* money

dough/doe Don't confuse **dough** with **doe**, which is the female of animals such as deer, rabbits and kangaroos.

doughnut

noun a ring-shaped cake which is fried and covered in sugar or icing

Word use: Another spelling is **donut**.

dour

adjective gloomy: *He looks dour and unfriendly.*

Word use: The more usual word is **stern**.
Word history: from a Latin word meaning 'hard'

douse   (*rhymes with* house)

verb to throw water on: *to douse a fire to put it out*

dove   (*say* duv)

noun a bird like a pigeon

dowdy

adjective shabby and unfashionable: *She wore dowdy old clothes.*

Word building: **dowdily** *adverb* **dowdiness** *noun*

down[1]

adverb **1** from higher to lower: *Climb down from there!* **2** on or to the ground: *She fell down.*
preposition **3** to or at a lower place on or in: *She hurried down the stairs*
adjective **4** downwards: *The track is down for about a kilometre.* **5** in bed or resting because you are sick: *I was down with the flu for a week.* **6** *Informal* unhappy: *She's been feeling a bit down since her best friend transferred to a different school.*
noun **7** a time of bad luck or depression: *Life has many ups and downs.*

down[2]

noun fine soft hair or feathers: *down on his face | a duck's down*

Word building: **downy** *adjective*

downfall

noun **1** disgrace or ruin: *Greediness was her downfall.* **2** a heavy fall of rain or snow

download

verb to copy (a file) from one computer or the internet to another computer, or to another storage device: *We found we were able to download sheet music from the web — and it's absolutely free!*

Word building: **download** *noun*

downpour

noun a heavy fall of rain

downs

plural noun open hilly country, usually covered with grass

downstairs

adverb **1** on or towards a lower storey or storeys of a house, and so on: *Is there a downstairs toilet?*
noun **2** a lower storey or storeys

Down syndrome   (*say* <u>down</u> sin-drohm)

noun a condition that some people are born with that means that they look a bit different from other people and have different abilities

downtime

noun **1** the time when a machine is not working **2** a time of relaxation: *After doing her homework, she felt like a bit of downtime.*

downwards

adverb towards a lower position or level: *Even in the dark, I could tell the track was moving downwards.*

Word building: **downward** *adverb*

dowry

noun money or property that a woman in some cultures brings to her husband when she marries

Word building: The plural is **dowries**.

doze

verb to fall into a light sleep, often without meaning to

Word building: **doze** *noun*

dozen

noun a group of twelve

Word building: The plural is **dozen** or **dozens**.

drab

adjective **1** dull grey or brown: *drab clothes* **2** dull or uninteresting: *drab life*

Word building: Other forms are **drabber**, **drabbest**.

draft

noun **1** a rough sketch or piece of writing **2** a letter instructing a bank to pay money: *a draft for $200*
phrase **3 the draft**, the forcing of people to join the armed forces

Word building: **draft** *verb*

draft/draught Don't confuse **draft** with **draught**, which is a current of air or wind. It is also a rather old-fashioned word for a drink.

draftsman

noun someone who makes drawings of the plans or designs of things such as bridges, roads and buildings

Word use: Another spelling is **draughtsman**.

drag

verb **1** to pull or move slowly and heavily along: *to drag a cupboard across the room | My feet were dragging after walking so far.* **2** to pass so slowly as to seem endless: *The speech dragged on.* **3** to search with nets: *The police dragged the river for the body.*
noun **4** something that holds you back **5** *Informal* someone or something very boring: *The party was a drag so we left early.* **6** *Informal* women's clothes when worn by men: *to be dressed in drag* **7** *Informal* a car race to see which car can accelerate fastest from a standstill

Word building: Other verb forms are **I dragged**, **I have dragged**, **I am dragging**.

dragon

noun **1** an imaginary fire-breathing monster which was supposed to look like a huge lizard with wings and fierce claws **2** a very strict and bossy woman **3** a type of lizard like the frill-necked lizard or bearded dragon

Word history: from a Greek word meaning 'serpent'

dragonfly

noun a large harmless insect with a long thin body and four long delicate wings of the same length

Word building: The plural is **dragonflies**.

drain

verb **1** to draw or flow away gradually: *to drain water from the swimming pool* | *The colour drained from her face.* **2** to make or become dry by water flowing away: *The dishes are draining on the sink.*
noun **3** a pipe or channel which carries liquid away **4** anything which uses up or exhausts: *Buying that new car was a drain on our bank account.*

Word building: **drainage** *noun*

drake

noun a male duck

Word use: The female is a **duck** and the young is a **duckling**.

drama

noun **1** an exciting, sad or serious play acted on stage, radio or television **2** any exciting event: *the drama of a bank robbery* **3** a piece of writing intended to be acted out. See the 'Types of writing and speaking' table at the end of this book.

Word building: **dramatic** *adjective* **dramatically** *adverb* **dramatics** *noun*

dramatise

verb **1** to take a story and make it into a play **2** to express or show in an exaggerated way: *Don't dramatise your sadness.*

Word use: Another spelling is **dramatize**.
Word building: **dramatisation** *noun* **dramatist** *noun*

drape

verb **1** to hang in loose folds: *to drape a blanket around your shoulders* | *That material drapes nicely.* **2** to put casually: *Don't drape your legs over the arm of the sofa.*
noun **3 drapes**, curtains

Word history: from a French word meaning 'cloth'

draper

noun a shopkeeper who sells material, such as cotton or linen

drapery

noun **1** material or cloth **2** a shop selling material or cloth

Word building: The plural is **draperies**.

drastic

adjective violent, harsh or extreme: *In an emergency we may need to take drastic action.*

Word building: **drastically** *adverb*

draught   (*rhymes with* craft)

noun **1** a current of air or wind **2** *Old-fashioned* a drink: *a long draught of water* **3** the depth of water which a ship needs so that it can float: *a draught of 30 metres* **4 draughts**, a game played by two people each with twelve pieces which they move diagonally across a chequered board

Word use: Definition 4 is also called **checkers**.
Word building: **draughty** *adjective* (**draughtier**, **draughtiest**) windy or breezy

draught/draft Don't confuse **draught** with **draft**, which is a rough sketch or piece of writing.

draught horse

noun a big strong horse used to pull heavy loads

draughtsman

noun **1** another spelling of **draftsman** **2** one of the pieces used in the game of draughts

draw

verb **1** to sketch or make a picture with a pen or pencil **2** to pull, move or take in a particular direction: *to draw your hand away* | *The ship draws near.* | *The crowd drew together.* | *to draw money from the bank* **3** to attract: *The tennis match drew a big crowd.*
noun **4** the act of drawing or picking: *a lottery draw* **5** something that is picked or drawn: *a lucky draw* **6** a contest where neither side wins: *The match ended in a draw.*
phrase **7 draw a blank,** to be unsuccessful, especially when looking for someone or something, or trying to find out about something: *I thought my watch was in lost property but I drew a blank.* **8 draw out, a** to make longer: *to draw out a conversation* **b** to encourage somebody to talk: *Try and draw that shy new girl out.*

Word building: Other verb forms are **I drew**, **I have drawn, I am drawing**. | **drawing** *noun* a sketch or picture **drawer** *noun* **drawn** *adjective*

drawback

noun a disadvantage or inconvenience: *The plan is excellent except for one drawback.*

drawbridge

noun a bridge which can be raised or lowered: *After the knights rode into the castle, they pulled up the drawbridge.*

drawer

noun **1** a container shaped like a box that slides in and out of furniture such as cupboards or desks **2 drawers**, *Old-fashioned* roomy underpants

drawl

verb to speak very slowly so that the sounds are long and drawn out

Word building: **drawl** *noun*

dray

noun a low horse-drawn cart without sides, used for carrying heavy loads

Word history: from a Middle English word meaning 'sledge without wheels'

dread

verb **1** to be very much afraid of: *to dread the exams*
noun **2** great fear or deep awe

Word building: **dread** *adjective* deeply feared and respected

dreadful

adjective **1** causing great dread or terror: *a dreadful giant*
Other words: **ghastly, horrendous, terrible**
2 extremely bad or unpleasant: *The film was dreadful so we left early.*
Other words: **atrocious, awful, terrible**

Word building: **dreadfully** *adverb* **dreadfulness** *noun*

dream

noun **1** the thoughts and pictures that pass through your mind when you are sleeping **2** a hope or ambition: *My dream is to sing in a band.*
verb **3** to imagine or have a dream
phrase **4 dream up**, *Informal* to invent or plan in your imagination

Word building: Other verb forms are **I dreamed** or **dreamt, I have dreamed** or **dreamt, I am dreaming**. | **dreamy** *adjective* (**dreamier, dreamiest**) vague or lost in dreams **dreamer** *noun* **dreamless** *adjective*
Word history: from an Old English word meaning 'gaiety' or 'noise'

Dreaming

noun in Aboriginal tradition, the time in which the earth came to have its present form, and in which the patterns of life and nature began

Word use: Another name is the **Dreamtime**.

dreary

adjective dull or depressing: *a dreary afternoon* | *a dreary sight*
Other words: **gloomy**

Word building: Other forms are **drearier, dreariest**. | **drearily** *adverb* **dreariness** *noun*

dredge

noun **1** a machine for drawing up sand or mud from the bottom of a river or harbour
verb **2** to use a dredge to clear out the bottom of: *to dredge the harbour*
phrase **3 dredge up**, to find with difficulty: *She finally dredged up some ideas for her story.*

dregs

plural noun **1** the solid part that settles at the bottom of a drink: *She drank the cup of tea down to the dregs.*
Other words: **sediment**
2 a useless or worthless part of something: *the dregs of society*

drench

verb to soak or make very wet: *The rain drenched my clothes.*

Word history: from an Old English word meaning 'make drink'

dress

noun **1** a piece of clothing worn by a woman, which covers her body from her shoulders to her legs **2** clothing in general: *The pictures in that book show the dress of the Middle Ages.*
verb **3** to put clothes on: *Please dress now.* | *Wait while I dress the baby.* **4** to treat by cleaning and bandaging: *The nurse dressed the wound.* **5** to arrange or decorate: *They dressed the shop window for Christmas.*
phrase **6 dress up, a** to put on your best clothes **b** to put on fancy dress or a costume that disguises you

Word building: The plural form of the noun is **dresses**. | **dress** *adjective*: *a dress suit* **dressy** *adjective* smart or stylish

dress circle

noun a curved section of seats upstairs in a theatre or cinema

dresser

noun a piece of furniture with shelves and drawers for dishes, knives and forks

dressing

noun **1** an act of getting dressed: *Dressing takes her hours.* **2** a sauce for foods: *salad dressing* **3** a bandage for a wound

dressing-gown

noun a coat that is worn over your nightclothes

dressing table

noun a piece of furniture for your bedroom, usually with drawers and a mirror

dribble

verb **1** to flow in small drops: *Blood dribbled from the wound.*
Other words: **drip, leak, seep, trickle**
2 to let spit flow from your mouth: *Babies are always dribbling.* **3** to move a ball along by a series of kicks or bounces, used in basketball or soccer

Word building: **dribble** *noun*

drift

verb **1** to be carried along by the movement of water or air **2** to wander without any particular aim or direction: *I have spent the last three years just drifting about.*
noun **3** a general movement or trend: *The drift of public opinion is towards the government.* **4** the general meaning: *Did you get the drift of the speech?*

Word building: **drifter** *noun* someone who wanders through life without aims or goals

driftwood

noun wood that is floating on water or has been washed ashore

drill

noun **1** a tool for making or boring holes **2** a strict way of training or exercise that is repeated regularly: *The soldiers were doing their marching drill.* | *We must do fire drill once a month.*
verb **3** to pierce using a drill **4** to train by giving repeated exercises: *She drilled them in their lines for the play.*

drink

verb **1** to swallow liquid **2** to drink alcohol
noun **3** any liquid that can be drunk **4** an alcoholic drink: *We had a drink to celebrate.*
phrase **5 drink in,** to take in by paying attention: *We drank in every word.*
Other words: **absorb**

Word building: Other verb forms are **I drank, I have drunk, I am drinking.** | **drinker** *noun*

drip

verb **1** to let drops fall: *That tap drips all the time.* **2** to fall in drops: *Rain is dripping from the leaves.*
noun **3** a falling drop of liquid or the sound it makes **4** a slow injection of liquid into the veins of a sick person **5** *Informal* a dull or boring person

Word building: Other verb forms are **I dripped, I have dripped, I am dripping.**

dripping

noun fat that has dripped from meat during cooking and which is kept to be used again

drive

verb **1** to force to go: *to drive the mice away* | *Don't drive yourself too hard.* **2** to control the movement of: *Can you drive a car?* **3** to take, go or travel in a car or other vehicle: *I will drive you home.* | *We are driving from Perth to Broome.*
noun **4** a trip in a car or other vehicle **5** a road up to a private house: *The car was parked in the drive.* **6** energy: *She has a lot of drive.* **7** an effort by many people to get something done: *The club is having a drive to get more members.*

Word building: Other verb forms are **I drove, I have driven, I am driving.** | **driver** *noun*

drive-in

noun **1** an outdoor cinema where people watch films from their cars
adjective **2** serving customers in their cars: *a drive-in bank*

driven

adjective pursuing a goal with fanatical determination: *She is absolutely driven in her desire to get into the best team.*

drizzle

verb to rain lightly

Word building: **drizzle** *noun*   **drizzly** *adjective*

drone[1]

noun **1** a male bee which does not make honey and has no sting **2** someone who is lazy and won't work

drone[2]

verb to make a dull continuous sound: *The lecturer's voice droned on and on.*

Word building: **drone** *noun* a humming sound

drool

verb **1** to let spit fall from your mouth: *He was drooling with hunger.*
phrase **2 drool over**, to have a greedy interest in: *She drooled over her friend's new car.*

droop

verb **1** to bend or hang down: *The flowers began to droop in the hot weather.* **2** to lose courage: *Their spirits drooped when the boat's engine stopped.*

Word building: **droop** *noun* **drooping** *adjective* **droopy** *adjective*

drop

noun **1** a small rounded amount of liquid which falls **2** a small amount of anything, especially liquid: *a drop of milk* **3** the distance or length by which anything falls: *That cliff has a big drop. | What is the drop of those curtains?* **4** a fall in amount or value: *There has been a drop in prices.*
verb **5** to fall or let fall: *He dropped onto the chair. | She dropped her pencil.* **6** to set down from a car or other vehicle: *I'll drop you at the corner.* **7** to make lower: *to drop your voice | to drop the hem of the dress*
phrase **8 drop in** or **drop by**, to visit for a short time

Word building: Other verb forms are **I dropped, I have dropped, I am dropping.**

drop-down menu

noun a computer menu which offers a choice of actions or screen pages

drought   (*rhymes with* out)

noun a long period of dry weather which is so long that plants die and water runs out

drove

verb to drive cattle or sheep over long distances: *He was droving in Queensland for many years.*

Word building: **drover** *noun* someone who droves cattle

drown

verb **1** to die from being under water for too long: *He drowned in the river.* **2** to kill by holding under water **3** to cover up by making a louder sound: *The noise of the traffic drowned her cries.*

drowse

verb to be almost asleep

Word building: **drowsy** *adjective* (**drowsier, drowsiest**) **drowsily** *adverb* **drowsiness** *noun*
Word history: from an Old English word meaning 'droop' or 'become slow'

drudge

noun someone who does boring or hard work

Word building: **drudge** *verb* **drudgery** *noun*

drug

noun **1** a chemical substance given to someone to prevent or cure a disease **2** a substance that is habit-forming
verb **3** to mix a drug with: *Someone had drugged Nick's drink.* **4** to poison or make unconscious with a drug

Word building: Other verb forms are **I drugged, I have drugged, I am drugging.**
Word history: from a Dutch word meaning 'dry thing'

drug mule

noun someone who carries illegal drugs for someone else, usually from one country to another

drum

noun **1** a musical instrument with a round hollow body covered with a tightly stretched skin, which makes a deep sound when it is hit **2** a container for petrol or other liquid, in the shape of a drum **3** *Informal* information or advice: *I'm new here so you'd better give me the drum.*
verb **4** to beat or play a drum **5** to beat on anything continuously: *She drummed on the desk with her fingers.*

Word building: Other verb forms are **I drummed, I have drummed, I am drumming. | drummer** *noun*

drunk

adjective **1** having had too much alcoholic drink
noun **2** someone who is drunk

Word building: **drunkard** *noun* someone who is often drunk   **drunken** *adjective*: *a drunken sleep*

dry

adjective **1** not wet or damp **2** having little or no rain: *The land was very dry because of the drought.*
Other words: **arid**
3 thirsty or making thirsty: *This is dry work.* **4** not sweet: *a dry wine* **5** dull or boring: *Her speech was very dry and several people fell asleep.*
Other words: **dreary, tedious**
6 funny and able to be expressed in a few words: *She has a dry sense of humour.*
verb **7** to make or become dry

Word building: Other verb forms are **I dried, I have dried, I am drying.** | **dryly, drily** *adverb* **dryness** *noun*

dry-clean

verb to clean (clothes) with chemicals rather than water

Word building: **dry-cleaning** *noun* **dry-cleaner** *noun*

dry dock

noun a dock from which water can be emptied so that the underneath of ships can be repaired or cleaned

dry ice

noun solid frozen carbon dioxide which is used to keep things cold

dryland farming

noun a method of cultivation of land which receives little rainfall, such as leaving the stubble of some plants on the ground to provide nutrients and preserve water

dual   (*say* <u>dyooh</u>-uhl)

adjective having to do with two or having two parts: *That plane has dual controls.* | *This book has a dual purpose — to teach you and to entertain you.*

Word building: **duality** *noun*

> **dual/duel** Don't confuse **dual** with **duel**, which is a fight or contest between two people using swords or pistols.

dub[1]

verb **1** to tap with a sword when making a knight: *The queen dubbed him Sir James.*
2 to give a name to: *We dubbed him 'The Rat' after he betrayed us.*

Word building: Other forms are **I dubbed, I have dubbed, I am dubbing.**

dub[2]

verb to give a new soundtrack in a different language to: *They dubbed the French film so that it could be understood in Australia.*

Word building: Other forms are **I dubbed, I have dubbed, I am dubbing.**

dubious   (*say* <u>dyooh</u>-bee-uhs)

adjective **1** uncertain or doubtful: *I feel dubious about my chances in the exam.*
2 open to suspicion or question: *Your excuse sounds dubious.*
Other words: **questionable**

Word building: **dubiously** *adverb* **dubiousness** *noun*

duchess

noun **1** a princess who rules a small country **2** a noblewoman of the next highest rank to a princess **3** the wife or widow of a duke

duck[1]

noun a waterbird with a flat bill, short legs and webbed feet

Word use: The male is a **drake**, the female is a **duck** and the young is a **duckling**.
Word history: from an Old English word meaning 'diver'

duck[2]

verb **1** to lower suddenly: *She ducked her head just in time to avoid being hit.*
2 to push under water for a moment: *You are not allowed to duck people in this pool.*
phrase **3 duck out** or **duck off**, *Informal* to go away for a short time: *I am just ducking out to the shop.*

Word building: **duck** *noun*

duck[3]

noun a batsman's score of zero in cricket

duct

noun **1** any tube or channel by which liquids are carried **2** a tube in your body that carries liquid: *a tear duct*

dud

noun *Informal* someone or something which turns out to be a failure

Word building: **dud** *adjective*

due

adjective **1** owing and waiting to be paid: *This bill will be due in a month's time.* **2** proper or suitable: *Please treat these disks with due care.* **3** expected to be ready or arrive: *The train is due at 7 o'clock.*
noun **4** something that is owed or deserved, especially praise or credit: *We must give Mum her due.* **5 dues,** payment or fees: *Members must pay their dues next meeting.*
adverb **6** directly or straight: *We sailed due east.*
phrase **7 due to,** caused by: *There was a traffic delay due to an accident.*

due/dew Don't confuse **due** with **dew. Dew** appears as beads of water on the grass in the early morning.

duel   (*say* dyooh-uhl)

noun **1** an arranged fight with special rules, between two people with weapons such as pistols and swords **2** any fight or contest between two sides
Word building: **duel** *verb* (**duelled, duelling**) **duellist** *noun*

duel/dual Don't confuse **duel** with **dual,** which has to do with two, or having two parts: *This computer game has dual controls so you can play too!*

duet   (*say* dyooh-et)

noun a musical piece for two voices or two performers

duffer

noun Informal a stupid person

duke

noun **1** a prince who rules a small country **2** a nobleman of the next highest rank to a prince
Word building: **dukedom** *noun*

dulcimer   (*say* dul-suh-muh)

noun an old-fashioned musical instrument with metal strings that you strike with light hammers

dull

adjective **1** boring or uninteresting: *a dull talk | a dull trip*
Other words: **dreary, monotonous, tedious**
2 stupid or unintelligent
Other words: **dense, dumb, obtuse**

3 not bright or clear: *a dull light*
4 not sunny: *a dull rainy afternoon*
Other words: **cloudy, grey, overcast**
5 not sharply felt: *a dull pain*
Other words: **faint, weak**
Word building: **dull** *verb* **dullness** *noun* **dully** *adverb*

duly   (*say* dyooh-lee)

adverb **1** properly or as deserved: *He was duly awarded the prize.* **2** at the proper time: *The train duly arrived.*

dumb   (*say* dum)

adjective **1** not able to speak **2** silent: *She was dumb with surprise.* **3** *Informal* stupid or unintelligent: *That was a dumb answer.*
Word building: **dumbly** *adverb* **dumbness** *noun*

dumbfound

verb to make unable to speak, usually because of amazement

dummy

noun **1** a copy or model of something used for display or to show off clothes: *He was dressing the dummy in the shop window.* **2** a rubber teat given to a baby to suck
Word building: The plural is **dummies.**

dump

verb **1** to throw down or put down heavily **2** to hand over or get rid of: *He dumps all the worst jobs on me. | They decided to dump the captain when the team kept on losing.*
noun **3** a place where something is dumped or stored: *a rubbish dump | an ammunition dump* **4** *Informal* a place or a house that is untidy and in bad condition
Word building: **dumper** *noun* a wave that dumps surfers to the bottom

dumpling

noun **1** a small ball of dough cooked with stewed meat or soup **2** a type of fruit pudding

dumpy

adjective short and fat: *She has a dumpy figure.*
Word building: Other forms are **dumpier, dumpiest.**

dunce

noun a stupid or unintelligent person

Word history: from John *Duns* Scotus, who lived from about 1265 to about 1308, and whose writing about religion was attacked as being foolish

dune

noun a sandhill formed by wind, near the beach or in deserts

dung

noun waste product from the bowels of animals

Other words: **manure**

dungarees (*say* dung-guh-<u>reez</u>)

plural noun work clothing, usually overalls, made from a rough cotton cloth

dungeon (*say* <u>dun</u>-juhn)

noun a dark small prison or cell, usually underground: *The prisoners were thrown into the dungeon of the castle.*

dunk

verb to dip into a liquid: *I like to dunk biscuits in my coffee.*

dunnart (*say* <u>dun</u>-aht)

noun a type of mouse found only in Australia. It is endangered. See the table at the end of this book

Word history: from an Aboriginal language of Western Australia called Nyungar. See the map of Australian Aboriginal languages at the end of this book.

dunny

noun *Informal* a toilet, especially an outside one

Word building: The plural is **dunnies**.

duo

noun a pair, especially of musicians: *a new singing duo*

dupe

verb to trick or deceive: *They duped me into believing that they would share the money with me.*

Word building: **dupe** noun someone who has been tricked or deceived

duple

adjective having two beats to the bar: *That piece of music is in duple time.*

duplex

noun a block of two flats or home units

duplicate (*say* <u>dyooh</u>-pluh-kuht)

adjective **1** exactly like another thing: *I would like a duplicate copy of this letter.*
noun **2** something which is exactly the same as something else, usually a copy: *Get me a duplicate of this letter please.*
verb (*say* <u>dyooh</u>-pluh-kayt) **3** to make an exact copy: *The secretary duplicated each letter.*

Word building: **duplication** noun

durable

adjective lasting for a long time: *School clothes should be made of durable material.*

Word building: **durability** noun **durably** adverb

duration

noun the length of time that anything continues for: *They went away for the duration of the holidays.*

duress (*say* dyooh-<u>res</u>)

noun the use of force or threats to get someone to do something: *She only admitted to the crime under duress.*

Word use: This word usually has **under** in front of it.

during (*say* <u>dyooh</u>-ring)

preposition for the given length of time of: *They paid careful attention during the president's speech.*

dusk

noun the time of the evening when it is half light and half dark

Word use: Another word for this is **twilight**.
Word history: from a Latin word meaning 'dark brown'

dusky

adjective **1** darkish in colour **2** dim or without much light

Word building: Other forms are **duskier**, **duskiest**. | **duskiness** noun

dust

noun **1** a fine dry powder of earth or other matter
verb **2** to wipe dust away from
3 to cover lightly with a fine powder: *She dusted her arms with talcum powder.*

Word building: **duster** noun **dusty** adjective (**dustier**, **dustiest**)

duty

noun **1** what someone feels is the right thing to do: *She decided it was her duty to stay with her sick mother.*
Other words: **obligation, responsibility**
2 what someone has to do because of their position: *These are your duties as leader of the group.*
Other words: **chore, job, responsibility, role, task**
3 a tax charged by the government: *customs duty*
Other words: **levy, tariff**
phrase **4 off duty**, not at work **5 on duty**, at work

Word building: The plural form of the noun is **duties**. | **dutiful** *adjective* **dutifully** *adverb*

dux

noun the top student at a school

DVD   (*say* dee-vee-<u>dee</u>)

noun a high-capacity disk, usually 12 cm in diameter, used to store in digital form, audio, video or text data, especially films, television shows, and so on

dwarf   (*say* dwawf)

noun **1** someone or something much shorter than normal **2** a small manlike creature in fairy stories: *Snow White and the Seven Dwarfs*
verb **3** to make seem small: *The tower dwarfed the surrounding buildings.*

Word building: **dwarfish** *adjective*

dwell

verb **1** to live: *They dwell in peace and harmony.*
phrase **2 dwell on**, to continue thinking, speaking or writing about: *It does no good to dwell on your troubles.*

Word building: Other verb forms are **I dwelt, I have dwelt, I am dwelling.** | **dwelling** *noun*

dwindle

verb to become smaller or less: *Our hopes are dwindling.*

dye

noun **1** a liquid that is used to colour cloth, hair and other things
verb **2** to colour with a dye: *I think I will dye this shirt red.*

Word building: Other verb forms are **I dyed, I have dyed, I am dyeing.** | **dyeing** *noun* **dyer** *noun*

dye/die Don't confuse **dye** with **die**. To **die** is to stop living.

dyke

noun a bank built to hold back the water of a sea or river

Word use: Another spelling is **dike**.

dyna-

prefix a word part meaning 'power': *dynamite* / *dynamo*

Word use: Another spelling is **dynam-**.
Word history: from Greek

dynamic   (*say* duy-<u>nam</u>-ik)

adjective **1** having to do with dynamics **2** energetic and forceful: *a dynamic person*

Word building: **dynamically** *adverb* **dynamism** *noun*

dynamics

plural noun **1** the science that studies the forces that make things move **2** the forces that are at work in any situation: *the dynamics of government*

dynamite

noun **1** a substance that makes a powerful explosion when set off: *We will blow up the building with dynamite.* **2** *Informal* anyone or anything likely to be dangerous or cause trouble

dynamo   (*say* <u>duy</u>-nuh-moh)

noun a machine which produces electrical energy

Word building: The plural is **dynamos**.

dynasty   (*say* <u>din</u>-uh-stee)

noun a series of rulers who are members of the same family

Word building: The plural is **dynasties**. | **dynastic** *adjective* **dynastical** *adjective*
Word history: from a Greek word meaning 'lord' or 'chief'

dys-

prefix a word part often used in medicine meaning 'difficulty' or 'poor condition': *dyslexia*

Word history: from Greek

dyslexia   (*say* dis-<u>lek</u>-see-uh)

noun a disability that makes it difficult to learn to read

Word building: **dyslectic** *adjective* **dyslexic** *adjective*

Ee

each
adjective **1** every: *each book in the library*
pronoun **2** every one: *Each of them went away sad.*
adverb **3** for every one: *They cost a dollar each.*

eager
adjective keenly wanting or longing: *an eager helper*
Other words: **enthusiastic, keen**

Word building: **eagerly** *adverb* **eagerness** *noun*
Word history: from a Latin word meaning 'sharp'

eagle
noun a large, sharp-sighted, hunting bird with a strong curved beak and claws

Word building: **eaglet** *noun* a young eagle

ear¹
noun **1** the part of the body used for hearing **2** the ability to notice differences of sound: *Marina has a good ear.*

ear²
noun the top part of a plant such as corn, on which the grain grows

earl (*rhymes with* girl)
noun a British nobleman

Word building: **earldom** *noun*

early
adverb **1** before the set time **2** at or near the beginning: *Early in her talk she showed slides.*

Word building: Other forms are **earlier, earliest.** | **earliness** *noun* **early** *adjective*

earn (*rhymes with* fern)
verb **1** to receive in return for working: *They earn $10 an hour.* **2** to deserve to get: *She earned her reputation as a hard worker.*

Word building: Other forms are **I earned** or **earnt, I have earned** or **earnt, I am earning.**

earn/urn Don't confuse **earn** with **urn**, which is a kind of vase. It is also a container with a tap, for heating water.

earnest (*say* er-nuhst)
adjective serious or sincere: *I think Simon is earnest in his desire to help.*

Word use: The opposite of this is **frivolous.**
Word building: **earnestly** *adverb* **earnestness** *noun*

earphone
noun a small listening device placed in or over the ear

earring
noun a ring or other ornament that you wear on or through the lobe of your ear

earth
noun **1** the planet we live on **2** dry land: *Sea used to cover some parts of the earth.* **3** soil, rather than rocks or sand **4** a wire connecting an electrical appliance to the ground, for added safety

Word building: **earthly** *adjective*

earthenware
noun goods, such as pots, made of baked clay

earthquake

noun a shaking of the ground caused by movement of rock under the earth's surface

earthworm

noun a worm with a body divided into segments, which burrows in soil and feeds on soil and rotting plants and animals

ease

noun **1** freedom from any problem or discomfort: *I learned to ride with ease.* **2** a free and relaxed manner: *Her ease with people overcame their shyness.*
verb **3** to give relief or comfort **4** to make less difficult **5** to move slowly and carefully: *They eased the old person into a chair.*

easel

noun a stand for holding an artist's canvas or a blackboard

east

noun the direction from which the sun rises
Word use: The opposite direction is **west**.
Word building: **east** *adjective* **east** *adverb* **eastern** *adjective*

Easter

noun a Christian festival held each year to celebrate the story that Jesus Christ rose from the dead, after he had been killed on the cross and buried
Word history: named after the Old English goddess of the dawn

easy

adjective **1** able to be done or understood without difficulty: *an easy question | an easy task*
Other words: **simple, uncomplicated**
2 able to be done without a lot of effort or energy: *an easy climb*
Other words: **undemanding**
Word building: Other forms are **easier, easiest.** | **easily** *adverb* **easiness** *noun*

eat

verb **1** to chew and swallow **2** to have a meal: *We eat at twelve.* **3** to wear away
Word building: Other forms are **I ate, I have eaten, I am eating.**

eating disorder

noun a pattern of eating which involves over-eating or not eating enough to such an extent that it affects a person's physical and mental health: *She was so skinny we thought she must have an eating disorder.*

eaves

plural noun the overhanging lower edges of a roof: *Pigeons have built a nest under the eaves.*

eavesdrop

verb to listen secretly
Word building: Other forms are **I eavesdropped, I have eavesdropped, I am eavesdropping.** | **eavesdropper** *noun*

ebb

verb **1** to flow back or away: *The tide turned and began to ebb.* **2** to fade away: *Her strength was quickly ebbing.*
Word building: **ebb** *noun*

ebony   (*say* eb-uh-nee)

noun a hard, black, shiny wood which is valuable for carving

e-book

noun a book that can be read in digital form: *You can read an e-book in bed if you have an e-reader.*

eccentric   (*say* uhk-sen-trik)

adjective not usual or normal: *eccentric behaviour*
Word use: The opposite of this is **conventional**.
Word building: **eccentric** *noun* an eccentric person **eccentrically** *adverb* **eccentricity** *noun*
Word history: from a Greek word meaning 'out of the centre'

ecclesiastical

(*say* uh-kleez-ee-as-tik-uhl)
adjective having to do with the church
Word building: **ecclesiastic** *noun* a member of the clergy

echidna   (*say* uh-kid-nuh)

noun a spiny, ant-eating animal found only in Australia, which lays eggs and feeds its young with its own milk
Word use: Another name is **spiny anteater**.
Word history: from a Greek word meaning 'viper'

echo   (*say* ek-oh)

noun **1** a repeating sound, when the sound waves bounce off something hard
verb **2** to repeat or act as an echo: *Our voices echoed in the bare room.* **3** to imitate or repeat: *You are just echoing someone else's ideas.*
Word building: Other verb forms are **it echoed, it has echoed, it is echoing.** | The plural form of the noun is **echoes**.

eclipse

noun **1** the darkness caused when the sun's or moon's light is blocked from the earth
verb **2** to do very much better than: *The brilliant pianist eclipsed everyone else's performance.*

eco *(say ee-koh)*

adjective of or relating to environmentally friendly practices, materials, technology, and so on: *an eco house*

ecological footprint

noun a measure of the demands that humans make on their environment by adding up the effects caused by the production of their food, the building and the heating and cooling of their homes, the making and the use of their cars, and so on

ecology

noun the study of the relationship between living things and their environment

Word building: **ecological** *adjective*
ecologically *adverb*   **ecologist** *noun*

e-commerce

noun buying and selling on the internet: *E-commerce has led to a downturn in trade for shops like antique stores.*

economical *(say ek-uh-nom-ik-uhl)*

adjective not wasteful: *She is an economical housekeeper.*

Word building: **economically** *adverb*

economy *(say uh-kon-uh-mee)*

noun **1** careful management of money or materials
Other words: **thrift**
2 the finances, trade, and so on, of a country and the system by which these are managed

Word building: **economics** *noun* the science of how money is used   **economic** *adjective*
economise *verb* to manage money or materials carefully

ecstasy *(say eks-tuh-see)*

noun a sudden feeling of great joy

Word building: **ecstatic** *adjective*   **ecstatically** *adverb*

eczema *(say ek-suh-muh)*

noun an itchy or painful rash in which the skin becomes red and flaky

eddy

noun a current moving in a circle, especially in a river

Word building: The plural is **eddies**. | **eddy** *verb* (**eddied, eddying**)

edge

noun **1** a border or a line where two parts or surfaces meet: *the horizon's edge | the edge of a box* **2** the thin cutting part of something sharp, such as a knife
verb **3** to move slowly and gradually: *to edge your way through the crowd* **4** to put an edge on
phrase **5 on edge, a** excited and nervous: *He was on edge about starting school.* **b** cross and annoyed: *Your constant arguing made me on edge.*

Word building: **edgy** *adjective* cross or nervous

edible

adjective able or fit to be eaten: *an edible mushroom*

edict *(say ee-dikt)*

noun an order given by a ruler or someone else in authority

edifice *(say ed-uh-fuhs)*

noun a building, especially a large or impressive one

edit

verb **1** to be in charge of the publication of: *My mother edits a science magazine.* **2** to read and correct the mistakes of: *I found a lot of spelling mistakes when I edited your story.*

Word building: Other forms are **I edited, I have edited, I am editing.** | **editor** *noun*

edition

noun one printing of a book or newspaper: *The afternoon edition of the paper has not come out yet.*

editorial

noun a newspaper article written by an editor, which expresses the editor's or the paper's views

Word use: Another word for this is **leader**.
Word building: **editorial** *adjective*

educate

verb **1** to instruct or give knowledge to: *Kim also educates the girls in skills such as fencing.* **2** to train: *I have educated my taste away from sweet foods.*

Word building: **educated** *adjective*   **education** *noun*   **educator** *noun*

eel
noun an edible snakelike fish

eerie   (*rhymes with* cheery)
adjective frighteningly strange: *The thick fog produced an eerie atmosphere in the mountains.*

Word building: Other forms are **eerier**, **eeriest**. | **eerily** *adverb* **eeriness** *noun* Word history: from an Old English word meaning 'cowardly'

effect
noun **1** something which is produced by some cause: *Wrinkles are an effect of age.* **2** the power to produce results: *Threats have no effect on us.*

Word building: **effect** *verb* to make happen: *to effect a change in the program*

> **effect/affect** Don't confuse **effect** with **affect**. They are rather alike in meaning but **effect** is usually a noun and **affect** is usually a verb.
> *The effect of the warm weather is to make me sleepy.*
> *Warm weather affects me and makes me sleepy.*

effective
adjective having the intended result: *an effective way of doing a job*

Word building: **effectively** *adverb* **effectiveness** *noun*

effeminate   (*say* uh-**fem**-uh-nuht)
adjective having qualities thought to be more suited to a woman: *That actor has an effeminate way of speaking.*

Word use: This word is used only of a man, and usually in a disapproving way.

effervescent   (*say* ef-uh-**ves**-uhnt)
adjective fizzy

Word building: **effervesce** *verb* **effervescence** *noun*

efficient   (*say* uh-**fish**-uhnt)
adjective able to do something quickly and easily: *an efficient housekeeper*

Word building: **efficiency** *noun* **efficiently** *adverb*

effigy   (*say* **ef**-uh-jee)
noun a picture or statue of a person

Word building: The plural is **effigies**.

effluent   (*say* **ef**-looh-uhnt)
noun something flowing out, such as the liquid waste from industry, sewage works, and so on

Word building: **effluent** *adjective* flowing out   **effluence** *noun*

effort
noun **1** the use of physical strength: *It takes a great deal of effort to push a car.* **2** a serious attempt: *If you made an effort you could learn these words.*

Word building: **effortless** *adjective*

effrontery   (*say* uh-**frun**-tuh-ree)
noun cheeky rudeness or impudence: *She had the effrontery to tell me I was an old prune!*

Word use: The more usual word is **cheek**.

EFTPOS   (*say* **eft**-pos)
noun a machine in supermarkets and shops that allows you to pay using a coded plastic card and a PIN

e.g.
short for *exempli gratia*, Latin words meaning 'for example': *Australia has many wildflowers, e.g. the flannel flower.*

egg
noun **1** a roundish object produced by a female animal, bird or fish, which contains or grows into its young: *There was a mass of frog's eggs in the pond.* **2** a bird's egg, especially a hen's: *eggs for breakfast*

eggplant
noun a large, dark purple, more or less egg-shaped fruit used as a vegetable

Word use: Another name is **aubergine** (*say* oh-buh-zheen).

ego   (*say* **ee**-goh)
noun **1** the 'I' or self of someone: *The ego plays a part in all our thoughts.* **2** conceit or self-importance: *Nothing you say can damage his ego.*

Word building: The plural is **egos**.

egotism
noun the habit of thinking and talking about yourself all the time: *Your egotism will lose you many friends.*

Word building: **egotist** *noun* **egotistical**, **egotistic** *adjective*

eiderdown
noun a quilt filled with feathers

eight   (*say* ayt)
noun **1** the number 8 **2** the Roman numeral VIII

Word building: **eight** *adjective*: *eight legs*   **eighth** *adjective*: *the eighth player*

eighteen
noun **1** the number 18 **2** the Roman numeral XVIII

Word building: **eighteen** *adjective*: *eighteen holes*   **eighteenth** *adjective*: *your eighteenth birthday*

eighty
noun **1** the number 80 **2** the Roman numeral LXXX

Word building: The plural is **eighties**. | **eighty** *adjective*: *eighty years old*   **eightieth** *adjective*: *his eightieth birthday*

eisteddfod   (*say* uh-<u>sted</u>-fuhd)
noun a competition of singing, playing music and reciting poetry

Word use: The second plural is unusual because the word comes from Welsh.
Word building: The plural is **eisteddfods** or **eisteddfodau** (*say* uh-<u>sted</u>-fuh-duy)).

either   (*say* <u>uy</u>-dhuh, <u>ee</u>-dhuh)
adjective **1** one or other of two: *Sit on either chair.* **2** both of two: *There are trees on either side of the path.*
pronoun **3** one or the other but not both: *Take either.*
conjunction **4** used with **or** to show one of two equal choices: *Either come or stay at home.*

Word building: **either** *adverb*: *If you don't come, she won't come either.*

ejaculate   (*say* uh-<u>jak</u>-yuh-layt)
verb **1** to say or shout suddenly, often because you are surprised: *'Stop right now!', ejaculated the teacher.* **2** to send or come out quickly, especially semen from the penis

Word use: The more usual word for definition 1 is **exclaim**. | Another word for definition 2 is **discharge**.
Word building: **ejaculation** *noun*

eject
verb to put or send out: *They ejected me from the assembly because I was laughing too much.*

Word building: **ejection** *noun*

elaborate   (*say* uh-<u>lab</u>-uh-ruht)
adjective **1** worked out in great detail: *an elaborate scheme* | *an elaborate pattern*
phrase (*say* uh-<u>lab</u>-uh-rayt) **2 elaborate on**, to add details to: *Sam elaborated on the story.*

Word building: **elaborately** *adverb* **elaboration** *noun*

elapse
verb to pass: *Two weeks elapsed before I saw her again.*

elastic
adjective able to be stretched and go back into shape again: *an elastic band*

Word building: **elasticity** *noun*

elastics
noun a game played with a very long cord of elastic which is joined together at both ends and stretched around people who act as posts that the players must jump around while also jumping over the elastic: *Let's play elastics at lunchtime!*

elated
adjective in high spirits: *She was elated at the thought of the trip to Hong Kong.*

Word building: **elation** *noun*

elbow
noun the joint between the upper and lower arm

elder
adjective **1** older: *Michael is Con's elder brother.*
noun **2** an older or senior person: *Listen carefully to your elders.* | *The elders of the tribe teach the young people.*

Word use: For other forms see **old**.

elderly
adjective old or aged: *You should speak clearly to elderly people.*

elect
verb to choose by vote: *to elect a member of parliament*

Word building: **election** *noun* **elector** *noun*

elective
adjective **1** filled by an election: *an elective position* **2** not required but optional: *an elective subject at school*

Word building: **elective** *noun* an elective subject

electorate (*say* uh-<u>lek</u>-truht)

noun the area, or the people in it, which a member of parliament represents

electrician

noun someone who works with electrical appliances and wiring

electricity

noun a form of energy from electrons, which can be used for heating, lighting, driving a motor, and other things

Word building: **electric** *adjective* **electrical** *adjective* **electrically** *adverb*

electrify

verb 1 to charge with electricity: *to electrify a fence* 2 to equip for use with electricity: *The railway line has been electrified.* 3 to thrill or excite: *Her news electrified us.*

Word building: Other forms are **it electrified, it has electrified, it is electrifying.** | **electrification** *noun*

electrocute

verb to kill by electricity: *A faulty electric toaster could electrocute you.*

Word building: **electrocution** *noun*

electrode

noun a conductor through which electric current enters or leaves a battery, circuit or valve

electromagnet

noun a magnet with wire coiled around an iron or steel core, through which an electric current is passed

Word building: **electromagnetic** *adjective* **electromagnetically** *adverb* **electromagnetism** *noun*

electron

noun a very tiny particle inside an atom which has a type of energy that balances the energy of a proton

Word use: The energy of an electron is called **negative.**

electronic

adjective worked or produced by small changes in voltage: *an electronic calculator*

Word use: This word does not mean the same as **electric**, which relates to electric current or energy.

Word building: **electronically** *adverb*

elegant

adjective graceful or stylish: *elegant manners | elegant clothes*
Other words: **chic, refined**

Word building: **elegance** *noun* **elegantly** *adverb*

elegy (*say* <u>el</u>-uh-jee)

noun a poem expressing sorrow over someone's death

Word building: The plural is **elegies.** | **elegist** *noun* someone who writes elegies

element

noun 1 something that is a part of a whole: *Kindness is one of the main elements of his character.*
Other words: **component, constituent**
2 a substance that can't be broken down into anything else: *The compound copper sulfate can be broken down into the elements copper and sulfur.* 3 a wire that is the heating unit of an electric heater, jug or similar electric appliance

Word building: **elemental** *adjective* simple or basic **elementally** *adverb*

elementary

adjective simple or basic

elephant

noun a very large animal of Africa or India, with a thick skin and a long nose or trunk used for getting hold of things or sucking up water

Word use: The male is a **bull**, the female is a **cow** and the young is a **calf.**

elevate

verb to lift or raise: *The idea of an outing elevated her spirits.*

Word building: **elevation** *noun*

elevator

noun 1 a building for storing grain 2 an American word for a **lift** (def. 2)

eleven (*say* uh-<u>lev</u>-uhn)

noun 1 the number 11 2 the Roman numeral XI

Word building: **eleven** *adjective*: *eleven lamingtons* **eleventh** *adjective*: *my friend's eleventh birthday*

elf

noun a small being in fairy stories who often plays tricks on people

Word building: The plural is **elves.** | **elfin** *adjective* small, bright, or mischievous, like an elf

eligible   (*say* el-uh-juh-buhl)
adjective **1** ready or qualified: *You are eligible to vote when you are eighteen years old.* **2** suitable to be chosen, especially as a husband or wife: *an eligible bachelor*

Word building: **eligibility** *noun*   **eligibly** *adverb*
Word history: from a Latin word meaning 'pick out'

eliminate
verb to get rid of or remove: *The early rounds of the tournament will eliminate the weakest players.*

Word building: **elimination** *noun*

elite   (*rhymes with* beat)
noun the group of people with the most money, power, and other advantages

Word building: **elitism** *noun* the idea that a certain group of people should have special advantages   **elite** *adjective*

elixir   (*say* uh-liks-uh)
noun a sweet liquid medicine: *a cough elixir*

Word history: from a Greek word for 'a drying powder for wounds'

elk
noun a large deer found in Europe and Asia

ellipse
noun an oval shape

Word building: **elliptical** *adjective*

ellipsoid
noun a solid oval, the shape of a football

Word building: **ellipsoidal** *adjective*

elm
noun a European tree which loses its leaves in winter

El Niño   (*say* el neen-yoh)
noun a climatic event involving a rapid warming of the surface of the southern Pacific Ocean causing a change in normal wind and current movements, having often disastrous effects on the world's weather, and marked in Australia by drought on the eastern coast

Word use: Compare this with **La Niña**.
Word history: from the Spanish word for 'the (Christ) child', referring to the appearance of the current off South America near Christmas

elocution
noun the study of good clear speaking

Word building: **elocutionary** *adjective*
elocutionist *noun*

elope
verb to run away with a lover, usually so that you can get married without the permission of your parents

Word building: **elopement** *noun*   **eloper** *noun*

eloquent   (*say* el-uh-kwuhnt)
adjective able to speak in a flowing, expressive manner

Word building: **eloquence** *noun*   **eloquently** *adverb*

else
adverb **1** instead: *someone else | who else?* **2** in addition: *What else shall I sing? | Who else is going?* **3** otherwise: *Run, or else you'll miss the train.*

elsewhere
adverb in or to some other place: *My friend lives elsewhere now.*

elusive
adjective hard to find or get hold of: *an elusive person | an elusive memory*

Word building: **elusiveness** *noun*

email   (*say* ee-mayl)
noun messages sent, by computer, from one person to another person

Word use: Another spelling is **e-mail.** | This word is a short way of saying **electronic mail.**
Word building: **email** *verb*: *I'll email the program to you.*

emancipate   (*say* uh-man-suh-payt)
verb to set free: *to emancipate a slave*

Word building: **emancipist** *noun* a convict pardoned by the governor in early colonial times   **emancipation** *noun*

embalm   (*rhymes with* harm)
verb to treat a corpse with chemicals in order to preserve it

embankment
noun a mound of earth and stones to keep back water or to carry a road or railway

embargo
noun a ban, usually placed by a government on trade of some kind: *an embargo on the export of parrots*

Word building: The plural is **embargoes.**

embark

verb **1** to go on board for a voyage: *They embarked on the passenger liner.* **2** to start: *They embarked on a new project.*

Word building: **embarkation** *noun*

embarrass

verb to cause to feel uncomfortable: *My mother's old-fashioned ideas embarrassed me in front of my friends.*

Word building: **embarrassment** *noun*

embassy

noun the office and house of an ambassador

Word building: The plural is **embassies**.

embellish

verb to make beautiful by decorating: *Carved figures embellished the box.*

Word use: The more usual word is **decorate**.
Word building: **embellishment** *noun*

embers

plural noun small pieces of live coal or wood remaining from a fire

embezzle

verb to steal, usually by making false entries in accounts: *The clerk embezzled $1000.*

Word building: **embezzlement** *noun* **embezzler** *noun*

emblem

noun a badge or something that serves as a sign or symbol: *A horseshoe is an emblem of good luck.*

Word building: **emblematic** *adjective*

emboss

verb to decorate with a design which stands out from its background

embrace

verb to hug or cuddle

Word building: **embrace** *noun*

embroider

verb **1** to sew decorative patterns on: *to embroider a cushion-cover* **2** to make more interesting with untruthful additions: *to embroider a story*

Word building: **embroidery** *noun*

embryo   (*say* em-bree-oh)

noun a young animal or human in the very early stages of growing in the womb

Word use: Compare this with **foetus**.
Word building: The plural is **embryos**. | **embryonic** *adjective*

emerald

noun **1** a green precious stone
adjective **2** clear bright green

emerge

verb to come out into view: *She emerged from behind the trees.*

Word building: **emergence** *noun*

emergency

noun an unexpected serious happening that needs action at once

Word building: The plural is **emergencies**.

emergency exit

noun an exit from a vehicle or building used as a way out in an emergency like a fire or accident

emigrate

verb to leave your own country to go to live in another

Word building: **emigrant** *noun* someone who emigrates   **emigration** *noun*

emigrate/immigrate Don't confuse **emigrate** with **immigrate**, which is to come to live in a new country.

eminence

noun **1** a high rank or standing: *She was in a position of eminence in her profession.* **2** a high place: *The house stood on an eminence.*

eminent

adjective important or high in rank

Word building: **eminently** *adverb*

eminent/imminent Don't confuse **eminent** with **imminent**, which means 'likely to happen at any moment'.

emission   (*say* uh-mish-uhn, ee-mish-uhn)

noun a substance, especially a gas, which is discharged into the atmosphere: *Burning coal gives off carbon dioxide emissions into the atmosphere.*

emit   (*say* uh-mit)

verb to send or give out: *The fire emits heat.* | *The child emitted a scream.*

Word building: Other forms are **I emitted, I have emitted, I am emitting.** | **emission** *noun*

emotion

noun a feeling, such as love, hate, happiness, misery or anger

Word building: **emotional** *adjective*
emotionally *adverb*
Word history: from a French word meaning
'excite'

emperor

noun a man who rules over a group of
countries or peoples: *Augustus was the first
Roman Emperor.*

Word building: **empress** *noun*

emphasis   (*say* <u>em</u>-fuh-suhs)

noun stress or importance: *The manager
placed great emphasis on punctuality.*

Word building: The plural is **emphases** (*say*
<u>em</u>-fuh-seez). | **emphasise** *verb* **emphatic**
adjective **emphatically** *adverb*

empire

noun **1** a group of countries or peoples
ruled by an emperor or empress **2** a large
and powerful business group controlled by
a single person or group of people

Word building: **imperial** *adjective*

employ

verb **1** to provide work for: *The factory
employs 100 people.* **2** to use: *to employ a
spade for digging* | *to employ your spare time
in reading*

Word building: **employee** *noun* someone
who works for an employer   **employer**
noun   **employment** *noun*

empty

adjective containing nothing

Word building: Other forms are **emptier**,
emptiest. | **empty** *verb* (**emptied**,
emptying)   **emptily** *adverb*   **emptiness** *noun*

emu

noun a large Australian bird which can't fly,
related to the cassowary

Word history: from a Portuguese word for an
ostrich or a cassowary

emulate

verb to try to be like: *She wanted to emulate
the great inventors of the past.*

Word use: The more usual word is **imitate**.
Word building: **emulation** *noun*   **emulative**
adjective   **emulator** *noun*

emulsion   (*say* uh-<u>mul</u>-shuhn)

noun a milk-like mixture, often rather oily

Word building: **emulsify** *verb* (**emulsified**,
emulsifying)
Word history: from a Latin word meaning
'milked out'

en-

prefix a word part meaning 'in' or 'into':
engrave | *engulf*

Word use: Another spelling is **em-**, as in
embalm.
Word history: from Latin

enable

verb to make able: *The bridge enables you to
cross the harbour.*

enamel

noun **1** a very hard coating applied to
metal **2** a glossy paint

enchant

verb **1** to cast a magic spell on **2** to delight
or charm: *Her singing enchanted us.*

Word building: **enchanter** *noun*   **enchanting**
adjective   **enchantingly** *adverb*   **enchantment**
noun

enclose

verb **1** to shut or close in on all sides:
A wall enclosed the orchard. **2** to put in:
I enclose a photograph with this letter.

Word building: **enclosure** *noun*

encore   (*say* <u>on</u>-kaw)

interjection **1** once more!
noun **2** an extra piece of music performed
in answer to continued clapping by the
audience

Word history: from a French word meaning
'again'

encounter

verb to meet: *to encounter an old enemy* | *to
encounter an unexpected problem*

Word building: **encounter** *noun* a meeting

encourage

verb to cheer up or cheer on: *The
coach encouraged us after our defeat.* | *We
encouraged the team with shouts and flag-
waving.*
Other words: **boost, hearten, inspire, rally,
reassure**

Word building: **encouragement** *noun*
encouraging *adjective*   **encouragingly**
adverb

encroach

verb to go beyond your own area and
onto someone else's: *The neighbours'
garage encroaches on our land.*

Word building: **encroachment** *noun*

encyclopedia

noun a book, usually in several volumes, of information arranged thematically

Word use: Another spelling is **encyclopaedia**.
Word building: **encyclopedic** *adjective*

end

noun **1** the finishing point **2** aim or purpose: *To what end are you doing this?* *phrase* **3 make both ends meet**, to spend no more than you earn

Word building: **end** *verb* to stop or finish **ending** *noun*

endanger   (*say* en-<u>dayn</u>-juh)

verb to cause somebody or something to be in danger or at risk: *If you go swimming in those big waves you could endanger your life.*

endangered species

noun a species of plant or animal that faces a high risk of dying out in the wild in the near future

Word use: Compare this with **critically endangered species** and **vulnerable species**.

endeavour   (*rhymes with* never)

verb to try or attempt: *We endeavour to do our best.*

Word use: Another spelling is **endeavor**.
Word building: **endeavour** *noun*

endorse

verb **1** to sign your name on: *to endorse a cheque* **2** to approve of or support: *to endorse an action | to endorse a candidate*

Word building: **endorsable** *adjective* **endorsement** *noun* **endorser** *noun*

endow   (*rhymes with* cow)

verb **1** to give money, especially to a school, hospital, and so on **2** to give or equip: *You have been endowed with great ability.*

Word building: **endowment** *noun*

endure

verb **1** to put up with, especially for a long time **2** to last well: *This car is so strong it should endure for years.*

Word building: **endurance** *noun* **enduring** *adjective*

enemy

noun **1** someone who hates someone else, or wishes to harm them **2** an unfriendly armed force which is prepared to fight: *The country was invaded by the enemy.*

Word building: The plural is **enemies**. | **enemy** *adjective*: *enemy territory* **enmity** *noun* **inimical** *adjective*

energetic   (*say* en-uh-<u>jet</u>-ik)

adjective strong and active: *Puppies are very energetic.*

Word building: **energetically** *adverb*

energy   (*say* <u>en</u>-uh-jee)

noun **1** ability to be vigorous and active: *I haven't the energy for another game.* Other words: **drive, verve, vitality** **2** electrical or other power: *It's wasting energy to leave the lights on.*

enforce

verb to make people obey: *to enforce a law | to enforce a school rule*

Word building: **enforceable** *adjective* **enforcedly** *adverb* **enforcement** *noun* **enforcer** *noun*

engage

verb **1** to employ: *Our neighbour has engaged a gardener.* **2** to attract or hold the attention of: *Sue engaged everyone with her witty conversation.* **3** to connect or interlock: *Have you engaged the gears?* **4** to fight: *The two armies engaged in battle.*

Word building: **engagement** *noun* **engaging** *adjective* **engagingly** *adverb*

engaged

adjective **1** busy or occupied: *Her telephone is giving the engaged signal.* **2** going to be married: *an engaged couple*

Word building: **engagement** *noun*

engine   (*say* <u>en</u>-juhn)

noun **1** a machine which changes energy from sources like petrol or steam into movement: *The factory replaced its old steam engines with electric motors.* **2** a railway locomotive

Word history: from a Latin word meaning 'invention'

engineer   (*say* en-juhn-<u>ear</u>)

noun someone who is trained to design and build things and to use machinery: *My cousin was an engineer who built roads and bridges. | an electrical engineer | a chemical engineer*

Word building: **engineer** *verb* to plan or arrange **engineering** *noun*

engrave

verb **1** to cut with a sharp tool: *The jeweller engraved my name on my watch.* **2** to fix firmly: *The words of the song are engraved in our memory.*

Word building: **engraver** *noun* **engraving** *noun*

engross   (*say* en-<u>grohs</u>)

verb to be so interesting as to hold the attention of completely: *That book engrossed her for days.*

Word building: **engrossing** *adjective*: *an engrossing film* **engrossed** *adjective*: *engrossed in her work*

engulf

verb to swallow up: *The tidal wave engulfed the coastal village.* | *Darkness engulfed the houses.*

enhance

verb to increase or improve: *A coat of paint should enhance the value of the house.*

Word building: **enhancement** *noun*

enigma   (*say* uh-<u>nig</u>-muh)

noun someone or something difficult or impossible to understand

Word building: **enigmatic** *adjective* puzzling **enigmatically** *adverb*
Word history: from a Greek word meaning 'riddle'

enjoy

verb **1** to get happiness from: *They enjoyed their meal.*
Other words: **like, love**
2 to have: *He enjoys a reputation for hard work.*
Other words: **possess**
phrase **3 enjoy yourself**, to have a good time

Word use: Definition 2 is used only with things that people like to have.
Word building: **enjoyable** *adjective* **enjoyably** *adverb* **enjoyment** *noun*

enlarge

verb **1** to increase in size: *She wants to enlarge the photos.* **2** to give more details: *Could you please enlarge on your first point?*

Word building: **enlargement** *noun*

enlighten

verb to make something clear to: *Would you care to enlighten me?*

Word building: **enlightened** *adjective* having knowledge or information **enlightenment** *noun*

enlist

verb to join the army, navy or air force

Word building: **enlistment** *noun*

enmity

noun strong dislike or hatred

enormous

adjective of an unusually large size: *an enormous house with many rooms*
Other words: **colossal, gigantic, huge, immense, mammoth, massive**

Word building: **enormity** *noun* **enormously** *adverb* **enormousness** *noun*

enough   (*say* uh-<u>nuf</u>, ee-<u>nuf</u>)

adjective as much as you want or need: *I've had enough ice-cream.* | *Are there enough kids to make a team?*

Word building: **enough** *pronoun* **enough** *adverb*

enquire

verb another way of spelling **inquire**

Word building: **enquirer** *noun* **enquiring** *adjective* **enquiringly** *adverb*

enquiry

noun another way of spelling **inquiry**

Word building: The plural is **enquiries**.

enrage

verb to make very angry: *Her cheeky questions enraged the guest speaker.*
Other words: **anger, incense, infuriate**

enrich

verb **1** to supply with more money **2** to improve the quality of: *Farmers enrich the soil with fertiliser.*

Word building: **enrichment** *noun*

enrol

verb **1** to put your name down: *He enrolled to study Italian.* **2** to record the name of: *The teachers enrol everyone on the first day.*

Word building: Other forms are **I enrolled, I have enrolled, I am enrolling.** | **enrolment** *noun*

ensign   (*say* <u>en</u>-suhn, <u>en</u>-suyn)

noun a flag or banner

ensuite   (*say* <u>on</u>-sweet)

noun a small bathroom joined to a bedroom
Word use: This word comes from French.

ensure   (*say* en-<u>shaw</u>)

verb to make certain

entangle
verb to twist or catch: *The horse entangled its tail in wire.*

Word building: **entanglement** *noun*

enter
verb **1** to come or go in: *We entered the house.* | *They entered after us.* **2** to start in: *She entered the race.* **3** to write on a list **4** to type (data, text, and so on) into a computer file

enterprise
noun **1** something to be done, especially something which involves effort or courage: *Running the school fete was quite an enterprise.* **2** the energy and skill you need to do something like that: *She is full of enterprise.*

Word building: **enterprising** *adjective* resourceful **enterprisingly** *adverb*

entertain
verb **1** to interest and amuse **2** to have as a guest: *They are entertaining us on Friday night.*

Word building: **entertainer** *noun* **entertaining** *adjective* **entertainment** *noun*

enthral (*say* en-<u>thrawl</u>)
verb to be so interesting, exciting or beautiful as to hold the attention of completely: *The lovely scenery enthralled us* | *The film enthralled me.*

Word building: Other forms are **I enthralled, I have enthralled, I am enthralling.** | **enthralled** *adjective* **enthralling** *adjective*

enthusiasm (*say* en-<u>thooh</u>-zee-az-uhm)
noun lively interest: *She is full of enthusiasm for her new job.*
Other words: **eagerness, excitement, fervour, zeal**

Word building: **enthuse** *verb* **enthusiast** *noun* **enthusiastic** *adjective*

entice
verb to tempt or persuade with promises of money or other advantages

Word building: **enticement** *noun* **enticing** *adjective* **enticingly** *adverb*

entire
adjective whole or unbroken: *She bought the entire set.*

Word building: **entirely** *adverb* quite **entirety** *noun*

entitle
verb to give someone a right or claim to something: *This kind of ticket entitles you to travel on public transport for the whole day.*

Word building: **entitled** *adjective* **entitlement** *noun*

entrails
plural noun the intestines

Word history: from a Latin word meaning 'within'

entrance¹ (*say* en-truhns)
noun **1** the act of entering: *to make an entrance at a party* **2** the way in: *The entrance was bolted.*

entrance² (*say* en-<u>trans</u>)
verb to fill with delight: *The dancers entranced the crowds with their grace.*

entrant
noun someone who takes part in a competition: *an entrant in the race*

entreaty
noun a serious request: *The doctor came as a result of their entreaty.*

Word building: The plural is **entreaties.** | **entreat** *verb* to beg

entree (*say* <u>on</u>-tray)
noun the small serving of tasty food you eat at dinner before the main course

Word use: Another spelling is **entrée.**

entrepreneur (*say* on-truh-pruh-<u>ner</u>)
noun someone who organises a business enterprise, especially a risky one

Word building: **entrepreneurial** *adjective*
Word history: from a French word meaning 'undertake'

entry
noun **1** the act of coming or going in: *The space shuttle made a safe entry into the earth's atmosphere.* **2** the way in: *The entry was blocked by a car.* **3** a written record: *In her diary there were few entries for that month.* **4** someone entered in a competition: *How many entries are there in the essay competition?*

Word building: The plural is **entries.**

envelop (*say* en-<u>vel</u>-uhp)
verb to wrap or cover: *He enveloped the baby in a large blanket.*

Word building: **enveloping** *adjective* **envelopment** *noun*

envelope (*say* <u>en</u>-vuh-lohp, <u>on</u>-vuh-lohp)
noun a folded paper cover for a letter

environment
noun **1** the whole surroundings of your life: *He grew up in a country town environment.* **2** the physical conditions of a place, such as weather, water and vegetation

Word building: **environmentalist** *noun* someone who is concerned about protecting the natural environment **environmental** *adjective*

environs (*say* en-<u>vuy</u>-ruhnz)
plural noun the surrounding districts: *the environs of Brisbane*

envoy
noun someone sent as a representative: *Envoys from each country met to discuss trade.*

envy
noun the desire for someone else's possessions or success: *Instead of enjoying what he has, he is full of envy of others.*

Word building: **enviable** *adjective* worth wanting **envious** *adjective* full of envy **envy** *verb* (**envied, envying**) **enviably** *adverb*

enzyme (*say* <u>en</u>-zuym)
noun an animal protein which produces a chemical change: *Enzymes help to digest the food we eat.*

eon
noun another way of spelling **aeon**

epaulet (*say* <u>ep</u>-uh-let)
noun a fancy shoulder piece worn on uniforms

ephemeral (*say* uh-<u>fem</u>-uh-ruhl)
adjective not lasting long: *She gets cross quickly but her anger is ephemeral.*

Word use: The more usual word is **passing**.
Word building: **ephemerally** *adverb*

epi-
prefix a word part meaning **1** in addition to: *epilogue* **2** near: *epidemic* **3** on: *epitaph* **4** against

Word use: Other spellings are **ep-** or **eph-**.
Word history: from Greek

epic
noun **1** a long poem about heroic deeds
adjective **2** grand or heroic: *an epic journey across the desert*

epidemic
noun a lot of cases of an illness in a short period of time: *There is an epidemic of measles at the school.*

Word building: **epidemic** *adjective* **epidemically** *adverb*

epigram
noun a short and witty saying

Word building: **epigrammatic** *adjective* **epigrammatically** *adverb*

epilepsy
noun an illness which produces fits of unconsciousness and uncontrollable movements of the body

Word building: **epileptic** *adjective* **epileptic** *noun* **epileptically** *adverb*

epilogue (*say* <u>ep</u>-uh-log)
noun a short section at the end of a play or written work which acts as a conclusion: *The author has added more recent facts as an epilogue to the book.*

episode
noun **1** an event in your life: *an episode from my past* **2** one in a series of scenes or chapters: *They watched the last episode of the serial on TV last night.*

Word building: **episodic** *adjective* **episodical** *adjective* **episodically** *adverb*
Word history: from a Greek word meaning 'coming in besides'

epistle (*say* uh-<u>pis</u>-uhl)
noun *Old-fashioned* a letter

epitaph (*say* <u>ep</u>-uh-tahf)
noun the words, sometimes in verse, written on a gravestone in memory of the dead person

epitome (*say* uh-<u>pit</u>-uh-mee)
noun the most typical example of: *With fair hair and a suntan, Ashley is the epitome of a surfer.*

Word building: **epitomise** *verb*

epoch (*say* <u>ee</u>-pok)
noun a period of time in history or geology: *in the epoch of the Napoleonic wars*

equal (*say* <u>ee</u>-kwuhl)

adjective **1** of the same number, value, or other quality: *Everyone's share is equal.* **2** evenly matched: *It's an equal fight.*
verb **3** to add up to the same number as: *I know that 5 plus 3 equals 8.* **4** to match: *The hurdler couldn't equal the record.*

Word building: Other verb forms are **I equalled, I have equalled, I am equalling.** | **equal** *noun* **equally** *adverb* **equalise** *verb* **equality** *noun*

equation

noun a mathematical expression in which two quantities are said to be equal, such as $12 \times \frac{1}{4} = 3$
Word building: **equate** *verb*

equator (*say* uh-<u>kway</u>-tuh)

noun the imaginary circle around the earth, halfway between the poles, where the climate is mostly hot and wet
Word building: **equatorial** *adjective*

equestrian (*say* uh-<u>kwes</u>-tree-uhn)

adjective having to do with horses or horse-riding

equi-

prefix a word part meaning 'equal': *equilateral* | *equilibrium*
Word history: from Latin

equilateral (*say* eek-wuh-<u>lat</u>-ruhl)

adjective equal-sided: *an equilateral triangle*

equilibrium (*say* eek-wuh-<u>lib</u>-ree-uhm)

noun **1** equal balance: *The children kept the see-saw in equilibrium.* **2** steadiness of feelings: *At first she was upset but soon recovered her equilibrium.*

equip

verb to provide with whatever is needed to do something: *to equip with camping gear*
Word building: Other forms are **I equipped, I have equipped, I am equipping.** | **equipment** *noun*

equivalent (*say* uh-<u>kwiv</u>-uh-luhnt)

adjective equal or matching: *An admiral in the navy is equivalent to a general in the army.*
Word building: **equivalence** *noun* **equivalently** *adverb*

era (*rhymes with* nearer)

noun any long period of time with a special characteristic: *the era of the steam train*

eradicate

verb to root out or destroy: *to eradicate crime*
Word building: **eradicable** *adjective* **eradication** *noun* **eradicator** *noun*

erase

verb to rub out or wipe off: *Use a rubber to erase your mistakes.*
Word building: **eraser** *noun* **erasure** *noun*

e-reader

noun an electronic device for reading publications in electronic form: *a handheld e-reader*
Word use: You can also use **e-book reader**.

erect

adjective **1** upright: *to sit with an erect back*
verb **2** to build: *They have erected a house on the spare block.*
Word building: **erectly** *adverb* **erection** *noun* **erectness** *noun*

ermine (*say* <u>er</u>-muhn)

noun the white winter fur of the stoat

erosion

noun the cracking and wearing away of the soil by weather
Word building: **erode** *verb*

erotic

adjective having to do with sexual love
Word building: **erotically** *adverb* **eroticism** *noun*

err

verb **1** to make a mistake: *I must have erred about the street number.* **2** to do wrong: *He admitted that he had erred by telling a lie.*
Word building: **erring** *adjective*

errand

noun a small task you are sent to do: *I went to town on an errand for my father.*

erratic

adjective unsteady and irregular in behaviour or movement
Word building: **erratically** *adverb*

error

noun **1** a mistake
Other words: **blunder, slip**
2 wrongdoing: *She has seen the error of her ways.*

Word building: **erratum** *noun* a mistake in printing or writing   **erroneous** *adjective* incorrect   **erroneously** *adverb*

erupt
verb **1** to explode or burst out: *The volcano has erupted.* **2** to break out suddenly: *A burst of laughter erupted in the cinema.*

Word building: **eruption** *noun*   **eruptive** *adjective*

escalate (*say* es-kuh-layt)
verb to make or become larger or greater: *to escalate a war | to escalate prices*

Word building: **escalation** *noun*

escalator (*say* es-kuh-lay-tuh)
noun a continuously moving stairway

escapade (*say* es-kuh-payd)
noun a reckless adventure

escape
verb **1** to get away: *He escaped from prison.* **2** to avoid: *She escaped injury.*

Word building: **escape** *noun*   **escapee** *noun*   **escaper** *noun*

escapee (*say* es-kuh-pee)
noun someone who has escaped from a place where they have been locked up: *The escapee had scaled the wall and run into the bush.*

escort
noun **1** someone who goes along with someone else as a guard or to show respect: *a police escort* **2** someone who goes with you to a dance or party: *Her escort for the dinner was late.*

Word building: **escort** *verb*: *to escort her home*

Eskimo
noun another word for **Inuit**

Word use: This is not used much nowadays.
Word building: The plural is **Eskimos** or **Eskimo**.
Word history: from an Algonquian (a language of some Native American peoples) name for these people, meaning 'eaters of raw flesh'

especially
adverb particularly or more than usually: *to be especially careful | to do especially well*

Word building: **especial** *adjective*: *a painting of especial importance | to take especial care*

espionage (*say* es-pee-uhn-ahzh)
noun the practice of spying

espresso
noun coffee made in a machine which forces steam through crushed coffee beans

Word use: This word comes from Italian.

esquire
noun the polite title after a man's name, usually shortened to *Esq.*, which is sometimes used instead of 'Mr' or 'Dr': *Robert Jones, Esq.*

essay
noun a short piece of writing on a particular subject: *The teacher hasn't marked our essays on the causes of World War I.*

Word building: **essayist** *noun* someone who writes essays
Word history: from a Latin word meaning 'a weighing'

essence
noun **1** the basic nature: *The artist has caught the essence of the Prime Minister in that portrait.* **2** the concentrated liquid from a substance: *vanilla essence*

essential (*say* uh-sen-shuhl)
adjective absolutely necessary: *Flour is an essential ingredient in bread.*

Word building: **essential** *noun* the main part   **essentially** *adverb*

establish
verb **1** to set up: *They have established a new school.* **2** to settle: *We have established ourselves in the new neighbourhood.* **3** to prove: *We can't establish the truth of what he says.*

Word building: **establishment** *noun*

estate
noun **1** an area of land in the country, especially a large and valuable one: *Her uncle has an estate where he breeds racehorses.* **2** the possessions and property of a person who has died

esteem
verb to respect or think highly of: *The judge always esteemed your father greatly.*

Word building: **esteem** *noun* high opinion

estimate (*say* es-tuh-mayt)
verb **1** to roughly work out the value, size, or other qualities: *We estimated the cost to be $20.*
noun (*say* es-tuh-muht) **2** a rough valuation

Word building: **estimation** *noun*

estuary   (*say* <u>es</u>-chooh-uh-ree)
noun the mouth or lower part of a river
which is affected by high tides
Word building: The plural is **estuaries**. |
estuarine *adjective*

e-tag
noun a small object attached to the
windscreen of a car which transmits
information to an electronic reader causing
a toll to be taken from the car owner's
account when they drive on a toll road

etc.   (*say* et-<u>set</u>-ruh)
short for *et cetera*, Latin words meaning
'and other things': *I need pens, papers,
ink, etc.*

etch
verb **1** to cut or eat into metal, as acid
does **2** to print from a design which has
been etched **3** to produce a clear and
therefore lasting effect: *Fear has etched those
events on my memory.*
Word building: **etching** *noun*

eternal
adjective lasting forever: *eternal life*
Word building: **eternally** *adverb*

eternity
noun **1** time without end: *A lifetime seems
short when you try to imagine eternity.*
2 a very long time: *We had to wait an
eternity.*
Word use: Definition 2 is used jokingly.

ethanol
noun an alcohol produced from crops and
used as a biofuel

ether   (*say* <u>ee</u>-thuh)
noun a chemical which used to be used to
put a patient to sleep during an operation,
but is now used to dissolve other
substances
Word history: from a Greek word meaning
'upper air' or 'sky'

ethics
plural noun the system of beliefs and rules
that we live by: *My big sister is a very
honourable person who always acts according
to her ethics.*
Word building: **ethical** *adjective* morally
right   **ethically** *adverb*

ethnic
adjective having to do with the history,
language and customs of a particular
group: *ethnic dancing*
Word building: **ethnically** *adverb*

etiquette   (*say* <u>et</u>-ee-kuht)
noun behaviour which is thought of as
polite and correct: *business etiquette*

etymology   (*say* et-uh-<u>mol</u>-uh-jee)
noun **1** the study of the changes in
words over a long period of time
2 an explanation of the history of a
word, showing all the changes it has gone
through
Word building: The plural is **etymologies**. |
etymological *adjective*   **etymologist** *noun*

eucalyptus   (*say* yooh-kuh-<u>lip</u>-tuhs)
noun a type of tree with many different
varieties, used for its timber and its strong
oil
Word use: You can also use **eucalypt**,
eucalyptus tree or **gum tree**.
Word building: The plural is **eucalyptuses** or
eucalypti. | **eucalyptus** *adjective*
Word history: from a Greek word meaning
'covered' (referring to the cap covering the
buds)

euro¹   (*say* <u>yooh</u>-roh)
noun a type of wallaroo with short, red-
coloured fur
Word building: The plural is **euros**.
Word history: from an Aboriginal language of
South Australia called Adnyamathanha. See the
map of Australian Aboriginal languages at the
end of this book.

euro²   (*say* <u>yooh</u>-roh)
noun a unit of money, issued as a coin
and used in many countries in Europe,
including France, Germany, Italy and
Spain

euthanase   (*say* <u>yooh</u>-thuh-nayz)
verb to help or let (someone) die who has
a disease that cannot be treated, and who
wishes to die, either by giving them a
special drug or by taking away machines
and other drugs that are keeping them alive

euthanasia   (*say* yooh-thuh-<u>nay</u>-zhuh)
noun the act of helping or letting someone
die when they want to, because their pain
or suffering has become too great

evacuate

verb to leave in order to escape danger: *They evacuate their house during earthquakes.*

Word building: **evacuation** *noun* **evacuee** *noun*

evade

verb **1** to get round or escape from by trickery: *He evaded pursuit.* **2** to avoid doing: *She evades work.*

Word building: **evasion** *noun* **evasive** *adjective* **evasively** *adverb*

evaluate ,

verb to test and find the value or quality of: *to evaluate your answer*

Word building: **evaluation** *noun*

evangelist (*say* uh-<u>van</u>-juh-luhst)

noun someone who travels from place to place teaching from the Bible

Word building: **evangelistic** *adjective*

evaporate

verb to dry up: *The water has evaporated.* | *The sun evaporates the puddles.*

Word building: **evaporation** *noun* **evaporator** *noun*

eve

noun **1** the day before: *Today is Christmas eve.* **2** the time just before an event takes place: *They left the country on the eve of war.*

even

adjective **1** able to be divided by two: *Four, six, eight and ten are even numbers.* **2** equal in size: *She cut the cake in even slices.* **3** fairly matched: *It is an even contest.* **4** calm and steady: *He has an even temper.* **5** smooth or level: *The cricket pitch is not even.*
adverb **6** still or yet: *School is even better now.* **7** however unlikely it may seem: *Even my little brother was quiet when the beautiful music began.*

Word building: **even** *verb* (**evened, evening**) to make even **evenly** *adverb* **evenness** *noun*

evening

noun the late afternoon and early night

Word building: **evening** *adjective*: *evening dress*

event

noun **1** something which happens, especially something important: *The fete is a big event.* | *the day's events* **2** one of the items in a sports competition: *The last event was an egg-and-spoon race.*

Word building: **eventful** *adjective* **eventfully** *adverb*

eventual

adjective final or last: *The eventual result was a draw.*

Word building: **eventuality** *noun* **eventually** *adverb*

ever (*say* <u>ev</u>-uh)

adverb at any time: *Have you ever felt like this before?*

evergreen

adjective having leaves all year long: *an evergreen tree*

Word use: Compare this with **deciduous**.
Word building: **evergreen** *noun* an evergreen plant

every

adjective **1** each of a group referred to one by one: *We go to school every day of the week.*
phrase **2 every other**, one out of two, or every second: *We catch the bus to school every other day.*

everyday

adjective having to do with ordinary or casual situations, rather than formal ones: *everyday language*

everyone

pronoun every person: *I invited everyone in my class to my party.*

everything

pronoun **1** every thing or detail of a group or total **2** something very important: *That photo of her grandmother means everything to her.*

everywhere

adverb in all places: *I've looked everywhere that I can think of.*

evict

verb to turn out or remove: *The landlord evicted the tenants for not paying the rent.*

Word building: **eviction** *noun*

evidence

noun **1** something seen or heard that shows something else to be true **2** a clear sign of something: *The daffodils are the first evidence of spring.*

evident

adjective clear, or easily seen or understood: *It's evident you don't know what you are talking about.*

Word building: **evidently** *adverb*

evil

adjective wicked and harmful
Other words: **diabolical, immoral, villainous, vile**

Word building: **evil** *noun* anything evil   **evilly** *adverb*

evolution   (*say* ev-uh-<u>looh</u>-shuhn, eev-uh-<u>looh</u>-shuhn)

noun **1** the gradual continuous change of plants and animals over time to adapt to the environment **2** any process in which something grows or develops over time: *the evolution of the public education system*

Word building: **evolutionary** *adjective*

evolve   (*say* uh-<u>volv</u>, ee-<u>volv</u>)

verb **1** to develop gradually: *A brilliant new idea evolved in his mind. | Doctors are evolving a new way of treating the disease.* **2** of plants and animals, to develop over time into a more complex or advanced state

ewe   (*say* yooh)

noun a female sheep

Word use: The male is a **ram** and the young is a **lamb**.

ewe/you Don't confuse **ewe** with **you**. **You** is the person being spoken to.

ex-

prefix a word part meaning **1** out of: *export* **2** former: *ex-wife*

Word use: Other spellings are **e-** or **ef-**.
Word history: from Latin

exact

adjective **1** absolutely right in every detail: *She wants an exact fit.*
verb **2** to demand, sometimes by force: *The government exacts tax from everyone.*

Word building: **exacting** *adjective* demanding   **exactly** *adverb*   **exactness** *noun*

exaggerate   (*say* uhg-<u>zaj</u>-uh-rayt)

verb **1** to say more than is true about: *You always exaggerate a story!* **2** to increase even more: *Tiredness exaggerates my stutter.*

Word building: **exaggerated** *adjective* **exaggeration** *noun*

exalt   (*say* uhg-<u>zawlt</u>, eg-<u>zawlt</u>)

verb **1** to raise in importance or power: *to exalt someone to the position of president* **2** to praise: *to exalt someone to the skies*

Word building: **exaltation** *noun*   **exalted** *adjective*

examination

noun **1** an act of careful looking and testing: *The dentist's examination of her teeth revealed a broken filling.* **2** a test of knowledge or skill which often has to be passed before the next stage of learning begins

Word use: The short form of definition 2 is **exam**.
Word building: **examinee** *noun* the person doing an exam   **examiner** *noun* the person who sets an exam   **examine** *verb*

example

noun **1** a sample which makes something clear: *He gave an example of what he wanted us to do.*
Other words: **case, instance, specimen**
2 a model to be followed: *You aren't setting a very good example to the younger children.*
Other words: **pattern**

exasperate

verb to annoy very much

Word building: **exasperation** *noun*
Word history: from a Latin word meaning 'roughened'

excavate   (*say* <u>eks</u>-kuh-vayt)

verb **1** to make a hole or cavity in by removing earth: *to excavate the ground for a building site* **2** to uncover by digging: *to excavate an ancient city*

Word building: **excavation** *noun*   **excavator** *noun*

exceed

verb to go beyond: *You shouldn't exceed the speed limit.*

Word building: **exceedingly** *adverb* extremely   **exceeding** *adjective*

excel   (*say* uhk-<u>sel</u>)

verb to be very good: *He excels at swimming.*

Word building: Other forms are **I excelled, I have excelled, I am excelling.**

excellent   (*say* <u>ek</u>-suh-luhnt)

adjective very good or of a very high quality: *Patrick is an excellent cook.*
Other words: **brilliant, exceptional, fabulous, fantastic, great, marvellous, outstanding, sensational, superb, terrific, tremendous, wonderful**

Word building: **excellence** *noun* **excellently** *adverb*

except (*say* uhk-<u>sept</u>)
preposition excluding or leaving out: *They all had shoes on except me.*

except/accept Don't confuse **except** with **accept**, which means 'to take or receive willingly'.

exception (*say* uhk-<u>sep</u>-shuhn)
noun someone or something which doesn't follow the general rule or pattern: *They behaved themselves, with only a few exceptions.*

Word building: **exceptional** *adjective* very unusual **exceptionally** *adverb*

excerpt (*say* <u>ek</u>-serpt)
noun a piece quoted from a book or shown from a film

excess
noun an extreme amount

Word building: **excessive** *adjective* **excessively** *adverb* **excessiveness** *noun*

exchange
verb **1** to give one thing in return for another: *We'll exchange with you* **2** to give to each other: *They exchanged insults.*
noun **3** the act of exchanging **4** a central office where letters and calls are received and sorted: *a telephone exchange*

excite (*say* uhk-<u>suyt</u>)
verb to cause eager feelings in: *Your visit has excited them.*

Word building: **excitement** *noun* **exciting** *adjective*
Word history: from a Latin word meaning 'call forth' or 'rouse'

exclaim
verb to cry out suddenly in fright or pleasure

Word building: **exclamatory** *adjective* **exclaimer** *noun*

exclamation
noun something said or cried out suddenly in fright or pleasure

exclamation mark
noun a punctuation mark (!) used after an exclamation

You use an **exclamation mark** when you write down an utterance to show that it has been said:

1 as a command:
Look out!
Come here!

2 as an expression of pleasure, surprise, fright, or some other strong feeling:
Oh no!
What a pity!
How lovely!

Note that if you are using an exclamation mark, you don't use a full stop as well.

If you have an exclamation which is also a question, the exclamation mark comes after the question mark:
You mean you're going to the party?!

exclude
verb to shut or keep out: *Blinds exclude light from rooms. | All children under ten are excluded from our club.*

Word building: **exclusion** *noun*

exclusive
adjective **1** fashionable: *an exclusive club | an exclusive suburb* **2** not shared with others: *an exclusive interview*

Word building: **exclusively** *adverb* **exclusiveness** *noun*

excommunicate
verb to cut off from receiving communion or being a member of a church

Word building: **excommunication** *noun*

excrete
verb to pass out from the body: *The caterpillar excreted a green slime after I trod on it.*

Word building: **excrement** *noun* waste matter from your body **excretion** *noun* **excretive** *adjective*

excruciating
(*say* uhks-<u>krooh</u>-shee-ay-ting)
adjective very painful or causing great suffering

Word building: **excruciatingly** *adverb*

excursion
noun a short journey or trip usually taken for a special reason: *Our class went on an excursion to the zoo.*

Word building: **excursive** *adjective* wandering

excuse   (*rhymes with* choose)

verb **1** to pardon or forgive **2** to free from duty or let off: *He excused her from the washing up.*

noun (*rhymes with* goose) **3** a reason, sometimes a pretended one, for being excused

Word building: **excusable** *adjective*

execute

verb **1** to do or carry out: *to execute a plan* **2** to put to death

Word building: **execution** *noun*

executive   (*say* uhg-<u>zek</u>-yuh-tiv)

noun **1** someone responsible for carrying out plans, especially in a business

adjective **2** having to do with managing things

exempt

verb to make free from a duty or rule: *She was exempted from sport because she was sick.*

Word building: **exempt** *adjective*   **exemption** *noun*

exercise

noun **1** an activity of the body or mind to train or improve it **2** a putting into practice: *It will be an exercise of your willpower to stop eating cake.*

Word building: **exercise** *verb*

exert   (*say* uhg-<u>zert</u>)

verb to use or put into action: *She exerted all her strength to lift the bricks.*

exertion

noun effort: *The exertion of her long swim was too much for her.*

exhale

verb to breathe out

Word building: **exhalation** *noun*

exhaust   (*say* uhg-<u>zawst</u>)

verb **1** to tire or wear out: *I have exhausted myself working.* **2** to empty or use up completely: *I have exhausted all my patience.*

noun **3** the used gases given off by an engine

Word building: **exhaustive** *adjective* thorough   **exhaustion** *noun*   **exhaustively** *adverb*

exhibit   (*say* uhg-<u>zib</u>-uht)

verb **1** to show or display

noun **2** something shown or displayed to the public

Word building: **exhibitor, exhibiter** *noun* someone who exhibits   **exhibition** *noun*

exhilarate   (*say* uhg-<u>zil</u>-uh-rayt)

verb to fill with energy or excitement: *The swim in the cold surf exhilarated me.*

Word building: **exhilarating** *adjective*   **exhilaratingly** *adverb*   **exhilaration** *noun*

exile

verb **1** to force to leave your home or country: *The king exiled her for treason.*

noun **2** someone who has been forced to leave their country or home **3** a long separation from your country or home

exist

verb **1** to be: *The earth has existed for millions of years.* **2** to have life or be real: *Do ghosts exist?* **3** to continue to live: *We cannot exist without water.*

Word building: **existence** *noun* the fact of existing   **existent** *adjective*

exit

noun **1** a way out: *The building had a number of exits.* **2** a going away or a departure: *Anne said 'goodbye' and made a quick exit.*

Word building: **exit** *verb* to go away or out

exit strategy

noun a plan a person has to remove themselves from some situation which does not leave them being disadvantaged or harmed: *If I was you, I would work out an exit strategy right now!*

exodus

noun a going out or a departure, usually of a large number of people

exorcise   (*say* <u>ek</u>-saw-suyz)

verb to free from evil spirits by prayers or a religious ceremony: *to exorcise a haunted house*

Word use: Another spelling is **exorcize**.

Word building: **exorcism** *noun*   **exorcist** *noun*

exotic

adjective **1** foreign or not belonging to your own country: *an exotic plant* **2** strange, or unusually colourful or beautiful: *When we were overseas we saw many exotic places and ate exotic food.*

Word building: **exotic** *noun* anything exotic, especially a plant   **exotically** *adverb*

expand

verb **1** to increase in size or to swell: *Daniel expanded the sentence into a whole paragraph.* | *The balloon expanded with air.* **2** to spread, stretch out or unfold: *A bird expands its wings to fly.*

Word building: **expansion** *noun*

expanse

noun a large open space or widespread area: *Australia has vast expanses of desert.*

expatriate *(say* eks-<u>pat</u>-ree-uht)*

noun someone who has left their own country to live in another

expect

verb **1** to look forward to **2** to look for with good reason: *I expect you to do your duty.* **3** to be pregnant: *My mother is expecting.*

Word building: **expectancy** *noun* **expectant** *adjective* **expectantly** *adverb* **expectation** *noun*

expedient

adjective useful or suitable for a particular purpose: *It would be expedient for you to go to the meeting.*

Word building: **expedience** *noun* **expediency** *noun* **expediently** *adverb*

expedite *(say* <u>eks</u>-puh-duyt)*

verb to hurry up or to do quickly: *We must expedite this matter so it will be ready on time.*

Word building: **expeditious** *adjective* quick **expeditiously** *adverb*

expedition

noun **1** a journey made for a special purpose, such as a war or exploration **2** the group of people and the transport used to go on such a journey

Word building: **expeditionary** *adjective*: *an expeditionary force*

expel

verb **1** to drive out or away with force: *When you blow up a balloon you expel air from your lungs.* **2** to dismiss or send away from a club or a school

Word building: Other forms are **I expelled, I have expelled, I am expelling.** | **expulsion** *noun* **expulsive** *adjective*

expend

verb **1** to use up: *I expended all my energy climbing the hill.* **2** to pay out or spend

Word building: **expendable** *adjective* **expenditure** *noun*

expense

noun cost or charge: *the expense of our holiday* | *We had our meal at the company's expense.*

Word building: **expensive** *adjective* **expensively** *adverb*

experience

noun **1** something that happens to you: *I had many strange experiences on my trip.* **2** the knowledge or practice you get from doing or seeing things
verb **3** to meet with, or have happen to you: *She experienced a lot of friendliness on her trip.*

Word building: **experienced** *adjective* wise or skilful

experiment

verb **1** to try or test to find something out: *Doctors are experimenting with drugs to find a cure.*
noun **2** a test or a trial carried out to discover something

Word building: **experimental** *adjective* **experimentally** *adverb* **experimentation** *noun*

expert

noun someone who has a lot of skill or knowledge about a special thing
Other words: **authority, professional, specialist**

Word building: **expert** *adjective* having a lot of special skill or knowledge **expertise** *noun* expert skill or knowledge

expire

verb **1** to come to an end: *The contract has almost expired.* **2** to die

Word building: **expiration** *noun* **expiry** *noun*

explain

verb **1** to make clear or easy to understand **2** to give the reason for or cause of: *Please explain your absence.*

Word building: **explanatory** *adjective* used to explain **explicable** *adjective* able to be explained
Word history: from a Latin word meaning 'make plain' or 'flatten out'

explanation

noun a talk or piece of writing which explains how or why something happens. See the 'Types of writing and speaking' table at the end of this book.

explicit   (*say* uhk-<u>splis</u>-uht)

adjective clearly and fully set out: *The recipe was so explicit that even I could understand it.*

Word building: **explicitly** *adverb*

explode

verb **1** to blow up or burst into pieces with a loud noise: *The bomb exploded.* **2** to burst out with a sudden expression of feeling: *She exploded with laughter when she saw it.*

Word history: from a Latin word meaning 'drive out by clapping'

exploit¹   (*say* <u>eks</u>-ployt)

noun a notable or daring deed

exploit²   (*say* uhks-<u>ployt</u>)

verb **1** to use unfairly or selfishly: *She exploits her little brother.* **2** to put to good use: *The earth is exploited for its oil and minerals.*

Word building: **exploitation** *noun*   **exploitative** *adjective*   **exploiter** *noun*

explore

verb **1** to travel over an area to discover things or places: *They explored the bush to see if it had any caves.* **2** to examine or go over carefully: *The doctor explored every symptom in order to make a diagnosis.*

Word building: **exploration** *noun*   **exploratory** *adjective*   **explorer** *noun*

explosion

noun **1** a blowing up or exploding: *The explosion scattered rubbish everywhere.* **2** a sudden burst of noise: *There was an explosion of laughter around the dinner table.*

Word building: **explosive** *noun* a substance that can explode, such as dynamite   **explosive** *adjective*   **explosively** *adverb*

export   (*say* uhk-<u>spawt</u>)

verb **1** to send to other countries for sale: *Australia exports a lot of wool every year.* *noun* (*say* <u>ek</u>-spawt) **2** something exported: *Sugar is one of Australia's exports.*

Word building: **exportation** *noun*   **exporter** *noun*

expose

verb **1** to uncover **2** to let light onto, when taking a photograph: *By mistake, I opened the back of the camera and exposed the film.*

Word building: **exposure** *noun*

exposition   (*say* ex-po-<u>zish</u>-on)

noun **1** a show or display that everyone can come and see **2** writing which gives only one opinion on something. See the 'Types of writing and speaking' table at the end of this book.

Word use: Definition 1 is sometimes shortened to **expo**.

express

verb **1** to put into words: *I expressed my opinion.* **2** to show or make known: *Your face expressed your surprise.* **3** to make known your feelings or thoughts: *Alexandre expresses himself well in English.*
adjective **4** sent or travelling direct without stopping: *an express parcel* **5** clearly stated or definite: *an express purpose*
noun **6** an express train or bus

Word building: **expressive** *adjective* showing how you feel   **expressively** *adverb*   **expressiveness** *noun*

expression

noun **1** the act of putting into words: *an expression of opinion* **2** the look on someone's face

expressway

noun a road on which traffic can travel fast

Word use: Other words for this are **freeway** and **motorway**.

exquisite

adjective delicately beautiful: *an exquisite vase*

Word building: **exquisitely** *adverb*   **exquisiteness** *noun*

extend

verb **1** to stretch out: *We will extend the coil of rope to its full length.* | *This road extends for miles.* **2** to make longer or larger: *to extend shopping hours* | *to extend a house*

Word building: **extent** *noun*: *to its full extent*

extension

noun **1** a stretching out or lengthening **2** something added on: *an extension to our house* **3** an extra telephone connected to the one you already have

Word building: **extension** *adjective*: *an extension ladder*

extensive

adjective **1** large in amount or size: *extensive knowledge | an extensive wheat farm* **2** carried out as far as possible: *an extensive search*

Word building: **extensively** *adverb*

exterior

adjective being on the outside of: *the exterior walls of the house*

Word use: The opposite of this is **interior**.
Word building: **exterior** *noun: the exterior of the building*

exterminate

verb to get rid of, especially by destroying: *to exterminate white ants*

Word building: **extermination** *noun*
exterminator *noun*
Word history: from a Latin word meaning 'driven beyond the boundaries'

external

adjective **1** on the outside: *Her external injuries included a black eye.* **2** coming from outside: *The external support for the school's project came mainly from local businesses.*

Word use: The opposite of this is **internal**.
Word building: **externally** *adverb*

extinct

adjective **1** no longer existing: *Dinosaurs are an extinct type of reptile.* **2** no longer active: *an extinct volcano*

Word building: **extinction** *noun*

extinguish

verb to put out: *Always extinguish your camp fire before leaving.*
Other words: **douse, quench, smother**

Word building: **extinguisher** *noun: a fire extinguisher*

extra

adjective **1** more than usual
noun **2** something added **3** someone playing a minor part in a film, usually as part of a crowd

extra-

prefix a word part meaning 'outside' or 'beyond': *extraordinary*

Word history: from Latin

extract   (*say* eks-<u>trakt</u>)

verb **1** to pull or take out: *to extract a tooth*
noun (*say* eks-trakt) **2** something taken out or separated: *I read an extract from her latest book. | a drink made from beef extract*

Word building: **extraction** *noun*

extraordinary   (*say* uhk-<u>straw</u>-duhn-ree)

adjective **1** more than ordinary: *Our leader is a woman of extraordinary strength.*
Other words: **exceptional, notable, outstanding, phenomenal, remarkable**
2 unusual: *We have been having extraordinary weather.*
Other words: **abnormal, exceptional, odd, peculiar, queer**

Word building: **extraordinarily** *adverb*

extrasensory perception

noun being able to know or find out things without using the usual senses like seeing and hearing, and so on

extravagant   (*say* uhk-<u>strav</u>-uh-guhnt, ek-<u>strav</u>-uh-guhnt)

adjective **1** spending more than you need to: *He is very extravagant when he goes shopping.* **2** costing a lot or more than you can afford: *an extravagant purchase*
Other words: **excessive, lavish**

Word building: **extravagance** *noun*
extravagantly *adverb*

extreme

adjective **1** very great: *I was in extreme pain.* **2** outermost: *We saw you at the extreme edge of the cricket field.*

Word building: **extremity** *noun* the extreme point or part of something   **extremely** *adverb*

extreme sport

noun a sport involving a lot of risk to the person who does it, such as bungee jumping

extrovert   (*say* <u>eks</u>-truh-vert)

noun someone who does not concentrate on himself or herself, and who is confident and likes being with other people: *The new girl was popular because she was such an extrovert and made friends easily.*

Word use: Compare this with **introvert**.
Word building: **extroverted** *adjective*

exuberant   (*say* uhg-<u>zyooh</u>-buh-ruhnt, eg-<u>zyooh</u>-buh-ruhnt)

adjective full of energy or warm feelings: *The team members were exuberant after their win. | What an exuberant welcome!*

Word building: **exuberance** *noun*   **exuberantly** *adverb*

exult (*say* uhg-<u>zult</u>, eg-<u>zawlt</u>)

verb to show pleasure or feel happy that you have achieved or won something: *He exulted to find that he had triumphed after all.*

Word building: **exultant** *adjective*   **exultantly** *adverb*   **exultation** *noun*   **exultingly** *adverb*

eye

noun **1** the organ or part of the body with which we see **2** the iris or coloured part of this organ: *She has blue eyes.* **3** a close or careful watch: *Keep an eye on my books for me.* **4** an ability to use your eyes effectively: *You have a good eye for ball games.*

phrase **5 see eye to eye,** to agree: *We see eye to eye on most things.*

eyeball

noun the round, ball-shaped object that forms your whole eye, including the part inside your head

eyebrow

noun the hair on the bony ridge over your eye

eyelash

noun one of the short curved hairs growing on the edge of an eyelid

eyelid

noun the lid of skin which moves up and down over your eye when you blink

eyesight

noun the power of seeing

eyesore

noun something unpleasant to look at: *The shabby picnic shed was an eyesore in the park.*

eyewitness

noun someone who actually sees a particular action or happening

Word building: **eyewitness** *adjective*: *an eyewitness account*

Ff

fable

noun a short story, often about animals, that teaches a lesson about how to behave: *the fable of the tortoise and the hare*

fabric

noun cloth made by weaving, knitting or pressing fibres together: *wool fabric | felt fabric*

fabulous

adjective **1** very good or wonderful: *We had a fabulous time.* **2** told about in fables or myths: *a fabulous creature*

Word building: **fabulously** adverb **fabulousness** noun

facade (say fuh-sahd)

noun the front of a building

Word use: This word comes from French.

face

noun **1** the front of your head from the forehead to the chin **2** a look or expression: *a sad face* **3** a surface of something: *the face of a cube | the face of a watch*
verb **4** to look towards **5** to come into contact with or meet: *to face difficulties*

Word building: **facial** adjective: *a facial expression*

facet (say fas-uht)

noun **1** a side or part of something complicated like a personality, an argument or a structure: *The conservation argument has many facets.* **2** one of the small, flat, polished surfaces of a gemstone

Word history: from a French word meaning 'little face'

facetious (say fuh-see-shuhs)

adjective meant to be or trying to be amusing, at the wrong time or in an unsuitable way: *a facetious remark | a facetious person*

Word building: **facetiously** adverb **facetiousness** noun

face value

noun **1** the value shown on a coin, ticket, price tag, and so on: *The face value of the ticket was $10 but we got three for $20.*
phrase **2 at face value**, according to the way a situation or a person appears to be: *She's not prepared to take people at face value — she doesn't really trust people until she has known them for a while.*

face washer

noun a small piece of soft cloth for washing your face or body

facility (say fuh-sil-uh-tee)

noun **1** something that makes doing a job easier: *He was given every facility to complete it in time.* **2** skill or cleverness: *Her facility with words impressed us.*

Word building: The plural is **facilities**. | **facilitate** verb to make easier

fact

noun **1** something that is true or real
phrase **2 in fact**, really: *In fact, the truth was far worse than we could have imagined.*

Word building: **factual** adjective **factually** adverb **factualness** noun

227

faction

noun a small group of people within a larger group, who hold a different opinion to the larger group

Word building: **factional** *adjective* **factionalism** *noun*

factor

noun **1** one of the things that brings about a result: *Hard work was a factor in her success.* **2** one of two or more numbers which, when multiplied together, give the product: *Factors of 18 are 3 and 6.*

Word history: from a Latin word meaning 'doer' or 'maker'

factory

noun a building or group of buildings where goods are made

faculty

noun **1** one of the powers that you are born with: *the faculty of hearing | My grandmother has just turned 100 and she's still got all her faculties.* **2** the ability to do something in particular: *a faculty for getting into trouble*

Word building: The plural is **faculties**.

fad

noun something that is popular for a short time: *Yoyos are a fad that comes and goes.*

Word building: **faddish** *adjective*

fade

verb **1** to lose colour or strength: *The carpet has faded over the years.* **2** to disappear slowly: *The smile faded from her face.*
Other words: **evaporate, vanish**
3 to cause to fade: *Sunshine faded the carpet.*

faeces (*say* <u>fee</u>-seez)

plural noun waste matter discharged from the intestines

Word use: Another spelling is **feces**. | Another word is **excrement**.

Fahrenheit (*say* <u>fa</u>-ruhn-huyt)

adjective relating to a scale of temperature in which the melting point of ice is 32° above zero and the boiling point is 212° above zero

Word history: named after a German scientist, Gabriel *Fahrenheit*, who thought up this scale and was the first to put mercury into thermometers

fail

verb **1** to be unsuccessful in: *He failed Maths.* **2** to be less than expected: *The wheat crop failed this year.*

Word building: **failing** *noun* a weakness **failure** *noun* lack of success

faint

adjective **1** lacking strength: *a faint light | a faint sound* **2** weak and dizzy: *I feel faint.*
verb **3** to lose consciousness for a short time
noun **4** a short loss of consciousness

Word building: **faintly** *adverb* **faintness** *noun*

fair[1]

adjective **1** not showing favouritism: *The judge in the trial was fair.*
Other words: **just, impartial, reasonable, unbiased**
2 done according to the rules: *It wouldn't be fair to take it without asking.*
Other words: **decent, honest, proper, right**
3 not cloudy: *fair weather*
Other words: **clear, fine, sunny**
4 of light colour: *fair hair | fair skin*

Word building: **fair** *adverb*: *to play fair* **fairly** *adverb* **fairness** *noun*

fair/fare Don't confuse **fair** with **fare**, which is the money you pay for a ticket on a bus or train.

fair[2]

noun **1** a group of sideshows and similar entertainments set up for a short time in one place **2** a regular gathering of buyers and sellers of a particular type of goods: *a book fair | a cattle fair*

fair dinkum

adjective Informal true or genuine: *a fair dinkum Australian*

fairway

noun the part of a golf course between a tee and the green where the grass is kept short, designed for the player to hit the ball along

fairy

noun a tiny imaginary creature with magical powers

Word building: The plural is **fairies**.

fairytale

noun **1** a story about fairies **2** a story that's untrue or hard to believe: *Her excuse was a bit of a fairytale.*

Word building: **fairytale** *adjective*

faith

noun **1** trust in someone or something
2 the collection of beliefs of a religion: *the Christian faith | the Jewish faith*

faithful

adjective loyal or trustworthy: *a faithful friend | a faithful worker*

Word building: **faithfully** *adverb*   **faithfulness** *noun*

fake

verb **1** to make in such a way as to trick other people: *to fake money* **2** to pretend: *to fake illness*

Word building: **fake** *noun* someone who fakes or something faked   **fake** *adjective*: *fake watches*   **faker** *noun*

falafel   (*say* fuh-<u>luf</u>-uhl, fuh-<u>laf</u>-uhl)

noun fried balls of ground chickpeas and spices, often eaten with a sauce, bread and salad

Word use: Another spelling is **felafel**.

falcon   (*say* <u>fal</u>-kuhn, <u>fawl</u>-kuhn)

noun a kind of hunting bird which captures its prey in flight

Word building: **falconry** *noun* the training and use of these birds   **falconer** *noun*
Word history: from a Latin word meaning 'sickle'

fall

verb **1** to drop from a higher to a lower place **2** to become less or lower: *Prices fall when there is a glut. | The temperature fell today.* **3** to come to be: *to fall asleep | to fall in love*
noun **4** an act of falling or dropping
phrase **5 fall back on**, to use when something else hasn't worked: *If I forget a line, I'll have to fall back on my notes.* **6 fall in with**, to agree to: *I'll fall in with your plans.* **7 fall out**, to quarrel **8 fall through**, to be unsuccessful: *Our plans fell through.*

Word building: Other verb forms are **I fell, I have fallen, I am falling**.

fallible   (*say* <u>fal</u>-uh-buhl)

adjective likely to make a mistake

Word building: **fallibility** *noun*   **fallibly** *adverb*

fallout

noun dangerous radioactive dust falling from the air, after a nuclear explosion

fallow

adjective ploughed but left unseeded to improve its quality: *If we leave this land fallow, we should get a good crop next season.*

false

adjective **1** not true or correct: *a false statement*
Other words: **deceitful, dishonest, untrue**
2 not faithful: *a false friend* **3** not real: *false teeth*
Other words: **artificial, counterfeit, fake, sham**

Word building: **falsify** *verb* (**falsified, falsifying**)   **falsely** *adverb*   **falseness** *noun*   **falsity** *noun*

falsehood

noun a statement that is not true

falsetto   (*say* fawl-<u>set</u>-oh)

noun a very high-pitched voice

Word building: The plural is **falsettos**. | **falsetto** *adjective*: *a falsetto voice*

falter

verb to move or speak weakly or unsteadily

Word building: **falteringly** *adverb*

fame

noun the state of being widely known: *Her fame spread after she won an Olympic medal.*

Word building: **famous** *adjective*   **famously** *adverb*

familiar

adjective **1** well-known: *a familiar story*
phrase **2 familiar with**, having knowledge of: *I am familiar with the success he has achieved.*

Word building: **familiarisation** *noun*   **familiarise** *verb*   **familiarity** *noun*   **familiarly** *adverb*

family

noun **1** parents and their children
2 a wider group of related people including grandparents, uncles, aunts and cousins **3** a group of related things: *the human family | a tree of the acacia family*
adjective **4** having to do with the family **5** suitable for a family
phrase **6 family tree**, the branching plan or diagram of your family, including all your relations and ancestors

Word building: The plural form of the noun is **families**. | **familial** (*say* fuh-<u>mil</u>-ee-uhl) *adjective* having to do with a family

famine (*say* <u>fam</u>-uhn)
noun a serious shortage of food, usually caused by drought

famished
adjective very hungry

famous
adjective well-known
Other words: **acclaimed, celebrated, distinguished, illustrious, legendary, notable, noted, prominent, renowned**

fan¹
noun **1** something designed to move the air and make you feel cooler
verb **2** to cool by moving the air: *We fanned her with a folded paper.*

Word building: Other verb forms are **I fanned, I have fanned, I am fanning.**

fan²
noun someone who is an eager supporter: *a football fan*

Word history: a shortened form of **fanatic**, although the meaning has now changed

fanatic (*say* fuh-<u>nat</u>-ik)
noun someone who is too enthusiastic, often in an unthinking way, about something they believe in: *a fanatic about health foods*

Word building: **fanatical** *adjective*   **fanatically** *adverb*   **fanaticism** *noun*
Word history: from a Latin word meaning 'having to do with a temple', 'inspired by a god', or 'frantic'

fanbelt
noun the belt which drives the cooling fan of a motor

fancy
noun **1** a liking: *She took a fancy to me.*
2 something imagined: *It was only a fancy though it seemed real at the time.*
verb **3** to imagine: *I fancied I saw myself in a beautiful palace.* **4** to like or want: *I fancy fish for tea.* **5** to believe without being certain: *I fancied she said she would come.*
adjective **6** ornamental: *fancy gold braid*

Word building: Other verb forms are **I fancied, I have fancied, I am fancying.** | Other adjective forms are **fancier, fanciest.** | **fanciful** *adjective*: *fanciful ideas*

fanfare
noun a short, loud piece of music usually played on trumpets, used to mark the beginning of an event or the arrival of someone important

fang
noun **1** one of the long, sharp, hollow teeth of a snake, by which it injects venom **2** a canine tooth

fantastic
adjective **1** strange or unusual: *fantastic ornaments*
Other words: **bizarre, crazy, eccentric, odd, outlandish, peculiar, weird**
2 imaginary: *fantastic fears*
Other words: **fanciful**
3 very good or wonderful: *a fantastic party*
Other words: **amazing, brilliant, excellent, exceptional, fabulous, great, marvellous, outstanding, phenomenal, terrific, tremendous**

Word building: **fantastically** *adverb*

fantasy
noun **1** imagination: *the world of fantasy* **2** the making of pleasant mental pictures: *a fantasy in which I'm a famous pilot*
Other words: **daydream**

Word building: The plural is **fantasies.** | **fantasise** *verb*

far
adverb **1** at or to a great distance or point: *He went far away.*
adjective **2** distant: *a far city* **3** the more distant of two: *the far side of the river*
phrase **4 as far as,** to the distance or degree that: *as far as I am concerned*

Word building: Other adjective forms are **farther** or **further, farthest** or **furthest.**

faraway
adjective **1** distant or remote: *a faraway country* **2** dreamy: *a faraway look*

farce
noun **1** a comedy in which the humour depends on a ridiculous and unlikely situation **2** foolish show or mockery: *Her unkindness made a farce of our friendship.*

Word building: **farcical** *adjective*: *a farcical situation*   **farcically** *adverb*

fare

noun **1** the price of travelling on a public vehicle: *a bus fare | a train fare* **2** food: *The fare at the hotel was good.*
verb **3** to get on or manage: *We fared well.*

fare/fair Don't confuse **fare** with **fair**. Someone who is **fair** does not show favouritism. For other meanings look up **fair**.

farewell

noun **1** a saying of goodbye: *a sad farewell*
verb **2** to say goodbye to

farm

noun an area of land used for growing crops or raising animals
Word building: **farm** *verb* **farmer** *noun* **farming** *noun*
Word history: from a French word meaning 'fix''

fascinate (*say* fas-uh-nayt)

verb to attract and hold the interest of completely: *She fascinated us with her stories.*
Word building: **fascinating** *adjective* **fascinatingly** *adverb* **fascination** *noun*
Word history: from a Latin word meaning 'enchanted'

fashion

noun **1** a style of dress: *Modern fashions are comfortable to wear.* **2** a custom or way of doing things: *The fashion of entertaining at a barbecue is popular.* **3** manner or way: *He spoke to me in a rude fashion.*
verb **4** to shape or form: *He fashioned a crib for the baby.*
Word building: **fashionable** *adjective* **fashionably** *adverb*

fast¹

adjective **1** able to move quickly: *a fast runner*
Other words: **quick, rapid, speedy, swift**
2 finished in a short time: *a fast race*
Other words: **quick**
3 ahead of the correct time: *My clock is fast.* **4** fixed firmly in place: *He made the boat fast to the wharf.*
adverb **5** tightly: *Hold fast to that rope.*
Other words: **firmly, securely**
6 soundly: *I was fast asleep.* **7** quickly or swiftly: *He ran fast.*
Other words: **briskly, rapidly, speedily**

fast²

noun a period of time when no food is eaten, usually for religious or health reasons
Word building: **fast** *verb*

fasten (*say* fah-suhn)

verb **1** to fix firmly in place by tying or attaching: *to fasten a boat to its mooring | Fasten your seatbelts.* **2** to close and make secure a window, door, and so on
Other words: **bar, bolt, lock**
Word building: **fastener** *noun*

fastidious (*say* fas-tid-ee-uhs)

adjective hard to please: *He is fastidious about cleanliness.*
Word use: The more usual word is **fussy**.
Word building: **fastidiously** *adverb* **fastidiousness** *noun*

fat

noun **1** the white or yellowish greasy substance found in or around the flesh of animals and in some plants: *Cut the fat from the chops.*
adjective **2** plump or obese **3** having much edible flesh: *a fat lamb*
Word building: Other adjective forms are **fatter, fattest.** | **fatten** *verb* **fatty** *adjective*

fatal

adjective **1** causing death: *a fatal injury*
Other words: **deadly, deathly, lethal, mortal**
2 likely to have very important results: *a fatal decision*
Other words: **critical, crucial, fateful**
Word building: **fatality** *noun* **fatally** *adverb*

fate

noun **1** the cause beyond your control that seems to control the things that happen to you: *It was fate that we should meet.*
2 the end, outcome or final result: *the fate of our plans*
Word building: **fateful** *adjective*: *the fateful day of the earthquake* **fatefully** *adverb*

fate/fete Don't confuse **fate** with **fete**. A **fete** is a kind of fair to raise money for a school or charity. Note that this can also be written **fête**.

father

noun **1** a male parent **2** someone who shows the interest of a father: *a father to the neighbourhood children* **3** someone who invents or begins something: *King Alfred was the father of the English navy.* **4** a title given to priests in the Catholic Church and the Church of England
verb **5** to be the father of **6** to act as a father towards
Word building: **fatherhood** *noun* **fatherly** *adjective*.

father-in-law

noun the father of your husband or wife

Word building: The plural is **fathers-in-law**.

fathom

noun **1** an old-fashioned measure of the depth of water equal to 6 feet, or nearly 2 metres in the metric system
verb **2** to understand completely: *I couldn't fathom maths until my brother helped me.*

fatigue (*say* fuh-<u>teeg</u>)

noun **1** severe mental or physical tiredness **2** weakening of material, especially metal, as a result of strain put on it after long use

Word building: **fatigue** *verb* (**fatigued, fatiguing**)

fatuous (*say* <u>fat</u>-chooh-uhs)

adjective foolish without knowing it

Word use: The more usual word is **silly**.
Word building: **fatuously** *adverb* **fatuousness** *noun*

fault

noun **1** responsibility or cause for blame: *It was my fault we were late.* **2** a mistake or blemish: *I returned the shirt to the shop because there was a fault in the collar.* **3** a failure to serve a ball according to the rules in tennis and similar games
phrase **4 at fault**, open to blame: *If the battery's flat we'll all know who's at fault.*

Word building: **fault** *verb*: *They couldn't fault his wonderful singing.* **faulty** *adjective* having faults **faultily** *adverb* **faultiness** *noun*
Word history: from a Latin word meaning 'deceive'

fault line

noun the line in the earth where the movement caused by an earthquake is likely to occur

fauna (*say* <u>faw</u>-nuh)

noun the animals of a particular area or period of time: *Australian fauna includes koalas, kookaburras and blue-tongue lizards.*

Word use: Compare this with **flora**.
Word building: **faunal** *adjective*
Word history: named after the Roman goddess *Fauna*, the sister of *Faunus*, god of the woodlands

favour

noun **1** a kind act: *Will you do me a favour?* **2** a state of being thought well of: *in favour with the teacher*
verb **3** to think of with approval: *to favour an idea* **4** to prefer unfairly: *A teacher shouldn't favour one student over another.* **5** to show favour to: *Will you favour us by coming to our meeting?*
phrase **6 in favour of**, **a** supportive of: *Are you in favour of our idea?* **b** payable to: *a cheque in favour of the Red Cross*

Word use: Another spelling is **favor**.
Word building: **favoured** *adjective*

favourable

adjective **1** giving help: *a favourable wind for the boats* **2** saying what you want to hear: *a favourable answer*

Word use: Another spelling is **favorable**.
Word building: **favourably** *adverb*

favourite

noun **1** someone or something most highly thought of: *This picture is my favourite.* **2** a competitor who is expected to win **3** someone who is treated as being better than others without really deserving it: *the teacher's favourite*

Word use: Another spelling is **favorite**.
Word building: **favourite** *adjective* **favouritism** *noun*

fawn[1]

noun **1** a young deer, under a year old
adjective **2** pale yellowish-brown

Word use: A male deer is a **buck** or **hart** and the female is a **doe** or **hind**.

fawn[2]

verb to try to get special treatment from someone by flattery

fax

noun **1** a way of sending documents or pictures along a telephone line **2** a document or picture sent this way
verb **3** to send by fax: *to fax a document*

Word use: You can also use **facsimile** (*say* fak-<u>sim</u>-uh-lee) for definitions 1 and 2.
Word history: a respelling of the first part of *facs(imile)*, which means 'an exact copy'

fear

noun **1** a feeling that danger or something unpleasant is near

Other words: **alarm, anxiety, apprehension, dread, fright, horror, nervousness, panic, terror**

verb **2** to be afraid of
Other words: **dread**
3 to feel anxious: *I fear for your safety.*
Other words: **worry**

Word building: **fearsome** *adjective*: *a fearsome storm*   **fearful** *adjective*   **fearless** *adjective*   **fearlessness** *noun*

feasible   (*say* <u>feez</u>-uh-buhl)

adjective likely to work: *a feasible plan*

Word building: **feasibility** *noun*   **feasibly** *adverb*

feast

noun **1** a large meal set out for many guests
Other words: **banquet**
2 a large quantity of anything eaten or giving pleasure: *a feast of ice-cream | a feast of music* **3** something very pleasant: *a feast for the eyes*

Word building: **feasting** *noun*: *It was a night of feasting.*   **feast** *verb*

feat

noun a deed of great skill, courage or strength

feather

noun **1** one of the growths that make up the covering of a bird's body
phrase **2 a feather in your cap**, an honour or mark of merit you have earned

Word building: **feathered** *adjective*   **feathery** *adjective*

feature

noun **1** any part of your face: *Your eyes are your best feature.* **2** an outstanding part or quality: *Climbing Uluru was the feature of our holiday.*
verb **3** to give special importance to: *to feature a tenor on a concert program* **4** to be an outstanding or distinguishing part: *Gum trees always feature in my paintings.*

Word building: **featured** *adjective*

February   (*say* <u>feb</u>-yooh-uh-ree, feb-rooh-uh-ree)

noun the second month of the year, with 28 days, but 29 days in leap years

Word use: The abbreviation is **Feb.**
Word history: from the Latin name for the Roman festival of purification, held on 15 February

federal

adjective having to do with a central government rather than state governments: *federal politics*

Word building: **federally** *adverb*

federation

noun the forming of a nation by a number of states who give some of their powers and responsibilities to a central government

Word building: **federate** *verb* to join in a league or federation

fee

noun the money you owe, such as to a doctor, lawyer or private school for their services

feeble

adjective **1** weak in body or mind
Other words: **delicate, frail, shaky**
2 lacking strength or brightness: *a feeble voice | feeble light*
Other words: **soft, weak**

Word building: **feebleness** *noun*   **feebly** *adverb*

feed

verb **1** to give food to **2** to supply with the means of growth: *to feed a fire | Two creeks feed the river.* **3** to be food for: *This leg of lamb will feed six people.* **4** to supply to: *to feed corn to chickens*
noun **5** food, especially for animals: *horses' feed* **6** *Informal* a meal

Word building: Other verb forms are **I fed, I have fed, I am feeding.** | **feeder** *noun*

feedback

noun **1** information passed back about something that has been done or said: *I've had a lot of feedback about my new book.* **2** the return of part of the sound put out by a loudspeaker into the microphone so that a high-pitched noise is made

feel

verb **1** to know or examine by touching: *Feel the wool. | We felt our way in the dark.* **2** to sense or experience: *She feels the cold. | She felt sadness at the news.* **3** to know that you are: *She feels happy. | I felt ill.* **4** to believe: *I feel that you are wrong.*
noun **5** the way something is sensed when you touch it: *a silky feel*

Word building: Other verb forms are **I felt, I have felt, I am feeling.**

feeler

noun **1** a thin, armlike growth on some animals, especially those without a backbone, which is used for touching or grasping **2** a remark made to find out what someone else is thinking

feeling

noun **1** a particular sensation or emotion: *a feeling of warmth | a feeling of fear* **2** a belief or idea: *I have a feeling it will turn out well.*

feet

noun plural of **foot**

feign (*rhymes with rain*)

verb **1** to pretend to have: *to feign illness* **2** to make up or invent: *to feign an excuse*

feline (*say* fee-luyn)

adjective having to do with cats or the cat family

Word building: **feline** *noun*

fell

verb to cut down or cause to fall: *to fell a tree | The champion boxer felled the opponent.*

fellow

noun **1** a man or a boy **2 Fellow**, a member of a professional society: *a Fellow of the Royal College of Surgeons*

Word building: **fellow** *adjective* having the same position or occupation: *my fellow workers* **fellowship** *noun*

felony (*say* fel-uh-nee)

noun a serious crime such as murder or burglary

Word building: **felon** *noun* a criminal **felonious** *adjective*

felt

noun cloth made of wool, fur or hair which is not woven but pressed firmly together: *soft toys made of felt*

Word building: **felt** *adjective*

felt pen

noun a thick, brightly coloured pen that is used to fill in the blank parts of a picture

Word use: This is sometimes called a **texta**.

female

noun **1** a woman or girl **2** any animal that belongs to the sex which is able to give birth to young

Word use: The opposite is **male**.
Word building: **female** *adjective*

feminine (*say* fem-uh-nuhn)

adjective **1** female **2** having qualities such as softness and gentleness, thought to be typical of women

Word use: The opposite is **masculine**.
Word building: **femininity** *noun*

feminism

noun the principle that women deserve the same rights and opportunities as men: *The rise of feminism has meant that women now have a better chance of getting good jobs than 40 years ago.*

Word building: **feminist** *noun* someone who holds these beliefs

fence

noun **1** a wall or barrier put up around something to separate it from its surroundings **2** *Informal* someone who earns a living by buying and selling stolen goods
verb **3** to enclose or separate by a fence: *to fence a garden* **4** to fight with a sword: *to fence as a sport*
phrase **5 sit on the fence**, to avoid taking sides in an argument

Word building: **fencer** *noun*

fencing

noun **1** the sport of sword fighting **2** material, such as wood or wire, used to build fences

fend

phrase **1 fend off**, to fight off or resist: *He fended off the savage dog.* **2 fend for**, to look after or protect

feng shui (*say* feng shway, fung shway)

noun the correct balance between people and their physical environment so as to increase good luck, achieved by following a practice in Chinese culture, especially by following rules in relation to the design and location of buildings, the position of objects and furniture in a room, and so on: *The feng shui of this room is wrong because the door is opposite the window.*

feral　(*say* fe̲-ruhl)

adjective wild or untamed: *Feral dogs roamed the countryside.*

Word history: from a Latin word meaning 'wild beast'

ferment　(*say* fuh-me̲nt)

verb **1** to change in taste and appearance, because yeast or bacteria has turned sugar into alcohol and gas: *Yeast ferments grape juice and turns it into wine.* | *The apple juice was standing there so long it fermented.*
noun (*say* fe̲r-ment) **2** a state of excitement and activity

Word building: **fermentation** *noun*

fern

noun a green leafy plant that does not have flowers and grows in damp shady places

Word building: **fernery** *noun* a place for growing ferns　**ferny** *adjective*

ferocious　(*say* fuh-ro̲h-shuhs)

adjective fierce, savage and cruel: *ferocious animals*

Word building: **ferociously** *adverb*　**ferocity** *noun*

ferret

noun **1** an animal with a long thin body used in hunting rabbits
phrase **2 ferret out**, to search out: *We ferreted out the truth.*

ferry

noun a boat that carries people or cars across a river or harbour

Word building: The plural is **ferries**. | **ferry** *verb* (**ferried, ferrying**) to transport from one place to another

fertile

adjective **1** richly productive and abundant: *Fertile land grows healthy crops.* | *Her stories are most interesting because of her fertile imagination.* **2** able to have babies

Word use: The opposite is **sterile**.
Word building: **fertility** *noun*
Word history: from a Latin word meaning 'fruitful'

fertilise

verb **1** to make fertile or enrich: *to fertilise the vegetable garden with cow manure* **2** to combine with in order to create new life: *The male sperm fertilises the female egg to start the development of a baby.*

Word use: Another spelling is **fertilize**.
Word building: **fertilisation** *noun*　**fertiliser** *noun*

fervour　(*say* fe̲r-vuh)

noun great enthusiasm or passion: *She spoke with fervour against nuclear bombs.*

Word use: Another spelling is **fervor**.
Word building: **fervent** *adjective*　**fervently** *adverb*

festival

noun **1** a joyful celebration with processions, exhibitions and performances of music, dance and drama
Other words: **carnival, fair, fete, gala, show**
2 a time of religious celebration: *the festival of Christmas*

festive

adjective merry and joyful: *to be in a festive mood*

Word building: **festivity** *noun* (**festivities**)

festoon

noun a streamer, or ribbon hung as a decoration

Word building: **festoon** *verb*: *to festoon the Christmas tree with lights*
Word history: from an Italian word meaning 'festival' or 'feast'

fetch

verb **1** to go and bring back: *Fetch the ball, Fido!* **2** to sell for or bring in: *That gold watch should fetch a high price.*

fetching

adjective charming and attractive: *a fetching smile*

Word building: **fetchingly** *adverb*

fete　(*sounds like* fate)

noun **1** a small fair held to raise money for a school or charity
verb **2** to treat as special and important: *We feted the overseas visitors with champagne.*

Word use: This word is sometimes spelt **fête** because it was originally French.

fete/fate Don't confuse **fete** with **fate**, which is the cause beyond your control that seems to control the things that happen to you.

fetlock

noun the part of a horse's leg with a tuft of hair just above the hoof

fetta   (*say* fet-uh)

noun a soft white cheese from Greece, which has been preserved by being soaked in salted water

Word use: Another spelling is **feta**.
Word history: from a Latin word meaning 'mouthful' or 'bite'

fetter

noun **1** a chain or shackle tied around the ankles **2** anything that restricts or stops you from doing what you want

Word use: Definition 2 is often used in the plural form, as in *to shake off your fetters*.
Word building: **fetter** *verb* to confine or restrict

fettuccine   (*say* fet-uh-chee-nee)

noun pasta that has been cut into wide strips

feud   (*rhymes with* stewed)

noun a bitter, long-lasting quarrel, especially between two families: *I've never met my cousins because of a family feud.*

Word building: **feud** *verb*

feudal   (*say* fyoohd-uhl)

adjective having to do with a way of life in which ordinary people lived on and used the land of nobility, giving them military and other service in return

Word use: We usually talk about the **feudal system** which was in force in medieval Europe.
Word building: **feudalism** *noun*

fever

noun **1** an unusually high body temperature caused by illness **2** great excitement: *The crowd waiting for the pop group worked itself up into a fever.*

Word building: **feverish** *adjective* hot or restless   **feverishly** *adverb*   **feverishness** *noun*

few

adjective **1** not many: *Few people go swimming in winter.*
phrase **2 a good few** or **quite a few**, a fairly large number **3 the few**, a small number or minority: *In the old days, education was only for the few.*

fiancée   (*say* fee-on-say)

noun the woman to whom a man is engaged to be married: *She is Tony's fiancée.*

Word use: The accent over the 'e' is there because this word was originally French.
Word building: **fiancé** *noun* the man to whom a woman is engaged

fiasco   (*say* fee-as-koh)

noun an embarrassing or ridiculous failure

fib

noun a lie about something that's not very important

Word building: **fib** *verb* (**fibbed**, **fibbing**)   **fibber** *noun*

fibre   (*say* fuy-buh)

noun **1** a fine thread of wool, cotton or other material **2** the part of food that can't be digested: *Celery has a lot of fibre.*

Word building: **fibrous** *adjective* stringy or indigestible

fibreglass

noun material made of fine glass fibres which is used to insulate buildings against heat and cold or mixed with plastic and used to make surfboards and boats

fibro

noun strong building material made of asbestos and cement

fickle

adjective changeable or likely to have changes of mind: *a fickle wind* | *a fickle friend*
Word building: **fickleness** *noun*

fiction

noun a story which isn't true but is made up from the imagination

Word use: The opposite is **nonfiction** or **fact**.
Word building: **fictitious** *adjective* not real or genuine   **fictional** *adjective*   **fictionally** *adverb*

fiddle

verb **1** to move your hands around restlessly **2** to play a violin
noun **3** a violin
phrase **4 fit as a fiddle**, in very good health

Word building: **fiddly** *adjective* needing to be done with care and patience   **fiddler** *noun*

fidelity   (*say* fuh-del-uh-tee)

noun **1** faithfulness or loyalty: *fidelity in marriage* | *fidelity to your friends* | *fidelity to the things you believe* **2** the ability to reproduce a sound exactly as it should be: *the fidelity of a radio or amplifier*

Word building: The plural is **fidelities**.

fidget   (*say* f̲ij̲-uht)
verb **1** to move about restlessly
noun **2** someone who fidgets
phrase **3 the fidgets,** restlessness because
you're bored or nervous

Word building: **fidgety** *adjective*

field
noun **1** a piece of open ground or space: *a
field of wheat | a football field* **2** an area of
interest or activity: *to study in the field of
chemistry*
verb **3** to stop or catch the ball in cricket
and other similar sports
adjective **4** happening on a sports field
rather than on a running track: *Long jump
is a field event.*

Word building: **fielder** *noun*

field glasses
plural noun another word for **binoculars**

fiend   (*say* feend)
noun **1** the devil or any evil spirit **2** a
nuisance or troublemaker **3** someone who
spends a lot of time or energy in playing a
game or sport: *a chess fiend*

Word building: **fiendish** *adjective* evil or
cruel   **fiendishly** *adverb*

fierce
adjective **1** wild or violent: *fierce animals*
Other words: **aggressive, dangerous,
ferocious, savage, vicious**
2 very strong or violent: *fierce winds*
Other words: **powerful, turbulent**
3 intense: *fierce competition for the prize*

Word building: **fiercely** *adverb*   **fierceness**
noun

fiery   (*say* f̲uy̲-uh-ree)
adjective **1** like fire: *fiery red* **2** showing
strong feelings: *a fiery speech*

fiesta   (*say* fee-e̲s̲-tuh)
noun a holiday or festival, especially on a
religious occasion

Word use: This word comes from Spanish.

fife
noun a high-pitched flute often played in
military bands

fifteen
noun **1** the number 15 **2** the Roman
numeral XV

Word building: **fifteen** *adjective*: *fifteen
children*   **fifteenth** *adjective*: *the fifteenth student*

fifty
noun **1** the number 50 **2** the Roman
numeral L

Word building: The plural is **fifties.** | **fifty**
adjective: *fifty singers*   **fiftieth** *adjective*: *his
fiftieth birthday*

fig
noun a small, soft, pear-shaped fruit
containing many tiny seeds which is eaten
fresh or dried

fight
noun **1** a contest between people or animals
involving a physical struggle: *I was hurt in
a fight in the playground.*
Other words: **brawl, scuffle, tussle**
2 a verbal disagreement: *My brother and I
had a fight over whose turn it was to do the
washing up.*
Other words: **argument, quarrel, row, squabble**
verb **3** to try to defeat: *to fight the enemy*
Other words: **assault, attack, oppose**
4 to take part in a battle: *We fought to the
end.*

Word building: Other verb forms are **I fought,
I have fought, I am fighting.** | **fighter** *noun*

figment
noun something that's only imaginary: *a
figment of your imagination*

figure
noun **1** a symbol that stands for a number:
the figure 3 **2** an amount or sum of money:
They paid a large figure for the new car.
3 a shape, form or pattern: *The dancer
has a graceful figure. | The figures on my
socks are squares and triangles.* **4** a person
or character: *The Prime Minister is an
important figure.*
verb **5** to work out or calculate: *to figure the
cost to be $150*
phrase **6 figure out,** to understand or
decide: *I can't figure out where I made the
mistake in this sum.*

Word building: **figures** *plural noun* calculations
or sums

figurehead
noun **1** someone who has an important
position in an organisation but has no real
power **2** a carved figure which decorates
the bow of a sailing ship

figure of speech

noun an expression in which words are used out of their usual meaning for special effect, like a metaphor or simile: *Calling it a one-horse town was just a figure of speech.*

figurine

noun a small statue or model

Word history: from an Italian word meaning 'little figure'

filament

noun a very thin thread: *a filament of cotton | The wire filament in a light bulb glows when electricity passes through it.*

Word building: **filamentous** *adjective*

file¹

noun **1** an orderly collection of papers or the folder they are kept in **2** an ordered collection of data stored on tape or disk for a computer **3** a line of people or things one behind the other: *to stand in single file* verb **4** to put or arrange in a file: *to file letters in order according to the date they were received* **5** to walk or march one after the other

file²

noun a steel tool whose surface is covered with ridges for smoothing or cutting metal and other materials

Word building: **file** *verb*

filigree (*say* fil-uh-gree)

noun a delicate lacelike design made out of metal thread, used in jewellery

Word building: **filigree** *adjective* **filigreed** *adjective*

fill

verb **1** to supply or have as much of something as can be held: *to fill the bath to the top* **2** to take up all the space or time: *Smoke filled the room. | The movie was filled with excitement.* **3** to take or occupy: *to apply to fill the position of caretaker* noun **4** earth and rocks used to fill a hole in the ground phrase **5 fill in, a** to complete by writing in the blank spaces: *to fill in an entry form for the competition* **b** to stand in for or replace: *The principal filled in for our teacher when he was away sick.* **6 fill the bill**, to be just what is needed

Word building: **filling** *noun: The pie has a lemon filling. | I have a filling in one of my teeth.* **filler** *noun*

fillet

noun a slice of fish or meat without the bone

Word building: **fillet** *verb*
Word history: from a French word meaning 'little thread'

filly

noun a female horse less than four years old

Word use: The plural is **fillies**. | A young male horse is a **colt**.

film

noun **1** a thin sheet or layer of material: *to wrap sandwiches in plastic film | a film of oil on water* **2** thin plastic material which is sensitive to light and is used in older types of cameras to take photographs: *Dad still uses film in his old camera, but I have a digital camera.* **3** a moving picture which is shown on a screen: *to see a film about life in China*

Word use: Another word for definition 3 is **movie**.
Word building: **film** *verb*

filmy

adjective light and transparent: *The dancers' costumes were made of filmy material.*

Word building: Other forms are **filmier**, **filmiest**. | **filminess** *noun*

filo pastry (*say* fee-loh pay-stree, fuy-loh pay-stree)

noun a very thin pastry made from flour and water, often used in Greek cookery

filter

noun a device for straining liquids or air to remove unwanted material: *A filter in a swimming pool keeps the water clean.*

Word building: **filtrate** *noun* the liquid which has been strained through a filter **filtration** *noun* the process of filtering **filter** *verb*

filth

noun something that is disgustingly dirty, repulsive or obscene

Word building: **filthy** *adjective* very dirty or unpleasant **filthy** *adverb* very or extremely: *filthy rich* **filthiness** *noun*

fin

noun **1** one of the flap-like structures on the body of a fish which is used for moving through the water **2** a small triangular or fin-shaped part on a surfboard, plane or boat to help with steering or balancing

final

adjective **1** last or coming at the end: *the final match of the season | I say 'no', and my word is final.*
noun **2** the one at the end of a series, especially of races or competitions: *to play in the grand final*

Word building: **finalise** *verb* to end or conclude   **finalist** *noun* a competitor who takes part in the last round of a contest   **finality** *noun*   **finally** *adverb*

finale *(say* fuh-<u>nah</u>-lee*)*

noun the last part of a concert, opera or ballet

finance

noun **1** the management of money: *an expert in banking and finance* **2 finances**, money supplies or revenue: *I'm sorry I can't lend you any money as my finances are rather low.*

Word building: **finance** *verb* to fund or pay for   **financier** *noun* someone whose business is lending money   **financial** *adjective*   **financially** *adverb*

finch

noun a type of small bird with a large beak for eating seeds

find

verb **1** to come upon by chance or after a search: *to find shells at the beach | to find a lost umbrella*
Other words: **discover, uncover**
2 to discover or learn: *to find the answer to a question*
Other words: **ascertain, determine**

Word building: Other forms are **I found, I have found, I am finding.** | **find** *noun* a valuable discovery   **findings** *plural noun* data or information   **finder** *noun*

fine¹

adjective **1** excellent or of high quality: *a fine musician* **2** sunny, or without rain: *fine weather* **3** very thin or slender: *a fine thread* **4** made up of tiny particles: *You have to grind the seeds into a very fine powder.* **5** sharp: *a fine point on a pencil* **6** well or healthy

Word building: **finely** *adverb*   **fineness** *noun*

fine²

noun a sum of money paid as a penalty for doing something wrong

Word building: **fine** *verb*

finesse *(say* fuh-<u>nes</u>*)*

noun fine skill or clever management: *to conduct business dealings with finesse*

finger

noun **1** any one of the five, long, end parts of your hand, especially one that's not your thumb
2 something shaped like a finger: *the finger of a glove | a finger of toast*

Word building: **finger** *verb* to touch lightly

fingerprint

noun the pattern made by the curved lines on the tips of your fingers

finicky

adjective **1** very fussy or choosy **2** fiddly or full of small, unimportant detail: *This embroidery is very finicky.*

finish

verb **1** to bring or come to an end
Other words: **complete, conclude, end**
noun **2** the end or conclusion
Other words: **close, completion, ending, termination**
3 the surface layer of wood or metal or the substance put on it: *to polish the car to give it a brilliant finish*
Other words: **appearance, polish, surface, texture, varnish**
phrase **4 finish off, a** to totally use up or complete: *to finish off your dinner*
b to kill or destroy

finite *(say* <u>fuy</u>-nuyt*)*

adjective having limits which can be measured or counted: *Is the number of stars in the universe finite?*

Word use: The more usual word is **limited.** | The opposite of this is **infinite.**
Word building: **finitely** *adverb*   **finiteness** *noun*

fiord *(say* <u>fee</u>-awd*)*

noun another spelling for **fjord**

fir

noun a tree, like a traditional Christmas tree, which has needle-like leaves and produces cones

fir/fur Don't confuse **fir** with **fur**, which is hair on an animal.

fire

noun **1** the heat, light and flames produced by burning: *You could see the fire from far away.* **2** a mass of burning material, such as in a fireplace: *to light a fire to keep warm* **3** enthusiasm or passion: *a speech full of fire* **4** the shooting of guns: *to open fire on the enemy soldiers*

verb **5** to set on fire or make very hot: *to fire the furnace* | *to fire pottery in a kiln* **6** to shoot: *to fire a gun* **7** to dismiss or sack from a job: *The boss fired me for not doing my work properly.* **8** to inspire or excite: *The speaker's words fired the audience with enthusiasm.*

Word building: **fiery** *adjective* (**fierier, fieriest**)　**firefighter** *noun* someone who fights fires

firearm

noun any type of gun

firebreak

noun a strip of land which has been cleared of grass and trees to stop a fire from spreading

firefighter

noun someone whose job is to put out or prevent fires

fireplace

noun an open place, built of brick or stone, for lighting fires in

fireproof

adjective not able to burn or be set on fire easily: *fireproof walls* | *fireproof clothing*

firestick farming

noun the burning of areas of bush using a lighted stick, traditionally used by Aboriginal people, to make way for new grass to grow as a food source for kangaroos, wallabies, and so on

firestorm

noun a phenomenon caused by a huge fire, where a rising body of air above the fire draws in strong winds which then create an inferno: *After the city was bombed, a large part of it was demolished in the firestorm that followed.*

fireworks

plural noun **1** containers filled with a powder that burns or explodes giving out brilliantly coloured sparks **2** an outburst of anger or bad temper

firey

noun Informal a person who fights fires

firm¹

adjective **1** solid, hard or stiff
Other words: **compacted, rigid, unyielding**
2 not moving or shaking
Other words: **secure, stable**
3 strong, definite and unchanging: *to speak in a firm voice* | *a firm belief*
Other words: **certain, definite, determined, fixed, resolute, steadfast, strong**

Word building: **firm** *verb* to make or become firm　**firmly** *adverb*　**firmness** *noun*

firm²

noun a business company
Other words: **business, corporation, organisation**

first

adjective **1** being number one or coming before all others in time, order or importance: *She was the first one to arrive.*
adverb **2** before anyone or anything else in time, order or importance: *He arrived first.* **3** for the first time: *They first met at a party.*

Word building: **first** *noun*　**firstly** *adverb*

first aid

noun emergency treatment given to someone hurt in an accident

first-class

adjective of the best quality, best-equipped or most expensive: *a first-class restaurant*

Word building: **first-class** *adverb*: *to travel first-class*

firsthand

adverb directly from the source: *We got the information firsthand.*

Word building: **firsthand** *adjective*

fish

noun **1** a cold-blooded animal which lives in water, breathes through gills, swims by means of fins and has scales on its body
verb **2** to catch or try to catch fish **3** to feel around for and find: *to fish some money out of your pocket*
phrase **4 fish for**, to try to get indirectly: *to fish for information*

Word building: The plural form of the noun is **fish** or **fishes**. | **fishmonger** *noun* someone who sells fish

fisherman

noun someone who fishes, either as a job or for pleasure
Other words: **angler**

Word building: The plural is **fishermen**.

fishy

adjective **1** having a fishlike smell or taste **2** *Informal* strange or causing suspicion: *There was something fishy about his disappearance, so I wondered what he was up to.*

Word building: Other forms are **fishier**, **fishiest**.

fissure   (*say* fish-uh)

noun a split: *The rock had a deep fissure in it.*

Word use: The more usual word is **crack**.

fist

noun your hand when the fingers are closed tightly into the palm

Word building: **fistful** *noun* a handful

fit[1]

adjective **1** suitable or good enough: *Those clothes are not fit to be worn.* **2** right or proper: *Picking up papers is a fit punishment for littering.* **3** healthy
verb **4** to be suitable or the right size or shape for **5** to make or have space for: *We can fit five people in the car.* **6** to put into place: *I am fitting a new handle on to this door.*
noun **7** the way in which something fits: *This shirt is a perfect fit.*
phrase **8 fit in**, to be or become suited: *Do you think this chair fits in with the rest of the furniture?* **9 fit out**, to provide with clothing or equipment

Word building: Other adjective forms are **fitter**, **fittest**. | Other verb forms are **I fitted**, **I have fitted**, **I am fitting**. | **fitter** *noun*   **fitness** *noun*

fit[2]

noun **1** a sudden outburst: *She hit him in a fit of rage.* | *I had a fit of coughing last night.* **2** a sudden sickness in which your body twists uncontrollably and you sometimes become unconscious

Word building: **fitful** *adjective* stopping and starting   **fitfully** *adverb*

fitting

adjective **1** suitable or proper
noun **2** a trying on of clothes for a proper fit **3** the size of clothes or shoes: *What is your fitting?* **4 fittings**, furnishings or equipment: *Their house has beautiful fittings.*

Word building: **fittingly** *adverb*

five

noun **1** the number 5 **2** the Roman numeral V

Word building: **five** *adjective*: *five candles*   **fifth** *adjective*: *her fifth birthday*

fix

verb **1** to make firm or put securely in place: *We've got to fix the poles into the ground before we put up the tent.* **2** to settle or decide: *Let's fix a price for this car.* **3** to mend or repair
noun **4** *Informal* a difficult situation: *I'm in such a fix that I don't know what to do.*
phrase **5 fix on**, to decide on **6 fix up**, **a** to arrange properly: *Please fix up the books on your desk.* **b** to put right: *This medicine will soon fix you up.*

Word building: **fixed** *adjective*   **fixedly** *adverb*   **fixer** *noun*

fixture

noun **1** something fixed in place, especially in a house or other building **2** a sporting event that is to be held on a particular date

fizz

verb to bubble and make a hissing sound: *I like it when lemonade fizzes up your nose.*

Word building: **fizz** *noun*   **fizzy** *adjective*

fizzle

verb **1** to make a hissing or spluttering sound
phrase **2 fizzle out**, *Informal* to fail after a good start: *Our plans have fizzled out.*

Word building: **fizzle** *noun*

fjord   (*say* fee-awd)

noun a deep, narrow inlet of the sea with steep cliffs on each side: *Norway is famous for its fjords.*

Word use: Another spelling is **fiord**.

flabbergasted

adjective very surprised or astonished: *We were flabbergasted by the news of the fortune he'd won.*
Other words: **amazed, astounded, shocked, stunned**

Word building: **flabbergast** *verb*

flabby

adjective having soft fatty flesh: *flabby arms* | *a flabby man*

Word building: **flabbily** *adverb*   **flabbiness** *noun*

flaccid   (*say* <u>flas</u>-uhd)

adjective soft and loose: *flaccid muscles*

Word use: The more usual word is **limp**.
Word building: **flaccidity** *noun*   **flaccidly** *adverb*   **flaccidness** *noun*

flag[1]

noun **1** a piece of cloth with a particular design used as a symbol of a country or an organisation, or as a signal: *The Australian flag has the Southern Cross on it.* | *A red flag is used to signal danger.*
verb **2** to signal, mark or warn with a flag

Word building: Other verb forms are **I flagged, I have flagged, I am flagging**.

flag[2]

verb to grow weak or tired: *The walkers began to flag at the end of the day.*

Word building: Other forms are **I flagged, I have flagged, I am flagging**.

flagon

noun a large bottle

flagrant   (*say* <u>flay</u>-gruhnt)

adjective obvious in a shameless way: *a flagrant lie* | *flagrant disobedience*

Word use: The more usual word is **blatant**.
Word building: **flagrancy** *noun*   **flagrantly** *adverb*
Word history: from a Latin word meaning 'blazing' or 'burning'

flair

noun **1** natural talent: *She has a flair for maths.* **2** smart style: *He dresses with flair.*

flair/flare Don't confuse **flair** with **flare**, which is a kind of light, usually short-lived and very bright.

flake[1]

noun **1** a small, flat, thin piece of anything: *a flake of skin* | *a flake of snow*
verb **2** to peel off in flakes: *This paint is flaking.*
phrase **3 flake out**, *Informal* to lie down or fall asleep from tiredness: *I flaked out after the race.*

Word building: **flaky** *adjective*   **flakily** *adverb*   **flakiness** *noun*

flake[2]

noun shark meat sold as food

flamboyant

adjective dazzlingly bright and showy

Word building: **flamboyance** *noun* **flamboyantly** *adverb*
Word history: from a French word meaning 'small flame'

flame

noun a tongue of fire: *Flames licked around the base of the tree.* | *The candle burnt with a low flame.*

Word building: **flame** *verb*

flameproof

adjective **1** not easily burnt: *flameproof clothing* **2** safe for use over flames: *a flameproof dish*

flamingo   (*say* fluh-<u>ming</u>-goh)

noun a water bird with a very long neck, long legs and dark pink feathers

Word building: The plural is **flamingos** or **flamingoes**.

flammable

adjective easily set on fire: *Be careful not to wear a flammable dressing gown.*

Word use: Another word for this is **inflammable**.

flan

noun a large tart with a sweet or savoury filling

flank

noun **1** the side of an animal between the ribs and hip **2** the side of anything
verb **3** to be at the side of: *The president was flanked by two guards.*

flannel

noun **1** a warm soft cloth, usually made of wool: *a flannel suit* **2** a face washer

flannelette

noun a cotton cloth treated on one side to look and feel like flannel

flannel flower

noun an Australian plant with light cream flowers and leaves that feel like flannel

flap

verb **1** to swing about loosely, especially with a noise: *The curtain is flapping in the wind.* **2** to move up and down: *The bird flapped its wings.*

noun **3** something flat and thin that is joined to something else on one side only and hangs loose **4** *Informal* a feeling of nervousness or excitement: *Don't get yourself into a flap.*

Word building: Other verb forms are **I flapped, I have flapped, I am flapping.**

flare

verb **1** to burn brightly and suddenly: *The fire flared up.* **2** to burst with a sudden strong feeling **3** to curve outwards like the end of a trumpet: *Jira's pants flared at the bottom.*

Word building: **flare** *noun* a bright light used as a signal

flare/flair Don't confuse **flare** with **flair**, which is natural talent.

flash

noun **1** a sudden short burst of flame or light: *a flash of lightning* **2** a short moment: *He was gone in a flash.* **3** a short, important piece of news on radio or television: *We heard about the accident on a radio news flash.*

Word building: **flash** *adjective*: *a flash flood* **flash** *verb* to flame or light up **flashy** *adjective* bright and showy

flashback

noun a part of a film or story that shows an event that happened at an earlier time

flashforward

noun a representation during a film, and so on, of an event or scene from a time in the future: *We knew the hero was going to die because we kept getting flashforwards of all his girlfriends crying around a dead body.*

flashlight

noun a bulb that gives a flash of very bright light, used when taking photographs inside or at night

flask   (*say* flahsk)

noun a small flat bottle

flat¹

adjective **1** even or smooth: *It is easier to run on flat ground.*

Other words: **horizontal, level, plane**

2 lying spread out: *I found you flat on the floor.* **3** not high: *a shoe with flat heels* **4** emptied of air: *a flat tyre*
Other words: **deflated**

5 clear and absolute: *Sabiti answered with a flat refusal.*
Other words: **definite, firm, outright**

6 boring or dull: *a flat performance*
Other words: **dreary, lifeless, monotonous, tedious, uninteresting**

7 no longer bubbly or fizzy **8** not shiny: *flat paint* **9** lowered in pitch by a semitone: *The musical note B flat is a semitone lower than the note B.*

adverb **10** in a flat position: *Please lay the paper out flat.*

noun **11** a flat side or part of anything: *She hit him with the flat of her hand.* **12** flat ground: *Be careful to stay on the flat.* **13 a** a note that is one semitone below a given note **b** the music sign (♭) which lowers the note by a semitone when it is placed before it

phrase **14 flat out, a** as fast or hard as possible: *We ran flat out and just caught the last train.* **b** very busy

Word use: The opposite of definitions 9 and 13 is **sharp.**
Word building: **flatly** *adverb* **flatness** *noun* **flatten** *verb* to make flat

flat²

noun a group of rooms for living in, usually part of a larger building and usually rented
Other words: **apartment, home unit, unit**
Word building: **flat** *verb* (**flatted, flatting**) to live in a flat

flatter

verb **1** to try to please by compliments or praise even if you do not mean them **2** to show or describe as being more attractive than is really so: *This photo flatters her.*

Word building: **flatterer** *noun* **flattery** *noun*

flaunt   (*say* flawnt)

verb to show off boldly: *She was always flaunting her parent's wealth.*

flaunt/flout Don't confuse **flaunt** with **flout**, which means 'to show no respect for'.

flautist   (*say* <u>flaw</u>-tuhst)

noun someone who plays the flute
Word history: from an Italian word meaning 'flute'

flavour

noun **1** taste, especially the special taste that something has: *Do you like the flavour of the sauce?* **2** the nature or quality of something: *The outdoor tables gave the restaurant a French flavour.*
Other words: **air, aspect, character, feel, feeling, quality, spirit**
verb **3** to add flavour to: *She flavoured the stew with salt and pepper.*
Other words: **season**

Word use: Another spelling is **flavor**.
Word building: **flavouring** *noun*

flaw

noun **1** a fault: *Laziness is the biggest flaw in my character.* **2** a crack or scratch: *There is a flaw in this plate.*

Word building: **flaw** *verb* to make or become cracked or spoilt   **flawless** *adjective*

flax

noun a plant with narrow leaves and blue flowers, grown for its fibre which is made into linen and for its seeds which contain oil

Word building: **flaxen** *adjective* pale yellow

flea

noun a small wingless insect which moves by jumping and which sucks blood from mammals and birds

fleck

noun a spot or small patch of something
Word building: **fleck** *verb*

fledgling

noun **1** a young bird that has just become able to fly **2** someone who is young or new to something

Word use: Another spelling is **fledgeling**.

flee

verb to run away or escape
Word building: Other forms are **I fled, I have fled, I am fleeing**.

fleece

noun **1** the coat of wool that covers a sheep or other animal
verb **2** to take money or belongings from by cheating: *They fleeced me of all my earnings.*

Word building: **fleecy** *adjective*   **fleeciness** *noun*

fleet[1]

noun **1** a large group of naval ships, usually under the command of one officer **2** a group of other boats, aeroplanes or vehicles: *a fleet of company cars*

Word use: Compare this with **flotilla**.

fleet[2]

adjective very fast or swift
Word building: **fleetly** *adverb*   **fleetness** *noun*

fleeting

adjective passing very quickly: *I only saw her for a fleeting moment.*

Word building: **fleetingly** *adverb*

flesh

noun **1** the soft part of an animal body, which is made up of fat and muscle **2** the human body when you think of it as separate from the mind or the spirit: *Meat feeds the flesh and books feed the mind.* **3** the soft part of a fruit or vegetable

Word building: **fleshy** *adjective* plump or fat   **fleshiness** *noun*

flex

verb **1** to bend or stretch: *She flexed her muscles.*
noun **2** a cord containing an electric wire

flexible

adjective **1** easily bent or stretched: *flexible wire*
Other words: **elastic, pliable, supple**
2 able to be changed easily: *My plans are flexible.*
Other words: **adaptable**

Word building: **flexibility** *noun*   **flexibly** *adverb*

flexitime

noun an arrangement in which workers can choose their starting and finishing times, as long as they work the right number of hours altogether

flick

noun a sudden light blow: *The teacher gave the table a flick with the duster.*
Word building: **flick** *verb*

flicker

verb **1** to burn unsteadily: *The candle flickered.* **2** to move quickly to and fro
Word building: **flicker** *noun*

flight[1]

noun **1** an act of flying or the way in which something flies: *The flight of my paper plane wasn't what I expected.* **2** a number of things flying together: *A flight of gulls landed on the water.* **3** a journey by aeroplane **4** a series of steps or stairs

flight[2]

noun **1** a running away or fleeing
phrase **2 take flight**, to run away

flight attendant

noun a person who works on a plane and looks after the passengers

flighty

adjective often changing your mind or feelings: *I wish you'd stop being so flighty.*
Other words: **temperamental**

Word building: Other forms are **flightier, flightiest.** | **flightiness** *noun*

flimsy

adjective **1** not strongly made: *a flimsy fence* **2** weak or not carefully thought out: *a flimsy excuse*

Word building: Other forms are **flimsier, flimsiest.** | **flimsiness** *noun*
Word history: made by changing around the letters of the word *film* and adding the ending *-sy*

flinch

verb to draw back from something dangerous, difficult or unpleasant: *They did not flinch when they saw the enemy.*

fling

verb **1** to throw, usually forcefully or impatiently: *The child flung the blunt pencil to the floor.* **2** to move quickly or violently: *Don't fling out of the room when you are annoyed.*
noun **3** a time of pleasure or fun: *Let's have a last fling before the exams.* **4** an attempt or try: *I will have one more fling at jumping that height.*

Word building: Other verb forms are **I flung, I have flung, I am flinging.**

flint

noun a hard kind of stone, which can start a fire when struck with steel

Word building: **flintily** *adverb* **flintiness** *noun* **flinty** *adjective*

flip

verb **1** to move or throw with a snap of a finger and thumb: *I'll flip the coin to see who goes first.* **2** to move with a jerk: *The student flipped over the pages of the book.*
noun **3** a flipping movement: *a flip of the wrist* **4** a somersault: *a backwards flip*

Word building: Other verb forms are **I flipped, I have flipped, I am flipping.**

flippant   (*say* flip-uhnt)

adjective not suitably serious: *This is not the time to make flippant remarks.*

Word building: **flippancy** *noun* **flippantly** *adverb*

flipper

noun **1** the broad flat limb of an animal such as a seal or whale that is used for swimming **2** a piece of rubber shaped like a flipper and worn on your foot to help in swimming

flirt

verb to amuse yourself by pretending to be romantically interested in someone

Word building: **flirt** *noun* **flirtation** *noun* **flirtatious** *adjective* **flirtatiously** *adverb*

flit

verb to move lightly and quickly: *The birds flitted from tree to tree.*

Word building: Other forms are **I flitted, I have flitted, I am flitting.**

float

verb **1** to rest or move gently on the top of a liquid: *Can you dive in and float on your back?* **2** to move freely and easily: *The idea floated through my mind.*
noun **3** something that floats, such as an air-filled rubber mattress that you lie on in the water, or the cork on a fishing line **4** a platform on wheels that carries a display in a procession **5** a van or trailer for carrying horses

flock

noun **1** a number of animals of the same kind that live and feed together, especially sheep and birds
verb **2** to gather together or go in a flock: *Everyone flocked around Teresa to hear the story.*

floe

noun a large piece of ice floating on the sea

flog

verb **1** to beat hard with a whip or stick: *The soldier flogged the convict.* **2** *Informal* to sell or try to sell: *He flogs used cars.* **3** *Informal* to steal: *Did you flog that money?*
Word building: Other forms are **I flogged, I have flogged, I am flogging.**

flood (*say* flud)

noun **1** a great overflow of water, especially over land which is usually dry: *Many houses were washed away in the flood.*
Other words: **deluge**
2 any great outpouring: *a flood of words | a flood of tears*
Other words: **rush, stream, torrent**
verb **3** to cover with water, as in a flood
Other words: **deluge, engulf, swamp**
4 to rise or flow in a flood **5** to supply in great numbers: *They flooded us with gifts.*

floodlight

noun **1** a light that gives a strong beam, used especially outside
verb **2** to light up with a floodlight: *to floodlight a sportsground at night*
Word building: Other verb forms are **I floodlit, I have floodlit, I am floodlighting.**

floor

Informal
noun **1** the lowest flat part of a room or other place: *Don't drop crumbs on the floor. | The ship sank to the floor of the sea.* **2** one of the different levels of a building: *That office block has thirty floors.*
Other words: **storey**
verb **3** to knock down or defeat: *The boxer floored the opponent.* **4** to confuse or puzzle completely: *This question will floor you.*
Word building: **flooring** *noun* material used to make floors

flop

verb **1** to fall or drop suddenly, especially with a noise: *I'm going to flop onto the couch and fall asleep.* **2** *Informal* to fail or break down
noun **3** the movement or sound of flopping: *I sat down with a flop.* **4** *Informal* something that is a failure: *Our school play was a complete flop.*
Word building: Other verb forms are **I flopped, I have flopped, I am flopping. | floppily** *adverb* **floppiness** *noun* **floppy** *adjective*

floppy disk

noun a flexible plastic disk used for storing information in a computer
Word use: Compare this with **hard disk.**

flora (*say* flaw-ruh)

noun the plants of a particular area or period of time: *Australian flora includes waratahs and banksias.*
Word use: Compare this with **fauna.**
Word history: named after *Flora*, the Roman goddess of flowers

floral (*say* flo-ruhl)

adjective having to do with or made of flowers

florid

adjective **1** red-coloured: *florid cheeks*
Other words: **ruddy**
2 too showy or flowery: *florid music | florid writing*
Other words: **ornate**
Word history: from a Latin word meaning 'flowery'

florist

noun someone who arranges and sells flowers

floristry

noun the art of arranging flowers

floss

noun **1** Look up **dental floss**
verb **2** to clean with dental floss: *Did you remember to floss your teeth this morning?*

flotilla

noun a group of small naval ships, or a small group of any boats
Word use: Compare this with **fleet.**

flounce¹

verb to move with an impatient or angry jerk of your body: *Habiba flounced out of the room in a rage.*
Word building: **flounce** *noun*

flounce²

noun a strip of material gathered together and used to decorate the bottom of a skirt or other clothing
Word building: **flouncing** *noun* **flouncy** *adjective*

flounder¹

verb **1** to struggle along with stumbling movements: *They floundered through the mud.* **2** to struggle helplessly because of embarrassment or confusion

flounder²

noun a kind of fish, eaten as food
Word building: The plural is **flounder.**

flour
noun a fine powder made by grinding wheat or other grains and used in cooking

Word building: **floury** *adjective*

flourish   (*say* fl<u>u</u>-rish)
verb **1** to grow strongly
Other words: **thrive**
2 to wave about in a showy way: *Kate flourished her prize.*
Other words: **brandish**
noun **3** a waving movement: *The knight gave a flourish of his sword.* **4** anything used for show such as a curve used to decorate handwriting

Word building: **flourishing** *adjective*
Word history: from a Latin word meaning 'bloom'

flout   (*say* flowt)
verb to show no respect for: *You always flout the rules.*

Word building: **flouter** *noun*   **floutingly** *adverb*

---

flout/flaunt Don't confuse **flout** with **flaunt**, which means 'to show off boldly'.

---

flow
verb **1** to move along in a stream: *The river flows out to the sea.* **2** to go along continuously and smoothly like a stream: *Her thoughts flowed smoothly onto the page.* **3** to fall or hang loosely: *Dale's hair flowed in the breeze.*

Word building: **flow** *noun*

flow chart
noun a diagram showing how something works or develops, stage by stage

flower
noun the blossom or part of a plant that produces the seed

Word building: **flower** *verb*

flowerbed
noun a small plot of ground in a garden where flowers are grown

flowery
adjective **1** covered with flowers **2** using a lot of fancy words: *a flowery speech*

Word building: Other forms are **flowerier**, **floweriest**. | **floweriness** *noun*

flu
noun a shortened form of **influenza**

fluctuate   (*say* fl<u>uk</u>-chooh-ayt)
verb to change all the time: *The temperature keeps fluctuating.*

Word use: The more usual word is **vary**.
Word building: **fluctuation** *noun*

flue   (*say* flooh)
noun a tube or pipe or any space for air or smoke to pass through

fluent   (*say* fl<u>ooh</u>-uhnt)
adjective **1** flowing smoothly and easily: *to speak fluent French* **2** able to speak easily: *to be fluent in French*

Word building: **fluency** *noun*   **fluently** *adverb*

fluff
noun **1** light, soft, tiny pieces from materials like cotton or wool: *Woollen jumpers often have fluff on them.*
2 *Informal* an error or mistake

Word building: **fluff** *verb*   **fluffy** *adjective*

fluid
noun **1** a substance that can flow, either a liquid or a gas
adjective **2** changing easily or not fixed

Word building: **fluidity** *noun*   **fluidly** *adverb*   **fluidness** *noun*

fluke[1]
noun **1** any accidental advantage or stroke of good luck, especially in sport
verb **2** *Informal* to get or win by a fluke: *to fluke the right answer*

Word building: **fluky** *adjective* (**flukier, flukiest**)

fluke[2]
noun **1** one of the flat triangular pieces on an anchor which catch in the ground **2** one of the triangular halves of a whale's tail

fluorescent
adjective giving off light when hit by a stream of particles such as electrons: *a fluorescent tube*

Word building: **fluorescence** *noun*

fluoride
noun a chemical compound which protects your teeth from decay

Word building: **fluoridate** *verb*   **fluoridation** *noun*

fluoro (say <u>flu</u>-ro)

adjective a very bright colour: *My favourite coloured pen is my fluoro green one.*

Word use: This word is a short way of saying **fluorescent**.

flurry

noun **1** sudden excitement or confusion: *In all the flurry I forgot my bag.* **2** a sudden gust of wind

Word building: **flurry** *verb* (**flurried, flurrying**)

flush[1]

verb **1** to blush or become red in the face **2** to flood with water, especially for cleaning: *to flush the toilet*

flush[2]

adjective **1** even or level: *That brick should be flush with this one.* **2** having plenty of something, especially money: *Let's eat out tonight, I'm flush at the moment.*

Word building: **flush** *adverb*

fluster

verb to make nervous or confused

Word building: **fluster** *noun* confusion

flute

noun **1** a musical wind instrument played by blowing across a hole near its end *verb* **2** to make long grooves in: *The potter fluted the edges of the new clay pot.*

Word building: **fluted** *adjective* having grooves: *a fluted glass*
Word history: from a Latin word meaning 'blown'

flutter

verb **1** to flap or wave: *The flags fluttered in the breeze.* **2** to move with quick uneven movements: *Nick's heart fluttered with excitement.*
noun **3** a flapping movement **4** a wave of nervous excitement or confusion: *A flutter of excitement went through the class when the visitor arrived.*

fly[1]

verb **1** to move through the air with the help of wings, wind or some other force **2** to move very quickly: *The runner was flying down the track.* **3** to make fly: *The children were flying a kite.* **4** to operate, or travel in, an aircraft or spacecraft
noun **5** a flap of material hiding a zipper in clothing, especially in trousers **6** a piece of material that forms the door or outer roof of a tent

Word building: Other verb forms are **I flew, I have flown, I am flying**. | The plural form of the noun is **flies**.

fly[2]

noun **1** an insect with two wings **2** a fish hook made to look like an insect

Word building: The plural is **flies**.

flying fox

noun **1** a large bat which has a foxlike head and feeds on fruit **2** a machine which is worked by an overhead cable and is used to carry you over water or rough land

flying saucer

noun a disc-shaped flying object said to be a spaceship from outer space

Word use: This is sometimes called a **UFO**.

flyleaf

noun a blank page at the beginning or end of a book

Word building: The plural is **flyleaves**.

foal

noun a young horse or donkey, either male or female

Word use: A male horse is a **stallion** and a female is a **mare** or **dam**. | A male donkey is a **jackass** and a female is a **jennet**.

foam

noun **1** a collection of very small bubbles **2** a spongy material made by putting gas bubbles into plastic or rubber

Word building: **foam** *verb* to froth **foaminess** *noun* **foamy** *adjective*

focus

noun **1** a point at which rays of light meet after they have been reflected or bent **2** the adjustment of something like a camera lens to get a clear, sharp picture **3** the main point of interest or attraction: *The new student was the focus of attention.*
verb **4** to adjust a lens so that the image is made clear: *I focused my camera.* **5** to bring rays of light together to a point: *I used my magnifying glass to focus the sun's rays onto the paper to burn it.* **6** to concentrate

Word use: Plural forms of the noun are **foci** and **focuses**.
Word building: Other verb forms are **I focused** or **focussed, I have focused** or **focussed, I am focusing** or **focussing**. | The plural form of the noun is **focuses** or **foci**. | **focal** *adjective*: *the focal point of the argument*

fodder

noun food like hay or straw for cattle and horses

foe

noun an enemy

foetus   (*say* <u>fee</u>-tuhs)

noun a young human or animal during its development in an egg or in its mother's womb, especially in the later stages

Word use: Another spelling is **fetus**. | Compare this with **embryo**.
Word building: **foetal** *adjective*

fog

noun a cloudlike layer that forms close to the earth's surface and is made up of drops of water
Other words: **mist, smog**

Word building: **fog** *verb* (**fogged, fogging**) **fogginess** *noun*   **foggy** *adjective*

fogey   (*say* <u>foh</u>-gee)

noun an old-fashioned person

Word use: Another spelling is **fogy**.
Word building: The plural is **fogies** or **fogeys**.

foghorn

noun a loud horn or siren used for warning ships in foggy weather

foible

noun a slight weakness in someone's character: *He has several foibles but no major faults.*

foil¹

verb to stop from being successful: *They foiled Mab's plan to run away.*

foil²

noun **1** metal which has been beaten, hammered or rolled out into very thin sheets: *aluminium foil* **2** anything that shows up the good qualities of something else by contrast with it

foil³

noun a light thin sword with a button on the point which prevents injury in fencing

foist   (*say* foyst)

verb to sell or get rid of things that are damaged or of low quality, using trickery: *The shop assistant tried to foist the soiled goods onto me.*

fold¹

verb **1** to bend over on itself: *They folded their blankets neatly on the bed.* **2** to wrap up: *Can you please fold the gift in paper?* **3** to cross: *to fold your arms*
noun **4** a part that is folded or a layer of something folded **5** a crease made by folding

fold²

noun a closed-off pen for keeping animals like sheep

folder

noun a holder or cover for papers usually made of a folded sheet of cardboard

foliage   (*say* <u>foh</u>-lee-ij)

noun the leaves of a plant

folk   (*rhymes with* coke)

noun **1** people in general **2** the people of a particular group: *City folk and country folk should understand each other.*
adjective **3** belonging to ordinary people: *folk music*
phrase **4 your folks**, *Informal* your own family

folklore   (*say* <u>fohk</u>-law)

noun the beliefs, stories and customs of a people or a tribe passed down from each generation

follow

verb **1** to come or go after: *You go ahead and I'll follow.* **2** to accept as a guide: *I'll follow your instructions.* **3** to move forward or go along: *Follow this path through the woods.* **4** to come after as a result: *It follows from this that the defendant must be innocent.* | *If you do that, disaster will follow.* **5** to understand: *Do you follow this lesson?* **6** to watch the movements of something or the way something is developing: *I follow the news carefully.*

folly

noun **1** foolishness **2** a foolish or silly act
Word building: The plural is **follies**.

fond

adjective **1** loving or affectionate: *a fond look*
phrase **2 fond of**, liking: *fond of children*
Word building: **fondly** *adverb*   **fondness** *noun*

fondle
verb to stroke or caress lovingly

fondue   (*say* <u>fond</u>-yooh)
noun a meal cooked at the table in which pieces of food are speared on the end of long forks and cooked in melted cheese or hot oil

Word history: from a French word meaning 'melt'

font[1]
noun a large stone bowl in a church which holds the water used in baptism

font[2]
noun a style of printing type: *Let's use a different font for this title.*

food
noun **1** anything that can be eaten to keep your body alive and help it grow
phrase **2 food for thought**, something that might inspire new ideas

food mile
noun a unit of measurement used to work out how far a food product has to travel before it is consumed: *Food grown locally travels fewer food miles than food imported from overseas.*

fool
noun **1** someone who is silly or without common sense
verb **2** to trick or deceive: *I fooled them into believing I was older than I really am.* **3** to play around or waste time: *Stop fooling around and come and finish your homework.*

Word history: from a Latin word meaning 'bellows'

foolhardy
adjective foolishly adventurous

Word use: The more usual word is **reckless**.
Word building: **foolhardily** *adverb* **foolhardiness** *noun*

foolish
adjective silly or unwise: *a foolish person | a foolish action*

Word building: **foolishly** *adverb* **foolishness** *noun*

foolproof
adjective designed not to fail or break even when wrongly used

foot
noun **1** the part of your body at the end of your leg, which is used for standing and walking **2** the end or bottom part, rather than the top part: *the foot of a hill* **3** a unit of measurement in the imperial system equal to about 30 centimetres
verb **4** to pay: *to foot the bill*
phrase **5 put your foot down**, to be strict

Word building: The plural form of the noun is **feet**.

football
noun **1** a game in which a ball is kicked or thrown, such as soccer, Australian Rules, Rugby Union and Rugby League **2** the ball used in these games

Word building: **footballer** *noun*

footlights
plural noun the row of lights at the front of the stage in a theatre

footnote
noun a note at the bottom of a page, usually in small printing, which tells you more about something in the main text

footpath
noun a strip, usually laid with concrete, for walking on next to a road or street

footprint
noun **1** a track or mark made by a foot **2** the surface area covered by a structure or device, as a building on an area of land, a computer on a desk, and so on **3** → **ecological footprint**

footstep
noun **1** the sound made by a step of the foot **2** the track or mark made by a foot
phrase **3 follow in someone's footsteps**, to copy or follow someone in their work or way of life

for
preposition **1** with the purpose or intention of: *to go for a walk* **2** meant to be used by or in connection with: *a book for children | a basket for cats* **3** in order to get: *money for lunch* **4** during: *for a very long time*

forage   (*say* <u>fo</u>-rij)
verb to search around for food or other supplies: *to forage in the refrigerator*

Word building: **forage** *noun* fodder for animals

foray

noun **1** a raid or attack in order to steal: *to make a foray into the enemy camp* **2** a first attempt: *to make a foray into a different kind of work*

Word building: **foray** *verb*

forbid

verb to not allow: *I forbid you to go.*

Word building: Other forms are **I forbade, I have forbidden, I am forbidding.** | **forbidding** *adjective* unpleasant, dangerous, or frightening

force

noun **1** strength or power: *the force of the wind* | *to use force to get your own way* **2** an organised group of people working together: *the police force* *verb* **3** to make or compel, often by using threats or violence: *The thief forced them to hand over the money.* **4** to use, move or do with force or effort: *to force the lid off a box* *phrase* **5 in force**, **a** operating or effective: *The new rules are in force from today.* **b** all together: *Her friends came to see her in force.*

Word building: **forceful** *adjective* strong and powerful **forcible** *adjective* using force

forceps   (*say* <u>faw</u>-suhps)

noun a pair of tongs or tweezers used for grasping and holding objects, especially in operations

Word building: The plural is **forceps.**

ford

noun a shallow part of a river where you can walk or ride across

Word building: **ford** *verb*: *to ford a stream*

fore

noun **1** the front part *adverb* **2** at or towards the bow of a ship *phrase* **3 to the fore**, to or at the front or best position: *Anne always pushes herself to the fore.*

Word use: The opposite of definition 2 is **aft**.

fore-

prefix a word part meaning **1** front: *forehead* **2** ahead of time: *forecast* **3** superior: *foreman*

Word history: from Middle English and Old English

forearm

noun the part of your arm between the elbow and the wrist

forecast

verb to predict or warn about for the future: *The Weather Bureau forecasts rain for the weekend.*

Word building: Other forms are **I forecast, I have forecast, I am forecasting.** | **forecast** *noun* a prediction, especially about the weather   **forecaster** *noun*

forefinger

noun the finger next to your thumb

foreground

noun the part of a view or picture nearest the front or the viewer

Word use: The opposite is **background**.

forehead   (*rhymes with* horrid)

noun the part of your face above your eyes and below your hair

Other words: **brow**

foreign   (*say* <u>fo</u>-ruhn)

adjective **1** from a country other than your own: *a foreign language* **2** not belonging in the place where it is found: *a foreign substance in your eye*

Word building: **foreigner** *noun* someone born in another country

foreman

noun **1** a worker who is placed in charge of other workers in a factory **2** the person who is chosen as the leader of a jury in a court of law

Word building: The plural is **foremen.** | **forewoman** *noun* (**forewomen**)   **foreperson** *noun* (**forepersons**)

foremost

adjective first or top: *The world's foremost athletes compete in the Olympic Games.*

Word building: **foremost** *adverb*

foresee

verb to expect or see in advance: *to foresee trouble*

Word building: Other forms are **I foresaw, I have foreseen, I am foreseeing.** | **foresight** *noun* care or thought for the future   **foreseeable** *adjective*

forest

noun land thickly covered with trees

Word building: **forester** *noun* someone trained to care for forests   **forestry** *noun* the science of planting and taking care of forests   **afforestation** *noun* the planting of forests

forever

adverb **1** without ever ending: *I will love you forever.* | *This road seems to go on forever.* **2** continually: *He's forever complaining.*

Word use: Another spelling is **for ever**.

forfeit   (*say* <u>faw</u>-fuht)

noun something paid or lost because of carelessness, disobedience or crime: *According to the rules of the game, you pay a forfeit if you give the wrong answer.*

Word building: **forfeit** *verb*: *You'll have to forfeit your turn.*   **forfeit** *adjective*

forge[1]

verb **1** to copy in order to trick or deceive: *to forge a signature* **2** to form or make by hard work: *A blacksmith forges horseshoes by heating and hammering metal* | *I didn't like Alex much at first, but over the years we've forged a firm friendship.*
noun **3** a furnace for softening metal before shaping it to make tools and other things

Word building: **forgery** *noun* the crime of making an imitation and passing it off as genuine   **forger** *noun*

forge[2]

verb to move forward with great effort: *to forge ahead through thick bush*

forget

verb to not remember: *I forgot to clean my teeth.*

Word building: Other forms are **I forgot, I have forgotten, I am forgetting.** | **forgetful** *adjective*   **forgetfulness** *noun*   **forgetfully** *adverb*

forgive

verb to excuse without holding any bad feelings: *He will forgive you if you say you are sorry.*
Other words: **pardon**

Word building: Other forms are **I forgave, I have forgiven, I am forgiving.** | **forgiveness** *noun*   **forgiving** *adjective*   **forgivingly** *adverb*

fork

noun **1** an instrument with prongs for lifting food, digging the garden and other things **2** a place in a tree, road, or river where it divides into several parts: *Turn left at the fork in the road.*

Word building: **forked** *adjective*: *the forked tongue of a snake*   **fork** *verb*

forklift

noun a small truck with two horizontal arms or prongs for lifting and carrying heavy loads

forlorn   (*say* fuh-<u>lawn</u>)

adjective left all alone and miserable: *a forlorn puppy*

Word building: **forlornly** *adverb*
Word history: from an Old English word meaning 'lose' or 'destroy'

form

noun **1** shape or appearance: *a birthday cake in the form of a '6'* **2** condition or fitness: *They were in good form for the big netball final.* **3** a printed paper with blank spaces to fill in: *an entry form for the competition* **4** behaviour or conduct: *It is not good form to talk with your mouth full.* **5** the set of classes in high school for students of about the same age **6** a long seat or bench
verb **7** to make, build or produce: *to form an idea* | *to freeze water to form ice* **8** to develop or be made: *Buds are forming on the trees.*

Word building: **formative** *adjective* shaping or moulding

formal

adjective **1** not relaxed or casual: *The principal greeted us in a formal manner.* **2** following the official or proper procedure: *to make a formal complaint in writing*
Other words: **official, proper**

Word building: **formally** *adverb*

formality

noun **1** a way of thinking and behaving that is formal and not relaxed **2** something done only because it fits in with formal or polite behaviour: *Everybody knew she'd win, so the announcement was just a formality.*

Word building: The plural is **formalities**.

format   (*rhymes with* doormat)
noun **1** shape, plan or style: *The book is now available in a new format with a soft cover and bigger print.*
verb **2** to organise information in a computer into files, and so on: *to format data*

Word building: Other verb forms are **it formatted, it has formatted, it is formatting.**

formation
noun **1** the process of making or producing: *the formation of ice from water* **2** something which has formed: *a rock formation* **3** a planned arrangement or pattern: *planes flying in formation*

former
adjective **1** earlier or past: *a former marriage* **2** being the first one of two: *They served both tea and coffee but I chose the former.*

Word use: The opposite of definition 2 is **latter.**
Word building: **formerly** *adverb* in the past

formidable   (*say* faw-muh-duh-buhl)
adjective **1** very difficult and needing much hard work: *To clean up such a messy bedroom is a formidable task.* **2** frightening: *a formidable enemy*

Word building: **formidably** *adverb*

formula   (*say* faw-myuh-luh)
noun **1** a rule or recipe to be followed: *The formula for mixing the baby's milk is one part milk powder to five parts water.* **2** in chemistry, the representation of the atoms in a molecule by symbols: *The formula for water is H_2O.*

Word building: The plural is **formulas** or **formulae.** | **formulate** *verb* to state clearly or exactly   **formulation** *noun*

forsake
verb to give up or abandon

Word building: Other forms are **I forsook, I have forsaken, I am forsaking.** | **forsaken** *adjective*   **forsakenly** *adverb*

fort
noun **1** a place like a castle, which is strongly built and armed against enemy attack
Other words: **citadel, fortress**
phrase **2 hold the fort,** to look after things for someone while they are away

Word history: from a Latin word meaning 'strong'

forte¹   (*say* faw-tay)
noun something that you do particularly well: *Maths is her forte.*

forte²   (*say* faw-tay)
adverb loudly: *This passage of music is played forte.*

Word use: This instruction in music written as **f.** | The opposite is **piano.**
Word building: **fortissimo** *adverb* very loudly
Word history: from an Italian word

forthcoming
adjective **1** happening or coming soon: *our forthcoming visit to the zoo* **2** ready when needed: *We wanted to buy a boat but the money was not forthcoming.*

Word use: The more usual word for definition 1 is **approaching.**

forthright
adjective speaking your mind openly and honestly

Word building: **forthrightly** *adverb* **forthrightness** *noun*

fortify   (*say* faw-tuh-fuy)
verb to make strong so as to resist attack, damage and other harmful things: *to build strong walls to fortify the castle* | *to drink hot soup to fortify yourself against the cold*

Word building: Other forms are **I fortified, I have fortified, I am fortifying.** | **fortifications** *plural noun* a fort or a wall built to protect against enemy attack

fortnight
noun two weeks or fourteen days and nights

Word building: **fortnightly** *adjective*   **fortnightly** *adverb*

fortress
noun another word for **fort**

fortunate
adjective lucky or having good fortune: *You were fortunate to find the money you lost.*

Word building: **fortunately** *adverb*

fortune
noun **1** a great amount of money or property: *to make a fortune buying and selling land* **2** luck: *We had the good fortune to have fine weather for the sports carnival.* **3** fate or destiny: *to tell someone's fortune*

Word use: The opposite of definition 2 is **misfortune.**

forty (say <u>faw</u>-tee)

noun **1** the number 40 **2** the Roman numeral XL

Word building: The plural is **forties**. | **forty** *adjective: forty years* **fortieth** *adjective: my fortieth birthday*

forum

noun **1** a public meeting to discuss matters of general interest **2** a gathering of comments and opinions on a particular subject, as on the internet, a radio program and so on **3** the main square or marketplace of an ancient Roman town

Word building: The plural is **forums** or **fora**.

forward

adjective **1** ahead or towards the front: *a forward step* | *the forward part of a boat* **2** behaving boldly usually in order to be noticed by others: *Kate is quite forward but her brother is very shy.*
verb **3** to send on: *to forward a letter to the new address*
noun **4** someone who plays in an attacking position in sports such as football and hockey

Word use: The more usual word for definition 2 is **bold**.
Word building: **forward** *adverb* **forwards** *adverb*

forward slash

noun a short diagonal line (/) either printed or on a computer screen: *Use a forward slash to separate the upper and lower parts of the fraction.*

fossick

verb **1** to try to find gold or precious stones in ground that has already been worked over by others **2** to search or hunt: *to fossick through a drawer for a pencil*

Word building: **fossicker** *noun*

fossil

noun **1** the remains of an animal or plant from long ago, preserved as rock **2** *Informal* someone who has old-fashioned ideas

Word building: **fossilise** *verb* **fossilised** *adjective*
Word history: from a Latin word meaning 'dug up'

fossil fuel

noun a fuel like coal, oil or natural gas, which have formed deep in the earth from the remains of living organisms millions of years old

foster

verb **1** to take into a family and care for: *to foster an orphan child* **2** to help or encourage to grow: *to foster friendship between nations*

Word use: Compare definition 1 with **adopt**.
Word building: **foster** *adjective: a foster child* | *a foster home*

foul

adjective **1** very nasty, dirty or unpleasant: *a foul smell* | *foul weather* | *foul language*
verb **2** to make or become dirty or unpleasant **3** to make or become jammed or caught: *Our propeller fouled on a fishing line.* **4** to play unfairly or break the rules in sport

Word building: **foul** *noun* an unfair action in sport **foully** *adverb* **foulness** *noun*

foul/fowl Don't confuse **foul** with **fowl** which is a bird kept for eating or for its eggs, such as a hen, duck or turkey.

found

verb to set up or start: *to found a new settlement*

Word building: **founder** *noun* **founding** *adjective*

foundation

noun **1** the founding or setting up of something **2** a base on which something rests or stands: *the stone foundations of a building* | *the foundations of society*

Word use: Definition 2 is often used in the plural.
Word building: **foundation** *adjective: a foundation member of the club*

founder[1]

noun someone who begins or starts up something: *She is the founder of the art gallery.*

founder[2]

verb **1** to fill with water and sink: *The ship began to founder off the jagged reef.* **2** to go lame, trip, or break down: *The horse foundered during the steeplechase.*

fountain

noun **1** a place where water spurts upward or streams downward from a water pipe **2** the origin or source: *the fountain of wisdom*

fountain pen
noun a pen which has a small container inside for supplying ink to the nib

four   *(say* faw)
noun **1** the number 4 **2** the Roman numeral IV

Word building: **four** *adjective*: *four angles*   **fourth** *adjective*: *the fourth child*

fourteen
noun **1** the number 14 **2** the Roman numeral XIV

Word building: **fourteen** *adjective*: *fourteen friends*   **fourteenth** *adjective*: *fourteenth birthday*

four-wheel drive
noun a car or truck which can travel over rough country or soft ground because all four wheels are driven by the engine

Word use: The abbreviation is **4WD**.

fowl
noun a bird kept for eating or for its eggs, such as a hen, duck or turkey

fowl/foul Don't confuse **fowl** with **foul**. Something is **foul** if it is very nasty, dirty or unpleasant.

fox
noun **1** a small wild dog with red-brown fur, a long bushy tail and pointed ears **2** someone who is sly or cunning

Word use: The male is a **dog**, the female is a **vixen** and the young is a **cub**.
Word building: The plural is **foxes**. | **foxy** *adjective* sly and cunning   **foxily** *adverb* **foxiness** *noun*

foyer   *(say* foy-uh)
noun the large entrance hall of a theatre or hotel

fracas   *(say* frak-ah, frak-uhs)
noun a disturbance or fight with a lot of noise: *The party was ruined by a fracas in the street afterwards.*

Word use: The first pronunciation is unusual because this word came from French (from an earlier Italian word meaning 'make an uproar').

fraction
noun **1** a part of a whole number: $\frac{3}{4}$ *is a fraction* **2** a small piece or amount: *to open the door a fraction*

Word building: **fractional** *adjective* **fractionally** *adverb*
Word history: from a Latin word meaning 'break'

fractious   *(say* frak-shuhs)
adjective uncooperative: *a fractious child*

Word use: The more usual word is **bad-tempered**.
Word building: **fractiously** *adverb*

fracture
verb to crack or break: *to fall over and fracture your arm* | *The rock fractured when we hit it.*

Word building: **fracture** *noun*

fragile
adjective delicate and easily damaged or broken: *a fragile china cup*
Other words: **breakable, brittle**

Word building: **fragilely** *adverb* **fragility** *noun*

fragment
noun a part that has been broken off or left unfinished: *a fragment of glass* | *a fragment of a poem*

Word building: **fragment** *verb* to break into small pieces   **fragmentary** *adjective*   **fragmentation** *noun*

fragrant
adjective sweet-smelling: *a fragrant perfume*

Word building: **fragrance** *noun*   **fragrantly** *adverb*

frail
adjective weak or delicate: *to be frail after a long illness*

Word building: **frailty** *noun* (**frailties**) weakness   **frailly** *adverb*   **frailness** *noun*

frame
noun **1** the structure which fits around or supports something and gives it shape: *a picture frame* | *a house with a wooden frame* | *the human frame* **2** one of the small pictures that make up a strip of film
verb **3** to form or put together: *to frame a plan* **4** to put into a frame or surround like a frame: *to frame a picture* | *Curly hair framed the child's face.* **5** *Informal* to make seem guilty: *The gangster framed her innocent partner.*
phrase **6 frame of mind,** mood: *to be in a good frame of mind*

Word building: **framer** *noun* **framework** *noun* a supporting frame

franchise   (*say* <u>fran</u>-chuyz)

noun **1** a citizen's right to vote
2 permission given by a manufacturer to a shopkeeper to sell the manufacturer's products

Word history: from a French word meaning 'free'

frank

adjective **1** open and honest in what you say: *to give a frank answer*
noun **2** a mark put on a letter in place of a postage stamp to show that postage has already been paid

Word building: **frank** *verb*: *to frank a letter* **frankly** *adverb* openly   **frankness** *noun*

frankfurt

noun a spicy red-coloured sausage, usually eaten with a bread roll

Word use: Other names are **frankfurter** and **saveloy**.
Word history: named after *Frankfurt*, a city in Germany

frantic

adjective wild with excitement, fear, worry or pain

Word building: **frantically** *adverb*

fraternal

adjective of or like a brother

Word building: **fraternity** *noun* a group of people with the same interests or goals: *the legal fraternity*   **fraternise** *verb* to be friendly   **fraternally** *adverb*

fraud   (*rhymes with* cord)

noun **1** deliberate trickery or cheating
2 someone or something that is not what they pretend to be

Word building: **fraudulent** *adjective* **fraudulently** *adverb*

fray[1]

noun a noisy fight or quarrel: *When the older children joined the fray the whole playground was in an uproar.*

fray[2]

verb to wear out: *My shirt collar is fraying.* | *A hard day's work frays my temper.*

frazzled

adjective weary or tired out: *I'm frazzled after a day looking after a screaming baby.*

Word building: **frazzle** *noun* the state of being worn out or burnt: *worn to a frazzle* | *burnt to a frazzle*   **frazzle** *verb*

freak

noun someone or something that is extremely strange or unusual

Word building: **freak** *adjective* unusual: *a freak storm*   **freakish** *adjective* weird: *freakish behaviour*   **freakishly** *adverb*

freckle

noun a small brown spot on your skin caused by the sun: *People with red hair usually have freckles.*

Word building: **freckle** *verb*   **freckled** *adjective*

free

adjective **1** costing nothing: *free tickets to the pictures* **2** not confined or restricted: *The bird flew out of the cage and is free.* | *a free choice* **3** not being used: *The room is free now.*

Word building: **free** *verb* (**freed**, **freeing**)   **free** *adverb*: *to set the bird free*   **freely** *adverb*

freedom

noun the right to act or speak out as you wish

Other words: **liberty**

freehand

adjective drawn by hand, and not traced or drawn with a ruler, compass or other instruments: *a freehand drawing*

Word building: **freehand** *adverb*

freelance

noun someone, especially a writer, who doesn't work for a wage but who sells work to more than one employer

Word building: **freelance** *verb*   **freelance** *adjective*

free-range

adjective able to walk around and feed freely, rather than being kept in a cage: *free-range chickens*

freestyle

noun a fast style of swimming in which your head and the front of your body are kept flat to the water, with legs kicking and your arms used in turn

Word use: Other names are **crawl** or **Australian crawl**.
Word building: **freestyle** *adjective*

free verse

noun poetry without regular rhythms or rhymes

freeway

noun a road on which traffic can travel fast

Word use: Other words for this are **expressway** and **motorway**.

freeze

verb **1** to turn to ice: *We freeze our drink bottles so they're still cold at lunchtime.* **2** to be or feel very cold **3** to keep fresh by putting in a freezer: *We freeze the meat.* **4** to keep very still, as with fear: *Thinking he heard footsteps, he froze.*
noun **5** a period of very cold weather **6** a period in which no change is allowed in something, such as prices or wages

Word building: Other verb forms are **I froze, I have frozen, I am freezing.** | **frozen** *adjective*

freeze-dry

verb to preserve food by quickly freezing it, then removing the liquid from it in a vacuum: *to freeze-dry meals*

Word building: Other forms are **I freeze-dried, I have freeze-dried, I am freeze-drying.** | **freeze-dried** *adjective*: *freeze-dried strawberries*

freight *(rhymes with rate)*

noun **1** goods sent by air, sea or land **2** the charge for sending goods

Word building: **freighter** *noun* a ship or plane that carries goods   **freight** *verb*

French horn

noun a brass wind instrument with a mellow tone

frenetic *(say fruh-net-ik)*

adjective insane or frantic: *frenetic activity*

Word use: This is sometimes spelt **phrenetic**.
Word building: **frenetically** *adverb*

frenzy

noun a wildly or furiously excited state: *The dog was in a frenzy barking at all the cars.*

Word building: **frenzied** *adjective*

frequency *(say free-kwuhn-see)*

noun **1** the fact of happening often: *I was annoyed by the frequency of Scott's visits.* **2** the rate at which something happens: *the frequency of a pulse* **3** the rate of cycles or vibrations of a wave movement: *My radio only picks up stations on a high frequency.*

Word building: The plural is **frequencies**.

frequent *(say free-kwuhnt)*

adjective **1** happening often: *They make frequent visits to the beach.*
Other words: **many, recurrent, regular, repeated**
verb (say fruh-kwent) **2** to visit often: *I frequent the cinema.*
Other words: **patronise**

Word building: **frequently** *adverb*

fresco

noun a painting done on a freshly plastered wall or ceiling before it has dried, so that the colours sink in

Word building: The plural is **frescoes** or **frescos**.
Word history: from an Italian word meaning 'cool'

fresh

adjective **1** in a natural state: *Sometimes we have fresh fruit and sometimes stewed fruit.* **2** new: *fresh footprints* **3** cool: *It's a fresh morning.* **4** not salt: *fresh water* **5** strong and not tired or faded: *You look fresh after your holiday.* **6** just arrived: *fresh from home* **7** cheeky: *Don't get fresh with me!*

Word building: **fresh** *noun*   **freshen** *verb* **freshly** *adverb*   **freshness** *noun*

freshwater crocodile

noun a small crocodile that lives in permanent freshwater areas such as lakes, billabongs and swamps in northern Australia: *Freshwater crocodiles are not interested in eating humans.*

fret[1]

verb to be worried or annoyed: *I fret about things not being done properly.*

Word building: Other forms are **I fretted, I have fretted, I am fretting.**

fret[2]

noun one of the bars across the neck of a stringed instrument, such as a guitar, which marks off the notes

friar

noun a member of a religious order, such as the Dominicans or the Franciscans, who lives a simple life of prayer

Word building: **friary** *noun* a place where friars live
Word history: from a Latin word meaning 'brother'

friction

noun **1** the rubbing of one thing against another: *There is some friction where the wheel touches the mudguard.* **2** a clash or struggle: *There was friction between the two children.*

Friday

noun the sixth day of the week

Word use: The abbreviation is **Fri.**

fridge

noun short for **refrigerator**

fried rice

noun rice that is fried with egg, pork, onion and soy sauce. This dish is from China.

friend   (*rhymes with* bend)

noun someone you like and who likes you

Word building: **friendliness** *noun*   **friendly** *adjective*   **friendship** *noun*

frieze   (*rhymes with* breeze)

noun a band around the top of a wall which is often decorated with a painted or sculpted pattern

frigate   (*say* frig-uht)

noun a warship, often used as an escort vessel

fright

noun **1** a sudden feeling of fear or shock: *Danny crept up to give me a fright.* **2** someone or something of a shocking or silly appearance: *to look a fright*

Word building: **frighten** *verb*   **frightened** *adjective*

frightful

adjective **1** alarming or unpleasant: *They had a frightful time trying to cross the flooded river.* **2** very bad: *We saw a frightful film.*

Word building: **frightfully** *adverb* very

frigid   (*say* frij-uhd)

adjective **1** very cold: *a frigid climate* **2** stiff or unfriendly: *Shen's frigid manner puts people off.*

Word use: The more usual word for definition 2 is **cold**.
Word building: **frigidity** *noun* coldness   **frigidly** *adverb* stiffly

frill

noun a ruffled edge, used to decorate something like the hem or neck of a dress

Word building: **frill** *verb* to add a frill to   **frilly** *adjective*

fringe

noun **1** a border of loose or bunched threads on something like a scarf or rug **2** hair which has been cut across the forehead **3** the edge or outer part: *We live on the fringe of the town.*
adjective **4** extra: *A fringe benefit of the job is the use of a car.*

Word building: **fringe** *verb*

frisbee

noun a flat plastic disc with a rim, designed to stay in the air for some time when thrown with horizontal spin, usually as part of a game

Word history: a trademark

frisk

verb **1** to leap around playfully, as a lamb or kitten does **2** *Informal* to search for hidden weapons: *After the bomb scare, guards frisked the visitors.*

Word building: **frisky** *adjective* lively   **friskily** *adverb*   **friskiness** *noun*

frittata   (*say* fri-tah-tuh)

noun a thick omelette containing vegetables, cheese, seasonings, and so on

Word history: from an Italian word meaning 'fried'

fritter¹

verb to waste gradually: *I fritter my money away on useless things.*

fritter²

noun a small piece of food, often fruit, fried in batter: *banana fritter*

frivolous   (*say* friv-uh-luhs)

adjective not serious: *I was in trouble for giving frivolous answers to the questions.*

Word building: **frivolity** *noun*   **frivolously** *adverb*

frock

noun a dress

frog

noun a tailless creature with webbed feet and long back legs for jumping, which lives in water or on land

frogman

noun a diver, especially one with a wetsuit, flippers, mask and snorkel or air tank

Word building: The plural is **frogmen**.

frolic

noun happy play: *After school they had a good frolic outside.*

Word building: **frolic** *verb* (**frolicked, frolicking**) **frolicsome** *adjective*
Word history: from a Dutch word meaning 'joyful'

from

preposition a word that marks a starting point, used to express **1** distance in regard to space, time, order, and so on: *the train from the mountains | from that day on | to stop himself from falling* **2** difference or distinction: *to sort the good from the bad* **3** source or origin: *to buy fruit from the shop | I learned that song from my grandfather.* **4** cause or reason: *to be fit from training*

frond

noun the divided leaf of plants such as ferns and palms

front   (*rhymes with* blunt)

noun **1** the part or surface facing forward or most often seen: *The door is at the front.* **2** the battle line: *Many soldiers died at the front.* **3** land facing a road or shore: *No-one owns the lake front.*

Word building: **front** *adjective*

frontier   (*say* frun-<u>tear</u>)

noun **1** the border of a country or state **2** the end of known territory: *The early settlers explored the frontier.*

frost

noun **1** extreme cold **2** the covering of ice formed when dew freezes
verb **3** to ice: *The baker frosted the cake.*

Word building: **frosted** *adjective* **frostily** *adverb* **frostiness** *noun* **frosty** *adjective*

frostbite

noun damage done by the freezing of exposed parts of your body in very cold conditions

Word building: **frostbitten** *adjective*

frosting

noun **1** a fluffy cake icing **2** a frostlike coating on glass, metal or other surfaces

froth

noun the mass of tiny bubbles that rise to the top of some liquids

Word use: A word with the same meaning is **foam**.
Word building: **froth** *verb* **frothily** *adverb* **frothiness** *noun* **frothy** *adjective*

frown

verb **1** to wrinkle your forehead in a look of worry or displeasure
phrase **2 frown on**, to disapprove of

Word building: **frown** *noun*

frugal   (*say* <u>frooh</u>-guhl)

adjective **1** very careful not to waste anything **2** poor or cheap: *They had a frugal meal of bread and tomatoes.*

Word use: The more usual word is **economical**.
Word building: **frugality** *noun* **frugally** *adverb*

fruit

noun **1** the edible part which grows from the flowers of trees and plants, such as apples, oranges, pineapples, and many others **2** the result: *This book is the fruit of years of work.*

Word building: **fruit** *verb* to bear fruit

frustrate

verb to put difficulties in the way of, or prevent: *I frustrate Lin's attempts to help by doing everything myself.*

Word building: **frustrated** *adjective* **frustration** *noun*

fry

verb to cook in a pan, using fat or oil

Word building: Other forms are **I fried, I have fried, I am frying.** | **fried** *adjective*

fudge

noun a soft sweet made from sugar, butter and milk

fuel

noun anything, such as wood, petrol or kerosene, which is burnt to give heat or to make an engine work

Word building: **fuel** *verb* (**fuelled, fuelling**) to get or supply with fuel
Word history: from a Latin word meaning 'hearth' or 'fireplace'

fugitive   (*say* <u>fyooh</u>-juh-tiv)

noun someone who is running away

Word building: **fugitive** *adjective*

fugue (*say* fyoohg)

noun a piece of music in which a short melody is played or sung and then copied by other instruments or voices

Word history: from a Latin word meaning 'flight'

fulcrum (*say* fool-kruhm)

noun the point on which something balances or turns: *A bent pipe made a fulcrum for the seesaw.*

Word building: The plural is **fulcrum** or **fulcra**.

fulfil

verb **1** to carry out: *I will fulfil my promise to pay.* **2** to satisfy: *I hope to fulfil my need to paint at the weekend.*

Word building: Other forms are **I fulfilled, I have fulfilled, I am fulfilling.** | **fulfilled** *adjective* **fulfilment** *noun*

full

adjective **1** filled up: *My knapsack is already full.*
Other words: **brimming, bulging, bursting, overflowing, packed**
2 whole or complete: *Su Li has collected the full series of cards.*
Other words: **entire, total**
3 wide or loose: *Kelly is wearing a full shirt.*

Word building: **full** *adverb* completely **fully** *adverb*

full stop

noun a punctuation mark (.) which is used at the end of a sentence or, sometimes, to show that a word has been shortened

You use a **full stop** at the end of a sentence except where a question mark or an exclamation mark is needed:
Our dog bit the visitor.

Sometimes, if you are reporting a conversation, you may use a short phrase which, although it is not a sentence, can make sense on its own and can have a full stop:
'Which watch do you like?'
'This one.'
'Did you see Jo?'
'No.'

Note that a full stop can also be called a **period.**

full-time

adjective working most of the week at any job: *a full-time actor*

fumble

verb to handle clumsily: *Unfortunately, I fumbled the catch and dropped the ball.*

Word building: **fumbler** *noun* **fumbling** *adjective*

fume

noun **1 fumes,** smoke or gas which can be easily seen or smelt
verb **2** to give out fumes **3** to be very angry: *Don't go near her because she is fuming.*

Word building: **fuming** *adjective*

fumigate (*say* fyooh-muh-gayt)

verb to treat with chemical fumes to get rid of insect pests

Word building: **fumigation** *noun* **fumigator** *noun*

fun

noun **1** enjoyment **2** playfulness: *to feel full of fun*
adjective **3** *Informal* providing enjoyment or entertainment; lively: *a fun place to be* | *a fun person*
phrase **4 make fun of,** to tease

function

noun **1** what someone or something is meant to do: *one of the functions of a treasurer* | *the function of a vehicle* **2** a social or official occasion, such as a dinner to raise money
verb **3** to work or go: *The heater isn't functioning.*

Word building: **functional** *adjective* useful **functionally** *adverb*

function key

noun one of a set of keys on a computer keyboard, usually ten or twelve, which you can program to perform complicated tasks when you press the key down once

fund

noun **1** a supply of money: *They have a fund which pays for their holidays.* **2** a supply: *My grandmother's fund of experience is helpful.*

Word building: **fund** *verb* to pay for

fundamental

adjective **1** most important: *You have to learn the fundamental rules of the road before you can get a licence.*
noun **2** the rule or principle underlying any system: *I am learning the fundamentals of computer programming.*

Word use: The more usual word is **basic**.
Word building: **fundamentally** *adverb* basically
Word history: from a Latin word meaning 'foundation'

funeral

noun a ceremony held to honour someone who has died, followed by the burial or cremation of the body

Word building: **funereal** *adjective* gloomy as a funeral

fungus

noun a simple plant, such as the mushroom, mould or yeast, which grows in dark or damp places

Word building: The plural is **fungi** or **funguses**.

funnel

noun **1** an open-ended cone used for pouring liquid or dry goods into a container with a narrow opening **2** the wide tube which forms the chimney of a ship or steam engine

Word building: **funnel** *verb* (**funnelled, funnelling**) to pour through a funnel

funnel-web

noun a large black venomous spider of eastern Australia, which builds a funnel-shaped web

funny

adjective **1** amusing or comical
Other words: **hilarious, humorous**
2 strange: *There's something funny about this recipe.*
Other words: **odd, peculiar, perplexing, queer, unusual, weird**

Word building: Other forms are **funnier, funniest**.

funny bone

noun the point of your elbow which tingles when it is hit

fun run

noun a long running race for amateur runners, usually used to raise money

fur

noun **1** the hairy coat of some animals, such as dogs, cats and possums **2** the skin of some animals, such as rabbits, minks and foxes, which is treated and made into a garment: *The opera singer wore fur.*

Word building: **furrier** *noun* a maker or seller of furs   **furriness** *noun*   **furry** *adjective*

fur/fir Don't confuse **fur** with **fir**, which is a kind of tree.

furious

adjective **1** extremely angry
Other words: **enraged, fuming, incensed, infuriated, irate, livid, mad**
2 strong or violent: *A furious wind knocked the trees over.*
Other words: **ferocious, fierce, wild**

Word building: **furiously** *adverb*   **fury** *noun*   **infuriate** *verb*

furl

verb to roll up: *The sailors lowered and furled the flag.*

furlong

noun an old-fashioned unit of distance just over 200 metres long

furnace

noun a structure for producing heat, as in the steel industry or for heating buildings

furnish

verb **1** to decorate with furniture and other fittings: *They have furnished the sitting room with cane chairs.* **2** to provide: *The attendant will furnish you with pens and paper.*

Word building: **furnishings** *plural noun* the carpets, furniture, and so on used to furnish a room

furniture

noun the chairs, beds, tables and other fittings of a room or house

furore   (*say* fyooh-raw)

noun an outburst of noisy disorder

furphy   (*say* fer-fee)

noun a piece of gossip

Word history: named after a Victorian man, John *Furphy*, who made water and sanitation carts, which used to be centres of gossip

furrow

noun **1** a groove, especially one made by a plough
verb **2** to wrinkle: *A frown furrowed the writer's brow.*

further

adverb **1** at or to a greater distance: *I ran further than you.* **2** in addition
adjective **3** more distant: *The further house is ours.* **4** more: *Do you want further advice?*

Word use: For definitions 1 and 3 the form **farther** can be used this word is part of the set **far, further, furthest**.

Word building: **further** *verb* to help to advance

furtive

adjective stealthy or sly: *The thief took a furtive look to see if anyone was watching.*

Word building: **furtively** *adverb*

fury

noun extreme or violent anger: *The loser threw the bat in a fury.*

fuse¹

noun **1** the wick which sets off an explosive when it is lit **2** the safety wire in an electrical circuit which cuts off the power if there is a fault

Word building: **fuse** *verb*: *The lights fused, and everything went dark.*

fuse²

verb to melt into one: *We can fuse the two metals by heating them.*

Word building: **fusion** *noun*

fuselage   (*say* fyooh-zuh-lahzh)

noun the body of an aircraft

Word history: from a French word meaning 'shaped like a spindle'

fuss

noun **1** unnecessary bother: *Alison does everything without fuss.* **2** a noise or disturbance: *When they couldn't get the seats they wanted, they made a great fuss.*

Word building: **fussily** *adverb*   **fussiness** *noun*   **fussy** *adjective*

futile

adjective useless and ineffective: *The dog made futile jumps at the cat up in the tree.*

Word building: **futility** *noun* uselessness   **futilely** *adverb*

future

noun the time which has not yet come: *Everyone worries about the future.*

Word building: **future** *adjective*: *future plans*   **futuristic** *adjective* in a modern style, especially of the space age

future tense

noun the form of a verb, using *will* or *shall*, which shows that something is going to happen, such as *will run* in *I will run in the race tomorrow.*

fuzz

noun **1** a fluffy mass or coating **2** *Informal* the police

Word building: **fuzzy** *adjective* blurred   **fuzzily** *adverb*   **fuzziness** *noun*

Gg

gabble
verb to talk so quickly that it is hard to understand you: *Stop gabbling and tell us calmly what happened.*

Word building: **gabbler** *noun*

gaberdine (*say* gab-uh-<u>deen</u>)
noun closely woven cloth made of wool, cotton, or spun rayon

Word use: Another spelling is **gabardine**.

gable
noun the triangular part of a wall between the two slopes of a roof

Word building: **gabled** *adjective*

gadget
noun a small invention or useful piece of machinery which performs a particular job: *a gadget for slicing carrots*

Word building: **gadgetry** *noun*: *The kitchen was equipped with all kinds of gadgetry.*

gag¹
verb **1** to cover someone's mouth to stop them from speaking or making a sound *noun* **2** something pushed into or tied round your mouth to prevent you from speaking

Word building: Other verb forms are **I gagged, I have gagged, I am gagging.**

gag²
noun a joke or trick

Word building: **gag** *verb* (**gagged, gagging**) **gagster** *noun*

gaggle
noun a flock of geese

Word history: the word imitates the noise that geese make

gaiety (*say* <u>gay</u>-uh-tee)
noun cheerfulness or high spirits

Word building: **gaily** *adverb*

gain
verb **1** to get or win: *to gain top marks in an exam* **2** to catch up: *We gained rapidly on the slow swimmer in the relay.*
noun **3** a profit: *a gain of $2 on the sale*
phrase **4 gain ground**, to go forward or get an advantage: *The party has gained ground in its goal to save the environment.* **5 gain time,** to delay: *The lawyer needs to gain time in the court case to find another witness.*

Word building: **gainful** *adjective*

gait (*say* gayt)
noun way of walking or moving: *an old man's gait* | *a horse's gait*

gala (*say* <u>gah</u>-luh)
noun a celebration or special occasion: *a swimming gala*

Word history: from a Dutch word meaning 'riches'

galah (*say* guh-<u>lah</u>)
noun **1** an Australian cockatoo with pink and grey feathers **2** a foolish person

Word use: Definition 2 is more suited to everday language.
Word history: from an Aboriginal language of New South Wales called Yuwaalaraay. See the map of Australian Aboriginal languages at the end of this book.

galaxy

noun **1** a large group of stars separated from any other similar group by great areas of space **2 the Galaxy**, our particular galaxy which contains several billion stars as well as our solar system

Word use: Another name for definition 2 is the **Milky Way**.
Word building: The plural is **galaxies**. | **galactic** *adjective*
Word history: from a Greek word meaning 'milk'

gale

noun a very strong wind

gallant   (*say* gal-uhnt, guh-<u>lant</u>)

adjective **1** brave and noble **2** very polite and courteous

Word building: **gallantry** *noun*
Word history: from a French word meaning 'magnificent'

gall bladder   (*say* <u>gawl</u> blad-uh)

noun a part of your body attached to your liver, which stores bile

galleon

noun a kind of large sailing ship with three masts, used in former times by Spain and other countries

gallery

noun **1** an upper floor or balcony where you can sit, especially in a theatre **2** a room or building where you can see paintings and sculptures

Word building: The plural is **galleries**.

galley

noun **1** a long low ship propelled by oars **2** the kitchen in a ship or aeroplane

Word building: The plural is **galleys**.

gallon

noun a unit of measure of liquid in the imperial system equal to about 4.5 litres

gallop

noun **1** the fastest movement of a horse
verb **2** to ride a horse at full speed: *The drovers galloped after the cattle.*

Word building: Other verb forms are **I galloped, I have galloped, I am galloping**.
Word history: from a German word meaning 'run well'

gallows

noun a wooden frame for hanging criminals

galore   (*say* guh-<u>law</u>)

adverb in great numbers: *There were cakes galore at the party.*

Word use: This word is only used after nouns.

galvanise

verb **1** to cause to move by, or as if by, an electric current: *to galvanise into action* **2** to coat with zinc to prevent rust: *to galvanise iron*

Word use: Another spelling is **galvanize**.
Word building: **galvanisation** *noun*

gamble   (*say* <u>gam</u>-buhl)

verb **1** to play a game in which you risk losing something, especially money **2** to take a chance: *I gambled on Kim's being away that day.*

Word building: **gamble** *noun*   **gambler** *noun*   **gambling** *noun*

gambol   (*say* <u>gam</u>-buhl)

verb to jump about in play: *The children gambolled in the shallow water.*

Word building: Other forms are **I gambolled, I have gambolled, I am gambolling.**

game

noun **1** something you can play, usually with set rules: *a game of football* | *a game of cards* **2** wild animals, including birds and fish, hunted for food or as a sport: *a book of recipes for cooking game*
adjective **3** brave and courageous: *as game as Ned Kelly* **4** *Informal* willing to do something difficult or dangerous: *I'm game if you are.*
phrase **5 off your game**, not giving your best performance **6 play the game**, to act fairly

Word building: **gamely** *adverb* bravely   **gameness** *noun*

gamelan   (*say* <u>gum</u>-uh-lun, <u>gam</u>-uh-lan)

noun **1** a South-East Asian tuned percussion instrument **2** an orchestra comprising a number of gamelans, with some woodwind and strings

gamut   (*say* <u>gam</u>-uht)

noun the whole scale or range: *A good actor can express the whole gamut of emotions.*

gander

noun a male goose

Word use: The female is a **goose** and the young is a **gosling**.

gang

noun **1** a band or group: *a gang of children* **2** a group of people working together: *a gang of labourers*
phrase **3 gang up on**, to join together or take sides against: *Don't gang up on me!*

gangling (*say* gang-gling)

adjective awkwardly tall and thin: *a gangling youth who had grown out of the school uniform*

Word use: Another spelling is **gangly**.

gangly

adjective tall and thin and moving awkwardly: *Even gangly creatures like stick insects find mates.*

gangplank

noun a movable board used as a bridge for going on and off a ship

gangrene (*say* gang-green)

noun the rotting of flesh caused by the blood supply being cut off

Word building: **gangrenous** adjective

gangster

noun a member of a gang of criminals

gangway

noun **1** a passageway, especially on a ship **2** another word for **gangplank**

gaol

noun another spelling for **jail**

Word building: **gaoler** noun   **gaol** verb

gap

noun **1** a break or opening: *a gap in the fence* **2** a blank or unfilled space: *a gap in my memory* | *a gap between words*

gape

verb **1** to stare with your mouth wide open: *They all gaped at George's green hair.* **2** to split or become open: *Your jeans are gaping at the seams.*

Word building: **gape** noun   **gaper** noun   **gapingly** adverb

garage

noun **1** a building for keeping a car, bus or truck **2** a place where cars are mended and petrol is sold

Word use: Another name for definition 2 is **service station**.
Word building: **garage** verb
Word history: from a French word meaning 'put in shelter'

garbage

noun rubbish or waste material
Other words: **refuse, trash**

garble

verb to mix up and so make hard to understand: *to garble a message*

Word building: **garbler** noun   **garbled** adjective

garden

noun **1** an area, usually with trees and plants, used for pleasure and as a place to relax: *the front garden* | *a botanical garden* **2** a flower bed: *a herb garden*
phrase **3 lead up the garden path**, *Informal* to trick or lead away from the truth

Word building: **garden** verb   **gardener** noun

gargle

verb to move a liquid around inside your throat without swallowing

Word building: **gargle** noun

gargoyle (*say* gah-goyl)

noun a spout, often carved in the shape of an ugly head with an open mouth, which carries rainwater off a roof

garish (*say* gair-rish, gah-rish)

adjective very bright in an unpleasant way: *garish colours*
Other words: **glaring, gaudy, loud, lurid, showy**

Word building: **garishly** adverb   **garishness** noun

garland

noun a string of flowers or leaves you wear as an ornament

garlic

noun a plant with a strong flavour like an onion, used in cooking

garment

noun a piece of clothing, such as a dress or shirt

garnish

verb to make more pleasing to taste or look at: *Garnish the fish with parsley and lemon.*

Word use: This word is used mostly in cookery.
Word building: **garnish** noun

garret

noun a room just under the roof of a house
Other words: **attic, loft**

garrison

noun **1** a group of soldiers who are ready to defend a fort or town **2** a place that has been strengthened against attack

Word building: **garrison** *verb*

garrulous　(*say* ga-ruh-luhs)

adjective very talkative

Word building: **garrulity** *noun* talkativeness **garrulously** *adverb* **garrulousness** *noun*

garter

noun a band made of elastic worn around your leg to hold up your long socks

gas¹

noun **1** any air-like substance that will take up the whole of the space that contains it **2** coal gas or natural gas used as a fuel: *We use gas for cooking.*
verb **3** to make sick or kill with a poisonous gas

Word use: Compare definition 1 with **solid** and **liquid**.
Word building: The plural form of the noun is **gases**. | Other verb forms are **I gassed, I have gassed, I am gassing**. | **gaseous** *adjective* like gas　**gassy** *adjective* full of gas
Word history: made up by a Flemish chemist who based it on a Greek word meaning 'chaos'

gas²

noun an American word for **petrol**

Word history: short for **gasoline**

gash

noun a long deep cut: *a gash in my leg*

Word building: **gash** *verb*

gasket

noun a metal or rubber fitting used to seal a joint, especially one in a car engine

gasp

noun **1** a sudden short intake of breath: *Everyone gave a gasp of horror.*
verb **2** to catch your breath or struggle for breath with your mouth open

Word building: **gasper** *noun*

gastr-

prefix a word part meaning 'stomach': *gastric*

Word use: Other spellings are **gastero-** and **gastro-**.
Word history: from Greek

gastric

adjective of or in your stomach: *gastric pains*

gastroenteritis

(*say* gas-troh-en-tuh-<u>ruy</u>-tuhs)
noun an illness in which the intestines become inflamed

Word use: A shortened form of this word is **gastro**.

gate　(*say* gayt)

noun **1** a movable frame for closing an entrance or blocking a passageway **2** the number of people who pay for admission to a sporting event

gatecrash

verb to enter or be present at without paying or being invited: *to gatecrash the tennis tournament | to gatecrash a party*

Word building: **gatecrasher** *noun*

gateway

noun a passage or entrance which is closed by a gate

gather

verb **1** to collect or pick: *to gather fruit* **2** to understand: *I gather that she is an expert.* **3** to draw into small folds on a thread: *to gather a skirt at the waist* **4** to come together: *A crowd gathered to see the fire.*

Word building: **gathering** *noun* a crowd of people　**gatherable** *adjective*　**gatherer** *noun*

gauche　(*say* gohsh)

adjective clumsy: *gauche manners*

Word use: The more usual word is **awkward**.
Word building: **gaucherie** *noun* clumsiness **gaucheness** *noun*

gaudy　(*say* <u>gaw</u>-dee)

adjective bright and attracting attention: *a gaudy beach towel*

Word building: Other forms are **gaudier, gaudiest**. | **gaudily** *adverb*　**gaudiness** *noun*

gauge　(*say* gayj)

verb **1** to judge or make a guess at: *to gauge the public reaction* **2** to measure: *to gauge the height of the building*
noun **3** thickness, especially of thin objects: *wire of a fine gauge* **4** an instrument for measuring: *a pressure gauge* **5** the distance between the two lines of a railway track

gaunt　(*say* gawnt)

adjective very thin and tired-looking in appearance

Word building: **gauntly** *adverb*   **gauntness**
noun
Word history: from a French word meaning
'rather yellow'

gauze (*say* gawz)
noun thin transparent cloth similar material
with an open weave, such as wire

Word building: **gauzy** *adjective* (**gauzier,**
gauziest)   **gauziness** *noun*

gawky
adjective tall and awkward: *the gawky body
of a baby giraffe*

Word building: Other forms are **gawkier,**
gawkiest.

gay
adjective **1** homosexual: *gay marriage*
2 cheerful or bright: *gay music | gay colours*

Word building: **gay** *noun*

gaze
verb to look long and steadily

Word building: **gaze** *noun*

gazelle (*say* guh-<u>zel</u>)
noun a small antelope with large eyes

Word building: **gazelle-like** *adjective*

gazette (*say* guh-<u>zet</u>)
noun an official government magazine
containing lists of people the government
has appointed

Word building: **gazette** *verb* to list or announce
in a gazette
Word history: from the Italian name for a coin
(the price of the gazette)

gear
noun **1** a group of toothed wheels, or
one of the wheels, that connect with each
other to pass on or change the movement
of a machine, such as those that carry
power from the engine to the wheels of
a car **2** equipment: *climbing gear | cricket
gear* **3** *Informal* clothes

Word building: **gear** *verb*

gearbox
noun a case in which gears of a motor are
enclosed

gearstick
noun a lever for connecting and
disconnecting gears in a car

gecko
noun a small lizard which is mostly active
at night

Word building: The plural is **geckos** or
geckoes.
Word history: from a Malay word that imitates
the sounds these lizards make

Geiger counter (*say* <u>guy</u>-guh kown-tuh)
noun an instrument for measuring
radioactivity, especially after the explosion
of an atom bomb

Word history: named after the German
physicist, Hans *Geiger*

gel (*say* jel)
noun a type of jelly that you can use to
help shape your hairstyle

Word building: **gel** *verb* (**gelled, gelling**)
Word history: short for **gelatine**

gelatine
noun a colourless, tasteless substance, used
to make jellies and glues

gelato (*say* juh-<u>lah</u>-toh)
noun an Italian iced dessert made from
cream, milk or water and with fruit or nut
flavouring

Word building: The plural is **gelatos** or **gelati**.
Word history: from an Italian word meaning
'frozen' or 'ice-cream'

gelding (*say* <u>gel</u>-ding)
noun a male horse that has had its sex
organs removed

Word building: **geld** *verb* to remove the sex
organs of

gelignite (*say* <u>jel</u>-uhg-nuyt)
noun an explosive substance used in mining

gem
noun **1** a stone used in jewellery, after it
has been cut and polished **2** any person
or thing that is as beautiful or valuable as
a gem

gender (*say* <u>jen</u>-duh)
noun **1** a set of groups in the grammar
of languages such as Latin, into which
all nouns can be divided. These groups
include masculine nouns like 'boy',
feminine nouns like 'girl', and neuter
nouns in which the object has no sex or
the sex isn't known. **2** sex, either male or
female: *Do you know the gender of these pet
mice?*

gene (*say* jeen)

noun one of the units in your body which is responsible for passing on characteristics, like blue eyes, from parents to their children

Word building: **genetic** *adjective* **genetically** *adverb*
Word history: from a Greek word meaning 'breed' or 'kind'

genealogy (*say* jee-nee-<u>al</u>-uh-jee)

noun a study or record of the ancestors and relations in your family

Word building: The plural is **genealogies**. | **genealogist** *noun* **genealogical** *adjective*

general

adjective **1** concerning all or most people: *a general election* **2** common or widespread: *a general feeling of unhappiness* **3** not limited to particular details or information: *general instructions*
noun **4** an officer of the highest rank in the Australian army **5** a military commander: *Julius Caesar was a great general.*
phrase **6 in general, a** as a whole, with everything included: *to discuss things in general* **b** usually: *In general, there is snow on the mountains at this time of year.*

Word building: **generalise** *verb* to make up a general rule from a limited number of examples **generally** *adverb* **generality** *noun*

generate

verb to bring into existence: *The sun generates heat.*

Word use: The more usual word is **produce**.

generation

noun **1** all of the people born about the same time: *the younger generation* **2** the period of years, usually about 25 to 30, thought of as the difference between one generation of a family and another

generation Z

adverb the generation born in the early 2000s, who are seen as able to use technology like computers and mobile phones, and often have both parents working

generator

noun a machine for producing electricity

generous

adjective unselfish or ready to give freely: *a generous person*

Other words: **charitable, kind, magnanimous, noble, unselfish**

Word use: The opposite of this is **selfish**.
Word building: **generosity** *noun* **generously** *adverb*
Word history: from a Latin word meaning 'of noble birth'

genesis (*say* <u>jen</u>-uh-suhs)

noun a coming into being: *the genesis of the Australian nation*

Word building: The plural is **geneses**.
Word history: from a Greek word meaning 'creation'

genetically-modified

adjective (of a plant or an animal) with genes added or changed to suit a particular purpose: *The genetically-modified rabbit glowed in the dark.*

genetics

noun the science which studies the passing on of special characteristics from parents to their offspring

Word use: This word is singular, like **mathematics**.
Word building: **geneticist** *noun*

genial (*say* <u>jee</u>-nee-uhl)

adjective having a warm and friendly manner

Word building: **geniality** *noun* **genially** *adverb*

genie (*say* <u>jee</u>-nee)

noun a spirit in Arabian stories

genitals

plural noun the parts of your body which are used for sexual intercourse and reproduction, especially the penis in males and the vagina in females

Word use: Another name is **genitalia**.
Word building: **genital** *adjective*

genius

noun a very talented or clever person
Other words: **prodigy**

Word building: The plural is **geniuses**.
Word history: from a Latin word meaning 'guardian spirit'

genocide (*say* <u>jen</u>-uh-suyd)

noun the planned killing of all the people belonging to one people or nation

Word building: **genocidal** *adjective*

genre (*say* zhon-ruh)
noun a kind, group, or sort, especially the different kinds of writing, films, and art that we recognise

genteel (*say* jen-teel)
adjective very careful in your manners, speech and behaviour
Word use: The more usual word is **polite**.
Word building: **genteelly** *adverb* **gentility** *noun*

gentile (*say* jen-tuyl)
noun someone who is not Jewish, especially a Christian

gentle
adjective **1** kind and patient
Other words: **compassionate, humane, mild, tender**
2 not rough or violent: *a gentle wind | a gentle tap*
Other words: **light, slight, soft**
3 gradual: *a gentle slope*
Other words: **moderate, slight**
4 soft or low: *a gentle sound*
Word building: **gentleness** *noun* **gently** *adverb*

gentleman
noun **1** any man: *Good morning, ladies and gentlemen.* **2** a man with polite manners: *I want you to behave like a gentleman.*
Word use: Definition 1 is used as a polite form of speech. | This word used to mean 'a man born into a family with a high social standing' and a woman of the same kind was called a **gentlewoman**.
Word building: The plural is **gentlemen**.

genuine (*say* jen-yoo-uhn)
adjective **1** true or real: *genuine sorrow | a genuine diamond*
Other words: **authentic**
2 having real, not pretended, feelings: *a genuine person*
Other words: **candid, frank, honest, sincere, unaffected**
Word building: **genuinely** *adverb* **genuineness** *noun*

geo-
prefix a word part meaning 'the earth': *geography | geology*
Word history: from Greek

geography (*say* jee-og-ruh-fee)
noun the study of the earth, including its land forms, peoples, climates, soils and plants

Word building: **geographer** *noun* **geographic** *adjective* **geographical** *adjective* **geographically** *adverb*

geology (*say* jee-ol-uh-jee)
noun the study of the rocks which form the earth
Word building: **geological** *adjective* **geologically** *adverb* **geologist** *noun*

geometry (*say* jee-om-uh-tree)
noun the part of mathematics that studies shapes such as squares and triangles
Word building: **geometric** *adjective* **geometrical** *adjective* **geometrically** *adverb*

geranium (*say* juh-ray-nee-uhm)
noun a common garden plant with red, pink or purple flowers
Word history: from a Greek word meaning 'crane's bill'

geriatric (*say* je-ree-at-rik)
adjective **1** having to do with old people or their care: *a geriatric hospital*
noun **2** someone who is old, especially if they are sick
Word building: **geriatrics** *noun* the medical care of old people **geriatrician** *noun* **geriatrist** *noun*

germ (*say* jerm)
noun **1** a tiny living thing that can only be seen with a microscope and which causes disease **2** the beginning of anything: *The germ of an idea came into my mind while I was in the shower.*

German measles
noun a disease which gives you a temperature and a rash and is usually not serious except for a woman who is having a baby
Word use: This is also called **rubella**.

German shepherd
noun another name for an **Alsatian**

germinate (*say* jerm-uh-nayt)
verb to begin to grow or develop: *Plant seeds germinate when they are watered. | The idea germinated in Sophie's mind.*
Word building: **germination** *noun*

gesticulate (*say* jes-tik-yuh-layt)
verb to make movements with part of your body, especially your hands, in order to express a feeling or idea
Word building: **gesticulation** *noun*

gesture (*say* jes-chuh)

noun **1** a movement of part of your body to express a feeling or idea: *He tossed his head in a gesture of impatience.* **2** something done to express a feeling or idea: *a gesture of friendship*

Word building: **gesture** *verb*

get

verb **1** to obtain or receive: *to get a new dress | to get a present* **2** to bring or fetch: *I'll go and get it.* **3** to hear or understand: *I didn't get what you said.* **4** to reach: *I've phoned Yumiko's house but I can't get her.* **5** to cause to be or do: *I must get my hair cut. | I can't get the car to start.* **6** to prepare or make ready: *Dad's getting the dinner.* **7** to arrive: *When did you get here?* **8** to become or grow: *I am getting tired.*

phrase **9 get away with**, to escape punishment for: *They got away with the crime.* **10 get by**, to manage: *I don't know how I'll get by without a car.* **11 get off**, to escape punishment **12 get on**, **a** to become old **b** to make progress **c** to be friendly: *Anna gets on well with the rest of the class.* **13 get over**, **a** to defeat or find a way around **b** to recover from

Word building: Other verb forms are **I got, I have got, I am getting.**

geyser (*say* gee-zuh, guy-zuh)

noun a hot spring that sometimes sends up jets of water and steam into the air

Word history: from an Icelandic word meaning 'gush'

ghastly (*say* gahst-lee)

adjective very bad or unpleasant: *a ghastly smell*

Word building: Other forms are **ghastlier, ghastliest.**

gherkin (*say* ger-kuhn)

noun a small, pickled cucumber

ghetto (*say* get-oh)

noun the part of a city where a group of people, such as poor people or people from another country, live together

Word building: The plural is **ghettos** or **ghettoes.**
Word history: from the Italian name given to the Jewish quarter of Venice in the 16th century

ghost (*say* gohst)

noun **1** the spirit of someone who has died, imagined as visiting living people
Other words: **apparition, phantom, spectre**
2 a very small amount or trace: *Ashley hasn't a ghost of a chance.* **3** an annoying double image on a television picture

Word building: **ghostly** *adjective* (**ghostlier, ghostliest**) **ghostliness** *noun*

giant (*say* juy-uhnt)

noun **1** an imaginary creature that looks like a human but is much bigger and stronger **2** someone or something of great size, importance or ability: *a sporting giant* *adjective* **3** huge or gigantic: *a giant plant*

Word building: **giantess** *noun*

gibber[1] (*say* jib-uh)

verb to speak quickly and without making much sense

Word building: **gibberish** *noun*

gibber[2] (*say* gib-uh)

noun a stone or rock

Word history: from an Aboriginal language of New South Wales called Dharug. See the map of Australian Aboriginal languages at the end of this book.

gibbon

noun a kind of small ape with long arms

giblets (*say* jib-luhts)

plural noun the inside parts of a fowl, such as the heart and liver, usually cooked separately

giddy (*say* gid-ee)

adjective having a feeling of whirling or spinning

Word building: Other forms are **giddier, giddiest.** | **giddily** *adverb* **giddiness** *noun*

gift

noun **1** something that is given as a present
Other words: **offering**
2 a special ability: *Ling has a gift for singing.*
Other words: **aptitude, faculty, flair, genius, knack, talent**

Word building: **gifted** *adjective* having special natural abilities

gig[1]

noun a light, two-wheeled carriage pulled by one horse

gig²

noun a job for a musician, usually a booking for one show

gigabyte (*say* gig-uh-buyt)

noun a unit for measuring the size of computer information, equal to 1024 megabytes

Word use: This word is often shortened to **gig**.

gigantic (*say* juy-gan-tik)

adjective very large or huge: *a gigantic monster | a gigantic rock*

Word building: **gigantically** *adverb* **giganticness** *noun*

giggle

verb to laugh in a silly way

Word building: **giggle** *noun* **giggler** *noun* **giggly** *adjective*

gild

verb to cover with a layer of gold or something gold-coloured

Word building: Other forms are **I gilded** or **gilt**, **I have gilded** or **gilt**, **I am gilding**. | **gilding** *noun*

gill

noun the part of the body that fish and other sea creatures use for breathing

gilt

adjective **1** golden-coloured or covered with gold: *a gilt vase*
noun **2** the gold or other material used in gilding

gilt/guilt Don't confuse **gilt** with **guilt**, which is the feeling you have when you know you've done something wrong.

gimmick

noun an unusual action or trick, usually used to get attention

Word building: **gimmicky** *adjective*

gin (*say* jin)

noun a strong alcoholic drink

ginger

noun **1** a plant root which is used in cooking as a spice and in medicine
adjective **2** reddish-brown: *ginger hair*

Word building: **gingery** *adjective*: *a gingery taste*

gingerly

adverb with great care: *They walked gingerly over the slippery rocks.*

Word use: The more usual word is **carefully**.

gingham (*say* ging-uhm)

noun a cotton cloth with a striped or checked pattern

Word history: from a Malay word meaning 'striped'

gipsy

noun another spelling of **gypsy**

giraffe (*say* juh-rahf)

noun an African animal with spots, a very long neck, and long legs

Word use: The male is a **bull**, the female is a **cow** and the young is a **calf**.

girder (*say* ger-duh)

noun a thick beam used as a support in building

girdle

noun a belt or cord worn around your waist a piece of elastic underwear that supports your stomach and hips

Word building: **girdle** *verb*

girl

noun a female child

Word building: **girlhood** *noun* **girlish** *adjective* **girlishly** *adverb* **girlishness** *noun*

girlfriend

noun **1** a woman or girl with whom someone has a romantic relationship: *My brother has a new girlfriend.* **2** a female friend: *Janine invited some girlfriends to her place for the weekend.*

girth (*say* gerth)

noun **1** the measurement around anything: *My girth is 75 centimetres, measured at the waist.* **2** a band placed under the stomach of a horse to hold a saddle or pack onto its back

gist (*say* jist)

noun the most important part: *I understand the gist of your argument.*

give

verb **1** to hand over freely: *to give someone a present* **2** to pay: *I'll give you $1 for those stamps.* **3** to allow or grant: *Give me one more chance.* **4** to present or organise: *to give a concert* | *to give a party* **5** to provide with: *to give help* | *to give a baby a name* **6** to make, especially a movement: *Con gave a jump.*

phrase **7 give away, a** to give as a present **b** to betray or allow to become known **8 give in,** to admit defeat **9 give out, a** to become worn out or used up **b** to hand out or distribute **10 give up, a** to lose all hope **b** to stop: *You should give up smoking.* **c** to surrender

Word building: Other verb forms are **I gave, I have given, I am giving.** | **gift** *noun* **giver** *noun*

glacial (say glay-shuhl, glay-see-uhl)

adjective **1** having ice **2** icy or cold as ice

Word building: **glacially** *adverb* **glaciate** *verb* **glaciation** *noun*

glacier

noun a large area of ice which moves slowly down a valley or mountain

Word building: **glaciered** *adjective*

glad

adjective **1** delighted or pleased

phrase **2 glad of,** grateful for: *I would be glad of a little help.*

Word building: Other adjective forms are **gladder, gladdest.** | **gladden** *verb* **gladly** *adverb* **gladness** *noun*

glade

noun an open space in a forest

gladiator

noun a man in ancient Rome who fought as a public entertainment

Word building: **gladiatorial** *adjective*

glamour

noun an exciting charm or beauty: *That job has a lot of glamour.* | *Tiffany's clothes always have glamour.*

Word use: Another spelling is **glamor.**
Word building: **glamorise** *verb* **glamorous** *adjective* **glamorously** *adverb*

glance

verb **1** to look quickly **2** to hit and go off at an angle: *The ball glanced off the cricket bat.*

Word building: **glance** *noun* **glancing** *adjective*: *a glancing blow*

gland

noun a part of your body that makes a substance that is used by another part of your body: *Sweat is made by glands.*

Word building: **glandular** *adjective*

glare

noun **1** a strong bright light: *the glare of car headlights* **2** an angry look

Word building: **glaring** *adjective* very obvious: *a glaring mistake* **glare** *verb* **glaringly** *adverb* **glaringness** *noun*

glass

noun **1** a hard transparent substance used for such things as windows, bottles and drinking containers **2** something made of glass, such as a drinking container or a mirror **3 glasses,** two lenses in a frame which are worn over your eyes to help you see more clearly

Word use: Another word for definition 3 is **spectacles.**
Word building: The plural is **glasses.** | **glassy** *adjective* (**glassier, glassiest**) **glassily** *adverb* **glassiness** *noun*

glaze

verb **1** to fit or cover with glass: *to glaze windows* **2** to cover with a thin coat of a clear shiny substance: *to glaze pottery* *noun* **3** a smooth, shiny coating or surface *phrase* **4 glaze over,** to become glassy: *His eyes glazed over as he sat daydreaming.*

Word building: **glazier** *noun* someone who fits glass into windows

gleam

noun **1** a flash of light **2** a dim light: *the gleam of polished wood* **3** a short burst: *When the teacher started talking about skateboarding, a gleam of interest came into Robin's eyes.*

Word building: **gleam** *verb* **gleaming** *adjective*

glean

verb to gather, usually slowly and bit by bit: *to glean grain after it has been reaped* | *to glean information*

Word use: The more usual word is **obtain.**
Word building: **gleaner** *noun*

glee

noun a feeling of joy

Word building: **gleeful** *adjective* **gleefully** *adverb* **gleefulness** *noun*

glen

noun a small narrow valley

glide

verb to move or make to move along smoothly

Word building: **glide** *noun* **glidingly** *adverb*

glider

noun **1** an aeroplane without an engine that flies by using wind and currents of air **2** a possum with thick skin stretched between its front and back legs to help it fly smoothly through the air. Some species are endangered. See the table at the end of this book.

glimmer

noun **1** a faint or flickering light **2** a faint hint or suggestion: *a glimmer of hope*

Word building: **glimmer** *verb* **glimmering** *noun* **glimmeringly** *adverb*

glimpse

noun a quick sighting: *Did you catch a glimpse of the thieves as they ran past?*

Word building: **glimpse** *verb*

glint

noun **1** a flash or glow of light: *the glint of metal* **2** a look showing amusement or a secret idea: *a glint in his eyes*

Word building: **glint** *verb*

glisten (*say* glis-uhn)

verb to shine with a sparkling light: *Georgina's gold ring glistened in the sunlight.*

glitter

verb to shine with a bright sparkling light: *Mei's eyes glittered with excitement.*
Other words: **gleam, sparkle, twinkle**

Word building: **glitter** *noun* **glitteringly** *adverb* **glittery** *adjective*

gloat

verb to look at or think about something or someone in a very satisfied way: *They gloated over their enemy's defeat.*

Word building: **gloater** *noun* **gloating** *adjective* **gloatingly** *adverb*

globalisation

noun the processes by which any system becomes international, such as businesses, governments, languages, and so on

global warming

noun the significant rise in temperature of the whole of the earth's atmosphere

globe

noun **1** a round ball-shaped map of the earth **2** anything shaped like a round ball
Other words: **sphere**
3 an electric light bulb
phrase **4 the globe**, the earth: *They travelled all over the globe.*

Word building: **global** *adjective* **globally** *adverb*
Word history: from a Latin word meaning 'round body', 'mass', or 'ball'

glockenspiel (*say* glok-uhn-speel, glok-uhn-shpeel)

noun a musical instrument with steel bars set in a frame, which you hit with hammers

Word history: from the German words for 'bell' and 'play'

gloom

noun a feeling of unhappiness or depression

Word building: **gloomy** *adjective* (**gloomier, gloomiest**) **gloomily** *adverb* **gloominess** *noun*

glorious

adjective **1** beautiful, wonderful, or delightful: *It is a glorious day.* | *We had a glorious time.* **2** giving or having glory: *a glorious victory*

Word use: The more usual word for definition 1 is **great**.
Word building: **gloriously** *adverb* **gloriousness** *noun*

glory

noun **1** praise and honour
Other words: **acclamation, distinction, fame, kudos, prestige, renown**
2 something that is a cause of pride or honour: *The beaches are one of the glories of Australia.*
Other words: **splendour, wonder**
3 splendid or divine beauty: *the glory of heaven*

Word building: The plural is **glories**. | **glorify** *verb* (**glorified, glorifying**) to praise or honour **glorification** *noun*

gloss

noun **1** the shine on the outside of something: *the gloss of satin*
verb **2** to put a gloss on
phrase **3 gloss over**, to cover up or try to make seem unimportant: *Brad glossed over his mistakes.*

Word building: **glossy** *adjective* (**glossier, glossiest**) **glossily** *adverb* **glossiness** *noun*

glossary

noun a list of special or difficult words about a particular subject, with their definitions: *This textbook has a glossary at the back.*

Word building: The plural is **glossaries.**

glove

noun a covering for your hand, usually with a separate part for each finger and for the thumb

Word building: **glover** *noun* someone who makes or sells gloves   **glove** *verb*

glow

noun **1** the light given out by something extremely hot
Other words: **radiance**
2 brightness of colour **3** a pleasant warm feeling: *a glow of happiness*

Word building: **glow** *verb* **glowing** *adjective* **glowingly** *adverb*

glow-worm

noun a kind of insect whose body glows in the dark

glucose

noun a natural sugar which is found in plants and which gives energy to living things

Word history: from a Greek word meaning 'sweet'

glue

noun **1** a paste used to stick things together *verb* **2** to stick with glue

Word building: **gluey** *adjective* (**gluier, gluiest**)   **glueyness** *noun*

glum

adjective unhappy or depressed

Word building: Other forms are **glummer, glummest.** | **glumly** *adverb* **glumness** *noun*

glut

noun an oversupply: *a glut of tomatoes*
Word building: **glut** *verb* (**glutted, glutting**)

glutton

noun someone who eats too much
Word building: **gluttonous** *adjective* **gluttonously** *adverb* **gluttony** *noun*

gnarled   (*say* nahld)

adjective **1** twisted and having many woody lumps: *a gnarled old tree* **2** rough and worn by the weather: *gnarled hands*

Word building: **gnarl** *noun* **gnarl** *verb*

gnash   (*say* nash)

verb to grind together: *She gnashed her teeth in anger.*

gnat   (*say* nat)

noun a kind of small insect with only one pair of wings

gnaw   (*say* naw)

verb to chew or bite: *The lion gnawed at its food.*

Word building: **gnawing** *adjective* **gnawing** *noun* **gnawingly** *adverb*

gnome   (*say* nohm)

noun a small being in fairy stories, usually imagined as a little old man

Word building: **gnomish** *adjective*

gnu   (*say* nooh)

noun a kind of antelope with curved horns and a long tail

Word building: The plural is **gnus** or **gnu.**

go

noun **1** to move or pass along: *Where are you going?* **2** to move away or depart: *I want you to go now.* **3** to work properly: *The engine won't go.* **4** to become: *He goes quiet when you mention her name.* **5** to reach or lead: *That road goes to Brisbane.* **6** to pass or happen: *Time goes quickly.* | *The party went well.* **7** to belong or have a place: *Where do the knives and forks go?* **8** to fit or be contained: *Two litres of milk will go into this jug.* **9** to be used up or finished: *The food went quickly.* **10** to make a particular sound or movement: *The gun went bang.* **11** energy: *She has plenty of go.* **12** a turn or try: *It's my go on the swing.* *phrase* **13 go in for**, to be interested in: *Jane goes in for surfing.* **14 go off**, **a** to explode: *The gun went off.* **b** to become bad: *The meat has gone off.* **c** to stop liking **15 on the go**, active and energetic

Word building: Other verb forms are **I went, I have gone, I am going.** | The plural form of the noun is **goes.**

goad

noun **1** a stick with a pointed end used to prod cattle and other animals into moving *verb* **2** to drive with a goad **3** to tease or anger

goal   (*say* gohl)

noun **1** an area, basket or something similar at which you aim the ball, in sports such as football, basketball and others **2** the score made by doing this: *We got three goals.* **3** something you aim towards: *My goal is to be a doctor.*

Other words: **aim, ambition, mission, objective, target**

Word building: **goalkeeper** *noun* the player whose job is to stop the ball going into, over, or through a goal

goanna   (*say* goh-<u>an</u>-uh)

noun any of a number of large Australian lizards

goat

noun a small cud-chewing animal with horns, which is able to live in rocky mountainous areas

Word use: The male is a **billy goat**, the female is a **nanny goat** and the baby is a **kid**.

gobble

verb to swallow or eat quickly in large pieces: *to gobble food*

goblet

noun a cup or glass with a stem and a base

goblin

noun an ugly elf who is supposed to make trouble for people

go-cart

noun **1** a small cart with wheels, which children use to ride in **2** another spelling for **go-kart**

god

noun **1** a supernatural being who is worshipped because of power to control human affairs and the world of nature: *Thor was the god of thunder.* **2** an idol or statue of a god **3** someone or something which is given too much attention: *Don't make money your god.* **4** **God**, the supreme maker and ruler of the universe worshipped by people who believe in one god

Word building: **goddess** *noun*

goddess   (*say* <u>god</u>-ess)

noun a female person or thing that is worshipped

godly

adjective deeply religious: *a godly person*

Word building: Other forms are **godlier, godliest**. | **godliness** *noun*

goggles

plural noun glasses with rims and side pieces used to protect your eyes from wind, dust, glare or water

Word building: **goggle** *verb* to stare with your eyes wide open

go-kart

noun a small, light, low-powered car for racing

Word use: Another spelling is **go-cart**.

gold

noun **1** a precious yellow metal **2** money or wealth **3** something highly valued: *a heart of gold*

adjective **4** made of gold, or like gold **5** yellow in colour, like gold

Word building: **goldsmith** *noun* someone who makes or sells articles of gold   **golden** *adjective*

goldfish

noun small fish often kept in aquariums or pools

Word building: The plural is **goldfish** or **goldfishes**.

goldmine

noun **1** a place where gold is mined **2** a source of something very useful: *My mother is a goldmine of information.*

Word building: **goldminer** *noun*   **goldmining** *noun*

golf

noun an outdoor game in which a small ball is hit with special clubs around a set course

Word building: **golf** *verb*   **golfer** *noun*

gondola   (*say* gon-duh-luh)

noun **1** a long narrow boat with high pointed ends, used on the canals of Venice in Italy **2** the basket beneath a balloon, for carrying passengers

Word building: **gondolier** *noun* the person who rows a gondola

gong

noun a bronze disc which is struck with a soft-headed stick to give a loud ringing sound

good

adjective **1** excellent or right
Other words: **fair, fine, satisfactory**
2 of fine quality
Other words: **precious, valuable**
3 well-behaved **4** helpful or useful: *a knife good for cutting* **5** enjoyable or pleasant: *a good holiday* **6** sufficient or ample: *a good supply*
Other words: **abundant, adequate, plentiful**
7 clever or skilful: *a good farmer*
Other words: **able, capable, proficient**
noun **8** advantage or benefit: *It's for your own good.* **9** excellent qualities or proper actions: *Look for good in others.*
Other words: **merit, virtue, worth**
10 goods, a possessions **b** products or articles that you can buy: *goods from a factory*
phrase **11 as good as,** almost: *I'm as good as finished.* **12 for good,** forever

Word building: Other adjective forms are **better, best.** | **goodness** *noun*

goodbye

interjection a word you use when you leave someone
Word history: a shortened form of 'God be with you'

google

verb to search for information on the internet, especially using Google search engine: *We googled to find out how to breed snails for cooking.*

goose

noun **1** a large bird with webbed feet and a long neck, sometimes kept on farms **2** a silly person: *Don't be a goose.*
Word use: The male is a **gander**, the female is a **goose** and the young is a **gosling**.
Word building: The plural is **geese**.

gooseberry   *(say* gooz*-buh-ree)*

noun a small, sour-tasting, round berry
Word building: The plural is **gooseberries**.

goose pimples

plural noun small lumps on your skin that appear when you are cold or frightened
Word use: Sometimes called **goose bumps** or **goose flesh**.

goosestep

noun an unusual marching step in which your legs are swung high while your knees are kept straight and stiff

gore[1]   *(say* gaw*)*

noun blood from a wound, especially when it has clotted
Word building: **gory** *adjective* (**gorier, goriest**)

gore[2]   *(say* gaw*)*

verb to pierce with horns or tusks: *The bull gored the matador.*

gorge   *(say* gawj*)*

noun **1** a narrow valley with steep rocky walls, often with a river running through it *verb* **2** to stuff by over-eating: *We gorged ourselves on the cake.*
Word history: from a French word meaning 'throat'

gorgeous

adjective very beautiful, especially in colouring: *a gorgeous sunset*
Word building: **gorgeously** *adverb* **gorgeousness** *noun*
Word history: from a French word meaning 'fashionable' or 'colourful'

gorilla

noun the largest kind of ape

gorilla/guerilla/griller Don't confuse **gorilla** with **guerilla** or **griller**.
A **guerilla** is a member of a small band of soldiers that makes surprise raids and attacks on the enemy. This may also be spelt **guerrilla**.
A **griller** is the part of a stove or kitchen appliance which cooks meat by direct heat.

gosling

noun a young goose
Word use: The female is a **goose** and the male is a **gander**.

gospel

noun **1** one of the first four books of the New Testament of the Christian bible: *the gospel of St Luke* **2** anything that is considered to be completely true
Word use: Definition 1 is often written **Gospel**.
Word building: **gospel** *adjective*: *a gospel story*

gossamer   *(say* gos*-uh-muh)*

noun **1** a fine cobweb lying on grass or bushes or floating in the air **2** any very fine material
Word building: **gossamer** *adjective*

gossip

noun **1** silly, and sometimes unkind, chatter about other people's business **2** someone who talks gossip
Word building: **gossip** *verb* **gossiper** *noun* **gossipy** *adjective*

gouge (*say* gowj)

noun **1** a sharp curved tool used for making grooves in wood **2** a hole made by this tool

Word building: **gouge** *verb*

goulash (*say* <u>gooh</u>-lash)

noun a meat stew containing onions and paprika

gourd (*say* gawd)

noun **1** the fruit of a climbing plant **2** the shell of this plant, dried and used as a bottle, bowl, or container

gourmet (*say* <u>gaw</u>-may)

noun someone who knows a lot about good food

Word history: from a French word meaning a 'wine merchant's man'

govern

verb to rule by laws

Word building: **governable** *adjective*

governess

noun a woman who teaches children in their own homes, usually because they live too far from a school

Word building: The plural is **governesses**.

government

noun **1** the group of people who rule or govern a country or state: *the Labor government | the government of Tasmania* **2** rule or control: *A country prospers under good government.*

Word building: **governmental** *adjective* **governmentally** *adverb*

governor

noun the representative of the king or queen in a state of the Commonwealth of Australia

Word building: **governorship** *noun*

governor-general

noun the main representative of the king or queen in Australia and some other British Commonwealth countries

Word building: The plural is **governor-generals** or **governors-general**.

gown

noun **1** a dress worn on important occasions **2** a loose, flowing garment worn by judges, lawyers, clergy and others

GPS (*say* jee pee <u>es</u>)

noun an invention which someone carries that uses information from satellites to tell the person exactly where they are

Word use: This is a short way of writing **global positioning system**.

grab

verb **1** to take suddenly
Other words: **clutch, snatch**
2 *Informal* to affect or impress: *How does that grab you?*

Word building: Other forms are **I grabbed, I have grabbed, I am grabbing.** | **grab** *noun* **grabber** *noun*

grace

noun **1** beauty of appearance or movement **2** favour or goodwill **3** a short prayer of thanks said before or after a meal

Word building: **graceful** *adjective* **gracefully** *adverb* **gracefulness** *noun*

gracious (*say* <u>gray</u>-shuhs)

adjective showing kindness and courtesy: *a gracious hostess | a gracious act*

Word building: **graciously** *adverb* **graciousness** *noun*

grade

noun **1** a stage or step on a scale of positions, quality or value: *What grade of clerk are you? | to sell eggs according to grade* **2** a class in a school arranged according to age and ability, in some states of Australia
verb **3** to arrange or sort according to grade **4** to make level and smooth: *to grade a road*

grader

noun **1** someone or something that sorts or groups: *a fruit grader* **2** a vehicle with a blade in front used for levelling roads

gradient

noun **1** the amount of slope or steepness in a road, railway or path **2** a sloping surface

gradual

adjective taking place little by little

Word building: **gradually** *adverb* **gradualness** *noun*

graduate   (*say* <u>graj</u>-ooh-uht)

noun **1** someone who has passed a course of study at a university or college

verb (*say* <u>graj</u>-ooh-ayt) **2** to receive a degree after passing such a course of study **3** to divide into regular divisions: *to graduate a thermometer*

Word building: **graduate** *adjective*   **graduation** *noun*

graffiti   (*say* gruh-<u>fee</u>-tee)

plural noun drawings or words written on walls in public places

Word use: You usually use a singular verb with **graffiti**: *Some graffiti is quite funny.*
Word building: The singular form is **graffito**.
Word history: from an Italian word meaning 'a scratch', which came from a Greek word meaning 'mark', 'draw', or 'write'

graft   (*say* grahft)

noun **1** part of a plant placed in a slit in another plant so that it is fed by the second plant and becomes part of it **2** a piece of living tissue cut by a doctor from one part of your body and placed somewhere else in your body: *a skin graft | a bone graft*

Word building: **graft** *verb*   **grafter** *noun* **grafting** *noun*

grain

noun **1** a small hard seed of one of the cereal plants: *wheat grain* **2** any small hard particle: *a grain of gold | a grain of sand* **3** a very small amount of something: *There might be a grain of truth in their story.* **4** the direction of the fibres in wood or cloth

Word building: **grainy** *adjective* (**grainier, grainiest**)   **granular** *adjective*   **granulate** *verb*

gram

noun one thousandth of a kilogram

grammar

noun **1** the parts of a language such as sounds and words, and the way they are combined into phrases and sentences **2** the description of this or a book containing such a description

Word building: **grammarian** *noun* **grammatical** *adjective*   **grammatically** *adverb*

gramophone

noun a machine that reproduces sound from a record

Word use: A more up-to-date word for this is **record-player**.

granary   (*say* <u>gran</u>-uh-ree)

noun a storehouse for grain

Word building: The plural is **granaries**.

grand

adjective **1** important-looking **2** noble or fine: *a grand old woman* **3** complete: *the grand total* **4** highest in importance

Word building: **grandeur** *noun*   **grandly** *adverb*   **grandness** *noun*

grandchild

noun the child of someone's daughter or son

Word building: The plural is **grandchildren**.

granddaughter

noun a daughter of someone's son or daughter

Word use: Another spelling is **grand-daughter**.

grandfather

noun the father of someone's father or mother

grandiose   (*say* <u>gran</u>-dee-ohs)

adjective too grand or splendid: *grandiose schemes*

Word building: **grandiosely** *adverb* **grandiosity** *noun*

grandmother

noun the mother of someone's father or mother

grandparent

noun a parent of one of your parents

grandson

noun a son of someone's son or daughter

grandstand

noun a building with seats rising in tiers, at a sports field or similar outdoor entertainment area

granite   (*say* <u>gran</u>-uht)

noun a hard rock used for carving monuments and for buildings

Word history: from a Latin word meaning 'grain'

grant

verb **1** to give or allow: *I grant you permission to leave early. | to grant land to the true owners* **2** to agree to: *to grant a request*

Word building: **grant** *noun*

grape

noun a small, round, green or purple fruit which grows in bunches on a vine and is used for eating or making wine

grapefruit

noun a large, round, yellow-skinned fruit with sour juicy flesh

graph (*say* graf, grahf)

noun a diagram which shows the relationship between two or more things by dots, lines or bars

Word building: **graph** *verb*

graph-

prefix a word part meaning 'writing': *graphics*

Word use: Another spelling is **grapho-**.
Word history: from Greek

graphic

adjective **1** vivid or true to life: *a graphic description* **2** having to do with the use of diagrams or graphs

Word building: **graphics** *noun* the art of drawing or producing patterns **graphically** *adverb*

graphic designer

noun a person who designs how the text and pictures will look on an advertisement or in a book or magazine

graphite (*say* graf-uyt)

noun a soft blackish form of carbon used in lead pencils

grapple

noun **1** a tool with one or more claws used for hooking or holding something
verb **2** to wrestle or struggle: *He grappled with the thief.* | *to grapple with a problem*

Word history: from an Old English word meaning 'seize'

grasp

verb **1** to seize and hold with your hands **2** to understand or take into your mind: *I grasped the meaning.*

Word building: **grasping** *adjective* greedy **grasp** *noun*

grass

noun **1** a plant which you can grow to make a lawn **2** any of a number of plants with long narrow leaves, including wheat, oats and bamboo **3** *Informal* another word for **marijuana**

Word building: **grassy** *adjective* (**grassier**, **grassiest**)

grasshopper

noun a type of plant-eating insect with large back legs for jumping

grate¹

noun **1** a frame of metal bars for holding wood or coal when burning in a fireplace **2** a frame of parallel or crossing bars used as a cover or guard: *a grate over a drain*

Word use: You can also use **grating** for definition 2.

grate/great Don't confuse **grate** with **great**, meaning 'large', as in *a great crowd of people*, or 'very good', as in *a really great film*.

grate²

verb **1** to rub together making a rough sound: *Chalk grates on the blackboard.* **2** to rub into small pieces against a surface with many sharp-edged openings: *to grate cheese* *phrase* **3 grate on**, to irritate or annoy

Word building: **grater** *noun* **grating** *adjective* **gratingly** *adverb*

grateful

adjective feeling thankful or showing thanks

Word building: **gratefully** *adverb* **gratefulness** *noun*

grave¹

noun a hole dug in the earth for burying a dead body

grave²

adjective **1** solemn or without humour: *a grave expression* **2** dangerous: *a grave situation* **3** important: *a grave decision*

Word use: The more usual word is **serious**.
Word building: **gravely** *adverb*

gravel

noun small stones mixed with sand

Word building: **gravelly** *adjective*
Word history: from a French word meaning 'little sandy shore'

gravity

noun **1** the force that attracts or causes everything to fall towards the centre of the earth **2** seriousness or solemnity: *the gravity of the occasion*

Word history: from a Latin word meaning 'heaviness'

gravy (*say* gray-vee)

noun a sauce made from the juices that drip from meat during cooking, mixed with flour and water

graze[1]

verb to feed on growing grass

graze[2]

verb **1** to touch lightly in passing
2 to scratch the skin of: *I fell and grazed my knee.*

Word building: **graze** *noun*

grazier

noun a farmer who usually has a large area of land on which cattle or sheep graze

grease   (*say* grees)

noun **1** melted animal fat **2** any fatty or oily substance **3** a substance used to keep machinery running smoothly
verb (*say* greez) **4** to put grease on

Word building: **greasy** *adjective* (**greasier, greasiest**)   **greasily** *adverb*   **greasiness** *noun*

great

adjective **1** large: *a great wave of water | a great crowd of people*
Other words: **colossal, enormous, gigantic, huge, immense, tremendous**
2 unusual or extreme: *You showed great strength in being able to do that.*
Other words: **exceptional, extraordinary, remarkable**
3 notable or important: *a great composer*
Other words: **celebrated, distinguished, eminent, famous, illustrious, prominent, remarkable, outstanding, venerable**
4 *Informal* very good or fine: *We had a great time.*
Other words: **enjoyable, excellent, fantastic, marvellous, terrific, wonderful**

Word building: **greatly** *adverb*   **greatness** *noun*

great/grate Don't confuse **great** with **grate**, which has several meanings. Look up **grate**.

greed

noun great or unreasonable desire for food or money

Word building: **greedy** *adjective* (**greedier, greediest**)   **greedily** *adverb*   **greediness** *noun*

green

adjective **1** of the colour of growing leaves **2** not ripe: *a green plum* **3** *Informal* jealous **4** having or showing a concern for environmental issues
noun **5** a green colour **6** the part of a golf course surrounding a hole **7** the smooth level lawn on which bowls is played **8 greens**, green vegetables

Word building: **green** *verb* to become or make green   **greenery** *noun* green plants   **greenness** *noun*

greengrocer

noun someone who sells fresh vegetables and fruit

greenhouse

noun a building used for growing plants, which is made mainly of glass so that it will store the sun's heat

greenhouse effect

noun the warming in the temperature of the earth caused by the atmosphere around the earth acting like the glass of a greenhouse and trapping heat, this warming becoming greater as more carbon gases build up in the atmosphere

greenhouse gas

noun a gas that contributes to the greenhouse effect

greenie

noun *Informal* someone who believes that the environment should be conserved, that our food should be produced without chemicals, and that we should live more simply

Word building: **greenie** *adjective*: *Everything is recycled in a greenie household.*

greet

verb to welcome or receive, usually with friendly words

greeting

noun **1** the act or words of someone who greets **2 greetings**, a friendly message: *to send greetings*

gregarious   (*say* gruh-**gair**-ree-uhs)

adjective fond of the company of other people

Word use: The more usual word is **sociable**.
Word building: **gregariously** *adverb*   **gregariousness** *noun*

gremlin

noun something that causes mischief or trouble: *a gremlin in the engine*

grenade   (*say* gruh-**nayd**)

noun a small bomb thrown by hand or fired from a rifle

Word history: from a Spanish word meaning 'pomegranate'

grevillea   (*say* gruh-<u>vil</u>-ee-uh)
noun any of a number of types of
Australian shrubs or trees, many of which
have spiky bright-coloured flowers
Word history: from the name of a Scottish
botanist, CF *Greville*, who died in 1809

grey
adjective **1** of a colour between black and
white **2** dark and overcast: *a grey day*
Word building: **grey** *noun*   **grey** *verb*

greyhound
noun a type of tall slender dog used for
racing

greywater
noun water that has been used in houses
and industry which can be used again for
things like watering gardens

grid
noun **1** a grating of crossed bars **2** a
network of cables and pipes supplying
electricity, gas or water **3** a network of
crossed lines on a map

griddle
noun a flat heavy pan for cooking on top of
the stove
Word building: **griddle** *verb*

grief   (*say* greef)
noun deep suffering in your mind because
of sorrow or loss
Other words: **grieving, lamentation, mourning**
Word building: **grievous** *adjective* causing grief
or sorrow

grievance
noun a feeling of anger or annoyance
caused by something unfair that has
happened

grieve   (*say* greev)
verb to feel or cause to feel grief: *I grieved
when my aunt died.* | *Your unkindness grieves
me.*
Word use: The more usual word is **sadden**.

grill
noun **1** a meal, mainly of meat, which has
been grilled **2** a griller
verb **3** to cook under or in a griller
4 *Informal* to question harshly and closely

grille   (*say* gril)
noun a screen of metal bars, sometimes
ornamental, for a window, gate, or the
front of a motor car

griller
noun the part of a stove or kitchen
appliance for cooking meat by direct heat

griller/gorilla/guerilla Don't confuse
griller with **gorilla** or **guerilla**.
A **gorilla** is the largest kind of ape.
A **guerilla** is a member of a small band of
soldiers that makes surprise raids and attacks
on the enemy. This may also be spelt **guerrilla**.

grim
adjective **1** having a fierce or forbidding
appearance **2** causing fear or disgust: *the
grim facts of war*
Word building: Other forms are **grimmer,
grimmest.** | **grimly** *adverb*   **grimness** *noun*

grimace   (*say* <u>grim</u>-uhs)
noun an unnatural or twisted look on your
face showing fear, hatred and other such
emotions
Word building: **grimace** *verb*
Word history: from a Spanish word meaning
'panic'

grime
noun dirt or filth, especially on a surface:
the grime on the walls
Word building: **grimy** *adjective* (**grimier,
grimiest**)   **grimily** *adverb*   **griminess** *noun*

grin
verb **1** to smile broadly
phrase **2 grin and bear it,** *Informal* to
suffer without complaining
Word building: Other verb forms are **I grinned,
I have grinned, I am grinning.** | **grin** *noun*

grind
verb **1** to crush into fine particles: *to grind
wheat* **2** to produce by grinding: *to grind
flour* **3** to grate together: *to grind your
teeth* **4** to smooth, shape or sharpen by
rubbing with a tool: *to grind a lens* | *to grind
an axe*
noun **5** *Informal* hard or boring work
Word building: Other verb forms are
I ground, I have ground, I am grinding. |
grinder *noun*

grip

noun **1** a firm hold **2** control: *John is in the grip of his emotions.*
verb **3** to grasp or seize firmly **4** to hold the interest of: *Your stories always grip us.*

Word building: Other verb forms are **I gripped, I have gripped, I am gripping.**

gripe

verb *Informal* to complain or grumble

Word building: **gripe** *noun*

grisly   (*say* griz-lee)

adjective horrible or frightening: *a grisly murder*

Word building: Other forms are **grislier, grisliest.** | **grisliness** *noun*

gristle   (*say* gris-uhl)

noun a firm elastic tissue in animals or humans
Other words: **cartilage**

Word building: **gristly** *adjective*

grit

noun **1** fine, hard, stony particles **2** strength of character or courage: *Carolyn showed a lot of grit in overcoming the injuries.*
verb **3** to clamp tightly: *to grit your teeth*

Word building: Other verb forms are **I gritted, I have gritted, I am gritting.** | **gritty** *adjective* (**grittier, grittiest**)   **grittiness** *noun*

grizzle

verb to whimper or whine

grizzled   (*say* griz-uhld)

adjective grey-haired or grey: *He's getting grizzled at the temples.*

Word building: **grizzle** *verb*   **grizzly** *adjective*

groan

noun **1** a low sad sound, usually expressing pain or sorrow
Other words: **moan**
verb **2** to utter a groan
Other words: **moan**

grocer

noun a shopkeeper who sells flour, tea, canned and other foods, as well as other household goods

Word use: This word is going out of use in Australia, except in the term **greengrocer.** This is probably because other types of shops, such as supermarkets, are now common.
Word building: **grocery** *noun*

groceries

plural noun food and other household goods bought at a shop or supermarket

Word use: **Groceries** used to be sold at a **grocer's** shop but now you usually buy them at a supermarket.

grog

noun *Informal* alcoholic drink, particularly when cheap and of poor quality

groggy

adjective staggering from tiredness, injury, or too much alcoholic drink

Word building: Other forms are **groggier, groggiest.** | **groggily** *adverb*   **grogginess** *noun*

groin   (*say* groyn)

noun the hollow where your thigh joins your abdomen

grommet   (*say* grom-uht)

noun a small tube put into the ear by a doctor to prevent ear infections: *I can't swim today because I have a grommet in my ear.*

groom

noun **1** someone who looks after horses **2** another word for **bridegroom**
verb **3** to brush, comb and generally keep clean and neat in appearance: *to groom a horse | to groom yourself*

groomsman

noun a man who accompanies a bridegroom at his wedding

Word building: The plural is **groomsmen.**

groove

noun **1** a long narrow cut made by a tool: *a groove in wood* **2** the track in a gramophone record in which the needle moves

Word building: **groove** *verb*

groovy

adjective Informal exciting or satisfying

grope

verb **1** to feel about with your hands **2** to search uncertainly: *I groped for an answer.*

Word building: **gropingly** *adverb*

groper

noun a large fish found in warm seas

gross (*say* grohs)

adjective **1** whole or total, without anything having been taken out: *gross income* **2** very bad or shocking: *gross injustice*
noun **3** twelve dozen or 144
verb **4** to earn a total of: *The company grossed ten million dollars last year.*

Word building: The plural form of the noun is **gross.** | **grossly** *adverb* **grossness** *noun*

grotesque (*say* groh-<u>tesk</u>)

adjective odd or unnatural in shape, form or appearance: *the grotesque figures in a nightmare*

Word building: **grotesquely** *adverb* **grotesqueness** *noun*

grotto

noun a cave

Word building: The plural is **grottoes** or **grottos.**

grotty

Informal
adjective **1** dirty **2** useless

Word building: Other forms are **grottier, grottiest.**

grouch

verb Informal to be sulky or bad-tempered

Word building: **grouchy** *adjective* (**grouchier, grouchiest**) **grouch** *noun* **grouchiness** *noun*

ground

noun **1** firm or dry land: *high ground* **2** earth or soil: *stony ground* **3** the land surrounding a building or group of buildings: *school ground* | *hospital grounds* **4** basis or reason: *He has no ground for complaint.*
verb **5** to run on to the shore: *The boat grounded in the storm.* **6** to stop from flying: *to ground a pilot*
phrase **7 gain ground**, to make progress **8 stand your ground**, to keep to your opinion

group

noun **1** a number of people or things gathered together and thought of as being connected in some way **2** a number of musicians who play together: *a pop group*

Word building: **group** *verb* **grouping** *noun*

grouse (*rhymes with* house)

verb to grumble or complain

Word use: This is more suited to everday language.
Word building: **grouse** *noun*

grout (*say* growt)

noun a thin coarse cement poured into the joint between tiles and brickwork

Word building: **grout** *verb*

grove

noun a small group of trees

grovel (*say* <u>grov</u>-uhl)

verb **1** to humble yourself in an undignified way **2** to lie or crawl face down, especially in fear

Word building: Other forms are **I grovelled, I have grovelled, I am grovelling.**

grow

verb **1** to increase in size
Other words: **enlarge, expand, multiply**
2 to develop: *These plants are growing well.*
Other words: **bloom**
3 to become gradually: *to grow older* | *to grow richer* **4** to cause to grow: *I grow roses.*

Word building: Other forms are **I grew, I have grown, I am growing.** | **growth** *noun*

growl

verb **1** to make a deep angry sound **2** to complain or grumble angrily

Word building: **growl** *noun*

grown-up

noun someone who is fully grown or mature

grub

noun **1** the young or larva of some insects **2** *Informal* a person, especially a child, covered with dirt: *You little grub!* **3** *Informal* food

Word building: **grub** *verb* (**grubbed, grubbing**)
Word history: from a Middle English word meaning 'dig'

grubby

adjective dirty or untidy: *Your shirt and hands are grubby — please clean up before dinner.*

Word building: Other forms are **grubbier, grubbiest.**

grudge

noun a feeling of anger caused by someone hurting or insulting you: *to bear a grudge*

Word building: **grudge** *verb* **grudgingly** *adverb*

gruel (*say* grooh-uhl)

noun a thin mixture of cereal, usually oatmeal, cooked in water or milk

gruelling (*say* grooh-uh-ling)

adjective very tiring: *a gruelling race*

Word use: The more usual word is **exhausting**.

gruesome

adjective causing feelings of horror: *a gruesome story*

gruff

adjective **1** hoarse or low and harsh **2** rough or unfriendly: *He had a gruff, cranky manner.*

Word building: **gruffly** *adverb* **gruffness** *noun*

grumble

verb to complain crankily

Word building: **grumble** *noun* **grumbler** *noun* **grumblingly** *adverb*

grumpy

adjective bad-tempered

Word building: Other forms are **grumpier**, **grumpiest**. | **grumpily** *adverb* **grumpiness** *noun*

grunt

verb **1** to make a deep sound like a pig *noun* **2** the sound of grunting

guacamole (*say* gwok-uh-moh-lee)

noun a dip made of mashed avocado with lemon or lime juice, and sometimes sour cream and mayonnaise

guarantee (*say* ga-ruhn-tee)

noun **1** a promise to replace or repair something if it is faulty: *My new television set has a guarantee for the next four years.* **2** a promise: *Wealth is no guarantee of happiness.*
verb **3** to give a promise or guarantee

Word building: **guarantor** *noun* someone who makes or gives a guarantee

guard (*say* gahd)

verb **1** to protect or keep safe from harm

Other words: **defend**
2 to keep from escaping **3** to keep in control: *to guard your tongue* **4** to make safe: *The pool fence guards the pool.*
noun **5** someone who protects or keeps watch
Other words: **guardian, protector**
6 a careful watch: *That prisoner should be kept under close guard.* **7** something that guards from harm or injury
Other words: **defence, protection, safeguard, shield**

Word building: **guarded** *adjective* careful **guardedly** *adverb* **guardedness** *noun*

guardian

noun **1** someone who guards, protects or takes care of someone or something **2** someone who is appointed by law to take care of another person and their property
adjective **3** guarding or protecting: *a guardian angel*

Word building: **guardianship** *noun*

guava (*say* gwah-vuh)

noun an American tree or shrub with a fruit used for making jam and jelly

guerilla (*say* guh-ril-uh)

noun a member of a small band of soldiers which continually annoys the enemy by surprise raids and attacks

Word use: Another spelling is **guerrilla**.
Word building: **guerilla** *adjective*: *guerilla warfare*
Word history: from the Spanish word for 'war'

guerilla/gorilla/griller Don't confuse **guerilla** with **gorilla** or **griller**.
A **gorilla** is the largest kind of ape.
A **griller** is the part of a stove or kitchen appliance which cooks meat by direct heat.

guess (*say* ges)

verb **1** to give an answer when you don't really know **2** to think or believe: *I guess I can get there in time.*
noun **3** a judgement or opinion formed without really knowing

guest (*say* gest)

noun **1** a visitor or someone who is entertained at your house **2** someone well-known who visits and performs at a club or show **3** someone who stays at a hotel or motel

Word building: **guest** *adjective*: *a guest artist*

guffaw (*say* gu-<u>faw</u>)
noun **1** a noisy laugh
verb **2** to laugh loudly and noisily

guidance
noun advice, guiding, or leadership

guide (*say* guyd)
verb **1** to show the way
noun **2** someone who guides, often for money **3** a book with information for travellers or tourists **4** a member of an international youth movement for girls which organises activities which promote outdoor adventure, community service and care for the environment
Word use: Definition 4 is sometimes spelt with a capital letter.

guide dog
noun a dog specially trained to lead or guide a vision-impaired person

guild (*say* gild)
noun an organisation or society of people who have similar jobs or interests

guile (*say* guyl)
noun cleverness in the way you deceive somebody
Word use: The more usual word is **cunning**.
Word building: **guileful** *adjective* clever and deceitful **guileless** *adjective* frank or honest

guillotine (*say* gil-uh-teen)
noun **1** a machine with a heavy blade that falls between two grooved posts and is used for cutting off someone's head **2** a machine with a long blade used for trimming paper
Word building: **guillotine** *verb*
Word history: named after the French doctor, JI *Guillotin*, who wanted it to be used in France

guilt (*say* gilt)
noun **1** the position of having committed a crime or being wrong: *The thief's guilt was proved by the court.* **2** a feeling that something is your fault: *I share the guilt in this matter.*
Word building: **guilty** *adjective* (**guiltier, guiltiest**) **guiltily** *adverb* **guiltiness** *noun*

guilt/gilt Don't confuse **guilt** with **gilt**, which is the gold or other material used to decorate precious objects like vases.

guinea pig (*say* <u>gin</u>-ee pig)
noun **1** a short-eared short-tailed animal kept as a pet and also used for scientific experiments **2** someone used in experiments: *The children were used as guinea pigs to test the new soft drink.*

guise (*say* guyz)
noun the outside appearance, usually only pretended, of someone or something: *The robber walked into the bank in the guise of a clergyman.*

guitar (*say* guh-<u>tah</u>)
noun a violin-shaped musical instrument with a long neck and strings which you pluck
Word building: **guitarist** *noun* someone who plays the guitar

gulf
noun **1** a part of an ocean which is partly bounded by land **2** a deep hollow or split in the earth **3** any wide separation: *The gulf between the two boys widened after the fight.*

gull
noun another word for **seagull**

gullet
noun the tube-like part of your body by which the food and drink you swallow pass to your stomach

gullible
adjective easily deceived or cheated
Word building: **gullibly** *adverb* **gullibility** *noun*

gully
noun **1** a small valley cut out of the earth by running water **2** a ditch or a gutter
Word building: The plural is **gullies**.

gulp
verb **1** to swallow quickly: *to gulp water | to gulp with fear*
noun **2** an amount swallowed at one time

gum[1]
noun **1** a sticky liquid which oozes from plants or trees **2** a tree or shrub which gives out this liquid, especially a eucalyptus tree **3** a sticky flavoured sweet for chewing **4** a glue
verb **5** to cover or stick together with gum
Word use: Another name for definition 3 is **chewing gum**.
Word building: Other verb forms are **I gummed, I have gummed, I am gumming. | gummy** *adjective*

gum²

noun the firm flesh around the bottom of your teeth

Word use: Often used as a plural **gums**.

gumboot

noun a rubber boot sometimes reaching to your knee or thigh

gun

noun **1** a weapon with a long metal tube for firing bullets or other ammunition **2** anything which is similar to a gun in its shape or in the way it is used: *a spray gun for paint*
verb **3** to shoot: *The thief gunned down the policeman.*

Word building: Other verb forms are **I gunned, I have gunned, I am gunning.** | **gunsmith** *noun* someone who makes or repairs guns

gunpowder

noun a mixture of chemical powders that explodes when set off by a gun or by fire

gunwale   (*say* gun-uhl)

noun the upper edge of the side of a ship or boat

Word use: Another spelling is **gunnel**.

gunyah   (*say* gun-yuh)

noun an Aboriginal hut or temporary shelter made from tree branches and bark

Word use: Another spelling is **gunya**. | Another word is **humpy**.
Word history: from an Aboriginal language of New South Wales called Dharug. See the map of Australian Aboriginal languages at the end of this book.

guppy

noun a small brightly coloured fish which is often kept in home aquariums

Word building: The plural is **guppies**.
Word history: named after a Trinidad clergyman, RJL *Guppy*, who sent the first recorded specimen to the British Museum

gurgle

verb **1** to flow with a noisy bubbling sound **2** to make or imitate this sound

Word building: **gurgle** *noun*   **gurglingly** *adverb*

guru   (*say* gooh-rooh)

noun a wise and powerful teacher

gush

verb **1** to flow suddenly in large amounts: *The sea gushed through the hole the torpedo had made.* **2** to have a large sudden flow of something: *The wound gushed blood.* | *Her eyes gushed tears.* **3** *Informal* to express yourself in a rush of emotional talk

Word building: **gush** *noun*   **gusher** *noun*   **gushingly** *adverb*   **gushy** *adjective*

gust

noun a sudden strong blast or rush: *a gust of wind*

Word building: **gusty** *adjective* (**gustier, gustiest**)   **gustily** *adverb*   **gustiness** *noun*

gusto

noun hearty enjoyment

Word use: The more usual word is **enthusiasm**.

gut

noun **1** another word for **intestine** **2** the tough string made from the gut of an animal and used for things like violin strings or tennis racquet strings **3 guts**, *Informal* **a** your stomach **b** courage **c** most important part or contents: *the guts of the motor*
verb **4** to take out the guts of something **5** to destroy the inside of something: *Fire gutted the inside of the building.*

Word building: Other verb forms are **I gutted, I have gutted, I am gutting.** | **gut** *adjective*: *a gut response*   **gutless** *adjective* cowardly   **gutsy** *adjective* full of courage

gutter

noun **1** a channel, usually along the side of a street, for carrying away water **2** a channel along the eaves or roof of a building for carrying off rainwater

Word use: Another word for definition 2 is **guttering**.

guttural   (*say* gut-uh-ruhl)

adjective **1** having to do with your throat **2** harsh and throaty

guy¹

Informal
noun **1** a man or a boy **2** any person

Word history: from *Guy* Fawkes, the leader of the Gunpowder Plot to blow up the British Houses of Parliament

guy²

noun a rope or wire attached to something to guide, steady or secure it

guzzle

verb to eat or drink noisily and greedily

Word building: **guzzler** *noun* someone who guzzles

gym   (*say* jim)

noun **1** a centre providing fitness equipment and classes **2** short for **gymnasium 3** short for **gymnastics**

Word building: **gymnast** *noun*

gymkhana   (*say* jim-<u>kah</u>-nuh)

noun horse-riding events with games and contests

Word history: from a Hindustani word meaning 'ball house' or 'racquet-court'

gymnasium   (*say* jim-<u>nay</u>-zee-uhm)

noun a building or room specially equipped for gymnastics and sport

Word use: The short form of this is **gym**.
Word building: The plural is **gymnasiums** or **gymnasia**.
Word history: from a Greek word meaning 'naked' (in ancient times athletes were naked when they trained)

gymnast   (*say* <u>jim</u>-nuhst)

noun someone especially trained and skilled in gymnastics

gymnastic   (*say* jim-<u>nas</u>-tik)

adjective having to do with physical exercises which develop your muscle strength and tone up your body

gymnastics   (*say* jim-<u>nas</u>-tiks)

noun the performance of gymnastic exercises

Word use: The short form of this is **gym**.

gyn-

prefix a word part meaning 'woman' or 'female': *gynaecology*

Word use: Another spelling is **gyno-**.
Word history: from Greek

gynaecology   (*say* guy-nuh-<u>kol</u>-uh-jee)

noun the type of medical practice that is concerned with diseases that affect only women

Word use: Another spelling is **gynecology**.
Word building: **gynaecological** *adjective*
gynaecologist *noun*

gypsy   (*say* <u>jip</u>-see)

noun someone who belongs to a group of people, once from India but now found mainly in Europe, who do not live in any one place but travel about

Word use: Another spelling is **gipsy**.
Word building: The plural is **gypsies**.
Word history: from a form of the word *Egyptian*

gyrate   (*say* juy-<u>rayt</u>)

verb to whirl or move in a circle

Word use: The more usual word is **rotate**.
Word building: **gyration** *noun*

gyro-

prefix a word part meaning 'ring', 'circle', or 'spiral': *gyroscope*

Word history: from Greek

gyroscope   (*say* <u>juy</u>-ruh-skohp)

noun a rotating wheel inside a frame which lets the wheel's axis keep its original direction even though the frame is moved around, used to help make such instruments as stabilisers in ships

Word building: **gyroscopic** *adjective*

Hh

habit

noun **1** a certain usual way of behaving: *It is a habit of mine to read in bed.* **2** the dress of someone in a religious order, like a nun or a monk

Word building: **habitual** *adjective* **habitually** *adverb*

habitat

noun the place where a plant or animal naturally lives or grows

habitation

noun a home or a place of living

Word building: **habitable** *adjective*

hack¹

verb **1** to cut or chop with rough heavy blows
noun **2** a rough cut or gash

hack²

noun **1** an old or worn-out horse **2** a riding horse kept for hire or ordinary riding **3** someone who does poor quality writing for a living
verb **4** *Informal* to put up with

Word building: **hack** *adjective*

hackles

plural noun the hair on the back of a dog's neck

haemo-

prefix a word part meaning 'blood': *haemorrhage*

Word use: Other spellings are **haem-** and **hemo-**.
Word history: from Greek

haemophilia   (*say* hee-muh-<u>fil</u>-ee-uh)

noun a disease which makes you bleed for a long time if you cut yourself

Word use: Another spelling is **hemophilia**.
Word building: **haemophiliac** *noun*

haemorrhage   (*say* <u>hem</u>-uh-rij)

noun a sudden flow of blood like one from a burst blood vessel

Word use: Another spelling is **hemorrhage**.
Word building: **haemorrhage** *verb*
Word history: from a Greek word meaning 'a violent bleeding'

hag

noun an ugly old woman

Word use: This word will offend people.

haggard   (*say* <u>hag</u>-uhd)

adjective looking worn out from hunger, sickness or worry

haggle

verb to bargain or argue about the price of something

haiku   (*say* <u>huy</u>-kooh)

noun a Japanese form of poem which has three lines

hail¹

verb **1** to greet or welcome **2** to attract attention by calling out: *to hail a taxi*
noun **3** a shout or call to attract attention

hail²

noun **1** a shower of small balls of ice from the clouds, like frozen rain **2** a shower of anything hard: *a hail of bullets*
verb **3** to pour down hail or to fall like hail

hair

noun **1** a fine threadlike growth from the skin of people and animals: *A single hair found at the crime scene provided the DNA of the killer.* **2** the mass of these which cover the human head or the body of an animal: *Please get your hair cut.*

hair/hare Don't confuse **hair** with **hare**, which is a rabbit-like animal.

hairdresser   (*say* hair-dress-er)

noun someone whose job it is to wash hair, cut it, and sometimes arrange it in a special way

hairy

adjective **1** covered with hair **2** *Informal* difficult: *a hairy problem* **3** *Informal* frightening: *a hairy drive*

Word building: Other forms are **hairier**, **hairiest**.

haj   (*say* hahj)

noun the pilgrimage to Mecca which every Muslim is supposed to make at least once

Word use: Other spellings are **hadj** or **hajj**.

hakea   (*say* hay-kee-uh)

noun a type of Australian shrub or tree that has hard woody fruit

halal   (*say* hal-al)

adjective having to do with meat from animals that have been killed according to the special food rules of Islamic religious practice: *halal meat | halal butcher*

Word history: from an Arabic word meaning 'lawful'

half   (*say* hahf)

noun **1** one of two equal parts into which anything can be divided
adjective **2** being about half the full amount: *half speed*
adverb **3** in part or partly: *The house was only half built.*

Word building: The plural form of the noun is **halves**.

half-brother

noun a brother who is related to you through one parent only

half-hearted

adjective having not much interest or willingness: *I made a half-hearted attempt to join in.*

half-sister

noun a sister who is related to you through one parent only

halfway

adverb **1** with half the distance covered: *He stopped halfway for a rest.* **2** to or at half the distance: *My belt only reaches halfway around Dad.*
adjective **3** in the middle, between two places or points: *The river is the halfway point between the two towns.*

hall

noun **1** a corridor or passage inside the front door of a house, from which you can get to the other rooms **2** a large building or room used for such things as public meetings or dances

hall/haul Don't confuse **hall** with **haul**. To **haul** something is to drag it along. A **haul** is something you grab or drag in:
We went fishing and got a good haul of whiting.

hallelujah   (*say* hal-uh-looh-yuh)

interjection a cry which expresses praise to God

Word history: a Hebrew word meaning 'praise ye Jehovah'

Halloween   (*say* hal-o-ween)

noun the night of 31 October, when children dress up in costumes and ask people for treats. If they don't get a treat, then they play a trick.

hallucination

(*say* huh-looh-suh-nay-shuhn)
noun something which someone imagines they have seen or heard: *Some drugs can make you have hallucinations.*
Other words: **delusion, fantasy, illusion**

Word building: **hallucinate** *verb*

halo   (*say* hay-loh)

noun **1** a ring of light surrounding the head of a holy person in paintings of saints or angels **2** a circle of light seen around the sun or moon

Word building: The plural is **haloes** or **halos**.

haloumi   (*say* huh-looh-mee)

noun a soft, firm cheese from Greece, which has been preserved by being soaked in salted water

Word use: Another spelling is **halloumi**.

halt

verb to stop

Word building: **halt** *noun*

halter

noun a rope or a strap for leading or tying horses or cattle

halve   (*say* hahv)

verb **1** to divide in halves: *Dad halved the apple for the two of us.* **2** to cut down or reduce to half

ham

noun **1** salted or smoked meat from the upper part of a pig's leg **2** *Informal* an actor who overacts **3** *Informal* someone whose hobby is sending and receiving radio messages around the world
verb **4** to overact or act in an exaggerated way

Word building: Other verb forms are **I hammed, I have hammed, I am hamming.**

hamburger

noun a bread roll containing a round, flat piece of fried minced beef, and often other things like lettuce and tomato

Word history: named after *Hamburg*, a town in Germany

hamlet

noun a very small village

hammer

noun **1** a tool with a heavy metal head and a handle, used for banging nails into wood and for beating things **2** anything shaped or used like a hammer
verb **3** to hit or work with a hammer **4** to hit with force, or to pound: *She hammered the table with her fist.*

hammock

noun a hanging bed made of canvas or netlike material

hamper[1]

verb to hold back or hinder: *Her heavy shoes hampered her swimming.*

hamper[2]

noun **1** a large cane basket, sometimes with a cover **2** such a basket filled with food, and so on, and given as a gift

hamster

noun a small short-tailed animal belonging to the rat family, which looks like a guinea pig

hand

noun **1** the end part of your arm below your wrist, used for touching and holding things **2** something like a hand: *the hands of a clock* **3** a worker or labourer: *On Friday nights I work as a kitchen hand.* **4** help or cooperation: *Give me a hand.* **5** a side or a point in an argument: *on the other hand* **6** a unit of measurement, about 10 centimetres, for giving the height of horses: *This horse is sixteen hands.* **7** a burst of clapping or applause for a performer: *Give them a big hand.* **8 hands,** power or control: *Your fate is in my hands.*
verb **9** to deliver or pass with your hand: *Hand me the jam please.*
phrase **10 at hand,** near or ready **11 in hand,** under control **12 old hand,** an experienced person

handbag

noun a small bag which can be carried in your hand, used for holding money and small articles

handcuff

noun one of a pair of connected steel rings or bracelets put around someone's wrists to stop them using their hands

Word building: **handcuff** *verb*

handicap

noun **1** a physical disability **2** any disadvantage that makes success harder **3** a race or contest in which the better competitors are given a disadvantage, such as a greater distance to run **4** the disadvantage given to these competitors, such as the extra distance: *Last year's winner was given a handicap of three metres.*

Word building: **handicap** *verb* (**handicapped, handicapping**) **handicapped** *adjective* disabled or crippled

handicraft

noun an occupation or art in which you use your hands: *Pottery and weaving are handicrafts.*

handkerchief   (*say* hang-kuh-cheef)

noun a small, usually square piece of cloth used for wiping your nose

handle

noun **1** a part of something, used to hold it by or open it with: *the handle of a knife | a door handle*
verb **2** to touch or feel with your hand **3** to use: *You handle a paintbrush with skill.* **4** to manage or control: *The guide cannot handle more than eight people in each tour.*

handlebars

plural noun the curved bar at the front of a bike that you steer it with

handsome

adjective **1** good-looking
Other words: **attractive**
2 large or generous: *a handsome gift*
Other words: **considerable, liberal, sizeable, substantial**
Word use: Definition 1 is used mostly of men.
Word building: **handsomely** *adverb* **handsomeness** *noun*

handwriting

noun writing done with your hand, especially your own style of writing: *very neat handwriting*
Word building: **handwritten** *adjective*

handy

adjective **1** close at hand: *Is the glue handy?* **2** skilful with your hands **3** useful or convenient: *a handy tool*
Word building: Other forms are **handier, handiest.** | **handily** *adverb* **handiness** *noun*

hang

verb **1** to fix or be fixed at the top but not at the bottom: *Hang the picture on that hook. | The vine is hanging from the top of the fence.* **2** to put to death by dropping with a rope around the neck **3** to bend downwards: *I hung my head in shame.*
phrase **4 hang around**, to spend time, sometimes with nothing to do **5 hang on**, to wait **6 hang up**, to break off a phone conversation
Word use: **I hung, I have hung, I am hanging,** except for definition 2, where you have to say **hanged** instead of **hung**

hangar

noun a large shed that planes are kept in

hang-glider

noun a large type of kite which you hang on to and guide as you glide through the air

Word building: **hang-glide** *verb* **hang-gliding** *noun*

hangover

Informal
noun **1** the feeling of sickness and headache that you get after drinking too much alcohol **2** something remaining or left over

hang-up

noun Informal something which worries you and which you can't get off your mind

Hanukkah *(say* <u>han</u>-ooh-kah*)*

noun a Jewish festival known as the Feast of the Dedication, lasting eight days

haphazard *(say* hap-<u>haz</u>-uhd*)*

adjective not planned, or happening by chance: *a haphazard remark*
Word building: **haphazardly** *adverb*

happen

verb **1** to take place or occur, sometimes by chance **2** to have the luck or the occasion: *I happened to see you just in time.*

happy

adjective **1** delighted, pleased or glad about something
Other words: **cheerful, ecstatic, joyful, thrilled**
2 fortunate or lucky: *a happy coincidence*
Word building: Other forms are **happier, happiest.** | **happily** *adverb* **happiness** *noun*

harangue *(say* huh-<u>rang</u>*)*

noun a long, noisy and scolding speech
Word building: **harangue** *verb*

harass *(say* <u>ha</u>-ruhs, huh-<u>ras</u>*)*

verb **1** to trouble by attacking or raiding again and again: *The enemy harassed the small towns regularly.* **2** to continually annoy or worry
Word building: **harassment** *noun*
Word history: from a French word meaning 'set a dog on'

harbour *(say* <u>hah</u>-buh*)*

noun **1** a sheltered part of the sea, deep enough for ships to be protected from wind and waves
verb **2** to give shelter to
Word use: Another spelling is **harbor**.

hard

adjective **1** solid and firm to the touch:
Rocks and wood are hard.
Other words: **rigid, stiff, tough**
2 difficult to do or explain: *a hard problem*
Other words: **awkward, complex,
complicated, tricky**
3 needing much effort or energy: *hard work*
Other words: **demanding, exhausting,
taxing, tiring**
4 (of water) containing salts from minerals
which make it difficult for soap to lather
adverb **5** with a lot of effort or energy: *to
work hard*
Other words: **energetically, forcefully,
intently, strongly**
phrase **6 hard up,** *Informal* urgently in
need of something, especially money
Other words: **broke** (*Informal*), **penniless, poor**

Word building: **hardness** *noun*

hard disk

noun a computer disk that is built into the
computer and is not easily removed

Word use: Compare this with **floppy disk.**

hard drive

noun a computer disk drive for a hard disk

harden

verb **1** to make or become hard or harder:
*The cold air hardened the wax. | The glue
slowly hardened.* **2** to make or become
unfeeling or unkind: *I hardened my heart
against the poor animal. | Joan's feelings
hardened when she saw the evidence.*

hardly

adverb **1** almost not at all: *The fog was so
thick, we could hardly see.* **2** probably not:
He would hardly come now, would he?

hardship

noun unpleasantness or suffering in the way
you live: *Being poor involves much hardship.*

hardware

noun **1** building materials or tools **2** the
mechanical parts of a computer

Word use: The opposite of definition 2 is
software.

hardy

adjective able to stand up to hard or severe
treatment or conditions

Word building: Other forms are **hardier,
hardiest. | hardily** *adverb* **hardiness** *noun*

hare

noun a rabbit-like animal with long ears
and long back legs

hare/hair Don't confuse **hare** with **hair. Hair**
is what grows on your head.

harebrained

adjective reckless or without sense

harm

noun damage or hurt

Word building: **harm** *verb* **harmful**
adjective **harmfully** *adverb* **harmless**
adjective **harmlessly** *adverb*

harmonica   (*say* hah-<u>mon</u>-ik-uh)

noun a small wind instrument with metal
reeds, which you play by blowing

Word use: Another name for this is **mouth
organ.**

harmony

noun **1** agreement in feelings, actions or
ideas **2** a pleasing combination of musical
notes sounding together

Word building: The plural is **harmonies. |
harmonisation** *noun* **harmonise**
verb **harmonious** *adjective* **harmoniously**
adverb
Word history: from a Greek word meaning 'a
joining', 'concord', or 'music'

harness

noun **1** the leather straps, bands and so on
used to control a horse, or to attach a cart
or load to it **2** a similar arrangement worn
by people for safety: *a parachute harness*
verb **3** to put a harness on **4** to put to
work: *We have harnessed water to produce
electricity.*

harp

noun a musical instrument with a
triangular frame and strings which are
plucked with the fingers

Word building: **harpist** *noun* a harp player

harpoon

noun a spearlike weapon attached to a
rope, used to catch large fish

Word building: **harpoon** *verb*

harpsichord   (*say* <u>hahp</u>-suh-kawd)

noun an old-fashioned musical instrument
like a piano

Word building: **harpsichordist** *noun* a
harpsichord player
Word history: from the French words for
'harp' and 'string'

harsh

adjective **1** rough and unpleasant: *a harsh voice* **2** cruel or severe: *a harsh winter*

Word building: **harshly** *adverb* **harshness** *noun*

hart

noun a male deer

hart/heart Don't confuse **hart** with **heart**, which is the organ in your body that pumps the blood and keeps it circulating.

harvest

noun the gathering or picking of crops

Word building: **harvest** *verb* **harvester** *noun* a machine for harvesting crops, especially wheat

hash[1]

noun a mixture of chopped cooked meat, reheated in a sauce

Word history: from a French word meaning 'axe'

hash[2]

noun the symbol (#) on a computer keyboard, telephone keypad, and so on

hassle

verb Informal to worry or annoy: *Don't hassle me about money.*

haste

noun action in a hurry

Word building: **hasty** *adjective* (**hastier**, **hastiest**) **hastily** *adverb* **hastiness** *noun*

hasten   (*say* hay-suhn)

verb to hurry: *He hastened to her side.*

hat

noun a shaped covering for the head, usually worn outdoors

hatch[1]

verb **1** to break out of an egg: *Two new chicks hatched this morning.* **2** to make up or arrange: *They have hatched a plan.*

Word building: **hatchery** *noun* a place for hatching eggs

hatch[2]

noun **1** an opening in a floor, a roof or a ship's deck **2** a cover for this opening

Word building: The plural is **hatches**.

hatchet

noun a small short-handled axe
Other words: **tomahawk**

Word history: from a French word meaning 'little axe'

hate

verb to strongly dislike: *I hate cleaning my room.*

Other words: **abhor, despise, detest, loathe**

Word building: **hate** *noun*   **hatred** *noun*   **hateful** *adjective* inspiring hate: *a hateful job*

haughty   (*say* haw-tee)

adjective too proud of yourself and scornful of others

Word building: Other forms are **haughtier**, **haughtiest**. | **haughtily** *adverb* **haughtiness** *noun*

Word history: from a French word meaning 'high'

haul

verb **1** to pull hard: *to haul a load of rubbish* | *to haul on the rope*
noun **2** a strong pull **3** the amount won, taken or caught at one time: *a haul of fish*

haul/hall Don't confuse **haul** with **hall**, which is a large assembly room.

haunch

noun **1** the part of your body around your hip **2** the back part of an animal

haunt

verb **1** to keep visiting as a ghost or spirit **2** to continually return to: *My memories haunt me whenever I visit here.*
noun **3** a place visited often: *The cave had been one of my favourite haunts in my childhood.*

Word building: **haunted** *adjective* worried, or visited by ghosts   **haunting** *adjective* fascinating, or repeating: *a haunting melody* | *a haunting memory*

have

verb **1** to own, or possess: *to have a ruby ring* | *to have a sister in Tasmania* | *to have red hair* **2** to get or receive: *Can I have your attention?* **3** to experience: *We had a great holiday.* **4** **Have** is used as an auxiliary or 'helping' verb with another verb: *They have eaten.* | *The storm has passed.*

Word building: Other forms are **I have; he, she, it has; I had; I have had; I am having.**

haven

noun a place of shelter or safety

haven't

verb a short form of **have not**

haversack

noun a old-fashioned word for **knapsack** or **rucksack**

havoc

noun great damage or devastation

hawk[1]

noun a hunting bird with a hooked beak and large claws

Word building: **hawkish** *adjective* fierce

hawk[2]

verb to offer things for sale in the street or by calling at people's homes

Word building: **hawker** *noun* a travelling seller of goods

hay

noun grass which has been cut and dried to use as animal feed

hay fever

noun an allergic reaction to pollen or other plant or animal material which causes sneezing and watery eyes

haywire

adjective crazy or out of control

hazard   (*say* <u>haz</u>-uhd)

noun **1** a risk or danger: *Smoking is a health hazard.*
verb **2** to risk or take a chance on: *to hazard a guess*

Word building: **hazardous** *adjective* dangerous or risky **hazardously** *adverb*
Word history: from an Arabic word for the die in a game of chance

haze

noun bits of dust, smoke and so on which combine and look like a thin mist

Word building: **hazy** *adjective* (**hazier**, **haziest**)

hazel

noun **1** a small tree which has light brown nuts that people eat
adjective **2** greenish-brown in colour: *hazel eyes*

he

pronoun the male being talked about: *He said he'd come.*

Word use: Other forms are **his** (*his hat, That book is his*), **him** (*Give it to him*), **himself** (*He hurt himself*).

head

noun **1** the top part of your body where your brain, eyes, ears, nose and mouth are, joined to the rest of your body by your neck **2** a similar part of an animal's body **3** the brain or mind: *a good head for figures* **4** the top or front part of anything: *the head of a page | the head of a procession* **5** a leader or a chief **6** a person or animal as one of a number: *ten head of cattle | She charged $10 a head for dinner.* **7 heads**, the side of a coin with a picture of a head on it: *Heads or tails?*
verb **8** to go or be at the head of or in front of: *She heads the list of winners.* **9** to turn towards a certain direction: *Head your horse down the other track. | Let's head for home.* **10** to give a heading or title to
phrase **11 come to a head**, to reach an important point or crisis **12 go to your head**, **a** to make you confused **b** to make you too proud or pleased with yourself **13 lose your head**, to panic, especially in an emergency

Word building: **head** *adjective*: *the head man*

headache

noun **1** a pain in your head **2** *Informal* a troublesome or worrying problem

heading

noun the words written as a title at the top of a page or at the beginning of a piece of writing

headland

noun a high piece of land which juts out into a sea or lake
Other words: **promontory**

head lice

plural noun very small insects that can live in your hair and make your head itchy. They lay eggs called nits.

Word use: This is often shortened to **lice**.

headlight

noun one of the powerful lights on the front of a car or truck

headline

noun **1** a line in big print at the top of a newspaper article, saying what it is about **2 headlines**, important news: *Drought is in the headlines again.*

headlong

adverb at great speed and in a foolhardy manner: *He raced headlong into the surf.*

headmaster
noun the male teacher in charge of a school

headmistress
noun the female teacher in charge of a school

headphones
plural noun a listening device for a radio made of earphones held on by a band over your head

Word use: Another name for this is **headset**.

headquarters   (*say* hed-kwaw-tuhz)
noun the place where the people in charge of a large organisation work: *police headquarters*

headscarf
noun **1** a scarf worn around the head **2** See **hijab**

Word building: The plural is **headscarfs** or **headscarves**.

head start
noun an advantage gained or given at the start of a race or competition: *The littlest children had a head start of 20 metres.*

headstrong
adjective hard to control or determined to have your own way

headway
noun forward motion: *The car made little headway in the heavy fog.*

heal
verb to make or become whole or well again

Word building: **healing** *adjective* able to heal   **healer** *noun*

heal/heel Don't confuse **heal** with **heel**, which is the rounded back of your foot.

health
noun **1** freedom from disease or sickness **2** the general state of your body: *in poor health*

Word building: **healthy** *adjective* (**healthier, healthiest**)   **healthily** *adverb*   **healthiness** *noun*

heap
noun **1** a group of things lying one on top of the other: *a heap of stones*
Other words: **mass, mound, pile, stack**
2 *Informal* a great quantity or number: *Their family has a heap of money.*

Other words: **abundance, lot, mass**
3 *Informal* something very old and broken down: *My first car was a real heap.*
phrase **4 give someone heaps,** *Informal* to give someone a lot of insults or trouble

Word building: **heap** *verb*

hear
verb **1** to be able to sense sounds through your ear **2** to be informed of or to receive information: *Have you heard the news yet?*

Word building: Other forms are **I heard, I have heard, I am hearing.**

hear/here Don't confuse **hear** with **here**. If you are **here**, you are in or at this place.

hearing
noun **1** the process by which sounds are sensed by your ear **2** the opportunity to speak or be heard: *Give our next speaker a decent hearing.* **3** the distance or range within which a sound can be heard: *I must tell you this while he is out of hearing.*

hearsay
noun gossip or rumour

hearse   (*rhymes with* verse)
noun a special car used in a funeral for carrying a coffin

heart
noun **1** the organ in your body that pumps the blood and keeps it circulating through your body **2** emotions, affections or feelings: *You've won my heart.* **3** courage or enthusiasm: *She showed plenty of heart when she went on to win.* **4** the middle part of something: *the heart of a lettuce* **5** the most important part: *the heart of the matter* **6** a figure said to be shaped like a heart, as on playing cards
phrase **7 by heart,** from memory: *to learn a poem off by heart*

Word use: **cardiac** is a medical word meaning 'having to do with the heart'.

heart/hart Don't confuse **heart** with **hart**, which is a male deer.

hearten
verb to cheer up or give courage to

hearth   (*rhymes with* bath)
noun the floor of a fireplace, which usually extends a little way onto the floor of the room

heart-rending

adjective causing great sorrow

hearty

adjective **1** warm-hearted, enthusiastic and sincere: *a hearty welcome | hearty approval* **2** large and satisfying: *a hearty meal*

Word building: Other forms are **heartier**, **heartiest**. | **heartily** *adverb* **heartiness** *noun*

heat

noun **1** warmth or the quality of being hot **2** excitement or anger: *the heat of an argument* **3** a race or competition run to decide who will be in the final: *If you come in the first three in your heat you have to run in the final.*

Word building: **heat** *verb* **heated** *adjective* **heater** *noun*

heath *(rhymes with teeth)*

noun **1** an area of open land with a lot of low shrubs growing on it **2** a small low shrub which grows on such land

heathen *(say hee-dhuhn)*

noun **1** someone who does not believe in the god of Christianity, Judaism, or Islam **2** someone who is not religious or who shows disrespect and dislike for religion

Word use: This word is usually used in an offensive way.
Word building: The plural is **heathen** or **heathens**. | **heathen** *adjective*
Word history: from an Old English word for someone who lived on a heath

heather *(rhymes with weather)*

noun any of the shrubs called heaths, usually with small light purple flowers

heave

verb **1** to raise or lift using effort or force **2** to drag, haul or pull: *The sailors heaved the ropes on board. | They heaved on the ropes.* **3** to rise and fall: *The athlete's chest heaved with the effort of breathing after the race.*

Word building: **heave** *noun*

heaven

noun **1** (in many religions) a place where people, who are chosen by a god or gods, live on after death in happiness **2** a place or condition of great happiness or pleasure

Word use: **Celestial** is a word meaning 'having to do with heaven'.
Word building: **heavenly** *adjective*

heavens

interjection an exclamation expressing surprise

heavy

adjective **1** of great weight and, as a result, hard to lift or carry **2** larger or greater than usual: *heavy rain* **3** serious: *a heavy responsibility* **4** filled or weighed down: *air heavy with moisture | Her heart was heavy with sorrow.*
noun **5** *Informal* someone important in a particular area: *He is one of the heavies of the television world.*

Word building: Other adjective forms are **heavier, heaviest**. | **heavily** *adverb* **heaviness** *noun*

heavy metal

noun a type of loud, fast rock music with a strong beat and long solos on electric guitars

heckle

verb to torment and bother a speaker with annoying questions and comments

hect-

prefix a word part indicating a hundred times a given unit: *hectare*

Word use: Another spelling is **hecto-**.
Word history: from Greek

hectare *(say hek-tair)*

noun a unit of measurement of land in the metric system equal to 10 000 square metres, or about $2\frac{1}{2}$ acres

hectic

adjective full of excitement, activity and confusion: *a hectic day*

Word building: **hectically** *adverb*

he'd

a short form of **he had** or **he would**

hedge

noun **1** a row of bushes or small trees planted close together to form a fence
verb **2** to enclose or separate by a hedge or barrier **3** to avoid making a direct answer: *Stop hedging and say what you want.*

hedgehog

noun a spiny, insect-eating animal found mostly in Europe, which is active at night

heed
verb to pay attention to, or to notice

Word building: **heed** *noun* careful attention　**heedless** *adjective* careless

heel
noun **1** the rounded back part of your foot below your ankle **2** the part of a sock or shoe that fits over your heel
verb **3** to follow by walking close to your heels: *to train a dog to heel*
phrase **4 down at heel**, shabby and poor-looking **5 take to your heels**, to run away quickly

heel/heal Don't confuse **heel** with **heal**. If you **heal**, you make or become well again.

heeler
noun a dog trained to round up sheep or cattle by chasing them and biting at their heels

hefty
adjective *Informal* big, strong and heavy

Word building: Other forms are **heftier**, **heftiest**. | **heftiness** *noun*

heifer (*say* hef-uh)
noun a young cow that has not had a calf

height (*rhymes with* kite)
noun **1** the distance from bottom to top **2** a cliff or mountain peak or other very high place **3** the greatest part or amount: *the height of her career | the height of stupidity*

Word use: **height** is the noun from the adjective **high**.
Word building: **heighten** *verb* to increase or make higher

heir (*sounds like* air)
noun someone who inherits a dead person's money, property or title

Word building: **heiress** *noun*

heir/air Don't confuse **heir** with **air**, which is what we breathe.

heirloom (*say* air-loohm)
noun something valuable that is handed down from generation to generation in a family

helicopter
noun an aircraft without wings which flies by means of a large propeller mounted on the top

heliport
noun a place for helicopters to take off and land

helium (*say* hee-lee-uhm)
noun a gas which is lighter than air and is often used to fill balloons

Word history: from a Greek word meaning 'sun'

hell
noun a dreadful place where evil people are said to go for punishment after death

Word building: **hellish** *adjective*

he'll
a short form of **he will**

hello
interjection a word you use when you meet someone you know

Word use: Other spellings are **hallo** and **hullo**.

helm
noun **1** the wheel or handle which is used to steer a boat
phrase **2 at the helm**, in charge: *The company has a new manager at the helm.*

Word building: **helmsman** *noun*

helmet
noun a hard hat worn to protect your head

help
verb **1** to aid or give assistance
Other words: **assist, support**
2 to avoid or keep from: *We couldn't help laughing.*
noun **3** someone or something that aids or assists: *He was no help at all.*
Other words: **aid, assistance, support**
phrase **4 help yourself to**, to take for yourself

Word building: **helper** *noun* someone who helps　**helpful** *adjective* willing to help　**helping** *noun* a serving of food

help desk
noun a section in a company or organisation which provides computer help to people: *Ring up the help desk — they might be able to tell you how to find the file.*

helpless
adjective **1** weak or unable to do anything **2** without help or assistance: *helpless victims of the earthquake*

Word building: **helplessly** *adverb* **helplessness** *noun*

helter-skelter

adverb with great haste and confusion: *The crowds ran helter-skelter from the surf when the shark alarm sounded.*

hem

verb **1** to fold back and sew the edge of: *to hem a dress*
phrase **2 hem in**, to surround or enclose: *Enemy soldiers hemmed the prisoners in.*

Word building: Other verb forms are **I hemmed, I have hemmed, I am hemming.** | **hem** *noun* a folded and sewn edge of material

hemi-

prefix a word part meaning 'half': *hemisphere*

Word history: from Greek

hemisphere   (*say* hem-uhs-fear)

noun half of a round or spherical shape such as the earth: *When it is spring in the southern hemisphere it is autumn in the northern hemisphere.*

Word building: **hemispherical** *adjective*

hemp

noun a plant which is grown for its strong fibres which are used to make rope and sacks, and also for the leaves which are used as a drug

hen

noun a female bird, especially a domestic chicken

Word use: The male is a **cock** or, for domestic chickens, a **rooster**.

henna

noun a reddish-orange dye which is used to colour hair

hepatitis   (*say* hep-uh-tuy-tuhs)

noun a disease of the liver which makes your skin and the whites of your eyes turn yellow

hepta-

prefix a word part meaning 'seven': *heptagon*

Word use: Another spelling is **hept-**.
Word history: from Greek

heptagon   (*say* hep-tuh-gon)

noun a flat shape with seven sides

Word building: **heptagonal** *adjective*

her

pronoun **1** a form of the pronoun **she** used as the object of the verb in a sentence: *I can't talk to her.* **2** a form of **she** that shows something belongs to her: *her book*

Word building: **hers** *pronoun*: *That book is hers.*   **herself** *pronoun*: *She cut herself.*

herald

noun somebody or something that carries messages or announces coming events

Word building: **herald** *verb* to announce

heraldry   (*say* he-ruhl-dree)

noun the investigation and recording of coats of arms and the histories of the families to which they belong

Word building: **heraldic** *adjective*

herb

noun a flowering plant used in cooking or medicines

Word building: **herbal** *adjective*: *a herbal remedy*   **herbicide** *noun* a chemical that kills plants   **herbalist** *noun*
Word history: from a Latin word meaning 'grass'

herbivore   (*say* her-buh-vaw)

noun an animal that eats plants

Word use: Compare this with **carnivore**, **insectivore** and **omnivore**.

herbivorous   (*say* her-biv-uh-ruhs)

adjective feeding on plants: *Cows are herbivorous animals.*

herd

noun a large group of animals: *a herd of cattle being driven to new pasture*

Word building: **herd** *verb* to drive or move together as a group

herd/heard Don't confuse **herd** with **heard**, which is the past form of the verb **hear**: *Don't shout I heard you the first time.*

here

adverb **1** in, at, or to this place: *Put it here.* | *Come here.* **2** at this point: *Here I paused for breath.*

Word use: Compare this with **there**.

here/hear Don't confuse **here** with **hear**. If you can **hear**, you are able to sense sounds through your ear.

hereditary   (*say* huh-<u>red</u>-uh-tree)
adjective inherited or passing down from
parent to offspring: *a hereditary disease |
hereditary ownership of land*

heredity   (*say* huh-<u>red</u>-uh-tee)
noun the passing on of characteristics from
parents to offspring: *Heredity is to blame for
my big nose.*

heresy   (*say* <u>he</u>-ruh-see)
noun a belief, especially about religion,
which goes against the things that people
generally believe
Word building: The plural is **heresies**. |
heretic *noun*   **heretical** *adjective*   **heretically**
adverb

heritage
noun something which is passed on to you
because you have been born of a particular
family or country
Other words: **inheritance, legacy**

hermit
noun someone who lives alone and keeps
away from other people
Word building: **hermitage** *noun* a place where
hermits live
Word history: from a Greek word meaning 'of
the desert'

hernia
noun the pushing out of an organ in your
body, through a tear or opening in the
tissue that surrounds it
Word use: This is also called a **rupture**.

hero
noun **1** a person who has done a very brave
thing **2** the character who has the main
part in a book, film or play
Word use: **hero** always used to refer to men
or boys, but nowadays women and girls can be
heroes as well.
Word building: The plural is **heroes**. | **heroic**
adjective   **heroism** *noun*

heroin
noun a dangerously addictive, illegal drug
made from morphine
Word history: from a Greek word for **hero**
(the effect of the drug is supposed to make
someone feel like a hero)

heroine
noun **1** a woman who has done a very
brave thing **2** the woman who has the main
part in a book, film or play

heron
noun a water bird with long legs, a long
neck and a long bill

herpes   (*say* <u>her</u>-peez)
noun an infection which causes small
blisters to break out on your skin

herring
noun small fish which are caught in the
seas of the northern hemisphere and eaten
either fresh or pickled

he's
a short form of **he is** or **he has**

hesitate
verb to wait or pause before doing
something, as if you are not sure if you
should go on: *to hesitate before you speak*
Word building: **hesitancy** *noun*   **hesitant**
adjective   **hesitantly** *adverb*   **hesitation** *noun*

hessian   (*say* <u>hesh</u>-uhn)
noun strong rough cloth often used to
make sacks

hetero-
prefix a word part meaning 'other' or
'different': *heterosexual*
Word use: Another spelling is **heter-**.
Word history: from Greek

heterosexual
(*say* het-uh-roh-<u>sek</u>-shooh-uhl)
noun someone who has sexual feelings for
people of the opposite sex to themselves
Word use: Compare this with **homosexual**.
Word building: **heterosexual** *adjective*
heterosexuality *noun*

hew   (*say* hyooh)
verb to cut: *to hew wood for the fire*
Word use: The more usual word is **chop**.
Word building: Other forms are **I hewed,
I have hewn, I am hewing**.

hex
noun an evil spell

hexa-
prefix a word part meaning 'six': *hexagon*
Word use: Another spelling is **hex-**.
Word history: from Greek

hexagon
noun a flat shape with six straight sides
Word building: **hexagonal** *adjective*

hibernate   (*say* huy-buh-nayt)
verb to hide away and sleep through the
winter: *Many animals in cold climates
hibernate when food is scarce during the winter.*
Word building: **hibernation** *noun*

hibiscus   (*say* huy-bis-kuhs)
noun a small tree with large brightly
coloured flowers

hiccup
noun a sudden movement in your chest
which causes a quick intake of breath and
a short sharp sound
Word use: Another spelling is **hiccough**.
Word building: **hiccup** *verb* (**hiccupped,
hiccupping**)

hide¹
verb to keep from being seen
Other words: **conceal**
Word building: Other forms are **I hid, I have
hidden, I am hiding.**

hide²
noun **1** the skin of an animal: *Cow hide is
used to make leather shoes.*
Other words: **pelt**
phrase **2 neither hide nor hair,** not even
the smallest trace: *We could see neither hide
nor hair of them.*

hideous   (*say* hid-ee-uhs)
adjective **1** very ugly: *a hideous
face* **2** shockingly dreadful: *a hideous crime*
Word building: **hideously** *adverb*
hideousness *noun*

hiding
noun **1** a severe beating as a punishment
2 a thorough defeat or loss in a game: *They
gave their opponents a hiding in the final.*

hierarchy   (*say* huy-uh-rah-kee)
noun a system which arranges people or
things in grades from the highest to the
lowest
Word building: The plural is **hierarchies.** |
hierarchical *adjective*

hieroglyphics   (*say* huy-ruh-glif-iks)
plural noun writing in which words or
sounds are represented by pictures:
Egyptian hieroglyphics

hi-fi
noun a record-player or tape recorder
which can produce sounds almost the same
as the original

Word building: **hi-fi** *adjective*
Word history: short for *high-fidelity*

high
adjective **1** tall or far above the
ground **2** from bottom to top: *a wall two
metres high* **3** being above the normal level
or amount: *The river is high after the rain.* |
high prices **4** sharp or shrill in sound: *to
sing in a high voice* **5** excited or happy: *The
children are in high spirits.* **6** bad-smelling:
This fish is high.
Word building: **highly** *adverb* very: *highly
dangerous*   **height** *noun*   **high** *adverb*

highlands
plural noun the high, mountainous part of
a country: *the New Guinea highlands*
Word building: **highlander** *noun*

highlight
noun the best, brightest or most
outstanding part: *The highlight of the trip
was seeing Uluru.*
Word building: **highlight** *verb* to emphasise or
make stand out

highlighter
noun a fluoro coloured pen used to colour
over special words or pictures that you
want to be noticed

high-rise
adjective having to do with a building that
has many storeys: *My aunt lives in a high-
rise apartment.*

highway
noun a main road built to carry a lot of
traffic

highwayman
noun a bandit, usually on horseback, who
used to hold up travellers on the road
Word building: The plural is **highwaymen.**

hijab   (*say* huh-jahb)
noun a scarf worn by many Muslim
women which covers the head and
sometimes part of the shoulders, leaving
the face uncovered
Word use: Another spelling is **hejab.** |
Another name for this is **headscarf.**

hijack
verb to seize by using threats or violence:
to hijack a plane
Word building: **hijacker** *noun*

hike

noun **1** a very long walk, usually for pleasure: *We went on a hike through the mountains.* **2** a sudden increase: *a hike in the price of petrol*

Word building: **hike** *verb*   **hiker** *noun*

hilarious   (*say* huh-<u>lair</u>-ree-uhs)

adjective **1** noisily cheerful **2** very, very funny: *a hilarious story*

Word building: **hilariously** *adverb*   **hilarity** *noun*

hill

noun **1** a naturally raised part of the earth's surface, smaller than a mountain: *We ran down the hill.* **2** a heap or mound made by humans or animals: *an ant hill | a hill of beans*

hillbilly

noun someone living in the country, especially in the mountains away from other people

Word use: This word was first used in North America. | An Australian word with a similar meaning is **bushie**.
Word building: The plural is **hillbillies**.

hilt

noun **1** the handle of a sword or dagger
phrase **2 to the hilt**, completely

him

pronoun a form of **he** used after the verb in a sentence: *The hat belongs to him.*

Word building: **himself** *pronoun*: *He can't do that by himself.*

him/hymn Don't confuse **him** with **hymn**, which is a song praising God, a deity, a nation, and so on.

hind¹

adjective behind or back: *Kangaroos have very strong hind legs.*

hind²

noun a female deer

Word use: Another word is **doe**. | The male is a **hart** or a **buck** and the young is a **fawn**.

hinder   (*say* <u>hin</u>-duh)

verb to slow down or make difficult: *Fog hindered our progress.*

Word building: **hindrance** *noun*
Word history: from an Old English word meaning 'behind' or 'back'

hindsight   (*say* <u>huynd</u>-suyt)

noun the ability to understand what you should have done in an event, after it has happened

Hinduism   (*say* <u>hin</u>-dooh-iz-uhm)

noun the main religion of India, in which followers worship many gods and goddesses. Followers of Hinduism are called Hindus, and worship in a temple.

Word building: **Hindu** *adjective*: *the Hindu system of castes or social ranks*

hinge

noun **1** a movable joint like the one which attaches a door to a door post, allowing the door to swing backwards and forwards
verb **2** to join by a hinge **3** to depend: *Everything hinges on your decision.*

hint

noun **1** a roundabout or indirect suggestion: *to drop a hint that you would like an invitation to the party* **2** a piece of helpful advice

Word building: **hint** *verb*: *to hint at his latest plan*

hinterland

noun the land lying just inland from the coast: *Very few people settled in the hinterland.*

hip

noun the part at each side of your body, just below the waist

hippie

noun a person who is part of a general movement that promotes peace and living with nature and rejects narrow social conventions, especially such a person living in the 1960s

Word use: Another spelling is **hippy**.

hippopotamus

noun a large mammal with short legs and a heavy hairless body, that lives around lakes and rivers in Africa

Word use: The short form of this is **hippo** and is a more informal word.
Word building: The plural is **hippopotamuses** or **hippopotami**.
Word history: from a Greek word meaning 'horse of the river'

hire

verb to pay money to use, or employ: *to hire a car | to hire a butler*

Word building: **hire** *noun*

hire-purchase

noun a way of buying expensive things like cars or furniture by making regular payments of money after you take the goods home

his

pronoun **1** the form of **he** you use when something belongs to him: *That car is his.* **2** belonging to him: *That is his cat.*

hiss

verb to make the sound 'ssss', like a snake, especially as a way of showing you don't like something: *The play was so boring that the audience hissed and booed the actors.*

Word building: **hiss** *noun*

historian

noun someone who studies history and writes about it

history

noun **1** the events which have happened in the past, or the study of them **2** a description of important things which have happened in the past

Word building: The plural is **histories.** | **historic** *adjective* important or well-known **historical** *adjective* **historically** *adverb* Word history: from a Greek word meaning 'inquiry' or 'observation'

hit

verb **1** to strike or give a blow to Other words: **bash, beat, knock, thump** **2** to reach or arrive at: *The school building fund hit $1000.* noun **3** a blow or stroke **4** a great success phrase **5** **hit it off**, *Informal* to get on well together: *I can't seem to hit it off with the new neighbours.* **6** **hit on**, to find by chance: *to hit on a good idea*

Word building: Other verb forms are **he hit, he has hit, he is hitting.** | **hit** *adjective: a hit record*

hitch

verb **1** to tie or fasten: *to hitch a horse to a cart* noun **2** a kind of knot that can be undone easily **3** something that obstructs or makes things difficult: *a hitch in our plans* phrase **4** **hitch up**, to pull or tug up: *to hitch up your trousers*

Word building: The plural form of the noun is **hitches.**

hitchhike

verb to travel free of charge by getting lifts in passing cars or trucks

Word use: This is sometimes shortened to **hitch.** Word building: **hitchhiker** *noun*

HIV

noun the virus that causes AIDS

Word history: made by joining the first letters of *human immunodeficiency virus*

hive

noun **1** a place that bees live in **2** a place full of busy people

hives

noun a rash, usually due to eating or touching something to which you are allergic: *Oranges give me hives.*

hoard

verb to save up and hide away in a secret place: *My little sister hoards every cent of money that she gets.*

Word building: **hoard** *noun* a secret store   **hoarder** *noun*

---

hoard/horde Don't confuse **hoard** with **horde,** which is a large group of people or animals.

---

hoarding

noun **1** a large board for putting up advertisements or notices **2** a temporary fence made of boards around a building site

hoarse (say haws)

adjective rough or croaky: *to shout until your voice becomes hoarse*

Word building: **hoarsely** *adverb* **hoarseness** *noun*

---

hoarse/horse Don't confuse **hoarse** with **horse,** which is a large, four-legged animal with hoofs, which is easily trained for riding, racing or pulling loads.

---

hoax

noun a trick or practical joke

Word building: **hoax** *verb* **hoaxer** *noun*

hobble

verb to walk with difficulty: *to hobble around with a sprained ankle*

hobby

noun something that you enjoy doing in your spare time: *My hobby is collecting stamps.* Other words: **interest, pastime**

Word building: The plural is **hobbies.**

hock

noun the joint in the hind leg of a horse or similar animal, which is like the ankle

hockey

noun a game played on a field or on ice in which two teams compete to hit a ball into a goal using a stick with a curved end

hoe

noun a garden tool with a long handle and flat thin blade, which you use to break up the soil

Word building: **hoe** *verb* (**hoed, hoeing**)

hog

noun **1** a pig **2** *Informal* someone who is greedy or dirty
phrase **3 go the whole hog**, *Informal* to do something completely: *I went the whole hog and spent all my pocket money on lollies.*
verb **4** *Informal* to take more than your share of: *to hog the biscuits*

Word use: The male of definition 1 is a **boar**, the female is a **sow** and the young is a **piglet** or a **shoat**.
Word building: Other verb forms are **I hogged, I have hogged, I am hogging**.

hoist

verb **1** to lift up or raise: *to hoist a flag*
noun **2** a lift or other machine that raises things off the ground

hold¹

verb **1** to have or keep in your arms or hands **2** to own: *to hold land in the country* **3** to contain: *The petrol tank holds 50 litres.* **4** to fasten or stay fastened: *A paperclip holds pages together.* | *The anchor will not hold in rough seas.* **5** to have or conduct: *to hold a meeting*
noun **6** a grip: *The wrestler locked the opponent in a firm hold.* **7** control or influence: *to have a hold on your audience*
phrase **8 hold up**, **a** to delay **b** to rob

Word building: Other verb forms are **I held, I have held, I am holding**. | **holder** *noun*

hold²

noun the part of a ship, below the deck, where cargo is carried

hold-up

noun **1** a robbery **2** a delay

hole

noun **1** an opening through something **2** a hollow space **3** *Informal* a dirty or unpleasant place: *This restaurant is a hole.*

Word building: **hole** *verb*   **holey** *adjective*

hole/whole Don't confuse **hole** with **whole**. Something is **whole** if it is complete or entire: *I have a whole packet of biscuits to myself.*

holiday

noun **1** a day's break from work or school, usually to celebrate or remember an important event: *a public holiday on Anzac Day* **2 holidays**, a much longer break from your daily work
Other words: **vacation**

Word building: **holiday** *verb*: *We holiday at the beach.*
Word history: from an Old English word meaning 'holy day' (the first holidays were special days in the church's calendar)

hollow

adjective **1** having empty space inside: *a hollow log* **2** empty of meaning: *hollow promises*
noun **3** a hole or a dip, especially in the ground

Word building: **hollow** *verb*   **hollowly** *adverb* **hollowness** *noun*

holly

noun a small tree with shiny prickly leaves and bright red berries in winter

holo-

prefix a word part meaning 'whole' or 'entire': *holocaust*

Word history: from Greek

holocaust   (*say* <u>hol</u>-uh-kost)

noun **1** great loss of life, especially when caused by a bad fire **2 the Holocaust**, the mass murder of Jews by the Nazis during the Second World War

Word history: from a Greek word meaning 'burnt offering'

holster

noun a leather case for a gun, worn on a belt

holy

adjective **1** specially recognised as set aside to a god: *a holy day* **2** religious or pious: *a holy person*

Word building: Other forms are **holier, holiest**. | **holiness** *noun*

holy/wholly/holey Don't confuse **holy** with **wholly** or **holey**.
Wholly means 'entirely':
    I am wholly committed to this new project.
Something is **holey** if it is full of **holes**:
    Your socks are so holey it's a wonder they don't fall apart.

homage   (*say* <u>hom</u>-ij)

noun respect or honour: *to pay homage to a leader*

home

noun **1** the place where you live or were born: *Australia is my home.* **2** a house or other dwelling **3** a place where people can be cared for: *an old people's home* **4** the base on a softball or baseball field where the batter stands to hit the ball, and then tries to run back to in order to score a point

adverb **5** to or at home: *to come straight home after school*

Word building: **home** *adjective*: *the home team* **homeward** *adverb* towards home **homing** *adjective*: *a homing pigeon*

homely

adjective **1** plain and simple: *homely food* **2** not pretty or good-looking: *a homely face*

Word building: Other forms are **homelier,** **homeliest.** | **homeliness** *noun*

homeopathy   (*say* hoh-mee-<u>op</u>-uh-thee)

noun the method of treating disease with tiny amounts of a substance which would, if you gave it in larger amounts, cause symptoms just like those of the disease being treated

Word use: Another spelling is **homoeopathy.** Word building: **homeopath** *noun* **homeopathic** *adjective*

home page

noun a short example of what a website contains

homesick

adjective unhappy and wanting to be at home

Word building: **homesickness** *noun*

homestead

noun the main house on a sheep or cattle station or a large farm

home unit

noun one out of a number of separately owned homes in the same building

Word use: You can also use **unit.**

homework

noun school work that is done at home

homicide   (*say* <u>hom</u>-uh-suyd)

noun the crime of killing someone on purpose

Word building: **homicidal** *adjective*: *a homicidal maniac* **homicidally** *adverb*

hommos   (*say* <u>hom</u>-uhs, <u>hoom</u>-uhs)

noun another spelling for **hummus**

homo-

prefix a word part meaning 'same': *homonym*

Word history: from Greek

homogeneous

(*say* hom-uh-<u>jee</u>-nee-uhs)

adjective made up of parts which are all of the same kind: *a homogeneous mixture*

Word building: **homogenise** *verb* to mix evenly so that all parts are alike **homogeneously** *adverb*

homonym   (*say* <u>hom</u>-uh-nim)

noun a word which has the same sound or the same spelling as another but has a different meaning

Word use: If two homonyms are spelt the same, like *bear* (the animal) and *bear* (to carry), they're called **homographs;** if two homonyms sound the same, like *heir* and *air*, they're called **homophones.**
Word history: from a Latin word meaning 'having the same name'

homosexual

(*say* hoh-muh-<u>sek</u>-shooh-uhl)

noun someone who has sexual feelings for people of the same sex as themselves

Word use: Compare this with **heterosexual.** Word building: **homosexual** *adjective* **homosexuality** *noun*

honest   (*say* <u>on</u>-uhst)

adjective truthful and fair

Word building: **honestly** *adverb* **honesty** *noun*

honey   (*rhymes with* funny)

noun a sweet sticky liquid made by bees from the nectar of flowers

honeycomb

noun a wax structure made up of many rows of tiny compartments, made by bees for holding eggs, honey and pollen in the hive

honeydew

noun a small round melon with sweet-flavoured white flesh and smooth, pale green or yellow skin

honeymoon

noun a holiday spent by a bride and groom straight after their wedding

Word building: **honeymoon** *verb*

honorary (*say* on-uh-ruh-ree)

adjective not paid for what you do: *the honorary secretary of the club*

honour (*say* on-uh)

noun **1** fame or glory: *to bring honour to the school* **2** respect or esteem: *to be treated with honour* **3** honesty and high morals: *a person of honour*

Word use: Another spelling is **honor**.
Word building: **honour** *verb* to show respect for **honourable** *adjective* **honourably** *adverb*

hood

noun **1** a loose kind of hat, usually attached to a coat, which covers your head and neck **2** a folding roof for a car or baby's pram

Word building: **hooded** *adjective*

hoodlum (*say* hoohd-luhm)

noun a rough destructive young person

hoodwink

verb to trick or deceive

hoof

noun the hard covering which protects the feet of some animals such as horses, cows and pigs

Word building: The plural is **hoofs** or **hooves**.

hook

noun **1** a piece of metal or some other material bent or curved so as to hold or catch something **2** a punch in boxing, made with the arm bent
verb **3** to hold or be fastened by a hook **4** to hit a ball so that it curves to the left if you are right-handed
phrase **5 by hook or by crook**, by any way possible

Word use: The opposite of definition 4 is **slice**.

hook-up

noun a link-up or connection between radio or television stations or telephones

hooligan

noun a rough and noisy young person who causes trouble

Word building: **hooliganism** *noun*

hoop

noun a ring or circular band made of wire, wood or plastic

hop¹

verb to jump, especially on one foot

Word building: Other forms are **I hopped, I have hopped, I am hopping**. | **hop** *noun*

hop²

noun a climbing plant whose flowers are used to flavour beer

hope

verb **1** to look forward to or expect, especially something good
noun **2** a wish or desire that something good will happen: *We all expressed a hope for their safety.* **3** an expectation or likelihood: *no hope of finding the lost money*

Word building: **hopeful** *adjective* **hopefulness** *noun* **hopeless** *adjective* **hopelessness** *noun*

hopscotch

noun a children's game in which a player throws a stone or other small flat object into a pattern of numbered squares drawn on the ground and then hops from one square to another without touching a line

horde

noun a large group: *a horde of flies buzzing around the barbecue*

horde/hoard Don't confuse **horde** with **hoard**, which is a secret supply collected over some period of time:
I have a private hoard of biscuits in my room.

horizon (*say* huh-ruy-zuhn)

noun **1** the line where the earth or sea appears to meet the sky **2** the limit or boundary to knowledge: *Reading broadens your horizons.*

horizontal (*say* ho-ruh-zon-tuhl)

adjective **1** parallel, or in line, with the horizon **2** lying down flat

Word use: Compare this with **vertical**.
Word building: **horizontally** *adverb*

hormone

noun a chemical substance made by a gland in the body which travels through the blood and affects other parts of the body

Word building: **hormonal** *adjective*
Word history: from a Greek word meaning 'setting in motion'

horn

noun **1** a hard pointed growth on the forehead of animals like cows, sheep and deer **2** the bonelike material making up horns or hoofs **3** a musical wind instrument: *a French horn* **4** a device for sounding a warning signal: *to blow the car's horn*

Word building: **horn** *verb* to wound or stab with the horns   **horny** *adjective* tough or hardened, as if made from horn

hornet

noun a large wasp with a very painful sting

horoscope   (*say* ho-ruh-skohp)

noun a diagram showing the position of the planets in the sky at a particular time and thought by some people to be an aid in forecasting the future

horrendous

adjective horrible and dreadful

horrible

adjective terrible, dreadful or very unpleasant
Other words: **awful, nasty, shocking**
Word building: **horribly** *adverb*

horrid

adjective nasty or horrible

horrify

verb to shock or fill with horror: *The violent film horrified me.*

Word building: Other forms are **I horrified, I have horrified, I am horrifying.** | **horrific** *adjective* shocking   **horrifying** *adjective*

horror

noun **1** a strong feeling of fear or disgust: *a horror of spiders* **2** *Informal* someone or something thought to be bad or ugly: *Her brother is a little horror.*

hors d'oeuvre   (*say* aw derv)

noun a small piece of food such as an olive, a nut or a savoury, served before a main meal

Word use: We pronounce these words like this because they come from French.

horse

noun **1** a large, four-legged animal with hoofs, which is easily trained for riding, racing or pulling loads
phrase **2 eat like a horse**, to have a big appetite **3 hold your horses**, to wait and not rush ahead

Word use: The female is a **mare**, the male is a **stallion** and the young is a **foal**.

> **horse/hoarse** Don't confuse **horse** with **hoarse**. If your voice is **hoarse**, then it sounds rough and distorted.

horsepower

noun a unit for measuring power in the imperial system: *a 50 horsepower engine*

horseradish

noun a plant whose strongly flavoured root is used in cooking

horticulture   (*say* haw-tuh-kul-chuh)

noun the growing of garden plants for their fruit, vegetables and flowers

Word building: **horticultural** *adjective*
horticulturalist *noun*   **horticulturist** *noun*

hose

noun **1** a flexible tube for carrying water **2** another word for **hosiery**

Word building: **hose** *verb* to water or wet with a hose

hosiery

noun clothing for your legs and feet, such as socks or stockings

hospice

noun a hospital for patients who are dying, often run by a church

hospital

noun a place where sick and injured people are given medical treatment

Word building: **hospitalise** *verb* to put into hospital

hospitality   (*say* hos-puh-tal-uh-tee)

noun kindness and generosity shown to guests

Word building: **hospitable** *adjective*
hospitably *adverb*

host[1] (*rhymes with* most)

noun **1** someone who entertains guests: *The host of a party* **2** an animal or plant on which a parasite lives: *A dog is host to many fleas.*

Word building: **host** *verb* **hostess** *noun*

host[2] (*rhymes with* most)

noun a great number or crowd: *a host of household chores | a host of angels*

hostage (*say* hos-tij)

noun someone held prisoner by an enemy until certain conditions are met or ransom money is paid

hostel

noun a place where people can get meals and a room to sleep for the night at a low cost

Word history: from a French word meaning 'guest'

hostile

adjective unfriendly or acting like an enemy

Word building: **hostility** *noun*
Word history: from a Latin word meaning 'enemy'

hot

adjective **1** having a high temperature and giving out heat
Other words: **blistering, burning, fiery, scorching, searing**
2 strong or burning to taste: *a hot curry*
Other words: **fiery, peppery, spicy**
3 angry, violent or passionate: *a hot temper*
phrase **4 not so hot,** *Informal* **a** not very good: *He's not so hot at maths.* **b** not very well: *I'm not feeling so hot.*

hot dog

noun a long red sausage served hot in a bread roll, usually with tomato sauce and sometimes mustard

hotel

noun a place which provides rooms and meals for paying guests, and which has special rooms where people can go to drink beer and other alcoholic drinks

Word building: **hotelier** *noun* someone who runs a hotel

hotline

noun a telephone line which connects people directly to special services that can give advice or organise help, as in times of emergency

hotplate

noun a metal plate on an electric stove or barbecue which can be heated and used to cook food

hound

noun **1** a dog, especially a hunting dog
verb **2** to hunt or pursue continually: *The dogs hounded the fox into the trap. | Her parents always have to hound her to do her homework.*

hour

noun **1** a unit of measurement of time equal to 60 minutes **2** a particular time: *The hour has come.* **3 hours,** the usual times for work or business: *School hours are 9 a.m. to 3.30 p.m. | office hours*
phrase **4 the eleventh hour,** the very last possible moment: *They were rescued at the eleventh hour.* **5 the wee** (or **small**) **hours,** the hours just after midnight

Word building: **hourly** *adjective*: *an hourly broadcast* **hourly** *adverb*: *to broadcast the news hourly*

hourglass

noun an instrument for measuring time, with sand running from one glass bulb to another in exactly an hour

Word building: The plural is **hourglasses.** | **hourglass** *adjective* shaped like an hourglass: *an hourglass figure*

house (*say* hows)

noun **1** a building where people live **2** a building for any purpose: *Parliament House | a house of worship* **3** a section of a school, made up of children from all classes, formed for sport and other competitions **4** the group of people forming a parliament or one of its divisions: *the upper house | the lower house* **5** a family seen as consisting of ancestors and descendants: *the royal house of Windsor* **6** an audience in a theatre: *The performers played to a full house.*
verb (*say* howz) **7** to provide space or accommodation for: *to house refugees*

Word building: **housing** *noun* a protective covering or support for a machine

houseboat

noun a boat which is fitted up for people to live on

household
noun **1** all the people who live together in a house
adjective **2** belonging to, or having to do with, a house or family: *household furniture | household chores*
Word building: **householder** *noun*

housie-housie
noun another name for **bingo**

hovel
noun a small dirty house or hut

hover *(say* hov-uh*)*
verb **1** to stay in one spot in the air as if hanging: *The bees were hovering over the flowers.* **2** to linger or stay close to: *The children hovered around a bowl of chocolates.*

hovercraft
noun a vehicle without wheels which can travel quickly over land or water, supported on a cushion of air

how
adverb in what way, or condition: *How did it happen? | How are you?*

however
adverb no matter how much, or in what way: *He'll never be able to sing however hard he tries. | Go there however you like.*

howl
verb to make a long, loud, wailing noise like a dog or wolf
Word building: **howl** *noun* **howler** *noun* a very stupid mistake

hub
noun **1** the centre part of a wheel **2** any busy or important centre: *The city is a hub of activity.*

huddle
verb **1** to crowd closely together: *to huddle by the fire to keep warm*
noun **2** a few people crowded together to discuss something in private

hue
noun a colour or shade of colour: *the hues of the rainbow*

huff
noun a fit of anger or resentment: *He left the room in a huff.*
Word building: **huffy** *adjective*

hug
verb **1** to put your arms around, especially in an affectionate way: *She hugged the crying boy and he soon settled down.* **2** to keep very close to: *During the storm, the boat hugged the coastline.*
Word building: Other forms are **I hugged, I have hugged, I am hugging.** | **hug** *noun*

huge
adjective very, very large: *a huge mountain*
Other words: **colossal, enormous, gigantic, mammoth, mighty, vast**
Word building: **hugely** *adverb* **hugeness** *noun*

hulk
noun someone or something that is bulky, heavy or clumsy
Word building: **hulking** *adjective*

hull
noun the body of a ship or boat: *to paint the hull*

hullabaloo *(say* hul-uh-buh-looh*)*
noun an uproar or loud noisy disturbance

hum
verb **1** to make a buzzing or droning sound **2** to sing with your lips closed **3** to be busy and active: *The factory hummed all day and night.*
Word building: Other forms are **I hummed, I have hummed, I am humming.** | **hum** *noun*

human
noun a woman, man or child
Word building: **human** *adjective*: *the human form* **humanly** *adverb*: *as soon as humanly possible*
Word history: from a Latin word meaning 'of a man'

humane *(say* hyooh-mayn*)*
adjective showing feelings of pity and tenderness: *It would be humane to help a dying person.*
Word building: **humanely** *adverb*

humanity
noun **1** all humans **2** sympathy and kindness towards other people and animals
Word building: **humanitarian** *adjective*

humankind
noun all human beings

humble

adjective **1** modest and meek: *She was too humble to expect the famous writer to speak to her.* **2** poor and lowly: *He came from a humble home.*

Word building: **humbly** *adverb* **humility** *noun*

humdrum

adjective dull and ordinary: *a humdrum existence*

humid

adjective moist and damp, especially when it's also warm: *a humid day*

Word building: **humidly** *adverb* **humidity** *noun*

humiliate

verb to cause to feel ashamed or foolish: *Your rude remarks humiliated me, and I refuse to be treated like that.*

Word building: **humiliation** *noun*

hummus   (*say* hoo-muhs, hom-uhs)

noun a Middle Eastern dip made from chickpeas, oil, lemon and garlic: *Would you like some hummus with your kebab?*

Word use: Another spelling is **hommus** or **hommos**.

humour

noun the quality of being funny or amusing: *a sense of humour | Standing there dripping wet, he couldn't see the humour in the situation.*

Word use: Another spelling is **humor**.
Word building: **humorous** *adjective*

hump

noun **1** a bulge on the back: *a camel's hump* **2** a rounded rise in the ground or on a road: *a speed hump*
verb **3** to carry: *to hump a swag*

humpy

noun an Aboriginal bush shelter

Word history: from an Aboriginal language of Queensland called Yagara. See the map of Australian Aboriginal languages at the end of this book.

humus   (*say* hyooh-muhs)

noun dark nourishing material in soil, formed by the rotting of animal and vegetable matter

hunch

verb **1** to push out or up: *to hunch your shoulders*
noun **2** *Informal* a belief, usually without the knowledge of the facts: *I had a hunch that something would happen.*

hundred

noun **1** the number 100, or 10 times 10 **2** the Roman numeral C

Word building: **hundred** *adjective: a hundred men* **hundredth** *adjective: a hundredth part of the money*

hunger

noun an uncomfortable feeling of the need for food

Word building: **hungry** *adjective* (**hungrier, hungriest**) **hungrily** *adverb*

hunk

noun a large rough piece: *They ate hunks of bread with the cheese.*

hunt

verb **1** to chase, for food or sport **2** to search: *I hunted everywhere for my pencil.*

Word building: **hunt** *noun* **hunter** *noun*

huntsman

noun another name for **tarantula** (def. 1)

hurdle

noun a movable fence over which horses or people have to jump in a race

Word building: **hurdle** *verb: to hurdle a fence* **hurdler** *noun*

hurl

verb to throw

hurricane

noun a violent tropical storm with a very strong wind

hurry

verb to act quickly to save time: *Hurry or you will be late!*
Other words: **dash, hasten, rush**

Word building: Other forms are **I hurried, I have hurried, I am hurrying.** | **hurried** *adjective* **hurriedly** *adverb* **hurry** *noun*

hurt

verb **1** to cause pain or damage to: *I hurt my leg. | My thoughtlessness hurt Jan.* **2** to be painful: *My leg hurts.*

Word building: **hurt** *noun* **hurtful** *adjective* **hurtfully** *adverb*

hurtle
verb to rush noisily: *We hurtled along in the train.*

husband
noun the man to whom a woman is married
Other words: **partner, spouse**

hush
verb **1** to make quiet or silent: *Hush your voice.* | *Hush the baby.* **2** to become quiet: *Hush!*
Word building: **hush** *noun*

husk
noun the dry outside covering of grain

husky[1]
adjective **1** low and hoarse: *a husky voice* **2** big and strong: *a husky lifesaver*
Word building: Other forms are **huskier, huskiest.** | **huskily** *adverb* **huskiness** *noun*

husky[2]
noun a dog used by people in Arctic regions for pulling sleds
Word building: The plural is **huskies.**

hustle　　(*say* hus-uhl)
verb **1** to push along roughly or hurriedly: *They hustled us out of the room.* **2** to hurry
Word building: **hustler** *noun* someone who gets easy money by gambling, or something like this

hut
noun a small house-like shelter: *a beach hut*

hutch
noun a coop or house for small animals: *a rabbit hutch*
Word building: The plural is **hutches.**

hybrid　　(*say* huy-bruhd)
noun an animal or plant that is the result of breeding between different types
Word building: **hybridise** *verb*
Word history: from a Latin word for the young of a tame sow and a wild boar

hybrid car
noun a car which uses electricity at lower speeds and fuel, like petrol or diesel, only at higher speeds: *I was very proud of my parents when they bought a hybrid car.*

hydrangea　　(*say* huy-drayn-juh)
noun a shrub which has large blue or pink flowers and loses its leaves in winter

hydrant
noun a point where a hose can be connected to a water main

hydraulic　　(*say* huy-drol-ik)
adjective worked by the pressure of water, oil or other liquid: *hydraulic brakes*
Word building: **hydraulically** *adverb* **hydraulics** *noun*

hydro-
prefix a word part meaning 'water': *hydroplane*
Word use: Another spelling is **hydr-.**
Word history: from Greek

hydro-electric
adjective having to do with the making of electricity by water power: *a hydro-electric scheme*
Word building: **hydro-electricity** *noun* the electricity made by water power

hydrofoil
noun **1** a ski-like attachment which raises the hull of a boat above the surface of the water when a certain speed has been reached **2** a boat with hydrofoils

hydrogen
noun a gas which combines with oxygen to make water

hydroplane
noun a light high-powered boat designed to skim along the surface of the water at high speed

hydroponics
noun the growing of plants in water rather than soil

hyena
noun a doglike animal that eats the flesh of dead animals
Word history: from a Greek word meaning 'hog'

hygiene　　(*say* huy-jeen)
noun **1** the science of preserving health **2** the cleanliness necessary for preserving health
Word building: **hygienic** *adjective* **hygienically** *adverb*

hymn　　(*sounds like* him)
noun a song praising God, a deity, a nation, and so on

Word building: **hymnal** (*say* <u>him</u>-nuhl) *noun* a book of hymns   **hymnbook** *noun*

hymn/him Don't confuse **hymn** with **him**, which is a form of the pronoun **he**:
I saw him going down the street.

hyper-
prefix a word part meaning 'over': *hyperactive*

Word history: from Greek

hyperactive
adjective so active that you are restless and cannot settle down: *a hyperactive child*

Word building: **hyperactivity** *noun*

hyperlink
noun (in computers) an image or text that you can click on to go to another document or website, or to another place in the same document

hyphen
noun a short line (-) used to join the parts of some compound words, as in *part-time*, or the parts of a word when it has to be split at the end of a line

Word building: **hyphenate** *verb* to write or join by a hyphen   **hyphenation** *noun*

Hyphens often link the two parts of a compound, as in *monkey-wrench, icy-cold* and (*to*) *spin-dry*.

With adjective and verb compounds (like *icy-cold* and *spin-dry*) the hyphen has an important role to play in making sure that both parts are read in the right grammatical 'slot' in the sentence. Compare the following sentences:
With icy cold turkey soup, it was a queer meal.
With icy-cold turkey soup, it was a queer meal.

If the hyphen is missing, you're not sure at first which word 'cold' goes with. It's the same in these examples:
You should only spin dry clean clothes.
You should only spin-dry clean clothes.

The hyphen helps to show that 'spin' is part of a compound verb.

With noun compounds the hyphen is usually less important:
You will need a monkey wrench for this job.
You will need a monkey-wrench for this job.

The compound won't suffer from misreading if there is no hyphen there.

Hyphens can also help to keep apart the two parts of a compound or complex word which would otherwise be misread. You may be puzzled or misled by the following:
sealegs
shakeout
reice
But with hyphens, their meaning is plain:
sea-legs
shake-out
re-ice
Hyphens and wordbreaks. Hyphens are also used when we divide a word at the end of a line because the whole word won't fit in. The hyphen shows that the rest of the word is on the next line.

Note that hyphens are the punctuation mark we use within words. The similar but longer mark we use in punctuating sentences is the **dash**. Look up **dash**.

hypno-
prefix a word part meaning 'sleep': *hypnosis*

Word history: from Greek

hypnosis
noun a sleeplike state brought about by cooperating with someone who is then able to control your mind and actions

Word building: **hypnotic** *adjective*

hypnotise
verb to put under hypnosis: *The doctor hypnotised the patient.*

Word use: Another spelling is **hypnotize**.
Word building: **hypnotism** *noun*

hypo-
prefix a word part meaning 'under': *hypodermic*

Word history: from Greek

hypochondria
(*say* huy-puh-<u>kon</u>-dree-uh)
noun the state of being very anxious about your health or imagining yourself ill

Word building: **hypochondriac** *noun*

hypocrite   (*say* <u>hip</u>-uh-krit)
noun someone who pretends to be better than they are

Word building: **hypocrisy** (*say* hip-<u>ok</u>-ruh-see) *noun*   **hypocritical** *adjective*

hypodermic
adjective injecting under the skin: *a hypodermic needle*

hypotenuse   (*say* huy-<u>pot</u>-uhn-yoohz)
noun the side opposite the right angle in a
right-angled triangle

hypothermia   (*say* huy-puh-<u>therm</u>-ee-uh)
noun a dangerous condition, often caused by
being exposed to cold weather, in which your
body temperature is lower than normal

Word building: **hypothermal** *adjective*

hypothesis   (*say* huy-<u>poth</u>-uh-suhs)
noun an idea which is taken as a useful
starting point for a discussion or scientific
investigation

Word building: The plural is **hypotheses**. |
hypothesise *verb*   **hypothetical**
adjective   **hypothetically** *adverb*

hysterical
adjective **1** extremely and wildly
emotional **2** laughing uncontrollably

Word building: **hysterics** *plural noun* a
violent emotional outburst   **hysteria**
noun   **hysterically** *adverb*
Word history: from a Greek word meaning
'suffering in the uterus' (women were the ones
believed to suffer from emotion like this)

Ii

I

pronoun the word that the speaker of a sentence uses about himself or herself: *I walked to the station.*

Word use: Other forms are **my** (*my hat*), **mine** (*That book is mine*), **me** (*Give it to me*), **myself** (*I hurt myself*).

ibis (*say* <u>uy</u>-buhs)

noun a wading bird with a long, thin, down-curved beak

Word building: The plural is **ibises**.

ice

noun **1** frozen water
verb **2** to become frozen: *The pond has iced over.* **3** to cover with icing: *to ice a cake*

Word building: **icy** *adjective*: *an icy road | an icy wind* **icily** *adverb* **iciness** *noun*

iceberg

noun a large mass of ice broken off from a glacier and floating in the sea

ice-cream

noun a sweet frozen food made with cream or milk

ice skate

noun a special boot with a blade running from the front of the sole to the back of the sole

Word use: This word is often shortened to **skate**. Word building: **ice-skate** *verb* to move swiftly on ice, wearing ice skates **ice-skater** *noun* person who ice-skates

icicle

noun a hanging tapering piece of ice formed by the freezing of dripping water

icing

noun a mixture of sugar and water or other ingredients for covering cakes

icon (*say* <u>uy</u>-kon)

noun **1** a picture, especially one used in religious worship **2** a small picture or symbol on a computer screen, that stands for a process, a group of files, or some other such thing, and can be clicked on to be opened or accessed **3** a person or thing that is so strongly associated with a particular place or way of life that it is seen as a symbol of it: *Uluru, kangaroos and surfers are all Australian icons.*

I'd

a short form of **I would** or **I had**

idea

noun a thought or picture in the mind

ideal

noun **1** an idea of something at its most perfect: *She is my ideal of a doctor.* **2** a high ambition or standard: *You must work hard towards your ideals.*

Word building: **ideal** *adjective* **idealise** *verb* **idealism** *noun* **ideally** *adverb*

identical

adjective exactly alike: *identical twins*

Word building: **identically** *adverb*

identify

verb to recognise or prove as being a particular thing or person: *Can you identify your keys?*

Word building: Other forms are **I identified, I have identified, I am identifying.** | **identifiable** *adjective* **identification** *noun*

identity

noun **1** the condition of being a certain person or thing: *The group kept its identity under different leaders.* **2** a well-known personality: *an identity in the cricket club*

Word building: The plural is **identities**.

identity theft

noun stealing information about a person so as to use their bank accounts or their credit cards

idiom   (*say* id-ee-uhm)

noun a saying that is only used in one particular language, especially one that does not mean exactly what the words themselves mean: *'It's raining cats and dogs' is an idiom in English for 'It's raining very heavily'.*

Word building: **idiomatic** *adjective* **idiomatically** *adverb*

idiosyncrasy

(*say* id-ee-oh-sink-ruh-see)

noun a peculiarity of someone's character or behaviour: *Lee's idiosyncrasy is writing with purple ink.*

Word building: The plural is **idiosyncrasies**. | **idiosyncratic** *adjective* **idiosyncratically** *adverb*

idiot

noun **1** someone who is very mentally deficient **2** a very stupid person

Other words: **dunce, fool, imbecile, moron, simpleton**

Word building: **idiotic** *adjective* **idiotically** *adverb*

idle

adjective **1** not doing or wanting to do anything: *idle workmen* **2** not being used: *idle machinery | idle time*

Word building: **idleness** *noun* **idler** *noun* **idly** *adverb*

idol

noun a statue worshipped as a god

Word building: **idolatry** *noun* **idolise** *verb*

i.e.

short for *id est*, Latin words meaning 'that is': *Please bring to the exam all your stationery needs, i.e. pencils, paper and ruler.*

if

conjunction **1** supposing that: *I'll go if you want me to.* **2** whether: *I don't know if I can stand on my head.*

igloo

noun a dome-shaped Inuit hut built of blocks of hard snow

ignite

verb to set on fire

ignition

noun **1** the act of setting on fire **2** a system for setting on fire, especially that of the electrical sparks which ignite the fuel in the cylinders in a car engine

ignoble

adjective of low character and behaviour

Word use: This is the opposite of **noble**. Word building: **ignobly** *adverb*

ignoramus   (*say* ig-nuh-ray-muhs)

noun someone who knows little or nothing

Word building: The plural is **ignoramuses**.

ignorant

adjective **1** uneducated **2** having no knowledge: *ignorant of Russian*

Word building: **ignorance** *noun* **ignorantly** *adverb*

ignore

verb to take no notice of

iguana   (*say* ig-wah-nuh)

noun a large lizard of tropical America

Word history: from a Native South American language

ill

adjective **1** sick **2** bad: *ill feeling* *adverb* **3** badly: *to treat someone ill* *noun* **4** an evil: *the ills of our society*

Word building: **illness** *noun*

I'll

a short form of **I will**

illegal

adjective not allowed by the law

Word building: **illegality** *noun* **illegally** *adverb*

illegible

adjective not able to be read: *illegible writing*

Word building: **illegibility** *noun* **illegibly** *adverb*

illegitimate
adjective **1** born to parents who are not legally married **2** against the law or not allowed

Word building: **illegitimacy** *noun* **illegitimately** *adverb*

illicit   (*say* i-<u>lis</u>-uht)
adjective forbidden or not legal: *illicit alcohol*

illiterate
adjective unable to read and write

Word building: **illiteracy** *noun*

illuminate
verb **1** to light up **2** to give knowledge to or inform: *Would you care to illuminate me on this point?*

Word building: **illumination** *noun*

illusion
noun a false idea or daydream: *illusions of becoming a rock singer*

illustrate
verb **1** to make clear by giving examples: *I'll illustrate my theory about leadership with accounts of the lives of some famous explorers.* **2** to provide with pictures: *The author illustrated the book with photographs.*

Word building: **illustrator** *noun* someone who illustrates books   **illustration** *noun* **illustrative** *adjective*

illustrious
adjective famous or distinguished: *an illustrious family in the nation's history*

Word building: **illustriously** *adverb*

im-
prefix a word part meaning **1** in or into: *immigrate* **2** not: *immortal*

I'm
a short form of **I am**

image
noun **1** a picture in the mind: *I have an image of the perfect house.* **2** reflection: *your image in the mirror* **3** an exact likeness: *She is the image of her mother.*

Word building: **imagery** *noun* all the metaphors, similes, and other figures of speech we use to express ourselves

imagination
noun the ability to form pictures in your mind or to make up interesting stories

Word building: **imaginative** *adjective*

imagine
verb **1** to form a picture of in the mind: *to imagine a scene at the beach*
Other words: **visualise**
2 to think something is true or real when it is not: *There was no-one outside so I must have imagined I heard footsteps.*
Other words: **dream, fancy**
3 to think or believe: *I imagine she'll be happy when she hears the good news.*
Other words: **assume, expect, presume, suppose**

Word building: **imaginary** *adjective* only in the mind

imam   (*say* im-<u>ahm</u>)
noun an Islamic religious leader

imbecile   (*say* <u>im</u>-buh-seel)
noun someone who is mentally deficient

Word building: **imbecile** *adjective*

imitate
verb to copy or use as a model

Word building: **imitation** *noun*   **imitative** *adjective*   **imitator** *noun*

immaculate
adjective spotlessly clean

Word building: **immaculately** *adverb*

immediate
adjective happening straight away: *an immediate reply*

Word building: **immediacy** *noun*   **immediately** *adverb*

immense
adjective extremely large

Word building: **immensely** *adverb*   **immensity** *noun*

immerse
verb to put below the surface of a liquid: *I immersed my feet in the warm water.*

Word building: **immersion** *noun*
Word history: from a Latin word meaning 'dipped'

immigrate
verb to come to live in a new country

Word building: **immigrant** *noun* someone who immigrates   **immigration** *noun*

immigrate/emigrate Don't confuse **immigrate** with **emigrate**, which is to leave your own country to go to live in a new country.

imminent

adjective likely to happen at any moment

Word building: **imminence** *noun*   **imminently** *adverb*

imminent/eminent Don't confuse **imminent** with **eminent**, which means 'important' or 'high in rank'.

immoral

adjective wrong or wicked

Word use: Compare this with **moral**.
Word building: **immorality** *noun*   **immorally** *adverb*

immortal

adjective living or lasting forever: *the immortal works of Banjo Paterson*

Word building: **immortalise** *verb*   **immortality** *noun*   **immortally** *adverb*

immune

adjective protected from a disease: *She is immune to mumps now.*

Word building: **immunology** *noun* the science that deals with protection from diseases   **immunise** *verb*   **immunity** *noun*

imp

noun **1** a little devil **2** a child who misbehaves a bit

Word building: **impish** *adjective*   **impishly** *adverb*

impact

noun the hitting of one thing against another: *I heard the impact of the cars at the corner.*

impair

verb to make worse: *Sickness impaired her performance.*

Word building: **impairment** *noun*

impartial

adjective not taking one side or the other: *an impartial judge*
Other words: **fair, neutral, unbiased**

Word building: **impartiality** *noun*   **impartially** *adverb*

impasse   (*say* im-pahs)

noun a situation from which there is no escape: *When they ran into a dead end with high walls around it, they realised they had reached an impasse.*

impassive

adjective not showing any emotion: *Hua's face remained impassive as I told my story.*

Word building: **impassively** *adverb*   **impassivity** *noun*

impatient

adjective **1** not wanting to wait: *They were impatient to start on the trip.*
Other words: **eager, enthusiastic, keen**
2 short-tempered or unwilling to be patient: *The children were noisy and he became impatient with them.*
Other words: **cranky, cross, crotchety, grumpy, irritable**

Word building: **impatience** *noun*   **impatiently** *adverb*

impeccable

adjective without any faults: *Your work was impeccable.*

Word use: The more usual word is **perfect**.
Word building: **impeccably** *adverb*

impede

verb to slow down or block the way of: *The demonstration impeded the traffic.*

Word building: **impediment** *noun*

imperfect

adjective faulty or not perfect

Word building: **imperfection** *noun*   **imperfectly** *adverb*

imperial

adjective **1** belonging to an empire: *the imperial throne* **2** having to do with a system of measurement set up in Britain and used in Australia before the metric system was introduced

imperial system

noun a former system of measurement for weight, length and area: *Inches and feet were units of measurement in the imperial system.*

imperious

adjective arrogant or bossy: *The director had an imperious manner.*

Word building: **imperiously** *adverb*

impersonal

adjective not showing any personal feelings: *Her remarks were cool and impersonal.*

Word building: **impersonally** *adverb*

impersonate

verb to pretend to be: *The thief impersonated a detective to persuade the guard to open the door.*

Word building: **impersonator** *noun* someone who acts the part of another, often on stage or on TV   **impersonation** *noun*

impertinent

adjective cheeky or rude

Word building: **impertinence** *noun* **impertinently** *adverb*

impetuous

adjective acting hastily and thoughtlessly

Word building: **impetuosity** *noun* **impetuously** *adverb*

impetus

noun **1** a moving force, stimulus, or impulse: *a fresh impetus to study hard* **2** the force or energy of a moving object

Word building: The plural is **impetuses**.

implement   (*say* im-pluh-muhnt)

noun **1** a tool: *a kitchen implement*
verb (*say* im-pluh-ment) **2** to put into effect: *to implement a plan*

Word building: **implementation** *noun*

implicit   (*say* im-plis-uht)

adjective **1** suggested or implied but not actually stated: *an implicit understanding* **2** absolute or unquestioning: *implicit reliance on a friend*

Word building: **implicitly** *adverb*

implore

verb to beg or plead

Word building: **imploringly** *adverb*

imply   (*say* im-pluy)

verb **1** to mean: *What do these words imply?* **2** to suggest without actually stating: *She did not say it was urgent but her manner implied it.*

Word building: Other forms are **I implied, I have implied, I am implying.** | **implication** *noun*

imply/infer Don't confuse **imply** with **infer**, which means 'to understand from information you've been given', as in *I infer from the expression on your face that you don't like broccoli.*

impolite

adjective having bad manners

Word building: **impolitely** *adverb*

import

verb to bring in from another country: *Australia imports clothing from Hong Kong.*

Word building: **import** *noun*   **importation** *noun*   **importer** *noun*

important

adjective **1** having great meaning or effect: *an important message* | *an important event*
Other words: **critical, crucial, key, major, momentous, significant**
2 leading or powerful: *an important visitor*
Other words: **eminent, influential, notable, prominent**

Word building: **importance** *noun*   **importantly** *adverb*

impose

verb **1** to set officially as something to be obeyed or paid: *to impose a tax* | *to impose a new law* **2** to push or force yourself on others: *We don't want to impose on you by staying the night.*

Word building: **imposition** *noun*

imposing

adjective making an impression on your mind: *an imposing building* | *an imposing person*

impossible

adjective **1** not able to be done or performed: *It is impossible to hold your breath for that long.* **2** not able to be, exist, or happen: *It's impossible for him to have done it — he was overseas the whole week.* **3** not able to be true: *an impossible story* **4** very difficult to manage or put up with: *an impossible situation*

Word building: **impossibility** *noun*

impostor   (*say* im-pos-tuh)

noun someone who deceives other people by pretending to be someone else

impotent   (*say* im-puh-tuhnt)

adjective not having the power to do things

Word use: The more usual word is **powerless**.
Word building: **impotence** *noun*   **impotently** *adverb*

impress

verb **1** to fill with admiration: *My sister's musical talent impressed everyone in the audience.* **2** to fix firmly in the mind: *She impressed her news on us.*

Word building: **impressive** *adjective*

impression

noun **1** a mark made by pressure: *the impression of a rubber stamp.* **2** a strong effect made on the mind or feelings: *Your story made an impression on the audience.* **3** a vague feeling or indication: *I had the impression she was unhappy.* | *The picture gave an impression of sunlight and leaves.*

Word building: **impressionable** *adjective* **impressionistic** *adjective*

imprint

verb to fix firmly: *The warning imprinted itself on my mind.*

impromptu

adjective made up or done on the spur of the moment: *an impromptu speech* | *an impromptu party*

Word history: from a Latin word meaning 'in readiness'

improve

verb to make or become better

Word building: **improvement** *noun*

improvise (say im-pruh-vuyz)

verb **1** to make do with what is available: *He improvised a meal from the leftovers in the fridge.* **2** to invent or compose on the spot: *to improvise a little tune*

Word building: **improvisation** *noun* **improviser** *noun*

impudent (say im-pyuh-duhnt)

adjective cheeky or insolent

Word building: **impudence** *noun* **impudently** *adverb*

impulse

noun a sudden desire: *He felt an impulse to run.*

Word building: **impulsive** *adjective* **impulsively** *adverb* **impulsiveness** *noun*

in

preposition **1** inside or within: *in the house* | *in the music business* | *in ten minutes* *adjective* **2** in fashion or in season: *Short hair is in this year.* | *Grapes are in now.*

in-

prefix a word part meaning **1** in or into: *inhale* | *inland* **2** not: *inadequate*

Word history: from Old English and Middle English

inadequate

adjective not enough to fill a need: *inadequate food*

Word building: **inadequacy** *noun* **inadequately** *adverb*

inane

adjective silly or senseless: *an inane remark*

Word building: **inanity** *noun* (**inanities**) **inanely** *adverb*

inanimate

adjective not living: *inanimate objects*

inaugurate

verb to bring into public use with an opening ceremony

Word building: **inaugural** *adjective*: *the inaugural meeting of the new club* **inauguration** *noun*

incandescent (say in-kan-des-uhnt)

adjective glowing with white heat

Word building: **incandescence** *noun*

incapacitate

verb to make unable or unfit: *Illness incapacitated the patient.*

Word building: **incapacitation** *noun*

incarnate (say in-kah-nuht)

adjective with a human body: *the devil incarnate*

Word building: **incarnation** *noun*

incense¹ (say in-sens)

noun a substance which gives off a sweet smell when burnt

incense² (say in-sens)

verb to make angry

incentive

noun something that encourages and gives a motive: *The scholarship was an incentive for her to work hard.*

incessant

adjective continuing without stopping: *an incessant noise*

Word building: **incessantly** *adverb*

incest

noun sexual intercourse between people from the same family

Word building: **incestuous** *adjective* **incestuously** *adverb*

inch

noun **1** a unit of length in the imperial system equal to 25.4 millimetres
verb **2** to move by a short distance at a time: *to inch along the cliff*

Word history: from a Latin word meaning 'twelfth part'

incident

noun an event or happening

Word building: **incidental** *adjective* happening at the same time as something more important   **incidentally** *adverb*

incinerate   (*say* in-<u>sin</u>-uh-rayt)

verb to burn to ashes: *We incinerated the rubbish. | The house was incinerated in the bushfire.*

Word building: **incinerator** *noun* a container for burning things in   **incineration** *noun*

incisor   (*say* in-<u>suy</u>-zuh)

noun a tooth in the front part of the jaw, used for cutting or biting

incite

verb to urge on or stir up: *He incited the crowd to riot.*

Word building: **incitement** *noun*

incline   (*say* in-<u>kluyn</u>)

verb **1** to slant or lean **2** to lean or tend towards in your mind
noun (*say* <u>in</u>-kluyn) **3** a slope

Word building: **inclination** *noun*: *They showed little inclination to do as they were told.*

include

verb to consist of or contain as a part: *Education includes what we learn both at home and at school.*

Word building: **inclusion** *noun*   **inclusive** *adjective*   **inclusively** *adverb*

incognito   (*say* in-kog-<u>nee</u>-toh)

adverb with your name or appearance changed so you won't be recognised: *He's travelling incognito.*

Word history: from a Latin word meaning 'unknown'

income

noun the money someone earns from their work or investments

income tax

noun a tax which the government sets each year, based on how much money you earn

incongruous   (*say* in-<u>kon</u>-grooh-uhs)

adjective out of place or unsuitable: *The man in the business suit looked incongruous at the barbecue.*

Word building: **incongruity** *noun*   **incongruously** *adverb*   **incongruousness** *noun*

inconvenient

adjective awkward or causing trouble: *an inconvenient time | an inconvenient way to travel*

Word building: **inconvenience** *noun*   **inconveniently** *adverb*

incorporate   (*say* in-<u>kaw</u>-puh-rayt)

verb to include and make part of: *We incorporated several ideas into the design of the house.*

Word building: **incorporation** *noun*

incorrigible   (*say* in-<u>ko</u>-ruh-juh-buhl)

adjective too bad to ever improve: *an incorrigible liar*

Word building: **incorrigibly** *adverb*

increase

verb to make or become greater or more in number: *to increase your knowledge | Australia's population increases every year.*

Word building: **increase** *noun*: *an increase in the price of bread*   **increasingly** *adverb* more and more: *increasingly sad*

incredible

adjective hard to believe: *incredible bravery | an incredible story*

Word building: **incredibility** *noun*   **incredibly** *adverb*

incredulous   (*say* in-<u>krej</u>-uh-luhs)

adjective not able to believe something, usually because it is too surprising or shocking: *I am incredulous that you have left the baby alone.*

Word use: You use **incredulous** to describe the way a person feels about something, but you use **incredible** to describe something that is unbelievable or very good.
Word building: **incredulity** *noun* refusal or inability to believe   **incredulously** *adverb*   **incredulousness** *noun*

incubate (*say* in-kyooh-bayt)

verb to hatch by keeping warm naturally or artificially: *The hen incubated the eggs by sitting on them for three weeks.* | *We are incubating these eggs under a warm lamp.*

Word building: **incubator** *noun* a machine that looks like a plastic box, for keeping premature babies at a constant temperature   **incubation** *noun*
Word history: from a Latin word meaning 'hatched' or 'sat on'

incur

verb to bring upon yourself: *to incur someone's anger* | *to incur debts*

Word building: Other forms are **I incurred, I have incurred, I am incurring.**
Word history: from a Latin word meaning 'run into'

indebted (*say* in-det-uhd)

adjective **1** owing money **2** feeling that you owe a debt of gratitude for help, a favour, or the like: *I am indebted to you for helping me with my studies.*

Word building: **indebtedness** *noun*

indecent

adjective not proper or in good taste: *indecent language*

Word building: **indecently** *adverb*

indeed

adverb truly or in fact: *Indeed he did it.*

indelible (*say* in-del-uh-buhl)

adjective **1** not able to be removed: *He made an indelible impression on us.* **2** making marks which can't be removed or rubbed out: *an indelible pencil*

Word building: **indelibly** *adverb*

indent

verb to set in or back from the margin: *to indent the first line of a paragraph*

Word building: **indentation** *noun*

independent

adjective **1** able to make up your own mind **2** not needing or relying on the help of others

Word building: **independence** *noun*   **independently** *adverb*

index

noun an alphabetical list of names, places or subjects in a book, showing their page numbers

Word building: The plural is **indexes** or **indices.** | **index** *verb*: *to index a book*   **indexation** *noun*

index finger

noun another name for **forefinger**

indicate

verb **1** to point out or point to: *I indicated the right way to go.* **2** to be a sign of: *Ajay's tiredness indicates he is not well.*

Word building: **indicative** (*say* in-dik-uh-tiv) *adjective*   **indication** *noun*

indicator

noun something that points to or shows something: *The car's indicator showed it was going to turn right.*

indifferent

adjective **1** showing no interest or concern: *He was indifferent to my pain.* **2** not very good: *She is an indifferent actress.* | *He is in indifferent health.*

Word building: **indifference** *noun*   **indifferently** *adverb*

indigenous (*say* in-dij-uhn-uhs)

adjective **1** native to a particular area or country: *Kangaroos are indigenous to Australia but rabbits are not.* **2** **Indigenous**, having to do with Aboriginal and Torres Strait Islander people: *Indigenous issues*

Word building: **indigene** *noun* a native inhabitant of a country   **indigenously** *adverb*

indigestion (*say* in-duh-jes-chuhn)

noun pain in your stomach caused by difficulty in digesting food

Word building: **indigestible** *adjective*: *Unripe fruit is indigestible.*

indignation

noun anger at something you think is unjust or wicked

Word building: **indignant** *adjective*   **indignantly** *adverb*

indignity (*say* in-dig-nuh-tee)

noun treatment which makes you feel embarrassed and foolish: *the indignity of being sent from the room*

Word building: The plural is **indignities.**

indigo (*say* in-dig-oh)

noun a blue dye

Word building: **indigo** *adjective* dark blue

indiscretion   (*say* in-dis-<u>kresh</u>-uhn)
noun an action which shows poor
judgement: *Joy-riding in his father's car was
a major indiscretion.*

indispensable
adjective absolutely necessary
Word building: **indispensability** *noun*
indispensably *adverb*

indisposed
adjective slightly sick or unwell: *indisposed
with a cold*
Word building: **indisposition** *noun*

individual
adjective **1** single or separate: *the individual
members of the class* **2** meant for one
person or thing only: *individual servings |
individual attention*
Word building: **individuality** *noun* the
quality that makes you different from other
people   **individual** *noun*   **individually** *adverb*

indoctrinate   (*say* in-<u>dok</u>-truh-nayt)
verb to instruct so thoroughly that the
ideas are accepted without question
Word building: **indoctrination** *noun*

indoors
adverb inside a building: *The children
played indoors while it was raining.*
Word building: **indoor** *adjective*: *indoor games*

induce
verb **1** to persuade or cause to decide: *I
will induce him to go.* **2** to cause or bring
on: *This drug induces sleep.*
Word building: **inducement** *noun*

indulge
verb **1** to give in to: *I indulged his wish for a
lazy afternoon.*
phrase **2 indulge in,** to satisfy your own
desire for: *to indulge in chocolates*
Word building: **indulgence** *noun*   **indulgently**
adverb

industrial
adjective **1** having to do with industry
or industries: *industrial waste | industrial
training | industrial worker* **2** having many
manufacturing industries: *an industrial nation*
Word building: **industrialist** *noun* someone
who owns or manages an industrial
business   **industrialise** *verb*   **industrialisation**
noun

industrious
adjective hardworking: *He is an industrious
student.*
Other words: **conscientious, diligent**
Word building: **industriously** *adverb*

industry   (*say* <u>in</u>-duhs-tree)
noun **1** all businesses that produce
or manufacture things: *the growth of
industry in Australia* **2** a particular type
of manufacturing business: *the steel
industry* **3** any large-scale business activity:
the tourist industry | the pastoral industry
4 hard, careful and conscientious work
Word building: The plural is **industries**.

inept
adjective awkward or unskilful: *an inept
attempt to chop wood*
Word building: **ineptitude** *noun*   **ineptly**
adverb   **ineptness** *noun*

inertia   (*say* in-<u>er</u>-shuh)
noun sluggishness or lack of energy:
Inertia overcame us in the midday heat.
Word history: from a Latin word meaning 'lack
of skill' or 'inactivity'

inevitable
adjective not able to be avoided: *an
inevitable result*
Word building: **inevitability** *noun*   **inevitably**
adverb

inexpensive
adjective not costing much: *an inexpensive
toy*
Word building: **inexpensively** *adverb*

infallible   (*say* in-<u>fal</u>-uh-buhl)
adjective **1** never being wrong or making a
mistake: *an infallible judge of character*
2 able to be relied on completely: *an
infallible law of nature | an infallible cure for
hiccups*
Word building: **infallibility** *noun*   **infallibly**
adverb

infamous   (*say* <u>in</u>-fuh-muhs)
adjective deserving or causing a very bad
name or reputation: *an infamous crime*
Word building: **infamously** *adverb*   **infamy**
noun

infant
noun a baby or very young child
Word building: **infancy** *noun* the time of being
an infant

infantile (*say* in-fuhn-tuyl)
adjective **1** having to do with infants:
infantile diseases **2** childish or like an
infant: *infantile behaviour*

infantry
noun soldiers who fight on foot with hand
weapons

infatuated (*say* in-fat-chooh-ayt-uhd)
adjective blindly or foolishly in love
Word building: **infatuate** *verb* **infatuation**
noun

infect
verb **1** to give germs or a disease to: *to
infect a wound* | *Last year, I got measles and
infected the whole family.* **2** to affect by
spreading from one to another: *Bernard's
restlessness infected the class.*
Word building: **infection** *noun* **infectious**
adjective **infectiousness** *noun*

infer (*say* in-fer)
verb to form an opinion after considering
all the facts and information: *He inferred
from the spy's report that the enemy would
attack.*
Word use: The more usual word is **gather**.
Word building: Other forms are **I inferred, I
have inferred, I am inferring.** | **inference** *noun*

infer/imply Don't confuse **infer** with **imply**,
which means 'to suggest without actually
stating' or 'to mean'.

inferior (*say* in-fear-ree-uh)
adjective **1** lower in rank or position: *an
inferior officer* **2** lower in value or quality:
inferior work
Word building: **inferiority** *noun*

inferno
noun a place that seems like hell because
of great heat or fire
Word building: The plural is **infernos**.
Word history: from an Italian word meaning
'hell' and before this from a Latin word
meaning 'underground'

infest
verb to spread or swarm over in great
numbers: *Snakes infest this part of the bush.*
Word building: **infestation** *noun*

infidel (*say* in-fuh-del)
noun someone who doesn't accept a
particular religious faith

Word use: This is an old-fashioned word that
Christians and Muslims used of each other in
the past.
Word building: **infidel** *adjective*

infiltrate
verb to secretly join or enter, usually to
work against: *She infiltrated the enemy
camp.*
Word building: **infiltration** *noun* **infiltrator**
noun

infinite (*say* in-fuh-nuht)
adjective endless or having no limits: *The
desert seemed infinite to the weary travellers.*
Word building: **infinitely** *adverb*

infinitive (*say* in-fin-uh-tiv)
noun the grammatical form of a verb that
you use after certain other verbs or after *to*,
such as *come* in *I didn't come* and *I wanted
to come*
Word building: **infinitive** *adjective*: *an infinitive
verb*

infirm
adjective weak in body or health
Word building: **infirmity** *noun*

infirmary
noun a kind of hospital: *the school's infirmary*
Word building: The plural is **infirmaries**.

inflame
verb to make angry or passionate: *The
Prime Minister inflamed the crowd with a
fiery speech.*
Word building: **inflammatory** *adjective*

inflammable
adjective easily set on fire: *inflammable
clothing*
Word use: Nowadays, the more usual word
is **flammable**. This is because many people
thought **inflammable** meant *not* easily set on
fire because *in-* at the beginning of a word
often does mean 'not', as in *inactive* and
insensitive. This misunderstanding could have
placed people in danger, so it was decided to
use **flammable** to mean easily set on fire and
nonflammable as its opposite, meaning not
likely to burn easily.
Word building: **inflammability** *noun*

inflammation
noun a red, painful, and often swollen area
on the body, caused by an infection
Word building: **inflamed** *adjective*

inflate
verb **1** to swell with gas or air: *to inflate a balloon* | *The rubber boat inflated.* **2** to cause a large rise in: *to inflate prices*

Word building: **inflation** *noun* a large rise in prices and cost of living   **inflatable** *adjective*   **inflationary** *adjective*

inflict
verb to cause to be experienced or suffered: *to inflict a wound*

Word building: **infliction** *noun*

influence
noun some force or power that affects or produces a change in someone or something else: *I try to be a good influence on my little brother.*

Word building: **influence** *verb*   **influential** *adjective*

influenza
noun a sickness caused by a virus which affects the nose and throat and causes high temperatures and tiredness

Word use: A shortened form of this word is **flu**.

influx
noun a flowing in: *influx of water* | *There was an influx of migrants to Australia when gold was discovered.*

Word building: The plural is **influxes**.

inform
verb to give news or knowledge to: *I informed them of your success.*

Word building: **informant** *noun* someone who informs   **informer** *noun* someone who tells on someone else, especially to the police   **informative** *adjective*

informal
adjective **1** casual or without ceremony or formality: *an informal visit* **2** not correct or usual: *an informal vote*

Word building: **informality** *noun*   **informally** *adverb*

information
noun knowledge or news: *tourist information*

information report
noun writing which gives facts on something. See the 'Types of writing and speaking' table at the end of this book.

information technology
noun the use of technology and computers to produce, save, find and share information

Word use: A shortened form of this is **IT**.

infra-
prefix a word part meaning 'below' or 'beneath': *infra-red*

Word history: from Latin

infra-red
noun the invisible part of the spectrum of light which has a wavelength longer than that of visible red light

Word building: **infra-red** *adjective*

infringe
verb to disobey: *to infringe a law* | *They infringed the rules of the club.*

Word use: The more usual word is **break**.
Word building: **infringement** *noun*
Word history: from a Latin word meaning 'break off'

infuriate
verb to make very angry

Word building: **infuriating** *adjective* **infuriatingly** *adverb*   **infuriation** *noun*

infuse
verb to soak in hot water to draw out the flavour: *to infuse tea*

Word building: **infuser** *noun*   **infusion** *noun*

ingenious   (*say* in-jeen-ee-uhs)
adjective **1** cleverly made or invented: *an ingenious machine* **2** clever at working out ways of doing and making things: *an ingenious inventor*

Word building: **ingeniously** *adverb*   **ingenuity** *noun*

ingot   (*say* ing-guht)
noun a block of metal which has been melted and poured into a mould

Word history: from a Middle English word for a 'mould for metal'

ingrained
adjective fixed firmly and deep: *ingrained habits* | *ingrained dirt*

ingratitude
noun failure to be grateful

Word building: **ingrate** *noun* an ungrateful person

ingredient

noun one of the parts of a mixture or a whole: *an ingredient in a cake | An ingredient of my success was hard work.*

inhabit

verb to live or dwell in: *Aboriginal people inhabited Australia long before Europeans came.* Other words: **populate**

Word building: **inhabitable** *adjective* **inhabitant** *noun*

inhale

verb to breathe in: *to inhale the fresh country air | Inhale deeply for good health.*

Word building: **inhaler** *noun* a device for puffing medicine into the mouth to help make breathing easier **inhalant** *noun* **inhalation** *noun*

inherit

verb **1** to receive as a gift from someone who has died: *Jess and I inherited some money and a stamp collection from our aunt.* **2** to get, as a family characteristic, through your parents: *My brother inherited Mum's blue eyes.*

Word building: **inheritance** *noun*

inhibit

verb to hold back or hinder: *Black plastic spread over your garden should inhibit the growth of weeds.*

Word building: **inhibited** *adjective* shy **inhibition** *noun*

inimical

adjective acting as an enemy or unfavourable: *an inimical attitude | a climate inimical to health*

Word building: **inimically** *adverb*

iniquity   (*say* in-<u>ik</u>-wuh-tee)

noun wickedness: *He will be punished for his iniquity.*

Word building: The plural is **iniquities.** | **iniquitous** *adjective*

initial

adjective **1** having to do with the beginning: *The initial plan was later changed.*
noun **2** the first letter of a word or name
verb **3** to mark or sign with the initials of your name

Word building: Other verb forms are **I initialled, I have initialled, I am initialling.** | **initially** *adverb* at first

initiate   (*say* in-<u>ish</u>-ee-ayt)

verb **1** to begin or set going: *I want to initiate an annual fun run at our school.* **2** to admit into a society or club with a formal ceremony

Word building: **initiate** *noun* someone who has been initiated   **initiation** *noun*   **initiator** *noun*

initiative   (*say* in-<u>ish</u>-ee-uh-tiv)

noun **1** a first act or step: *to take the initiative* **2** readiness or ability to set something going

Word use: Another word for definition 2 is **enterprise.**

inject

verb to use a syringe and needle to force a fluid into: *The doctor injected me with a pain-killing drug.*

Word building: **injection** *noun*

injure

verb to hurt or cause harm to: *The sharp rock injured me when I slipped. | Gossip often injures innocent people.*

Word building: **injury** *noun* (**injuries**)   **injured** *adjective*   **injurious** *adjective*

injustice

noun **1** something that is unfair or unjust **2** unfairness or lack of justice

ink

noun a dark fluid used for writing or printing

Word building: **ink** *verb*

inkling

noun a vague or uncertain idea: *I had an inkling of what might happen.*

inlaid

adjective set in the surface of something: *an inlaid pattern in wood*

Word building: **inlay** *noun*

inland

adjective having to do with, or situated in parts of a country away from the coast or border: *inland towns*

Word building: **inland** *adverb*: *We went inland.* **inland** *noun*: *We went to the inland for our trip.*

inlet

noun a small narrow bay or cove

inmate

noun someone who has to stay in a hospital, prison or other institution

inn

noun a small hotel, especially one for travellers

Word building: **innkeeper** *noun* someone who looks after an inn
Word history: from an Old English word meaning 'house'

innate

adjective existing in a person from their birth: *Will I ever get over my innate shyness?*

Word building: **innately** *adverb* **innateness** *noun*

inner

adjective **1** further in: *an inner door* **2** private or personal: *inner thoughts*

Word building: **innermost** *adjective* furthest inwards

innings

noun **1** the turn of a member of a cricket team to bat **2** the whole team's turn at batting: *The first innings was interrupted by rain.*

innocent

adjective **1** free from guilt or from having done anything wrong **2** harmless: *innocent fun*

Word building: **innocence** *noun* **innocently** *adverb*

innocuous   (*say* in-<u>ok</u>-yooh-uhs)

adjective not harmful: *an innocuous remark*

Word building: **innocuously** *adverb* **innocuousness** *noun*

innovation   (*say* in-uh-<u>vay</u>-shuhn)

noun a new method, practice or custom

Word building: **innovate** *verb* **innovator** *noun*

innovative   (*say* <u>in</u>-uh-vuh-tiv)

adjective new and original: *She had some fantastically innovative ideas for improving publicity for the band.*

innuendo   (*say* in-yooh-<u>en</u>-doh)

noun a remark that suggests something unpleasant about someone without actually saying it

Word building: The plural is **innuendos** or **innuendoes**.

innumerable

(*say* in-<u>yooh</u>-muh-ruh-buhl)
adjective too many to be counted

Word building: **innumerably** *adverb*

inoculate   (*say* in-<u>ok</u>-yuh-layt)

noun to protect from a disease, by introducing germs which give you a very mild form of the disease
Other words: **vaccinate**

Word building: **inoculation** *noun* **inoculator** *noun*

inpatient

noun a patient who stays in hospital while they are having their treatment

input

noun anything that is put in to be used, especially by a machine

inquest

noun an official inquiry to find out how someone died

inquire

verb to ask for information: *'Do you know how to get to the city?' he inquired.* | *Let's inquire about the singing lessons.*

Word use: Another spelling is **enquire**.
Word building: **inquirer** *noun* **inquiring** *adjective* **inquiringly** *adverb*

inquiry

noun **1** a question **2** an investigation: *There will be an official inquiry into what caused the fire.*

Word use: Another spelling is **enquiry**.
Word building: The plural is **inquiries**.

inquisition   (*say* in-kwuh-<u>zish</u>-uhn)

noun a thorough investigation and questioning

Word building: **inquisitor** *noun*

inquisitive   (*say* in-<u>kwiz</u>-uh-tiv)

adjective wanting to find out all about something: *inquisitive onlookers*

Word building: **inquisitively** *adverb*

insane

adjective mentally ill or mad: *He's insane.* | *an insane act*

Word building: **insanely** *adverb* **insanity** *noun*

insatiable (*say* in-<u>say</u>-shuh-buhl)

adjective never having enough: *an insatiable appetite*

Word building: **insatiably** *adverb*

inscribe

verb to write or cut: *I inscribed my name on the metal plaque.*

Word building: **inscription** *noun*

inscrutable (*say* in-<u>skrooh</u>-tuh-buhl)

adjective mysterious or not easily understood: *an inscrutable expression*

Word building: **inscrutability** *noun* **inscrutably** *adverb*

insect

noun a small creature with its body clearly divided into three parts with three pairs of legs and usually two pairs of wings

Word use: Bees, ants and flies are insects; spiders and ticks are not, even though some people call them insects.
Word history: from a Latin word meaning 'cut in' or 'cut up' (from the way insects' bodies have three segments)

insecticide (*say* in-<u>sek</u>-tuh-suyd)

noun any chemical substance used to kill insects

Word building: **insecticidal** *adjective*

insectivore

noun a bird or animal that eats insects

Word use: Compare this with **herbivore, carnivore** and **omnivore.**
Word building: **insectivorous** *adjective*: *Lizards are insectivorous.*

insecure

adjective **1** not firm or safe: *He had an insecure hold on the rope.* **2** afraid or unsure: *She feels insecure if she can't see her mother.*

Word building: **insecurely** *adverb* **insecurity** *noun*

insensitive

adjective lacking in feeling

Word building: **insensitively** *adverb* **insensitivity** *noun*

insert

verb to put or set inside: *Insert the key in the lock.* | *to insert an advertisement in a newspaper*

Word building: **insert** *noun* **insertion** *noun*

inside

noun **1** the inner part or side **2 insides,** *Informal* your stomach and intestines and other inner parts of your body
adjective **3** being on or in the inside: *inside walls* **4** coming from within a place: *inside information*
adverb **5** indoors, or into the inner part: *She's working inside.*

insight

noun an understanding of the inner nature of someone or something: *I gained an insight into the working of her mind.*

insignia (*say* in-<u>sig</u>-nee-uh)

plural noun badges or special marks of a position someone holds: *The insignia of office are passed on from one mayor to the next.*

insinuate

verb **1** to suggest something unpleasant without saying so outright: *By asking where my sales docket was, he insinuated that I had stolen the shoes.* **2** to get into gradually and slyly: *Jasper insinuated himself into the boss's favour.*

Word building: **insinuation** *noun*

insipid

adjective **1** without much flavour: *an insipid cup of tea* **2** boring, dull: *I thought the famous painting was rather insipid.*

insist

verb to demand firmly: *I insist that you come.*

Word building: **insistence** *noun* **insistent** *adjective* **insistently** *adverb*

insolent (*say* <u>in</u>-suh-luhnt)

adjective insulting and rude

Word building: **insolence** *noun* **insolently** *adverb*

insomnia (*say* in-<u>som</u>-nee-uh)

noun sleeplessness

Word building: **insomniac** *noun* someone who has trouble sleeping at night **insomniac** *adjective*

inspect

verb **1** to look carefully at or over
Other words: **examine, review, scrutinise, study, survey**
2 to look at formally or officially: *The general inspected the soldiers.*
Other words: **review**

Word building: **inspection** *noun* **inspector** *noun*

inspire

verb **1** to have an encouraging and uplifting effect on: *The leader's courage inspired the followers.* **2** to produce or give rise to: *I seem to inspire love in all my friends.*

Word building: **inspired** *adjective*: *an inspired idea* **inspiration** *noun* **inspirer** *noun*

install

verb **1** to put into place for use: *to install a new stove* **2** to place in an official position with a ceremony: *to install the new club president*

Word building: **installation** *noun*

instalment

noun **1** a single payment in a series which is meant to pay off a debt **2** a single part of a story being published in several parts in a magazine or newspaper

instance

noun an example or case: *Looking after his friend's dog was another instance of his kindness.*

instant

noun **1** a very short space of time
Other words: **minute, moment, second**
2 a particular point of time: *At that instant the door slammed.*
Other words: **juncture, moment**
adjective **3** happening immediately: *instant relief*
Other words: **immediate, instantaneous, sudden**
4 in a form that makes preparation quick and easy: *instant coffee*

Word building: **instantaneous** *adjective* happening or done in an instant **instantly** *adverb*

instead

adverb in place of someone or something else: *She sent me instead.*

instep

noun the upper part of your foot between your toes and ankle

instinct

noun **1** a natural urge or tendency that is there when you are born: *a bird's instinct to migrate in winter* **2** a natural knowledge or skill: *He has an instinct for making friends.*

Word building: **instinctive** *adjective* **instinctively** *adverb*

institute

verb **1** to set up or establish: *to institute a new government department* | *to institute rules of conduct*
noun **2** an organisation or society set up to carry on a particular activity: *a literary institute*

Word building: **institutor** *noun*

institution

noun **1** an organisation set up for a worthwhile cause: *an institution for the care of the aged* **2** a building used by an organisation like this **3** a setting up or establishing: *the institution of democratic government*

Word building: **institutional** *adjective* **institutionalise** *verb* **institutionally** *adverb*

instruct

verb **1** to teach or train **2** to order or command

Word building: **instructive** *adjective*: *an instructive booklet* **instruction** *noun* **instructively** *adverb* **instructor** *noun*

instrument   (*say* in-struh-muhnt)

noun **1** a mechanical device or tool: *a doctor's instrument* **2** something made to produce musical sounds: *Horns and clarinets are wind instruments.* **3** an electrical device which gives information about the state of some part of an aeroplane, car or other vehicle: *The pilot checked the instruments on the panel.*

Word building: **instrumental** *adjective*: *instrumental music* **instrumentalist** *noun* a performer on a musical instrument

insubordinate

(*say* in-suh-baw-duh-nuht)
adjective not obeying those in authority

Word building: **insubordination** *noun*

insufferable

adjective unbearable or not able to be tolerated: *He is an insufferable gossip.*

Word building: **insufferably** *adverb*

insulate   (*say* in-shuh-layt)

verb **1** to cover with something to stop the escape of electric current: *to insulate the electric toaster cord* **2** to put a special material in the roof to keep in warmth in winter and keep out heat in summer: *We insulated our house.*

Word building: **insulation** *noun* **insulator** *noun*
Word history: from a Latin word meaning 'made into an island'

insulin (*say* in-syuh-luhn)
noun a substance your body produces to help it use the sugar in the food you eat

Word use: **Diabetes** is the illness that you get if your body does not make enough insulin.
Word history: from a Latin word meaning 'island' (the gland in the body where insulin is made has lumps of tissue that look like islands)

insult (*say* in-sult)
verb **1** to act or speak rudely or offensively to
Other words: **abuse, affront, offend, slight, snub**
noun (*say* in-sult) **2** a rude or offensive action or remark
Other words: **affront, snub, taunt, tease**

Word building: **insulting** *adjective* **insultingly** *adverb*

insurance
noun a system of paying money to a company that says it will pay you a sum of money if you suffer a loss from fire, burglary, accident or the like

Word building: **insured** *noun* the person who takes out insurance **insurer** *noun* the company that provides insurance **insure** *verb*

intact
adjective unharmed, unchanged or whole: *The parcel arrived intact.*

integer (*say* in-tuh-juh)
noun any whole number

Word use: Compare this with **fraction**.
Word history: from a Latin word meaning 'untouched', 'whole', or 'entire'

integral (*say* in-tuh-gruhl)
adjective necessary to the completeness of: *Saliva is an integral part of the digestive system.*

Word building: **integrally** *adverb*

integrate
verb to bring together to make a united whole: *I've tried to integrate all these facts into one powerful argument. | The government is working to integrate the two races to bring harmony to the nation.*

Word building: **integration** *noun*

integrity (*say* in-teg-ruh-tee)
noun honesty and trustworthiness

intellect (*say* in-tuh-lekt)
noun the power of your mind to think, reason and understand: *to have a fine intellect*
Other words: **intelligence**

intellectual (*say* in-tuh-lek-chooh-uhl)
adjective **1** of interest to the mind or intellect: *He prefers intellectual hobbies such as chess.* **2** making much use of the mind: *an intellectual writer*

Word building: **intellectual** *noun* **intellectuality** *noun* **intellectually** *adverb*

intelligence (*say* in-tel-uh-juhns)
noun **1** the ability to learn, understand and reason: *Your intelligence enables you to solve problems.* **2** good mental ability: *a woman of intelligence*

Word building: **intelligent** *adjective* **intelligently** *adverb*

intend
verb to have in mind or to mean: *I intended to do it. | I intend no harm.*

Word building: **intended** *adjective*: *a tool intended for cutting* **intention** *noun*

intense
adjective **1** very great or strong: *intense pain | intense joy* **2** showing strong feeling: *an intense expression*

Word building: **intensify** *verb* (**intensified, intensifying**) **intensely** *adverb* **intenseness** *noun*

intensity
noun **1** great strength, especially of feeling: *the intensity of the wind | the intensity of his emotions* **2** high degree: *the intensity of the cold*

intensive
adjective with a lot of attention or work: *intensive care of a seriously ill person | intensive farming*

Word building: **intensively** *adverb*

intent¹
noun purpose, or what you intend: *He acted with criminal intent.*

intent²
adjective having your mind firmly fixed: *Zoe was intent on watching the end of the movie before starting her homework.*

Word building: **intently** *adverb*

intention
noun a firm plan or purpose

Word building: **intentional** *adjective*
intentionally *adverb*

inter-

prefix a word part meaning 'between' or 'among': *intercom* | *international*

Word history: from Latin

interact

verb to act on or have an effect on each other: *Some chemicals interact to form gases.*

Word building: **interaction** *noun*　**interactive** *adjective*

intercept　(*say* in-tuh-<u>sept</u>)

verb to take or seize on the way from one place to another: *to intercept a letter*

Word building: **interception** *noun*　**interceptor** *noun*

interchange

verb **1** to cause to change places: *I interchanged the two names on the list.*　*noun* **2** a point at which travellers can change direction, as in a public transport system, or where major roads meet

Word building: **interchange** *noun*: *interchange of ideas*　**interchangeable** *adjective*　**interchangeably** *adverb*

intercom

noun a system for sending spoken messages throughout a place such as a school or office

Word history: short for **intercommunication system**

intercourse

noun **1** exchange of ideas, thoughts and feelings between people **2** short for **sexual intercourse**

interest

noun **1** the feeling you have when your attention is held by something: *to have an interest in stamp collecting* **2** importance: *The results of the election were of great interest to us all.* **3** money paid to you by a bank or building society for the use of the money you have put into your account *verb* **4** to hold the attention of

Word building: **interested** *adjective*
interestedly *adverb*　**interesting** *adjective*　**interestingly** *adverb*

interface

noun **1** the point where a connection is made between a computer and another piece of equipment, or between a computer and the person using it **2** a piece of software that makes this connection

interfere　(*say* in-tuh-<u>fear</u>)

verb **1** to take a part in someone else's affairs without being asked: *Our neighbours interfere all the time.* **2** to clash or get in the way: *Your plans interfere with mine.*

Word building: **interference** *noun*

intergalactic　(*say* in-tuh-guh-<u>lak</u>-tik)

adjective existing or happening between different galaxies in space: *intergalactic warfare*

interim　(*say* <u>in</u>-tuh-ruhm)

noun a time coming between: *Tony's between jobs at the moment — he goes surfing in the interim.*

Word building: **interim** *adjective* temporary
Word history: from a Latin word meaning 'in the meantime'

interior　(*say* int-<u>ear</u>-ree-uh)

adjective being within: *the interior rooms*

Word use: The opposite is **exterior**.
Word building: **interior** *noun*: *the interior of the country*

interjection

noun a remark made to interrupt a conversation or a speech

Word building: **interject** *verb*　**interjector** *noun*

interlude

noun **1** a short period of time, especially of restfulness: *Our picnic by the river was a pleasant interlude.* **2** a short performance, especially of music between two acts of a play

intermediate

adjective being or happening between two times, places or stages

interminable　(*say* in-<u>term</u>-uhn-uh-buhl)

adjective without end: *interminable talks*

Word building: **interminably** *adverb*

intermission

noun an interval, especially at the pictures

intermittent

adjective stopping and starting: *There was intermittent rain all day.*

Word building: **intermittently** *adverb*

intern¹ (*say* in-<u>tern</u>)
verb to keep in an enclosed and guarded area, especially during wartime

Word building: **internment** *noun*

intern² (*say* <u>in</u>-tern)
noun a doctor who has recently finished university and is working full-time in a hospital

internal
adjective **1** having to do with the inside: *the internal organs of our bodies* **2** happening within: *the internal affairs of a country*

Word use: The opposite of this is **external**.
Word building: **internally** *adverb*

international
adjective between or among nations: *international sporting events*

Word building: **internationally** *adverb*

internet
noun the linking of computers all around the world so that you can share information

Word use: This word is often shortened to **the net**.

internet cafe
noun a place like a shop where a person can access the internet by paying a fee and which sometimes provides refreshments

internet service provider
noun a company that provides access to the internet, usually for a fee: *Most internet service providers get rid of any spam before it hits your computer.*

interplay
noun the effect of actions on each other

Word building: **interplay** *verb* to have an effect on each other

interpret (*say* in-<u>ter</u>-pruht)
verb **1** to explain the meaning of: *to interpret dreams* **2** to translate what is said in a foreign language

Word building: Other forms are **I interpreted, I have interpreted, I am interpreting.** | **interpretation** *noun* **interpreter** *noun*

interrogate (*say* in-<u>te</u>-ruh-gayt)
verb to question closely to find out something: *The police interrogated the suspect.*

Word building: **interrogation** *noun* **interrogator** *noun*

interrupt (*say* in-tuh-<u>rupt</u>)
verb to stop or break into in the middle of: *She interrupted my speech.* | *to interrupt someone's work*

Word building: **interruption** *noun* **interruptive** *adjective*

intersect
verb **1** to cut or divide by passing through or across: *This line intersects the circle.* **2** to cross: *There is a signpost where the streets intersect.*

Word building: **intersection** *noun* a place where streets cross

intersperse
verb to scatter here and there among other things

Word building: **interspersion** *noun*

interstate
adjective **1** between states: *an interstate competition*
adverb **2** to or from another state: *She wants to send a letter interstate.*

interval
noun **1** the length of time between events: *an interval of 50 years* **2** a pause or break, especially halfway through a program of films or music **3** the space between things **4** the difference in pitch between two notes

intervene
verb to step in, in order to change or solve: *The government intervened in the industrial dispute.*

Word building: **intervention** *noun*

interview
noun a meeting in which someone is asked questions about something: *The Prime Minister gave an interview about the election.* | *a job interview*

Word building: **interview** *verb* **interviewer** *noun*

intestine (*say* in-<u>tes</u>-tuhn)
noun the long tube that carries food from your stomach to your anus

Word use: This word usually occurs in the plural form **intestines**.
Word building: **intestinal** *adjective*

intimate

adjective **1** very close: *intimate friends* **2** secret or deep: *intimate thoughts* **3** very thorough: *an intimate knowledge*

Word building: **intimate** *noun* a close friend **intimacy** *noun* **intimately** *adverb*

intimidate

verb **1** to make frightened or nervous **2** to frighten in order to force someone into doing something

Word building: **intimidation** *noun*

into

preposition **1** towards or at the inside or inner part: *to run into the room* | *to be well into a comic* **2** to a new or changed condition: *to turn into a frog* **3** being the divisor of, in maths: *2 into 10 equals 5*

intolerance

noun a person's inability to accept behaviour, beliefs or opinions different to their own: *Her intolerance made other people wary of speaking to her.*

intonation

noun the pattern of changes of pitch in speech or music

Word building: **intone** *verb*

intoxicate

verb to make drunk

Word building: **intoxicant** *noun* something that intoxicates **intoxication** *noun*

intra-

prefix a word part meaning 'within': *intravenous*

Word history: from Latin

intransitive verb

noun a verb like *come* that needs no object for it to make sense

Word use: The opposite is a **transitive verb**.

intravenous   (*say* in-truh-**vee**-nuhs)

adjective into a vein: *The sick baby had intravenous feeds through a tube in her arm.*

Word building: **intravenously** *adverb*

intrepid   (*say* in-**trep**-uhd)

adjective very brave: *an intrepid explorer*

Word building: **intrepidly** *adverb*

intricate   (*say* **in**-truh-kuht)

adjective finely detailed: *intricate lace*

Word building: **intricacy** *noun* **intricately** *adverb* **intricateness** *noun*

Word history: from a Latin word meaning 'entangled'

intrigue   (*say* in-**treeg**)

verb **1** to interest or make curious because of puzzling or unusual qualities: *The strange sounds intrigued her.* **2** to plan secretly

Word building: Other forms are **I intrigued, I have intrigued, I am intriguing.** | **intrigue** *noun* a secret scheme or plot **intriguing** *adjective*

intrinsic

adjective belonging to a basic nature of something or someone: *a metal with intrinsic strength* | *a person with intrinsic honesty*

introduce

verb **1** to bring two people that you know together and make them known to each other: *I'll introduce you to my friend Rachael.* **2** to speak or write about a topic for the first time **3** to bring in a new thing, idea, system or way of doing things: *to introduce a foreign species of bird into the rainforest* | *to introduce meat into the baby's diet* | *to introduce a new payment system into the business*

introduced species

noun a species of plant or animal which has been brought to an area where it does not occur naturally, often resulting in the loss of a native species

Word use: Compare this with **native species**.

introduction

noun **1** the act of making known for the first time: *We had our introduction to sailing during the holidays.* **2** the first part of a book or essay which leads up to the main subject

Word building: **introduce** *verb* **introductory** *adjective*

introvert   (*say* **in**-truh-vert)

noun someone who is concerned mainly with their own thoughts and does not like being with other people all the time: *An introvert is often a thoughtful person who is interesting once you get to know them.*

Word use: Compare this with **extrovert**.
Word building: **introverted** *adjective*

intrude

verb to enter or force yourself in when you are not wanted or invited

Word building: **intruder** *noun*: *The intruder stole our TV.* **intrusion** *noun* **intrusive** *adjective* **intrusively** *adverb*

intuition (*say* in-tyooh-<u>ish</u>-uhn)

noun a strong feeling about something without any real reason that you know of: *My intuition tells me that she's not well.*

Word building: **intuitive** *adjective* **intuitively** *adverb*

Inuit

noun **1** one of the people who originally lived in Greenland, northern Canada, Alaska and north-eastern Siberia **2** a member of this people **3** the language of this people

Word use: Another spelling for this is **Innuit**. | Another name is **Eskimo**, although this is not used much nowadays.

invade

verb **1** to attack and enter: *Caesar invaded Britain.* **2** to force yourself in on: *to invade someone's privacy*

Word building: **invader** *noun* **invasion** *noun*

invalid[1] (*say* <u>in</u>-vuh-lid)

noun someone who is sick or weak

Word building: **invalid** *adjective*: *an invalid son*

invalid[2] (*say* in-<u>val</u>-uhd)

adjective not correct, especially legally: *invalid arguments* | *an invalid will*

Word building: **invalidate** *verb* to make invalid **invalidation** *noun* **invalidly** *adverb*

invaluable

adjective with a value too great to be measured: *an invaluable painting* | *invaluable help*
Other words: **precious, priceless, treasured**
Word building: **invaluably** *adverb*

invent

verb to make or think up: *She invented a machine for cleaning windows.* | *He invented an excuse.*
Other words: **conceive, concoct, create, design, develop, devise**
Word building: **invention** *noun* **inventive** *adjective* **inventively** *adverb* **inventor** *noun*

inverse

adjective turned in the opposite position or direction

Word building: **inverse** *noun* the opposite **inversely** *adverb* **invert** *verb*

invertebrate (*say* in-<u>ver</u>-tuh-bruht)

adjective without a backbone: *A worm is an invertebrate animal.*

Word building: **invertebrate** *noun*

inverted comma

noun another name for **quotation mark**

invest

verb **1** to spend money on something in the hope of making more money: *She invested in real estate and made a big profit.* **2** to use or spend: *to invest time and effort*

Word building: **investor** *noun* someone who invests **investment** *noun*

investigate

verb to look into or examine closely: *She heard a noise and went to investigate.* | *The police investigated the crime.*

Word building: **investigation** *noun* **investigator** *noun*

invigorate

verb to fill with energy and strength: *The exercises should invigorate you.*

Word building: **invigorating** *adjective* **invigoratingly** *adverb*

invincible (*say* in-<u>vin</u>-suh-buhl)

adjective unable to be defeated or beaten

Word building: **invincibly** *adverb*

invisible

adjective unable to be seen

Word building: **invisibility** *noun* **invisibly** *adverb*

invite

verb **1** to ask to visit or take part: *We invited Ben for dinner.* | *They invited us to help in the garden.* **2** to act so as to produce a certain result: *to invite danger*

Word building: **inviting** *adjective* tempting **invitation** *noun* **invitingly** *adverb*

in vitro (*say* in <u>vit</u>-roh)

adjective in artificial surroundings, like a test tube: *in vitro fertilisation*

Word history: from Latin words meaning 'in glass'

invoice

noun a bill for things you've bought, listing all their prices separately

Word building: **invoice** *verb*

involve

verb to include as a necessary part of something: *The job of an art gallery guide involves a knowledge of art history.*

involved

adjective **1** complicated, or very difficult to sort out: *an involved plan* **2** deeply interested: *involved in music* **3** closely connected or associated, especially romantically

Word building: **involvement** *noun*

inward

adjective **1** directed towards the inside: *an inward gaze*
adverb **2** towards the inside: *Look inward for strength.*

iodine   (*say* uy-uh-deen)

noun a chemical element which produces a purple antiseptic when heated

ion

noun a tiny particle, such as an atom, which has an electric charge

ion/iron Don't confuse **ion** with **iron**, which has many meanings. Look up **iron**.

IP address

noun a unique identifying number for any computer connected to the internet

irate

adjective angry

Word building: **ire** *noun* anger

iris

noun **1** the coloured part of the eye around the pupil **2** a large brightly coloured flower

Word building: The plural is **irises**.
Word history: named after *Iris*, a messenger of the gods and goddess of the rainbow in Greek myths

irk

verb to annoy or trouble: *It irked me to wait so long.*

Word building: **irksome** *adjective*

iron

noun **1** a metallic element used in the making of tools and machinery, and which is also found in some foods and is used by the body in the making of blood **2** a tool with a handle which can be heated and used to remove the creases from clothes **3** a golf club with an iron head
adjective **4** made of iron **5** strong and unyielding: *an iron will*

Word building: **iron** *verb* to remove creases with an iron

iron/ion Don't confuse **iron** with **ion**, which is a small particle of matter with an electric charge.

ironbark

noun a gum tree with hard dark-grey bark

ironman

noun a contestant in a sporting event in which male competitors first swim, then ride bikes and finally run

irony   (*say* uy-ruh-nee)

noun a humorous way of speaking in which the real meaning is the opposite of what is said: *'How nice!' he said with irony when he saw the ugly coat.*

Word building: **ironic** *adjective*   **ironically** *adverb*

irrational

adjective absurd or unreasonable: *Jan has an irrational fear of water.*

Word use: This is the opposite of **rational**.
Word building: **irrationally** *adverb*

irregular

adjective **1** uneven: *The sick man's pulse was irregular.* | *irregular walls* **2** not usual or normal

Word use: This is the opposite of **regular**.
Word building: **irregularity** *noun*   **irregularly** *adverb*

irrelevant

adjective having nothing to do with what is being discussed: *an irrelevant remark*

Word use: The opposite of this is **relevant**.
Word building: **irrelevance** *noun*   **irrelevancy** *noun*   **irrelevantly** *adverb*

irresistible   (*say* ir-uh-<u>zist</u>-uh-buhl)
adjective so tempting that you cannot fight against it: *an irresistible impulse* / *irresistible food*

Word use: The opposite is **resistible**.
Word building: **irresistibility**
noun   **irresistibleness** *noun*   **irresistibly** *adverb*

irresponsible   (*say* ir-uh-<u>spons</u>-uh-buhl)
adjective not careful or able to be trusted: *an irresponsible ruler*

Word use: The opposite is **responsible**.
Word building: **irresponsibility**
noun   **irresponsibleness** *noun*   **irresponsibly** *adverb*

irrigate
verb to supply with water using a system of canals and pipes: *to irrigate a farm*

Word building: **irrigation** *noun*

irritable
adjective easily annoyed: *I am tired and irritable.*

Word building: **irritability** *noun*   **irritably** *adverb*

irritate
verb **1** to annoy or make angry: *The audience's chatter irritated the musicians.*
Other words: **aggravate, bother, exasperate, irk, rankle**
2 to make sore: *She irritates the mosquito bites by scratching them.*
Other words: **aggravate, chafe, inflame**

Word building: **irritant** *noun* something which irritates   **irritating** *adjective*   **irritation** *noun*

Islam
noun a world religion based on the teachings of the prophet Mohammed and set down in the holy book of Islam, the Koran, which teaches that its followers should live their lives according to the wishes of Allah (God). Followers of Islam are called Muslims, and worship in a mosque.

Word building: **Islamic** *adjective*: *Islamic teachings*

island   (*say* <u>uy</u>-luhnd)
noun a piece of land completely surrounded by water

Word building: **islander** *noun* someone who lives on an island

isle   (*rhymes with* mile)
noun a small island

iso-
prefix a word part meaning 'equal': *isobar*
Word history: from Greek

isobar   (*say* <u>uy</u>-suh-bah)
noun a line drawn on a weather map, connecting all the places that have the same air pressure

isolate
verb **1** to keep quite separate or apart: *Distance isolates the farmers.* **2** to track down: *They isolated the fault.*

Word building: **isolated** *adjective*   **isolation** *noun*

isosceles   (*say* uy-<u>sos</u>-uh-leez)
adjective with two sides equal: *an isosceles triangle*

issue
noun **1** something sent or given out **2** something published or sent out at a certain time: *the November issue of our school magazine* **3** a lively or important topic of discussion **4** a complaint: *Do you have an issue with the new rules?*
verb **5** to give or send out: *The teachers issued pens and paper.* **6** to publish

Word building: Other verb forms are **I issued, I have issued, I am issuing**.

isthmus   (*say* <u>is</u>-muhs)
noun a narrow strip of land, with water on both sides, joining two larger pieces of land

Word building: The plural is **isthmuses**.
Word history: from a Greek word meaning 'narrow passage' or 'neck'

it
pronoun someone or something being talked about whose sex is not known or that does not have a sex: *Do you know who it was?* / *I don't know who wrote it.*

Word use: Other forms are **its** (*I don't know its name*), **itself** (*The dog hurt itself*).

IT
noun a short form of **information technology**

italics   (*say* uh-<u>tal</u>-iks)
plural noun printing which slopes to the right, often used for emphasis

Word building: **italic** *adjective*

itch

verb **1** to have a feeling on the skin which makes you want to scratch: *My leg itches.* **2** to want very much: *He is itching to play.*

Word building: **itch** *noun*   **itchy** *adjective*   **itchiness** *noun*

item

noun **1** one thing, especially among a number: *I have five items on my list.* **2** a piece of news: *Here is an interesting item on page one.*

Word building: **itemise** *verb* to list one by one

itinerant   *(say* uy-<u>tin</u>-uh-ruhnt)*

adjective travelling from place to place, especially to find work: *an itinerant fruit picker*

itinerary   *(say* uy-<u>tin</u>-uh-ree)*

noun the program or plan of a trip, listing places to be visited, times of journeys and so on

Word building: The plural is **itineraries**.

it'll

a short form of **it will** or **it shall**

it's

a short form of **it is** or **it has**

I've

a short form of **I have**

ivory

noun **1** the valuable creamy white tusk of elephants, used for carving ornaments *adjective* **2** made of ivory **3** creamy white

ivy

noun a climbing plant with smooth, shiny, evergreen leaves

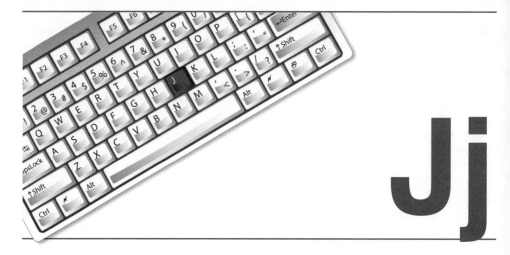

Jj

jab

verb to push or poke with something sharp: *Your hockey stick jabbed me in the ribs.*

Word building: Other forms are **I jabbed, I have jabbed, I am jabbing.** | **jab** *noun*: *a jab with a needle*

jabiru (say jab-uh-rooh)

noun a type of white stork found in Australia that has a green-black head, neck and tail

jacaranda

noun a tall tree with pale purple flowers

Word history: from a Native South American word

jack

noun **1** a tool used for lifting up heavy weights, such as a car **2** a playing card that has a picture of the knave or prince on it *phrase* **3 jack up, a** to lift with a jack **b** *Informal* to refuse to do something: *We asked him to help but he jacked up.*

jackal

noun a wild dog of Asia and Africa which hunts in packs at night

jackaroo

noun a young man working on a cattle or sheep station, usually in order to gain experience in the skills needed to own or manage a station

Word use: Another spelling is **jackeroo.**
Word building: **jackaroo** *verb*

jacket

noun **1** a short coat **2** a book's paper cover which can be taken off

jackhammer

noun a handheld machine used for drilling rocks and concrete

jack-in-the-box

noun a toy figure on a spring which pops out of its box when the lid is opened

jackknife

noun **1** a large knife whose blade folds into its handle **2** a dive in which you bend your body so that your hands touch your toes

Word building: The plural is **jackknives.** | **jackknife** *verb* to fold up or bend

jackpot

noun the biggest prize that you can win in a lottery or other competition

jade

noun **1** a precious, usually green, stone used for carving and jewellery *adjective* **2** green like jade

jaded

adjective worn out with tiredness

jaffle

noun a sandwich cooked by being pressed between two hot metal plates

jagged (say jag-uhd)

adjective rough and sharp-edged: *I cut my hands on the jagged rocks.*
Other words: **pointed, rough, serrated, uneven**

jaguar

noun a large, fierce, spotted cat found in tropical America

jail (say jayl)

noun the place where prisoners are kept while they serve their sentence

Word use: Another spelling is **gaol**.
Word building: **jailer** *noun*   **jail** *verb* to imprison

jam[1]

verb **1** to become stuck: *The door jammed in the wet weather.* **2** to push or force into a space tightly
noun **3** people or things crowded together: *a traffic jam* **4** *Informal* a difficult situation: *He got into a bit of a jam.*

Word building: Other verb forms are **I jammed, I have jammed, I am jamming**.

jam[2]

noun a food made of fruit and sugar which you spread on bread or scones

jamb   (*sounds like* jam)

noun the side piece of a doorway or window

jamboree

noun a large gathering of scouts

janitor

noun a North American word for **caretaker**

January   (*say* jan-yooh-uh-ree)

noun the first month of the year, with 31 days

Word use: The abbreviation is **Jan.**
Word history: from a Latin word meaning 'the month of Janus'; Janus was the Roman god of doors and gates, who was drawn with two faces looking in opposite directions.

jar[1]

noun a glass container with a lid

jar[2]

verb **1** to make a harsh unpleasant grating sound **2** to jolt or shake about roughly or painfully **3** to upset or shock

Word building: Other forms are **it jarred, it has jarred, it is jarring**.

jargon

noun the words and phrases used only by people in a particular job or group: *computer jargon*

jarrah

noun a large tree found in western Australia with a hard dark red wood

Word history: from an Aboriginal language of Western Australia called Nyungar. See the map of Australian Aboriginal languages at the end of this book.

jaunt

noun a short trip, usually for fun: *They had a jaunt on the harbour.*

Word building: **jaunt** *verb*

jaunty

adjective **1** lively and confident: *a jaunty step* **2** smart: *She is wearing a jaunty outfit.*

Word building: Other forms are **jauntier, jauntiest**. | **jauntily** *adverb*   **jauntiness** *noun*

javelin

noun a spear which is thrown in sporting contests

jaw

noun one of the two bones between your chin and nose which contain your teeth

jaywalk

verb to cross a street carelessly, taking no notice of traffic lights and so on

jazz

noun **1** a type of music with strong rhythms, first played by African Americans
phrase **2 jazz up**, *Informal* to make brighter or more lively: *She has jazzed up her room with new curtains.*

Word building: **jazz** *adjective*: *jazz music*   **jazzy** *adjective*: *a jazzy version of the song* | *jazzy colours*

jealous   (*say* jel-uhs)

adjective wanting what other people have, or not wanting to lose what you've already got: *Jenny is jealous of my popularity.* | *a jealous husband*

Word building: **jealously** *adverb*   **jealousy** *noun*

jeans

plural noun trousers made of denim or other strong material

jeans/genes Don't confuse **jeans** with **genes**. **Genes** are the units in your body which are responsible for passing on physical characteristics, like blue eyes, from parents to their children.

jeep

noun a small strong car for driving in rough conditions

jeer

verb to mock or insult

Word building: **jeer** *noun*   **jeeringly** *adverb*

jelly

noun a soft food, set with gelatine so that it wobbles when it is moved

Word building: The plural is **jellies**. | **jelly** *verb* (**jellied, jellying**)

jellyfish

noun a soft-bodied sea animal, especially one with an umbrella-shaped body and long tentacles

Word building: The plural is **jellyfishes** or **jellyfish**.

jeopardy   (*say* jep-uh-dee)

noun danger: *A very bad illness could put your life in jeopardy.*

Word building: **jeopardise** *verb* to risk

jerk

noun a sudden rough movement

Word building: **jerk** *verb* to move with a jerk   **jerkily** *adverb*   **jerkiness** *noun*   **jerky** *adjective*

jersey

noun **1** a long-sleeved knitted pullover **2 Jersey**, a breed of cattle which produces rich milk

Word history: from the island of *Jersey*, in the English Channel, where the cows came from and where the machine-knitted cloth has been produced for a long time

jest

noun a joke

Word building: **jest** *verb* to speak jokingly

jester

noun a clown who entertained royalty and nobility in medieval times

jet¹

noun **1** a fast-flowing spurt or stream of liquid or gas: *The fountain sent a jet of water into the air.* **2** the opening for a stream of liquid or gas: *She lit the gas jets.* **3** a plane which is powered by engines that work by having hot gas forced at high speed through an opening at the back

Word building: **jet** *verb* (**jetted, jetting**)

jet²

noun a hard black coal which is polished and used to make buttons, jewellery and the like

jet set

noun a wealthy and fashionable group of people who can afford to spend their time flying from one part of the world to another for pure enjoyment

jetty

noun a long structure, jutting out into a river or the sea, that boats or ships can be tied to

Word building: The plural is **jetties**.

Jew

noun **1** a person descended from the Hebrews **2** a person whose religion is Judaism

Word building: **Jewish** *adjective*

jewel

noun **1** a precious stone, such as a diamond, a ruby or an emerald, which has been cut and polished **2** an ornament, such as a brooch or ring, made of precious stones, pearls, gold or other valuable materials

Word building: **jeweller** *noun* someone who works with or sells jewels   **jewellery** *noun* jewels

jib

verb **1** to stop suddenly, like a horse when it is frightened
phrase **2 jib at**, to be unwilling to do: *He will wash up but he jibs at cooking.*

Word use: Another word for definition 1 is **baulk**.
Word building: Other verb forms are **I jibbed, I have jibbed, I am jibbing**.

jiffy

noun *Informal* a very short time: *I'll have it done in a jiffy.*

Word building: The plural is **jiffies**.

jig

noun a very lively dance
Word building: **jig** *verb* (**jigged, jigging**)

jigsaw

noun a narrow saw for cutting curves

jigsaw puzzle

noun a puzzle made up of many differently shaped pieces which fit together to form a picture

jillaroo (say jill-a-roo)

noun a young woman who is learning to work on a cattle or a sheep station

Word building: **jillaroo** *verb*

jingle

verb **1** to clink or tinkle: *Su Li's keys jingle when she runs. | Bruno jingled his coins impatiently.*
noun **2** a tinkling sound
Other words: **clink, rattle, tinkle**
3 a bright simple song of the sort used in radio or TV commercials

jinx

noun someone or something which is supposed to bring bad luck

Word building: The plural is **jinxes.** | **jinx** *verb*

job

noun **1** a piece of work or a task **2** paid employment

jockey

noun someone who rides horses in races

jocular

adjective joking or playful: *a jocular mood*
Word building: **jocularity** *noun* **jocularly** *adverb*

jodhpurs (say jod-puhz)

plural noun riding trousers which are close fitting below the knee

joey

noun a young animal, especially a young kangaroo which is carried in its mother's pouch

jog

verb **1** to run or go along at a slow regular pace **2** to push or nudge: *to jog someone's elbow*

Word building: Other forms are **I jogged, I have jogged, I am jogging.** | **jog** *noun*

jogger

noun **1** someone who jogs for exercise **2** a type of sports shoe worn for jogging and some other types of exercise

join

verb **1** to put or come together: *She joined the pieces with glue. | This is where the two parts join.*

Other words: **combine, connect, couple, link, unite**
2 to meet up with: *I'll join you for lunch.*
3 to become a member of

Word building: **join** *noun*

joiner

noun someone who makes wooden furniture and house fittings such as window frames

Word building: **joinery** *noun* the work a joiner does

joint

noun **1** the place where two things or parts are joined: *She hurt her elbow joint.* **2** a cut of meat: *She put a joint of lamb in the oven.*

Word building: **joint** *adjective* shared: *a joint account* **jointly** *adverb*

joist

noun a length of wood or metal used to support floors, ceilings or other structures

joke

noun **1** something which is said or done to make people laugh
phrase **2 practical joke,** a prank or trick played on someone with the intention of causing embarrassment

Word building: **joke** *verb* **joker** *noun* **jokingly** *adverb*

jolly

adjective **1** good-humoured and full of fun: *She is a jolly old woman.*
adverb **2** *Informal* very: *You've done jolly well.*

Word building: **jolliness** *noun* **jollity** *noun*

jolt

verb to bump or shake roughly

Word building: **jolt** *noun*

jostle (say jos-uhl)

verb to push roughly or rudely: *People were jostling to see the parade.*

jot

verb **1** to write briefly or scribble down: *I'll jot down a few thoughts.*
noun **2** a little bit: *He doesn't care a jot.*

Word building: Other verb forms are **I jotted, I have jotted, I am jotting.** | **jotter** *noun* **jotting** *noun*

joule

noun a measure of work or energy

Word history: named after a British physicist, JP *Joule,* who lived from 1818-89

journal (*say* jer-nuhl)

noun **1** a newspaper or magazine
2 a daily record of events

journalism (*say* jer-nuhl-iz-uhm)

noun the work of writing and running
newspapers and magazines, or news
programs on television or radio
Word building: **journalist** *noun*

journey (*say* jer-nee)

noun a trip, especially by land: *We made a*
car journey to the mountains.
Word building: **journey** *verb*

joust (*say* jowst)

noun a contest between two knights on
horseback to see which can unseat the
other with a spear

jovial

adjective cheerful and friendly
Word building: **joviality** *noun* **jovially** *adverb*

jowl

noun a fold of flesh which hangs below the
cheek or jaw

joy

noun great happiness or delight
Other words: **bliss, ecstasy, joyfulness**
Word building: **joyful** *adjective* **joyfully** *adverb*
joyous *adjective* **joyously** *adverb* **overjoyed**
adjective

joystick

noun **1** the control stick of a plane
2 a device with a lever that looks like
a plane's joystick, used to change the
position of the cursor on a computer
screen

jube

noun a chewy fruit-flavoured lolly made
with gelatine

jubilant

adjective extremely happy or joyful: *He was*
jubilant at winning the race.
Word building: **jubilantly** *adverb* **jubilation**
noun

jubilee

noun a celebration, especially of the
anniversary of something which happened
a long time ago

Judaism (*say* jooh-day-iz-uhm)

noun the religion of the Jewish people,
based on the writings of the Old Testament
and the teaching of the rabbis, which say
that there is only one God. Followers of
Judaism are called Jews, and worship in a
synagogue
Word building: **Judaic** *adjective*: *the Judaic*
tradition

judge

noun **1** someone whose job is to hear and
decide cases in a court of law **2** someone
who gives an opinion or a decision on the
winner of a contest or competition
verb **3** to make a decision or calculation,
or form an opinion, based on information
that you have: *I'll judge the distance from my*
place to your place based on how long it takes
me to walk there. | *I will judge the talent*
contest.

judgement

noun **1** an opinion or conclusion: *Your*
judgement of her is too harsh. **2** the ability
to make right decisions: *That driver has*
good judgement. **3** the decision in a court
case: *The judgement was 'guilty'.*
Word use: Another spelling is **judgment**.

judicial (*say* jooh-dish-uhl)

adjective having to do with judges or law
courts: *There is to be a judicial inquiry.*
Word building: **judiciary** *noun* the system of
courts and judges **judicially** *adverb*

judicious (*say* jooh-dish-uhs)

adjective showing good judgement
Word use: The more usual word is **wise**.
Word building: **judiciously** *adverb*

judo

noun a Japanese type of self-defence
without weapons, based on jujitsu
Word history: from a Japanese word meaning
'soft way'

jug

noun a container with a handle and
pouring lip

juggle

verb to throw several things into the air and
keep them moving, without dropping any
Word building: **juggler** *noun* an entertainer
who juggles

juice

noun **1** the liquid part of a plant, especially fruit: *orange juice* **2** *Informal* petrol: *We're out of juice.*

Word building: **juicy** *adjective* (**juicier, juiciest**) **juiciness** *noun*

jujitsu   (*say* jooh-jit-sooh)

noun a Japanese way of self-defence without weapons

Word history: from a Japanese word meaning 'soft or supple art'

jukebox

noun a coin-operated machine which plays music that you choose

July

noun the seventh month of the year, with 31 days

Word use: The abbreviations are **Jul** or **Jy**.
Word history: named after the Roman general and statesman, *Julius* Caesar, who was born in this month

jumble

verb to muddle or confuse

Word building: **jumble** *noun* confusion or disorder

jumbo

Informal
noun **1** an elephant **2** a very large jet plane, or anything bigger than usual

Word building: **jumbo** *adjective* very large

jumbuck

noun a sheep

Word use: This is a very old-fashioned word that we know only because it's in the song 'Waltzing Matilda'.

jump

verb **1** to leap or spring from the ground **2** to make a sudden movement due to fear or surprise: *She jumped at the noise.* **3** to move irregularly: *Her argument jumps from one point to another.*
noun **4** a leap **5** something to be leapt over **6** a sudden move from one state or thing to another: *a jump in price* **7** a sudden nervous movement

jumper

noun a piece of clothing, usually made of wool, and worn on the top half of the body, often over other clothes
Other words: **pullover, sweater**

jumpsuit

noun trousers and top which are joined at the waist

jumpy

adjective nervous or frightened in mood or behaviour: *The storm makes the animals jumpy.*

Word building: Other forms are **jumpier, jumpiest**. | **jumpily** *adverb* **jumpiness** *noun*

junction   (*say* junk-shuhn)

noun the place where two or more things, especially roads or railway tracks, meet or cross

juncture   (*say* junk-shuh)

noun **1** a particular point in time: *At this juncture let us finish.* **2** the junction or joining point of two things

June

noun the sixth month of the year, with 30 days

Word use: The abbreviation is **Jun**.
Word history: named after the Roman goddess *Juno*, the wife of Jupiter

jungle

noun the thick trees and vegetation which grow in warm, damp, tropical conditions

junior

adjective younger or smaller: *the junior members of the family*

Word building: **junior** *noun*

junk[1]

noun old or unwanted things

junk[2]

noun a Chinese flat-bottomed boat

junket

noun a milk pudding made by setting sweetened warm milk

junk food

noun food that is not healthy: *Chips are my favourite junk food.*

junkie

noun *Informal* a drug addict

junta   (*say* jun-tuh)

noun a small group of people ruling a country, especially as the result of a revolution

jurisdiction (*say* jooh-ruhs-<u>dik</u>-shuhn)
noun the legal power to settle matters: *The soldiers come under military jurisdiction.*

jury
noun **1** the group of people chosen to hear and try to decide the outcome of a court case **2** a group chosen to judge a competition and award prizes

Word building: **juror** *noun* a member of a jury

just
adjective **1** fair or rightly judged: *a just decision*
adverb **2** by a very little: *You have just missed him.* **3** exactly: *That's just what I think.* **4** only: *Sam is still just a child.*

Word building: **justly** *adverb*

justice
noun **1** what is right and fair: *We must continue to fight for justice.* **2** judgement by a court of law

justify
verb to try to defend or show to be right: *She can justify her argument.*

Word building: Other forms are **I justified, I have justified, I am justifying.** | **justifiable** *adjective* **justifiably** *adverb* **justification** *noun*

jut
verb to stick out: *A shelf juts from the wall.* | *The rock juts out sharply here.*

Word building: Other forms are **I jutted, I have jutted, I am jutting.**

jute
noun a strong fibre which is used for making rope or sacks

Word history: from a Sanskrit word meaning 'a braid of hair'

juvenile
adjective **1** young or for the young **2** childish

Word building: **juvenile** *noun* a young person

juxta-
prefix a word part meaning 'near' or 'close by': *juxtapose*

Word history: from Latin

juxtapose
verb to place close together

Word building: **juxtaposition** *noun*

Kk

kaftan
noun another spelling for **caftan**

kaleidoscope (*say* kuh-<u>luy</u>-duh-skohp)
noun a tube with mirrors and pieces of coloured glass in one end, which shows different patterns when it is turned around

Word building: **kaleidoscopic** *adjective*

kanga cricket (*say* kang-guh <u>krik</u>-uht)
noun a type of cricket for children that uses a softer ball and a plastic bat

kangaroo
noun an Australian animal with a small head, short front limbs, and a large tail and back legs for leaping

Word use: The male is a **buck**, the female is a **doe** and the young is a **joey**. | The kangaroo belongs to a class of animals called **marsupials**. Word history: from an Aboriginal language of Queensland called Guugu Yimidhirr. See the map of Australian Aboriginal languages at the end of this book.

karaoke (*say* ka-ree-<u>oh</u>-kee)
noun singing along to a video of a song. The singer reads the words to the song displayed on a video screen.

karate (*say* kuh-<u>rah</u>-tee)
noun a Japanese form of self-defence which uses only hands, elbows, feet and knees as weapons

Word history: from a Japanese word meaning 'empty hand'

karri
noun a western Australian gum tree with hard, long-lasting wood

Word history: from an Aboriginal language of Western Australia called Nyungar. See the map of Australian Aboriginal languages at the end of this book.

kauri (*say* <u>kow</u>-ree)
noun a tall New Zealand cone-bearing tree, which is valued for its wood and its resin

Word history: from a Maori word

kayak (*say* <u>kuy</u>-ak)
noun a light canoe, like the watertight skin-covered hunting canoe made by Inuit people

kebab (*say* kuh-<u>bab</u>)
noun a short form of **doner kebab** or **shish kebab**

keel
noun **1** a long piece of timber or metal which stretches along the bottom of a ship, holding it together
phrase **2 keel over**, to turn over or upside down: *The yacht keeled over in the strong breeze.*

keen
adjective **1** strong or clear in feelings or senses: *a keen disappointment* | *a keen eye*
Other words: **acute, fine, sensitive, sharp**
2 full of enthusiasm: *He's keen to start the job.* | *a keen swimmer*
Other words: **ardent, avid, eager, enthusiastic**
3 sharp: *a keen blade*
phrase **4 keen on**, fond of: *She's keen on cakes.*

Word building: **keenly** *adverb* **keenness** *noun*

keep

verb **1** to continue or make continue in the same way or state: *to keep calm | to keep the house clean* **2** to retain or hang on to: *I'll keep one dress and send the others back.* **3** to have and look after: *to keep hens* **4** to obey, follow or carry out: *to keep a promise | to keep the law*

noun **5** the basic needs of living, like food and shelter: *to earn your keep*

Word building: Other verb forms are **I kept, I have kept, I am keeping.** | **keeper** *noun*

keeping

noun **1** care or possession: *They gave their watches into my keeping while they went swimming.*

phrase **2 in keeping with**, suitable for: *clothes in keeping with the event*

keepsake

noun something kept to remember a person or event by: *She took the program as a keepsake of the concert.*

keg

noun a barrel, especially for beer

kelp

noun a greenish-brown seaweed which grows in thick strands

kelpie

noun a breed of Australian sheepdog

kennel

noun a house or shelter built for a dog

kerb

noun the line of stones or concrete at the edge of a street

kernel

noun **1** the inner part of a nut which you can eat **2** a grain, as of wheat or corn

kerosene

noun a liquid used as a fuel for lamps, engines and heaters

ketchup

noun a sauce: *tomato ketchup*

Word use: This word is used more in America.

kettle

noun a pot with a spout, a lid and a handle, used for boiling water

kettledrum

noun a drum with a skin stretched over a brass or copper bowl

key

noun **1** a small, specially-shaped piece of metal that can open a lock **2** something which helps you to read or understand such things as a map, a code, or a puzzle **3** one of the notes on a piano **4** the set of notes, starting and ending on one particular note, used to make up a piece of music: *This piece is in the key of C major.* **5** one of a set of parts pressed in working a typewriter or computer terminal

phrase **6 key in**, to type information into a computer: *To log on you must first key in your name.*

Word use: When you key in you use a **keyboard.**

Word building: Other verb forms are **I key in, I keyed in, I am keying in.** | **key** *adjective* main or important

key/quay Don't confuse **key** with **quay**, which is a wharf where ships load or unload passengers and cargo.

keyboard

noun the row or set of keys such as on a piano, typewriter or computer

key signature

noun the sharps or flats placed after the clef to show what key a piece of music is in

Word use: Compare this with **time signature.**

keystone

noun the wedge-shaped stone at the top of an arch which is thought to hold the other stones in place

khaki (*say* kah-<u>kee</u>, <u>kah</u>-kee)

adjective dull greenish-brown, used especially for soldiers' uniforms

Word building: **khaki** *noun*

kibbutz (*say* kib-<u>oots</u>)

noun an Israeli farming settlement whose management, work and products are shared

Word building: The plural is **kibbutzim.** | **kibbutznik** *noun* someone who lives and works on a kibbutz

Word history: from a Modern Hebrew word meaning 'gathering'

kick

verb **1** to hit, move or drive with the foot: *That horse kicks. | to kick a ball* **2** to spring back: *The rifle kicked into her shoulder.*

noun **3** a hit or thrust with the foot
4 a sudden strong movement backwards, especially of a gun **5** *Informal* a feeling of pleasure or satisfaction: *She gets a kick out of dancing.*

kid¹
noun **1** a young goat **2** *Informal* a child
Word use: The male is a **billy goat** and the female is a **nanny goat**.

kid²
verb to tease or trick: *He's only kidding.*
Word building: Other forms are **I kidded, I have kidded, I am kidding.**

kidnap
verb to take someone away by force and hold them prisoner until money is paid, or some other condition is met
Word building: Other forms are **they kidnapped, they have kidnapped, they are kidnapping.** | **kidnapper** *noun*

kidney
noun one of the two bean-shaped organs in your body which get rid of waste from the blood

kikuyu (*say* kuy-<u>kooh</u>-yooh)
noun a tough grass which is used for lawns and pasture

kill
verb **1** to cause the death of **2** to stop or destroy: *He will kill any suggestion you make.*
Word building: **kill** *noun* **killer** *noun*

kiln
noun a big oven or furnace for baking bricks or pottery

kilo
noun short for **kilogram**
Word building: The plural is **kilos.**

kilo-
prefix a word part indicating a thousand times a given unit: *kilogram* | *kilometre*
Word history: from Greek

kilobyte (*say* <u>kil</u>-uh-buyt)
noun a unit for measuring computer information equal to 1024 bytes

kilogram
noun a weight equal to 1000 grams

kilojoule
noun 1000 joules of energy or the amount of food needed to produce it

kilometre (*say* <u>kil</u>-uh-mee-tuh, kuh-<u>lom</u>-uh-tuh)
noun a length equal to 1000 metres

kilowatt
noun 1000 watts

kilt
noun a pleated skirt of tartan cloth, sometimes worn by men in the Scottish Highlands

kimono (*say* <u>kim</u>-uh-noh, kuh-<u>moh</u>-noh)
noun a wide-sleeved Japanese robe which is tied at the waist

kin
noun your relatives: *Her mother's kin were Irish.*
Word building: **kin** *adjective*

kind¹
adjective warm-hearted, friendly and well-wishing
Other words: **compassionate, considerate, good, kindly, thoughtful**
Word use: The opposite is **unkind.**
Word building: **kindly** *adverb* **kindness** *noun*

kind²
noun **1** a group of things or people of the same nature or type
Other words: **category, class, genre, sort, type, variety**
2 something not quite exact: *They used the shed as a kind of house.*
Other words: **sort, type**

kindergarten
noun a school or class for very young children which prepares them for primary school
Word history: from the German words for 'children' and 'garden'

kindle
verb **1** to set alight or ablaze: *I kindled the fire with dry leaves.* **2** to light up: *The sticks began to kindle.* | *William's eyes kindled.*

kindling
noun the twigs and other material used to start a fire

kindred
noun your relatives
Word building: **kindred** *adjective* like or related

kinetic   (*say* kuh-<u>net</u>-ik)
adjective having to do with movement

king
noun **1** a man from a royal family who rules over a country or empire **2** someone who is powerful or outstanding: *a cattle king* **3** a playing card with a picture of a king on it **4** the chess piece whose capture ends the game
Word building: **king** *adjective* large: *king size* **kingly** *adjective*

kingdom
noun **1** a country or government ruled over by a king or queen **2** one of the large divisions of nature: *the animal, vegetable and mineral kingdoms*

kingfisher
noun a brilliantly coloured bird which eats fish or insects in water

kink
noun **1** a wrinkle or fault **2** an unusual taste or whim
Word building: **kinky** *adjective* (**kinkier, kinkiest**)

kinship
noun relationship by family or other ties: *He claims kinship with my cousin.* | *The girls found a kinship in collecting stickers.*

kiosk   (*say* <u>kee</u>-osk)
noun a small shop or stall which sells such things as newspapers, souvenirs and light refreshments
Word history: from a Turkish word meaning 'pavilion'

kipper
noun a dried fish, usually herring or salmon, which has been salted and smoked

kit
noun **1** a set of tools, supplies or parts for a special purpose: *climbing kit* | *first-aid kit* **2** a set of parts to be put together: *We bought the furniture as a kit.*

kitchen
noun the room or place where food is cooked and prepared

kite
noun **1** a light frame covered by a thin material, which is flown in the wind at the end of a long string **2** a medium-sized hawk with long wings and tail

kitten
noun a young cat

kiwi
noun **1** a New Zealand bird with thick legs and a long thin bill, and which cannot fly **2** *Informal* someone from New Zealand

kiwifruit
noun a small, oval, hairy fruit with a gooseberry-like flavour
Word use: Another name for this is **Chinese gooseberry**.

klaxon
noun a loud horn once used in motor cars

kleptomania   (*say* klep-tuh-<u>mayn</u>-ee-uh)
noun an uncontrollable urge to steal things
Word building: **kleptomaniac** *noun*

knack   (*say* nak)
noun the skill for doing a particular thing

knacker   (*say* <u>nak</u>-uh)
noun someone who buys old or useless horses to kill for pet meat
Word building: **knackery** *noun*

knapsack   (*say* <u>nap</u>-sak)
noun a leather or canvas bag for clothes and supplies which is carried on the back, especially by hikers and climbers

knave   (*say* nayv)
noun *Old-fashioned* a dishonest man or boy
Other words: **rascal**
Word building: **knavish** *adjective*   **knavishly** *adverb*

knead   (*say* need)
verb to press and push with your hands: *The baker kneaded the dough.*

knead/need Don't confuse **knead** with **need**. To **need** something is to want it urgently: *I need help. Quick!*

knee   (*say* nee)
noun the joint between the upper and lower leg

kneecap
noun the flat movable bone which covers the knee joint

kneejerk
adjective immediate and without thinking: *My kneejerk reaction was to drop the hot cup.*

kneel (*say* neel)
verb to go down on your knees
Word building: Other forms are **I knelt** or **kneeled, I have knelt** or **kneeled, I am kneeling.**

knell (*say* nel)
noun a slow bell ringing for a death or funeral

knickerbockers (*say* <u>nik</u>-uh-bok-uhz)
plural noun loose short trousers which are gathered in at the knees
Word history: named after Diedrich *Knickerbocker*, the imaginary author of Washington Irving's book *The History of New York* which had illustrations of people wearing baggy pants like the ones Dutch people wore in about 1800

knickers (*say* <u>nik</u>-uhz)
plural noun underpants, usually for women

knick-knack (*say* <u>nik</u>-nak)
noun a small ornament

knife (*say* nuyf)
noun **1** a tool with a sharp blade for cutting
verb **2** to wound with a knife
Word building: The plural form of the noun is **knives.**

knight (*say* nuyt)
noun **1** a nobleman who pledged to serve and fight for a king or queen in Medieval times **2** an honour, with the title 'Sir', given to a man by a king or queen for service to his country **3** a chess piece shaped like a horse's head
Word building: **knight** *verb* **knighthood** *noun* **knightly** *adjective*

knight/night Don't confuse **knight** with **night.** **Night** is the time between sunset and sunrise, when it is dark.

knit (*say* nit)
verb **1** to make out of long strands of wool, using a pair of long needles: *to knit a jumper* **2** to join together: *I have to wait for the bones to knit after my fracture.* **3** to wrinkle up: *Emma knits her brow when she is thinking.*
Word building: Other forms are **I knitted, I have knitted, I am knitting.** | **knitter** *noun*

knit/nit Don't confuse **knit** with **nit**, which is the egg or young of an insect, such as a louse, living in human hair.

knob (*say* nob)
noun **1** a round handle, as on a drawer or door **2** a rounded lump: *a knob of butter*
Word building: **knobby** *adjective* **knobbly** *adjective*

knock (*say* nok)
verb **1** to tap or beat: *Knock on the door.*
Other words: **bang, rap, strike, thump**
2 to bump or strike: *She knocked the leg of the table.* | *He knocked the nail in.*
Other words: **hit**
3 *Informal* to criticise or find something wrong with: *She is always knocking their efforts.*
Other words: **belittle, deride, ridicule**
Word building: **knock** *noun*

knockout
noun **1** the act of knocking someone unconscious **2** *Informal* something or someone who is extremely attractive or successful

knot (*say* not)
noun **1** a piece of thread, rope or the like, tied or tangled **2** a fault or join in the grain of wood **3** a measure of speed, used especially for ships, equal to about 1.85 kilometres per hour
Word building: **knot** *verb* (**knotted, knotting**) **knotty**

knot/not Don't confuse **knot** with **not.** You use **not** to express something negative, or to deny or refuse something:
I am not going to the dance.

know (*say* noh)
verb **1** to feel certain that something is a fact or the truth **2** to have learned and understood **3** to have met before: *I know that face.*
Word building: Other forms are **I knew, I have known, I am knowing.** | **knowable** *adjective* that can be known **knowing** *adjective* shrewd **knowingly** *adverb*

know/no Don't confuse **know** with **no,** which is the opposite of *yes.* We use it to deny, disagree with or refuse something.

know-all
noun someone who says they know everything, or everything about a particular subject

knowledge (*say* <u>nol</u>-ij)
noun what is or can be known: *Do you have any knowledge of what took place?* | *She passed on her knowledge to her daughters.*
Word building: **knowledgeable** *adjective*

knuckle (*say* <u>nuk</u>-uhl)
noun a finger joint, especially the bottom joint where the finger meets the rest of the hand

koala (*say* koh-<u>ah</u>-luh)
noun a furry, grey, Australian animal without a tail, which lives and feeds in certain types of gum tree
Word use: The koala belongs to a class of animals called **marsupials**.
Word history: from an Aboriginal language of New South Wales called Dharug. See the map of Australian Aboriginal languages at the end of this book.

komodo dragon
noun a large lizard from Komodo, an island in Indonesia

kookaburra
noun an Australian kingfisher whose call sounds like human laughter
Word use: Other names are **laughing kookaburra** and **laughing jackass**.
Word history: from an Aboriginal language of New South Wales called Wiradjuri. See the map of Australian Aboriginal languages at the end of this book.

Koori (*say* <u>koo</u>-ree)
noun an Aboriginal person from New South Wales or Victoria
Word use: Another spelling is **Koorie**.
Word building: **Koori** *adjective*: *Koori music*
Word history: from an Aboriginal language of New South Wales called Awabakal. See the map of Australian Aboriginal languages at the end of this book.

Koran (*say* kaw-<u>rahn</u>, kuh-<u>rahn</u>)
noun the holy book of Islam, which Muslims believe came directly from Allah through the prophet Mohammed
Word history: from an Arabic word meaning 'reading' or 'recitation'

kosher (*say* <u>koh</u>-shuh)
adjective prepared according to the special food rules of the Jewish religion: *a kosher meal*
Word history: from Hebrew

kowari (*say* kuh-<u>wah</u>-ree)
noun a small, yellow-brown animal with a black bushy tail that lives in the Australian desert. It is endangered. See the table at the end of this book
Word history: from an Aboriginal language of South Australia called Diyari. See the map of Australian Aboriginal languages at the end of this book.

kowtow
verb **1** to kneel touching the forehead to the ground in respect or worship **2** to try very hard to please, especially in an over-eager way
Word history: from a Chinese word meaning 'knock-head'

kris
noun a short sword or heavy knife, used in Malaysia
Word history: from a Malay word

Krishna
noun the most popular Hindu god
Word history: from a Sanskrit word meaning 'black'

kudos (*say* <u>kyooh</u>-dos)
noun glory or fame: *She only does something if it will bring her kudos.*

kumquat (*say* <u>kum</u>-kwot)
noun another spelling for **cumquat**

kung-fu (*say* koong-<u>fooh</u>, kung-<u>fooh</u>)
noun a Chinese form of karate

kurrajong
noun a flowering tree of eastern Australia whose bark was traditionally used by Aboriginal people to make fishing line and fishing nets
Word history: from an Aboriginal language of New South Wales called Dharug. See the map of Australian Aboriginal languages at the end of this book.

kylie (*say* <u>kuy</u>-lee)
noun a boomerang with one side flat and the other curved
Word history: from an Aboriginal language of Western Australia called Nyungar. See the map of Australian Aboriginal languages at the end of this book.

Ll

label

noun **1** a piece of paper put on something to show what it is, who owns it, or where it is going: *a label for a suitcase | a label for a jar*

verb **2** to mark or describe with a label: *The bottle was labelled poison.*

Word building: Other verb forms are **I labelled, I have labelled, I am labelling.**

laboratory (*say* luh-<u>bo</u>-ruh-tree)

noun a building or room for doing scientific tests or for making chemicals or medicines

Word building: The plural is **laboratories.**

laborious (*say* luh-<u>baw</u>-ree-uhs)

adjective needing a lot of effort: *laborious work*

Word building: **laboriously** *adverb*

labour

noun **1** hard or tiring work: *the labour of building a house* **2** people who are employed to do such work, especially when organised into trade unions: *Organised labour will push for reform.* **3** the pain and effort of giving birth to a baby

Word use: Another spelling is **labor.**
Word building: **labour** *verb* **labourer** *noun*

labrador

noun a kind of large dog with short black or golden hair

Word history: named after *Labrador*, a peninsula in Canada, where the breed first came from

labyrinth (*say* <u>lab</u>-uh-rinth)

noun a twisting set of passages in which it is hard to find your way
Other words: **maze**

lace

noun **1** a material with a fine netlike design of threads: *a wedding dress made of lace* **2** a cord for pulling and holding something together: *shoelaces*

verb **3** to tie together with a lace: *to lace your shoe*

Word building: **lacy** *adjective* (**lacier, laciest**)

lacerate (*say* <u>las</u>-uh-rayt)

verb to tear roughly or cut: *Be careful, the broken glass could lacerate your feet.*

Word building: **lacerated** *adjective* **laceration** *noun*

lack

noun **1** a shortage or absence of something you need or want: *a lack of food | a lack of interest*
Other words: **deficiency, insufficiency, scarcity, want**

verb **2** to be without: *to lack strength*
Other words: **need, want**

laconic (*say* luh-<u>kon</u>-ik)

adjective using few words: *She gave a laconic reply.*

Word building: **laconically** *adverb*

lacquer (*say* <u>lak</u>-uh)

noun a clear coating put on something to protect it or to make it shiny

Word building: **lacquer** *verb* **lacquered** *adjective*

lacrosse (*say* luh-<u>kros</u>)

noun a game played by two teams with ten players in each, who try to hit a ball through a goal using racquets with long handles

lact-

prefix a word part meaning 'milk': *lactate*

Word use: Another spelling is **lacto-**.
Word history: from Latin

lactate

verb to produce milk

Word building: **lactation** *noun*

lad

noun a boy or young man

ladder

noun **1** a structure made of wood, metal or rope, with rungs or steps you use to climb up or down **2** a line in a stocking or pair of tights where the stitches have come undone

ladle

noun a cup-shaped spoon with a long handle, for serving liquids: *a soup ladle*

Word building: **ladle** *verb*

lady

noun a woman

Word use: This word may offend some women.
Word building: The plural is **ladies**.

ladybird

noun a small beetle whose orange or red back is spotted with black

lag

verb **1** to become less or decrease: *My interest in work is beginning to lag.*
phrase **2 lag behind**, to fall behind or drop back: *He's always lagging behind when we go for a walk.*

Word building: Other verb forms are **I lagged, I have lagged, I am lagging**.

lager (*say* <u>lah</u>-guh)

noun a kind of light beer

lagerphone

noun a homemade percussion instrument made of beer bottle tops loosely nailed to a broom handle

lagoon

noun a pond of shallow water, often separated from the sea by low banks of sand

lair

noun the den or shelter of a wild animal

lake

noun a large area of water surrounded by land

laksa

noun a spicy Malaysian dish of thin rice noodles, vegetables, meat or tofu, and so on, served in a soup

lama (*rhymes with* farmer)

noun a Buddhist priest or monk

Word history: from a Tibetan word

lamb

noun a young sheep or its meat

Word use: The male is a **ram** and the female is a **ewe**.

lame

adjective **1** having something wrong with your foot or leg that causes you to limp
Other words: **crippled, disabled, handicapped**
2 weak or poor: *a lame excuse*

Word building: **lame** *verb* **lamely** *adverb* **lameness** *noun*

lament (*say* luh-<u>ment</u>)

verb **1** to feel or show sorrow for: *She lamented her husband's death.*
noun **2** a poem or song expressing sorrow

Word building: **lamentable** *adjective* **lamentably** *adverb* **lamentation** *noun*

laminate

verb **1** to separate into thin sheets or layers **2** to cover with thin layers

Word building: **laminate** *adjective* **laminated** *adjective* **lamination** *noun*

lamington

noun a square of sponge cake covered with chocolate icing and grated coconut

Word history: thought to be named after Baron *Lamington*, governor of Queensland 1895-1901

lamp

noun a kind of light, often one which you can move or carry around: *a kerosene lamp*

lance

noun **1** a long spear
verb **2** to cut open with a sharp instrument: *The doctor lanced my boil.*

land

noun **1** the part of the earth's surface not covered by water **2** a particular area of ground: *We own the house and the land around it.* **3** a country or nation: *Our land is called Australia.*
verb **4** to come or bring to land or shore **5** to come to rest in any place or position: *Where did the ball land?* **6** *Informal* to gain or obtain: *He landed a good job.*

landcare

noun the sustainable management of the environment and natural resources in agriculture

landing

noun **1** the act of landing **2** the area at the top or bottom of a flight of stairs **3** the end of an aeroplane's journey

landlady

noun a woman who owns and rents out land, houses, flats or rooms

landline

noun a telephone that works by receiving electromagnetic signals passed through cables under or above the ground from another telephone: *Why don't you use the landline instead of your mobile — it might be a bit cheaper.*

landlord

noun a person who owns and rents out land, houses, flats or rooms

landlubber

noun someone who is not used to boats or sailing

landmark

noun **1** something on land that is easily seen and is used as a guide to travellers **2** an event that stands out as important: *The Eureka Stockade was a landmark in Australia's history.*

landmass

noun a large body of land surrounded by water, like an island or a continent

landscape

noun **1** a view of country scenery **2** a painting of country scenery
verb **3** to arrange to make look like a landscape: *to landscape a garden*

landslide

noun **1** the sliding down of a mass of rocks and soil from a steep slope **2** an easy win in an election: *The government won in a landslide.*

lane

noun **1** a narrow passage or road between fences, walls or houses
Other words: **alley**
2 a strip of road marked out for a single line of vehicles **3** a strip marked out on a running track or swimming pool for one runner or swimmer in a race

lane/lain Don't confuse **lane** with **lain**, which is a past form of the verb **lie**:
I felt refreshed after I had lain down for half an hour.

language

noun **1** the arrangement of words we use when we speak and write **2** any set of signs or symbols used to pass on information: *sign language / computer language* **3** the language of a particular country or group of people: *French is the language of France.*
Other words: **tongue**

languid   (*say* lang-gwuhd)

adjective weak, tired or slow-moving
Word building: **languidly** *adverb*

languish   (*say* lang-gwish)

verb to become weak or without interest

La Niña   (*say* lah neen-yuh)

noun the reverse of an El Niño, marked in Australia by heavy rain on the eastern coast
Word use: Compare this with **El Niño.**
Word history: from Spanish; the feminine form of *El Niño*, to indicate the contrast of heavy rain to drought

lank

adjective **1** too long and thin: *Your plants will grow very lank without sunlight.* **2** straight and dull: *lank hair*
Word building: **lankly** *adverb*   **lankness** *noun*

lanky

adjective tall, thin and often awkward: *My lanky neighbour insisted he could fit into our cubby house, but when he tried, the door broke.*
Word building: Other forms are **lankier, lankiest.** | **lankiness** *noun*

lantana (*say* lan-<u>tah</u>-nuh)

noun a plant with yellow or orange flowers, which has become an annoying weed in warm, wet parts of Australia

lantern

noun a glass case that holds a light and protects it from wind and rain

lap¹

noun the front of your body from your waist to your knees, when you are sitting down: *She sat the child on her lap.*

lap²

noun a single round of a racing track or a single length of a swimming pool
Other words: **circuit, course**

lap³

verb **1** to hit with a gentle splashing: *The water lapped against the side of the boat.* **2** to drink using the tongue: *The cat lapped the milk.*

Word building: Other forms are **I lapped, I have lapped, I am lapping.**

lapel (*say* luh-<u>pel</u>)

noun the part of a coat collar that is folded back over your chest

lapse

noun **1** a mistake or failure: *a lapse of memory* **2** the passing of time: *We saw each other again after a lapse of two years.*
verb **3** to pass slowly or gradually: *The sick child lapsed into unconsciousness.* **4** to fall or sink into a bad habit or way of life

laptop

noun a microcomputer, small enough to be carried around, that is designed to rest on the user's lap

larceny (*say* <u>lah</u>-suh-nee)

noun the stealing of someone else's goods
Word building: The plural is **larcenies.** | **larcenous** adjective

lard

noun pig fat prepared for use in cooking

larder

noun a room or cupboard where food is kept
Other words: **pantry**

large

adjective **1** of more than usual size, amount or extent: *a large dog* | *a large family*
phrase **2 at large, a** free: *The murderer is at large.* **b** as a whole: *This is important for the school at large.*

Word building: **largely** adverb to a great extent **largeness** noun

lark¹

noun a kind of bird that lives in northern areas of the world and sings while flying

lark²

noun something done for fun or as a joke: *We hid under the bed for a lark.*

larrikin

noun someone, usually young, who behaves in a noisy, wild way
Word building: **larrikinism** noun

larva

noun the young of any insect which changes the form of its body before becoming an adult: *A caterpillar is the larva of a butterfly.*

Word building: The plural is **larvae** (*say* <u>lah</u>-vee). | **larval** adjective
Word history: from a Latin word meaning 'ghost', 'skeleton' or 'mask'

larva/lava Don't confuse **larva** with **lava. Lava** is molten rock from a volcano.

laryngitis (*say* la-ruhn-<u>juy</u>-tuhs)

noun a soreness and swelling in your larynx that often makes you lose your voice for a while

larynx (*say* <u>la</u>-rinks)

noun the box-like space at the top of your windpipe that contains the vocal cords which you use to speak

Word use: The larynx is sometimes called the **voice box** in informal language.
Word building: The plural is **larynges** or **larynxes.**

lasagne (*say* luh-<u>sahn</u>-yuh)

noun **1** a type of pasta cut into rectangular sheets **2** a dish made with this, often with mince meat, tomato and cheese

laser (*say* <u>lay</u>-zuh)

noun a device which produces a very narrow beam of intense light

Word history: an acronym made by joining the first letters of the words *light amplification* by *stimulated emission* of *radiation*

lash

noun **1** the cord part of a whip
Other words: **strap, switch**
2 a blow with a whip or something similar: *He got six lashes.* **3** short for **eyelash**
verb **4** to strike with a whip or something similar **5** to tie with a rope or cord
Other words: **bind, cable, fasten, rope, secure**
6 to beat violently against: *Waves lashed the side of the ship.*

Word building: The plural form of the noun is **lashes**.

lass

noun a girl or young woman

Word building: The plural is **lasses**.

lasso   (*say* las-<u>ooh</u>)

noun a long rope with a loop at one end which tightens when pulled, used to catch horses and other animals

Word building: The plural is **lassos** or **lassoes**. | **lasso** *verb* (**lassoed, lassoing**)

last¹

adjective **1** coming after everything else in time, order or place **2** latest or most recent: *last night*
adverb **3** after all the others: *I came last in the race.*
noun **4** something that is at the end: *This is the last of the questions*
phrase **5 at last**, eventually or after a long time: *We waited patiently and at last the bus arrived.*

Word building: **lastly** *adverb*

last²

verb to go on or continue: *This lesson will last half an hour.*

Word building: **lasting** *adjective*

latch

noun **1** a bar which slides or falls into a slot, used to keep a door or gate closed
verb **2** to close or fasten with a latch
phrase **3 latch on to**, *Informal* to understand: *He latched on to what she meant.*

Word building: The plural form of the noun is **latches**.

late

adjective **1** coming or continuing after the usual or proper time: *a late arrival* | *a late dinner*

Other words: **belated, overdue, slow**
2 far advanced in time: *a late hour* | *the late afternoon* **3** having recently died: *the late king*
adverb **4** after the usual or proper time: *They came late.*
phrase **5 of late**, recently: *She has been working hard of late.*

Word building: **lately** *adverb* recently **lateness** *noun*

latent

adjective present but not active or able to be seen: *a latent disease* | *a latent talent*
Other words: **dormant**

Word building: **latency** *noun*

lateral

adjective of or having to do with the side: *a lateral view* | *a lateral root of a plant*

Word building: **laterally** *adverb*

lathe

noun a machine which holds and turns a piece of wood or metal while it is being cut or shaped

lather   (*rhymes with* gather)

noun **1** foam made from soap and water **2** froth caused by heavy sweating
verb **3** to become covered with a lather

latitude

noun **1** the distance by which a point on the earth is north or south of the equator, measured in degrees **2** freedom, or room to move: *Give your horse a bit of latitude and it'll find its own way home.*

Word building: **latitudinal** *adjective*

latter

adjective **1** the second out of two things mentioned: *I prefer the latter idea.* **2** recent or, in a period of time, towards the end: *Things have been going well in latter days.* | *the latter years of his life*

Word use: The opposite of definition 1 is **former**.
Word building: **latterly** *adverb*

lattice   (*say* <u>lat</u>-uhs)

noun a frame made of crossed wooden or metal strips with diamond-shaped spaces in between, used as a screen or as a support for plants

laugh

verb **1** to make the sounds that show amusement, happiness or scorn
Other words: **cackle, chortle, chuckle, giggle, guffaw, snicker, snigger**
phrase **2 laugh off**, to treat lightly or with scorn: *I laughed off her accusations.*
Other words: **discount, dismiss, disregard**

Word building: **laughable** *adjective* funny or foolish **laugh** *noun* **laughter** *noun*

launch¹

noun a strong open boat, usually with a motor

launch²

verb **1** to send into the water: *to launch a ship* **2** to send up into the air: *to launch a rocket* **3** to set going or start: *to launch an attack* | *to launch out on a new career*

Word building: **launch** *noun*

laundromat

noun a public laundry with washing machines and spin-driers which you operate by putting coins in the slot of each machine

Word history: a trademark

laundry

noun **1** a room for washing clothes **2** clothes that are ready to be washed or have been washed

Word building: **launder** *verb* to wash and iron

laurel   (*say* lo-ruhl)

noun **1** a small evergreen tree with leaves that are used as a herb in cooking **2** the leaves of this tree made into a wreath, used as a sign of victory
phrase **3 rest on your laurels**, to be happy with what you have already done and not want to try for any more achievements

lava   (*say* lah-vuh)

noun **1** the hot liquid rock which comes out of a volcano **2** the hard rock formed when this becomes cool and solid

lava/larva Don't confuse **lava** with **larva**, which is the young of any insect that changes the form of its body before becoming an adult.

lavatory

noun a toilet or a room with a toilet in it
Word building: The plural is **lavatories**.

lavender

noun **1** a small shrub with pale purple flowers that have a strong but pleasing smell
adjective **2** pale bluish-purple

lavish   (*say* lav-ish)

adjective **1** plentiful or abundant: *lavish gifts* **2** generous in giving or using: *You are too lavish with your money.*

Word building: **lavish** *verb* **lavishly** *adverb* **lavishness** *noun*

law

noun **1** a rule or set of rules, especially those made by a government or ruler
Other words: **act, decree, edict, ordinance, regulation**
2 the area of knowledge or the occupation that has to do with these rules: *to study law* | *to practise law in a law court*
3 a statement describing what always happens under certain conditions: *the law of gravity*
Other words: **principle**

Word building: **lawful** *adjective* allowed by law **lawless** *adjective* not controlled by or not obeying the law **lawfully** *adverb* **lawlessly** *adverb*

law/lore Don't confuse **law** with **lore**. **Lore** is learning or knowledge about a particular subject, as in *the lore of herbs.*

lawn

noun an area of mown, grass-covered land, usually part of a garden

Word history: from a French word meaning 'wooded ground'

lawyer

noun someone whose work is to give advice about the law and to argue on behalf of people in law courts
Other words: **attorney, barrister, solicitor**

lax

adjective **1** careless or not strict: *lax behaviour* | *lax rules* **2** loose or slack: *lax muscles*

Word building: **laxity** *noun* **laxness** *noun*

laxative

noun a medicine for helping you pass waste matter from your bowels easily and without pain

Word building: **laxative** *adjective*

lay¹

verb **1** to put down or place: *to lay the book on the table | Lay your towel on the sand.* **2** to produce an egg **3** to prepare: *to lay the table | to lay plans*

phrase **4 lay off, a** to dismiss from a job: *The boss laid off five workers.* **b** *Informal* to stop: *Let's lay off work early today.* **5 lay out, a** to arrange in order, or prepare **b** to spend: *to lay out a fortune* **c** *Informal* to knock unconscious

noun **6** the way in which something lies or is laid: *the lay of the land*

Word building: Other verb forms are **I laid, I have laid, I am laying.**

lay/lie Don't confuse **lay** with **lie²**, which is similar in meaning, but used in a different way. While you usually **lay** *something*, as in *to lay a towel on the sand, to lay an egg* and *to lay the table*, you **lie** somewhere (*to lie in bed*), in a certain condition (*to lie dormant*), and so on. Note that the past form of **lie** is **lay** (*The dog lay on the bed all day yesterday*), while the past form of **lay** is **laid** (*He laid the table earlier*).

lay²

verb the past tense of **lie²**

lay-by

noun **1** a system of buying something by paying out part of the cost and then making further payments until it has been fully paid for and may be collected: *I'll put this shirt on lay-by.* **2** something bought in this way

Word building: **lay-by** *verb*

layer

noun a single thickness or coating: *a cake with three layers | a layer of paint*

Word building: **layer** *verb*

layout

noun the way something is arranged: *the layout of a newspaper page | the layout of a kitchen*

lazy

adjective **1** not liking work or effort: *a lazy student* **2** slow-moving: *a lazy stream* **3** not spent in work or effort: *a lazy afternoon*

Word building: Other forms are **lazier, laziest.** | **laze** *verb* to be lazy or spend time lazily   **lazily** *adverb*   **laziness** *noun*

lead¹   (*say* leed)

verb **1** to guide, often in a particular direction or to a particular place **2** to go or be at the front of **3** to command or be in charge of: *to lead an army | to lead a discussion*

phrase **4 lead to,** to be a way of getting to: *The next track leads to the river.*

noun (*say* leed) **5** the front position: *Bao Yu is in the lead.* **6** amount or distance ahead: *a lead of five metres* **7** a strap for holding an animal: *Put the dog on its lead.*

Other words: **cord, leash, tether, rein**

8 a clue: *The police haven't got any leads about the murder.*

Word building: Other verb forms are **I led, I have led, I am leading.**

lead²   (*say* led)

noun **1** a heavy bluish-grey metal used to make pipes, petrol, paint and bullets **2** a thin stick of carbon used in pencils

Word building: **leaden** *adjective* heavy and grey like lead   **lead** *adjective*   **leadenly** *adverb*

leaded petrol

noun petrol that contains tiny bits of lead which can harm you and the environment

leader   (*say* leed-uh)

noun **1** someone or something that leads **2** an article in a newspaper that gives the opinion of the newspaper or its editor on events happening at the moment **3** the main violinist in an orchestra, who helps the conductor

Word use: Another word for definition 2 is **editorial.**

Word building: **leadership** *noun*

leaf

noun **1** the flat, usually green, part of a plant that grows out from its stem **2** a page of a book **3** a thin sheet of metal: *gold leaf*

Other words: **foil, plate**

phrase **4 turn over a new leaf,** to begin new and better behaviour

Word building: The plural form of the noun is **leaves.** | **leafy** *adjective* (**leafier, leafiest**)   **leafless** *adjective*

leaflet

noun a small sheet of printed information: *They handed out leaflets advertising the school fete.*

Other words: **brochure, pamphlet**

league (*say* leeg)

noun **1** a group of people, countries or organisations who have made an agreement between themselves
Other words: **alliance, association, bloc, coalition, confederation, federation, union**
2 League, *short for* **Rugby League**
phrase **3 in league**, having an agreement: *They are in league with each other.*

Word history: from a Latin word meaning 'bind'

leak

noun **1** a hole or crack that lets liquid or gas in or out accidentally: *This bucket has a leak.* **2** the amount of liquid or gas that escapes through a leak: *There has been a huge leak from this bucket.* **3** the giving out of secret information: *a government leak*
verb **4** to let a substance in or out through a leak: *The roof leaks.* **5** to pass in or out through a leak: *Gas is leaking.*

Word building: **leaky** *adjective* (**leakier, leakiest**)   **leakage** *noun*   **leakiness** *noun*

leak/leek Don't confuse **leak** with **leek**. A **leek** is a vegetable that is related to the onion.

lean¹

verb **1** to be or to put in a sloping position: *She leaned over her work.* | *She leaned her head out the window.* **2** to rest against or on something for support
Other words: **prop**

Word building: Other forms are **I leaned** or **leant, I have leaned** or **leant, I am leaning.**

lean²

adjective **1** thin: *a lean person*
Other words: **skinny, slender, slight, slim**
2 with little or no fat: *lean meat*

Word building: **leanness** *noun*

leap

verb **1** to jump or move quickly: *to leap over a puddle* | *to leap away from burning fat* **2** to jump over: *He leapt the fence.*
noun **3** a jump **4** a sudden rise: *a leap in prices*
phrase **5 leap at**, to accept eagerly: *He leapt at the chance to go horse riding.*

Word building: Other verb forms are **I leapt** or **leaped, I have leapt** or **leaped, I am leaping.**

leap year

noun a year of 366 days every fourth year, with the extra day on 29 February

learn

verb **1** to come to have knowledge of or skill in: *to learn Italian* | *to learn piano*
Other words: **acquire, grasp, master**
2 to get knowledge or skill: *She learns quickly.*

Word building: Other forms are **I learned** or **learnt, I have learned** or **learnt, I am learning.** | **learning** *noun* the gaining of knowledge by study or the knowledge gained this way   **learner** *noun*

learned (*say* lern-uhd)

adjective having a lot of knowledge from study: *a learned woman*

Word building: **learnedly** *adverb*

lease (*rhymes with* peace)

noun **1** a written agreement which gives someone the right to use land or live in a building in return for rent
verb **2** to give or have the use of by a lease

leash

noun a strap for holding a dog

Word building: **leash** *verb*

least

adjective **1** smallest: *Our geography teacher gives us the least amount of homework.*
Other words: **lowest, minimum, slightest**
noun **2** the smallest in amount, extent or importance: *That is the least of my problems.*
phrase **3 at least**, **a** at the lowest calculation or judgement: *He must be at least fifty years old.* **b** at any rate: *I feel awful but at least I don't have to go to school.*

Word use: For other forms of the adjective see **little**.

leather (*rhymes with* feather)

noun the skin of animals prepared by tanning and used to make such things as shoes and bags

Word building: **leathery** *adjective*

leave¹

verb **1** to go away from: *I left the room.* **2** to depart or go away: *When do we leave?* **3** to allow to stay or remain in a particular place or condition: *to leave the books on the table* | *to leave the door unlocked*
phrase **4 leave alone**, to stop interfering with: *Leave me alone.* **5** to give for use after you have died: *Did your grandmother leave you anything in her will?*
Other words: **bequeath**

Word building: Other verb forms are **I left, I have left, I am leaving.**

leave²

noun **1** permission: *Can I have leave to go home?* **2** the time during which someone has permission to be absent: *My teacher is away on six weeks' leave.*

phrase **3 take leave of,** to say goodbye to

lecture

noun **1** a speech that you prepare and give before an audience or a class in order to teach or inform: *a lecture on Australian history*

Other words: **address, talk**

2 a long talk that's a warning or a scolding: *She gave me a lecture about my lateness.*

Word building: **lecturer** *noun* someone who gives lectures   **lecture** *verb*
Word history: from a Latin word meaning 'read'

ledge

noun a narrow flat shelf sticking out from something upright: *a window ledge*

ledger

noun an account book used to record money that is paid out and paid in

lee

noun a side or part that is sheltered or turned away from the wind: *the lee of a hill*

Word building: **lee** *adjective*   **leeward** *adjective*   **leeward** *adverb*

leech

noun a small worm that sucks the blood of humans or animals and was once used by doctors to take blood from sick people

Word building: The plural is **leeches.**

leek

noun a vegetable that tastes like an onion and has a white bulb and wide green leaves

leek/leak Don't confuse **leek** with **leak**. A **leak** is a hole or crack that lets liquid or gas in or out accidentally.

leer

noun an unpleasant kind of smile that suggests thoughts of sex, cruelty or cunning

Word building: **leer** *verb*

leeway

noun **1** the distance by which a ship or plane is blown off course by the wind **2** extra space, time or money that allows freedom of action and choice

left

adjective **1** having to do with the side of a person or thing which is turned toward the west when they are facing north: *Raise your left hand.*

noun **2** the left side: *Turn to the left.* **3** a political party or group that believes in the equal distribution of wealth and supports workers rather than companies

Word use: The opposite is **right.** | Definition 3 is sometimes spelt with a capital letter.

leg

noun **1** one of the parts of a body which is used for support and for walking **2** one of the supports of a piece of furniture: *the leg of a table* **3** one of the sections of a journey, race or competition: *The first leg of the flight was to Singapore.*

legacy

noun **1** a gift of money or property made after someone's death through their will: *He left her a legacy of $500.* **2** anything that is handed down from the past or happens as a result of something in the past: *The refugee problem is a legacy of war.*

Word building: The plural is **legacies.** | **legatee** *noun* someone who is given a legacy

legal   (*say* lee-guhl)

adjective **1** allowed or decided by law: *a legal action* **2** having to do with law: *a legal secretary*

Word building: **legalise** *verb* to make legal **legality** *noun*   **legally** *adverb*

legend   (*say* lej-uhnd)

noun a story that comes from long ago in the past and which is thought by many people to be at least partly true: *the legend of King Arthur and the Knights of the Round Table*

Word building: **legendary** *adjective*

legible

adjective able to be read easily: *legible handwriting*

Word use: The opposite is **illegible.**
Word building: **legibility** *noun*   **legibly** *adverb*

legion

noun **1** a unit of soldiers in the ancient Roman army **2** any large group of soldiers **3** any great number: *She has a legion of friends.*

Word building: **legionary** *noun*   **legionary** *adjective*

legislation

noun **1** the making of laws: *Parliament is responsible for legislation.* **2** a law or all the laws made: *Parliament passed new legislation to increase parking fines.*

Word building: **legislate** *verb*   **legislator** *noun*

legislature   (*say* lej-uhs-lay-chuh)

noun an organisation, such as a parliament, that makes laws

Word building: **legislative** *adjective*

legitimate   (*say* luh-jit-uh-muht)

adjective **1** in accordance with law: *a legitimate document* **2** born to parents who are legally married: *a legitimate child*

Word building: **legitimacy** *noun*   **legitimately** *adverb*

leisure   (*rhymes with* measure)

noun **1** time that is free from work
phrase **2 at leisure,** without hurry

Word building: **leisurely** *adjective* unhurried

lemon

noun **1** a yellow fruit with a sour taste
adjective **2** clear light-yellow

lemonade

noun a fizzy soft drink made with lemons, sugar and water

lend

verb **1** to give the use of, for a short time
Other words: **loan**
phrase **2 lend itself to,** to be well suited for: *This room lends itself to study.*

Word use: Compare definition 1 with **borrow.**
Word building: Other verb forms are **I lent, I have lent, I am lending.** | **lender** *noun*

length

noun **1** the measure from end to end: *This room is four metres in length.*
Other words: **extent**
2 a piece of something long: *a length of rope*
phrase **3 at length, a** in full detail: *She told the story at length.* **b** at last or finally: *At length the train arrived.*

Word building: **lengthen** *verb*   **lengthiness** *noun*   **lengthy** *adjective*

lenient   (*say* lee-nee-uhnt)

adjective gentle or not hard in treatment: *a lenient punishment*

Word building: **lenience** *noun*   **leniency** *noun*   **leniently** *adverb*

lens

noun a piece of glass or other material with one or more curved surfaces, used to make objects look larger or used in glasses to correct bad eyesight

Word building: The plural is **lenses.**

lentil

noun a kind of plant with a seed that is used as food, similar to peas and beans

leopard   (*say* lep-uhd)

noun a large, fierce, spotted animal of the cat family

Word use: The male is a **leopard,** the female is a **leopardess** and the young is a **cub.**

leotard   (*say* lee-uh-tahd)

noun a close-fitting piece of clothing worn for dancing or doing exercises

Word history: named after a French acrobat, Jules *Léotard*

leper   (*say* lep-uh)

noun someone who has leprosy

leprechaun   (*say* lep-ruh-kawn)

noun a fairy in Irish folk stories, in the shape of a little man

Word history: from an Irish word meaning 'little body'

leprosy

noun a disease you can catch from other people, which can cause sores on your skin, the loss of your fingers and toes, and the loss of feeling in parts of your body

lesbian

noun a woman who has sexual feelings for other women

Word building: **lesbian** *adjective*   **lesbianism** *noun*

less

adjective **1** smaller in size, amount or extent: *I want less talking.*
adverb **2** to a smaller extent or in a smaller amount: *Choose a less expensive present.*

Word use: Many people say that **fewer** should be used with things you can count and **less** with things you can't, as in *You should eat less sugar and fewer biscuits.* | For other forms see **little.**

lessen

verb to make or become less: *This medicine will lessen the pain.*

lesson

noun **1** the time during which a pupil or a class is taught one subject **2** anything that you learn or from which you learn: *a lesson in crossing roads | The accident taught me a lesson.*

let

verb **1** to allow or permit **2** to rent or hire out: *We have a room to let.*
Other words: **lease**
phrase **3 let down**, to disappoint: *You will let us down if you don't come.*
Other words: **fail**
4 let know, to inform or tell: *I'll let you know the news.* **5 let off**, **a** to excuse **b** to make explode: *We have a whole bag of fireworks to let off.*

Word building: Other verb forms are **I let, I have let, I am letting**.

lethal *(say* leeth*-uhl)*

adjective causing death: *a lethal poison*

Word building: **lethally** *adverb*

lethargy *(say* leth*-uh-jee)*

noun a state of sleepy laziness: *The hot weather has filled me with lethargy.*

Word building: **lethargic** *adjective* **lethargically** *adverb*

letter

noun **1** a message in writing or printing addressed to a person or group
Other words: **dispatch, note**
2 one of the signs used in writing and printing to stand for a speech sound: *'A' is the first letter of the alphabet.*

lettuce

noun a plant with large green leaves which are used in salads

leukaemia *(say* looh-kee*-mee-uh)*

noun a disease in which your body produces too many white blood cells and which often causes death

Word use: Another spelling is **leukemia**.
Word history: from a Greek word meaning 'white'

levee *(say* lev*-ee)*

noun **1** a raised bank of earth and sand built up by a river during floods **2** a bank built to keep a river from overflowing

level

adjective **1** even or having no part higher than another: *a level surface* **2** not sloping or horizontal: *level ground*

Other words: **even, flat**
3 equal: *They are level in intelligence.*
noun **4** a horizontal or level position or surface **5** a ranking whether high or low: *She was given a job at the top level of the company.* **6** an instrument for finding out whether something is exactly flat or horizontal
verb **7** to make or become level or equal
Other words: **flatten, smooth**
8 to aim or point: *Michael levelled the gun at the target.*
phrase **9 on the level**, *Informal* honest: *Are you sure he is on the level?*

Word building: **leveller** *noun* **levelly** *adverb*

lever *(say* lee*-vuh)*

noun **1** a bar supported at one point along its length, which lifts a weight at one end when you press or pull down the other
verb **2** to move with a lever: *to lever a rock out of the ground*
Other words: **force, prise**

Word building: **leverage** *noun*

levitate

verb to rise or float in the air as if by magic

Word building: **levitation** *noun*

levity

noun a lack of seriousness in the way you think and behave

levy *(say* lev*-ee)*

verb **1** to place or impose by law: *to levy a tax on cigarettes and beer*
noun **2** a fee or a tax which has to be paid: *The club imposed a levy on members to pay for the Christmas party.*

Word building: Other verb forms are **they levied, they have levied, they are levying.** | The plural form of the noun is **levies**.

liability

noun **1** something or someone that causes difficulty rather than being helpful: *New shoes are a liability on a long walk because they can make your feet sore.* **2** legal responsibility: *He accepted liability for the accident.* **3 liabilities**, debts, especially money that is owed

Word building: The plural is **liabilities**.

liable

adjective **1** likely: *Problems are liable to come up.* **2** having a legal responsibility: *He was liable for the accident and had to pay the repair costs.*

liaison (*say* lee-<u>ay</u>-zuhn)

noun a connection or communication between people or groups: *The school captain acted as a liaison between teachers and pupils.*

Word building: **liaise** *verb* to communicate and act together with

liar

noun someone who tells lies
Other words: **fibber, storyteller**

liar/lyre Don't confuse **liar** with **lyre**, which is a stringed musical instrument like a harp, used in ancient Greece.

libel (*say* <u>luy</u>-buhl)

noun a written or printed statement which damages someone's reputation: *The politician sued the newspaper for libel.*

Word use: Compare this with **slander**.
Word building: **libel** *verb* (**libelled, libelling**) **libeller** *noun* **libellous** *adjective* **libellously** *adverb*
Word history: from a Latin word meaning 'book'

liberal

adjective **1** happy to see change and development, especially in social and religious matters **2** broad-minded or accepting a wide range of ideas: *a liberal thinker* **3** generous: *a liberal gift | a liberal giver*

Word building: **liberality** *noun* **liberalism** *noun* **liberally** *adverb*

liberate

verb to set free: *The army liberated the country from enemy control.*

Word building: **liberation** *noun* **liberator** *noun*

liberty

noun **1** freedom from imprisonment, or from a cruel or foreign government **2** freedom to do, think, or speak as you choose **3** a rude or disrespectful freedom in behaviour or speech: *Don't think that you can take liberties with me.*
phrase **4 at liberty**, free, or having permission to do a particular thing

Word building: The plural form of the noun is **liberties**.

library

noun **1** a room or building where books and other reading or study materials are kept for people to use or borrow **2** a collection of books, or of films or music: *She has a good library at home.*

Word building: The plural is **libraries**. | **librarian** *noun* a person in charge of a library

lice

plural noun very small insects that can live in your hair and make your head itchy. They lay eggs called nits.

Word use: This word is a short way of saying **head lice**.
Word building: The singular form is **louse**.

licence

noun **1** official permission to do something or a certificate showing this permission: *a driving licence* **2** uncontrolled freedom of behaviour: *That babysitter allows the children too much licence.*

license

verb to give official permission to: *One day the Government might license all teachers.*

Word building: **licensee** *noun* someone who has a licence, usually to sell alcohol

lichen (*say* <u>luy</u>-kuhn)

noun a moss-like plant that grows in patches, usually on rocks or tree trunks

lick

verb **1** to pass your tongue over: *David licked the back of the stamp.* **2** to pass over or touch lightly: *Flames licked the logs of wood.* **3** *Informal* to defeat: *We licked the other team.*

Word building: **lick** *noun*

licorice (*say* <u>lik</u>-uh-rish)

noun a sweet-tasting substance made from the root of a plant and used in making sweets and some medicines

Word use: Another spelling is **liquorice**.

lid

noun **1** a movable top for covering a container **2** short for **eyelid**

lie[1]

noun a deliberate untruth
Other words: **falsehood, fib, half-truth, invention**

Word building: **lie** *verb* (**lied, lying**)

lie²

verb **1** to be or rest in a flat horizontal position: *I would like to lie in bed all day. | A book is lying on the table.* **2** to remain in a certain position or condition: *The money lay forgotten in the bank for many years.* **3** to be found or to be located: *The trouble with the bike lies with the gears. | Our land lies beside the river.*

phrase **4 lie low**, to be in hiding

Word building: Other verb forms are **I lay, I have lain, I am lying**.

lie/lay Don't confuse **lie** with **lay¹**, which is similar in meaning, but used in a different way. Unlike **lie**, you usually **lay** *something*, as in *to lay a towel on the sand*, *to lay an egg* and *to lay the table*. Note that the past form of **lie** is **lay** (*The dog lay on the bed all day yesterday*), while the past form of **lay** is **laid** (*He laid the table earlier*).

lieutenant (*say* lef-<u>ten</u>-uhnt)

noun an officer in the army or navy, lower in rank than a captain

Word history: from a French word meaning 'holding a place'

life

noun **1** the condition that makes animals and plants different from dead things and from other objects like rocks, liquids, machines and so on **2** the time you are alive, from your birth to your death **3** living things as a group: *life on earth* **4** lively activity or interest: *Her speech was full of life.*

Word building: The plural is **lives**.

lifeboat

noun a boat carried on a large ship and used if the ship sinks or catches fire

life cycle

noun the development of a living thing from the beginning of its life to the time it becomes an adult

lifeguard

noun someone who is paid to patrol a place where people swim, such as a public pool, and to rescue people if necessary and give them first aid

lifesaver

noun someone who makes sure that people swim at the safe part of a beach and who rescues swimmers in difficulty, often working as a volunteer rather than being paid

lifesaving

noun the techniques to deal with emergency situations in and near the water, such as methods of rescue and mouth-to-mouth resuscitation: *She wants to get a certificate for lifesaving as well as for swimming.*

lift

verb **1** to raise or bring upwards *noun* **2** a moving platform or cage for bringing people from one level of a building to another **3** a free ride in a vehicle: *Can you give me a lift home?*

Word use: Another word for definition 2, mainly used in America, is **elevator**.

lift-off

noun the moment when a space shuttle or rocket leaves the ground

light¹

noun **1** a form of radiation produced by some objects such as the sun or fire, which bounces off other things and so lets us see them **2** one of those things which give off light, such as an electric light globe or the sun **3** one of the set of coloured lights that is used to control traffic at intersections **4** new knowledge or information: *Can you throw any light on this mystery?*

adjective **5** having light, rather than darkness: *a light room* **6** pale in colour: *light blue*

verb **7** to set burning or start to burn: *He lit a fire. | The match won't light.* **8** to give light to: *They took a torch to light their way.*

phrase **9 light up**, **a** to make brighter: *A smile lit up her face.* **b** to become light or without colour: *The city lights up at night.*

Word building: Other verb forms are **I lit** or **lighted, I have lit** or **lighted, I am lighting.** | **lighting** *noun* **lightness** *noun*

light²

adjective **1** of little weight: *a light load* **2** small in amount, force or depth: *a light meal | light rain | light sleep* **3** not heavy or serious: *light reading* **4** cheerful: *a light heart*

phrase **5 make light of**, to treat as being of little importance: *Dimitri always makes light of his troubles.*

Word building: **lightly** *adverb* **lightness** *noun*

lighthouse

noun a tower with a strong light that guides ships at sea and warns them of any dangerous rocks nearby

lightning

noun a sudden flash of light in the sky caused by electricity in the air during a thunderstorm

light-year

noun the distance travelled by light in one year, used in measuring distances between stars

like¹

adjective **1** similar or able to be compared in some way
noun **2** something that is similar: *oranges, lemons and the like* **3** a similar person or thing: *No-one has seen your like around here before.*
Word building: **liken** *verb* **likeness** *noun*

like²

verb **1** to find pleasant or agreeable: *I like picnics. | I like her.*
Other words: **appreciate, enjoy, love**
2 to wish or want: *Do it whenever you like.*
Other words: **desire, fancy, prefer**
Word building: **likeable** *adjective* easy to like
likes *plural noun*: *to have likes and dislikes*
liking *noun*: *I have a liking for chocolate cake.*

likely

adjective **1** probable: *a likely account of what happened*
adverb **2** probably: *He was very likely right.*
Word building: **likelihood** *adjective* chance

lilac   (*say* luy-luhk)

noun **1** a purple or white flower with a pleasant smell, which grows in clusters on a shrub
adjective **2** pale reddish-purple

lilt

verb to sing or play in a light rhythmic manner
Word building: **lilt** *noun* **lilting** *adjective*

lily

noun a plant with a bulb and a funnel-shaped flower which can be found in many colours, although most people think of lilies as being white
Word building: The plural is **lilies**.

lima bean   (*say* luy-muh been)

noun a kind of bean with a broad flat seed that you can eat

limb

noun **1** your arm or leg, or the similar part of an animal's body, such as a wing
Other words: **member**
2 the large main branch of a tree
Other words: **bough**

limber

phrase **limber up**, to exercise or warm up in order to make yourself flexible and relaxed: *Always remember to limber up before a race.*

limbo

phrase **in limbo**, in an uncertain situation, where nothing is decided: *Our holiday plans are in limbo until Dad's health improves.*

lime¹

noun **1** a white powder obtained by heating limestone, that is used in making cement **2** a calcium mixture used to improve crop-growing soil

lime²

noun **1** a small greenish-yellow citrus fruit
adjective **2** greenish-yellow

limelight

noun a situation where a person gets a lot of attention from other people, the media, and so on: *After he released his first album, he suddenly found himself in the limelight.*

limerick   (*say* lim-uh-rik)

noun a funny rhyming poem of five lines
Word history: named after *Limerick*, a county in the Republic of Ireland

limestone

noun a soft, white, chalky rock

limit

noun **1** the end or furthest part: *to reach the limit of your patience* **2** a boundary or line that you should not pass: *You may only ride up to the limit I have set you.*
verb **3** to keep within a certain amount or space: *to limit your pocket money | to limit the playing area*
Word building: Other verb forms are **I limited, I have limited, I am limiting. | limitation** *noun*

limousine   (*say* lim-uh-zeen)

noun any large comfortable car, especially one driven by a paid driver

limp[1]
verb to walk with difficulty because of an injured leg or foot
Word building: **limp** *noun*

limp[2]
adjective not stiff or firm: *limp material*
Word building: **limply** *adverb* **limpness** *noun*

limpet
noun a cone-shaped shellfish that sticks very firmly to rocks

limpid
adjective clear or transparent: *limpid pools of water*
Word building: **limpidly** *adverb*

line[1]
noun **1** a thin mark or stroke made on paper, wood or some other surface **2** something arranged like a line: *a line of trees | a line of words on a page*
Other words: **chain, column, file, procession, row, string**
3 a wrinkle on someone's face **4** a strip of railway track: *the railway line* **5** a type of goods which a shop sells: *We don't stock that line.* **6 lines**, the words of an actor's part in a play: *Have you learned your lines?*
verb **7** to form a line along: *Trees lined the street.*
phrase **8 line up**, **a** to take a position in a line or queue **b** to bring into a line
Other words: **align, arrange, order**
Word building: **lineage** (*say* lin-ee-ij) *noun* descent from a line of ancestors **linear** *adjective* stretched in a line

line[2]
verb to cover the inside of: *to line a coat with silk*
Word building: **lining** *noun* a covering for an inside surface

linen
noun **1** cloth made from flax **2** articles made from linen or cotton, such as sheets and tablecloths

liner
noun a large passenger ship

linesman
noun **1** a sports official who helps a referee or umpire decide if the ball has landed inside or outside one of the lines on the field of play **2** someone who puts up or repairs telephone or electric power lines
Word building: The plural is **linesmen**.

linger
verb to stay on in a place because you don't want to leave
Word building: **lingering** *adjective*: *a lingering illness* **lingeringly** *adverb*

lingerie (*say* lon-zhuh-ray)
noun women's underwear or nightwear
Word use: This comes from a French word and in English we have tried to give it a French sound.

linguistics (*say* ling-gwis-tiks)
noun the study of language, including sounds, words and grammar: *Linguistics is a subject studied at university.*
Word building: **linguist** *noun* someone who studies language **linguistic** *adjective*: *linguistic knowledge*

liniment
noun an oily liquid for rubbing on bruises, sprains or sore muscles

link
noun **1** one of the separate rings which make up a chain **2** anything which connects: *Our love of football is a strong link between us.*
Other words: **bond, connection, tie**
verb **3** to join together, like the rings of a chain: *to link up* **4** to join one thing to another so that they work together: *Our school is going to link our computers to the internet soon.*
Other words: **connect**
Word building: **link** *verb* **linkage** *noun*

linoleum (*say* luy-noh-lee-uhm)
noun a floor covering made of a mixture of oil, cork and rosin pressed into a strong cloth backing
Word use: This is sometimes shortened to **lino**.

linseed
noun the seed of the flax plant from which an oil is made

lion
noun a large, honey-coloured member of the cat family, that lives in Africa and southern Asia, the male of which has a mane
Word use: The male is a **lion**, the female is a **lioness** and the young is a **cub**.

lip

noun **1** one of the two folds of skin around the mouth **2** the edge of something: *There was a chip in the lip of the cup.*
Other words: **rim**

lipstick

noun a cosmetic for colouring your lips

liquefy   (*say* l<u>ik</u>-wuh-fuy)

verb to make or become liquid

Word building: Other forms are **I liquefied, I have liquefied, I am liquefying.** | **liquefier** *noun*

liqueur   (*say* luh-<u>kyooh</u>-uh)

noun a type of strong alcoholic liquor made in many flavours

liquid

adjective **1** flowing like water
Other words: **fluid, running, runny**
2 having to do with liquids: *a liquid measuring jug*

Word building: **liquid** *noun* any liquid substance

liquidate

verb **1** to settle or pay: *to liquidate a debt* **2** to pay off debts and finish doing business **3** to get rid of, especially by killing: *to liquidate political prisoners*

Word building: **liquidation** *noun*: *The company went into liquidation.*   **liquidator** *noun*

liquid paper

noun a thin white paint that is used to cover written mistakes on paper

Word use: Another word for this is **white-out**.

liquor   (*sounds like* licker)

noun a strong alcoholic drink such as brandy or whisky

liquorice   (*say* l<u>ik</u>-uh-rish)

noun another spelling for **licorice**

lisp

noun the inability to pronounce 's', making it sound like the 'th' in *thin*

Word building: **lisp** *verb*

list¹

noun **1** a set of the names of things written down one under the other, so that you'll remember them: *a shopping list* **2** any set of names, words, and so on, written down: *She had to keep a list of all the parcels that were sent out that day.*
Other words: **catalogue, record, register**

Word building: **list** *verb*   **listing** *noun*

list²

verb to lean to one side: *The ship listed to starboard.*
Other words: **bank, incline, slant, slope, sway, tilt, tip**

Word building: **list** *noun*

listen   (*say* l<u>is</u>-uhn)

verb to pay attention so that you are able to hear something

Word building: **listener** *noun*

listless

adjective having no energy or interest in anything

Word building: **listlessly** *adverb*   **listlessness** *noun*

literal

adjective **1** true to fact and not exaggerated: *a literal account of what happened* **2** following or referring to the exact or actual words that are written or spoken: *a literal translation*

Word building: **literally** *adverb*

literary

adjective having to do with books and literature of a high standard: *a literary critic*

literate   (*say* l<u>it</u>-uh-ruht)

adjective able to read and write

Word use: The opposite is **illiterate**.
Word building: **literacy** *noun*

literature

noun **1** books, poems, plays and other forms of writing of a high standard: *Australian literature* **2** what is written about a particular subject: *the literature of home decorating*

lithe   (*say* luydh)

adjective supple or bending easily: *She has a lithe figure.*

Word building: **lithely** *adverb*   **litheness** *noun*

litmus

noun a colouring which is often soaked onto strips of paper and used to tell whether a liquid is an acid or an alkali. The paper turns red when you dip it in acid and blue in an alkali.

Word building: **litmus paper** *noun*

litre   (*rhymes with* beater)

noun a measure of liquid in the metric system

Word history: from a Greek word meaning 'pound'

litter

noun **1** things, especially rubbish, scattered about, especially in a public place
2 a number of baby animals born at the same time: *a litter of puppies*
Other words: **brood**
verb **3** to make untidy by scattering rubbish: *The picnickers littered the beach with cans.* **4** to be scattered around: *Bottles littered the park.*

Word building: **litterbug** *noun* someone who drops litter in public places

little

adjective **1** small in size: *There's a little hole in my shirt.*
Other words: **microscopic, minute, tiny**
2 not much or small in amount: *of little use*
Other words: **minimal, minor, slight**
3 short or brief: *a little time*

Word building: Other forms for definitions 2 and 3 are **less, least.**

live¹   *(rhymes with* give)

verb **1** to be alive or have life
Other words: **breathe**
2 to keep life going: *to live on bread and water* **3** to have your home in a particular place: *to live in Australia*
Other words: **dwell, inhabit, reside**

live²   *(rhymes with* dive)

adjective **1** living or alive **2** broadcast or televised as it is being performed: *a live broadcast of the town hall concert* **3** charged with electricity: *a live wire* **4** unexploded: *a live bullet*

Word building: **live** *adverb*: *a cricket match televised live*

livelihood   *(say* luyv-lee-hood)

noun a way of earning money to live: *He makes a livelihood from fishing.*

lively   *(say* luyv-lee)

adjective full of energy or spirit: *a lively puppy*

Word building: **liven** *verb* to make more lively or energetic   **liveliness** *noun*

liver   *(rhymes with* giver)

noun the part of your body that makes bile which helps digest your food

livestock

noun all the animals kept on a farm or station property

livid   *(say* liv-uhd)

adjective **1** very angry: *My parents were livid when I told them.* **2** discoloured by bruises

living

adjective **1** alive
Other words: **animate, breathing, existent, live**
2 in existence or use: *German is a living language.* **3** having to do with living beings: *The floods were the worst in living memory.*
noun **4** livelihood: *to earn a living*
Other words: **income**
phrase **5 the living image,** the exact likeness or copy: *You're the living image of your aunty.*

living room

noun a room in a home with comfortable seats, for relaxing or entertaining guests

Word use: Another term for this is **lounge room.**

lizard

noun a reptile with a long thin body, four legs and a long tail

llama   *(rhymes with* farmer)

noun a South American animal related to the camel and used for carrying loads

load

noun **1** something carried
Other words: **cargo**
2 the quantity carried: *a load of soil*
verb **3** to put a load on or in **4** to take on as a load: *The ship is loading wheat now.* **5** to put bullets into or a film into: *to load a gun | to load a camera*

Word building: **loaded** *adjective*: *a loaded ship | a loaded gun*

loaf¹

noun **1** an amount of bread or cake baked in a particular shape **2** any food made into a loaf shape: *a meat loaf*

Word building: The plural is **loaves.**

loaf²

verb to be lazy or do nothing: *I loafed all day.*
Other words: **idle, laze, lounge around, rest**

Word building: **loaf** *noun* a restful lazy time

loam

noun loose, very fertile soil

Word building: **loamy** *adjective*

loan

noun **1** the giving of something to be used for a short time before being returned to the owner: *I'll give you a loan of my book.* **2** money given for a short time, usually to be repaid with interest: *a bank loan*
Other words: **advance, credit**

Word building: **loan** *verb* to lend

loan/lone Don't confuse **loan** with **lone**, which means 'not with anyone', as in *a lone traveller.* It can also mean 'standing apart', as in *a lone tree.*

loath   (*rhymes with* both)

adjective unwilling or not inclined: *I am loath to lend her anything.*

Word use: The more usual word is **reluctant**.

loathe   (*rhymes with* clothe)

verb to hate or detest very much

Word building: **loathsome** *adjective*

lob

verb to hit or throw a ball so that it has a very high bounce, as in tennis

Word building: Other forms are **I lobbed, I have lobbed, I am lobbing.** | **lob** *noun*
Word history: from a Middle English word for a kind of fish, and later meaning 'clumsy person'

lobby

noun **1** an entrance hall **2** a group of people trying to get support for a particular cause: *a lobby for cancer research*

Word building: The plural is **lobbies.** | **lobby** *verb* (**lobbied, lobbying**): *to lobby for the conservation of rainforests* **lobbyist** *noun*

lobe

noun the soft, hanging, lower part of your ear

lobster

noun a large shellfish with ten legs and a long tail, which turns pink when cooked

local

adjective **1** having to do with a particular place: *a local custom* **2** having to do with the area you are living in rather than the whole town or state: *local government | the local school*
Other words: **community, district, municipal, neighbourhood, regional**
3 acting on only part of the body: *a local anaesthetic*
noun **4** someone who lives in a particular place: *He's one of the locals.*

Word building: **localise** *verb* **locally** *adverb*

locality   (*say* loh-<u>kal</u>-uh-tee)

noun a particular place or area: *We are now in the locality where Ned Kelly lived.*

Word building: The plural is **localities**.

locate

verb **1** to find the place of: *to locate the fault in the engine* **2** to put in a place or area: *to locate the Post Office near the shops*

Word building: **location** *noun*

locavore   (*say* <u>loh</u>-kuh-vaw)

noun a person who eats only food that is produced locally: *He says being a locavore means his food tastes better because it is fresher.*

loch   (*sounds like* lock)

noun a Scottish word for **lake**

lock¹

noun **1** a device for fastening a door, gate, lid or drawer, which needs a key to open it **2** a part of a canal with gates at each end allowing ships to be raised from one level to another
verb **3** to fasten or become fastened with a key **4** to shut or put into a place of safety or imprisonment

lock²

noun a short length or curl of hair
Other words: **ringlet, strand**

locker

noun a cupboard that may be locked, especially one for your own use

locket

noun a small case for a small picture or lock of hair, usually worn on a chain hung around your neck

locksmith

noun someone who makes or mends locks and keys

locomotive   (*say* loh-kuh-<u>moh</u>-tiv)

noun the engine which pulls railway carriages or trucks

Word building: **locomotion** *noun* the act or power of moving around

locust   (*say* <u>loh</u>-kuhst)

noun a type of grasshopper which moves from one place to another in large numbers and destroys crops

lodge

noun **1** a building used as a holiday house: *a ski lodge* **2** a meeting place of a branch of a secret society
verb **3** to board or live for a while in someone else's home: *I lodge at Mrs Smith's house.* **4** to be put, caught or placed: *A speck of dirt lodged in my eye.* **5** to put for safe keeping: *to lodge valuables with a bank*

Word building: **lodger** *noun* **lodgings** *noun* **lodgement** *noun*

loft

noun **1** the space in a building between the roof and the ceiling **2** an upper level of a church or hall made for a special purpose: *a choir loft*

lofty

adjective **1** reaching high into the air: *lofty mountains* **2** noble or high in character: *He has lofty ideals.* **3** proud or haughty: *a lofty manner*

Word building: Other forms are **loftier, loftiest.**

log

noun **1** a large branch or the trunk of a tree which has fallen or been cut down **2** the daily record of a voyage or flight kept by the captain of a ship or plane
Other words: **account, diary, journal**
phrase **3 log off**, to exit from a computer network **4 log on**, to enter your name and password into the computer so that you can begin using it: *You must log on before you can access the network.*

Word use: You can also say **log out** for definition 3, and **log in** for definition 4.
Word building: **log** *verb* (**logged, logging**) **logger** *noun* **logging** *noun*

loganberry

noun a large, dark-red berry you can eat, or the plant it grows on

Word building: The plural is **loganberries.**
Word history: named after the Californian man who first grew them, JH *Logan*, 1841–1928

logbook

noun a book in which the record of a journey made by a ship or plane is entered

logic　　(say loj-ik)

noun correct reasoning: *My argument was based on logic.*

Word building: **logical** *adjective* **logically** *adverb* **logician** *noun* someone who studies the art of logic

logo

noun a symbol or other design that identifies a brand or a company

loin

noun **1** the part of your body between your lowest rib and the top of either thigh **2** the similar part of a four-legged animal: *a loin of lamb*
phrase **3 gird up your loins**, to get ready for action

loiter

verb to move about aimlessly or stay in the one place: *I loitered on the street corner waiting for my friend.*

Word building: **loiterer** *noun*

loll

verb **1** to lean in a lazy manner: *He lolled against the post.* **2** to hang loosely: *The dog's tongue lolled from its mouth as it panted.*

lollipop

noun a kind of boiled sweet, often fixed to the end of a stick

lolly

noun any sweet, especially a boiled one
Other words: **candy**

Word building: The plural is **lollies.**

lone

adjective **1** being alone or not with anyone: *a lone traveller* **2** standing apart from others: *a lone tree*

Word building: **loner** *noun* someone who likes to be alone

lone/loan Don't confuse **lone** with **loan**, the giving of something to be used for a short time and then returned to the owner:
Can I have a loan of your ruler?

lonely

adjective **1** alone or without friendly company: *A lighthouse keeper's job is a lonely one.* **2** far away from where people are: *lonely beaches* **3** feeling sad because of being alone: *The old man was lonely when his wife died.*

Word building: **loneliness** *noun*

long¹

adjective **1** having a great distance from one end to the other
Other words: **extended, extensive, lengthy**
2 lasting a great amount of time
Other words: **drawn-out, interminable, lengthy, prolonged, protracted**
3 having a stated distance or time: *a road two miles long | a speech an hour long*
phrase **4 the long and short of**, the main part of: *The long and short of it is that we decided to go.*
adverb **5** for a great amount of time: *Did he stay long?* **6** for or throughout a certain amount of time: *How long did he stay?*
Word building: **length** *noun*

long²

phrase **long for**, to want or desire very much: *I long for a pet.*
Word building: **longing** *noun* **longingly** *adverb*

longitude   (*say* long-guh-tyood)

noun the distance, measured in degrees, by which a point on the earth is east or west of Greenwich in England
Word building: **longitudinal** *adjective* **longitudinally** *adverb*

longwinded

adjective talking for too long or using more words than necessary: *You are always so longwinded in your explanations.*
Word building: **longwindedness** *noun*

look

verb **1** to use your eyes in order to see **2** to examine by searching: *to look through papers* **3** to appear or seem: *He looked happy.* **4** to face towards: *The house looks east.*
phrase **5 look after**, to take care of **6 look down on**, to despise or scorn **7 look for**, to search for **8 look out**, to be on guard or be watchful: *to look out for danger* **9 look up to**, to admire or respect
Word building: **looks** *noun* general appearance: *good looks* **look** *noun*

lookout

noun **1** a watch kept for something that may come or happen **2** someone who keeps such a watch or the place from which they watch **3** a place on a mountain from which you can admire the view

loom¹

noun a machine or apparatus for weaving cloth
Word history: from an Old English word meaning 'tool' or 'implement'

loom²

verb to appear, often in a large or frightening form: *The hedge suddenly loomed in front of the young horse rider.*
Other words: **arise, emerge, materialise**
Word history: from a Swedish word meaning 'move slowly'

loop

noun **1** a more or less oval shape twisted in a piece of string, ribbon or something similar
Other words: **circle, ring, coil, twist**
2 anything shaped like this: *a loop in a railway track*
Word building: **loop** *verb*

loophole

noun **1** an opening, especially in a wall to allow light in or to fire weapons through **2** a way or means of escape

loose   (*say* loohs)

adjective **1** free from being fastened: *a loose end of string* **2** not bound together: *a loose bundle of papers* **3** not in a container: *loose peanuts* **4** not firm: *a loose rein* **5** not fitting tightly: *a loose sweater*
phrase **6 at a loose end**, having nothing to do
Word building: **loose** *verb* to let loose **loosen** *verb* to make or become looser **loosely** *adverb*

loot

noun anything that has been stolen, especially from an enemy in war
Word building: **loot** *verb* **looter** *noun*

lop

verb **1** to cut off: *to lop branches from a tree* **2** to cut branches from: *to lop trees*
Word building: Other forms are **I lopped, I have lopped, I am lopping.** | **lopper** *noun*

lope

verb to move with long easy steps
Word building: **lope** *noun*

lopsided

adjective **1** leaning to one side **2** larger or heavier on one side than the other

Word building: **lopsidedly** *adverb*
lopsidedness *noun*

lord

noun **1** a British nobleman with a title in front of his name **2** someone who has power over others

Word building: **lord** *verb*: *to lord it over someone* **lordly** *adjective*

lore

noun learning or knowledge, especially on a particular subject: *family lore | the lore of herbs*

lore/law Don't confuse **lore** with **law**, a set of rules made by a government or a ruler.

lorikeet

noun a small brightly coloured parrot that has a brush-like tongue for feeding on nectar

lorry

noun another name for **truck**

Word building: The plural is **lorries**.

lose *(say loohz)*

verb **1** to come to be without for some reason, and not be able to find
Other words: **mislay, misplace**
2 to have taken away from you by death: *to lose an uncle* **3** to fail to get or win

Word building: Other forms are **I lost, I have lost, I am losing.** | **loser** *noun*

loss

noun **1** the losing of something: *the loss of my wallet | the loss of his friends*
2 something that is lost
phrase **3 a dead loss**, a completely useless person or thing **4 at a loss**, confused or uncertain: *I was at a loss as to what to do.*

lost

adjective **1** no longer in your possession **2** not knowing the way **3** wasted or not used: *lost time*

lot

noun **1** a large number **2** your fate in life: *Illness seems to be her lot.* **3** the drawing of an object from a hat or box to decide something by chance: *We decided by lot who would go first.*
phrase **4 the lot**, the whole amount

lotion *(say loh-shuhn)*

noun a liquid that you use to heal, clean or feed your skin

Word history: from a Latin word meaning 'a washing'

lottery

noun a kind of raffle in which the prize is usually money

Word building: The plural is **lotteries**.

lotto

noun another name for **bingo**

lotus *(say loh-tuhs)*

noun a kind of waterlily which grows in Asia and Egypt

loud

adjective **1** producing a lot of sound so that you can hear it easily: *a loud radio | loud knocking*
Other words: **booming, deafening, noisy, thunderous**
2 very colourful, usually in an unpleasant way: *a loud tie*
Other words: **garish, gaudy, glaring, lurid, ostentatious**

Word building: **loudly** *adverb*: *to knock loudly* **loudness** *noun*

loudspeaker

noun a device which turns electronic signals into sounds, as in a radio or public address system

Word use: The short form of this is **speaker**.

lounge

verb **1** to lie back lazily: *to lounge in a chair*
noun **2** the most expensive seats in a theatre **3** another name for a **couch**

lounge room

noun another word for **living room**

louse

noun **1** a small wingless insect which lives in the hair or skin and sucks blood
2 *Informal* someone who is hateful or not to be trusted

Word use: The plural of definition 1 is **lice**.

lousy *(say low-zee)*

adjective **1** having many lice **2** *Informal* mean or hateful
phrase **3 feel lousy**, *Informal* to be sick or unwell

Word building: Other adjective forms are **lousier, lousiest**.

lout

noun a rough, rude and sometimes violent young man

Word building: **loutish** *adjective*

love

noun **1** strong or warm feelings of affection: *love for a parent | love for a friend* Other words: **adoration, devotion, fondness** **2** sexual desire **3** strong liking: *love of reading* **4** no score in tennis and similar games: *The score is 30 love.*
verb **5** to have strong or warm feelings of affection for: *I love my Grandma.* Other words: **adore, care for, cherish** *phrase* **6 in love with,** feeling deep passion for: *They are in love with each other.* **7 make love,** to have sexual intercourse

Word building: **beloved** *adjective* dearly loved **lovable** *adjective* inspiring love **lover** *noun* **loving** *adjective*

lovely

adjective **1** having a beautiful appearance or personality **2** very pleasant: *a lovely day*

Word building: Other forms are **lovelier, loveliest.** | **loveliness** *noun*

low¹

adjective **1** not far above the ground, floor or base **2** lying below the average level: *low ground | The river is low because of the drought.* **3** small in amount: *a low number* **4** deep in pitch: *a low buzz | a low voice* **5** of lesser rank, quality or importance: *low birth*

Word building: **low** *adverb* **lowly** *adjective*

low²

verb to make the sound that cattle make

Word use: This is an old-fashioned word for **moo.**
Word building: **low** *noun* **lowing** *noun*

lower

verb **1** to make or become less: *to lower the price of bread | Prices lowered when supplies increased.* **2** to make less loud: *to lower the voice* **3** to let down: *to lower a rope*

Word use: The opposite is **raise.**

lower case

noun the printing type that makes small, not capital, letters

Word use: The opposite is **upper case.**
Word building: **lower-case** *adjective*

loyal

adjective faithful and true: *a loyal friend* Other words: **dedicated, dependable, devoted, reliable, steadfast, trustworthy**

Word building: **loyally** *adverb* **loyalty** *noun*

lozenge   (*say* <u>loz</u>-uhnj)

noun a small sweet, usually used to soothe a sore throat

Word history: from a Persian word meaning 'stone slab'

Ltd

short for *Limited*; used after the name of a company to show that the shareholders lose only what they have put in if the company gets into debt

Word use: See also **Pty**, which often comes before **Ltd.**

lubricate

verb to oil or grease the moving parts of, so that they will move more easily: *to lubricate an engine*

Word building: **lubricant** *noun* **lubrication** *noun* **lubricative** *adjective*

lucerne   (*say* <u>looh</u>-suhn)

noun a plant used to feed cattle

Word use: Another name for this is **alfalfa.**

lucid   (*say* <u>looh</u>-suhd)

adjective **1** clear or easy to understand: *a lucid explanation* **2** having clear understanding: *The player was still lucid despite a severe blow to the head.*

Word building: **lucidity** *noun* **lucidly** *adverb*

luck

noun **1** something which happens to a person by chance **2** good fortune: *She wished me luck.*
phrase **3 no such luck,** unfortunately not **4 push your luck,** to take another risk in the hope that you'll be lucky yet again

Word building: **lucky** *adjective* (**luckier, luckiest**) **luckily** *adverb* **luckiness** *noun*

lucrative   (*say* <u>looh</u>-kruh-tiv)

adjective producing good profits or paying well: *a lucrative business*

ludicrous   (*say* <u>looh</u>-duh-kruhs)

adjective so silly as to cause laughter: *a ludicrous remark*

lug

verb to pull along or carry with effort

Word building: Other forms are **I lugged, I have lugged, I am lugging.**

luggage

noun the suitcases and other containers you use when travelling

Word use: Another word is **baggage.**

lukewarm

adjective **1** a bit warm **2** not very enthusiastic: *a lukewarm response*

lull

verb **1** to put to sleep by singing or rocking **2** to calm or quiet: *to lull someone's fears*

Word building: **lull** *noun* a period of calm

lullaby

noun a song sung to put a baby to sleep

Word building: The plural is **lullabies**.

lumber¹

noun **1** timber sawn into boards **2** a number of useless objects stored away

lumber²

verb to move heavily and slowly, or clumsily: *Dad woke up when the alarm went off and lumbered down the hallway to the kitchen.*

lumberjack

noun someone who cuts down trees

Word use: This is mostly used in America and Canada.

luminous   (*say* <u>looh</u>-muhn-uhs)

adjective giving off or reflecting light: *a luminous clock face*

Word building: **luminosity** *noun*   **luminously** *adverb*

lump

noun **1** a mass of solid matter: *a lump of clay* **2** a swelling: *a lump on the head* *adjective* **3** including a number of things taken together: *a lump sum of money* **4** in the form of a lump: *lump sugar* *phrase* **5 have a lump in the throat**, to feel as if you're about to cry

Word building: **lumpily** *adverb*   **lumpiness** *noun*   **lumpy** *adjective* (**lumpier, lumpiest**)

lunar   (*rhymes with* sooner)

adjective having to do with the moon

lunatic   (*say* <u>looh</u>-nuh-tik)

noun someone who is mad

Word building: **lunatic** *adjective*: *a lunatic idea* Word history: at one time it was thought that people were sent mad by the full moon, which is called *luna* in Latin

lunch

noun a light midday meal

Word building: The plural is **lunches**. | **lunch** *verb*

luncheon   (*say* <u>lunch</u>-uhn)

noun a formal word for **lunch**

lung

noun one of two parts in your body that you use for breathing

lunge

verb to make a sudden forward movement or attack: *I lunged at him with a stick.*

Word building: **lunge** *noun*

lurch¹

noun a sudden or unsteady movement, especially to one side

Word building: The plural is **lurches**. | **lurch** *verb* to stagger or make a lurch

lurch²

noun a helpless situation: *They were left in the lurch.*

lure

noun **1** something that attracts: *The shop offered free child-minding as a lure to customers.* **2** a device used to attract fish

Word building: **lure** *verb*

lurid   (*say* <u>looh</u>-ruhd)

adjective **1** shining with an unnatural glare: *the lurid city lights* **2** horrifying or frightening: *lurid tales | lurid crimes*

lurk

verb **1** to stay or move about secretly: *to lurk in the darkness* *noun* **2** an easy and often sly way of doing a job or earning a living

luscious   (*say* <u>lush</u>-uhs)

adjective tasting very pleasant: *a luscious pie*

Word building: **lusciously** *adverb* **lusciousness** *noun*

lush

adjective with strong-growing plants and trees: *the lush undergrowth of the forest*

Word building: **lushly** *adverb* **lushness** *noun*

lust

noun **1** strong desire: *to have a lust for power* **2** uncontrolled sexual desire

Word building: **lust** *verb* **lustful** *adjective* **lustfully** *adverb*

lustre (*rhymes with* duster)
noun **1** shining brightness: *the lustre of a new silver coin* **2** brightness or glory: *Your good results have added lustre to your name.*
Word building: **lustrous** *adjective*   **lustrously** *adverb*

lute (*rhymes with* boot)
noun an old-fashioned musical instrument with strings like a guitar
Word building: **lutenist** *noun*

luxuriant (*say* lug-<u>zhooh</u>-ree-uhnt)
adjective strong in growth: *luxuriant vines*
Word building: **luxuriance** *noun*   **luxuriantly** *adverb*

luxury (*say* <u>luk</u>-shuh-ree)
noun **1** anything that makes life extremely pleasant or comfortable **2** enjoyment of costly food, clothing and living generally: *He lives a life of luxury.*
Word building: The plural is **luxuries.** | **luxuriate** *verb* to enjoy as a luxury   **luxurious** *adjective*: *a luxurious home*   **luxuriously** *adverb*

lychee (*say* <u>luy</u>-chee)
noun a small Chinese fruit with a thin shell covering a sweet jelly-like pulp
Word history: from a Chinese word

lynch (*rhymes with* finch)
verb to put to death, usually by hanging, without a trial: *The mob lynched the murderer before the police arrived.*

Word building: **lynching** *noun*
Word history: named after Captain William *Lynch*, 1742–1820, of the US, who was the first to do this

lynx (*sounds like* links)
noun a type of wildcat with long limbs and a short tail
Word building: The plural is **lynxes** or **lynx**.

lyre (*sounds like* liar)
noun a stringed musical instrument of ancient Greece

lyre/liar Don't confuse **lyre** with **liar**, someone who tells lies.

lyrebird
noun a type of Australian bird which can mimic other sounds and is known for the long beautiful tail feathers which the males display when courting the females

lyric (*say* <u>li</u>-rik)
adjective **1** having the form and musical quality of a song: *lyric poetry*
noun **2** a lyric poem **3** the words of a song
Word use: You can also use **lyrical** for definition 1. | Definition 3 is often used in the plural.
Word building: **lyricist** (*say* <u>li</u>-ruh-suhst) *noun* someone who writes lyrics   **lyrically** *adverb*   **lyricism** *noun*

macabre (*say* muh-<u>kahb</u>, muh-<u>kah</u>-buh, muh-<u>kah</u>-bruh)
adjective horrible in a gruesome way: *macabre crimes*

macadamia
noun a nut with a hard shell, which you can eat and which grows on a native Australian tree

macaroni
noun thick short tubes of pasta which are boiled and served in a sauce

Word history: from an Italian word; and before this from a Greek word meaning 'food of broth and pearl barley'

macaw (*say* muh-<u>kaw</u>)
noun a colourful, tropical American parrot with a long tail and a harsh voice

machete (*say* muh-<u>shet</u>-ee)
noun a large knife with a broad blade used for slashing thick plants

machine (*say* muh-<u>sheen</u>)
noun a device which is made up of parts that work together and which is used to perform a task: *a washing machine*

Word building: **machine** *verb* to make or do by machine: *Could you machine this hem for me?* **machinist** *noun* someone who works a machine

machine gun
noun a gun which can fire a rapid stream of bullets

machinery
noun **1** machines in general: *Farm machinery such as the plough has made work on the land easier.* **2** the parts of a machine: *the machinery of a clock*

macho (*say* <u>mach</u>-oh)
adjective strongly masculine

mackerel
noun a shiny greenish fish which is used for food

macramé (*say* muh-<u>krah</u>-mee)
noun the craft of making things by knotting thread or cord in patterns

macro-
prefix a word part meaning 'large' or 'great'

Word use: Compare this with **micro-**.
Word history: from Greek

mad
adjective **1** insane or mentally unbalanced: *Do you think he is mad?*
Other words: **crazy, demented, deranged**
2 *Informal* angry: *I am mad because you teased me.*
Other words: **annoyed, cross, furious**
3 wild or excited: *I have a mad urge to travel.*
Other words: **crazy, impulsive**

Word building: **madden** *verb* to make mad or angry **madly** *adverb* **madness** *noun*

madam
noun a respectful or formal word used when speaking to a woman: *May I help you, madam?*

Word use: When you begin a letter 'Dear Madam', you usually use a capital letter.
Word building: The plural is **madams** or **mesdames**.
Word history: it comes from the French words *ma dame* which mean 'my lady'

magazine

noun **1** a paper or journal containing stories, articles and advertisements, usually issued once a week or once a month
Other words: **bulletin, periodical, review**
2 a place where explosives are kept
Other words: **arsenal**

maggot

noun the small white grub which turns into a fly or other insect

Word building: **maggoty** *adjective* full of maggots

magic

noun **1** power which is supernatural or which can't be explained normally
Other words: **sorcery, witchcraft, wizardry**
2 a performance in which seemingly impossible tricks are done for entertainment

Word building: **magic** *adjective*   **magical** *adjective*   **magically** *adverb*

magic bullet

noun a single, remarkably effective remedy for a problem: *There is no magic bullet for pollution.*

magician   (*say* muh-jish-uhn)

noun someone who practises magic or magic tricks

magistrate

noun someone who acts as a judge in some less important court cases: *She had to appear before a magistrate for not paying her fines.*

magma

noun the very hot molten or liquid rock under the solid crust of the earth's surface

magnanimous   (*say* mag-nan-uh-muhs)

adjective nobly unselfish and generous: *He is too magnanimous to hold a grudge.*

Word building: **magnanimity** (*say* mag-nuh-nim-uh-tee) *noun*   **magnanimously** *adverb*

magnate   (*say* mag-nayt)

noun someone who is very powerful and successful, especially in business

magnesium

noun a light silver-white metal

magnet

noun **1** a piece of iron or steel which draws iron objects to it **2** anything that attracts something else

Word building: **magnetic** *adjective*   **magnetically** *adverb*   **magnetism** *noun*

magnetic tape

noun tape which is used to record sound for a tape recorder, pictures for a video cassette, or data for a computer

magnificent

adjective **1** grand in appearance: *magnificent robes* **2** excellent: *a magnificent dinner*

Word building: **magnificence** *noun*   **magnificently** *adverb*

magnify

verb to make larger or greater: *This lens magnifies very strongly.* / *This will magnify the trouble that you're in.*
Other words: **enlarge**

Word building: Other forms are **it magnified, it has magnified, it is magnifying.** / **magnifier** *noun* someone or something that magnifies   **magnification** *noun*

magnitude

noun **1** size: *They measured the magnitude of the angles.* **2** greatness or importance: *She finally realised the magnitude of her loss.*

magnolia

noun a type of tree or shrub with fragrant white, dark pink or red flowers

Word history: named after a French botanist, P *Magnol* (1638–1715)

magpie

noun a black and white bird with a large beak, which is found throughout Australia and New Guinea

mahjong   (*say* mah-zhong)

noun a game played with many tiles, counters and dice, usually for four players, and originally played in China

mahogany   (*say* muh-hog-uh-nee)

noun a hard reddish-brown wood, used for making furniture

maid

noun **1** *Old-fashioned* an unmarried woman **2** a female servant

maid/made Don't confuse **maid** with **made**, which is the past tense and past participle of **make**.

maiden

noun **1** *Old-fashioned* a young unmarried woman
adjective **2** unmarried: *my maiden aunt*
3 done or used for the first time: *a maiden voyage*

maiden name

noun a woman's surname before she is married

mail[1]

noun **1** letters and packages sent by post
2 a train or boat which carries mail, often at night: *the North Coast Mail*
Word building: **mail** *verb*   **mail** *adjective*

mail/male Don't confuse **mail** with **male**, which is an animal of the masculine gender. A man is a **male**, and so is a boy.

mail[2]

noun armour made of linked metal rings, which was worn in medieval times

maim

verb to damage or cripple
Word building: **maimed** *adjective*

main

adjective **1** most important or biggest: *the main course | the main reason*
noun **2** the largest pipe in a gas or water system
Word building: **mainly** *adverb*

main/mane Don't confuse **main** with **mane**, which is long hair growing on the neck of an animal like a horse or a lion.

mainland

noun a large landmass, as distinct from the islands around it: *Tasmanians sometimes go to the mainland for a holiday.*

mainstream

noun the chief trend or tendency in an area: *in the mainstream of rock music*
Word building: **mainstream** *adjective*: *mainstream ideas*

maintain

verb **1** to keep up or keep in good condition: *to maintain a correspondence | to maintain the roads* **2** to hold onto: *to maintain a lead*
Word building: **maintenance** *noun*

maize

noun a tall cereal plant with heads of yellow grain
Word history: from a West Indian language called Taino

majesty

noun **1** the title given to a king or queen: *Your Majesty* **2** greatness or dignity: *The majesty of the view left them speechless.*
Word building: The plural is **majesties**. | **majestic** *adjective* dignified or grand **majestically** *adverb*

major

noun **1** an officer in the army
adjective **2** greater in size or importance: *My major work was on the language of teenagers.*

majority   (*say* muh-jo-ruh-tee)

noun **1** the greater number or more than half: *The majority of people stayed at home.*
Other words: **most, bulk**
2 the age at which the law says you are an adult and can vote in elections
Word use: The opposite of this is **minority**.
Word building: The plural is **majorities**.

major scale

noun any musical scale which has semitones between the third and fourth notes and between the seventh and eighth notes
Word use: Such a scale is said to be in a **major** key. | Compare this with **minor scale**.

make

verb **1** to bring into being or create: *He makes his own clothes. | Who makes the laws?* **2** to produce an effect: *The rain makes the road slippery.* **3** to prepare for use: *to make a bed* **4** to win or get: *to make a friend* **5** to be or become: *The box will make a useful container.* **6** to add up to: *I know that 3 and 3 make 6.* **7** to reach or attain: *They made the shore at last. | She will make the finals.*
phrase **8 make for**, to try to reach: *Let's make for home.* **9 make up**, **a** to form or complete: *Six games make up a set.* **b** to invent: *He makes up stories.* **c** to become friendly again after a quarrel **d** to apply cosmetics to: *The actor made up his face.*
Word building: Other verb forms are **I made, I have made, I am making**. | **make** *noun* a type or brand

makeshift

noun something used in place of something else: *He broke the hammer and had to use a brick as a makeshift.*

Word building: **makeshift** *adjective*

make-up

noun **1** any cosmetic substance you put on your face to try to make it attractive-looking. Lipstick and mascara are two types of make-up: *Gina wore lots of make-up to her formal.* **2** all the things that go together to make something whole: *the make-up of the company | the make-up of a personality*

mal-

prefix a word part meaning 'bad': *maltreat | malnutrition*

Word history: from Latin

malady   (*say* mal-uh-dee)

noun an illness or disease

malapropism   (*say* mal-uh-prop-iz-uhm)

noun a word used by mistake for a similar-sounding word, so that the effect is funny: *It is a malapropism to say 'Beethoven wrote nine sympathies' since the right word is 'symphonies'.*

Word history: named after Mrs *Malaprop*, a character in a play, who misuses words in this way

malaria

noun an illness which gives you fever, chills and sweating, and which is spread by mosquitoes

male

noun **1** a man or boy **2** any animal that belongs to the sex which fertilises the female egg

Word use: The opposite is **female**.
Word building: **male** *adjective*

male/mail Don't confuse **male** with **mail**, which is all the letters and parcels that are sent by post.

malevolent   (*say* muh-lev-uh-luhnt)

adjective full of ill will: *a malevolent sneer*

Word building: **malevolence** *noun*
malevolently *adverb*

malice

noun the desire to harm or hurt someone: *Did you break my pen out of malice?*

Word building: **malicious** *adjective*
maliciously *adverb*

malignant

adjective **1** dangerous or deadly: *a malignant cancer* **2** nasty or evil: *a malignant look*

Word building: **malign** *verb* to speak ill of
malignancy *noun*   **malignantly** *adverb*

mall   (*say* mawl, mal)

noun an area without traffic where people can stroll and shop
Other words: **arcade, plaza**

mall/maul Don't confuse **mall** with **maul**. To **maul** something or someone is to attack them savagely.
The lion mauls a carcass.

malleable   (*say* mal-ee-uh-buhl)

adjective easily worked into a different shape: *Some metals are more malleable than others.*

Word building: **malleability** *noun*

mallee

noun a wiry Australian gum tree which has several thin trunks which grow from a large underground root

Word building: **the mallee** *noun* country where these trees grow
Word history: probably from an Aboriginal language of Victoria called Wembawemba. See the map of Australian Aboriginal languages at the end of this book.

mallet

noun **1** a hammer made of wood **2** the wooden stick used to hit the ball in croquet or polo

malnutrition

noun illness caused by not having enough food

malt

noun grain which is used in making beer and whisky

maltreat

verb to treat roughly or cruelly

Word use: The more usual word is **abuse**.
Word building: **maltreatment** *noun*

mammal

noun an animal whose young feeds on its mother's milk

Word building: **mammalian**
(*say* muh-<u>may</u>-lee-uhn) *adjective*
Word history: from a Latin word meaning 'of the breast'

mammoth

noun **1** a type of large hairy elephant with long curved tusks, that died out a long time ago
adjective **2** huge: *a mammoth sale*

man

noun **1** a grown-up male human being **2** a piece in a game such as chess or draughts

Word building: The plural is **men**. | **man** *verb* (**manned, manning**) to provide with workers   **manly** *adjective* (**manlier, manliest**): *Bravery is seen as a manly quality.*   **manhood** *noun*

manage

verb **1** to be able to: *Can you manage to carry them all by yourself?* **2** to take charge of or control: *The young student teacher cannot manage the class very well.*

Word building: **manageable** *adjective* **manager** *noun*

management

noun **1** the running of something: *He leaves the management of the business to her.* **2** the people who run something, such as a business or hotel

manager

noun **1** someone who runs a business **2** someone who looks after the business interests of an entertainer or a sporting team

Word building: **manageress** *noun*   **managerial** *adjective*

mandarin

noun a small, soft-skinned, orange-coloured citrus fruit

Word use: Another spelling is **mandarine**.

mandatory

adjective necessary, compulsory: *Voting is mandatory for all adults in Australia.*
Other words: **obligatory**

mandolin

noun a musical instrument with a pear-shaped wooden body and metal strings which you pluck

mane

noun the long hair on a male lion's head or along the neck of a horse

mane/main Don't confuse **mane** with **main**, which means 'the most important or biggest'.

mange   (*say* maynj)

noun a skin disease, mainly of animals, in which the skin becomes rough and red and loses its hair

Word building: **mangy** *adjective* (**mangier, mangiest**)

manger   (*say* <u>mayn</u>-juh)

noun a box from which cattle or horses eat

mangle

verb to crush, cut or ruin

mango

noun a sweet yellow tropical fruit

Word building: The plural is **mangoes** or **mangos**.

mangrove

noun a tree which grows thickly along the water's edge sending up roots through the mud or sand

manhole

noun a covered hole, as in a footpath or ceiling, that you can climb through to get at pipes and wires

mania

noun **1** great enthusiasm or excitement: *He has a mania for collecting matchboxes.* **2** a violent or excitable form of insanity

Word building: **manic** *adjective*

maniac

noun someone who is mad, or who acts wildly or dangerously

Word building: **maniacal** (*say* muh-<u>nuy</u>-uh-kuhl) *adjective*

manicure

noun treatment of your hands and fingernails

Word building: **manicurist** *noun* someone who does manicures

manifesto

noun a public statement by a government or group, setting out its ideas or goals: *the Communist manifesto*

Word building: The plural is **manifestos** or **manifestoes**.

manipulate (*say* muh-<u>nip</u>-yuh-layt)
verb **1** to use, especially with skill: *to manipulate the puppets with strings* **2** to influence cleverly and unfairly: *She manipulates people.* **3** to use the hands to treat as a chiropractor does: *to manipulate the spine*
Word building: **manipulation** *noun* **manipulative** *adjective* **manipulator** *noun*

mankind
noun **1** men, as distinguished from women; the male sex **2** humankind

mannequin
(*say* <u>man</u>-uh-kuhn, <u>man</u>-uh-kwuhn)
noun **1** someone who wears new clothes to show them to customers **2** a human-sized figure used by dressmakers and window dressers to fit or model clothes
Word history: from a Dutch word meaning 'little man'

manner
noun **1** a way of being or doing: *a pleasant manner* **2 manners**, behaviour or way of behaving: *good manners | bad manners*

manner/manor Don't confuse **manner** with **manor**.
A **manor** is a mansion surrounded by a large estate.

mannerism
noun a habit of doing something a little strange: *He has a funny little mannerism — he pulls his ear every time he starts to speak.*

manoeuvre (*say* muh-<u>nooh</u>-vuh)
noun **1** a clever move: *She won the game by an unbeatable manoeuvre.* **2 manoeuvres**, military exercises: *The soldiers are out on manoeuvres.*
Word building: **manoeuvre** *verb* **manoeuvrability** *noun* **manoeuvrable** *adjective*

manor
noun a large British country house with its land, originally the home of a lord

manor/manner Don't confuse **manor** with **manner**.
Your **manner** is your way of being or doing things:
    The new boy has a pleasant manner.

manse
noun the house that a member of the clergy lives in

mansion
noun a large or grand house

manslaughter (*say* <u>man</u>-slaw-tuh)
noun the accidental killing of someone

mantelpiece
noun the shelf above a fireplace

mantis
noun a long, stick-like, brown or green insect which holds its front legs doubled up as if in prayer
Word use: Another name for this is **praying mantis**.
Word building: The plural is **mantises** or **mantes**.

mantle
noun a loose cloak or cover
Word building: **mantle** *verb* to cover

manual
adjective **1** done by hand: *manual work* *noun* **2** a book which tells you how to do or use something **3** a car which has gears that you change by hand
Word building: **manually** *adverb*

manufacture
verb to make or produce by hand or machine, especially in large numbers
Word building: **manufacture** *noun* **manufacturer** *noun* **manufacturing** *noun*

manure
noun animal waste, especially when used as fertiliser

manuscript
noun a book, letter or piece of music, written by hand
Word building: **manuscript** *adjective*

many
adjective **1** a large number of things or of people: *There are many different species of birds where I live | There were many people at the beach on Sunday.* **2** relatively large in number: *Many of his CDs are scratched. | I think I ate too many pancakes.*
Word building: Other forms are **more**, **most**.

Maori (*say* <u>mow</u>-ree, <u>mah</u>-uh-ree)
noun **1** the indigenous people of New Zealand **2** a member of this people **3** the language of this people

Word history: from a Maori word meaning 'of the usual kind'

map

noun a drawing or diagram of an area showing where certain things are, such as towns, roads, mountains and borders
Other words: **chart**

Word building: **map** *verb* (**mapped, mapping**)

maple

noun a tree that grows in cold countries, used for its wood and its sap which produces a sweet syrup

mar

verb to spoil: *Too much cake could mar your performance in the swimming race.*

Word building: Other forms are **I marred, I have marred, I am marring.**

marathon

noun a long-distance foot race, officially of 42 195 metres

Word history: named after the Greek plain of *Marathon* from which a runner took news of a Greek victory in 490 BC to Athens, 42 kilometres away

marauding

adjective going from place to place to raid, steal and attack people: *Marauding pirates used to rule the seas.*

marble

noun **1** a hard mottled limestone of various colours, used in building and sculpture
2 a small glass ball used in a game

Word building: **marble** *verb* to mottle   **marble** *adjective*

march

verb **1** to walk like a soldier, with even steps and swinging arms
Other words: **parade, stride**
2 to make someone march: *She marched them out to the playground.*
noun **3** the act of marching, as when soldiers walk from one place to another
Other words: **parade**
4 an event when a lot of people walk together to protest about something or ask for something: *a peace march*
Other words: **demonstration, protest**
5 the distance covered by a march: *The town is three days' march away.* **6** a lively rhythmical piece of music suited to marching

Word building: **marcher** *noun*

March

noun the third month of the year, with 31 days

Word use: The abbreviation is **Mar.**
Word history: from a Latin word meaning 'the month of Mars', after the planet *Mars*

mare   (*rhymes with* hair)

noun a fully-grown female horse

Word use: Another word is **dam.** | The male is a **stallion** and the young is a **foal.**

mare/mayor Don't confuse **mare** with **mayor**, which is the chief official of a local government.

margarine

noun a butter-like spread made from vegetable oil

margin

noun **1** an edge or border, such as the blank space beside the writing on a page
phrase **2 margin of error**, an extra amount allowed in calculations, such as of time or money, to cover mistakes

Word building: **marginal** *adjective*   **marginally** *adverb*

marijuana   (*say* ma-ruh-<u>wah</u>-nuh)

noun the dried leaves and flowers of the Indian hemp plant which contain a drug

marinate

verb to add flavour to a food by soaking it in an oily spicy liquid before cooking

Word building: **marinade** *noun* the liquid used for marinating

marine

adjective **1** having to do with the sea: *marine creatures*
noun **2** a soldier who serves on ship and on land

Word building: **mariner** *noun* a seaman

marionette

noun a puppet which is worked by strings attached to its limbs

maritime

adjective having to do with the sea or shipping: *maritime law*

mark

noun **1** something like a spot, line, scratch or stain on anything
Other words: **blemish, smudge, spot**
2 a sign or label which tells something about an object, such as who made it or who owns it
Other words: **brand**
3 a symbol, such as a letter of the alphabet, used to judge behaviour or work: *a good mark for an essay*
Other words: **assessment, score**
4 a target: *Did your dart hit the mark?*
Other words: **goal, object**
verb **5** to make marks on
Other words: **blemish, scratch, smudge, stain**
6 to be a special feature of: *It was a day marked by happy surprises.* **7** to be a sign of: *A sudden drop in temperature marked the end of summer.*
Other words: **denote, indicate, signify**
8 to judge, by a number or other sign, the value of work: *The teacher marked our work and handed it back to us.*
Other words: **assess, evaluate, grade**
Word building: **marked** *adjective* noticeable **markedly** *adverb* **marker** *noun*

market

noun **1** a place where things are bought and sold, often at many different stalls **2** the demand for goods: *There is no market for typewriters any longer.*
Word building: **market** *verb* to sell **marketable** *adjective* easy to sell

marketing

noun the organised selling of a product or service, including advertising

marlin

noun a large powerful fish with an upper jaw like a spear

marmalade

noun a jam made of citrus fruits, such as oranges and grapefruit
Word history: from a Greek word meaning 'honey apple'

maroon¹   (*say* muh-<u>rohn</u>)

noun a dark brownish-red
Word building: **maroon** *adjective*

maroon²   (*say* muh-<u>roohn</u>)

verb **1** to force (someone) to leave a ship, leaving them in a deserted place **2** to leave behind without a way out
Word building: **marooned** *adjective*

marquee   (*say* mah-<u>kee</u>)

noun a big tent used for outdoor parties, circuses and so on

marriage celebrant

noun someone who is authorised by the government to marry people

marrow

noun **1** the soft tissue inside bones which is important in producing red blood cells
2 a large white, yellow or green vegetable

marry

verb **1** to join together as husband and wife
Other words: **wed**
2 to take as a husband or wife: *My sister is marrying my best friend's brother.*
Word building: Other forms are **I married, I have married, I am marrying.** | **marriage** *noun* **marriageable** *adjective*

marsh

noun low-lying wet land
Other words: **bog, swamp**
Word building: **marshy** *adjective*

marshal

noun someone who organises the activities at a show or other public occasion
Word building: **marshal** *verb* (**marshalled, marshalling**) to organise in rows or ranks

marshal/martial Don't confuse **marshal** with **martial**, which means 'to do with fighting or war', as in *martial arts*.

marshmallow

noun a soft sweet made from gelatine, sugar and flavouring

marsupial   (*say* mah-<u>syooh</u>-pee-uhl)

noun a mammal such as a kangaroo which keeps and feeds its young in a pouch for a few months after birth
Word building: **marsupial** *adjective*: *a marsupial mouse*
Word history: from a Latin word meaning 'pouch'

martial   (*say* <u>mah</u>-shuhl)

adjective having to do with war or fighting

martial arts

plural noun sports such as judo and kung-fu, which are based on self-defence without the use of weapons

martyr (*say* <u>mah</u>-tuh)
noun **1** someone who is killed or suffers a great deal for the sake of their beliefs **2** someone who goes without, just so that they can feel better than other people
Word building: **martyr** *verb*　**martyrdom** *noun*

marvel
noun something which causes delight and wonder
Word building: **marvel** *verb* (**marvelled, marvelling**): *I marvel at your skill.*　**marvellous** *adjective* wonderful　**marvellously** *adverb*

marzipan
noun a sweet made of crushed almonds and sugar

mascara
noun a substance used to colour the eyelashes
Word history: from a Spanish word meaning 'a mask'

mascot
noun something which is supposed to bring good luck

masculine (*say* <u>mas</u>-kyuh-luhn)
adjective having qualities thought to be typical of a male
Word use: The opposite is **feminine**.
Word building: **masculinity** *noun*

mash
verb to pound down or crush

mask
noun **1** a covering for your face, worn as a disguise or for protection
verb **2** to hide or disguise
Other words: **cloak, conceal, cover, veil**

mason
noun someone who builds or works with stone
Word building: **masonry** *noun*

masquerade (*say* mas-kuh-<u>rayd</u>)
noun **1** a party at which the guests wear masks and fancy dress **2** a false outward show
Word building: **masquerade** *verb*

mass[1]
noun **1** a quantity of matter of no particular shape or size: *a mass of snow | a cloud mass* **2** a large number or quantity: *a mass of papers | a mass of water* **3** the amount of matter in a body
phrase **4 the masses**, the common people
Word use: The plural is **masses**.

mass[2]
noun a religious service in the Roman Catholic and some other Christian churches
Word use: Another spelling is **Mass**.
Word building: The plural is **masses**.

massacre (*say* <u>mas</u>-uh-kuh)
noun the killing of a large number of people: *Hitler's massacre of the Jews*
Other words: **carnage, slaughter**
Word building: **massacre** *verb*

massage (*say* <u>mas</u>-ahzh)
noun the act of rubbing and pressing the body, to relax or ease pain
Word building: **masseur** *noun* a man skilled in massage　**masseuse** *noun* a woman skilled in massage　**massage** *verb*

massive
adjective large and heavy: *a massive load*
Word building: **massively** *adverb*

mass media
plural noun radio, television, newspapers and magazines, by which information is passed on to large numbers of people

mass-produce
verb to make in large quantities with machines in factories
Word building: **mass-production** *noun*

mast
noun **1** a tall pole rising from the deck of a ship **2** any upright pole: *a radio-transmitting mast*

master
noun **1** someone who has control or special skill: *He is a master of several languages.* **2** the owner of a dog or other animal **3** a male teacher, especially one who is head of a department
verb **4** to get control of: *He struggled to master his feelings.*
Word building: **master** *adjective* main: *a master plan*　**masterly** *adjective* showing great skill　**mastery** *noun*

masterpiece

noun the most excellent piece of work of an artist, musician or writer

masturbate

verb to rub the genitals to produce a pleasant sensation

Word building: **masturbation** *noun*

mat

noun **1** a piece of material of some kind used to cover the floor or part of it: *a bath mat / a rubber mat*
Other words: **carpet, rug**
2 a small piece of cork or fabric for putting under a plate or ornament
verb **3** to make or become a thick and tangled mass
Other words: **knot, tangle**

Word building: Other verb forms are **it matted, it has matted, it is matting.** | **matting** *noun*

matador

noun the bullfighter who kills the bull

Word use: Compare this with **picador.**
Word history: from a Latin word meaning 'slayer'

match¹

noun a short thin piece of wood tipped with a chemical substance which produces fire when you scrape it on a rough surface

Word building: The plural is **matches.**

match²

noun **1** someone or something that equals or looks like another in some way
2 a contest or game: *a football match*
Other words: **bout, competition, event, fixture**
verb **3** to agree exactly: *These colours don't match.* **4** to place in opposition: *They are matched in the semi-final.*

Word building: The plural form of the noun is **matches.** | **matchless** *adjective* without an equal   **matchlessly** *adverb*

mate

noun **1** a friend: *Thanh is a real mate.* **2** the male or the female of a pair of animals: *the fox and its mate*

material

noun **1** the substance which is used to make something: *building materials* **2** cloth: *curtain material*
Other words: **fabric, textile**
adjective **3** existing in a form you can touch

Other words: **concrete, physical, solid, tangible**

materialise

verb to appear in a physical shape: *Her figure materialised out of the mist.*

Word use: Another spelling is **materialize.**

maternal

adjective belonging to or like a mother: *maternal feelings*

Word building: **maternity** *noun*
motherhood   **maternally** *adverb*

mathematics

noun the science dealing with numbers and the size of things: *Mathematics is fun.*

Word building: **mathematical** *adjective*
mathematically *adverb*   **mathematician** *noun*

maths

noun a shortened form of **mathematics**

matilda

noun a swag

Word use: This is used only in the expression 'waltzing Matilda', meaning 'going about as a swagman'.

matinee   (*say* <u>mat</u>-uh-nay)

noun an afternoon performance of a play or showing of a film

Word history: from a French word meaning 'morning'

matri-

prefix a word part meaning 'mother': *matriarch*

Word history: from Latin

matriarch   (*say* <u>may</u>-tree-ahk)

noun a woman leader in a family, tribe or any field of activity

Word building: **matriarchal**
adjective   **matriarchy** *noun*

matriculation

(*say* muh-trik-yuh-<u>lay</u>-shuhn)
noun (in some countries) an examination which must be passed before you can enrol at a university

Word building: **matriculate** *verb*

matrimony   (*say* <u>mat</u>-ruh-muh-nee)

noun marriage

Word building: **matrimonial** *adjective*

matron

noun **1** a middle-aged married woman
2 the most important nurse in a
hospital **3** a woman in charge of household
arrangements in a school or other
institution

Word use: Definition 1 may offend some
women.
Word building: **matronly** *adjective*

matt

adjective having a dull surface: *matt paint*

Word use: Another spelling is **mat**.
Word history: from a French word meaning
'dead'

matter

noun **1** the substance of which things are
made **2** a particular kind of substance:
colouring matter **3** an affair or subject:
*a matter of fact | a matter of life and
death* **4** trouble or difficulty: *What is the
matter?*
verb **5** to be of importance

matter-of-fact

adjective ordinary, not excited or
imaginative: *a matter-of-fact voice*

mattock

noun a tool for loosening the soil, like a
pick but with a blade instead of a point

mattress

noun a soft and springy covering for the
base of a bed

mature

adjective **1** fully grown or developed: *a
mature tree | a mature adult* **2** ripe: *mature
fruit* **3** having the understanding and
attitudes which an adult should have

Word building: **maturation** *noun* **maturely**
adverb **maturity** *noun*

matzo *(say* mat-soh*)*

noun a biscuit made of bread without
yeast, eaten by Jewish people during the
Feast of the Passover

Word use: Another name for bread made
without yeast is **unleavened bread**.
Word building: The plural is **matzos**.

maul

verb to handle roughly

maul/mall Don't confuse **maul** with **mall**,
which is an area without traffic where people
can stroll and shop.

mauve *(say* mohv*)*

adjective light purple

maxim

noun a saying containing a general truth or
rule: *'Look before you leap' is a wise maxim.*

maximum

noun the greatest number or amount
possible: *The hall holds a maximum of
500 people. | The bottle is filled to the
maximum.*

Word use: The opposite is **minimum**.
Word building: The plural is **maximums** or
maxima. | **maximise** *verb* **maximum** *adjective*

may

verb **1** to be allowed to: *You may go now.*
2 could possibly: *They may arrive this
afternoon.*

Word use: This verb is a helping verb, always
used with another one in the form **I may** or
I might.

May

noun the fifth month of the year, with
31 days

maybe

adverb possibly: *The dog's not outside —
maybe Mum took him for a walk.*

mayhem

noun disorder or confusion

Word history: from a French word meaning
'injury'

mayonnaise *(say* may-uh-nayz*)*

noun a thick cold sauce made from eggs
and oil and eaten with salad

mayor *(say* mair*)*

noun the head of a city or suburban
council

Word building: **mayoress** *noun* the wife of a
mayor

mayor/mare Don't confuse **mayor** with **mare**,
which is a female horse.

maze

noun a confusing and complicated
arrangement of many crossing paths or
lines that you have to find a way through

me

pronoun the form of the pronoun **I** you use
after a verb: *Give me the book, please.*

meadow

noun a paddock

Word use: This word is used mostly in England.

meagre   (*say* mee-guh)

adjective small or of poor quality: *a meagre meal*

meal[1]

noun food served at more or less fixed times each day: *Breakfast is my favourite meal.*

meal[2]

noun grain which has been ground or crushed

Word building: **mealy** *adjective* soft, dry and crumbly

mean[1]

verb **1** to intend or have the purpose: *I mean to talk to him.*
Other words: **aim, plan, want**
2 to signify or indicate: *'Vermicelli' means 'little worms'. | The naughty student's arrival means trouble.*
Other words: **denote, represent**

Word building: Other forms are **I meant, I have meant, I am meaning.**

mean[2]

adjective **1** stingy or not willing to give anything away
Other words: **miserly, selfish, ungenerous**
2 nasty: *mean motives*
Other words: **cruel, malicious, spiteful, unkind**

mean[3]

noun **1** something halfway between two end points **2** an average

Word building: **mean** *adjective*

meander   (*say* mee-an-duh)

verb to wind or wander about: *The river meandered through the valley.*

meaning

noun what is indicated or referred to by something: *Do you know the meaning of this word? | Dad explained the meaning of the story.*

Word building: **meaningful** *adjective* **meaningless** *adjective*

means

plural noun **1** a method or way used to reach an end: *a means of transport* **2** a supply of money: *Our means are not enough for our needs.*

Word use: Although this is a plural noun definition 1 is usually followed by a singular verb.

meanwhile

adverb at the same time as something just mentioned: *We packed our camping gear into the car. Meanwhile, storm clouds began to gather in the sky.*

measles

noun a type of infectious disease with fever and a rash

Word history: from a German word meaning 'a spot'

measure

noun **1** the size or quantity of something **2** an agreed unit or standard: *A metre is a measure of length.* **3** a means to an end: *to take measures to prevent illness*
verb **4** to decide the size or quantity of, usually by using a special instrument such as a ruler or scales
Other words: **calculate, determine, evaluate**

Word building: **measurement** *noun*

meat

noun the soft flesh of animals that is used for food

meat/meet Don't confuse **meat** with **meet**. To **meet** someone is to come across them, either by accident or by arrangement.

mechanic

noun some who fixes machinery, especially cars and engines

mechanical

adjective **1** having to do with or worked by machinery or tools **2** like a machine: *to answer in a mechanical way*

Word building: **mechanically** *adverb*

mechanise

verb to change over to the use of machines in: *to mechanise the furniture industry*

Word use: Another spelling is **mechanize**.
Word building: **mechanisation** *noun*

mechanism   (*say* mek-uhn-iz-uhm)

noun a piece of machinery

medal

noun a metal disc or cross given as a reward for bravery or as a prize

Word building: **medallist** *noun* someone who receives a medal, especially for sport

medal/meddle Don't confuse **medal** with **meddle**, which is to interfere with something that doesn't concern you.

medallion
noun a large medal, especially one given as a prize, or something shaped like one, used as part of a design such as on a building

meddle
noun to interfere with something that doesn't concern you
Other words: **intrude, pry**

Word building: **meddlesome** *adjective* tending to meddle   **meddler** *noun*

media
plural noun the means of communication, including radio, television, newspapers and magazines: *The media have been full of the news of the floods.*

Word use: This word is the plural of **medium** but is often used as if it were singular.

mediaeval
adjective another way of spelling **medieval**

median
adjective coming in the middle: *a median strip on a six lane highway*

mediate
verb to come between people or groups who are arguing to try to get them to agree: *to mediate in a dispute*

Word building: **mediator** *noun* someone who mediates   **mediation** *noun*

medical
adjective having to do with medicine or its practice: *a medical examination | a medical book*

Word building: **medically** *adverb*

medication
noun another word for **medicine** (def. 1)
Word building: **medicate** *verb*

medicine
noun **1** a substance used in treating disease: *cough medicine* **2** the art or science of treating disease: *skilled in medicine*
Other words: **healing**

Word use: Another word for definition 1 is **medication**.
Word building: **medicinal** (*say* muh-dis-uh-nuhl) *adjective*

medicine man
noun a man who has power over a tribe because they think he can do magic

medieval   (*say* med-ee-eev-uhl)
adjective belonging to or having to do with the Middle Ages, that is, from about the fifth to the fifteenth century

Word use: Another spelling is **mediaeval**.

mediocre   (*say* mee-dee-oh-kuh)
adjective neither good nor bad: *mediocre abilities*

Word building: **mediocrity** (*say* mee-dee-ok-ruh-tee) *noun*

meditate
verb to think long and deeply: *to meditate on a problem*

Word building: **meditation** *noun*   **meditative** *adjective*   **meditatively** *adverb*

medium
noun **1** the way in which something is done or communicated: *a painting medium | an advertising medium | the mass media* **2** someone who claims to be able to communicate with the spirits of dead people

Word building: The plural for definition 1 is **media**. | The plural for definition 2 is **mediums**. | **medium** *adjective* middle or average

medley
noun a mixture: *Kate played a medley of songs on her guitar.*

meek
adjective patient and obeying readily: *She was too meek to object to the unfair arrangements.*

Word building: **meekly** *adverb*   **meekness** *noun*

meet
verb **1** to come face to face with: *I met Laura in the street. | I felt I could meet any objection.* **2** to welcome on arrival: *to meet a friend at the airport* **3** to come together: *The paths met near the river.*

Word building: Other forms are **I met, I have met, I am meeting**.

meet/meat Don't confuse **meet** with **meat**. **Meat** is the flesh of animals.

meeting
noun an arrangement to come together for a purpose: *a meeting of the chess club* | *a business meeting*

mega-
prefix a word part meaning 'great' or 'huge': *megalomania* | *megaphone*
Word history: from Greek

megabyte   (*say* <u>meg</u>-uh-buyt)
noun a unit for measuring the size of computer information equal to 10 000 000 bytes: *The file we downloaded was 3.5 megabytes.*

megafauna   (*say* meg-a-faw-nuh)
noun a group of very large animals: *Australia's megafauna such as giant kangaroos no longer exist.*

megalomania
(*say* meg-uh-luh-<u>may</u>-nee-uh)
noun a mental illness in which the patients falsely believe they are great and powerful
Word building: **megalomaniac** *noun*

megaphone
noun a funnel-shaped device for increasing or directing sound

megawatt
noun a unit of electrical power: *The new wind farm will generate 500 megawatts of power.*

melancholy   (*say* <u>mel</u>-uhn-kol-ee)
noun a feeling of sadness or depression
Word building: **melancholy** *adjective*

melee   (*say* mel-<u>ay</u>)
noun a confused and noisy fight

mellow
adjective **1** soft and rich: *a mellow voice* | *a mellow flavour* **2** softened by time: *a mellow attitude to life*
Word building: **mellow** *verb*   **mellowness** *noun*

melodrama
noun a play that is too dramatic to be real
Word building: **melodramatic** *adjective*
Word history: from a Greek word meaning 'music drama'

melody
noun a tune
Other words: **air**

Word building: **melodic** *adjective*   **melodically** *adverb*   **melodious** *adjective*   **melodiously** *adverb*

melon
noun a large, juicy fruit with a thick skin

melt
verb **1** to make or become liquid by heating: *Melt the fat in the pan.* | *You left the ice-cream out and it began to melt.* **2** to fade gradually: *The mountain ridge melted into the clouds.* **3** to fill with tender feeling: *My heart melted as soon as I saw you.*

member
noun **1** each of the people forming a society, parliament or other group **2** a part of a whole, such as a limb of your body
Word building: **membership** *noun*: *the membership of a club*

membrane
noun a thin sheet or film: *The eardrum is a membrane between the outer and middle ear.*
Word building: **membranous** *adjective*

memento
noun something that acts as a reminder of what is past: *She gave them a book as a memento of her visit.*
Word building: The plural is **mementos** or **mementoes**.

memo
noun a shortened form of **memorandum**
Word building: The plural is **memos**.

memoirs   (*say* <u>mem</u>-wahz)
plural noun a record of the life and times of somebody based on the personal experience of the writer
Other words: **autobiography**

memorable
adjective worth remembering

memorandum
noun a note of something to be remembered
Word building: The plural is **memorandums** or **memoranda**.

memorial
noun something to remind people of a person or event: *a memorial to Burke and Wills*
Other words: **commemoration, monument**

memorise

verb to put into the memory or learn by heart: *I finally memorised the poem.*

Word use: Another spelling is **memorize**.
Word building: **memorisation** *noun*

memory

noun **1** the ability to store things in your mind and recall them when needed **2** something remembered: *a memory of home*
Other words: **recollection, remembrance**
3 part of a computer in which information is stored until needed
phrase **4 in memory of**, to help people remember or remind them of: *a monument in memory of Captain Cook*

memory stick

noun a small, portable information storage device that plugs into a computer: *He lost the memory stick but luckily the information was on the computer too.*

menace

noun **1** something dangerous **2** a threatening attitude: *to speak with menace* **3** *Informal* a nuisance
Word building: **menace** *verb* to threaten

menagerie   (*say* muh-<u>naj</u>-uh-ree)

noun a collection of wild animals in cages for show

mend

verb **1** to make right or put into working order again **2** to get better: *My broken arm is beginning to mend.*

menial

adjective having to do with or fit for servants: *menial work*
Word building: **menial** *noun* a servant

meningitis   (*say* men-uhn-<u>juy</u>-tuhs)

noun a disease that causes swelling in the lining of the brain

menopause

noun the time in a woman's life when her monthly periods stop altogether
Word building: **menopausal** *adjective*

menstrual cycle

noun the cycle in which a womb prepares for pregnancy and which ends in menstruation if there is no pregnancy

menstruate

verb to have a flow of blood and mucus from the womb, usually monthly
Word building: **menstrual** *adjective*
menstruation *noun*

menstruation

noun the process occurring once a month in a woman's body in which blood passes out of her uterus when she has a period

mental

adjective having to do with the mind
Other words: **cerebral, intellectual, psychological**
Word building: **mentally** *adverb*   **mentality** *noun*

mention

verb to briefly speak or write about
Word building: **mention** *noun*

mentor

noun a wise and trusted adviser: *Her father has been her mentor for many years.*
Word history: from *Mentor*, friend of the Greek hero Odysseus and guardian of his household when he went to Troy

menu

noun **1** a list of the dishes served at a meal or in a restaurant **2** a list of options you can choose from when you are using a computer

mercenary   (*say* <u>mers</u>-uhn-ree)

adjective **1** working or caring only for money: *She has a mercenary attitude to her art.*
noun **2** a soldier who is paid to fight in a foreign army
Word building: The plural form of the noun is **mercenaries**.

merchandise   (*say* <u>mer</u>-chuhn-duys)

noun goods for sale
Word building: **merchandise** *verb* to sell   **merchandiser** *noun*

merchant

noun someone who buys and sells goods
Word building: **merchantman** *noun* a trading ship   **merchant** *adjective*

mercury

noun a silvery metallic element which is liquid instead of solid at ordinary temperatures

Word use: An old-fashioned word for this is **quicksilver**.
Word building: **mercurial** *adjective* rapidly changing in mood
Word history: named after the planet *Mercury* because long ago the symbol for the planet was used for the metal as well

mercy

noun kindness shown by not punishing or not being cruel
Other words: **compassion, grace, leniency, pity**

Word building: The plural is **mercies**. | **merciful** *adjective*   **merciless** *adjective*

mere

adjective being nothing more than: *You are a mere child.*

Word building: **merely** *adverb* only or just

merge

verb to unite or blend together: *The colours merged.*

Word building: **merger** *noun* a joining of two companies in business

meridian

noun a line of longitude

meringue   (*say* muh-<u>rang</u>)

noun a mixture of sugar and beaten egg whites used in cakes and sweets

merino   (*say* muh-<u>ree</u>-noh)

noun a type of sheep that has very fine wool

Word building: The plural is **merinos**.
Word history: from a Latin word meaning 'of the larger sort'

merit

noun **1** excellence: *a painting of merit* **2 merits**, the qualities or features of something or someone, whether good or bad: *Let's take each case on its merits.*

Word building: **merit** *verb* (**merited, meriting**) to deserve   **meritorious** *adjective*

mermaid

noun an imaginary sea creature, a woman from the waist up and a fish from the waist down

Word building: **merman** *noun*
Word history: from the Latin word for 'lake' added to the word **maid**

merry

adjective cheerful or happy
Other words: **festive, jolly, jovial, joyous**

Word building: **merriment** *noun*   **merrymaking** *noun*

merry-go-round

noun a revolving circular platform with wooden horses or similar things on it, which people ride on for fun
Other words: **carousel, roundabout**

mesh

noun **1** a net or network: *nylon mesh for an insect screen | caught in the meshes of the law* **2** the space between the threads of a net, wire netting and so on: *This net has a wide mesh.*

Word building: **mesh** *verb*   **enmesh** *verb*

mesmerise

verb to completely hold the attention of: *The beauty of the scenery mesmerised me.*

Word use: Another spelling is **mesmerize**. | This word once used to mean **hypnotise**.
Word building: **mesmeric** *adjective* **mesmerisation** *noun*

mess

noun **1** a dirty or untidy state **2** a difficult or confused state: *My life is in a mess.* **3** a dining room, especially in the army *phrase* **4 mess about** (or **around**), *Informal* to waste time doing useless things

Word building: **messily** *adverb*   **messiness** *noun*   **messy** *adjective*

message

noun **1** information sent from one person to another
Other words: **communication, note, notification, word**
2 the meaning of something such as a book or what it tries to teach you

messenger

noun someone who carries a message

meta-

prefix a word part indicating change: *metabolism | metamorphosis*
Word history: from Greek

metabolism   (*say* muh-<u>tab</u>-uh-liz-uhm)

noun all the processes and chemical changes happening in your body or any living thing

Word building: **metabolise** *verb* to change by metabolism   **metabolic** *adjective*

metal

noun an element such as iron, copper or gold which is shiny, able to be shaped or worked, and is a good conductor of electricity

Word building: **metallurgy** *noun* the study of metals   **metallic** *adjective*   **metalwork** *noun*

metal/mettle Don't confuse **metal** with **mettle**. To be on your **mettle** is to try to do your very best. Something that tests your **mettle** is something that tests your courage or spirit.

metamorphosis

(*say* met-uh-**maw**-fuh-suhs)
noun a change from one form to another: *the metamorphosis of a caterpillar into a butterfly*

Word building: The plural is **metamorphoses**. | **metamorphic** *adjective*

metaphor   (*say* met-uh-faw)

noun a figure of speech in which something is spoken of as if it were something else: *'Knowledge is a key that opens many doors' is a metaphor.*

Word use: Compare this with **simile**.
Word building: **metaphorical** *adjective* **metaphorically** *adverb*

meteor   (*say* mee-tee-aw)

noun a small rocklike object from outer space which enters the earth's atmosphere making a fiery streak across the sky

Word building: **meteoric** *adjective* brilliant, fast or passing quickly, like a meteor   **meteorically** *adverb*

meteorite

noun a mass of stone or metal that has reached the earth from outer space

meteorology

(*say* mee-tee-uh-**rol**-uh-jee)
noun the study of weather and climate

Word building: **meteorological** *adjective* **meteorologist** *noun*

meter

noun an instrument that measures, especially one that measures the amount of gas, electricity or water passing through it
Other words: **dial, gauge**

meter/metre Don't confuse **meter** with **metre** which is a unit of measurement of length. **Metre** can also mean 'the regular arrangement of stressed and unstressed syllables in poetry'.

method

noun a way of going about something, especially an orderly way: *a method for doing a sum*
Other words: **means, mode, procedure, technique**

Word building: **methodical** *adjective* **methodically** *adverb*

methylated spirits

noun a liquid used for cleaning and sometimes as a fuel

meticulous   (*say* muh-**tik**-yuh-luhs)

adjective careful about small details: *It is good to be meticulous in your school work.*

Word building: **meticulously** *adverb*
Word history: from a Latin word meaning 'fearful'

metre¹

noun a unit of measurement of length in the metric system

metre²

noun the arrangement of words in poetry into patterns of rhythm

Word building: **metrical** *adjective*

metric

adjective belonging to the system of measurement based on the metre

Word building: **metrically** *adverb*   **metricate** *verb*   **metrication** *noun*

metric system

noun a decimal system of measurement originally based on the metre

metronome

noun an instrument that can be set to beat at a fixed rate and so give the right speed of performance for a piece of music

metropolitan   (*say* met-ruh-**pol**-uh-tuhn)

adjective having to do with a large city

Word building: **metropolis** (*say* muh-**trop**-uh-luhs) *noun* a large city

mettle

noun **1** the quality of someone's character, especially when spirited or brave: *We need a lad of mettle for this job.*
phrase **2 on your mettle,** eager to do your best

Word building: **mettlesome** *adjective* full of courage

mettle/metal Don't confuse **mettle** with **metal**, which is a hard substance like gold, silver, copper or iron.

mezzanine   (say mez-uh-neen)
noun a balcony-like floor in a building, usually between the ground floor and the next

micro-
prefix a word part meaning **1** very small: *microbe* | *microcomputer* **2** making bigger or stronger: *microscope* | *microphone*
Word use: Compare this with **macro-**.
Word history: from Greek

microbe
noun a tiny living creature which is so small that it can only be seen under a microscope, and which usually carries disease

microchip
noun a minute square which contains electronic circuits, used in a computer, watch, or electronic game
Word use: The prefix *micro-* meaning 'very small' indicates that this is even smaller than an ordinary electronic **chip**.

microcomputer
noun a small computer that will fit on your desk, and is meant for only one person to use at a time

microfiche   (say muy-kroh-feesh)
noun a sheet of transparent plastic about the size of a filing card which may have many pages of print on it that can be read with a special projector

microfilm
noun a photographic film with very small images which can be enlarged when projected and is used for storing information

microorganism
noun an extremely small animal or vegetable organism that can only be seen with a microscope

microphone
noun an instrument which changes sound waves into electrical waves, often used in equipment that makes sounds louder or records them on a tape recorder

microprocessor
noun the most important electronic chip in a microcomputer

microscope
noun an instrument used for looking at extremely tiny things that you normally can't see
Word building: **microscopic** *adjective* extremely small
Word history: from the Greek word for 'small' added to the Greek word for 'view'

microwave oven
noun a type of oven which heats or cooks food very quickly by passing high-speed waves through it

midday
noun twelve o'clock in the middle of the day
Other words: **noon**

middle
noun a halfway point: *the middle of the road* | *the middle of the discussion*
Word building: **middle** *adjective*

midget
noun a very small person or thing

midnight
noun twelve o'clock at night

midriff
noun the part of your body between the chest and the waist

midwife
noun a nurse specially trained to help a woman while she is having a baby
Word building: The plural is **midwives**. | **midwifery** (say mid-wif-uh-ree) *noun*

might¹
noun power or force

might/mite Don't confuse **might** with **mite**, which is a small insect.

might²
verb could possibly: *He might be lost.*
Word use: This verb is a helping verb, always used with another one. It is the past tense of **may**.

mighty
adjective **1** powerful: *a mighty king* **2** huge: *a mighty forest*

Word building: Other forms are **mightier,
mightiest**.

migraine

noun a very bad headache which makes
you feel ill

migrant

noun someone who leaves their own
country to go and live in another
Other words: **emigrant, immigrant**

migrate

verb **1** to change the place of living at
regular times each year, as some birds
do **2** to go to live in another country:
*Many people have migrated from South-East
Asia to Australia.*

Word building: **migration** *noun* **migratory**
adjective

mild

adjective **1** gentle: *a mild voice* **2** not severe:
mild pain **3** not sharp or strong: *a mild flavour*

Word building: **mildly** *adverb* **mildness** *noun*

mildew

noun a coating or growth which appears
on damp cloth, paper, leather and other
materials

mile

noun a unit of length in the imperial
system equal to about 1.6 kilometres

Word building: **mileage** *noun*
Word history: from a Latin word meaning 'a
thousand'

militant

adjective fighting or ready to fight,
especially for a cause: *a militant supporter
of Aboriginal land rights*

Word building: **militancy** *noun* **militant**
noun **militantly** *adverb*

military

adjective **1** having to do with soldiers: *a
military hospital*
phrase **2 the military**, all the soldiers in a
country

militia (*say* muh-<u>lish</u>-uh)

noun a group of part-time citizen soldiers

milk

noun the white liquid produced by female
mammals to feed their young, especially
cow's milk

Word building: **milky** *adjective*

mill

noun **1** a building with machinery for
grinding grain into flour **2** a small grinding
machine: *a coffee mill | a pepper mill*
3 a factory, especially one for spinning or
weaving: *a woollen mill*

Word building: **mill** *verb* **miller** *noun*

millennium

noun a period of 1000 years

millet

noun a cereal grain grown in Asia and
southern Europe

milli-

prefix a word part indicating one
thousandth of a given unit: *millibar*

millibar

noun a unit of measurement for air
pressure, especially in the atmosphere

milligram

noun a weight equal to one thousandth of
a gram

millilitre

noun a unit of measurement equal to one
thousandth of a litre

millimetre

noun a unit of measurement equal to one
thousandth of a metre

milliner (*say* <u>mil</u>-uh-nuh)

noun someone who makes or sells hats

million

noun a number, one thousand times one
thousand, 1 000 000 or 10^6

Word building: **million** *adjective*: *A million
copies of the book have been sold.* **millionth**
adjective: *the millionth baby born in the city*

millionaire

noun someone who has a million dollars or
more

millipede

noun a small creature like a caterpillar with
a long body made up of many parts most
of which have two pairs of legs

Word history: from a Latin word meaning
'wood louse'

mime

noun **1** a form of acting in which the actors tell the story by using movements of their body and face instead of words **2** a play in which the performers use this form of acting

Word building: **mime** *verb*

mimic

verb **1** to copy or imitate
noun **2** someone who is good at imitating the voice and movements of others

Word building: Other verb forms are **I mimicked, I have mimicked, I am mimicking.** | **mimicry** (*say* <u>mim</u>-uh-kree) *noun*

mince

verb **1** to cut or chop into very small pieces **2** to soften so as not to be so forceful: *to mince words* **3** to speak, walk or move in a dainty way
noun **4** meat that has been minced

mind

noun **1** the part of you that thinks and feels, using judgement, memory and so on **2** intelligence, understanding or mental ability
Other words: **awareness, intellect**
3 memory: *Keep this in mind.* **4** your opinion or what you think or feel: *Feel free to speak your mind.*
verb **5** to look after: *Will you mind the baby?*
Other words: **care for, tend, watch**
6 to dislike or feel bad about: *Do you mind the cold weather?*

Word building: **mindful** *adjective* careful or aware **mindless** *adjective* senseless

mind game

noun a contest where psychological factors are more important than physical ones or where the people in the contest may be put under psychological pressure

mine¹

noun **1** a large hole dug in the earth to remove precious stones, coal and so on **2** a rich store of anything: *This book is a mine of information.* **3** a bomb placed underground or in the sea to blow up the enemy or their ships

mine²

pronoun one of the forms of **I** and **me** you use to show that something belongs to you: *That book is mine.* | *a friend of mine*

miner¹

noun someone who works in a mine

miner/minor Don't confuse **miner** with **minor**.
Minor means 'lesser in size, extent, or importance' as in *a minor share* or *a minor weakness*.

miner²

noun a type of bird with a yellow beak and yellow or yellow-brown legs: *noisy miner*

mineral

noun a substance such as stone, ore or coal which is obtained by mining

Word building: **mineral** *adjective*

mineral water

noun water containing dissolved mineral salts and gases

minestrone (*say* min-uh-<u>stroh</u>-nee)

noun a soup made with vegetables, herbs, pasta, and so on

Word history: from a Latin word meaning 'serve' or 'wait on'

mingle

verb **1** to become mixed: *Her tears mingled with the rain on her face.* **2** to take part with others or to associate with: *She mingled with the rest of the guests.*

mini

noun **1** another word for **miniskirt**
adjective **2** very small or miniature

mini-

prefix a word part meaning 'small' or 'miniature': *miniskirt*

Word history: a short form of *miniature*, from Latin

miniature (*say* <u>min</u>-uh-chuh)

noun **1** a very small copy or model of something: *Some model aeroplanes are exact miniatures of the real thing.* **2** a very small painting, especially a portrait
adjective **3** on a very small scale or much reduced in size

minibus

noun a motor vehicle that is big enough to carry between five and ten passengers

Word building: The plural is **minibuses.**

minim

noun a note in music equal to half a semibreve in length

Word history: from a Latin word meaning 'least' or 'smallest'

minimum

noun **1** the smallest number or amount possible: *You have to get a minimum of four points to qualify.* **2** the lowest number

Word use: The opposite is **maximum**.
Word building: The plural is **minimums** or **minima**. | **minimise** *verb* **minimum** *adjective* **minimal** *adjective*

miniskirt

noun a very short skirt

Word use: Another word for this is **mini**.

minister

noun **1** a member of the clergy who conducts services in a church **2** a member of parliament who is in charge of a government department
verb **3** to give service, care or help: *He ministered to the sick people.*

Word building: **ministerial** *adjective* **ministry** *noun*

mink

noun **1** an animal that looks like a weasel and lives part of the time in water **2** the valuable fur of this animal

minor

adjective **1** lesser in size or importance: *a minor share | You only have to fix a few minor things and then it will be perfect.*
Other words: **insignificant, minimal, slight, small, trivial**
noun **2** someone who is under the legal adult age

minor/miner Don't confuse **minor** with **miner**. Look up **miner**.

minority

noun **1** the smaller part or number, or less than half **2** a group of people whose views are different to the views of most other people: *There will always be a minority which does not agree.*

Word use: The opposite of this is **majority**.
Word building: The plural is **minorities**.

minor scale

noun any musical scale which has a semitone between the second and third notes

Word use: Such a scale is said to be in a **minor** key. | Compare this with **major scale**.

minstrel

noun a musician in the Middle Ages who sang or said poetry while playing an instrument

Word history: from a French word meaning 'servant'

mint¹

noun **1** a herb with leaves that are used in cooking **2** a peppermint

mint²

noun **1** a place where money is made by the government
verb **2** to make money in a mint
phrase **3 in mint condition**, new or looking like new: *The second-hand car was in mint condition.*

minus

adjective having to do with subtraction or taking away: *the minus sign*

minuscule   (*say* <u>min</u>-uhs-kyoohl)

adjective extremely small: *You can be sure that if he gets to the chocolate first, there'll only be a minuscule amount left for everyone else.*

minute¹   (*say* <u>min</u>-uht)

noun **1** a sixtieth part of an hour **2** any short space of time: *Wait a minute.*
Other words: **instant, moment**
3 minutes, the official record of what has been discussed in a meeting

minute²   (*say* muy-<u>nyooht</u>)

adjective extremely small: *She got a minute piece of dirt in her eye.*
Other words: **microscopic, minuscule, tiny**

miracle

noun **1** an event which can't be explained by natural or scientific evidence or arguments **2** a wonderful or remarkable thing: *It was a miracle that the lost child was found.*
Other words: **marvel, wonder**

Word building: **miraculous** *adjective* **miraculously** *adverb*

mirage   (*say* muh-<u>rahzh</u>)

noun an illusion or false vision in which someone sees distant things as much closer than they really are, or even sees things that are not there at all

Word history: from a French word meaning 'look at (yourself) in a mirror'

mire   (*rhymes with* buyer)

noun **1** wet swampy ground **2** deep mud

Word building: **miry** *adjective*

mirror

noun **1** glass that has been treated so that you can see yourself reflected in it **2** something that gives a true picture of something else: *This story is a mirror of my true feelings.*

Word building: **mirror** *verb*

mirth

noun amusement and laughter: *The audience bubbled with mirth.*

mis-

prefix a word part meaning **1** failure: *misfire* **2** wrong: *mislay | mislead* **3** not: *mistrust*

Word history: from Old English

misadventure

noun **1** bad luck or a piece of ill fortune **2** an accident or mishap

misbehave

verb to behave badly: *If you misbehave in the car, we won't be stopping for ice-cream.*

Word building: **misbehaviour** *noun*

miscarriage

noun **1** the failure to get the right result or decision: *a miscarriage of justice* **2** the birth of a dead baby, especially early in a pregnancy

Word building: **miscarry** *verb* (**miscarried, miscarrying**)

miscellaneous   (*say* mis-uh-<u>lay</u>-nee-uhs)

adjective made up of a mixture of different kinds: *I keep a miscellaneous collection of items like bottle tops, pens and clips in my top drawer.*

Word building: **miscellaneously** *adverb* **miscellany** *noun*

mischief   (*say* <u>mis</u>-chuhf)

noun **1** behaviour meant to tease or annoy **2** harm, injury or trouble

Word building: **mischievous** (*say* <u>mis</u>-chuh-vuhs) *adjective* **mischievously** *adverb*

miser   (*say* <u>muy</u>-zuh)

noun **1** someone who lives very poorly so as to save and store up money **2** someone who is mean and greedy

Word building: **miserly** *adjective*

miserable   (*say* <u>miz</u>-ruh-buhl)

adjective **1** very unhappy or uncomfortable **2** causing unhappiness or discomfort: *miserable weather* **3** mean and stingy

misery   (*say* <u>miz</u>-uh-ree)

noun great unhappiness

Word building: The plural is **miseries**.

misfire

verb **1** to fail to fire or explode properly **2** to go wrong or to fail: *Your plan to disrupt the assembly misfired.*

misfit

noun someone who does not fit in or get along well in their job or with other people

misfortune

noun bad luck

misgiving

noun a feeling of doubt or worry

mishap   (*say* <u>mis</u>-hap)

noun an unfortunate accident

misjudge

verb to judge or calculate incorrectly: *He misjudged the width of the creek and tumbled into the water. | He misjudged his sister's mood and they got into an argument.*

Word building: **misjudgement** *noun*

mislay

verb to put in a place which you forget afterwards: *I have mislaid my pen again.*

Word use: Another word is **misplace**.
Word building: Other forms are **I mislaid, I have mislaid, I am mislaying**.

mislead

verb **1** to lead or guide wrongly **2** to influence badly or to lead into error or wrongdoing: *My friends are misleading me into bad habits.*

Word building: Other forms are **I misled, I have misled, I am misleading. | misleading** *adjective* **misleadingly** *adverb*

miss[1]

verb **1** to fail to hit, meet, catch, see, hear and so on **2** to fail to attend **3** to notice or feel sad about the absence or loss of: *She missed her sister when she went away.* **4** to escape or avoid

Word building: **miss** *noun*

miss²

noun **1** a young unmarried woman
2 Miss, a title put before an unmarried woman's name

Word use: Some women prefer **Ms** because it makes no reference to whether they are married or not.

missile   (*say* <u>mis</u>-uyl)

noun an object or weapon that can be thrown or shot
Other words: **projectile**

missing

adjective absent or not found

mission   (*say* <u>mish</u>-uhn)

noun **1** a group of people sent out, usually to another country, to do government or religious work **2** a duty someone is sent to carry out

Word history: from a Latin word meaning 'a sending'

missionary   (*say* <u>mish</u>-uhn-ree)

noun someone sent out, often to another country, on religious work

Word building: The plural is **missionaries.**

mist

noun a cloud-like collection of water vapour, like a very thin fog

Word building: **misty** *adjective*   **mistily** *adverb*

mistake

noun **1** an error or misunderstanding
verb **2** to believe to be someone or something different: *He always mistakes me for my sister.* **3** to misunderstand: *She mistook my meaning.*

Word building: Other verb forms are
I mistook, I have mistaken, I am mistaking.

mister

noun **1** *Informal* a form of address for a man: *Hello mister, what's your name?*
2 Mister, a title put before a man's name

Word use: **Mister** is usually written **Mr.**

mistletoe   (*say* <u>mis</u>-uhl-toh)

noun a plant with small white berries which feeds and grows on the branches of other trees, and is often used for Christmas decorations

mistress

noun **1** a woman in charge of a household, servants and so on **2** a female owner of an animal like a dog or a horse **3** a female teacher in charge of a particular subject or department at school **4** a woman who has a sexual relationship with a man who is married to someone else

mistrust

noun suspicion, or a lack of trust or confidence

Word building: **mistrust** *verb*   **mistrustful** *adjective*   **mistrustfully** *adverb*

misunderstanding

noun **1** a failure to understand correctly: *There seems to be some misunderstanding about the date of the birthday party.*
2 a disagreement or quarrel

Word building: **misunderstand** *verb* **(misunderstood, misunderstanding)**

misuse   (*say* mis-<u>yoohs</u>)

noun **1** wrong use: *Misuse of some medicines can be dangerous.*
verb (*say* mis-<u>yoohz</u>) **2** to use in the wrong way **3** to treat badly

mite

noun a tiny insect-like creature which lives in food like cheese or flour or feeds off plants and animals

mite/might Don't confuse **mite** with **might**, which is power, as in the phrase *with all your might.*

mitre   (*say* <u>muy</u>-tuh)

noun **1** the tall headdress worn by a bishop **2** the angle cut at the ends of two pieces of wood which are then joined together

mitten

noun a kind of glove which covers the four fingers together and the thumb separately

mix

verb **1** to combine or blend together: *You can mix flour and water to make paste.* | *He mixes business with pleasure.*
Other words: **incorporate, fuse, merge, unite**
2 to make by combining different things: *She mixed a cake.*
phrase **3 mix with**, to be friends with or associate with

Word building: **mix** *noun*   **mixer** *noun*

mixture

noun something made up of mixed or combined things

mix-up

noun a muddle or confused state of things

moan

noun **1** a long low sound of sorrow or pain **2** any similar sound: *the moan of the wind* **3** *Informal* a complaint

Word building: **moan** *verb*

moat

noun a deep wide trench or ditch, usually filled with water, surrounding a town or castle to help protect it from invaders

mob

noun **1** a large crowd which is sometimes rowdy or violent **2** a group of friends **3** a group of animals
verb **4** to crowd around: *The fans mobbed the pop star at the concert.* **5** to surround and attack violently: *The people mobbed the bus and destroyed it.*

Word building: Other verb forms are **they mobbed, they have mobbed, they are mobbing.**

mobile

adjective **1** able to be moved
Other words: **movable, portable**
2 changing easily: *The clown had a mobile face which he could change from happy to sad.*
noun **3** a hanging decoration made up of delicately balanced movable parts
4 a mobile phone

Word building: **mobility** *noun*

mobile phone

noun a telephone without a cord that you can use anywhere

mobilise

verb to get ready for duty or use: *The general mobilised the troops.*

Word use: Another spelling is **mobilize**.
Word building: **mobilisation** *noun*

moccasin   (*say* mok-uh-suhn)

noun a shoe made completely of soft leather

Word history: from a Native North American language

mock

verb **1** to make fun of
Other words: **deride, ridicule, tease**
adjective **2** being a copy or imitation: *a mock battle*

Other words: **artificial, counterfeit, fake, pretend, sham**

Word building: **mockery** *noun*

modal verb

noun a type of auxiliary verb that shows how likely or how necessary something is, as in 'She *might* come', 'The sun *will* set', 'He *should* apologise', 'I *must* walk the dog.'

mode

noun a method or way: *a mode of travel*

model

noun **1** an example used for copying or comparing: *Her work was used as a model by the teachers.* **2** a small copy: *a model of an aeroplane* **3** someone who poses for a painter or photographer **4** someone employed to wear and show new clothes to customers **5** a particular style or form: *This bike is the latest model.*
adjective **6** excellent or worthy to serve as a model: *She was a model student.*
verb **7** to form, shape or make: *He modelled a vase out of clay* **8** to be employed as a model

Word building: Other verb forms are
I modelled, I have modelled, I am modelling.

modem

noun a device that allows one computer to be linked to another through the telephone system

Word history: made from part of the words *modulator demodulator*

moderate   (*say* mod-uh-ruht)

adjective **1** reasonable or not extreme: *a moderate request* **2** fair, average or medium: *a moderate income*
noun **3** someone who is moderate in opinions or actions
verb (*say* mod-uh-rayt) **4** to make or become less violent or severe

Word building: **moderator** *noun* someone or something that moderates   **moderately** *adverb*   **moderation** *noun*

modern

adjective belonging to or used in the present time
Other words: **contemporary, current, new, recent**

Word building: **modernise** *verb*

modest

adjective **1** having a moderate opinion of yourself and your abilities **2** moderate or reasonable **3** behaving in a proper or decent way

Word building: **modestly** *adverb*   **modesty** *noun*

modify

verb **1** to change a little bit: *I can easily modify my plans to fit in with the new rules.* **2** to reduce or make less severe or extreme: *Annabelle modified her strong language in front of her parents.* **3** to limit or add more detail to the meaning of a word: *Adverbs modify verbs.*

Word building: Other forms are **I modified, I have modified, I am modifying.** | **modification** *noun*: *a modification to the house* **modifier** *noun*

modulate

verb **1** to tone down or adjust **2** to change the pitch or loudness of your voice when you speak

Word building: **modulation** *noun*

module

noun a part of something which can be separated from the rest and be used on its own

Word building: **modular** *adjective*: *modular furniture*

mohawk

noun a type of hairstyle, with a long strip of upright hair along the middle of the head, and the sides of the head shaved

Word history: from the name of a Native American people

moist

adjective damp or slightly wet
Other words: **clammy, soggy**

Word building: **moisten** *verb* to make moist **moistly** *adverb*   **moisture** *noun*

molar

noun one of the large teeth at the back of your mouth used for grinding

Word building: **molar** *adjective*

molasses

noun the syrup taken from raw sugar

mole[1]

noun a small spot, usually dark, on your skin

mole[2]

noun a small furry animal that feeds on insects and lives mainly underground

molecule   *(say* mol-uh-kyoohl*)*

noun the smallest unit or particle into which something can be divided without changing its features: *A molecule of water has two hydrogen atoms and one oxygen atom.*

Word building: **molecular** *adjective*

molest   *(say* muh-lest*)*

verb to annoy or interfere with so as to hurt

Word building: **molestation** *noun*

mollify

verb to make calmer or less angry: *He managed to mollify her with apologies.*
Other words: **appease, pacify, placate, soothe**

Word building: Other forms are **I mollified, I have mollified, I am mollifying.**
Word history: from a Latin word meaning 'soften'

mollusc

noun an animal with a soft body, no backbone, and sometimes a hard shell, such as a snail or octopus

Word history: from a Latin word meaning 'soft' (used about a thin-shelled nut)

mollycoddle

verb to treat too carefully or tenderly: *Her mother mollycoddled her even when she was a teenager.*

molten

adjective made into liquid by heat: *molten steel*

moment

noun **1** a very short space of time: *I'll be there in a moment.*
Other words: **flash, instant, minute, second**
2 the present or another particular time: *I can't come at the moment.* | *I was going out the door at that moment.* **3** importance: *This is a decision of great moment.*

Word building: **momentous** *adjective* of great importance **momentously** *adverb*

momentary

adjective **1** lasting for only a moment: *a momentary flash of light* **2** happening at every moment: *He lives in momentary fear of discovery.*

Word building: **momentarily** *adverb*

momentum
noun the force of something's movement: *If I build up enough momentum, I bet I can leap right over that creek!*

monarch   (*say* mon-uhk)
noun a ruler of a country who inherits the position, such as a king or queen
Other words: **sovereign**
Word building: **monarchist** *noun* a supporter of the monarchy   **monarchy** *noun*

monastery   (*say* mon-uhs-tree)
noun a place where a group of monks live and work
Word building: The plural is **monasteries**. | **monastic** *adjective* having to do with monasteries or monks

Monday
noun the second day of the week
Word use: The abbreviation is **Mon**.
Word history: from an Old English word meaning 'moon's day'

money
noun **1** metal coins or banknotes
Other words: **cash, currency**
2 property or wealth: *That is a family with lots of money.*
Other words: **assets, capital, fortune**
Word building: The plural is **moneys** or **monies**. | **monetary** *adjective*

money order
noun an order for payment which can be exchanged for money at a post office

mongrel   (*say* mun-gruhl)
noun a plant or animal, especially a dog, that is a mix of different breeds or kinds

monitor
noun **1** the part of the computer that you look at to read the words and pictures. It looks like a TV screen. **2** a kind of television set used in TV studios to check the quality of the broadcast, or with computers to display data **3** something that keeps a check or gives warning **4** a kind of large lizard which is supposed to warn that crocodiles are near **5** a pupil who has particular jobs to help the teacher
verb **6** to watch or measure carefully: *We must monitor our spending.*
Other words: **audit, check**

monk   (*rhymes with* sunk)
noun a male member of a religious group living a life of religious devotion away from the rest of the world

monkey
noun a kind of animal that has a long tail and lives in trees in tropical areas
Word building: The plural is **monkeys**.

monkey-wrench
noun a spanner or wrench with an opening that can be changed so that it can be used on things of different size

mono-
prefix a word part meaning 'alone' or 'single': *monologue* | *monolith*
Word history: from Greek

monocle
noun a glass lens for one eye only

monogamy   (*say* muh-nog-uh-mee)
noun marriage to one person at a time
Word use: Compare this with **polygamy** and **bigamy**.
Word building: **monogamous** *adjective*

monogram
noun a design made up of two or more letters, usually your initials

monolith
noun a single huge rock or stone, such as Uluru
Word building: **monolithic** *adjective*

monologue   (*say* mon-uh-log)
noun a long talk by one person

monopoly   (*say* muh-nop-uh-lee)
noun the complete control of something, especially the supply of a product or service
Word building: The plural is **monopolies**. | **monopolise** *verb*   **monopolisation** *noun*

monorail   (*say* mon-o-rail)
noun a train that runs on one rail which is usually on top of the carriages

monotone
noun a series of spoken or sung sounds in one unchanging tone: *She spoke in a dreary monotone.*

monotony   (*say* muh-not-uh-nee)
noun lack of change or variety producing boredom

Word building: **monotonous** *adjective*: *a monotonous day* **monotonously** *adverb*

monotreme

noun an egg-laying mammal. The platypus and the echidna, found in Australia and nearby regions, are the only examples.

Word history: from a Greek word meaning 'one hole' (their eggs and the waste matter from their bodies come out of the same opening)

monsoon

noun **1** a strong wind of the Indian Ocean and Indonesia **2** a rainy season associated with a monsoon wind

Word building: **monsoonal** *adjective*
Word history: from an Arabic word meaning 'season' or 'seasonal wind'

monster

noun **1** someone or something that is frighteningly horrible or cruel **2** someone or something of huge size

monstrous

adjective **1** huge or great: *a monstrous amount of money* **2** frightful or shocking: *a monstrous face* | *a monstrous idea*

Word building: **monstrosity** *noun* **monstrously** *adverb*

montage   (*say* mon-<u>tahzh</u>)

noun **1** the method of arranging different pictures, or parts of pictures, into one image **2** a film-editing technique in which a few different shots are put together to form a single image, or a few images are shown one after the other to express one idea

Word history: French word meaning 'mounting', 'putting together'

month

noun **1** any of the twelve parts into which the year is divided **2** a period of about four weeks or 30 days

Word building: **monthly** *adjective*: *a monthly magazine* **monthly** *adverb*: *They come monthly.*

monument

noun **1** something made in memory of a person or event, such as a statue **2** something from the past, such as an ancient building: *the monuments of ancient Greece*

monumental

adjective great in size or importance
Word building: **monumentally** *adverb*

mood

noun the way you feel at a particular time: *Dad's been in a bad mood since the car broke down* | *I'm in the mood to watch a funny movie.*
Other words: **disposition, frame of mind, humour, spirit**

moody

adjective **1** angry or unhappy **2** changeable in mood or feelings
Other words: **temperamental**

Word building: Other forms are **moodier, moodiest.** | **moodily** *adverb* **moodiness** *noun*

moon

noun **1** the round body that circles the earth every month and can be seen as a light in the sky at night **2** this body as it appears at different stages of the month: *the new moon* | *the full moon*

Word use: The adjective from **moon** is **lunar.**

moor[1]

noun an open area of damp wild land, usually covered with low, rough, plant growth usually found in Britain

moor/more Don't confuse **moor** with **more**, which is the opposite of **less**:
Can I please have some more cake?

moor[2]

verb to make stay in the same position with ropes or an anchor: *to moor a ship*
Word building: **mooring** *noun* **moorings** *plural noun*

moose

noun a large animal of the deer family
Word building: The plural is **moose.**

moot point

noun an issue which does not have a clear or straightforward answer, and so is often argued about: *Whether war is ever the right thing is a moot point.*

mop

noun **1** a loose bundle of cloth or strings fixed to the end of a stick, and used for washing floors or dishes **2** a thick mass: *a mop of hair*
verb **3** to clean or wipe up with a mop or something similar

Word building: Other verb forms are **I mopped, I have mopped, I am mopping.**

mope

verb to be in an unhappy mood

mopoke

noun a kind of owl found in Australia and New Zealand

Word history: named after the sound it makes

moral

adjective **1** having to do with the knowledge of what is right and wrong: *This is a moral question.* **2** acting according to the rules of what is thought to be right, especially in sexual behaviour: *a moral person*
noun **3** the lesson taught by story or experience: *The moral is 'Slow and steady wins the race'.* **4 morals**, beliefs or ways of behaviour that have to do with right and wrong

Word use: Compare this with **immoral**.
Word building: **moralise** *verb* to make moral judgements **moralistic** *adjective* **morally** *adverb*

morale   (*say* muh-<u>rahl</u>)

noun a cheerful and confident state of mind: *We must keep the cricket team's morale high.*

moratorium

noun any official delay, such as in making a political decision

Word building: The plural is **moratoria** or **moratoriums**.

morbid

adjective **1** showing an unhealthy interest in gruesome things **2** caused by or having to do with disease

Word building: **morbidity** *noun*   **morbidly** *adverb*   **morbidness** *noun*

more

adjective **1** in greater quantity, measure, degree or number: *more apples to eat* **2** to a greater degree: *more slowly*

more/moor Don't confuse **more** with **moor**, which is an open area of damp, wild land usually found in Britain.

morgue   (*say* mawg)

noun a place where the bodies of dead people are kept until their funerals

morning

noun the beginning or first part of the day, before noon

morning/mourning Don't confuse **morning** with **mourning**. Someone is in **mourning** if they are grieving over the death of someone they love.

moron

noun Informal someone who is stupid

Word building: **moronic** *adjective*
Word history: from the Greek word *moros* meaning 'dull', 'foolish'

morose   (*say* muh-<u>rohs</u>)

adjective bad-tempered or unfriendly because of unhappiness

Word building: **morosely** *adverb*   **moroseness** *noun*

morphine   (*say* <u>maw</u>-feen)

noun a drug used to stop pain and to help you to sleep

Word history: from a Greek word for 'the strange forms people see in dreams'; *Morpheus* was the Greek god of dreams

morse code

noun a system of signalling in which different groups of short and long sounds or flashes of light, called dots and dashes, stand for each letter in a word

Word history: named after Samuel FB *Morse*, the US inventor of the telegraph system and of morse code

morsel

noun a very small piece or amount

mortal

adjective **1** having to die eventually: *All humans are mortal.* **2** causing death: *a mortal wound* **3** deadly or extreme: *a mortal enemy*
noun **4** a human being

Word building: **mortally** *adverb*

mortality

noun **1** the condition of being mortal or human: *Her death made me think about my own mortality.* **2** death or rate of death: *Child mortality is high in some countries.*

mortar[1]

noun **1** a heavy bowl in which food or other substances are ground to a powder with a pestle **2** a short cannon designed to fire shells to a great height

mortar²

noun a mixture of lime or cement, sand and water, used for joining bricks together

mortarboard

noun a square-shaped cap sometimes worn by teachers and university students

mortgage   (*say* <u>maw</u>-gij)

noun a promise that a property will be given over if a loan is not repaid to a bank or the like: *We have a mortgage on our house.*

Word building: **mortgagee** *noun* someone to whom property is mortgaged   **mortgagor** *noun* someone who mortgages property   **mortgage** *verb*

mortify

verb to severely embarrass or hurt the feelings or pride of: *My mother mortified me by treating me like a baby in front of my friends.*

Word building: Other forms are **I mortified, I have mortified, I am mortifying.** | **mortification** *noun*

mortuary

noun a place where the bodies of dead people are kept until their funerals

Word building: The plural is **mortuaries.**

mosaic   (*say* moh-<u>zay</u>-ik)

noun a picture or pattern made of small pieces of different coloured stone or glass

mosque   (*say* mosk)

noun a Muslim place of worship

mosquito

noun a small flying insect, the female of which sucks the blood of animals and humans, and by this passes on some diseases, such as malaria

Word building: The plural is **mosquitoes** or **mosquitos.**
Word history: a Latin word meaning 'fly'

moss

noun a plant with very small leaves that grows in patches on damp ground, tree trunks or rocks

Word building: The plural is **mosses.** | **mossy** *adjective* (**mossier, mossiest**)

most

adjective **1** the greatest amount, quantity or degree of: *I ate the most ice-cream.* | *Mum caught the most fish.* | *You got the most sunburnt.*
pronoun **2** the greatest amount, quantity or degree: *Ahmed laughed the most.*
adverb **3** in or to the greatest degree or range: *It was the most difficult thing I've ever had to do.*

Word building: **mostly** *adverb*

motel

noun a roadside hotel which provides accommodation for travellers and parking for their cars

moth

noun a flying insect, similar to a butterfly, that is active at night

mothball

noun a small ball of a chemical substance which is stored with clothes to kill moths

mother

noun **1** a female parent **2** the head of a convent of nuns
verb **3** to be the mother of **4** to act as a mother to

Word building: **motherhood** *noun* **motherliness** *noun*   **motherly** *adjective*

mother-in-law

noun the mother of your husband or wife

Word building: The plural is **mothers-in-law.**

mother-of-pearl

noun the hard shiny lining of some shells, used for ornaments

motif   (*say* moh-<u>teef</u>)

noun **1** an idea that is repeated in various ways throughout a piece of writing or music or in the work of an artist **2** a part of a design that is repeated, such as in wallpaper

motion

noun **1** movement or the power of movement **2** an idea put forward at a meeting to be voted on: *He moved a motion in Parliament.*
verb **3** to direct by a movement of the hand or head: *He motioned her to leave the room.*

motive

noun a strong reason for doing something: *Jealousy was the motive for the murder.*

Word building: **motivate** *verb*: *Ambition motivates her to work hard.* **motivated** *adjective*   **motivation** *noun*

motley

adjective made up of different parts or colours: *a motley collection of people*

motocross

noun cross-country motorcycle racing

motor

noun an engine, especially that of a car or boat

motorcycle

noun a large heavy bicycle with an engine

Word use: This is also called a **motorbike**.
Word building: **motorcyclist** *noun*

motorist

noun someone who owns and drives a car

motorway

noun a road on which traffic can travel fast

Word use: Other words for this are **expressway** and **freeway**.

mottled

adjective covered with different coloured spots or patches: *a mottled book jacket | mottled skin*

Word building: **mottle** *verb*

motto

noun a short saying, often taken as summing up the aims or beliefs of a particular organisation or group: *The motto of the scouts is 'Be prepared'.*

Word building: The plural is **mottoes** or **mottos**.

mould¹   (*rhymes with* bold)

noun **1** a hollow form which gives shape to melted or soft material which hardens inside it: *a pottery mould | a jelly mould*
verb **2** to give a particular shape or character to

mould²

noun a furry growth on something that is too damp or is decaying: *This bread has mould on it.*

Word building: **mouldy** *adjective* (**mouldier, mouldiest**)

moult   (*rhymes with* bolt)

verb to lose or throw off old feathers, fur or skin: *Some birds moult in spring.*

mound

noun **1** a heap: *a mound of earth* **2** a small hill

mount

verb **1** to go up: *She mounted the stairs.*
2 to get up on: *He mounted the horse.*
3 to fix on or in a position or setting: *to mount a painting on a wall | to mount a jewel* **4** to rise or increase: *Prices are mounting.*
noun **5** a horse for riding **6** a backing or setting: *We should put this photograph on a white mount.*

mountain

noun **1** a large natural raised part of the earth, higher than a hill
Other words: **elevation, peak**
2 something like this in size, shape or amount: *a mountain of reading*

Word use: This is sometimes called a **mount**, especially in a name as in *Mount Kosciuszko*.
Word building: **mountaineer** *noun* someone who climbs mountains   **mountainous** *adjective*

mourn   (*say* mawn)

verb to feel or show sorrow over, especially over someone's death or the loss of something: *They are mourning the death of their father.*

Word building: **mourner** *noun*   **mournful** *adjective*   **mournfully** *adverb*   **mourning** *noun*

mouse

noun **1** a small furry animal with sharp teeth and a long tail, usually brown, white or grey coloured **2** a small object which you hold and move on the desk to position the cursor on the visual display unit of a computer

Word building: The plural is **mice**. | **mousy** *adjective* shy and quiet

moussaka   (*say* mooh-sah-kuh)

noun a dish from Greece, Turkey and other countries near them, with layers of minced lamb, tomatoes and eggplant, with a thick white sauce on top

mousse   (*say* moohs)

noun **1** a food made of whipped cream, beaten eggs, gelatine and a sweet or savoury flavouring: *chocolate mousse | fish mousse* **2** a foam-like substance, as one used to style the hair, cleanse the skin, and so on: *shaving mousse | shower mousse.*

Word history: from a French word meaning 'froth'

moustache (*say* muh-<u>stahsh</u>)

noun the hair that grows on the upper lip of a person

Word history: from a French word meaning 'upper lip'

mouth (*say* mowth)

noun **1** the opening in the face used for eating, drinking and talking **2** an opening in anything **3** the place where a river flows into the sea

verb (*say* mowdh) **4** to move the lips as if talking, but make no sound

mouthful

noun as much as you can fit into your mouth at one time

mouth organ

noun another word for **harmonica**

mouthpiece

noun the part of a wind instrument which you blow into or the part of a telephone which you speak into

mouth-to-mouth resuscitation

noun an attempt by a person to help someone who is having trouble breathing by breathing into their mouth: *They dragged the man out of the sea and tried mouth-to-mouth resuscitation.*

Word use: Another word for this is **kiss of life**.

move

verb **1** to change from one place or position to another: *to move the chair across the room*
Other words: **relocate, shift**
2 to cause strong feelings in: *The sad movie moved me.* **3** to make a formal request at a meeting
noun **4** a movement or change of position **5** a player's turn in a game: *Throw the dice and make your move.*
phrase **6 move in**, to settle into a house **7 move out**, to leave a house

Word building: **movable** *adjective*

movement

noun **1** a moving or changing from one place or position to another **2** an organised group of people working towards a particular goal: *the movement against uranium mining* **3** one of the sections of a long piece of music: *This symphony has four movements.*

movie

noun another word for **film** (def. 3)

mow

verb **1** to cut off or down: *to mow the lawn*
phrase **2 mow down**, to knock down: *The runaway car mowed down people on the footpath.*

Word building: Other verb forms are **I mowed, I have mown, I am mowing**.

mozzarella (*say* mot-suh-<u>rel</u>-uh)

noun a soft, white cheese which melts easily and is often used on pizzas and in other Italian foods

Word history: from an Italian word meaning 'a slice'

MP3 (*say* em-pee-<u>three</u>)

noun a computer file, especially a sound file and most often of music, that is compressed so that it can be sent quickly by email or over the internet: *We downloaded some free MP3s from our favourite website.*

MP3 player

noun a piece of equipment for downloading, storing and playing MP3s: *I wouldn't mind an MP3 player for my birthday so that I can listen to music as I go to school.*

Mr (*say* <u>mis</u>-tuh)

a title put before a man's name

Mrs (*say* <u>mis</u>-uhz)

a title put before a married woman's name

Ms (*say* muhz, miz)

a title put before a woman's name

much

adjective **1** in great amount, quantity or degree: *We had so much fun!*
pronoun **2** a great quantity or amount: *Much of this needs to be redone.*

Word building: Other adjective forms are **more, most**.

muck

noun **1** dirt or mud: *The dog was covered in muck after its walk.*
phrase **2 muck about** (or **around**), *Informal* to play around or waste time doing unimportant things **3 muck out**, *Informal* to remove muck from: *I have to muck out the stables.* **4 muck up**, *Informal* **a** to spoil: *You've mucked up my painting.* **b** to misbehave: *Stop mucking up or you'll get into trouble.*

Word building: **mucky** *adjective*

muck-up

noun Informal a mess or muddle

mucus   (*say* <u>myooh</u>-kuhs)

noun **1** thick slimy liquid which builds up in your nose and throat when you have a cold **2** thick liquid which builds up in other parts of the body

Word building: **mucous** *adjective*

mud

noun wet, soft, sticky earth

Other words: **bog, mire, slush**

Word building: **muddy** *adjective* (**muddier, muddiest**)

muddle

verb to mix up or confuse

Word building: **muddle** *noun* a confused mess **muddler** *noun*

mudguard

noun a cover for the wheel of a car or bicycle to stop mud and water splashing up

muesli   (*say* <u>myoohz</u>-lee, <u>moohz</u>-lee)

noun breakfast cereal made from oats, chopped fruit and nuts

Word history: from the German that is spoken in Switzerland

muff

noun **1** a rolled up piece of fur or woollen material into which you can put your hands to keep them warm

verb **2** *Informal* to bungle or miss: *to muff an easy catch*

muffin

noun **1** a small cake, often containing fruit **2** a flat, bread-like roll, eaten toasted and buttered

muffle

verb **1** to wrap in scarves, shawls and other warm clothes **2** to deaden the sound of: *to muffle drums*

Word building: **muffled** *adjective*

muffler

noun **1** a device which fits onto the exhaust pipe of a car to deaden the noise of the engine **2** a thick warm scarf

mug

noun **1** a large drinking cup **2** *Informal* your face **3** *Informal* someone who is easily fooled

verb **4** *Informal* to attack and rob

Word building: **mugger** *noun*

muggy

adjective unpleasantly warm and humid: *muggy weather*

Word building: Other forms are **muggier, muggiest.**

mulberry   (*say* <u>mul</u>-bree)

noun **1** a tree which has sweet, dark-purple fruit like blackberries, and leaves which are eaten by silkworms **2** the fruit of this tree

Word building: The plural is **mulberries.**

mulch

noun straw, grass clippings, leaves or similar material spread on gardens to protect and feed the plants

Word building: **mulch** *verb*

mule

noun **1** the offspring of a female horse and a male donkey **2** *Informal* someone who is stupid or stubborn

Word use: The male is a **jackass**, the female is a **mare** and the young is a **foal**.

Word building: **muleteer** *noun* a driver of mules **mulish** *adjective*

mulga

noun **1** a type of wattle tree found in dry inland areas of Australia. Cattle like to eat its leaves

phrase **2 up the mulga**, away out in the bush or outback

Word history: from Aboriginal languages of New South Wales called Yuwaalaraay and Kamilaroi. See the map of Australian Aboriginal languages at the end of this book.

mulgara   (*say* mul-<u>gah</u>-ra)

noun a small marsupial that looks like a mouse with a black hairy tail. It lives in the Australian desert and is endangered. See the table at the end of this book

Word history: from an Aboriginal language of South Australia called Wangganguru. See the map of Australian Aboriginal languages at the end of this book.

mull

phrase **mull over**, to think about: *She mulled over the problem.*

mullet

noun a type of fish commonly found in the rivers and sea around Australia

multi-
prefix a word part meaning 'many': *multinational | multiracial*
Word history: from Latin

multicultural
adjective having to do with a society which contains several large groups of people of different cultures or races
Word building: **multiculturalism** *noun*

multimeter (*say* <u>mul</u>-tee-mee-tuh)
noun an instrument for testing electrical equipment, which measures voltage, current and resistance

multinational
adjective involving many different countries: *a multinational business company*

multiple
adjective **1** having many parts
noun **2** a number formed by multiplying one number by another: *6, 9 and 12 are multiples of 3*
Word building: **multiplicity** *noun* a large number

multiply
verb **1** to increase in amount or number: *to multiply your savings by putting them in the bank | Rabbits multiply quickly.* **2** to add a number to itself a number of times to get a total or product: *Multiply 4 by 3 to get 12.*
Word building: Other forms are **I multiplied, I have multiplied, I am multiplying.** | **multiplier** *noun* a number by which another number is multiplied **multiplication** *noun*

multiracial
adjective having people of many different races or nationalities: *a multiracial society*

multitude
noun a great number or crowd: *a multitude of people*
Word building: **multitudinous** *adjective*

mum¹
noun an informal word for **mother**

mum²
adjective saying nothing: *to keep mum about the plan*

mumble
verb to speak softly and unclearly

mumbo jumbo
noun meaningless words, especially when thought to have a magical effect

mummy¹
noun an informal word for **mother**

mummy²
noun a dead body that has been specially treated to stop it from decaying: *Mummies were found in the pyramids of Egypt.*
Word building: **mummify** *verb* (**mummified, mummifying**)
Word history: from a Persian word meaning 'asphalt'

mumps
noun a disease caused by a virus which makes the glands around your mouth and neck very sore and swollen: *Mumps is a disease which can be serious if not properly treated.*

munch
verb to chew noisily: *Cows munch grass.*

mundane
adjective ordinary or boring: *to lead a very mundane life*
Word history: from a Latin word meaning 'of the world'

municipality
(*say* myooh-nuh-suh-<u>pal</u>-uh-tee)
noun a district which has its own local government: *The council collects the garbage from all houses in the municipality.*
Word building: **municipal** *adjective*: *the municipal library*

munitions
plural noun weapons and ammunition used in war

mural
noun a picture painted on a wall or ceiling

murder
noun **1** the crime of deliberately killing someone
Other words: **assassination, homicide, slaughter, slaying**
2 *Informal* a very hard or unpleasant job: *It's murder trying to comb the knots out of your hair.*
Word building: **murder** *verb* **murderer** *noun* **murderess** *noun* **murderous** *adjective*

murky
adjective dark and gloomy: *a murky cave | murky water*
Word building: **murk** *noun* **murkiness** *noun*

murmur

noun a whispering sound or conversation: *the murmur of the wind in the trees | the murmur of the children in school assembly*

Word building: **murmur** *verb* (**murmured, murmuring**)   **murmuring** *adjective*

Murri   (*say* mu-ree)

noun an Aboriginal person from northern New South Wales or Queensland

Word building: **Murri** *adjective*: *Murri traditions*
Word history: from the Kamilaroi language of New South Wales

muscle   (*say* mus-uhl)

noun **1** one of the parts of the body which give it the strength and power to move **2** strength or force: *You need to put some muscle into sawing wood.*

Word building: **muscly** *adjective*   **muscular** *adjective*   **muscularity** *noun*
Word history: from a Latin word meaning 'little mouse' (because some muscles have the same shape as a mouse)

muscle/mussel Don't confuse **muscle** with **mussel**, which is a type of shellfish that you can eat.

muse¹

verb to meditate or be lost in thought: *to muse on what might happen*
Other words: **contemplate, ponder, wonder**

muse²

noun one of nine goddesses who appear in stories of Ancient Greece and who were in charge of writing, painting and science

museum

noun a place where rare and interesting things are displayed
Other words: **gallery**

mush

noun **1** something thick and soft like porridge **2** *Informal* something very sentimental, such as a film or book

Word building: **mushy** *adjective* (**mushier, mushiest**)

mushroom

noun a type of fungus shaped like an umbrella which grows very quickly in damp soil and which you can eat

Word use: Compare this with **toadstool**.
Word building: **mushroom** *verb* to grow or spring up everywhere

music

noun **1** sounds combined together using melody, rhythm and harmony to express ideas and feelings **2** written notes and signs which represent sounds which can be sung or played on a musical instrument

musical

adjective **1** producing music or like music: *musical instruments | a musical voice* **2** fond of music or able to play an instrument or sing well

Word building: **musical** *noun* a play or film with a lot of singing and dancing   **musically** *adverb*

musician

noun someone who plays or composes music

Word building: **musicianship** *noun*

music sticks

plural noun two wooden sticks which are hit together rhythmically to make music, often used in Aboriginal music

Word use: They are also known as **song sticks**.

musk

noun a strong perfume produced by a type of deer

Word building: **musky** *adjective* (**muskier, muskiest**)

musket

noun an old-fashioned type of gun from which the modern rifle has developed

Word building: **musketeer** *noun* a soldier armed with a musket

Muslim

noun a person whose religion is Islam

Word use: Another spelling is **Moslem**.
Word building: **Muslim** *adjective*: *Muslim law*
Word history: from an Arabic word meaning 'submission' or 'someone who accepts Islam'

muslin   (*say* muz-luhn)

noun a soft, fine, cotton material

mussel

noun a type of shellfish which has two black shells hinged together and which you can eat

mussel/muscle Don't confuse **mussel** with **muscle**. Your **muscles** are the parts of your body which give it the ability to move.

must

verb **1** to have to: *I must tidy my room.* **2** to be definitely: *She must be nearly 90.*
noun **3** something that is thought to be necessary: *This new book is a must for all children.*
Other words: **essential, necessity, requirement**
Word use: This verb is a helping verb, always used with another one.

mustard

noun **1** a yellow-brown powder made from the seeds of a herb, which is used as a hot spice in cooking
phrase **2 keen as mustard**, very eager

muster

verb **1** to gather into a group: *to muster sheep | The soldiers mustered on the parade ground.*
noun **2** a gathering up or rounding up into a group
phrase **3 pass muster**, to come up to a certain standard: *Those dirty fingernails certainly won't pass muster.*
Word building: **musterer** noun **mustering** noun
Word history: from a Latin word meaning 'show'

musty

adjective smelling stale: *Femi opened the windows to air the musty room.*
Word building: Other forms are **mustier, mustiest.**

mutate

verb to change or alter
Word building: **mutant** noun a new type of organism produced by mutation **mutant** adjective

mutation

noun **1** a plant or animal which becomes different in appearance or nature because of a change in genes **2** the process of changing

mute

noun **1** someone who is unable to speak **2** something which can be put in or on a musical instrument to soften the sound
Word building: **mute** adjective silent **mute** verb **mutely** adverb

mutilate   (say myooh-tuh-layt)

verb to injure, damage or disfigure very badly
Word building: **mutilation** noun **mutilator** noun

mutiny   (say myooh-tuh-nee)

noun rebellion against authority, especially of sailors or soldiers against their officers
Word building: The plural is **mutinies.** | **mutiny** verb (**mutinied, mutinying**) **mutineer** noun someone who rebels or mutinies **mutinous** adjective

mutter

verb to speak or grumble in a low voice that is hard to understand
Other words: **mumble, murmur**
Word building: **mutter** noun

mutton

noun the meat from a sheep

mutual

adjective shared or common: *our mutual friend*
Word building: **mutuality** noun **mutually** adverb

muzzle

noun **1** the jaws, mouth and nose of an animal
Other words: **snout**
2 a small wire cage which can be fastened over an animal's mouth to stop it biting **3** the open front end of a gun
Word building: **muzzle** verb

my

pronoun the form of the pronoun **I** and **me** that you use before a noun to show that something belongs to you: *my new boyfriend*

myopia   (say muy-oh-pee-uh)

noun a condition of the eyes which stops you from clearly seeing things in the distance
Word building: **myopic** adjective

myriad   (say mi-ree-uhd)

noun a very great number: *myriad stars*
Word building: **myriad** adjective
Word history: from the Greek word for 'ten thousand'

myrrh   (say mer)

noun a sticky gum which tastes bitter but which can be used to make incense and perfume

mysterious   (*say* muh-<u>stear</u>-ree-uhs)
adjective puzzling or full of mystery: *a mysterious smile*
Word building: **mysteriously** *adverb*

mystery   (*rhymes with* history)
noun something that is puzzling or secret or can't be explained: *the mystery of UFOs*
Other words: **enigma, puzzle**
Word building: The plural is **mysteries**.

mystic   (*say* <u>mis</u>-tik)
noun someone who prays or meditates in order to know the mysteries of the universe
Word building: **mysticism** *noun*

mystical   (*say* <u>mis</u>-tik-uhl)
adjective giving a sense of spiritual mystery or wonder: *There was a mystical beauty in the landscape.*

mystify   (*say* <u>mis</u>-tuh-fuy)
verb to bewilder or puzzle
Word building: Other forms are **it mystified, it has mystified, it is mystifying.** | **mystification** *noun*

myth   (*rhymes with* pith)
noun an ancient story about gods, heroes and supernatural happenings, which may try to explain natural events like the weather, sunrise and sunset and so on
Other words: **fable, legend**
Word building: **mythical** *adjective*: *The bunyip is a mythical creature.*   **mythology** *noun* all the myths of a particular culture **mythological** *adjective*
Word history: from a Greek word meaning 'word' or 'speech'

myxomatosis
(*say* mik-suh-muh-<u>toh</u>-suhs)
noun a very infectious disease which kills rabbits

Nn

naan (*say* nahn)
noun a flat, round bread used in Indian cooking

nab
verb *Informal* to catch or seize suddenly

Word building: Other forms are **I nabbed, I have nabbed, I am nabbing**.

nachos
noun a snack made from corn chips with tomato, chilli, and melted cheese on top

Word history: from Mexican Spanish (spoken in Mexico)

nag¹
verb to keep on finding fault, complaining, or making demands
Other words: **badger, harass, pester**

Word building: Other forms are **I nagged, I have nagged, I am nagging**. | **nagger** *noun*

nag²
noun *Informal* a horse, especially one that is old or worn out

nail
noun **1** a small metal spike, usually with a flattened end, used to fasten pieces of wood together **2** the thin horny end of your finger or toe
verb **3** to fasten with nails

naive (*say* nuy-**eev**)
adjective simple, innocent and ignorant: *a naive comment*

Word building: **naively** *adverb* **naivety** *noun*

naked (*say* **nay**-kuhd)
adjective unclothed or bare: *a naked body* | *the naked truth*

Word building: **nakedly** *adverb* **nakedness** *noun*

name
noun **1** what someone or something is called **2** reputation or fame: *Catriona has made her name as a trumpet player.*
verb **3** to give a name to: *We named the baby Isabella.* **4** to mention by name: *The report named three prominent businesspeople.*

Word building: **namely** *adverb* that is to say **namesake** *noun* someone having the same name as someone else

naming ceremony
noun an occasion where a child is formally given a name, and where people are sometimes appointed to be their guardians

nanny
noun a person who lives in your house to look after your children

Word building: The plural is **nannies**.

nanny goat
noun a female goat

Word use: The male is a **billy goat** and the young is a **kid**.

nap
verb to have a short sleep

Word building: Other forms are **I napped, I have napped, I am napping**. | **nap** *noun*

napalm (*say* **nay**-pahm)
noun a substance which is mixed with petrol and used in flame throwers and fire bombs

nape

noun the back of your neck

napkin

noun **1** another name for **serviette**
2 another name for **nappy**

nappy

noun a piece of cloth or a pad of paper tissue fastened round a baby's waist and legs to soak up its urine and contain the waste matter from its bowels

Word building: The plural is **nappies**.

narcissism   (*say* nah-suhs-iz-uhm)

noun self love, especially love of your own appearance

Word building: **narcissistic** *adjective*
Word history: from *Narcissus*, a handsome young man in Greek myths, who fell in love with his own reflection in water and was changed into a narcissus plant

narcotic

noun any drug which can relieve pain and make you sleepy

Word building: **narcotic** *adjective*
Word history: from a Greek word meaning 'making stiff or numb'

narrate

verb to tell a particular story in speech or writing
Other words: **recount, relate, report**

Word building: **narration** *noun* story-telling
narrative *noun* a story   **narrator** *noun*

narrative   (*say* na-ruh-tiv)

noun writing which tells a story. See the 'Types of writing and speaking' table at the end of this book.
Other words: **tale**

narrow

adjective **1** not wide: *a narrow opening*
Other words: **constricted, cramped, restricted, tight**
2 only just succeeding: *a narrow victory* **3** small-minded and lacking understanding of other people or the world: *a narrow person*
Other words: **biased, bigoted, closed-minded, intolerant, narrow-minded, prejudiced**

Word building: **narrowly** *adverb*   **narrowness** *noun*

nasal

adjective **1** of or having to do with your nose: *a nasal spray* **2** sounded through your nose: *a nasal voice*

Word building: **nasality** *noun*   **nasally** *adverb*

nasturtium   (*say* nuh-ster-shuhm)

noun a garden plant with red, yellow or orange flowers and round leaves

Word history: from the Latin name for a type of cress

nasty

adjective **1** unpleasant or disgusting: *nasty weather | a nasty smell*
Other words: **awful, disagreeable, dreadful, foul, horrible, horrid**
2 unkind or cruel: *You were very nasty to my little brother.*
Other words: **disagreeable, mean**

Word building: Other forms are **nastier, nastiest**. | **nastily** *adverb*   **nastiness** *noun*

nation

noun a large group of people living in one country under one government

Word building: **national** *adjective*   **nationally** *adverb*

nationalise

verb to bring under public ownership or government control: *to nationalise the health system*

Word use: Another spelling is **nationalize**.
Word building: **nationalisation** *noun*

nationalism

noun **1** patriotism or love of your own country: *Their nationalism took the form of singing bush ballads.* **2** a strong wish for the growth, freedom and independence of your country or nation

Word building: **nationalist** *noun*   **nationalistic** *adjective*

nationality

noun membership or connection that someone has with a country: *I have Australian nationality.*
Other words: **citizenship**

Word building: The plural is **nationalities**.

native

adjective **1** of your birth: *your native land* **2** belonging to the place you were born: *native language* **3** belonging to the country it is in: *a native plant*
noun **4** someone born in a particular place: *a native of Adelaide* **5** one of the people who have lived in a country for hundreds of years: *a native of New Guinea* **6** a plant or animal in its own country

native species

noun a species of plant or animal which occurs naturally in an area: *The brushtail possum is a native species in Australia, but in New Zealand it is an introduced species and has become a pest.*

Word use: Compare this with **introduced species**.

native title

noun an Aboriginal or Torres Strait Islander person's right to land or water that they have maintained connection with

nativity

noun birth

Word building: The plural is **nativities**.

natural

adjective **1** found in or formed by nature: *the lion's natural habitat* **2** given by nature: *natural talent*
Other words: **inborn, innate, uncultivated, untaught**
3 real and without pretence: *a natural manner*
Other words: **straightforward, unaffected**
noun **4** **a** a note that is not a sharp or flat **b** the sign in music (♮) that is placed before a note to show it is a natural

Word building: **naturally** *adverb*

naturalise

verb to make a full citizen of a country

Word use: Another spelling is **naturalize**.
Word building: **naturalisation** *noun*

nature

noun **1** the world around us made up of earth, sky and sea, especially when untouched by human beings: *Lovers of nature enjoy bush-walking.* **2** the make-up and qualities of a person or thing: *The little children enjoy riding that horse because it has a kind nature. | The nature of glue is to stick.* **3** kind or sort: *These books are of the same nature.*

Word building: **naturalist** *noun* a person who studies nature

naught *(say nawt)*

noun Old-fashioned
1 nothing **2** destruction, ruin or complete failure: *to bring to naught | to come to naught*
phrase **3 set at naught**, to regard or treat as of no importance

Word history: from Old English *na* no + *wiht* thing

naught/nought Don't confuse **naught** with **nought**, the sign in maths (0) which stands for zero.

naughty

adjective badly-behaved
Other words: **disobedient, mischievous**

Word building: Other forms are **naughtier, naughtiest**. | **naughtily** *adverb* **naughtiness** *noun*

nausea *(say* naw-see-uh)

noun a feeling of wanting to vomit

Word building: **nauseate** *verb* **nauseous** *adjective*

nautical

adjective of or belonging to ships, sailors or sailing

Word building: **nautically** *adverb*

nautilus

noun a kind of squid or octopus with a spiral shell divided into many sections

Word building: The plural is **nautiluses** or **nautili**.
Word history: from a Greek word meaning 'sailor'

naval

adjective of or belonging to a navy: *a naval battle | naval uniform*

naval/navel Don't confuse **naval** with **navel**, the small, round hollow in your stomach.

navel

noun **1** the small round hollow in the middle of your stomach, which was where the umbilical cord was attached when you were born
phrase **2 navel orange**, a kind of seedless orange that has a hollow at the top rather like a navel

navigate

verb to steer or direct on a course: *to navigate a ship*

Word building: **navigable** *adjective* **navigation** *noun* **navigator** *noun*

navy

noun the part of a country's armed forces that is trained to fight at sea

Word building: The plural is **navies**. | **naval** *adjective*

NB

short for *nota bene*, Latin words meaning 'note well'

Word use: This is usually used in writing to make you notice a particular piece of important information.

near

adverb **1** at or to a short distance: *Stand near. | Come near.*
adjective **2** being at a short distance in place or time: *The shops are near. | Christmas is near.* **3** less distant: *the near side*
verb **4** to come close or to approach: *Our boat neared the wharf. | The storm is nearing.*

Word building: **nearby** *adjective*   **nearby** *adverb*

nearly

adverb **1** almost: *We nearly reached the top.* **2** closely: *nearly related*

neat

adjective **1** tidy and ordered: *a neat room*
Other words: **orderly, shipshape**
2 well thought out and put together: *a neat plan*
Other words: **clever, effective**

Word building: **neatly** *adverb*   **neatness** *noun*

nebula   (*say* neb-yuh-luh)

noun a cloudlike patch in the night sky, usually consisting of a group of stars

Word building: The plural is **nebulas.**
Word history: from a Latin word meaning 'mist', 'cloud' or 'vapour'

nebulous

adjective cloudy or vague: *a nebulous shape | a nebulous idea*

Word building: **nebulously** *adverb*

necessary   (*say* nes-uh-se-ree)

adjective **1** unable to be done without: *Water is necessary for life.*
Other words: **essential, indispensable, needed, required, vital**
2 that must happen: *It is necessary that you fill in all the boxes on the form.*
Other words: **compulsory, mandatory, obligatory**

Word building: **necessary** *noun*
(**necessaries**)   **necessarily** *adverb*

necessity   (*say* nuh-ses-uh-tee)

noun **1** something that cannot be done without: *A four-wheel drive is a necessity in the outback.* **2** the state of being poor: *Necessity caused them to steal.*

Word building: The plural is **necessities.** |
necessitate *verb* to make necessary

neck

noun **1** the part of your body that joins your head to your shoulders **2** any narrow connecting part: *the neck of a bottle | the neck of a violin*

necklace   (*rhymes with* reckless)

noun a string of beads or other ornament worn round your neck

nectar

noun a sweet liquid produced by plants and made into honey by bees

nectarine

noun a kind of peach with a smooth skin

need

noun **1** something that you have to have: *The immediate needs of the bushfire victims are food and shelter.*
Other words: **necessity, requirement**
2 a necessity brought about by a particular situation: *Do you think there is any need to worry about the fact that they are so late?* **3** a situation or time when you want something: *a friend in need*
verb **4** to have a need for: *You need help.*
Other words: **require**
5 to have to do: *I need to cut my nails for the netball match.*
Other words: **must, should**

Word building: **needy** *adjective* (**needier, neediest**)   **needful** *adjective*   **needless** *adjective*

need/knead Don't confuse **need** with **knead,** which means 'to press and push something with your hands':
The pastry chef kneaded the dough.

needle

noun **1** a small, thin, pointed tool, usually made of steel and with a hole at one end for thread, used for sewing **2** a thin rod for knitting, or one hooked at the end for crocheting **3** a pointer on a dial: *a compass needle* **4** a thin tube sharp enough to pierce your skin, used for giving injections **5** anything sharp and shaped like a needle: *a pine needle*

negative

adjective **1** saying or meaning no: *a negative answer* **2** minus or smaller than nothing: *a negative number* **3** having an excess of electrons: *the negative poles of an electric cell*
noun **4** an answer or opinion that says or means no **5** a photographic film which is used to make prints and has the light and dark of the picture reversed

Word building: **negate** *verb* **negation** *noun* **negatively** *adverb*

neglect

verb **1** to pay no attention to: *You mustn't neglect your piano practice.*
Other words: **disregard, forget, ignore, overlook, shirk**
2 to fail to look after: *to neglect a dog*
Other words: **abuse, maltreat**

Word building: **neglect** *noun* **neglectful** *adjective* **neglectfully** *adverb*

negligee (*say* neg-luh-zhay)

noun a woman's dressing-gown, especially one made of thin material

Word history: from a French word meaning 'neglected'

negligent (*say* neg-luh-juhnt)

adjective careless or neglectful

Word building: **negligence** *noun* **negligently** *adverb*

negligible (*say* neg-luh-juh-buhl)

adjective unimportant enough to be ignored: *The amount of juice spilt was negligible.*

Word building: **negligibly** *adverb*

negotiate (*say* nuh-goh-shee-ayt)

verb to arrange by discussion: *The government has negotiated a treaty.*

Word building: **negotiable** *adjective* **negotiation** *noun*

neigh (*say* nay)

noun the sound a horse makes

Word building: **neigh** *verb*

neighbour (*say* nay-buh)

noun someone who lives near you

Word use: Another spelling is **neighbor**.
Word building: **neighbourhood** *noun* **neighbourly** *adjective*

neither (*say* nuy-dhuh, nee-dhuh)

adjective **1** not one or the other: *Neither statement is true.*
pronoun **2** not the one or the other: *Neither of the magazines belong to me.*
conjunction **3** not either: *Neither you nor I will ever know the true story.*

Word use: Definition 3 is always used with **nor**.

neo-

prefix a word part meaning 'new' or 'recent': *Neo-Gothic*

Word history: from Greek

neon

noun a gas which glows when an electric current is put through it, and so is used in lights

nephew (*say* nef-yooh)

noun the son of your brother or sister, or of your husband's or wife's brother or sister

nepotism (*say* nep-uh-tiz-uhm)

noun the favouring of a relation or friend by giving them a job or promotion

nerd

noun Informal a person who does not have much social ability, often someone who spends a lot of time on the computer

nerve

noun **1** a fibre or bundle of fibres that carries messages from your brain to other parts of your body so that you can move and feel **2** courage, especially when you are facing a difficult situation: *You need nerve to walk a tightrope.* **3 nerves**, nervousness or shakiness: *I had an attack of nerves before the school play.*

nervous

adjective **1** excited, uneasy or frightened, especially about something that is going to happen: *I'm nervous about singing in front of the whole school.*
Other words: **agitated, anxious, apprehensive, edgy, fearful, jumpy, tense, worried**
2 having to do with the system of nerves in the body

Word building: **nervously** *adverb* **nervousness** *noun*

nest

noun a shelter built or a place used by a bird to lay its eggs and bring up its young

Word building: **nest** *verb* **nestling** *noun*

net[1]

noun **1** a material made of fine threads knotted or woven together with holes in between: *a mosquito net* **2** a fabric like this, made of cord or rope: *a fishing net* **3** a piece of net used in some sports, such as tennis
verb **4** to catch in a net
phrase **5 the net**, the linking of computers all around the world so that you can share information: *Let's surf the net!*

Word building: Other verb forms are **I netted, I have netted, I am netting.**
Word history: Definition 5 is a short way of saying **the internet**.

net²

adjective **1** not counting packaging: *The net weight of these baked beans is 250 grams.* **2** after expenses have been paid: *net profit*

Word use: Another spelling is **nett**.

netball

noun **1** a ball game played by two teams of seven. Players must not bounce the ball and they must try to 'shoot a goal' by throwing the ball into a ring on top of a tall post. **2** the ball used in this game

nett

adjective another spelling of **net²**

nettle

noun **1** a common weed with hairs on its leaves and stem, which cause a rash if you touch them
verb **2** to irritate: *My friend's criticisms nettle me.*

network

noun **1** a netlike arrangement of connected lines or passages: *a network of drainage ditches* **2** a group of radio or television stations, sometimes having the same owner, that can broadcast the same programs **3** a system in which computers in different places, often quite far apart, can be linked together and share information

Word building: **network** *verb* to link by computer network **networked** *adjective* linked on a computer network **networking** *noun*

neurotic

adjective on edge and behaving strangely, because of a disorder of the mind

Word building: **neurotic** *noun* a neurotic person **neurotically** *adverb*
Word history: from a Greek word for a type of nerve

neuter

adjective being neither feminine nor masculine

neutral

adjective **1** not taking one side or the other: *Sweden was neutral in the second World War.* **2** greyish or of no particular colour
noun **3** the position of gears in a car where they are not ready to be driven by the engine

Word building: **neutralise** *verb* to counteract or cause to have no effect **neutrally** *adverb*

neutron

noun a tiny particle which is part of an atom

Word use: See also **electron** and **proton**.

never

adverb not ever: *I'll never eat in this restaurant again! | I've never been to Uluru.*

never-never

noun desert country where hardly anyone lives

new

adjective **1** recently arrived, obtained or come into being **2** fresh or unused: *Turn to a new page.*

Word building: **newly** *adverb* **newness** *noun*

new/knew Don't confuse **new** with **knew**, which is the past tense of the verb **know**, to feel certain that something is true, or to have learned and understood it:
I knew all the answers.

news

noun a report of something that has just happened

newsagency   (*say* news-age-en-see)

noun a shop where you can buy newspapers, pens, magazines and books

Word building: **newsagent** *noun* someone who runs a newsagency

newspaper

noun a publication printed on large sheets of paper, which is put out at regular times, usually daily or weekly, and which contains news, comment, feature articles, and advertisements

newt

noun a small animal with a long tail that can live both on land and in the water

New Year

noun the time at the beginning of a year, when people celebrate the end of one year and the beginning of the next year

next

adjective **1** straight after this one: *Can I have the next ride?* **2** nearest: *the next room*
adverb **3** in the nearest place: *Can I sit next to you?*

next of kin

noun your nearest relation or relations

nib

noun the writing point of a pen

nibble

verb **1** to bite off small bits from: *I nibbled the chocolate.* **2** to bite gently: *The fish nibbled the bait.*

Word building: **nibble** *noun*

nice

adjective **1** delightful: *We've had a nice day.*
Other words: **enjoyable, good, splendid, terrific, wonderful**
2 kind or pleasant: *The new student is a really nice person.*
Other words: **agreeable, considerate, thoughtful**
3 showing accuracy, skill or exactness: *Zoltan hit a nice shot.*
Other words: **accurate, deft, skilful**
4 delicious: *This cake is nice.*
Other words: **appetising, delectable, luscious, scrumptious**

Word building: **nicety** *noun* (**niceties**) a fine or small point: *a nicety in the small print of the contract* **nicely** *adverb* **niceness** *noun*

niche (*say* neesh, nitch)

noun **1** a small hollow set into a wall: *A lovely statue stood in the niche.* **2** a place or position suitable for a person or thing: *Everyone has their niche in society.*

nick

noun **1** a small cut or notch
verb **2** to cut slightly **3** *Informal* to steal
phrase **4 in good nick**, in good condition
5 in the nick of time, at the last possible moment **6 nick off**, *Informal* to leave or disappear

nickel

noun a hard silvery-white metal

nickname

noun a name used instead of your real name
Word building: **nickname** *verb*

nicotine (*say* nik-uh-<u>teen</u>)

noun a poisonous substance in tobacco

Word history: named after the Frenchman, Jacques *Nicot*, who introduced tobacco into France in 1560

niece (*say* nees)

noun the daughter of your brother or sister, or of your husband's or wife's brother or sister

nifty

Informal
adjective **1** smart or clever: *a nifty trick* **2** stylish: *a nifty outfit*

Word building: Other forms are **niftier, niftiest**.

night

noun the time of darkness between sunset and sunrise

night/knight Don't confuse **night** with **knight**. A **knight** is a nobleman who pledged to serve and fight for a king or queen in Medieval times.

nightcap

noun **1** a drink, especially a hot one, you have before going to bed **2** a cap people used to wear to bed

nightingale (*say* <u>nuy</u>-ting-gayl)

noun a small bird known for the beautiful singing of the male, especially at night

nightly

adjective **1** coming, happening or active at night: *a nightly visit*
adverb **2** every night: *The play is performed nightly during May.*

nightmare

noun **1** a very frightening dream **2** any very upsetting or frightening experience

Word building: **nightmarish** *adjective*

nil

noun nothing: *The result of my efforts was nil.*

nimble

adjective **1** able to move quickly and easily: *a nimble acrobat* | *nimble fingers* **2** quick in understanding: *a nimble mind*

Word building: **nimbleness** *noun* **nimbly** *adverb*

nimbus

noun **1** a rain cloud **2** another word for **halo**

Word building: The plural is **nimbuses**.
Word history: from a Latin word meaning 'rainstorm' or 'thunder-cloud'

nine

noun **1** the number 9 **2** the Roman numeral IX

Word building: **nine** *adjective*: *nine candles* **ninth** *adjective*: *his ninth birthday*

nineteen

noun **1** the number 19 **2** the Roman numeral XIX

Word building: **nineteen** *adjective*: *nineteen players* **nineteenth** *adjective*: *their nineteenth wedding anniversary*

ninety

noun **1** the number 90 **2** the Roman numeral XC

Word building: The plural is **nineties**. | **ninety** *adjective*: *ninety students* **ninetieth** *adjective*: *Grandma's ninetieth birthday*

nip

verb **1** to pinch or take a small bite: *The puppy nipped my ankle.*
noun **2** a pinch or a small bite

Word building: Other verb forms are **I nipped, I have nipped, I am nipping**.

nipple

noun part of your breast and in women the part from which a baby may suck milk

nippy

adjective **1** very chilly or cold: *a nippy breeze* **2** active or nimble: *For eighty, he's still pretty nippy on his feet.*

Word building: Other forms are **nippier, nippiest**.

nirvana   (*say* ner-<u>vah</u>-nuh)

noun in Buddhism, the final state of happiness someone reaches when they are free from human emotions and worries

nit

noun **1** the egg of an insect such as a louse **2** the young of such an insect especially when it is living in human hair **3** *Informal* a foolish or stupid person

Word use: Sometimes **nitwit** is used for this definition.

nit/knit Don't confuse **nit** with **knit**, which means 'to make something out of long strands of wool, using a pair of long needles'.

nitrogen   (*say* <u>nuy</u>-truh-juhn)

noun a colourless gas with no smell, which forms part of the earth's atmosphere

Word building: **nitric** *adjective*

nix

noun *Informal* nothing

no

interjection **1** a word used when answering a question to express that a statement is not correct, or that you do not agree to a request or offer: *No, it's not a shark.* | *No, you cannot have any more chocolate.* | *No, thanks, I won't be able to come.*
adjective, adverb **2** not any: *I have no spare clothes with me.* | *He's not well but he's feeling no worse.*

No.

short for **number**

noble

adjective **1** belonging to the aristocratic or ruling class of a country: *a noble family*
Other words: **aristocratic, titled**
2 having high principles: *My teacher has a noble character.*
Other words: **honourable, lofty, moral, principled**
3 stately in appearance: *a noble monument*

Word building: **nobility** *noun* aristocracy **noble** *noun* an aristocrat **nobleman** *noun* **noblewoman** *noun* **nobly** *adverb*

nobody

pronoun **1** no person: *There was nobody in the playground.*
noun **2** a person of no importance: *He's a real nobody.*

Word use: Another word for definition 1 is **no-one**.

nocturnal   (*say* nok-<u>ter</u>-nuhl)

adjective **1** active by night: *Possums are nocturnal animals.* **2** done, happening or coming by night: *a nocturnal adventure*

Word building: **nocturnally** *adverb*

nod

verb **1** to move your head up and down slightly to show that you agree with something, to answer 'yes' to something or as a greeting: *Maya nodded when I asked if she was coming.* | *I nodded to my neighbour as we passed each other in the street.*
phrase **2 nod off**, to go to sleep

Word building: Other verb forms are **I nodded, I have nodded, I am nodding**. | **nod** *noun*: *He gave a nod.*

node

noun **1** a knot, lump or knob: *a lymph node in your body* **2** a joint in the stem of a plant, especially where a leaf grows

Word building: **nodal** *adjective* **nodose** *adjective*

nodule

noun a small rounded mass or lump

Word building: **nodular** *adjective*

noise

noun any kind of sound, especially a sound which is too loud or which you don't like
Other words: **clamour**, **commotion**, **din**, **racket**

Word building: **noisily** *adverb* **noisiness** *noun* **noisy** *adjective*

nomad

noun **1** a member of a group of people or tribe that moves from one area to another hunting, food-gathering or grazing their animals **2** any wanderer

Word building: **nomadic** *adjective*
Word history: from a Greek word meaning 'roaming' (like cattle)

nominate

verb to name as a candidate in an election: *I have nominated you as school captain.*

Word building: **nomination** *noun* **nominator** *noun* **nominee** *noun*

non-

prefix a word part meaning 'not': *nonfiction | nonflammable*

Word history: from Latin

nonagon

noun a flat shape with nine straight sides

nonchalant (*say* non-shuh-luhnt)

adjective calm and not worried: *The leader faced the angry crowd with a nonchalant air.*

Word building: **nonchalance** *noun* **nonchalantly** *adverb*

noncommittal

adjective not showing your opinion or decision so that you won't be held to it: *a noncommittal answer*

nonconformist

(*say* non-kuhn-fawm-uhst)
noun a person who refuses to accept the usual or expected ideas, customs or ways of living

Word building: **nonconformity** *noun*

nondescript

adjective very ordinary-looking, without any easily recognised qualities

none (*rhymes with* bun)

pronoun **1** not one: *None of my friends came to help.* **2** not any: *That is none of your business.*

nonentity (*say* non-en-tuh-tee)

noun someone of no importance: *He was a nonentity in the organisation.*

nonfiction

noun something written about real people and facts, rather than made-up stories

nonflammable

adjective not easily set alight or burnt

nonplussed (*say* non-plust)

adjective puzzled

Word building: **nonplus** *verb* (**nonplussed**, **nonplussing**)

non-renewable resource

noun something needed in everyday life like oil or gas for power which, once they run out, cannot be replaced or restored

nonsense

noun words that are silly or without meaning

Word building: **nonsensical** *adjective*

noodle

noun a type of pasta cut in long thin strips

nook

noun **1** a corner, especially in a room **2** any small, private or hidden place

noon

noun midday or twelve o'clock in the daytime

no-one

pronoun no person: *No-one was at home, so I wrote a note and slipped it under the front door.*

Word use: Another word for this is **nobody**.

noose

noun a loop with a sliding knot which tightens as the rope is pulled

nor

conjunction a word used after *neither*, or after a negative statement, to mention something else that is also negative: *I can neither sing nor dance. | I don't eat meat, nor does my brother.*

norm

noun a standard or model that you judge everything else by

normal

adjective ordinary or usual: *the normal way of doing it | normal behaviour*
Other words: **common, customary, general, regular, standard, typical**

Word use: The opposite of this is **abnormal**.
Word building: **normal** *noun*: *Everything is back to normal now.* **normalcy** *noun* **normality** *noun* **normally** *adverb*

north

noun the direction which is to your right when you face the setting sun or the west

Word use: The opposite direction is **south**.
Word building: **north** *adjective* **north** *adverb* **northern** *adjective*

nose

noun **1** the part of your face you use for breathing and smelling **2** a sense of smell: *This cat has a good nose for mice.*
verb **3** to move or push forward: *The car nosed through the flock of sheep.* **4** to interfere or pry: *He likes to nose into other people's business.*
phrase **5 turn your nose up at**, to reject something you don't like, especially when you really ought to be grateful

Word building: **nasal** *adjective*

nostalgia   (*say* nos-<u>tal</u>-juh)

noun a longing for the past and all the things that belonged to it

Word building: **nostalgic** *adjective* **nostalgically** *adverb*

nostril

noun one of the two openings of your nose

nosy

adjective interested in things that aren't your business

Word building: Other forms are **nosier, nosiest**. | **nosily** *adverb* **nosiness** *noun*

not

adverb a word which shows a negative or opposite: *I will not do that. | The movie was not very good.*

notable

adjective **1** important or worthy of noticing: *a notable success*
noun **2** an important person

Word building: **notability** *noun* **notably** *adverb*

notation

noun a way of writing down things like music or dance by using signs or symbols, such as notes or lines to stand for sounds or marks to stand for movement

notch

noun a small sharp cut on an edge or surface

Word building: The plural is **notches**. | **notch** *verb*

note

noun **1** something written down as a reminder to yourself **2** a short letter **3** paper money: *a $10 note* **4** importance or fame: *The mayor is a person of note in our town.* **5** notice: *Take note of what I tell you.* **6** a musical sound, or the sign or symbol you use to write it down on paper
verb **7** to write down **8** to notice or pay attention to

Word use: Another word for definition 3 is **banknote**.

noted

adjective famous or honoured: *a noted author*

nothing

noun **1** not anything: *I have nothing to do. | There's nothing left in the biscuit tin. | She had nothing to say.*
phrase **2 for nothing**, free of charge **3 next to nothing**, not much at all

notice

noun **1** a sign or note giving a warning or some information **2** a statement that an agreement of some sort is to end: *The landlady gave notice to her tenant to leave. | The boss gave a fortnight's notice to the workers because the company was closing down.* **3** interested attention: *The new film is worthy of notice.*

Word building: **notice** *verb* **noticeable** *adjective* **noticeably** *adverb*

noticeboard

noun a board where people put notes and general information for others to see, such as at a school, in an office, or in another public place

notify

verb to inform or tell, especially in an official way: *The School Committee notified the parents that the meeting time had changed.*

Word building: Other forms are **I notified, I have notified, I am notifying.** | **notifiable** *adjective* **notification** *noun*

notion

noun **1** an idea, often not very clear in your mind: *I have a notion of what life in the year 2030 may be like.* **2** a foolish or fanciful idea: *He's full of notions about ways to make a fortune.*

Word building: **notional** *adjective*

notorious   (*say* nuh-<u>taw</u>-ree-uhs)

adjective famous or well-known for something bad: *He's a notorious liar.*

Word building: **notoriety** *noun* **notoriously** *adverb* **notoriousness** *noun*

nougat   (*say* <u>nooh</u>-gah)

noun a hard paste-like sweet containing almonds or other nuts

nought   (*rhymes with* fort)

noun the symbol '0', or zero

nought/naught Don't confuse **nought** with **naught**, which is an old-fashioned word for 'nothing':
Don't be scared, it was naught but the wind.
It can also mean 'ruin', or 'complete failure', as in *to bring to naught* or *come to naught.*

noun

noun a type of word which names something, commonly divided into proper nouns like *Australia* and common nouns like *beauty* or *dog*

nourish   (*say* <u>nu</u>-rish)

verb to give enough food to encourage or ensure growth

Word building: **nourishing** *adjective* **nourishment** *noun*

novel[1]

noun a long imaginative story which fills a whole book

Word building: **novelist** *noun*

novel[2]

adjective new or different: *a novel idea*

novelty

noun **1** newness or strangeness: *the novelty of going to the beach instead of to the mountains* **2** a new or different experience **3** a new or unusual article in a shop

Word building: The plural is **novelties.**

November

noun the 11th month of the year, with 30 days

Word use: The abbreviation is **Nov.**
Word history: from a Latin word for the ninth month of the early Roman year

novice   (*say* <u>nov</u>-uhs)

noun **1** someone who is new to the type of work or job they are doing **2** someone who is living in a religious order for a time of testing before taking final vows

now   (*rhymes with* <u>cow</u>)

adjective at this time: *Don't wait till later, do it now!*

nowadays

adverb in these times, rather than in the past: *Nowadays, we use the internet as well as the library to do research for our projects.*

nowhere

adverb no place, not anywhere: *There's nowhere in the world with nicer beaches than Australia, in my opinion.*

noxious   (*say* <u>nok</u>-shuhs)

adjective **1** harmful or hurtful: *noxious gases* **2** declared harmful by law and meant to be destroyed: *noxious plants*

Word building: **noxiously** *adverb*

nozzle

noun the end of a pipe or hose through which you can spray water

nuance   (*say* <u>nyooh</u>-ons)

noun a slight variation of colour, meaning, expression or feeling: *the nuances of the game of cricket* | *the nuances of the pianist's performance*

nuclear   (*say* <u>nyooh</u>-klee-uh)

adjective **1** having to do with or forming a nucleus **2** having to do with or powered by atomic energy **3** armed with atomic weapons: *America is a nuclear power.*

nuclear disarmament
noun the getting rid of nuclear weapons from countries committed to making and storing them

nuclear energy
noun another name for **atomic energy**

nuclear power
noun **1** power created using the nucleus of an atom **2** a country which uses nuclear energy or nuclear weapons

nuclear reactor
noun a machine for producing nuclear energy

nuclear waste
noun dangerous substances remaining after the production of nuclear energy

nuclear weapon
noun any weapon that uses atomic energy

nucleus   (*say* <u>nyooh</u>-klee-uhs)
noun **1** the central part or thing about which other parts or things are grouped: *Keiko and Toshi were the nucleus of a new rock band.* **2** the central part of an atom made of protons and neutrons

Word building: The plural is **nucleuses**.

nude
adjective **1** unclothed or naked
noun **2** an unclothed human figure, especially one that an artist has painted

Word building: **nudism** *noun* **nudist** *noun* **nudity** *noun*

nudge
verb to give a small push to, especially with your elbow

Word building: **nudge** *noun*

nugget
noun a lump of something, especially of gold found in the ground

nuisance   (*say* <u>nyooh</u>-suhns)
noun someone or something that's very annoying
Other words: **annoyance, bother, pest, trial**

null
adjective **1** of no importance or use
phrase **2 null and void,** having no legal force or effect: *The contract was declared null and void.*

Word building: **nullify** *verb* (**nullified, nullifying**)   **nullification** *noun*

nulla-nulla
noun a heavy wooden club traditionally used by Aboriginal people in fighting and hunting

Word history: from an Aboriginal language of New South Wales called Dharug. See the map of Australian Aboriginal languages at the end of this book.

numb   (*rhymes with* sum)
adjective unable to feel anything: *My fingers were numb with cold.*

Word building: **numb** *verb*   **numbly** *adverb*

numbat
noun a small Australian marsupial which feeds on insects, especially termites. It has red and brown fur with white stripes on its back, a long bushy tail and a long pointed nose. It is endangered. See the table at the end of this book.

Word history: from an Aboriginal language of Western Australia called Nyungar. See the map of Australian Aboriginal languages at the end of this book.

number
noun **1** the sum or total of a collection of things: *What is the number of people coming?* **2** a collection or quantity, usually large: *A number of people came.* **3** another name for **integer 4** another name for **numeral 5** the particular numeral or figure given to something to fix its place in a list or series: *Our house number is 67.* **6** a song, especially on a concert program: *Hans will sing the next number.*
verb **7** to mark with a number **8** to count saying the numbers one by one: *We numbered off as we stood in line.*

numberplate
noun a flat metal strip which shows the registration number of your car

numeral
noun a figure or letter, or a group of figures or letters, which represent a number: *The number of days in the week is expressed by the numeral 7.*

Word building: **numeral** *adjective*

numerate
adjective having basic skills in maths
Word building: **numeracy** *noun*

numerator

noun the number which is written above the line in a fraction to show how many parts of the whole are taken: *In the fraction $\frac{3}{4}$, 3 is the numerator.*

Word use: Compare this with **denominator**.

numerical   (*say* nyooh-<u>me</u>-rik-uhl)

adjective having to do with numbers

Word building: **numerically** *adverb*

numerous

adjective very many: *Numerous people went to the concert.*

nun

noun a female member of a religious group living a life of religious devotion, usually in a convent

Word building: **nunnery** *noun* a convent

Nunga   (*say* nung-guh)

noun an Aboriginal person from southern South Australia

Word building: **Nunga** *adjective*: *Nunga traditions*
Word history: from an Aboriginal language of South Australia

nuptial   (*say* <u>nup</u>-shuhl)

adjective having to do with marriage or the marriage ceremony: *nuptial vows*

Word building: **nuptials** *noun* a marriage or wedding ceremony

nurse

noun **1** someone who looks after sick people, usually in a hospital **2** someone employed to care for children
verb **3** to look after in time of sickness: *to nurse a patient* **4** to hold in your arms: *to nurse a baby* **5** to look after carefully so as to help growth: *to nurse seedlings | to nurse an ambition* **6** to breastfeed: *My mum nursed me until I was one year old.*

Word use: Other words for definition 2 are **nursemaid** and **nanny**.

nursery

noun **1** a room or place for babies **2** a school for very young children **3** a place where young plants can be bought

Word building: The plural is **nurseries**.

nursery rhyme

noun a short simple poem or song for young children

nurture   (*say* <u>ner</u>-chuh)

verb to feed and look after when young: *to nurture children*

Word building: **nurture** *noun*

nut

noun **1** a dry fruit consisting of a kernel that you can eat inside a hard shell **2** the kernel itself **3** a small metal block with a hole which has a thread in it, enabling it to be screwed on the end of a bolt **4** *Informal* your head **5** *Informal* someone who is odd or foolish

nutmeg

noun a spice made from the seed of a tree that grows in tropical countries

nutrient   (*say* <u>nyooh</u>-tree-uhnt)

noun a substance that provides food and energy: *Vitamins and minerals are important nutrients.*

Word building: **nutrient** *adjective*

nutrition   (*say* nyooh-<u>trish</u>-uhn)

noun **1** eating or eating habits: *healthy nutrition* **2** the process by which food is changed to nourish our bodies

Word building: **nutritionist** *noun* **nutritious** *adjective*

nuzzle

verb to touch or rub with the nose: *The horse nuzzled me as I walked past.*

nylon

noun a strong material made from coal, which gives elastic threads that are useful in making fabrics or bristles and so on

Word building: **nylons** *plural noun* stockings made out of nylon

nymph   (*say* nimf)

noun **1** a goddess, pictured as a beautiful young woman living in the sea, woods or mountains **2** a young wingless insect

Nyungar   (*say* <u>nyoong</u>-ah)

noun an Aboriginal person from south-western Australia

Word use: Another spelling is **noongar**.
Word building: **Nyungar** *adjective*: *Nyungar culture*
Word history: from the Nyungar language of Western Australia

Oo

oaf

noun someone who is clumsy, stupid or rude

Word building: **oafish** *adjective*: *oafish behaviour*
Word history: from an Old English word meaning 'elf'

oak

noun a tree that bears acorns and is famous for its hard wood

Word building: **oaken** *adjective* made of oak

oar (*rhymes with* for)

noun a long pole with a wide flattened end, used for rowing a boat

> **oar/or/ore/awe** Don't confuse **oar** with the other three words that sound the same.
> You use **or** to connect alternative words, phrases or clauses:
> *I don't know which colour to choose — red, yellow or green.*
>
> **Ore** is a rock or mineral which is mined for the metal it contains.
> **Awe** is a feeling of great respect mixed with fear:
> *The men were in awe of her bad temper.*

oasis (*say* oh-<u>ay</u>-suhs)

noun a place in the desert where there is water and trees can grow

Word building: The plural is **oases**.

oath

noun **1** a promise you make, such as in a court of law, that what you say will be true: *She said it under oath.* **2** a saying which uses the name of your god or anything holy to give importance to your words

Word use: An oath as in definition 2 can offend people when it is done in anger or for silly reasons.

oats

plural noun a cereal which is used to make porridge and to feed horses: *Give the horses some oats.*

obedient

adjective following someone else's wishes or commands: *an obedient dog*

Word building: **obedience** *noun* **obediently** *adverb*

obelisk

noun a tall pillar of stone, put up as a monument

Word history: from a Greek word meaning 'a pointed pillar'

obese (*say* oh-<u>bees</u>)

adjective very fat

Word building: **obesely** *adverb* **obesity** *noun*

obey (*say* oh-<u>bay</u>)

verb to do as you are told

obituary (*say* uh-<u>bich</u>-uh-ree)

noun a notice, usually in a newspaper, saying that someone has died and which often includes a short account of their life and achievements

object (*say* <u>ob</u>-jekt)

noun **1** something which can be seen or felt: *The shelf was crowded with objects.* **2** the reason or purpose: *What is the real object of your visit?* **3** the person or thing which receives the action of a verb, as 'ball' does in *I hit the ball.*

phrase (*say* uhb-<u>jekt</u>) **4 object to, a** to say you don't like, or that you disapprove of, something: *I object to that idea.* **b** to argue against: *He objected to a picnic being held on a rainy day.*

Word building: **objector** *noun* someone who objects

objection

noun an argument against something

objectionable

adjective unpleasant or offensive: *objectionable behaviour*

Word building: **objectionably** *adverb*

objective

noun **1** something to work towards: *Their objective is to grow all the food they need.* *adjective* **2** real and not just in your mind: *Unicorns belong to the world of myth, not to the objective world.* **3** fair and free of prejudice: *He finds it hard to be objective.*

Word use: The opposite of definition 2 is **subjective**.
Word building: **objectively** *adverb* **objectivity** *noun*

objective case

noun the form of a noun or pronoun which shows it is the object of a verb, such as 'him' in *I can hear him.*

obligation

noun something which should be done out of duty or gratitude: *You have an obligation to be obedient to your parents.*

Word building: **obligatory** *adjective* required

oblige   (*say* uh-<u>bluyj</u>)

verb **1** to do a favour: *He will oblige.* *phrase* **2 be obliged**, to be grateful for someone's kindness: *I am deeply obliged to you.* **3 be obliged to**, to have to, out of duty or need, or by law: *He was obliged to change the tyre.*

Word building: **obliging** *adjective* **obligingly** *adverb*
Word history: from a Latin word meaning 'bind' or 'tie around'

oblique   (*say* uh-<u>bleek</u>)

adjective **1** indirect: *There was only an oblique reference to what had happened.* **2** slanting or sloping: *an oblique line*

Word building: **obliquely** *adverb*

obliterate

verb to wipe out or destroy: *The waves obliterated their footprints.*

Word building: **obliteration** *noun*

oblivious

adjective **1** forgetful or not remembering: *oblivious of her promise* *phrase* **2 oblivious of**, not noticing: *oblivious of the cold*

Word building: **oblivion** *noun*   **obliviously** *adverb*

oblong

noun a rectangle with two sides longer than the opposite two

Word building: **oblong** *adjective*: *an oblong box*

obnoxious   (*say* uhb-<u>nok</u>-shuhs)

adjective disagreeable or nasty: *an obnoxious person*

Word building: **obnoxiously** *adverb*
Word history: from a Latin word meaning 'exposed to harm'

oboe

noun a tube-shaped woodwind instrument with a double reed that you blow through

Word building: **oboist** *noun*

obscene   (*say* uhb-<u>seen</u>)

adjective indecent or disgusting: *obscene violence*

Word building: **obscenity** *noun* (**obscenities**)   **obscenely** *adverb*

obscure

adjective **1** dark or shadowy: *an obscure corner* **2** uncertain or unclear: *obscure meaning*

Word building: **obscure** *verb* to darken **obscurity** *noun*   **obscurely** *adverb*

observant

adjective watchful or alert: *The observant child noticed where the sweets were kept.*

Word building: **observantly** *adverb*

observatory

noun a building equipped with powerful telescopes for observing the stars, planets and weather patterns

Word building: The plural is **observatories**.

observe

verb **1** to see, notice or watch: *Observe the detail.* | *He just goes along to observe.*
2 to study: *He's observing the bird life.*
3 to keep or follow: *Observe the rules.*
4 to comment or remark: *'You're quite late',* *she observed.*

Word building: **observation** *noun*   **observer** *noun*

obsession

noun a strong idea or feeling which controls someone's behaviour

Word building: **obsess** *verb*   **obsessed** *adjective*   **obsessive** *adjective*   **obsessively** *adverb*

obsessive-compulsive disorder

adjective a confused state of mind where a person cannot stop thinking irrational thoughts and keeps repeating actions to try to get some relief

obsolete

adjective out of date: *an obsolete weapon*

Word building: **obsolescent** *adjective* going out of date   **obsolescence** *noun*

obstacle

noun something which is in your way or which holds you up

obstetrics

noun the type of medical practice that is concerned with caring for pregnant women before, during and after the birth of their babies

Word building: **obstetric** *adjective* **obstetrician** *noun*

obstinate

adjective stubborn or not willing to change your mind, even though you may be wrong

Word building: **obstinacy** *noun*   **obstinately** *adverb*

obstreperous

adjective resisting control in a noisy way: *obstreperous behaviour* | *obstreperous children*

Word building: **obstreperously** *adverb*

obstruct

verb **1** to block or close off: *A landslide obstructed the road.* **2** to prevent or make difficult: *She obstructed our efforts to open the gate.*

Word building: **obstruction** *noun* a blockage

obtain

verb to get or acquire: *She managed to obtain fresh bread.*

obtuse

adjective **1** stupid or slow to understand
2 having more than 90° and less than 180°: *an obtuse angle*

Word building: **obtusely** *adverb*   **obtuseness** *noun*

obvious

adjective clearly understood or seen

Word building: **obviously** *adverb* clearly
Word history: from a Latin word meaning 'in the way' or 'meeting'

occasion

noun **1** a particular time or event: *I remember the occasion when I met you.*
2 an opportunity: *I want to take the occasion to thank you.*

Word building: **occasion** *verb* to give cause for or bring about

occasional

adjective happening sometimes: *occasional showers*
Other words: **infrequent, intermittent, sporadic**

Word building: **occasionally** *adverb* sometimes

occult   (*say* <u>ok</u>-ult)

adjective having to do with so-called sciences, such as magic or astrology, which say they use secret ways to gain knowledge

occupant

noun someone who lives in or occupies a house or a room

Word building: **occupancy** *noun*

occupation

noun **1** your usual job or employment: *What is her occupation?* **2** the possession of a place, either legally or illegally: *The tenant is in occupation.* **3** the taking over of a country by force

occupy

verb **1** to fill or pass: *How do you occupy your time?* **2** to be in or live in: *Who occupies the house?* **3** to seize or possess by force: *to occupy a country*

Word building: Other forms are **I occupied, I have occupied, I am occupying.**

occur

verb **1** to happen: *Tell me what has occurred.*
Other words: **take place**

phrase **2 occur to,** to come into the mind of:
It occurs to me that you might not want to come.
Other words: **strike**

Word building: Other verb forms are
I occurred, I have occurred, I am occurring. |
occurrence *noun*

ocean   (*say* <u>oh</u>-shuhn)

noun one of the large areas of salt water
between continents, such as the Atlantic
Ocean or the Pacific Ocean

Word building: **oceanic** *adjective*

ochre   (*say* <u>oh</u>-kuh)

noun a yellowish clay used in paints and
dyes

ocker

Informal

noun **1** the Australian working man
thought of as not having much education
and with rather rough manners **2** an
Australian person who has the qualities
that people think of as being Australian,
such as good humour, helpfulness, and
being able to overcome difficulties

Word building: **ocker** *adjective* very Australian:
an ocker sense of humour

o'clock

adverb of or by the clock: *It will be twelve
o'clock in five minutes.*

octagon

noun a flat shape with eight straight sides

octave   (*say* <u>ok</u>-tiv)

noun **1** the eight note distance between
two musical notes of the same name but
different pitch **2** these two notes played
together

octet

noun **1** a group of eight **2** a piece of music
for eight voices or eight performers

October

noun the tenth month of the year, with
31 days

Word use: The abbreviation is **Oct.**
Word history: from the Latin name for the
eighth month of the early Roman year

octopus

noun a soft-bodied sea animal which has
eight arms with suckers on them

Word building: The plural is **octopuses** or
octopi.
Word history: from a Greek word meaning
'eight-footed'

odd

adjective **1** strange or unusual: *odd
behaviour*
Other words: **abnormal, atypical, peculiar,
weird**

2 unable to be exactly divided by two:
*Seven is an odd number, and eight is an even
number.* **3** part-time or casual: *odd jobs*
4 not matching, or left over: *odd socks* | *an
odd glove*

Word building: **oddity** *noun* (**oddities**) **oddly**
adverb

odds

plural noun **1** the chances of something
happening, such as a horse winning a race:
The odds are five to one on Black Prince. |
The odds are against you.
phrase **2 at odds,** in disagreement: *They
are always at odds.*

ode

noun a song or poem praising something:
an ode to love

odious

adjective hateful or disgusting: *He's an
odious character.*

Word building: **odium** *noun* hatred

odour

noun a smell: *an unpleasant odour*

Word use: Another spelling is **odor**.

oesophagus   (*say* uh-<u>sof</u>-uh-guhs)

noun the tube that connects the back of
your mouth with your stomach

Word use: Another spelling is **esophagus**. |
Another word is **gullet**.
Word building: The plural is **oesophagi** (*say*
uh-<u>sof</u>-uh-guy). | **oesophageal** *adjective*

of

preposition a word indicating: **1** contents
or substance: *a bucket of water* | *a lump
of coal* **2** cause or reason: *to die of
thirst* **3** distance or separation from:
*The house was within metres of the
beach.* **4** belonging, possession or
association: *the prime minister of Australia* |
the responsibility of us all

off

adverb **1** away from or unattached from something: *The lid was off the jar.* | *The handle came off.* **2** to or at a distance away: *The holidays are only two weeks off.* **3** less: *50 per cent off* **4** away from your school or your job: *I had to take two weeks off when I broke my leg.* | *Mum has three weeks off at Christmas.*

preposition **5** away from: *She fell off the bed!* **6** distant from: *off the main road* *adjective* **7** stopped or no longer working: *The radio is off.* | *Our agreement is off.* **8** *Informal* unwell: *I feel a bit off, I think I need some fresh air.* **9** bad or unfit for eating: *The milk's gone off.*
phrase **10 be off**, to leave

offal

noun animal intestines and other parts which are thrown away, or other organs such as the brain, liver and tripe which are used as food

off-colour

adjective **1** unwell or sick **2** in bad taste: *an off-colour joke*

Word use: Another spelling is **off-color**.

offence

noun **1** a wrongdoing or crime: *a traffic offence* **2** an insult, or other wrong: *an offence against decency*

offend

verb **1** to annoy or displease **2** to do wrong or commit a crime

Word building: **offender** *noun*

offensive

adjective **1** displeasing or disgusting: *an offensive book* | *an offensive smell* **2** insulting: *an offensive gesture* **3** attacking: *offensive movements*

Word building: **offensive** *noun* an attack **offensively** *adverb*

offer

verb **1** to put forward hoping that it will be accepted: *She offered the plate of cakes.* **2** to show willingness: *She offered to help.* **3** to bid or suggest: *He is offering $100.*
noun **4** a suggestion or proposal: *an offer of marriage* | *an offer of $10*

Word building: **offering** *noun* something offered

offhand

adjective vague or casual, sometimes in a rude way: *He nodded in an offhand manner.*

office

noun **1** a place where people work or do business, usually at desks **2** a place where you go to buy tickets or get information **3** rank or duty: *She holds the office of deputy manager.*

Word building: **officiate** *verb* to do the duties of any office

officer

noun **1** someone who holds a rank in the army, navy, air force or police force **2** someone chosen to do an important job in a particular organisation: *The society has to elect its officers.*

official   (*say* (uh-<u>fish</u>-uhl)

noun **1** someone with a rank or who has authority to do a particular job *adjective* **2** properly approved or arranged: *an official statement*

Word building: **officially** *adverb*

offline

adjective not connected to a computer network: *The bank's computers were offline for a couple of hours and there was chaos.*

off-peak

adjective having to do with a time when there is less activity or lower demand: *an off-peak hot water service*

off-putting

adjective discouraging or unfriendly: *The new student has an off-putting manner.*

offset

verb to balance the bad result of doing one thing by doing something else that has a good result: *We will offset our carbon emissions by planting more trees.*

Word building: Other forms are **I offset, I have offset, I am offsetting**.

offsider

noun a partner or friend

offspring

noun the young of a particular parent

often

adverb happening many times: *I often walk the dog before school.*

ogle

verb to look at, especially with sexual interest

ogre   (*say* o̲h-guh)

noun an imaginary monster of fairy tales and legends, that likes to eat people

ohm   (*rhymes with* gnome)

noun a measure of electrical resistance

Word history: named after a German scientist, GS *Ohm*, 1787–1854

oil

noun **1** a fatty liquid made from animal or vegetable fats, which is used in cooking **2** a thick black liquid made from petroleum which is used to run and care for machinery

verb **3** to cover or fill with oil

Word building: **oily** *adjective* (**oilier, oiliest**)

oilskin

noun a cloth treated with oil to make it waterproof so that it can be used for rain wear

ointment

noun a soft greasy mixture used to heal your skin

okay

Informal

adjective **1** all right or satisfactory: *Are you okay now?*

adverb **2** well or correctly: *The car performed okay.*

verb **3** to pass or accept: *Will you okay this?*

Word use: This is also written **OK**.

Word building: **okay** *noun* approval

okra

noun a tall plant which produces pods that are used in soups and chutneys

Word history: from a West African language

old

adjective **1** having lived for a long time: *an old person*

Other words: **aged, elderly, senior**

2 having existed for a long time: *old artefacts in a museum*

Other words: **ancient, antique**

3 aged in appearance: *He suddenly looks old.* **4** having reached a certain age: *five years old* **5** worn out: *I think it's about time these old clothes were thrown out* **6** of an earlier time: *in the old days* | *old girls of the school*

Other words: **former, past, previous**

Word building: **olden** *adjective* having to do with the past

old-fashioned

adjective belonging to an earlier time or style: *old-fashioned clothes*

oleander   (*say* oh-lee-a̲n-duh)

noun a poisonous pink or white flowering shrub with dark green leaves

oligarchy   (*say* o̲l-uh-gah-kee)

noun a type of government in which a few people have all the power

olive

noun **1** a tree which grows in warm countries, or its fruit which can be eaten or crushed for its oil

adjective **2** yellowish-green or brownish-green

ollie

noun a manoeuvre using a skateboard or snowboard in which the board is driven into the air from a flat surface without holding the board, often in order to perform a jump over stairs or other obstacles: *Jo can do a ten-stair ollie.*

Olympic Games

noun a big sporting competition between most countries of the world, held every four years in a different country

ombudsman   (*say* o̲m-buhdz-muhn)

noun an official whose job is to look into people's complaints against the government

omelette   (*say* o̲m-luht)

noun a food made of eggs beaten up and fried in a pan

Word history: from a French word meaning 'a thin plate'

omen   (*say* o̲h-muhn)

noun a sign of good or bad luck to come

ominous

adjective threatening: *an ominous silence* | *ominous clouds*

Word building: **ominously** *adverb*

omit

verb **1** to leave out: *You have omitted a word.*

Other words: **exclude, overlook**

2 to fail to do: *He omits to knock.*

Other words: **forget, neglect**

Word building: Other forms are **I omitted, I have omitted, I am omitting**. | **omission** *noun*

omni-

prefix a word part meaning 'all': *omnipotent*

Word history: from Latin

omnibus

noun **1** an old-fashioned word for **bus**
2 a book of collected stories or writings by
one writer or about one particular subject

Word building: The plural is **omnibuses**.

omnipotent (*say* om-<u>nip</u>-uh-tuhnt)

adjective having the power to do all things:
an omnipotent god

Word building: **omnipotence** *noun*

omniscient (*say* om-<u>nis</u>-ee-uhnt)

adjective knowing everything: *the
omniscient author*

Word use: The more usual word is **all-
knowing**.
Word building: **omniscience** *noun*

omnivore

noun an animal that eats both animal and
plant foods

Word use: Compare this with **carnivore,
herbivore** and **insectivore**.

omnivorous (*say* om-<u>niv</u>-uh-ruhs)

adjective **1** eating both animal and plant
foods: *Humans are omnivorous.* **2** taking in
everything, as with your mind: *She is an
omnivorous reader.*

Word building: **omnivore** *noun*

on

preposition **1** above but touching something
acting as a support: *on the table* **2** at the
time or occasion of: *on Sunday | on my
birthday* **3** about: *He asked my views on
watching TV.* **4** near or close to: *a house on
the coast*
adverb **5** on yourself or itself: *to put your
tights on* **6** tight: *to hold on*

Word building: **on** *adjective: The heater is on
already.*

once (*say* wuns)

adverb **1** at one time in the past **2** a single
time: *once a day*
phrase **3 once upon a time,** long ago

Word building: **once** *conjunction: We can leave
once I find my car keys.*

oncology (*say* ong-<u>kol</u>-uh-jee)

noun the branch of medicine which deals
with tumours

Word building: **oncologist** *noun*

one (*say* wun)

noun **1** the first number, 1 **2** the Roman
numeral I **3** a single person or thing: *to
come one at a time*

Word use: Something that is number one or
comes before all others is the **first**.
Word building: **one** *adjective: one apple | one of
our friends*

onion

noun a strong-smelling bulb vegetable used
in cooking and salads

online

adjective **1** directly linked to a computer:
an online printer **2** connected to the
internet: *I can't surf the net at home yet
because we're still not online.* **3** having a site
on the internet: *Macquarie Dictionary is
online. Have you checked out their site yet?*

onlooker

noun someone who watches something
happen: *A crowd of onlookers gathered
around the scene of the accident.*
Other words: **observer, spectator, viewer**

only (*say* <u>ohn</u>-lee)

adverb **1** alone: *Only one goldfish
remained.* **2** no more than: *If you would
only go away.*
conjunction **3** but or except: *I would have
gone, only you didn't want me to.*
phrase **4 only too,** very: *She was only too
pleased to come.*

onomatopoeia

(*say* on-uh-mat-uh-<u>pee</u>-uh)
noun the use of a word or words which
sound like what they are describing, such
as *crunch, splash* or *buzz*

Word building: **onomatopoeic** *adjective*

onset

noun a beginning: *the onset of a disease*

onslaught (*say* <u>on</u>-slawt)

noun a fierce rush or attack

onto

preposition to a place or position on: *I
moved the chairs onto the verandah. |
The cat leapt onto the table.*

onus (*say* <u>oh</u>-nuhs)

noun a responsibility or duty: *The onus is
on you to organise the dance.*

Word history: from a Latin word meaning
'load' or 'burden'

onwards

adverb in a direction ahead or towards a point in front: *The troops marched onwards to their camp for the night.*

Word use: Another word for this is **onward**.

ooze[1]

verb **1** to seep or leak slowly: *Gas oozed from the crack in the pipe.* **2** to give out slowly: *The wound is oozing blood.* | *She oozes charm.*

ooze[2]

noun soft mud, such as on the bottom of the ocean

opal

noun a valuable gem of various colours, streaked with red and blue

opaque (*say* oh-payk)

adjective not able to be seen through: *The water was muddy and opaque.*

Word use: Compare this with **transparent** and **translucent**.
Word building: **opaquely** *adverb*

open

adjective **1** not shut or locked **2** not limited or enclosed: *open fields* **3** not blocked or obstructed: *an open view* **4** friendly: *She has an open nature.* **5** able to be entered in, such as a competition, or applied for, such as a job
verb **6** to make or become open: *She opened the window.* | *The door opened.* **7** to begin or start: *She opened the book at page ten.* | *Has school opened?*
noun **8** a clear space: *Dinner is served in the open.* **9** a competition in which both amateur and professional athletes can take part

Word building: **opening** *noun* **openly** *adverb* **openness** *noun*

open-minded

adjective able to accept new and different ideas

opera

noun a play which is sung to music

Word building: **operatic** *adjective*
Word history: from a Latin word meaning 'service', 'work' or 'a work'

operate

verb **1** to work: *He can't operate the levers.* | *The escalator isn't operating.* **2** to perform surgery: *The doctor will have to operate on her leg.*

operating system

verb the central program in a computer which enables all the other programs to work

operation

noun **1** the way that something works **2** working order: *The lift isn't in operation.* **3** a medical treatment on someone's body, using surgery **4** a military mission

Word building: **operational** *adjective*

operative

adjective **1** working or functional: *an operative life of two years* **2** having force or effect: *The law is only operative in this State.*

operator

noun **1** someone who works a machine: *a lift operator* **2** someone who runs a big business: *the operators of a tourist resort*

opinion

noun what you think or decide: *My opinion is that we should all help.* | *public opinion*

Word building: **opinionated** *adjective* full of your own ideas

opium

noun a drug made from the juice of the poppy, which is used to relieve pain and to put you to sleep

Word building: **opiate** *noun* a medicine containing opium, that puts you to sleep
Word history: from a Greek word meaning 'juice'

opponent

noun someone who is on the opposite side to you in a fight or contest
Other words: **adversary, challenger, rival**

opportunistic

adjective making the most of a chance that presents itself, without any previous planning: *The money was left lying on the table so the theft was opportunistic.*

opportunity

noun a suitable time or occasion: *She never had the opportunity to sing at a concert.*

Word building: The plural is **opportunities**.

oppose

verb to resist or fight: *They opposed her marriage.*

opposite

adjective **1** completely different: *We hold opposite views on everything.* **2** facing: *She lives in the opposite house.*

Word building: **opposite** *noun* the contrary

opposition

noun **1** resistance or a fight: *They put up strong opposition.* **2** the opposing side: *She met the opposition in a debate.*

oppress

verb **1** to cause hardship to or weigh heavily upon: *Their poverty oppressed them.* **2** to be cruel to: *The soldiers oppressed their prisoners.* Other words: **tyrannise**

Word building: **oppression** *noun* **oppressive** *adjective* **oppressor** *noun*

opt

verb **1** to choose: *He opted to join.* *phrase* **2 opt out**, to decide not to join in

optical

adjective having to do with seeing: *optical glasses* / *optical illusion*

optician   *(say* op-<u>tish</u>-uhn*)*

noun someone who makes or sells glasses

optimise

verb to achieve the best result possible: *The team optimised their chances of winning by training very hard very early.*

optimism

noun hopefulness or the habit of expecting that things will turn out well: *She's not well but she's full of optimism.*

Word use: The opposite is **pessimism**.
Word building: **optimist** *noun* someone who looks on the bright side   **optimistic** *adjective* **optimistically** *adverb*

option

noun a choice or the right to choose

Word building: **optional** *adjective*

optometrist   *(say* op-<u>tom</u>-uh-truhst*)*

noun someone who tests your eyesight and, if necessary, makes glasses to improve it

Word building: **optometry** *noun*

opulent   *(say* <u>op</u>-yuh-luhnt*)*

adjective rich or wealthy

Word building: **opulence** *noun* wealth **opulently** *adverb* richly

opus   *(say* <u>oh</u>-puhs*)*

noun a work, especially a musical composition

Word use: The plural is **opera** but it is not often used for this.

or

conjunction showing a connection between words, phrases, and clauses expressing choices: *blue or red* / *in love or in hate* / *to be or not to be*

or/oar/ore/awe Don't confuse **or** with the other three words that sound the same.
You use an **oar** for rowing a boat.
Ore is a rock or mineral which contains a metal that is valuable enough to be mined.
Awe is a feeling of great respect mixed with fear: *The class was in awe of the teacher's ability to know when someone was misbehaving.*

oracle

noun **1** someone, especially a priest or priestess in ancient Greece, who answers difficult questions or reveals the future **2** a difficult saying given by such an oracle

Word building: **oracular** *adjective*

oral

adjective **1** spoken: *an oral test in French* **2** having to do with your mouth or taken by mouth

oral/aural Don't confuse **oral** with **aural**, which means 'having to do with hearing or listening'.

orange

noun **1** a round reddish-gold citrus fruit *adjective* **2** reddish-gold

orangutan   *(say* uh-<u>rang</u>-uh-tan*)*

noun a large ape found in Indonesia, which climbs trees

Word use: Another spelling is **orang-outang**.
Word history: from a Malay word meaning 'man of the woods'

orator

noun a public speaker, especially a skilful one

Word building: **oration** *noun* a formal speech   **oratorical** *adjective* **oratory** *noun*

orbit

noun the curved path or line of flight followed by a planet or satellite around the earth or sun

Word building: **orbit** *verb* to travel around

orchard

noun a paddock or farm where fruit trees are grown

Word building: **orchardist** *noun*

orchestra   (*say* <u>aw</u>-kuhs-truh)

noun a large group of musicians who play their instruments together

orchid   (*say* <u>aw</u>-kuhd)

noun a plant that grows in warm climates and the beautiful waxy flower it produces

ordain

verb **1** to appoint to the church as a priest or minister **2** to declare: *The king ordained that the prisoner be banished for life.*

Word use: The more usual word for definition 2 is **order**.

Word building: **ordination** *noun*

ordeal

noun a severe test or hardship: *The funeral was an ordeal for her.*

order

noun **1** a command

Other words: **decree, direction, edict**

2 the proper arrangement of things: *Restore order to your room.* **3** a request for goods: *an order at the shop* **4** the way things are placed in relation to each other: *Did they come in that order?* **5** working condition: *It's out of order.* **6** a division into a particular group or kind: *the order of mammals* **7** a religious group living under the same rules: *the Dominican order* **8** a lawful state or behaviour: *The police tried to restore order.*

Other words: **calm, peace, stability**

verb **9** to command or give an instruction

Other words: **bid, demand, tell**

10 to request or ask for: *Let us order tea.*

Word building: **orderly** *adjective*

ordinal number

noun a number which tells you the place of a thing in a series, such as *first* in *the first child* or *fourteenth* in *the fourteenth week*

Word use: Compare this with **cardinal number**.

ordinance

noun a rule or regulation: *an ordinance of the governor*

ordinary

adjective **1** usual or normal: *an ordinary working day*

Other words: **conventional, regular, standard**

2 of poor quality or inferior: *It looks rather ordinary.*

Other words: **average, mediocre**

Word use: The opposite of definition 1 is **extraordinary**.

Word building: **ordinarily** *adverb* usually **ordinariness** *noun*

ore

noun a rock or mineral which contains a metal that is valuable enough to be mined

Word history: from an Old English word meaning 'brass'

---

ore/or/oar/awe Don't confuse **ore** with the other three words that sound the same.

You use **or** to connect alternative words, phrases or clauses:

> *I don't know which colour to choose — red, yellow or green.*

You use an **oar** for rowing a boat.

Awe is a feeling of great respect mixed with fear:

> *The men were in awe of her bad temper.*

---

oregano   (*say* o-ruh-<u>gah</u>-noh)

noun a herb of the mint family, used in cooking

organ

noun **1** a musical instrument with pipes and one or more keyboards **2** a part of your body which has a particular job, such as your heart which pumps blood or your liver which makes bile **3** something which can be used to express a particular viewpoint: *This newsletter is the official organ of our society.*

organdie

noun a fine but stiff cotton material

organic

adjective **1** having to do with living things or their organs **2** having to do with the way parts are organised in a complete structure **3** relating to farming without chemicals: *They only use organic fertilisers.*

Word building: **organically** *adverb*

organisation

noun **1** the skilful arrangement or running of something **2** a group which runs something **3** something which is run or managed

Word use: Another spelling is **organization**.

Word building: **organisational** *adjective*

organise

verb **1** to form, especially into a group which works or does things together: *to organise a chess club* **2** to order or arrange neatly: *to organise my books* **3** to arrange or plan: *He organised the holiday.*

Other words: **coordinate, manage**

Word use: Another spelling is **organize**.

organism
noun a living thing: *She saw the tiny organism under the microscope.*

orgasm
noun the moment of greatest pleasure in sexual intercourse

orgy (*say* <u>aw</u>-jee)
noun wild or drunken feasting, or other uncontrolled behaviour
Word building: The plural is **orgies**.

orient
verb **1** another word for **orientate**
noun **2 the Orient**, the countries of Asia, east of the Mediterranean

oriental
adjective of or from an Asian country
Word use: You can also use **Oriental**.

orientate
verb **1** to aim or direct: *We have orientated the course to include everybody.* **2** to adjust or adapt: *You orientated yourself quickly in your new surroundings.*
Word building: **orientated** *adjective* **orientation** *noun*

orienteering
noun a sport in which you have to find your way as quickly as possible over a difficult course, using maps and compasses

origami
noun the art of folding paper into interesting shapes, first developed in Japan
Word history: from a Japanese word

origin
noun where something or someone comes from: *the origin of an idea* / *of Irish origin*

original
adjective **1** first or earliest: *The original models are in the museum.* **2** newly thought up or invented, especially without a model: *an original design*
noun **3** the earliest or first form from which copies are made: *He has kept the original.* **4** a work which has not been copied from anything else
Word building: **originality** *noun* **originally** *adverb*

originate
verb to start: *Who originated the idea?* / *The idea originated with Bill.*

ornament
noun an object or a decoration which is meant to be beautiful rather than useful
Word building: **ornament** *verb* to decorate **ornamental** *adjective* **ornamentation** *noun*

ornate
adjective covered with ornaments, showy or fine: *ornate chairs*
Word building: **ornately** *adverb*

ornitho-
prefix a word part meaning 'bird': *ornithology*
Word use: Another spelling is **ornith-**.
Word history: from Greek

ornithology
noun the study of birds and bird life
Word building: **ornithologist** *noun*

orphan
noun someone, especially a child, whose parents have died
Word building: **orphan** *verb*: *He was orphaned by a car accident.*

orphanage
noun a place where children without parents live

orthodontist
noun someone whose job is to straighten your teeth
Word building: **orthodontics** *noun*

orthodox
adjective **1** usual or accepted: *orthodox dress* **2** according to usual religious teaching
Word building: **orthodoxly** *adverb* **orthodoxy** *noun*

orthopaedics (*say* awth-uh-<u>pee</u>-diks)
noun the type of medical treatment that corrects or cures any problems or diseases of your spine and bones
Word use: Another spelling is **orthopedics**.
Word building: **orthopaedic** *adjective* **orthopaedist** *noun*

orthotic (*say* aw-<u>thot</u>-ik)
noun a device made to improve the position or way of moving of some part of the body, especially the foot: *He even had to wear his orthotics with his gym shoes.*

oscillate   (*say* os-uh-layt)
verb to move or swing to and fro

Word building: **oscillation** *noun*   **oscillator** *noun*

osmosis
noun the movement of liquid from a cell in which there is a strong solution across the cell wall to a cell in which there is a weak solution, so that in the end the solutions will be of equal strength on each side of the wall

Word history: from a Greek word meaning 'a thrusting'

ostentatious
noun meant to be impressive, but too showy: *He is an ostentatious dresser.*

Word use: Words of opposite meaning are **modest** and **discreet**.
Word building: **ostentation** *noun*
ostentatiously *adverb*   **ostentatiousness** *noun*

osteopathy   (*say* os-tee-op-uh-thee)
noun the method of treating disease by pressing bones and muscles in your body

Word building: **osteopath** *noun*   **osteopathic** *adjective*

ostracise
verb to keep away from, or send away, especially as a punishment

Word use: Another spelling is **ostracize**.
Word building: **ostracism** *noun*

ostrich
noun a large bird of Africa which runs fast but can't fly

other   (*say* udh-uh)
adjective **1** additional or extra: *He and one other person were there.* **2** different: *at some other school | I don't like it any other way.*

otherwise
adverb **1** if the circumstances were different: *I have to babysit, otherwise I'd come to the movies with you.* **2** in other ways: *It's a bit slow to load, but it's an otherwise awesome game.*

otter
noun a furry water mammal with webbed feet and a flattened tail like a ship's rudder

ottoman   (*say* ot-uh-muhn)
noun a low padded seat without a back or arms

ought   (*say* awt)
verb to be required, or to have a responsibility: *I ought to help Mum wash the car.*

ouija   (*say* wee-juh)
noun a board used in seances, which is supposed to tap out messages from dead people

Word history: from the French word for 'yes' (*oui*) added to the German word for 'yes' (*ja*)

ounce
noun a unit of weight in the imperial system equal to about 29 grams

our
pronoun the form of **we** and **us** that expresses ownership and is used before a noun: *our house*

Word building: **ours** *pronoun*: *Those clothes are ours.*

oust
verb to push out or expel: *The rebels ousted the king from the palace.*

out
adverb **1** away from: *The family ran out of the burning house.* **2** so that it can be seen: *After the rain the sun came out.* **3** not alight or burning: *The fire was out.* **4** not switched on: *The lights were out.*

outback
noun the remote parts of the country or bush, far from the cities and the coast

Word building: **outback** *adjective*   **outback** *adverb*

outboard
adjective on the outside of a boat or plane: *an outboard motor*

outbreak
noun a sudden beginning or happening: *the outbreak of war | an outbreak of measles*

outburst
noun a sudden bursting or pouring out: *an outburst of violence | an outburst of laughter*

outcast
noun someone who is not accepted by people in a society

outcome
noun a result or consequence: *the outcome of the elections*

outcry
noun a loud noise or an uproar: *a public outcry against nuclear bombs*

Word building: The plural is **outcries**.

outdoors

adverb **1** outside, in the open air: *Let's sit outdoors.*
noun **2** the natural world outside houses: *the great outdoors | I like to spend a lot of time in the outdoors.*
Word building: **outdoor** *adjective*: *outdoor furniture*

outer

adjective outside of, or on the outside edge of, something: *Jess lives in the outer suburbs of Melbourne. | The spider crept up the outer surface of the windscreen.*
Word building: **outermost** *adjective*

outfit

noun **1** a set of clothes or equipment needed for an activity: *A skiing outfit consists of skis, poles, boots and warm clothes.* **2** a business or group of people working together: *a military outfit*
Word building: **outfit** *verb* (**outfitted, outfitting**) to equip or fit out

outgoing

adjective **1** friendly and sociable: *He is outgoing and has lots of friends.* **2** departing or going out: *outgoing trains*

outing

noun a trip taken for fun: *an outing to the beach*

outlandish

adjective incredibly strange and unusual: *outlandish behaviour | an outlandish costume.*

outlaw

noun someone who has broken the law and is wanted by the police
Word use: This word was used especially of highwaymen and bandits in the old days.
Word building: **outlaw** *verb* to forbid by law

outlay

noun money, time or energy spent in getting something
Word building: **outlay** *verb* (**outlaid, outlaying**) to spend

outlet

noun **1** an opening or way for letting something out: *A power point is an outlet for electricity. | Stamping your feet is an outlet for anger.* **2** a shop or market: *an outlet for handcrafts*

outline

noun **1** a line showing the shape of something: *the outline of a circle* **2** a short description giving only the most important points: *an outline of a story*
Word building: **outline** *verb*

outlook

noun **1** a view: *an outlook over the park from the verandah* **2** an attitude or point of view: *a gloomy outlook on life* **3** what is likely to happen in the future: *The weather outlook for tomorrow is good.*

outpatient

noun a patient who comes to a hospital for medical treatment but does not have to stay

outpost

noun **1** a group of soldiers stationed away from the main army **2** a settlement far away from the main town: *a desert outpost*

output

noun **1** something that is produced: *to increase the output of a factory* **2** the information that a computer puts out

outrage

noun **1** something that shocks or offends people **2** a feeling of very strong anger
Word building: **outrageous** *adjective*

outright

adverb **1** completely or totally: *to refuse outright* **2** immediately: *to be killed outright*
Word building: **outright** *adjective*: *an outright failure*

outset

noun the beginning or start: *Our team looked set to win from the outset.*

outside

noun **1** the outer part or side: *to paint the outside of the house | She seems calm on the outside but inside she's angry.*
adjective **2** on the outer side or part: *the outside walls* **3** coming from somewhere else: *a business funded by outside money*
adverb **4** on or to the outside: *It's cold outside. | Go outside.*
phrase **5 an outside chance,** scarcely any chance at all
Word use: The opposite is **inside**.
Word building: **outsider** *noun* someone who doesn't fit in to a group

outskirts

plural noun the outer areas: *small farms on the outskirts of the city*

outspoken

adjective saying openly what you think even if it offends people

Word building: **outspokenly** *adverb*

outstanding

adjective **1** standing out from all others: *an outstanding swimmer* **2** not settled or finished: *outstanding debts*

Word building: **outstandingly** *adverb*

outward

adjective **1** able to be seen: *outward signs of fear* **2** outside or outer: *the outward surface* **3** away from a place: *a bus making an outward journey*
adverb **4** towards the outside: *to look outward over the sea*

Word use: Another form of the adverb is **outwards**. | The opposite is **inward**.
Word building: **outwardly** *adverb* on the outside: *outwardly shy*

outwit

verb to beat by being more cunning or clever: *If you can't be stronger than your opponents you must outwit them.*

Word building: Other forms are **I outwitted, I have outwitted, I am outwitting**.

oval

adjective **1** shaped like an egg
noun **2** an oval shape **3** a field for playing sport on

ovary

noun the part of a woman's body that produces eggs for reproduction

Word building: The plural is **ovaries**. | **ovum** *noun* (*plural* **ova**) the egg produced by an ovary
Word history: from a Latin word meaning 'egg'

ovation

noun cheers and enthusiastic applause: *The audience gave the orchestra an ovation.*

oven   (*say* uv-uhn)

noun a closed-in space, usually part of a stove, used for cooking, heating and drying

Word building: **ovenproof** *adjective* not damaged by being heated in an oven   **ovenware** *noun* ovenproof dishes

over

preposition **1** above in place or position: *Let's hang the streamers over the table.* **2** on top of: *I'll hit you over the head.* **3** across: *You drive over the bridge and then turn left.* **4** more than: *We had to walk over a kilometre to reach the station.* **5** during: *I'm having horse riding lessons over the holidays.*
adverb **6** through: *Read it over and tell me what you think.* **7** down or upside down: *Try to knock over the can with this stone.*

overall

adjective **1** from one extreme limit of a thing to another: *the overall length of the road* **2** with everything included: *What's the overall cost?*

Word building: **overall** *adverb*: *the problem considered overall*

overalls

plural noun a pair of trousers with a flap covering your chest, fastened by shoulder straps

overawe

verb to fill with fear and respect: *The presence of the famous actor overawed them.*

overbalance

verb to fall or trip over: *to overbalance while skating*

overbearing

adjective bossy and arrogant

Word building: **overbear** *verb* (**overbore, overborne, overbearing**) to overcome or force aside

overboard

adverb **1** over the side of a boat or ship into the water: *to fall overboard and have to be rescued*
phrase **2 go overboard**, *Informal* to be overly enthusiastic: *He's really going overboard about computers.*

overcast

adjective cloudy and grey: *overcast skies*

overcome

verb **1** to win the battle against: *to overcome an enemy | to overcome the fear of heights* **2** to make weak or helpless: *Weariness finally overcame the travellers.*

Word building: Other forms are **I overcame, I have overcome, I am overcoming**.

overdo

verb to do more than is sensible: *to overdo exercise*

Word building: Other forms are **I overdid, I have overdone, I am overdoing.** | **overdone** *adjective* cooked too much

overdose

noun a dose of a drug large enough to either kill you or make you seriously ill: *an overdose of heroin*

Word use: In informal language this is known as an **OD.**

overdue

adjective late or past the proper time: *overdue library books*

overflow

verb **1** to spill or flow over
noun **2** a flood: *the overflow of a river* **3** the area of land covered by water in times of flood

Word building: **overflowing** *adjective*

overgrown

adjective covered with weeds and long grass

Word building: **overgrow** *verb*   **overgrowth** *noun*

overhang

verb **1** to hang over: *A tree overhangs the cliff.* | *We can shelter where the cliff overhangs.* **2** to loom over or threaten: *Danger overhung their journey.*

Word building: Other forms are **I overhung, I have overhung, I am overhanging.** | **overhang** *noun* a part which sticks out

overhaul

verb to check, take apart, and repair: *to overhaul an engine*

Word building: **overhaul** *noun*

overhead

adverb **1** straight above: *birds flying overhead*
noun **2 overheads,** the costs involved in running a business

Word building: **overhead** *adjective* above your head: *overhead telephone wires*

overhear

verb to hear, especially by accident: *They were talking so loudly I couldn't help overhearing what was said.*

Word building: Other forms are **I overheard, I have overheard, I am overhearing.**

overlap

verb to partly cover: *Place the tiles on the roof so that one overlaps the other.*

Word building: Other forms are **they overlapped, they have overlapped, they are overlapping.** | **overlap** *noun: an overlap of ten centimetres*

overlook

verb **1** to miss or ignore: *to overlook a spelling mistake* | *I shall overlook your lateness this time.* **2** to look down over: *The house overlooks the park.*

overpass

noun a bridge for cars or pedestrians, which crosses over a busy road

overpower

verb to overcome by greater strength: *We overpowered the opposition easily.*

Word building: **overpowering** *adjective* very strong: *an overpowering perfume*

overrun

verb to spread or swarm over: *The Pied Piper got rid of the rats which were overrunning the city.*

Word building: Other forms are **I overran, I have overrun, I am overrunning.**

overseas

adverb over or beyond the sea: *to travel overseas*

Word building: **overseas** *adjective*

oversee

verb to supervise or manage: *to oversee workers*
Word building: Other forms are **I oversaw, I have overseen, I am overseeing.** | **overseer** *noun* a supervisor or person in charge

overt   (*say* oh-<u>vert</u>)

adjective not secret: *He treated me with overt hostility and anger.*

Word use: The more usual word is **open.**
Word building: **overtly** *adverb*

overtake

verb **1** to catch up and pass: *The police overtook the speeding car.* | *It is dangerous to overtake on a bridge.* **2** to come upon suddenly: *A storm overtook the yacht.*

Word building: Other forms are **I overtook, I have overtaken, I am overtaking.**

overthrow

verb **1** to defeat or put an end to by force: *The army overthrew the government.* **2** to throw too far: *The fielder overthrew the ball and it missed the wicket.*

Word building: Other forms are **I overthrew, I have overthrown, I am overthrowing.** | **overthrow** *noun*

overtime

noun extra time worked before or after the usual working hours: *to get extra pay for overtime*

Word building: **overtime** *adjective*

overture

noun **1** music played before the start of an opera, ballet or musical show **2** a first attempt to be friends with someone

overturn

verb **1** to turn over on its side, back or face: *to overturn the wheelbarrow* | *The car overturned.* **2** to reverse or turn the other way: *The High Court overturned the lower court's decision.*

overwhelm

verb to crush or bury

Word building: **overwhelming** *adjective*

overwrought (*say* oh-vuh-rawt)

adjective worked up with excitement or worry

ovulate

verb to release eggs from your ovary: *Women ovulate every month.*

Word building: **ovulation** *noun*

ovum (*say* oh-vuhm)

noun one of the cells produced by a female which can join with a sperm to develop into a new individual

Word building: The plural is **ova.**
Word history: from the Latin word meaning 'egg'

owe

verb **1** to have to pay back: *I owe you $2.* **2** to have a duty to give: *I owe her an apology.*

owing

adjective **1** due to be paid or given back: *the amount owing*
phrase **2 owing to,** because of: *I was late owing to the heavy traffic.*

owl

noun **1** a bird with large eyes and a hooting call, which feeds mostly at night on small animals like birds and frogs **2** a solemn-looking or wise person

own

verb **1** to possess or have for yourself
noun **2** something belonging to yourself: *She has a bike of her own.*
phrase **3 get your own back,** to have revenge **4 on your own,** alone and without help **5 own up,** to admit or confess

Word building: **own** *adjective* belonging to yourself **owner** *noun* **ownership** *noun*

ox

noun another word for **bullock**

Word building: The plural is **oxen.**

oxyacetylene torch

noun a device used for welding or cutting steel by burning a mixture of acetylene and oxygen in a special jet

Word use: Another name for this is **oxyacetylene burner.**

oxygen (*say* ok-suh-juhn)

noun a gas with no colour or smell which is an essential part of the air we breathe

oyster

noun a shellfish you can eat, often found clinging to rocks

Oz

noun Informal Australia

Word use: You can also use **oz.**

ozone

noun a poisonous form of oxygen which is found in the air in tiny quantities, formed when lightning passes through the atmosphere

Word history: from a Greek word meaning 'smell'

ozone depletion

noun a thinning in the ozone layer above the earth caused by chemicals in the air breaking down and releasing chlorine gas which destroys the ozone

ozone layer

noun a layer of ozone in one of the outer parts of the atmosphere, which partly blocks the harmful rays of the sun

Word use: Another word for this is **ozonosphere.**

Pp

pace

noun **1** a single step or the distance covered by it **2** speed or rate of movement

verb **3** to set the pace for: *A car will go beside the runners to pace them.* **4** to walk with regular steps: *He paced backwards and forwards.* **5** to measure by paces: *We paced the oval and found it to be about 50 metres long.*

phrase **6 put someone through their paces**, to make someone perform or show their abilities

pacemaker

noun **1** someone or something that sets the pace usually in a race **2** a medical instrument placed in someone's body when their heart is diseased and needs help to keep it beating at the right rate

pacific (say puh-<u>sif</u>-ik)

adjective peaceful

Word use: The more usual word is **peace-loving**.
Word building: **pacification** noun

pacifism (say <u>pas</u>-uh-fiz-uhm)

noun opposition to war or violence of any kind

Word building: **pacifist** noun

pacify (say <u>pas</u>-uh-fuy)

verb to make peaceful or calm: *She quickly pacified the frightened horse.*

Word building: Other forms are **I pacified, I have pacified, I am pacifying**.

pack

noun **1** a parcel or bundle of things wrapped or tied up **2** a load carried on the back of people or animals: *The hikers put their packs on.* **3** a group of animals living and hunting together: *a pack of wolves* **4** a group of people or things: *a pack of thieves | a pack of lies* **5** a complete set: *a pack of playing cards*

verb **6** to put into a suitcase, parcel or box
Other words: **cram, fill, stow**
7 to press together or crowd: *The people packed into the hall.*

phrase **8 pack off**, to send away in a hurry: *Dad packed us off to school.*

Word building: **packer** noun a person or machine that packs   **packed** adjective

package

noun a parcel or a bundle
Other words: **pack, packet**
Word building: **package** verb

packet

noun a small pack or package of anything

pact

noun an agreement: *The two friends made a pact to help each other.*

pad¹

noun **1** a wad or mass of soft material used to give comfort, protection or shape to something **2** a number of sheets of paper held together at one edge **3** a soft block of material soaked in ink used for inking a rubber stamp **4** the soft, cushion-like part on the underside of the feet of animals like dogs, foxes, and so on **5** a flat area that helicopters, and sometimes spaceships, take off from

Word use: Another term for definition 2 is **writing pad**.
Word building: **pad** verb (**padded, padding**)

pad[2]

verb to walk with soft footsteps: *I'm padding around trying not to wake anyone.*

Word building: Other forms are **I padded, I have padded, I am padding.**

paddle[1]

noun a short oar which you use in guiding a canoe through the water

Word building: **paddle** *verb*

paddle[2]

verb to walk or play with bare feet in shallow water

paddock

noun a large area of land which has been fenced and is usually used for grazing sheep or other animals

pademelon   (*say* pad-ee-mel-uhn)

noun a type of small wallaby

padlock

noun a removable lock with a curved metal bar which passes through something and is then snapped shut

paediatrics   (*say* pee-dee-at-riks)

noun the study and treatment of the diseases and illnesses of young children

Word use: Another spelling is **pediatrics.**
Word building: **paediatrician** (*say* pee-dee-uh-trish-uhn) *noun* a doctor who specialises in children's illnesses **paediatric** *adjective*

paedophile

(*say* ped-uh-fuyl, peed-uh-fuyl)
noun an adult who engages in sexual activities with children

pagan   (*say* pay-guhn)

noun someone who does not follow one of the major accepted religions

Word building: **pagan** *adjective* **paganism** *noun*

page[1]

noun **1** one of the sheets of paper making up a book, magazine, letter, and so on **2** one side of one of these sheets

page[2]

noun **1** a uniformed boy employee of a hotel or something similar
verb **2** to try to find someone in a hotel, hospital, shop, and so on by calling out their name on a microphone or public address system

pageant   (*say* paj-uhnt)

noun **1** a colourful public show, often including a procession of people in costume **2** any showy display

Word building: **pageantry** *noun*

pagoda   (*say* puh-goh-duh)

noun a sacred building or temple shaped like a tower and usually found in eastern countries such as India and China

pail

noun another word for **bucket**

pail/pale Don't confuse **pail** with **pale**, which means 'whitish, colourless or not very bright'.

pain

noun **1** hurt felt in a part of your body when you are injured or sick
Other words: **ache, discomfort**
2 suffering felt when you are unhappy
Other words: **affliction, distress**
3 pains, very careful efforts: *Great pains were taken to make the wedding a happy occasion.*
Other words: **care, trouble**
verb **4** to cause pain or suffering to
Other words: **afflict, distress, hurt, torment, upset**
phrase **5 a pain in the neck**, *Informal* someone or something annoying or unpleasant

Word building: **painful** *adjective* **painfully** *adverb* **painless** *adjective* **painlessly** *adverb*

pain/pane Don't confuse **pain** with **pane**, which is a single plate or sheet of glass, usually in a window.

painkiller

noun a medicine which lessens pain

painstaking

adjective extremely careful: *painstaking work*

paint

noun **1** a liquid colouring substance that you can put on a surface to give it colour
verb **2** to make a picture of someone or something using paint **3** to cover with paint: *She painted the ceiling red.*

Word building: **painting** *noun*

painter[1]

noun **1** an artist who paints pictures **2** someone whose work is painting walls, fences, and so on

painter²

noun a rope for tying a boat to a ship, wharf, and so on

pair

noun **1** two things of the same kind that go together: *a pair of shoes* **2** a combination of two parts joined together to make a single thing: *a pair of scissors* **3** two people, things or animals thought of as connected to each other in some way: *a happily married pair*

Word building: The plural is **pairs** or **pair**.
Word history: from a Latin word meaning 'equal'

pair/pear/pare Don't confuse **pair** with **pear** or **pare**.

A **pear** is a kind of fruit.

You **pare** an apple when you peel off the skin.

pal

noun *Informal* a friend

Word building: **pally** *adjective* friendly
Word history: from a Gypsy word meaning 'brother'

palace

noun the official home of a king, queen, bishop or other very important person

palatable (*say* pal-uh-tuh-buhl)

adjective pleasant to taste

palate (*say* pal-uht)

noun **1** the roof of your mouth **2** the sense of taste

palatial (*say* puh-lay-shuhl)

adjective like a palace

Word building: **palatially** *adverb*

pale

adjective **1** having a whitish or colourless appearance: *a pale face* **2** not very bright in colour
verb **3** to become pale **4** to become less in importance or strength: *Her unhappiness paled beside that of her friend.*

Word building: **palely** *adverb* **paleness** *noun*

pale/pail Don't confuse **pale** with **pail**, which is another word for 'bucket'.

palette (*say* pal-uht)

noun a thin board, usually with a thumb hole at one end, used by painters to mix colours on

palindrome (*say* pal-uhn-drohm)

noun a word or sentence which reads the same either backwards or forwards, such as the sentence *Madam, I'm Adam.*

Word history: from a Greek word meaning 'running back'

paling (*say* pay-ling)

noun a long pointed piece of wood, often used to build a fence

palisade (*say* pal-uh-sayd)

noun a fence of tall pointed sticks set firmly in the ground as a defence around a fort or camp

pall¹ (*say* pawl)

noun **1** a cloth for spreading over a coffin **2** something that covers with darkness or gloominess: *A pall of smoke hung over the city.*

pall² (*say* pawl)

verb to become tiring or boring

pallbearer

noun someone who carries the coffin at a funeral

pallet

noun **1** a tool with a flat blade and a handle used for shaping and smoothing in pottery **2** a movable platform on which things are placed when being stored or moved from place to place in a factory

pallid

adjective pale or lacking in colour

Word building: **pallor** *noun* unusual paleness caused by fear, illness, and so on

palm¹ (*say* pahm)

noun the part of the inside of your hand that reaches from your wrist to the beginning of your fingers

palm² (*say* pahm)

noun a tall plant with no branches, but a crown of large fan-shaped leaves at the top

palmistry (*say* pah-muh-stree)

noun the art of telling someone's fortune or character by the length and pattern of the lines on the palm of their hand

Word building: **palmist** *noun* someone who reads palms

palmtop (*say* pahm-top)

noun a small personal computer that can be held in the hand

palomino   (*say* pal-uh-<u>mee</u>-noh)

noun a tan or cream-coloured horse with a white mane and tail

Word use: Another spelling is **palamino**.
Word building: The plural is **palominos**.
Word history: from a Spanish word meaning 'like a dove'

palpitate

verb **1** to beat much faster than normal: *Her heart was palpitating with the effort of the long run.* **2** to shake slightly or to tremble: *He palpitated with fear.*

Word building: **palpitation** *noun*

palsy   (*say* <u>pawl</u>-zee)

noun another word for **paralysis**

paltry   (*say* <u>pawl</u>-tree)

adjective small or worthless: *a paltry sum of money | a paltry coward*

pamper

verb to treat too kindly: *He pampers the dogs by giving them beef ravioli.*

pamphlet   (*say* <u>pam</u>-fluht)

noun **1** a very small paper-covered book **2** a single sheet of paper with advertisements printed on it, which is handed out to you or put in your letterbox

Word building: **pamphleteer** *noun* someone who writes pamphlets

pan

noun **1** a broad, shallow, open dish, which is usually used for cooking **2** any container shaped liked this: *Gold can be separated from gravel and sand by washing it in a pan.*
verb **3** to wash gravel or sand in a pan to separate gold or other heavy metals **4** *Informal* to criticise severely: *The critics panned the new film.*

Word building: Other verb forms are **I panned, I have panned, I am panning.**

pancake

noun a thin flat cake made of batter cooked in a frying pan

pancreas   (*say* <u>pan</u>-kree-uhs)

noun a gland near your stomach which produces important hormones and helps your digestion

Word building: **pancreatic** *adjective*: *pancreatic juices*

panda

noun a large, black-and-white, bear-like animal which is found mainly in China

pandemonium

(*say* pan-duh-<u>moh</u>-nee-uhm)
noun wild and noisy confusion

Word history: from *Pandemonium*, the name the poet John Milton (1608–74) gave to the capital of Hell

pander

verb If you **pander** to someone, you let them have their way: *I think that my parents pander to my little sister.*

Word building: **panderer** *noun*

pane

noun a single plate or sheet of glass, usually part of a window

pane/pain Don't confuse **pane** with **pain**, which is the hurt or suffering you feel when you are injured, sick or unhappy.

panel

noun **1** a separate section set into a ceiling, door or wall, that is sometimes raised above or sunk below the main surface **2** a thin flat piece of wood **3** a separate section of material set into a dress **4** a board or section of a machine on which controls are fixed: *the instrument panel of a car* **5** a group of people selected to form a jury, or brought together to discuss matters, judge competitions and so on

Word building: **panel** *verb* (**panelled, panelling**) **panellist** *noun* a member of a small group formed to discuss things, often on TV   **panelling** *noun*

pang

noun a sudden, short, sharp feeling of pain

panic

noun **1** a sudden terror, sometimes without an obvious reason
verb **2** to feel or cause to panic: *She panicked when she saw the gun. | The falling branch panicked the horse.*

Word building: Other verb forms are **I panicked, I have panicked, I am panicking.** | **panicky** *adjective*   **panic-stricken** *adjective* **panic-struck** *adjective*
Word history: from a Greek word meaning 'having to do with or caused by *Pan*', the god of the forests in Greek myths

panorama   (*say* pan-uh-<u>rah</u>-muh)
noun **1** a view over a wide area
2 a continually changing scene: *the panorama of city life*
Word building: **panoramic** *adjective*

panpipe
noun a musical instrument made up of pipes of different lengths which are played by blowing across their open ends

pansy
noun a garden plant with white, yellow or purple flowers
Word building: The plural is **pansies**.

pant
verb **1** to breathe hard and quickly because of effort or emotion
noun **2** a sudden short breath
Word building: **pantingly** *adverb*

panther
noun a leopard, especially a black one
Word use: The male is a **panther**, the female is a **pantheress** and the young is a **cub**.

pantihose
noun women's tights, usually made out of stocking material
Word use: This word is always used as a plural, with a plural verb: *My pantihose have a ladder in them.*

pantomime
noun a play in which the actors use actions and not words to tell the story
Other words: **mime**

pantry
noun a room or cupboard in which food is kept
Word building: The plural is **pantries**.
Word history: from a Latin word meaning 'bread'

pants
plural noun **1** another name for **trousers**
2 underpants, especially women's

papacy   (*say* <u>pay</u>-puh-see)
noun **1** the office or position of the pope in the Roman Catholic church **2** the period during which a particular pope rules
Word use: The plural is **papacies**.

papal   (*say* <u>pay</u>-puhl)
adjective having to do with the pope: *papal authority*

paparazzo   (*say* pa-puh-<u>raht</u>-soh, pah-puh-<u>raht</u>-soh)
noun a newspaper photographer who persistently seeks celebrities in order to photograph them and sell the photographs to the media
Word building: The plural is **paparazzi**.

papaya   (*say* puh-<u>puy</u>-uh)
noun a pawpaw, especially of the smaller kind with reddish-pink flesh

paper
noun **1** a material made from straw, wood, and so on, usually in thin sheets for writing or printing on, or wrapping things in **2** a newspaper **3** a written examination **4** **papers**, documents identifying who you are, what country you come from and so on

paperback
noun a book with a soft paper cover, usually cheaper than one with a hard cover

papier-mâché   (*say* pay-puh-<u>mash</u>-ay)
noun a substance made of paper pulp sometimes mixed with glue and other materials and used when wet to make models, boxes, and so on which become hard and strong when dry
Word history: from a French word meaning 'chewed paper'

pappadum
noun a thin, crisp, Indian wafer bread, made from spiced potato or rice flour
Word use: Other spellings are **pappadam** or **poppadum**.

paprika   (*say* <u>pap</u>-ri-kuh, puh-<u>pree</u>-kuh)
noun powder made from a red pepper, used as a spice

papyrus   (*say* puh-<u>puy</u>-ruhs)
noun **1** a tall water plant **2** material for writing on made out of this plant **3** an ancient document written on this material
Word building: The plural is **papyri** (*say* puh-<u>puy</u>-ruy).

par
noun **1** an equal level: *Her tennis playing is on a par with her sister's.* **2** an average or normal amount: *below par / above par*

parable   (*say* <u>pa</u>-ruh-buhl)
noun a short story used to teach a truth or moral lesson

parabola   (*say* puh-<u>rab</u>-uh-luh)
noun a special kind of even curve, like the path of an object when it is thrown forward into the air and falls back to the earth
Word use: This word is used in geometry.
Word building: **parabolic** *adjective*: *parabolic equations*

parachute   (*say* <u>pa</u>-ruh-shooht)
noun a large piece of cloth shaped like an umbrella and used to slow down the fall of someone jumping from an aircraft
Word building: **parachute** *verb*   **parachutist** *noun*

parade
noun **1** a gathering of troops, scouts, and so on for inspection or display **2** a group of people marching in the street to celebrate something
Other words: **march, pageant, procession**

paradigm   (*say* <u>pa</u>-ruh-duym)
noun a pattern or example

paradise
noun **1** heaven **2** a place of great beauty or delight
Word history: from a Persian word meaning 'enclosure'

paradox
noun **1** a statement which is true although it contains two seemingly opposite ideas, such as the statement 'You have to be cruel to be kind' **2** someone or something which seems to show contradictions
Word building: The plural is **paradoxes**. | **paradoxical** *adjective*   **paradoxically** *adverb*

paragon   (*say* <u>pa</u>-ruh-guhn)
noun someone or something good enough to copy: *She is a paragon of virtue.*

paragraph
noun a section of writing dealing with a particular subject or point, beginning on a new line

parakeet
noun a kind of small parrot, such as the budgerigar, usually with a long pointed tail

parallel   (*say* <u>pa</u>-ruh-lel)
adjective **1** being the same distance from each other at every point: *A railway track is made up of two parallel lines.*
noun **2** a line parallel with another **3** a comparison showing likeness: *You can draw a parallel between her and many great musicians before her.*

parallelogram   (*say* pa-ruh-<u>lel</u>-uh-gram)
noun a four-sided figure whose opposite sides are parallel to each other

parallel universe
noun another world that some people imagine might exist in another space and time next to our own world

paralysis   (*say* puh-<u>ral</u>-uh-suhs)
noun an inability to move
Word building: The plural is **paralyses** (*say* puh-<u>ral</u>-uh-seez). | **paralyse** *verb*

paramedical
adjective helping the medical profession: *ambulances and other paramedical services*

parameter
noun one of a set of variable qualities or factors: *If you change a parameter, such as temperature in the experiment, the results will vary.*

paramount
adjective above others in rank, authority or importance
Word use: The more usual word is **chief**.

paranoid
adjective full of fears about things which are imagined
Word building: **paranoia** (*say* pa-ruh-<u>noy</u>-uh) *noun*   **paranoiac** *adjective*

parapet
noun a wall or barrier at the edge of a balcony, roof or bridge

paraphernalia
(*say* pa-ruh-fuh-<u>nay</u>-lee-uh)
plural noun goods, equipment, baggage or other articles, especially unnecessary ones

paraphrase
verb to put in different words so that it's easier to understand
Word building: **paraphrase** *noun*

paraplegic   (*say* pa-ruh-<u>plee</u>-jik)
noun someone who has lost the use of both arms or both legs
Word building: **paraplegia** *noun*   **paraplegic** *adjective*

parasite

noun **1** an animal or plant which lives on or in another from which it obtains its food: *Fleas are parasites.* **2** someone who lives on the money earned by other people without doing anything in return

Word building: **parasitic** *adjective* **parasitism** *noun*

parasol

noun a small sun umbrella

Word history: from Latin words meaning 'guard against the sun'

paratrooper

noun a soldier who reaches a battle by landing from an aeroplane by parachute

parcel

noun a package or wrapped bundle of goods

Word building: **parcel** *verb* (**parcelled, parcelling**) to make up into a parcel

parch

verb to make or become very dry

Word building: **parched** *adjective*

parchment

noun **1** the skin of sheep, goats or similar animals prepared as a material to write on **2** paper which looks like this

pardon

noun **1** forgiveness, especially for a crime *verb* **2** to forgive and not punish **3** to excuse: *'Pardon me', I said when I walked in front of her.*

Word building: **pardonable** *adjective*

pare   (*rhymes with* hair)

verb **1** to peel or cut off the outer layer of: *to pare apples* **2** to cut down or make less: *to pare expenses*

pare/pair/pear Don't confuse **pare** with **pair** or **pear**.

Two things that go together, like shoes, are a **pair**.

A **pear** is a kind of fruit.

parent

noun a father or a mother

Word building: **parentage** *noun*   **parental** *adjective*   **parentally** *adverb*   **parenthood** *noun*

parenthesis   (*say* puh-<u>ren</u>-thuh-suhs)

noun **1** one of the upright brackets ( ) often used to mark off a phrase or clause **2** a descriptive or explanatory phrase or clause put into a sentence and marked off by commas, brackets or dashes, such as 'the blue one' in *He took your bag — the blue one — when he left.*

Word building: The plural is **parentheses** (*say* puh-<u>ren</u>-thuh-seez). | **parenthesise** *verb* **parenthetic** *adjective*

parish

noun **1** a district which has its own church and clergy **2** the people of a parish

Word building: The plural is **parishes**. | **parishioner** *noun*

park

noun **1** an area of land set aside for public use and kept in good order by the council or government: *Hyde Park | a national park verb* **2** to put or leave a car, bicycle or other vehicle in a particular spot, such as at the side of the road

parka

noun a warm waterproof jacket with a hood

parley

noun a talk or discussion, especially between people who are fighting each other

Word building: The plural is **parleys**. | **parley** *verb*

parliament   (*say* pah-luh-muhnt)

noun the group of people elected to make the laws for a country or state

Word building: **parliamentarian** *noun* **parliamentary** *adjective* Word history: from an Old French word meaning 'talking'

parlour

noun **1** a formal room where you entertain visitors **2** a room where customers of certain businesses are attended to: *a beauty parlour*

Word use: Another spelling is **parlor**.

parmesan

noun a hard, dry, pale yellow cheese, often used for grating

Word history: named after the city of *Parma* in Northern Italy

parody (say pa-ruh-dee)

noun a humorous imitation of a serious piece of writing or music

Word building: The plural is **parodies**. | **parody** *verb* (**parodied, parodying**)

parole

noun the early freeing of a prisoner on the condition of good behaviour: *He is out on parole.*

Word building: **parole** *verb*
Word history: from a French word meaning 'word'

paroxysm (say pa-ruhk-siz-uhm)

noun a sudden violent fit: *a paroxysm of coughing | a paroxysm of anger*

parquet (say pah-kay)

adjective made of short pieces of wood fitted together to form a pattern: *a parquet coffee table*

Word building: **parquet** *noun* **parquetry** *noun*

parrot

noun a hook-billed, often brightly coloured bird which can be taught to talk

Word building: **parrot** *verb* to repeat or imitate like a parrot

parry

verb to turn aside or avoid: *She was able to parry my question.*

Word building: Other forms are **I parried, I have parried, I am parrying**.

parse (rhymes with bars)

verb to describe by telling the part of speech and so on: *to parse all the words in the sentence*

parsley

noun a herb used in cooking

parsnip

noun a whitish root vegetable that is shaped like a carrot

parson

noun a member of the clergy

Word building: **parsonage** *noun* a parson's house

part

noun **1** a piece or portion: *a part of a meal | a part of a book*
Other words: **section**
2 something is essential in making up a whole: *Kindness is part of his character. | Oxygen is an important part of the air we breathe.*
Other words: **component, constituent, element, ingredient**
3 a replacement piece for something worn out or broken: *We always carry spare parts for our bicycles.*
Other words: **component**
4 a share in something, such as work or a musical performance **5** an actor's role: *a part in a play*
verb **6** to separate
Other words: **divide, segment, detach, disconnect**

Word building: **partly** *adverb*: *The house is partly brick.*

partial (say pah-shuhl)

adjective **1** not total or general: *My cousin suffers from partial deafness.* **2** showing unfair support or favouritism: *Everyone could see the umpire was being partial in most decisions.*
phrase **3 partial to,** having a strong liking for: *I am partial to cake.*

Word building: **partiality** *noun* **partially** *adverb*

participate (say pah-tis-uh-payt)

verb to take part

Word building: **participant** *noun* **participation** *noun*

participle (say pah-tuh-sip-uhl)

noun **1** a word formed from a verb and used as an adjective, such as *burning* in *a burning candle* or *added* in *added work*
2 a word formed from a verb and used in compound verbs, such as *burning* in *the candle has been burning* or *added* in *I have added*

Word building: **participial** *adjective*

particle

noun a very small bit: *a particle of dust*

particular

adjective **1** single, or one, rather than all: *I am interested in that particular book on dogs.* **2** more than usual or special: *Take particular care of that book.*
noun **3** a point or detail: *The report was right in every particular.*
phrase **4 in particular,** especially: *There is one book in particular that I want to read.*

Word building: **particularly** *adverb*

partition

noun **1** a separating wall **2** a division into shares or parts: *The partition of the city into East Berlin and West Berlin occurred in 1945.*

Word building: **partition** *verb* to divide into parts

partner

noun someone who shares or takes part in something with someone else: *a business partner* | *a dancing partner*

Word building: **partner** *verb* **partnership** *noun*

part of speech

noun any of the main grammatical types of words in a language such as *noun, pronoun, verb, adjective, adverb, preposition, conjunction* or *interjection*

partridge

noun a European bird that is hunted and eaten

Word building: The plural is **partridge** or **partridges**.

part-time

adjective taking or working fewer than all the usual working hours: *a part-time job* | *a part-time gardener*

Word building: **part-time** *adverb*: *I work part-time.*

party

noun **1** a social gathering, often to celebrate something: *a birthday party* **2** a group of people who work for the same political ideals: *the Australian Labor Party*

Word building: The plural is **parties**.

pass

verb **1** to go by or beyond **2** to do successfully: *to pass a test* **3** to send or hand to: *to pass a message* | *Pass me that book.*
Other words: **give, transfer**
4 to approve or make: *to pass laws*
noun **5** a narrow path or road through a low part in a mountain **6** a piece of paper that shows you are allowed to do something or go somewhere: *a special pass* | *a train pass*
Other words: **authorisation, licence, permission, permit, ticket**
7 the handing or tossing of a ball to another player in some ball games **8** the passing of an examination
phrase **9 pass away,** to die

Word building: **passable** *adjective*

passage

noun **1** a corridor, channel, or a way for going: *a passage between rooms* | *a passage between islands* **2** a part of a story or piece of music

passbook

noun another word for **bankbook**

passenger

noun someone who travels on a ship, plane, bus or other vehicle

passion (*say* pash-uhn)

noun **1** any strong feeling or emotion, especially love, anger or grief **2** a strong interest or enthusiasm: *He has a passion for football.*

Word building: **passionate** *adjective*
Word history: from a Latin word meaning 'suffering'

passionfruit

noun a small purplish fruit, the seeds and pulp of which you can eat

Word use: The plural is **passionfruit**.

passive

adjective **1** letting things happen without taking any action yourself **2** having to do with a verb, the subject of which is having the action done to it rather than doing the action itself, such as 'was punished' in *I was punished by my parents.*

Word use: Compare definition 2 with **active**.
Word building: **passively** *adverb* **passivity** *noun*

passive aggressive

adjective annoying somebody by deliberately not cooperating, frustrating what they are trying to do by not doing anything to help: *When she saw she was getting nowhere by screaming she gave him the passive aggressive treatment.*

Passover

noun a feast of the Jews held each year to celebrate the escape of the Hebrews from Egypt and to remember when God saved the Hebrew children while all the firstborn Egyptian children were killed

Word history: from the phrase *pass over*

passport

noun a government document which identifies you and which you need to travel to foreign countries

password

noun a secret word that lets you get into a place where others are not allowed

past

adjective **1** gone by in time: *The old lady's past activities included bushwalking.*
noun **2** time gone by: *in the past*
adverb **3** by: *The troops marched past.*

pasta (*say* <u>pahs</u>-tuh, <u>pas</u>-tuh)
noun a food made from flour, water and sometimes egg, such as spaghetti or macaroni

paste
noun **1** a mixture of flour and water used for sticking paper onto other surfaces
Other words: **adhesive, glue, gum**
2 something made into a soft smooth mass: *toothpaste | almond paste*

Word building: **paste** *verb: to paste pictures in a project book*

pastel (*say* <u>pas</u>-tuhl)
noun **1** a soft pale colour **2** a crayon, or a drawing made with crayons

Word building: **pastel** *adjective*

pasteurise (*say* <u>pahs</u>-chuh-ruyz)
verb to destroy germs in, by heating to a very high temperature: *to pasteurise milk*

Word use: Another spelling is **pasteurize**.
Word building: **pasteurisation** *noun*
Word history: named after Louis *Pasteur*, 1822–1895, a French chemist

pastie (*say* <u>pas</u>-tee, <u>pahs</u>-tee)
noun a type of pie filled with meat and vegetables

Word use: Another spelling is **pasty**.
Word building: The plural is **pasties**.

pastime
noun something you do to make time pass pleasantly: *Reading is a good pastime.*

pastor
noun a member of the clergy

Word building: **pastorate** *noun*
Word history: from a Latin word meaning 'shepherd'

pastry
noun a mixture of flour, water and fat cooked as a crust for pies and tarts

Word building: The plural is **pastries**.

past tense
noun the form of a verb which shows that something has already happened such as *ran* in *I ran away* and *have run* in *I have run away*

pasture (*say* <u>pahs</u>-chuh)
noun land suitable for grazing cattle or sheep: *There is good pasture on the property.*

Word building: **pastoral** *adjective: pastoral land* **pasture** *verb* to graze **pastoralist** *noun*

pasty[1] (*say* <u>pay</u>-stee)
adjective whitish or sick-looking: *a pasty complexion*

pasty[2] (*say* <u>pas</u>-tee, <u>pahs</u>-tee)
noun another spelling for **pastie**

pat[1]
verb **1** to strike lightly with your hand **2** to stroke gently

Word building: Other forms are **I patted, I have patted, I am patting**. | **pat** *noun*

pat[2]
adjective **1** exactly to the point: *He gave a pat reply.*
adverb **2** exactly or perfectly: *I want to know it pat. | Learn it off pat.*

patch
noun **1** a piece of material used to mend a hole or a weak place **2** a piece of material used to cover a wound **3** a small piece: *a patch of land | a patch of sunlight*

Word building: The plural is **patches**. | **patch** *verb* **patchy** *adjective* (**patchier, patchiest**)

patchwork
noun a type of work in which pieces of differently coloured or shaped cloth are sewn together

pâté (*say* <u>pat</u>-ay)
noun a paste or spread made out of finely minced liver, meat, fish, and so on

Word history: from a French word, which is why it has accents

patent (*say* <u>pay</u>-tuhnt)
noun permission given by the government to be the only person allowed to make or sell an invention

patent leather
noun leather with a very shiny surface

Word building: **patent-leather** *adjective*

paternal
adjective having to do with or being like a father: *paternal love*

Word building: **paternalism** *noun* **paternalistic** *adjective* **paternally** *adverb* **paternity** *noun*

path
noun **1** a narrow way for walking: *a path down to the river*
Other words: **track, trail, way**
2 a direction which someone or something follows: *the path to success | a flight path*
Other words: **course, route, way**

pathetic (*say* puh-<u>thet</u>-ik)
adjective **1** causing feelings of pity or
sadness: *a pathetic sight* **2** *Informal*
showing a great lack of ability: *It was a
pathetic attempt.*
Word building: **pathetically** *adverb*

pathologist (*say* puh-<u>thol</u>-uh-juhst)
noun a doctor who is an expert in the
effects of diseases on the body
Word building: **pathological** *adjective*
pathology *noun*

patient (*say* <u>pay</u>-shuhnt)
noun **1** someone who is being treated by a
doctor or is in a hospital
adjective **2** putting up with delay,
annoyance, and so on, without getting
annoyed or without complaining: *a patient
customer* | *He is very patient with young
children even when they are noisy.*
Word building: **patience** *noun*
patiently *adverb*

patio (*say* <u>pat</u>-ee-oh, <u>pay</u>-shee-oh)
noun an outdoor living area next to a
house
Word building: The plural is **patios.**

patriarch (*say* <u>pay</u>-tree-ahk)
noun a male leader in a family, tribe or any
field of activity
Word building: **patriarchal** *adjective*
patriarchy *noun*

patriot (*say* <u>pay</u>-tree-uht)
noun someone who loves their country and
is loyal to it
Word building: **patriotic** *adjective*
patriotically *adverb*   **patriotism** *noun*

patrol (*say* puh-<u>trohl</u>)
verb to go around regularly to make sure
there is no trouble: *The police car patrolled
the streets.*
Word building: Other forms are **I patrolled,
I have patrolled, I am patrolling.** | **patrol** *noun*

patron (*say* <u>pay</u>-truhn)
noun **1** a regular customer of a hotel, shop,
cinema or similar place **2** a supporter or
helper: *a patron of art*
Word building: **patronage** *noun*

patronise (*say* <u>pat</u>-ruh-nuyz)
verb **1** to be a customer of: *I've been
patronising that shop for years.* **2** to treat
in a kindly fashion, but as if inferior:
*Older children often patronise the younger
ones.*
Word use: Another spelling is **patronize.**

patter[1]
verb to strike or move with quick, light,
tapping sounds: *She pattered down the
hallway in bare feet.*
Word building: **patter** *noun*

patter[2]
noun rapid speech or chatter, especially of
a salesperson or entertainer

pattern
noun **1** an ornamental design **2** a model or
guide: *a paper pattern for a dress*
Word building: **pattern** *verb*

paunch (*rhymes with* launch)
noun the belly or abdomen, usually a
particularly large and rounded one: *He's got
a paunch from drinking too much beer.*
Word building: **paunchiness** *noun*
paunchy *adjective*

pause (*say* pawz)
noun a short rest or stop when you're
speaking or doing something
Other words: **break, interlude, lull, recess**
Word building: **pause** *verb*

pave
verb to make a firm level surface by laying
concrete, stones or bricks on: *to pave a
path*

pavement
noun a paved footpath at the side of a road

pavilion (*say* puh-<u>vil</u>-yuhn)
noun an open shelter in a park or
amusement area

pavlova
noun a dessert made of a large round
meringue filled with cream and topped
with fruit
Word history: named after Anna *Pavlova*,
1885–1931, a Russian ballerina

paw

noun the foot of an animal with nails or claws

Word building: **paw** *verb* to strike or scrape with the paws

paw/pour/poor/pore Don't confuse **paw** with **pour**, **poor**, or **pore**.

You can **pour** a liquid from one container to another.

Someone is **poor** if they don't have much money or property.

A **pore** is a small hole. Sweat comes out through the **pores** in your skin. To **pore** over something is to read or study it carefully:
He watched the pirates pore over the secret treasure map.

pawn[1]

verb to leave with a pawnbroker when you borrow money, to make sure that you repay your debt: *I pawned my watch.*

pawn[2]

noun one of the pieces of lowest value in chess

pawnbroker

noun someone who lends you money, but only if you leave something that can be sold if you don't return the money

pawpaw

noun a large, yellow, fleshy fruit which grows in tropical Australia

Word use: A smaller kind of pawpaw, with reddish-pink flesh is the **papaya**.

pay

verb **1** to give money in return for something: *I paid for the milk yesterday.* **2** to give or offer: *to pay a compliment* **3** to be worthwhile: *It pays to be honest.* **4** to suffer or be punished: *to pay for your mistakes* *noun* **5** wages or salary

Word building: Other verb forms are **I patrolled, I have patrolled, I am patrolling.** | **payable** *adjective* **payment** *noun*

PC

noun a short form of **personal computer**

PE *(say* pee <u>ee</u>)

noun sport and other forms of exercise, usually done at school

Word use: This word is a short way of saying **physical education**.

pea

noun a small, round, green seed which grows in a pod, used as a vegetable

peace

noun **1** freedom from war **2** calm, quiet or stillness: *peace of mind | the peace of the countryside*
Other words: **serenity, tranquillity**

Word building: **peaceable** *adjective* loving peace **peaceful** *adjective: a peaceful scene*

peace/piece Don't confuse **peace** with **piece**, which is a bit or part of something, as in a *piece of cake.* It can also be a single or individual thing, as in *a piece of fruit.*

peach

noun a round, sweet, pinkish-yellow fruit with a single seed and furry skin

Word building: The plural is **peaches**.

peacock

noun a type of pheasant noted for the colourful eye-like pattern on its tail feathers

Word use: The male is a **peacock**, the female is a **peahen** and the young is a **chick**.

peak

noun **1** the pointed top of a mountain **2** the highest or greatest point: *the peak of her achievements*

Word building: **peak** *verb*

peak/peek/pique Don't confuse **peak** with **peek** or **pique**.

To **peek** is to snatch a quick look, often when you are not supposed to.

Pique is a feeling of mild annoyance. To be **piqued** is to be a bit annoyed.

peal

noun **1** a loud, long, drawn-out sound of bells **2** any other loud long sound: *a peal of laughter*

Word building: **peal** *verb*

peal/peel Don't confuse **peal** with **peel**. To **peel** an apple is to remove the skin from it.

peanut

noun a small nut which ripens in a pod underground and which you can eat

pear

noun a thin-skinned, pale green or brownish fruit, round at its base and growing smaller towards the stem

pear/pair/pare Don't confuse **pear** with **pair** or **pare**.

Two things that go together, like shoes, are a **pair**.

You **pare** an apple when you peel the skin off.

pearl   (*rhymes with* curl)

noun a shiny, round, usually white growth, found in some oysters and used in jewellery

Word building: **pearly** *adjective*

peasant   (*say* <u>pez</u>-uhnt)

noun someone who lives and works on a farm and is regarded as an inferior sort of person

Word use: This word is only used about olden times or of people in developing countries.
Word building: **peasantry** *noun* all peasants taken as a group

peat

noun **1** soil which consists of partially rotted leaves, roots, grasses and similar matter in marshy areas **2** blocks of this, dried and used as fuel

pebble

noun a small, smooth, rounded stone

Word building: **pebbly** *adjective*

pecan   (*say* <u>pee</u>-kan, pee-<u>kan</u>)

noun a sweet oily nut which grows on trees in America, and which you can eat

peck

verb **1** to strike or eat with the beak: *The bird pecked the branch. | The chickens pecked the corn.* **2** to pick or nibble at food **3** to kiss quickly on the cheek

Word building: **peck** *noun*

peculiar   (*say* puh-<u>kyooh</u>-lee-uh)

adjective **1** strange, odd or queer
Other words: **abnormal, atypical, unusual, weird**
phrase **2 peculiar to,** having to do with one particular person or thing: *Gathering shiny objects is a habit peculiar to magpies and bowerbirds.*

Word building: **peculiarity** *noun*
(**peculiarities**)   **peculiarly** *adverb*

pedal

noun a lever worked by the foot: *an organ pedal | a sewing machine pedal | a bicycle pedal*
Word building: **pedal** *verb* (**pedalled, pedalling**)

pedal/peddle Don't confuse **pedal** with **peddle**. To **peddle** something is to sell it, usually in small quantities, to individual buyers. The person who peddles is a **pedlar** or **peddler**.

peddle

verb to take around from place to place in order to sell

pedestal

noun **1** a support for a statue or ornament **2** the supporting base of a column

pedestrian   (*say* puh-<u>des</u>-tree-uhn)

noun someone who walks: *A pedestrian must be careful when crossing a busy street.*

Word history: from a Latin word meaning 'on foot'

pedigree

noun a line of direct relationship, showing, for example, the mother, and her mother before her, and so on: *My cat has a long pedigree.*

Word building: **pedigreed** *adjective*

pedlar

noun someone who travels round selling things

peek

verb to peep or peer

peek/peak/pique Don't confuse **peek** with **peak** or **pique**.

A **peak** is the pointed top of a mountain.

Pique is a feeling of mild annoyance. To be **piqued** is to be a bit annoyed.

peel

verb **1** to take off the skin, rind or outer layer of **2** to come off: *My skin is peeling where I was sunburnt.*

Word building: **peel** *noun*: *an orange peel* **peeler** *noun*: *a potato peeler* **peeling** *noun*

peel/peal Don't confuse **peel** with **peal**. Bells **peal** when they ring out.

peep

verb **1** to look through a small opening or from a hiding place **2** to come briefly or partly into view: *The sun peeped over the horizon.*

Word building: **peep** *noun*

peer[1]

noun **1** someone in your own age group **2** a nobleman

Word building: **peerage** *noun* the nobility **peeress** *noun* a noblewoman **peerless** *adjective* having no equal

peer/pier Don't confuse **peer** with **pier**. A **pier** is a jetty.

peer²

verb **1** to look closely in order to see clearly **2** to peep: *to peer through a window*

peer/pier Don't confuse **peer** with **pier**. A **pier** is a jetty.

peevish

adjective cross or easily annoyed

peg

noun **1** a small wooden, metal or plastic pin used to fasten things, to hang things on, or to mark a place: *a clothes peg | a tent peg | a hat peg | a surveyor's peg* *verb* **2** to fasten with a peg *phrase* **3 peg away**, to work steadily

Word building: Other verb forms are **I pegged, I have pegged, I am pegging**.

pejorative   (*say* puh-jo-ruh-tiv)

adjective expressing disapproval: *a pejorative statement*

Word use: The more usual word is **disapproving**. Word building: **pejoratively** *adverb*

pelican

noun a large, web-footed seabird with a pouch hanging beneath its bill for holding the fish it catches

pellet

noun **1** a small rounded piece of anything: *a paper pellet | a pellet of food* **2** a small bullet fired from a shotgun

pelmet

noun an ornamental covering which hides a curtain rail

pelt¹

verb **1** to throw: *to pelt stones at a post* **2** to come down heavily: *Rain pelted down.* **3** to hurry: *He pelted down the hill.*

pelt²

noun the skin taken from a dead animal to be made into leather

pelvis

noun the ring of bone made up of the lower part of your backbone and your two hip bones, and the cavity it forms

Word building: **pelvic** *adjective*

pen¹

noun an instrument for writing with ink: *a ballpoint pen*

Word building: **pen** *verb* (**penned, penning**) to write

pen²

noun an enclosure for animals on a farm

Word building: **pen** *verb* (**penned** or **pent**, **penning**) to put in a pen

penal   (*say* pee-nuhl)

adjective having to do with the punishment of crimes: *the penal laws*

penalty   (*say* pen-uhl-tee)

noun **1** the price you pay for breaking a law or rule **2** a free kick or shot allowed in some sports to one team or player because an opponent has broken a rule

Word building: The plural is **penalties**. | **penalise** *verb*

penance   (*say* pen-uhns)

noun a punishment you agree or offer to accept to show you are sorry for doing wrong

pencil

noun a thin pointed piece of wood enclosing a stick of graphite or crayon and used for writing or drawing

Word building: **pencil** *verb* (**pencilled, pencilling**)

pendant

noun a hanging piece of jewellery such as a necklace

Word building: **pendant** *adjective* hanging

pendulum   (*say* pen-juh-luhm)

noun a weight swinging backward and forward which makes some clocks work

penetrate   (*say* pen-uh-trayt)

verb **1** to go into or through, especially with a sharp instrument: *The arrow penetrated my arm. | The army penetrated the enemy's defences.* **2** to enter, reach or pass through, as if by piercing: *The knife penetrated to the bone.*

Word building: **penetrating** *adjective*: *a penetrating look* **penetrable** *adjective* **penetration** *noun* **penetratingly** *adverb*

penfriend

noun someone, usually in another country, you have become friends with through writing letters

penguin *(say* pen-gwuhn)

noun a bird which cannot fly, has webbed feet and lives in or near the cold southern parts of the world

Word history: from Old French words meaning 'white head'

penicillin *(say* pen-uh-sil-uhn)

noun a strong germ-fighting substance used in medicines and ointments

peninsula *(say* puh-nin-shuh-luh)

noun a long piece of land jutting out into the sea

Word building: **peninsular** *adjective*
Word history: from Latin words meaning 'almost an island'

penis *(say* pee-nuhs)

noun the part of a male's genitals with which he urinates and has sexual intercourse

penitent *(say* pen-uh-tuhnt)

adjective sorry for wrongdoing and willing to put things right
Other words: **repentant**

Word building: **penitence** *noun*   **penitently** *adverb*

penitentiary *(say* pen-uh-ten-shuh-ree)

noun a jail or prison

penknife

noun a small knife with one or more blades that fold into the handle so that it can be carried safely in a pocket

Word use: The plural is **penknives**. | This used to be used to clean and mend quill pens. | It can also be called a **pocket-knife**.

pennant

noun a triangular flag, used as a signal on ships or as an award in a sporting event

penny

noun a bronze or copper coin worth only a small amount, that used to be used in Australia and still is in Britain and some other countries

Word building: The plural is **pennies** or **pence**. | **penniless** *adjective* having no money

pension

noun a regular payment made by the government to someone who is old, sick or poor, or by a private company to someone who has retired from working for it

Word building: **pensioner** *noun*

pensive

adjective seriously or sadly thoughtful: *a pensive stare*

Word building: **pensively** *adverb*

pentagon

noun a flat shape with five straight sides

Word building: **pentagonal** *adjective*

penthouse

noun a separate flat on the roof or top storey of a building

people

noun **1** human beings in general **2** all the members of a tribe, ethnic group or nation: *a peace-loving people | a nomadic people* **3** the members of a particular group or community: *the people of a neighbourhood | working people* **4** your family or relatives: *Some of my people are coming to visit.*

Word use: This word is usually thought of as plural (*People are arriving already*, *The people have voted*). However, when it is used as in definition 2, it is singular, and has a plural form **peoples** (*the different peoples of southern Africa*).

pepper

noun **1** a spice with a hot taste, made from the dried berries of a tropical plant **2** a capsicum: *a green pepper | a red pepper*

Word building: **peppery** *adjective*

peppermint

noun a lolly made with a strong-tasting, strong-smelling oil from a plant

pepperoni *(say* pep-uh-roh-nee)

noun a kind of salami often used on pizzas

Word use: Another spelling is **peperoni**.

perceive

verb **1** to come to know of through one of the senses, such as sight or hearing: *He perceived a glimmer of light at the top of the well.* **2** to understand: *I perceive that you do not agree.*

Word building: **perceivable** *adjective* **perceptible** *adjective*

per cent

adverb in every hundred: *My bank pays ten per cent interest so if I have $100 in my account for a year, I get paid $10 interest.*

Word use: This can also be written **percent**. | The symbol is %.

percentage

noun **1** a number which shows the rate in every hundred: *The percentage of dark-haired children in this class is 65.* **2** a part or proportion: *A large percentage of children at our school live nearby.*

perception

noun **1** the act of perceiving or the ability to perceive: *My perception of colour is not good.* **2** the ability to understand the inner nature of something quickly and clearly: *She has a lot of perception.* **3** understanding or knowledge

Word building: **perceptive** *adjective* quick in perceiving   **perceptively** *adverb*

perch¹

noun **1** a rod for birds to roost on
verb **2** to settle or rest on a perch or something similar: *The birds perched on the roof.* | *I perched the vase on the top shelf.*

perch²

noun a kind of fish that you can eat

percolate   (*say* per-kuh-layt)

verb **1** to make a liquid pass through a substance **2** to spread or become known gradually: *The news percolated through the classroom.*

Word building: **percolator** *noun* a coffee-maker in which boiling water is percolated through ground coffee   **percolation** *noun*

percussion   (*say* puh-kush-uhn)

noun the hitting of one thing against another

percussion instrument

noun a musical instrument, such as a drum, cymbal, or piano, which produces notes when it is struck

Word building: **percussionist** *noun*

perennial   (*say* puh-ren-ee-uhl)

adjective **1** lasting for a long time or continually coming back: *a perennial joke* | *a perennial trouble-maker* **2** having a life cycle of more than two years: *a perennial plant*

Word building: **perennial** *noun* a perennial plant   **perennially** *adverb*

perfect   (*say* per-fuhkt)

adjective **1** with nothing missing and no faults **2** completely suited for a particular purpose: *He is a perfect husband for her.* **3** complete or absolute: *a perfect stranger* **4** having to do with the form of a verb which shows that something continues up to the present (*I have run*), to some point in the past (*I had run*), or in the future (*I will have run*)
verb (*say* per-fekt) **5** to make complete or perfect

Word building: **perfection** *noun*   **perfectly** *adverb*

perforate   (*say* per-fuh-rayt)

verb to make a hole or holes in: *He used the point of a pencil to perforate the paper.*

Word building: **perforated** *adjective*   **perforation** *noun*

perform

verb **1** to do or carry out: *The dancer performed a graceful arm movement.* | *I performed my duty.*
Other words: **effect, execute, fulfil**
2 to do an act in front of an audience

Word building: **performance** *noun*   **performer** *noun*

performance-enhancing drug

noun a substance taken by a person to improve their performance in sport: *He was suspended for three years for taking a performance-enhancing drug.*

perfume

noun **1** a liquid prepared so that it gives out a pleasant smell **2** a pleasant smell

Word building: **perfume** *verb*: *to perfume a handkerchief*   **perfumer** *noun* someone who makes or sells perfume   **perfumery** *noun*

pergola   (*say* per-guh-luh, puh-goh-luh)

noun a shelter made of bars supported on posts, over which climbing plants are grown

perhaps

adverb maybe: *Perhaps there will be a storm tonight.*

peril

noun danger or risk: *Our lives are in peril.*

Word building: **perilous** *adjective*   **perilously** *adverb*

perimeter (say puh-<u>rim</u>-uh-tuh)
noun **1** the outside edge of a shape or area: *the perimeter of a football field* **2** the length of this edge

period
noun **1** any division or portion of time: *We will have a period of work and then a period of play.* **2** a particular division of time or history: *the colonial period in Australia* **3** the monthly flow of blood from the uterus of a woman, or the time when this happens **4** another word for **full stop**
adjective **5** having to do with a particular period of history: *period costumes*

Word building: **periodic, periodical** *adjective* happening or appearing at regular intervals **periodical** *noun* a magazine that comes out at regular intervals **periodically** *adverb*

periphery (say puh-<u>rif</u>-uh-ree)
noun the outside edge of an area or thing: *The chairs were arranged around the periphery of the room.*

Word building: **peripheral** *adjective* not central in importance **peripherally** *adverb*

periscope
noun an instrument made of a tube with an arrangement of mirrors, used to see something from a position below or behind it: *the periscope of a submarine*

perish
verb **1** to die: *The explorers perished in the desert.* **2** to rot or decay: *Rubber perishes.*

Word building: **perishable** *adjective* **perishable** *noun*

perjury
noun the crime of telling a lie while under an oath: *The witness in the court case committed perjury.*

Word building: **perjure** *verb* **perjurer** *noun*

perk
noun Informal an extra benefit or bonus that someone gets in a job, in addition to their pay: *One of the perks of the job is a company car with free petrol.*

perky
adjective active and lively: *I'm feeling quite perky today after a good night's sleep.*

Word building: Other forms are **perkier, perkiest.**

permanent
adjective lasting for a very long time or forever: *a permanent dye | permanent snow on a mountain top*

Word use: The opposite is **temporary.**
Word building: **permanence** *noun* **permanency** *noun* **permanently** *adverb*

permeate (say <u>per</u>-mee-ayt)
verb to pass or spread through: *A strange smell permeated the room.*

Word building: **permeable** *adjective* able to be passed through, especially by liquids **permeation** *noun*

permission
noun the act of permitting or allowing someone to do something
Other words: **authority, liberty, licence**

Word building: **permissible** *adjective* **permissibly** *adverb*

permissive
adjective allowing freedom, especially in sexual or moral matters: *a permissive society*

Word building: **permissively** *adverb* **permissiveness** *noun*

permit (say puh-<u>mit</u>)
verb **1** to say that someone can do something
Other words: **allow**
2 to give the chance for: *This oven door permits heat to escape.*
Other words: **allow**
noun (say <u>per</u>-mit) **3** an official certificate that gives permission
Other words: **authorisation, licence, pass**

Word building: Other verb forms are **I permitted, I have permitted, I am permitting.**

permutation
noun the changing of the order of the elements in a group or set: *ACB and BAC are some of the permutations of ABC.*

Word use: The more usual word is **variation.**

peroxide (say puh-<u>rok</u>-suyd)
noun a chemical that is often used to bleach or lighten hair

Word building: **peroxide** *adjective*: *a peroxide blonde* **peroxide** *verb*

perpendicular
(say per-puhn-<u>dik</u>-yuh-luh)
adjective **1** upright or vertical: *a perpendicular post* **2** meeting a line or surface at right angles

perpetrate
verb to do or carry out: *to perpetrate a crime*
Word building: **perpetration** *noun*
perpetrator *noun*

perpetual   (*say* puh-<u>pet</u>-chooh-uhl)
adjective **1** lasting forever **2** continuing without a break: *There has been a perpetual stream of visitors.*
Word building: **perpetuate** *verb* to make last for a very long time   **perpetually** *adverb*

perplex
verb to make puzzled: *This question perplexes me.*
Other words: **baffle, bewilder, confuse, mystify**
Word building: **perplexed** *adjective*
perplexing *adjective*   **perplexity** *noun*

persecute
verb **1** to constantly treat unfairly or cruelly **2** to harm or punish for having certain ideas or religious beliefs
Word building: **persecution** *noun*
persecutor *noun*

persevere
verb to continue in spite of difficulty: *I am tired but I will persevere with my work.*
Other words: **persist**
Word building: **perseverance** *noun*

persimmon
noun a red or orange plumlike fruit
Word history: from an Algonquian (a language of some Native North American tribes) word meaning '(artificially) dried fruit'

persist
verb **1** to continue doing something, often in spite of difficulty: *I persisted with my questions until I got an answer.*
Other words: **persevere**
2 to go on and on: *My toothache persisted for hours.*
Word building: **persistence** *noun*
persistent *adjective*

person
noun **1** a human being **2** a type of verb or pronoun form that shows the difference between the speaker to or 'first person', the person spoken to or 'second person', and anyone or anything spoken about or 'third person', such as, in their order, the pronouns 'I', 'you' and 'her' in *I will tell you about her.*
phrase **3 in person**, with the person actually present: *He brought the letter in person.*

personage
noun a person, especially someone important

personal
adjective **1** private or having to do with a particular person: *a personal matter* | *personal attention* **2** directed to a particular person in a rude way: *You shouldn't make personal remarks about someone's appearance.*
Word building: **personally** *adverb*

personal computer
noun a small computer that can be placed on a desk or table and is meant for use in the home or by small businesses
Word use: The short form of this is **PC**.

personalise
verb to mark property in some way, such as with a name or initials, to show who owns it: *Annabel personalised a towel for every member of her exercise group.*
Word use: Another spelling is **personalize**.
Word building: **personalised** *adjective*: *a personalised numberplate*

personality
noun **1** the qualities of character that make someone an individual: *My baby already has a personality.* **2** strong or lively character: *She has plenty of personality.* **3** someone who is well-known: *a television personality*
Other words: **celebrity, star**
Word building: The plural is **personalities**.

personify
verb **1** to give a human nature or form to: *Some stories personify animals by making them talk.* **2** to be a perfect example of: *She personifies beauty.*
Word building: Other forms are **I personified, I have personified, I am personifying.** |
personification *noun*

personnel   (*say* per-suh-<u>nel</u>)
noun the group of people working for a particular organisation

perspective
noun **1** the appearance of distance as well as height and width, produced on a flat surface, such as in a painting: *The artist has achieved perspective in painting that row of trees.* **2** a mental point of view: *She has a new perspective on this problem.*
phrase **3 in perspective**, with a proper balance

perspire

verb to get rid of a salty liquid through the pores of your skin
Other words: **sweat**

Word building: **perspiration** *noun*

persuade

verb to cause to do or believe something by advice, argument or influence: *They persuaded me to go.* | *She persuaded him that he was wrong.*
Other words: **coax, convince, induce**

Word building: **persuasive** *adjective* **persuasively** *adverb*

persuasion

noun **1** the act or power of persuading **2** a belief, especially religious: *people of the Buddhist persuasion*

pert

adjective **1** bold or impudent **2** attractive in a lively way: *a pert hat*

Word building: **pertly** *adverb* **pertness** *noun*

pertinent

adjective having to do with the matter being discussed or thought about: *a pertinent comment*
Other words: **applicable, connected, related, relevant**

Word building: **pertinence** *noun* **pertinently** *adverb*

perturb

verb to disturb or worry greatly

Word building: **perturbation** *noun*

peruse   (*say* puh-<u>roohz</u>)

verb **1** to read through something in a careful or thorough way: *She promised to peruse the contract and see if there were any problems with it.* **2** to read over something in a leisurely way: *She perused the newspaper headlines while she waited.*

Word building: **perusal** *noun*

perverse

adjective deliberately going against what is expected or wanted: *a perverse answer* | *a perverse mood*
Other words: **contrary**

Word building: **perversely** *adverb* **perverseness** *noun* **perversity** *noun*

pervert   (*say* puh-<u>vert</u>)

verb **1** to make turn away from what is right, either in behaviour or in beliefs
noun (*say* <u>per</u>-vert) **2** someone who has unusual or unpleasant sexual habits

Word building: **perversion** *noun* **perverted** *adjective*

pessimism

noun the habit of expecting that things will turn out badly

Word use: The opposite is **optimism**.
Word building: **pessimist** *noun* someone who looks on the gloomy side   **pessimistic** *adjective*   **pessimistically** *adverb*

pest

noun someone or something that is annoying or harmful

Word building: **pestilent** *adjective*

pester

verb to annoy continually

pesticide

noun a chemical for killing pests, such as insects

pestle   (*say* <u>pes</u>-uhl)

noun a club-shaped tool for grinding substances in a mortar

Word history: from a Latin word meaning 'pounded'

pesto

noun a thick green sauce made of basil, pine nuts, garlic, parmesan cheese and oil, used in Italian cooking

Word history: from an Italian word meaning 'paste'

pet

noun **1** an animal that is kept because it is loved rather than because it is useful **2** a person who is given special attention: *teacher's pet*
verb **3** to treat in a special way, giving kisses and loving pats to, as if to a pet

Word building: Other verb forms are **I petted, I have petted, I am petting**.

petal

noun any of the leaflike parts of a flower which are usually of a colour different to green

petite   (*say* puh-<u>teet</u>)

adjective small and slim: *a petite ballet dancer*

petition

noun a formal request, especially to someone or a group in power: *to sign a petition to the local council asking for more parks*

Word building: **petition** *verb* **petitioner** *noun*

petrify

verb **1** to make stiff or unable to move with fear **2** to turn into stone or something like stone: *Millions of years have petrified the tree trunk.*

Word building: Other forms are **it petrified, it has petrified, it is petrifying.** | **petrifaction** *noun*

petrol

noun a liquid made from petroleum, used widely as a fuel in engines

petroleum

noun an oily liquid, usually obtained by drilling under the ground, and used to make petrol or other fuels

petticoat

noun a light skirtlike undergarment worn by women

Word use: Another word for this is **slip.**

petty

adjective **1** of little importance: *petty details* Other words: **insignificant, trivial** **2** concerned with unimportant things or showing narrow ideas and interests: *a petty mind*

Word building: Other forms are **pettier, pettiest.** | **pettily** *adverb* **pettiness** *noun*

petulant

adjective showing or feeling impatient annoyance, especially over something unimportant: *a petulant toss of the head*

Word building: **petulance** *noun* **petulantly** *adverb*

petunia

noun a kind of plant with funnel-shaped flowers of different colours

Word history: from a Guarani (South American) word meaning 'tobacco'

pew

noun a long benchlike seat in a church

pewter

noun a mixture of metals, including tin, used for making dishes, mugs and so on

phalanger

(*say* fuh-<u>lan</u>-juh)

noun one of the Australian marsupials which live in trees and which have tails that can wrap around branches, such as cuscuses and brush-tailed possums

phantom

noun **1** an image appearing in a dream or in the mind only **2** a ghost or ghostly appearance

Word building: **phantasmal** *adjective*

pharmacy

noun **1** the preparing and giving out of drugs used in medicine: *She is studying pharmacy.* **2** a chemist's shop

Word building: The plural is **pharmacies.** | **pharmaceutical** *adjective* **pharmacist** *noun*

pharynx

(*say* <u>fa</u>-rinks)

noun the tube which connects your mouth and nose passages with your throat

Word use: The plural is **pharynxes.**

phase

noun **1** a stage of change or development: *the phase of childhood*

verb **2** to gradually introduce or take out: *We are phasing in a new method of work.* | *We are phasing out all the old computer system for the new one.*

pheasant

(*say* <u>fez</u>-uhnt)

noun a kind of large long-tailed bird, often eaten as food

phenomenon

noun **1** anything which is seen or able to be seen: *The growth of new leaves in spring is a phenomenon of nature.* **2** something or someone that is beyond the ordinary

Word building: The plural is **phenomena.** | **phenomenal** *adjective* extraordinary **phenomenally** *adverb*

phial

(*say* <u>fuy</u>-uhl)

noun a small glass container for liquids: *a phial of medicine*

philately

(*say* fuh-<u>lat</u>-uh-lee)

noun the collecting and studying of postage stamps

Word building: **philatelic** *adjective* **philatelist** *noun*

philharmonic

adjective fond of music

Word use: This is used especially in the names of musical societies, choirs or orchestras.

philistine (*say* fīl-uh-stuyn)

noun someone who doesn't like beautiful things such as paintings, sculpture or music, and is proud to be that way

Word building: **philistine** *adjective* **philistinism** *noun*
Word history: named after the people of *Philistia*, an ancient country on the east coast of the Mediterranean Sea, who were thought to be barbarians

philosophy (*say* fuh-<u>los</u>-uh-fee)

noun **1** the search for truth and wisdom and the answers to questions such as 'Why do I exist?' and 'What is the purpose of life?' **2** a system of rules or principles by which you live: *a philosophy of life*

Word building: The plural is **philosophies.** | **philosophical** *adjective* sensible and calm when faced with difficulties **philosopher** *noun* **philosophically** *adverb* **philosophise** *verb*

phishing (*say* <u>fish</u>-ing)

noun a type of internet fraud where an email that is supposed to be from a reputable source is actually from somebody trying to discover personal details that they can then use to their own advantage: *We warned our grandmother about phishing and told her never to reveal her credit card details in an email.*

phlegm (*say* flem)

noun thick mucus in your nose, throat or lungs

Word building: **phlegmy** *adjective*

phlegmatic (*say* fleg-<u>mat</u>-ik)

adjective calm and even-tempered

phobia (*say* <u>foh</u>-bee-uh)

noun an overpowering fear: *a phobia about spiders*

Word use: This word is often joined with another word part to mean 'fear of a particular thing', as in *claustrophobia* which means 'fear of being shut in a small space'.
Word building: **phobic** *adjective*

phoenix (*say* <u>fee</u>-niks)

noun a beautiful, mythical bird, said to rise again as a healthy young bird after being burnt to ashes

phone

noun a shortened form of **telephone**

Word building: **phone** *verb*

phonetics

noun the study of the sounds used in speaking

Word building: **phonetic** *adjective*: *the phonetic alphabet* **phonetically** *adverb*

phoney

adjective false or not genuine: *a phoney $20 note*

Word building: **phoney** *noun*

phosphorescent (*say* fos-fuh-<u>res</u>-uhnt)

adjective shining or giving out light without getting hot

Word building: **phosphoresce** *verb* **phosphorescence** *noun*

phosphorus (*say* <u>fos</u>-fuh-ruhs)

noun a chemical element which is used in making match heads, detergents and garden fertilisers

Word building: **phosphate** *noun* a garden fertiliser made from phosphorus
Word history: from a Greek word meaning 'bringer of light'

photo

noun a shortened form of **photograph**

Word building: The plural is **photos.**

photocopy

noun an exact copy of a page of writing or pictures, made by a machine using a special camera and paper which reacts to light

Word use: Another word for this is **photostat.**
Word building: The plural is **photocopies.** | **photocopier** *noun* a machine which makes these copies **photocopy** *verb* (**photocopied, photocopying**)

photogenic

adjective looking attractive in photographs

photograph

noun a picture produced when a film is exposed to light in a camera

Word building: **photograph** *verb* **photographic** *adjective*

photography

noun the art of taking photographs

Word building: **photographer** *noun*

photosynthesis
(*say* foh-toh-<u>sin</u>-thuh-suhs)
noun the process by which green plants are able to use sunlight to make sugars from carbon dioxide and water

phrase
noun **1** a small group of words that go together, usually without a verb **2** a group of musical notes which go together to form part of a tune
verb **3** to say or write in a particular way: *Could you phrase your question differently?*

phylum   (*say* <u>fuy</u>-luhm)
noun one of the main groups into which biologists classify animals and plants: *All animals with backbones are in the same phylum.*

Word building: The plural is **phyla.**

physical
adjective **1** having to do with the human body: *physical exercise* **2** having to do with the material things in the world rather than spiritual things

Word building: **physically** *adverb*

physician   (*say* fiz-<u>ish</u>-uhn)
noun a medical doctor, especially one who does not do surgery

physics
noun the science of heat, light, electricity, magnetism, motion and other forms of matter and energy

Word building: **physicist** *noun*

physiology   (*say* fiz-ee-<u>ol</u>-uh-jee)
noun the science that has to do with the bodies of living things and how they work

Word building: **physiological** *adjective* **physiologist** *noun*

physiotherapy
noun the treatment of disease and injuries by massage and exercise

Word building: **physiotherapist** *noun*

physique   (*say* fuh-<u>zeek</u>)
noun the shape of someone's body: *a muscular physique*

pi   (*rhymes with* my)
noun the number you always get, 3.141 592+, when you divide the circumference of a circle by its diameter, expressed by the symbol π

pianist   (*say* <u>pee</u>-uh-nuhst)
noun someone who plays the piano

piano[1]
noun a large musical instrument played by striking keys which are connected to hammers which then strike metal strings

Word building: The plural is **pianos.**
Word history: short for the Italian words *pianoforte* or *fortepiano*

piano[2]
adverb softly: *This music should be played piano.*

Word use: This instruction in music is written as **p.** | The opposite is **forte.**
Word building: **pianissimo** *adverb* very softly
Word history: from an Italian word

piano accordion
noun a kind of accordion which has keys like a piano

picador   (*say* <u>pik</u>-uh-daw)
noun a bullfighter on horseback who makes the bull angry by poking it with sharp sticks

Word use: Compare this with **matador.**

piccolo   (*say* <u>pik</u>-uh-loh)
noun a small flute with a very high sound

Word building: The plural is **piccolos.**
Word history: from an Italian word meaning 'small'

pick[1]
verb **1** to choose or select **2** to take or gather **3** to use a sharp object to break open or dig into
noun **4** a choice or selection: *Take your pick.* **5** a plectrum, used to play a guitar or banjo
phrase **6 pick at,** to eat hardly any of: *to pick at your food* **7 pick on,** to annoy or criticise **8 pick up, a** to call for: *I'll pick you up at 8.30.* **b** to learn easily, without special teaching: *Children pick up foreign languages quickly.* **c** to get well again **9 the pick,** the best one

Word building: **picker** *noun*

pick[2]
noun a tool made up of a metal bar with sharp ends, fitted to a wooden handle and used for breaking up hard ground

Word use: It is also called a **pickaxe.**

picket

noun **1** a pointed wooden fence post **2** members of a trade union who stand guard outside their workplace during a strike, to stop people from going in to work

Word building: **picket** verb (**picketed, picketing**): to picket a factory

pickle

noun **1** an onion, cucumber or other vegetable preserved in vinegar or salt water **2** a spot of trouble: to get yourself into a pickle

Word building: **pickle** verb to preserve in salt or vinegar

pickpocket

noun someone who steals things out of people's pockets or handbags

picnic

noun **1** an outing to the beach, park and so on, during which you eat a meal in the open air **2** Informal an easy thing to do: It's no picnic doing all your Christmas shopping in one day.

Word building: **picnic** verb (**picnicked, picnicking**)

picture

noun **1** a drawing, painting, photo or something similar **2** someone or something that looks very beautiful: She looks a picture in her new dress.

phrase **3 the pictures**, another word for **cinema**

verb **4** to imagine: I can't picture myself being old.

Word building: **pictorial** adjective illustrated: a pictorial history of Australia

picture/pitcher Don't confuse **picture** with **pitcher**, which is a large jug. It can also be the baseball player who throws the ball to the batter.

picturesque (say pik-chuh-resk)

adjective pretty or charming: a picturesque village

Word building: **picturesquely** adverb

pidgin (say pij-uhn)

noun a language based on a mixture of other languages and used by people who have no other language in common

pie

noun a pastry case filled with fruit, vegetables or meat and baked in an oven

piebald

adjective covered with patches of black and white or other colours: a piebald horse

Word use: Compare this with **skewbald**.

piece

noun **1** a bit or part of something **2** a single or individual thing: a piece of fruit

verb **3** to fit or join: to piece together a jigsaw

piece/peace Don't confuse **piece** with **peace**, which is freedom from war, as in a march for peace. It can also be calm or quiet, as in peace of mind.

piecemeal

adverb bit by bit or piece by piece

Word building: **piecemeal** adjective

pied (rhymes with side)

adjective covered with different coloured patches: the Pied Piper

Word history: from the word magpie, as this bird has black-and-white feathers

pier (rhymes with here)

noun **1** a jetty built out into the water, that you can tie a boat to or fish from
Other words: **dock, quay, wharf**
2 one of the wooden or concrete supports which are driven into the ground to hold up a bridge
Other words: **pile**

pier/peer Don't confuse **pier** with **peer**. To **peer** at something is to look at it closely in an effort to see. Your **peers** are your equals, in age or rank.

pierce

verb to go into or through sharply: The needle was not sharp enough to pierce the thick material.
Other words: **perforate, puncture**

Word building: **piercing** adjective loud and sharp: piercing screams **piercingly** adverb

piety (say puy-uh-tee)

noun deep honour and respect for religion

pig
noun **1** a farm animal with a flat snout and curly tail, which is kept for its meat
Other words: **hog, swine**
2 someone who is dirty, selfish or greedy
Word use: The male is a **boar**, the female is a **sow** and the young is a **piglet**.
Word building: **piggery** *noun* a place where pigs are kept

pigeon   (*say* pij-uhn)
noun a plump small-headed bird which is easily tamed

pigeonhole
noun a small compartment for papers in an old-fashioned desk

piggyback
noun a ride on the back or shoulders
Word building: **piggyback** *verb*

pig-headed
adjective stupidly stubborn or obstinate

piglet
noun a baby pig

pigment
noun **1** a coloured powder which can be mixed with water to make paint **2** the substance which gives animals and plants colour
Word building: **pigmentation** *noun*

pigsty
noun **1** an enclosure where pigs are kept **2** *Informal* any dirty or untidy place: *Clean your room — it's a real pigsty!*
Word building: The plural is **pigsties**.

pigtail
noun a plait or bunch of tied-up hair hanging from the side or back of your head

pike¹
noun a large fierce fish with a long pointed snout, found in northern countries

pike²
verb Informal to let someone down by not keeping to an arrangement, especially by cancelling at the last minute or not going out somewhere with them: *I'm really annoyed that she keeps piking every time we agree to meet up.*
Word building: **piker** *noun*

pikelet
noun a small sweet pancake, often eaten with butter and jam

pile¹
noun **1** a number of things heaped up in one place **2** a large amount or number: *I have a pile of homework.*
verb **3** to load or stack
phrase **4 pile up**, to heap up or accumulate

pile²
noun a long heavy beam driven into the ground to support a bridge or building
Other words: **pier**

pile³
noun the raised surface of carpet, towels, velvet and similar material

pilfer
verb to steal in small amounts: *to pilfer biscuits from the tin*
Word building: **pilferer** *noun*

pilgrim
noun someone who makes a long journey to visit a holy place
Word building: **pilgrimage** *noun*: *to make a pilgrimage to Mecca*
Word history: from a Latin word meaning 'foreigner'

pill
noun a very small disc of medicine, which you swallow whole
Word use: Another word for this is **tablet**.

pillage
verb to rob brutally and violently: *The enemy soldiers pillaged the city.*
Other words: **loot, plunder**
Word building: **pillage** *noun*   **pillager** *noun*

pillar
noun a column which supports part of a building

pillion
noun the passenger seat behind the driver's seat on a motorcycle
Word building: **pillion** *adjective*
Word history: from a Latin word meaning 'skin' or 'pelt'

pillow
noun a soft cushion to rest your head on when you are in bed

pilot

noun **1** someone who flies a plane
2 someone who steers a ship into or out of port
adjective **3** done as an experiment: *a pilot film for a new television series*

Word building: **pilot** *verb*

pimple

noun a pus-filled swelling, usually on the face

Word building: **pimply** *adjective*

pin

noun **1** a thin piece of metal with a sharply pointed end, used to fasten things together **2** any type of fastener that looks or works like a pin: *Grandma broke her hip and had to have a pin put in it.*
verb **3** to fasten or hold securely in position: *to pin papers together | The fallen branch pinned him to the ground.*

Word building: Other verb forms are **I pinned, I have pinned, I am pinning.**

PIN

noun a group of numbers or letters you use to show who you are when you are doing something like getting money from an automatic teller machine

Word use: This word is an acronym made by joining the first letters of the words *Personal Identification Number.*

pinafore

noun a dress with no sleeves and a low neck, worn over a blouse or jumper, often as a school uniform or apron

pinball

noun a game in which you pull levers and push buttons to shoot a ball up a sloping board and score points when the ball hits various objects on the board

pincers

plural noun **1** a tool with a pair of hinged, pinching jaws, used for pulling nails out of wood **2** the pinching claws of crabs, lobsters and some insects

pinch

verb **1** to press or squeeze tightly and painfully between two surfaces, such as your thumb and finger: *He pinched her arm.* **2** *Informal* to steal

noun **3** a painful nip or squeeze **4** the very small amount that you can hold between your finger and thumb: *a pinch of salt*
phrase **5 at a pinch,** if absolutely necessary: *Eight people can fit into the car at a pinch.*

Word building: **pincher** *noun*

pincushion

noun a small cushion in which pins can be stuck to keep them handy when sewing

pine¹

noun an evergreen tree with needle-like leaves and cones instead of flowers

pine²

verb **1** to have an intense longing, or to yearn: *to pine for home*
phrase **2 pine away,** to become sick from grief and longing

pineapple

noun a large, yellow, tropical fruit which is sweet and juicy inside and has a rough outer skin

pine nut

noun a small edible nut, found in the cone of some kinds of pine tree

ping-pong

noun a game rather like tennis but played indoors on a table, using small bats and a very light, hollow, plastic ball

Word use: It is also known as **table tennis.**

pinion¹

noun a small toothed wheel which locks together with a toothed bar or larger wheel, used in machinery

pinion²

noun **1** a bird's wing or feather
verb **2** to cut off part of a bird's wing to stop it flying away **3** to prevent escape by tying back the arms or hands

pink¹

adjective **1** pale red
phrase **2 in the pink,** *Informal* feeling bright and healthy

pink²

verb to cut in a zigzag pattern

Word building: **pinking shears** *noun* scissors with notched blades for cutting a zigzag line

pinnacle

noun **1** a high, pointed mountain peak, or a tall, pointed spire on the roof of a building **2** the highest point of anything

pint

noun a unit of measure of liquid in the
the imperial system equal to almost
600 millilitres

pin-up

noun a picture of a favourite person,
pinned or stuck up on a wall

pioneer

noun someone who first explores an area,
going ahead of others and opening the way
for them: *pioneers opening up the Australian
bush* | *a pioneer of modern music*

Word building: **pioneer** *verb*

pious   (*say* puy-uhs)

adjective deeply religious

Word building: **piously** *adverb*

pip¹

noun the small seed of an apple, orange or
similar fruit

pip²

noun a short high sound such as the ones
used as time signals on the phone or on
radio

pipe

noun **1** a hollow tube for carrying water,
gas and so on **2** a small bowl with a hollow
tube or stem for smoking tobacco **3** a tube
through which you can pump air to make
musical notes, such as in an organ
verb **4** to transport or carry using a pipe: *to
pipe water from the dam to the house*
phrase **5 pipe down**, to keep quiet **6 pipe
up**, to start talking suddenly

Word building: **pipeline** *noun* a pipe for
carrying gas, oil or water over a long distance

pipi

noun a shellfish that burrows in the sand
and that is good to eat

piping

noun **1** a system of pipes such as for the
plumbing of a house **2** the shrill sound
made by birds **3** a thin strip of material
for trimming the edges of cushions or
clothes
phrase **4 piping hot**, very hot

pipsqueak

noun *Informal* someone thought to be small
and unimportant

piquant   (*say* peek-uhnt)

adjective **1** pleasantly spicy and sharp
in flavour: *Adding the little bit of
red vinegar made the sauce agreeably
piquant.* **2** interesting or stimulating: *His
piquant humour entertained us.*

pique   (*rhymes with* week)

verb **1** to annoy and upset: *Maria's
refusal to see Evan piqued him.* **2** to excite
or stimulate: *The large parcel piqued my
curiosity.*

Word building: **pique** *noun* anger or hurt
feelings

pique/peak/peek Don't confuse **pique** with
peak or **peek**.

A **peak** is the top of a mountain.

To **peek** is to snatch a quick look, often when
you are not supposed to.

piranha   (*say* puh-rah-nuh)

noun a small South American fish which
swims in schools that viciously attack
animals, including people, and eat their
flesh at great speed

pirate

noun **1** someone who attacks and robs
ships at sea
verb **2** to take and use without permission:
*to pirate someone's ideas and pretend they are
your own*

Word building: **piracy** *noun*

pirouette   (*say* pi-rooh-et)

noun a quick turn in a dance, often on
tiptoe

Word building: **pirouette** *verb*
Word history: from a French word meaning
'top' or 'whirligig'

pistil

noun the seed-bearing part of a flower

pistol

noun a gun with a short barrel that fits into
a holster or pocket

piston

noun a rod or disc inside a tube which
is pumped up and down and used in
engines

pit¹

noun **1** a large hole in the ground, such as a mine **2** a small hollow in the surface: *That big pimple has left a pit in my skin.* **3** the space in front of and beneath the stage in a theatre where the orchestra sits **4** an area beside a car racing track where the cars are repaired and filled with petrol
verb **5** to make hollows or holes in: *Meteors have pitted the moon with craters.* **6** to set in opposition: *I was pitted against their strongest player.*

Word building: Other verb forms are **I pitted, I have pitted, I am pitting.** | **pitted** *adjective*

pit²

noun the stone of a fruit such as a peach or a date

Word building: **pit** *verb* (**pitted, pitting**)

pita

noun a small, flat, round pocket of bread which you can open up and fill with food

Word use: Another spelling is **pitta.** | Another name is **pita bread.**
Word history: from a Greek word meaning 'a cake'

pitch

verb **1** to set up: *to pitch a tent* **2** to throw **3** to make a sudden falling movement: *He tripped and pitched forward.* **4** to rise and fall, as a ship does **5** to set at a certain level of musical pitch: *She pitched her instrument too high.*
noun **6** a throw or toss **7** the quality of a musical note thought of in terms of its highness or lowness **8** the area for playing sport, particularly the area between the wickets in cricket **9** the degree of slope: *the steep pitch of the roof*

pitcher¹

noun the baseball player who throws the ball to the batter

pitcher/picture Don't confuse **pitcher** with **picture**, which is a drawing, painting or photo.

pitcher²

noun a large jug

pitcher/picture Don't confuse **pitcher** with **picture**, which is a drawing, painting or photo.

pitchfork

noun a large fork used for lifting and tossing hay

pitfall

noun an unexpected trap

pith

noun **1** any soft spongy substance such as that between the skin and the flesh of an orange **2** the most important part

Word building: **pithy** *adjective* (**pithier, pithiest**)

pitiable

adjective **1** deserving pity **2** worthless

Word building: **pitiably** *adverb*

pitiful

adjective **1** causing or deserving pity **2** unsuccessful or worthless: *pitiful efforts*

Word building: **pitifully** *adverb*

pitta

noun another spelling for **pita**

pittance

noun a very small amount of money

pity

noun **1** deep sympathy for the suffering or sorrow of other people **2** a cause for sorrow: *It's a pity she can't come too.*
Other words: **shame**

Word building: **pity** *verb* (**pitied, pitying**)

pivot

noun someone or something on which something turns or depends

Word building: **pivot** *verb* (**pivoted, pivoting**) to turn, as on a pivot **pivotal** *adjective*

pixel

noun the smallest part of a graphic image which can be produced on a computer screen

pixie

noun an elf or fairy

pizza (*say* <u>peet</u>-suh)

noun a thin dough base covered with tomato, salami, cheese or similar savoury foods and baked in an oven

Word history: from an Italian word meaning 'pie'

placard

noun a large notice or poster

placate

verb to make calm or happy: *They placated the baby with toys.*
Other words: **appease, mollify, pacify**
Word building: **placatory** *adjective*

place

noun **1** a particular area or part of space: *He's gone to a place I don't know.*
2 situation: *I wouldn't do it if I were in your place.* **3** the page or passage you are up to when reading: *Mark your place with a bookmark.* **4** a short street, court or square **5** position in a race: *second place*
verb **6** to put or set: *She placed it on the table.* **7** to remember: *I can't place her.*
phrase **8 in place of,** instead of **9 take place,** to happen
Word building: **placement** *noun*

placenta   (*say* pluh-<u>sen</u>-tuh)

noun the organ which gives food and oxygen to a baby in its mother's womb
Word building: **placental** *adjective*: *placental mammals*
Word history: from a Greek word meaning 'flat cake'

placid   (*say* <u>plas</u>-uhd)

adjective calm or peaceful
Word building: **placidity** *noun*   **placidly** *adverb*

plagiarism   (*say* <u>play</u>-juh-riz-uhm)

noun the copying of someone else's ideas or way of expressing them, as in writing or art, and using them as if they were your own
Word building: **plagiarise** *verb*

plague   (*say* playg)

noun **1** any serious disease which spreads very quickly **2** a huge number of any pest: *a plague of mice*
Word building: **plague** *verb*

plaid   (*rhymes with* dad)

noun tartan cloth

plain

adjective **1** clearly seen, heard or understood
Other words: **apparent, clear, conspicuous, distinct, evident, obvious**
2 simple and uncomplicated
Other words: **basic, straightforward**
3 not beautiful
noun **4** a large flat area of land
Word building: **plainly** *adverb*

plain/plane Don't confuse **plain** with **plane**, which is a tool for smoothing wood. It is also a shortened form of **aeroplane**.

plaintiff

noun a person who brings a court case against someone else known as the defendant

plaintive

adjective complaining or sorrowful: *a plaintive cry*
Word building: **plaintively** *adverb*

plait   (*rhymes with* mat)

verb to weave or braid together three or more strands or bunches, as of hair
Word building: **plait** *noun*

plan

noun a program or design for how something should be done or made: *He has a plan for our next outing. | Have you finished the plans for the house?*
Word building: **plan** *verb* (**planned, planning**)

plane¹

noun **1** a flat or level surface **2** a level: *Her writing is on a higher plane than mine.* **3** a winged machine which is driven through the air by its propellers or jet engines
Word building: **plane** *adjective*
Word history: Definition 3 is a shortened form of **aeroplane**.

plane²

noun a tool for smoothing wood
Word building: **plane** *verb*

planet

noun any of the large bodies in space revolving around the sun or around any star
Word building: **planetary** *adjective*

plank

noun a flat length of wood, such as one used in building

plankton

noun the mass of very tiny plants and animals which float in water

plant

noun **1** a living thing which grows in the ground and which cannot move around **2** the machinery and equipment connected with an industry
verb **3** to put in the ground to grow **4** to put or fix: *to plant an idea*

plantation

noun a farm, especially in tropical areas where crops such as coffee, sugar or cotton are grown

plaque *(rhymes with* mark)

noun **1** a metal plate, such as one fastened to a wall, with a name, profession or memorial date on it **2** a coating on teeth which causes decay

plasma

noun the liquid part of blood which contains the blood cells

plaster

noun **1** a thick mixture of lime, sand and water, used to cover walls and ceilings **2** a fine white powder which swells and sets rapidly when mixed with water and is used in making moulds **3** a bandage soaked in such a mixture, which is put around a broken limb to hold it in place **4** a covering for a minor wound

Word use: Another name for definition 2 is **plaster of Paris.**
Word building: **plaster** *verb*: *to plaster walls* **plasterer** *noun* someone whose job is to plaster walls and ceilings

plastic

noun **1** a substance which can be shaped when soft and then hardened *adjective* **2** made of plastic: *a plastic cup* **3** having to do with surgery done to repair or replace badly formed or injured parts of the body

Word building: **plasticity** *noun*

plasticine *(say* plas-tuh-seen)

noun a soft substance like clay that can be shaped into figures

Word history: a trademark

plate

noun **1** a flat round dish for food **2** cutlery or dishes made of, or coated with, gold or silver **3** a thin flat sheet of metal **4** a colour illustration in a book **5** a support for false teeth

Word building: **plate** *verb* to coat with precious metal

plateau *(say* plat-oh)

noun a large flat stretch of high ground

Word building: The plural is **plateaus** or **plateaux.**

platelet

noun one of many tiny discs in the blood which help it to clot around wounds

platform

noun **1** a raised floor, as in a hall or theatre, for public speakers or performers **2** the raised area beside the tracks at a railway station **3** in computers, an operating system

platinum

noun a greyish-white metallic element used in making scientific equipment and jewellery

Word history: from a Spanish word meaning 'silver'

platitude

noun an expression which has been used too many times, especially one spoken as if it were fresh and wise

Word building: **platitudinous** *adjective*

platonic

adjective having to do with a love that is deep but does not involve sex: *platonic love*

Word building: **platonically** *adverb*
Word history: named after the Greek philospher *Plato*, who lived from about 427 to 347 BC

platoon

noun a group or unit of soldiers

platter

noun a large plate used for serving food

platypus

noun an Australian web-footed animal with a bill like a duck's, which lays eggs and feeds its young with its own milk

Word building: The plural is **platypuses.**
Word history: from a Greek word meaning 'flat-footed'

plausible *(say* plawz-uh-buhl)

adjective believable or reasonable: *a plausible story*

Word building: **plausibility** *noun* **plausibly** *adverb*

play

noun **1** activity for fun or relaxation
Other words: **amusement, entertainment, recreation**
2 a story which can be acted out by actors in a theatre
Other words: **drama**
3 light, rapid movement: *the play of reflections on water*
verb **4** to act the part of: *He is playing Hamlet.*
Other words: **perform**
5 to do or take part in for sport or amusement: *Do you play cards?* **6** to take part in a game **7** to pretend to be or imitate, as in children's games: *They are playing pirates.* **8** to perform on: *He plays the flute.* **9** to cause to produce music or sound: *to play a CD.*

player

noun **1** someone who takes part in or is skilled in a game: *The players were still in the change rooms.* **2** someone who acts a part on the stage: *The audience continued to clap until the players came out again.* **3** someone who plays a musical instrument: *The players waited until the conductor's baton rose.*

playground

noun **1** an outside area with equipment like swings, slides and so on, for children to play in **2** an outside area at a school, where students can play at recess and lunch

playwright

noun someone who writes plays
Other words: **dramatist**

plaza

noun an open space or square in a town

plea

noun an earnest request

plead

verb **1** to beg or earnestly ask **2** to say whether you are innocent or guilty in a court case **3** to use as an excuse: *He pleaded tiredness.*

pleasant   (*say* plez-uhnt)

adjective agreeable or pleasing: *a pleasant outing | a pleasant manner*
Other words: **enjoyable, lovely, nice**
Word building: **pleasantly** *adverb*

please

verb **1** to make happy or satisfied: *The gift pleased them greatly.*

Other words: **cheer, delight, gladden**
interjection **2** if you are willing: *Come here please.*

Word building: **pleasing** *adjective* **pleasingly** *adverb*

pleasure   (*say* plezh-uh)

noun enjoyment or happiness
Other words: **delight, gladness, joy**

Word building: **pleasurable** *adjective* **pleasurably** *adverb*

pleat   (*rhymes with* meet)

noun a pressed or stitched fold in trousers or a skirt

Word building: **pleat** *verb*

plectrum

noun a small piece of wood, plastic or metal, used to pluck the strings of instruments such as the guitar or banjo

Word building: The plural is **plectrums**.

pledge

noun **1** a promise made very seriously **2** something given as a guarantee that you will return a loan: *He left $10 as a pledge.*

Word use: Another word for definition 1 is **vow**.
Word building: **pledge** *verb*

plentiful

adjective great in amount or number: *a plentiful supply*

Word building: **plentifully** *adverb*

plenty

noun an amount or supply which is large or sufficient: *Take some, we have plenty.*

Word building: **plenteous** *adjective*

pliable

adjective flexible or easily bent: *a pliable stem | a pliable nature*

Word building: **pliability** *noun* **pliably** *adverb*

pliers   (*say* pluy-uhz)

plural noun a tool used for gripping, and for twisting or cutting wire

plight

noun a state or situation, usually bad: *She left them in an awful plight.*

plod

verb to go or continue in a slow, steady and unexciting way: *He plods off to work every day.*

Word building: Other forms are **I plodded, I have plodded, I am plodding.** | **plodder** *noun*

plot¹

noun **1** a secret plan or scheme **2** the story of a novel or play
verb **3** to plan secretly **4** to mark out or map: *to plot a route*

Word building: Other verb forms are **I plotted, I have plotted, I am plotting.** | **plotter** *noun*

plot²

noun a small piece of ground: *a vegetable plot*

plough (*rhymes with* now)

noun **1** a tool with a curved blade for digging the soil
verb **2** to dig with a plough
phrase **3 plough through,** to work steadily at: *He ploughs through the housework.*

ploy (*rhymes with* toy)

noun a scheme or trick to gain an advantage over someone: *The ploy I used on my mother worked — she's letting me go to the school disco.*

pluck

verb **1** to pull at and remove: *to pluck an apple from the tree* **2** to play notes on the strings of an instrument by pulling at them with your fingers or by using a plectrum
noun **3** courage

Word building: **plucky** *adjective* (**pluckier, pluckiest**) brave   **pluckily** *adverb*
pluckiness *noun*

plug

noun **1** a stopper to prevent liquid escaping, as from a basin **2** something used to block a hole **3** the connection at the end of an electrical wire which you put into a power point
verb **4** to stop up: *He plugged the leak.*
5 *Informal* to mention often, as a kind of advertisement: *He is plugging their show.*

Word building: Other verb forms are
I plugged, I have plugged, I am plugging.

plum

noun a soft, smooth-skinned fruit related to but larger than the cherry

Word building: **plum** *adjective* choice: *a plum job*

plumage (*say* ploohm-ij)

noun the feathers covering a bird's body

plumb (*rhymes with* mum)

noun **1** a lead weight on a string, used in measuring depth or as a test of uprightness **2** an exactly upright or perpendicular line or position: *The post is out of plumb, so we'll have to straighten it.*
adverb **3** in an upright position **4** exactly: *plumb in the middle*

Word use: Another word for definition 1 is **plumbline.**
Word building: **plumb** *verb*: *to plumb the depths of the ocean*

plumber (*say* plum-uh)

noun someone who puts into a building the pipes which are used to carry water and waste, and fixes them when something goes wrong

Word building: **plumbing** *noun*

plume

noun a feather, especially a long or showy one

plummet

verb to fall straight and fast, as something heavy does

plump

adjective rather fat and well-rounded

plunder

verb to rob violently, as in war
Other words: **loot, pillage**

Word building: **plunder** *noun*

plunge

verb **1** to dip or thrust: *She plunged her bucket into the river.* | *The storm plunged the town into darkness.* **2** to dive or fall, as into water
Other words: **drop, plummet**
3 to move quickly or suddenly: *to plunge into action*
noun **4** a sudden rush or move **5** a dive or fall
Other words: **jump, leap**

plural

adjective indicating more than one person or thing such as the words 'children' and 'hear' in *The children hear the bell.*

Word building: **plurality** *noun*

plus

adjective **1** having to do with addition: *the plus sign*
noun **2** an added advantage: *another plus*

plush

adjective rich, fine or costly

plutonium
noun a radioactive element which is obtained from uranium, and is a powerful source of energy

ply¹
verb **1** to use or do, especially busily: *to ply the oars | to ply a trade* **2** to supply continuously: *She plied us with sandwiches.* **3** to travel or cross often: *to ply the harbour | to ply between Sydney and Auckland*

Word building: Other forms are **I plied, I have plied, I am plying.**

ply²
noun a strand or a thickness

Word building: The plural is **plies.**

plywood
noun board made of layers of wood stuck together

p.m.
short for *post meridiem*, Latin words meaning 'after noon': *I go to bed at 9 p.m.*

pneumatic   (*say* nyooh-<u>mat</u>-ik)
adjective worked by air or air pressure: *a pneumatic pump*

Word building: **pneumatically** *adverb*
Word history: from a Greek word meaning 'of a wind'

pneumonia   (*say* nyooh-<u>mohn</u>-yuh)
noun an illness caused by an infection or inflammation of the lungs, which gives you a fever and makes breathing difficult

poach¹
verb to cook in liquid just below boiling point

poach²
verb to hunt or fish without permission on someone else's property

Word building: **poacher** *noun* someone who poaches

pocket
noun **1** a cloth fold or pouch sewn into a garment, for holding things **2** a small area of something: *a pocket of coal | a pocket of resistance*
verb **3** to put into your own pocket, especially dishonestly

pocket money
noun **1** money that children are regularly given by their parents or carers, often in return for doing chores **2** small amounts of money used to pay for personal items

pod
noun the long container in which seeds grow: *a pea pod*

podcast
verb to present information (like a radio program) over the internet as a computer file so it can be stored and played later on a computer or an MP3 player

Word building: **podcast** *noun* **podcast** *adjective* **podcasting** *noun, adjective*

poddy
noun a young animal, especially a calf, which needs to be fed by hand

Word building: The plural is **poddies.** | **poddy** *adjective*

podium
noun a small platform for speakers or conductors

Word building: The plural is **podia.**
Word history: from a Greek word meaning 'foot'

poem
noun a piece of poetry

Word building: **poet** *noun* someone who writes poems

poetry
noun **1** writing or speaking which expresses feelings and thoughts on people and things that happen, especially your own feelings and thoughts. See the 'Types of writing and speaking' table at the end of this book. **2** beauty or harmony

Word building: **poetic** *adjective* **poetically** *adverb*

poignant   (*say* <u>poyn</u>-yuhnt)
adjective deeply or keenly felt: *poignant sorrow*

Word building: **poignancy** *noun*

point

noun **1** a sharp end: *the needle's point*
2 a written dot, as in punctuation or decimals **3** the level or place in a process at which something happens: *boiling point* **4** any of the 32 compass positions **5** a fact, idea or opinion put forward in a discussion, speech, piece of writing, and so on: *I'll make one last point before finishing.* **6** the main fact, idea, and so on: *I didn't understand the point of the story.*
Other words: **meaning, message**
7 reason or intention: *The point of this exercise is to strengthen your leg muscles.* | *I don't see the point of doing this any longer.*
Other words: **purpose**
8 a unit for scoring in a game: *We won by only a single point.*
verb **9** to show by a finger or sign: *The sign points north.* **10** to aim: *to point a gun*
Word building: **pointed** *adjective* sharp: *a pointed weapon* | *a pointed comment* **pointedly** *adverb*

point-blank

adjective **1** aimed or fired at very close range: *a point-blank shot* **2** plain or straight-forward: *a point-blank answer*
Word building: **point-blank** *adverb*

pointy

adjective being pointed at the end: *The pencil has a pointy end and a round end.*

poise

noun **1** confidence or ease when dealing with people and situations: *The school captain greeted the visitors with poise.*
verb **2** to hold steady or balanced
Word building: **poised** *adjective* dignified

poison

noun **1** a substance which causes death or illness if you swallow it
verb **2** to kill or harm with poison
Word building: **poisonous** *adjective*

poke

verb **1** to push or prod: *to poke someone with your finger* **2** to show or appear, especially from behind something: *I poked my head around the door, but no-one was there.*
Word building: **poke** *noun*

poker¹

noun a metal rod for stirring the fire in a fireplace or oven

poker²

noun a card game in which the players bet money on the value of the cards they are holding

poky

adjective cramped: *a poky little room*
Word building: Other forms are **pokier, pokiest**.

pole¹

noun a long thin piece of wood or other material: *a flag pole*

pole²

noun an opposite end or force: *the north and south poles*
Word building: **polar** *adjective* **polarity** *noun*

> **pole/poll** Don't confuse **pole** with **poll**. When someone takes a **poll** they count and record the number of people, votes or opinions in favour of or opposed to an important issue.

police

noun members of a force employed by the state or nation to keep order and to protect life and property: *The police were at the scene of the accident within minutes.*
Word building: **police** *verb* **policeman** *noun* **policewoman** *noun*

policy¹ (*say* pol-uh-see)

noun a plan of action: *What is their foreign policy?* | *It's good policy to save.*
Word building: The plural is **policies**.

policy² (*say* pol-uh-see)

noun a signed agreement with an insurance company
Word building: The plural is **policies**.

poliomyelitis

(*say* poh-lee-oh-muy-uh-luy-tuhs)
noun a disease, now rare, causing paralysis
Word use: A shortened form of this is **polio**.

polish

verb **1** to make shiny by rubbing **2** to put the final touches to: *She just needs to polish her performance.*
noun **3** a paste or liquid which gives a shine when it is rubbed on: *shoe polish* **4** fineness or elegance: *He sings with polish.*
phrase **5 polish off**, to finish: *Let's polish off those cakes.*
Word building: **polished** *adjective* **polisher** *noun*

polite

adjective **1** having good manners
Other words: **civil, courteous, gracious, proper**
2 refined: *polite society*

Word use: Words having the opposite meaning
are **impolite** and **rude**.
Word building: **politely** *adverb* **politeness** *noun*

political asylum

noun the protection that a country gives
to a person who has fled from their own
country because they have been persecuted
or because of war

politics

noun **1** the leading and management of
the affairs of a country or state **2** methods
used to gain power or success: *I hate the
politics of my job.*

Word use: You can treat this noun as singular
or plural.
Word building: **political** *adjective*
politically *adverb* **politician** *noun*

polka

noun a quick and lively dance

Word building: **polka** *verb* (**polkaed, polkaing**)

poll

noun **1** a counting of people, votes or
opinions **2 the polls**, the place where
votes are taken
verb **3** to ask and record the opinions of: *to
poll the nation on an important matter* **4** to
receive a number of votes: *to poll badly in
an election* **5** to cut off the hair or horns of

poll/pole Don't confuse **poll** with **pole**.
One kind of **pole** is a long thin piece of wood.

The other kind of **pole** is one of the
extremities of the axis of the earth.

A **Pole** (with a capital letter) is a person from
Poland.

pollen

noun the yellowish seed dust of flowers

Word history: a Latin word meaning 'fine
flour' or 'dust'

pollinate

verb to cause to produce seeds by adding
pollen: *Bees pollinate flowers as they collect
nectar.*

Word building: **pollination** *noun*

pollute

verb to spoil or make dirty: *The heavy
traffic pollutes the air.*

Other words: **adulterate, contaminate,
poison, taint**

Word building: **pollutant** *noun* something
which pollutes   **polluted** *adjective*
pollution *noun*

pollution   (*say* puh-<u>loo</u>-shuhn)

noun **1** the act of polluting
2 environmental pollutants, such as
motor vehicle emissions, industrial waste,
and so on **3** the results of these pollutants,
as city smog, chemicals in the water,
and so on

polo

noun a ball game on horseback, between
two teams using long wooden mallets and a
wooden ball

poltergeist   (*say* <u>pol</u>-tuh-guyst)

noun a troublesome ghost or spirit who is
supposed to move things and make noises

Word history: from German words for 'noise'
and 'ghost'

poly-

prefix a word part meaning 'much' or
'many': *polygon*

Word history: from Greek

polygamy   (*say* puh-<u>lig</u>-uh-mee)

noun marriage to more than one person at
a time

Word use: Compare this with **monogamy** and
bigamy.
Word building: **polygamist** *noun* **polygamous**
adjective

polygon

noun a flat shape with many straight sides

polythene

noun a firm light plastic which is used for
containers, packing and insulation

Pom

adjective Informal an English person

Word use: This word may offend some
people. | Another word for this is **Pommy**.

pomegranate   (*say* <u>pom</u>-uh-gran-uht)

noun a thick-skinned pinkish fruit which
splits open when it is ripe to reveal many
seeds and flesh that you can eat

pommel

noun **1** the front peak of a saddle **2** a knob
at the end of a sword or knife handle

pomp

noun splendid display, as in a ceremony or parade

pompom

noun a ball made of wool or other thread, often put on hats or caps as an ornament

pompous

adjective showing too much sense of your own importance: *a pompous speech*

Word building: **pomposity** *noun*
pompously *adjective*

poncho

noun a cloak with a hole in the centre to put your head through

Word building: The plural is **ponchos**.

pond

noun an area of water smaller than a lake

ponder

verb to think about deeply or carefully: *to ponder the question*

ponderous

adjective **1** large and heavy **2** serious and dull: *a ponderous discussion*

Word building: **ponderously** *adverb*

pontiff

noun a pope

Word building: **pontifical** *adjective*

pontificate   (*say* pon-<u>tif</u>-uh-kuht)

noun **1** the time during which a pontiff holds office
verb (*say* pon-<u>tif</u>-uh-kayt) **2** to speak in an important-sounding manner

Word use: The more usual word for definition 2 is **lecture**.

pontoon

noun a floating structure used to support a temporary bridge or dock

pony

noun a small horse

Word building: The plural is **ponies**.

ponytail

noun a hairstyle in which the hair is tied in a loose bunch at the back of the head

poodle

noun a dog with thick curly hair often trimmed in special shapes

pool¹

noun **1** a small area of still water, especially one made for swimming in **2** a small collection of any liquid: *a pool of blood*

pool²

noun **1** a combination of possessions, money or services for the use of everyone in a group: *All the managers can get a letter typed by a typist in the typing pool.* **2** the sum of money that can be won in some gambling games **3** a kind of billiards game
verb **4** to put together for the use of everyone in a group: *Let's pool our money and buy her a present from us all.*

poop   (*rhymes with* loop)

noun a deck at the back part of a ship, above the main deck

poor

adjective **1** having little money, property or means of producing wealth: *a poor person | a poor country* **2** low in quality or skill: *a poor piece of work* **3** small in amount or number: *a poor wage* **4** unfortunate or unlucky: *You poor thing!*
noun **5** poor people as a group: *I am collecting money for the poor.*

Word building: **poorly** *adverb*   **poorness** *noun*   **poverty** *noun*

poor/pour/paw/pore Don't confuse **poor** with **pour**, **paw**, or **pore**.

You can **pour** a liquid from one container to another.

A **paw** is the foot of an animal with nails or claws.

A **pore** is a small hole. Sweat comes out through the **pores** in your skin. To **pore** over something is to read or study it carefully:
   He watched the pirates pore over the secret treasure map.

pop¹

verb **1** to make a short explosive sound **2** to come, go or put quickly or suddenly: *I'll pop in and visit you. | Pop the books on my desk.*
noun **3** a short explosive sound

Word building: Other verb forms are **I popped, I have popped, I am popping**.

popcorn

noun maize grain which bursts open and puffs up when heated and is then eaten

pope
> *noun* the bishop of Rome as head of the Roman Catholic Church
>
> Word use: This is often spelt with a capital letter.
> Word building: **papal** *adjective* having to do with a pope

poplar (*say* pop-luh)
> *noun* a tall, fast-growing tree

pop music
> *noun* music that is very popular at a certain time, especially among young people, usually having a strong rhythm

poppadum
> *noun* another spelling for **pappadum**

poppy
> *noun* a kind of brightly coloured flower
> Word building: The plural is **poppies**.

populace (*say* pop-yuh-luhs)
> *noun* the people who live in an area

popular
> *adjective* **1** widely liked by a particular group or people in general: *a popular song | a girl who is popular with her class* **2** having to do with the people in general: *popular beliefs*
> Word building: **popularity** *noun* **popularly** *adverb*

populate
> *verb* **1** to live in: *Australia was populated by Aboriginal people before the coming of Europeans.*
> Other words: **inhabit**
> **2** to fill up with people

population
> *noun* the people living in a country, town or other area

populous
> *adjective* having a large number of people: *a populous city*

porcelain (*say* paw-suh-luhn)
> *noun* a kind of fine china, used for dishes and ornaments

porch
> *noun* a covered area at the entrance of a building
> Word building: The plural is **porches**.

porcupine
> *noun* a small animal covered with stiff sharp spines

pore¹
> *verb* to read or study carefully: *The students pored over their books.*

pore²
> *noun* a very small opening, especially in the skin, for liquid to be taken in or come out through: *Sweat comes out through your pores.*

> **pore/pour/paw/poor** Don't confuse **pore** with **pour**, **paw** or **poor**.
>
> You can **pour** a liquid from one container to another.
>
> A **paw** is the foot of an animal with nails or claws.
>
> Someone is **poor** if they don't have much money or property.

pork
> *noun* the meat of a pig

pornography
> *noun* art, photography or writing that is thought to be indecent or obscene
> Word building: **pornographer** *noun* **pornographic** *adjective*

porous
> *adjective* having lots of small holes or spaces that allow air or water to pass through: *These plants will grow best in porous soil. | Water will eventually pass through sandstone because it is a porous type of rock.*
> Word building: **porousness** *noun*

porpoise
> *noun* a sea mammal with a rounded snout, usually blackish on top and paler beneath, which often leaps from the water
> Word building: The plural is **porpoises** or **porpoise**.
> Word history: from a Latin word meaning 'hogfish'

porridge
> *noun* oats cooked with water or milk, often eaten for breakfast

port¹
> *noun* **1** a harbour where ships load and unload **2** a town with a harbour

port²
> *noun* the left-hand side of a ship or plane when you are facing the front
> Word use: The opposite is **starboard**.

port³

noun a sweet dark red wine

port⁴

noun **1** an opening, such as a porthole in a ship **2** a connection point in a computer for the entry or exit of data

port⁵

noun a suitcase or school bag

portable

adjective able to be easily carried or moved: *a portable television*

Word building: **portability** *noun*

porter

noun someone whose job is carrying bags or other loads: *a railway porter*

portfolio

noun **1** a case for carrying loose papers or letters **2** the duties of a minister in a government: *The Premier gave her the Education portfolio.*

porthole

noun a round opening like a window in the side of a ship that gives light and air

portion

noun a part or share of something

Word building: **portion** *verb*

portly

adjective large and fat

Word building: **portliness** *noun*

portmanteau   (*say* pawt-<u>man</u>-toh)

noun a suitcase for travelling which opens into two halves

Word building: The plural is **portmanteaus** or **portmanteaux**.
Word history: from a French word meaning 'cloak-carrier'

portmanteau word

noun a word in which the start of one word is joined up with the end of another word to make a new word: *'Smog' is a portmanteau word made from 'smoke' and 'fog'.*

Word history: from the book *Through the Looking Glass* by Lewis Carroll: 'You see it's like a portmanteau ... there are two meanings packed up in one word.'

portrait   (*say* <u>pawt</u>-ruht)

noun **1** a painting, drawing or photograph of someone, especially of their face **2** a written or spoken description: *a portrait of life in the Middle Ages*

Word building: **portraiture** *noun*

portray

verb **1** to make a painting or drawing of **2** to act the part of: *I portrayed a queen in the class play.* **3** to describe in words

Word building: **portrayal** *noun*

pose

verb **1** to take up a particular position: *The model posed for the camera.* **2** to pretend to be something or someone **3** to present or put forward: *The teacher posed a hard question.*

Word building: **pose** *noun*   **poser** *noun*

posh

adjective *Informal* smart, expensive-looking, or high-class: *a posh car*

position

noun **1** a place or location: *Take any position in the back row.* **2** proper place: *I am putting these chairs into position.* **3** the manner in which something is placed or arranged **4** a situation or state: *My lack of money puts me in a difficult position.* **5** rank or standing: *a high position in society* **6** a job **7** a point of view: *What is your position in this argument?*

Word building: **position** *verb*

positive

adjective **1** absolutely sure or certain **2** expressing agreement: *a positive answer* **3** actual or real: *This has been of positive good to us.* **4** tending to see what is good or gives hope: *positive criticism of a pupil's work | a positive attitude towards a problem* **5** greater than zero in quantity **6** having a deficiency or lack of electrons: *the positive pole of an electric cell*

Word building: **positively** *adverb* **positiveness** *noun*

posse   (*say* <u>pos</u>-ee)

noun a group of people that helps a sheriff keep peace

Word use: This word is mainly used in America.

possess

verb **1** to own or have: *to possess a lot of books | to possess courage* **2** to take over and control: *Rage possessed her.*
Other words: **seize**

Word building: **possessor** *noun*

possessed

adjective taken over by a strong feeling, madness or an apparently supernatural force: *She screamed like someone possessed.*

possession

noun **1** ownership or the act of possessing: *I took possession of my new car yesterday.* **2** something possessed: *This watch is my favourite possession.*

possessive

adjective wanting to possess or control all by yourself
Word building: **possessively** *adverb*
possessiveness *noun*

possessive case

noun the form of a noun or pronoun which shows ownership, such as *her*, in *her book*, which is the possessive case of *she*

possible

adjective able to be, happen, be done or be used: *a possible cure for a disease | Is it possible to drive there in one day?*
Word building: **possibility** *noun*
(**possibilities**) **possibly** *adverb*

possum

noun an Australian marsupial that lives in trees and has long arms and legs and a long tail for climbing and is active at night. Some species are endangered or vulnerable. See the table at the end of this book.

post¹

noun **1** an upright piece of wood or metal used as a support: *a fence post* **2** a post marking the start or finish of a race
verb **3** to put up on a post or wall for public attention: *They posted a list of the new prices.*

post²

noun **1** a job or duty: *She has a teaching post.* **2** the place where a job or duty is done, especially guard duty
Word building: **post** *verb*: *to post a guard at the gate*

post³

noun **1** delivery of letters or other mail **2** the letters themselves **3** the system of carrying letters and other mail
verb **4** to send by post: *I am posting a letter to you tomorrow.*

Word building: **postage** *noun* the cost of sending something by post **postal** *adjective*

post-

prefix a word part meaning 'behind' or 'after': *posterior | post-mortem*
Word history: from Latin

postcard

noun a card for sending by post with a picture on one side and a space for a message on the other side

postcode

noun a group of numbers added to your address to help speed the delivery of mail

poster

noun a large notice, often illustrated

posterior

adjective **1** from or at the back: *a posterior view of the spine*
noun **2** *Informal* your bottom

posterity (say po-ste-ruh-tee)

noun the people who will live in the future: *Your work will be remembered by posterity.*

posthumous (say pos-chuh-muhs)

adjective published, given or happening after someone's death: *a posthumous publication of Patrick's last novel | a posthumous award*
Word building: **posthumously** *adverb*

post-mortem

noun the medical examination of a dead body
Other words: **autopsy**
Word building: **post-mortem** *adjective*

postpone

verb to put off to a later time: *They postponed the game because of rain.*
Other words: **adjourn, defer, delay, suspend**
Word building: **postponement** *noun*

postscript

noun an extra message written on the end of a finished and signed letter
Word use: The short form of this is **PS**.

posture

noun position of your body: *a kneeling posture*

posy

noun a small, neatly arranged bunch of flowers

Word building: The plural is **posies**.

pot

noun **1** a container, usually round and deep: *a cooking pot | a flower pot*
verb **2** to put or plant in a pot

Word building: Other verb forms are **I potted, I have potted, I am potting**.

potato

noun a white plant root which you can eat as a vegetable

Word building: The plural is **potatoes**.

potent

adjective powerful or strong: *a potent king | a potent medicine*

Word building: **potency** noun

potential

adjective **1** capable of becoming in the future: *I think this song is a potential hit.*
noun **2** possible or likely ability: *She is a pianist with a lot of potential.*

Word building: **potentiality** noun **potentially** adverb

pothole

noun a hole in the ground, especially one in a road

potion

noun Old-fashioned a drink, especially medicine, or one that's poisonous or magical in some way

pot luck

noun a situation where a person is not sure what to expect but is hoping for the best: *It was a case of pot luck when the bus finally arrived — we all just grabbed whatever seat we could.*

potoroo

noun a small, long-nosed animal with a pointed head that lives in thick grass, and sleeps during the day and comes out at night. It is endangered. See the table at the end of this book.

Word history: from an Aboriginal language of New South Wales called Dharug. See the map of Australian Aboriginal languages at the end of this book.

potpourri (*say* pot-<u>poo</u>-ree, poh-poo-<u>ree</u>)

noun **1** a mixture of dried flower petals used to give a perfume **2** any collection or mixture of different things: *This book is a potpourri of stories, poems and plays.*

Word history: from a French word meaning 'rotten pot'

potter[1]

noun someone who shapes pots, dishes and so on out of clay, and then hardens them by baking

Word building: **pottery** noun the things a potter makes

potter[2]

verb to busy or occupy yourself without getting much done: *I spent the day pottering about the house.*

potty[1]

adjective Informal foolish or crazy

Word building: Other forms are **pottier, pottiest**.

potty[2]

noun a pot used as a toilet, especially for small children

pouch

noun **1** a small bag or sack, used for carrying things like money **2** a part of the body shaped like a bag or pocket: *the pouch of a kangaroo | pouches of skin beneath the eyes*

Word building: The plural is **pouches**.

poultry

noun birds such as chickens, turkey, ducks and geese, which are used as food or for egg production

pounce

verb to move or leap suddenly and seize: *The lion pounced on the zebra.*

Word building: **pounce** noun

pound[1]

verb **1** to hit hard and many times **2** to crush into a powder or small pieces **3** to beat or throb violently: *My heart was pounding with excitement.* **4** to go with quick heavy steps: *They pounded along the corridor.*

pound[2]

noun **1** a unit of weight in the imperial system equal to just under half a kilogram **2** a unit of money used in Australia until 1966 and still used in Britain and some other countries

pound[3]

noun a place where animals are sheltered or kept, especially if they are homeless

pour

verb **1** to send flowing or falling: *She poured milk into a glass.* **2** to move or flow in great numbers: *The children poured out of the bus.* **3** to rain heavily

> **pour/poor/paw/pore** Don't confuse **pour** with **poor**, **paw**, or **pore**.
>
> Someone is **poor** if they don't have much money or property.
>
> A **paw** is the foot of an animal with nails or claws.
>
> A **pore** is a small hole. Sweat comes out through the **pores** in your skin. To **pore** over something is to read or study it carefully:
> *He watched the pirates pore over the secret treasure map.*

pout

verb to push out the lips showing disappointment or sulkiness
Word building: **pout** *noun*

poverty

noun **1** the condition of being poor: *They lived in poverty for years.* **2** a shortage of something needed or wanted: *a poverty of ideas*

powder

noun **1** the very small loose bits of something dry that has been crushed or ground: *talcum powder | a powder of dust | tablets crushed to a powder*
verb **2** to crush into a powder
Other words: **pulverise**
3 to cover with a powder: *to powder your face*
Word building: **powdery** *adjective*

power

noun **1** the ability to do something
Other words: **capability, capacity, faculty**
2 control over others, especially the control that rulers or governments have: *The election put a new government into power.*
Other words: **authority, command, dominion**
3 strength or force: *a punch with a lot of power*

Other words: **forcefulness, might, muscle**
4 someone who is very powerful: *Dominique is the power behind the project.* **5** a country that has a lot of power: *There was a meeting of world powers in London.* **6** the number that is the result of multiplying a number by itself one or more times: *Four is the second power of two, and eight is the third power of two.* **7** energy or force that can be used for doing work: *electrical power*
verb **8** to supply with electricity or another kind of power: *to power a machine*
Word building: **powerful** *adjective*
powerfully *adverb*

power board

noun a plastic unit on which there are a number of power points: *There are not enough power points in this room — we need a power board.*

power play

noun the use of tactics in any situation to intimidate the person who is on an opposing side

power point

noun a device, usually on a wall, to plug electrical power leads into

practical

adjective **1** having to do with actual practice or action, rather than ideas: *an invention with a practical use | You need practical experience for this job.* **2** interested in and good at useful work: *a practical person* **3** sensible and realistic: *He always has a practical answer.*
Word building: **practicality** *noun*

practically

adverb **1** in a practical way **2** nearly or almost: *We're practically there.*

practice

noun **1** actual action or performance: *The idea sounded good but didn't work in practice.* **2** an action or performance that is repeated regularly to improve skill **3** the usual way of doing something: *It is the practice at our school to have assembly every Wednesday.* **4** the business of someone such as a doctor or lawyer

practise

verb **1** to do or carry out as a usual habit: *You should always practise truthfulness.* **2** to work in as a profession: *to practise law* **3** to do or perform repeatedly in order to improve skill: *I was practising my tennis strokes.*
Word building: **practised** *adjective*

practitioner

noun someone working in a practice, particularly a doctor: *a medical practitioner*

pragmatic

adjective thinking about the results or usefulness of actions: *She is too pragmatic to waste time wanting what she can't have.*

Word building: **pragmatically** *adverb*

prairie

noun a flat, grassy, treeless plain, especially in America and Canada

Word history: from a Latin word meaning 'meadow'

praise

verb to say that you admire and approve of: *The police praised the citizen who rescued the old man.*

Word building: **praise** *noun*

pram

noun a four-wheeled carriage for pushing a baby in

prance

verb to leap about

prank

noun a playful trick

prattle

verb to chatter in a stupid way

Word building: **prattle** *noun*

prawn

noun a small shellfish used for food

pray

verb **1** to talk to your god to thank, praise or ask for something **2** to ask earnestly: *I prayed them to let me go.*

Other words: **appeal, beg, beseech, plead**

pray/prey Don't confuse **pray** with **prey**. To **prey** on something is to hunt and eat it. It can also mean 'to affect something harmfully':
> *Cats prey on mice.*
> *The cause of his death still preys on my mind.*

prayer *(say* prair*)*

noun **1** a communication someone makes with the god they believe in, often a request for help or forgiveness: *He said a prayer for his sister's safety.* **2** the act or practice of praying: *They joined together in prayer for the victims of the earthquake.*

praying mantis

noun another word for **mantis**

pre-

prefix a word part meaning 'before': *prehistoric*

Word history: from Latin

preach

verb **1** to give a sermon: *She preaches every Sunday.* **2** to give advice in a boring way: *He is always preaching about keeping the place tidy.*

preamble *(say* pree-<u>am</u>-buhl*)*

noun an introduction explaining the purpose of the book or document which follows

precarious *(say* pruh-<u>kair</u>-ree-uhs*)*

adjective **1** uncertain or depending on conditions you can't control: *Jerry's position in the company is precarious.* **2** unsafe or risky: *a precarious position on top of a ladder*

Word building: **precariously** *adverb*

precaution

noun something done in advance to prevent problems: *precautions against burglary*

Word building: **precautionary** *adjective*

precede

verb to go before: *He preceded her into the room.*

Word building: **precedence** *noun* the right to go before something or someone else

precede/proceed Don't confuse **precede** with **proceed**. To **proceed** is to go on or forward:
> *The winners will proceed to the victory stand.*

precedent

noun an event or case which may be used as an example for future action: *She set a precedent when she joined the soccer team, and soon lots of girls were signing up.*

precept *(say* <u>pree</u>-sept*)*

noun a rule of action: *'Look before you leap' is a wise precept.*

precinct *(say* <u>pree</u>-singkt*)*

noun **1** a place or area with definite limits: *shopping precinct* **2** the surrounding area: *the precincts of the city*

precious

adjective **1** costing a lot or having great value: *precious stones*
Other words: **valuable**
2 deeply loved: *a precious friend*
Other words: **dear, cherished, treasured**

precipice   (*say* pres-uh-puhs)

noun a steep cliff
Word building: **precipitous** *adjective*

precipitate

verb **1** to bring about quickly: *Your arrival precipitated the quarrel.* **2** to change from vapour into dew, rain or snow

precipitation

noun **1** the water which forms as vapour, changes into liquid and falls to earth as dew, rain or snow **2** the amount of dew, rain or snow in any one time and place

precis   (*rhymes with* lacy)

noun a brief piece of writing containing the main points of a larger work
Other words: **summary, synopsis**

precise   (*say* pruh-suys)

adjective exact: *precise measurement | precise instructions*
Word building: **precision** *noun*

preclude

verb to rule out or exclude: *The new rules will not preclude anybody from joining.*

precocious

adjective more advanced than others of the same age: *a precocious child*
Word building: **precociously** *adverb* **precociousness** *noun* **precocity** *noun*

predatory   (*say* pred-uh-tree)

adjective hunting other animals for food: *An eagle is a predatory bird.*
Word building: **predator** *noun*

predecessor

noun someone who had the job before you: *He was my predecessor as captain of the team.*

predicament   (*say* pruh-dik-uh-muhnt)

noun a difficult or dangerous situation

predicate   (*say* pred-uh-kuht)

noun the word or words which say something about the subject of a sentence, such as 'lived in a cottage' in the sentence *The Williams family lived in a cottage.*

predict

verb to tell what is going to happen in the future
Word building: **predictable** *adjective* **prediction** *noun*

predominate

verb **1** to be stronger or more important **2** to control or lead: *She predominates in class discussions.*
Word building: **predominance** *noun* **predominant** *adjective*

pre-eminent

adjective superior to or better than others: *My aunt is pre-eminent in science.*
Word building: **pre-eminence** *noun* **pre-eminently** *adverb*

preen

verb to trim or arrange feathers with the beak

prefabricate

verb to make in a factory in parts, ready for putting together somewhere else at a later time: *The house was prefabricated to save money.*
Word building: **prefabrication** *noun*

preface   (*say* pref-uhs)

noun an introduction or statement at the front of a book, explaining its purpose
Word building: **preface** *verb* **prefatory** *adjective*

prefect

noun a senior pupil with certain responsibilities in a school

prefer

verb to like better
Word building: Other forms are **I preferred, I have preferred, I am preferring.** | **preferable** *adjective* **preferably** *adverb* **preference** *noun*

prefix

noun a word part which is put in front of a word to change the meaning, such as 'un-' in *unkind*
Word history: from a Latin word meaning 'fixed before'

pregnant

adjective having a baby growing in the womb
Word building: **pregnancy** *noun*

prehistoric

adjective belonging to the time before history was written or records were kept

prejudice (*say* prej-uh-duhs)

noun **1** an opinion unfairly formed beforehand, without reason or evidence **2** harm or unfair treatment which is caused by an opinion like this
verb **3** to influence without sensible reason: *Their cute uniforms prejudiced the judge in their favour.*

preliminary

adjective coming before and leading up to the main matter: *a preliminary test*

prelude (*say* prel-yoohd)

noun **1** something that comes before: *Thought should be a prelude to action.* **2** a short piece of music written for an instrument

premature (*say* prem-uh-chuh, prem-uh-tyooh-uh)

adjective coming or happening too soon: *a premature baby* | *a premature decision*

Word building: **prematurely** *adverb*

premeditate

verb to plan beforehand

Word building: **premeditation** *noun*

premenstrual

adjective happening in the days before menstruation

premier (*say* prem-ee-uh)

noun **1** the leader of a State government
adjective **2** first or leading: *the premier team in the championship*

Word building: **premiership** *noun*

premiere (*say* prem-ee-air)

noun the first public performance of a play, film or something similar

Word building: **premiere** *verb*

premises (*say* prem-uh-suhz)

plural noun a building or house with the land belonging to it

premium (*say* pree-mee-uhm)

noun **1** a bonus, gift or additional sum **2** a payment made for insurance

premonition (*say* prem-uh-nish-uhn)

noun a feeling that something bad is about to happen: *I had a premonition about the accident.*

preoccupied

adjective completely taken up in thought: *She seemed preoccupied and did not listen to a word I said.*

Word building: **preoccupation** *noun*

prepare

verb to make or get ready: *to prepare a garden for planting* | *to prepare for a trip*

Word building: **preparation** *noun* **preparatory** *adjective*

preposition (*say* prep-uh-zish-uhn)

noun a word placed before a noun to show its relation to other words in the sentence, such as 'to' and 'from' in *I gave an apple to Joseph and he took a sandwich from me.*

preposition/proposition Don't confuse **preposition** with **proposition**, which is a suggestion or proposal:
Your proposition that we should have a picnic lunch is a good one.

preposterous

adjective absurd or far from what is normal or sensible: *a preposterous scheme for recycling oyster shells*

Word use: The more usual word is **ridiculous**.
Word building: **preposterously** *adverb*

prerogative

noun a right or privilege: *It is the captain's prerogative to choose the team.*

preschool

noun a place where some young children go for a year or so before they start primary school

prescribe

verb to order for use as a treatment: *The doctor prescribed some cough medicine.*

prescription

noun a written order by a doctor to a chemist for medicine

presence

noun attendance or being in a place: *Your presence is requested at the party.*

present[1] (*say* prez-uhnt)

adjective **1** happening or existing now: *the present Prime Minister* **2** being in a place: *Is everyone present?*
noun **3** the present time

present² (*say* pruh-<u>zent</u>)

verb **1** to give, especially in a formal way: *The mayor presented the prizes.*
noun (*say* <u>prez</u>-uhnt) **2** something given: *birthday presents*

Word building: **presentation** *noun*

presentable

adjective fit to be seen: *Have a shower and make yourself presentable.*

Word building: **presentably** *adverb*

presently

adverb **1** in a short time: *The manager will see you presently.* **2** at this time: *He is presently living in Bendigo.*

present tense

noun the form of a verb which shows that something is happening or exists now, such as 'run' in *I run every day* and 'am running' in *I am running for the bus.*

preservative

noun a substance that prevents something, such as food, from going bad

preserve

verb **1** to keep something safe from harm or damage so that it can continue: *The aim of the new laws is to preserve the rainforests.*
Other words: **conserve, maintain, save, sustain**
2 to keep from going bad: *to preserve fruit*

Word building: **preservation** *noun*
preserve *noun*

preside

verb to be in charge of a meeting or gathering, and to control what happens: *The judge presided in the courtroom.* | *The club's chairperson presided at the meeting.*

president

noun **1** the elected head of a republic **2** someone chosen to have control over the meetings of a society or something similar

Word building: **presidential** *adjective*

press

verb **1** to act upon with weight or force: *Press down the lid.* **2** to squeeze: *Was that you pressing my hand under the table?* **3** to urge: *Georgina pressed us to stay.* **4** to use an iron to remove creases from clothes
noun **5** a machine used for printing **6** newspapers, magazines and so on, or the people who write for them

pressure (*say* <u>presh</u>-uh)

noun **1** the weight or force with which you press on something: *to put pressure on a lever* **2** a force applied to something, measured as so much weight on a unit of area: *air pressure* **3** continual worry: *He is under pressure at work.*

pressurise

verb to keep normal air pressure in: *to pressurise the cabin of a plane*

Word use: Another spelling is **pressurize**.

prestige (*say* pres-<u>teezh</u>)

noun high reputation or standing: *Don Bradman has enormous prestige in the world of cricket.*

Word building: **prestigious** *adjective*

presume

verb **1** to take for granted: *I presume you're tired after your walk.* **2** to dare: *I would not presume to tell you how to do it.*

Word use: Some people think that **assume** is better for definition 1.
Word building: **presumptuous** *adjective* taking something for granted without reasonable cause **presumption** *noun*

pretence

noun **1** a false show: *a pretence of friendship* **2** a pretended reason

pretend

verb **1** to make a false claim: *It was difficult to pretend to be interested in the boring speech.* | *The burglar pretended to be reading the sign.* **2** to make believe

pretentious (*say* pruh-<u>ten</u>-shuhs)

adjective having an exaggerated outward show of importance, wealth and so on

Word building: **pretentiously** *adverb*

pretty

adjective **1** pleasant or attractive
Other words: **attractive, cute, lovely**
adverb **2** rather or quite: *pretty good*
Other words: **fairly**

Word building: Other adjective forms are **prettier, prettiest**. | **prettiness** *noun*

pretzel

noun a small crisp salted biscuit, often in the shape of a knot

Word history: from a German word

prevail

verb **1** to win or triumph: *In spite of the objections, good sense prevailed.* **2** to be most numerous or strong: *Stunted gum trees prevail on these dry hillsides.*
phrase **3 prevail upon**, to persuade successfully: *I prevailed upon them to change their minds.*

prevalent   (*say* prev-uh-luhnt)

adjective widespread: *a prevalent weed*

Word building: **prevalence** *noun*
prevalently *adverb*

prevaricate   (*say* pruh-va-ruh-kayt)

verb to speak in a way which tries to avoid the point by trickery

Word building: **prevarication** *noun*

prevent

verb **1** to stop: *Prevent the baby from swallowing those beads.* **2** to keep from happening: *She was just in time to prevent an accident.*

Word building: **prevention** *noun*
preventive *adjective*

preventive medicine

noun a strategy of medical examinations, treatments or advice designed to prevent sickness occurring: *Having fluoride in the water supply is an example of preventive medicine.*

preview

noun a showing of a film or exhibition before the public is allowed to see it

previous

adjective happening before: *the previous day*
Word building: **previously** *adverb*

prey   (*rhymes with* may)

noun **1** an animal hunted for food by another: *Mice are the prey of cats.*
2 a victim
phrase **3 prey on**, **a** to hunt and eat: *Cats prey on mice.* **b** to affect harmfully: *The problem is preying on my mind.*

prey/pray Don't confuse **prey** with **pray**. **Pray** means 'to talk to a god'.

price

noun the amount of money for which something is bought or sold
Word building: **price** *verb* to give or guess the price of

priceless

adjective having a value beyond all price: *a priceless talent*

prick

noun **1** a small hole made by a needle, thorn or something sharp **2** the feeling of being pricked
verb **3** to pierce with a sharp point

prickle

noun a sharp point or thorn
Word building: **prickly** *adjective* (**pricklier, prickliest**)

pride

noun **1** well-earned pleasure or satisfaction: *I take pride in my projects.* **2** a high, or too high, opinion of your own dignity or importance
phrase **3 pride yourself on**, to take well-earned pleasure or satisfaction in: *Toakase prided herself on a job well done.*

priest

noun someone whose job is to perform religious ceremonies
Word building: **priestess** *noun*
priesthood *noun*   **priestly** *adjective*

prig

noun someone who is too concerned about duty and who always thinks they are right
Word building: **priggish** *adjective*
priggishly *adverb*

prim

adjective stiff and very proper in manner
Word building: Other forms are **primmer, primmest**.

primary

adjective first in order or importance: *primary education | the primary reason for her success*

primate

noun **1** any mammal of the group that includes humans, apes and monkeys **2** the head bishop of a country

prime

adjective of the first importance or quality: *prime time | prime beef*

prime minister

noun the leader of the government in some countries, including Australia

prime number

noun a number which cannot be divided exactly except by itself and 1

primer¹   (*say* <u>pruy</u>-muh, <u>prim</u>-uh)

noun a simple book for teaching the beginnings of any subject, especially reading

primer²   (*say* <u>pruy</u>-muh)

noun a coat of paint used to prepare a surface for the next coat

primeval   (*say* pruy-<u>meev</u>-uhl)

adjective belonging to the earliest period of the earth

Word building: **primevally** *adverb*
Word history: from a Latin word meaning 'young' with the ending '-al' added

primitive

adjective **1** being the earliest in existence: *primitive forms of life* **2** belonging to an early stage of civilisation: *primitive art*

prince

noun a son or near male relation of a king or queen

Word building: **princely** *adjective*

princess

noun **1** a daughter or near female relation of a king or queen **2** someone married to a prince

principal   (*say* <u>prin</u>-suh-puhl)

adjective **1** main or leading: *the principal thing to remember*
Other words: **chief, first, foremost, major, prime**
noun **2** the head of a school
Other words: **head, headmaster, headmistress**

Word building: **principally** *adverb*

> **principal/principle** Don't confuse **principal** with **principle**, which is a general truth or rule.

principle   (*say* <u>prin</u>-suh-puhl)

noun **1** a general truth or rule: *the principle of good behaviour | political principles* **2** a sense of what is right and wrong: *a person of principle*

print

verb **1** to make copies of by pressing an inked surface on to paper or other material: *to print newspapers* **2** to write in separate letters rather than in running writing: *Please print your name and address.*

Word building: **print** *noun*

printer   (*say* <u>print</u>-er)

noun a machine that is attached to your computer and prints what is on your computer screen so that you can read it on paper

printout

noun information printed by a computer so that it can be read

prior¹

adjective **1** earlier: *a prior engagement*
phrase **2 prior to**, before: *prior to my going away*

prior²

noun a head monk or friar

Word building: **priory** *noun* (**priories**) **prioress** *noun*

priority   (*say* pruy-<u>o</u>-ruh-tee)

noun the right to go before someone or something else, because of urgency or importance

prise   (*sounds like* prize)

verb to raise, move or force with a lever: *Prise open the lid with a screw driver.*

> **prise/prize** Don't confuse **prise** with **prize**, which is a reward for success.

prism

noun a transparent object, usually of glass and with triangular ends, used for breaking light down into the colours of the rainbow

Word building: **prismatic** *adjective*
Word history: from a Greek word meaning 'something sawed'

prison

noun a place where criminals are kept locked up

Word building: **prisoner** *noun* someone who is kept somewhere against their will **imprison** *verb*

private

adjective **1** belonging to someone in particular: *private property*
Other words: **personal**
2 concerned with personal affairs: *My diary is private.*

Word building: **privacy** *noun* **privately** *adverb*

privet

noun an evergreen tree or shrub introduced into Australia from Europe, which is now thought to be a pest because it grows over areas of native bushland

privilege   (say priv-uh-lij)

noun 1 a special right or advantage enjoyed by only a limited number of people: *We had the privilege of meeting the great poet.* 2 a special right or protection given to people in authority or office: *parliamentary privilege*

Word building: **privileged** *adjective*

prize

noun 1 a reward for winning a race or competition 2 something won in a lottery or raffle
verb 3 to value highly

prize/prise Don't confuse **prize** with **prise**. To **prise** something open is to force it open, usually with a lever.

pro-

prefix a word part meaning 'in favour of': *pro-Australian*

Word history: from Latin

probable

adjective likely or expected to happen or be true

Word building: **probability** *noun*   **probably** *adverb*

probation

noun 1 a period of trial: *She is new in the job and still on probation.* 2 a system of punishment in which certain people who have broken the law can stay free on condition of good behaviour: *He has been put on probation for shoplifting.*

Word building: **probationary** *adjective*

probe

verb to examine or search thoroughly: *to probe a wound | to probe evidence*

Word building: **probe** *noun*

problem

noun 1 something which is difficult or uncertain: *Your inability to concentrate is a problem.*
Other words: **complication, difficulty, trouble**
2 a question to be answered: *a maths problem*

Other words: **conundrum, puzzle**

Word building: **problematic** *adjective*

procedure   (say pruh-see-juh)

noun 1 a way of doing something: *the usual procedure for applying for a job | parliamentary procedure* 2 the piece of writing which tells you how to do or make something. See the 'Types of writing and speaking' table at the end of this book.

proceed

verb 1 to move forward, especially after stopping 2 to go on or continue

Word building: **proceeds** *plural noun* money from a sale

proceed/precede Don't confuse **proceed** with **precede**. To **precede** someone is to go in front of them.

proceeding

noun 1 behaviour or way of acting: *This is a strange proceeding.* 2 **proceedings**, records of the activities and meetings of a club or society

process

noun 1 a series of actions carried out for a particular purpose: *the process of making butter*
verb 2 to treat, prepare or deal with in a certain way: *to process iron ore | to process film | to process data*

Word building: **processor** *noun*

procession

noun an orderly line of people, cars or floats moving along in a ceremony or as a show
Other words: **parade**

proclaim

verb to announce publicly: *The Governor-General proclaimed three new laws this morning.*

Word building: **proclamation** *noun*

procrastinate

verb to put off doing something till another time

Word building: **procrastination** *noun*

procreate

verb to produce offspring

Word use: The more usual word is **breed**.
Word building: **procreation** *noun*

procure

verb to obtain: *to procure food | to procure a result*

Word building: **procurable** *adjective*

prod

verb to poke or jab

Word building: **prod** *noun*

prodigal

adjective wasteful or extravagant: *a prodigal use of materials | the prodigal son*

Word building: **prodigal** *noun* **prodigality** *noun*

prodigious   (*say* pruh-<u>dij</u>-uhs)

adjective extraordinary in size, amount or force: *a prodigious noise*

Word use: The more usual word is **great**.

prodigy   (*say* <u>prod</u>-uh-jee)

noun **1** someone, especially a child, who has extraordinary talent: *Mozart was a musical prodigy.* **2** an extraordinary or wonderful thing

Word building: The plural is **prodigies**.

produce   (*say* pruh-<u>dyoohs</u>)

verb **1** to bring into being: *This soil produces good crops.* **2** to pull out and present: *The magician produced a rabbit from a hat.* **3** to assemble the cast for and generally organise and control: *to produce a play*
noun (*say* <u>proj</u>-oohs) **4** things that are grown: *Farmers take their produce to market.*

Word building: **producer** *noun* **production** *noun*

product

noun **1** something made or brought into existence: *the product of labour | household products* **2** the result you get by multiplying two or more numbers together

Word building: **productive** *adjective* **productively** *adverb* **productivity** *noun*

profane

adjective showing deep lack of respect for religion: *profane language*

Word building: **profanely** *adverb* **profanity** *noun*
Word history: from a Latin word meaning 'in front of the temple'

profess

verb to declare or show, often insincerely: *He professed great sorrow.*

profession

noun **1** an occupation in which advanced and special knowledge of a subject is needed: *She is a lawyer by profession.* **2** the people in a profession taken as a whole: *the legal profession* **3** a declaration, whether true or false: *a profession of love*

professional

adjective **1** following an occupation to earn a living from it: *a professional golfer* **2** belonging to a profession

Word use: The opposite of definition 1 is **amateur**.
Word building: **professional** *noun* **professionalism** *noun* **professionally** *adverb*

professor

noun a university teacher of the highest rank

Word building: **professorial** *adjective*

proffer

verb to place before someone, for them to accept: *I proffered my resignation to the board.*

Word use: The more usual word is **offer**.

proficient

adjective skilled or expert: *a proficient carpenter*

Word building: **proficiency** *noun* **proficiently** *adverb*

profile

noun **1** an outline drawing of a face, especially a side view **2** a short account of someone's life and character: *There is a profile of the Treasurer in today's paper.*
phrase **3 keep a low profile**, to act so as not to be noticed

profit

noun **1** money made from selling something at a higher price than you paid for it **2** advantage or benefit: *There is no profit in regretting the past.*

Word building: **profit** *verb* **profitable** *adjective* **profitably** *adverb*

profit/prophet Don't confuse **profit** with **prophet**. A **prophet** is someone who speaks on behalf of a god. It can also mean a great teacher or leader.

profiterole   (*say* pruh-<u>fit</u>-uh-rohl)
noun a small shaped piece of pastry, cooked and filled with cream and chocolate: *Her diet plan was to give up profiteroles and other delicious things.*

profound
adjective very deep: *profound sleep* | *a profound thought*
Word building: **profoundly** *adverb* **profundity** *noun*

profuse   (*say* pruh-<u>fyoohs</u>)
adjective plentiful: *a profuse flow of blood* | *profuse apologies*
Word building: **profusely** *adverb* **profusion** *noun*

progeny   (*say* <u>proj</u>-uh-nee)
noun offspring or descendants: *the progeny of my pet rabbits* | *the progeny of kings*
Word building: **progenitor** *noun* an ancestor

prognosis   (*say* prog-<u>noh</u>-suhs)
noun a doctor's opinion on how a disease will develop
Word building: The plural is **prognoses** (*say* prog-<u>noh</u>-seez).

program   (*say* <u>proh</u>-gram)
noun **1** a plan to be followed: *a program of study* **2** a list of items and performers in a concert or play **3** a particular entertainment or production: *There's a good program on TV tonight.* **4** a set of instructions that makes a computer deal with certain data and solve problems in a particular way
Word use: Another spelling for definitions 1, 2 and 3 is **programme**.
Word building: **program** *verb* (**programmed, programming**) **programmer** *noun*
Word history: from a Greek word meaning 'a public notice in writing'

progress
noun **1** moving forward or improvement: *progress along a road* | *progress in your studies*
Other words: **advance, advancement, headway, progression**
phrase **2 in progress**, going on or under way: *work in progress*
Word building: **progress** *verb* **progression** *noun*

progressive
adjective favouring or making change, improvement or reform: *a progressive policy* | *a progressive school*
Word building: **progressively** *adverb*

prohibit
verb to forbid by law: *The government has prohibited smoking on trains.*
Word building: **prohibition** *noun* **prohibitive** *adjective*

project   (*say* <u>proh</u>-jekt)
noun **1** a plan or scheme: *a project for making money* **2** a special piece of work that you do for school, usually by researching something: *a project on wheat*
verb (*say* pruh-<u>jekt</u>) **3** to throw: *to project your voice* **4** to show on a screen: *to project a film* **5** to jut out
Word building: **projection** *noun*

projectile   (*say* pruh-<u>jek</u>-tuyl)
noun **1** something thrown: *Stones and other projectiles were hurled at the speaker.* **2** something fired from a gun
Word use: The more usual word is **missile**.

projector
noun a piece of equipment for showing a film or a slide on a screen

proliferate   (*say* pruh-<u>lif</u>-uh-rayt)
verb to grow by multiplying: *The weeds have proliferated since the rain.*
Word building: **proliferation** *noun*

prolific
adjective producing plentifully: *a prolific tree* | *a prolific writer*

prologue   (*say* <u>proh</u>-log)
noun **1** a speech at the beginning of a play **2** anything that introduces something else

prolong
verb to make last longer: *to prolong a speech* | *to prolong a pleasure*
Word building: **prolongation** *noun*

promenade   (*say* prom-uh-<u>nahd</u>)
noun **1** an unhurried walk, especially in a public place **2** a place where people walk to and fro, especially next to a beach
Word use: The more usual word for definition 1 is **stroll**. | Another word for definition 2 is **esplanade**.
Word building: **promenade** *verb*

prominent
adjective **1** sticking out: *prominent teeth*
2 outstanding or important: *a prominent citizen*

Word building: **prominence** *noun*
prominently *adverb*

promiscuous   (*say* pruh-<u>mis</u>-kyooh-uhs)
adjective having many sexual partners

Word building: **promiscuity** *noun*
promiscuously *adverb*

promise
noun **1** a declaration or statement that you will do, or keep from doing something
Other words: **commitment, guarantee, oath, pledge, undertaking, vow**
2 signs of future excellence: *to show promise*
Other words: **potential**

Word building: **promise** *verb*

promontory   (*say* <u>prom</u>-uhn-tree)
noun a high point of land or rock jutting out into the sea

Word building: The plural is **promontories**.

promote
verb **1** to raise or advance in rank or position: *You have been promoted to general manager.* **2** to try to increase the sales of by advertising: *They are promoting the new product on television.*

Word building: **promoter** *noun* the organiser of an event   **promotion** *noun*

prompt
adjective **1** immediate: *a prompt reply to a letter*
verb **2** to encourage or urge to action: *A desire for justice prompted me to interrupt.* **3** to remind of the next words in a play
noun **4** a message on a computer, in words or symbols on the screen, letting you know that the computer is ready for more instructions

Word building: **prompter** *noun*   **promptly** *adverb*   **promptitude** *noun*

prone
adjective **1** liable or likely to have or do: *prone to headaches* **2** lying flat with your face downwards

prong
noun a thin sharp point on a fork

pronoun
noun a word which stands for a noun, such as *we, her, they, it, that* or *who*

pronounce
verb **1** to make the sound of: *Australians pronounce 'dance' in two ways.* **2** to declare formally: *to pronounce a judgement*

Word building: **pronouncement** *noun*: *the pronouncement of a new law*
pronunciation *noun*: *the pronunciation of a name*

pronounced
adjective strongly marked: *a pronounced tendency*

proof
noun **1** something that shows a thing is true
adjective **2** strong enough to resist: *It is proof against fire.*

proofread
verb to read in order to find and mark mistakes to be corrected

Word building: Other forms are **I proofread, I have proofread, I am proofreading.** |
proofreader *noun*

prop
phrase **prop up**, to support or prevent from falling: *to prop up a wall | to prop up someone on cushions*

Word building: Other forms are **I propped, I have propped, I am propping.** | **prop** *noun*

propaganda
noun information which is used to try and convince you of a certain point of view: *political propaganda*

Word building: **propagandise** *verb*
Word history: from the Latin name of a committee of cardinals set up in 1622 by Pope Gregory XV to help spread the Christian faith

propagate
verb **1** to increase or multiply: *Some plants can be propagated by cuttings.* **2** to spread: *to propagate ideas*

Word building: **propagation** *noun*

propel
verb to drive forwards: *The boat was propelled by oars.*

Word building: Other forms are **I propelled, I have propelled, I am propelling.**

propellant
noun the fuel used to propel a rocket

propeller

noun a device with revolving blades used for driving a plane or ship

proper

adjective **1** accepted or right: *the proper way to write | the proper time to sleep* **2** correct in behaviour: *She is always very proper when she comes to tea.* **3** real or genuine: *I need some proper tools, not these toys.*

proper noun

noun a noun that is the name of one particular place, person or thing, such as *Perth*, *Sally* or *the Indian Pacific*

Word use: Proper nouns are spelt with a capital letter. | Compare this with **common noun**.

property

noun **1** something that is owned: *This book is my property.* | *National parks are public property.* **2** a piece of land or building that may be owned **3** a station or farm: *a cattle property*

Word building: The plural is **properties**.

prophecy   (*say* prof-uh-see)

noun **1** a statement telling what is going to happen in the future **2** a message from a god, or the act of proclaiming such a message

Word building: The plural is **prophecies**.

prophesy   (*say* prof-uh-suy)

verb to deliver a prophecy, or to predict: *He prophesied a terrible storm.*

Word building: Other forms are **I prophesied, I have prophesied, I am prophesying.**

prophet

noun **1** someone who speaks on behalf of a god **2** someone who predicts the future **3** a great teacher or leader

Word building: **prophetic** *adjective*

prophet/profit Don't confuse **prophet** with **profit**, which is the money you make from selling something at a higher price than you paid for it. It can also be an advantage or benefit:

There is no profit in regretting the mistakes you made in your youth.

proportion

noun **1** the relation or comparison of one thing to another according to its size, number, and so on: *the proportion of girls to boys in the class* **2** a proper or correct relationship between things: *The dog's small head was not in proportion to its large body.* **3** a part, compared to the whole: *a large proportion of the total*

Word building: **proportion** *verb* **proportionate** *adjective*

propose

verb **1** to put forward or suggest **2** to plan or intend **3** to suggest marriage: *He proposed to her.*

Word use: The more usual word for definition 1 is **suggest**. The more usual word for definition 2 is **intend**.

Word building: **proposal** *noun* **proposition** *noun*

propound

verb to put forward to be considered, accepted, or acted on: *He propounded a theory.*

proprietor   (*say* pruh-pruy-uh-tuh)

noun the owner of a business or a property

Word building: **proprietary** *noun*

propriety   (*say* pruh-pruy-uh-tee)

noun good manners or proper behaviour

propulsion   (*say* pruh-pul-shuhn)

noun a driving or propelling force: *Many planes are driven by jet propulsion.*

prosaic   (*say* proh-zay-ik)

adjective dull and unimaginative

Word building: **prosaically** *adverb*

proscribe

verb to forbid

prose

noun ordinary written or spoken language rather than poetry

prosecute

verb to accuse before a court of law

Word building: **prosecution** *noun*

proselyte   (*say* pros-uh-luyt)

noun a convert or someone who has changed from one opinion to another

prospect
noun **1** something looked forward to or expected, especially something successful: *A holiday is a pleasant prospect.* | *If you keep doing well at school, you'll have good prospects of being school captain next year.* **2** someone who may be a customer, contestant, and so on: *Try him, he looks a likely prospect.* **3** a view or a scene
verb **4** to search for gold or other minerals

Word building: **prospective** *adjective* **prospector** *noun*

prospectus
noun a statement or pamphlet which advertises something new or gives more details about things like a school, university or commercial company

prosper
verb **1** to do well: *Their new business is prospering.* **2** to grow strongly: *These shrubs will prosper if you plant them in a sunny position.*

prosperous
adjective successful or wealthy: *a prosperous business*
Other words: **blooming, booming, flourishing, thriving**

Word building: **prosperity** *noun* **prosperously** *adverb*

prostitute
noun someone who has sexual intercourse with someone else for money

Word building: **prostitution** *noun*

prostrate
phrase **prostrate yourself,** to lie face down on the ground: *The prisoners prostrated themselves at the feet of the general.*

Word building: **prostrate** *adjective*

protagonist   (*say* pruh-<u>tag</u>-uh-nuhst)
noun the main character in a story or play

protect
verb to guard or defend from injury, danger or annoyance
Other words: **shield**

Word building: **protected** *adjective* **protection** *noun* **protective** *adjective* **protector** *noun*

protection
noun **1** the act of keeping someone or something safe: *The bus shelter gave some protection from the pouring rain.* **2** the state of being protected: *The asylum seekers were seeking protection.*

protectorate   (*say* pruh-<u>tek</u>-tuh-ruht)
noun a country protected and controlled by another stronger state

protégé   (*say* <u>proh</u>-tuh-zhay)
noun someone who is protected or supported by someone else

Word history: from a French word meaning 'protect'

protein   (*say* <u>proh</u>-teen)
noun any of a group of substances which are present in such foods as milk, meat and cheese and which are important to our diet

protest   (*say* <u>proh</u>-test)
noun **1** an expression of disagreement or disapproval
Other words: **complaint, dissent, objection, opposition**
verb (*say* pruh-<u>test</u>) **2** to express disagreement or disapproval
Other words: **complain, object**
3 to state strongly and positively: *She protested her innocence to the end.*
Other words: **affirm, assert, declare, maintain**

Word building: **protestation** *noun*

protocol   (*say* <u>proh</u>-tuh-kol)
noun the rules of behaviour used on official occasions involving kings, queens or other important people

proton
noun a tiny positive particle inside an atom which has a type of energy that balances the energy of an electron

Word use: The energy of a proton is called **positive**.

prototype   (*say* <u>proh</u>-tuh-tuyp)
noun the original or the model of something which is later copied

protract
verb to draw out or lengthen in time

protractor
noun an instrument used to measure or mark off angles

protrude

verb to jut out

proud

adjective **1** feeling pleased or satisfied: *She was proud that her father had won first place in the garden show.* **2** having too high an opinion of your own importance
Other words: **arrogant, conceited, egotistical, haughty, smug, vain**

prove   (*rhymes with* groove)

verb **1** to show to be true or genuine **2** to show to be capable of something: *Raenan proved himself an expert driver.* **3** to turn out: *The report proved to be false.*
Word building: Other forms are **I proved, I have proved** or **proven, I am proving**.

proverb

noun a short, popular, usually wise saying that has been used by people for a long time, such as *A stitch in time saves nine.*
Other words: **adage, motto**
Word building: **proverbial** *adjective*

provide

verb **1** to make available or to supply: *I will provide the food.* | *He will provide us with the drink.* **2** to supply what is needed to live: *Parents usually provide for their children.*
Word building: **provider** *noun*

providence   (*say* prov-uh-duhns)

noun the careful management of things like money, in preparation for the future
Word building: **provident** *adjective*

province

noun **1** a section or division of a country, territory or region **2** a range or field of knowledge: *The history of South Australia is outside the province of the course.*
Word building: **provincial** *adjective*

provision

noun **1** a section of a document which sets out a condition **2** the providing or supplying of something such as food **3** an arrangement made beforehand **4 provisions**, supplies of food and other necessities

provisional

adjective for the time being only: *a provisional government*
Word use: The more usual word is **temporary**.
Word building: **provisionally** *adverb*

provoke

verb **1** to make angry or annoyed: *They provoked the dog by teasing it.* **2** to stir up or cause: *Our behaviour provoked our parents' anger.*
Word building: **provocation** *noun* **provocative** *adjective*

prowess   (*say* prow-es, prow-es)

noun **1** bravery **2** outstanding ability
Word use: The more usual word is **skill**.

prowl

verb to go about quietly, as if in search of prey or something to steal
Word building: **prowl** *noun*

proximity

noun nearness in place, time and so on

proxy

noun someone who is officially allowed to act for someone else: *I acted as proxy for my father at the ceremony.*
Word building: The plural is **proxies**.

prude

noun someone who is too modest or proper

prudence

noun careful practical wisdom or good sound judgement
Word building: **prudent** *adjective*

prune¹

noun a dried plum

prune²

verb to cut off twigs or branches from

pry

verb to look or search with too much curiosity: *He is always prying into our affairs.*
Word building: Other forms are **I pried, I have pried, I am prying**. | **prying** *adjective*

PS

short for *postscript*, a Latin word meaning 'written after'
Word use: This is often used at the end of a letter to show something has been added.

psalm   (*say* sahm)

noun a sacred song, hymn or poem
Word history: from a Greek word meaning 'a song sung to the harp'

pseudonym (*say* <u>syooh</u>-duh-nim)
noun an invented name used by a writer
Word use: Another word for this is **pen-name**.

psych (*say* suyk)
verb Informal to persuade somebody to do something by using psychological strategies such as praise, shame, and so on: *The coach psyched them into moving faster and better than they ever had before.*

psychiatry (*say* suh-<u>kuy</u>-uh-tree)
noun the study and treatment of mental illness
Word building: **psychiatric** *adjective* **psychiatrist** *noun*

psychic (*say* <u>suy</u>-kik)
adjective **1** having to do with the human soul or mind **2** having the power to tell the future or what others are thinking
Word building: **psychic** *noun*

psychology (*say* suy-<u>kol</u>-uh-jee)
noun the study of the mind, how it works, and why people behave as they do
Word building: **psychological** *adjective* **psychologically** *adverb* **psychologist** *noun*

psychosomatic
(*say* suy-koh-suh-<u>mat</u>-ik)
adjective having to do with an illness of your body which is caused by or made worse by your emotional state

p.t.o.
short for *please turn over*

Pty (*say* pruh-<u>pruy</u>-uh-tree)
short for *proprietary* which is added to the name of a company to show that there is only a small number of shareholders
Word use: See also **Ltd** which often comes after **Pty**.

pub
noun Informal a hotel
Word history: short for **public house**

puberty (*say* <u>pyooh</u>-buh-tee)
noun the stage of life or physical development when someone is first capable of producing children

pubic (*say* <u>pyooh</u>-bik)
adjective having to do with the lower part of your abdomen where the genitals are: *pubic hair*

public
adjective **1** having to do with or used by the people of a community or the people as a whole: *public affairs* | *public transport*
noun **2** the people of a community

publican
noun the owner or manager of a hotel

publication
noun **1** the publishing of a book, magazine, newspaper or other printed work **2** something which is published

publicity (*say* pub-<u>lis</u>-uh-tee)
noun any advertisement, information and so on which is meant to attract the attention of the public

public relations
noun the methods used to give the public a good impression of a particular business or company

publish
verb **1** to prepare and issue a book, magazine, and so on, in printed copies for sale to the public **2** to announce to the public
Word building: **publisher** *noun* a person or company that publishes books

puce (*say* pyoohs)
adjective dark purplish-brown
Word history: from a French word meaning 'flea'

pucker
verb to gather into small folds or wrinkles
Word building: **pucker** *noun*

pudding
noun a soft sweet dish usually served as a dessert

puddle
noun a small pool of liquid, such as dirty water left after rain

puff
noun **1** a short, quick, sending out of air, wind or breath **2** a light pastry with a filling of jam, cream, and so on: *a cream puff*
verb **3** to blow with puffs: *The smoke puffed into the air.* | *The train puffed steam out of its funnel.* **4** to breathe quickly after violent exercise **5** to smoke a cigarette, cigar or pipe
phrase **6 puff up**, to become swollen

puffin

noun a seabird found in the northern Atlantic, with a ducklike body and a narrow brightly coloured bill

pug

noun a small dog with a smooth coat, a very wrinkled face, a snub nose and a tightly curled tail

pugnacious   (*say* pug-<u>nay</u>-shuhs)

adjective tending to quarrel or fight

Word use: The more usual word is **aggressive**.
Word building: **pugnaciously** *adverb*

pull

verb **1** to move something by drawing it towards you
Other words: **drag, haul, lug, tug**
2 to tear apart: *to pull something to pieces*
3 to strain: *to pull a muscle*
phrase **4 pull in,** to move your vehicle to the side of the road to stop **5 pull up,** to stop

Word building: **pull** *noun*

pullet   (*rhymes with* bullet)

noun a hen less than one year old

pulley   (*rhymes with* bully)

noun a wheel or system of wheels with ropes or chains, used to lift heavy things

pullover

noun another word for **jumper**

pulmonary   (*say* <u>pul</u>-muhn-ree, <u>pool</u>-muhn-ree)

adjective having to do with the lungs: *The pulmonary artery takes blood from the heart to the lungs.*

pulp

noun **1** the soft juicy part of a fruit **2** any soft wet mass: *Paper is made out of the pulp from wood, linen and similar materials.*
Word building: **pulp** *verb*

pulpit

noun a raised platform in a church where the priest or minister stands to give a sermon

pulsate   (*say* pul-<u>sayt</u>)

verb to beat or throb like your heart
Word building: **pulsation** *noun*

pulse

noun the regular beating in your arteries caused by the pumping of blood by your heart
Word building: **pulse** *verb*

pulverise

verb **1** to pound or grind into dust or powder: *He pulverised the rock into sand.* **2** to destroy completely
Word use: Another spelling is **pulverize**.

puma   (*say* <u>pyooh</u>-muh)

noun a large animal of the cat family found in America
Word use: It is sometimes called a **cougar** or a **mountain lion**.

pumice   (*say* <u>pum</u>-uhs)

noun a light spongy form of volcanic stone used for polishing things

pummel

verb to beat with rapid blows of the fists
Word building: Other forms are **I pummelled, I have pummelled, I am pummelling**.

pump

noun **1** a device that forces a liquid or gas in or out of something
verb **2** to move by using a pump: *to pump water out of the dam* **3** to move or operate by an up-and-down hand action
phrase **4 pump up,** to fill with air: *to pump up your tyres*

pumpkin

noun a large, roundish, yellow-orange vegetable

pun

noun a play on words which sound alike but are different in meaning, as in '*What do cannibals eat for tea? Human beans!*'
Word building: **pun** *verb* (**punned, punning**)

punch[1]

noun **1** a hit or blow, especially with your fist **2** a strong or forceful effect
Word building: **punch** *verb*

punch[2]

noun a device for making holes in tickets, leather or similar materials

punch[3]

noun a drink made of water, fruit juice, pieces of fruit and sometimes wine, rum or other spirit

punchline

noun the last line of a joke which is the part that makes the whole joke funny: *I am hopeless at telling jokes because I always forget the punchline.*

punctilious   (*say* punk-<u>til</u>-ee-uhs)

adjective being very exact about doing things correctly: *The new secretary was punctilious in carrying out all duties.*

Word use: The more usual word is **careful**.

punctual   (*say* <u>punk</u>-chooh-uhl)

adjective careful about being on time

Word building: **punctuality** *noun* **punctually** *adverb*

punctuation   (*say* punk-chooh-<u>ay</u>-shuhn)

noun commas, semi-colons, colons, full stops and so on used in writing to make the meaning clear

Word building: **punctuate** *verb*

puncture   (*say* <u>pungk</u>-chuh)

verb to prick or make a hole in: *to puncture the skin with a pin | to puncture a tyre*

Word building: **puncture** *noun*

pundit   (*say* <u>pun</u>-duht)

noun Informal someone who knows a lot about a subject

pungent   (*say* <u>pun</u>-juhnt)

adjective having a sharp taste or smell: *the pungent odour of vinegar*

Word building: **pungency** *noun* **pungently** *adverb*
Word history: from a Latin word meaning 'pricking'

punish

verb to make suffer in some way because of wrongdoing

Word building: **punishment** *noun*

punk

adjective **1** worthless or of poor quality **2** having to do with punk rock and the people interested in it

punk rock

noun a type of rock music with a very fast beat, which often has aggressive or unconventional lyrics

Word use: Other terms for this are **punk** and **punk music.**

punnet

noun a small shallow box or basket for small fruits, especially strawberries

punt¹

noun a shallow-bottomed boat with square ends

Word building: **punt** *verb* to work a punt or carry in a punt

punt²

noun a kick which you give to a dropped football before it has hit the ground

Word building: **punt** *verb*

punt³

noun a chance to bet: *to take a punt*

puny   (*say* <u>pyooh</u>-nee)

adjective **1** small and weak **2** of little importance: *puny efforts*

Word building: Other forms are **punier, puniest.**

pup

noun a young dog or some other animal less than one year old

Word use: Another word for this is **puppy.**

pupa   (*say* <u>pyooh</u>-puh)

noun an insect in the cocoon between the larva and mature adult stages

Word building: The plural is **pupae** (*say* <u>pyooh</u>-pee). | **pupal** *adjective* **pupate** *verb*
Word history: from a Latin word meaning 'girl', 'doll' or 'puppet'

pupil¹

noun someone who is being taught

pupil²

noun the small dark spot on the iris of your eye, which expands to allow more light into the retina

puppet

noun **1** a doll or figure of some kind which is moved by wires or your hand, usually on a small stage
Other words: **marionette**
2 someone who is controlled by others

Word building: **puppeteer** *noun* **puppetry** *noun*

purchase   (*say* <u>per</u>-chuhs)

verb to pay for or buy

Word building: **purchase** *noun* something bought

purdah

noun an outfit of black clothing, shoes and gloves, and a covering for the face, worn by some Muslim women

pure

adjective **1** having nothing mixed with it, especially anything which might spoil it: *pure gold | pure silk*
Other words: **unadulterated, untainted**
2 clear and true: *the pure notes of a flute* **3** clean and spotless: *a pure reputation*
Other words: **flawless, immaculate, impeccable**

Word building: **purify** *verb* (**purified, purifying**) **purely** *adverb* **purification** *noun* **purity** *noun*

puree (*say* pyooh-ray)

noun vegetables or fruit cooked and then sieved or blended

Word use: Another spelling is **purée**. It can be spelt like this because it comes from French.
Word building: **puree** *verb*

purgative (*say* per-guh-tiv)

noun a medicine causing emptying or cleansing of the bowels

Word building: **purgative** *adjective* cleansing or purging

purgatory (*say* per-guh-tree)

noun **1** a place of temporary punishment where some Christians believe you go after death but before you go to heaven **2** any place or situation in your life which causes a lot of suffering

Word use: Definition 1 often has a capital 'P' and is part of the belief of the Roman Catholic Church.

purge (*say* perj)

verb to purify or get rid of what is unwanted or not good

Word building: **purge** *noun*

puritan (*say* pyooh-ruh-tuhn)

noun someone who tries to be very pure and strict in moral and religious matters

Word building: **puritan** *adjective* having to do with puritans **puritanical** *adjective* behaving like a puritan **puritanism** *noun*

purl

noun a stitch used in knitting

Word building: **purl** *verb*

purple

adjective dark reddish-blue

purpose

noun **1** the reason something is done or made: *The purpose of this device is to make potato peeling easier.*
Other words: **aim, function, intention, object, point**
phrase **2 on purpose**, intentionally
Other words: **deliberately**

Word building: **purposeful** *adjective*

purr

verb to make a low, continuous, murmuring sound as a cat does

Word building: **purr** *noun*

purse

noun **1** a small bag for carrying money
verb **2** to draw into folds or wrinkles: *She pursed her lips in annoyance.*

purser

noun a ship's officer who looks after the accounts

pursue (*say* puh-syooh)

verb **1** to follow so as to catch
Other words: **chase, hunt, tail**
2 to try hard for or seek: *to pursue happiness | to pursue a career*

Word building: **pursuit** *noun*

pus (*rhymes with* bus)

noun the yellowish-white substance in a boil or sore

Word building: **pussy** (*rhymes with* fussy) *adjective*

push

verb **1** to move by pressing or leaning against **2** to force from behind: *We pushed our way through the crowd.* **3** to recommend or to insist on earnestly: *She pushed me to agree with her. | I pushed my ideas.*
phrase **4 push on**, to continue or go forward

Word building: **push** *noun*

pushover

noun something easily done

push-up

noun an exercise in which you raise your body from a lying down position by pushing against the floor, leaving your feet on the ground and keeping your body and legs in a straight line

Word use: Another name for this is **press-up**.

puss
noun a cat

Word use: You can also use **pussy**.

pussyfoot
verb to act timidly as if afraid to make a decision

pustule (*say* <u>pus</u>-tyoohl)
noun a pimple

Word building: **pustulant** *adjective* **pustular** *adjective*

put
verb **1** to place or set down **2** to cause to suffer: *The king put the villain to death.* **3** to cause to begin: *I put Sam to work.* **4** to express in words: *to put a question phrase* **5 put down, a** to stamp out: *to put down a rebellion* **b** to kill as an act of mercy: *We had to put down our old sick dog.* **6 put off,** to postpone **7 put on,** to pretend to have or to be: *My little brother puts on a sore ankle whenever Dad asks him to do something.* **8 put out,** to annoy or make difficulties for **9 put up with,** to bear or endure

Word building: Other verb forms are **I put, I have put, I am putting.**

putrid (*say* <u>pyooh</u>-truhd)
adjective decaying or rotten, especially when foul-smelling

Word building: **putrefy** *verb* (**putrefied, putrefying**)

putt (*rhymes with* but)
verb to strike a golf ball gently along the green towards the hole

Word building: **putter** *noun* a golf club for putting **putt** *noun*

putty
noun a kind of cement used for fixing glass into frames or filling holes in wood

Word building: **putty** *verb* (**puttied, puttying**)
Word history: from a French word meaning 'a potful'

puzzle
noun **1** a toy or game which entertains by giving you an interesting problem to solve **2** something that is difficult to understand: *Her rudeness is a puzzle to me.*

Other words: **conundrum, enigma, mystery, riddle**

Word building: **puzzle** *verb* **puzzlement** *noun*

pygmy (*say* <u>pig</u>-mee)
noun **1** a member of a tribe of African people who are mostly under 1.5 metres tall **2** any small dwarf-like person or thing

Word use: Another spelling is **pigmy**.
Word building: The plural is **pygmies**.

pyjama party
noun a party you go to in your pyjamas and stay the whole night

Word use: Another word for this is **slumber party**.

pyjamas
plural noun loose trousers and jacket worn in bed

Word history: from a Persian word meaning 'leg garment'

pylon (*say* <u>puy</u>-lon)
noun **1** a tall steel tower carrying electric or telephone wires **2** one of the two tall structures on either side of the end of a bridge or of a gateway

pyramid (*say* <u>pir</u>-uh-mid)
noun a structure with a square base and with sides sloping to a point, such as the huge stone ones built by the ancient Egyptians

pyre (*rhymes with* fire)
noun a pile of wood used for burning dead bodies in some countries

pyromania (*say* puy-ruh-<u>mayn</u>-ee-uh)
noun a great desire to set things on fire

Word building: **pyromaniac** *noun* **pyromaniacal** *adjective*

pyrotechnics
noun the art of making and using fireworks

Word building: **pyrotechnic** *adjective* **pyrotechnist** *noun*

python (*say* <u>puy</u>-thuhn)
noun a large snake which crushes its prey but is not venomous

Qq

quack[1]
noun the sound a duck makes

Word building: **quack** *verb*
Word history: an imitation of the sound

quack[2]
noun someone with no proper medical training who tricks sick people into believing he can cure them
Other words: **charlatan**

Word building: **quackery** *noun*

quad bike
noun a four-wheeled motorcycle designed to go over rough terrain

quadrangle
noun a square or rectangular courtyard surrounded by buildings

quadrant
noun **1** a quarter of a circle **2** an instrument for measuring altitudes, especially in astronomy and navigation

Word use: Compare definition 2 with **sextant**.

quadriceps   (*say* <u>kwod</u>-ruh-seps)
noun the large muscle on the front of the thigh

Word history: from a Latin word meaning 'four-headed', as this muscle is joined to the bone in four places

quadrilateral
noun a flat shape with four sides

Word building: **quadrilateral** *adjective*

quadrille   (*say* kwuh-<u>dril</u>)
noun a dance where four couples dance in a square pattern

Word history: from a Spanish word meaning 'company' or 'troop'

quadruped   (*say* <u>kwod</u>-ruh-ped)
noun an animal with four feet

Word building: **quadruped** *adjective*

quadruple   (*say* kwod-<u>rooh</u>-puhl)
verb **1** to multiply by four
adjective **2** made up of four parts **3** four times bigger

Word building: **quadruple** *noun*

quadruplet
noun one of four children born at the same time to the same mother

Word use: A shortened form of this is **quad**.

quaff   (*say* kwof)
verb to drink thirstily

quagmire   (*say* <u>kwog</u>-muy-uh)
noun a muddy patch of ground: *The rain has turned the yard into a quagmire.*
Other words: **bog, marsh, swamp**

quail[1]
noun a small bird that builds its nest on the ground and is hunted for sport and food

Word building: The plural is **quails** or **quail**.

quail[2]
verb to show fear when danger threatens: *The cat quailed under the chair when the big dog entered the room.*

quaint
adjective charmingly strange or old-fashioned: *a quaint little country town*

Word building: **quaintly** *adverb* **quaintness**
noun

quake

verb to tremble or shake: *to quake with fear | The city quaked with the force of the explosion.*
Other words: **quiver, shiver, shudder**

Word building: **quake** *noun* earthquake

qualify (*say* kwol-uh-fuy)

verb **1** to make or become suitable for: *Her teaching experience qualifies her for the job. | To qualify for the final you must do well in the heats.* **2** to change or limit the meaning of: *to qualify a remark | An adjective qualifies a noun.*

Word building: Other forms are **I qualified, I have qualified, I am qualifying.** | **qualification** *noun* **qualified** *adjective*

quality (*say* kwol-uh-tee)

noun **1** a feature or characteristic: *The sound of an echo has a hollow quality.* **2** value or worth: *clothes of good quality*

Word building: The plural is **qualities.** | **quality** *adjective* fine or good

qualm (*rhymes with* farm)

noun a slightly guilty feeling: *They had some qualms about being late.*

Word history: from an Old English word meaning 'torment', 'pain' or 'plague'

quandary (*say* kwon-dree)

noun confusion about what is the best thing to do: *I'm in a quandary about this invitation.*

Word building: The plural is **quandaries.**

quandong (*say* kwon-dong)

noun an Australian tree with fruit which you can eat raw or make into jams and jellies

quantity (*say* kwon-tuh-tee)

noun an amount or measure: *What quantity does this bottle hold?*

Word building: The plural is **quantities.** | **quantify** *verb* (**quantified, quantifying**) to measure

quarantine (*say* kwo-ruhn-teen)

noun the isolating of people or animals for a certain period of time to make sure they don't spread a disease to others

Word building: **quarantine** *verb*

quarrel (*say* kwo-ruhl)

noun an angry argument
Other words: **altercation, disagreement, dispute, fight, row, squabble, wrangle**

Word building: **quarrel** *verb* (**quarrelled, quarrelling**) **quarrelsome** *adjective*

quarry[1] (*rhymes with* sorry)

noun a large open pit where stone used for building is cut or blasted out of the ground: *a sandstone quarry*

Word building: The plural is **quarries.** | **quarry** *verb* (**quarried, quarrying**)

quarry[2] (*rhymes with* sorry)

noun an animal or bird that is being hunted or chased: *The hounds tracked down their quarry.*

Word building: The plural is **quarries.**

quarter (*say* kwaw-tuh)

noun **1** one of the parts you get when you divide something equally into four: *a quarter of an apple* **2** a district in a town: *the business quarter* **3** **quarters**, a place to live: *the nurses' quarters*

Word building: **quarter** *verb*

quarterdeck

noun the part of the top deck of a ship between the mast and the stern, used by the officers

quartermaster

noun an army officer in charge of food, clothing, housing and equipment

quartet

noun **1** a group of four people, especially musicians or singers **2** a musical piece for four voices or four performers: *a quartet for string instruments*

quartz (*say* kwawts)

noun a common mineral which has many different forms and colours, and which can be used to help make very accurate clocks and watches

quasi-

prefix a word part meaning 'resembling' or 'as though': *quasi-official*

Word history: from Latin

quaver

noun **1** a shaking or trembling voice: *The old man spoke in a quaver.* **2** a musical note which is half as long as a crotchet

Word building: **quaver** *verb* to say or sing in a trembling voice   **quavery** *adjective*

quay (*say* kee)

noun a wharf where ships and ferries load or unload passengers and cargo

quay/key Don't confuse **quay** with **key**, which is most often a small, specially shaped piece of metal that can open a lock.

queasy

adjective feeling as if you are going to vomit

Word building: Other forms are **queasier**, **queasiest**. | **queasily** *adverb*   **queasiness** *noun*

queen

noun **1** a woman who is the lifelong ruler of a country **2** the wife of a king **3** the large egg-laying female of such creatures as bees, ants and termites **4** a playing card with a picture of a queen on it **5** the most powerful chess piece

Word building: **queenly** *adverb*

queer

adjective **1** strange or odd: *a queer idea*
Other words: **abnormal, atypical, peculiar, unusual, weird**
2 unwell: I feel queer.
Other words: **nauseous, queasy, sick**
3 *Informal* homosexual

Word building: **queerly** *adverb*
Word history: from a Greek word meaning 'cross' or 'oblique'

quell

verb to stop or calm: *to quell riots* | *to quell your fears*

quench

verb **1** to put out: *to quench a fire* **2** to satisfy or make less: *A cool drink will quench your thirst.*

querulous (*say* kwe-ruh-luhs)

adjective irritable and complaining

Word building: **querulously** *adverb*

query (*say* kwear-ree)

noun **1** a question or inquiry **2** a doubt or problem: *a query about the electricity bill*

Word building: The plural is **queries**. | **query** *verb* (**queried, querying**) to ask questions about or doubt

quest

noun a search: *a talent quest* | *a quest for gold*

question

noun **1** a request for information: *The police asked the witnesses many questions about the accident.* **2** a doubt or problem: *There is no question about her honesty.*
phrase **3 out of the question**, impossible

Word building: **questionable** *adjective* uncertain   **question** *verb*   **questionably** *adverb*

question mark

noun a punctuation mark (?) put at the end of a written question

A **question mark** can be used in a number of ways to indicate a question:
1. *How are you going?*
2. *Well? What?*
3. *That's all you've got to say?*
4. *I said, 'How are you going?'*
5. *'Are you going to answer me?' I asked.*

Example 1 shows the most common use of the question mark, at the end of a sentence which is a question.

Example 2 shows that you can use a question mark for a question that isn't a complete sentence — it may only be one word.

Questions sometimes use the same word order as statements. But when they are spoken, you know they are questions by the special pitch of the voice of the speaker. When such questions are written, the only indication that they <u>are</u> questions is the question mark at the end, as in example 3.

Examples 4 and 5 show how to use question marks with quotation marks. The question mark comes just before the final quotation mark, and there is no need for a comma if the sentence continues after the quotation.

Note that there is no need for a question mark when you write an indirect question:
I asked how she was going.

Note also that it is not necessary to use a question mark when the sentence is a request:
Would you pass the butter, please.

questionnaire (*say* kwes-chuhn-air)

noun a list of questions set out on a printed form with spaces for the answers to be written in

queue (*say* kyooh)

noun a single line of people, cars or animals waiting in turn for something: *a queue for tickets*

Word building: **queue** *verb*

quibble

verb to argue, especially over things that don't matter: *to quibble over a few cents change*

quiche   (*say* keesh)

noun a tart filled with a mixture of cooked eggs, cream and cheese, often eaten cold

quick

adjective **1** fast, rapid or impatient: *a quick movement | a quick temper*
Other words: **speedy, swift, hasty**
2 done, completed or happening in a short time: *a quick job*
Other words: **brief, fleeting, short**
noun **3** the sensitive skin under your nails: *nails bitten down to the quick*

Word building: **quicken** *verb* to make or become fast   **quick** *adverb*   **quickly** *adverb*

quicksand

noun wet sand which traps anyone who falls into it and sucks them down

quicksilver

adjective **1** changing quickly
noun **2** an old-fashioned word for **mercury**

quid

noun *Informal* one pound in money, used before decimal currency

quiet

adjective **1** still or silent
Other words: **hushed**
2 calm and peaceful: *a quiet weekend | a quiet street*
Other words: **serene, tranquil**
3 shy: *The new student is rather quiet.*
Other words: **reserved, subdued**

Word building: **quiet** *noun* calmness or peace   **quieten** *verb* to make or become quiet   **quietly** *adverb*

quill

noun **1** a large feather **2** an old-fashioned pen, made from a goose's feather **3** a sharp spine of an echidna or porcupine

quilt

noun a light warm cover for a bed, sometimes filled with feathers

quince

noun a sour yellow fruit, rather like a large pear, which is so hard it has to be cooked before you can eat it

quinine   (*say* kwin-een)

noun a bitter medicine used to treat malaria

quintessential   (*say* kwin-tuh-sen-shuhl)

adjective being the perfect example of something or someone: *She thought he was the quintessential gentleman.*

quintet

noun **1** a group of five people, especially musicians or singers **2** a musical piece for five voices or five performers

quintuple   (*say* kwin-tup-uhl, kwin-tyoohp-uhl)

verb **1** to multiply by five
adjective **2** made up of five parts **3** five times bigger

Word building: **quintuple** *noun*

quintuplet   (*say* kwin-tup-luht)

noun one of five children born at the same time to the same mother

quip

noun a clever or sarcastic remark

Word building: **quip** *verb* (**quipped**, **quipping**) **quipster** *noun*

quirk

noun **1** a particular habit or way of acting: *a quirk of his nature* **2** a sudden twist or turn: *quirk of fate*

Word building: **quirky** *adjective* (**quirkier**, **quirkiest**) odd or eccentric

quit

verb **1** to give up or leave: *to quit a job | The wages were very low so she quit.*
phrase **2 call it quits, a** to decide to stop doing something **b** to end an argument by agreeing that both sides are even

Word building: Other verb forms are **I quit** or **quitted, I have quit** or **quitted, I am quitting**.

quite

adverb **1** completely or entirely: *to be quite right* **2** fairly or reasonably: *quite pretty*

quiver[1]

verb to tremble or shake slightly: *to quiver with fear* | *The leaves quiver in the breeze.*

Word building: **quiver** *noun*

quiver[2]

noun a case for holding arrows

quixotic   *(say* kwik-<u>sot</u>-ik)

adjective having romantic ideas about doing brave and wonderful deeds

Word history: from *Don Quixote*, the hero of a Spanish novel, who was always trying to do good

quiz

noun a test to see who knows the most about a particular subject: *a general knowledge quiz on TV* | *a spelling quiz*

Word building: The plural is **quizzes**. | **quiz** *verb* (**quizzed**, **quizzing**) to ask many questions

quizzical

adjective teasing, or suggesting you know something the other person doesn't: *a quizzical smile*

quoits   *(say* koyts)

plural noun a game played by throwing rings made of stiff rope over a peg on the ground

quokka   *(say* <u>kwok</u>-uh)

noun a small wallaby found in Western Australia

quoll

noun a marsupial with a long tail and spots, about the size of a cat. It is endangered. See the table at the end of this book

Word use: Another word for this is **native cat**.
Word history: from an Aboriginal language of Queensland called Guugu Yimidhirr. See the map of Australian Aboriginal languages at the end of this book.

quorum   *(say* <u>kwaw</u>-ruhm)

noun the number of people that have to be at a meeting before decisions can be made

quota

noun the share that you are entitled to: *Because of the drought, the farmers needed more than their quota of water.*

quotation

noun a passage copied exactly from a book or speech

quotation mark

noun one of the punctuation marks (" ") or (' ') used before and after a quotation, as in *"We learned 'Advance Australia Fair' at school"*, she said.

Quotation Marks are also known as **quote marks, quotes** and **inverted commas**. Their main use is to show that you are quoting someone exactly, and especially to show that you are quoting someone's spoken words:

Sam told them to 'get lost'.

This shows that 'get' and 'lost' are exactly the words that Sam spoke.
Compare:

Sam told them to get lost.

Here Sam still tells the people to go away, but because there are no quotation marks it may be that he used some expression other than 'get lost'.

Quotation marks can sometimes be used to indicate the titles of short pieces of writing — for example, essays, poems, or the chapters of a book. The names of planes, trains and other vehicles can similarly be written with quotation marks.

Another use for quotes is to highlight a word or to show that you've made it up:

I think the word 'ocker' is a bit old-fashioned. Why don't we call them 'yappies' — for yokelish Australian people?

When using quotation marks, there are two things to consider: **(1)** whether to use double quotes (" ") or single quotes (' '), and **(2)** how to punctuate with quotation marks.

1 Double quotes or single quotes?
In your writing you must choose one or the other as your basic system. There are good arguments in favour of each.

Double quotes are useful because you can tell them apart easily from apostrophes:

'I've visited all my friends' houses,' Maria said.
"I've visited all my friends' houses," Maria said.

The main argument for single quotes is that they are less fussy, both to look at and to write. Once you have chosen one style as your basic quotation marks, you should use it throughout your written work. The second style can then be used for quotations within quotations:

She told me, 'Sam saw them and said "get lost" to them.'
She told me, "Sam saw them and said 'get lost' to them."

2 Punctuation with quotations. When you are writing speech you often introduce a quotation with a phrase like *he said*, *she replied* and so on. There are three common ways to punctuate between the phrase and the quote. You can simply leave a space, add a comma, or add a colon:

Sam said 'Get lost'
Sam said, 'Get lost'
Sam said: 'Get lost'

Once you are inside the quotation marks you should use exactly the same punctuation as you would in your normal writing. If the quotation is a sentence, it should start with a capital letter, and should usually end with a full stop:

Sam said 'You've all got to get lost.'

If the sentence continues after the quotation is ended, the full stop changes to a comma:

Sam said 'You've all got to get lost,' and went home.

quote

verb **1** to repeat exactly: *to quote a phrase from Shakespeare* **2** to name a price: *The mechanic quoted $100 to fix the car.*

Word building: **quotable** *adjective* worth repeating   **quote** *noun* quotation

quotient   (*say* <u>kwoh</u>-shuhnt)

noun the number or result you get when one number is divided by another: *In the sum 12 ÷ 4, the quotient is 3.*

Word use: Compare this with **divisor** and **dividend**.

Qwerty keyboard

noun a keyboard on a typerwiter or computer which has the keys arranged so that the letters *q, w, e, r, t* and *y* are the first six of the top row of letters

Word use: Another way of writing this is **QWERTY keyboard**.

Rr

rabbi (*say* <u>rab</u>-uy)
noun a Jewish priest or leader

rabbit
noun **1** a small, long-eared, burrowing animal
verb **2** to hunt rabbits
phrase **3 rabbit on**, *Informal* to talk a lot of nonsense
Word use: The male is a **buck**, the female is a **doe** and the young is a **kit**.

rabble
noun a noisy crowd or mob

rabies
noun a fatal disease that is spread to people by the bite of a dog or some other animal which has the disease
Word building: **rabid** *adjective*
Word history: from a Latin word meaning 'madness' or 'rage'

race[1]
noun **1** a contest of speed **2** any kind of competition: *the arms race* **3** a narrow passageway for animals, such as one leading to a sheep dip
verb **4** to run or move very quickly **5** to compete with in running: *I'll race you to the shop.*

race[2]
noun a group of people with the same ancestors, the same language and culture, or the same skin colour

racial (*say* <u>ray</u>-shuhl)
adjective **1** having to do with or typical of a race: *White skin is a racial characteristic of English people.* **2** having to do with relations between people of different races: *racial harmony*
Word building: **racially** *adverb*

racism (*say* <u>ray</u>-siz-uhm)
noun **1** the belief that your own race is better than any other **2** unpleasant or violent behaviour towards members of another race
Word use: This is also called **racialism**.
Word building: **racist** *noun* **racist** *adjective*

rack
noun **1** a framework of bars, wires or pegs for holding things **2** a frame on which people used to be tortured by having their bodies stretched
verb **3** to cause great pain to: *Fever racked her body.*

racket[1]
noun **1** a loud confused noise
Other words: **clamour, commotion, din, ruckus, uproar**
2 an illegal business or way of making money: *an organised car-stealing racket*
Other words: **fraud, swindle**
Word building: **racketeer** *noun* someone involved in a racket

racket[2]
noun another spelling for **racquet**

raconteur (*say* rak-on-<u>ter</u>)
noun someone who is very good at telling interesting and amusing stories, especially true ones

racquet (*say* <u>rak</u>-uht)
noun a bat with a network of nylon or cord stretched across an oval frame, which is used in tennis and similar games

radar
noun a device which tells you the position and speed of objects like cars, ships or planes by sending out radio waves and measuring the time the echo takes to come back and the direction it comes from

Word history: an acronym made by joining the first letters of the words ra(*dio*) d(*etecting*) a(*nd*) r(*anging*)

radial (*say* <u>ray</u>-dee-uhl)
adjective arranged like rays or radii

radiant (*say* <u>ray</u>-dee-uhnt)
adjective **1** shining or sending out rays: *the radiant sun* **2** bright with joy: *a radiant smile*

Word building: **radiance** *noun* **radiantly** *adverb*

radiate
verb **1** to spread out like rays from a centre **2** to send out in rays: *The stove radiated heat.*

radiation
noun the sending and spreading out of rays, particles or waves, especially by a radioactive substance

radiator
noun **1** an electric room heater with a rod or rods which become red-hot **2** a device which cools the engine of a motor vehicle

radical (*say* <u>rad</u>-ik-uhl)
adjective **1** being in favour of extreme social or political reforms: *a radical political party* **2** going to the root or bottom of things: *a radical change in education*

Word building: **radical** *noun* **radically** *adverb*
Word history: from a Latin word meaning 'root'

radicle (*say* <u>rad</u>-i-kuhl)
noun the largest and most important root of a young plant

radio
noun **1** the sending of electrical signals through the air **2** a device for picking up radio broadcasts
verb **3** to send a message by radio: *We radioed for help.*

Word building: Other verb forms are **I radioed, I have radioed, I am radioing.** | The plural form of the noun is **radios.**

radioactivity
noun the ability of some atomic elements, like uranium, to release harmful radiation

Word building: **radioactive** *adjective*

radish
noun a hot-tasting red-skinned vegetable eaten raw in salads

radium
noun a naturally occurring radioactive element sometimes used to treat cancer

radius
noun **1** a straight line going from the centre of a circle to its circumference or edge **2** a circular area around some point: *every house within a radius of ten kilometres of the school*

Word building: The plural is **radii** (*say* <u>ray</u>-dee-uy) or **radiuses.**

raffia
noun a fibre obtained from the leaves of a palm tree that you use in weaving baskets and in other crafts

raffle
noun a lottery in which the prizes are usually goods, not money

Word building: **raffle** *verb*

raft
noun a floating platform, often made of logs, for carrying goods or people on the water

rafter
noun a sloping piece of wood forming part of the framework of a roof

rag
noun **1** an old torn piece of cloth that you use for cleaning **2** a newspaper or magazine that's badly written **3 rags,** worn and shabby clothing

ragamuffin
noun someone who is ragged and dirty, especially a child

rage

noun **1** violent anger: *to get into a rage*
Other words: **fury, temper, wrath**
verb **2** to act or speak angrily
Other words: **fume, seethe**
3 to move or happen violently: *The storm raged for days.* **4** *Informal* to set about enjoying yourself
phrase **5** all the rage, fashionable or popular

ragged (*say* rag-uhd)

adjective **1** wearing old and torn clothes **2** torn or worn to rags: *ragged clothing*

raid

noun a sudden invasion or attack: *a police raid on a gambling house | a raid on an enemy airfield*

rail

noun **1** a rod or bar used as a support or barrier **2** the railway: *We will travel by rail.* **3 rails**, the railway lines that a train runs on

railway

noun **1** the track or way laid with parallel metal rails for trains to run on **2** all these tracks together with their trains, buildings and land

rain

noun **1** water falling from the sky in drops **2** a large quantity of anything which keeps on falling for some time: *a rain of confetti*
verb **3** to come down from the sky in drops of water **4** to fall constantly like rain: *Tears rained down her cheeks.*
phrase **5 rain cats and dogs**, to rain heavily

rain/reign/rein Don't confuse **rain** with **reign** or **rein**.

The **reign** of a king or queen is the period during which they rule.

A rider uses a **rein** to guide a horse.

rainbow

noun an arc of colours that appears in the sky when the sun is shining after rain

Word building: **rainbow** *adjective* having many colours

rainbow lorikeet

noun a brightly coloured, noisy, sociable parrot: *The rainbow lorikeets were screeching in the trees.*

rainforest

noun thick forest in moderately warm to very hot areas which have heavy rainfall and high humidity

raise

verb **1** to lift up
Other words: **elevate**
2 to bring up or produce: *to raise a family | to raise cattle*
Other words: **foster, nurture, rear**
3 to gather together or collect: *to raise an army | to raise money*
Other words: **make, source**
4 to cause to stick out: *The sun raised blisters on my arms.* **5** to increase in amount: *to raise prices*
Other words: **boost, hike, inflate**

Word building: **raise** *noun* an increase in wages

raisin

noun a dried sweet grape

Word history: from a Latin word meaning 'cluster of grapes'

rake

noun **1** a long-handled gardening tool used for gathering cut grass and leaves or for levelling and smoothing the ground
verb **2** to clear or level with a rake: *to rake the lawn* **3** to use a rake: *He's out in the garden raking.*
phrase **4 rake in**, to gather or collect: *to rake in donations*

rally

verb **1** to bring together: *to rally an army*
2 to come together: *The people rallied behind their leader.* **3** to revive or recover: *They rallied my spirits. | The patient rallied briefly before falling unconscious.*
noun **4** a public meeting to discuss an important or worrying topic **5** a recovery from illness **6** a long exchange of strokes in tennis and similar games **7** a car competition testing skill rather than speed

Word building: The plural form of the noun is **rallies**.

ram

noun **1** a male sheep **2** a device for battering or forcefully pushing something
verb **3** to strike with great force: *The car rammed the wall.* **4** to drive or force by heavy blows: *to ram the earth down*

Word use: The female is a **ewe** and the young is a **lamb**.
Word building: Other verb forms are
I rammed, I have rammed, I am ramming.

RAM (*say* ram)
noun computer memory from which each item can be accessed or found equally quickly

Word history: an acronym made from the first letters of *Random Access Memory*

Ramadan (*say* ram-uh-<u>dahn</u>)
noun the ninth month of the Muslim year during which there is a daily fast from sunrise to sunset

Word history: from an Arabic word

ramble
verb **1** to wander about in an unhurried way **2** to talk or write without keeping to the subject
noun **3** a pleasant slow walk, especially in the country

Word building: **rambler** *noun* **rambling** *adjective*

ramp
noun a sloping surface connecting two levels: *a pedestrian ramp | a loading ramp*

Word history: from a French word meaning 'creep', 'crawl', or 'climb'

rampage (*say* ram-payj)
noun **1** violent or angry behaviour
verb (*say* ram-<u>payj</u>) **2** to move or act violently and angrily

Word building: **rampageous** *adjective*

rampant (*say* <u>ram</u>-puhnt)
adjective **1** violent or raging **2** unchecked: *Looting was rampant in the bombed city.*

rampart (*say* <u>ram</u>-paht)
noun a mound of earth used as a fortification or defence

ram raid
noun a robbery where a car is driven into the front window of a shop or service station to gain access to goods

ramshackle
adjective shaky or likely to collapse: *a ramshackle old building*

ranch
noun a large farm or station for grazing cattle, horses or sheep

Word use: This word is especially used in America.
Word building: The plural is **ranches**. | **rancher** *noun*

rancid (*say* <u>ran</u>-suhd)
adjective having a stale sour smell or taste: *rancid fat*

Word building: **rancidity** *noun*

random
adjective **1** happening or being done without a plan or purpose: *a random choice*
phrase **2 at random**, without a plan, purpose or pattern

random drug test
noun a test given at random to people such as athletes to see if they have drugs in their body by checking their saliva, blood or urine: *He failed the random drug test and was suspended from play for a year.*

range
noun **1** a line or row of mountains **2** a large area of land, especially one used for shooting practice: *a rifle range* **3** the distance that a bullet or rocket can travel **4** the limits within which there can be differences: *You are within the normal range for height.* **5** a collection or variety: *a range of goods | a range of opinions* **6** a cooking stove
verb **7** to vary or change within stated limits: *Prices ranged from $5 to $10.* **8** to go, move or wander: *We ranged over a wide area on our holidays.*

ranger
noun someone who looks after a national park, a nature reserve, and so on

rank[1]
noun **1** social class: *people of every rank* **2** official position or grade: *the rank of colonel* **3** a row or line: *The soldiers stood in ranks.*

Word building: **rank** *verb*

rank[2]
adjective **1** growing too tall or coarse: *rank weeds* **2** having a strong unpleasant taste or smell: *a rank cigar*

Word building: **rankly** *adverb*

rankle
verb to irritate or upset for some period of time: *It still rankles that I had to wash the car last week even though it was your turn to do it.*

ransack
verb to search and rob: *to ransack a house*

ransom

noun money which must be paid for the return of someone who has been kidnapped or captured in a battle

Word building: **ransom** *verb* (**ransomed, ransoming**)

rant

verb to speak loudly or angrily

Word building: **ranter** *noun*

rap[1]

verb to strike with a quick light blow: *She rapped my knuckles.* | *to rap on the door*

Word building: Other forms are **I rapped, I have rapped, I am rapping.** | **rap** *noun*

rap/wrap Don't confuse **rap** with **wrap**. To **wrap** something is to fold paper or material around it:

I'll wrap the present for you.

rap[2]

noun **1** another word for **rap music**
verb **2** to perform rap music

Word building: Other verb forms are **I rapped, I have rapped, I am rapping.**

rapacious (*say* ruh-<u>pay</u>-shuhs)

adjective very greedy: *The rapacious behaviour of the banks was a major cause of the collapse.*

Word building: **rapaciously** *adverb* **rapacity** (*say* ruh-<u>pas</u>-uh-tee) *noun*

rape

noun the crime of having sexual intercourse with someone against their will

Word building: **rape** *verb* **rapist** *noun*

rapid

adjective fast or quick: *rapid growth* | *a rapid worker*
Other words: **speedy, swift**

Word building: **rapidity** *noun* **rapidly** *adverb*

rapier (*say* <u>ray</u>-pee-uh)

noun a sword with a long, thin, pointed blade

rap music

noun a type of music that has strong rhythms in which the words rhyme and are spoken, not sung

Word use: Another word for this is **rap**.

rapport (*say* ruh-<u>paw</u>)

noun a friendly feeling between people: *I seem to have a good rapport with my new teacher.*

rapt

adjective **1** deeply occupied with your own thoughts and unaware of what is going on around you: *He was rapt in the music.* **2** overpowered by strong feelings: *She was rapt with joy.*

rapt/rapped/wrapped Don't confuse **rapt** with **rapped** or **wrapped**.
Rapped is the past form of the verb **rap**, to hit or knock sharply or lightly:

She rapped my knuckles.

Wrapped is the past form of the verb **wrap**, to fold material or paper around someone or something:

I wrapped the blanket around the baby wallaby.

When someone says that they're really **wrapped** in someone or something, it means that they're very enthusiastic about them. You can also spell this **rapt**.

Note that **wrapped** implies being <u>wrapped</u> up in someone and **rapt** describes being <u>enraptured</u> by someone. When used in this way, both these words are part of informal language, and you should try to avoid them in your essay writing.

rapture

noun great joy or happiness

Word building: **rapturous** *adjective* **rapturously** *adverb*

rare[1]

adjective **1** unusual or uncommon: *a rare disease*
Other words: **infrequent, occasional**
2 thin: rare mountain air

Word building: **rarefy** *verb* (**rarefied, rarefying**) to make or become thin **rarely** *adverb*

rare[2]

adjective underdone or cooked so that it is still very red inside: *a rare grilled steak*

Word building: **rareness** *noun* **rarity** *noun*

rascal (*say* <u>rahs</u>-kuhl)

noun **1** a dishonest person **2** a mischievous child or scamp

Word history: from a Latin word meaning 'scratch'

rash¹

adjective **1** acting too quickly and without thought: *a rash person*
Other words: **foolhardy, headstrong, reckless**
2 done without thought about what might happen: *a rash move*
Other words: **foolhardy, hasty, reckless**

Word building: **rashly** *adverb* **rashness** *noun*

rash²

noun red itchy spots or patches on your skin

rasher

noun a thin slice of bacon

rasp

noun **1** a coarse metal file
verb **2** to use a rasp: *to rasp wood* **3** to scrape or rub roughly: *The cat's tongue rasped my hand.* **4** to make a grating sound: *The door rasped on its hinges.*

raspberry   (*say* <u>rahz</u>-bree)

noun a soft, juicy, reddish-purple berry

Word building: The plural is **raspberries.** | **raspberry** *adjective*

rat

noun **1** a long-tailed animal similar to, but larger than, a mouse **2** *Informal* someone who leaves a friend who is in trouble
phrase **3 smell a rat**, *Informal* to be suspicious

rate

noun **1** speed: *to work at a steady rate* | *to travel at a rate of 100 kilometres an hour* **2** a charge or payment: *The bank's loan interest rate is variable.* **3 rates**, the tax paid by people who own land to their local council
verb **4** to set a value on, or consider as: *Our project has been rated as the best.* | *I rate you as a very good friend.*
phrase **5 at any rate**, in any case **6 at this rate**, if things go on like this

rather

adverb **1** quite, or fairly: *I'm rather hungry.*
phrase **2 rather than**, instead of: *I'd prefer to stay in and watch DVDs rather than go to the movies.*

ratify

verb to confirm or approve

Word building: Other forms are **I ratified, I have ratified, I am ratifying.** | **ratification** *noun* **ratifier** *noun*

rating

noun the value or standing that someone or something has

ratio   (*say* <u>ray</u>-shee-oh)

noun the relationship between two amounts or quantities expressed in the lowest possible whole numbers: *The pupil-teacher ratio at our school is 30 to 1.* | *The ratio of good apples to bad in the bag was 11 to 2.*

ration   (*rhymes with* fashion)

noun **1** a fixed amount allowed to one person or group: *a ration of sultanas*
verb **2** to share out as a ration: *to ration tea when it is in short supply*

rational   (*say* <u>rash</u>-uh-nuhl)

adjective **1** sensible or reasonable: *a rational decision* **2** sane or in possession of your reason: *He was quite rational when he regained consciousness.*

Word building: **rationalise** *verb* to bring into an order **rationality** *noun* **rationally** *adverb*

rattle

verb **1** to make, or cause to make, a series of short, sharp, clattering sounds: *The window rattled.* | *The burglar rattled the door-knob.* **2** to confuse or upset: *The examiner rattled me with difficult questions.*
noun **3** a number of short, sharp, clattering sounds **4** a baby's toy which makes such a noise

Word building: **rattly** *adjective*

rattlesnake

noun a venomous American snake that has a tail with horny rings which make a rattling sound

raucous   (*say* <u>raw</u>-kuhs)

adjective harsh-sounding: *a raucous laugh*
Word building: **raucously** *adverb*

ravage

verb to damage badly: *Sorrow ravaged her face.*

Word building: **ravages** *plural noun*: *the ravages of war*

rave

verb **1** to talk wildly making little sense, especially when you are very ill **2** *Informal* to talk or write excitedly

Word building: **rave** *noun*

raven

noun **1** a large, shiny, black bird with a harsh call
adjective **2** shiny black: *raven hair*

ravenous   (*say* rav-uh-nuhs)

adjective very hungry

Word building: **ravenously** *adverb*

ravine   (*say* ruh-veen)

noun a long, deep, narrow valley, especially one made by a river

ravioli   (*say* rav-ee-ohl-ee)

plural noun small squares of pasta wrapped around minced meat, cooked, and served in a sauce

Word history: from a Latin word meaning 'turnip' or 'beet'

ravishing

adjective very beautiful

Word building: **ravishingly** *adverb* **ravishment** *noun*

raw

adjective **1** not cooked **2** not treated or processed: *raw leather* **3** inexperienced or untrained: *a raw recruit* **4** very painful: *a raw wound* **5** very cold: *a raw wind*

Word building: **rawly** *adverb*   **rawness** *noun*

---

raw/roar Don't confuse **raw** with **roar**. Lions **roar** when they make a loud deep sound.

---

ray

noun **1** a beam of light **2** a small amount: *a ray of hope*

rayon

noun an artificial fabric, similar to silk

raze

verb to knock down level to the ground: *The wreckers had to raze the building after the fire.*

razor

noun a sharp-edged instrument or a small electrical instrument for shaving hair from your skin

Word history: from a French word meaning 'scrape' or 'shave'

re-

prefix a word part meaning **1** again: *repeat* **2** back: *repay*

Word history: from Latin

reach

verb **1** to get to or arrive at **2** to succeed in touching: *I can reach the high shelf.*
noun **3** the distance you can reach: *She left the water within the patient's reach.*
4 a straight part of a river between bends

Word building: The plural form of the noun is **reaches.**

react   (*say* ree-akt)

verb **1** to act in answer or reply: *We all react to danger in different ways.* **2** to act upon each other, as chemicals do when combined

reaction   (*say* ree-ak-shuhn)

noun **1** something done as a result of an action by someone else: *Her reaction to my rudeness was to walk away.* **2** a chemical change

read   (*say* reed)

verb **1** to look at and understand: *to read a sign | to read French* **2** to look at and say aloud **3** to understand: *to read her character from her face* **4** to translate and understand information from: *My computer can't read that disk.*
phrase **5 read between the lines,** to see the hidden truth or meaning

Word building: Other verb forms are **I read, I have read, I am reading.** | **readable** *adjective* easy to read   **reader** *noun*

---

read/reed Don't confuse **read** with **reed**, which is a tall kind of grass growing in marshes and swamps.

---

ready

adjective **1** completely prepared
Other words: **equipped, organised, set**
2 quick: *a ready answer*
Other words: **prompt**
3 likely at any moment: *a tree ready to fall*
verb **4** to prepare
Other words: **arm, equip, organise**

Word building: Other verb forms are **I readied, I have readied, I am readying.** | **readily** *adverb* **readiness** *noun*

real

adjective **1** true or actual: *the real reason | a story from real life* **2** genuine or not artificial: *real diamonds*

Word building: **really** *adverb*: *really good*

real/reel Don't confuse **real** with **reel**, which is a cylinder onto which thread or something similar is wound. To **reel** is to sway or stagger, often from a blow. A **reel** can also be a lively Scottish dance.

real estate
noun land and the buildings on it

realise
verb **1** to come to understand
Other words: **comprehend, see**
2 to make real or bring to pass: *Our worst fears were realised.*

Word use: Another spelling is **realize**.
Word building: **realisation** *noun*

realism
noun **1** the facing of life as it really is
2 painting nature or writing about life as it really is

Word use: The opposite of this is **idealism**.
Word building: **realist** *noun*   **realistic** *adjective*

reality   (*say* ree-<u>al</u>-uh-tee)
noun **1** the state of being real: *I need to face the reality of the situation.* **2** a real thing: *My dream of being a racing car driver could become a reality!*

Word building: The plural is **realities**.

reality TV
noun a type of television program, usually starring ordinary people instead of actors, which shows actual events as they occur, often in a situation that has been set up especially for the program

really
adverb **1** in reality: *He said he made the cake himself, but really he bought it from the supermarket.* **2** truly: *a really funny book* **3** indeed: *Really, that's what she said!* **4** extremely: *really cold*

realm   (*say* relm)
noun **1** a kingdom **2** a particular area of interest or knowledge: *the realm of literature*

ream
noun **1** a packet, bundle or stack of 500 sheets of paper **2 reams**, *Informal* lots: *The DVD player came with reams of confusing instructions.*

reap
verb **1** to cut with a sickle or machine: *to reap the wheat* **2** to get as a return for work: *to reap the benefit*

Word building: **reaper** *noun*

rear¹
noun **1** the back of anything **2** your buttocks
adjective **3** situated at or having to do with the rear: *a rear window*

rear²
verb **1** to look after and support: *to rear a family* **2** to rise up on the hind legs: *The horse reared when it saw the snake.*

reason
noun **1** the cause of an action or happening
Other words: **impetus, incentive, motive**
2 a statement or explanation of these causes
Other words: **excuse, justification**
3 the ability to use your mind to form opinions **4** sound judgement or good sense
Other words: **common sense, intelligence, logic**
verb **5** to argue in a sensible way: *I will try to reason with him.*
Other words: **debate**
phrase **6** it stands to reason, it is obvious

Word building: **reasoned** *adjective* logically thought out   **reasoning** *noun*

reasonable
adjective **1** sensible or showing sound judgement: *a reasonable choice | a reasonable person* **2** fair or moderate: *a reasonable price*

Word building: **reasonably** *adverb*

reassure   (*say* ree-uh-<u>shaw</u>)
verb to give confidence to

Word building: **reassurance** *noun*

rebate   (*say* <u>ree</u>-bayt)
noun the return of an amount of money you have already paid out for something: *We got a rebate on our electricity bill.*

Word building: **rebate** *verb*

rebel   (*say* <u>reb</u>-uhl)
noun **1** someone who fights the government or resists those in authority or refuses to obey laws, rules, and so on
verb (*say* ruh-<u>bel</u>) **2** to fight against the government or resist those who rule or have power

Word building: Other verb forms are **I rebelled, I have rebelled, I am rebelling**. | **rebel** *adjective*   **rebellious** *adjective*

rebellion (*say* ruh-<u>bel</u>-yuhn)
noun an event when people fight the government or refuse to obey those in authority or to follow rules, laws, and so on
Other words: **resistance, revolt, revolution, uprising**

rebound (*say* ruh-<u>bownd</u>)
verb **1** to bounce or spring back: *The ball rebounded off the wall.*
noun (*say* <u>ree</u>-bownd) **2** the action of rebounding: *to catch a ball on the rebound*

rebuff
noun a refusal to accept offers or suggestions: *Your rebuff hurt my feelings.*
Other words: **snub**
Word building: **rebuff** *verb*

rebuke
verb to scold or show you disapprove of
Word building: **rebuke** *noun*

recall (*say* ruh-<u>kawl</u>)
verb **1** to remember **2** to bring or order back: *to recall an ambassador*
noun (*say* <u>ree</u>-kawl) **3** ability to remember

recede (*say* ruh-<u>seed</u>)
verb to move back and become more distant
Word building: **recessive** *adjective*

receipt (*say* ruh-<u>seet</u>)
noun **1** a signed piece of paper proving that you have received goods sent or have paid money **2** the receiving of something: *On receipt of your letter I sent the parcel.* **3 receipts**, money received, especially in a shop

receive
verb **1** to get or be given: *to receive a gift | to receive news* **2** to admit or allow to enter: *to receive into a club*

receiver
noun **1** someone or something that receives **2** someone who receives things which they know have been stolen **3** someone who is appointed to take over a bankrupt company **4** the player receiving the balls served in tennis and similar games

recent
adjective happening or done not long ago
Word building: **recently** *adverb*

receptacle (*say* ruh-<u>sep</u>-tik-uhl)
noun a container or something that holds things: *a receptacle for rubbish*

reception
noun **1** a formal party in honour of someone **2** an office or desk where hotel guests or callers are met and looked after **3** the result or act of receiving or being received: *Reception on our TV is not very clear. | Her friends gave her a warm reception when she came.*

receptionist
noun someone employed in an office or hotel to look after callers or guests

receptive
adjective quick to take in new ideas or knowledge: *a receptive mind*

recess
noun **1** a part of a room where the wall is set back for shelves or cupboards **2** a short time or break when work stops: *morning tea recess*
Word building: The plural is **recesses**. | **recess** *verb*

recession
noun a time when business affairs in a nation are bad and many people do not have a job

recipe (*say* <u>res</u>-uh-pee)
noun a list of ingredients and the instructions telling you how to cook something

reciprocal (*say* ruh-<u>sip</u>-ruh-kuhl)
adjective given, felt or done by one person to another: *reciprocal aid | reciprocal love*
Word building: **reciprocally** *adverb* **reciprocate** *verb*

recital (*say* ruh-<u>suy</u>-tuhl)
noun **1** a concert or entertainment given by one performer or by the pupils of one teacher **2** a long explanation or statement: *We listened to a recital of Annabelle's problems.*

recite
verb **1** to repeat from memory the words of: *She recited a poem in class on Open Day.* **2** to repeat poetry or something similar from memory: *He is going to recite now.*
Word building: **recitation** *noun*

reckless
adjective not caring about danger, especially in a foolish way: *He's a reckless climber.*

Word building: **recklessly** *adverb* **recklessness** *noun*

reckon
verb **1** to say what you think or believe: *I reckon she is clever.* **2** to calculate or count up: *I reckon our stall at the fete made $200.* **3** *Informal* to think or suppose: *I reckon we ought to go now.* **4** to depend or rely: *We can reckon on their help I am sure.*

Word building: **reckoning** *noun* an accounting

reclaim
verb **1** to make suitable for farming or some other use: *We reclaimed the swamp land for a park.* **2** to get back: *I reclaimed my cases at the airport.*

Word building: **reclamation** *noun*

recline
verb to lean or lie back

recluse (*say* ruh-<u>kloohs</u>)
noun someone who lives alone and does not mix with other people

Word building: **reclusive** *adjective*

recognise (*say* <u>rek</u>-uhg-nuyz)
verb **1** to know again: *I hardly recognised her when she came back.* **2** to understand or realise: *I recognise the truth of what you say.*

Word use: Another spelling is **recognize**.
Word building: **recognisable** *adjective* **recognisably** *adverb* **recognition** *noun*

recoil
verb **1** to draw back: *I recoiled from the snake in fear.* **2** to spring back: *The rifle recoiled against my shoulder when I fired it.*

Word building: **recoil** *noun*

recollect (*say* rek-uh-<u>lekt</u>)
verb to remember or bring back to your mind

Word building: **recollection** *noun*

recommend
verb **1** to suggest as being good or worthwhile **2** to urge strongly: *I recommend that you be very careful.*

Word building: **recommendation** *noun*

recompense (*say* <u>rek</u>-uhm-pens)
verb to make a repayment to: *I will recompense you for the trouble you have had.*
Other words: **compensate, reimburse**

Word building: **recompense** *noun*

reconcile (*say* <u>rek</u>-uhn-suyl)
verb **1** to cause to agree or make friendly: *to reconcile the two opinions | to reconcile the quarrelling brothers*
Other words: **conciliate**
2 to be no longer opposed: I am reconciled to moving to another town.

Word building: **reconciliation** *noun*

recondition
verb to repair or bring back to a good condition: *to recondition a motor*

reconnoitre (*say* rek-uh-<u>noy</u>-tuh)
verb **1** to look carefully at in order to gain useful information: *The scouts reconnoitred the area before the army attacked.* **2** to study or examine an area or situation before taking action: *The scouts were sent out to reconnoitre.*

Word building: **reconnoitre** *noun*
Word history: from a French word meaning 'recognise'

record (*say* ruh-<u>kawd</u>)
verb **1** to write down so that the information can be kept: *to record a conversation* **2** to put music or other sounds on a tape or compact disc
noun (*say* <u>rek</u>-awd) **3** something that has been recorded in writing or print **4** a disc, usually plastic, on which music has been recorded: *a gramophone record* **5** the best performance so far in a sport or any other activity: *She broke the record for the long jump.* **6** a self-contained group of data on a computer, such as an employee's name, address and salary

Word building: **record** *adjective* **recording** *noun*

recorder
noun **1** an official who keeps records **2** a machine for recording sound, especially on magnetic tape **3** a type of wooden or plastic flute with a soft sound

record-player
noun a machine on which gramophone records are played

recount (*say* ruh-<u>kownt</u>)
verb **1** to narrate or tell about: *to recount the events of the day*
noun **2** a piece of writing which explains exactly how things happened. See the 'Types of writing and speaking' table at the end of this book.

recover
verb **1** to regain or get again: *to recover lost property* **2** to get well again after being sick
Word building: **recovery** *noun*

recreation (*say* rek-ree-<u>ay</u>-shuhn)
noun a game, hobby or sport which is an enjoyable change from your daily work

recruit (*say* ruh-<u>krooht</u>)
noun **1** someone who has just joined the army, navy or air force **2** someone who has just joined an organisation or group: *a new recruit to the choir*
verb **3** to enlist or enrol: *We are recruiting new members for our club.* **4** to enlist people for service: *The army is recruiting now.*

rectangle
noun a four-sided shape with all its angles right angles. An oblong is a rectangle, and so is a square.
Word building: **rectangular** *adjective*

rectify (*say* <u>rek</u>-tuh-fuy)
verb to make or put right: *to rectify a mistake*
Word building: Other forms are **I rectified, I have rectified, I am rectifying.** | **rectification** *noun*

rector
noun a member of the clergy in charge of a parish, congregation or college
Word building: **rectory** *noun* a rector's house
Word history: from a Latin word meaning 'ruler'

rectum
noun the short final section of your large intestine leading to your anus
Word building: The plural is **recta.** | **rectal** *adjective*

recuperate (*say* ruh-<u>kooh</u>-puh-rayt)
verb to recover from sickness or tiredness
Word building: **recuperation** *noun* **recuperative** *adjective*

recur (*say* ruh-<u>ker</u>)
verb to happen again
Word building: Other forms are **I recurred, I have recurred, I am recurring.** | **recurrence** *noun* **recurrent** *adjective*
Word history: from a Latin word meaning 'run back'

recycle
verb to use again, usually in another form: *to recycle waste paper into cardboard*
Word building: **recyclable** *adjective*

red
adjective **1** of the colour of a ripe tomato **2** having communist or radical political views
phrase **3 see red**, to become very angry
Word building: **red** *noun* **redden** *verb*

red/read Don't confuse **red** with **read** (rhymes with *bed*), which is the past form of the verb **read** (rhymes with *feed*):
I read Sam a fairy story last night.

red-back
noun a small, very venomous Australian spider with a red or orange streak on it

red blood cell
noun a red corpuscle in the blood, which carries oxygen to cells in the body

red card
noun a red card that a referee shows to a player who has broken the rules to tell them to leave the field until the end of the game: *He'd better watch his step or he'll be getting a red card.*

redeem
verb **1** to pay off: *to redeem a debt* **2** to claim (an item) by presenting a coupon, voucher, and so on **3** to get back by paying: *to redeem a pawned watch* **4** to make up for past misbehaviour: *Michiko redeemed herself in my opinion by apologising.*
Word building: **redeemable** *adjective* **redeemer** *noun* **redemption** *noun*

red-handed
adjective in the very act of doing something wrong: *They caught me red-handed.*
Word use: This adjective follows the noun it describes.
Word building: **red-handedly** *adverb*

red herring

noun a false clue or something that takes your attention away from what is really important: *The blood-stained knife was a red herring.*

reduce

verb **1** to make lower, less or fewer: *to reduce the price of milk | to reduce speed | to reduce the number of pupils in a class*
Other words: **cut, decrease, diminish, drop, lessen, minimise**
2 to bring to another condition: to reduce someone to tears

Word building: **reduction** *noun*

redundant

adjective no longer needed

Word building: **redundancy** *noun*
redundantly *adverb*

reed

noun **1** a tall straight-stemmed grass growing in marshes or swamps **2** a musical pipe made from a reed or something like it **3** a vibrating piece of cane or metal set in the mouthpiece of some wind instruments such as an oboe

reed/read Don't confuse **reed** with **read**. Children learn to **read** books at school.

reef

noun a narrow ridge of rock, sand or coral at or near the ocean surface

reef knot

noun a kind of double knot which does not slip

reek

verb to have a strong unpleasant smell: *He reeks of stale tobacco.*

Word building: **reek** *noun*

reek/wreak Don't confuse **reek** with **wreak**. To **wreak** your revenge on someone is to carry out a vengeful act against them. To **wreak** havoc is to bring about ruinous damage.

reel¹

noun **1** a cylinder or wheel-like device onto which something is wound: *a reel of thread* **2** a roll or spool of film
verb **3** to wind on a reel
phrase **4 reel off**, to say or write in a smooth rapid way: *to reel off instructions*

reel/real Don't confuse **reel** with **real**. Something is **real** if it is true or genuine.

reel²

verb to sway or stagger, especially from a blow or an attack of giddiness

reel/real Don't confuse **reel** with **real**. Something is **real** if it is true or genuine.

reel³

noun a lively Scottish dance or the music for it

reel/real Don't confuse **reel** with **real**. Something is **real** if it is true or genuine.

refer   (*say* ruh-<u>fer</u>)

verb **1** to go or send for information or help: *to refer to a map for directions | to refer a patient to a specialist*
phrase **2 refer to**, to mention: *to refer to past events*

Word building: Other verb forms are **I referred, I have referred, I am referring. | referral** *noun*

referee

noun someone who decides or settles matters which could be argued about, especially in sport
Other words: **judge, umpire**

Word building: **referee** *verb* (**refereed, refereeing**): *to referee a football game*

reference

noun **1** a mention **2** a book or a place in a book or other writing where information may be found **3** the act of looking for information: *to make reference to an encyclopedia | a library for public reference* **4** a letter giving a description of someone's character and abilities: *You will need two references to apply for this job.*
adjective **5** used to give information: *reference books*
phrase **6 with reference to**, having to do with: *I will ask you some questions with reference to your family.*

referendum

noun a public vote taken on a question of government or law

Word building: The plural is **referendums** or **referenda**.

refine

verb **1** to make more fine or pure: *to refine sugar* **2** to make more elegant or polite: *to refine your manners*

Word building: **refinery** *noun* (**refineries**) **refined** *adjective* **refinement** *noun*

reflect

verb **1** to throw back: *Metal reflects light.* **2** to show an image of: *The mirror reflected her dirty face.*
Other words: **mirror, reproduce**
3 to show: The children's good results reflected their hard work.
Other words: **demonstrate, display, exhibit**
4 to think carefully: I will reflect on what she said.
Other words: **consider, contemplate**

Word building: **reflection** *noun* **reflective** *adjective* **reflector** *noun*

reflex (*say* ree-fleks)

noun an action done without thinking as a response to something: *Sneezing and blinking are reflexes.*

Word building: The plural is **reflexes.** | **reflex** *adjective*

reflexive pronoun

noun a pronoun which is the object of a reflexive verb, such as 'herself' in *She washes herself.*

reflexive verb

noun a verb whose subject and object are identical, such as 'wash' in *She washes herself.*

reform

verb to improve by changing what is wrong or bad: *You need to reform your behaviour.*

Word building: **reform** *noun* **reformation** *noun* **reformer** *noun*

refrain¹

verb to keep yourself back: *to refrain from eating more cake*

Word history: from a Latin word meaning 'to bridle'

refrain²

noun a line or verse that is repeated regularly in a song or poem
Other words: **chorus**

refresh

verb to make fresh and strong again: *That cold drink has refreshed me.*

Word building: **refreshing** *adjective*

refreshment

noun something that refreshes, especially food and drink or a light meal: *The refreshments are in the next room.*

refrigerate

verb to make or keep cold or frozen: *to refrigerate food*

Word building: **refrigeration** *noun*

refrigerator

noun a cabinet or room where food and drink are kept cool

Word use: A shortened form of this is **fridge.**

refuge (*say* ref-yoohj)

noun **1** shelter or protection from danger or trouble: *They took refuge from the storm in a cave.* **2** a place that gives shelter or protection: *a refuge for the homeless*

refugee (*say* ref-yooh-jee)

noun someone who escapes to another country for safety, especially during a war

refund (*say* ruh-fund)

verb **1** to give back or repay: *I asked the shop to refund my money because the toy I bought was broken.*
noun (*say* ree-fund) **2** a repayment of money

refurbish

verb to make clean or new-looking: *to refurbish an old armchair*

refuse¹ (*say* ruh-fyoohz)

verb to say you will not accept, give or do: *He refused her invitation to the party.* | *He refused to go.*
Other words: **decline, reject**

Word building: **refusal** *noun*

refuse² (*say* ref-yoohs)

noun rubbish: *The gutters were filled with refuse.*
Other words: **garbage, junk, litter, trash**

refute

verb to prove to be false: *I refuted all her arguments.*

Word building: **refutation** *noun*

regain

verb to get back again: *I stopped at the top of the hill to regain my breath.*

regal

adjective having to do with or like a king or queen: *a regal visit | regal appearance*

Word building: **regality** *noun*   **regally** *adverb*

regard

verb **1** to think of or consider: *I regard you as a hard worker.* **2** to look at or observe: *The principal regarded us with a smile.*
noun **3** thought or attention: *You give no regard to what I say.* **4** a feeling of kindness or liking: *I held you in high regard.* **5 regards**, expressions of respect or friendship: *Please give your sister my regards.*
phrase **6 with** or **in regard to**, having to do with or concerning: *I am writing with regard to your party.*

Word building: **regardless** *adjective*
regardlessly *adverb*

regatta

noun a meeting for boat races

regenerate

verb to make or develop again, especially in a better form: *The town has been regenerated and now has more shops and a new park.*

Word building: **regeneration** *noun*: *a campaign for bush regeneration.*

regent

noun someone who rules a kingdom while the king or queen is sick or too young

Word building: **regency** *noun*
Word history: from a Latin word meaning 'ruling'

reggae   (*say* reg-ay)

noun a kind of pop music which started in the West Indies

regime   (*say* ray-zheem)

noun **1** a system of rule or government: *The new school principal brought in a different regime.* **2** a particular government: *This regime has not done much for unemployed people.*

Word use: This is also spelt **régime** because it comes from French.

regiment   (*say* rej-uh-muhnt)

noun **1** a division of an army consisting of two or more battalions
verb (*say* rej-uh-ment) **2** to group together and treat with strict discipline: *The camp leaders regimented us too much.*

Word building: **regimental** *adjective*
regimentation *noun*

region

noun **1** any part or area: *a region of your body | a country region* **2** an area of the earth with particular features: *the tropical regions*

Word building: **regional** *adjective*   **regionally** *adverb*

register

noun **1** a list of names, belongings, or events, kept as a record: *a register of births and marriages* **2** a book for keeping such lists: *a hotel register* **3** a machine which records information: *a cash register* **4** the musical range of a voice or instrument
verb **5** to write down or have written down in a register: *I registered my name on the waiting list. | You have to register your car every year.* **6** to show or indicate: *The thermometer registered a very low temperature. | Alexia's face registered surprise.*

Word building: **registration** *noun*

registrar

noun **1** someone who keeps records **2** a doctor in a hospital who is training to be a specialist

Word building: **registry** *noun* (**registries**)

regress

verb to move or go back: *Don't regress to your old rude manners.*

Word building: **regress** *noun*   **regression** *noun*   **regressive** *adjective*   **regressively** *adverb*

regret

verb **1** to feel sorry or sad about: *I regret that I got angry with you. | She regretted the end of the holiday.*
noun **2** a feeling of loss or disappointment or of being sorry about something you have done **3 regrets**, polite expressions of being sorry: *Please give her my regrets that I cannot come.*

Word building: Other verb forms are
I regretted, I have regretted, I am regretting. | regretful *adjective*   **regretfulness** *noun*
regrettable *adjective*

regular

adjective **1** usual or normal: *Let's go to school the regular way.* **2** arranged evenly: *regular teeth* **3** following a rule or pattern, especially having to do with fixed times: *My grandfather is regular in his habits. | regular meals | a regular visitor*
noun **4** *Informal* a regular visitor or customer

Word building: **regularity** *noun* **regularly** *adverb*

regulate

verb to control or change so that a rule or standard is kept to: *to regulate behaviour | to regulate the temperature of a room*

Word building: **regulative** *adjective* **regulator** *noun* **regulatory** *adjective*

regulation

noun **1** a rule or law: *school regulations* **2** control, or correction and adjustment: *the regulation of traffic*

rehabilitate

verb to help return to normal activities, especially after an illness or accident

Word building: **rehabilitation** *noun*

rehearse (*say* ruh-<u>hers</u>)

verb to practise in private before giving a public performance

Word building: **rehearsal** *noun*

reign (*sounds like* rain)

noun **1** the time during which a king or queen rules: *the reign of Queen Elizabeth* *verb* **2** to rule as a king or queen **3** to be in control: *Peace reigned throughout the world.*

reign/rain/rein Don't confuse **reign** with **rain** or **rein**.

Rain is water falling from the sky in drops.

A rider uses a **rein** to guide a horse.

reimburse (*say* ree-im-<u>bers</u>)

verb to pay back: *I will reimburse your expenses.*
Other words: **compensate, refund, repay**

Word building: **reimbursement** *noun*

rein (*sounds like* rain)

noun **1** a long thin strap which a rider uses to guide a horse or other animal **2** any kind of control or check: *She keeps a tight rein on her feelings.*

Word building: **rein** *verb*
Word history: from a Latin word meaning 'hold back'

reincarnation

(*say* ree-in-kah-<u>nay</u>-shuhn)
noun the belief that the soul, when the body dies, moves to a new body or form

reindeer (*say* <u>rayn</u>-dear)

noun a kind of deer with large antlers, that lives in the cold northern areas of the world

Word building: The plural is **reindeers**.

reinforce (*say* ree-in-<u>faws</u>)

verb to strengthen, by adding someone or something: *Extra soldiers were sent to reinforce the army. | These facts will reinforce my argument.*

Word building: **reinforcements** *plural noun* additional men or ships sent to an army or navy **reinforcement** *noun*

reject (*say* ruh-<u>jekt</u>)

verb **1** to refuse to accept or use: *I rejected the invitation. | They rejected my work.* *noun* (*say* <u>ree</u>-jekt) **2** someone or something that has been rejected: *We will use these pictures and throw out the rejects.*

Word building: **rejection** *noun*

rejoice

verb to be glad or delighted: *They rejoiced over her success.*
Other words: **celebrate, cheer**

Word building: **rejoicing** *noun*

rejoinder

noun a spoken answer or response: *a quick rejoinder*

rejuvenate (*say* ruh-<u>jooh</u>-vuh-nayt)

verb to make young again: *I need a holiday to rejuvenate me.*

Word building: **rejuvenation** *noun*

relapse

verb to return or fall back: *to relapse into sickness | to relapse into bad behaviour*
Word building: **relapse** *noun*

relate

verb **1** to tell: *to relate a story* **2** to connect, in your mind: *The police related our neighbour's presence to the time of the burglary.* **3** to be friends or understand each other: *Some parents and teenagers find it hard to relate.*

related

adjective **1** associated or connected: *The two questions are related.* **2** part of the same family

relation

noun **1** the way things or people are connected: *the relation between two numbers | the relation between husband and wife* **2** a family relative

Word building: **relationship** *noun*

relative

noun **1** someone who is part of your family: *Cousins, aunts and uncles are some of our relatives.*
Other words: **kin, relation**
adjective **2** thought about in comparison with something else: *They live in relative poverty.*
Other words: **comparative**
phrase **3 relative to,** having a connection with: *How well you do in the exam is relative to how much you study.*

Word building: **relatively** *adverb*: *She is relatively happy.* **relativity** *noun*

relax

verb **1** to loosen or make less firm: *to relax your arm* **2** to make or become less strict: *to relax the level of discipline*
Other words: **ease, slacken**
3 to rest and feel at ease: *You can sit down and relax for an hour.*
Other words: **unwind**

Word building: **relaxation** *noun*

relay   (*say* ree-lay)

noun **1** a group which takes its turn with others to keep some activity going: *to work in relays* **2** a team race in which each member runs or swims a part of the distance
verb (*say* ruh-lay, ree-lay) **3** to pass or carry forward: *to relay a message*

release

verb **1** to set free: *to release the prisoner | to release from pain*
Other words: **free, liberate, emancipate**
2 to make public: *to release a news story*

Word building: **release** *noun*

relent

verb to soften or become more forgiving than you meant to be: *I relented when I saw how sorry he was.*

Word building: **relentless** *adjective* never stopping or becoming softer   **relentlessly** *adverb*   **relentlessness** *noun*

relevant

adjective connected with what is being discussed: *a relevant remark*
Other words: **applicable, pertinent, related**

Word building: **relevance** *noun*   **relevancy** *noun*   **relevantly** *adverb*

reliable

adjective trusted or able to be relied on: *a reliable friend | a reliable encyclopedia*
Other words: **dependable, trustworthy**

Word building: **reliability** *noun*   **reliably** *adverb*

reliant

adjective having trust, or depending: *I am reliant on them for money.*

Word building: **reliance** *noun*

relic

noun something left over from the past: *These statues are relics of a great civilisation.*

relief

noun **1** freedom or release from pain, unhappiness or worry
Other words: **deliverance, reprieve, rest**
2 something that gives relief or help
Other words: **aid, assistance**
3 someone who replaces someone else in a job or on a duty
Other words: **replacement**
4 a figure or shape in a sculpture carved so that it stands out above its background

relieve

verb **1** to remove or lessen: *to relieve pain* **2** to free from pain, unhappiness or worry: *Her safe arrival relieved them.* **3** to free from duty by coming as a replacement: *He relieved the soldier on guard.* **4** to bring help to: *Food was sent to relieve the drought victims.*

religion

noun **1** belief in a supernatural power or powers thought to control the world **2** the way this belief is expressed in thoughts and actions

Word building: **religious** *adjective* **religiously** *adverb*
Word history: from a Latin word meaning 'fear of the gods' or 'sacredness'

relinquish   (*say* ruh-ling-kwish)

verb to give up or put aside: *to relinquish a possession | to relinquish all hope*

Word building: **relinquisher** *noun* **relinquishment** *noun*

relish

noun **1** a liking or enjoyment of something: *I look forward to my holidays with relish.* **2** something that adds taste to food, such as a sauce
verb **3** to like or enjoy: *I relish the idea of going on the school trip to Uluru.*

Word history: from a French word meaning 'what is left' or 'remainder'

reluctant

adjective unwilling or not prepared: *She was reluctant to help.*

Word building: **reluctance** *noun*
reluctantly *adverb*

rely   (*say* ruh-**luy**)

phrase **rely on**, to depend upon or put trust in: *I am relying on you to help me.*

Word building: Other forms are **I relied, I have relied, I am relying**.

remain

verb **1** to stay: *to remain at home | to remain happy*
Other words: **continue**
2 to be left: *Some food remained after the party.*

remainder

noun what remains or is left: *How will we spend the remainder of the day? | If you subtract 4 from 6 the remainder is 2.*

remains

plural noun **1** what is left: *the remains of a meal* **2** someone's dead body: *They buried the remains.*

remark

verb **1** to comment or say casually: *He remarked that it was a fine day.*
noun **2** the act of taking notice: *an event worthy of remark* **3** a comment

Word building: **remarkable** *adjective* worthy of notice: *a remarkable achievement*
remarkably *adverb*

remediation   (*say* ruh-mee-dee-**ay**-shuhn)

noun the process of improving or fixing a situation where there is a problem

remedy   (*say* **rem**-uh-dee)

noun **1** a cure for a disease **2** something that corrects anything that is wrong or bad: *a remedy for unemployment*
verb **3** to cure or put right: *to remedy a disease | to remedy a fault*

Word building: The plural form of the noun is **remedies**. | Other verb forms are **I remedied, I have remedied, I am remedying**. | **remedial** *adjective*: *remedial teaching*

remember

verb to bring back to or keep in your mind: *I can't remember the answer. | Please remember to bring your books.*

Word building: **remembrance** *noun*

remind

verb to make remember: *I always have to remind you to take your key.*

Word building: **reminder** *noun*

reminiscence   (*say* rem-uh-**nis**-uhns)

noun **1** a remembering of the past **2** something remembered: *Tell me reminiscences about your childhood.*

Word building: **reminisce** *verb*
reminiscent *adjective*

remiss

adjective careless or negligent: *We've been remiss in looking after the garden.*

remnant

noun a part or amount that is left: *a remnant of material*

remorse

noun the feeling of being sorry that you have when you have done something wrong: *She felt deep remorse when she looked at the beautiful cup she had smashed.*
Other words: **penitence, regret, repentance, sorrow**

Word building: **remorseful** *adjective*
remorseless *adjective*

remote

adjective **1** far away in distance: *a remote outback town*
Other words: **distant, isolated**
2 far away in time: *the remote past*
Other words: **distant**
3 slight: *There was a remote chance that he would come.*
Other words: **faint, negligible**

Word building: **remotely** *adverb*
remoteness *noun*

remove

verb **1** to take off or away: *Please remove your shoes. | Someone has removed my book.* **2** to dismiss from a job or official position: *to remove a prime minister*

Word building: **removalist** *noun* someone whose job is to transport furniture for people who are moving to a new house or office   **removal** *noun*

renal
adjective having to do with your kidneys

rend
verb to pull or tear violently

Word building: Other forms are **I rent, I have rent, I am rending.**

render
verb **1** to cause to be or become: *My jokes rendered them helpless with laughter.* **2** to give: *to render help | to render payment* **3** to perform: *to render a song* **4** to cover with a coat of plaster: *to render a wall*

Word building: **rendering** *noun* **rendition** *noun*

rendezvous   (*say* <u>ron</u>-day-vooh)
noun **1** a meeting arranged beforehand: *a rendezvous between spaceships* **2** a meeting place

Word building: **rendezvous** *verb* (**rendezvoused, rendezvousing**) Word history: from a French word which is why the 's' is not sounded

renew
verb **1** to begin again: *They renewed their friendship.* **2** to build up again: *to renew supplies*

Word building: **renewal** *noun*

renewable resource
noun something in nature such as the sun or the wind which can generate power and which does not run out, unlike other resources like oil which do

renounce
verb to give up or put aside: *to renounce their evil ways | to renounce a legal claim*

Word building: **renunciation** *noun*

renovate
verb to repair or restore to good condition: *to renovate an old house*

Word building: **renovation** *noun*   **renovator** *noun*

renown
noun fame: *a singer of great renown*

Word building: **renowned** *adjective*

rent
noun **1** payment that you make regularly for a house, flat or other property that you use
verb **2** to allow the use of in return for regular payment: *I have decided to rent my house to them.* **3** to have the use of in return for regular payment: *I have rented a flat in the city.*

Word building: **rental** *noun*

repair
verb **1** to bring back to good condition: *to repair an old bike*
Other words: **fix, mend, restore, recondition**
2 to put right: *I will repair the damage.*
noun **3** the work of repairing
Other words: **renovation, restoration**
4 condition: *a house in good repair | a car in bad repair*
Other words: **shape, state**

Word building: **repairable** *adjective*

reparation
noun **1** the making up for doing something wrong or harmful: *injury for which there can be no reparation* **2** something done or money paid as reparation

repay
verb to pay back or return: *to repay a loan | to repay a visit*

Word building: Other forms are **I repaid, I have repaid, I am repaying.** | **repayment** *noun*

repeal
verb to officially put an end to: *to repeal a law*

Word building: **repeal** *noun*

repeat
verb **1** to say or do again: *to repeat a sentence | to repeat a piece of music*
noun **2** something that is repeated, such as a television program that has been shown before

Word building: **repeated** *adjective* **repeatedly** *adverb*

repel
verb **1** to drive back: *They repelled the enemy.* **2** to disgust: *Her cruelty repels. | The smell repelled them.* **3** to keep away: *This spray repels mosquitoes.*

Word building: Other forms are **it repelled, it has repelled, it is repelling.** | **repellent** *adjective* **repelling** *adjective*

repent

verb to regret or feel sorry: *Do you repent your harsh words? | I repent that I was so cruel.*

Word building: **repentance** *noun* **repentant** *adjective*

repertoire (*say* rep-uh-twah)

noun the plays, musical pieces or other items which an entertainer such as an actor or musician is prepared to perform in public: *She has a huge repertoire of songs.*

Word history: from a Latin word meaning 'inventory' or 'catalogue'

repetition

noun **1** the act of repeating: *Repetition becomes tedious.* **2** the thing which is repeated: *Your speech was just a repetition of mine.*

Word building: **repetitious** *adjective* **repetitive** *adjective* **repetitively** *adverb*

replace

verb **1** to take the place of: *Someone else will replace me tomorrow.* **2** to renew or exchange, especially something damaged: *I have to replace the old tyre.* **3** to put back: *I replaced the toys in the cupboard.*

Word building: **replacement** *noun*

replay

noun **1** a previously tied match or game that is played again to decide the winner **2** a repeat, especially on television, of the important parts of a game, often straight after they have happened

replenish

verb to refill or restore: *to replenish a jug | to replenish your strength*

Word building: **replenishment** *noun*

replica

noun an exact copy: *He made a small replica of the rocket.*

Word building: **replicate** *verb* **replication** *noun*

reply

verb to give an answer or response: *Did you reply to the letter? | She replied with a nod.*

Word building: Other forms are **I replied, I have replied, I am replying.** | **reply** *noun* (**replies**)

report

noun **1** an account of the important facts, especially of a meeting, an event, or someone's progress at work or school **2** a loud sudden noise, like a gun firing *verb* **3** to describe or give an account of: *I reported my discovery.* **4** to complain about or tell on: *I am going to report them.* **5** to appear for duty: *At the start of each day, you must report to your supervisor.* **6** to act as a reporter: *My big sister reports for a newspaper.*

reporter

noun **1** someone who works for radio, television or a newspaper, gathering and describing the news **2** someone who makes a report of what is said, such as in a law court

repose

noun peaceful rest: *to lie in repose*

Word building: **repose** *verb* to rest

repossess

verb to take back again, usually because payments have not been made when they should: *The store repossessed their television set.*

Word building: **repossession** *noun*

represent

verb **1** to stand for or mean: *A yellow flag represents sickness on board a ship.* **2** to act on behalf of: *She represents her country.* **3** to show or portray: *The painting represents a country scene.*

Word building: **representation** *noun* **representative** *adjective*

repress

verb to keep under control by effort or force: *She repressed her anger.*

Word building: **repressed** *adjective* **repression** *noun* **repressive** *adjective*

reprieve

noun a delay, especially in carrying out a punishment: *The judge granted the criminal a reprieve from execution.*

Word building: **reprieve** *verb*

reprimand

noun a scolding or rebuke, especially from someone in charge

Word building: **reprimand** *verb*

reprisal

noun an act which causes hurt or damage to someone as punishment for what they have done

reproach

noun blame or disapproval: *She was full of reproach for our misbehaviour.*

Word building: The plural is **reproaches**. | **reproach** *verb* to blame   **reproachful** *adjective*   **reproachfully** *adverb*

reproduce

verb **1** to copy: *to reproduce a picture* **2** to produce offspring or young

Word building: **reproducer** *noun*   **reproducible** *adjective*   **reproduction** *noun* **reproductive** *adjective*

reprove   (*say* ruh-proohv)

verb to blame: *She reproved them for being impatient.*

Word use: The more usual word is **scold**. Word building: **reproof** *noun*

reptile

noun an animal such as a lizard, snake, turtle or crocodile that is covered with scales, breathes air through lungs, and whose body temperature changes as the surrounding air or water changes

Word building: **reptilian** *adjective*

republic

noun a nation which has an elected president, not a monarch

Word history: from a Latin word meaning 'public matter'

republican

adjective **1** relating to a republic: *a republican government* **2** favouring a republican form of government

Word building: **republican** *noun*

repugnant

adjective unpleasant or distasteful: *a repugnant job* | *She finds the idea repugnant.*

Word use: The more usual word is **disgusting**. Word building: **repugnance** *noun*

repulse

verb **1** to drive back: *They repulsed the attack.* Other words: **avert**, **repel** **2** to reject or refuse: *He repulsed her offer of help.* **3** to cause a feeling of strong dislike; disgust

Word building: **repulse** *noun*

repulsive

adjective dreadful, horrible and disgusting

Word building: **repulsion** *noun*

reputable   (*say* rep-yuh-tuh-buhl)

adjective able to be trusted: *a reputable firm of lawyers*

Word building: **reputably** *adverb*

reputation

noun **1** the way in which people regard someone or something *a good reputation as an actor* **2** honesty or good name: *She spoiled her reputation.*

reputed

adjective supposed or thought to be: *He's a reputed champion.*

Word building: **repute** *noun*   **reputedly** *adverb*

request

noun **1** the act of asking **2** the thing asked for

Word building: **request** *verb* to ask

requiem   (*say* rek-wee-uhm)

noun a church service, especially in the Roman Catholic Church, where prayers are said for someone who has died

Word history: from a Latin word meaning 'rest' (the first word in the Latin mass for the dead)

require

verb **1** to need: *Skiing requires practice.* **2** to demand or insist on: *He will do as you require.* | *She requires an early start.*

Word building: **requirement** *noun* **requisition** *noun*

rescue

verb to save from danger or set free from confinement

Word building: **rescue** *noun*   **rescuer** *noun*

research

noun close study or scientific experiment in order to understand or learn more about a subject

Word building: **research** *verb* **researcher** *noun*

resemble

verb to be like: *She resembles her mother.*

Word building: **resemblance** *noun* similarity or likeness

resent

verb to feel jealous, hurt or angry about: *They resent my success. | I resent your rudeness.*

Word building: **resentful** *adjective* **resentfully** *adverb* **resentment** *noun*

reservation

noun **1** something which has been held or set aside for you, such as seats in a theatre or a room in a motel **2** a doubt: *She has reservations about her ability to do the job.*

reserve

verb **1** to save or keep for later **2** to book in advance: *You have to reserve your seat.* *noun* **3** someone or something kept as a replacement, especially an extra member of a sports team **4** public land set aside for a special use, especially as a park or wildlife sanctuary

Word building: **reserve** *adjective*

reserved

adjective **1** kept or set aside: *reserved seats* **2** shy and not wanting to talk about yourself: *He has a very reserved nature.*

reservoir (say rez-uh-vwah)

noun **1** a place where water is stored: *the town reservoir* **2** a container, especially for oil or gas

reshuffle

verb to change around: *The Prime Minister will reshuffle cabinet.*

Word building: **reshuffle** *noun*

reside

verb to live, especially over a long period: *He resides in Australia now.*

residence

noun **1** the place where someone lives, especially a large house **2** the time you live in a place: *They threatened to cut short Dhin's residence in Australia.*

Word building: **resident** *noun* **residential** *adjective*

residue

noun what is left
Other words: **remainder, remains**

Word building: **residual** *adjective* remaining

resign

verb **1** to give up or step down: *Jenny resigned from her job. | I want to resign from the committee.* **2** to surrender or give in to: *We resigned ourselves to whatever might happen.*

Word building: **resignation** *noun* **resigned** *adjective* **resignedly** *adverb*

resilient

adjective able to bounce back: *Rubber is a resilient material. | She has a resilient nature.*

Word building: **resilience** *noun* **resiliently** *adverb*

resin

noun a sap produced by some plants, which can be used in medicines and varnishes

Word building: **resinous** *adjective*

resist

verb to withstand or fight against: *to resist temptation*

Word building: **resistance** *noun* **resistant** *adjective*

resolute

adjective firm or determined: *a resolute character | a resolute approach*

Word building: **resolutely** *adverb*

resolution

noun **1** a decision, especially one made by a group or committee: *They passed a resolution to meet every month.* **2** determination or firmness: *She wore an expression of stubborn resolution.* **3** the quality of an image, as a photograph, computer screen, and so on: *The photo was of such high resolution that you could see the bee's stinger.*

resolve

verb **1** to decide **2** to solve or settle: *They couldn't resolve the problem. | to resolve doubts*

Word building: **resolve** *noun* determination

resonant

adjective **1** resounding or ringing: *She played a resonant chord on the piano.* **2** deep and rich in tone: *He has a resonant baritone voice.*

Word building: **resonance** *noun* **resonantly** *adverb*

resonate

verb to ring or resound: *The strings on her cello resonated when she plucked them.*

Word building: **resonation** *noun*

resort   (*say* ruh-<u>zawt</u>)

verb **1** to fall back on, in time of need: *He resorted to begging for money.*
noun **2** a holiday place: *a seaside resort* **3** someone or something turned to for help: *a last resort*

resound

verb to boom, ring or echo: *The hills resounded with their voices.*

Word building: **resounding** *adjective* **resoundingly** *adverb*

resource

noun **1** something very useful, such as money or wealth: *Our mineral resources are running out.* **2** the ability to manage in a difficult situation

Word building: **resourceful** *adjective*

respect

noun **1** admiration or high regard **2** politeness or consideration: *You should show more respect.* **3 respects,** friendly greetings: *Give my respects to your wife.* **4** a matter or detail: *In some respects it would have been better.*

Word building: **respect** *verb*

respectable

adjective **1** good or worthy of respect, especially in the sense of being socially acceptable: *a respectable person | a respectable job* **2** fairly good: *a respectable mark in the test*

Word building: **respectability** *noun* **respectably** *adverb*

respective

adjective having to do with each one: *They went their respective ways.*

Word building: **respectively** *adverb*

respiration

noun breathing: *The patient's respiration is very rapid.*

respond

verb **1** to answer, using words or actions: *She responded 'yes'. | He responded with a nod.* **2** to react: *He did not respond to my pleas.*

response

noun **1** a reply in words or actions: *They had a big response to their appeal for clothes.* **2** a reaction: *The sunflower turns in response to light.*

Word building: **responsive** *adjective*

responsibility

noun a duty or care: *It is her responsibility to lock up. | He shares in the responsibility of looking after the children.*

Word building: The plural is **responsibilities**.

responsible

adjective **1** reliable or capable: *a responsible person* **2** answerable for something or to someone: *Who is responsible for this mess? | I am responsible to my boss if anything goes wrong.*

Word building: **responsibly** *adverb*

rest¹

noun **1** a time of sleep or recovery **2** time off, especially from something tiring or troubling **3** a stopping of movement: *The wheels came to rest.* **4** the time of silence between notes in music **5** a support: *a foot rest*
verb **6** to sleep or relax **7** to stop or have a break **8** to lie or lean: *to rest your arm on the table* **9** to depend or let depend: *The outcome rests on you. | They rest their case on new evidence.* **10** to stay or let stay: *The torch light rested on one spot. | Isabella rested her gaze on the clock.*
phrase **11 at rest, a** dead: *He is at rest in his grave.* **b** peaceful or unworried: *My mind is at rest now.* **12 let rest,** to leave alone: *He let the matter rest.*

Word building: **restful** *adjective*

rest²

noun everyone or everything left: *The rest had to go.*

restaurant   (*say* <u>res</u>-tuh-ront)

noun a place where you can buy and eat a meal

Word history: from a French word meaning 'restore'

restless

adjective unable to keep still or calm because you are nervous, bored, anxious, and so on: *The children grew restless towards the end of the long speech.*

restore

verb **1** to give or bring back: *to restore lost property to its owner* | *to restore order* **2** to bring back to good condition: *to restore a building* | *to restore the colour to her cheeks*

Word building: **restoration** *noun*   **restorer** *noun*

restrain

verb to control or prevent: *I was able to restrain myself from eating another piece of chocolate cake.* | *The teacher restrained me from sitting with my friends.*

Word building: **restraint** *noun*

restrict

verb to limit or confine: *Bill restricts his food intake.* | *The doctor has restricted me to bed.*

Word building: **restricted** *adjective*   **restrictive** *adjective*   **restriction** *noun*

result

noun **1** the effect of an action or event **2** the answer to a sum
verb **3** to end in a particular way: *The match resulted in a draw.*

resume

verb **1** to continue: *They resumed their journey after a break.* | *Now that you are quiet, let us resume.* **2** to take back, or go back to: *The council resumed our land.* | *Please resume your seats.*

Word building: **resumption** *noun*

resurrect

verb **1** to bring back from the dead **2** to bring back into use: *We resurrected our old clothes.*

Word building: **resurrection** *noun*

resuscitate   (*say* ruh-<u>sus</u>-uh-tayt)

verb to bring back to life, especially from unconsciousness: *to resuscitate the drowning man*

Word building: **resuscitation** *noun*

retail

noun **1** the sale of goods to the public, not to shops
verb **2** to sell to the user **3** to be sold: *It retails at $5.*

Word use: Compare this with **wholesale**.
Word building: **retail** *adjective*   **retailer** *noun*

retain

verb **1** to keep or keep on: *She is managing to retain her old home.* | *to retain an old servant* **2** to remember: *She doesn't retain names.* **3** to hold in place: *Her hair is retained by a net.*

Word building: **retainer** *noun*

retaliate

verb to strike back: *If you tease me, I will retaliate.*

Word building: **retaliation** *noun*

retard

verb to slow down: *The muddy road retarded our progress.*

Word building: **retardation** *noun*   **retarded** *adjective*

retch

verb to try to vomit

Word building: **retching** *noun*

retina   (*say* <u>ret</u>-uh-nuh)

noun the coating on the back part of your eyeball which receives the image of what you see

Word building: The plural is **retinas** or **retinae**. | **retinal** *adjective*
Word history: from a Latin word meaning 'net'

retire

verb **1** to leave work, especially because you are getting old **2** to go away from other people, especially to go to bed **3** to leave the sports field or ring early, usually because you are injured: *The cricketer had to retire.*

Word building: **retiring** *adjective* shy   **retired** *adjective*   **retirement** *noun*

retort

noun a quick or sharp reply

Word building: **retort** *verb*

retrace

verb to go over again: *She retraced her steps.* | *He tried to retrace the events of that day long ago.*

Word building: **retraceable** *adjective*

retract

verb **1** to go back in: *The TV retracts into the wall.* **2** to take back something you have said by stating that it was untrue or you should not have said it: *The politician retracted his statement about climate change.*

Word building: **retractable** *adjective*
retraction *noun*

retread

verb to renew the part of a wheel or tyre that touches the road

Word building: **retread** *noun*

retreat

noun **1** withdrawal from a difficult or dangerous situation, usually in war: *The troops had to make a retreat before the enemy.* **2** withdrawal from people or activity **3** a place which is sheltered or remote: *They have a retreat in the bush.*

Word building: **retreat** *verb*

retrench

verb to dismiss, in order to save money: *The factory has to retrench half its workers.*

Word building: **retrenchment** *noun*

retrieve

verb **1** to get or bring back: *I retrieved my watch from the office.* | *The dog retrieved the ball.* **2** to save: *to retrieve a difficult situation*

Word building: **retrievable** *adjective*
retrieval *noun*

retriever

noun a type of dog that can be trained to bring birds and small animals back to the hunter

retro-

prefix a word part meaning 'backwards': *retrospective*

Word history: from Latin

retrospective

adjective **1** having to do with or coming from the past: *a retrospective exhibition of paintings* **2** taking effect from a date before the present: *a retrospective wage rise*

Word building: **retrospective** *noun*
retrospectively *adverb*

return

verb **1** to go or come back: *They have to return home now.* | *She continually returns to the same idea.* **2** to give or send back: *He returned the insult.* | *She will return the books.*
noun **3** an act of returning: *An effective return of service is an asset in tennis.*
4 a repetition or recurrence: *Many happy returns of the day!* **5** something received,

such as a profit from an investment or a reply to a question **6** a report or paper which has to be sent: *a tax return*

Word building: **return** *adjective*

reunion

noun a special meeting, usually of a family, or of people who have not seen each other for a long time

rev

noun **1** a turning round or revolution, usually of an engine
verb **2** to make turn over faster: *to rev your engine*

Word building: Other verb forms are **I revved, I have revved, I am revving.**
Word history: a shortened form of **revolution**

Rev

a shortened form of **Reverend**

reveal

verb **1** to show: *She drew back the curtain and revealed the painting.*
Other words: **uncover**
2 to make known: *to reveal a secret* | *to reveal the truth*
Other words: **disclose, divulge**

Word building: **revealing** *adjective*
revelation *noun*

reveille *(say* ruh-<u>val</u>-ee)*

noun the signal sounded on a bugle or drum to wake up soldiers in the morning

Word history: from a French word meaning 'awaken'

revenge

noun the hurt or damage done to pay someone back for the bad things they have done to you
Other words: **retaliation, vengeance**

Word building: **revenge** *verb*

revenue

noun the money a government makes from taxes and other sources

reverberate

verb to echo over and over again

Word building: **reverberation** *noun*

revere *(say* ruh-<u>vear</u>)*

verb to feel deep respect for

Word building: **reverence** *noun*
reverent *adjective* **reverential** *adjective*

Reverend

noun a title of respect for a member of the clergy: *See you on Sunday, Reverend!*

reverse

noun **1** the opposite: *No, the reverse is true.* **2** the back or rear of anything **3** a gear which drives a car backwards
verb **4** to turn back or drive backwards or put in the opposite direction: *He took two steps forward then reversed.* | *She reversed the car into the drive.* **5** to cancel or wipe out: *The judge reversed the decision.*

Word building: **reversal** noun **reverse** adjective

reverse-cycle

adjective having the capacity to make an area cool in summer and warm in winter: *Our family bought a reverse-cycle air conditioner.*

revert

verb to go back to: *to revert to an old habit*

review

noun **1** a newspaper or magazine article which describes and gives you an opinion of a book, a film, a performance or an art exhibition **2** a magazine which contains articles about recent happenings or discoveries often in a particular area of interest: *a scientific review* **3** an inspection or examination: *The matter is under review.*
verb **4** to look over: *The general reviewed the troops.* **5** to write about: *to review a book* **6** to reconsider or think about again: *She reviewed her decision.*

Word building: **reviewer** noun

revise

verb **1** to check or correct: *I revised the manuscript.* **2** to go back over in order to learn: *Have you revised your maths for the test?*
Word building: **revision** noun

revive

verb **1** to return to life or energy: *She revived when she had finished her rest.* **2** to set going again or bring back into use: *to revive an argument* | *to revive a play*
Word building: **revival** noun

revoke   (say ruh-vohk)

verb to take back or cancel: *to revoke the mayor's decree*
Word building: **revocation** noun **revocatory** adjective

revolt

verb **1** to rebel or rise up against those with power over you: *The prisoners revolted against their jailers.* **2** to disgust: *The food revolted her.*

Word building: **revolt** noun **revolting** adjective **revoltingly** adverb

revolution

noun **1** a complete change: *There's been a revolution in the business.* **2** the complete overthrow of a government or a form of government **3** one complete turn, usually in a circle: *The wheel made two revolutions.*

Word building: **revolutionise** verb

revolutionary

adjective **1** having to do with a complete change or revolution: *a revolutionary invention* | *a revolutionary government*
noun **2** someone who supports a revolution

Word building: The plural form of the noun is **revolutionaries**.

revolve

verb **1** to turn in a circle or move in an orbit: *He revolved the wheel.* | *The moon revolves around the earth.* **2** to move in a cycle: *The seasons revolve.*

revolver

noun a pistol with a revolving section for bullets, which can be fired without having to reload between shots

revue

noun a musical show with songs, dances and items which make fun of recent events or popular fashions

reward

noun **1** something given or received in return for work or help **2** money offered to encourage people to give information about a crime or lost property

Word building: **reward** verb **rewarding** adjective

rhapsody   (say rap-suh-dee)

noun a romantic poem or piece of music

Word building: The plural is **rhapsodies**. | **rhapsodic** (say rap-sod-ik) adjective

rhesus monkey

(say ree-suhs mung-kee)
noun a monkey from India that is used a lot in medical research

rhetoric (*say* <u>ret</u>-uh-rik)

noun speaking or writing that is exaggerated in style

Word building: **rhetorical** (*say* ruh-<u>to</u>-rik-uhl) *adjective*

rheumatism (*say* <u>rooh</u>-muh-tiz-uhm)

noun a disease affecting your joints or muscles

Word building: **rheumatic** *adjective*

rhinoceros

noun a large thick-skinned mammal of Africa and Asia, with one or two horns on its nose

Word use: A shortened form of this is **rhino**.
Word building: The plural is **rhinoceroses** or **rhinoceros**.

rhododendron

noun a large shrub with pink, purple or white flowers

Word history: from a Greek word meaning 'rose tree'

rhombus

noun a parallelogram with four equal sides and angles that are not right angles

Word building: The plural is **rhombuses** or **rhombi**.

rhubarb

noun a plant whose stalks are cooked with sugar and water to make a dessert

rhyme

noun **1** an agreement or a likeness in the sounds at the end of words, as in *cat* and *bat* **2** a word which rhymes with another **3** a poem or verse that has rhymes

Word building: **rhyme** *verb*
Word history: from a German word meaning 'series' or 'row'

rhythm

noun **1** the pattern of beats in music or speech **2** an even or regular movement: *He has no sense of rhythm.*

Word building: **rhythmical** *adjective* **rhythmically** *adverb*

rhythm and blues

noun a type of music originally based on blues, but often with a faster tempo and more complex rhythms

Word use: The short form of this is **R & B**.

rib

noun **1** one of the set of curved bones partly enclosing your chest **2** the main vein of a leaf **3** a raised or ridged pattern in knitting

Word building: **rib** *verb* (**ribbed, ribbing**) **ribbed** *adjective*

ribbon

noun **1** a band of thin material used for tying or decorating: *Her hair was tied with ribbons.* **2** the ink-soaked tape used in a typewriter

rice

noun white or brown seeds or grain grown in warm wet climates and widely used for food

rich

adjective **1** having a great deal of anything, especially money: *a rich woman | a rich country*
Other words: **affluent, prosperous, wealthy**
2 of fine full quality, such as materials, sounds, smells and colours: *a rich tone | a rich velvet* **3** fatty or hard to digest: *rich foods*

Word building: **riches** *noun* wealth **richly** *adverb*

rickety

adjective weak or shaky: *a rickety old chair*

rickshaw

noun a light cart drawn by one or two people, which is used in some Asian countries as a car or taxi

Word use: The long form of this is **jinrikisha**.
Word history: from a Japanese word meaning 'man-powered carriage'

ricochet (*say* <u>rik</u>-uh-shay)

noun the movement of an object, such as a bullet, when it hits something, bounces off, and keeps travelling in another direction

Word building: **ricochet** *verb* (**ricocheted, ricocheting**)

ricotta

noun a soft, white cottage cheese with a mild taste, made from whey and used in cooking

Word history: from an Italian word meaning 'cooked again'

rid

verb **1** to clear of something unwanted: *to rid the house of white ants*
phrase **2 get rid of,** to get free of

Word building: Other verb forms are **I rid, I have rid, I am ridding.** | **riddance** *noun* a freeing or clearing: *She's gone and good riddance!*

riddle¹

noun **1** a cleverly worded question usually asked as a joke **2** any puzzling thing or person

riddle²

verb to pierce with many holes, like those of a sieve

ride

verb **1** to sit on and control: *to ride a horse | to ride a bike* **2** to travel or be carried along: *to ride in a train*
noun **3** a short journey: *a ride on a horse | a bus ride*

Word building: Other verb forms are **I rode, I have ridden, I am riding.** | **rider** *noun*

ridge

noun **1** a long narrow range of mountains **2** any long narrow strip: *ridges of earth left by a plough*

Word building: **ridge** *verb*

ridicule

verb to make fun of: *to ridicule their strange way of speaking*

Word building: **ridicule** *noun*

ridiculous

adjective funny or causing people to laugh: *a ridiculous hat*

Word building: **ridiculously** *adverb*

rife

adjective common or widespread: *Dishonesty is rife in our society.*

rifle

noun a gun that you support against your shoulder, with a long barrel which is specially designed to give spin to the bullet so its flight will be more accurate

rift

noun **1** a narrow opening made by splitting: *a rift in the earth* **2** a breaking down in the friendly relations between people or countries

rig

verb **1** to equip with the necessary ropes and lines: *to rig a yacht* **2** to control dishonestly: *to rig an election*
phrase **3 rig up,** to put together or in proper working order: *to rig up a dance floor | to rig up a tent*

Word building: Other verb forms are **I rigged, I have rigged, I am rigging.** | **rig** *noun* **rigging** *noun*

right

adjective **1** fair and good **2** correct **3** not left: *your right hand* **4** straight or upright: *to put things right | a right angle*
noun **5** what is fair and good: *We must hope that right will win.* **6** a fair claim: *I have a right to some time off.* **7** the right side: *the third house on the right* **8** a political party or group that believes in the private ownership of land, business and money rather than the equal distribution of wealth
adverb **9** to the right side: *Turn right at the post office.* **10** directly or straight: *Go right home.* **11** exactly or immediately: *right here | right now*
verb **12** to correct or make up for: *to right a wrong*

Word use: Definition 8 often has a capital letter.

right/write/rite Don't confuse **right** with **write,** or **rite.**

To **write** is to form letters or words with a pen or something similar. You **write** a poem when you create it using words.

A **rite** is a ceremony, often a religious one.

right angle

noun an angle of 90°

Word building: **right-angled** *adjective*: *a right-angled triangle*

righteous   (*say* ruy-chuhs)

adjective **1** good and upright: *a righteous person* **2** having a good cause or reason: *righteous indignation*

Word building: **righteously** *adverb* **righteousness** *noun*

rigid

adjective **1** stiff and unmoving: *The handrail should be rigid.* **2** strict or unbending: *rigid discipline*

Word building: **rigidity** *noun*   **rigidly** *adverb*

rigour

noun **1** strictness: *He trained with the utmost rigour.* **2** hardship or severity: *Some animals can survive the rigours of desert life.*

Word use: Another spelling is **rigor**.
Word building: **rigorous** *adjective*

rim

noun the outer edge, especially of a circular or round object: *the rim of a glass | the rim of a wheel*

rind

noun a fairly thick and firm skin: *lemon rind | the rind of cheese*

ring¹

noun **1** a circular band for wearing on your finger: *a wedding ring* **2** anything shaped like a ring: *a key ring* **3** a circular line or shape: *to draw a ring* **4** an enclosed area, not necessarily circular: *a circus ring | a boxing ring*

Word building: **ring** *verb*

ring/wring Don't confuse **ring** with **wring**. To **wring** is to twist and squeeze something: *I'll wring the water out of my wet socks. I saw her wring her hands in grief.*

ring²

verb **1** to give out a clear musical sound: *The bells are ringing. | Jesse's voice rang out.* **2** to make a bell sound, especially as a signal: *to ring a doorbell* **3** to telephone: *Ring me on Wednesday.*

Word building: Other forms are **I rang, I have rung, I am ringing. | ring** *noun*

ring/wring Don't confuse **ring** with **wring**. To **wring** is to twist and squeeze something: *I'll wring the water out of my wet socks. I saw her wring her hands in grief.*

ringbark

verb to cut away a ring of bark from a tree trunk or branch in order to kill it by cutting off the flow of sap

ringer¹

noun a station hand, especially a stockman or drover

ringer²

noun **1** the fastest shearer of a group **2** anyone who is the fastest or best at anything

ring-in

noun someone or something taking the place of another at the last moment

ringlet

noun a long curl of hair shaped like a corkscrew

ringmaster

noun someone in charge of a circus performance

ringtone

noun **1** the noise you hear when you are ringing someone that tells you their telephone is ringing: *There was no ringtone at all — maybe the phone has been cut off.* **2** the noise, usually a tune, that a mobile phone makes when someone is ringing in: *She spent a long time looking for an especially cool ringtone for her mobile.*

ringworm

noun a skin disease with ring-shaped patches, caused by fungi

rink

noun **1** a sheet of ice prepared for skating **2** a smooth floor for rollerskating

rinse

verb **1** to wash lightly in clean water to remove scraps of food or soap
noun **2** a liquid for colouring your hair

riot

noun **1** a disturbance of the peace by a group of people **2** wild disorder or confusion

Word building: **riot** *verb*   **rioter** *noun* **riotous** *adjective*   **riotously** *adverb*
Word history: from a Latin word meaning 'roar'

rip¹

verb **1** to tear or become torn in a rough way
phrase **2 rip off**, *Informal* to charge too much

Word building: Other verb forms are **I ripped, I have ripped, I am ripping. | rip** *noun*

rip²

noun a disturbance in the sea resulting in a fast current, especially one at a beach

ripe

adjective ready for harvesting, picking or eating: *ripe wheat | ripe fruit*

Word building: **ripen** *verb*   **ripeness** *noun*

ripper

noun **1** a digging tool, usually on the back of a bulldozer, used for breaking up rock **2** *Informal* someone or something that you admire a lot: *That skateboard is a ripper!*

ripple

verb **1** to make small waves on: *The wind is rippling the water.*
noun **2** a small wave **3** a sound coming as though in a wave: *a ripple of laughter*

rise

verb **1** to get up or get out of bed
Other words: **arise**
2 to extend or go upwards, or swell up: *The tower rises to a great height.* | *Her voice rose.* | *The cake has risen.* **3** to rebel: *The people rose against the tyrant.*
noun **4** an upward movement: *a rise in temperature* | *a rise in prices*
Other words: **escalation, increase, jump**
5 an upward slope: *a rise in the ground*

Word building: Other verb forms are **I rose, I have risen, I am rising.** | **rising** *noun*

risk

noun the possibility of being injured, hurt or losing something
Other words: **chance, danger**

Word building: **risky** *adjective* (**riskier, riskiest**) **risk** *verb*

risotto

noun rice cooked slowly with meat, fish or vegetables and flavoured with cheese and herbs, originally an Italian dish

rissole

noun a fried ball or small cake of minced food: *a meat rissole*

rite

noun a ceremony, especially a religious one

rite/right/write Don't confuse **rite** with **right**, or **write**.

Something is **right** if it is good or fair.

To **write** is to form letters or words with a pen or something similar. You **write** a poem when you create it using words.

ritual

noun **1** a set procedure for a religious or other ceremony **2** an often repeated series of actions: *the ritual of getting up in the morning*

rival

noun **1** someone who is aiming at the same thing as another person: *He was her rival for the championship.*
verb **2** to compete with

Word building: Other verb forms are **I rivalled, I have rivalled, I am rivalling.** | **rivalry** *noun* (**rivalries**)

river

noun a large natural stream of water flowing in a definite course or channel

rivet

noun **1** a bolt for holding pieces of metal together
verb **2** to fasten with a rivet **3** to fix firmly: *He was riveted to the spot.* | *The scene riveted her attention.*

Word building: Other verb forms are **I riveted, I have riveted, I am riveting.**

road

noun a way or track suitable for cars, people and animals to travel along

road/rode/rowed Don't confuse **road** with **rode** or **rowed**.

Rode is the past tense of the verb **ride**, to sit on and control something:
I fell off that horse the first time I rode it.

Rowed is the past form of the verb **row**, to move using oars:
I rowed the boat right around the island.

roadie

noun someone who looks after the sound equipment for a pop group on tour

road kill

noun the remains of an animal or animals that have been run over by a car and left lying on the road: *On our holiday we saw eagles feeding on road kill.*

road train

noun a truck towing trailers, usually used for carrying cattle

roadway

noun another word for **road**

roam

verb to walk or travel with no particular purpose

roan

adjective of a reddish-brown colour with splashes of grey or white: *a roan horse*

roar

verb **1** to make a loud deep sound: *A lion roared.* | *The wind roared.* **2** to speak very loudly: *The commander roared an instruction to the troops.*

Other words: **bawl, bellow, shout, yell**

3 to laugh loudly

Other words: **guffaw, howl**

Word building: **roar** *noun*

roar/raw Don't confuse **roar** with **raw**. Food is **raw** if it hasn't been cooked.

roast

verb **1** to cook over a fire or bake in an oven

noun **2** a piece of meat that has been or is going to be roasted

rob

verb to steal from, often using force

Word building: Other forms are **he robbed, he has robbed, he is robbing.** | **robbery** *noun* (**robberies**)

robe

noun a long, loose gown

robin

noun **1** any of a group of Australian birds with brightly coloured breasts **2** a European bird with a red breast, often painted on Christmas cards

robot   (*say* <u>roh</u>-bot)

noun a machine programmed to do a job usually done by a person

Word history: first used in the play *RUR* by the Czech writer Karel Capek, 1890-1938

robust   (*say* <u>roh</u>-bust)

adjective strong: *a robust frame* | *in robust health*

rock¹

noun a large mass of stone

rock²

verb **1** to move from side to side: *The boat is rocking on the waves* | *to rock a cradle*

noun **2** another word for **rock'n'roll** or **rock music**

rocker

noun **1** one of the curved pieces on which a cradle or a rocking chair rocks **2** a rocking chair

rockery

noun part of a garden where you grow plants in between rocks

Word building: The plural is **rockeries**.

rocket

noun **1** a cylinder full of gunpowder or something similar, fired into the air as a signal or as a firework **2** a space vehicle driven by hot gas that shoots out from its rear

rockmelon

noun a small round melon with orange-coloured flesh

Word use: Another word for this is **cantaloupe**.

rock music

noun a kind of loud popular music with a strong rhythm and electronically amplified sound, usually more complicated than rock-and-roll

rock'n'roll

noun **1** a simple kind of popular music with a strong beat **2** a dance performed to this music

Word use: This is sometimes written **rock and roll**.

rod

noun a long stick of wood, metal or other material

rodent

noun one of a group of animals with sharp teeth for gnawing, including rats, mice and guinea pigs

Word history: from a Latin word meaning 'gnawing'

rodeo   (*say* roh-<u>day</u>-oh, <u>roh</u>-dee-oh)

noun an event in which there are competitions in riding horses and lassoing cattle

Word history: from a Spanish word meaning 'cattle ring'

roe

noun **1** the mass of eggs inside a female fish **2** the sperm of the male fish

rogue   (*say* rohg)

noun **1** a dishonest person **2** someone who plays tricks for fun

Word building: **roguish** *adjective* mischievous **roguery** *noun*

role

noun **1** the part or character that an actor plays **2** the expected or usual part played in life: *a mother's role* | *a husband's role*

roll

verb **1** to move or cause to move by turning over and over like a ball or a wheel: **2** to be carried along on wheels: *The truck rolled down the hill.* **3** to press or flatten with a particular tool made for the purpose: *to roll pastry | to roll a cricket pitch* **4** to sway or cause to sway from side to side

noun **5** a piece of paper, material or food made into the shape of a cylinder: *a roll of carpet | a sponge roll* **6** a list or register: *a class roll* **7** a low continuous sound: *a roll of thunder*

phrase **8 roll up**, **a** to make into the shape of a cylinder: *to roll up a map* **b** to come along: *A big crowd rolled up to the meeting.*

roller

noun **1** a cylinder used for flattening: *a road roller | the rollers in a mangle* **2** a cylinder around which something is rolled: *a hair roller* **3** a long swelling wave advancing steadily

rollerblade

noun **1** a type of rollerskate with narrower wheels that are positioned in a straight line from the front of the sole to the back of the sole

verb **2** to move swiftly on the ground, wearing rollerblades

Word use: Another word for this is **in-line skate**.
Word building: **rollerblader** *noun* someone who rollerblades

roller-coaster

noun a fast and thrilling ride at amusement parks, with open cars that travel at high speeds around a twisting track

rollerskate

noun **1** a type of skate with two wheels on the front of the sole and two wheels on the back of the sole

verb **2** to move swiftly on the ground, wearing rollerskates

Word building: **rollerskater** *noun* someone who rollerskates

rollicking

adjective jolly and carefree: *a rollicking song*

rollout

noun the launch of a new product: *The company was gearing up for the rollout of the new software.*

ROM   (*say* rom)

noun computer memory which can be read but not changed

Word history: an acronym made from the first letters of *Read Only Memory*

romance

noun **1** a story of adventure, often not much like real life **2** a love affair

Word building: **romantic** *adjective*

Roman numerals

plural noun the numbers used by the ancient Romans, and still used for some purposes, like royal titles and chapter headings in books

romp

verb **1** to play in an active noisy way

phrase **2 romp in**, to win easily

roo

noun a shortened form of **kangaroo**

roof

noun **1** the top covering of a building or car **2** the overhead or upper surface of a hollow space: *the roof of a cave | the roof of your mouth*

Word building: The plural is **roofs**.

rook[1]

noun a large black European bird like a crow that nests in groups in tall trees

rook[2]

noun a chess piece which can only travel in straight lines

Word use: Another name for this is **castle**.

rookery

noun **1** a place where there are a lot of rooks' nests **2** a breeding place for other birds or animals: *a penguin rookery*

Word building: The plural is **rookeries**.

room

noun **1** a part of a building separated by walls from other parts **2** space: *Move up and give me some room.*

Word building: **roomy** *adjective* (**roomier, roomiest**) spacious

roost

noun a resting place for birds at night

Word building: **roost** *verb*

rooster

noun a type of male domestic fowl

Word use: The female is a **hen** and the young is a **chicken**.

root

noun **1** the part of a plant which usually grows downwards into the soil and supplies the plant with food and water **2** the origin or beginning: *Money is the root of all evil.* **3** a number which, when multiplied by itself a certain number of times, produces a given quantity: *2 is the square root of 4 and the cube root of 8* **4 roots**, a feeling of belonging: *I have lived here for ten years but my roots are in Hong Kong.*
verb **5** to send down roots and begin to grow: *A strange plant has rooted in our garden.* **6** to fix as if by roots: *I was rooted to the spot.*
phrase **7 root out**, **a** to pull up by the roots: *to root out weeds* **b** to remove completely: *to root out wickedness*

Word use: For definition 3 see **square root** and **cube root**.
Word building: **rootless** *adjective*

rope

noun a strong thick cord made of twisted fibre or wire

Word building: **rope** *verb* to tie up with a rope

ropeable

adjective *Informal* angry

rosary

noun **1** a string of beads used for counting a series of prayers, usually in the Roman Catholic Church **2** the series of prayers that are said

Word building: The plural is **rosaries**.

rose

noun **1** a wild or garden shrub with attractive, usually sweet-smelling, flowers and thorny stems
adjective **2** deep pink

rosella

noun a parrot with bright red, green and blue feathers, common in Australia

Word history: from *Rosehill*, an early settlement in NSW

rosemary

noun a bushy plant with strongly-scented leaves used as a herb

Word history: from a Latin word meaning 'dew of the sea'

rosette

noun a decoration made of ribbons tied so as to look like the petals of a rose

rosin   *(say* roz-uhn)

noun resin made from the dried sap of pine trees, used for rubbing on violin bows

roster

noun a list of people's names and the times they are on duty: *a roster for the school tuckshop*

rostrum

noun a raised platform for a speaker or the conductor of an orchestra

Word building: The plural is **rostrums** or **rostra**.

rosy

adjective **1** pink and healthy-looking: *rosy cheeks* **2** likely to turn out well: *a rosy future*

Word building: Other forms are **rosier, rosiest**.

rot

verb **1** to make or go bad: *Sweets rot your teeth.* | *The garbage is rotting.*
noun **2** a type of disease that makes things decay or go bad: *This timber has dry rot.* | *The cow has foot rot.* **3** *Informal* nonsense or rubbish: *He talks a lot of rot.*

Word building: Other verb forms are **it rotted, it has rotted, it is rotting**.

rotate

verb **1** to turn round like a wheel **2** to go, or cause to go, through a series of changes: *to rotate the crops each year*

Word building: **rotary** *adjective* turning round and round: *a rotary clothes hoist*   **rotation** *noun*

rote

phrase **learn by rote**, to learn something by repeating it over and over until you memorise it: *I find that I have to learn my times tables by rote.*

rotisserie   *(say* roh-tis-uh-ree)

noun a skewer which turns round and round in an oven, for cooking chickens and other food

Word history: from a French word meaning 'roasting place'

rotten

adjective **1** gone bad or decaying: *a rotten apple*
Other words: **off, putrefied, spoiled**
2 *Informal* sick or unhappy: *to feel rotten*
Other words: **awful, dreadful, terrible, wretched**
3 *Informal* dishonest or bad: *a rotten liar*

rotund   (*say* roh-<u>tund</u>)

adjective plump and rounded: *a rotund belly*
Word building: **rotundity** *noun*   **rotundness** *noun*

rouge   (*say* roohzh)

noun pinkish-red make-up used to make your cheeks look rosy
Word use: This word comes from French.
Word building: **rouge** *verb*: *I rouged my cheeks.*

rough   (*say* ruf)

adjective **1** not smooth or even
Other words: **bumpy, uneven**
2 wild or violent: *rough weather | a rough football match* **3** not exact or without full details: *Do you have a rough idea of when you'll arrive? | a rough description*
Other words: **approximate**
4 basic and without refinement: *a rough bush shelter | rough manners*
Other words: **crude**
phrase **5** rough it, to make do without the usual home comforts: *to rough it camping in the bush* **6** rough on, difficult for: *It was rough on the family when their dog died.*
Word building: **roughly** *adverb* approximately **roughen** *verb*

roughage

noun the fibre in food that you can't digest

roulette   (*say* rooh-<u>let</u>)

noun a gambling game in which players bet on a small ball which runs around a spinning wheel

round

adjective **1** shaped like a circle or ball
Other words: **circular, spherical**
2 completed by returning to the place you started: *a round trip*
Other words: **return**
3 whole or complete: *a round dozen*
noun **4** an outburst: *a round of applause*
5 a period of boxing or wrestling: *He was knocked out in the third round.* **6** a song for several singers, each joining in at a different time
adverb **7** in a circular direction: *to spin round | a tree 40 centimetres round* **8** here and there: *to travel round* **9** in some other direction: *to turn round*

phrase **10** round up, to gather in one place: *to round up sheep*
Word use: Another word for the adverb **round** is **around**.

roundabout

noun **1** a circular intersection for controlling traffic **2** another word for **merry-go-round**
adjective **3** going the long way round: *a roundabout way home*

rounders

plural noun a game like baseball, played with a soft ball
Word use: This word takes a singular verb, as in *Rounders is a good game.*

rouse[1]   (*rhymes with* cows)

verb **1** to wake up: *The phone roused her.* **2** to stir up: *to rouse her anger*
Word use: Another word is **arouse**.
Word building: **rousing** *adjective*: *a rousing song*

rouse/rows Don't confuse **rouse** with **rows**. If people have lots of **rows** (rhyming with *cows*), they have many noisy fights or quarrels.

Rows (rhyming with *hose*) means 'lines of people or things', as in *rows of potatoes*. **Rows** with this pronunciation can also be a form of the verb **row**:

> *She often rows the boat.*

rouse[2]   (*rhymes with* mouse)

phrase **rouse on**, to be angry with: *to rouse on the children for getting home late*

rouseabout   (*say* rows-uh-bowt)

noun someone hired to do odd jobs for which not much skill is needed

rout   (*rhymes with* out)

verb to defeat and force to run away: *to rout an army*
Word building: **rout** *noun* a total defeat

route   (*sounds like* root)

noun **1** a way or road from one place to another: *The bus takes the long route home.*
2 (*say* rowt) in computers, a path between parts of a computer network
Word building: **route** *verb* (**routed, routeing** or **routing**) to send by a particular route

routine   (*say* rooh-<u>teen</u>)

noun something which is always done in the same way or at the same time or place: *a dance routine*
Word building: **routine** *adjective*: *Routine work gets boring.*

rove
verb to wander or roam

Word building: **rover** *noun*

row[1] (*rhymes with* go)
noun a line of people or things

row[2] (*rhymes with* go)
verb to move using oars: *to row a boat | to learn how to row*

Word building: Other forms are **I rowed, I have rowed, I am rowing.** | **rower** *noun*

row[3] (*rhymes with* how)
noun **1** a noisy quarrel or fight **2** shouting and loud noise: *I can't sleep with that row going on.*

Word building: **row** *verb* to quarrel loudly

rowdy (*rhymes with* cloudy)
adjective wild and noisy: *a bunch of rowdy kids*

Word building: Other forms are **rowdier, rowdiest.** | **rowdily** *adverb* **rowdiness** *noun*

rowlock (*say* rol-uhk)
noun one of the metal rings that support the oars in a rowing boat

royal
adjective having to do with a king or queen: *a royal visit*

Word building: **royally** *adverb*

royalty
noun **1** kings, queens and members of their families **2** a share of the profits made from their work, paid to an inventor, author or composer

RSVP
short for French words meaning 'please reply'

Word use: This expression is used in written invitations.

rub
verb **1** to move back and forth while pressing down: *to rub polish on your shoes | I have blisters where my shoes rubbed.*
phrase **2 rub it in,** to keep on reminding someone about their mistakes **3 rub out,** to clean off by rubbing: *to rub out a pencil mark*

Word building: Other verb forms are **I rubbed, I have rubbed, I am rubbing.**

rubber
noun **1** stretchy material made from the thick sap of some tropical trees, used to make things like car tyres, bouncing balls and elastic bands **2** another word for an **eraser**

Word building: **rubbery** *adjective* soft and stretchy

rubbish
noun **1** useless left-over material or matter
Other words: **debris, garbage, junk, litter, refuse, trash, waste**
2 nonsense: *Don't talk rubbish.*

Word building: **rubbish** *verb* to scoff at **rubbishy** *adjective* worthless

rubble
noun rough pieces of broken stone or brick

rubella (*say* rooh-bel-uh)
noun another name for **German measles**

Word history: from a Latin word meaning 'reddish'

ruby
noun a precious stone of a rich red colour

Word building: The plural is **rubies.** | **ruby** *adjective*

rucksack
noun a bag with shoulder straps worn by hikers on their backs

rudder
noun a flat movable plate at the back of a boat or plane, used for steering

ruddy
adjective having a healthy red colour: *a ruddy face*

Word building: Other forms are **ruddier, ruddiest.**

rude
adjective **1** bad-mannered or impolite
Other words: **cheeky, impertinent, impolite, impudent, insolent**
2 made in a basic and simple way: *a rude bush hut*

Word use: For definition 1 the opposite is **polite.**
Word building: **rudely** *adverb* **rudeness** *noun*

ruffian
noun someone who is rough or rowdy

ruffle

verb **1** to spoil the calmness or smoothness of: *Don't ruffle Nick's temper.* | *Birds ruffle their feathers.*

noun **2** a frill on a skirt, blouse or curtains

Word building: **ruffled** *adjective*

rug

noun **1** a thick warm blanket **2** a small carpet

Rugby League

noun a type of football, played by two teams of 13 players each. It is similar to Rugby Union.

Word use: The short form of this is **League**.

Rugby Union

noun a type of football played by two teams of 15 players each. It is similar to Rugby League.

Word use: The short form of this is **Union**.

rugged   (*say* rug-uhd)

adjective **1** rough or uneven: *a rugged mountain range* **2** tough and strong: *a rugged mountain climber*

Word building: **ruggedly** *adverb*

ruin

verb **1** to wreck or destroy: *The rain ruined the harvest.*

noun **2** complete destruction: *the ruin of my hopes* **3** **ruins**, the remains of fallen buildings: *the ruins of an ancient castle*

Word building: **ruination** *noun*   **ruined** *adjective*

rule

noun **1** an instruction telling you what to do: *to play according to the rules*

verb **2** to govern, control or reign: *The queen ruled her country wisely.* **3** to decide or direct: *The referee ruled that I was out.* **4** to draw, using a ruler: *to rule a straight line*

phrase **5 as a rule**, usually: *We walk to school as a rule.*

Word building: **ruling** *noun* a decision made by someone in charge   **ruling** *adjective* in charge

ruler

noun **1** someone who rules or governs **2** a strip of wood or plastic with a straight edge, used for measuring and drawing straight lines

rum

noun a strong alcoholic drink made from sugar cane

rumble

noun **1** a deep rolling sound: *the rumble of thunder* **2** *Informal* a gang fight

Word building: **rumble** *verb*: *The train rumbled along the track.*

rumbustious   (*say* rum-bus-chuhs)

adjective rowdy or boisterous

Word building: **rumbustiously** *adverb*

ruminate   (*say* rooh-muh-nayt)

verb **1** to chew the cud, like a cow **2** to consider very carefully or meditate: *to ruminate on a problem*

Word building: **ruminant** *noun* an animal that chews its cud

rummage

verb to search by moving everything around: *to rummage through a bag to find a pen*

Word history: from a French word meaning 'stow goods in the hold of a ship'

rummy

noun a card game in which you put cards into matching sets and ordered groups

rumour   (*rhymes with* boomer)

noun a story that spreads round which may or may not be true

Other words: **gossip, hearsay, talk**

Word use: Another spelling is **rumor**.
Word building: **rumour** *verb*: *It is rumoured that you are going overseas.*

rump

noun **1** the back part of a cow, horse or similar animal **2** meat taken from this part: *grilled rump*

rumple

verb to crush or mess up: *Please don't rumple the bed cover.*

Word building: **rumple** *noun* a crease or wrinkle

rumpus

noun a loud noise and commotion

run

verb **1** to move quickly on your feet **2** to go or make go: *The bus runs every half hour.* | *to run a car* **3** to pass quickly: *to run your fingers through your hair* | *to have ideas running through your mind* **4** to flow or fill with water: *to leave a tap running* | *to run a bath* **5** to extend or continue: *to run a net across the river* | *A crack runs down the wall.* **6** to conduct or manage: *to run a business*
noun **7** the action of running: *to go for a run* **8** a trip or journey: *a run in the car* **9** a pen for animals: *a chicken run* **10** a score in cricket: *Our team made 120 runs.* **11** a series of happenings: *a run of good luck*
phrase **12 in the long run**, in the end: *It turned out well in the long run.* **13 run out**, to be all used up: *The food has run out.* **14 run through**, **a** to practise: *to run through a speech* **b** to stab with a sword

Word building: Other verb forms are **I ran, I have run, I am running**.

runaway

adjective **1** running out of control: *a runaway horse* **2** very easy: *a runaway win over the other team*

Word building: **runaway** *noun* someone who has escaped or run away

rung

noun one of the steps of a ladder

run-in

noun Informal a disagreement or argument

runner

noun **1** someone who runs well and competes in races **2** a messenger **3** one of the smooth strips of wood on which a drawer slides

runner-up

noun someone who comes second in a contest

running

adjective **1** able to run or suitable for running: *a machine in running order* | *running shoes* **2** flowing: *running water* **3** in a row: *to be late three days running*
noun **4** management or organisation: *the running of a shop*
phrase **5 out of the running**, with no chance of winning **6 running writing**, writing where all the letters of a word are joined together

runny

adjective flowing or pouring out liquid: *runny custard* | *a runny nose*

Word building: Other forms are **runnier, runniest**.

run-off

noun **1** a deciding contest or race held after a tie or dead heat **2** something that runs off, such as water that drains off land in streams, or rain that flows off a roof after rain

runt

noun a person or animal that is the smallest in their group: *This piglet is the runt of the litter.*

Word use: This word is used to insult people.

runway   (*say* run-way)

noun the strip of land that an aeroplane takes off from and lands on

rupture

verb to break or burst: *to rupture a friendship* | *Her appendix ruptured.*

rural

adjective having to do with the countryside or farming: *rural land*

Word building: **rurally** *adverb*

ruse   (*rhymes with* shoes)

noun a dishonest trick or scheme

rush¹

verb **1** to move or do in a great hurry: *The river rushed over the rocks.* | *Don't rush your dinner.* **2** to hurry into doing something or making a decision: *Don't rush me.*
noun **3** a time of great hurry and movement: *the gold rush* | *a rush of wind*

rush²

noun a type of long grass that grows in wet ground along river banks

rust

noun **1** the red or orange coating which forms on the surface of iron when it reacts to air and water
verb **2** to become covered with this orange coating

Word building: **rusty** *adjective* (**rustier, rustiest**)

rustic

adjective having to do with, or suitable for, the country rather than the city: *a rustic lifestyle* | *a rustic style of architecture*

rustle   (say rus-uhl)

verb **1** to make quiet sounds, like leaves or papers rubbing against each other: *The leaves rustled in the breeze. | The folds of her skirt rustled as she skipped along.*

phrase **2 rustle up**, *Informal* to make out of what is available: *I'll rustle up some lunch.*

Word building: **rustle** *noun*

rut

noun **1** a groove made in the ground by the wheels of a car

phrase **2 in a rut**, doing the same thing all the time

ruthless

adjective showing no pity or mercy: *a ruthless tyrant*

Word building: **ruthlessness** *noun* **ruthlessly** *adverb*

rye

noun a grain which grows like wheat and is ground into flour

Word building: **rye** *adjective*: *rye bread*

Sabbath

noun **1** the seventh day of the week, Saturday, which is the day of worship for Jews and for some Christians **2** the first day of the week, Sunday, which is the day of worship for most Christians

sabotage (*say* sab-uh-tahzh)

noun damage done on purpose to stop somebody else being successful: *the sabotage of the enemy's arms factory*

Word building: **sabotage** *verb*

sabre (*say* say-buh)

noun a heavy, slightly curved, one-edged sword

saccharin (*say* sak-uh-ruhn)

noun a sweet chemical used instead of sugar

Word building: **saccharine** *adjective*

sachet (*say* sash-ay)

noun a small sealed packet or bag used to contain small servings of food, or shampoo for your hair, or perfumed herbs to keep your cupboards smelling fresh

Word history: from a French word, which is why the 't' is not sounded

sack

noun **1** a large bag made of strongly woven material **2** dismissal from your job: *I've been given the sack.*

Word building: **sack** *verb*

sacrament (*say* sak-ruh-muhnt)

noun a Christian religious ceremony which is the outward show of a spiritual event or change: *the sacrament of baptism*

Word use: This is often spelt with a capital letter.
Word building: **sacramental** *adjective*

sacred (*say* say-kruhd)

adjective **1** holy or worthy of religious respect: *a sacred city* **2** having to do with religion: *sacred music*
Other words: **religious, spiritual**

Word building: **sacredly** *adverb* **sacredness** *noun*

sacrifice

verb **1** to give up at a loss to yourself: *I sacrificed my chance of winning to help my friend.* **2** to offer to a god, especially your life or your goods

Word building: **sacrifice** *noun* **sacrificial** *adjective*

sacrilege (*say* sak-ruh-lij)

noun disrespect shown to something sacred

Word building: **sacrilegious** *adjective* **sacrilegiously** *adverb*

sad

adjective unhappy or sorry: *I'm sad that my friend has gone away.*
Other words: **forlorn, gloomy, glum, miserable, mournful, sorrowful, upset**

Word use: The opposite of this is **happy**.
Word building: Other forms are **sadder, saddest.** | **sadly** *adverb* **sadness** *noun*

saddle

noun **1** a seat for the rider of a horse **2** the seat on a bicycle **3** a piece of meat including part of the backbone and the ribs: *a saddle of mutton*
verb **4** to put a saddle on **5** to load or burden: *He saddled me with a nasty job.*

Word building: **saddler** *noun*   **saddlery** *noun*

safari   (*say* suh-<u>fah</u>-ree)

noun a long journey, usually for hunting wild animals

Word building: The plural is **safaris**.
Word history: from Swahili, an African language

safe

adjective **1** removed from danger or risk: *You are safe now.*
Other words: **all right, immune, protected, secure, sheltered**
2 careful in avoiding danger: *a safe driver*
Other words: **cautious, wary**
3 free of or away from danger or risk: *A Safety House is a safe place where you can go if you are in trouble.* **4** harmless, or not dangerous: *That kind of mushroom is perfectly safe to eat.*
noun **5** a steel or iron box that you keep money, jewels or valuable papers in

Word building: **safely** *adverb*   **safety** *noun*

safe sex

noun sexual practices in which precautions are taken to prevent the spread of disease, especially AIDS, through sexual intercourse

safety belt

noun **1** a belt or strap fastening someone working up high to a fixed object to prevent them from falling **2** another term for **seatbelt**

safflower

noun a plant with large orange-red flowers which is grown for the oil you can get from its seeds

saffron

noun an orange-coloured powder made from flowers, which is used to colour food

sag

verb **1** to bend down, especially in the middle: *The mattress sagged from the weight of the body.* **2** to droop or hang loosely: *Her shoulders sagged.*

Word building: Other forms are **I sagged, I have sagged, I am sagging.** | **sag** *noun*

saga   (*say* <u>sah</u>-guh)

noun **1** a long novel about the lives of a family or group of people **2** any long story

sage[1]

noun a very wise person

Word building: **sage** *adjective*: *sage comments*

sage[2]

noun a herb used in cooking

sago   (*say* <u>say</u>-goh)

noun a starchy food made from the soft inside of the trunk of some palm trees

sail

noun **1** a sheet of canvas or nylon which catches the wind and makes a boat move through the water **2** a voyage in a ship or boat
verb **3** to travel in a ship or boat **4** to move or be carried along on water: *Ships sail to Hobart from Melbourne.* **5** to move along quickly: *Clouds sailed overhead.* **6** to cause to sail: *We normally sail our boat on the harbour every Saturday.*

Word building: **sailor** *noun* a member of a ship's crew

sail/sale Don't confuse **sail** with **sale**. A **sale** is when something such as a house is sold. If you go to a **sale**, you can buy things at a specially low price.

sailboard

noun a light-weight surfboard with a mast and sail, on which the rider stands to control the sail

saint

noun **1** someone who has been declared to be holy by the Christian church **2** a very good person

Word use: Definition 1 is shortened to *St* and used as a title as in *St John.*
Word building: **sainthood** *noun*   **saintly** *adjective*

sake

noun **1** purpose: *For the sake of peace, let's not argue.* **2** benefit or good: *For your own sake, do your best.*

salad

noun **1** a dish of raw vegetables such as lettuce, tomatoes and celery **2** a dish of raw or cooked food served cold, usually with a dressing: *rice salad | fruit salad*

salamander (*say* <u>sal</u>-uh-man-duh)
noun a type of amphibian with a tail, which lives in the water when very young, but later lives on land

salami (*say* suh-<u>lah</u>-mee)
noun a kind of sausage with a strong salty taste

salary
noun the regular pay you get for your job, especially for office work
Word use: Compare this with **wage**.
Word building: The plural is **salaries**.

sale
noun **1** the act of selling: *the sale of a house* **2** a special selling at a low price: *a sale of summer clothes*
phrase **3 for sale** or **on sale**, able to be bought: *Our house is for sale. | Her latest book is on sale now.*

sale/sail Don't confuse **sale** with **sail**, which is the part of a boat which catches the wind and makes it move through the water.

saline (*say* <u>say</u>-luyn)
adjective containing or tasting like salt: *a saline solution*
Word building: **salinity** *noun*

saliva (*say* suh-<u>luy</u>-vuh)
noun the watery liquid in your mouth, which helps you swallow and begin to digest food
Word building: **salivary** *adjective*: *the salivary glands*   **salivate** *verb*

sallow
adjective having a sickly yellowish colour: *sallow skin*

salmon (*say* <u>sam</u>-uhn)
noun a fish with pink flesh, which is good to eat
Word building: The plural is **salmon**.

salon (*say* <u>sal</u>-on)
noun a fashionable shop: *a beauty salon*

saloon
noun a well-furnished bar room in a hotel

salsa
noun **1** a spicy sauce made from tomatoes and chilli, used in Mexican cooking **2** a type of dance music from Central America which blends lively rhythms with jazz and rock music

salt
noun **1** white crystals obtained from sea water and used to flavour or preserve food **2** a chemical compound formed from an acid and an alkali
Word building: **salty** *adjective* (**saltier**, **saltiest**)

saltbush
noun a plant which can grow in very dry parts of Australia and which horses and cattle eat

saltcellar
noun a container for salt, used at a meal table

saltwater crocodile
noun a large crocodile that inhabits the coast and near-coastal waters of north-eastern Australia: *Saltwater crocodiles can eat just about any animal that comes into their territory.*

salutary (*say* <u>sal</u>-yuh-tree)
adjective **1** health-giving or wholesome **2** doing good: *salutary advice*
Word use: The more usual word is **beneficial**.

salute
verb **1** to greet **2** to raise your right hand to the side of your head as a mark of respect for: *The soldier saluted the queen.*
Word building: **salutation** *noun*   **salute** *noun*

salvage (*say* <u>sal</u>-vij)
noun the saving of a ship or its cargo from fire, shipwreck or other damage
Word building: **salvage** *verb*

salvation
noun **1** the act of saving **2** the cause or means of saving: *The ladder against the wall of the burning house was their salvation.*

salvo
noun the firing of guns a number of times, often as a salute
Word building: The plural is **salvoes**.
Word history: from a Latin word meaning 'be in good health'

same

adjective **1** exactly alike: *I have the same jacket as you.* **2** referring to one particular thing, time or place, not to different ones: *They go to the same school.* **3** referring to something that has already been mentioned: *I suggested going to the beach, and Rania said she'd had the same idea.*
pronoun **4** the same person or thing: *She's the same as ever.*

sample

noun **1** a part or piece which shows what the whole is like: *a sample of her writing*
Other words: **example, specimen**
verb **2** to test or judge by a sample: *to sample a cake*

Word building: **sample** *adjective*: *a sample packet*

samurai   (*say* sam-yuh-ruy)

noun a Japanese warrior who lived in medieval times

Word building: The plural is **samurai**.

sanatorium

noun a hospital for sick people who need to rest and live for a time in a healthy climate

Word use: Another spelling is **sanitarium**.
Word building: The plural is **sanatoriums** or **sanatoria**.

sanctify

verb to make holy or set apart as holy

Word building: Other forms are **I sanctified, I have sanctified, I am sanctifying.** | **sanctification** *noun*

sanction

verb to give approval or support to

Word use: The more usual word is **approve**.
Word building: **sanction** *noun*

sanctuary   (*say* sang-chuh-ree)

noun **1** a holy place **2** a place of safety: *a bird sanctuary* **3** protection given to someone running away from ill-treatment

Word building: The plural is **sanctuaries**.

sand

noun **1** fine grains of rocks that have been broken up or worn away
verb **2** to smooth or polish with sand or sandpaper

Word building: **sandhill** *noun* a low hill of piled up sand   **sandy** *adjective* (**sandier, sandiest**)

sandal

noun a kind of shoe made of a flat sole fastened to the foot with straps

sandalwood

noun a sweet-smelling wood used for carving ornaments, or burnt as incense

sandpaper

noun a strong paper coated with a layer of sand and used for smoothing rough surfaces

Word building: **sandpaper** *verb*

sandshoe

noun a canvas shoe with a rubber sole, usually worn for sport

sandstone

noun a rock made of sand held together with one of several minerals

sandwich

noun **1** two slices of bread with a cold filling between them
verb **2** to crowd or place between two other things: *We sandwiched the child between the two adults on the small seat.*

Word building: The plural form of the noun is **sandwiches**.
Word history: named after the fourth Earl of *Sandwich*, 1718–92, who invented them

sane

adjective **1** having a healthy mind
2 sensible or based on common sense: *a sane decision*

Word building: **sanely** *adverb*   **sanity** *noun*

sanitary

adjective having to do with cleanliness or care in preventing disease

Word building: **sanitation** *noun* the protection of public health using sanitary methods

sap¹

noun the juice circulating in a plant

sap²

verb to weaken or destroy gradually: *Worry sapped her health.*

Word building: Other forms are **I sapped, I have sapped, I am sapping.**

sapling

noun a young tree

sapphire   (*say* saf-uy-uh)

noun a clear blue gemstone

Word building: **sapphire** *adjective*

sarcasm

noun the saying of harsh and bitter things, using the trick of saying the opposite of what you really mean, so as to hurt someone's feelings

Word building: **sarcastic** *adjective* **sarcastically** *adverb*

sarcophagus (*say* sah-<u>kof</u>-uh-guhs)

noun a stone coffin

Word building: The plural is **sarcophagi** or **sarcophaguses**.

sardine

noun a young sea-fish usually cooked in oil and tinned

sardonic

adjective sarcastic or mockingly scornful: *a sardonic remark*

Word use: The more usual word is **mocking**.

sari (*say* <u>sah</u>-ree)

noun a long piece of cotton or silk material worn by a Hindu woman, which she drapes around her body with one end over her head or shoulders

sarong (*say* suh-<u>rong</u>)

noun a length of cloth wrapped around the body like a skirt and worn by both men and women in Malaysia and some Pacific islands

sash[1]

noun a long band of cloth worn round your waist or over your shoulder

Word use: The plural is **sashes**.

sash[2]

noun a window frame which slides up and down

Word use: The plural is **sashes**.

sashimi (*say* suh-<u>shee</u>-mee)

noun a Japanese food made of strips of fish eaten raw, usually with a tasty sauce

satanic (*say* suh-<u>tan</u>-ik)

adjective extremely evil: *The villain had a satanic smile.*

Word history: from *Satan*, the name of the devil

satay

noun cubes of spiced meat cooked on a skewer and covered with hot peanut sauce

satchel

noun a school bag with straps, carried on your back

satellite

noun **1** an object in space, such as a moon, which moves around a larger one, such as a planet **2** a human-made object sent into orbit around the earth or another planet to transmit information back to earth

satin

noun **1** a very smooth shiny cloth *adjective* **2** made of satin **3** smooth and shiny: *a satin finish*

satire

noun **1** the use of sarcasm or humour to draw people's attention to something which is silly or bad **2** any poem, book or play which does this

Word building: **satiric** *adjective* **satirical** *adjective* **satirically** *adverb* **satirise** *verb* **satirist** *noun*

satisfy

verb **1** to please or make happy: *to satisfy an employer* **2** to bring to an end by supplying what is needed: *to satisfy someone's hunger*
Other words: **appease**
3 to convince: *to satisfy yourself that a job has been done*

Word building: Other forms are **I satisfied, I have satisfied, I am satisfying.** | **satisfaction** *noun* **satisfactory** *adjective*

saturate

verb to soak thoroughly: *The rain saturated the ground.*

Saturday

noun the seventh day of the week
Word use: The abbreviation is **Sat.**
Word history: from an Old English word meaning 'day of Saturn'

satyr (*say* <u>sat</u>-uh)

noun a god, pictured in old stories as part goat and part human

sauce

noun **1** a thick cooked liquid put on food as a flavouring **2** *Informal* rudeness or impertinence
Word building: **saucy** *adjective*

sauce/source Don't confuse **sauce** with **source**. The **source** of something is the place, thing or person from which it comes:
The Murray River has its source in the Snowy Mountains.
Which book was the source of your information?
My mother is the source of that rumour.

saucepan
noun a cooking pot with a lid and a long handle

saucer
noun a small round plate used under a cup

sauna (*say* saw-nuh)
noun a room with a kind of steam bath in which you become clean by perspiring a lot

saunter (*say* sawn-tuh)
verb to walk in an unhurried way

Word building: **saunter** *noun*

sausage
noun finely minced meat packed into a thin skin

sausage roll
noun a roll of baked pastry filled with sausage meat

sauté (*say* soh-tay)
verb to brown or cook gently in a pan with a little fat

Word building: Other forms are **I sautéed, I have sautéed, I am sautéing.**
Word history: from a French word, which is why there is an accent over the 'e'

savage
adjective **1** untamed or wild **2** fierce or cruel: *savage punishment*
noun **3** a person who has no experience of the modern world **4** a rude or cruel person

Word building: **savagery** *noun*

savanna (*say* suh-van-uh)
noun a grassland area with some trees scattered about

Word use: Another spelling is **savannah**.

save
verb **1** to rescue from danger or harm **2** to avoid spending or using up: *to save $100 | to save electricity*
Other words: **budget, conserve, economise**
phrase **3 save up**, to put aside money: *to save up for a bicycle*

saveloy (*say* sav-uh-loy)
noun another word for **frankfurt**

saviour (*say* sayv-yuh)
noun someone who saves or rescues

Word use: Another spelling is **savior**.

savour (*sounds like* saver)
verb to taste or smell, especially with pleasure

Word use: Another spelling is **savor**.
Word building: **savour** *noun*

savoury (*say* say-vuh-ree)
adjective **1** having a delicious taste or smell **2** salty or sharp-tasting rather than sweet: *a savoury filling*

Word use: Another spelling is **savory**.

saw
noun **1** a cutting tool with sharp teeth on a thin blade
verb **2** to cut with a saw **3** to cut as a saw does: *Kim sawed at the meat with the blunt old knife.*

Word building: Other verb forms are **I sawed, I have sawn** or **sawed, I am sawing**.

saw/sore/soar Don't confuse **saw** with **sore** or **soar**.

If your leg is **sore**, it hurts or feels painful. If you feel **sore** about something, you are annoyed or offended.

To **soar** is to fly upwards, or to rise to a great height:
Jets soar into the air.
House prices are about to soar.

saxophone
noun a wind instrument with a curved brass body

Word building: **saxophonist** *noun*

say
verb **1** to speak or utter **2** to express in words: *to say that you are happy* **3** to assert or declare: *They said he would go.*
noun **4** a turn to speak: *You can have your say now.*

Word building: Other verb forms are **I said, I have said, I am saying.**

saying
noun **1** something wise that's often said
Other words: **adage, expression, proverb**
phrase **2 go without saying**, to be very obvious

scab
noun **1** the crust which forms over a sore when it is healing **2** someone who goes on working during a strike

Word building: **scab** *verb* (**scabbed, scabbing**)

scabbard (say skab-uhd)
noun a holder for the blade of a sword or dagger

scaffold
noun **1** a framework to stand on when you are doing work on a building **2** a raised platform on which criminals are executed

scald (rhymes with called)
verb **1** to burn with hot liquid or steam **2** to heat to almost boiling point: to scald milk
noun **3** a burn caused by hot liquid or steam

scale¹
noun **1** one of the thin, flat, fingernail-like plates which form the covering of fish and some other animals **2** any thin flaky coating or flake that peels off from a surface

Word building: **scale** verb to remove scale or scales from **scaly** adjective

scale²
noun **1** a set of marks along a line for measuring: the scale of a thermometer **2** a marked line on a map showing how to measure distances **3** size, compared to something else: Our new house is on a larger scale than our old one. **4** a series of musical notes going up or down at fixed intervals, usually one that begins on a particular note: the scale of C major
verb **5** to climb: to scale a mountain | to scale a wall **6** to arrange according to a scale: to scale exam marks

scales
plural noun a weighing machine

scallop (say skol-uhp)
noun **1** a type of shell-fish which has two wavy shells and is good to eat **2** one of the regular curves along the edge of pastry, a garment or cloth

Word building: **scallop** verb (**scalloped, scalloping**)

scalp
noun **1** the skin of your head where the hair grows
verb **2** to cut the scalp from

scalpel
noun a small, very sharp knife used by surgeons in operations

scam
noun Informal a trick, especially one involving money: Be careful of email scams when you use the internet.

scamp
noun a rascal or mischievous person

scamper
verb to run or hurry away quickly

Word building: **scamper** noun

scan
verb **1** to look at closely **2** to look over quickly: to scan a page **3** to read the information contained in the barcode of supermarket items, library books, and so on, the way a computer does **4** to read an image, or text with a scanner in order to reproduce it

Word building: Other forms are **I scanned, I have scanned, I am scanning.** | **scan** noun **scanner** noun

scandal
noun **1** talk or gossip that harms someone's reputation **2** a disgraceful or dreadful happening

Word building: **scandalise** verb to shock or horrify **scandalous** adjective **scandalously** adverb

scanner (say skann-er)
noun a machine that looks at written information and puts it directly into a computer

scant
adjective **1** hardly enough: There is scant time in which to finish. **2** barely as much as there's supposed to be: a scant cup of flour

Word building: **scanty** adjective: a scanty supply **scantily** adverb **scantiness** noun

scapegoat
noun someone who is made to take the blame for others

scar
noun a mark left on your skin by a healed sore or burn

Word building: **scar** verb (**scarred, scarring**) to leave a scar

scarce
adjective **1** not enough to fill the need **2** rarely seen or found: Leather-covered books are scarce now.

Word building: **scarcity** noun

scarcely
> *adverb* barely or not quite

scare
> *verb* to frighten or become frightened:
> *to scare everybody with fearful stories* | *The horse scares easily so be careful.*
>
> Word building: **scare** *noun* **scared** *adjective* **scary** *adjective* (**scarier, scariest**)

scarecrow
> *noun* a figure dressed in old clothes, put up to frighten birds away from crops

scarf
> *noun* a piece of material worn around your neck or head for warmth or ornament
>
> Word building: The plural is **scarfs** or **scarves**.

scarlet
> *adjective* bright red
>
> Word history: from a Persian word meaning 'a rich cloth'

scarlet fever
> *noun* a disease that spreads easily, causing a high fever and a scarlet rash

scathing (*say* skay-dhing)
> *adjective* meant to hurt your feelings by criticising you: *a scathing remark*
>
> Word use: The more usual word is **scornful**.
> Word building: **scathingly** *adverb*

scatter
> *verb* **1** to throw loosely about
> Other words: **distribute, spread**
> **2** to drive off or go in different directions:
> *The runaway car scattered the crowd.* | *The crowd scattered.*
> Other words: **disperse**
>
> Word building: **scattering** *noun* a small spread-out number or quantity **scatter** *noun*

scavenger
> *noun* **1** someone who searches in rubbish for useful things **2** an animal which eats flesh from dead animals
>
> Word building: **scavenge** *verb*

scene (*sounds like* seen)
> *noun* **1** a place where something happens: *the scene of the crime* **2** a view or a picture of a view **3** one of the divisions of a play **4** a real or imaginary event, especially one described in writing **5** a noisy outburst of excitement or anger in front of other people
>
> Word building: **scenic** *adjective*

scene/seen Don't confuse **scene** with **seen**. **Seen** is a past form of the verb **see**, to take things in with your eyes or mind. It is the past participle:
> *Have you seen the circus?*
> *He hasn't seen the joke yet.*

scenery (*say* seen-uh-ree)
> *noun* **1** the natural features of a place: *beautiful coastal scenery* **2** paintings, hangings and structures put on a stage to show the place where a play is meant to take place

scent (*sounds like* sent)
> *noun* **1** a pleasant smell: *the scent of flowers*
> Other words: **aroma, bouquet, odour, perfume**
> **2** the particular smell of an animal or person which enables other animals to follow them **3** perfume: *a bottle of scent*
> Other words: **fragrance**
>
> Word building: **scent** *verb* **scented** *adjective*

scent/sent/cent Don't confuse **scent** with **sent** or **cent**.

Sent is the past form of the verb **send**:
> *My cousin in Indonesia sent me this postcard.*

A **cent** is one-hundredth of a dollar.

sceptic (*say* skep-tik)
> *noun* someone who doesn't believe things that most other people accept without question
>
> Word building: **sceptical** *adjective* **sceptically** *adverb* **scepticism** *noun*

sceptre (*say* sep-tuh)
> *noun* a rod carried by a king or queen, as a symbol of royal power

schedule (*say* shed-joohl, sked-joohl)
> *noun* **1** a plan which shows you how a project is to be done and sets out a timetable for it **2** a list of things to be done
>
> Word building: **schedule** *verb*

scheme (*say* skeem)
> *noun* **1** a plan of action: *a scheme for raising money* **2** a secret plot: *a scheme to kidnap the president*
>
> Word building: **scheming** *adjective* crafty or cunning **scheme** *verb*

schizophrenia (*say* skit-suh-<u>free</u>-nee-uh)
a serious mental illness where the way a
person thinks and feels does not relate to
what is really happening in the world

Word building: **schizophrenic** *adjective*

scholar (*say* <u>skol</u>-uh)
noun **1** a student or pupil **2** a learned
person: *a Latin scholar*

Word building: **scholarly** *adjective*

scholarship (*say* <u>skol</u>-uh-ship)
noun **1** a sum of money won by a student
which helps to pay school or university
fees **2** knowledge gained by study: *Jeanette
is a woman of great scholarship.*

scholastic (*say* skuh-<u>las</u>-tik)
adjective having to do with schools, students
or education: *scholastic achievements*

school¹
noun **1** a place where children are taught
2 the children who go to a school: *The
school went to the zoo today.* **3** any place or
time of teaching: *a dancing school | a tennis
school*

Word building: **school** *verb* to train or
teach　**schooling** *noun* education or training

school²
noun a large number of fish, whales or
porpoises swimming together

Word history: from a Dutch word meaning
'school' or 'multitude'

schooner (*say* <u>skooh</u>-nuh)
noun **1** a sailing ship with two or more
masts **2** a large beer glass

science
noun **1** the study of the physical world in
an organised way, by measuring, testing
and experimenting **2** knowledge gained
in this way **3** a particular branch of this
study: *the science of botany*

Word building: **scientific** *adjective*　**scientist**
noun

science fiction
noun a genre of fiction that uses scientific
knowledge imaginatively in its story,
setting and so on

scissors (*say* <u>siz</u>-uhz)
plural noun a cutting instrument made of
two blades joined together: *My scissors are
blunt.*

Word use: The term *a pair of scissors* is often
used.

scoff
verb to mock or jeer

scold
verb to find fault with: *She scolded me for
being careless.*

scoliosis (*say* sko-lee-<u>oh</u>-suhs)
noun a condition that can happen, especially
in adolescents, where a person's spine bends
sideways

scone (*rhymes with* gone)
noun a light plain cake split open and
spread with butter

Word history: from a Dutch word meaning
'fine bread'

scoop
noun **1** a small spoon-like ladle: *a flour
scoop* **2** the bucket of a dredge **3** a hollow
made or an amount taken by a scoop
4 a news story published or broadcast
before any other newspaper or radio or
television station

Word building: **scoop** *verb*

scooter
noun a child's toy with two wheels, one in
front of the other, and a board between
them on which you stand

scope
noun **1** range or reach: *This comes within
the scope of my work.* **2** space or room:
scope for improvement

scorch
verb **1** to burn slightly, often with an
iron **2** to cause to dry up with heat: *The
sun scorched the desert.*

Word building: **scorch** *noun* a burn on the
surface

score
noun **1** the total of points made by a
competitor or team in a game **2** a scratch,
especially a deep one in wood or metal
3 a set of twenty: *to live three score
years* **4** a written or printed piece of music
with all parts included and written one
under the other

Word building: **score** *verb*

scorn
noun an open show of disgust or contempt

Word building: **scorn** *verb*

scorpion

noun a spider-like invertebrate with a long narrow tail that ends in a venomous stinger

scoundrel　(*say* skown-druhl)

noun a wicked or dishonourable person

scour　(*rhymes with* flower)

verb to clean by rubbing hard, usually in soap and water

scout　(*say* skowt)

noun **1** someone sent to find out information, especially about an enemy **2** a member of an international youth movement which organises activities which promote outdoor adventure, community service and care for the environment

Word use: Definition 2 is sometimes spelt with a capital letter.
Word building: **scout** *verb*

scowl

verb to have an angry look on your face
Other words: **frown, grimace**

Word building: **scowl** *noun*

scrabble

verb to scratch or scrape with claws or your hands: *to scrabble in the dirt*

scramble

verb **1** to climb or walk quickly and awkwardly
noun **2** a hurried climb or movement over rough ground **3** a disorderly struggle to get something: *a scramble for seats in the back row*
phrase **4 scramble eggs**, to cook eggs by mixing yolks and whites with milk, and heating

scrap[1]

noun **1** a small piece **2** anything useless or worn out, especially old metal **3 scraps**, bits of food left over from a meal
adjective **4** consisting of scraps: *a scrap heap*
verb **5** to make into scrap: *to scrap a ship for its metal* **6** to put aside as useless

Word building: Other verb forms are
I scrapped, I have scrapped, I am scrapping.

scrap[2]

noun a fight or quarrel

Word building: **scrap** *verb* (**scrapped, scrapping**)

scrape

verb **1** to drag or rub something sharp or rough over, usually to remove a layer: *We scraped the wall to remove the old paint.* **2** to scratch: *The knife scraped the table.* **3** to rub harshly or noisily: *The chalk scraped on the blackboard.*
phrase **4 scrape up**, to gather together **5 scrape through**, to manage with difficulty

Word building: **scrape** *noun*

scratch

verb **1** to mark or cut roughly: *to scratch polished wood | The kitten scratched my skin.* **2** to draw a pen or pencil through: *to scratch a mistake from a page* **3** to withdraw: *to scratch a horse from a race* **4** to lessen itching by rubbing with the nails or claws: *That dog is always scratching.* **5** to make a slight grating noise

Word building: **scratch** *noun* (**scratches**)
scratchy *adjective*　**scratchily** *adverb*

scrawl

verb to write untidily

Word building: **scrawl** *noun*

scrawny

adjective thin or bony: *the scrawny neck of a hen*

Word building: Other forms are **scrawnier, scrawniest.** | **scrawniness** *noun*

scream

verb **1** to make a loud piercing cry or sound: *The hyena screamed with pain.*
noun **2** such a cry or sound **3** *Informal* someone or something that is very funny: *He's a real scream.*

screech

verb to make a harsh high-pitched cry or noise: *The owl screeched overhead. | The tyres screeched on the wet road.*

Word building: **screech** *noun* (**screeches**)

screen

noun **1** a large, flat surface on which a film can be shown **2** the part of a TV set or the video terminal of a computer or the front of a mobile phone or any device like that on which the picture appears **3** a frame covered with wire mesh, placed over a window to keep out insects **4** a covered frame or a curtain used to hide something or to protect something **5** anything that shelters or hides: *They stood behind a screen of shrubs.*

Word building: **screen** *verb*

screw

noun **1** a kind of a nail with a slot in its flat end and a spiral thread above its point
verb **2** to turn: *to screw a lid on* **3** to twist or wrinkle: *The baby screwed up its face when it tasted the lemon juice.*

screwdriver

noun a tool which fits into the end of a screw and is turned to drive the screw in or take it out

scribble

verb **1** to write hastily or carelessly **2** to make meaningless marks with a pen or pencil

Word building: **scribble** *noun* **scribbler** *noun*

scribe

noun **1** a writer or author **2** someone who used to make copies of books before the invention of printing **3** someone who writes or types something which another person dictates

script

noun **1** the words written down for the actors to say in a play or film **2** handwriting

scripture

noun any holy writing or book

Word building: **scriptural** *adjective*
Word history: from a Latin word meaning 'writing'

scroll

noun **1** a roll of parchment or paper with writing on it
verb **2** to make text roll by on a computer screen: *From this point you can scroll either up or down.*

scrotum

noun the pouch of skin in males which contains their testicles

Word building: The plural is **scrota**.

scrounge

verb Informal to obtain by borrowing, begging or stealing

Word building: **scrounger** *noun*

scrub¹

verb **1** to rub hard with a brush, soap and water in order to clean **2** Informal to get rid of or cancel: *We have to scrub the Christmas concert.*

Word building: Other forms are **I scrubbed, I have scrubbed, I am scrubbing.** | **scrub** *noun*

scrub²

noun a bush area of low trees or shrubs

scruff

noun the back of your neck

scruffy

adjective dirty, shabby and uncared for

scrum

noun **1** a way of restarting the play in a game of Rugby League or Rugby Union, in which some of the players pack together and push, one side against the other, until the ball is thrown in and someone kicks it out to other team-mates **2** the formation of players in a scrum

Word use: Another word is **scrummage**.

scrumptious (*say* skrum-shuhs)

adjective very tasty or delicious: *a scrumptious dinner*

scrupulous (*say* skroohp-yuh-luhs)

adjective **1** careful or exact in every detail: *I try to be scrupulous in my work.* **2** being strict about doing what is right: *Yumiko is scrupulous in her dealings with the customers.*

Word building: **scruple** *noun* a doubt that you have about a matter of deciding between right and wrong **scrupulously** *adverb*

scrutinise (*say* skrooh-tuh-nuyz)

verb to examine closely and carefully

Word use: Another spelling is **scrutinize**. | The more usual word is **inspect**.
Word building: **scrutiny** *noun* (**scrutinies**)

scuba (*say* skooh-buh)

noun a system that lets a diver breathe air through a mouthpiece connected by tubes to an air tank

Word history: an acronym made from the first letters of *self-contained underwater breathing apparatus*

scuff

verb **1** to scrape with your feet **2** to make a mark on by scraping: *to scuff your shoes* | *to scuff furniture*

scuffle

verb to struggle or fight in a confused way

Word building: **scuffle** *noun*

scullery

noun a small room where the rough, dirty, kitchen work is done

Word building: The plural is **sculleries**.

sculpture

noun **1** the art or work of making figures or designs in marble, clay, bronze or similar materials **2** something made this way

Word building: **sculpt** *verb* to carve   **sculpture** *verb* to form sculptures   **sculptor** *noun*   **sculptural** *adjective*

scum

noun **1** a thin layer of froth or dirt on the top of a liquid **2** someone who is low or worthless: *the scum of the earth*

Word use: Definition 2 will offend the person it is used about.

scurry

verb to move quickly: *The children scurried back to bed.*
Other words: **dart, dash, fly, hurry, race, run, scamper**

Word building: Other forms are **I scurried, I have scurried, I am scurrying.** | **scurry** *noun* (**scurries**)

scurvy

noun a disease caused by lack of vitamin C in your diet

scuttle

verb to run with quick steps: *The mice scuttled away.*

Word building: **scuttle** *noun*

scythe   (*say* suydh)

noun a tool with a long curved blade joined at an angle to a long handle: *He used a scythe to cut the long grass.*

sea

noun **1** the salt waters that cover most of the earth's surface **2** a particular part of these waters, usually near or almost surrounded by land: *the Tasman Sea* **3** a large quantity: *a sea of troubles* *phrase* **4 at sea, a** sailing or on the ocean **b** uncertain or confused

sea/see Don't confuse **sea** with **see**. You **see** things with your eyes. **See** can also mean 'to understand'.

sea anemone   (*say* <u>see</u> uh-nem-uh-nee)

noun a sea animal which stays in one place and catches food with one or more tentacles growing on top of its tube-shaped body

seafarer

noun a traveller on the sea

Word building: **seafaring** *adjective*

seafood

noun food which comes from the sea, such as fish, squid and shellfish

seagull

noun a bird which lives near or on the sea and is usually white with a grey back and wings and has a harsh cry

seahorse

noun a small fish with a curved tail and a head shaped like a horse's

seal[1]

noun **1** a design pressed into a piece of wax, or a stamp engraved with such a design, used for making a document official **2** a piece of wax for closing an envelope or document, which has to be broken before the contents can be read **3** anything used to close something *verb* **4** to close so that entry is impossible except by force: *I sealed the envelope.* | *The king sealed the tomb.* **5** to cover with tar: *to seal a road* **6** to decide finally: *to seal someone's fate*

seal[2]

noun a sea mammal with smooth fur, a long rounded body and large flippers

Word use: The male is a **bull**, the female is a **cow** and the young is a **pup**.

sea level

noun the average level of the sea, used as a base to measure height: *The town is 1000 metres above sea level.*

sea lion

noun a type of large Australian seal which has white hair on the back of its neck

seam

noun **1** the line where two pieces of material have been joined together: *The seam isn't sewn straight.* **2** a thin layer of a different kind of rock or mineral in the ground: *a coal seam*

seam/seem Don't confuse **seam** with **seem**.
To **seem** is to appear to be a certain way:
They seem happy together.

seaman

noun a sailor

Word building: The plural is **seamen**. |
seamanship *noun*

seance (*say* say-ons)

noun a meeting of people who are trying to
contact the spirits of dead people

Word history: from a Latin word meaning 'sit'

seaplane

noun a plane with floats, which can land
on water

sear

verb **1** to burn or blacken the outside of: *to
sear a piece of meat* **2** to cause to dry up or
wither: *The sun seared the wheat.*

Word building: **searing** *adjective*

search

verb **1** to go through or look through
thoroughly in order to find something
or someone: *I searched the house for my
watch.* **2** to examine, usually for hidden or
illegal objects: *Guards searched everyone's
bags.*

Word building: **search** *noun* (**searches**)

search warrant

noun an order by a court which allows the
police to search your house, usually for
stolen goods

seasickness

noun a feeling of sickness in your stomach,
or vomiting caused by the movement of a
ship at sea

Word building: **seasick** *adjective*

season

noun **1** one of the four divisions of the
year into spring, summer, autumn and
winter **2** a period of time, especially when
it is connected with some event or activity:
*the Christmas season | the football season |
It's been a good season for strawberries.*
verb **3** to add flavour or interest to:
*She seasons her cooking with pepper and
herbs.* **4** to treat or let stand until ready for
use: *to season timber*

Word building: **seasonal** *adjective*
seasonally *adverb*

seasoning

noun something like salt, herbs or spices,
which adds flavour

seat

noun **1** something for sitting on: *a garden
seat* **2** a part for sitting on: *the seat of a
chair | the seat of your pants* **3** a centre
of some activity: *a seat of learning*
4 a large country house **5** the right to sit
in parliament: *She won a seat in the last
election.*

Word use: The more usual word for definition 3
is **place**.
Word building: **seat** *verb*   **seated** *adjective*

seatbelt

noun a belt attached to the seat of a vehicle
or plane which you put around you to
secure you in case there is a sudden stop or
an accident

Word use: Another term for this is **safety belt**.

sea urchin

noun a sea animal with a round, spiky shell

seaweed

noun any plant that grows in the ocean

secateurs (*say* sek-uh-tuhz, sek-uh-terz)

plural noun gardening shears for clipping
and pruning

seclude

verb to shut away: *My big sister secludes
herself in her room.*

Word building: **secluded** *adjective* quiet and
private   **seclusion** *noun*

second¹

adjective **1** next after the first **2** another:
a second chance **3** alternate: *every second
weekend*
verb **4** to express support of: *Who will
second this proposal so we can vote on it?*

Word building: **second** *noun*   **seconder** *noun*

second²

noun one sixtieth part of a minute of time

secondary

adjective **1** next after the first in order or
importance: *secondary school | a secondary
matter* **2** taken from something else: *a
secondary source* **3** having to do with the
processing of primary products, such as
meat, wheat, coal and wool: *a secondary
industry*

second-hand

adjective bought or got from someone else: *a second-hand car | a second-hand jumper*
Other words: **old, pre-owned, used**

seconds

noun a second serving of the food that has already been eaten: *If you eat seconds all the time, you will get larger.*

secret

adjective **1** done or made without others knowing: *a secret plan* **2** designed to escape notice: *a secret door*
Word building: **secretive** *adjective* liking to keep things to yourself **secrecy** *noun* **secret** *noun* **secretly** *adverb*

secretary

noun someone whose job is to write letters, keep records or make phone calls for an employer
Word building: The plural is **secretaries.** | **secretarial** *adjective*

secrete   (*say* suh-<u>kreet</u>)

verb **1** to produce, such as by a gland: *to secrete saliva* **2** to hide away: *He has secreted the treasure under the floor.*

sect

noun a religious group, especially one which has broken away from a larger group
Word building: **sectarian** *adjective*

section

noun **1** a part of something
Other words: **compartment, division**
2 a picture of how something would look if you cut it from top to bottom and showed the inside

sector

noun **1** a division of a circle, shaped like a wedge of cake **2** a large division or an area of activity: *the public sector*

secular   (*say* <u>sek</u>-yuh-luh)

adjective worldly, as opposed to religious or spiritual: *She doesn't like to hear secular music in church.*

secure

adjective **1** free from care or danger
Other words: **protected, safe**
2 firmly fastened or in place
Other words: **fast, firm, fixed**
3 in safe keeping: *Your money will be secure in the bank.*
verb **4** to get: *He was unable to secure tickets.*

Other words: **acquire, gain, obtain, procure**
5 to tie up tightly: *to secure a boat to its mooring*
Other words: **fasten, fix**
6 to be or make safe
Word building: **securely** *adverb* **security** *noun*

sedan   (*say* suh-<u>dan</u>)

noun a car with four doors, which seats from four to six people
Word history: from a Latin word meaning 'seat'

sedate

adjective calm and steady: *They walked at a sedate pace.*
Word building: **sedate** *verb* to calm with a sedative **sedation** *noun*

sedative

noun a drug which lessens pain or excitement
Word building: **sedative** *adjective* calming or soothing

sediment

noun solid material that falls to the bottom of a liquid
Other words: **dregs**
Word building: **sedimentary** *adjective* **sedimentation** *noun*

seduce

verb to persuade or entice to do something considered wrong
Word building: **seducer** *noun* **seduction** *noun* **seductive** *adjective* **seductively** *adverb*

see

verb **1** to take things in with your eyes or your mind: *to see clearly | I see what you mean.* **2** to consider or think of: *We shall see. | I see it like this.* **3** to find out: *See who it is.* **4** to meet or visit: *to see a friend | to see the doctor* **5** to go with: *She'll see you to the door.* **6** to imagine or remember: *I can just see her laughing the way she used to.* **7** to know or experience: *He must have seen a lot.*
phrase **8 see through, a** to detect: *She saw through the disguise.* **b** to stay until the end of: *He always sees a job through.*
Word building: Other verb forms are **I saw, I have seen, I am seeing.**

see/sea Don't confuse **see** with **sea**, which is a large stretch of water.

seed

noun **1** the part produced by a plant from which a new plant grows **2 seeds**, the beginnings or start: *the seeds of their quarrel*

Word building: **seed** *verb*

seedling

noun a young plant

seedy

adjective **1** shabby and untidy: *a seedy appearance* **2** unwell: *I'm feeling quite seedy this morning.*

Word building: Other forms are **seedier**, **seediest**.

seek

verb **1** to try to find or get: *to seek an answer | to seek fame* **2** to try: *She seeks to help.*

Word building: Other forms are **I sought**, **I have sought**, **I am seeking**.

seem

verb to have the look of being: *She seems happy.*

Word building: **seeming** *adjective* **seemingly** *adverb*

> **seem/seam** Don't confuse **seem** with **seam**. A **seam** is the line where two pieces of material like fabric or metal have been joined together. It can also be a layer of rock or mineral in the ground, as in *a coal seam*.

seep

verb to leak or drip slowly: *Water seeps from the pipe.*

Word building: **seepage** *noun*

seer

noun someone who can see into the future

seesaw

noun a plank balanced in the middle, so that the child sitting at one end rises when the child at the other end goes down

Word building: **seesaw** *verb* to move like a seesaw

seethe

verb **1** to bubble and foam: *The sea was seething far below.* **2** to be excited or disturbed: *She is seething with rage.*

segment

noun a piece or section: *a segment of orange*

Word building: **segment** *verb* to separate into pieces **segmentation** *noun*

segregate

verb to set or keep apart, especially one group of people from another

Word use: The more usual word is **separate**.

Word building: **segregation** *noun*

seize (*say* seez)

verb **1** to take hold of suddenly, or by force: *to seize an idea or an opportunity | to seize a knife*

Other words: **clasp, clutch, grab, grasp, snatch** **2** to become stuck or jammed: *The engine seized.*

Word building: **seizure** *noun*

seldom

adverb rarely or not often: *He seldom takes part.*

select

verb **1** to choose: *Select your favourite recipe.*

Other words: **pick**

adjective **2** carefully chosen: *a select few* **3** of special value or excellence

Other words: **choice, deluxe, premium, prime**

Word building: **selection** *noun* **selective** *adjective* **selectively** *adverb*

selective

adjective being very careful about the choices that you make: *My dog is very selective and won't eat anything out of a can.*

self

noun Your **self** is you, and everything that makes you who you are: your body, your mind, your personality and your intelligence.

Word building: The plural is **selves**.

self-

prefix a word part indicating action directed towards yourself: *self-control*

self-confidence

noun belief in your own ability: *to be full of self-confidence*

Word building: **self-confident** *adjective*

self-contained

adjective **1** keeping your thoughts to yourself **2** having within yourself or itself all that is necessary; independent

self-control

noun the ability to stop yourself from doing something: *I don't have much self-control when it comes to sweets.*

Word building: **self-controlled** *adjective*

self-defence

noun the ability to protect yourself against attack

selfish

adjective thinking only of your own interests: *a selfish act*
Other words: **egotistical, thoughtless**

Word building: **selfishly** *adverb*
selfishness *noun*

self-raising flour

noun flour with baking powder already added to it, so that it makes bread or cakes rise

self-service

adjective having to do with a shop or restaurant where the customers serve themselves and then pay a cashier

sell

verb **1** to give up for money: *Did you sell your skateboard?* **2** to have for sale: *Do you sell goldfish here?*

Word building: Other forms are **I sold, I have sold, I am selling.** | **seller** *noun* someone who sells

sell/cell Don't confuse **sell** with **cell**, which is a small bare room, like a *prison cell*. A **cell** is also a small unit of living matter, as in a *plant cell*.

sellout

noun **1** a betrayal: *What a sellout — she promised us an early mark, and then forgot about it!* **2** a performance like a sporting event for which all the tickets are sold: *The final was a sellout weeks before the event!*

semaphore   (*say* <u>sem</u>-uh-faw)

noun a system for signalling messages using flags

Word building: **semaphore** *verb*

semen   (*say* <u>see</u>-muhn)

noun liquid containing sperm, which is produced by the testicles

Word history: from a Latin word meaning 'seed'

semi-

prefix a word part meaning 'half': *semicircle*
Word history: from Latin

semibreve

noun a musical note which is four crotchets long

semicircle

noun a half circle
Word building: **semicircular** *adjective*

semicolon

noun a punctuation mark (;) which is used to show more of a break between parts of a sentence than a comma does, as in *I entered the house; I picked up the bag; I left the house.*

You generally use a **semicolon** to divide parts of a sentence which could each stand on their own as separate sentences. The **semicolon** shows that the separate parts are related in some way:
The telephone rang; my friend ran inside.
The telephone rang. My friend ran inside.

The first example suggests much more strongly than the second that the two events are related (perhaps the friend ran inside <u>because</u> the telephone rang.)

Note that it is quite acceptable to use connecting words like *and, but* and *however* after a **semicolon**:
The telephone rang; and my friend ran inside.

Semicolons can also be used to separate lists of different sets of things — that is, to form a large list made up of smaller lists:
At the jumble sale there were books, magazines and newspapers; CDs and DVDs; and tables, chairs and sofas.

The small lists in this sentence are the lists of printed works, recordings and furniture. The individual items in these small lists are separated by a comma. The small lists together make up the larger list of 'kinds of things sold', and the three kinds of things are separated by a **semicolon**.

semidetached

adjective partly separate, used especially about two houses sharing one wall while remaining separate from other buildings

seminary   (*say* <u>sem</u>-uhn-ree)

noun a college for training Roman Catholic priests
Word building: **seminarian** *noun*

semiquaver

noun a musical note which is equal to half a quaver

semitone

noun half a tone, or the difference between the notes which are next to each other on the piano

semitrailer

noun a large truck which consists of a long trailer connected to the cabin and a powerful engine

semolina   (*say* sem-uh-<u>lee</u>-nuh)

noun the large hard bits of wheat grains left over after the fine flour has been separated

Word history: from a Latin word meaning 'fine flour'

senate   (*say* <u>sen</u>-uht)

noun one of the decision-making bodies in the government of a country

Word building: **senator** *noun*

send

verb **1** to cause to go: *They sent me away.* | *I send a letter every week.* **2** to cause to become: *You send me mad with rage.* **3** to send a message: *I will send for you.* *phrase* **4 send up**, to mock, usually by imitating in an exaggerated way: *The kids at school send up my accent.*

Word building: Other verb forms are **I sent, I have sent, I am sending.** | **sender** *noun*

senile

adjective weak in body or mind because of old age

Word building: **senility** *noun*

senior

adjective of greater age or importance: *She was a bit taller, since she was the senior of the two girls.* | *My mum is a senior lecturer at the university.*

Word building: **senior** *noun*   **seniority** *noun*

sensation

noun **1** feeling: *The accident has left her with no sensation in her hand.* | *He had the sensation that he was being followed.* **2** a cause or feeling of excitement: *The pop star was a sensation.* | *The news flash caused a sensation.*

Word building: **sensational** *adjective* **sensationally** *adverb*

sense

noun **1** one of the powers or abilities by which we taste, touch, hear, see and smell: *My sense of smell is impaired.* **2** any physical or mental feeling or ability: *a sense of tiredness* | *a sense of humour* **3** the ability to think and act sensibly and intelligently: *You have no sense.* | *Sally has plenty of common sense.* **4** meaning: *Could you explain the sense of this remark?* *verb* **5** to notice or feel with your senses: *You could sense the tension between the players.*

Word building: **senseless** *adjective* not having any **sense** (definition 3): *a senseless action*

sensible

adjective **1** full of good sense: *a sensible move* **2** *Old-fashioned* knowing or aware: *She is sensible of her responsibility.*

Word building: **sensibility** *noun* (**sensibilities**) the ability to feel   **sensibly** *adverb*

sensitive

adjective **1** having feeling: *sensitive to the cold* **2** easily affected by something: *He has a sensitive nature.* | *The film is sensitive to light.* **3** causing strong feelings: *a sensitive matter*

Word building: **sensitivity** *noun* (**sensitivities**)   **sensitively** *adverb*

sensory

adjective having to do with feeling: *Tentacles are the sensory organs of some animals.*

sensual

adjective having to do with feeling or with your senses: *Listening to the music was a sensual pleasure.*

Word building: **sensualist** *noun*   **sensuality** *noun*   **sensually** *adverb*

sentence

noun **1** a group of words which form a complete statement, question, comment or exclamation, such as *He hit the ball.* **2** the punishment of a criminal: *The judge passed a sentence of five years' jail.*

Word building: **sentence** *verb* to condemn to punishment

sentiment

noun **1** an attitude or opinion: *What is the public sentiment about this new law?* **2** an emotion

Word use: The more usual word is **feeling**.

sentimental

adjective showing or having to do with tender feelings: *sentimental tears | a sentimental song*

Word building: **sentimentality** *noun* **sentimentally** *adverb*

sentinel

noun a soldier who acts as a lookout

sentry

noun a soldier who stands guard to keep people out

Word building: The plural is **sentries**.

separate

verb **1** to put or keep apart **2** to stop living with a marriage partner, without actually divorcing

Word building: **separate** *adjective* not connected

September

noun the ninth month of the year, with 30 days

Word use: The abbreviations are **Sep** and **Sept**.
Word history: from a Latin word for the seventh month in the early Roman calendar

septet

noun **1** any group or set of seven **2** a musical piece for seven voices or seven performers

septic

adjective infected with germs: *a septic wound*

sepulchre   (*say* sep-uhl-kuh)

noun *Old-fashioned* a tomb or a grave

sequel   (*say* see-kwuhl)

noun **1** a book or film which continues on from an earlier work **2** anything which follows or results from something

sequence   (*say* see-kwuhns)

noun a series of things following each other

Word building: **sequential** *adjective*

sequin   (*say* see-kwuhn)

noun a small shiny disc sewn as a decoration onto bags, evening clothes or fancy dress

Word building: **sequined** *adjective*

serenade   (*say* se-ruh-nayd)

noun music traditionally played or sung by a lover under the beloved's window at night

Word building: **serenade** *verb*

serene

adjective calm and peaceful
Word building: **serenely** *adverb*   **serenity** *noun*

serf

noun someone who in feudal times was not free but was thought of as belonging to the land that a lord owned, and was sold with it

serf/surf Don't confuse **serf** with **surf**, which is the waves which break along the shore making foamy water.

sergeant   (*say* sah-juhnt)

noun **1** an officer in the army who ranks next above a corporal **2** a police officer ranking between a constable and an inspector

serial   (*say* sear-ree-uhl)

noun a story that is published or broadcast one part at a time at regular intervals

serial/cereal Don't confuse **serial** with **cereal**, which is grain, such as wheat or rice. A **cereal** is the breakfast food made from this.

series   (*say* sear-reez)

noun **1** a number of things or events arranged or happening in a certain order or sequence **2** a set of something: *This coin will now complete the series in my collection.* **3** a number of programs on radio or television which are linked in some way, either by subject matter or by being about the same group of people

Word building: The plural is **series**.

serious   (*say* sear-ree-uhs)

adjective **1** solemn or thoughtful: *The judge had a serious expression when giving the verdict.*
Other words: **earnest, grave**
2 sincere and not joking: *Are you serious?*

Other words: **genuine, honest, straightforward**

3 important or needing a lot of thought: *Buying a new house is a serious matter.*
Other words: **significant, weighty**

4 giving cause for concern or worry: *Dad's condition after the operation was serious.*
Other words: **grave**

Word building: **seriously** *adverb*

sermon

noun **1** a serious talk, usually one preached in church: *Sunday's sermon was about loving your neighbour. | Her father gave her a sermon about riding her bike on the busy road.* **2** a long boring speech

serpent

noun **1** an old-fashioned word for **snake**
2 someone who is cunning, untrustworthy or evil: *Satan, or the Devil, is often described as a serpent.*

serrated   (*say* suh-<u>ray</u>-tuhd)

adjective having notches or teeth along the edge: *A saw has a serrated blade.*

Word building: **serrate** *verb*   **serration** *noun*

serum   (*say* <u>sear</u>-ruhm)

noun **1** a clear, pale yellow liquid that separates from your blood when it clots **2** this liquid used as a base for vaccines

Word use: The plural forms are **sera** and **serums**.

servant

noun **1** someone who works for or is in the service of someone else: *a public servant* **2** someone who is employed to live in your house and help look after it

serve

verb **1** to work for **2** to put on a table: *to serve the dinner* **3** to supply or answer the needs of: *The shop assistant served me.*
Other words: **assist, help**
4 to give help or assistance: *to serve in a shop* **5** to go through a term of service such as in the army or in a jail **6** to be of use: *That tree will serve as a shelter from the rain.*
Other words: **act, do, function, operate, suffice**
7 to start playing for a point in tennis by hitting the ball over the net
noun **8** the act of serving a ball in tennis

server

noun a program which provides services to numbers of computers through a network

service

noun **1** a helpful act: *to perform a service for someone* **2** the supplying of something either useful to, or needed by, a large group of people: *a telephone service | a bus service* **3** a department of public employment or the group of people in it: *the diplomatic service* **4** the way you serve food: *The service in this restaurant is bad.* **5** the act of getting a car or other machinery into good order: *I put my car in the garage for a service.* **6** a religious ceremony: *a marriage service* **7** a set of dishes for a particular use: *a dinner service* **8** the act of serving a ball in tennis
verb **9** to make fit for use: *The garage serviced my car.*
phrase **10 the services**, the military armed forces

serviceable

adjective useful: *My old sandshoes are still serviceable.*

Word building: **serviceably** *adverb*

service station

noun a place where you can buy petrol and oil for motor vehicles, and where mechanical repairs are carried out

serviette

noun a piece of cloth or paper, used during a meal to wipe your lips and hands and to protect your clothes

Word use: Other words are **napkin** or **table napkin**.

serving

noun **1** the act of someone or something that serves **2** a portion or helping of food or drink
adjective **3** having to do with dishing out food: *a serving spoon*

sesame   (*say* <u>ses</u>-uh-mee)

noun a tropical herb, whose small oval seeds are used for food and oil

session   (*say* <u>sesh</u>-uhn)

noun **1** the sitting or meeting together of a court, council or parliament **2** a period of time for any particular activity: *a dancing session*

set

verb **1** to put in a particular place or position: *I set the vase in the middle of the table.* **2** to cause to begin: *The accident really set me thinking.* **3** to fix or appoint: *The officials set a time for the race.* **4** to provide for others to follow: *Karen set an excellent example.* **5** to give, assign or make up: *The teacher set the homework. | Have you set the maths exam yet?* **6** to arrange in proper order: *Whose turn is it to set the table for dinner?* **7** to adjust or regulate: *I set the clock.* **8** to put something into a fixed place or position: *The doctor set my broken leg.* **9** to become hard or solid: *The jelly set in the bowl.* **10** to pass or sink below the horizon: *The sun sets every evening.*

noun **11** a number of things that are used together, or form a collection: *a set of dishes* **12** a radio or television receiver **13** a group of games that make up one of the sections of a tennis match **14** a number of pieces of scenery arranged together, used for a play or film **15** any collection of numbers or objects in maths which have something in common

adjective **16** fixed beforehand: *a set time | set rules* **17** fixed or rigid: *a set smile | set in your ways* **18** ready and prepared: *all set to go*

phrase **19 set off, a** to explode: *to set off a bomb* **b** to begin a journey **20 set out, a** to arrange **b** to explain carefully **c** to start a journey **21 set up, a** to build or erect **b** to provide with: *My parents have set me up with a new modem.* **c** to claim to be: *Bruno sets himself up as an expert.*

Word building: Other verb forms are **it set, it has set, it is setting.**

setback

noun something that hinders or slows down your progress

set square

noun a flat piece of wood or plastic in the shape of a right-angled triangle, used in drawing technical things like plans for buildings

settee (*say* set-<u>ee</u>)

noun a seat or sofa for two or more people

setting

noun **1** the surroundings of anything: *The house was situated in a pretty country setting.* **2** the time and place in which a play or film takes place **3** a group of things such as a knife, fork, and plate used to set someone's place at the table

settle

verb **1** to decide or agree: *They settled on a suitable time.* **2** to put in order or arrange: *She settled all her affairs before she went away.* **3** to pay: *He settled the bill.* **4** to set up a home: *The family settled in Tasmania.* **5** to sink down gradually: *The dust slowly settled.*

phrase **6 settle down, a** to put to bed **b** to begin to do serious work **c** to begin to live an ordered life, especially after marrying

Word building: **settlement** *noun*

settler

noun someone who settles in a new country: *British settlers came to Australia two hundred years ago.*

set-up

noun **1** organisation or arrangement: *The set-up of the library is clear.* **2** *Informal* something which has been arranged dishonestly **3** *Informal* a trap

Word building: **set-up** *adjective*

seven

noun **1** the number 7 **2** the Roman numeral VII

Word building: **seven** *adjective*: *seven swans* **seventh** *adjective*: *That's your seventh biscuit!*

seventeen

noun **1** the number 17 **2** the Roman numeral XXVII

Word building: **seventeen** *adjective*: *seventeen red roses* **seventeenth** *adjective*: *her seventeenth birthday*

seventy

noun **1** the number 70 **2** the Roman numeral LXX

Word building: The plural is **seventies.** | **seventy** *adjective*: *seventy boats* **seventieth** *adjective*: *his seventieth birthday*

sever (*say* <u>sev</u>-uh)

verb **1** to cut or separate **2** to break off: *The countries have severed all friendly relations.*

several
adjective **1** more than two, but not
many **2** individual, different, or respective:
They went their several ways.

severe   (*say* suh-<u>vear</u>)
adjective **1** harsh or extreme: *severe
punishment* **2** unsmiling or stern: *a severe face*
Other words: **grim, hard, serious**
3 serious or grave: *a severe illness*
4 simple, plain and without decoration:
She wears severe clothes.
Other words: **austere**

Word building: **severity** *noun*

sew   (*sounds like* so)
verb **1** to join with stitches, using a needle
and thread **2** to make or repair clothes
with a needle and thread

> **sew/so/sow** Don't confuse **sew** with **so** or **sow**.
> **So** means 'therefore'.
>
> To **sow**, rhyming with go, is to scatter seed on
> the ground. But a **sow**, rhyming with *cow*, is a
> female pig.

sewage
noun the waste matter which passes
through drains and sewers

sewer
noun a pipeline, usually underground, made
to carry away waste water and waste matter

sewerage
noun the removal of waste water and waste
matter using sewers

sex
noun **1** one of the two divisions of
either female or male in humans and
animals **2** the characteristic or condition of
being either female or male **3** the instinct
which causes sexual attraction between
two people **4** the arousal of sexual interest
by the way people are portrayed in films,
books, and so on: *sex on TV* **5** another
name for **sexual intercourse**

sexist
adjective having to do with an attitude
which judges someone by their sex rather
than by their own individual qualities or by
how qualified or experienced they are

Word building: **sexism** *noun*   **sexist** *noun*

sextant
noun an instrument which measures the
angles between the sun, moon, stars and
earth to help sailors work out their position

sextet
noun **1** any group or set of six **2** a musical
piece for six voices or six performers

sexual
adjective having to do with sex

Word building: **sexuality** *noun*   **sexually** *adverb*

sexual harassment
noun unwanted sexual advances, suggestive
remarks, and so on, especially when made
by someone in a more powerful position in
a workplace

sexual intercourse
noun a sexual act between two people,
usually one in which a man's penis enters a
woman's vagina

Word use: The more usual word is **sex**.

sexy
adjective **1** having a great concern with
sex: *a sexy book* **2** having an attractiveness
or charm that attracts others sexually

Word building: Other forms are **sexier,
sexiest**. | **sexily** *adverb*

shabby
adjective **1** very worn: *shabby clothes* |
shabby furniture
Other words: **ragged, threadbare, used,
weathered**
2 wearing old or very worn clothes **3** mean
or unfair: *It was a shabby trick to play on a
friend.*
Other words: **dishonourable**

Word building: Other forms are **shabbier,
shabbiest**. | **shabbily** *adverb*

shack
noun a rough cabin or hut

shackle
noun **1** a ring of iron, usually one of a pair,
for holding the wrist or ankle of a prisoner
or slave **2** anything that stops someone's
free thought or action

shade
noun **1** a slight darkness or an area of
slight darkness caused by the blocking off
of rays of light **2** something that shuts
out, or protects from, light or heat: *Pull
down the shades on those windows.*
3 a darker or lighter kind of one colour:
Her dress was in three shades of green.
verb **4** to dim or darken **5** to protect from
heat or light

Word building: **shady** *adjective* (**shadier,
shadiest**)

shadow

noun **1** the dark figure or area of shade made by something blocking out light **2** shade or slight darkness
verb **3** to shade, or protect from heat or light **4** to follow secretly

Word building: **shadowy** *adjective*

shaft

noun **1** a long pole or rod: *the shaft of a spear | the shaft of an arrow* **2** a ray or beam: *a shaft of sunlight* **3** a passage that is like a well, or an enclosed vertical or sloping space: *a lift shaft | a mine shaft*

shaggy

adjective **1** covered with or having long rough hair: *a shaggy dog* **2** rough, coarse or untidy: *The lion had a shaggy appearance.*

Word building: Other forms are **shaggier**, **shaggiest**.

shake

verb **1** to move backwards and forwards with quick short movements **2** to fall or scatter by using such movements: *Sand shakes off easily.* **3** to tremble with fear or cold **4** to make unsteady or unsettled: *My faith in your honesty has been shaken by your behaviour.*
noun **5** the act of shaking or an unsteady movement **6** a drink made by shaking ingredients together: *a milk shake*
phrase **7 no great shakes**, *Informal* of no particular importance **8 shake hands**, to grip hands as a greeting, or to show agreement

Word building: Other verb forms are **I shook**, **I have shaken, I am shaking.** | **shaky** *adjective* (**shakier, shakiest**) **shakily** *adverb*

shale   (*rhymes with* hail)

noun a rock made of many thin layers, which is easy to split and which was made when clay or other very tiny particles were pressed firmly together

shall

verb will or should: *I shall come to your party. | Shall I make you a sandwich?*

shallot   (*say* shuh-lot)

noun an onion-like plant used for flavouring in cooking and as a vegetable

shallow

adjective **1** not deep: *shallow water* **2** without any serious thought: *a shallow mind | a shallow argument*

Word building: **shallowness** *noun*

sham

noun something that is not what it appears to be
Other words: **fake, fraud, pretence**

Word building: **sham** *verb* (**shammed, shamming**): *to sham illness*

shame

noun **1** a mentally painful feeling that comes after you know you have said or done something wrong or silly **2** a disgrace or dishonour: *Her crime brought shame to her family.* **3** a pity or something to be sorry about: *It's a shame he can't come today.*
phrase **4 put to shame, a** to disgrace or make ashamed **b** to do better than: *Juan puts Richard to shame in swimming.*

Word building: **shame** *verb*: *to cause to feel shame* **shameful** *adjective* **shamefully** *adverb* **shameless** *adjective* **shamelessly** *adverb*

shampoo

noun a liquid soap, especially for the hair

Word building: **shampoo** *verb* (**shampooed, shampooing**): *to shampoo your hair | to shampoo a carpet*

shamrock

noun a bright green plant with three small leaves grouped on one stem: *The shamrock is the national emblem of Ireland.*

shandy

noun a drink which is a mixture of beer with either ginger beer or lemonade

Word building: The plural is **shandies.**

shanghai[1]   (*say* shang-huy)

verb **1** to force someone to join a ship as a member of the crew **2** *Informal* to get someone to do something, usually either without their knowledge, or against their wishes: *My mother shanghaied me into washing the car.* **3** *Informal* to steal

Word building: Other forms are **I shanghaied, I have shanghaied, I am shanghaiing.**
Word history: short for 'to ship to *Shanghai*' (a seaport in China)

shanghai[2]   (*say* shang-huy)

noun a child's catapult or slingshot

shanty¹

noun a roughly-built hut, cabin, or house

Word building: The plural is **shanties**.

shanty²

noun a sailors' song, usually sung in rhythm to the work they are doing

Word building: The plural is **shanties**.

shape

noun **1** the outline or form of something or someone **2** proper order: *The house is now in shape for our visitors.* **3** condition: *Their business affairs were in bad shape.*
verb **4** to give definite form, shape or character to: *The potter carefully shaped the pot.*
phrase **5 shape up**, to develop: *The new worker is shaping up well.*

Word building: **shapely** *adjective* (**shapelier, shapeliest**) having a pleasing shape **shapeless** *adjective*

share (*rhymes with* hair)

noun **1** the part given to or owned by someone **2** each of the equal parts into which the ownership of a company is divided: *to buy 500 shares in BHP*
verb **3** to divide into parts with each person receiving a part **4** to use or enjoy together: *The whole family shares the car.*

shark

noun any of a number of large fish which are very fierce and possibly human-eaters, and which have soft skeletons and five to seven pairs of gill openings

sharp

adjective **1** having a thin cutting edge or a fine point: *a sharp knife | a sharp needle* **2** sudden or abrupt: *a sharp rise in temperature | a sharp bend in the road* **3** clearly outlined or distinct: *a sharp picture on TV*
Other words: **clear, precise**
4 strong or biting in taste **5** very cold or piercing: *a sharp wind* **6** mentally quick and alert: *a sharp mind* **7** keen or sensitive: *a sharp ear* **8** higher in pitch by a semitone, or too high in pitch: *B sharp | Your recorder is a bit sharp in the low notes.*
adverb **9** precisely: *at one o'clock sharp*
Other words: **exactly, promptly, punctually**
noun **10 a** a note that is one semitone above a given note **b** the music sign (♯) which raises a note by a semitone when it is placed before it

Word use: The opposite of definitions 8 and 10 is **flat**.
Word building: **sharpen** *verb* **sharply** *adverb* **sharpness** *noun* **sharpener** *noun* an implement that sharpens

shashlik

noun another name for **shish kebab**

shatter

verb **1** to break into pieces **2** to weaken or destroy: *My confidence at riding has been shattered since the accident.*

shave

verb **1** to remove hair with a razor **2** to take thin slices from, especially so as to smooth: *The carpenter shaved the wood.* **3** to graze or come very near: *The car just shaved the corner.*
noun **4** the act or process of shaving
phrase **5 a close shave**, a narrow miss or escape

Word building: Other verb forms are **I shaved, I have shaved** or **shaven, I am shaving**.

shaving

noun a very thin piece, especially of wood: *The shavings from the door covered the floor.*

shawl

noun a piece of material worn as a covering for your shoulders or head

she

pronoun the female being talked about: *She was reading a book.*

Word use: Other forms are **her** (*her hat, Give it to her*), **hers** (*That book is hers*), **herself** (*She hurt herself*).

sheaf

noun **1** one of the bundles into which cereal plants like wheat and rye are bound after they are cut in the field **2** any bundle, group or collection: *a sheaf of papers*

Word building: The plural is **sheaves**.

shear

verb **1** to remove by cutting with a sharp instrument: *He sheared all the wool from the sheep.* **2** to cut hair or fleece from something: *to shear sheep*
noun **3 shears**, large scissors or another similar cutting tool

Word building: Other verb forms are **I sheared, I have sheared** or **shorn, I am shearing**. | **shearer** *noun*

sheath

noun **1** a covering for the blade of a sword, dagger or bayonet **2** any similar covering **3** a close-fitting dress which follows the shape of your body

Word building: The plural is **sheaths**. | **sheathe** *verb*

shed¹

noun a simple or roughly-built building used for storage or sheltering animals

shed²

verb **1** to pour forth or let fall: *to shed blood | to shed tears* **2** to give forth or send out light, sound or smell: *This lamp sheds a soft glow of light.* **3** to cast or throw off: *A snake regularly sheds its skin and grows another one.*

Word building: Other forms are **I shed, I have shed, I am shedding.**

she'd

a short form of **she would** or **she had**

sheep

noun **1** an animal, closely related to the goat, which is kept for its meat and thick wool **2** someone who is shy, timid or stupid

Word use: The male is a **ram**, the female is a **ewe** and the young is a **lamb**.
Word building: The plural is **sheep**.

sheep dip

noun a deep trough containing a liquid which kills harmful insects on sheep as they are driven through it

sheepish

adjective awkwardly shy or embarrassed

sheer¹

adjective **1** very thin so that you can see through: *The curtains on the window were almost sheer.* **2** absolute, or unmixed with anything else: *You won by sheer luck.* **3** very steep: *a sheer cliff*

Word building: **sheer** *adverb* very steeply

sheer²

verb to swerve or change course: *The ship sheered away from the rocks.*

sheet

noun **1** one of two large pieces of cloth used on a bed, one under you and the other over you **2** any layer or covering: *a sheet of water* **3** a broad thin piece of something: *a sheet of glass | a sheet of paper*

shelf

noun **1** a thin flat piece of wood, glass or something similar, fixed horizontally to a wall or in a frame and used for holding things like books or ornaments **2** a ledge: *a shelf of rock*

Word building: The plural is **shelves**.

shell

noun **1** the hard outer covering of things like nuts, eggs and certain animals **2** something like a shell: *Just the shell of the building remained after the fire.* **3** a hollow bullet-like case filled with explosives, to be fired from a large gun
verb **4** to take out of the shell: *to shell peas* **5** to fire shells on: *The soldiers shelled the enemy.*
phrase **6 shell out**, *Informal* to hand over or pay up

she'll

a short form of **she will**

shellfish

noun an animal like an oyster or lobster that is not a fish but lives in water and has a shell

Word building: The plural is **shellfish** or **shellfishes**.

shelter

noun **1** protection from bad weather, danger and so on: *We took shelter from the rain.* **2** a place of safety and protection: *a bomb shelter*

Word building: **shelter** *verb* **sheltered** *adjective*

shelve

verb **1** to place on a shelf or shelves **2** to stop considering or thinking about: *He shelved the problem for a few days.*

shepherd   (*say* shep-uhd)

noun **1** someone who looks after sheep
verb **2** to take care of or to guard, especially when moving along: *The police shepherded the pop star through the crowd.*

sherbet

noun **1** a sweet fizzy powder that you can eat dry or use to make a fizzy drink **2** a frozen fruit-flavoured dessert
Other words: **sorbet**

Word history: from an Arabic word meaning 'a drink'

sheriff

noun **1** an officer in some courts of law who has duties such as organising juries **2** the chief law enforcement officer of a North American county

sherry

noun a strong sweet or dry wine

Word building: The plural is **sherries**.

she's

a short form of **she is** or **she has**

shield

noun **1** a flat piece of metal, leather or wood, carried to protect your body in a battle **2** anything used for protection: *She held her hands to her eyes as a shield against the sun.*

Other words: **defence**

Word building: **shield** *verb*

shift

verb **1** to move from one place or position to another: *Can you please shift the vase so that I can see the TV?*
noun **2** a change or a move: *a shift in the wind* **3** the period of time worked by someone in a place of work which operates 24 hours a day: *I have to do the night shift at the hospital tomorrow.* **4** the people who work during this time: *The day shift takes over now.* **5** a loose-fitting dress

shifty

adjective deceitful and looking as if you've got something to hide: *The burglar had shifty eyes.*

Word building: Other forms are **shiftier, shiftiest**. | **shiftily** *adverb*

shilling

noun a silver coin used in Australia before decimal currency

shimmer

verb to shine or gleam with a dim unsteady light

shin

noun **1** the front part of your leg between your knee and your ankle
verb **2** to climb by gripping with your hands and your feet: *He shinned quickly up the rope.*

Word building: Other verb forms are **I shinned, I have shinned, I am shinning**.

shine

verb **1** to glow or give out light
Other words: **beam, flash, glimmer, radiate**
2 to polish: *Shine your shoes for the class photo.* **3** to be very good: *Cathy shines at tennis.*
Other words: **excel, succeed, triumph**
4 to direct the light of: *Shine the torch over here.*
noun **5** polished brightness
Other words: **brilliance, dazzle, gloss, glossiness, lustre, polish**

Word building: Other verb forms are **it shone, it has shone, it is shining**. For definition 2 the verb forms can also be **I shined, I have shined, I am shining**. | **shiny** *adjective* (**shinier, shiniest**)

shingle

noun a thin piece of wood, slate and so on used in rows to cover the roofs and sides of houses

Word building: **shingle** *verb* to cover with shingles

shingles

noun a painful skin disease which affects the nerves in your body

Shinto

noun a religion of Japan in which nature and ancestors are worshipped and held sacred

Word building: **Shintoist** *noun*

ship

noun **1** a large boat for carrying people or goods over deep water
verb **2** to send by ship, train, truck and so on

Word building: Other verb forms are **I shipped, I have shipped, I am shipping**.

shipment

noun a load of goods shipped at one time

shipshape

adjective neat and tidy

shire

noun a local government area

shirk

verb to get out of doing: *to shirk your job*

Word building: **shirker** *noun*

shirt

noun a piece of clothing for the top part of your body, with long or short sleeves, and usually with a collar, and buttons down the front

shish kebab

noun cubes of meat cooked on a skewer, sometimes with vegetables such as onion and capsicum

Word use: A shortened form is **kebab**.
Word history: from the Turkish words for 'skewer' and 'roast meat'

shiver

verb to shake with fear, cold or excitement
Other words: **quiver, shudder, tremble**

Word building: **shiver** *noun* **shivery** *adjective*

shoal¹

noun a sandbank under shallow water

shoal²

noun a group of fish swimming together

shock¹

noun **1** a sudden and violent fright or upset **2** pain and injury caused by an electric current passing through the body

Word building: **shocking** *adjective*: *shocking news* **shock** *verb*

shock²

noun a thick bushy mass: *a shock of hair*

shoddy

adjective **1** bad or made badly: *shoddy work | a shoddy house* **2** mean: *a shoddy thing to do*

Word building: Other forms are **shoddier, shoddiest**. | **shoddily** *adverb* **shoddiness** *noun*

shoe

noun **1** a covering for your foot **2** a curved steel bar to protect the bottom of the hoof of a horse or similar animal
verb **3** to adjust the shoes on a horse's hooves, or to attach new ones
phrase **4 in someone's shoes**, in the position or situation that someone else is: *I wouldn't like to be in your shoes.*

Word building: Other verb forms are **he shod, he has shod, he is shoeing.**

shoehorn

noun a long piece of metal or plastic that you put into the heel of your shoe to make it go on more easily

shoot

verb **1** to hit or kill with a bullet, arrow or something else fired from a weapon: *The policeman shot the bank robber.* **2** to fire from a weapon: *to shoot an arrow* **3** to send out quickly and accurately like an arrow or bullet: *to shoot questions | to shoot a ball into goal* **4** to move quickly: *He shot along the path.* **5** to photograph or film: *to shoot a scene* **6** to put out new growths: *Plants shoot in spring.*
noun **7** a new growth on a plant

Word building: Other verb forms are **I shot, I have shot, I am shooting.** | **shooter** *noun*

shop

noun **1** a building where you buy things: *I'm just going to have a look in the shops.*
verb **2** to buy things: *Dad likes to shop at the organic market rather than at the big supermarket.*

Word building: Other verb forms are **I shopped, I have shopped, I am shopping.** | **shopping** *noun* **shopkeeper** *noun*

shoplift

verb to steal from a shop while pretending to be shopping

Word building: **shoplifter** *noun* **shoplifting** *noun*

shopping centre

noun a very big building that has many different shops inside it

Word use: Another word for this is **shopping mall**.

shore

noun the land along the edge of the sea or a lake

shore/sure Don't confuse **shore** with **sure**. If someone is **sure** of something, they are certain or confident of it, as in *sure of success.*

short

adjective **1** not long **2** not tall **3** rude and abrupt: *He was short with me.* **4** not having enough: *We are short of water.*
adverb **5** suddenly: *to stop short* **6** without going the full length: *The ball fell short of the goal.*
noun **7** a short film advertising a program or a film to be shown later
Other words: **trailer**
8 shorts, short trousers ending above the knees

phrase **9 short for**, being a shortened form of: *'Phone' is short for 'telephone'*.

Word use: Definition 8 is sometimes used in the plural.

Word building: **shortly** *adverb* **shortness** *noun*

shortage
noun a lack in amount: *a shortage of food*

shortbread
noun a thick biscuit made with a lot of butter

short circuit
noun a fault in an electrical circuit causing the current to flow between two points only instead of through the whole circuit

shortcoming
noun a failure or fault: *Laziness is my worst shortcoming.*

short cut
noun a shorter or quicker way: *We took a short cut through the park to get to Justin's house.*

shortening
noun fat, such as butter or margarine, used in making pastry

shorthand
noun a system of fast handwriting using lines, curves and dots instead of letters

Word building: **shorthand** *adjective*

shorthanded
adjective not having enough helpers or workers

shortly
adverb soon: *I am coming shortly.*

short-sighted
adjective **1** not able to clearly see things that are far away
Other words: **myopic**
2 not thinking about the future: *a short-sighted answer to a problem*

Word building: **short-sightedness** *noun*

short-tempered
adjective becoming angry easily

shot
noun **1** the shooting of a gun, bow or other weapon: *She took three shots at the target.* | *I think I heard a shot.* **2** bullets or other lead ammunition **3** the heavy metal ball thrown in shot-put contests **4** a stroke or throw in sports: *a shot at goal* **5** a try, attempt or guess **6** an injection: *The doctor gave me a tetanus shot.* **7** *Informal* a photograph: *We took some shots of our house.*

shotgun
noun a gun that fires small shot and is used for shooting animals for sport

shot-put   (*say* <u>shot</u>-poot)
noun **1** the sport of throwing a heavy metal ball as far as possible **2** the ball itself

Word building: **shot-putter** *noun* **shot-putting** *noun*

should   (*rhymes with* <u>wood</u>)
verb to have a duty to: *You should say sorry for hitting your brother.*

shoulder   (*rhymes with* holder)
noun **1** the part of your body that joins your neck to your arm
verb **2** to push with the shoulders: *I shouldered my way through the crowd.* **3** to support or carry on the shoulders: *to shoulder the load of wood* **4** to take upon yourself: *to shoulder a responsibility*

shoulderblade
noun the flat bone that forms the back part of the shoulder

shout
verb **1** to call or cry out loudly
Other words: **bawl, bellow, roar, scream, yell**
2 *Informal* to buy or pay for: *I'll shout the ice-creams.*

Word building: **shout** *noun*

shove   (*say* shuv)
verb to push roughly

Word building: **shove** *noun*

shovel   (*say* <u>shuv</u>-uhl)
noun **1** a tool or machine with a wide blade for moving things like soil or rubbish
verb **2** to move with a shovel: *to shovel sand into a truck*

Word building: Other verb forms are **I shovelled, I have shovelled, I am shovelling.**

show

verb **1** to cause or allow to be seen: *Seung showed his drawing to his mother.* **2** to point out or explain: *Please show me how to do it.* **3** to guide: *Show me the bathroom.* **4** to prove by demonstrating: *I'll show that it is true.*
noun **5** a public showing or exhibition: *an art show* **6** an entertainment, such as a play or television series **7** a false showing or pretence: *I was bored but pushed myself to make a show of interest.*
phrase **8 show off, a** to show proudly: *Sophie showed off her new computer game.* **b** to behave so as to get attention or praise for yourself: *Stop showing off.* **9 show up, a** to make stand out clearly: *White clothes show up dirt.* **b** to appear or arrive: *My partner didn't show up till after dinner.*
Word building: Other verb forms are **I showed, I have shown, I am showing.** | **showy** *adjective* attracting attention **showily** *adverb*   **showiness** *noun*

showdown

noun an open showing of disagreements, in order to clear up a situation: *I've decided to have a showdown with the boss this week.*

shower

noun **1** a brief fall of rain **2** a fall of anything in large numbers: *a shower of sparks* | *a shower of questions* **3** a spout that sends out fine streams of water for washing your body **4** the use of such a shower to wash yourself
verb **5** to wet with a shower: *He showered us with the hose.* **6** to wash yourself under a shower **7** to fall in a shower: *Bullets showered down on us.*
phrase **8 shower on,** to give generously to: *He showered presents on her.*
Word building: **showery** *adjective*

show-off

noun someone who behaves so as to get attention or praise

showroom

noun a room where goods for sale are shown

shrapnel

noun the small parts of an exploded cannon shell: *He was wounded by shrapnel.*

Word history: named after the inventor H *Shrapnel*, 1761–1842, an officer in the British army

shred

noun **1** a narrow strip cut or torn off: *a dress torn to shreds* **2** a very small bit: *There was not a shred of food left.* | *He did not feel a shred of pity for her.*
verb **3** to tear into small pieces: *We can shred this material and use it to stuff cushions.*
Word building: Other verb forms are **I shredded** or **shred, I have shredded** or **shred, I am shredding.**

shrew

noun **1** a small, long-nosed mammal that looks like a mouse, and eats insects **2** a very bad-tempered woman
Word building: **shrewish** *adjective*

shrewd

adjective clever, and with good practical judgement: *a shrewd business executive*
Other words: **astute, sharp, smart**
Word building: **shrewdly** *adverb* **shrewdness** *noun*

shriek   (*say* shreek)

noun a loud, sharp, high-pitched cry or noise: *a shriek of fright* | *the shriek of a whistle*
Word building: **shriek** *verb*

shrill

adjective loud and high-pitched: *a shrill voice*
Word building: **shrilly** *adverb*   **shrillness** *noun*

shrimp

noun a kind of prawn

shrine

noun a sacred or holy place: *a shrine of remembrance for those killed in the war*

shrink

verb **1** to become or make smaller: *The number of children at our school is shrinking.* | *Hot water shrinks woollen clothes.* **2** to draw back: *The frightened child shrank into a corner.*
Word building: Other forms are **I shrank, I have shrunk** or **shrunken, I am shrinking.** | **shrinkable** *adjective*   **shrinkage** *noun*

shrivel

verb to shrink and wrinkle: *Heat shrivels grass.* | *He is shrivelling with age.*

Word building: Other forms are **I shrivelled,
I have shrivelled, I am shrivelling.**

shroud

noun **1** a cloth for wrapping a dead body
in **2** something which covers and hides like
a cloth: *a shroud of rain*
verb **3** to cover or hide: *Darkness shrouded
the town. | Mystery shrouded her past life.*

shrub

noun a small, low, tree-like plant

Word building: **shrubby** *adjective*

shrug

verb to raise and lower your shoulders to
show doubt, scorn or lack of interest

Word building: Other forms are **I shrugged,
I have shrugged, I am shrugging. | shrug** *noun*

shudder

noun to shake suddenly from fear, cold or
horror

Word building: **shudder** *noun*

shuffle

verb **1** to walk slowly without lifting the
feet **2** to move about: *Su Li shuffled the
papers on her desk. | They shuffled me from
one class to another.* **3** to mix up the order
of cards in a pack

Word building: **shuffle** *noun*   **shuffler** *noun*

shun

verb to keep away from deliberately: *He
shunned me for a week after our fight.*

Word building: Other forms are **I shunned,
I have shunned, I am shunning.**

shunt

verb **1** to move aside or turn aside or out
of the way **2** to move from one line of
rails to another: *The train was shunted onto
the northern line.*

Word building: **shunt** *noun*

shush

interjection **1** a command to be quiet or
silent
verb **2** to make or become silent

shut

verb **1** to close or put something in or
across an opening: *to shut a book | to shut
a door*
adjective **2** closed
phrase **3 shut down**, to close down or stop
for a while: *Schools shut down during the*

holidays. **4 shut in**, to keep in or confine:
to shut a bird in a cage **5 shut off**, to stop
the flow of: *to shut off electricity* **6 shut
out**, to keep out or bar: *My sister shut me
out of her room.* **7 shut up**, **a** to keep in
or hide from view: *to shut up your prize
dog* **b** *Informal* to stop talking

Word building: Other verb forms are **it shut,
it has shut, it is shutting.**

shutter

noun **1** a movable wooden cover for the
outside of a window **2** a part of a camera
which opens and shuts over the lens to
allow light through to the film

Word building: **shutter** *verb*

shuttle

noun the part of a loom that carries the
thread backwards and forwards in weaving

Word history: from an Old English word
meaning 'a dart' or 'an arrow'

shuttlecock

noun **1** a piece of cork, rubber or light
plastic with feathers stuck in it that is hit
backwards and forwards in games such
as badminton **2** a game played with a
shuttlecock

shy

adjective **1** bashful or not feeling relaxed
with other people
Other words: **diffident, reserved**
2 easily frightened away
Other words: **timid**
verb **3** to move suddenly back or aside: *The
horse shied when the car went past.*

Word building: Other verb forms are **it shied,
it has shied, it is shying. | shyly** *adverb*

sibling

noun a brother or sister

sick

adjective **1** ill or having a disease
Other words: **ailing, off-colour, unwell, sickly**
2 vomiting or feeling like vomiting
Other words: **nauseous**
3 for sick people: *sick leave* **4** having to do
with something horrible or disgusting: *a
sick joke*
Other words: **off-colour, tasteless**
phrase **5 be sick**, to vomit **6 be sick of**,
to be annoyed or fed up with: *I am sick of
your untidiness.*

Word building: **sicken** *verb* to make sick
sickening *adjective*   **sickness** *noun*

sick bay

noun the place that you go to if you are feeling ill while you are at school

sickie

noun *Informal* a day taken off work with pay because of real or pretended sickness

sickle

noun a curved short-handled tool for cutting grass or grain

sickly

adjective **1** unhealthy or getting sick easily: *a sickly child* **2** having to do with sickness: *a sickly colour of the face* **3** making you feel sick: *sickly food*

Word building: Other forms are **sicklier**, **sickliest**. | **sickliness** *noun*

side

noun **1** one of the outer edges or lines of something usually not the top, bottom, front or back: *the side of a house | the side of a rectangle* **2** one of the two surfaces of a material like paper or cloth: *Write on one side only.* **3** either half of your body: *I've got a stitch in my side.* **4** the space next to someone or something: *You stand at my side.* **5** one of two or more groups that are against each other: *Which side are you on?* **6** a position or way of thinking about something: *to look at a question from all sides* **7** a part or area: *the north side of a city* *adjective* **8** at the side: *a side door* **9** from the side: *a side view*

sideboard

noun a piece of furniture with shelves and drawers for holding things like plates and cups

sideline

verb **1** to cause a player to be unable to play: *The injury sidelined her for a month.* **2** to put somebody outside the main action of an activity: *They sidelined him because he wasn't contributing much.* *noun* **3** something additional to a main activity, product, and so on: *The farmer tried growing macadamias as a sideline to his usual crops.*

sideshow

noun a small show that is part of a larger fair or circus

sidestep

verb **1** to step to one side to avoid: *to sidestep a puddle* **2** to avoid: *He sidestepped making a decision.*

Word building: Other forms are **I sidestepped**, **I have sidestepped**, **I am sidestepping**.

sideways

adverb **1** from or to the side of something: *to look sideways* **2** with the side going first: *The crab scuttled sideways across the rock.*

Word building: **sideways** *adjective*: *a sideways glance*

sidle

verb to move sideways, usually hoping not to be noticed: *He sidled into the room late.*

siege   (*say* seej)

noun the surrounding of a place in order to capture it: *The city was under siege for three days during the war.*

siesta   (*say* see-<u>es</u>-tuh)

noun a midday or afternoon rest

Word history: from Spanish and before that from a Latin word meaning 'sixth (hour)' or 'midday'

sieve   (*say* siv)

noun **1** a container with mesh or holes at the bottom used for straining liquids or separating thick from thin, or large from small *verb* **2** to separate or strain with a sieve Other words: **sift**

sift

verb **1** to separate the thick or coarse parts of with a sieve: *to sift flour* Other words: **sieve** **2** to scatter with a sieve: *to sift icing sugar onto a cake* **3** to sort through carefully: *I sifted all the information to find the piece of evidence I wanted.*

sigh

verb to let out your breath slowly and with a soft sound, from tiredness, sadness or relief

Word building: **sigh** *noun*

sight

noun **1** the ability to see Other words: **vision** **2** something which is seen or should be seen: *They were a beautiful sight in their costumes. | the sights of the city* **3** something that looks odd or unattractive: *My brother looked a sight wearing Mum's dress.*

verb **4** to get sight of*: They sighted a ship on the horizon.*
phrase **5 in sight of**, in a position where it is possible to see: *We are now in sight of land.*

---

sight/site/cite Don't confuse **sight** with **site** or **cite**.

A **site** is the land where something is built or will soon be built. It is also a short way of saying *website*.

To **cite** something is to mention or refer to it.

---

sightseeing (*say* site-see-ing)
noun travelling around a city looking at objects and places of interest: *We spent a wonderful week sightseeing in Paris.*

sign
noun **1** anything that shows that something exists or is likely to happen: *Clouds are a sign of rain.* **2** a mark, figure or symbol used to stand for a word, idea or mathematical value: *a dollar sign | a plus sign* **3** a movement that expresses an idea or feeling: *He made a sign for me to leave the room.* **4** a notice that gives information, warns or advertises: *a house with a 'For Sale' sign*
verb **5** to write your signature on: *to sign a letter* **6** to write as a signature: *She signed her name.*
phrase **7 in sight of**, in a position where it is possible to see: *We are now in sight of land.* **8 sign off**, to stop broadcasting a radio or television program **9 sign up, a** to enter the military services: *My grandfather signed up when he was just a teenager.* **b** to take on by a signed agreement: *The club signed up two new players.*

signal
noun **1** any action or object that warns, points a direction or gives an order: *He gave the signal for them to start. | We stopped at the traffic signals.* **2** the waves by which sound or pictures are sent in radio and television
verb **3** to make a signal to: *She signalled him to stop talking.* **4** to make known by signal: *We signalled the good news.*
Word building: Other verb forms are **I signalled, I have signalled, I am signalling.**

signature
noun **1** the way you write your own name **2** the sign or signs written at the beginning of a piece of music to tell its key and time

signet
noun a raised engraved design used as an official stamp or set into a finger ring

significant
adjective **1** important: *a significant event in Australia's history* **2** full of meaning: *a significant look*
Word building: **significance** *noun* **significantly** *adverb*

signify
verb **1** to be a sign of: *Black clouds signify a storm.* **2** to make known by signs: *You can signify anger by frowning.*
Word building: Other forms are **I signified, I have signified, I am signifying.** | **signification** *noun*

silence
noun **1** absence of any sound or noise
verb **2** to bring to silence: *She silenced the class.*
Word building: **silencer** *noun*

silent
adjective **1** making no sound or not talking: *He remained silent.*
Other words: **hushed, quiet, still**
2 having no sound: *a silent room | a silent movie* **3** not pronounced: *In the word 'know' the letter 'k' is silent.*

silhouette (*say* sil-ooh-et)
noun **1** an outline drawing filled in with black, like a shadow
verb **2** to show up like a silhouette or shadow: *The tree was silhouetted against the sky.*

silicon
noun an element found in minerals and rocks, used in making such things as glass and steel

silk
noun a soft shiny cloth made from the threads of the cocoon of the silkworm: *Before nylon was invented, stockings were made out of silk.*
Word building: **silk** *adjective* **silken** *adjective* **silkiness** *noun* **silky** *adjective*

silk-screen

noun a way of printing in which ink is passed over a stencil attached to a screen of silk or other fine cloth

Word building: **silk-screen** *verb*

silkworm

noun a kind of caterpillar which spins a fine soft thread to make a cocoon

sill

noun a flat piece of wood or other material beneath a window or door

silly

adjective foolish or stupid

Other words: **idiotic, inane, senseless**

Word building: Other forms are **sillier, silliest. | silliness** *noun*

silo

noun a tower-like building for storing grain

Word building: The plural is **silos.**
Word history: from a Greek word for a pit to keep grain in

silt

noun earthy matter like very fine sand which is carried by running water and then left behind on the river bottom

silver

noun **1** a white metal used for making things like jewellery, coins, mirrors and cutlery **2** things made from silver or similar metal, such as coins or knives and forks: *I have a $5 note but no silver. | We put the silver on the dining table on special occasions.*
adjective **3** made of silver or of a metallic mixture similar to it **4** producing silver: *a silver mine* **5** shiny whitish-grey

Word building: **silver** *verb* **silvery** *adjective*

silver bullet

noun a certain and effective remedy, often one that people have thought about but not been able to create: *Unfortunately there is no silver bullet for cancer.*

silverfish

noun a small wingless insect which feeds on paper and some fabrics, and so damages books and household goods

Word use: The plural is **silverfishes** or **silverfish.**

SIM card

noun a small piece of plastic issued by a mobile phone network that a person puts into a mobile phone to make it work

similar

adjective having a general likeness: *Their faces are similar. | My rollerblades are similar to yours.*

Word building: **similarity** *noun*

simile   (*say* sim-uh-lee)

noun a figure of speech which points out a likeness between two generally unlike things, as in *to sing like a bird* and *He's as strong as an ox.*

simmer

verb **1** to cook in a liquid just below boiling point **2** to be full of strong but controlled feelings: *She was simmering with rage.*
phrase **3 simmer down,** to become calm or calmer

simper

verb to smile in a silly or unnatural way: *She simpered when he said she looked pretty.*

Word building: **simper** *noun*

simple

adjective **1** easy to understand, do or use: *a simple explanation | a simple test | a simple tool* **2** plain and uncomplicated: *a simple writing style | simple clothes* **3** mentally weak **4** having to do with the most basic one-word form of a verb: *The verb 'ran' in 'I ran' is in the simple past tense.*

Word use: Compare definition 4 with **continuous** and **perfect** which talk about verbs of more than one word such as 'am running' and 'have run'.
Word building: **simpleness** *noun* **simplicity** *noun*

simpleton

noun a foolish person

simplify

verb to make easier or more simple

Word building: Other forms are **I simplified, I have simplified, I am simplifying.**

simplistic

adjective being so simple as to lose accuracy: *He gave a simplistic account of the causes of unemployment.*

Word building: **simplistically** *adverb*

simply

adverb **1** in a plain and straightforward way: *She answered simply.* | *He dressed simply.* **2** merely: *He is simply going for a walk.* **3** absolutely: *She was simply wonderful in the emergency.*

simulate   *(say* sim-yuh-layt*)*

verb **1** to make a pretence of: *He simulated admiration to flatter her.* **2** to imitate or make a copy of: *They simulated diamonds to make the cheap jewellery.*

Word building: **simulator** *noun* a device used in training or experiments that simulates movement or flight   **simulation** *noun*

simulcast   *(say* sim-uhl-kahst*)*

noun a program broadcast on television and radio at the same time

simultaneous   *(say* sim-uhl-tay-nee-uhs*)*

adjective happening at the same time

Word building: **simultaneously** *adverb*

sin

noun **1** an act of breaking a holy law **2** disobedience, especially towards the rules of what is thought to be right and wrong

Word building: **sin** *verb* (**sinned, sinning**) **sinful** *adjective*

since

adverb **1** from then until now: *I've been taking karate lessons since kindergarten.* **2** between a particular past time and the present time: *She agreed at first, but has since changed her mind.*
preposition **3** counting from: *since 10 o'clock last night*
conjunction **4** because: *Since you're so good with numbers, you can help Oscar with his maths homework.*

sincere

adjective having and expressing true feelings: *I was sincere in my wishes for your success.*
Other words: **genuine**

Word building: **sincerity** *noun*

sinew   *(say* sin-yooh*)*

noun a piece of tough tissue joining a muscle to a bone

sing

verb **1** to give out musical sounds with your voice **2** to perform in this way: *She sang a song.*

Word building: Other forms are **I sang, I have sung, I am singing.**

singe   *(say* sinj*)*

verb to burn slightly

single

adjective **1** one and only: *my single reason for going* **2** for one person: *a single bed* **3** unmarried
phrase **4 single out**, to choose alone: *They singled her out for promotion.*

Word building: **single** *noun*   **singleness** *noun*

single-handed

adverb by working alone: *Fiona built the house single-handed.*

Word building: **single-handedly** *adverb*

singlet

noun a garment with narrow shoulder straps, worn on the upper part of your body, usually under your other clothes

singsong

adjective with a regular up and down pattern in the tone: *a singsong voice*

singular

adjective **1** indicating one person or thing such as the words 'teacher', 'hears' and 'she' in the sentence *She hears the teacher.* **2** unusual: *He had a very singular appearance.*

Word use: The more usual word for definition 2 is **odd**.
Word building: **singularly** *adverb*

sinister

adjective suggesting a threat of evil: *a sinister remark*

sink

verb **1** to go down gradually, as in water: *The ship sank.* | *The sun is sinking.* **2** to cause to go down: *They sank an enemy ship.*
noun **3** a kitchen basin with a drain
phrase **4 sink in**, to become understood: *The importance of the letter at last sank in.*

Word building: Other verb forms are **I sank, I have sunk, I am sinking.**

sinker

noun a weight, usually of lead, for making a fishing line sink below the surface

sinuous   *(say* sin-yooh-uhs*)*

adjective winding like a snake: *a sinuous path*

Word use: The more usual word is **twisting**.

sinus (say <u>suy</u>-nuhs)

noun one of the air-filled holes in your skull, connecting with your nose

sip

verb to drink in small mouthfuls

Word building: Other forms are **I sipped, I have sipped, I am sipping.** | **sip** *noun*

siphon (say <u>suy</u>-fuhn)

noun a tube through which liquid flows up over the edge of a higher container to a lower one, using the force of gravity to draw the liquid out at the lower end

Word use: Another spelling for this is **syphon**.
Word building: **siphon** *verb*
Word history: from a Greek word meaning 'a pipe'

sir

noun a respectful or formal word used when speaking to a man: *May I help you, sir?*

sire

noun the male parent of an animal

siren

noun a device that makes a loud warning sound, used on ambulances, police cars and so on

sissy

noun Informal a coward

Word building: The plural is **sissies**.

sister

noun **1** a female relative who has the same parents as you **2** a senior nurse **3** a nun

Word building: **sisterhood** *noun*

sister-in-law

noun **1** the sister of your husband or wife **2** the wife of your brother **3** the wife of the brother of your husband or wife

Word building: The plural is **sisters-in-law**.

sit

verb **1** to rest on the lower part of your body **2** to rest or be placed: *The teapot is sitting on the table.* **3** to try to answer the questions in: *to sit an exam* **4** to pose: *to sit for a portrait* **5** to be in the process of meeting: *Parliament is sitting.*

Word building: Other forms are **I sat, I have sat, I am sitting.**

sitar (say <u>sit</u>-ah)

noun an Indian musical instrument which you play by plucking its three strings

Word history: from Hindi, a language of India

site

noun **1** the piece of land on which something is or will be built: *a house on a site overlooking the ocean* **2** a place where something happens or has happened: *the site of the annual picnic* **3** a place on the World Wide Web with an address that can be looked up for information and facts

Word use: Definition 3 is a short way of saying **website**.

---

site/sight/cite Don't confuse **site** with **sight** or **cite**.

Your **sight** is your ability to see things. It can also be something worth seeing.

To **cite** something is to mention or refer to it.

---

situate

verb to place in a position

situation

noun **1** a position in relation to the surroundings: *The shop has a good situation.* **2** a state of affairs: *The situation has been difficult since he left.*

situation comedy

noun a movie or television show that is based on the funny situations in ordinary life

six

noun **1** the number 6 **2** the Roman numeral VI **3** a score of six runs in cricket, obtained by hitting the ball over the field boundary without it bouncing

Word building: **six** *adjective*: *six canoes* **sixth** *adjective*: *their sixth trip to Vietnam*

sixteen

noun **1** the number 16 **2** the Roman numeral XVI

Word building: **sixteen** *adjective*: *sixteen candles* **sixteenth** *adjective*: *her sixteenth birthday*

sixty

noun **1** the number 60 **2** the Roman numeral LX

Word building: The plural is **sixties**. | **sixty** *adjective*: *sixty competitors* **sixtieth** *adjective*: *the sixtieth anniversary of the founding of the school*

size

noun the dimensions or extent of something

sizeable

adjective quite big

Word building: **sizeably** *adverb*

sizzle

verb to make a hissing sound while cooking: *The sausages are sizzling in the pan.*

skate

noun **1** a special boot with either a blade attached to the sole to move on ice, or wheels attached to the sole to move on the ground
verb **2** to move swiftly wearing skates

Word use: This word is a short way of saying **ice-skate** or **rollerskate**.
Word building: **skater** *noun* someone who skates

skateboard

noun **1** a narrow wooden or plastic board on rollerskate wheels which you usually ride standing up
verb **2** to move swiftly on the ground, riding a skateboard

skein   (*rhymes with* cane)

noun a length of thread or wool wound in a coil

skeleton

noun **1** all the bones of a human or animal body, connected together **2** a bare framework of something
adjective **3** cut back to the smallest number that can cope: *a skeleton staff*

Word building: **skeletal** *adjective*

sketch

noun **1** a drawing or painting done roughly or quickly **2** any rough plan or outline

Word building: **sketchy** *adjective* (**sketchier**, **sketchiest**) **sketch** *verb*

skewbald

adjective having patches of different colours, especially of white and brown: *a skewbald horse*

Word use: Compare this with **piebald**.

skewer

noun a long pin of wood or metal, especially one for holding meat while it is being cooked

Word building: **skewer** *verb*

ski

noun one of a pair of long narrow pieces of wood, metal or plastic, which you fasten to your shoes and use for moving on snow

Word building: **ski** *verb* (**ski'd** or **skied**, **skiing**)

skid

verb to slide forward when the wheels of your car or bike are no longer gripping the road surface: *The car skidded on the icy road.*

Word building: Other forms are **I skidded**, **I have skidded**, **I am skidding**. | **skid** *noun*

skill

noun the ability to do something well
Other words: **capability**, **competency**, **efficiency**, **proficiency**, **talent**

Word building: **skilful** *adjective* **skilfully** *adverb* **skilfulness** *noun* **skilled** *adjective*

skillet

noun a small frying pan

skim

verb **1** to remove floating matter from: *to skim soup stock* **2** to remove from the surface of something: *to skim fat from gravy* **3** to move lightly over the surface or top of: *The birds skimmed across the lake.* **4** to read quickly without taking everything in: *I have just skimmed the newspaper.*

Word building: Other forms are **I skimmed**, **I have skimmed**, **I am skimming**.

skim milk

noun milk from which the cream has been removed

skimpy

adjective **1** scanty or hardly enough: *a skimpy meal* **2** stingy or mean with money

Word building: Other forms are **skimpier**, **skimpiest**. | **skimp** *verb* **skimpily** *adverb* **skimpiness** *noun*

skin

noun **1** the outer covering of an animal or human **2** any surface layer: *banana skin*

Word building: **skin** *verb* (**skinned**, **skinning**) to remove the skin of

skindiving

noun underwater swimming for which you use a snorkel, mask and flippers

Word building: **skindiver** *noun*

skink

noun any of many different, usually smooth-scaled lizards

skinny

adjective thin

Word building: Other forms are **skinnier, skinniest.** | **skinniness** *noun*

skip

verb **1** to jump lightly from one foot to the other **2** to jump over a twirling rope **3** to leave out: *He often skips bits when he's reading.*

Word building: Other forms are **I skipped, I have skipped, I am skipping.** | **skip** *noun*

skipper

noun the captain of a ship or a team

skirmish

noun a small battle

Word building: **skirmish** *verb*
Word history: from a German word for 'shield'

skirt

noun **1** a piece of outer clothing, usually worn by women, that hangs from the waist
verb **2** to go round the edge of: *He skirted the dam.*

skirting board

noun a board running round a room at the base of the walls

skit

noun a short play or other piece of writing which makes fun of something

skite

noun someone who boasts a lot
Word building: **skite** *verb*

skittle

noun **1** a piece of wood shaped like a bottle, which people try to knock over with a ball as part of a game **2 skittles**, this game
verb **3** to knock something or someone over: *That skateboarder almost skittled me.*

skittles

plural noun a game played with bottle-shaped pieces of wood and a ball to knock them down

Word building: **skittle** *verb* to knock over

skivvy

noun a close-fitting piece of clothing of knitted material, with long sleeves and a high collar

Word building: The plural is **skivvies**.

skulk

verb to stay nearby, trying not to let anyone know you are there: *A man was skulking about the place before the burglary.*

skull

noun the bony framework of the head, enclosing the brain and supporting the face

skullcap

noun a close-fitting, brimless cap, especially one worn by a Jewish man or boy

Word use: Another word for this, when worn by a Jewish person, is **yarmulke**.

skunk

noun a small, furry, American animal that lets out a foul-smelling fluid when attacked

Word history: from a Native North American language

sky

noun the area of the clouds or the upper air

Word building: The plural is **skies**.

skydiving

noun the sport of falling from a plane for some distance before opening your parachute

skylight

noun a flat window in a roof

skyscraper

noun a very tall building, especially an office block

slab

noun a large flat piece: *a stone slab | a slab of cake*

slack

adjective **1** hanging loosely: *a slack rope*
Other words: **limp**
2 *Informal* lazy or neglectful: *It was slack of you to forget her birthday.*

Word building: **slack** *verb* **slacken** *verb* **slackly** *adverb* **slackness** *noun*

slacks

plural noun long trousers

slag

noun the waste material from a mine, or from metal-bearing rock when it is melted down

slalom (*say* slay-luhm, slah-luhm)

noun a downhill skiing race with a winding course

slam

verb **1** to shut hard with a loud noise: *to slam a door* **2** to hit or throw hard or noisily: *to slam a ball into a net*

Word building: Other forms are **I slammed, I have slammed, I am slamming.**

slander

noun a false spoken statement which damages someone's reputation or good name

Word use: Compare this with **libel.**
Word building: **slander** *verb*　**slanderous** *adjective*

slang

noun casual, informal language that is not fitting for formal use

Word building: **slangy** *adjective*

slant

noun **1** a slope or angle **2** an aspect or point of view: *This news gives a new slant to the problem.*

Word building: **slant** *verb*　**slantwise** *adverb*

slap

noun **1** a quick hit, especially with the open hand
verb **2** to hit smartly, especially with the open hand **3** to put carelessly: *to slap on paint | to slap a book on the table*

Word building: Other verb forms are **I slapped, I have slapped, I am slapping.**

slapstick

noun rough and noisy comedy

slash

verb **1** to cut violently and unevenly: *Vandals have slashed the train seats.* **2** to reduce greatly: *to slash prices*

Word building: **slash** *noun*

slat

noun a long strip of wood or metal: *the slats of a blind*

slate

noun a dark bluish-grey rock which splits easily into layers and is used on roofs and floors

slaughter (*say* slaw-tuh)

verb **1** to kill for food: *to slaughter cattle* **2** to kill violently in great numbers

Word building: **slaughter** *noun*

slave

noun **1** someone who works without being paid and is the prisoner of someone else
verb **2** to work very hard, like a slave

Word building: **slavery** *noun*　**slavish** *adjective*

slay

verb to kill

Word building: Other forms are **he slew, he has slain, he is slaying.**

slay/sleigh Don't confuse **slay** with **sleigh,** which is a sled, usually one pulled by animals.

sleazy

adjective untidy and dirty

Word building: Other forms are **sleazier, sleaziest. | sleazily** *adverb*　**sleaziness** *noun*

sled

noun a vehicle with runners for sliding over snow

Word use: You can also use **sledge.**

sledge

noun another name for **sled**

sledgehammer

noun a large heavy hammer

sleek

adjective smooth and shiny: *sleek hair*

Word building: **sleekness** *noun*

sleep

verb **1** to rest with your eyes closed and your mind unconscious: *Did you sleep well last night?* **2** to have beds for: *The caravan sleeps four.*

Word building: Other forms are **I slept, I have slept, I am sleeping. | sleepy** *adjective* (**sleepier, sleepiest**)　**sleep** *noun*　**sleepiness** *noun*　**sleepless** *adjective*

sleep apnoea (*say* sleep ap-nee-uh)

noun a condition where a person stops breathing for short periods while they are asleep

Word use: Another spelling is **sleep apnea.**

sleeper

noun **1** a wooden, concrete or steel beam on which railway lines rest **2** a small ring worn in a pierced ear to prevent the hole from closing

sleepover

noun a night spent sleeping at someone else's home: *Lena and I are going to go to Chloe's sleepover on Friday night.*

sleet

noun rain mixed with snow or hail

Word building: **sleet** *verb*

sleeve

noun **1** the part of a garment that covers the arm **2** a cover into which something slides

sleigh *(sounds like* slay*)*

noun a sled, especially one pulled by animals

sleigh/slay Don't confuse **sleigh** with **slay**, which is to kill.

slender

adjective slim or thin: *slender legs | a slender branch*

Word building: **slenderness** *noun*

sleuth *(rhymes with* tooth*)*

noun a detective

slice

verb **1** to cut into thin pieces: *to slice bread* **2** to hit or kick a ball so that it curves to the right if you are right-handed

Word use: The opposite of definition 2 is **hook.**

Word building: **slice** *noun* **sliced** *adjective*

slick

adjective **1** clever and smooth, but not sincere: *a slick salesman* **2** smart or skilful: *a slick answer*
noun **3** a shiny patch of oil on water

Word building: **slick down** *verb* to smooth down: *to slick down hair with oil*

slide

verb **1** to move along smoothly: *to slide a drawer in and out | to slide down a slippery dip*
noun **2** a sliding movement: *She slipped on a banana peel and went for a slide.* **3** a see-through photograph which can be shown on a screen using a projector **4** a thin sheet of glass used for holding things that you look at under a microscope

Word building: Other verb forms are **I slid, I have slid, I am sliding.**

slight

adjective **1** small: *a slight cough* **2** thin: *a man of slight build*
verb **3** to treat rudely: *They slighted me by not inviting me to the party.*

Word building: **slight** *noun* an insult **slightly** *adverb*: *You are only slightly taller than me.*

slim

adjective slender or slight: *slim legs | a slim chance*

Word building: Other forms are **slimmer, slimmest. | slim** *verb* (**slimmed, slimming**)

slime

noun slippery wet matter, usually unpleasant: *Snails leave a trail of slime.*

Word building: **slimy** *adjective* (**slimier, slimiest**) **sliminess** *noun*

sling

noun **1** a piece of cloth looped around your neck to hold your arm if it is hurt **2** an old-fashioned weapon for throwing stones, made of a leather strap which is swung quickly round and round before releasing the stone
verb **3** to throw or fling: *to sling a stone* **4** to hang loosely: *to sling a coat across your shoulders*

Word building: Other verb forms are **I slung, I have slung, I am slinging.**

slingshot

noun another word for **catapult**

slink

verb to creep quietly so as not to be noticed: *The dog slunk away with its tail between its legs.*

Word building: Other forms are **I slunk, I have slunk, I am slinking.**

slip

verb **1** to slide easily: *to slip a note under the door | The wet glass slipped from her hand.* **2** to fall over: *to slip on a polished floor* **3** to escape from: *The dog slipped its leash. | Your birthday slipped my mind.*
noun **4** a mistake: *to make a slip in adding up the bill* **5** a petticoat **6** a small sheet or piece: *a slip of paper*

Word building: Other verb forms are **I slipped, I have slipped, I am slipping.**

slipper

noun a soft comfortable shoe for wearing indoors

slippery

adjective too smooth or wet to get a hold on: *slippery ice*

slippery dip

noun a steeply-sloping smooth metal structure which is fun to slide down

slit

noun a long straight cut or opening

Word building: **slit** *verb* (**slit, slitting**): *to slit open an envelope*

slither

verb to slide along like a snake

sliver   (*rhymes with* river)

noun a small thin piece: *a sliver of wood*

Word building: **sliver** *verb*

slob

noun someone who is lazy and untidy

Word use: This word is used as an insult.
Word history: from an Irish word meaning 'mud'

slobber

verb to dribble or drool

Word building: **slobbery** *adjective*

slog

verb **1** to hit hard: *She slogged the ball.* **2** to plod along heavily: *The weary hikers slogged up the hill.*

Word building: Other forms are **I slogged, I have slogged, I am slogging.**

slogan   (*say* sloh-guhn)

noun a clever catchy saying used to advertise something

slop

verb to spill or splash: *Don't slop water over the side of the bath.* | *The milk slopped out of the cup.*

Word building: Other forms are **I slopped, I have slopped, I am slopping.**

slope

verb **1** to be higher at one end than the other: *The hill slopes steeply.*
noun **2** a slant or tilt: *the slope of a roof* **3 slopes**, a hilly area: *There will be snow on the southern slopes.*

Word building: **sloping** *adjective*

sloppy

adjective **1** wet and runny **2** too sentimental: *a sloppy love story* **3** loose or untidy: *a sloppy jumper* | *sloppy school work*

Word building: Other forms are **sloppier, sloppiest**. | **sloppily** *adverb*   **sloppiness** *noun*

slosh

verb to pour or splash sloppily: *to slosh water over the floor* | *to slosh around in the mud*

slot

noun a small narrow slit or opening: *Put a coin in the slot.*

sloth   (*rhymes with* both)

noun **1** great laziness **2** a slow clumsy mammal which lives in the jungles of South America

Word building: **slothful** *adjective*

slouch

verb to walk or sit without holding yourself up straight

Word building: **slouch** *noun*

slouch hat

noun an army hat with the brim designed to be turned up on one side

slovenly   (*say* sluv-uhn-lee)

adjective dirty careless and untidy

Word building: **slovenliness** *noun*

slow

adjective **1** taking a long time: *a slow train* **2** not hurrying: *to walk at a slow pace*
Other words: **leisurely, sluggish, unhurried** **3** behind the right time: *The clock is five minutes slow.*
phrase **4 slow down**, to make or become slower

Word building: **slowly** *adverb*   **slowness** *noun*

sludge

noun soft muddy substance: *The drain is clogged with sludge.*

Word building: **sludgy** *adjective*

slug[1]

noun **1** a slimy creature like a snail without its shell **2** a small bullet

slug²

Informal

verb **1** to punch hard: *to slug him in the eye* **2** to charge far too much: *They slugged me for fixing my bike.*

Word building: Other forms are **I slugged, I have slugged, I am slugging.** | **slug** *noun*

sluggish

adjective moving slowly with no energy

Word building: **sluggishly** *adverb*

sluice   *(rhymes with* loose*)*

noun **1** a channel for water, fitted with a gate to control the water flow
verb **2** to drain: *to sluice water from a pond* **3** to wash with running water

slum

noun a dirty overcrowded place in which poor people live

Word building: **slummy** *adjective*

slumber

noun deep sleep

Word building: **slumber** *verb*

slump

verb to drop heavily: *to slump into a chair*

Word building: **slump** *noun*

slur

verb **1** to pronounce unclearly: *Don't slur your words.* **2** to harm the good name of: *The newspaper article slurred the politician.*

Word building: Other forms are **I slurred, I have slurred, I am slurring.** | **slur** *noun*

slush

noun snow which is partly melted

Word building: **slushy** *adjective*

slushy

noun a half-frozen drink made of cordial with finely crushed ice added: *He asked for a berry slushy.*

Word use: Another spelling is **slushie.**

sly

adjective **1** cunning or deceitful
Other words: **calculating, crafty, guileful, sneaky, tricky, wily**
phrase **2** on the sly, secretly: *to take money on the sly*

Word building: **slyly** *adverb*

smack¹

phrase **smack of,** to have a touch of: *Your behaviour smacks of selfishness.*

Word building: **smack** *noun*

smack²

verb **1** to hit with the hand open
phrase **2** smack your lips, to make a noise with your lips as if you are looking forward to eating something good

Word building: **smack** *noun*

small

adjective **1** not big or great **2** ashamed or embarrassed: *to feel small*
phrase **3** small talk, conversation about things which are not important

Word building: **small** *adverb*: *to cut the fruit up small*

smallpox

noun a serious infectious disease with a rash which leaves deep scars

smart

adjective **1** clever or intelligent **2** quick **3** neat and fashionable: *a smart new suit*
verb **4** to sting or hurt: *A cut smarts if you bathe it with salt water.* | *to smart from an insult*

Word building: **smarten** *verb*   **smartly** *adverb*

smash

verb **1** to break loudly into pieces: *to smash a plate* **2** to hit with great force: *to smash the ball over the net* | *The car smashed into the fence.*
noun **3** a loud crash **4** an album, film or play that is a great success

Word use: Definition 4 is also called a **smash-hit.**

smear

verb **1** to rub or spread: *to smear grease over the walls*
noun **2** a dirty mark or stain: *a smear of paint* **3** a slur on your good name

smell

verb **1** to sense through the nose **2** to give off an odour: *The dinner smells delicious.*
noun **3** the ability to sense odours through the nose **4** an odour or scent: *flowers with a strong smell*

Word building: Other verb forms are **I smelt** or **smelled, I have smelt** or **smelled, I am smelling**. | **smelly** *adjective* (**smellier, smelliest**)

smelt

verb to melt or refine ore in order to obtain metal: *to smelt iron*

Word building: **smelter** *noun* the place where this is done

smile

verb to show you are happy or amused by widening your mouth and turning it up at the corners

Word building: **smile** *noun*

smirk

verb to smile in a smug way that annoys people

Word building: **smirk** *noun*

smith

noun someone who makes things out of metal: *Blacksmiths work with iron, silversmiths with silver.*

Word building: **smithy** *noun* a blacksmith's workshop

smithereens

plural noun tiny pieces: *The cup smashed into smithereens.*

smock

noun a long loose shirt worn on top of your clothes to stop them getting dirty

Word building: **smocking** *noun* a sort of embroidery used on baby's clothes   **smock** *verb*

smog

noun a dirty cloud of smoke and fog

Word building: **smoggy** *adjective* (**smoggier, smoggiest**)
Word history: a blended or portmanteau word made from *smoke + fog*

smoke

noun **1** the cloud of gas and tiny particles given off when something burns: *Bushfires filled the air with smoke.* **2** a cigarette: *a packet of smokes*
verb **3** to give off smoke: *The chimney is smoking.* **4** to breathe in the smoke of a cigarette while holding it between your lips **5** to treat with wood smoke as a preservative: *to smoke meat*

Word building: **smoky** *adjective* (**smokier, smokiest**)

smokescreen

noun anything used to hide the truth or what you are really doing: *Your excuse was simply a smokescreen.*

smoking ceremony

noun an Aboriginal ceremony in which green leaves from local plants are burnt, creating smoke which is said to cleanse and heal the area, sometimes after someone has died

smooth

adjective **1** even and without bumps or lumps
Other words: **flat, flush, level, plane**
2 very pleasant in manner, especially when insincere: *a smooth talker*
Other words: **suave**
verb **3** to make even or level
Other words: **even, flatten, level**

Word building: **smoothly** *adverb*
smoothness *noun*

smorgasbord

noun a meal where you help yourself to a great variety of meats and salads

Word use: This word comes from a Swedish word meaning 'sandwich table'.

smother   (*rhymes with* brother)

verb **1** to choke by keeping out air: *to smother a fire with sand* | *Don't cover your head with a plastic bag because you might smother.* **2** to cover all over: *She smothered her face with make-up.* **3** to protect too closely: *Her parents smother her and never allow her to play outside.*

smoulder   (*rhymes with* folder)

verb to burn slowly giving off smoke but no flame

SMS   (*say* es em es)

noun **1** a service which allows you to key in a message on a mobile phone and send it to another mobile phone where someone else can read it on the screen **2** the coded forms of words used in such a system

smudge

noun a dirty mark or smear

Word building: **smudge** *verb*

smug

adjective very pleased with yourself: *a smug grin*

Word building: **smugly** *adverb*
Word history: from a Dutch word meaning 'neat'

smuggle

verb to carry secretly and illegally: *to smuggle rare birds out of the country*

Word building: **smuggler** *noun* **smuggling** *noun*

smut

noun **1** a smudge of soot or dirt **2** offensive or obscene talk

Word building: **smutty** *adjective* (**smuttier, smuttiest**)

snack

noun **1** a small quick meal: *a snack after school* **2** *Informal* something that is very easy to do: *That test was a snack.*

snag¹

noun **1** something sharp sticking out or lying on the bottom of a river **2** a problem or difficulty: *a snag in our plans*

Word building: **snag** *verb* (**snagged, snagging**)

snag²

noun *Informal* a sausage

snail

noun a small slow-moving animal with a soft body and a coiled shell, often found in gardens

snake

noun **1** a long scaly creature without legs which slithers silently along the ground *phrase* **2 snake in the grass**, someone who secretly does you harm

Word building: **snaky** *adjective* (**snakier, snakiest**) spiteful or angry **snake** *verb* to twist and wind like the body of a snake

snap

verb **1** to break with a sudden sharp sound: *to snap a biscuit in two | The rubber band snapped.* **2** to make a sudden biting movement: *The dog will snap if you tease it.* **3** to speak angrily and sharply *noun* **4** a sudden sharp sound or movement **5** an easy card game in which you try to be the first to call out when you see two matching cards *phrase* **6 snap up**, to grab quickly: *to snap up a bargain*

Word building: Other verb forms are **I snapped, I have snapped, I am snapping.** | **snappy** *adjective* (**snappier, snappiest**) quick or brisk **snap** *adjective* sudden: *a snap decision*

snapper

noun a large fish of warm seas which is good for eating

Word use: Another spelling is **schnapper**.

snapshot

noun an informal photograph taken quickly

snare (*rhymes with* hair)

noun a trap for catching birds and small animals

Word building: **snare** *verb*

snarl¹

verb to growl angrily or fiercely

Word building: **snarl** *noun*

snarl²

noun a tangle or knot

Word building: **snarl** *verb*

snatch

verb **1** to take hold of suddenly: *to snatch a purse* *noun* **2** a sudden grab **3** a scrap or small part: *to overhear snatches of conversation*

sneak

verb **1** to make a movement: *to sneak in the room* **2** to take slyly and quietly: *to sneak a chocolate* *noun* **3** someone mean who tells tales and can't be trusted

Word building: Other verb forms are **I sneaked, I have sneaked, I am sneaking.** | **sneaky** *adjective* (**sneakier, sneakiest**) **sneakily** *adverb*

sneaker

noun a rubber-soled shoe made of canvas

sneer

verb to say or look in a nasty mocking way Other words: **leer, smirk**

Word building: **sneer** *noun*

sneeze

verb **1** to have a sudden noisy explosion of air, mostly through your mouth, because of irritation in your nose *phrase* **2 not to be sneezed at**, *Informal* worth thinking about: *This offer is not to be sneezed at.*

Word building: **sneeze** *noun*

snicker

verb to laugh or giggle in a rather rude way: *She snickered at his silly mistake.*
Other words: **snigger**

Word building: **snicker** *noun*

sniff

verb to breathe in through the nose in a short sharp burst: *to sniff the air | to sniff with a cold*

Word building: **sniff** *noun*

sniffle

verb **1** to sniff continually because you have a cold or are trying not to cry
phrase **2 the sniffles**, a cold with a runny nose

snigger

verb to give a rather rude laugh or giggle which you try to hide: *to snigger at a dirty joke*
Other words: **snicker**

Word building: **snigger** *noun*

snip

verb to cut using small quick strokes of the scissors

Word building: Other forms are **I snipped, I have snipped, I am snipping.** | **snip** *noun*

sniper

noun someone who shoots from a place which is hidden or a long way from the target

Word building: **snipe** *verb*

snivel

verb to sniffle noisily while you are crying

Word building: Other forms are **I snivelled, I have snivelled, I am snivelling.**

snob

noun someone who looks down on people who are not wealthy, important or clever

Word building: **snobbery** *noun*   **snobbish** *adjective*

snooker

noun a game like billiards, played with balls of many colours

snoop

verb to creep around, prying into things

Word building: **snoopy** *adjective*

snooze

noun Informal a rest or short sleep

Word building: **snooze** *verb*

snore

verb to breathe with a loud rumbling noise while you're asleep

Word building: **snore** *noun*

snorkel

noun a tube that lets you breathe fresh air as you swim face downwards in the water

Word building: **snorkel** *verb* (**snorkelled, snorkelling**)
Word history: from a German word

snort

verb to force your breath out of your nose so that it makes a rough rumbling sound: *to snort with anger*

snout

noun the front part of an animal's face where the nose and jaws are
Other words: **muzzle**

snow

noun frozen rain drops which fall to the ground as tiny white flakes

Word building: **snowy** *adjective* white **snow** *verb*

snowball

noun **1** a pile of snow pressed into a ball
verb **2** to pile up at a great rate: *The work is snowballing.*

snowboard

noun a board for gliding over the snow, which looks like a surfboard because the person using it stands up on it

snowman

noun a human-like figure made of hard packed snow

Word building: The plural is **snowmen.**

snub

verb **1** to show dislike or contempt for, especially by ignoring
noun **2** an instance of this: *a deliberate snub*
Other words: **rebuff**
adjective **3** short and turned up at the tip: *a snub nose*

Word building: Other verb forms are **I snubbed, I have snubbed, I am snubbing.**

snuff

noun powdered tobacco used for sniffing

snug

adjective comfortable and warm: *Our strong tent was snug despite the rain.*

Word building: Other forms are **snugger**, **snuggest**.

snuggle

phrase **snuggle up**, to lie closely together for warmth or comfort: *The kittens snuggled up in their basket.*

so

adverb **1** in the way shown or described: *Do it so.* **2** as told or described: *Is that so?* **3** to that extent: *Do not walk so fast.* **4** very: *You are so kind.* **5** for this reason: *Bananas are nutritious and so you should eat them often.* **6** about that number or amount: *a day or so ago*
phrase **7 and so forth**, and the rest **8 just so**, in perfect order **9 so-so**, only fair: *I'm feeling so-so today.* **10 so that**, **a** with the result that **b** in order that

so/sew/sow Don't confuse **so** with **sew** or **sow**. To **sew** is to stitch something with a needle and thread.

To **sow**, rhyming with *go*, is to scatter seed on the ground. But a **sow**, rhyming with *cow*, is a female pig.

soak

verb **1** to lie or leave in liquid for a long time: *I like to soak in a bath after sport.* | *She soaked the clothes to loosen the dirt.* **2** to wet thoroughly
phrase **3 soak up**, to take in or absorb
Word building: **soak** *noun*

soap

noun a substance made out of fat, used for washing yourself or cleaning things
Word building: **soap** *verb* **soapy** *adjective*

soap opera

noun *Informal* a television series which tells a story about people's lives and problems, often in an over-emotional way

Word history: from the fact that soap manufacturers used to sponsor this type of entertainment

soar

verb **1** to fly upwards
Other words: **ascend, climb, mount, rise**
2 to fly at a great height hardly moving the wings: *The eagle soared over the valley.*
3 to rise to a great height: *Our hopes soared.* | *Prices are soaring.*
Other words: **climb, mount**

soar/saw/sore Don't confuse **soar** with **saw** or **sore**.

A **saw** is a cutting tool. **Saw** is also the past tense of the verb **see**, to take things in with your eyes or your mind.

If your leg is **sore**, it hurts or feels painful.

sob

verb **1** to cry making a gulping noise as you breathe **2** to speak while doing this: *She sobbed her words of pity.*

Word building: Other forms are **I sobbed**, **I have sobbed, I am sobbing**. | **sob** *noun*

sober

adjective **1** not drunk **2** quiet and serious: *The sad news put us in a sober mood.*

Word building: **sober** *verb* **sobriety** *noun*

soccer

noun a form of football played with a round ball in which the players, except for the goalkeeper, are not allowed to use their hands or arms to play the ball

sociable (*say* soh-shuh-buhl)

adjective friendly, or wanting to be with other people

Word building: **sociability** *noun* **sociableness** *noun* **sociably** *adverb*

social

adjective **1** having to do with friendliness: *Our tennis club is as much a social club as a sporting one.* **2** having to do with fashionable people: *a social page in a newspaper* **3** having to do with human society, or the way it is organised: *social problems* | *social status*
noun **4** a party or gathering: *a church social*

Word building: **socially** *adverb*

socialise (*say* soh-shuhl-uyz)

verb **1** to train or educate so as to live according to the customs of society **2** to be friendly and mix with others at a party

Word use: Another spelling is **socialize**.
Word building: **socialisation** *noun*

socialism (*say* soh-shuhl-iz-uhm)

noun the political belief that all industry and wealth should be owned and controlled by the people as a whole

Word use: Compare this with **capitalism** and **communism**.
Word building: **socialist** *noun*

society (*say* suh-<u>suy</u>-uh-tee)
noun **1** people as a whole: *human society* **2** people as a group in which there are divisions according to birth, education and occupation: *the middle class of society* **3** a group of people with a common interest: *a society of orchid growers* **4** companionship or company: *I enjoy your society.* **5** rich people and their activities: *Some people enjoy reading about society in the social columns of newspapers.*
Word building: The plural is **societies**.

sociology (*say* soh-see-<u>ol</u>-uh-jee)
noun the study of the development and organisation of human society
Word building: **sociologist** *noun*

sock¹
noun **1** a garment that you wear under a shoe, covering the foot and the ankle and sometimes reaching up to the knee
phrase **2 pull your socks up**, to make more effort

sock²
verb *Informal* to hit hard
Word building: **sock** *noun*

socket
noun **1** a hollow area which holds some part or thing: *an eye socket* **2** a device on the wall into which you plug an electric cord

sod
noun a square or oblong piece of grass which has been cut or torn out of a lawn or other turf

soda
noun **1** a chemical compound containing sodium used for various purposes: *caustic soda | baking soda* **2** a shortened form of **soda water** **3** a drink made with soda water, fruit juices and ice-cream
Word history: from an Arabic word

soda water
noun a fizzy drink made by filling water with bubbles of carbon dioxide

sodden
adjective soaked with a liquid: *sodden washing hanging in the rain*

sodium (*say* <u>soh</u>-dee-uhm)
noun a soft, silver-white, metallic element found in salt

sofa
noun a long couch with a back and two sides

soft
adjective **1** easily cut or pressed out of shape **2** smooth and pleasant to touch: *the soft fur of a kitten* **3** low in sound: *We could hardly hear her soft voice.* **4** not harsh or glaring: *soft light* **5** gentle or pitying: *She has a soft heart.* **6** not able to bear hardship: *He's too soft for a farmer's life.* **7** (of water) having a low level of salts from minerals, so that soap lathers easily in it
Word building: **soften** *verb* **softly** *adverb*

softball
noun a form of baseball played with a larger softer ball which is bowled underarm

soft drink
noun a drink which has no alcohol in it

software
noun a collection of programs used to control a computer

soggy
adjective **1** soaked or thoroughly wet: *soggy ground* **2** damp and heavy like bread when it is not cooked enough
Word building: Other forms are **soggier**, **soggiest**.

soil¹
noun ground or earth, especially of the kind plants can grow in

soil²
verb to make or become dirty or stained
Word building: **soiled** *adjective*

solar
adjective **1** having to do with the sun: *a solar eclipse* **2** operated or produced by the heat of the sun: *solar energy*

solar heating
noun the use of energy from the sun to provide heating for air or water in a building

solar hot water panel
noun a device which uses the energy from the sun to heat water for a building

solar panel
noun a device which uses energy from the sun and turns it into electricity

solar system

noun the sun together with all the planets, moons and so on which revolve around it

solder

noun an alloy which can be melted easily and used to join metals together

Word building: **solder** verb

soldier

noun **1** someone who serves in an army **2** someone who serves any cause: a soldier against poverty
verb **3** to serve as a soldier
phrase **4 soldier on**, to continue doing something you have started, even though it may have become difficult

Word building: **soldierly** adjective

sole¹

adjective **1** being the only one: I am the sole remaining member of my family **2** not shared: the sole right to sell a property

sole²

noun the underneath or bottom of your foot or shoe

sole³

noun any of a number of types of flat-bodied fishes with both eyes on the upper side

sole/soul Don't confuse **sole** with **soul**. Your **soul** is the spiritual part of you, contrasted with your body.

solemn (say sol-uhm)

adjective **1** sincere: a solemn promise
Other words: **earnest, serious**
2 causing a grave mood: solemn music
Other words: **sombre**
3 marked by formality or ritual: a solemn ceremony

Word building: **solemnity** noun (**solemnities**) **solemnise** verb **solemnly** adverb

solenoid (say soh-luh-noyd, sol-uh-noyd)

noun a coil or wire in which a magnetic field is set up when electricity flows through it

solicitor (say suh-lis-uh-tuh)

noun a lawyer who advises clients and prepares cases for a barrister to present in court

solid

adjective **1** having length, breadth and thickness: a solid shape **2** having the inside filled: a solid rubber ball **3** consisting only of: solid gold
noun **4** something solid **5 solids**, food that is not in liquid form: The baby is almost ready to start eating solids.

Word building: **solidify** verb (**solidified, solidifying**) to make or become solid **solidity** noun **solidly** adverb

solidarity (say sol-uh-da-ruh-tee)

noun a united front presented by members of a group with strongly-held common ideas and interests

Word use: The more usual word is **unity**.

soliloquy (say suh-lil-uh-kwee)

noun a speech you make when you are alone or when you are pretending to be alone, such as in a play

Word building: The plural is **soliloquies**.

solitary (say sol-uh-tree)

adjective **1** quite alone **2** being the only one: a solitary exception

solitude (say sol-uh-tyoohd)

noun a state of being alone: to enjoy a brief time of solitude

solo

noun **1** a musical performance by one person
adjective **2** performed or done alone: a solo item | a solo flight
adverb **3** alone: He flew solo.

soloist (say soh-loh-uhst)

noun someone who performs a solo: The conductor hushed the orchestra as the soloist began playing.

solstice

noun one of the two times each year when the sun is furthest away from the equator and the longest or shortest day occurs. The first comes on about June 21, when the sun enters the sign of Cancer (the winter solstice) and the other comes on about December 22, when the sun enters the sign of Capricorn (the summer solstice).

soluble   (*say* <u>sol</u>-yuh-buhl)
adjective **1** able to be dissolved: *Sugar is soluble in water.* **2** able to be solved: *a soluble problem*

Word use: The opposite is **insoluble**.
Word building: **solubility** *noun*

solution
noun **1** the solving of, or answer to a problem **2** a substance which is made up of one chemical, usually a solid, spread perfectly throughout another chemical, usually a liquid: *Sugar can be dissolved in tea to make a solution.*

solve
verb to explain or find the answer to: *He solved the mystery.*

solvent
noun **1** a liquid substance that can dissolve other substances in it: *Water is a solvent for sugar.*
adjective **2** having enough money to be able to pay your debts

Word building: **solvency** *noun* the ability to pay your debts

sombre   (*say* <u>som</u>-buh)
adjective gloomily dark or dull: *the sombre interior of the deserted castle* / *sombre clothes*

sombrero   (*say* som-<u>brair</u>-roh)
noun a broad-brimmed hat worn in Spain, Mexico and some other countries

Word building: The plural is **sombreros**.
Word history: from a Spanish word meaning 'shade'

some
adjective **1** being a person or thing that has not been named: *some poor woman* **2** certain: *some friends of mine* / *some changes were made* **3** *Informal* great or important: *That was some storm!*

some/sum Don't confuse **some** with **sum**. A **sum** is a calculation in arithmetic:
   am doing my sums now
It is also an amount of money:
   That is a big sum to pay out.

somehow
adverb in some way that is not made clear: *I've got to get home somehow.*

someone
pronoun a person or any person: *He's someone who you can count on.* / *At last I can see someone I know.* / *Is someone there?*

Word use: Another word for this is **somebody**.

somersault   (*say* <u>sum</u>-uh-solt)
noun a gymnastic movement in which you roll completely, heels over head

Word building: **somersault** *verb*

something
pronoun **1** a certain thing that has not been named
noun **2** an important or valuable person or thing: *Your singing is really something.*

sometimes
adverb now and then, or at times: *Sometimes I think I'm the only one who really cares.*

somewhere
adverb **1** in or at some place that is not mentioned, or not known: *Somewhere over the rainbow.* **2** at some point in time: *The accident happened somewhere between three o'clock and five o'clock.*

son
noun **1** the male child of someone **2** a man looked upon as having been affected by a particular thing: *a son of the land*

sonar   (*say* <u>soh</u>-nah)
noun a device for finding depth under water by measuring the time it takes to receive an echo from a sound

sonata   (*say* suh-<u>nah</u>-tuh)
noun a musical composition usually for one instrument accompanied by a piano

song
noun **1** a short musical composition with words **2** musical sounds produced by birds
phrase **3 for a song**, at a very low price

sonic
adjective **1** having to do with sound waves **2** having to do with the speed of sound

son-in-law
noun the husband of your daughter

Word building: The plural is **sons-in-law**.

sonnet
noun a poem of fourteen lines in which the lines have to rhyme in a certain way

sonorous   (say son-uh-ruhs)
adjective sounding low, loud and rich: a sonorous voice
Word use: The more usual word is **deep**.
Word building: **sonority** noun

sook   (rhymes with book)
noun someone who is shy, timid or cowardly
Word use: This is mostly used about children.
Word building: **sooky** adjective (**sookier, sookiest**)

soon
adverb **1** within a short time **2** quickly or promptly: You came too soon.

soot   (rhymes with foot)
noun the black substance which sticks to the inside of a chimney when coal, wood, oil or other fuels are burnt
Word building: **sooty** adjective (**sootier, sootiest**)

soothe
verb **1** to calm or comfort: He soothed the frightened child.
Other words: **pacify, quiet, quieten**
2 to relieve or lessen: to soothe pain
Other words: **allay, alleviate, ease**
Word building: **soothing** adjective

sophisticated   (say suh-fis-tuh-kay-tuhd)
adjective **1** wise and experienced in the interests and pleasures of the world **2** intricate or complex: sophisticated machinery
Word building: **sophistication** noun

soporific   (say sop-uh-rif-ik)
adjective causing sleep or sleepiness

sopping
adjective very wet

soppy
adjective Informal too sentimental: a soppy love story
Word building: Other forms are **soppier, soppiest**. | **soppily** adverb **soppiness** noun

soprano   (say suh-prah-noh)
noun **1** the range of notes which can be sung by a woman or boy with a high voice **2** a woman or boy who sings in this range
Word use: **soprano** is the highest range of singing voices, with **alto** next below.
Word building: The plural is **sopranos**. | **soprano** adjective: a soprano cornet

sorbet   (say saw-bay, saw-buht)
noun a frozen dessert made with fruit and egg-whites, often used to refresh your mouth between courses of a meal

sorcery   (say saw-suh-ree)
noun magic, especially black magic using evil spirits
Word building: **sorcerer** noun   **sorceress** noun

sordid
adjective **1** morally mean or nasty: a sordid way of life **2** dirty or filthy: sordid surroundings
Word building: **sordidness** noun

sore
adjective **1** painful or hurting
Other words: **aching, sensitive, tender**
2 Informal annoyed or offended: What are you sore about?
Word building: **sore** noun

sore/saw/soar Don't confuse **sore** with **saw** or **soar**.
A **saw** is a cutting tool with sharp teeth on a thin blade. **Saw** is also the past tense of the verb **see**, to take things in with your eyes or your mind:
We saw your photo in the paper.
To **soar** is to fly upwards, or to rise to a great height:
Jets soar into the air.
House prices are about to soar.

sorrow
noun grief, sadness or the feeling of being sorry
Word building: **sorrowful** adjective

sorry
adjective **1** feeling sad because you have done something wrong
Other words: **contrite, penitent, regretful, remorseful, repentant**
2 feeling pity
Other words: **sympathetic**
Word building: Other forms are **sorrier, sorriest**.

sort

noun **1** a particular kind or type: *Cod are a sort of fish.*
verb **2** to arrange or group according to type or kind
phrase **3 of sorts**, of a kind that is neither good nor bad: *He is a friend of sorts.* **4 out of sorts**, not in good health or in a good humour **5 sort of**, in some way: *I sort of hoped he would come.*

SOS   (*say* es oh <u>es</u>)

noun an urgent call for help: *The ship sent an SOS by radio.*

Word history: probably chosen because the Morse code for these letters is clear and easy, but some people say the letters stand for 'Save Our Souls'

soufflé   (*say* <u>sooh</u>-flay)

noun a light baked dish, usually with fish or cheese to give it flavour, made fluffy with beaten egg-whites

Word history: from French, which is why it has an accent over the 'e'

soul

noun **1** the unseen or spiritual part of a person believed to survive after you die **2** human being: *She's a kind soul.* **3** another word for **soul music**

soul/sole Don't confuse **soul** with **sole**, which is the underneath part of your foot.

soul music

noun a type of modern African-American blues music with songs about emotions and personal experiences

Word use: Another word for this is **soul**.

sound¹

noun **1** something heard as a result of vibrations in the air reaching your ear
verb **2** to make a sound: *The trumpet sounded.* **3** to cause to make a sound: *Sound the trumpets.* **4** to give a certain feeling when heard or read: *That sounds strange.*

sound²

adjective **1** healthy or in good condition: *a sound heart* **2** unbroken or deep: *sound sleep* **3** reliable or good: *sound advice*
phrase **4 sound as a bell**, in perfect condition

sound³

verb **1** to measure or try the depth of by letting down a lead weight on the end of a line
phrase **2 sound out**, to try by indirect ways to find the feelings of: *Sound her out about going for a swim.*

sound⁴

noun a narrow stretch of water joining two larger bodies of water or between an island and the mainland

sound system

noun a machine that consists of a CD player, tape deck, radio, and so on

soundtrack

noun **1** the strip at the side of a cinema film which carries the sound recording **2** such a recording transferred to a CD or tape

soup

noun **1** a liquid food flavoured with meat, fish or vegetables
phrase **2 in the soup**, *Informal* in trouble

Word history: from a French word meaning 'soup' or 'broth'

sour

adjective **1** having an acid taste such as that of lemons
Other words: **astringent, bitter, sharp, tart**
2 cross or irritable: *He's in a sour mood today.*
Other words: **disagreeable, nasty, unpleasant**
Word building: **sour** *verb* **sourish** *adjective*

source

noun the place, thing or person from which something comes: *The Murray River has its source in the Snowy Mountains. | That book was the source of my information. | He is the source of that rumour.*
Other words: **beginning, origin, start**

source/sauce Don't confuse **source** with **sauce**, which is a thick cooked liquid used to flavour food, such as *tomato sauce.*

south

noun the direction which is to your left when you face the setting sun in the west

Word use: The opposite direction is **north**.
Word building: **south** *adverb* **south** *adjective* **southern** *adjective*

Southern Cross

noun the constellation you can see in the southern sky whose four chief stars are in the shape of a cross

souvenir (*say* sooh-vuh-<u>near</u>)

noun something you keep as a memory of a place or event

souvlaki (*say* soohv-<u>lah</u>-kee)

plural noun a Greek dish of diced lamb and vegetables cooked on skewers

sovereign (*say* <u>sov</u>-ruhn)

noun **1** a king or queen
Other words: **monarch**
adjective **2** having highest rank, power or authority

Word building: **sovereignty** *noun*

sow¹ (*rhymes with* go)

verb **1** to scatter in the earth for growth: *to sow wheat seeds* **2** to scatter seeds over: *to sow a field with wheat*

Word building: Other forms are **I sowed, I have sown** or **sowed, I am sowing.**

sow² (*rhymes with* how)

noun an adult female pig

Word use: The male is a **boar** and the young is a **piglet.**

sow/so/sew Don't confuse **sow** with **so** or **sew.**
So means 'therefore'.
To **sew** is to stitch something with a needle and thread.

soybean

noun a kind of plant seed which can be eaten as a bean or grown for its oil

Word use: This is also called **soy** or **soya bean.**

soy sauce

noun a dark brown sauce that tastes very salty, used in Chinese cooking

spa

noun **1** a place where there is a flow of mineral water from the earth **2** a bath or swimming pool which has heated, bubbly water pumped into it

space

noun **1** the continuous openness in which everything exists: *There is space all around us.* **2** the space outside the earth's atmosphere: *to send a rocket into space* **3** a part or area of space: *This table takes up a lot of space.*

Other words: **room**
4 the distance between things: *The trees were planted at equal spaces apart.*
5 a blank area on a surface: *We put a space between each word when we write.*
Other words: **gap**
6 a period of time: *He arrived after a space of two hours.*
Other words: **span**
verb **7** to arrange with spaces in between: *Space yourselves so that you have room to swing your arms.*

Word use: Definition 2 is also called **outer space.**

spacecraft

noun any vehicle that can travel through space

spaceship

noun a vehicle that can travel to outer space

space shuttle

noun a spaceship that carries people and equipment between earth and a satellite and which can land and be used again

spacious

adjective having a lot of space: *a spacious house*
Other words: **open, roomy**

Word building: **spaciousness** *noun*

spade¹

noun a tool for digging, with a long handle and a metal blade that you push into the ground with your foot

spade²

noun a black shape like an upside-down heart with a stem, used on playing cards

spaghetti (*say* spuh-<u>get</u>-ee)

noun a food made from flour, water and salt, formed into long thin strips and cooked by boiling

spam

noun emails sent to large numbers of people, often advertising things that people are not interested in

span

noun **1** the distance between the two furthest edges or ends of something: *the span of a bridge | the span of your hand* **2** the full stretch of anything: *Humans have a longer life span than animals.*
verb **3** to stretch over or across: *The bridge spans the river.*

Word building: Other verb forms are
I spanned, I have spanned, I am spanning.

spangle

noun a small piece of something that
glitters: *an evening dress covered with
spangles*

Word building: **spangled** *adjective*

spaniel

noun a kind of dog with a long silky coat
and drooping ears

spank

verb to hit as a punishment, usually with
the open hand

Word building: **spank** *noun*   **spanking** *noun*

spanner

noun a tool for gripping and turning
something, such as a nut on a bolt

spar¹

noun a strong pole, such as a mast on a
ship

spar²

verb to punch lightly or make punching
movements: *The boxers sparred at each other
for practice.*

Word building: Other forms are **I sparred,
I have sparred, I am sparring.** | **spar** *noun*

spare   *(rhymes with* hair*)*

verb **1** to stop yourself from destroying
or hurting: *The king spared his enemy's
life.* **2** to show consideration for: *Please
spare my feelings.* **3** to part with or let go:
Can you spare a few dollars?
adjective **4** extra: *a spare tyre* **5** free for
extra use: *spare time* **6** lean or thin: *a spare
physique*
noun **7** something that is extra: *This light
bulb is blown and we haven't a spare.*

spark

noun **1** a tiny piece of burning material
thrown up by a fire **2** a sudden letting
out of electricity, usually with a flash of
light
Other words: **flare, flash, flicker, sparkle**
3 a small showing of something: *a spark of
intelligence*
verb **4** to send out sparks
Other words: **flare, flash, flicker, sparkle**
5 to set going: *Your speech has sparked a lot
of interest.*
Other words: **initiate**

sparkle

verb **1** to burn or shine with little flashes
of light
Other words: **gleam, glint, glisten, glitter,
twinkle**
2 to be lively or brilliant: *The conversation
sparkled.*

Word building: **sparkle** *noun*

spark plug

noun a part in an engine that gives out an
electric spark which sets fire to the fuel in
each cylinder

sparrow

noun a small brown bird, common in many
parts of the world

sparse

adjective thinly spread out or scattered: *a
sparse population*

Word use: The more usual word is **scattered.**
Word building: **sparsely** *adverb*
sparseness *noun*   **sparsity** *noun*

spasm

noun **1** a sudden uncontrolled movement
of your muscles **2** a sudden short burst
of activity or feeling: *to work in spasms* / *a
spasm of rage*

Word building: **spasmodic** *adjective*

spastic

noun someone who is partly paralysed
because of a kind of brain damage

spate

noun a sudden pouring out: *a spate of
words*

Word use: The more usual word is **flood.**

spatial   *(say* spay-shuhl*)*

adjective having to do with space: *That
painter has a good spatial sense.*

spatula   *(say* spat-chuh-luh*)*

noun a tool with a flat bendable blade,
used for mixing or spreading such things as
paint or food

spawn

noun a mass of eggs given out by fish and
other water creatures

Word history: from a Latin word meaning
'expand'

speak

verb **1** to give out the sounds of words in an ordinary voice **2** to have a conversation or tell by speaking **3** to give a speech or lecture **4** to be able to use a particular language: *Can you speak Italian?*
Word building: Other forms are **I spoke, I have spoken, I am speaking**.

speaker

noun **1** someone who speaks, especially before an audience **2 the Speaker**, the person who controls the meeting of a house of parliament

spear

noun a weapon which consists of a long pole with a sharp pointed end
Word building: **spear** *verb*

spear gun

noun a gun that throws out a spear, used in underwater fishing

special

adjective **1** of a particular or distinct kind: *a special bus for schoolchildren | a new car with special fittings* **2** more important than or different from what is ordinary or usual: *special circumstances*
Other words: **exceptional**
noun **3** something which is special, particularly something sold at a special cheap price
Word building: **specially** *adverb* particularly

specialise

verb to concentrate on a special kind of work or study: *She specialises in Australian history.*
Word use: Another spelling is **specialize**.

specialist

noun someone who studies or is good at a particular subject or area of work, particularly a doctor: *to go and see a skin specialist*

speciality   (*say* spesh-ee-<u>al</u>-uh-tee)

noun another word for **specialty**

specialty   (*say* <u>spesh</u>-uhl-tee)

noun a particular kind of study, work or product that someone specialises in: *The surgeon's specialty is kidneys. | This restaurant's specialty is spaghetti.*

species   (*say* <u>spee</u>-seez, <u>spee</u>-sheez)

noun one of the groups into which animals and plants are divided according to their characteristics
Word building: The plural is **species**.

specific   (*say* spuh-<u>sif</u>-ik)

adjective **1** particular: *I want the specific kind of paper I mentioned, not something similar.* **2** giving definite details: *a specific description*
Word building: **specifically** *adverb*

specification

(*say* spes-uh-fuh-<u>kay</u>-shuhn)
noun **1** the act of specifying: *the specification of your requirements* **2** an item in a detailed description of the measurements and materials to be used for something you plan to make: *the builder's specifications for the extensions to our house*

specify   (*say* <u>spes</u>-uh-fuy)

verb to state with definite details: *You must specify how many chairs you will need.*
Word use: The more usual word is **say**.
Word building: Other forms are **I specified, I have specified, I am specifying**.

specimen   (*say* <u>spes</u>-uh-muhn)

noun a single thing or part taken as being typical of a whole group or mass: *This poem is a specimen of my work. | The doctor took a specimen of my blood for tests.*
Word use: The more usual word is **sample**.

speck

noun a very small spot or bit: *a brown dress with specks of green | a speck of dust*
Word building: **specked** *adjective*

speckle

noun **1** a small spot or mark
verb **2** to mark with speckles: *Dust speckled the coat.*
Word building: **speckled** *adjective*

spectacle

noun **1** anything seen, especially something that draws your attention: *The storm made a great spectacle.* **2** a large public show or display **3 spectacles**, another name for **glasses**

spectacular

adjective unusual to look at, in a very exciting and impressive way: *a spectacular performance | a spectacular view of the sea | The fireworks were spectacular.*
Word building: **spectacularly** *adverb*

spectator

noun someone who watches something: *spectators at a football game*
Other words: **observer, onlooker, viewer**

spectre (*say* spek-tuh)

noun another name for a **ghost** (definition 1)
Word building: **spectral** *adjective*

spectrum

noun **1** the band of colours which is produced when white light is split up **2** a range of ideas, beliefs or types: *the spectrum of public opinion*
Word history: from a Latin word meaning 'appearance' or 'form'

speculate

verb to have an opinion without certain knowledge: *She speculated on her chances of winning.*
Word use: The more usual word is **think**.
Word building: **speculation** *noun* **speculative** *adjective* **speculator** *noun*

speech

noun **1** the ability to speak **2** a talk given in front of an audience: *The principal made a long speech at assembly.* **3** the way someone speaks: *Your speech is not clear enough.*

speed

noun **1** quickness in moving, going, or doing something
verb **2** to move or make move quickly: *Harry sped on his way.* | *to speed plans* **3** to drive a vehicle faster than is allowed by law
phrase **4 speed up**, to go or do more quickly
Word building: Other verb forms are **I sped** or **speeded, I have sped** or **speeded, I am speeding**. | **speedy** *adjective* (**speedier, speediest**) **speedily** *adverb* **speedster** *noun*

speedometer

noun an instrument on a vehicle that shows how fast it is travelling

spell¹

verb **1** to say or write the letters of a word in order: *She can spell well.* **2** to be the letters that make up a word: *The letters 'm-a-t' spell 'mat'.* **3** to mean: *That noise in the engine spells trouble.*

Word building: Other forms are **I spelt** or **spelled, I have spelt** or **spelled, I am spelling**. | **spelling** *noun*

spell²

noun **1** a group of words that is supposed to have magic power: *The witch chanted a spell.* **2** a fascinating power: *You have me in your spell.*

spell³

noun **1** a period of work: *I will take a spell at digging now.* **2** a short period of anything: *a spell of cold weather* **3** a period of rest: *You should take a spell or you will get tired.*

spend

verb **1** to pay out: *I spent a lot of money today.* **2** to pass: *They spent the holidays at the beach.* **3** to use up: *I have spent all my energy.*
Word building: Other forms are **I spent, I have spent, I am spending**. | **spender** *noun*

spendthrift

noun someone who spends their money wastefully

sperm

noun one of the cells produced by a male that can join with an egg or ovum to develop into a new individual

spew

verb *Informal* to vomit

sphere (*say* sfear)

noun **1** something completely round in shape, such as a ball or a planet **2** an area of activity: *He works in the sphere of education.*
Word building: **spherical** *adjective*

spice

noun **1** a substance made from a plant which is used to flavour or preserve food: *Pepper and cinnamon are spices.* **2** something that adds interest: *You need to give your story some spice.*
Word building: **spicy** *adjective* (**spicier, spiciest**) **spiciness** *noun*
Word history: from a Latin word meaning 'species'

spider

noun an eight-legged creature, like an insect but without wings, which usually spins a web and is sometimes venomous
Word building: **spidery** *adjective*

spike¹

noun **1** a sharp pointed piece or part: *a fence with spikes on it* **2 spikes,** a pair of shoes with sharp metal pieces on the bottom, worn by runners or other athletes to stop them slipping

Word building: **spiky** *adjective* (**spikier, spikiest**)   **spike** *verb*

spike²

noun the part of a cereal plant, such as wheat, that contains the grains

spill

verb **1** to run or fall from a container: *The milk is spilling over.* **2** to make run or fall from a container: *I have spilt the cereal.*

Word building: Other forms are **I spilt** or **spilled, I have spilt** or **spilled, I am spilling.** | **spill** *noun*   **spillage** *noun*

spin

verb **1** to make thread by twisting and winding fibres, such as cotton or wool **2** to form by producing a long moist thread from the body: *Spiders spin webs.* **3** to turn or make turn around and around very fast: *The top is spinning.* | *She spun a coin.* *noun* **4** a spinning or whirling movement **5** a short quick journey: *Let's take the car for a spin.* *phrase* **6 spin out,** to make last a long time: *to spin out a story*

Word building: Other verb forms are **I spun, I have spun, I am spinning.** | **spinner** *noun* **spinning** *noun*

spinach   (*say* spin-ich)

noun a plant with large green leaves which is eaten as a vegetable

Word history: from an Arabic word

spindle

noun **1** a rod used to twist or wind the thread in spinning **2** a part of a machine which turns round or on which something turns

spindly

adjective long and thin: *a spindly plant*

spin-dry

verb to dry by spinning in a machine so that the moisture is taken out: *to spin-dry clothes*

Word building: Other forms are **I spin-dried, I have spin-dried, I am spin-drying.** | **spin-drier** *noun*   **spin-dryer** *noun*

spine

noun **1** the column of bones in your back **2** a thorn on a plant **3** a stiff pointed part on an animal, such as on an echidna **4** the part of a book's cover that holds the front and back together

Word building: **spiny** *adjective* (**spinier, spiniest**) having spines or leaves shaped like spines   **spinal** *adjective* having to do with your spine

spinifex   (*say* spin-uh-feks)

noun a kind of spiny grass

spinnaker   (*say* spin-uh-kuh)

noun a large triangular sail

spinning wheel

noun a machine for spinning consisting of a spindle turned around by a large wheel driven by your hand or foot

spin-off

noun something useful that has come into being as a result of something larger or more important: *The non-stick frying pan was a spin-off of space research.*

spinster

noun a woman who has not been married

spiny anteater

noun another name for an **echidna**

spiral

noun **1** a curve that winds around and around away from a centre: *a spring in the shape of a spiral* *verb* **2** to move in the shape of a spiral: *Smoke spiralled from the chimney*

Word building: Other verb forms are **it spiralled, it has spiralled, it is spiralling.** | **spiral** *adjective*: *a spiral staircase*

spire

noun a tall pointed part of a building, usually on a roof or tower: *the spire of a church*

spirit

noun **1** another name for **soul 2** a supernatural being **3** temper or character: *a person with a generous spirit* **4** feeling or mood: *team spirit* | *the spirit of Christmas* **5** general meaning or intention: *the spirit of an agreement* **6** lively courage: *I like Chris for her spirit.* **7 spirits, a** the state of your mind: *The principal seems in high spirits today.* **b** strong alcoholic drink *verb* **8** to carry mysteriously or secretly: *The culprit was spirited away by his friends before the police arrived.*

Word building: **spirited** *adjective* showing lively courage

spiritual

adjective **1** having to do with or interested in the spirit rather than the body: *a spiritual attitude | a spiritual person* **2** having to do with holy, religious, or supernatural things: *a spiritual leader*

Word use: The opposite of definition 1 is **worldly**.

Word building: **spirituality** *noun*

spit¹

verb **1** to force out saliva from your mouth: *Don't spit on the footpath.* **2** to send out from your mouth: *She spat her lolly out.* **3** to fall in light scattered drops: *It is spitting with rain.* **4** to make a noise like spitting: *Fat was spitting in the pan.*
noun **5** saliva, especially when spat out

Word building: Other verb forms are **I spat, I have spat, I am spitting.**

spit²

noun **1** a sharp pointed rod which is pushed through meat for roasting it over a fire or grilling it in an oven **2** a narrow area of land jutting out into the water

spite

noun **1** a bad-tempered wish to annoy or hurt someone else: *He had no reason for hitting her except spite.*
Other words: **malice**
phrase **2 in spite of**, without taking notice of: *We will play in spite of the bad weather.*

Word building: **spite** *verb* **spiteful** *adjective*

splash

verb **1** to wet by scattering with drops of liquid or mud **2** to fall in drops: *Rain splashed on the window.* **3** to make fly about in drops: *The baby splashed the bath water.*
noun **4** the act or sound of splashing **5** a mark made by splashing **6** a patch of colour or light: *a splash of red on a white background*
phrase **7 make a splash**, to be widely noticed: *She made a splash in her new clothes.*

Word building: **splashy** *adjective*

splendid

adjective **1** magnificent or grand: *a splendid sight | a splendid victory*

Other words: **glorious, impressive, magnificent**
2 extremely good: *a splendid performance*
Other words: **admirable, brilliant, excellent, fabulous, fantastic, fine, great, marvellous, wonderful**

Word building: **splendidly** *adverb* **splendour** *noun*

splice

verb to join by twisting threads together or overlapping timber: *to splice ropes | to splice pieces of wood*

splint

noun a thin piece of something hard and straight, such as wood, fastened on both sides of a broken or injured bone to hold it in position

splinter

noun a long, thin, sharp piece broken off from something hard, such as wood, metal or glass

Word building: **splinter** *verb*

split

verb **1** to separate or break apart, especially from end to end: *The ends of my hair are splitting. | He split the apple in two.* **2** to divide up in any way **3** to divide in opinion or feeling: *The argument split the family.*
noun **4** the act of splitting **5** a break or division caused by splitting: *a split in a dress | a split in public opinion*
phrase **6 split up**, to stop living together or stop being friends **7 the splits**, an exercise in which you spread your legs apart along the floor until they stretch out at right angles to your body

Word building: Other verb forms are **I split, I have split, I am splitting.**

splurge

verb to spend extravagantly or wastefully: *She splurged all her money on a taxi.*

Word building: **splurge** *noun*
Word history: a blended or portmanteau word made from *splash+ surge*

splutter

verb **1** to talk quickly or in a confused way: *He spluttered with rage.* **2** to make a popping noise, as boiling fat does

Word building: **splutter** *noun* **splutterer** *noun*

spoil

verb **1** to damage or ruin
Other words: **destroy, impair, wreck**
2 to damage the nature or character of by giving way to demands or temper: *to spoil a child*
Other words: **indulge, pamper**
3 to go bad: *The food will spoil if you don't put it away.*
Other words: **rot**
Word building: Other forms are **I spoiled** or **spoilt, I have spoiled** or **spoilt, I am spoiling**.

spoke

noun one of the rods, bars or wires that connect the rim of a wheel to the hub or centre, as on a bicycle or steering wheel

spokesperson

noun someone who speaks on behalf of someone else
Word building: The plural is **spokespersons** or **spokespeople**. | **spokeswoman** *noun* (**spokeswomen**) **spokesman** *noun* (**spokesmen**)

sponge (*say* spunj)

noun **1** a material with lots of holes for soaking up liquid, used especially for wiping and cleaning **2** a kind of sea creature whose rubbery absorbent skeleton can be used for washing and cleaning **3** a light cake made from well-beaten eggs, flour and sugar
verb **4** to wash, wipe and clean with a sponge **5** *Informal* to live at someone else's expense: *Wayne sponged on his uncle.*
Word building: **spongy** *adjective*

sponsor

noun a person or group who supports someone or something, often with money
Word building: **sponsor** *verb* **sponsorship** *noun*

spontaneous

adjective happening naturally and, often, unexpectedly: *spontaneous growth | spontaneous applause*
Word building: **spontaneity** *noun* **spontaneously** *adverb*

spoof

noun *Informal* a humorous imitation: *He did a spoof of the prime minister.*
Word building: **spoof** *verb* **spoofer** *noun*

spook

noun *Informal* a ghost: *The attic is full of spooks.*

Word building: **spook** *verb* **spooked** *adjective* **spooky** *adjective*

spool

noun a cylinder or bobbin on which something, such as wire, thread or film, is wound

spoon

noun a utensil with a rounded end attached to a handle, which is used for stirring or lifting food and other things

spoor

noun the track left by a wild animal

sporadic (*say* spuh-<u>rad</u>-ik)

adjective irregular and not very frequent: *Apart from the sporadic rain the weather was marvellous.*
Other words: **infrequent, intermittent, irregular, occasional**
Word building: **sporadically** *adverb*

spore

noun a seed or germ cell

sporran

noun the pouch of fur worn by Scottish Highlanders at the front of the kilt
Word history: from a Gaelic word, a language of the ancient Celtic people and their modern ancestors in Ireland and Scotland

sport

noun **1** something done for pleasure or exercise, usually needing some bodily skill **2** playful joking: *It was meant in sport.* **3** someone who is fair-minded or good-natured: *She's a good sport.*
Word building: **sporting** *adjective* **sportive** *adjective* **sporty** *adjective*

sports

noun athletics or other similar sporting activities
Word building: **sports** *adjective*: *sports day | sports coat* **sportsman** *noun* **sportswoman** *noun*

sports car

noun a fast car, usually a two-seater

sports store

noun a shop that sells the clothing and equipment used in sport

spot

noun **1** a small, usually round, mark: *There's a spot on your collar.* **2** a place: *We found a nice spot to have a picnic.*

verb **3** to mark or stain: *This material spots easily.* | *You have spotted your jacket.* **4** to see or notice: *I couldn't spot you in the crowd.*

phrase **5 on the spot, a** instantly: *I bought it on the spot.* **b** in an awkward situation: *Your question put me on the spot.*

Word building: Other verb forms are **I spotted, I have spotted, I am spotting.** | **spotted** *adjective* **spotty** *adjective*

spotlight
noun a lamp with a strong narrow beam, such as used in the theatre or attached to cars

Word building: **spotlight** *verb* (**spotlit** or **spotlighted, spotlighting**)

spouse (*rhymes with* house)
noun your husband or wife

spout
noun the tube or liplike part of a container from which water or other contents are poured

Word building: **spout** *verb* to pour out

sprain
verb to twist and bruise, without actually putting out of place or breaking: *I sprained my ankle.*

Word building: **sprain** *noun*

sprawl
verb **1** to lie or sit with your limbs stretched out: *He sprawled all over the couch.*
Other words: **loll, lounge, recline, repose, stretch out**

2 to spread out in an untidy or careless way: *Her writing sprawled all over the page.*

Word building: **sprawl** *noun*

spray¹
noun a fine stream of droplets, such as one thrown by a wave or jet of water

Word building: **spray** *verb*

spray²
noun a single stem, or a small bunch of flowers: *She had a spray of jasmine pinned to her dress.*

spread (*rhymes with* bed)
verb **1** to extend, or stretch out: *The rain is spreading south.* | *She spread the cloth on the table.* **2** to scatter, or send around: *to spread germs* | *to spread the news*
Other words: **distribute, pass on**

3 to put on in a thin layer: *to spread butter*
Other words: **apply, smear**

4 to cover with a thin layer: *She spread the bread with jam.*
Other words: **coat, smear**

noun **5** anything which is spread on bread, such as jam or soft cheese **6** *Informal* a large meal or feast

Word building: Other verb forms are **I spread, I have spread, I am spreading.**

spree
noun **1** a lively time of fun
2 an extravagant outing: *a shopping spree*

sprightly
adjective lively and merry: *a sprightly tune*

spring
verb **1** to move or leap upwards with sudden energy: *to spring into the air* | *The dog springs into her arms.*
Other words: **bounce, bound, jump**

2 to arise or happen: *Farms are springing up on the city's outskirts.*
Other words: **appear, develop, emerge, materialise**

3 to come: *All her troubles sprang from that one mistake.*
Other words: **originate**

noun **4** a leap or pounce
Other words: **bounce, bound, jump**

5 a coil of wire which bounces back when it is stretched
Other words: **spiral**

6 the season of the year after winter and before summer, when the weather starts to get warmer and new leaves and flowers begin to grow **7** the ability to bounce back: *The mattress hasn't much spring left.*
Other words: **bounce, elasticity, resilience**
8 a flow of water from the ground: *a hot spring*

Word building: Other verb forms are **I sprang** or **sprung, I have sprung, I am springing.** | **spring** *adjective* **springiness** *noun* **springy** *adjective*

springboard
noun a board with a lot of bounce in it, used for diving or vaulting

spring-clean
verb to clean thoroughly, as people used to do each spring: *to spring-clean a house*

Word building: **spring-clean** *noun* **spring-cleaning** *noun*

spring roll
noun **1** a deep-fried roll of thin dough with a savoury filling, originally a Chinese dish **2** a roll of raw vegetables and seafood or tofu, wrapped in rice paper and eaten cold, originally a Vietnamese dish

Word history: in Chinese tradition, this is eaten at the spring festival

sprinkle

verb **1** to scatter here and there, or in small quantities **2** to rain slightly

Word building: **sprinkle** *noun* **sprinkler** *noun*

sprint

verb to race at top speed, especially over a short distance

Word building: **sprint** *noun* **sprinter** *noun*

sprite

noun a small fairy

sprocket

noun a toothed wheel that meshes with the links of a chain such as the one on a bicycle

sprout

verb **1** to grow, or send up shoots: *He is trying to sprout plants from seed.* | *The bulb has sprouted.*
noun **2** a shoot **3** another name for a **brussels sprout**

spruce¹

noun an evergreen tree with fine needle-like leaves, and cones

spruce²

adjective stylish or smart: *You look very spruce in your new clothes.*

Word building: **spruce up** *verb* to smarten

spry

adjective nimble or active: *My grandparents are still very spry.*

Word building: Other forms are **spryer**, **spryest**. | **spryly** *adverb*

spud

noun **1** *Informal* a potato **2** a spade-like tool for digging up weeds

Word history: from a Middle English word for 'a kind of knife'

spunk

noun **1** courage **2** *Informal* someone who is good-looking

Word building: **spunky** *adjective* (**spunkier**, **spunkiest**)

spur

noun **1** a sharp instrument worn on the heel of a riding boot to urge a horse to go faster **2** anything which makes work go faster or urges you on **3** something looking like a spur, such as the horny piece on some birds' feet, or a ridge rising up to a mountain range

phrase **4 on the spur of the moment**, suddenly or without preparation

Word building: **spur** *verb* (**spurred**, **spurring**)

spurn (*say* spern)

verb to reject or scorn: *Ashley spurned the offer of help.*

spurt

verb to flow or release suddenly: *Blood spurted from the wound.* | *The chimney spurted a cloud of smoke.*

Word building: **spurt** *noun* a sudden rush

sputnik

noun a satellite placed in orbit around the earth, especially an early Soviet model

spy

noun **1** someone who secretly watches and reports others' activities
verb **2** to watch secretly, and report **3** to see: *I can't spy her yet.*

Word building: The plural form of the noun is **spies**. | Other verb forms are **I spied, I have spied, I am spying.** | **spying** *noun*

spyware

noun software that another person tries to install on your computer so that they can find out things about you that you might not want them to know

squabble (*rhymes with* wobble)

noun a small unimportant quarrel: *They are good friends in spite of their squabbles.*
Other words: **argument, disagreement, dispute**

Word building: **squabble** *verb*

squad (*rhymes with* rod)

noun a small group taking part in a shared activity: *a squad of cleaners* | *the football squad*

squadron (*say* skwod-ruhn)

noun a fighting unit in the navy or the air force

squalid (*say* skwol-uhd)

adjective dirty or filthy: *a squalid hovel*

squall

noun a sudden strong wind

Word building: **squall** *verb*

squalor (*say* skwol-uh)

noun dirt and poverty

squander (*say* skwon-duh)
verb to spend or use wastefully

square
noun **1** a shape with four equal sides and four right angles **2** an open public place in a town **3** an instrument which is used to draw and check right angles **4** a number multiplied by itself: *The square of 2 is 2 × 2, or 4.* **5** *Informal* someone who is conservative in their likes and appearance
verb **6** to make straight or square **7** to multiply by itself: *If you add 2 and 3 then square the result, you get 25.* **8** to agree: *It doesn't square with the facts.*
adjective **9** in the form of a right angle: *a square corner* **10** cube-shaped or nearly so: *a square box* **11** equal to a square with sides of the stated length: *a square kilometre* **12** even or level: *The two sides aren't quite square.* **13** paid up: *We are square now.* **14** fair: *a square deal* **15** full or complete: *a square meal* **16** *Informal* conservative in looks or behaviour

Word building: **square** *adverb*   **squarely** *adverb*

square dance
noun a country dance for couples, in which someone calls or sings the steps to be followed

square metre
noun a unit of measurement equal to a square which measures one metre on each side

square root
noun the number which, when multiplied by itself, gives the stated number: *The square root of 16 is 4.*

squash[1] (*say* skwosh)
verb **1** to flatten or crush: *The dog squashed my hat.* **2** to put down: *to squash the rebellion*
noun **3** a game for two players with racquets and a small rubber ball, played in a small court with walls **4** a fizzy fruit drink

squash[2] (*say* skwosh)
noun a round vegetable like a marrow

squat (*say* skwot)
verb **1** to sit in a crouching position **2** to live without permission on land or property which you don't own
adjective **3** short and thickset: *a squat figure*

Word building: Other verb forms are **I squatted, I have squatted, I am squatting.** | **squat** *noun*   **squatness** *noun*

squatter (*say* skwot-uh)
noun **1** a rich landowner **2** someone who lives without permission in a place they don't own

squawk
verb to make a loud unpleasant cry: *The chickens squawked when the fox chased them.*

Word building: **squawk** *noun*

squeak
verb to make a high-pitched cry or a creaking noise: *A mouse squeaked.* | *The gate squeaks.*

Word building: **squeaky** *adjective* (**squeakier, squeakiest**)   **squeak** *noun*   **squeakily** *adverb*

squeal
verb to make a sudden high-pitched cry, as if in pain or fear

Word building: **squeal** *noun*

squeeze
verb **1** to press hard, so as to remove something: *to squeeze an orange* **2** to cram: *to squeeze clothes into a bag* **3** to hug or hold close **4** to force a way: *They squeezed through the crowd.*
noun **5** a tight fit: *She's wearing the jacket but it's a bit of a squeeze.* **6** a small amount of something got by squeezing: *a squeeze of lemon*
phrase **7 a tight squeeze**, a difficult situation

squid
noun a sea animal with a soft body and no backbone, which has tentacles attached to its head

Word use: This is called **calamari** when it is cooked.

squint
verb **1** to have both your eyes turned towards your nose **2** to look indirectly, such as by a quick glance or with half-closed eyes

Word building: **squint** *noun*   **squinting** *adjective*

squire
noun **1** an English country gentleman **2** a young nobleman attending a medieval knight

Word building: **squire** *verb* to attend

squirm

verb to wriggle uncomfortably: *to squirm with embarrassment*

squirrel

noun a bushy-tailed animal found in Europe, Asia and North America, which lives in trees and hoards nuts and acorns

squirt

verb to wet with a jet of liquid: *They squirted each other with hoses.*

stab

verb **1** to wound, pierce or push, as if with a knife: *Timothy stabbed himself with the needle.* | *Don't stab at your food.*
noun **2** a sudden painful blow or feeling: *a stab of regret* **3** an attempt: *Now you have a stab at doing an eight-stair ollie.*

Word building: Other verb forms are **I stabbed, I have stabbed, I am stabbing.** | **stabbing** *adjective*: *a stabbing pain*

stable¹

noun a place where horses are kept and fed

Word building: **stable** *verb* to put or keep in a stable

stable²

adjective firm and steady: *a stable temperature*

Word building: **stability** *noun*

staccato (*say* stuh-kah-toh)

adjective an instruction in music to make notes sharply separate

stack

noun **1** a large pile of things on top of each other **2** a tall chimney **3** a large number or quantity: *There were a stack of people there.*
verb **4** to pile up: *to stack the plates* **5** to arrange unfairly: *to stack the cards*
phrase **6 stack a meeting**, to influence the decisions of a meeting unfairly by organising people to attend who will vote the way you want

Word building: **stacked** *adjective*

stadium

noun a large, often indoor, sports arena, with seats for spectators and parking available

staff

noun **1** the people who work in a business or an institution, such as a school or hospital **2** a large stick or rod

Word building: **staff** *verb* **staff** *adjective*

stag

noun a male deer

Word use: The female is a **doe** and the young is a **fawn**.

stage

noun **1** a raised floor, usually in a theatre, on which public performances take place **2** a step in a process: *Now we can go on to the next stage.* **3** a period of development: *an early stage* **4** a section of a rocket which drops off after firing
verb **5** to do or perform, especially on a stage: *to stage a play* **6** to plan or carry out: *to stage a riot*

stagecoach

noun a passenger and goods coach which used to cover a particular route, changing horses regularly on long trips

stagger

verb **1** to stand or go unsteadily **2** to arrange so that things don't occur at the same time: *They stagger their holidays.* **3** to shock: *The news staggered me.*

Word building: **staggered** *adjective* amazed **stagger** *noun*

stagnant

adjective still and dirty: *stagnant water*

Word building: **stagnancy** *noun*

stagnate

verb **1** to stop running or flowing: *The water has stagnated.* **2** to become dull and inactive: *She feels she is stagnating at home.*

Word building: **stagnation** *noun*

stain

noun **1** a mark or blemish
Other words: **blot, blotch, spot**
2 a clear colouring, as used on wood

Word building: **stain** *verb*

stair

noun one of a series of steps

stair/stare Don't confuse **stair** with **stare**. To **stare** at someone is to look directly at them for a long time with your eyes wide open.

staircase

noun a series of steps with its handrail or banister

stake¹

noun **1** a stick which is often pointed at one end: *We put in stakes to support the vine.*
verb **2** to put stakes in the ground as a marker, or for support **3** to make a claim for: *I have staked my share.*
phrase **4 stake out**, to surround, in order to keep watch or make a raid: *to stake out a building* **5 the stake**, death by burning while tied to a stake

stake²

noun **1** the amount bet in a race or game: *The stakes were high.* **2** a personal interest or involvement: *He has a stake in the shop, so he wants it to be successful.*
phrase **3 at stake**, at risk: *A lot is at stake.*
Word building: **stake** *verb* to bet

stake/steak Don't confuse **stake** with **steak**, which is a thick slice of meat or fish which is usually grilled or fried.

stalactite　(*say* stal-uhk-tuyt)

noun a deposit formed by dripping water, which hangs from the roof of a limestone cave

stalagmite　(*say* stal-uhg-muyt)

noun a deposit formed by dripping water, which builds up on the floor of a limestone cave

stale

adjective not fresh or new: *This bread is stale. | Her writing has become rather stale, I'm afraid.*

stalemate

noun a situation where no progress can be made
Word use: This comes from chess, where any move by the king would put him in check and conclude the game.

stalk¹　(*rhymes with* fork)

noun the stem of a plant

stalk²　(*rhymes with* fork)

verb **1** to follow quietly and carefully: *The cat was stalking a mouse.* **2** to walk slowly and proudly: *He stalked out of the room in a rage.*

stalk/stork Don't confuse **stalk** with **stork**, which is a large bird with long legs and a long beak.

stall

noun **1** a stand, tent or table where goods are sold, such as at a fete **2** a section of a stable or shed where one horse or cow is kept
verb **3** to stop, especially without wanting to: *She stalled the car. | The car stalled at the lights.*
phrase **4 the stalls**, the front seats on the ground floor of a theatre

stallion　(*say* stal-yuhn)

noun a male horse kept for breeding
Word use: The female is a **mare** and the young is a **foal**.

stamen

noun the part of a flower that produces the pollen
Word building: The plural is **stamens** or **stamina**.
Word history: from a Latin word meaning 'thread'

stamina　(*say* stam-uh-nuh)

noun physical strength or power, especially to fight off sickness or tiredness

stammer

noun another word for **stutter**
Word building: **stammer** *verb*

stamp

verb **1** to strike, beat, or crush by a downward push of your foot **2** to put a mark on something to show that it has been approved or is genuine: *The customs officer stamped my passport.* **3** to mark something with a pattern or design: *They stamped the emblem on the shirt.*
noun **4** a small sticky piece of paper printed by the government for attaching to letters or documents **5** an official mark showing something is genuine or has been approved **6** an engraved block or instrument, usually of rubber, used for making a mark on something

stampede

noun a sudden scattering or headlong flight of a group of animals or people, often in fright
Word building: **stampede** *verb*

stance

noun **1** a way of standing: *a boxer's stance* **2** your way of thinking: *My stance on saving rainforests is well-known.*
Word use: The more usual word is **position**.

stanchion (*say* stan-shuhn, stan-chuhn, stahn-shuhn, stahn-chuhn)

noun an upright post or support in part of a building or structure: *a window stanchion | a bridge stanchion*

stand

verb **1** to take or keep an upright position on your feet **2** to stop moving or halt: *Stand and deliver!* **3** to be placed or situated: *The house stands at the end of the street.* **4** to be unchanged or to continue the same: *The law still stands.* **5** to become a candidate: *She stood for the position of mayor.* **6** to undergo: *The suspect will stand trial.* **7** to bear or tolerate: *I can't stand you.*
noun **8** opposition to, or support for a cause: *My parents take a strong stand against smoking.* **9** a platform or raised place, such as for spectators or a display of goods **10** a framework to support something
phrase **11 stand by, a** to wait or be ready **b** to help: *I'll stand by you.* **c** to keep to: *I always stand by my promises.* **12 stand down, a** to go off duty **b** to withdraw, especially from a contest **c** to suspend from employment temporarily during a strike, etc.: *Ten more workers were stood down this morning.* **13 stand for,** to represent: *A police officer stands for the law.* **14 stand in,** to act in place of someone else
Word building: Other verb forms are **I stood, I have stood, I am standing.**

standard

noun **1** anything taken as a rule or basis for comparing other things
Other words: **criterion, model**
2 a grade or level of excellence or achievement: *a high standard of living*
3 a flag, emblem or symbol
adjective **4** used as a standard or rule: *standard spelling* **5** normal, acceptable or average: *The shirt was the standard size for a ten-year-old.*
Other words: **customary, ordinary, typical, usual**

standardise

verb **1** to make standard in size, weight or quality, and so on **2** to compare with or test by a standard: *This car has been standardised with the original model.*
Word use: Another spelling is **standardize.**
Word building: **standardisation** *noun*

stand-by

noun someone or something kept ready to be used when needed or in an emergency
Word building: The plural is **stand-bys.**

stand-in

noun any substitute, but especially one used to replace someone for a short time in a play or film

standing

noun **1** position, status or reputation: *a person of good standing* **2** duration or length of existence or membership: *a member of long standing*
adjective **3** in an upright position **4** continuing without stopping or changing: *a standing rule*

stand-out

adjective outstanding or obvious: *the stand-out choice for school captain*

standstill

noun a stop or halt: *Work came to a standstill.*

stanza

noun a group of lines of poetry arranged in a pattern or verse
Word history: from a Latin word meaning 'standing'

staple¹

noun **1** a bent piece of wire used to bind papers and similar things together **2** a U-shaped piece of metal with pointed ends for driving into a surface
Word building: **staple** *verb*

staple²

noun **1** a most important or main item, especially food which is used or needed continually **2** a fibre of wool or cotton
adjective **3** most important: *Rice is the staple food in India.*

stapler

noun a small machine used to join papers with staples

star

noun **1** any of the large bodies in space like our sun, which we see as bright points of light in the night sky **2** a shape resembling a star in the sky, with five or six points which look like rays of light **3** someone who is excellent in something or who is famous in an art or profession: *She is a swimming star. | He is a film star.*
adjective **4** brilliant or best: *She is the star swimmer in the team.*

verb **5** to put stars on, or to mark with stars **6** to appear as, or to present someone as, a leading performer: *She starred in the film.* | *The play starred the son of the director.*

Word building: Other verb forms are **I starred, I have starred, I am starring.** | **starred** *adjective* **starry** *adjective*

starboard (*say* stah-buhd)
noun the right-hand side of a ship when you are facing the front or bow of the ship
Word use: The opposite is **port**.

starch
noun **1** a white tasteless substance found in foods like potatoes, wheat and rice **2** a preparation of this used to make clothes and materials stiff
verb **3** to stiffen with starch

stare
verb **1** to look directly for a long time, especially with your eyes wide open
noun **2** a long fixed look with your eyes wide open

stare/stair Don't confuse **stare** with **stair**, which is one of a series of steps.

starfish
noun a sea animal with a body in the shape of a star

stark
adjective **1** complete or total: *stark madness* **2** harsh or barren: *A desert is a stark landscape.*
adverb **3** absolutely or utterly: *stark naked*

starling
noun a noisy bird with dark shiny feathers

start
verb **1** to begin to move or to set moving: *I started on my journey.* | *He started the engine.* **2** to begin: *When did you start on your career?* | *Will you start the letter?* **3** to move suddenly or with a sudden jerk from a position or place: *The rabbit started up from the undergrowth.* **4** to be among the competitors in a race or contest: *How many are starting in the long jump?*
noun **5** a beginning **6** the first part of anything: *the start of a book* **7** a sudden jerk of your body: *I woke with a start.* **8** a lead or advantage over other competitors: *They gave me a start of ten metres in the race.*

starter
noun **1** someone who gives the signal to start a race **2** anyone who is a competitor in a race or contest
phrase **3 for starters**, *Informal* **a** the first course of a meal **b** a first stage in anything: *We'll dig a hole for starters.*

startle
verb **1** to disturb, surprise or frighten suddenly
Other words: **alarm, disconcert, scare, shock**
2 to move with a sudden jerk, such as from a fright or surprise

starve
verb **1** to die or cause to die from hunger: *Many babies starve in poor countries.* | *Some people starve their pets.* **2** to be suffering severely from hunger **3** to cause to suffer from the lack of something needed: *The strike starved the city of petrol.*
Word building: **starvation** *noun*

state
noun **1** the condition of someone or something: *a state of unhappiness* **2** a tense, excited or nervous condition: *Don't get yourself into a state over this.* **3** a number of people living in a definite territory and organised under one government **4** the territory itself: *Tasmania is a State of Australia.*
adjective **5** having to do with ceremonies, special occasions, or the government
verb **6** to say or express in speech or writing: *State your reasons clearly if you want an early reply.*

stately
adjective formal, grand, or majestic: *a stately palace*
Word building: Other forms are **statelier, stateliest**.

statement
noun **1** the stating or declaring of facts or ideas **2** the thing or things stated: *I don't think that statement's true.*

statesman
noun someone who is skilled in, or whose work is, directing the affairs of the government
Word building: The plural is **statesmen.** | **statesmanship** *noun*

static

adjective **1** at rest or still **2** having to do with electricity which is not flowing, especially that caused by friction
noun **3** noise or interference with sound waves such as crackling caused by electrical activity in the air

station

noun **1** a place at which a train regularly stops **2** the end of a bus or coach route **3** a farm for raising sheep or cattle **4** a place set up for some particular kind of work or service: *a police station* **5** the place or the equipment used for broadcasting or transmitting for radio or television
verb **6** to place or post in a position for a particular reason: *The guard was stationed at the gate.*

stationary   (*say* stay-shuhn-ree)

adjective not moving: *The car was stationary at the red light.*

Word use: This should not be confused with **stationery**.

stationery   (*say* stay-shuhn-ree)

noun writing paper and writing materials such as pens and pencils

Word use: This should not be confused with **stationary**.
Word building: **stationer** *noun* someone who sells stationery

station wagon

noun a car which has extra space behind the back seat, and a door at the back

statistics

plural noun information collected together and presented in the form of figures, charts or graphs

Word building: **statistical** *adjective*

statue   (*say* stat-chooh)

noun an image of a person or animal made out of stone, wood or bronze

stature   (*say* stat-chuh)

noun **1** someone's height **2** achievement or distinction reached by someone: *Marie is a woman of high stature in the computing business.*

status   (*say* stay-tuhs)

noun **1** someone's social or professional position, rank, or importance **2** the state or condition of something

staunch[1]

verb to stop the flow of blood from: *to staunch a wound*

staunch[2]

adjective **1** loyal or steadfast: *a staunch friend* **2** strong or substantial

stave

noun **1** a thin, narrow, curved piece of wood that is part of the side of a barrel or tub **2** the set of five horizontal lines used in music, on which the notes are written
phrase **3** **stave in**, to break a hole in **4** **stave off**, to put off or prevent: *The berries staved off starvation for the lost hikers.*

Word use: Another word for definition 2 is **staff**.
Word building: Other verb forms are **I staved** or **stove**, **I have staved** or **stove**, **I am staving**.

stay[1]

verb **1** to remain in a place
Other words: **wait**
2 to continue to be: *Children cannot stay clean.*
Other words: **remain**
noun **3** a time of living somewhere: *We had a short stay in Queensland.*
Other words: **visit**

stay[2]

noun a support, especially used to keep something steady
Other words: **brace, prop**

stead   (*rhymes with* bed)

noun **1** place or position: *Since he couldn't come, he sent his brother in his stead.*
phrase **2** **stand in good stead**, to be useful: *My extra study stood me in good stead in the exam.*

steadfast   (*say* sted-fahst)

adjective firmly fixed, constant, or unchanging: *a steadfast gaze | a steadfast friend*
Other words: **firm, steady, unwavering**

steady   (*say* sted-ee)

adjective **1** firmly placed or fixed: *a steady ladder*
Other words: **secure, stable**
2 constant or regular: *steady progress at school*
Other words: **continuous, even, solid**
3 free from excitement or upset: *steady nerves*
Other words: **calm, composed, controlled**
4 reliable or having good habits: *Her friend seems a steady little boy.*
noun **5** a regular girlfriend or boyfriend
adverb **6** in a firm or regular manner

phrase **7 go steady**, to go out regularly with the same boyfriend or girlfriend

Word building: Other adjective forms are **steadier, steadiest**. | The plural form of the noun is **steadies**. | **steady** *verb* (**steadied, steadying**)   **steadily** *adverb*

steak   (*sounds like* stake)

noun a thick slice of meat or fish usually used for grilling or frying

steak/stake Don't confuse **steak** with **stake**. A **stake** is a stick with a pointed end. A **stake** can also be the amount bet in a race or game.

steal

verb **1** to take something that does not belong to you, especially secretly **2** to get, take, or do secretly: *I stole a nap during the class.* **3** to move or go secretly: *The prisoner stole away quietly in the night.*
noun **4** *Informal* something obtained cheaply or below its true cost: *This hat is a real steal.*

Word building: Other verb forms are **I stole, I have stolen, I am stealing.**

steal/steel Don't confuse **steal** with **steel**, which is iron mixed with other metals and carbon to make it very hard and strong.

stealth   (*say* stelth)

noun secret, hidden, or sly action or behaviour

steam

noun **1** a colourless gas or vapour produced by boiling water and used for driving machinery and for heating
verb **2** to give off steam: *The hot food was steaming.* **3** to treat with steam in order to cook, soften or heat
phrase **4 let off steam**, to release or let go of stored-up feelings **5 run out of steam**, to lose power or energy **6 steam up**, to become covered with steam: *The kitchen windows had all steamed up.*

Word building: **steamy** *adjective* (**steamier, steamiest**)

steam engine

noun an engine which is powered by steam, especially a locomotive

steamroller

noun **1** a heavy vehicle with a large roller, used for crushing and levelling rocks and earth in road-making **2** an overpowering force which crushes anything in its path

Word building: **steamroller** *verb*

steed

noun *Old-fashioned* a horse, especially one for fast riding

steel

noun **1** iron mixed with carbon and other metals so that it is very hard and strong
verb **2** to make hard, unfeeling, or determined: *I steeled myself against their rudeness.*

Word building: **steely** *adjective* (**steelier, steeliest**)   **steel** *adjective*

steel/steal Don't confuse **steel** with **steal**, which is to take something that does not belong to you.

steep[1]

adjective **1** having a sharp slope
Other words: **precipitous, sheer**
2 too high: *a steep price*
Other words: **excessive, high, unreasonable**
3 *Informal* extreme or extravagant: *It's a bit steep to do something like that.*

steep[2]

verb **1** to soak or lie soaking in water or other liquid
Other words: **brew, infuse, stand**
2 to be filled with: *a mind steeped in romance*
Other words: **infuse**

steeple

noun a tall tower attached to a church, often with a spire on top

steeplechase

noun a race over a course which has obstacles such as jumps and ditches

Word building: **steeplechase** *verb*

steer[1]

verb **1** to guide the course of by using a rudder or wheel: *He steered the boat.*
Other words: **direct, pilot**
2 to be guided in a particular direction: *This plane steers easily.*

steer[2]

noun a sterilised male of the cattle family, especially one raised for beef

stellar

adjective having to do with a star or stars

stem[1]

noun **1** the central stalk of a plant that grows upwards from the root **2** the stalk which supports or joins a flower, leaf, or fruit to a plant **3** a long thin part like the stem of a plant: *the stem of a pipe | the stem of a wineglass*
verb **4** to originate or come from: *This model stems from an earlier invention of mine.*

Word building: Other verb forms are **it stemmed, it has stemmed, it is stemming**.

stem[2]

verb to stop, check, or dam up: *She stemmed the flow of blood with a towel.*

Word building: Other forms are **I stemmed, I have stemmed, I am stemming**.

stem cell

noun a cell that is taken from an organism early in its development which can be changed into any cell type in the body, such as a blood cell or a muscle cell

stench

noun a very bad smell, especially of something decaying: *The stench was overpowering and we had to cover our noses.*

stencil   (*say* <u>sten</u>-suhl)

noun **1** a thin sheet of paper, cardboard or metal with designs or letters cut out of it: *The children painted over the stencils leaving colourful patterns on the paper underneath.* **2** the actual letters or designs produced
verb **3** to mark, paint or produce letters or designs by using a stencil

Word building: Other verb forms are **I stencilled, I have stencilled, I am stencilling.**
Word history: from a Latin word meaning 'spark'

stenographer   (*say* stuh-<u>nog</u>-ruh-fuh)

noun someone who can write in shorthand what someone else is saying and then type it out

step

noun **1** a movement made by lifting your foot and putting it down again in a new position **2** the distance measured by one such movement: *Move a step nearer.* **3** a move or action: *the first step towards peace* **4** a support for your foot in going up or coming down: *a step of a ladder or stair*
verb **5** to walk or tread: *Please step this way. | Don't step on my drawing!*

phrase **6 step on it,** *Informal* to hurry **7 watch your step,** to go or behave carefully

Word building: Other verb forms are **I stepped, I have stepped, I am stepping.**

step-

prefix a word part that indicates that you are related to someone because of the remarriage of a parent, rather than by birth

Word use: You can have a **step-parent, step-mother, step-father, step-sister, step-brother, step-child, step-daughter** and **step-son.**

stepladder

noun a ladder which has flat steps instead of rungs and has a pair of hinged legs to keep it upright

steppe   (*say* step)

noun a large plain, especially one without trees

stereo   (*say* <u>ste</u>-ree-oh, <u>stear</u>-ree-oh)

noun a radio, CD or record-player, or recording system equipped to reproduce stereophonic sound

Word building: The plural is **stereos.** | **stereo** *adjective*

stereophonic   (*say* ste-ree-uh-<u>fon</u>-ik)

adjective having to do with using two channels and two speakers to transmit and broadcast sound

stereotype

noun an overly simple idea or image, used to label or define people in very narrow terms: *She says that all teenagers are lazy and disrespectful, but that's just a stereotype.*

sterile   (*say* <u>ste</u>-ruyl)

adjective **1** free from living germs: *a sterile bandage* **2** barren or fruitless, or not able to have children: *Some fields are sterile and will not produce crops.*

Word building: **sterility** *noun*

sterilise

verb **1** to destroy germs in something, often by boiling it **2** to make unable to reproduce young, especially by surgery: *The vet sterilised my dog.*

Word use: Another spelling is **sterilize.**
Word building: **sterilisation** *noun*

sterling

adjective **1** having to do with British money **2** being of a certain standard quality of silver **3** made of this sterling silver: *a sterling cutlery set* **4** thoroughly excellent: *sterling character*

stern[1]

adjective **1** firm or strict: *stern discipline*
Other words: **harsh, stringent**
2 hard, harsh, or severe: *a stern warning*

stern[2]

noun the back part of anything, but especially of a ship or boat
Other words: **back, rear**

stethoscope   (*say* steth-uh-skohp)

noun an instrument used by doctors to listen to the sounds made by your heart and lungs

stew

verb **1** to cook by slow boiling **2** *Informal* to worry or fuss
noun **3** food cooked by stewing, especially a dish of meat and vegetables cooked together **4** *Informal* a condition or state of worrying or uneasiness

steward

noun **1** someone who looks after others in a club or on a ship or plane **2** someone who manages someone else's affairs or property

stick[1]

noun **1** a branch or long thin piece of wood, sometimes used for a special purpose: *a walking stick* **2** something shaped like a stick: *a stick of celery*
phrase **3 the sticks,** *Informal* the country, especially when thought of as backward and dull

stick[2]

verb **1** to pierce with a pointed instrument **2** to thrust something pointed in or through something: *If you stick a pin into a balloon it will burst.* **3** to put into a place or position: *Just stick your head out of the window.* **4** to fasten into position by piercing or gluing: *I stuck the photo on the cover of my diary.* **5** to prevent or be prevented from moving: *The car stuck in the mud.* **6** to stay attached as if by glue: *The mud sticks to your shoes.* **7** to remain firm in opinion, attachment and so on: *Jasmine sticks to her word. | I will stick by my friends.*

Word building: Other forms are **I stuck, I have stuck, I am sticking.** | **stick** *noun*

sticker

noun an adhesive or gummed label, usually with an advertisement or other message printed on it

stick insect

noun an insect, often without wings, with a long, thin, twig-like body

sticky

adjective **1** adhesive or gluey **2** hot and humid: *a sticky day* **3** *Informal* awkward or difficult to deal with: *a sticky situation*

Word building: Other forms are **stickier, stickiest.** | **stickily** *adverb*   **stickiness** *noun*

stickybeak

noun someone who is curious about things that aren't their business

Word building: **stickybeak** *verb*

stiff

adjective **1** hard or firm and not easily bent **2** not moving or working easily: *a stiff hinge* **3** not able to move easily: *Her legs were stiff with the cold.* **4** *Informal* unfortunate or unlucky: *That's stiff!* **5** strong and with steady force: *a stiff wind* **6** severe or hard to deal with: *He gave us a stiff punishment.* **7** unusually high in price or demand: *That's a stiff price for that vase.*
noun **8** *Informal* a dead body

Word building: **stiff** *adverb*   **stiffen** *verb*   **stiffness** *noun*

stifle

verb **1** to smother or prevent the breathing of **2** to keep back or to stop: *He stifled a yawn.* **3** to become stifled or be unable to breathe

Word building: **stifling** *adjective*

stigma

noun a mark of shame or a stain on your reputation

Word use: The more usual word is **blot**.

stile

noun a step or steps for climbing over a fence where there is no gate

stiletto (*say* stuh-<u>let</u>-oh)
noun **1** a dagger with a narrow thick blade **2** a high, very narrow heel on a woman's shoe

Word history: from the Latin word for a pointed instrument

still[1]
adjective **1** free from movement: *still water*
Other words: **motionless, unmoving, stationary**
2 free from sound or noise: *a still night*
Other words: **hushed, quiet, silent, tranquil**
noun **3** stillness or silence: *in the still of the night*
Other words: **peacefulness, quiet, quietness**
4 a single photographic picture
adverb **5** up to or even at this time: *Is she still here?* **6** without sound or movement: *She stood still.*
verb **7** to make or become quiet or silent

Word building: **stillness** *noun*

still[2]
noun equipment for distilling a liquid, especially a liquor

stilt
noun **1** one of a pair of poles used for walking on, each with a support for your foot at some distance above the ground **2** a high supporting post under a building

stilted
adjective not at ease or relaxed: *The new captain spoke in a very stilted manner.*

Word use: The more usual word is **unnatural**.

stimulant (*say* <u>stim</u>-yuh-luhnt)
noun something that increases wakefulness or quickens some bodily process, such as a medicine or food

stimulate (*say* <u>stim</u>-yuh-layt)
verb **1** to spur on or excite: *The dancers were stimulated by the music and bright lights.* **2** to act as a stimulus or stimulant

Word building: **stimulation** *noun* **stimulator** *noun*

stimulus (*say* <u>stim</u>-yuh-luhs)
noun something that starts action, effort, or thought: *Seeing the exhibition was the stimulus she needed to start painting again.*

Word building: The plural is **stimuli**.

sting
verb **1** to prick or wound with a sharp-pointed, often venomous organ which some animals have: *A bee stung me.* **2** to hurt the feelings of: *Her unkind words stung me.*
noun **3** an act of stinging **4** the wound or pain caused by stinging **5** a sharp-pointed, often venomous, organ of insects and other animals, able to cause painful wounds

Word building: Other verb forms are **it stung, it has stung, it is stinging**.

stingray
noun a type of fish with a wide, flat body and a long, spiny tail

stingy (*say* <u>stin</u>-jee)
adjective mean about spending money
Other words: **miserly**

Word building: Other forms are **stingier, stingiest**.

stink
verb **1** to give off a bad smell
noun **2** a bad smell **3** *Informal* a fuss: *She kicked up a stink when she heard the news.*

Word building: Other verb forms are **it stank, it has stunk, it is stinking**.

stir
verb **1** to mix something by moving a spoon, stick, or something similar around in it
Other words: **beat, blend, whisk**
2 to move: *The breeze stirred the leaves.* / *Not a leaf stirred.* **3** to bring about an emotion or feeling: *The old photographs stirred up memories of her youth.*
Other words: **activate, inspire, rouse**
4 *Informal* to deliberately mention things likely to cause an argument
Other words: **agitate**
noun **5** the act or sound of stirring or moving **6** excitement or commotion: *Her arrival caused quite a stir.*
Other words: **disturbance, fuss**

Word building: Other verb forms are **I stirred, I have stirred, I am stirring**.

stir-fry
verb **1** to fry food lightly while stirring it
noun **2** a dish prepared by stir-frying: *I'm making a stir-fry for dinner tonight.*

Word building: Other verb forms are **I stir-fried, I have stir-fried, I am stir-frying**.

stirrup
noun a loop or ring of metal hung from the saddle of a horse to support the rider's foot

stitch

noun **1** a complete movement of a threaded needle through a piece of material **2** the loop of thread left in the material **3** one complete movement with needles in knitting, crochet and so on **4** a sudden sharp pain, especially between your ribs *phrase* **5 in stitches**, laughing uncontrollably

Word building: **stitch** *verb*

stoat

noun a type of weasel which has a brown coat of fur in summer

Word use: The white winter coat of the stoat is called **ermine**.

stock

noun **1** the total quantity of goods kept by a business shop for selling to customers **2** a quantity of something kept for future use: *We kept a good stock of food in the house.* **3** another word for **livestock 4** ancestry: *He is of Italian stock.* **5** liquid in which meat, fish, vegetables, and so on have been cooked, often used as a base for sauces or soups **6** the shares of a business company *verb* **7** to provide with, or to collect a stock or supply **8** to provide with horses, cattle, and so on: *to stock the property with fine merinos* *adjective* **9** kept in store: *stock articles* **10** in common use or ordinary: *a stock argument*

stockade

noun a strong wooden fence built for defence

stocking

noun a tight-fitting item of clothing that covers the foot and leg

stockman

noun someone whose job is to look after the animals, especially the cattle, on a property

Word building: The plural is **stockmen**.

stockpile

verb to save up in large amounts for future use: *to stockpile wood for the winter*

Word building: **stockpile** *noun*

stock-still

adverb without moving at all: *to stand stock-still*

stocky

adjective short, solid and strong: *a stocky young footballer*

Word building: Other forms are **stockier**, **stockiest**.

stoke

verb to stir up and add fuel to: *to stoke a fire*

Word building: **stoker** *noun*: *a stoker on a steam train*

stole

noun a long wide scarf worn around your shoulders for warmth

stomach   (*say* <u>stum</u>-uhk)

noun the bag-like organ in the body that receives food after it is swallowed, and starts to digest it

Word history: from a Greek word meaning 'throat'

stone

noun **1** the hard substance which rocks are made of: *a house built of stone* **2** a piece of rock **3** a gem **4** the hard seed inside a cherry, peach, plum or similar fruit **5** an old-fashioned measure of weight, equal to a little more than six kilograms *verb* **6** to throw stones at **7** to take the stones out of: *to stone peaches*

Word building: **stony** *adjective* (**stonier**, **stoniest**): *stony ground | a stony heart*

stoned

adjective *Informal* completely drunk or drugged

stonefish

noun a venomous tropical fish, looking like a piece of coral or rock, with spines which can give you a painful sting, sometimes causing death

Word building: The plural is **stonefish** or **stonefishes**.

stool

noun a seat with no arms or back

stoop

verb **1** to bend forwards **2** to lower yourself: *to stoop to lying*

stop

verb **1** to end or finish **2** to bring or come to a halt **3** to prevent: *to stop them from leaving* **4** to close or block up: *to stop a leak* **5** to stay: *to stop overnight with friends* *noun* **6** a finish or end: *to put a stop to the noise* **7** the place where a bus, tram or other vehicle stops to pick up and set down passengers

Word building: Other verb forms are **I stopped, I have stopped, I am stopping.** | **stoppage** *noun*: *a traffic stoppage*

stopper

noun something that fits into the top of a bottle to close it

stop press

noun last minute news put into a newspaper after printing has already begun

stopwatch

noun a watch which can be stopped and started by pressing a button, used for timing races and so on

Word building: The plural is **stopwatches.**

storage

noun room to keep things: *The cupboard has plenty of storage.*

store

noun **1** things put away for use in the future: *a store of groceries* **2** a place for keeping a supply of things: *Get some pencils from the store.* **3** a shop: *the corner store* *phrase* **4 in store,** coming soon: *There is a surprise in store for you.*

Word building: **store** *verb*: *to store food*

storehouse

noun a building in which things are stored or kept

storey

noun one whole level of a building Other words: **floor**

Word building: The plural is **storeys.** Word history: from a French word meaning 'build'

stork

noun a large bird with long legs and a long beak, which feeds in shallow water

storm

noun **1** a violent change in the weather bringing wind, rain, thunder and lightning **2** a strong outburst: *a storm of applause* *verb* **3** to rush angrily: *He stormed out of the room.* **4** to attack suddenly and violently: *The warriors stormed the castle.*

Word building: **stormy** *adjective* (**stormier, stormiest**)

story

noun **1** the telling of something that has happened, either made up or in real life: *the story of Waltzing Matilda* **2** a lie or fib

Word building: The plural is **stories.**

stout

adjective **1** rather overweight **2** strong and heavy: *a stout stick* **3** brave and fearless: *a stout heart* *noun* **4** a strong dark-brown beer

stove

noun a device which uses wood, gas or electricity to produce heat for cooking or warming a room

stow   (*rhymes with* so)

verb to pack or store away: *Stow your luggage in the boot of the car.*

stowaway   (*say* stoh-uh-way)

noun someone who hides on a ship or plane to get a free trip

Word building: **stowaway** *verb*

straddle

verb to sit or stand on with one leg on each side: *to straddle a horse*

straggle

verb **1** to lag behind or walk out of line **2** to grow or spread untidily: *Overgrown vines straggled over the fence.*

Word building: **straggler** *noun*   **straggly** *adjective*

straight

adjective **1** not bent or curved **2** honest and reliable: *a straight answer* **3** serious: *to keep a straight face* | *to have a straight talk* *adverb* **4** without bending, curving or twisting: *The road runs straight for five* *kilometres.* **5** neatly and in the proper order: *to set your room straight* **6** directly or immediately: *I'll come straight over.*

Word building: **straighten** *verb*

straight/strait Don't confuse **straight** with **strait**, which is a narrow channel connecting two large bodies of water.

straight angle
noun an angle of 180°

straightaway
adverb at once: *I'll come straightaway.*

straightforward
adjective **1** honest and open **2** not difficult or complicated: *a straightforward problem*

strain¹
verb **1** to pull, push or stretch hard or too far: *to strain a muscle | The dog strained at its leash.* **2** to pour through a sieve: *to strain orange juice*
noun **3** great effort, pressure or stress: *He looked tired from the strain of work. | The strain on the rope made it snap.* **4 strains,** musical sounds: *the sweet strains of a violin*

strain²
noun breed or family line: *This strain of cat has no tail.*

strainer
noun a filter or sieve: *a tea strainer*

strait
noun a narrow channel connecting two large bodies of water: *Bass Strait*

strait/straight Don't confuse **strait** with **straight**, which is means 'not bent or curved'.

straitjacket
noun a coat which is wrapped around mentally ill people to restrain them, if they are acting violently enough to hurt themselves or others

Word use: Another spelling is **straightjacket.**

straitlaced
adjective rather strict and proper about the way people should behave

strand
noun **1** one of the threads which are twisted together to form a rope or cord **2** a lock of hair

stranded
adjective **1** washed up on the beach: *a stranded whale* **2** alone and helpless: *stranded in the middle of the desert*

strange
adjective **1** queer or odd: *a strange way of walking*
Other words: **abnormal, bizarre, extraordinary, peculiar, remarkable, unusual**
2 not seen or heard of before: *a strange part of town*
Other words: **foreign, unfamiliar, unknown**

stranger
noun **1** someone you haven't met before **2** someone who has not been in a place before: *I'm a stranger in town.*

strangle
verb to kill by squeezing the throat and cutting off the air supply

Word use: Another word is **strangulate.**
Word building: **stranglehold** *noun* a tight hold around the neck **strangler** *noun* **strangulation** *noun*

strap
noun **1** a strip of leather or cloth used for tying or holding things in place: *a watch strap*
verb **2** to fasten with a strap

Word building: Other verb forms are **I strapped, I have strapped, I am strapping.**

strapping
adjective tall and strong: *a strapping young athlete*

strategy   *(say* strat-uh-jee*)*
noun **1** a clever scheme **2** the planning and tactics used in war

Word use: The more usual word for definition 1 is **plan.**
Word building: The plural is **strategies.** | **strategic** *adjective* important in a strategy **strategist** *noun*

stratum   *(say* strah-tuhm*)*
noun a layer or level: *The cliff face shows several different rock strata.*

Word building: The plural is **strata.**
Word history: from a Latin word meaning 'something spread out'

straw
noun **1** a thin hollow tube through which you can suck a drink **2** cut dried stalks of wheat, oats, corn or other grain

strawberry

noun a small, juicy, red fruit which has many tiny seeds on its surface

Word building: The plural is **strawberries**.

stray

verb to wander off and get lost

Word building: **stray** *adjective: a stray puppy*   **stray** *noun: That puppy is a stray.*

streak

noun **1** a long thin mark or line: *a streak of paint*
Other words: **band, smear, strip, stripe**
verb **2** to mark with streaks
Other words: **smear, smudge**
3 to move very quickly: *The dog streaked across the road.*
Other words: **dash, flash, fly, hurtle, race, rush, speed**

Word building: **streaky** *adjective* (**streakier, streakiest**)

stream

noun **1** a small river or creek
2 a continuous flow: *a stream of air | a stream of words*
verb **3** to flow or run: *Tears streamed from his eyes.* **4** to group according to ability: *The school streamed the children into different classes.*

streamer

noun a long strip of brightly coloured paper

streaming

noun the process of data flowing to a computer and it being displayed at the same time, rather than being stored first and then displayed later

streamlined

adjective shaped to move quickly and smoothly through air or water

street

noun **1** a road lined with buildings **2** the people who live in a street: *The whole street gathered around the bonfire.*

streetwise

adjective able to cope with the sorts of challenges found in city life: *He's pretty streetwise — he'll get the money somehow.*

strength

noun the quality of being strong: *Do you have enough strength to move the piano?*
Other words: **force, might, muscle, power**

Word building: **strengthen** *verb* to make or grow stronger

strenuous   (*say* <u>stren</u>-yooh-uhs)

adjective needing a great effort: *strenuous exercise*

Word use: The more usual word, particularly if you are talking about work, is **hard**.
Word building: **strenuously** *adverb*

stress

noun **1** great importance: *to lay stress on the need for safety* **2** accent or emphasis: *to pronounce a word with the stress on the first syllable* **3** strain or pressure: *the stress of work*

Word use: The plural is **stresses**.
Word building: **stress** *verb*

stressful

adjective causing great anxiety to a person: *She found the idea of camping out for a couple of nights quite stressful.*

stretch

verb **1** to pull out or extend **2** to spread: *The desert stretches for miles.* **3** to widen or enlarge: *to stretch a jumper*
noun **4** the action of stretching: *to have a yawn and a stretch* **5** a continuous spread or period of time: *a stretch of land | a stretch of ten years*
phrase **6 stretch out,** to lie down at full length **7 stretch your legs,** to go for a walk

Word building: **stretchy** *adjective*

stretcher

noun a light frame covered with canvas for carrying sick people

strew

verb to scatter or throw everywhere: *to strew the floor with clothes*

Word building: Other forms are **I strewed, I have strewn, I am strewing**.

stricken

adjective struck down or overcome: *stricken with fear*

Word use: This word comes from the verb **strike**. | When talking about emotions, the more usual word is **overcome**.

strict

adjective **1** demanding that you behave well and obey the rules: *a strict teacher*

Other words: **exacting, firm, rigorous, severe, stern**
2 complete or total: *in strict secrecy*
Other words: **utter**

Word building: **strictly** *adverb*

stride
verb **1** to walk with long steps
noun **2** a big step forward: *to take ten strides to reach the end of the room* | *to make great strides in learning to read* **3 strides,** *Informal* trousers

Word building: Other verb forms are **I strode, I have stridden, I am striding.**

strife
noun **1** fighting and quarrelling: *a country torn with strife*
phrase **2 in strife,** in trouble: *You'll be in strife for being so late.*

strike
verb **1** to hit
Other words: **belt, clout, punch, smack, swipe, thump**
2 to attack: *A snake sometimes strikes without warning.* **3** to come across or find: *to strike gold*
Other words: **discover**
4 to affect strongly: *The ghost story struck them with terror.* **5** to sound by hitting a gong: *The clock struck three.* **6** to light: *to strike a match*
noun **7** a hit or blow **8** a work stoppage, usually in protest against low pay and poor working conditions

Word building: **striking** *adjective* impressive or noticeable

string
noun **1** a thread or cord **2** a row or line of things: *a string of cars* **3** one of the pieces of wire stretched across a violin, guitar or similar instrument, which produces musical sounds when it is made to vibrate **4 strings,** musical instruments with strings, especially those played with a bow
verb **5** to hang or thread on a string
phrase **6 string out,** to spread out or lengthen: *The people strung out along the beach to watch the surfers.* | *to string out a conversation*

Word building: **stringy** *adjective* (**stringier, stringiest**): *stringy meat*

stringent
adjective very strict: *stringent laws*

strip¹
verb **1** to remove or take away: *to strip the paint from a table* **2** to take off all your clothes

Word building: Other forms are **I stripped, I have stripped, I am stripping.** | **stripper** *noun*

strip²
noun **1** a long narrow piece or area: *a strip of paper* | *the coastal strip*
phrase **2 comic strip,** a series of cartoons telling a story

stripe
noun **1** a long narrow band of a different colour from the rest of a thing: *red stripes on a blue background* **2 stripes,** strips of braid worn on a military uniform to show rank

Word building: **striped** *adjective*

strive
verb to try hard or struggle: *to strive for success*

Word building: Other forms are **I strove, I have striven, I am striving.**

strobe
noun a device which gives out a series of brilliant flashes of light

stroganoff (*say* strog-uh-nof)
noun a Russian dish of meat cooked in a sauce of sour cream and mushrooms

Word history: from the name of Count Paul *Stroganoff*, a Russian diplomat in the 19th century.

stroke¹
noun **1** a hit or blow **2** a style of swimming **3** an action or event: *a stroke of good luck* **4** a sudden break in the circulation of blood in the brain which can cause paralysis or other disabilities

stroke²
verb to pass your hand over gently

Word building: **stroke** *noun*

stroll
verb to walk slowly

Word building: **stroll** *noun*

stroller
noun a chair on wheels used for carrying small children

strong

adjective **1** having a powerful body: *They asked Tim to lift it because he is very strong.*
Other words: **brawny, muscly, muscular, robust, sturdy**
2 having great power or effect: *a strong wind | a strong will*
Other words: **powerful**
3 not easily broken: *a strong fence*
Other words: **durable, resilient, sturdy, tough**
4 having a lot of flavour or smell: *strong coffee*
Other words: **concentrated, intense**
adverb **5** in number: *The army was 10 000 strong.*

Word building: **strongly** *adverb*

stronghold

noun a fortress

structure

noun **1** something that has been built or constructed: *Bridges and buildings are both structures.* **2** the way something is put together: *the structure of a sentence*

Word building: **structural** *adjective*
structure *verb*

struggle

verb **1** to fight physically against someone or something that is opposing you: *The robber struggled with the police before deciding to cooperate.*
Other words: **battle, grapple, scuffle, tussle, wrestle**
2 to try to do something difficult: *We struggled to get to the top of the hill.*
Other words: **battle, labour, strain, strive, toil**

Word building: **struggle** *noun* **struggler** *noun*

strum

verb to play by running your fingers across the strings of: *to strum a guitar*

Word building: Other forms are **I strummed, I have strummed, I am strumming.**

strut¹

verb to walk proudly or pompously, with your back straight and your chin pushed forward
Other words: **prance**

Word building: Other forms are **I strutted, I have strutted, I am strutting.**

strut²

noun a wooden or metal bar that supports part of a building

Word building: **strut** *verb* (**strutted, strutting**) to support with a strut

stub

noun **1** a short end piece: *the stub of a pencil*
verb **2** to bump against something hard: *to stub your toe*

Word building: Other verb forms are **I stubbed, I have stubbed, I am stubbing. | stubby** *adjective* short and thick

stubble

noun **1** the short stalks left in the ground after wheat or corn has been harvested **2** the short prickly hairs growing on the face of a man who hasn't shaved for a few days

Word building: **stubbly** *adjective*

stubborn   (*say* <u>stub</u>-uhn)

adjective determined not to give way or change your mind
Other words: **inflexible, obstinate, uncompromising, unyielding**

Word building: **stubbornness** *noun*

stuck-up

adjective Informal snobbish or conceited

stud¹

noun a small knob or button: *Football boots have studs underneath. | This shirt fastens with studs.*

stud²

noun a farm where horses or cattle are kept for breeding

student

noun someone who is studying or being taught, especially at a school, college or university

Word building: **studious** *adjective* hardworking and keen to study

studio   (*say* <u>styooh</u>-dee-oh)

noun **1** the workroom of an artist or musician **2** a place where films or radio and television programs are made

study   (*rhymes with* muddy)

verb **1** to spend time learning **2** to look at closely: *to study a document*
noun **3** the careful learning of a subject **4** a room with a desk and books for studying **5** a short piece of music often used for practising technique

Word use: The plural of the noun is **studies**.
Word building: Other verb forms are **I studied, I have studied, I am studying.**

stuff

noun **1** the material from which things are made: *cushions filled with soft stuff* **2** *Informal* belongings: *Put your stuff in your locker.*
verb **3** to fill tightly or cram: *to stuff clothes into a drawer*

stuffing

noun **1** material used for filling **2** a tasty mixture put inside a chicken or other poultry before it is cooked

stuffy

adjective **1** not having enough air: *a stuffy room* **2** prim or easily shocked

Word building: Other forms are **stuffier, stuffiest**. | **stuffily** *adverb* **stuffiness** *noun*

stumble

verb **1** to trip and nearly fall **2** to walk unsteadily **3** to act or speak in an unsteady and hesitating way

stump

noun **1** a short part left after the main part has been cut off: *a tree stump* | *the stump of a pencil* **2** one of the three upright sticks forming the wicket in cricket
verb **3** to baffle completely: *The question stumped me.*

Word building: **stumpy** *adjective* short and thick

stun

verb **1** to make unconscious: *The blow stunned me.* **2** to shock or astonish

Word building: Other forms are **I stunned, I have stunned, I am stunning**.
Word history: from an Old English word meaning 'resound' or 'crash'

stunt¹

verb to stop or slow down the growth of: *Lack of food stunts children in some countries.*

stunt²

noun **1** a spectacular and often dangerous performance **2** something done to attract publicity or attention

stunt double

noun someone who is paid to perform dangerous acts, especially as a stand-in for a film actor

stupefy   (*say* <u>styooh</u>-puh-fuy)

verb **1** to make senseless or unconscious: *The blow on her head stupefied her.* **2** to astound or overcome with amazement

Word building: Other forms are **it stupefied, it has stupefied, it is stupefying**. | **stupefaction** *noun*

stupendous

adjective amazingly good: *The singer's performance was stupendous.*

Word building: **stupendously** *adverb*

stupid

adjective **1** not clever or quick to understand: *a stupid dog*
Other words: **dull, dumb, slow, unintelligent**
2 showing a lack of good sense: *a stupid thing to do*
Other words: **crazy, dumb, foolish, idiotic, irresponsible, mad, rash, senseless, silly, unwise**

Word building: **stupidly** *adverb* **stupidity** *noun*

stupor   (*say* <u>styooh</u>-puh)

noun a state in which the mind or senses are deadened or not working, as a result of illness or drugs

sturdy

adjective strong or able to stand up to rough use or handling: *a sturdy garden tool*

Word building: Other forms are **sturdier, sturdiest**. | **sturdily** *adverb* **sturdiness** *noun*

sturgeon   (*say* <u>ster</u>-juhn)

noun a large fish found in the northern areas of the world, the eggs of which can be salted and eaten as caviar

stutter

noun a speech problem in which the rhythm of speech is blocked and sounds, especially the first consonants in words, are repeated

Word building: **stutter** *verb*

sty¹

noun a place to keep pigs in

Word building: The plural is **sties**.

sty²

noun a small, red and painful swelling on the eyelid

Word use: This word is also spelt **stye**.
Word building: The plural is **sties**.

style

noun **1** a kind of design or way of making: *The church is built in the Gothic style.* **2** a way of doing something: *Shakespeare's style of writing* | *a style of living*

Word building: **stylish** *adjective* fashionable or elegant   **style** *verb*

stylus

noun **1** a pointed tool for drawing or writing **2** a record-player needle

suave (*say* swahv)

adjective smooth and sophisticated in manner: *The famous actor was very suave.*

sub

noun a shortened form of several words such as **submarine, subscription** and **substitute**

sub-

prefix a word part meaning **1** under: *subway* **2** not quite: *subnormal*

Word history: from Latin

subconscious (*say* sub-<u>kon</u>-shuhs)

noun the part of your mind below consciousness or awareness: *Your dreams can come from your subconscious.*

Word building: **subconscious** *adjective*

subdivide

verb to divide again into smaller divisions, especially land

Word building: **subdivision** *noun*

subdue

verb **1** to overcome, usually by force **2** to calm

Word building: Other forms are **I subdued, I have subdued, I am subduing.**

subject (*say* <u>sub</u>-jekt)

noun **1** a matter under discussion: *the subject of a book* **2** a branch of study: *My favourite subject is maths.* **3** something chosen by an artist for painting **4** someone who is under the rule of a monarch or state: *a British subject* **5** the part of a sentence about which something is said, such as 'the roof of the house' in *The roof of the house was red.*
phrase **6 subject to, a** open to or likely to receive: *subject to teasing* **b** depending on: *The excursion to the beach is subject to the teacher's approval.* **c** (*say* suhb-<u>jekt</u>) to cause to undergo: *He was subjected to harsh treatment.*

subjective

adjective having to do with the thinker rather than the thing thought about: *a subjective opinion*

Word use: The opposite is **objective**.

subjective case

noun the form of a noun or pronoun which shows it is the subject of a verb such as 'I' in *I can hear you.*

sublime (*say* suh-<u>bluym</u>)

adjective noble, lofty, or awe-inspiring: *sublime poetry | a sublime view*

Word building: **sublimely** *adverb* **sublimeness** *noun* **sublimity** *noun*

submarine

adjective **1** being under water: *submarine cables*
noun **2** a type of ship that can travel under water

submerge

verb to sink or make sink: *The submarine submerged. | Submerge the clothes in the water.*

Word building: **submersion** *noun*

submissive

adjective giving in obediently or not standing up for yourself: *He is too submissive and often agrees to do more than his fair share of work.*

submit

verb **1** to yield or give in: *to submit to orders | to submit to punishment* **2** to hand in or offer for acceptance or judgement: *to submit an entry in a competition*

Word building: Other forms are **I submitted, I have submitted, I am submitting. | submission** *noun*

subordinate

adjective placed in or belonging to a lower order or rank: *a subordinate employee*

Word building: **subordinate** *noun* **subordination** *noun*

subscription

noun **1** a payment you make for club membership, a series of concert tickets, a regular magazine or such like **2** an amount of money given: *subscription to the bushfire appeal*

Word building: **subscribe** *verb*

subsequent (*say* <u>sub</u>-suh-kwuhnt)

adjective happening later: *subsequent events*

subside

verb to sink to a lower level: *The rain has made the road subside. | The laughter subsided.*

Word building: **subsidence** *noun*

subsidiary (*say* suhb-<u>sij</u>-uh-ree)
adjective less important: *a subsidiary role*

subsidy (*say* <u>sub</u>-suh-dee)
noun a supporting payment made by a government or other organisation: *a subsidy to farmers*

Word building: The plural is **subsidies.** | **subsidise** *verb*

subsist
verb to stay alive, especially when food and other needs are in short supply

Word use: The more usual word is **live.**
Word building: **subsistence** *noun*

substance
noun **1** anything of which a thing is made **2** a particular kind of matter: *This substance will remove paint.* **3** the main or basic part: *the substance of an argument*

substantial
adjective large or solid: *a substantial sum of money* | *a substantial building*

substantiate (*say* suhb-<u>stan</u>-shee-ayt)
verb to back up by providing evidence: *Can you substantiate your claims about a secret plot?* | *The suspect had solid evidence to substantiate her story.*

substitute
noun **1** someone or something acting in place of another
verb **2** to put in the place of: *She substituted margarine for butter.*

Word building: **substitution** *noun*

subterfuge (*say* <u>sub</u>-tuh-fyoohj)
noun a plan or trick used to hide or avoid something

subterranean (*say* sub-tuh-<u>ray</u>-nee-uhn)
adjective underground: *a subterranean passage*

subtitle
noun **1** a secondary title of a book or a play: *The subtitle of 'The Mikado' is 'The Town of Titipu'.* **2 subtitles,** a translation in words on the screen of what is being said in a foreign-language film

subtle (*say* <u>sut</u>-uhl)
adjective **1** so fine or slight as to not be obvious or clear: *a subtle difference* **2** skilful or clever: *subtle humour*

Word building: **subtlety** *noun* (**subtleties**) **subtly** *adverb*
Word history: from a Latin word meaning 'fine' or 'delicate'

subtract
verb to take away: *Subtract 2 from 7, and you get 5.*

Word building: **subtraction** *noun*

suburb
noun a district of a city with its own shopping centre, school and other facilities: *a bayside suburb* | *an industrial suburb*

Word building: **suburban** *adjective*

subway
noun a tunnel under a street or railway for people to walk through

succeed (*say* suhk-<u>seed</u>)
verb **1** to do or accomplish what you have attempted: *After an effort he succeeded in opening the box.*
Other words: **achieve, triumph**
2 to come after and take the place of: *She succeeded her father in the family business.*
Other words: **follow, replace**

success (*say* suhk-<u>ses</u>)
noun **1** a good or desired result **2** someone who has achieved much in their field

Word building: The plural is **successes.** | **successful** *adjective*   **successfully** *adverb*

successor (*say* suhk-<u>ses</u>-uh)
noun someone or something that comes after and takes the place of: *He is my successor as president of the debating society.*

succulent (*say* <u>suk</u>-yuh-luhnt)
adjective juicy: *a succulent steak*

Word building: **succulence** *noun* **succulently** *adverb*

succumb (*say* suh-<u>kum</u>)
verb to yield or give way: *She succumbed to the tiredness.* | *He succumbed to temptation.*

such
adjective a word used to **1** introduce things or qualities that are like others of that kind: *Such puzzles are very difficult.* **2** emphasise a quality or amount: *This is such a delicious ice-cream.* | *There were such a lot of people at the beach.*
phrase **3 such as,** for example: *She enjoys playing many sports, such as squash and volleyball.*

suck

verb **1** to draw in with the mouth: *to suck lemonade through a straw* **2** to hold and move about in the mouth until melted or dissolved: *to suck a lolly* **3** to draw in: *Cold air is sucked in through the window.*

Word building: **suck** *noun*

sucker

noun **1** *Informal* someone who is easily tricked: *Only a sucker would fall for this email scam.* **2** a part on the body of some insects and animals, such as frogs, that allows them to stick to surfaces

suckle

verb to nurse or feed milk to from the breast: *The woman suckled her baby.* | *The cow suckled the calf.*

suction

noun the power of sucking produced when the pressure of the air inside something is less than the outside pressure

sudden

adjective happening quickly and without warning
Other words: **abrupt, hasty, impromptu, unexpected**

Word building: **suddenness** *noun*

sudoku   (*say* suh-<u>doh</u>-kooh)

noun a puzzle where nine digits are placed in horizontal or vertical rows of a grid in such a way that no digit is used more than once in each row

suds

plural noun soapy water with bubbles

sue

verb to bring a legal action against: *He is suing the makers of the faulty machine.*

Word building: Other forms are **I sued, I have sued, I am suing.**

suede   (*say* swayd)

noun a soft leather with a slightly furry surface

suet   (*say* <u>sooh</u>-uht)

noun a hard dry fat surrounding the kidneys of animals and used in cooking

suffer

verb **1** to feel pain or unhappiness: *She suffers from asthma.* | *He has suffered for a long time.* **2** to put up with: *She suffered their insults quietly.*

suffice

verb to be enough: *Three lamingtons will suffice, thank you.*

sufficient

adjective enough

Word building: **sufficiency** *noun*

suffix

noun a word part added to the end of a word, such as *-ness* in *kindness*

suffocate

verb **1** to kill by stopping from breathing: *The murderer suffocated the victim with a pillow.* **2** to die from lack of air

Word building: **suffocation** *noun*

sugar

noun a sweet substance made mainly from cane and beet and used widely in food

Word building: **sugary** *adjective*

sugar cane

noun a tall, grassy plant that grows in warm, tropical areas, from which sugar is extracted

suggest   (*say* suh-<u>jest</u>)

verb to put forward the idea of: *She suggested a game of chess.*

Word building: **suggestion** *noun*

suggestible

adjective easily influenced

suggestion

noun **1** an idea or plan offered for someone to consider: *She made a suggestion about how I could improve my swimming technique.* | *He made the suggestion that we leave our car at home and go with him.* **2** a slight sign of something: *There was the faintest suggestion of sarcasm in her voice.* | *The cake was chocolate flavoured, with a suggestion of orange.*

suggestive

adjective suggesting something, especially something improper

suicide

noun **1** the act of killing yourself deliberately: *to commit suicide* **2** someone who does this

Word building: **suicidal** *adjective*   **suicide** *verb*

suit

noun **1** a set of clothes meant to be worn together **2** one of the four sets in a pack of cards
verb **3** to fit or be convenient: *Tomorrow will suit quite well.* **4** to be convenient to: *It suits me to go on Thursday.* **5** to look attractive on: *That colour suits you.*

suitable

adjective **1** fitting or convenient: *a suitable time* **2** appropriate or right for the occasion: *suitable clothes*

Word building: **suitability** *noun*

suitcase

noun an oblong bag for carrying clothes and other things when you travel

suite   (*say* sweet)

noun a series or set, especially of furniture or rooms

sukiyaki   (*say* soo-kee-<u>ah</u>-kee)

noun a Japanese food of fried meat, vegetables and so on, usually cooked with soy sauce

sulfur   (*say* <u>sul</u>-fuh)

noun a yellow non-metallic element used in gunpowder, matches and other things

Word use: This word used be spelt **sulphur** but nowadays this spelling is only used for the colour, as in *sulphur-crested cockatoo.*
Word building: **sulfuric** *adjective*   **sulfurous** *adjective*   **sulfureous** *adjective*

sulk

verb to be bad-tempered and silent because you feel that you have been unfairly treated

Word building: **sulky** *adjective* (**sulkier, sulkiest**)

sullen

adjective angry, silent and ill-mannered

Word building: **sullenness** *noun*

sulphur

noun an old-fashioned spelling of **sulfur**

sultan

noun a Muslim ruler

Word building: **sultanate** *noun*
Word history: from an Arabic word meaning 'king', 'ruler', or 'power'

sultana

noun **1** a small green seedless grape **2** dried fruit made from such a grape **3** a wife or any close female relative of a sultan

sultry

adjective hot and humid: *It was a sultry day, before the thunderstorm.*

Word building: **sultriness** *noun*

sum

noun **1** a total: *The sum of 183 and 17 is 200.* **2** an exercise or problem in arithmetic **3** an amount: *a sum of money*
phrase **4 sum up, a** to add up **b** to express in a shortened form: *It is difficult to sum up what she said.* **c** to form an opinion about: *She summed him up at once.*

Word building: Other verb forms are **I summed, I have summed, I am summing.**

sum/some Don't confuse **sum** with **some**, which means 'a few or a little'.

summary

noun a short statement in speech or writing giving the main points of something
Other words: **precis, synopsis**

Word building: The plural is **summaries.** | **summarise** *verb*: *She summarised the Prime Minister's speech for the newspapers.*

summer

noun the warmest season of the year

Word building: **summery** *adjective*

summit

noun the top or highest point: *the summit of a hill | the summit of her career*

summon

verb to send for officially: *They summoned me to appear before the committee.*

summons

noun an order to appear at a particular place, especially a court of law

Word building: The plural is **summonses.**

sumptuous   (*say* <u>sump</u>-chooh-uhs)

adjective rich and luxurious: *a sumptuous home*

sun

noun **1** the star which is the centre of our solar system and which gives light and warmth to the earth **2** sunshine: *a seat in the sun*

Word use: An adjective from **sun** is **solar**.
Word building: **sunny** *adjective* (**sunnier, sunniest**)   **sunless** *adjective*   **sunlight** *noun*

sunbake
verb to lie or sit in the sun in order to become tanned

sunburn
noun painful reddening of the skin caused by being burnt by the heat of the sun
Word building: **sunburnt** *adjective*

sundae
noun an ice-cream served with flavoured syrup and chopped nuts

Sunday
noun the first day of the week
Word use: The abbreviation is **Sun**.

sundial
noun an instrument which tells the time by a shadow cast on its face, which is marked in hours like a clock

sunflower
noun a tall plant with big yellow flowers and seeds which you can eat

sunglasses
plural noun spectacles with darkened lenses to protect your eyes from the glare of the sun

sunrise
noun the appearance of the sun above the horizon in the morning, or the time when this happens

sunscreen (*say* <u>sun</u>-screen)
noun a cream put on your skin to protect it from the sun
Word use: This is sometimes called **sunblock**.

sunset
noun the disappearance of the sun below the horizon at night, or the time when this happens

sunshine
noun **1** the light of the sun **2** cheerfulness or brightness

sunspot
noun one of the dark patches on the surface of the sun which are believed to affect some things on earth, such as the weather

sunstroke
noun a sickness with weakness and a high temperature caused by being in the sun for too long

suntan
noun brownness of the skin caused by being out in the sun
Word building: **suntanned** *adjective*

super
adjective Informal extremely good or pleasing: *a super effort* | *a super holiday*

super-
prefix a word part meaning 'over' or 'superior to': *supernatural*
Word history: from Latin

superannuation
(*say* sooh-puh-ran-yooh-<u>ay</u>-shuhn)
noun money that is put away for someone to live on when they retire from work

superb
adjective excellent or splendid: *a superb performance* | *superb beauty*

supercilious (*say* sooh-puh-<u>sil</u>-ee-uhs)
adjective proud and scornful: *a supercilious person* | *a supercilious look*
Other words: **condescending, contemptuous, disdainful, haughty**
Word building: **superciliously** *adverb* **superciliousness** *noun*

supercontinent
noun one of the huge masses of land existing millions of years ago which over time split into smaller continents

superficial
adjective **1** having to do with the outside or surface: *a superficial cut* **2** being on the outside only, rather than real or deep: *a superficial similarity between two people* | *superficial sorrow* **3** caring only about how things appear on the surface: *a superficial writer*
Word building: **superficially** *adverb* **superficiality** *noun*

superfluous (*say* sooh-<u>per</u>-flooh-uhs)
adjective more than is needed: *There were so many helpers that he was superfluous.*
Word building: **superfluity** *noun* **superfluously** *adverb* **superfluousness** *noun*

superintendent
noun someone who is in charge of work, a business, or a building
Word building: **superintend** *verb*

superior

adjective **1** higher in position or rank: *a superior officer* **2** better or of higher quality: *superior intelligence* **3** greater in amount: *They beat us because of superior numbers.*

noun **4** someone who is higher in rank than you: *You have to be careful how you speak to your superiors.*

Word building: **superiority** *noun*

superlative   (*say* sooh-<u>per</u>-luh-tiv)

adjective **1** of the highest or best kind: *a superlative voice | superlative skill* **2** having to do with the form of an adjective or adverb which expresses the greatest degree of comparison: *'Smoothest' is the superlative form of 'smooth' and 'most easily' is the superlative form of 'easily'.*

Word use: Compare definition 2 with **comparative**.

Word building: **superlatively** *adverb*

supermarket

noun a large self-service shop selling food and other household goods

supernatural

adjective not able to be explained in terms of the laws of nature: *A ghost is a supernatural being.*

Word building: **supernatural** *noun*

superpower

noun a very rich and powerful nation

supersonic

adjective moving faster than the speed of sound: *a supersonic jet*

superstar

noun a singer or actor who is very famous

superstition

noun a belief about the meaning of a thing or event that does not stem from reason or sensible thought: *There is a superstition that if you break a mirror you get seven years' bad luck.*

Word building: **superstitious** *adjective* **superstitiously** *adverb*

supervise

verb to direct or manage: *to supervise a class | to supervise a job*

Word building: **supervision** *noun* **supervisor** *noun* **supervisory** *adjective*

supper

noun a light meal eaten in the evening

supplant

verb to take the place of: *He has supplanted her as captain of the team.*

Word use: The more usual word is **replace**.

supple

adjective flexible or bending easily: *an athlete with a supple body | a supple cane*

Word building: **suppleness** *noun*

supplement   (*say* <u>sup</u>-luh-muhnt)

noun **1** something added for completion or correction: *Two hundred new words are listed in the supplement of the dictionary.* **2** an extra part of a newspaper on a particular subject: *an educational supplement*

verb (*say* <u>sup</u>-luh-ment) **3** to add to: *She supplements her pocket money by babysitting.*

Word building: **supplementary** *adjective* **supplementation** *noun*

supply

verb **1** to provide: *to supply a school with books | to supply books to a school*
Other words: **equip, furnish**

noun **2** an amount of something provided or available for use: *We have a good supply of paper.*
Other words: **quantity, stock, store**

3 supplies, a store of materials, food, and so on: *He was in charge of the army's supplies.*
Other words: **provisions**

Word building: Other verb forms are **I supplied, I have supplied, I am supplying.** | The plural form of the noun is **supplies.** | **supplier** *noun*
Word history: from a Latin word meaning 'fill up'

support

verb **1** to hold up: *to support a weight; a wall that supports a building* **2** to give help or strength to: *Thankyou for supporting me with kindness and advice. | I have information to support my argument.* **3** to believe in and help: *They support the Labor Party. | William supports the local netball team.* **4** to supply with money or other things needed for living: *Teresa works to support the family.*

noun **5** the providing of support: *I need your support.* **6** someone or something that gives support: *This pole is one of the supports of the tent. | Dad was a great support to Mum during her final exams.*

Word building: **supporter** *noun* **supportive** *adjective*

suppose

verb **1** to take as being a fact: *Let us suppose that everything will go well.* **2** to think or believe without actual knowledge: *I suppose that you are right.* | *Do you suppose it was an accident?*

Word building: **supposition** *noun*

supposed

adjective **1** thought to be probable: *their supposed victory*
phrase **2 supposed to**, expected or meant to: *You are supposed to be here at 9 o'clock every morning.*

Word building: **supposedly** *adverb*

suppress

verb **1** to abolish or put an end to: *The government suppressed cigarette advertisements at sporting events.* **2** to keep inside or hidden: *I suppressed a yawn.* | *They suppressed the news of his death.*

Word building: **suppression** *noun* **suppressive** *adjective* **suppressor** *noun*

supra-

prefix a word part meaning 'above'

Word history: from Latin

supreme

adjective **1** highest in position or power: *the supreme commander* **2** greatest: *supreme courage*; *supreme hatred*

Word building: **supremacy** *noun*

sure

adjective **1** certain or having no doubt about something you think: *I am sure she will win.*
Other words: **confident, convinced, positive**
2 certain to be the case: *She is a sure winner.* **3** able to be trusted: *a sure messenger*
Other words: **reliable, trustworthy**
4 firm: *to stand on sure ground* **5** never missing or slipping: *a sure aim with a gun*
Other words: **certain, reliable, steady**
adverb **6** *Informal* surely or certainly: *You sure were lucky.*
phrase **7 make sure**, to be certain: *Make sure that you lock the door when you leave.*

Word building: **sureness** *noun*

sure/shore Don't confuse **sure** with **shore**, which is the land along the edge of the sea or a lake.

surely

adverb **1** firmly or steadily: *He ran slowly but surely.* **2** almost certainly: *It will surely be fine tomorrow.*

surf

noun **1** the waves which break along the shore making foamy water
verb **2** to ride waves, usually using your body or a board **3** to explore (the internet) in a random way: *Most lunchtimes we just surf the net rather that play sport.*

surf/serf Don't confuse **surf** with **serf**, which was a peasant in medieval times.

surface

noun **1** the outer part or side of anything: *a polished surface* | *the six surfaces of a cube*
Other words: **exterior, outside**
2 the top, especially of water or other liquid: *I swam up to the surface.* **3** outside appearance: *He was calm on the surface but felt frightened inside.*
verb **4** to rise to the surface: *The diver surfaced.* **5** to give a surface to: *He surfaced the path with gravel.*
Other words: **coat, cover**

surfboard

noun a long narrow board used to ride waves towards the shore

surfing

noun the sport of riding waves towards the shore, either by standing on a surfboard or by allowing your body to be carried along by the wave

Word building: **surfer** *noun*

surge

noun **1** a wave-like rush or forward movement: *a surge of anger* | *the surge of a crowd*
verb **2** to rush forwards or upwards in waves or like waves: *The crowd surged around the prime minister's car.* | *Blood surged to the speaker's face.*

surgeon   (*say* ser-juhn)

noun a doctor who does surgery

surgery

noun **1** the treatment of diseases or injuries by using instruments to cut into the body **2** the room of a doctor or dentist where patients go for treatment

Word building: **surgical** *adjective*

surly

adjective unfriendly and bad-tempered: *a surly person* | *a surly voice*

Word building: Other forms are **surlier,
surliest.**

surname

noun someone's family name: *Her first
name is Jane and her surname is Brown.*

surpass

verb to be better than: *This painting
surpasses all your other ones.*

Word use: The more usual word is **outdo.**

surplice   (*say* <u>ser</u>-pluhs)

noun a loose white piece of outer clothing
worn in church by choir singers and by
some priests and ministers

Word history: from a French word meaning
'over-fur (garment)'

surplus   (*say* <u>ser</u>-pluhs)

noun an amount that is more than what
is needed or used: *Australia had a wheat
surplus after several seasons of good rainfall.*

Word building: **surplus** *adjective*: *surplus food*

surprise

verb **1** to fill with a feeling of shock and
wonder because of being unexpected or
very unusual: *Her sudden outburst of anger
surprised me.*
Other words: **amaze, astonish, astound, stun**
2 to come upon suddenly and
unexpectedly: *He surprised me as I was
creeping out the back door.*
Other words: **catch**
noun **3** something that surprises: *Your
present was a lovely surprise.* **4** the feeling
of being surprised: *She shouted with
surprise.*

Word building: **surprise** *adjective*: *a surprise
party* | **surprising** *adjective*: *a surprising event*

surrender

verb to give up to the ownership or power
of someone else or something: *The killer
surrendered the gun to the policeman.* | *I have
surrendered to despair.*

Word building: **surrender** *noun*

surround

verb to go around completely: *A wooden
fence surrounds our house.* | *A feeling of
sadness surrounded them.*

surroundings

plural noun everything that is around or
near someone or something: *Everyone is
affected by their surroundings.*
Other words: **environment, location**

surveillance   (*say* suh-<u>vay</u>-luhns)

noun a watch kept over someone to
find out what they are doing, especially
someone suspected of doing something
wrong: *The suspect didn't realise that the
police had him under surveillance.*

survey   (*say* ser-<u>vay</u>, <u>ser</u>-vay)

verb **1** to take a general view of: *We
surveyed the surrounding countryside from
the hill.* **2** to ask the views of, in order to
write a report about what people think
or do: *You need to survey the public on
this matter.* **3** to find out the form and
boundaries of land by measuring: *The
council surveyed the area.*
noun **4** an act of surveying: *They did a
survey to see what people thought about
daylight saving.* **5** a report or map made
after surveying

Word building: The plural form of the noun is
surveys. | **surveyor** *noun* someone whose job
is taking surveys, particularly of land

survive

verb to remain alive or in existence,
especially after someone else's death or
after some event: *Three were killed in the
expedition and only one survived.* | *The
singer's popularity has survived through many
music fads.*
Other words: **endure**

Word building: **surviving** *adjective*: *He has
three surviving children.* **survival** *noun*
survivor *noun*

susceptible   (*say* suh-<u>sep</u>-tuh-buhl)

phrase **susceptible to,** easily affected by:
He is susceptible to colds. | *She is susceptible
to praise.*

Word building: **susceptibility** *noun*

sushi

noun a Japanese food of slightly sweetened
rice rolled with toppings or fillings of raw
seafood, vegetables, seaweed, and so on

suspect   (*say* suhs-<u>pekt</u>)

verb **1** to think to be guilty or bad without
certain knowledge: *They suspected me of
being a thief.* **2** to think to be likely: *I
suspect that he is not very happy.*
noun (*say* <u>sus</u>-pekt) **3** someone who is
suspected, especially of a crime: *The police
have three suspects.*
adjective **4** open to being suspected: *Your
story is very suspect.*

suspend

verb **1** to hang by being joined to something above: *I will suspend the curtains from this rail.* **2** to put off until a later time: *The judge suspended the criminal's sentence for six months.* **3** to remove for a time from a position or membership: *The coach suspended me from the team.*

Word building: **suspended** *adjective*: *dust particles suspended in the air*

suspender

noun an elastic strap with fasteners to hold up a woman's stockings

suspense

noun an anxious state of mind caused by having to wait to find something out: *He was in suspense until he heard the results of the exams.*

Word building: **suspenseful** *adjective*

suspension

noun **1** a suspending or being suspended **2** a liquid in which very small parts of a solid substance are mixed but not dissolved **3** the system of springs and so on used in a vehicle to stop jolts being felt inside or damaging the engine

suspicion   (*say* suhs-<u>pish</u>-uhn)

noun **1** the feeling of suspecting: *He looked at her with suspicion.* **2** the condition of being suspected: *He is under suspicion.* **3** a slight trace showing: *She gave the suspicion of a smile.*

Word building: **suspicious** *adjective* **suspiciously** *adverb*

sustain

verb **1** to hold up or support: *I can't sustain your weight for long.* **2** to suffer or have happen to you: *I sustained a terrible injury in the car accident.* **3** to keep up: *It's hard to sustain a conversation with him. | This drink should sustain you until we get there.*

Word building: **sustenance** *noun* things that make living possible, such as food and money

sustainable

adjective designed to continue operating for a long time at the same level without having bad effects on the environment: *Their dream was to develop a more sustainable form of air transport.*

sustainable development

noun plans and actions that are mindful as to how development will affect the environment and natural resources in the future

swab   (*say* swob)

noun a piece of sponge, cloth, or cottonwool, often on a stick, used for cleaning parts of your body, such as your mouth, or applying a medicine and so on

swaddle   (*say* <u>swod</u>-uhl)

verb to wrap up tightly with clothes or strips of cloth: *to swaddle a newborn baby*

swag

noun a bundle or roll of belongings carried on the shoulders by someone travelling in the bush

Word building: **swagman** *noun*

swagger

verb to walk pompously and proudly
Other words: **prance**, **strut**

Word building: **swagger** *noun*

swagman

noun a man who camps and walks through the Australian bush, carrying everything he owns in a bundle on his shoulders: *Once a jolly swagman camped by a billabong*

Word building: The plural is **swagmen**.

swallow[1]   (*say* <u>swol</u>-oh)

verb **1** to take into the stomach through the throat **2** to take in and make disappear: *Darkness swallowed the hills. | My new car swallowed up most of my money.* **3** to believe without questioning: *Don't swallow everything he tells you.*

Word building: **swallow** *noun*

swallow[2]

noun a small bird with long wings and a forked tail

swamp   (*say* swomp)

noun **1** an area of wet soft ground
Other words: **bog**, **marsh**
verb **2** to flood: *Water swamped our tent.*

swan   (*say* swon)

noun a large waterbird with a long thin neck, either black or white in colour

Word use: The male is a **cob**, the female is a **pen** and the young is a **cygnet**.

swank

noun *Informal* showy smartness in appearance or behaviour: *a person with a lot of swank.*

Word building: **swanky** *adjective* (**swankier, swankiest**)

swap   (*say* swop)

verb to exchange: *We swapped beds for the night.*

Word building: Other forms are **I swapped, I have swapped, I am swapping.** | **swap** *noun*

swarm   (*rhymes with* form)

noun **1** a large group of bees **2** a large number of people or things, especially when moving together
verb **3** to move in great numbers: *People swarmed into the cinema.*
phrase **4 swarm with,** to be covered or filled with: *This grass is swarming with ants.*

swarthy   (*say* swaw-dhee)

adjective dark in skin-colour

Word use: Other forms are **swarthier, swarthiest.**
Word building: **swarthiness** *noun*

swastika   (*say* swos-tik-uh)

noun an ancient symbol or ornament in the form of a cross with its ends bent at right angles: *The swastika was the official symbol of the Nazi party under Adolf Hitler.*

Word history: from a Sanskrit word meaning 'wellbeing'

swat   (*say* swot)

verb to hit with a hard quick blow

Word building: Other forms are **I swatted, I have swatted, I am swatting.**

swathe   (*rhymes with* bathe)

verb to wrap up with strips of material or other wrappings: *She swathed her neck with a scarf.*

sway

verb **1** to move or swing from side to side: *The crowd swayed in time to the music.* | *The wind swayed the trees.* **2** to cause to think or act in a particular way: *Carmen's speech swayed most people to vote for her.*
noun **3** a swaying movement **4** control or rule: *The Prime Minister has held sway for many years.*

Word use: The more usual word for definition 2 is **persuade**.

swear

verb **1** to make a very serious promise or oath: *I swear that I am speaking the truth.* | *You swore to keep the secret.* **2** to make swear: *I swore Tom to secrecy.* **3** to use language that is generally thought unpleasant or rude

Word building: Other forms are **I swore, I have sworn, I am swearing.** | **swearer** *noun*

sweat   (*say* swet)

verb **1** to give out a salty liquid through the skin: *This work has made me sweat.*
Other words: **perspire**
noun **2** *Informal* to work hard **3** the liquid produced in sweating
phrase **4 sweat on,** *Informal* to feel worried or impatient about: *I was sweating on getting that job.*

Word building: **sweaty** *adjective*

sweater   (*say* swet-uh)

noun a knitted jumper

sweatshirt

noun a loose light jumper

sweep

verb **1** to clean or move away with a broom or brush: *to sweep a floor* | *to sweep dust away* **2** to push or touch with a light stroke: *Prasan swept the hair from his face.* | *The priest's long robes swept the floor.* **3** to pass over or make pass over with a continuous movement: *Fire swept the countryside.* | *Rob swept a brush over the table.* **4** to move quickly and smoothly: *Sam swept out of the room.* | *The student's glance swept over the page.* **5** to stretch continuously: *The mountains sweep down to the sea.*
noun **6** the act of sweeping: *This floor needs a sweep.* **7** a swinging movement: *He gave a sweep of his arm.* **8** steady forceful movement: *the sweep of the waves* **9** a continuous stretch: *a long sweep of sand* **10** someone whose job is sweeping, especially cleaning out chimneys

Word building: **sweeping** *adjective* wide-ranging

sweet

adjective **1** having a pleasant taste like that of sugar or honey **2** pleasant in any way: *sweet sounds* | *a sweet person* | *a sweet face*
noun **3** something that is sweet, such as a lolly or a chocolate **4 sweets,** a dessert

Word building: **sweeten** *verb* to make sweet   **sweetly** *adverb*   **sweetness** *noun*

sweet corn

noun the yellow kernels or seeds of maize, which you can eat as a vegetable

sweetheart

noun someone loved by someone

Word use: This is often used as a way of addressing someone.

sweet potato

noun a tropical plant with a root that you can eat as a vegetable

swell

verb **1** to grow or make grow in size, amount or force: *The music swelled and then died away.* | *Rain swelled the river till it overflowed.* **2** to bulge out or make bulge out: *Wind swelled the sails of the ship.*
noun **3** an increase in size, amount or force **4** the movement of the waves of the sea: *There is a big swell today.* **5** *Informal* someone who is rich and fashionably dressed
adjective **6** *Informal* excellent: *What a swell day for a picnic!*

Word building: Other verb forms are **it swelled, it has swollen, it is swelling.** | **swelling** *noun* a swollen part

swelter

verb to feel very hot: *We sweltered all summer.*

Word building: **sweltering** *adjective*

swerve

verb to turn aside suddenly: *The car swerved to miss the dog.*
Other words: **swing, twist, veer**

Word building: **swerve** *noun*

swift

adjective fast or quick: *a swift ship* | *He is always swift to help.*
Other words: **rapid, speedy**

Word building: **swiftly** *adjective* **swiftness** *noun*

swill

noun **1** any liquid or partly liquid food for animals, especially pigs
verb **2** to drink greedily **3** to clean by flooding with water: *to swill a kitchen floor*

swim

verb **1** to move through water by movements of the arms, legs, fins or tail **2** to move across or along by swimming: *to swim a river* **3** to be dizzy or giddy: *My head was swimming.* **4** to be covered or flooded with a liquid: *My meat was swimming in gravy.*

Word building: Other forms are **I swam, I have swum, I am swimming.** | **swim** *noun* **swimmer** *noun*

swimsuit

noun a piece of clothing to wear when you're swimming

swindle

verb to cheat out of money

Word building: **swindle** *noun* **swindler** *noun*

swine

noun **1** a pig **2** *Informal* someone who is unpleasant or nasty

Word building: The plural is **swine**.

swing¹

verb **1** to move or make move to and fro **2** to move or make move in a curve: *The car swung around the corner.* | *He swung open the door.*
noun **3** a swinging movement **4** a change, especially in the number of votes for a political party in an election: *a swing to Labor* **5** a seat hung from above on which you sit and swing to and fro for fun

Word building: Other verb forms are **I swung, I have swung, I am swinging.**

swing²

noun a kind of jazz music, often played by big bands

swipe

Informal
verb **1** to hit after taking a full swing with the arm: *He swiped me across the face.* **2** to steal: *She swiped my rubber.*

Word building: **swipe** *noun*

swirl

verb to move in a whirling way: *Water swirled around the rock.*

Word building: **swirl** *noun* **swirly** *adjective*

swish

verb to move or make move with a hissing sound: *The whip swished through the air.* | *The horse swished its tail.*

Word building: **swish** *noun*

switch

verb **1** to change or turn: *to switch classes | to switch directions | to switch a conversation to another subject*
noun **2** a changing or turning: *a switch of plans* **3** a button for turning electricity on or off **4** a thin cane used for whipping **5** a shortened form of **switchboard**
phrase **6 switch on**, to make an electrical appliance start: *to switch on a light* **7 switch off**, to make an electrical appliance stop: *to switch off a toaster*

switchboard

noun an arrangement of switches on a board, especially one that is used to connect telephone calls

swivel   (*say* <u>swiv</u>-uhl)

verb to turn around: *He swivelled around to have a better look.*

Word building: Other forms are **I swivelled, I have swivelled, I am swivelling**.

swoon

verb **1** to faint or become unconscious: *The pain made her swoon.* **2** to have such a strong feeling as to almost faint: *She swooned over her favourite rock star.*

swoop

verb **1** to sweep down through the air: *The eagle swooped on the mouse.* **2** to come down in a sudden attack: *The army swooped down on the town.*

Word building: **swoop** *noun*

sword   (*say* sawd)

noun a weapon with a long pointed blade fixed in a handle

swordfish

noun a large sea fish with a long, sharp upper jaw, like a sword

Word building: The plural is **swordfish** or **swordfishes**.

syllable   (*say* <u>sil</u>-uh-buhl)

noun a part of a word which consists of a vowel sound and possibly consonant sounds around the vowel: *'Along' has two syllables and 'wonderful' has three.*

syllabus

noun an outline of what is to be taught in a course of lessons

symbol

noun **1** something that stands for or means something else: *The dove is a symbol of peace.*

Other words: **emblem, sign**
2 a letter, number or other mark used to stand for something: *The symbol for degrees is °.*

Word building: **symbolise** *verb*: *This ring symbolises our friendship.*   **symbolic** *adjective*

symmetry   (*say* <u>sim</u>-uh-tree)

noun the arrangements of the parts of something so that they are all balanced in size and shape: *a design with perfect symmetry*

Word building: **symmetrical** *adjective*

sympathise

verb **1** to share in a feeling of sorrow or trouble with someone: *He sympathised with her when he heard of her mother's death.*
Other words: **commiserate**
2 to understand and agree with: *I sympathise with your ideas.*

Word use: Another spelling is **sympathize**.
Word building: **sympathiser** *noun*

sympathy   (*say* <u>sim</u>-puh-thee)

noun **1** a feeling shared with someone else, especially in sorrow or trouble: *I felt great sympathy for her.*
Other words: **compassion, kindness, understanding**
2 an agreement in ideas, likes or dislikes: *They were in sympathy on that matter.*

Word building: **sympathetic** *adjective* **sympathetically** *adverb*

symphony   (*say* <u>sim</u>-fuh-nee)

noun a musical composition for a full orchestra, usually with several movements or major sections

Word building: The plural is **symphonies**. | **symphonic** *adjective*

symposium   (*say* sim-<u>poh</u>-zee-uhm)

noun a meeting for discussion

Word building: The plural is **symposiums** or **symposia**.

symptom

noun **1** something that shows that you have a disease or illness of some kind: *A sore throat is a symptom of a cold.* **2** any sign that shows that something is happening: *Unemployment is a symptom of a weak economy.*

Word building: **symptomatic** *adjective*: *A high temperature is symptomatic of flu.*

synagogue   (*say* <u>sin</u>-uh-gog)

noun a Jewish place of worship

Word history: from a Greek word meaning 'meeting' or 'assembly'

synchronise (*say* sing-kruh-nuyz)
verb **1** to happen or make happen at
the same time: *Let's synchronise our
arrival.* **2** to make show the same time:
We'd better synchronise our watches.
Word use: Another spelling is **synchronize**.
Word building: **synchronisation** *noun*

syncopate (*say* singk-uh-payt)
verb to change the rhythm of, by putting
the beat in unexpected places: *to syncopate
a piece of music*
Word building: **syncopation** *noun*

syndicate (*say* sin-dik-uht)
noun **1** a group of people or business
companies who combine to carry out an
expensive project: *A syndicate is building a
big new hotel.*
verb (*say* sin-dik-ayt) **2** to form into a
syndicate

syndrome (*say* sin-drohm)
noun in medicine, a group of signs or types
of behaviour that shows that a disease or a
condition exists: *One feature of the syndrome
is a mild to severe intellectual disability.*

synonym (*say* sin-uh-nim)
noun a word having the same or very
similar meaning as another: *'Joyful' and
'glad' are synonyms.*
Word building: **synonymous** *adjective*

synopsis (*say* suh-nop-suhs)
noun a written outline of a longer piece of
writing: *a synopsis of an essay*
Word use: The more usual word is **summary**.
Word building: The plural is **synopses** (*say*
suh-nop-seez).

synoptic chart
noun a chart or map showing the weather
conditions over a large area at a particular
time

syntax
noun the pattern for forming sentences or
phrases in a particular language

synthesis (*say* sin-thuh-suhs)
noun the blending together of parts into a
whole: *The plan was the result of a synthesis
of our ideas.* | *This cloth is made by a
synthesis of different materials.*
Word use: Compare this with **analysis**.
Word building: **synthesise** *verb* to make up by
grouping parts together

synthesiser
noun a machine, usually a computer, which
makes speech or music

synthetic (*say* sin-thet-ik)
adjective **1** human-made or artificial:
synthetic rubber **2** having to do with
synthesis

syphon
noun another spelling for **siphon**

syringe (*say* suh-rinj)
noun a small tube with either a piston or a
rubber bulb for drawing in and squirting
out liquid, used to clean wounds or, when
fitted to a needle, to inject liquid into or
take it out of the body
Word building: **syringe** *verb*

syrup
noun a thick, sweet, sticky liquid:
strawberry syrup
Word building: **syrupy** *adjective*

system
noun **1** the way something is organised or
arranged: *the decimal system of currency* |
the parliamentary system of government | *a
new system of marking exam papers* **2** an
organised way of doing something: *You
must have more system in your work.* **3** a set
of connected parts: *a railway system* | *the
nervous system of the body*
Word building: **systematic** *adjective* orderly

Tt

tab

noun **1** a small flap or loop attached to a piece of clothing or something similar **2** a tag for a name or label
phrase **3 keep tabs on**, to keep a watch or a check on: *They keep tabs on promising players.*

tabby

noun a grey or brownish-yellow cat with a striped coat

Word building: The plural is **tabbies**. | **tabby** *adjective*

table

noun **1** a piece of furniture which has a flat top resting on one or more legs **2** a plan or chart setting out items or numbers: *a table of contents | a multiplication table*
verb **3** to set out a subject for discussion in parliament

tableau   (*say* <u>tab</u>-loh)

noun a group of people arranged to form a picture or scene: *They made a charming tableau.*

Word building: The plural is **tableaux** (*say* <u>tab</u>-loh, <u>tab</u>-lohz) or **tableaus**.
Word history: from a French word meaning 'table' or 'picture'

tablespoon

noun a large spoon used for measuring or serving

tablet

noun **1** a small, flat, solid piece of medicine or soap **2** a flat slab or surface that you can carve or write on: *People used to write on tablets made of stone.*

Word use: Another word for definition 1 is **pill**.

tabloid

noun a newspaper with many pictures and short articles that don't give you a lot of detail about what is being described and with pages that are one half the size of an ordinary newspaper

Word building: **tabloid** *adjective*: *a tabloid newspaper*

taboo   (*say* tuh-<u>booh</u>)

adjective strictly forbidden: *Kicking and biting are taboo.*

Word building: **taboo** *verb* (**tabooed, tabooing**) **taboo** *noun*

tabouli   (*say* tuh-<u>booh</u>-lee)

noun a salad of cracked wheat, chopped parsley, mint, tomato, oil and lemon juice

Word use: Other spellings are **tabouleh** and **tabbouli**.

tack

noun **1** a small nail, such as is used in shoemaking or for putting up pictures **2** a zigzag movement or sharp turn, as in sailing against the wind
verb **3** to fasten with tacks **4** to zigzag or change direction: *The yacht tacked across the harbour.* **5** to sew loosely with large stitches **6** to join loosely or roughly: *They've tacked a bathroom onto the laundry.*

tackle

noun **1** equipment, especially for fishing or sailing **2** the ropes and blocks used for lifting, lowering or moving heavy weights *verb* **3** to take on and struggle with: *to tackle a problem* **4** to seize and bring to a stop, especially in football: *He was heavily tackled by three opposing forwards.* **5** to try to get the ball from, especially in soccer and hockey

Word building: **tackler** *noun*

tacky

adjective sticky: *They wiped their tacky fingers.*

Word building: Other forms are **tackier, tackiest.** | **tackiness** *noun*

taco   (*say* tah-koh, tak-oh)

noun a flat piece of crisp Mexican corn bread folded around a spicy savoury filling

tact

noun a sense of the right time to do or say something: *She showed great tact in handling the situation.*

Word building: **tactful** *noun*   **tactfully** *adverb* **tactfulness** *noun*   **tactless** *adjective* **tactlessly** *adverb*

tactics

plural noun a plan of action, especially for placing and moving troops and ships during a battle: *They outwitted the enemy with their superior tactics.*

Word building: **tactical** *adjective*   **tactically** *adverb*   **tactician** *noun*

tactile

adjective **1** having a sense of touch: *The fingertips are especially tactile.* **2** inviting to the touch: *a tactile surface*

Word building: **tactility** *noun*

tadpole

noun a young frog or toad in the earliest stage of its life during which it develops legs and becomes able to leave the water

tag

noun **1** a small loop or label **2** something attached to the end of a cord such as on a shoelace *verb* **3** to put a label on **4** to label or describe someone with a word or phrase: *They tagged me a coward.* **5** to follow closely, especially without being invited: *The dog tagged along wherever we went.*

Word building: Other verb forms are **I tagged, I have tagged, I am tagging.**

tai chi   (*say* tuy chee)

noun a set of exercises in which it is important to move smoothly from one exercise to the next while keeping your balance. It can help keep your mind alert.

Word use: This word comes from the Chinese language and means 'fist of the Great Absolute'.

tail

noun **1** the end of the backbone which forms part of the body of animals such as the cat **2** the end or bottom of anything: *a shirt tail* **3 tails, a** a black formal suit for men with a long-tailed coat **b** the side of a coin opposite that with the picture of a head on it: *Heads or tails?* *verb* **4** to follow closely: *The police tailed the stolen car to the airport.*

tail/tale Don't confuse **tail** with **tale**, which is a story, as in *a fairy tale*.

tailor

noun **1** someone who mends or makes clothes, especially for men **2** an Australian fish, named because of its scissor-like teeth *verb* **3** to provide or design for a particular need or situation, as a tailor makes clothes to fit each customer: *We'll tailor our prices to suit the market.*

Word building: **tailor-made** *adjective*

taint

verb **1** to spoil slightly: *The baby's crying tainted our enjoyment of the film.* **2** to make or become bad or corrupt

Word building: **taint** *noun*

taipan   (*say* tuy-pan)

noun a venomous brown snake with long fangs, found in Australia and New Guinea

Word history: from an Aboriginal language of Queensland called Wik-Mungkan. See the map of Australian Aboriginal languages at the end of this book.

take

verb **1** to get or receive: *He took it from me.* | *They took $10 for the chair.* **2** to have or use: *to take a rest* **3** to subtract: *Take 2 from 4.* **4** to bring or carry: *Take your coat with you.* **5** to travel on or lead: *He takes a train.* | *Where will it*

take us? **6** to feel or experience: *to take pride | to take it personally* **7** to make use of: *to take an opportunity* **8** to use up: *This takes time.* **9** to write down: *Take a note.* **10** to make: *to take a photo* **11** to regard or consider: *They take me to be a fool.* **12** to require or need: *It takes nerve to do that.* **13** to have the desired effect: *The dye didn't take, and now the colour's all wrong.* **14** to become: *She took ill.*
phrase **15 take after**, to be or look like: *She takes after her aunt.* **16 take in, a** to deceive or trick
Other words: **fool, hoodwink**
b to make smaller: *She had to take in the waist.* **17 take off, a** to leave
Other words: **depart, exit, go**
b to imitate: *to take off an accent*
Other words: **ape, copy, mimic**

Word building: Other verb forms are **I took, I have taken, I am taking.**

takeaway

noun a hot or cold meal that you buy at a shop, but take to a different place to eat

Word use: This is also called **fast food.**

take-off

noun the moment when an aircraft leaves the ground and starts to fly

takeover

noun the gaining or taking of control, especially of another business or country

Word building: **takeover** *adjective*: *a takeover bid*

talcum powder

noun a scented powder, used after a bath or shower

tale

noun a story, which may be true or false

tale/tail Don't confuse **tale** with **tail**, which is the end or bottom of anything.

talent

noun skill or ability: *Her drawings show talent.*

Word building: **talented** *adjective*

talisman   (*say* tal-uhz-muhn)

noun something considered to be lucky or magical

talk

verb **1** to speak, or express in words **2** to give or reveal information: *They tried to make him talk.* **3** to be able to speak: *I talk Italian.* **4** to discuss: *They are talking politics.*
noun **5** an occasion for talking, such as a speech, lecture or conference **6** a conversation: *We had a good talk.* **7** gossip, or the topic of gossip: *the talk of the town*
phrase **8 talk someone into something**, to persuade someone to do something

Word building: **talkative** *adjective* **talkatively** *adverb* **talker** *noun*

tall

adjective **1** of more than the usual height: *a tall building | a tall boy* **2** having a particular height: *She is 1.6 metres tall.*

tally

noun **1** a record or account of an amount counted or owed: *The shearers keep a tally of the sheep they shear.*
verb **2** to count or record **3** to agree: *Your story doesn't tally with the facts.*

Word building: Other verb forms are **I tallied, I have tallied, I am tallying.** | The plural form of the noun is **tallies.**

talon

noun the claw, especially of birds of prey such as the eagle

tambourine   (*say* tam-buh-reen)

noun a small drum with a skin-covered frame which has metal discs set into it, played by hitting and shaking it

Word history: from a French word meaning 'little drum'

tame

adjective **1** used to being handled by humans: *a tame bird* **2** dull: *The film was very tame.*

Word building: **tame** *verb* to bring under human control **tamely** *adverb* **tameness** *noun* **tamer** *noun*

tamper

verb to interfere so as to change or damage

tampon

noun a cotton plug used to absorb the flow of blood from a wound or from the vagina during menstruation

tan

verb **1** to turn or become brown in the sun: *She sat in the sun to tan her legs.* | *Her back tans nicely.* **2** to change into leather by soaking and treating: *to tan a hide*
noun **3** a suntan
adjective **4** yellowish-brown

Word building: Other verb forms are **I tanned, I have tanned, I am tanning.** | **tanner** *noun*

tandem

adverb **1** one behind another
noun **2** a bicycle for two riders

Word building: **tandem** *adjective*

tandoori

adjective having to do with Indian food cooked in a very hot clay oven: *tandoori chicken*

tang

noun a strong, salty or sharp flavour or smell: *the tang of the sea*

Word building: **tangy** *adjective* (**tangier, tangiest**)

tangent   (*say* tan-juhnt)

noun **1** a straight line which touches a curve **2** a sudden new direction: *He keeps flying off at a tangent.*

Word building: **tangent** *adjective* touching

tangerine   (*say* tan-juh-reen)

noun **1** a type of mandarin
adjective **2** reddish-orange

Word history: named after the Moroccan seaport of *Tangier*

tangible   (*say* tan-juh-buhl)

adjective real, or able to be touched or felt

Word building: **tangibly** *adverb*

tangle

verb to put or get in a confused muddle: *The kitten has tangled the threads.*

Word building: **tangle** *noun*

tango

noun a South American ballroom dance

Word building: The plural is **tangos.** | **tango** *verb* (**tangoed, tangoing**)

tank

noun **1** a container for liquid, such as petrol or water **2** a heavy fighting vehicle armed with cannons and machine guns

tankard

noun a beer mug, or other large cup, sometimes with a lid

tanker

noun a large vehicle or vessel for carrying oil or other liquids in large quantities

tantalise

verb to tease or torment with the sight of something wished for but out of reach

Word use: Another spelling is **tantalize.**
Word building: **tantalising** *adjective* **tantalisingly** *adverb*

tantrum

noun a violent outburst of temper

Taoism   (*say* tow-iz-uhm)

noun a Chinese philosophy which encourages people not to interfere with nature and to be sincere and honest

Word building: **Taoist** *noun* a follower of Taoism

tap¹

verb to hit lightly

Word building: Other forms are **I tapped, I have tapped, I am tapping.** | **tap** *noun*

tap²

noun **1** something used to control the flow of liquid: *a bath tap*
verb **2** to draw on, as from a supply of water, or other resources: *I was able to tap my reserves of energy when I needed them.* **3** to connect with secretly, in order to overhear conversation: *The detectives tapped our phone.*

Word building: Other verb forms are **I tapped, I have tapped, I am tapping.**

tape

noun **1** a long strip of paper, cloth or a similar material such as you use in sewing or in typewriters **2** a plastic strip coated with magnetic powder, used to record sound and video signals and to store information from computers **3** another name for **tape measure**
verb **4** to record on tape: *He taped my record of the opera.*

tape measure

noun a long strip or ribbon made of linen or steel, marked with millimetres and centimetres for measuring

taper

verb **1** to gradually narrow or thin at one end: *The road tapers in to a track.* | *She tapered her nails to a point.*
noun **2** a very thin candle
Word building: **tapering** *adjective*

tape recorder

noun a machine which records sound on magnetic tape

tapestry

noun a piece of cloth with a design which has been woven or embroidered
Word building: The plural is **tapestries**.

tapeworm

noun a flat or tapelike worm which lives in the intestine of people and animals

tapioca   (*say* tap-ee-<u>oh</u>-kuh)

noun floury grains of cassava starch used for puddings and thickening sauce

taproot

noun the big main root of a plant from which the other roots branch

tar

noun a thick, black, sticky substance that you get from wood or coal, especially used for making roads
Word building: **tar** *verb* (**tarred, tarring**) to cover or smear with tar

tarantula   (*say* tuh-<u>ran</u>-chuh-luh)

noun **1** a large, furry, Australian spider which often shelters indoors when it's raining **2** a venomous spider of Europe
Word use: Another name for definition 1 is **huntsman**.
Word history: named after the Italian seaport of *Taranto*, where the European spider is common

target

noun **1** something which you aim at in order to hit or reach: *Her arrow hit the centre of the target.* | *They set a target of ten days to finish work.*
Other words: **goal**
2 a victim: *He is the target of their jokes.*
Other words: **butt**

tariff

noun **1** a charge for importing something into a country **2** the price charged for a room in a hotel

tarmac

noun **1** a mixture of tar and gravel used to seal roads **2** an airport runway
Word history: a short form of *tarmacadam* (*tar* + *macadam*, a road surface of broken stones)

tarnish

verb to dull, discolour or spoil: *Silver tarnishes in the salt air.* | *to tarnish a reputation*
Word building: **tarnish** *noun*   **tarnished** *adjective*

tarpaulin   (*say* tah-<u>paw</u>-luhn)

noun a large canvas or other waterproof cover

tarragon

noun a strong-smelling herb used in cooking and salads

tarry

verb *Old-fashioned* to linger or loiter
Word building: Other forms are **I tarried, I have tarried, I am tarrying.**

tart[1]

adjective sour or sharp: *a tart taste* | *a tart retort*
Word building: **tartly** *adverb*   **tartness** *noun*

tart[2]

noun a shallow fruit or jam pie, without a top

tartan

noun the checked woollen cloth in the colours of the different Scottish Highland clans, or any similar checked cloth
Word building: **tartan** *adjective*

task

noun **1** a piece of work, or a duty
Other words: **assignment, chore, job, mission**
phrase **2 take to task**, to blame or scold

Tasmanian devil

noun a fierce black-and-white meat-eating marsupial, found in Tasmania

Tasmanian tiger

noun a carnivorous, wolflike marsupial from Tasmania, now thought to be extinct, with tan-coloured fur and black stripes
Word use: Another word for this is **thylacine**.

tassel

noun a bunch of silk, or other threads, hanging as an ornament

taste

noun **1** the sense which experiences flavour **2** flavour: *It has a sweet taste.* **3** a liking or enjoyment: *I've acquired a taste for olives.* **4** a sense of what belongs or is attractive: *He has no taste.* **5** a first experience or sample: *She had a taste of city life.*

verb **6** to try by eating: *He tasted the soup to see if it was ready.* **7** to experience or feel, especially through your sense of taste **8** to have a certain flavour: *This tastes like chicken.*

Word building: **tasteful** *adjective*   **tasteless** *adjective*

tasty

adjective full of flavour: *a tasty sauce*

Word building: Other forms are **tastier, tastiest**. | **tastiness** *noun*

tatters

plural noun torn or ragged pieces, especially of clothing: *My shirt was in tatters after the riot.*

tattoo[1]

noun **1** a signal on a trumpet or drum: *to beat a tattoo* **2** an outdoor military display

tattoo[2]

noun an ink picture permanently printed into someone's skin with needles

Word building: **tattoo** *verb* (**tattooed, tattooing**)

taunt

verb to insult or tease cruelly

Word building: **taunt** *noun*   **taunting** *adjective*   **tauntingly** *adverb*

taut

adjective stretched tight: *They held the rope taut.*

Word building: **tautly** *adverb*   **tautness** *noun*

tavern

noun a place where food and alcoholic drink can be bought

tawdry

adjective cheap and showy: *tawdry jewellery*

tawny

adjective yellowish-brown, like a lion's coat

Word building: Other forms are **tawnier, tawniest**.
Word history: from a French word meaning 'tanned'

tax

noun **1** money people have to pay each year to support the government
verb **2** to put a tax on **3** to burden or exhaust: *The work taxes her strength.*

Word building: **taxable** *adjective*   **taxation** *noun*

taxi

noun **1** a car for hire, with a driver and a meter which calculates the fare
verb **2** to move along the runway before taking off, or after landing: *The pilot taxied the plane to the terminal.*

Word building: Other verb forms are **I taxied, I have taxied, I am taxiing.** | The plural form of the noun is **taxis**.

T-ball

noun a type of softball for children in which the ball is not thrown to the batter, but is hit from a pole at waist height

tea

noun **1** a drink made by pouring boiling water onto the dried leaves of a shrub grown in China, India and Ceylon **2** the dried leaves of this shrub **3** a late afternoon or evening meal: *They had tea at six.*

Word history: from the Chinese word *ch'a*

---

tea/tee Don't confuse **tea** with **tee**, which is a small support for the ball that you use in golf.

---

teach

verb to instruct or give knowledge of: *She teaches kindergarten children.* | *He teaches Maths.*

Word building: Other forms are **I taught, I have taught, I am teaching.** | **teacher** *noun*

teak

noun a hard long-lasting wood used for ship building and furniture

team

noun **1** a group of people who share an activity, such as sport or work: *A new doctor joined the team.* **2** a number of animals harnessed together to do work: *a team of oxen*

---

team/teem Don't confuse **team** with **teem**. To **teem** is to rain very hard. It can also mean 'to swarm with small animals':
This river teems with fish.

---

tear¹   (*rhymes with* here)
noun **1** a drop of water that falls from your
eye, caused by sadness or pain
phrase **2 in tears**, crying: *She is in tears
again.*
Word building: **tearful** *adjective*   **tearfully**
adverb

tear/tier Don't confuse **tear** with **tier**, which is
one level in a series of levels:
The wedding cake had three tiers in it.

tear²   (*rhymes with* bare)
verb **1** to rip: *I tore my shirt.* | *The paper
tears easily.* **2** to remove or pull away: *Be
careful, the dingo will tear the food from your
hands.* | *I couldn't tear myself from the game.*
phrase **3 tear off**, to hurry away
Word building: Other verb forms are **I tore,
I have torn, I am tearing.** | **tear** *noun* a rip

tease   (*say* teez)
verb **1** to mock or pester in a light-hearted
but embarrassing way **2** to separate the
strands of: *to tease wool*
Word building: **tease** *noun*   **teasing** *adjective*
teasingly *adverb*

teaspoon
noun a small spoon which holds about five
millilitres

teat
noun the rubber top on a baby's bottle
which is shaped like a nipple

tea-tree
noun a shrub with small leaves and red,
white or pink flowers, found in Australia
and New Zealand

techie   (*say* tek-ee)
noun *Informal* somebody who knows a lot
about technology or computers: *He's such a
techie it's sometimes hard to understand what
he's talking about.*

technical   (*say* tek-nik-uhl)
adjective **1** having to do with practical
science and machinery: *a technical education* |
technical expertise **2** using words or
covering topics that only an expert would
understand
Word building: **technicality** *noun*
technically *adverb*   **technician** *noun*

technique   (*say* tek-neek)
noun **1** the way of doing or performing:
*My technique is influenced by my
teacher.* **2** practical skill or knowledge: *You
have good ideas but not much technique.*

technology   (*say* tek-nol-uh-jee)
noun the study of the use of science in
industry
Word building: **technological** *adjective*:
technological advances   **technologically** *adverb*
technologist *noun*

tectonic
adjective having to do with the structure of
the earth's crust, and its movements

tectonic plate
noun one of the sections of the earth's
surface, beneath the land and the oceans,
which moves in relation to other sections:
*The tsunami was caused when one tectonic
plate moved under another one.*

tedious
adjective long and boring: *a tedious wait* | *a
tedious lecture*
Word building: **tediously** *adverb*   **tedium** *noun*

tee
noun **1** the starting place for each hole in
golf **2** a plastic or wooden holder from
which you drive a golf ball
phrase **3 tee off**, to strike the ball from a
tee **4 tee up**, to organise or arrange: *We've
teed up a partner for you.*

tee/tea Don't confuse **tee** with **tea**, which is a
drink made by pouring boiling water onto dry
leaves.

teem¹
phrase **teem with**, to be full of: *The park
teems with wildlife.*
Word building: **teeming** *adjective*

teem²
verb to rain very hard: *We had to go inside
because it was teeming.*

teem/team Don't confuse **teem** with **team**,
which is a group of people who share an
activity, such as sport or work.

teenager
noun someone who is aged between twelve
and twenty
Word building: **teenage** *adjective*

teepee

noun a kind of tent made of skins, typical of some Native North American tribes

teeter

verb to almost lose balance: *We watched in awe as the acrobat teetered on the ledge* | *The cup teetered on the edge of the table and then fell to the ground.*

teethe (*say* teedh)

verb to grow teeth: *The baby will soon start to teethe.*

Word building: Other forms are **he teethed, he has teethed, he is teething.**

teetotal

adjective opposed to the drinking of alcohol: *a teetotal organisation*

Word building: **teetotalism** *noun* **teetotaller** *noun*

telco

noun a company which enables people to communicate or receive information by telephone, radio or satellite

telecast

noun a television broadcast

telecommunications

plural noun the sending of messages by telephone, radio or satellite

telegram

noun a message sent by telegraph

telegraph

noun a system or device for sending messages by electric signals along wire

Word building: **telegraph** *verb* **telegraphic** *adjective* **telegraphy** *noun*

telepathy (*say* tuh-lep-uh-thee)

noun the sharing or passing on of information or thoughts between one person's mind and another's without speaking, writing or using actions: *We didn't tell him so he must have known by telepathy.*

Word building: **telepathic** *adjective* **telepathically** *adverb* **telepathist** *noun*

telephone

noun a device used for speaking to someone else over a long distance, usually powered by electricity

Word use: A shortened form of this is **phone.**
Word building: **telephone** *verb* **telephonic** *adjective* **telephonically** *adverb* **telephonist** *noun*

telephoto lens

noun a lens for a camera which gives a larger picture of distant objects

teleprinter

noun an instrument with a typewriter keyboard which sends and receives messages by changing typed information into electrical signals

telescope

noun a tube-shaped instrument with powerful lenses which make distant objects seem closer

Word building: **telescope** *verb* to shorten **telescopic** *adjective*

television

noun **1** the sending of pictures and sound by radio waves which are picked up by the receiving sets of viewers **2** a television set or receiver

Word use: A shortened form of this is **TV.**
Word building: **televise** *verb*

telex

noun **1** a postal service in which teleprinters are rented to businesses which can send and receive their own messages **2** the message sent or received

Word building: The plural is **telexes.** | **telex** *verb*

tell

verb **1** to give an account or description of **2** to express or say: *to tell a lie* **3** to know or recognise: *Can you tell which is yours?* **4** to order: *Tell him to go.* **5** to have or show an effect: *The strain is telling on your face.*
phrase **6 tell on**, to tell tales about **7 tell off**, to scold

Word building: Other verb forms are **I told, I have told, I am telling.**

teller

noun someone who works in a bank receiving and paying out the customers' money

telltale

adjective revealing, especially what is not meant to be known: *There were telltale footprints under the window.*

Word building: **telltale** *noun*

temper

noun **1** the particular state of mind or mood you are in: *She's in a good temper.* **2** an angry or resentful mood: *You're often in a temper.*

verb **3** to strengthen by changes of temperature: *to temper steel* **4** to make less severe: *She tempered her anger.*

temperament

noun a type of personality, especially a moody one: *She has a cheerful temperament.* | *He has such a temperament.*

Word building: **temperamental** *adjective* moody **temperamentally** *adverb*

temperance

noun **1** moderation and self-control, especially in drinking alcohol **2** the complete avoidance of alcohol

temperate   (*say* tem-puh-ruht)

adjective moderate and steady: *a temperate use of alcohol* | *a temperate winter*

Word building: **temperately** *adverb* **temperateness** *noun*

temperature   (*say* temp-ruh-chuh)

noun **1** a measure of the degree of heat or cold of something or someone **2** an abnormally high amount of heat in your body: *to have a temperature*

tempest

noun a violent storm or a violent disturbance: *The ship sank in the tempest.* | *a tempest of tears*

Word building: **tempestuous** *adjective* **tempestuously** *adverb*
Word history: from a Latin word meaning 'season'

temple¹

noun a large building where people worship

temple²

noun the flat part on either side of your forehead

tempo

noun speed, rhythm or pattern: *music with a fast tempo* | *the tempo of modern life*

temporary   (*say* temp-ree)

adjective lasting for a short time: *a temporary job*

Word use: The opposite is **permanent**.
Word building: **temporarily** *adverb*

tempt

verb **1** to attract or persuade, especially to something unwise or forbidden **2** to dare or provoke: *Don't tempt fate.*

Word building: **temptation** *noun* **tempter** *noun* **tempting** *adjective* **temptingly** *adverb* **temptress** *noun*

tempura   (*say* tem-pooh-ruh)

noun a Japanese food made from seafood or vegetables coated in a light batter and deep-fried in oil

ten

noun **1** the number 10 **2** the Roman numeral X

Word building: **ten** *adjective*: *ten tourists* **tenth** *adjective*: *his tenth trip this year*

tenacious   (*say* tuh-nay-shuhs)

adjective **1** holding on firmly: *a tenacious grip* **2** stubbornly persistent: *a tenacious person*

Word building: **tenaciously** *adverb* **tenacity** *noun*

tenant

noun someone who pays rent for the use of a house, land or a flat

Word building: **tenancy** *noun*

tend¹

verb **1** to be likely or inclined: *I tend to be cross when I'm tired.* **2** to move in a certain direction: *The sunflower tends toward the light.*

Word building: **tendency** *noun* (**tendencies**)

tend²

verb to watch or look after: *to tend a fire* | *The nurse is tending the patient.*

tender¹

adjective **1** not tough or hard: *tender steak* **2** warm and affectionate: *a tender heart* **3** gentle or delicate: *a tender touch* **4** painful to feel or discuss: *tender to the touch* | *It's a tender subject.*

Word building: **tenderly** *adverb* **tenderness** *noun*

tender²

verb **1** to offer: *I tendered my resignation.* *noun* **2** an offer, as of payment or to do a job for a certain price: *They will accept the lowest tender.*

tendon

noun a cord of tough body tissue joining a muscle to a bone

Word use: Another word is **sinew**.

tendril

noun a coiling threadlike part of a climbing plant

tenement (*say* ten-uh-muhnt)

noun a building divided into flats, especially one in the poorer crowded parts of a large city

tennis

noun a game in which two players, or two pairs of players, use racquets to hit a ball over a central net

tenor (*say* ten-uh)

noun **1** the range of musical notes which can be sung by a male singer with a high voice: *Scott sings tenor in the choir.* **2** a man with a high singing voice

Word use: **tenor** range is higher than **baritone** and **bass** and lower than **soprano** and **alto**.
Word building: **tenor** *adjective*: *a tenor saxophone*

tenpin bowling

noun an indoor sport in which the player bowls a heavy ball down a wooden alley at ten upright objects called pins, to knock down as many as possible

tense¹

adjective **1** rigid or stretched tight **2** suffering from nervous strain: *You have been very tense since your illness.*

Word building: **tense** *verb* **tensely** *adverb* **tenseness** *noun* **tension** *noun*

tense²

noun the form of a verb which shows the time of an action

Word use: See **present tense, past tense, future tense**.

tent

noun a movable shelter made of cloth, held up by poles

tentacle

noun a thin, easily bent, arm-like part on an animal such as an octopus, used for feeling and grasping

tentative

adjective unsure or cautious: *He made a tentative attempt to join in the conversation.*

Word building: **tentatively** *adverb*

tenuous

adjective weak or vague: *a tenuous connection*

Word building: **tenuously** *adverb*

tepid (*say* tep-uhd)

adjective lukewarm or slightly warm

Word building: **tepidly** *adverb*

teppanyaki (*say* te-pan-yah-kee)

noun a Japanese dish in which pieces of meat or fish are roasted on a hot iron plate

Word history: from the Japanese word for 'iron' added to the Japanese word for 'roast' or 'bake'

teriyaki (*say* te-ree-yah-kee)

noun a Japanese food consisting of meat, fish or chicken marinated in soy sauce and then grilled

term

noun **1** a division of the year in schools and colleges **2** a period of time: *in the long term* **3** a descriptive or naming word or group of words: *This book is full of technical terms.* **4 terms**, conditions of agreement

terminal

adjective **1** marking the end: *a terminal illness*
noun **2** the end of a railway line or other travel route where passengers and goods arrive and leave: *an air terminal* **3** a point where current enters or leaves in an electrical circuit **4** another name for **computer terminal**

terminate

verb **1** to bring to an end: *They have terminated my cousin's job at the factory.* **2** to come to the end of a journey at a certain place: *This train terminates here.*

Word building: **termination** *noun*

terminus

noun a station at the end of a railway line or bus route

termite

noun a pale-coloured insect which can destroy buildings and furniture by boring holes in wood

Word use: A termite is often called a **white ant**, though it is not really an ant.

terrace

noun **1** a narrow flattened area on the side of a hill: *a rice terrace* **2** a row of houses joined together **3** one of these houses

terracotta

noun **1** a clay used for pipes, roof tiles and other similar things
adjective **2** brownish-red

Word history: from an Italian word meaning 'baked earth'

terrain

noun a part of the land surface, with its natural features in mind: *rough terrain*

Word history: from a French word meaning 'earth'

terrestrial

adjective living or growing on land

terrible

adjective **1** causing great fear: *a terrible monster*
Other words: **bloodcurdling, dreadful, fearsome, formidable, frightening, frightful, horrible, horrific, nightmarish, scary, terrifying**
2 very bad: *a terrible noise*
Other words: **atrocious, awful, dreadful, horrendous**

Word building: **terribly** *adverb*

terrier

noun a kind of small dog, originally used for hunting

terrific

adjective **1** very great: *terrific speed* **2** very good: *a terrific game*

Word building: **terrifically** *adverb*

terrify

verb to frighten very much
Other words: **alarm, horrify, petrify, scare**

Word building: Other forms are **I terrified, I have terrified, I am terrifying.**

territory

noun land thought of as belonging to someone: *enemy territory*

Word building: The plural is **territories.** | **territorial** *adjective*

terror

noun an overpowering fear

terrorise

verb to fill with fear and alarm

Word use: Another spelling is **terrorize.**

terrorism

noun a way of fighting a government by acts of armed violence

Word building: **terrorist** *noun* someone who carries out acts of terrorism

terry towelling

noun a cotton cloth with loops on both sides

terse

adjective short and to the point: *a terse comment*

Word building: **tersely** *adverb* **terseness** *noun*

tertiary (*say* ter-shuh-ree)

adjective third in order or importance

tertiary education

noun education at college or university, which follows secondary education

test

noun **1** a trial to decide something: *a test of strength* **2** a set of questions to answer, designed to show how much you know about something: *a maths test* **3** another word for **test match**
verb **4** to try in order to find out: *to test if the water is hot enough | to test the class's knowledge*

testament

noun a will

Word use: This definition is used mostly in the phrase 'last will and testament'.
Word building: **testamentary** *adjective*

testicle

noun one of the two round male sex glands in the scrotum

testify

verb **1** to swear as true: *The witness testified that he had seen a blue Holden near the bank.* **2** to give evidence: *The barren land testifies to a hard winter.*

Word building: Other forms are **I testified, I have testified, I am testifying.**

testimonial

noun **1** a reference for a job **2** something given as an expression of appreciation: *I was given a pen as a testimonial from my workmates.*

testimony (*say* test-uh-muh-nee)

noun the statement of a witness under oath to tell the truth

Word building: The plural is **testimonies.**

test match

noun one of a series of international sporting events, usually cricket or Rugby Union

tetanus (say tet-uh-nuhs)

noun an infectious, often deadly, disease which causes extreme stiffness of the muscles of the jaw and other parts of the body

Word history: from a Greek word meaning '(muscle) spasm'

tether

noun a rope or chain for tying up an animal

Word building: **tether** verb

text

noun 1 the main body of words in a book, not including notes, the index and other extra material 2 another word for **textbook**

verb 3 to send a text message: He sat there texting all through dinner. | Text me when you arrive.

Word building: **textual** adjective

texta (say tex-tuh)

noun a thick, brightly coloured pen that is used to fill in the blank parts of a picture

Word use: This is sometimes called a **felt pen**.

textbook

noun a book setting out the information for a course of study in a subject

textile

noun any woven material used for clothing, curtains and so on

text message

noun a message sent through a mobile phone using SMS: There was a competition to see who was able to send text messages the fastest.

texture

noun the roughness or smoothness of a material: The pebbles next to the concrete give a contrast in texture.

than

conjunction 1 a word used after adjectives, adverbs and some other words to introduce the second part of a comparison: She is taller than I am.

preposition 2 in comparison with: Ayana is taller than Tamara.

thank

verb 1 to give thanks to: to thank them for their kindness

noun 2 **thanks**, words saying how grateful you are

Word building: **thankful** adjective **thankless** adjective

that

pronoun 1 You use **that** a to show a person, thing, or idea, and so on, which has been pointed out, mentioned, or suggested to you: That is my brother. b to show one of two or more people, things, and so on, already mentioned, referring to the one that is further away: That is riper than this. 2 if you are giving extra information about someone or something already mentioned: How old is the car that was stolen?

adjective 3 **That** is used to show a a particular person, thing, or idea: That man is my grandfather. b the one of two or more people, things, and so on, that is further away: It was that book I wanted, not this one.

adverb 4 You use **that** with other adverbs and adjectives to show the exact degree and so on: that much | that far.

thatch

verb to cover a roof with straw, reeds or palm leaves

Word building: **thatch** noun

thaw

verb to melt: The ice has thawed.

Word building: **thaw** noun

the

definite article You use the definite article before nouns: 1 to refer to a particular thing or person (instead of any thing or person): The DVD I watched last night was very funny. | Pass me the milk, please. 2 to mark a noun as being used to identify a whole class or type: The youth of today know a lot about technology. | The thylacine is an extinct species.

theatre (say thear-tuh)

noun 1 a building or hall for presenting plays, opera, ballet and so on 2 a cinema 3 a room in a hospital where operations are performed

theatrical (say thee-at-rik-uhl)
adjective **1** in or belonging to a theatre: *a theatrical presentation* **2** aiming to create an effect: *She made a theatrical entrance into the restaurant.*

Word building: **theatrically** adverb

theft
noun the act or crime of stealing

their
pronoun a form of **they** that shows something belongs to them: *The children are in their beds.*

Word building: **theirs** pronoun: *That umbrella is theirs.*

their/there/they're Don't confuse **their** with **there** or **they're**.

There is used to call attention to a particular place:

Please move over there.

They're is a form of *they are.*

them
pronoun the form of **they** you use after a verb: *I'll take them away.*

theme
noun the subject of a speech, a book, or a piece of music

then
adverb **1** at the time: *I was just a child then.* **2** immediately or soon afterwards: *He woke up, then got out of bed.* **3** next in order of time or place: *We lived in Melbourne for five years, then in Perth.* | *On the other side of the rainforest, there's a campsite, then a beach.* **4** at another time: *I'm getting paid on Thursday — I'll buy you dinner then.* **5** in that case: *If the restaurant's closed, then I'll cook us a nice dinner.*

theodolite (say thee-od-uh-luyt)
noun an instrument used in surveying land

theology
noun **1** the study of religion **2** a collection of beliefs held by a particular religion: *Hindu theology*

Word building: The plural is **theologies**. | **theologian** noun **theological** adjective **theologically** adverb

theorem (say thear-ruhm)
noun a statement containing something to be proved in mathematics

theory (say thear-ree)
noun **1** an explanation based on observation and reason: *atomic theory* **2** a suggested explanation with little or no basis in fact: *a theory about ghosts* **3** the part of a subject which deals with underlying principles rather than practice: *You can put a new element in an electric jug without knowing the theory of electricity.*

Word building: The plural is **theories**. | **theoretical** adjective **theoretically** adverb **theorise** verb

therapy
noun healing treatment: *water therapy* | *speech therapy*

Word building: The plural is **therapies**. | **therapeutic** adjective **therapist** noun

there
adverb **1** in or at that place: *Your book is there, where you left it.* **2** at that particular point: *He finished there, ready to start again.*

Word use: Compare this with **here**.

there/their/they're Don't confuse **there** with **their** or **they're**.

Their is a form of *they* that shows something belongs to them:

The boys are in their room.

They're is a form of *they are.*

therefore
adverb as a result: *That car uses less petrol and is therefore better for the environment.*

thermal
adjective having to do with heat: *This special thermal clothing is designed to keep you warm in the snow.*

thermometer
noun an instrument for measuring temperature

thermos flask
noun a container with two walls made of silver glass, for keeping cold substances cold and hot substances hot

Word use: The short form of this is **thermos**. Word history: a trademark, based on a Greek word meaning 'hot'

thermostat
noun a device for keeping a temperature steady: *an oven thermostat*

thesaurus (*say* thuh-<u>saw</u>-ruhs)

noun a book of words arranged in groups which have a similar meaning

Word building: The plural is **thesauruses**.
Word history: from a Greek word meaning 'treasure' or 'treasure house'

these

pronoun, adjective the plural of **this**: *These are your books.* | *These designs are more colourful than those.*

thesis (*say* <u>thee</u>-suhs)

noun **1** an idea, argument or explanation, especially one to be discussed and proved **2** a book-length essay presented by a student for a higher university degree

Word building: The plural is **theses** (*say* <u>thee</u>-seez).

thespian

noun an actor: *The old man spoke nostalgically of his days as a famous thespian on the London stage.*

Word building: **thespian** *adjective*

they

pronoun the plural of **he, she** and **it** that comes before a verb: *They sang sweetly.*

Word use: Other forms are **their** (*their hats*), **theirs** (*Those books are theirs*), **them** (*Give the books to them*), **themselves** (*They hurt themselves*).

they'd

a short form of **they had** or **they would**

they'll

a short form of **they will** or **they shall**

they're

a short form of **they are**

they're/their/there Don't confuse **they're** with **their** or **there**.

Their is a form of *they* that shows something belongs to them:
The boys are in their room.

There is used to call attention to a particular place:
Look at the kookaburra over there!

they've

a short form of **they have**

thick

adjective **1** measuring rather a lot from one surface to the other: *a thick slice of bread* | *a thick blanket* **2** measuring as stated between

opposite surfaces: *a board two centimetres thick* **3** dense or packed close together: *thick bush* | *a thick crowd* **4** not runny or pouring easily: *a thick sauce* **5** with the particles close together: *thick smoke*

Word building: **thicken** *verb*   **thickly** *adverb*   **thickness** *noun*

thicket

noun a thick growth of shrubs or small trees

thief

noun someone who steals

Word building: The plural is **thieves**.

thieve

verb to steal

thigh

noun the part of your leg between your groin and your knee

thimble

noun a protective metal cover for your finger, worn when sewing

thin

adjective **1** measuring not much from one surface to the other: *a thin slice of bread* **2** slim or lean: *She keeps thin by exercising.* **3** barely covering or scattered: *thin hair* | *a thin crowd* **4** runny or watery: *thin gravy* **5** easily seen through: *thin curtains* | *a thin excuse*

Word building: **thin** *verb* (**thinned, thinning**)   **thinly** *adverb*   **thinness** *noun*

thing

noun **1** a real object that is not alive **2** some object which is not or cannot be easily described: *The stick had a brass thing on it.* **3** a matter or affair: *Things are going well.* **4 things**, utensils or personal belongings: *the tea things* | *your things on the table*

think

verb **1** to form or turn over in your mind: *to think pleasant thoughts* | *He was thinking what to do.* **2** to imagine or have an idea of: *Think what it would be like to be rich.* **3** to have a purpose in mind: *She thought she would go home.* **4** to consider or have an opinion: *He thought the film was good.* **5** to take account: *Think of other people's feelings.*

Word building: Other forms are **I thought, I have thought, I am thinking.**

thirst

noun **1** an uncomfortable feeling of dryness in your mouth and throat caused by the need for a drink **2** an eager desire: *a thirst for knowledge*

Word building: **thirsty** *adjective* (**thirstier, thirstiest**) **thirst** *verb* **thirstily** *adverb*

thirteen

noun **1** the number 13 **2** the Roman numeral XIII

Word building: **thirteen** *adjective*: *thirteen computers* **thirteenth** *adjective*: *my thirteenth birthday*

thirty

noun **1** the number 30 **2** the Roman numeral XXX

Word building: The plural is **thirties.** | **thirty** *adjective*: *thirty magpies* **thirtieth** *adjective*: *my uncle's thirtieth birthday.*

this

pronoun **1** You use **this a** to show a person, thing, or idea, and so on, which has been pointed out, mentioned, or suggested: *This is your classroom.* **b** to show one of two or more people, things, and so on, already mentioned, referring to the one that is nearest: *This is riper than that.*
adjective **2 This** is used to show **a** a particular person, thing, or idea: *This colour is very drab.* **b** the one of two or more people, things, and so on, that is nearest: *This shirt looks better than that one.*
adverb **3** You use **this** with other adverbs and adjectives to show the exact degree and so on: *this much*

thistle

noun a plant with prickly leaves and purple or white flowers

thong

noun **1** a simple kind of sandal, usually made of rubber or leather **2** a narrow strip of leather

thorax

noun **1** the chest in human beings or a similar part in other animals **2** the part of an insect's body between its head and abdomen

Word building: The plural is **thoraces** or **thoraxes.**
Word history: from a Greek word meaning 'breastplate' or 'chest'

thorn

noun a sharp-pointed prickle on the stem of a plant

Word building: **thorny** *adjective* (**thornier, thorniest**)

thorough

adjective complete, careful or without missing anything: *a thorough search* | *a thorough wash*

Word building: **thoroughly** *adverb* **thoroughness** *noun*

thoroughfare

noun a public road or way open at both ends

those

pronoun, adjective the plural of **that**: *Those are your books.* | *Those designs are more colourful than these.*

though

conjunction **1** despite the fact that: *Though the other team won, we had a great time playing soccer.* **2** yet, but, or still: *I can come to the party, though I'll have to leave early.*

thought

noun **1** the forming of ideas in your mind **2** an idea **3** consideration or reflection: *Give it thought before you agree.*

Word building: **thoughtful** *adjective* **thoughtless** *adjective*

thoughtful

adjective **1** thinking hard about something in particular, or tending to do a lot of thinking in general: *After I explained the problem, Youssef was quiet and thoughtful for hours.* | *She's a thoughtful sort of person, always taking the time to think things through.* **2** kind and considerate, always thinking about other people's needs and feelings: *It was very thoughtful of you to send me a Christmas card.*

Word building: **thoughtfully** *adverb* **thoughtfulness** *noun*

thoughtless

adjective not kind or considerate of other people's needs and feelings: *It was very thoughtless of her to brag about all her new computer games when she knows we can't afford many things like that.*

Word building: **thoughtlessly** *adverb* **thoughtlessness** *noun*

thousand

noun **1** the number 1000 **2** the Roman numeral M

Word building: **thousand** *adjective*: *a thousand sheep* **thousandth** *adjective*: *You are the thousandth person through the gates.*

thrash

verb **1** to beat soundly as a punishment **2** to defeat utterly

thread   (*rhymes with* red)

noun **1** a very thin cord of cotton, wool or other fibre spun out to a great length and used for weaving cloth **2** a very thin cord of any fibre used for sewing **3** a thin strand **4** the spiral part on a screw
verb **5** to pass a thread through

threadbare

adjective worn and thin: *threadbare trousers* / *a threadbare argument*

threat   (*rhymes with* bet)

noun **1** a warning that you intend to hurt or rob someone: *Terrified by the threats, I handed over the money.* **2** a possible danger: *a threat of war*

Word building: **threaten** *verb*

three

noun **1** the number 3 **2** the Roman numeral III

Word building: **three** *adjective*: *three friends* **third** *adjective*: *This is the third time I've asked you.*

three-dimensional

adjective having, or seeming to have, length, breadth and height and therefore a solid look

thresh

verb to separate grain or seeds from, by beating: *to thresh corn*

threshold   (*say* thresh-hohld)

noun **1** the bottom part of an entrance or doorway: *He paused on the threshold.* **2** a beginning point: *the threshold of a career*

thrift

noun careful management of money and supplies

Word building: **thrifty** *adjective* (**thriftier, thriftiest**) **thriftless** *adjective*

thrill

verb **1** to feel a sudden wave of strong emotion: *to thrill with terror* **2** to excite very much: *She was thrilled at winning the prize.*

Word building: **thrill** *noun* **thrilling** *adjective* **thrilled** *adjective*

thriller

noun an exciting story, especially one about a crime

thrive

verb **1** to grow strongly **2** to do well or prosper: *The business is thriving.*

throat

noun **1** the front of your neck below your chin **2** the passage from your mouth to your stomach or lungs

throb

verb to beat regularly and strongly: *My heart throbbed.* / *The engine throbbed.*

Word building: Other forms are **I throbbed, I have throbbed, I am throbbing.** / **throb** *noun*

throne

noun **1** the special chair used by a king, queen or bishop on important occasions **2** the office or power of a king or queen: *to be loyal to the throne*

throne/thrown Don't confuse **throne** with **thrown**, which is a past form of the verb **throw**. It is the past participle:
My ball was thrown over the fence by my sister.

throng

noun a crowd: *Throngs of people watched the parade.*

Word building: **throng** *verb*: *People thronged to the show.*

throttle

verb **1** to choke or strangle
noun **2** a device such as a lever which controls the flow of petrol into an engine

through   (*say* throoh)

preposition in at one end or side and out the other: *through the tunnel* / *to stitch through material*

Word use: Another spelling is **thru** but this is not suited to formal writing.

throughout

preposition **1** at every part of, or at every time within: *There are chocolate chips throughout this cake.* | *There have been many wars throughout history.*
adverb **2** in every part, or at every time: *The magazine had errors throughout.* | *She has been very supportive throughout.*

throw

verb **1** to fling or send through the air **2** to arrange: *to throw a party*
phrase **3 throw up,** *Informal* to vomit

Word building: Other verb forms are **I threw, I have thrown, I am throwing.** | **throw** *noun*

thrust

verb to force or push hard: *to thrust a dagger into his back* | *to thrust through the crowds*

Word building: Other forms are **I thrust, I have thrust, I am thrusting.** | **thrust** *noun*

thud

noun a heavy bumping sound: *to fall to the ground with a thud*

Word building: **thud** *verb* (**thudded, thudding**)

thug

noun someone who is brutal and violent

Word history: from the name of a group of robbers and murders in India who strangled their victims

thumb   *(rhymes with* sum*)*

noun **1** the inner finger that is much shorter and thicker than the rest
verb **2** to turn over using your thumb: *to thumb through the pages of a book*
phrase **3 all thumbs,** clumsy and awkward

thumbnail sketch

noun a picture which is a very small version of a larger one, as on a computer picture file to give an idea of what the full-sized image is

thump

verb to hit heavily or beat: *to thump on the back* | *My heart is thumping.*
Other words: **bang, knock, pound**

Word building: **thump** *noun*

thunder

noun the loud booming noise that follows a flash of lightning in a storm

Word building: **thunder** *verb* **thunderous** *adjective* **thundery** *adjective*

thunderbolt

noun **1** a flash of lightning and thunder **2** something that suddenly frightens or surprises you

Thursday

noun the fifth day of the week

Word use: The abbreviation is **Thur** or **Thurs.**

thus

adverb as a result: *I am much healthier since I started to exercise and thus much happier.*

thwart   *(rhymes with* short*)*

verb to oppose or stop from succeeding: *to thwart their plans*

Word use: The more usual word is **block.**

thylacine   *(say* thuy-luh-seen*)*

noun another word for **Tasmanian tiger**

thyme   *(sounds like* time*)*

noun a common garden herb of the mint family

tiara   *(say* tee-ah-ruh*)*

noun a piece of women's jewellery that looks like a tiny crown

tick[1]

noun **1** the clicking sound made by a clock **2** a small mark (✓) used to show that something has been done correctly **3** *Informal* a moment or instant: *I'll be there in a tick.*
verb **4** to make ticking sounds **5** to mark correct with a tick
phrase **6 tick off,** to scold or speak crossly to

tick[2]

noun a tiny blood-sucking creature whose poison can paralyse dogs and cats

ticket

noun **1** a small printed card which shows that you have paid for something: *a bus ticket* **2** a label or tag showing how much something costs
Other words: **tab**

tickle

verb to stroke or poke lightly, causing itching or irritation

Word building: **tickle** *noun*

ticklish

adjective **1** sensitive to being tickled: *I'm ticklish under the arms.* **2** difficult and needing to be handled carefully: *a ticklish situation*

tidal wave

noun a huge ocean wave caused by a cyclone

tiddlywinks

noun a game in which you flick coloured discs into a cup

tide

noun **1** the rise and fall of the ocean, twice each day **2** a trend which comes and goes like a tide: *the tide of good fortune*

phrase **3 tide over**, to help through a difficult time: *This money will tide you over until pay day.*

Word building: **tidal** *adjective*

tidings

plural noun news or information: *to bring glad tidings*

tidy

adjective **1** neat, with everything in its right place: *a tidy desk*
Other words: **orderly, shipshape**
noun **2** a rubbish container: *a kitchen tidy*
Other words: **bin**

Word building: Other adjective forms are **tidier, tidiest.** | The plural form of the noun is **tidies.** | tidy *verb* (**tidied, tidying**)   **tidily** *adverb*   **tidiness** *noun*

tie

verb **1** to fasten with cord or string: *to tie a parcel*
Other words: **bind, lash, rope, secure, strap**
2 to loop into a knot or bow: *to tie a ribbon around your hair* **3** to get the same score in a contest: *They tied for first place.*
noun **4** a ribbon or string **5** a strip of cloth worn around your neck and knotted under your collar

Word building: Other verb forms are **I tied, I have tied, I am tying.**

tier   (*rhymes with* here)

noun a row or layer: *tiers of seats in a theatre*

tier/tear Don't confuse **tier** with **tear. Tears** are the drops that fall from your eyes when you are crying.

tiger

noun a large wild animal of the cat family which has yellow-brown fur with black stripes

Word use: The male is a **tiger**, the female is a **tigress** and the young is a **cub**.

tiger snake

noun a very venomous Australian snake with striped markings

tight

adjective **1** fitting very closely: *tight shoes*
Other words: **close, constricting, cramped, restrictive**
2 pulled or stretched as far as it can go: *a tight knot* **3** *Informal* drunk **4** *Informal* mean with money

Word building: **tight** *adverb*   **tighten** *verb*   **tightness** *noun*

tightrope

noun a wire stretched tightly above the ground for acrobats to balance on

tights

plural noun stockings that stretch from your waist to your feet

tile

noun a thin slab of baked clay for covering roofs, floors, walls and other surfaces

Word building: **tile** *verb*: *to tile a roof*

till[1]

verb to dig and prepare for planting crops: *to till the soil*
Other words: **cultivate, hoe, plough, work**

till[2]

noun a drawer for keeping money in, in a shop

tiller

noun a handle joined to a boat's rudder, used for steering

tilt

verb **1** to lean or slant: *to tilt the ladder against the wall* | *to tilt to the left*
Other words: **bend, tip**
2 to fight in a jousting tournament

Word building: **tilt** *noun*

timber

noun wood that has been sawn ready for building
Other words: **boards, lumber, planks**

Word building: **timber** *adjective*: *a timber house*   **timbered** *adjective* covered with trees

timbre (*say* <u>tam</u>-buh, <u>tim</u>-buh)
noun the particular sound an instrument makes: *The flute and clarinet have different timbres.*
Word history: from a Greek word meaning 'tambourine' or 'kettledrum'

time
noun **1** the passing of the hours, days, weeks, months and years **2** a particular moment shown by a clock: *What is the time?* **3** a particular period or moment: *It is time to go home.* **4** the rhythm or tempo of a piece of music
verb **5** to measure or record the time or speed of: *to time a race* **6** to choose the moment for: *She timed her arrival perfectly.*
phrase **7 from time to time**, occasionally **8 on time**, punctually or at the right time **9 time after time**, again and again **10 times**, lots of, or multiplied by: *I know that 5 times 4 is 20.*
Word building: **timeless** *adjective* everlasting **timer** *noun*

time line
noun a line marked with dates to show the order in which events have happened: *I drew a time line showing all the important events that have happened in my life.*

timely
adjective happening at just the right time: *a timely arrival*
Word building: **timeliness** *noun*

timepiece
noun a clock or watch, especially an old-fashioned one

time signature
noun a sign of two numbers written one above the other at the beginning of a piece of music showing the rhythm
Word use: Compare this with **key signature**.

timetable
noun **1** a list of the times when buses and trains arrive and depart **2** a list of the times when school lessons begin

timid
adjective easily frightened
Other words: **afraid, apprehensive, fearful**
Word building: **timidity** *noun* **timidly** *adverb*

timing
noun control of the best time for something to happen: *The timing of the announcement was perfect.*

timorous (*say* tim-uh-ruhs)
adjective timid or fearful
Word building: **timorously** *adverb*

timpani (*say* <u>tim</u>-puh-nee)
plural noun a set of kettledrums

tin
noun **1** a light silver-coloured metal that cans and cooking pots are made of **2** a metal container, such as a can or a pan: *a tin of apricots | a cake tin*
Word building: **tin** *verb* (**tinned, tinning**) to seal up and preserve in a tin

tinder
noun dry paper or twigs that catch fire easily

tinea (*say* <u>tin</u>-ee-uh)
noun a skin disease, caused by a fungus, which makes the skin between your toes red and sore
Word history: from a Latin word meaning 'gnawing worm'

tingle
verb to have a prickly feeling: *to tingle with cold | to tingle with excitement*
Word building: **tingle** *noun* **tingling** *adjective*

tinker
noun **1** someone who used to go from door to door mending old pots and pans
verb **2** to fiddle around trying to mend something without much success: *to tinker with the car engine*

tinkle
verb to jingle or ring lightly: *to tinkle a bell*
Word building: **tinkle** *noun*

tinnie
noun **1** *Informal* a can of beer **2** a small aluminium boat
Word use: It can also be spelt **tinny**.

tinny
adjective **1** not made strongly and likely to fall apart: *a tinny bicycle* **2** having a hollow metallic sound
Word building: Other forms are **tinnier, tinniest**.

tinsel

noun glittering metal strips used for decoration: *to hang tinsel on the Christmas tree*

Word building: **tinselly** *adjective*

tint

noun **1** a colour, especially a delicate or pale colour **2** a dye for your hair
verb **3** to dye or colour slightly: *to tint your hair*

tiny

adjective very small or minute

Other words: **diminutive, microscopic, miniature, minuscule**

Word building: Other forms are **tinier, tiniest**.

tip¹

noun the pointed part at the end: *the tip of my nose*

tip²

verb **1** to make slope, tilt or fall over: *If you tip the cup the milk will spill.*
Other words: **incline, lean, slant**
2 to fall or make fall: *My lunch tipped out of my bag.* | *I tipped the water out of the glass.*
noun **3** a rubbish dump

Word building: Other verb forms are **I tipped, I have tipped, I am tipping**.

tip³

noun **1** money given in thanks to someone who has done something for you: *to leave a tip for the waiter* **2** a piece of useful information: *a tip on how to solve a problem*
Other words: **clue, hint, idea, suggestion**
phrase **3 tip off,** *Informal* to warn of trouble or danger

Word building: Other verb forms are **I tipped, I have tipped, I am tipping**.

tip⁴

verb to touch lightly or tap

Word building: Other forms are **I tipped, I have tipped, I am tipping**.

tipsy

adjective a bit drunk: *She gets tipsy after only one glass of wine.*

Word building: **tipsily** *adverb*   **tipsiness** *noun*

tiptoe

verb to walk softly and carefully on the tips of your toes

tirade   (*say* tuy-**rayd**)

noun a long angry speech

tire

verb to make or become sleepy or weak: *The long walk tired the children* | *She has been ill and tires easily.*

Word building: **tiring** *adjective*: *Gardening in the heat is very tiring.*

tired

adjective **1** feeling sleepy, or that you need to rest: *I was so tired after the bushwalk that I fell asleep as soon as I got back to camp.*
phrase **2 tired of,** bored with: *I'm so tired of sausages — this is the fourth night in a row that we've had them for dinner!*

Word building: **tiredness** *noun*

tissue   (*say* <u>tish</u>-ooh)

noun **1** the substance of which living things are made: *muscle tissue* **2** soft thin paper, especially a piece used as a paper handkerchief: *Give me a tissue to blow my nose.*

titbit

noun **1** a delicious morsel of food **2** an especially interesting piece of gossip or other information

title

noun **1** the name of a book, film or piece of music **2** a name showing someone's occupation or rank in society, such as *Ms, Mr, Doctor, Sir,* or *Dame* **3** the legal right to own property or a certificate stating this: *the title to a house*

Word building: **title** *verb* to call or name **titled** *adjective*

titter

verb to giggle in a silly or nervous way

Word building: **titter** *noun*

to

preposition **1** towards or in the direction of: *from east to west* **2** showing a limit or extent: *rotten to the core* **3** touching or held against: *Apply varnish to your nails.* | *to hold your hand to your head* **4** with the aim, purpose, or intention of: *I'll go to the rescue.*
adverb **5** into a closed position: *to pull the door to*
phrase **6 to and fro,** backwards and forwards

to/too/two Don't confuse **to** with **too** or **two**. The most common meanings of the adverb **too** are 'also or in addition' and 'more than is required':

I want to come too
Your voice is too soft to hear

Two is a number and is a noun or an adjective.

toad

noun an animal like a big frog

toadstool

noun a type of fungus like a mushroom, but usually poisonous

toast[1]

noun sliced bread cooked till it is brown on both sides

Word building: **toast** *verb* **toaster** *noun*

toast[2]

noun **1** someone or something you honour with a special drink: *The Queen will be our next toast.* **2** the act of drinking in this way: *a toast to the Queen* **3** someone who suddenly becomes very popular and famous: *She was the toast of the town.*

Word building: **toast** *verb*

tobacco

noun **1** a plant whose leaves are dried and used for smoking in cigarettes, cigars and pipes **2** the dried leaves themselves

Word building: **tobacconist** *noun*

toboggan

noun a light sled

Word building: **toboggan** *verb* (**tobogganed**, **tobogganing**)

today

noun **1** this present day: *Today is our last day of school.* **2** this present time or age: *In the past, people had to travel to Europe by boat, but today's travellers can fly there.*

Word building: **today** *adverb*: *Let's pack our bags today.*

toddle

verb to walk slowly and unsteadily

Word building: **toddler** *noun* a very young child

toe (*rhymes with* no)

noun any one of the five end parts of your foot

toe/tow Don't confuse **toe** with **tow**, which is to drag or pull using a rope or chain.

toffee

noun a sticky sweet made from sugar, water and sometimes butter

tofu

noun a white curd made from soy bean milk, used in many Asian dishes

Word use: Another name is **bean curd**.
Word history: from a Chinese word meaning 'fermented bean'

toga (*say* toh-guh)

noun a robe worn by people in ancient Rome

together

adverb **1** with another person or other people: *My friend and I go fishing together.* | *All the kids in our group work together as a team.* **2** joined or fixed with each other: *to clasp your hands together* | *to sew pieces of cloth together*

Word building: **togetherness** *noun*

toggle

noun a type of fastener, made of a small bar or pin which fits through a loop of rope or chain

toil

verb **1** to work hard for a long time **2** to walk with great difficulty: *to toil up the hill*

Word building: **toil** *noun*

toilet

noun **1** a bowl, connected to a drain, for getting rid of urine and waste matter from the bowel **2** a room where people go to use a toilet **3** the process of washing, shaving and getting dressed

Word building: **toiletry** *noun* soap, toothpaste and other similar things
Word history: from a French word meaning 'cloth'

token

noun **1** a ticket or disc used instead of money to pay for something **2** a sign or symbol of something: *A wedding ring is a token of love.*

tolerate

verb to put up with or allow: *She can't tolerate loud noise.* | *He won't tolerate bad behaviour.*

Word building: **tolerable** *adjective* **tolerably** *adverb* **tolerance** *noun* **tolerant** *adjective* **tolerantly** *adverb*

toll[1]

verb to ring slowly: *to toll a bell*

toll[2]

noun **1** a fee paid for crossing a bridge or driving on an expressway **2** the price paid in terms of numbers of people dead: *the death toll in war | the road toll*

tollway   (*say* toll-way)

noun a road that you must pay money to travel on

tom

noun a male cat

tomahawk

noun a small axe, first used by the Native North Americans

Word history: from a Native North American word meaning 'war club' or 'ceremonial object'

tomato

noun a juicy red fruit which can be cooked or eaten raw in salads

Word building: The plural is **tomatoes**.

tomb   (*rhymes with* room)

noun a grave, especially a grand one where an important person is buried

tomboy

noun an adventurous high-spirited girl

tombstone

noun a stone over someone's grave with their name and dates of birth and death carved on it

tomorrow

noun the day after today

tom-tom

noun an African or Indian drum

ton

noun **1** a unit of weight in the imperial system equal to approximately 1016 kilograms **2** *Informal* any heavy weight: *My schoolbag weighs a ton.* **3 tons**, *Informal* lots of: *I've got tons of homework to do. | Tons of kids from my class will be going to the same high school as me.*

tone

noun **1** a musical sound: *a violin with a mellow tone* **2** a musical interval equal to two semitones **3** the lightness or darkness of a colour: *a blue tone* **4** the style or quality of something: *Bad behaviour lowers the tone of the school.*

phrase **5 tone up**, to make strong and fit: *Exercise tones up your body.*

tongs

plural noun a tool with two arms hinged together, used for picking up things

tongue   (*rhymes with* hung)

noun **1** the mass of muscle in your mouth that helps in eating food and shaping the sounds of human speech **2** a language or dialect: *a foreign tongue* **3** the loose flap of leather under the laces of some shoes **4** the clapper, or piece of metal, that hangs inside a bell and makes a sound when it hits the side

tonic

noun something that makes you stronger, healthier and more cheerful

tonight

noun the coming night of the present day: *Tonight's fireworks display is going to be amazing.*

Word building: **tonight** *adverb*: *Come and watch the fireworks tonight.*

tonne   (*rhymes with* on)

noun a measure of mass equal to 1000 kilograms

tonsil

noun either of the two oval-shaped masses of tissue at the back of your throat

Word building: **tonsillitis** *noun* an infection which makes your tonsils sore

too

adverb **1** also or in addition: *young, brainy, and beautiful too* **2** more than what is wanted or right: *you are talking too much*

too/to/two Don't confuse **too** with **to** or **two**. The most common way **to** is used is to indicate movement in the direction of a place or person: *Tomorrow I'm flying from Adelaide to Perth*
Two is a number and is a noun or an adjective.

tool

noun **1** any instrument used for doing some mechanical work, such as a hammer, saw or knife **2** anything used like a tool to do work or to cause some result: *Books are a tool for gaining knowledge.*

toot

verb to sound or cause to sound in short blasts, like a horn or whistle

Word building: **toot** *noun*

tooth

noun **1** one of the hard bonelike parts or growths inside the mouths of humans and animals, used for eating **2** any toothlike part of a comb, rake or saw

Word building: The plural is **teeth**.

top¹

noun **1** the highest point or surface of anything **2** the part of a plant above the ground: *carrot tops* **3** a part thought of as higher: *the top of the the street* **4** a covering or lid such as on a box or a jar **5** an outer piece of clothing for the upper part of your body **6 tops**, *Informal* the very best: *The film was the tops.*
adjective **7** highest or upper: *the top shelf* **8** *Informal* best or excellent: *He's a top student.*
verb **9** to give a top to or put a top on **10** to be at or reach the top of: *to top the class in maths*

Word building: Other verb forms are **I topped, I have topped, I am topping.**

top²

noun a cone-shaped toy which is made to spin on its pointed end

topic

noun the subject of a speech, discussion, conversation, or piece of writing
Other words: **theme**

topical

adjective dealing with things that are happening now

Word building: **topically** *adverb*

topple

verb **1** to fall forward or to tumble down **2** to make fall

topsy-turvy

adverb upside down, backwards, or back to front

Word building: **topsy-turvy** *adjective*

torch

noun **1** a light which is run by batteries and which you can carry around **2** something with a burning flame or flare which can be carried around or set into a holder **3** an instrument like a lamp which produces a very hot flame used for burning off paint or melting metal

toreador   (*say* to-ree-uh-daw)

noun a Spanish bullfighter

torment   (*say* taw-**ment**)

verb **1** to torture or give great pain to: *Headaches torment me day after day.* **2** to worry or annoy greatly: *My lost bag has been tormenting me all morning.*
noun (*say* **taw**-ment) **3** great pain or agony **4** something that causes pain or is a source of worry or trouble: *My bad knee is a torment to me.*

tornado

noun a violent whirlwind

Word building: The plural is **tornadoes** or **tornados**.
Word history: from a Spanish word meaning 'thunderstorm'

torpedo

noun **1** a cigar-shaped missile containing explosives, which can travel by itself under water when fired by a submarine or torpedo-boat
verb **2** to attack or destroy by torpedo or torpedoes

Word building: The plural form of the noun is **torpedoes**.

torrent

noun **1** a stream of water flowing with great speed or violence, or a violent downpour of rain **2** a violent stream or flow of anything: *a torrent of words*

torso

noun the main part of your body, without your head, arms or legs
Other words: **trunk**

Word building: The plural is **torsos**.

tortilla   (*say* taw-**tee**-yuh)

noun a Mexican flat bread made from ground corn

tortoise   (*say* **taw**-tuhs)

noun any of various reptiles which have feet with toes, a hard shell covering their bodies and most of which live on land

Word use: Compare this with **turtle**.

torture

noun **1** an act or method of causing severe pain, especially so as to gain information
verb **2** to cause severe pain to: *The soldiers tortured the spies to find out what they knew.*

toss

verb **1** to throw, fling or sway: *She tossed the paper into the bin.* | *The ship was tossing in the waves.* **2** to move around or mix: *He tossed the salad.* **3** to throw a coin to decide something according to which side falls face up: *Toss for it, and heads I win!*

Word building: **toss** *noun*

tot

noun a small child: *She patted the tot on the head.*

total

adjective **1** whole or entire: *This is the total bill.* **2** complete or absolute: *a total failure*
noun **3** the sum or whole amount
verb **4** to add up or find the total of **5** to reach an amount of: *The bills for the outfit total $200.*

Word building: Other verb forms are **I totalled, I have totalled, I am totalling.** | **totality** *noun* **totally** *adverb*

totalitarian   (*say* toh-tal-uh-<u>tair</u>-ree-uhn)

adjective having to do with a government which has complete control and doesn't allow any opposition

Word building: **totalitarianism** *noun*

totem

noun **1** something, often an animal, used as the token or emblem of a family or group **2** a statue or drawing of such an emblem

Word building: **totem** *adjective*: *totem pole*

totter

verb to sway or walk unsteadily

touch

verb **1** to feel with your hand or finger **2** to come into contact: *The two wires are touching.* **3** to strike or hit gently or lightly: *I touched you on your sleeve.* **4** to affect with a feeling or emotion: *Their sad story touched my heart.*
noun **5** the act of touching or being touched **6** the one of your five senses which is used to feel or handle things **7** close communication: *Have you been in touch with your mother lately?*

touchy

adjective **1** irritable or easily offended: *Be careful because he's very touchy today.* **2** likely to irritate or offend: *Don't talk about that because it's a touchy subject.*

Word building: Other forms are **touchier, touchiest.**

tough   (*say* tuf)

adjective **1** not easily broken or cut
Other words: **durable, sturdy, strong**
2 difficult to chew **3** strong or able to put up with bad conditions: *tough soldiers*
Other words: **hardy, resolute, staunch, steadfast, sturdy**
4 hard or difficult to deal with: *a tough exam*
Other words: **complicated, demanding, exacting**
5 rough or aggressive: *tough behaviour*

Word building: **toughly** *adverb* **toughness** *noun*

tour

verb to travel through a place or to travel from one place to another: *The band toured America.* | *They are touring all this summer.*

Word building: **tour** *noun*

tourist

noun someone who travels or tours for pleasure

Word building: **tourism** *noun*

tournament   (*say* <u>taw</u>-nuh-muhnt)

noun **1** a meeting for contests in sports, cards, and other similar things: *a tennis tournament* | *a bridge tournament* **2** a contest in medieval times where two knights on horseback fought for a prize

tourniquet   (*say* <u>taw</u>-nuh-kay)

noun a tight bandage or band, twisted or wrapped around your arm or leg to stop bleeding

tow   (*rhymes with* no)

verb to drag or pull using a rope or chain: *to tow a car*

Word building: **tow** *noun*

tow/toe Don't confuse **tow** with **toe**. People have **toes** at the end of their feet.

towards

preposition **1** in the direction of: *We rode towards the coast.* **2** regarding: *My attitude towards my job improved when I was assigned an interesting new project.* **3** just before: *towards noon* **4** as a help or contribution: *to give money towards a new team uniform*

Word use: Another form is **toward.**

towel

noun **1** a piece of cloth used for wiping and drying something wet
phrase **2 throw in the towel**, to give up or admit defeat

towelling

noun **1** a type of cloth used for making towels, clothes for the beach and so on **2** a rubbing with a towel

tower   (*rhymes with* flower)

noun **1** a tall narrow structure that is usually part of a building like a church, but sometimes stands alone
verb **2** to rise and stretch far upwards: *The mountain towers into the sky.*

town

noun **1** a large area of houses, shops and offices where many people live and work, larger than a village and smaller than a city **2** the main shopping and business centre or area of a city: *I'm going to town to do my shopping.* **3** the people of a town: *The whole town is worried about the traffic problem.*

town hall

noun a large public building belonging to a town, for meetings and gatherings

township

noun a small town or settlement

toxin

noun a poison produced by some animal or vegetable organisms which can cause diseases such as tetanus or diphtheria

Word building: **toxic** *adjective*

toy

noun **1** an object for children or others to play with
phrase **2 toy with**, **a** to handle aimlessly or carelessly: *Stop toying with your food.* **b** to think or act without plan or serious purpose: *to toy with an idea*

Word building: **toy** *adjective*: *a toy train.*

trace

noun **1** a mark that shows that something has been present, often a footprint or a track: *There was a trace of blood on Ivan's shirt.* | *The robbers left traces in the snow.* **2** a very small amount: *The earth contained only a trace of iron.*

Other words: **dab, dash, scrap, shadow, touch, vestige**
verb **3** to follow the footprints, or make out the course of: *They traced the robbers to their hideout.* | *She traced the history of the wool industry in Australia.* **4** to copy by following the lines of the original on transparent paper placed over it: *If you can't draw the map of Australia, you'd better trace one.*

Word building: **tracing** *noun*

trachea   (*say* truh-<u>kee</u>-uh)

noun the scientific word for **windpipe**

track

noun **1** a rough path or trail **2** a structure of metal rails and sleepers on which a train runs **3** a mark or series of marks like footprints, left by anything that has passed along **4** a path or course laid out for racing, such as the part of a playing field where running takes place **5** one of the separate sections on a recording such as a CD or a gramophone record, containing one song or piece of music
verb **6** to follow, or hunt by following, the tracks or footprints of **7** to follow the course of by radar or sonar
adjective **8** relating to athletic sports performed on a running track: *track events*

tracksuit

noun a loose two-piece set of clothing worn by athletes in training or between events

tract[1]

noun **1** a stretch of land or water **2** a system or series of connected parts in your body: *digestive tract*

tract[2]

noun a short piece of writing, often on a religious subject

traction

noun **1** the act of drawing or pulling something, especially along a surface **2** the force that prevents a wheel slipping: *These tyres have good traction.*

tractor

noun a powerful motor vehicle used to pull farm machinery and so on

trade

noun **1** the buying, selling or exchanging of goods
Other words: **commerce**
2 a particular kind of work, or sometimes the people who are involved in this work: *the trade of a carpenter* | *This magazine is for the electrical trade.*
verb **3** to buy, sell or exchange goods or other desirable things: *They traded in wheat.* | *They traded seats with each other.*
adjective **4** having to do with commerce or a particular job
phrase **5 trade in**, to give as a part payment in exchange for something new: *She traded in her old car for a new one.*

trademark

noun a name, sign or mark used to show that goods have been made by a particular manufacturer

trade union

noun an organisation or association of workers set up to help them with any work problems, especially with their employers
Word building: **trade unionism** *noun*
trade unionist *noun*

tradition

noun **1** the handing down of beliefs, customs and stories from one generation to another **2** the beliefs or customs that are handed down
Word building: **traditional** *adjective*

traffic

noun **1** the coming and going of people or vehicles along a road, waterway, railway line or airway **2** the people or vehicles that travel along such a route **3** the business, trade, or dealings carried out between countries or people, sometimes illegally: *traffic in drugs*
verb **4** to carry on trade or commercial dealings, often illegally
Word building: Other verb forms are
I trafficked, I have trafficked, I am trafficking. | **trafficker** *noun*

tragedy *(say* traj-uh-dee*)*

noun **1** a sad or serious play with an unhappy ending **2** any very sad or dreadful happening
Word building: **tragic** *adjective* **tragically** *adverb*
Word history: from a Greek word meaning 'goat song'

trail

verb **1** to drag or be dragged along the ground **2** to have floating or coming out behind: *The car was trailing clouds of smoke.* **3** to follow the track of **4** to hang down loosely from something **5** to follow: *The little boy trailed after his sister.*
noun **6** a path or a track made across rough country **7** footprints or smell left by a hunted animal or person **8** a stream of dust or smoke left behind something moving

trail/trial Don't confuse **trail** with **trial**. A **trial** is the testing of something, especially a case to test a person's guilt or innocence in a law court.

trail bike

noun another name for **dirt bike**

trailer

noun **1** a vehicle, made to be towed by a car or a truck, used to carry loads **2** an advertisement for a film soon to be shown, usually made up of scenes from it
Word use: Other words for definition 2 are **short** or **shorts**.

train

noun **1** a number of railway carriages joined together and pulled by an engine **2** a line of people, cars, or animals travelling together: *a camel train* **3** something that is drawn or trails along: *the train on a wedding dress* **4** a group of followers: *The Dalai Lama and his train entered.* **5** a series of connected ideas: *a train of thought*
verb **6** to teach a person or animal to know or do something **7** to become or make fit by exercise or diet for some sport or a contest
Word building: **training** *noun*

trainee

noun someone receiving training
Word building: **trainee** *adjective*: *a trainee pilot*

trainer

noun **1** someone who trains horses for racing **2** someone who trains athletes **3** a shoe suitable to wear when exercising or playing sport

trait *(say* tray, trayt*)*

noun that feature or quality that sets something apart from others: *a bad character trait*
Other words: **attribute, characteristic**

traitor

noun someone who betrays a person or a country

tram

noun a passenger car running on rails, usually powered by electricity from an overhead wire

tramp

verb **1** to tread or walk heavily or steadily: *The soldiers tramped down the road.* **2** to tread heavily: *Don't tramp on the daffodils!* *noun* **3** the act of tramping: *a tramp through the bush* **4** the sound of a firm heavy tread **5** someone who travels about from place to place on foot, with no fixed home

Other words: **vagrant**

trample

verb **1** to crush or tread heavily on **2** to treat cruelly: *Sarah trampled on his feelings.*

trampoline

noun a frame with tightly stretched material attached to it by springs, on which you can jump and tumble for pleasure or sport

Word building: **trampoline** *verb*
Word history: from an Italian word meaning 'springboard'

trance

noun **1** a dazed state in which you are not fully conscious **2** the condition of being completely lost in thought

tranquil   (*say* trang-kwuhl)

adjective peaceful, quiet or calm

Word building: **tranquillity** *noun*   **tranquilly** *adverb*

tranquilliser   (*say* trang-kwuh-luy-zuh)

noun a drug that calms you down

Word use: Another spelling is **tranquillizer**.

trans-

prefix a word part meaning 'across' or 'beyond': *transport*

Word history: from Latin

transact

verb to carry through to a successful conclusion: *It won't take long to transact our business.*

transaction

noun **1** a piece of business **2** the managing or carrying on of business

transfer

verb **1** to carry or send from one place or person to another **2** to take or move from one surface to another
noun **3** the act of transferring or the fact of being transferred: *The transfer of soldiers is complete.* **4** a drawing or pattern which can be put onto another surface: *These transfers can be put onto your T-shirt.*

Word building: Other verb forms are **I transferred, I have transferred, I am transferring.** | **transference** *noun* **transferral** *noun*

transfix

verb **1** to pierce through or fix fast with something sharp or pointed **2** to make unable to move, such as with amazement or terror: *I was absolutely transfixed at the sight of the shark.*

transform

verb **1** to change in form or appearance: *The dress transformed her into a real beauty.* **2** to change in condition or character: *The new job transformed Haruko's life.*

Word building: **transformation** *noun*

transformer

noun an electrical device used for changing one voltage to another

transfuse

verb **1** to pour in or spread through **2** to take from one person or animal and inject into another: *to transfuse blood*

Word building: **transfusion** *noun*

transistor

noun **1** a small electronic device used in computers, radios, and so on, for controlling the flow of current **2** a small radio equipped with these devices

transit

noun **1** passing across or through: *the transit of passengers from Sydney to Perth* **2** the state of being carried from one place to another: *The parcel was lost in transit.*

Word building: **transition** *noun*

transitive verb

noun a verb like *bring* that needs an object for it to make sense

Word use: The opposite is an **intransitive verb**.

translate

verb to change from one language into another: *He translated the book from Italian into English.*

Word building: **translation** *noun*   **translator** *noun*

translucent   (*say* tranz-<u>looh</u>-suhnt)

adjective allowing some light to come through

Word use: Compare this with **opaque** and **transparent**.
Word building: **translucence** *noun* **translucently** *adverb*

transmission

noun **1** the act of transmitting **2** something that is transmitted **3** the broadcasting of a radio or television program **4** the part of a motor which transmits the power from the engine to the wheels

transmit

verb **1** to send over or along: *The money was transmitted secretly.* **2** to pass on to someone else: *to transmit a disease* **3** to broadcast

Word building: Other forms are **I transmitted, I have transmitted, I am transmitting.** | **transmitter** *noun*

transmute

verb to change from one nature or form to another

Word building: **transmutation** *noun*

transparency

noun **1** the quality of being transparent or able to be seen through **2** something which is transparent, especially a transparent photograph projected onto a screen or looked at by light shining through from behind

transparent

adjective **1** allowing light to pass through so that you can see through: *transparent material* **2** easily understood or seen through: *She gave a transparent excuse.*

Word use: Compare definition 1 with **opaque** and **translucent**.
Word building: **transparently** *adverb*

transplant   (*say* trans-<u>plant</u>)

verb **1** to remove from one place to another: *to transplant carrots | to transplant a heart*
noun (*say* <u>trans</u>-plant) **2** the act of transplanting **3** something transplanted, such as a part of someone's body: *He died before a suitable transplant could be found.*

transport   (*say* trans-<u>pawt</u>, <u>trans</u>-pawt)

verb **1** to carry from one place to another **2** to carry away by strong emotion: *She was transported with happiness.* **3** to send to another country to live: *to transport criminals*
noun (*say* <u>trans</u>-pawt) **4** a system or method of transporting: *public transport* **5** a ship, plane or truck used to transport people or goods

Word building: **transportation** *noun*

transpose

verb **1** to change the position or order of: *to transpose a paragraph* **2** to make change places: *If you transpose the letters in the word 'on', you get 'no'.*

Word building: **transposition** *noun*

transverse

adjective lying or cutting across: *There was writing on the transverse part of the cross.*

transvestite

noun someone who gets sexual pleasure from wearing the clothing of the opposite sex

trap

noun **1** a device for catching animals
Other words: **hook, lure, net, snare**
2 a trick or any other way of catching someone by surprise
Other words: **ambush**
3 a two-wheeled carriage drawn by a horse **4** *Informal* your mouth
verb **5** to catch in a trap
Other words: **hook, net, snare**
6 to trick or lead by tricking: *She trapped him into telling the truth.*
Other words: **ambush, lure**

Word building: Other verb forms are **I trapped, I have trapped, I am trapping.**

trapdoor

noun a door cut into a floor, ceiling or roof

trapdoor spider

noun a type of spider with a painful bite that digs tunnels in the ground, sometimes fitted with a lid which it is able to open or stay tightly closed

trapeze (*say* truh-**peez**)

noun a short bar joined to the ends of two hanging ropes, on which gymnasts and acrobats perform

Word history: from a Latin word meaning 'small table'

trapezium

noun a four-sided figure, two of whose sides are parallel

trash

noun **1** rubbish or anything worthless or useless **2** nonsense or silly ideas or talk **3** people thought of as worthless

Word building: **trash** *verb* to destroy **trashy** *adjective*

trauma (*say* **traw**-muh)

noun **1** a wound or injury to your body **2** any experience which shocks you and has a lasting effect on your mind

Word building: The plural is **traumata** or **traumas**.

travel

verb **1** to go from one place to another or go throughout a place: *I travelled across India.* | *We travelled the world for two years.* Other words: **journey** **2** to go from place to place for a business firm **3** *Informal* to move with speed: *That snowboarder was really travelling!* noun **4** the act of travelling: *Travel is my main interest in life.* **5** **travels**, journeys

Word building: Other verb forms are **I travelled, I have travelled, I am travelling.**

traverse

verb to pass across, over or through

trawl

noun a strong net which is dragged along the sea bottom to catch fish

Word building: **trawler** *noun* a type of boat used in fishing with a trawl **trawl** *verb*

tray

noun a flat piece of wood, plastic or metal used for holding or carrying things: *He brought the tea on a tray.*

treacherous (*say* **trech**-uh-ruhs)

adjective disloyal or not to be trusted: *a treacherous enemy* | *treacherous weather*

Word building: **treacherously** *adverb* **treachery** *noun*

treacle

noun a dark, sticky liquid made from sugar

Word building: **treacly** *adjective*

tread (*rhymes with* led)

verb **1** to walk or step on: *We tread lightly so as not to damage the flowers.* | *I tread the same path every day to get to school.* noun **2** a step, or the sound it makes: *You could hear his tread on the stairs.* **3** the part, especially of a tyre, which touches the road or any other surface phrase **4** **tread water,** to keep your head above water by moving your arms and legs

Word building: Other verb forms are **I trod, I have trod** or **trodden, I am treading.**

treason

noun the crime of betraying your country, such as by spying for another country

Word building: **treasonable** *adjective*

treasure (*say* **trezh**-uh)

noun **1** something worth a lot of money, such as gold and jewels, or anything which is highly valued: *My bike is my greatest treasure.* Other words: **riches, valuables** verb **2** to value highly: *I'll treasure your letters.* Other words: **cherish, love, prize** **3** to store up for later use

Word building: **treasured** *adjective*

treasurer (*say* **trezh**-uh-ruh)

noun **1** someone in charge of the money belonging to a company, club or city: *The treasurer reported that funds were low.* **2 Treasurer,** the head of the Treasury: *The Treasurer announced the budget.*

treasury (*say* **trezh**-uh-ree)

noun **1** a place where money or valuables are kept **2 Treasury,** the government department which manages a country's finances

treat

verb **1** to behave towards, in a particular way: *They treated me kindly.* **2** to try to cure: *to treat a patient* **3** to deal with or discuss: *They are treating the matter seriously.* **4** to change by chemical or other process: *to treat sewage* **5** to pay for some special pleasure for: *Binh's father treated us to an ice-cream.* noun **6** the gift of a drink, dinner or entertainment: *It's my treat this time.*

Word building: **treatment** *noun*

treaty

noun an agreement: *After the war both countries signed the peace treaty.*

Word building: The plural is **treaties**.

treble

adjective **1** high-pitched: *a treble voice | a treble recorder* **2** three times as much as: *He paid treble the amount.*
noun **3** a piano part for the right hand **4** a high-pitched voice or sound

Word use: The opposite of definitions 1, 3 and 4 is **bass**.
Word building: **treble** *verb* to triple

tree

noun a plant with leaves and woody branches, trunk and roots

trek

verb to walk or travel especially over a long distance or with much difficulty: *We are going to trek across the mountains.*

Word building: Other forms are **I trekked, I have trekked, I am trekking.** | **trek** *noun* **trekker** *noun*
Word history: from a Dutch word meaning 'draw' or 'travel'

trellis

noun a support made of crossing wooden or other strips, such as for a vine or creeper
Other words: **framework, lattice**

tremble

verb to shake, especially from fear, weakness or cold
Other words: **quake, quiver, shiver**

Word building: **tremble** *noun* **trembly** *adjective*

tremendous

adjective **1** large or great: *a tremendous size* **2** wonderful or remarkable: *She's a tremendous character.*

Word building: **tremendously** *adverb*

tremolo   (*say* trem-uh-loh)

noun a trembling effect in someone's voice or in a musical instrument
Word building: The plural is **tremolos**.

tremor

noun a shaking movement or vibration: *She has a tremor in her hand. | The earth tremor damaged our wall.*

tremulous   (*say* trem-yuh-luhs)

adjective shaky or uncertain: *Danny's voice was tremulous with excitement.*

Word building: **tremulously** *adverb*

trench

noun a deep ditch, especially one dug to protect soldiers from enemy fire
Word building: The plural is **trenches**.

trend

noun a tendency or movement in a certain direction, which leads to a fashion: *There's a trend towards smaller cars.*

Word building: **trendy** *adjective* (**trendier, trendiest**) fashionable   **trendiness** *noun*

trespass

verb to enter a place illegally and without permission
Word building: **trespass** *noun*   **trespasser** *noun*

trestle   (*say* tres-uhl)

noun a plank supported by legs at each end

triad   (*say* truy-ad)

noun a group of three closely connected things, such as musical notes in a chord
Word building: **triadic** *adjective*

trial

noun **1** a hearing of the facts or a trying of someone's guilt or innocence in a law court **2** a test or contest: *a trial of strength* **3** an experiment: *The trial was unsuccessful.* **4** a cause of suffering: *My asthma is a trial to me.*
phrase **5 on trial**, undergoing a test or trial, especially in court

Word building: **trial** *adjective*   **trial** *verb* (**trialled, trialling**): *They are trialling a new method of teaching maths.*

trial/trail Don't confuse **trial** with **trail**, which is to drag or be dragged along the ground.

triangle

noun **1** a flat three-sided shape **2** a percussion instrument made of a steel rod bent into a triangle, which is struck with a small steel rod
Word building: **triangular** *adjective*

tribe

noun **1** a group of people who believe they have a common ancestor, have many of the same customs and usually live in the same area **2** any large group with something in common: *He brought a tribe of friends home.*

Word building: **tribal** *adjective* **tribally** *adverb*

tribunal   (*say* truy-byooh-nuhl)

noun a court of justice, or a place where judgements are made

tributary   (*say* trib-yuh-tree)

noun a stream flowing into a larger river

Word building: The plural is **tributaries.** | **tributary** *adjective*

tribute

noun a gift or speech made to show respect or regard for someone

triceps   (*say* truy-seps)

noun a muscle with three attachments to the bone, especially the muscle at the back of your upper arm

Word history: from a Latin word meaning 'three-headed', as this muscle is joined to the bone in three places

trick

noun **1** something done to deceive or amuse
Other words: **hoax, prank, ruse**
2 a skilful or clever act, such as juggling
Other words: **craft, gimmick, skill**
3 something which deceives your senses: *A mirage is just a trick of your eyes.*
Other words: **delusion, figment, illusion**
4 a habit or mannerism: *She has a trick of nodding while you speak.*
Other words: **idiosyncrasy, peculiarity, tendency, trait**
verb **5** to deceive or cheat by a trick
Other words: **bluff, delude, doublecross, fool, hoodwink**

Word building: **trickery** *noun* **trickster** *noun*

trickle

verb to flow in a very small or slow stream: *Tears trickled down her cheeks.*

Word building: **trickle** *noun*

tricky

adjective **1** difficult to handle or deal with: *a tricky question* **2** given to playing tricks, especially in order to cheat or deceive

tricycle   (*say* truy-sik-uhl)

noun a cycle with three wheels, usually two at the back

trifle

noun **1** a small or worthless amount or thing **2** a dessert usually made of sponge cake with sherry or wine, jelly, jam, fruit and custard
verb **3** to waste time: *She spends all day trifling.*
phrase **4** **trifle with,** to treat too lightly: *Can't you see she's trifling with you?*

Word building: **trifler** *noun*

trigger

noun the lever on a gun which you press to fire the bullet

Word building: **trigger** *verb* to start off: *trigger a reaction*
Word history: from a Dutch word meaning 'pull'

trill

noun a vibrating sound, especially when made up of two notes being rapidly repeated one after the other

Word building: **trill** *verb*

trillion

noun a number, one million times one million, 1 000 000 000 000, or 10^{12}

Word use: **Trillion** can be used to mean a million times a billion, but this is extremely rare nowadays.
Word building: **trillion** *adjective* **trillionth** *adjective*

trilogy   (*say* tril-uh-jee)

noun a series of three related works, such as novels or plays

trim

verb **1** to shorten, such as by cutting or tightening: *Samuel needs to trim his beard.* | *to trim a sail* **2** to decorate: *to trim a Christmas tree*

Word building: Other forms are **I trimmed, I have trimmed, I am trimming.** | **trim** *adjective* neat and smart

trimaran   (*say* truy-muh-ran)

noun a sailing boat with three hulls

trinity

noun a group of three

trinket

noun a cheap ornament

trio   (*say* tree-oh)

noun **1** a group of three **2** a group of three musicians **3** a musical piece for three voices or performers

trip

noun **1** a journey or outing: *We are going on a world trip.* | *We took a trip on a ferry.*
verb **2** to stumble or cause to fall: *I tripped and fell.* | *The wire tripped me.* **3** to set off: *You trod on the wire which trips the alarm.*
phrase **4 trip up**, to cause to make a mistake: *The lawyer's questions tripped me up.*

Word building: Other verb forms are **I tripped, I have tripped, I am tripping.**

tripe

noun **1** the stomach of cattle which is cleaned and sold to eat **2** *Informal* worthless rubbish

triple

verb **1** to multiply by three
adjective **2** having three parts: *a triple program* **3** three times as great: *a triple quantity*

Word use: A word with the same meaning as definition 3 is **treble.**

triplet

noun **1** one of three children born at the same time to the same mother **2** a three-line verse of poetry

tripod   (*say* truy-pod)

noun a three-legged stool or support

trite

adjective repeated too often to be interesting: *a trite remark*

Word building: **tritely** *adverb*   **triteness** *noun*

triumph   (*say* truy-umf)

noun a victory or success
Other words: **conquest, win**

Word building: **triumph** *verb*   **triumphant** *adjective*   **triumphantly** *adverb*

trivial

adjective unimportant: *trivial details*
Other words: **insignificant, petty**

Word building: **triviality** *noun*   **trivially** *adverb*

troll

noun an imaginary being in fairy stories, either a dwarf or a giant, who lives underground

trolley

noun **1** a cart on wheels, used for carrying goods in a supermarket **2** a small table on wheels for carrying food or crockery **3** a truck with low sides which runs on rails: *The miners loaded the trolley with coal.*

trombone

noun a brass wind instrument like a trumpet, on which you change the note by sliding a section of tube in or out

Word building: **trombonist** *noun*
Word history: from an Italian word meaning 'trumpet'

troop

noun **1** a group or band of people, animals or things: *a circus troop* | *a troop of scouts* **2 troops**, a large number of soldiers
verb **3** to come or go in large numbers

Word building: **trooper** *noun*

trophy   (*say* troh-fee)

noun **1** a prize won in a contest **2** a souvenir kept from a war or a hunting expedition

Word building: The plural is **trophies.**

tropic

noun **1** either of two lines of latitude 23½° north and south of the equator, known as the *Tropic of Cancer* and the *Tropic of Capricorn* **2 the tropics**, the area of land lying between these bands

Word building: **tropical** *adjective*   **tropically** *adverb*

trot

verb **1** to go at a fast but steady pace, as horses do when they move so that a front leg moves at the same time as the opposite back leg
noun **2** a fast but steady pace: *She set off at a trot.* **3 trots**, trotting races for horses

Word building: Other verb forms are **it trotted, it has trotted, it is trotting.** | **trotter** *noun* a horse bred for trotting races

troubadour   (*say* trooh-buh-daw)

noun a singer or song-writer, especially in medieval France

trouble   (*rhymes with* bubble)

verb **1** to disturb, bother or worry: *It's a shame to trouble her when she's tired.* **2** to put to inconvenience: *May I trouble you to ask the time?*
noun **3** a difficulty or an unhappy situation: *to make trouble* | *to be in trouble* **4** inconvenience: *I went to a lot of trouble to find it.* **5** any problem or disorder: *industrial trouble* | *heart trouble*

Word building: **troublesome** *adjective*   **troubled** *adjective*

trough   (*rhymes with* off)
noun **1** a long low container for animal feed or water, or any similar trench or hollow **2** an area of low pressure on a weather map

trounce
verb to completely defeat: *We trounced the other team in the finals.*

troupe   (*sounds like* troop)
noun a band or group of entertainers: *a troupe of actors*

Word building: **trouper** *noun*

trousers
plural noun clothing for the lower half of your body from waist to ankle, divided into two parts for your legs

trousseau   (*say* <u>trooh</u>-soh)
noun linen and clothes collected by a woman for her marriage

Word building: The plural is **trousseaux** or **trousseaus**.
Word history: from a French word

trout
noun a freshwater fish related to the salmon

Word building: The plural is **trout**.

trowel
noun **1** a flat tool with a handle used for spreading cement or plaster **2** a small garden spade

Word building: **trowel** *verb* (**trowelled, trowelling**)

truant
noun someone who stays away from school without permission

Word building: **truancy** *noun*   **truant** *adjective*

truce
noun an agreement to end fighting: *Both sides agreed to call a truce over Christmas.*
Other words: **armistice, ceasefire**

truck
noun **1** a motor vehicle with a back section for carrying goods **2** a railway goods carriage

Word building: **truck** *verb*

trudge
verb to tread heavily or slowly: *We trudged up the mountain in our boots.*

true
adjective **1** full of truth or not false: *a true story*
Other words: **accurate, correct, factual, right**
2 real or being what it seems: *true gold*
Other words: **actual, authentic, genuine, legitimate**
3 loyal or faithful: *a true friend* **4** exact: *She measured the sides to see if they were true.*

Word building: **true** *adverb*: *Tell me true.*   **truly** *adverb*

trump
verb **1** to take or win by having the best card in a game such as bridge: *He trumped my king with an ace.*
phrase **2 trump up**, to invent dishonestly: *She trumped up some story to get out of trouble.*

Word building: **trump** *noun*

trumpet
noun **1** a brass wind instrument with a curved tube and three valves
verb **2** to sound a trumpet or make a similar loud noise: *The elephants trumpeted in the forest.* **3** to tell far and wide: *He trumpeted the news all through the neighbourhood.*

Word building: **trumpeter** *noun*

truncheon   (*say* <u>trun</u>-shuhn)
noun a short stick or club, as used by police to keep order or defend themselves

Word history: from a Latin word meaning 'stump'

trundle
verb to roll along, or move on wheels: *to trundle a hoop* | *The trolley trundled along the aisle.*

trunk
noun **1** the main or central part: *the trunk of a tree* **2** the main part of your body without your head, legs or arms
Other words: **torso**
3 a box or chest for storing or transporting your possessions **4** the long flexible nose of an elephant **5 trunks**, shorts worn while playing sport, especially while swimming

Word building: **trunk** *adjective* main or central: *trunk line*

truss
verb **1** to bind or secure: *They trussed her hands tightly.* | *He trussed the turkey.* **2** to support, such as with bars and beams: *to truss a bridge*

Word building: **truss** *noun*

trust

noun **1** belief or confidence: *to lose someone's trust* **2** the expectation that someone can or will pay: *He will let you buy on trust.* **3** reliableness or responsibility: *a position of trust* **4** money or property held and managed by one person for another or others

verb **5** to believe or have confidence in **6** to hope or expect: *They trust you will come.*

trustee

noun someone who manages business or property for another

trustworthy

adjective deserving trust: *a trustworthy ally*

Word building: **trustworthiness** *noun*

truth

noun **1** what has really happened: *He doesn't always tell the truth.*
Other words: **facts, reality**
2 a fact or principle: *a scientific truth*
Other words: **axiom, certainty, law**
3 honesty or reliableness: *There's not much truth in what she says.*

Word building: **truthful** *adjective* **truthfully** *adverb*

try

verb **1** to make an effort or attempt to do: *You must try harder before you give it up.* | *Try it.* **2** to test or find out: *Did you try it for size?* **3** to examine in a court of law: *Don't judge her until she is tried.* **4** to strain or exhaust: *He tries my patience.*
noun **5** an attempt or effort **6** a score in Rugby League, worth four points, or in Rugby Union, worth five points

Word building: Other verb forms are **I tried, I have tried, I am trying.** | The plural form of the noun is **tries.** | **trying** *adjective* annoying: *His nagging is very trying.*

tsar (*say* zah)

noun the emperor of Russia in former times

Word use: Another spelling is **czar.**

T-shirt

noun a short-sleeved cotton shirt without a collar

Word use: Another spelling is **tee-shirt.**

tsunami (*say* tsooh-<u>nah</u>-mee)

noun a large, often destructive sea wave caused by an earthquake beneath the sea

Word history: from Japanese words meaning 'harbour wave'

tuan

noun a small marsupial that looks like a mouse with a hairy-tipped tail. It lives mainly in trees and is endangered. See the table at the end of this book

Word use: Another name for this is **phascogale.**
Word history: from an Aboriginal language of Victoria called Wathawurung. See the map of Australian Aboriginal languages at the end of this book.

tub

noun a round flat-bottomed container: *a wash tub* | *a tub of butter*

tuba (*say* <u>tyooh</u>-buh)

noun a very low-pitched brass wind instrument

tubby

adjective short and fat

Word building: Other forms are **tubbier, tubbiest.** | **tubbiness** *noun*

tube

noun **1** a narrow hollow pipe which liquid or gas can flow through **2** a soft narrow container, sealed at one end, with a screw top at the other: *a toothpaste tube* | *a tube of paint*

tuber (*say* <u>tyooh</u>-buh)

noun an underground stem, such as a potato, from which new plants may grow

Word history: from a Latin word meaning 'bump' or 'swelling'

tuberculosis

(*say* tuh-ber-kyuh-<u>loh</u>-suhs)
noun a disease of the lungs in which small lumps or swellings are produced

Word building: **tubercular** *adjective* **tuberculous** *adjective*

tuck

verb **1** to put into or fold away: *to tuck something in your pocket* **2** to sew in a narrow fold to improve the fit of a garment *phrase* **3 tuck in, a** to fold tightly into the bed clothes: *She tucked them in.* **b** *Informal* to eat heartily

Word building: **tuck** *noun* a narrow fold

tucker

noun *Informal* food: *The tucker's good.*

tuckshop
noun a shop, usually in a school, which sells lunches and snacks

Tuesday
noun the third day of the week

Word use: The abbreviation is **Tue** or **Tues**.
Word history: from a Latin word meaning 'day of Mars'

tuft
noun an upright bunch, such as of hair, grass or feathers

Word building: **tuft** *verb*   **tufted** *adjective*

tug
verb **1** to pull hard: *to tug on the reins* | *to tug the rope twice* **2** to tow, such as with a tugboat
noun **3** a hard pull **4** another name for **tugboat**

Word building: Other verb forms are **I tugged, I have tugged, I am tugging**.

tugboat
noun a small powerful boat which is used to tow other ships

tuition   (*say* tyooh-<u>ish</u>-uhn)
noun teaching: *She needs more tuition before the exam.*

tulip
noun a cup-shaped flower, which grows from a bulb

tumble
verb **1** to fall or roll: *Prices are tumbling.* | *to tumble downstairs* **2** to toss: *to tumble clothes in a drier*

Word building: **tumble** *noun*

tumbler
noun a drinking glass

tummy
noun *Informal* your stomach, where food is partly digested

Word building: The plural is **tummies**.

tumour
noun a swelling in someone's body, especially one made up of an unusual growth of cells

Word use: Another spelling is **tumor**.

tumult   (*say* <u>tyooh</u>-mult)
noun **1** a noisy disturbance or uproar **2** a mental or emotional disturbance: *These words caused a tumult in her breast.*

Word building: **tumultuous** *adjective*

tuna
noun a large sea fish with pink flesh, used for food

tundra
noun a treeless Arctic plain with mosses, lichens and dwarfed plants

Word history: from a Russian word meaning 'marshy plain'

tune
noun **1** a number of musical sounds of different pitch, one after the other, that form a pattern **2** correct adjustment of pitch: *Is your violin in tune?*
verb **3** to set to a correct or usual musical pitch: *to tune an instrument* **4** to put into smooth running order: *to tune an engine* **5** to adjust so as to get an incoming signal at its strongest: *to tune a radio*

Word building: **tuneful** *adjective*   **tuner** *noun*

tunic
noun **1** a soldier's or police officer's jacket **2** a sleeveless dress worn as part of a school uniform

tunnel
noun an underground passage, especially a large one for trains or cars

Word building: **tunnel** *verb* (**tunnelled, tunnelling**)

turban
noun a headdress in some Asian and African countries, made of a long piece of cloth wound round the head in folds

turbine
noun a revolving motor in which a wheel with blades is driven by a liquid or gas passing through it

turbulence
noun a violent commotion or storminess

Word building: **turbulent** *adjective*

tureen   (*say* tuh-<u>reen</u>, tyooh-<u>reen</u>)
noun a large deep dish with a cover, for holding soup at the table

turf

noun **1** a grass surface with its matted roots and the soil it is growing in **2** a piece of this

turkey

noun a large bird bred for eating

Word use: The male is a **cock**, the female is a **hen** and the young is a **poult**.

turmoil

noun wild disorder: *Everything is in turmoil because he is leaving at a moment's notice.*

turn

verb **1** to spin: *The wheels are turning slowly.* Other words: **revolve, rotate**
2 to go round: *The truck turned the corner.* **3** to point or aim in a certain direction: *They turned the ship into the wind.* | *Celeste turned her face to the wall.* **4** to move to the other side or the opposite position: *Turn the page quietly.* | *I tossed and turned all night.* **5** to become: *Kim turned red.* **6** to change or be changed: *The magician turned the rabbit into a pumpkin.* | *The caterpillar turned into a butterfly.*
noun **7** a movement of rotation, whether complete or not: *a slight turn of the handle* **8** a chance to do something or get something, coming in order to each of a number of people: *It's my turn to choose.* **9** a change of direction: *He made a turn to the right.*
phrase **10 turn on, a** to start the supply of: *to turn on the electricity* **b** to excite or interest: *Rock music really turns me on.* **11 turn out, a** to switch off: *Turn out the lights.* **b** to produce or make: *The factory turns out 3000 compact discs an hour.* **c** to force to go: *The landlord turned them out into the street.* **d** to empty: *I turned out my pockets.* **e** to become or develop: *Your student has turned out well.* **f** to come along: *A large crowd turned out to hear her speak.* **12 turn up, a** to fold, especially so as to shorten: *I turned up the hem of my jeans so that they wouldn't get wet.* **b** to be found: *That pen I lost has turned up at last.* **c** to increase the strength of: *Turn up the gas.* **d** to arrive: *Pallavi turned up unexpectedly.*

turnip

noun a plant with a thick white or yellow root which is eaten as a vegetable

turnstile

noun a revolving gate that allows one person to pass at a time

turntable

noun the turning surface on which a record in a gramophone rests

turpentine

noun **1** an oil used for dissolving paint, originally from a tree, now usually made from petroleum **2** a very tall Australian tree with stringy bark and leaves which are whitish underneath

Word use: Definition 1 is often shortened to **turps**.

turquoise   (*say* ter-kwoyz)

noun a greenish-blue stone used in jewellery

turret

noun a small tower at a corner of a building

turtle

noun any of various reptiles which have flippers and a hard shell covering their bodies, and most of which live in the sea

Word use: Compare this with **tortoise**.

tusk

noun the very long tooth, usually one of a pair, that certain animals such as the elephant or walrus have

tussle

verb to fight roughly

Word building: **tussle** *noun*

tussock

noun a tuft or clump of grass

tutor

noun a teacher, especially either a private one or one in a university

tutu

noun a short ballet skirt, usually made out of layers of net-like material

tuxedo   (*say* tuk-see-doh)

noun a man's black jacket, worn on formal occasions

Word history: named after a US country club at *Tuxedo* Park, in New York State

TV

noun a short form of **television**

tweed

noun a rough woollen cloth

tweezers

plural noun small pincers or nippers for plucking out hairs, or picking up small objects

twelve   (*say* twelv)

noun **1** the number 12 **2** the Roman numeral XII

Word building: **twelve** *adjective: twelve skaters*   **twelfth** *adjective: December is the twelfth month.*

twenty   (*say* <u>twen</u>-tee)

noun **1** the number 20 **2** the Roman numeral XX

Word building: The plural is **twenties.** | **twenty** *adjective: twenty children*   **twentieth** *adjective: This will be the twentieth card in my collection.*

24/7

adverb **1** without stopping: *The highway noise goes on 24/7.*

adjective **2** going on without stopping: *24/7 complaints from Mum about my room*

Word history: short for *twenty-four hours a day, seven days a week*

twice

adverb **1** two times: *Mum pays the rent twice a month.* | *I've been camping twice.* **2** doubly: *twice as many* | *twice as big*

twiddle

verb to turn round and round, especially in a pointless or irritating way: *to twiddle your thumbs*

twig

noun a small thin branch of a tree

twilight

noun the dim light from the sky after sunset

twin

noun **1** one of two children or animals born at the same birth **2** one of two things that match or look alike

Word building: **twin** *adjective*

twine

verb **1** to twist or wind
noun **2** string made of two or more strands twisted together

twinge

noun a pain that lasts only a moment: *a twinge of rheumatism*

twinkle

verb to shine with flickering gleams of light

Word building: **twinkle** *noun*

twirl

verb to spin rapidly

twist

verb **1** to combine by winding together: *fibres twisted to make a rope* **2** to turn about to face another direction: *The soldier twisted around immediately.* **3** to wring or squeeze out of place or shape **4** to sprain or put out of place: *I twisted my ankle during training.* **5** to change the meaning of: *You have twisted my argument unfairly.*

Word building: **twist** *noun*

twitch

verb **1** to jerk or give a short sudden pull at: *Caroline twitched the rope out of my hands.* **2** to give a slight but sudden movement: *My mouth twitched.*

Word building: **twitchy** *adjective* nervous   **twitch** *noun*

two

noun **1** the second number, 2 **2** the Roman numeral II

Word use: Something or someone that is number two or comes next after the first is the **second**.

Word building: **two** *adjective*

two/to/too Don't confuse **two** with **to** or **too**. **To** indicates movement in the direction of a place or person:

> *Can you walk over here to me?*

Too means 'also' or 'in addition', and 'more than is required'.

> *I want to come too.*
> *Your voice is too soft to hear.*

two-up

noun a game in which two coins are spun in the air and bets are laid on both falling either heads up or tails up

tycoon

noun a rich and powerful owner of a business

type

noun **1** a kind: *a type of music*
Other words: **branch, category, class,
fashion, genre, sort, style, variety**
2 metal letters for printing **3** printed
letters: *a headline in large type*
verb **4** to write with a typewriter

typewriter

noun a machine with a keyboard, which
produces numbers and letters like those
used in printing

typhoid   (*say* tuy-foyd)

noun a severe disease that can kill you and
that you can catch by eating or drinking
food or water made impure with a
particular kind of bacteria

Word use: The full name of this is **typhoid
fever.**

typhoon   (*say* tuy-foohn)

noun a violent storm like a cyclone or
hurricane

typical

adjective **1** agreeing with and belonging to
a particular kind: *typical desert plants*
2 expected, normal or characteristic:
typical behaviour

Word building: **typically** *adverb*

typist

noun someone who uses a typewriter

tyranny   (*say* ti-ruh-nee)

noun **1** complete or unchecked
power **2** unjustly harsh government

Word building: **tyrannise** *verb*

tyrant   (*say* tuy-ruhnt)

noun **1** a king or ruler with unlimited
power **2** anyone in a position of power
who uses it cruelly and unjustly

tyre

noun a band of metal or rubber, fitted
round the rim of a wheel

Uu

udder

noun the bag-like part of the body which produces milk in such animals as cows and goats

UFO

noun something unknown that you see in the sky, especially if you think it might be a spaceship

Word building: The plural is **UFOs** or **UFO's**.
Word history: short for *unidentified flying object*

ugg boot

noun a comfortable shoe made from sheepskin with the soft fleece being on the inside of the boot and the leather on the outside: *Grey and cold — just the weather for my old ugg boots!*

Word use: Another spelling is **ug boot** or **ugh boot**.

ugly

adjective **1** unpleasant in appearance
Other words: **frightful, grotesque, hideous, horrid, monstrous**
2 nasty or threatening: *an ugly situation*
Other words: **dangerous, intimidating, menacing, troublesome**

Word building: **ugliness** noun

ukulele (*say* yooh-kuh-<u>lay</u>-lee)

noun a musical instrument like a small guitar but with only four strings

Word history: from a Hawaiian word meaning 'flea'

ulcer

noun a sore which is hard to heal, on your skin or inside, in such a place as the lining of your stomach

Word building: **ulcerate** *verb* **ulcerous** *adjective*

ultimate

adjective final or most important: *my ultimate aim in life*

Word building: **ultimately** *adverb* finally

ultimatum (*say* ul-tuh-<u>may</u>-tuhm)

noun a final statement of terms or conditions: *After the third broken window our neighbour gave us an ultimatum.*

ultra-

prefix a word part meaning **1** beyond: *ultraviolet* **2** excessively: *ultrafashionable*

Word history: from Latin

ultrasound

noun sound vibrations sometimes used by doctors instead of X-rays

ultraviolet

adjective beyond the violet end of the visible spectrum of light: *The ultraviolet light rays from the sun can burn you.*

Uluru (*say* ool-luh-<u>rooh</u>)

noun a very big, red rock in the middle of Australia that is a very special place for Indigenous Australians

Word history: from an Aboriginal language of Northern Territory called Luritja. See the map of Australian Aboriginal languages at the end of this book.

umbilical cord (*say* um-<u>bil</u>-uh-kuhl kawd, um-buh-<u>luy</u>-kuhl kawd)

noun the tube which connects an unborn baby or animal to the lining of its mother's womb, and through which food passes

umbrella

noun a circular screen on a metal framework which you use for a shelter against rain or sun

Word history: from an Italian word meaning 'shade'

umpire

noun someone who makes sure that a game, like cricket or tennis, is played according to the rules
Other words: **referee**

Word building: **umpire** *verb*

un-

prefix a word part meaning **1** not: *uncertain* **2** the opposite: *unbend*

Word history: from Old English

unanimous   (*say* yooh-<u>nan</u>-uh-muhs)

adjective **1** all having the same opinion: *The committee members were unanimous in their support.* **2** showing complete agreement: *a unanimous vote*

Word building: **unanimously** *adverb* **unanimity** *noun*

unassuming

adjective modest or not making any special claims about yourself: *an unassuming manner*

unbelief

noun lack of belief in religion

unbending

adjective firm or determined: *He was quite unbending about the rules.*

unburden

verb to free from a load: *He unburdened himself of his worries by ringing me last night.*

uncanny

adjective weird or unnatural: *It was quite uncanny that we both had the same dream.*

Word building: **uncannily** *adverb* **uncanniness** *noun*

uncertain

adjective **1** not sure: *I am uncertain about the date today.* **2** not to be depended on: *The weather is so uncertain.*

Word building: **uncertainly** *adverb* **uncertainty** *noun*

uncle

noun **1** the brother of your father or mother **2** your aunt's husband

uncomfortable

adjective **1** lacking in comfort: *an uncomfortable chair* **2** uneasy: *Your staring makes me feel uncomfortable.*

Word building: **uncomfortably** *adverb*

unconscious   (*say* un-<u>kon</u>-shuhs)

adjective **1** unaware: *I am unconscious of my surroundings when reading.* **2** having fainted or lost consciousness: *The man lay unconscious at the foot of the cliff.*
Other words: **comatose**
3 below the level of awareness: *The unconscious mind holds a lot of information we cannot recall.*
Other words: **innate, instinctive, subconscious**

Word building: **unconsciously** *adverb*

uncouth

adjective rough and ill-mannered

Word building: **uncouthly** *adverb* **uncouthness** *noun*

under

preposition **1** covered by: *Your glasses are under your book.* **2** below the surface of: *There are a lot of fish under the water.* **3** less than: *How many lollies can I get for under a dollar?* **4** subject to the power or direction of: *We had to do the exam under strict supervision.*
adverb **5** in a place that is covered by: *Let's sit under the tree where it's cooler.* **6** beneath the surface: *If you open your eyes under the water, you can see all the fish.*

underarm

adverb with your arm remaining below the shoulder: *to bowl underarm*

undercarriage

noun the parts of an aeroplane under the body, supporting it on the ground or when taking off and landing

undercurrent

noun **1** a current under the surface **2** a hidden tendency or movement: *There was an undercurrent of feeling against the leader.*

underestimate

verb to work out or calculate at too low a rate, value or amount: *I underestimated the time needed for the job.*

undergo

verb **1** to experience or go through: *to undergo a medical examination* **2** to suffer: *He has undergone many hardships.*

Word building: Other forms are **I underwent, I have undergone, I am undergoing.**

undergraduate

noun a university student who has not yet received a degree

underground

adjective **1** lying under the ground: *an underground river*
Other words: **subterranean**
2 secret: *underground work for the cause*
Other words: **clandestine, hidden**

Word building: **underground** *adverb*

undergrowth

noun shrubs and low plants growing beneath or among trees

underhand

adjective secret and sly: *underhand dealings*

underline

verb **1** to draw a line underneath **2** to stress the importance of
Other words: **emphasise, highlight**

underneath

preposition under or beneath: *The wombat's burrow was underneath an old gum tree.*

underpants

plural noun an undergarment covering the lower part of your body from the waist to the top of the thighs

underpass

noun a road or pathway which goes under a railway or another road

understand

verb **1** to grasp the idea of: *I am trying to understand what you are saying.* **2** to know the nature of thoroughly: *We understand her very well.* **3** to get the idea of by knowing the meaning of the words used: *Do you understand Greek?* **4** to be sympathetic: *He knew that whatever he did she would understand.*

Word building: Other forms are **I understood, I have understood, I am understanding.**

understanding

noun **1** ability to understand or grasp ideas **2** knowledge: *He has a good understanding of the subject.* **3** a private agreement: *They came to an understanding about the profits.*

Word building: **understanding** *adjective* sympathetic

understate

verb to describe as less than is true: *My aunty understated her income to the Taxation Office and got into trouble. | To say the professor was knowledgeable is to understate the case.*

Word building: **understatement** *noun*

understudy

noun an actor or singer who stands by to replace someone who is unable to perform, usually because of illness

Word building: The plural is **understudies. | understudy** *verb* (**understudied, understudying**)

undertake

verb to promise: *He undertook to have the job finished within a year.*

Word building: Other forms are **I undertook, I have undertaken, I am undertaking.**

undertaker

noun someone who prepares bodies for burial or cremation and arranges funerals

undertaking

noun **1** a solemn promise to do something **2** a task: *a difficult undertaking*

underwear

noun clothing such as singlets, underpants and petticoats, worn under other clothes

underworld

noun **1** the world of criminals and criminal activities **2** according to myth, a world beneath the earth which is inhabited by the spirits of all the people who have died

undo

verb **1** to open or untie: *to undo a parcel* **2** to ruin or spoil: *The storm undid all our work in the garden.*

Word building: Other forms are **I undid, I have undone, I am undoing. | undoing** *noun* downfall

undress

verb to take clothes off: *to undress the baby | Please undress for bed.*

unearth

verb to dig up or find after searching: *Mother unearthed her old school photos.*

uneasy

adjective worried or uncomfortable

Word building: **uneasily** *adverb* **uneasiness** *noun*

unemployed
adjective out of work

Word building: **unemployment** *noun*

uneven
adjective **1** not flat, level or straight: *uneven ground* **2** not equally balanced: *an uneven contest*

Word building: **unevenly** *adverb* **unevenness** *noun*

unfair
adjective not fair or just
Other words: **biased, discriminatory, partial, prejudiced, unjust, unobjective**

Word building: **unfairly** *adverb* **unfairness** *noun*

unfamiliar
adjective **1** not having knowledge of: *I am unfamiliar with that writer.* **2** not known or seen before: *Your face is unfamiliar to me.*

Word building: **unfamiliarity** *noun*

unfeeling
adjective cold and hard-hearted

unfold
verb **1** to spread or open out **2** to become known little by little: *Listen as the story unfolds.*

unforeseen
adjective not expected: *an unforeseen delay*

unfortunate
adjective **1** unlucky **2** likely to turn out badly: *an unfortunate decision*

Word building: **unfortunately** *adverb*

ungainly
adjective clumsy or awkward

Word building: **ungainliness** *noun*

unhurried
adjective slow, deliberate and leisurely

unicorn   (*say* yooh-nuh-kawn)
noun an imaginary animal like a horse with a single horn growing in the middle of its forehead

Word history: from a Latin word meaning 'having one horn'

uniform
adjective **1** same in appearance: *bottles of uniform size and colour*
noun **2** special clothes worn by people to show they have a particular job or go to a particular school

Word building: **uniformity** *noun* **uniformly** *adverb*

unify   (*say* yooh-nuh-fuy)
verb to form into one whole

Word building: Other forms are **I unified, I have unified, I am unifying.** | **unification** *noun*

uninhibited
adjective behaving just as you like without worrying about what other people think

uninstall
verb to remove from a computer: *The new program was causing problems in the whole system so we uninstalled it.*

uninterested
adjective not wanting to know about something
Other words: **apathetic, bored, indifferent**

uninterested/disinterested Don't confuse **uninterested** with **disinterested**, which means 'not directly involved'.

union   (*say* yoohn-yuhn)
noun **1** a number of things joined together as one **2** short for **trade union**

Word building: **unionise** *verb* to organise into a trade union   **unionist** *noun* a member of a trade union

unique   (*say* yooh-neek)
adjective different from all the others: *Your fingerprints are unique.*

Word building: **uniquely** *adverb*

unisex
adjective suitable for both females and males: *a unisex hairstyle*

unison   (*say* yooh-nuh-suhn)
phrase **in unison**, singing or saying the same thing all together: *The choir sang in unison.*

unit
noun **1** a single person or thing or the whole of a group of people or things **2** an amount used in measurement: *A metre is a unit of length.* **3** one complete part of a school subject: *two units of maths* **4** short for **home unit**

unite
verb to join together as one: *The two clubs united.* | *The fight to save the koalas united the community.*

Word building: **united** *adjective*

unity
noun a feeling of belonging or harmony in a group

universal
adjective including and affecting everyone, everything and every place

Word building: **universality** *noun* **universally** *adverb*

universe
noun the whole of space and everything that exists in it
Other words: **cosmos**

university
noun a place where you can study to earn a degree and do research after you have left school

unknown
adjective unfamiliar or not known: *an unknown face*

unleaded petrol
noun petrol that does not contain tiny bits of lead and is therefore not as harmful to people and the environment

Word use: Compare this with **leaded petrol**.

unless
conjunction except if: *I'll have the last biscuit, unless you want it.*

unlike
preposition **1** different from: *The food at the restaurant was unlike the food they usually ate at home.* **2** not in the nature of: *It's unlike him to be late.*

unlikely
adjective **1** probably not true: *an unlikely story* **2** probably not going to happen: *Rain is unlikely.*

Word building: **unlikelihood** *noun*

unload
verb to take things off or out of: *to unload a truck | to unload a gun*

unnatural
adjective not normal, natural or usual: *an unnatural light in the sky*

Word building: **unnaturally** *adverb*

unnerve
verb to upset or make nervous: *The scornful crowd unnerved the speaker.*

Word building: **unnerving** *adjective*

unprepossessing
(*say* un-pree-puh-<u>zes</u>-ing)
noun ordinary or not impressive: *The restaurant looked unprepossessing but the food was delicious.*

unravel
verb to untangle or come undone: *to unravel a mystery | The knitting has unravelled.*

Word building: Other forms are **I unravelled, I have unravelled, I am unravelling**.

unreal
adjective **1** imaginary or non-existent **2** *Informal* amazing or unbelievable: *That song is unreal.*

Word building: **unreality** *noun*

unrest
noun an angry restless feeling: *unrest among the prisoners*

unruly
adjective disobedient or uncontrollable: *an unruly class*

unscathed
adjective not hurt or injured: *They survived the battle unscathed.*

unscrew
verb **1** to unfasten by taking the screws out of: *to unscrew the brass plate from the door* **2** to take off by turning round and round: *to unscrew the lid from a bottle*

unseemly
adjective not proper or decent: *unseemly behaviour*

Word building: **unseemliness** *noun*

unsettle
verb to disturb or upset: *The thunder unsettled the dogs.*

Word building: **unsettling** *adjective*

unsightly
adjective not pleasant to look at: *an unsightly scar*

unthinkable
adjective not deserving to be considered or thought about: *It is unthinkable that we would leave the children alone.*

untie
verb to loosen or set loose by undoing a knot: *She untied her scarf. | He untied the dog.*

Word building: Other forms are **I untied, I have untied, I am untying**.

until

conjunction **1** up to the time that or when: *We will wait until you get here.* **2** before: *Don't start the race until you hear the starting gun.*
preposition **3** up to the time of: *She stayed until midnight.* **4** before: *She did not go until midnight.*

untold

adjective **1** not told: *an untold story* **2** more than can be counted or measured: *a person of untold wealth*

untruth

noun a lie or falsehood

unusual

adjective not common or ordinary

Word building: **unusually** *adverb*

unwieldy

adjective **1** difficult to handle or manage: *an unwieldy load* **2** awkward: *an unwieldy movement of the arm*

unwitting

adjective **1** not meant or intended: *an unwitting insult* **2** not knowing, or unaware: *an unwitting victim*

Word building: **unwittingly** *adverb*

unzip

verb **1** to undo the zip on a piece of clothing **2** to return (computer data that has been put into a form that takes less storage) to its original form

Word building: Other forms are **I unzipped, I have unzipped, I am unzipping.**

up

adverb **1** to or in a higher place: *I'll race you up to the top of the hill! | The bird's nest is up in the highest branch.* **2** to or in an upright position: *Sit up.* **3** to, near, or at a higher rank or condition: *She's moving up in the company.*
preposition **4** to or at a higher place on or in: *We ran up the stairs.*
adjective **5** going upwards: *the up ramp in the carpark* **6** out of bed: *What time in the morning will you be up?*
phrase **7 up to, a** If something is **up to** someone, it is their responsibility to do it: *It is up to all of us to prevent bullying.* **b** If someone is **up to** a task or a position, they are able to do or perform it: *Are you up to playing the lead role in the play?*

upbraid

verb to speak angrily to about doing something wrong: *The coach upbraided us for our laziness.*
Other words: **chastise, rebuke, reprove, scold**

upbringing

noun the care and education that is given by parents or similar people to someone during their childhood

update

verb **1** to give the latest news to: *I will update you on what has happened recently.* **2** to make more modern: *They are updating the shop.*

Word building: Other forms are **I updated, I am updating.** | **update** *noun*

upgrade

verb **1** to promote or make more important: *Mum's boss upgraded her to a new job. | The company upgraded my position.* **2** to improve: *You must upgrade your work.*

upheaval

noun a complete change or great disturbance: *We were in a state of upheaval after we moved house.*

uphill

adjective **1** going upwards: *an uphill path* **2** very difficult: *an uphill task*

Word building: **uphill** *adverb*

uphold

verb to support or keep unchanged: *The principal upheld the rule that the teacher had made.*

Word use: The more usual word is **maintain**.
Word building: Other forms are **I upheld, I have upheld, I am upholding.**

upholster

verb to provide with coverings, stuffing and springs: *to upholster a chair*

Word building: **upholsterer** *noun* **upholstery** *noun*

upkeep

noun the work or cost of looking after something or someone

uplift

verb **1** to lift up **2** to cause to feel better, especially spiritually or mentally: *The beautiful singing uplifted the audience.*

Word building: **uplift** *noun*

upload
verb to copy from a personal computer to a larger system like a network

upon
preposition on: *upon the table* | *Upon their arrival, we all sat down for morning tea.*

upper
adjective **1** higher or highest in place, position or rank: *the upper slopes of a mountain* | *the upper class* **2** facing upwards: *the upper side of a coin*

upper case
noun the printing type that makes capital letters

Word use: The opposite is **lower case**.

upright
adjective **1** straight upward or vertical: *an upright position*
Other words: **erect, perpendicular, standing**
2 honest and just: *an upright person*
Other words: **decent, moral, principled, righteous, scrupulous, virtuous**

Word building: **upright** *adverb*

uprising
noun a violent rebellion against a government or other authority by a large number of people
Other words: **mutiny, revolt, revolution**

uproar
noun a noisy disturbance: *There was an uproar in the classroom before the teacher came.*

Word building: **uproarious** *adjective*

upset
verb **1** to turn or knock over: *to upset a boat* | *to upset a tray of drinks*
Other words: **overturn**
2 to put out of order: *to upset someone's plans* **3** to make feel sad or hurt: *Your insults upset me.*
Other words: **distress, disturb, grieve, hurt**
4 to make feel sick in the stomach: *That food upset me.*

Word building: Other forms are **I upset, I have upset, I am upsetting.** | **upset** *noun*
upset *adjective*

upstairs
adverb **1** on or towards a higher storey or storeys of a house, office building, and so on
noun **2** a higher storey or storeys

uptake
noun the act of understanding or grasping facts: *I am quick on the uptake so you won't have to tell me twice.*

uptight
adjective Informal nervous or worried: *I felt uptight before my music exam.*

up-to-date
adjective **1** including the most recent facts: *an up-to-date news report* **2** modern: *up-to-date clothes* | *up-to-date ideas*

upwards
adverb towards a higher position or level: *The smoke drifted upwards.*

Word building: **upward** *adverb*

uranium (*say* yooh-**rayn**-ee-uhm)
noun a white radioactive metal which comes from a yellow ore and which can be used to produce nuclear weapons and energy

urban
adjective having to do with a city or town: *the urban population*

urban sprawl
noun the outer parts of a city where houses spread out into surrounding areas often without much planning for how they look or for what facilities will be available: *We live on the western perimeter of Sydney's urban sprawl.*

urchin
noun a small person, especially one who is mischievous or poorly dressed

Word history: from the Latin word for 'hedgehog'

urge
verb **1** to try hard to persuade: *I urged you to be very careful.* **2** to push, drive or force: *I urged the horse along the path.* | *Hunger urged us to keep going.*
noun **3** a strong natural desire: *I felt an urge to eat some fruit.*

urgent
adjective needing immediate action or attention: *an urgent message*

Word building: **urgency** *noun*   **urgently** *adverb*

urinal (*say* **yooh**-ruh-nuhl, yuh-**ruy**-nuhl)
noun a building to urinate in, especially a men's toilet

urinate

verb to pass urine from the body

Word building: **urination** *noun*

urine   (*say* <u>yooh</u>-ruhn, <u>yooh</u>-ruyn)

noun liquid produced by the kidneys and passed from the body as a waste product

Word building: **urinary** *adjective*

URL

noun an internet address for a web page

Word history: short for *uniform resource locator*

urn

noun **1** a kind of vase, especially one for holding the ashes of someone who has been cremated **2** a container with a tap, used for heating water

urn/earn Don't confuse **urn** with **earn**. To **earn** is to receive something in return for working, or to deserve to get something.

us

pronoun the form of **we** that comes after a verb: *Don't worry about us.*

usage

noun **1** the way of using or treating: *rough usage* **2** a custom or practice **3** the way in which a language is used: *English usage.*

USB   (*say* yooh es <u>bee</u>)

noun a standard for connecting computers to other devices like digital cameras or scanners enabling data to be transferred between them

Word history: short for *universal serial bus*

USB stick

noun a data storage device with a USB interface

use   (*say* yoohz)

verb **1** to put into action for some purpose: *I will use a knife to cut this rope. | Do you know how to use this computer?*
Other words: **employ, utilise**
2 to take advantage of someone's feeling for you in order to get them to do something you want: *She doesn't love Brad — she is simply using him.*
Other words: **exploit**
noun (*say* yoohs) **3** the act of using: *This shows the use of common sense. | You should clean those brushes after each use.* **4** the state

of being used: *Is this seat in use?* **5** a way of being used: *You will find that this bag has a lot of uses.*
6 the ability to use something: *Mario lost the use of his legs after the accident.*
7 a need for using something: *Do you have any use for these old skates?*
Other words: **call, want**
8 the ability to be used in a helpful way: *This book is of use to me.*
phrase **9 use up,** to take or wear out the entire supply of: *I've used up the toothpaste. | They've used up their strength.*
Other words: **exhaust, expend, consume**

Word building: **usable** *adjective*   **useful** *adjective*   **useless** *adjective*   **user** *noun*

use/ewes Don't confuse **use** with **ewes**. **Ewes** is the plural of **ewe**, a female sheep.

used¹   (*say* yoohzd)

adjective another word for **second-hand**

used²   (*say* yoohst)

phrase **used to, a** was or were accustomed: *We used to go there every summer.* **b** in the habit of or accustomed to: *I am used to getting up early.*

usher

noun someone who shows people to their seats at a meeting in church or at another public gathering

usual

adjective normal or customary: *We went to school the usual way.*
Other words: **accepted, common, conventional, habitual, ordinary, regular, standard, traditional, typical**

Word building: **usually** *adverb*

utensil   (*say* yooh-<u>tens</u>-uhl)

noun an instrument, tool, or container, especially one of those used for cooking or eating: *Pots and pans are kitchen utensils.*

Word history: from a Latin word meaning 'useful'

uterus   (*say* <u>yooh</u>-tuh-ruhs)

noun the part of the body of a female in which a baby grows

Word use: The plural is **uteri** or **uteruses**. | Another word is **womb**.

utilise

verb to put into use: *We can utilise the sun's power to make electricity.*

Word use: Another spelling is **utilize**.
Word building: **utilisation** *noun*

utility

noun **1** usefulness **2** a service run by the government, such as public transport, gas or electricity supply **3** a small truck

Word use: Definition 3 is also called a **ute** in informal language.

utmost

adjective **1** greatest: *This is of the utmost importance.* **2** farthest: *He went to the utmost areas of the earth.*
noun **3** the greatest amount possible: *This is the utmost that can be said.* **4** the best that you can do: *Try your utmost.*

Word use: Another form of this word is **uttermost**.

utopia   (*say* yooh-<u>toh</u>-pee-uh)

noun a completely perfect place or society

utter¹

verb to speak: *He was sorry he had uttered angry words.*

Word building: **utterance** *noun*

utter²

adjective complete or total: *utter happiness* / *The room was utter luxury.*

Word building: **utterly** *adverb*

U-turn

noun a turn made by a car or other vehicle so that it faces the way it has just come

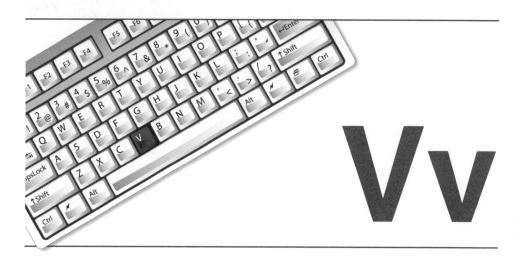

Vv

vacant (*say* <u>vay</u>-kuhnt)
adjective **1** empty: *vacant space* **2** not occupied by anyone: *a vacant chair | a vacant job*

Word building: **vacancy** *noun* **vacantly** *adverb*

vacate (*say* vuh-<u>kayt</u>)
verb to leave or make empty: *You must vacate your hotel room by 10 o'clock.*

vacation
noun **1** a holiday
Other words: **break, recess**
2 the time of the year when a place such as a university is closed

vaccine (*say* <u>vak</u>-seen)
noun a liquid made from the germs that give you a disease, which you take to stop you getting that disease

Word building: **vaccinate** *verb* to give a vaccine to **vaccination** *noun*
Word history: from a Latin word meaning 'having to do with cows'

vacuum (*say* <u>vak</u>-yoohm)
noun an empty space, especially a space that has been made empty of air: *A pump works by making a vacuum which fills up with liquid.*
Other words: **emptiness, void**

vacuum cleaner
noun a machine that sucks up dirt from floors

vagina (*say* vuh-<u>juy</u>-nuh)
noun the part of a female's genitals that leads from the uterus to the outside of the body

vagrant (*say* <u>vay</u>-gruhnt)
noun someone who wanders from place to place instead of having a settled home
Other words: **tramp**

vague (*say* vayg)
adjective not clear or certain: *vague shapes | vague feelings*

Word building: **vaguely** *adverb* **vagueness** *noun*

vain
adjective **1** very proud of yourself, especially about the way you look
Other words: **conceited, immodest**
2 useless or having no effect: *She made a vain attempt to stop the dogs fighting.*
phrase **3** in vain, uselessly or without effect: *They tried in vain to save the child.*

Word building: **vainly** *adverb* **vanity** *noun*

vain/vein/vane Don't confuse **vain** with **vein** or **vane**.

A **vein** is a blood vessel taking the blood back to the heart.

A **vane** is a flat piece of metal, or something similar, designed to move with the wind. A **weather vane** shows the direction the wind is blowing.

valedictory (*say* val-uh-<u>dik</u>-tuh-ree)
adjective saying farewell: *She will give the valedictory speech.*

valentine
noun **1** a present or message of love or friendship sent to someone on St Valentine's Day, 14 February **2** the person you choose to send this message to

valet (*say* <u>val</u>-ay, <u>val</u>-uht)

noun a male servant who looks after his employer's clothes and other personal things

valiant

adjective brave or courageous: *a valiant person | a valiant attempt to save his life*

Word building: **valiantly** *adverb*

valid

adjective **1** made with good reasons: *a valid excuse to leave the room* **2** having legal or official force: *This ticket is valid for two rides.*

Word building: **validity** *noun*   **validly** *adverb*

valley

noun the low land between hills or mountains, usually with a river flowing through it

Other words: **canyon, gorge, gully, ravine**

valour

noun braveness or courage

Word use: Another spelling is **valor**.

valuable

adjective **1** worth a lot of money: *valuable jewels*

Other words: **costly, expensive, precious**

2 of great use or importance: *valuable help*

noun **3** valuables, things that are valuable, such as jewellery: *Don't leave any valuables in the changing rooms.*

value

noun **1** the amount of money something is worth: *the value of your house* **2** what makes something worthwhile or useful: *The guest speaker talked about the value of education.* **3 values,** the beliefs and ideas about what is important, held by a person or community of people: *We like each other because we have the same values.*

verb **4** to decide the value of: *My cousin's job is to value antique furniture.* **5** to think to be valuable: *I value your friendship.*

Word building: **valuer** *noun*

valve

noun **1** the part of a pipe or other passage that opens and shuts to control the flow of liquid or gas **2** one of the parts of the shell of a sea animal, such as a mussel

vampire

noun an imaginary being, usually thought of as a dead person come back to life, believed to suck the blood from people while they are sleeping

Word history: from a Turkish word meaning 'witch'

van

noun a covered vehicle for carrying goods: *a removal van*

Word history: short for **caravan**

vandal

noun someone who deliberately destroys or damages things

vane

noun **1** a blade on a windmill **2** a flat piece of metal or other material on a roof, which turns with the wind to show which direction it is blowing from

Word use: Definition 2 is also called a **weathervane**.

vane/vain/vein Don't confuse **vane** with **vain** or **vein**.

You are **vain** if you are very proud of yourself, especially about the way you look.

A **vein** is one of the small tubes that carries blood through your body.

vanguard

noun **1** the front part of an army **2** any leading position: *She is in the vanguard of fashion.*

vanilla

noun a liquid made from a bean from a plant, used to flavour food

vanish

verb to disappear, especially quickly: *When I turned around she had vanished.*

vanity

noun **1** extreme pride in yourself: *She is too full of vanity.* **2** something that someone is vain about: *His hair was one of his vanities.*

Word building: The plural is **vanities**.

vanquish

verb to defeat: *The Roman army vanquished the enemy. | Our team vanquished all the others.*

vaporise

verb to change into vapour: *Liquid vaporises when it is boiled.*

Word use: Another spelling is **vaporize**.
Word building: **vaporisation** *noun* **vaporiser** *noun*

vapour

noun a cloud of a gas-like substance, such as fog, mist or steam

Word use: Another spelling is **vapor**.
Word building: **vaporous** *adjective*

variable

adjective **1** likely to vary or change: *variable weather | a person with variable moods* **2** able to be changed: *The length of this table is variable.*

Word building: **variably** *adverb*

variation

noun **1** a change or alteration: *There is a lot of variation in the weather at this time of the year.* **2** a different form of something: *This story is just a variation of all your other stories.*

variegated   (*say* vair-ree-uh-gayt-uhd)

adjective marked with different colours: *variegated leaves*

variety

noun **1** a variation or a change from what usually happens: *You enjoy work more if there is some variety in it.* **2** a number of things of different kinds: *a shop with a variety of cakes*

Other words: **assortment, diversity, mix, mixture**

3 kind or sort: *This variety of ice-cream is my favourite.*

various

adjective **1** different: *Your talents are many and various.* **2** several: *I visited various parts of the country.*

Word building: **variously** *adverb*
variousness *noun*

varnish

noun a liquid coating which, when dry, gives a hard glossy look to a surface

Word building: **varnish** *verb*

vary

verb **1** to change: *She never varies her habits.* **2** to be different or cause to be different: *Opinions vary as to whether this is a good idea. | You should vary what you read.*

Word building: Other forms are **I varied, I have varied, I am varying.**

vase   (*rhymes with* bars)

noun a container for flowers

vassal

noun someone in feudal times who lived on land owned by nobility and had to fight and work for them in return

vast

adjective very great: *a vast country | a vast amount of money*

Word building: **vastly** *adverb*   **vastness** *noun*

vat

noun a very large container for liquids

vaudeville   (*say* vaw-duh-vil)

noun a light theatrical entertainment, mainly with musical and comedy acts

vault¹

noun **1** an underground room, especially one for storing valuable things or one where dead people are buried **2** an arched roof or something thought to be similar: *the vault of a church | the vault of the sky*

Word building: **vaulted** *adjective*: *a vaulted roof*

vault²

verb **1** to leap or jump with your hands supported on something: *Jusef vaulted over the fence.* **2** to jump over in this way: *Nadya vaulted the fence.*

Word building: **vault** *noun*
Word history: from a Latin word meaning 'roll'

VCR

noun another word for **video** (definition 2)

Word history: short for *video cassette recorder*

veal

noun meat from a calf

veer

verb to change direction: *The road suddenly veered to the left. | I veered to avoid the dog.*

vegetable

noun **1** a plant or part of a plant which is used as food: *Tomatoes, beans and potatoes are vegetables.*

adjective **2** of or having to do with plants: *the vegetable kingdom*

vegetarian

noun someone who refuses to eat meat or fish and lives mainly on vegetable food

vegetation

noun the whole plant life of a particular area: *Tropical places usually have thick vegetation.*

vehement (*say* <u>vee</u>-uh-muhnt)
adjective strong or passionate: *a vehement dislike*
Word building: **vehemence** *noun*
vehemently *adverb*

vehicle (*say* <u>vee</u>-ik-uhl)
noun a form of transport, like a car or bicycle
Word building: **vehicular** *adjective*

veil (*rhymes with* pale)
noun **1** a piece of material worn to cover the head and face
verb **2** to hide or disguise: *The mountains were veiled in mist.*

vein (*sounds like* vain)
noun **1** one of the small tubes that carries blood through your body **2** a line on a leaf or insect's wing **3** a layer of coal or gold in the middle of rock

vein/vain/vane Don't confuse **vein** with **vain** or **vane**.

You are **vain** if you are very proud of yourself, especially about the way you look.

A **vane** is a flat piece of metal, or something similar, designed to move with the wind. A **weather vane** shows the direction the wind is blowing.

velcro
noun a type of fastening tape made of two fabric strips, one with many tiny nylon hooks and the other with a nylon pile, that stick firmly together when pressed
Word building: **velcro** *adjective*
Word history: a trademark

velocity (*say* vuh-<u>los</u>-uh-tee)
noun speed: *a wind velocity of 100 kilometres an hour*
Word building: The plural is **velocities**.

velvet
noun a kind of soft thick material that feels rather like fur
Word building: **velvet** *adjective* **velvety** *adjective*

vendetta
noun a feud in which the family of a murder victim tries to get revenge by killing the murderer or one of the murderer's family

veneer (*say* vuh-<u>near</u>)
noun **1** a thin layer of wood or plastic used to cover the surface underneath **2** outwardly pleasant behaviour, disguising what is really underneath: *a veneer of good manners*

venerable
adjective worthy of respect because of age or importance
Word building: **venerate** *verb* to respect

venereal disease (*say* vuh-<u>near</u>-ree-uhl duh-zeez)
noun any disease picked up by having sexual intercourse with someone who is infected, but not including AIDS
Word use: This is often shortened to **VD**.

vengeance (*say* <u>ven</u>-juhns)
noun **1** the act of paying someone back for harm they have done to you
Other words: **reprisal, retaliation, revenge**
phrase **2 with a vengeance**, very strongly or forcefully

venison
noun the meat of a deer, eaten as food

venom
noun the poison that spiders and snakes inject into their victims
Other words: **toxin**
Word building: **venomous** *adjective* poisonous

vent
noun **1** an opening to let smoke or fumes out
verb **2** to express or show: *to vent anger*

ventilate
verb to bring fresh air into and let stale air out of: *Open the windows to ventilate the room.*
Word building: **ventilation** *noun* **ventilator** *noun*

ventricle
noun either of the two lower cavities of the heart, from which blood is pumped out
Word use: Compare this with **atrium**.

ventriloquism
(*say* ven-<u>tril</u>-uh-kwiz-uhm)
noun a way of speaking without moving your lips so that your voice seems to come from somewhere else
Word building: **ventriloquist** *noun*

venture

noun **1** something risky or a bit dangerous: *a business venture*
verb **2** to risk or dare: *to venture an opinion*
Word building: **venturesome** *adjective* bold

venue   (*say* <u>ven</u>-yooh)

noun the place where a particular event is held: *The new hall is the venue for the school concert.*

verandah

noun a partly open section on the outside of a house, usually covered by the main roof
Other words: **balcony, deck, patio, porch**

Word use: Another spelling is **veranda**.
Word history: from a Portuguese word for 'railing', which came from a Latin word meaning 'rod'

verb

noun a word in a sentence which tells you what someone or something does or feels, such as 'heard' and 'flew' in *I heard the plane as it flew overhead.*

verbal

adjective **1** spoken rather than written: *a verbal message* **2** having to do with words: *verbal skills*
Word building: **verbally** *adverb*

verbatim   (*say* vuh-<u>bay</u>-tuhm)

adverb using exactly the same words: *to quote her words verbatim*

verdict

noun the judge's or jury's decision or answer in a law court

verge

noun **1** the very edge: *on the verge of tears* **2** the strip of dirt or grass at the edge of a road
phrase **3 verge on,** to come close to: *to verge on stupidity*

verger

noun the caretaker of a church

verify

verb to prove to be true or correct: *You can verify the spelling of a word by looking it up in the dictionary.*
Word building: **verification** *noun*

vermin

plural noun dirty pests such as rats, cockroaches and fleas

Word history: from a French word meaning 'worm'

versatile

adjective able to do a variety of things: *a versatile performer* | *a versatile tool*
Word building: **versatilely** *adverb* **versatility** *noun*

verse¹

noun **1** poetry: *a play written in verse* **2** a group of lines that go together in a song or poem **3** a short part, usually numbered, of a book such as the Bible or the Koran

verse²

verb *Informal* to play against someone in a game or competition: *We versed that team last week.*
Word history: from *versus*

version

noun **1** someone's description of what happened compared with someone else's: *What's your version of the accident?* **2** a particular form of something: *the film version of 'Alice in Wonderland'*

versus   (*say* <u>ver</u>-suhs)

preposition against: *an Australia versus England test match*

vertebra   (*say* <u>ver</u>-tuh-bruh)

noun one of the bones of your spine or backbone
Word building: The plural is **vertebrae** (*say* <u>ver</u>-tuh-bree).

vertebrate   (*say* <u>ver</u>-tuh-bruht)

noun an animal with a backbone: *Fish are vertebrates but prawns are not.*

vertex

noun **1** the top or highest point of something: *the vertex of a triangle* **2** the point where two sides of an angle or three or more sides of a solid meet: *A square-based pyramid has five vertices.*
Word building: The plural is **vertices** or **vertexes**.

vertical

adjective standing straight up or at right angles to the horizon: *a vertical line*
Other words: **perpendicular, upright**

Word use: Compare this with **horizontal** and **diagonal**.
Word building: **vertically** *adverb*

vertigo   (*say* <u>ver</u>-tuh-goh)
noun a feeling of sickness or dizziness, often caused by looking down from a height

verve
noun lively enthusiasm: *to speak with verve*

very
adverb **1** in a high degree: *very fast* | *very sorry* | *very quietly*
Other words: **decidedly, exceedingly, exceptionally, extremely, particularly, really, remarkably**
adjective **2** exact or actual: *That is the very thing you should not have done!* | *He shuddered at the very thought.*

vessel
noun **1** a ship or boat **2** a hollow container, such as a cup or bottle **3** a tube which carries fluid inside your body, such as a blood vessel

vest
noun **1** another word for **waistcoat** **2** another word for **singlet**

vestibule   (*say* <u>vest</u>-uh-byoohl)
noun an entrance hall

vestige   (*say* <u>vest</u>-ij)
noun the last trace of something that was once there
Word building: **vestigial** *adjective*

vestry
noun the room in a church where members of the clergy put on their robes and where sacred objects are kept
Word use: The plural is **vestries**.

vet
noun **1** a short form of **veterinary surgeon**
verb **2** to check or examine carefully: *to vet the people applying for a job*
Other words: **screen**

veteran
noun **1** someone who has worked for a long time in a particular job **2** a returned soldier
adjective **3** with long experience: *a veteran bushwalker*
phrase **4 veteran car**, a car built before 1919

veterinary surgeon
  (*say* <u>vet</u>-uh-ruhn-ree ser-juhn)
noun someone whose job is to treat sick animals

Word use: Another word is **veterinarian**. | The short form of this is **vet**.

veto   (*say* <u>vee</u>-toh)
verb to refuse to agree to: *to veto a plan*
Word building: Other forms are **I vetoed, I have vetoed, I am vetoing**. | **veto** *noun* (**vetoes**) the power or right to prevent something

vex
verb to annoy or worry: *to vex your parents*
Word building: **vexation** *noun* **vexatious** *adjective* **vexed** *adjective*

viable   (*say* <u>vuy</u>-uh-buhl)
adjective able to be done or put into practice: *a viable plan*
Word building: **viability** *noun*

viaduct   (*say* <u>vuy</u>-uh-dukt)
noun a bridge with many arches, which carries a road or railway over a valley

vibe
noun *Informal* the feeling you get, good or bad, just from being in a place: *I don't like the vibe in this empty old warehouse.*

vibes
plural noun a short form of **vibraphone**

vibrant
adjective **1** bright, lively and exciting: *a vibrant colour* | *a vibrant personality* **2** vibrating or quickly moving to and fro
Word building: **vibrancy** *noun* **vibrantly** *adverb*

vibraphone
noun an electronic musical instrument like a xylophone, often used in jazz

vibrate
verb **1** to keep on moving quickly up and down or to and fro
Other words: **pulsate, shudder, quiver, tremble**
2 to make a buzzing or quivering sound
Word building: **vibration** *noun*

vicar
noun a priest, especially one in charge of an Anglican parish
Word building: **vicarage** *noun* a vicar's house

vice[1]
noun **1** wickedness or evil **2** a fault or bad habit

vice²
noun a tool which closes around something and holds it tightly in place while you work on it

Word history: from a Latin word meaning 'vine'

vice-regal
adjective having to do with someone appointed as a deputy by a king or queen, such as a Governor-General or Governor of a State

vice versa　(*say* vuy-suh <u>ver</u>-suh)
adverb the other way round from what you've just said, as in *I like him and vice versa,* which means *I like him and he likes me.*

vicinity
noun neighbourhood or area nearby: *There is no swimming pool in our vicinity.*

Word building: The plural is **vicinities.**

vicious　(*say* <u>vish</u>-uhs)
adjective very cruel or harmful: *a vicious dog | a vicious attack*

Word building: **viciously** *adverb* **viciousness** *noun*

victim
noun someone who suffers harm or injury: *a victim of a car accident*
Other words: **casualty**

victimise
verb to punish or harm unfairly

Word use: Another spelling is **victimize.**
Word building: **victimisation** *noun*

victory
noun a win or success in a contest
Other words: **conquest, triumph**

Word building: The plural is **victories. |
victor** *noun* the winner **victorious** *adjective* **victoriously** *adverb*

video
adjective **1** having to do with television
noun **2** a tape recorder which records both images and sounds **3** a video recording **4** a video cassette

Word history: Definition 2 is short for a **video recorder** or **video cassette recorder.**

videotape
noun magnetic tape used for recording pictures and sound to be shown on television

vie
phrase **vie with,** to compete against or try to beat

Word building: Other forms are **I vied, I have vied, I am vying.**

view
noun **1** whatever you can see from a particular place: *a spectacular view from the top of the tower* **2** an idea or opinion: *What is your view on homework?*
verb **3** to look at or see: *I will view the new building tomorrow.*
phrase **4 in view of,** because of
5 on view, displayed for all to see

Word building: **viewer** *noun*

vigil　(*say* <u>vij</u>-uhl)
noun the act of keeping watch at night: *to keep vigil by a sick child's bed*

vigilant　(*say* <u>vij</u>-uh-luhnt)
adjective alert and watchful

Word building: **vigilance** *noun* **vigilantly** *adverb*

vigour
noun energy and strength

Word use: Another spelling is **vigor.**
Word building: **vigorous** *adjective* strong, energetic and full of life **vigorously** *adverb*

vile
adjective disgustingly bad: *a vile smell | vile language*

Word building: **vilely** *adverb* **vileness** *noun*

villa
noun **1** a large country house, especially in a Mediterranean country **2** a small house, usually one of a set of connected houses

village
noun a small town in the country
Other words: **hamlet, township**

Word building: **villager** *noun*

villain　(*say* <u>vil</u>-uhn)
noun a wicked person or scoundrel
Other words: **rascal, rogue**

Word building: **villainy** *noun* wickedness **villainous** *adjective*

villein　(*say* <u>vil</u>-uhn)
noun someone in feudal times, with a little more freedom than a serf

vindicate (*say* <u>vin</u>-duh-kayt)
verb to show to be right or innocent
Word building: **vindication** *noun*

vindictive
adjective spiteful or full of revenge: *a vindictive remark*
Word building: **vindictively** *adverb*

vine
noun a climbing plant, such as a grape

vinegar
noun a sour liquid made from wine or cider and used to flavour food
Word history: from the French word for 'wine' added to the French word for 'sour'

vineyard (*say* <u>vin</u>-yuhd)
noun a farm where grapevines are grown

vintage
noun **1** the wine or grapes grown in one particular year: *The 1976 vintage is Bernadette's favourite.*
adjective **2** very high quality, though perhaps in an old-fashioned way
phrase **3 vintage car**, a car built between 1919 and 1930

vinyl (*say* <u>vuy</u>-nuhl)
noun a type of plastic

viola
noun a stringed instrument, like a violin but a little bigger
Word use: The **viola** is lower in pitch than the **violin** and higher than the **cello** and **double bass**.

violate
verb **1** to disobey: *to violate the law* **2** to treat brutally, showing no respect: *to violate a holy place*
Word building: **violation** *noun*

violent
adjective powerful and causing damage: *a violent storm | a violent temper*
Other words: **destructive, furious, raging, severe, tempestuous, wild**
Word building: **violence** *noun* **violently** *adverb*

violet
noun a small plant with purplish-blue flowers
Word building: **violet** *adjective* purplish-blue

violin
noun a stringed instrument played with a bow and held between your shoulder and chin
Word use: The **violin** is higher in pitch than the **viola**, **cello** and **double bass**.
Word building: **violinist** *noun*

violoncello (*say* vuy-uh-luhn-<u>chel</u>-oh)
noun the full form of **cello**

VIP
short for **very important person**

viper
noun a type of very venomous snake

virgin
noun **1** someone who has never had sexual intercourse
adjective **2** completely natural or unspoiled: *virgin bush | virgin wool*
Word use: Definiton 1 is mostly used of girls and women.
Word building: **virginity** *noun*

virile (*say* <u>vi</u>-ruyl)
adjective strong, forceful and masculine
Word building: **virility** *noun*

virtual
adjective as if it were really so: *Cinderella's family made her a virtual slave.*
Word building: **virtually** *adverb* in effect: *The deputy was virtually the head of the school.*

virtue
noun **1** goodness or proper behaviour **2** a good quality: *Patience is a virtue.*

virtuoso (*say* ver-tyooh-<u>oh</u>-soh)
noun a highly skilled musician
Word building: The plural is **virtuosos** or **virtuosi**. | **virtuosity** *noun*

virtuous
adjective good, honourable and obedient
Word building: **virtuously** *adverb*

virulent (*say* <u>vi</u>-ruh-luhnt)
adjective **1** very harmful: *a virulent disease* **2** bitter and spiteful: *virulent criticism*
Word building: **virulence** *noun* **virulently** *adverb*

virus

noun **1** a very small organism that causes disease **2** any disease caused by a virus: *the common cold is a virus.* **3** a small program in computers, which is let loose in the operating system with the intention of causing as much damage as possible, usually destroying files

visa   (*say* vee-zuh)

noun a stamp or written notice put in your passport, giving you permission to enter a certain country

viscount   (*say* vuy-kownt)

noun a British nobleman ranking below an earl and above a baron

Word building: **viscountess** *noun*

visibility

noun the distance you can see, given the weather conditions or time of day: *Drive slowly because visibility is bad.*

visible

adjective able to be seen: *The lighthouse is visible from a long distance.*
Other words: **apparent, discernible, evident, perceivable**

Word building: **visibly** *adverb*

vision

noun **1** the power or sense of seeing: *The old man has good vision for his age.*
Other words: **eyesight, sight**
2 the power of imagining: *It was Colonel Light's vision that led to Adelaide being built.* **3** a mental image: *a vision of paradise*
Other words: **dream, image**

Word building: **visionary** *adjective*
visionary *noun*

vision-impaired

adjective not having very good sight or being completely blind

visit

verb **1** to call on to see: *to visit friends* **2** to stay with as a guest: *My cousin is visiting me this week.*

Word building: **visit** *noun*   **visitor** *noun*

visor   (*say* vuy-zuh)

noun the movable part of a helmet, which can be pulled down over your eyes

visual

adjective **1** of or having to do with sight: *visual ability* **2** able to be seen: *Teachers use pictures as visual aids.*

Word building: **visually** *adverb*

visual display unit

noun a computer terminal which shows information on a screen

Word use: This is also called a **VDU**.

visualise

verb to form a mental picture of: *I recognise her name, but I can't visualise her face.*

Word use: Another spelling is **visualize**.

vital

adjective **1** having to do with or necessary to life: *the vital parts of the body* **2** full of life: *She is a very vital person.* **3** absolutely necessary: *It is vital that we stick together.*

Word building: **vitally** *adverb*

vitality

noun energy or vigour

vitamin   (*say* vuy-tuh-muhn, vit-uh-muhn)

noun any of a number of substances present in very small quantities in food, and necessary for good health

vivacious   (*say* vuh-vay-shuhs)

adjective lively or energetic: *a vivacious talker*

Word building: **vivaciously** *adverb*
vivacity *noun*

vivid

adjective **1** bright or dazzling: *vivid colours* **2** strong and clear: *a vivid imagination*

Word building: **vividly** *adverb*   **vividness** *noun*

vixen

noun a female fox

Word use: The male is a **dog** and the young is a **cub**.

V-jay   (*say* vee-jay)

noun an announcer on commercial television who introduces video clips

Word use: Another spelling is **VJ** or **veejay**.

vocabulary   (*say* voh-kab-yuh-luh-ree)

noun the total number of words used by someone or by a particular group of people: *She has a large vocabulary.*

vocal

adjective **1** of or having to do with your voice: *the vocal cords* **2** talkative: *Henry was very vocal on the subject of music.* **3** sung or for singing: *vocal music*

Word building: **vocally** *adverb*

vocal cords

plural noun the folds of tissue lining your larynx which vibrate as air from your lungs passes them, making voiced sounds

vocalist

noun a singer

vocation

noun an occupation, business or profession, especially one which you seriously believe in: *a vocation to be a nurse*

vodka

noun a Russian alcoholic drink made from grain and potatoes

Word history: from a Russian word meaning 'little water'

vogue *(say* vohg*)*

noun fashion: *a style in vogue fifty years ago*

voice

noun **1** the sound or sounds you make with your mouth especially when you speak or sing **2** the right to express an opinion: *He had no voice in the matter.*
verb **3** to utter or give voice to: *to voice an opinion*
Other words: **articulate, declare, express, pronounce, speak, state**

voicemail

noun **1** a system of recording telephone messages **2** a telephone message recorded in this way

void

adjective **1** without legal force: *The contract is null and void.* **2** empty: *This statement is void of meaning.*
noun **3** an empty space: *They peered over the edge of the cliff into the void.*

volatile *(say* vol-uh-tuyl*)*

adjective evaporating quickly: *Methylated spirits is a volatile substance.*

volcano

noun a mountain with an opening in the top, through which molten rock, steam and ashes burst out when it is active

Word building: The plural is **volcanoes** or **volcanos**. | **volcanic** *adjective*
Word history: named after *Vulcan*, the Roman god of fire

volition *(say* vuh-lish-uhn*)*

noun an act of will or purpose: *I did it of my own volition.*

volley

noun **1** the firing of a number of guns together **2** an outpouring at one time: *a volley of words* **3** in tennis, the return of a ball before it bounces
verb **4** to return a ball before it bounces

volleyball

noun a team game in which a large ball is volleyed by hand or arm over a net

volt

noun a measurement of electric force

Word building: **voltage** *noun*

voluble

adjective marked by a ready and continuous flow of words: *a voluble child | a voluble explanation*

Word use: When referring to a person, the more usual word is **talkative**.
Word building: **volubility** *noun* **volubly** *adverb*

volume

noun **1** a book, especially one of a series **2** the space occupied by a body or substance, measured in cubic units **3** amount, especially a large amount: *the volume of traffic | volumes of smoke* **4** loudness: *Turn down the volume on the TV.*

voluminous *(say* vuh-loohm-uhn-uhs*)*

adjective **1** forming enough to fill a book: *voluminous letters* **2** large or full: *a voluminous skirt*

Word building: **voluminously** *adverb*

voluntary

adjective **1** done or made by free will or choice: *a voluntary decision* **2** unpaid: *voluntary work*

Word building: **voluntarily** *adverb*

volunteer

noun **1** someone who offers to do something, such as raise money for charity, of their own free will
verb **2** to offer without being asked: *He volunteered to make the tea.* **3** to join the army as a volunteer

Word building: **volunteer** *adjective*

vomit

verb to throw up the contents of the stomach through the mouth

Word building: Other forms are **I vomited, I have vomited, I am vomiting.** | **vomit** *noun*

vote

noun **1** a formal expression, such as putting your hand up or ticking a piece of paper, indicating a wish or choice
Other words: **ballot, election**
2 the total number of votes: *the Labor vote*

Word building: **vote** *verb*

vouch

phrase **vouch for,** to guarantee or make yourself responsible for: *I can vouch for her.*

voucher

noun **1** a piece of paper that proves how money has been spent: *a shopping voucher* **2** a ticket used instead of money: *a gift voucher*

vow

noun a solemn promise

Word building: **vow** *verb*

vowel

noun **1** a speech sound made by allowing air to pass through the middle of your mouth without being blocked by your tongue or lips **2** a letter, *a, e, i, o* or *u,* used to represent the sound of a vowel

Word use: Compare this with **consonant.**

voyage

noun a journey by sea or air to somewhere quite far away
Other words: **cruise, trip**

Word building: **voyage** *verb*

vulgar

adjective coarse, crude or ill-mannered: *vulgar manners*

Word building: **vulgarity** *noun*

vulnerable

adjective able or liable to be hurt; not strong or protected
Other words: **exposed, open, susceptible, unprotected**

Word building: **vulnerability** *noun* **vulnerably** *adverb*

vulnerable species

noun a species of plant or animals that is facing a high risk of dying out in the wild in the medium-term future

Word use: Compare this with **endangered species, critically endangered species.**

vulture

noun a large bird with a bald head, that eats dead flesh

vulva

noun the external female sexual organs

Ww

wad (*say* wod)

noun **1** a small lump or pad of anything soft: *a wad of cottonwool* **2** a roll or bundle: *a wad of banknotes*

waddle (*say* <u>wod</u>-uhl)

verb to walk with short steps, swaying from side to side like a duck

Word building: **waddle** *noun*

waddy (*rhymes with* body)

noun a heavy, wooden, war club traditionally used by Aboriginal people

Word building: The plural is **waddies**.

Word history: from an Aboriginal language of New South Wales called Dharug. See the map of Australian Aboriginal languages at the end of this book.

wade

verb to walk through water

wafer

noun **1** a thin crisp biscuit **2** a thin disc of bread made without yeast, used in some Christian church services

waffle[1] (*say* <u>wof</u>-uhl)

noun a crisp, flat cake, made from batter, with a pattern of squares left by the appliance in which it is cooked

waffle[2] (*say* <u>wof</u>-uhl)

verb Informal to talk or write at length without giving much clear information: *He would have waffled on for an hour if we hadn't interrupted him.*

waft (*rhymes with* soft)

verb to blow lightly: *The breeze wafted the leaves.* | *The sounds of music wafted across the lake.*

Word building: **waft** *noun*

wag

verb **1** to move from side to side **2** to play truant from: *to wag school*

Word building: Other forms are **I wagged, I have wagged, I am wagging**.

wage

noun **1** the money you are paid regularly for working, especially in a factory or as a labourer

verb **2** to carry on: *to wage war*

Word use: Compare definition 1 with **salary**.

wager

noun a bet

Word building: **wager** *verb*

waggle

verb to wag with short quick movements

wagon

noun **1** a four-wheeled heavy cart **2** a railway truck

waif

noun a homeless orphan

wail

verb to give a long sad cry or to cry continuously

Word building: **wail** *noun*

wail/whale Don't confuse **wail** with **whale**, which is a very large mammal that lives in the sea.

waist

noun the part of your body between your ribs and hips

waist/waste Don't confuse **waist** with **waste**. To **waste** something is to use it up or spend it without much result:
> *Try not to waste too much money on cheap gimmicks.*

waistcoat

noun a close-fitting sleeveless piece of clothing which reaches to the waist and buttons down the front, often worn under a jacket

wait

verb **1** to stay or rest until something happens **2** to be ready: *Your dinner is waiting.*
phrase **3 wait on**, to act as a waiter or waitress to: *to wait on someone*
Word building: **wait** noun

wait/weight Don't confuse **wait** with **weight**. **Weight** is how heavy something is. Your **weight** is how heavy you are.

waiter

noun someone who serves food and drink to you at your table in a restaurant or hotel
Word building: **waitress** noun

waive   (say wayv)

verb **1** to decide not to insist on: *to waive a parking fine* **2** to put off for the moment: *to waive a deadline for homework*

wake[1]

verb **1** to stop being asleep: *I like to wake to the sound of music.*
Other words: **awake, awaken**
2 to rouse from sleep: *My alarm always wakes me at seven.*
Word building: Other forms are **I woke, I have woken, I am waking.** | **wakeful** adjective **waken** verb **awake** verb **awaken** verb

wake[2]

noun the track left by a ship moving through the water
Other words: **wash**

walk

verb to go along by putting one foot after the other
Other words: **amble, march, pace, pad, saunter, step, stride, stroll, strut, swagger, toddle, tramp, troop**
Word building: **walk** noun

walkie-talkie

noun a light radio that you can carry, used by police, soldiers and so on to send and receive messages

walkover

noun an easy victory

wall

noun **1** one of the sides of a building or room **2** a brick or stone structure acting as a boundary fence or barrier
Other words: **barricade, partition, screen**
3 anything that closes off or divides

wallaby

noun any of several types of kangaroo-like animals. Some species are endangered or vulnerable. See the table at the end of this book.
Word use: The wallaby belongs to a class of animals called **marsupials**.
Word building: The plural is **wallabies**.
Word history: from an Aboriginal language of New South Wales called Dharug. See the map of Australian Aboriginal languages at the end of this book.

wallaroo

noun a large kangaroo with shaggy, dark fur that lives in rocky or hilly land
Word use: The wallaroo belongs to a class of animals called **marsupials**.
Word history: from an Aboriginal language of New South Wales called Dharug. See the map of Australian Aboriginal languages at the end of this book.

wallet

noun a small folding case for papers, banknotes and so on, carried in your pocket or handbag

wallop

verb Informal to beat soundly
Word building: **wallop** noun

wallow

verb to lie or roll about: *The hippopotamuses were wallowing in the mud.* | *I wallowed in a hot bath.*

walnut

noun **1** a type of nut which you can eat, grown on a European tree **2** the wood of this tree, used for making furniture

walrus

noun a large warm-blooded sea animal with flippers and large tusks

waltz (*say* wawls, wols)

noun **1** a type of dance in which you and your partner move in circles to music with a 1-2-3 beat **2** a piece of music for this dance

Word building: **waltz** *verb*

wan

adjective **1** pale or lacking in colour: *a wan complexion | a wan light* **2** sickly: *a wan smile*

wand (*rhymes with* bond)

noun a thin stick or rod, especially one used by a magician or fairy to work magic

wander (*say* won-duh)

verb **1** to go about with no definite aim or fixed course
Other words: **meander, ramble, range, roam, rove**
2 to move or turn away from: *My eyes wandered from the screen.*
Other words: **deviate, digress, diverge, stray**

wander/wonder Don't confuse **wander** with **wonder**. To **wonder** (rhymes with *under*) is to think about something with curiosity or surprise:
I wonder why she decided to change schools.

wane

verb to grow, or seem to grow, smaller or less: *Her enthusiasm has waned. | The moon is waning.*

Word use: The opposite of this is **wax²**.

wangle

verb Informal to do or get something by cunning or trickery: *He wangled an extra day's holiday.*

Word building: **wangle** *noun*

want

verb **1** to feel a need or a desire for something: *The cat wants its dinner. | He's always wanting something new.*
Other words: **covet, crave, desire, long for**
2 to feel a need or desire to do something: *I want to see you.*
Other words: **wish**
3 to require or need something: *The car wants cleaning.* **4** to wish or feel like doing something: *They can go out if they want.* **5** to have none or little of: *He wants common sense.*

noun **6** something wanted or needed: *They employed a nurse to see to the sick man's wants.* **7** an absence of something necessary: *The plants are dying for want of rain.* **8** a state of being poor: *They lived in want for many years.*

Word use: The more usual word for definition 5 is **lack**. | The more usual word for definition 6 is **need**. | The more usual word for definition 7 is **lack**. | The more usual word for definition 8 is **poverty**.

wanton (*say* won-tuhn)

adjective **1** done or behaving without thought or sense, often with bad results: *a wanton attacker of innocent people | wanton cruelty towards animals* **2** loose or not controlled in your sexual behaviour

Word building: **wantonly** *adverb* **wantonness** *noun*

war

noun **1** fighting with weapons between countries, or between groups within a nation
Other words: **battle, clash, combat, conflict, contest, fight, struggle**
2 any other fighting: *a war of words*

Word building: **war** *verb* (**warred, warring**) **warfare** *noun* **warlike** *adjective*

war/wore Don't confuse **war** with **wore**, which is the past tense of the verb **wear**, to carry or have on your body:
I wore a red wig to the fancy dress party.

waratah (*say* wo-ruh-tah)

noun an Australian shrub with large red flowers

Word history: from an Aboriginal language of New South Wales called Dharug. See the map of Australian Aboriginal languages at the end of this book.

warble

verb to sing with trills, like a bird

ward

noun **1** a division of a municipality, city or town used in elections: *Jones is standing for the East ward.* **2** a room or division in a hospital **3** a young person who has been legally placed under the care or control of a guardian: *a state ward*
phrase **4 ward off**, to turn aside: *to ward off a blow*

warden
noun someone who is given the care or responsibility of something

warder
noun a prison officer

wardrobe
noun **1** a cupboard for keeping clothes in **2** someone's clothes, or the costumes used by actors

ware
noun **1 wares**, articles for sale: *At the markets you can buy wares ranging from vegetables to jewellery.* **2** a particular kind of article produced to be sold: *kitchen ware*

Word use: This word as in definition 2 is now mainly joined with some other word to make one word, as in *glassware* or *silverware*.

ware/wear/where Don't confuse **ware** with **wear** or **where**.

To **wear** is to carry or have something on your body, as in *to wear a hat*.

Where asks the question 'at what place?':
Where are my rollerblades?

warehouse
noun a large building for storing goods

wares
plural noun things for sale: *The wares were displayed in the window.*

warhead
noun the section of a rocket, bomb or torpedo containing the explosive

warlock
noun a wizard or sorcerer

warm
adjective **1** having some heat that can be felt: *warm water* **2** keeping heat in: *warm clothes* | *a warm house* **3** kind and affectionate: *a warm welcome*

Word building: **warm** *verb*　**warmth** *noun*

warm-blooded
adjective having a body temperature which stays more or less the same regardless of the surrounding temperature: *warm-blooded animals*

Word use: The opposite is **cold-blooded**.

warn
verb to tell or signal of a possible danger: *They warned us that the road was icy.* | *Flashing lights warn of fog.*

Word building: **warning** *noun*

warn/worn Don't confuse **warn** with **worn**. Something is **worn** if it is shabby or damaged from frequent use, as in *a worn bedspread*. **Worn** is also a past form of the verb **wear**:
I have worn the same school jumper for four winters.

warp
verb **1** to bend or become bent out of shape: *Rain has warped the timber.* | *The records warped in the sun.*
noun **2** a bend or twist **3** the lengthwise threads in weaving

warrant　(*say* wo-ruhnt)
noun **1** a paper issued by a magistrate allowing a police officer to make an arrest or a search of a building
verb **2** to give a formal promise or guarantee: *The company has warranted to repair or replace the car if it breaks down in the first three months.* **3** to demand or require: *The circumstances warrant immediate action.*

warranty
noun a formal promise or assurance of reliability: *Do not buy an electric heater without a warranty.*

warren
noun a series of connecting burrows where many rabbits live

warrigal　(*say* wo-ruh-guhl)
noun **1** another word for **dingo**
adjective **2** wild or untamed

Word history: from an Aboriginal language of New South Wales called Dharug. See the map of Australian Aboriginal languages at the end of this book.

warrior
noun a soldier or fighter
Other words: **combatant**

wart
noun a small hard lump on the skin, caused by a virus

wary　(*say* wair-ree)
adjective watchful or careful

wasabi　(*say* wuh-sah-bee)
noun a green paste with a hot, spicy taste, eaten with Japanese food

wash

verb **1** to wet and rub, usually with soap or detergent, in order to clean **2** to carry along by water: *The bottle was washed ashore in New Zealand.*
noun **3** an act of washing **4** clothes which are ready to be washed, or have just been washed: *I have lost a sock in the wash.* **5** waves made by a ship: *The dinghy rocked in the liner's wash.*

Word building: **washable** *adjective*

washer

noun **1** a flat ring of rubber or metal to make a joint or a nut fit tightly **2** another word for **face washer**

washing machine

noun a machine that washes clothes automatically

wasp

noun a four-winged insect that stings

Word building: **waspish** *adjective* sharp and spiteful

waste

verb **1** to use up or spend without much result: *to waste food | to waste money buying junk food*
Other words: **squander**
2 to wear away: *Illness has wasted the patient's muscles.*

Word building: **wastage** *noun*   **waste** *noun*
wasteful *adjective*

waste/waist Don't confuse **waste** with **waist** which is the part of your body between your ribs and hips.

watch

verb **1** to look at attentively: *The students watched a film.* **2** to be careful of: *Watch your step.* **3** to guard: *They watch the place at night.*
noun **4** a lookout or guard: *to keep watch* **5** a small clock which you wear on your wrist

Word building: **watchful** *adjective*

watchman

noun someone who keeps guard over a building, usually at night, to protect it from fire and burglary

water

noun **1** the colourless transparent liquid which forms rain, rivers, lakes and oceans
verb **2** to pour water on: *to water the garden*
Other words: **dampen, hose, moisten, soak, spray, sprinkle, wet**
3 to supply with water: *to water a horse*
phrase **4 water down**, to make weaker by adding water

Word building: **watery** *adjective*

waterbomb

verb to drop large quantities of water from a plane onto an area to extinguish bushfires

watercolour

noun **1** paint made from colour diluted with water and gum instead of oil **2** a painting done in watercolour

Word use: Another spelling is **watercolor**.
Word building: **watercolourist** *noun*

watercress

noun a leafy salad vegetable with a peppery taste

water cycle

noun the cycle of water on earth through heating of sea water into steam (evaporation), collection of steam as clouds (condensation), rain falling (precipitation) on land and returning to the sea

waterfall

noun a steep fall or flow of a river or stream from a high place, as over a cliff or high rock

waterfront

noun **1** land next to the ocean or a lake **2** the wharves in a port

waterhole

noun a natural hole in which water collects, such as one in the dried-up bed of a river

waterlily

noun a water plant with large flowers and flat leaves that float

Word building: The plural is **waterlilies**.

waterlogged

adjective **1** completely soaked with water **2** flooded

watermark

noun **1** a line showing the greatest height that water has risen to **2** a mark, usually the maker's name or trademark, made in paper and able to be seen when held up to the light

watermelon

noun a large melon with green skin and dark pink flesh

water polo

noun a game played by two teams of seven swimmers each, in which the object is to pass a ball into the opposing team's goal

waterproof

adjective made of, or coated with, material which prevents water getting through

Word building: **waterproof** *verb*

watershed

noun the ridge line at the top of a range of hills dividing two drainage areas or river basins

waterski

verb to travel on special skis over water, towed by a speedboat

Word building: Other forms are **I waterskied, I have waterskied, I am waterskiing**.

watertight

adjective **1** completely sealed against water **2** having no fault or weakness: *a watertight argument*

waterway

noun a body of water, such as a river or canal, that boats and ships can travel on

watt

noun a unit of electrical power

wattle

noun **1** another word for **acacia** **2** rods or twigs interwoven and used for fences, walls or roofs **3** a coloured fleshy part hanging from the throat of certain birds such as the turkey

wattle and daub

noun interwoven sticks or twigs covered with mud, used as a building material

wave

noun **1** a movement in the form of a ridge on the surface of a liquid, especially the sea
Other words: **billow, surge, swell**
2 a vibration that travels through air or water and which we experience as light, sound and so on: *a sound wave* **3** a surge of feeling: *A wave of anger went through me.* **4** an up-and-down or side-to-side movement of the hand used as a sign of greeting or farewell

verb **5** to move up and down or from side to side: *to wave a flag*
Other words: **brandish, flourish**
6 to move the hand in greeting

Word building: **wavy** *adjective* (**wavier, waviest**)

wavelength

noun **1** one full wave movement, such as from the top of one wave to the top of the next **2** a way of thinking: *We're on the same wavelength.*

waver

verb **1** to sway backwards and forwards: *The flag wavered in the breeze.* **2** to feel or show doubt: *He made the decision to stay at home but then wavered.*

wax[1]

noun **1** a fairly hard greasy substance that is easy to melt
verb **2** to rub or polish with wax
Other words: **shine, varnish**

wax[2]

verb to grow, or seem to grow, bigger: *The moon is waxing.*

Word use: The opposite of this is **wane**.

way

noun **1** manner or means: *the right way to do it* **2** direction: *Come this way.* **3** passage or progress: *They made their way through the bush.* **4** road, path, route or passage: *a way through the wood*

way/weigh/whey Don't confuse **way** with **weigh** or **whey**. To **weigh** something is to measure how heavy it is:
The greengrocer weighed the apples on the scales.
Whey is the watery part of milk separated from the curd, formed in cheese-making.

wayfarer

noun a traveller, especially on foot

waylay

verb to lie in wait for, especially in order to attack: *They waylaid him outside his house.*

Word building: Other forms are **I waylaid, I have waylaid, I am waylaying**.

way-out

adjective *Informal* quite different from the usual: *way-out clothes*

wayward

adjective acting in a way that people don't think right or proper: *a wayward child*

we

pronoun the plural form of **I**: *We are not coming.*

Word use: Other forms are **our** (*our hats*), **ours** (*Those books are ours*), **us** (*Give them to us*), **ourselves** (*We hurt ourselves*).

weak

adjective **1** liable to break or fall down: *a weak framework*
Other words: **delicate, flimsy, fragile**
2 not healthy or strong
Other words: **feeble, frail, infirm, sickly**
3 lacking in force or strength: *a weak leader | a weak argument*
Other words: **ineffective**

Word building: **weaken** *verb* **weakness** *noun*

weak/week Don't confuse **weak** with **week**. A **week** is seven days.

weakling

noun a weak person or animal

weal

noun a mark or swelling on the skin made by a blow

Word use: Another word for this is **welt**.

wealth

noun **1** a large store of money and property
Other words: **fortune, riches**
2 a rich supply: *a wealth of ideas*
Other words: **abundance, profusion**

Word building: **wealthy** *adjective*

wean

verb to start feeding with food other than its mother's milk: *to wean a baby*

weapon   (*say* <u>wep</u>-uhn)

noun an instrument used in fighting

wear

verb **1** to carry or have on your body: *to wear a dress | to wear jewellery*
noun **2** a gradual using up: *The carpet shows signs of wear.* **3** clothing: *beach wear*
phrase **4 wear away**, to get rid of bit by bit: *The rain has worn away the paint.*
5 wear off, to gradually reduce or get less: *The effect of the aspirin is wearing off and my headache is returning.*

Other words: **decrease, diminish, ease, ebb, lessen, reduce**
6 wear out, a to wear or use until no longer fit for use: *to wear out clothes* **b** to tire out because of continuous strain: *You have finally worn out my patience.*
Other words: **deplete, exhaust**

Word building: Other verb forms are **I wore, I have worn, I am wearing.** | **wearable** *adjective*

wear/where/ware Don't confuse **wear** with **where** or **ware**.

Where asks the question 'at what place?':
Where are my rollerblades?

We usually use **ware** as part of a combination word. It is a particular kind of manufactured article that you can buy, such as *silverware, tinware* or *software*. The word **wares** means 'things for sale'.

weary

adjective tired

Word building: Other forms are **wearier, weariest.** | **weary** *verb* (**wearied, wearying**) | **wearily** *adverb*

weasel

noun a small, fierce, European animal that eats mice, rabbits and other small animals

weather

noun **1** the state of the atmosphere as far as heat and cold, wetness and dryness are concerned
Other words: **climate**
verb **2** to be affected by the weather: *The fence has weathered to a grey colour.* **3** to come safely through: *to weather a storm*
Other words: **endure, survive, withstand**

weather/whether/wether Don't confuse **weather** with **whether** or **wether**.

Whether is a word which introduces the first of two alternatives. For example:
I do not know whether to come or to go

A **wether** is a castrated ram.

weatherboard

adjective having a covering of overlapping boards: *a weatherboard cottage*

weathervane

noun a flat piece of metal fixed on a roof, which moves with the wind and shows its direction

weave

verb **1** to thread fibres together in order to make cloth, baskets or the like
Other words: **interlace, intertwine, knit**
2 to go by moving from side to side: *She weaved through the crowd.*

Word building: Other forms are **I wove, I have woven, I am weaving.**

web

noun **1** the fine, silk-like, sticky net that spiders make to catch insects **2** the system of storing information on the internet so that people all around the world can find it

Word use: Definition 2 is a short way of saying **the World Wide Web (WWW).**

webbed

adjective of the foot of an animal or bird, having skin between the toes, usually to help in swimming

Word use: An animal with webbed feet is a **web-footed** animal.

webcam

noun a video camera attached to a computer that you can use to send a video picture over the internet

Word history: short for *web camera*

web-footed

adjective having skin between the toes to help in swimming

web page

noun a section of a website that you can access on the internet

web portal

noun a website which gives information and sometimes direct links to other websites together with email facilities, online shopping, and so on

website

noun a place on the internet with an address that can be looked up for information and facts

Word use: This is often shortened to **site.**

wed

verb *Old-fashioned* to marry: *They will wed tomorrow morning. | The minister wed them.*

Word building: Other forms are **I wed, I have wed, I am wedding.**
Word history: from an Old English word meaning 'pledge'

wedding

noun a marriage ceremony

wedge

noun a piece of wood or metal, thinner at one end than the other and used when you want to split wood or make something secure: *She put a wedge in front of the wheel to stop the car sliding down the slope.*

Word building: **wedge** *verb*

wedlock

noun the state of being married

Wednesday (*say* <u>wenz</u>-day)

noun the fourth day of the week, after Tuesday

Word use: The abbreviation is **Wed.**
Word history: from an Old English word meaning 'Woden's day' (Woden was the chief Anglo-Saxon god)

wee

adjective very small

weed

noun **1** a useless plant growing where it is not wanted
verb **2** to pull weeds out of: *to weed the garden*

weedy

adjective thin and weak

Word building: Other forms are **weedier, weediest.**

week

noun a period of seven days, especially from Sunday to Saturday

week/weak Don't confuse **week** with **weak,** which means 'liable to break or fall down'.

weekday

noun any day of the week except Saturday or Sunday

weekend

noun the time from Friday evening to Sunday evening, when most people do not have to work or go to school

weekly

adjective **1** happening once a week: *the weekly wash*
adverb **2** once a week: *The garbage is collected weekly.*
noun **3** a paper or magazine that comes out once a week

Word building: The plural form of the noun is **weeklies**.

weep

verb to show sorrow or any emotion by crying
Other words: **bawl, blubber, cry, howl, sob, wail, whimper**
Word building: Other forms are **I wept, I have wept, I am weeping**.

weevil

noun a kind of beetle which destroys grain, nuts, fruit and trees

weft

noun the threads woven across the warp in cloth

weigh   (*sounds like* way)

verb **1** to measure the heaviness of by means of a scale or balance **2** to press heavily: *The affair weighed on her conscience.*
Other words: **burden, oppress, torment, worry**

weigh/way/whey Don't confuse **weigh** with **way** or **whey**.
A **way** of doing something is the manner or fashion in which you do it:
  Are you sure that's the right way to ride a skateboard?
Way can also mean 'direction':
  You should go that way.
Whey is the watery part of milk separated from the curd, formed in cheese-making.

weight   (*say* wayt)

noun **1** an amount of heaviness **2** a heavy object **3** something serious and worrying: *That lifts a weight from my mind.*
Word building: **weighty** *adjective*

weight/wait Don't confuse **weight** with **wait**. To **wait** is to stay or rest until something happens.

weir   (*rhymes with* ear)

noun a small dam across a river

weird

adjective very odd or strange
Other words: **abnormal, bizarre, peculiar, queer, unusual**
Word building: **weirdly** *adverb*   **weirdness** *noun*

welcome

noun a kindly greeting: *a warm welcome*

Word building: **welcome** *verb*   **welcome** *adjective*

weld

verb to join together by heat and pressure: *to weld metal*

welfare

noun the state of being healthy and having a good way of life: *He is interested in the welfare of old people.*

well¹

adverb **1** in a good way: *She sings well.* **2** thoroughly: *Shake the bottle well.* **3** clearly: *I can see it well.*
adjective **4** in good health **5** satisfactory: *All is well.*
Word building: Other adjective forms are **better, best**.

well²

noun **1** a hole drilled or dug in the ground to obtain water, oil, natural gas or other substances
verb **2** to spring or gush: *Tears welled up in my eyes.*

we'll

the short form of **we will** or **we shall**

wellbeing

noun the state of being healthy and contented
Word use: Another spelling is **well-being**.

well-meaning

adjective having good intentions

well-off

adjective wealthy or prosperous
Word use: Another word for this is **well-to-do**.

welt

noun a raised mark on the skin made by a blow with a stick or whip
Word use: Another word for this is **weal**.

we're   (*say* wair)

a short form of **we are**

werewolf

noun a man who, according to old superstition, changed into a wolf when there was a full moon
Word building: The plural is **werewolves**.
Word history: from the Old English word for 'man' added to **wolf**

west

noun the direction in which the sun sets

Word use: The opposite direction is **east**.
Word building: **west** adjective   **west** adverb

western

adjective **1** lying in or towards the west: western suburbs
noun **2** a film or story about cowboys and Indians in the American west

wet

adjective **1** covered or soaked with water or some other liquid **2** not yet dry: wet paint **3** rainy: a wet summer
verb **4** to make wet **5** to make wet by urinating: Baby has wet its nappy.
phrase **6 the wet**, the rainy season in central and northern Australia, from December to March

Word building: Other verb forms are **I wet, I have wet, I am wetting**. | The plural form of the noun is **werewolves**.

wet blanket

noun someone who stops you enjoying yourself

wether

noun a castrated ram

wether/weather/whether Don't confuse **wether** with **weather** or **whether**.

The **weather** is sunshine or rain.

Whether is the word that introduces the first of two alternatives. For example:
   I do not know whether to come or go.

wetland

noun an area where the soil is permanently under water and where plant life is adapted to live in those conditions

Word use: This word is often found in the plural **wetlands**.

wetsuit

noun a tight rubber garment worn by divers and surfers to keep in body heat

we've

a short form of **we have**

whack

noun a sharp blow
Word building: **whack** verb

whale

noun a very large sea mammal that used to be hunted for its valuable oil. Some species are endangered. See the table at the end of this book.

Word use: The male is a **bull**, the female is a **cow** and the young is a **calf**.
Word building: **whaler** noun   **whaling** noun

whale/wail Don't confuse **whale** with **wail**. To **wail** is to give a long sad cry or to cry continuously.

wharf   (say wawf)

noun a structure built along or out from the shore of a harbour, where ships can load and unload
Other words: **dock, jetty, pier, quay**

Word building: The plural is **wharves** or **wharfs**. | **wharfie** noun someone who works on the wharves
Word history: from an Old English word meaning 'dam'

what   (say wot)

pronoun used when asking for or about something: What time is lunch?

whatever

pronoun **1 a** anything that: You can eat whatever you like. **b** no matter what: Ring me tomorrow, whatever happens. **2** what ever? what?: Whatever did you do that for? adjective **3** any ... that: Whatever instruction she gives, you should obey her. **4** no matter what: Whatever the problem, just ignore it and keep going. **5** what or who ... it may be: For whatever reason, he did not come to meet us at the cinema.

Word use: In definition 2 whatever is used as a replacement for what to give emphasis to a question.

wheat

noun the grain of a widely-grown cereal plant, used for making flour

wheatgerm

noun a part of the wheat grain, rich in vitamins, which is removed when the wheat is ground

wheedle

verb to get by coaxing or persuasion: They wheedled some money from their mother for the movies.

wheel

noun **1** a circular frame or solid disc turning on an axle, used in machinery and on vehicles
verb **2** to roll or push on wheels: *to wheel a pram* **3** to turn around: *The horse wheeled around when it saw the snake.*

wheelbarrow

noun a small cart, usually with one wheel at the front and two legs, which you lift when you wheel it along

wheelchair

noun a chair on wheels, used by people unable to walk

wheeze

verb to breathe with difficulty, making a whistling sound
Word building: **wheeze** *noun* **wheezy** *adjective*

whelk

noun a shellfish with a spiral shell

when   (*say* wen)

adverb **1** at what time: *When are we going to the beach?*
conjunction **2** at the time that: *When I grow up I want to be a movie star.*

whenever

conjunction **1** at any time when: *You can go home whenever you like.*
adverb **2** when?: *Whenever did you think up that idea?*
Word use: In definition 2 *whenever* is used as a replacement for *when* to give emphasis to a question.

where   (*say* wair)

adverb at what place: *Where is my other shoe?*

where/wear/ware Don't confuse **where** with **wear** or **ware**.

To **wear** is to carry or have something on your body, as in *to wear a hat*.

We usually use **ware** as part of a combination word. It is a particular kind of manufactured article that you can buy, such as *silverware*, *tinware* or *software*. The word **wares** means 'things for sale'.

whereabouts

noun the place where someone or something is: *We didn't know your whereabouts.*

wherever

conjunction **1** in, at, or to, whatever place: *Sit down wherever you can.*
adverb **2** where?: *Wherever did you buy those shoes?*
Word use: In definition 2 *wherever* is used as a replacement for *what* to give emphasis to a question.

whet

verb to sharpen: *to whet a knife | to whet your appetite*
Word building: Other forms are **I whetted, I have whetted, I am whetting**.

whether

conjunction the word that introduces the first of two alternatives: *I don't know whether to go to the party or stay home and study.*

whether/weather/wether Don't confuse **whether** with **weather** or **wether**.

The **weather** is sunshine or rain.

A **wether** is a castrated ram.

whey

noun the watery part of milk separated from the curd, formed in cheese-making

whey/way/weigh Don't confuse **whey** with **way** or **weigh**.

A **way** of doing something is the manner or fashion in which you do it:
Are you sure that's the right way to ride a skateboard?

Way can also mean 'direction':
You should go that way.

To **weigh** something is to measure how heavy it is.

which   (*say* wich)

pronoun what one: *Which CD do you want to play?*

which/witch Don't confuse **which** with **witch**. A **witch** is the female equivalent of a wizard.

whichever

pronoun **1** any one that: *Look at these books and choose whichever you prefer.* **2** no matter which: *I always enjoy films, so I don't mind whichever we go to.*
adjective **3** no matter which: *Whichever day you want to go is fine with me.*

whiff

noun a slight puff: *a whiff of smoke | a whiff of perfume*

while   (*say* wuyl)
conjunction for the length of time that: *You can tell me the news while I prepare dinner.*

while/wile Don't confuse **while** with **wile**. A **wile** is a cunning trick. It is a rather old-fashioned word, although the adjective from it, **wily**, is still well-known.

whim
noun a sudden change of mind without an obvious reason

whimper
verb to cry weakly
Word building: **whimper** *noun*

whimsical
adjective amusingly odd

whine
verb to make a high-pitched complaining cry
Word building: **whine** *noun*

whinge
verb to complain in a tiresome way
Word building: Other forms are **I whinged, I have whinged, I am whingeing.**

whinny
noun the sound a horse makes
Word building: The plural is **whinnies.** | **whinny** *verb* (**whinnied, whinnying**)

whip
noun **1** a long piece of rope or leather attached to a handle, used to hit animals or people
verb **2** to beat with a whip **3** to beat with light, quick strokes: *to whip cream*
phrase **4 whip out**, to bring out with a sudden movement: *He whipped out a gun.*
5 whip up, to rouse: *to whip up enthusiasm*
Word building: Other verb forms are **I whipped, I have whipped, I am whipping.**

whirl
verb to turn round or spin rapidly
Word building: **whirl** *noun*

whirlpool
noun a circular current in a river or sea

whirlwind
noun a strong wind that blows in a spiral

whirr
verb to make a low buzzing sound while moving or working: *The machinery whirred constantly.*
Word building: **whirr** *noun*

whisk
noun **1** a light, sweeping stroke: *a whisk with a duster* **2** a kitchen tool used for beating eggs, cream and so on
verb **3** to move lightly and rapidly: *to whisk something out of the way* | *to whisk out of the room*

whisker
noun **1** one of the long bristles on the face of a cat or similar animal **2 whiskers**, a man's beard and moustache

whisky
noun an alcoholic drink distilled from grain, especially barley
Word building: The plural is **whiskies**.
Word history: from a Gaelic word meaning 'water of life'

whisper
verb to speak very softly with your breath rather than your voice
Other words: **murmur, mutter**
Word building: **whisper** *noun*

whist
noun a card game played by two pairs of people

whistle
verb **1** to make a shrill sound by forcing your breath through a small opening that you form between your lips and your teeth **2** to make a similar sound by blowing through a whistle **3** to make a shrill sound: *The wind whistles in the trees.*
noun **4** a small pipe which produces one or more notes when you blow through it **5** the sound produced by a whistle or by whistling

white
adjective **1** of the colour of milk **2** light or fairly light in colour: *white wine* | *white coffee* | *white meat* **3** having light skin like a European: *a white person*
Word building: **white** *noun*   **whiten** *verb*   **whiteness** *noun*

white ant
noun an insect which eats through wood
Word use: Scientists classify it as a **termite**, not as an ant.

white-ant
verb to make someone or something less successful or confident: *His efforts were deliberately white-anted by the party leader.*

white blood cell
noun a white or colourless corpuscle in the blood, which fights disease in the body

whiteboard
noun a large white plastic board used for writing or drawing on with a special felt pen

white elephant
noun something useless which can cost a lot of money to maintain: *The big new theatre is a white elephant because nobody uses it.*

white heat
noun heat great enough for metal to glow white

white lie
noun a lie told for reasons of kindness or politeness

white-out
noun a thin white paint that is used to cover written mistakes on paper

Word use: Another word for this is **liquid paper**.

whitewash
noun **1** a white liquid that people use to paint walls and ceilings with **2** anything used to cover up faults and give a good appearance on the surface

Word building: **whitewash** *verb*

whiting
noun a kind of small fish, which is good to eat

whittle
verb **1** to cut, trim or shape by taking off bits with a knife **2** to make less, a little at a time: *We've managed to whittle down our costs.*

whiz¹
verb to move with a humming or hissing sound: *A bullet whizzed past my ear.*
Other words: **zoom**

Word building: Other forms are **I whizzed, I have whizzed, I am whizzing**.

whiz²
noun Informal someone who is very good at something: *a whiz at maths*

who   (*say* hooh)
pronoun which person or people: *Who wants some ice-cream?*

whoever
pronoun **1** whatever person: *Whoever comes first will get the best position.* **2** who ever?, or who?: *Whoever is that very tall man over there?*

Word use: In definition 2 *whoever* is used as a replacement for *who* to give emphasis to a question.

whole   (*sounds like* hole)
adjective **1** making up the full quantity, number or thing **2** in one piece: *I swallowed the cherry whole.*

Word building: **whole** *noun*   **wholly** *adverb*

---

whole/hole Don't confuse **whole** with **hole**. You can have a **hole** in your pocket or dig a **hole** in the ground.

---

wholemeal
noun flour made from the whole grain of wheat

whole number
noun a number without fractions, such as 0, 1, 2, 3 and so on

Word use: Another name for this is **integer**.

wholesale
noun the sale of goods, usually in large quantities, to shop owners rather than directly to the public

Word use: Compare this with **retail**.
Word building: **wholesale** *adjective* **wholesale** *verb*   **wholesaler** *noun*

wholesome
adjective good for you

whom
pronoun the objective case of the pronoun **who**: *With whom did you go to the party?*

whoop   (*say* woohp)
noun a loud cry or shout: *She gave a whoop of glee.*

Word building: **whoop** *verb*

whooping cough   (*say* hooh-ping kof)
noun a disease caught mostly by children, in which they cough a lot and find it hard to breathe

whore   (*say* haw)
noun an old-fashioned word for **prostitute**

whose

pronoun **1** belonging to whom: *Whose is this coat?*

adjective **2** of, belonging or relating to whom: *Whose book is this?*

why   (*rhymes with* <u>eye</u>)

adverb for what reason: *Why do birds fly?*

wick

noun the twisted threads in a candle or lamp which absorb the melted wax or oil to be burnt

wicked   (*say* <u>wik</u>-uhd)

adjective **1** evil and harmful: *a wicked person* **2** bad or wrong: *Stealing is wicked.*

wickerwork

noun things made of twigs plaited or woven together

wicket

noun **1** one of the two sets of three stumps with two bails on top at which the bowler aims the ball in cricket **2** the ground between the two wickets: *a wet wicket* **3** the dismissal of a member of the batting team: *3 wickets for 90 runs*

wide

adjective **1** having a large size from side to side
Other words: **ample, broad, open, spacious**
2 having a certain size from side to side: *30 centimetres wide*
adverb **3** fully: *Open wide! | He is wide awake.* **4** far to the side: *The shot went wide.*

Word building: **widen** *verb*   **width** *noun*

widespread

adjective **1** spread over a wide space: *a widespread network of roads* **2** happening in many places or among many people: *a widespread belief*

widow

noun a woman whose husband is dead and who has not married again

widower

noun a man whose wife is dead and who has not married again

wield

verb to control and use: *to wield a weapon | to wield influence*

wife

noun the woman to whom a man is married

Other words: **partner, spouse**

Word building: The plural is **wives**.

wig

noun a specially made covering of hair for the head

wiggle

verb to move with short motions from side to side

wigwam   (*say* <u>wig</u>-wom)

noun a Native North American hut made of poles with bark, mats or skins laid over them

Word history: from a Native North American word meaning 'dwelling'

wild

adjective **1** living in a natural state without human interference or care: *wild animals*
Other words: **feral, undomesticated, untamed**
2 growing in a natural state: *wild strawberries* **3** unruly or disorderly: *wild hair | a wild party*
phrase **4 the wild**, natural surroundings, usually a long way from civilisation or other people: *She is fond of camping in the wild.*

wildcard

noun **1** in some card games, a playing card which can be given the value of any other card **2** in computer searches, a special character that is not a letter or number, used to stand for any character or set of characters

Word building: **wildcard** *adjective*: *a wildcard search*

wilderness

noun **1** an unoccupied and dismal stretch of country **2** a natural area of country without roads or houses, which may be very beautiful but difficult to reach

wildlife

noun animals, birds and insects living in their natural surroundings

wile

noun a trick or something done to persuade someone

wile/while Don't confuse **wile** with **while**. **While** is a conjunction meaning 'for the length of time that':
While I cook dinner you can tell me the news.

wilful

adjective **1** done on purpose: *a wilful act* **2** headstrong or obstinate: *a wilful child*

will¹

verb **1** to be going to: *I will cut your hair.* **2** to be willing to: *I will help you.* **3** to be accustomed or likely to: *He would sit for hours and hours.*

Word use: This is a helping verb, always used with another one in the form **will** or **would**.

will²

noun **1** the power of choosing your own actions **2** wish or desire: *against my will* **3** purpose or determination: *the will to win* Other words: **aim, intention** **4** a legal document stating what a person wants done with their property after their death

Word building: **will** *verb*

willing

adjective agreeing quite happily: *He was willing to help.*

willow

noun a tree with thin branches that hang down

willpower

noun control over your own actions: *It takes a lot of willpower to stay on a diet.*

willy-willy

noun a strong wind that moves around in circles

Word history: from an Aboriginal language of Western Australia called Yindjibarndi. See the map of Australian Aboriginal languages at the end of this book.

wilt

verb to become limp: *These flowers will wilt without water.*

wily

adjective crafty or cunning

Word building: Other forms are **wilier, wiliest**. | **wiliness** *noun*

wimp

noun Informal someone who is thought to be weak and afraid of doing anything at all dangerous

Word history: perhaps from *Wimpy*, a timid character in the comic strip *Popeye*

win

verb **1** to gain a victory **2** to get by effort: *to win fame* Other words: **achieve, attain, gain, secure** **3** to be successful in: *to win a game* | *to win a lottery*

Word building: Other forms are **I won, I have won, I am winning**. | **win** *noun*

wince

verb to start or flinch because of pain or a blow

Word building: **wince** *noun*

winch

noun a device for hauling or hoisting, consisting of a cable wound round a drum turned by a crank or motor

Word building: **winch** *verb*

wind¹ (*rhymes with* pinned)

noun **1** moving air **2** a gale or storm **3** breath: *I couldn't run because I was short of wind.* **4** gas coming from your stomach or bowel *verb* **5** to take away the breath of: *The blow winded me.*

Word building: **windy** *adjective* (**windier, windiest**)

wind² (*rhymes with* lined)

verb **1** to turn first one way and then another: *The path winds up the hill.* **2** to roll into a ball: *to wind wool* **3** to tighten the spring of: *to wind a clock*

Word building: Other forms are **I wound, I have wound, I am winding**.

windbreak

noun a protection from the wind such as a fence or row of trees

windcheater

noun a close-fitting jacket or jumper worn for protection against the wind

wind energy

noun the power from wind used for making electricity

windfall

noun **1** fruit blown off a tree by the wind **2** an unexpected piece of good luck

wind farm

noun a group of turbines set up in a windy location which can turn the energy from wind into electricity

wind instrument
noun a musical instrument that you play by blowing

windmill
noun a mill for grinding or pumping, worked by the wind turning a set of arms or sails

window
noun **1** an opening in a wall for letting in light and air and usually having panes of glass **2** part of the VDU screen of a computer, such as the area taken up by the pull-down menu, or the part of a large document that you can see on the screen

windpipe
noun the tube that carries air from your throat to your lungs

Word use: The scientific word for this is **trachea**.

windscreen
noun the sheet of glass forming the front window of a motor vehicle

windward
adverb **1** towards the wind: *to sail windward* adjective **2** facing the wind: *the windward side*

Word use: The opposite of this is **leeward**.
Word building: **windward** noun

wine
noun an alcoholic drink made from grapes and sometimes from other fruit

wing
noun **1** the part of the body of a bird or insect that is used for flying **2** one of the long flat parts that stick out from either side of an aeroplane **3** a part of a building which is joined to the main part: *A new wing was built on to the school.* **4** a political group within a larger group: *the left wing of the Labor Party* **5** the side part of a sports field on which football, hockey and similar games are played **6** someone who plays in this place on the field
verb **7** to fly: *The bird winged its way home.*

wink
verb to close and open one eye quickly: *He winked at me to show we were friends again.*

Word building: **wink** noun

winning
adjective **1** being the winner: *the winning team* **2** charming: *a winning smile* noun **3 winnings**, something won, especially money: *Let's count our winnings.*

winter
noun the coldest season of the year

Word building: **wintry** adjective

win-win
adjective describing a situation where each of two alternatives is a good outcome: *It was win-win for me — if I went to school, everyone would write on my plaster cast, and if I stayed at home, I'd have the internet to myself.*

wipe
verb **1** to rub lightly in order to clean or dry
Other words: **blot, mop, sponge, swab**
2 to remove by wiping: *He wiped the crumbs off the chair.*
phrase **3** wipe out, to destroy or defeat completely
Other words: **annihilate, obliterate**

Word building: **wipe** noun   **wiper** noun

wire
noun **1** a long piece of thin metal that can be bent: *a fence made of wire* | *an electric wire*
verb **2** to fasten with wire: *He wired the gate to the fence.* **3** to provide with an electric system of wiring such as for lighting

wireless
noun **1** an old-fashioned word for **radio**
adjective **2** not requiring a telephone line or cable: *a wireless internet connection*

wire tap
noun a connection made secretly to a telephone line, which enables a person to hear conversations they are not meant to hear

wiry
adjective **1** like wire in shape or stiffness: *wiry grass* | *wiry hair* **2** thin and strong: *a wiry person*

Word building: Other forms are **wirier, wiriest**.

wisdom
noun **1** the quality of being wise: *There is wisdom in what she says.* **2** knowledge or learning: *Books pass on the wisdom of the past.*

wise

adjective **1** able to judge what is true or right: *a wise person*
Other words: **judicious, perceptive, sage**
2 showing good judgement: *a wise decision*
3 having knowledge or information: *My mother is wise in the law.* | *The explanation did not make us any wiser.*
Word building: **wisely** *adverb*

wisecrack

noun a smart or amusing remark
Word building: **wisecrack** *verb*

wish

verb **1** to want or desire: *I wish to be a concert pianist.* **2** to express a desire for something, sometimes silently: *I wish we could go swimming.* | *to wish upon a star* **3** to say to as a greeting: *He wished her good morning.*
noun **4** something you wish for: *Did you get your wish?* **5** the act of wishing: *Shut your eyes and make a wish.*

wishbone

noun a bone shaped like a Y in the chest of birds such as chickens
Word history: from the belief that when two people pull the bone apart, the one getting the longer piece will have their wish come true

wishy-washy

adjective without strength or force: *a wishy-washy speech*

wisp

noun someone or something that is small or thin: *a wisp of a boy* | *a wisp of hair* | *a wisp of smoke*
Word building: **wispy** *adjective* (**wispier, wispiest**)

wistful

adjective thoughtful in a sad way: *a wistful stare*
Word building: **wistfully** *adjective*   **wistfulness** *noun*

wit

noun **1** the ability to be amusing in a clever way **2** someone with this ability **3 wits**, mental abilities or common sense: *She always has her wits about her.*
Word building: **witticism** *noun*   **wittily** *adverb*   **wittiness** *noun*   **witty** *adjective*

witch

noun a woman who practises magic, especially to do evil
Word building: **witchcraft** *noun*

witch/which Don't confuse **witch** with **which**. **Which** is a pronoun that introduces a question: *Which witch did you like best?*

witchdoctor

noun a person supposed to have magical powers for healing or harming others
Other words: **medicine man**

witchetty grub

noun a large white grub that can be eaten
Word history: from an Aboriginal language of South Australia called Adnyamathanha. See the map of Australian Aboriginal languages at the end of this book.

with

preposition **1** in the company of: *Some of my friends came with me.* **2** in some particular relation to: *You mix blue with red to get purple.* **3** understanding: *Before I move on to the next point, are you all still with me?* **4** by the use or means of: *to cut meat with a knife* **5** in the care or keeping of: *Leave it with me and I'll fix it tomorrow.*

withdraw

verb **1** to move back or away: *She withdrew to the kitchen.*
Other words: **depart, retreat**
2 to take back: *I withdraw what I said about you.* **3** to take out: *to withdraw some money from the bank*
Word building: Other forms are **I withdrew, I have withdrawn, I am withdrawing.** | **withdrawal** *noun*   **withdrawn** *adjective* not wanting to talk to people

wither

verb to make or become dried up and shrunken: *The sun withered the grass.* | *Our friendship has withered away.*

withhold

verb to hold back: *They will withhold payment until they are satisfied with the goods.*
Word building: Other forms are **I withheld, I have withheld, I am withholding.**

within

preposition **1** inside: *He found an old postcard within the pages of the book.* | *After a few minutes' drive, we were within the city.* **2** not outside of or beyond: *The small child made sure she kept her mother within view.*
adverb **3** inside: *She opened the old box, revealing the treasure within.* **4** inside yourself: *He was smiling but within he was very sad.*

without

preposition **1** lacking or not with: *She went out without her coat.* **2** free from: *The patient has been without pain for several days now.*
adverb **3** lacking: *She was too late for dinner and had to go without.*

withstand

verb to stand or hold firm against: *My parents withstood my sister's requests for more money.* | *This material will withstand heavy use.*

Word use: The more usual word is **resist**.
Word building: Other forms are **I withstood, I have withstood, I am withstanding**.

witness

noun **1** someone who sees or hears something by being present: *I was a witness to the accident.* **2** someone who gives evidence, especially in a law court
verb **3** to be present at and see: *We all witnessed the fight.*
Other words: **observe, view, watch**

wizard

noun **1** someone who practises magic
Other words: **enchanter, magician, sorcerer, warlock**
2 someone who is very good at something: *a wizard at maths*
Other words: **expert, genius**

Word building: **wizardry** *noun*

wizened   *(say* wiz-*uhnd)*

adjective dried up and shrunken: *the wizened face of an old man*

wobbegong   *(say* wob-ee-gong*)*

noun a type of shark with a flattened body and mottled colouring, found along the east coast of Australia as well as other parts of the Pacific Ocean

Word history: possibly from an Aboriginal language of New South Wales

wobble

verb **1** to move unsteadily from side to side: *The acrobat wobbled and almost fell off the tightrope.*
Other words: **sway, teeter, totter**
2 to make move from side to side: *She wobbled her loose tooth.*

Word building: **wobble** *noun*   **wobbly** *adjective*

woe

noun great sadness

Word building: **woeful** *adjective*

woebegone   *(say* woh-buh-gon*)*

adjective sad or miserable: *a woebegone look*

wog[1]

noun someone from another country, especially someone with olive-brown skin

Word use: This word will offend people.

wog[2]

noun *Informal* a germ that causes a sickness: *Almost everyone in our class has caught the wog.*

wok

noun a large, round-bottomed, metal bowl used in Chinese cookery

wolf

noun a large, wild, dog-like animal that eats flesh

Word building: The plural is **wolves**.

woman   *(say* woom-uhn*)*

noun an adult female human being

Word building: The plural is **women** *(say* wim-uhn*)*. | **womanhood** *noun*   **womanish** *adjective*   **womanly** *adjective*

womankind

noun women, as distinguished from men; the female sex

womb   *(rhymes with* room*)*

noun another word for **uterus**

wombat

noun a short-legged heavy marsupial that burrows holes. Some species are endangered. See the table at the end of this book.

Word history: from an Aboriginal language of New South Wales called Dharug. See the map of Australian Aboriginal languages at the end of this book.

wonder   (*say* <u>wun</u>-duh)

verb **1** to think about with curiosity or surprise: *I wonder why Su Li decided to go.* **2** to think about with admiration: *I wonder at her courage.*

noun **3** something strange and surprising: *It is a wonder that you arrived on time.* **4** the feeling caused by something strange and surprising: *He looked at her work with wonder.*

> **wonder/wander** Don't confuse **wonder** with **wander**. To **wander** (rhymes with *yonder*) is to go about with no definite aim or fixed course.

wonderful

adjective extremely good or excellent
Other words: **brilliant, exceptional, fabulous, fantastic, great, marvellous, outstanding, sensational, superb, terrific, tremendous**

won ton   (*say* <u>won</u> ton)

noun a small ball of spicy pork wrapped in thin dough, usually boiled and served in soup in Chinese cooking

woo

verb to try to win the love of, especially so as to marry: *He is wooing the new girl in class.*
Word building: **wooer** *noun*

wood

noun **1** the hard substance that makes up most of the trunk and branches of a tree **2** this substance cut up and used in various ways, such as building houses and making furniture
Other words: **lumber, timber**
3 an area covered thickly with trees: *I went for a walk in the wood.* **4** a golf club with a wooden head

> **wood/would** Don't confuse **wood** with **would**. **Would** is an auxiliary verb, so you will always find it used with another verb:
> *would like to help you*
> *would have helped you if you'd asked me*

woodblock

noun **1** a block of wood with a raised design on it for printing from **2** a print made in this way
Word use: Another word for this is **woodcut**.

wooden

adjective **1** made of wood: *a wooden table* **2** stiff and clumsy: *a wooden way of walking* **3** without interest or liveliness: *a wooden stare | a wooden performance*

woodpecker

noun a bird with a hard strong beak for digging into wood after insects

woodwind

noun the group of musical wind instruments that includes the flutes, clarinets, oboes and bassoons

woodwork

noun **1** things made of wood **2** the making of wooden things: *He is good at woodwork.*
Other words: **carpentry, joinery**

wool

noun **1** the soft curly hair of sheep and some other animals **2** thread or cloth made from sheep's wool: *a dress of wool*
Word building: **woollen** *adjective*

woolly

adjective **1** made of wool or something similar: *a woolly jumper* **2** not clear or firm: *woolly thinking*

woomera

noun a strong piece of wood with a notch at the end, traditionally used by Aboriginal people to help throw a spear
Word history: from an Aboriginal language of New South Wales called Dharug. See the map of Australian Aboriginal languages at the end of this book.

woozy

adjective *Informal* dizzy and faint: *She felt woozy for a few days after the operation.*
Word building: Other forms are **woozier, wooziest.** | **woozily** *adverb* **wooziness** *noun*

word

noun **1** a sound or group of sounds which stands for an idea, action or object and which is one of the building blocks of a language **2** the group of letters you use to write down these sounds **3** speech or talk: *Can I have a word with you?* **4** a short saying: *I will give you a word of warning.* **5** a promise: *You gave your word.*
Other words: **assurance, commitment, guarantee, oath, pledge, vow**
6 order or command: *Start moving when I give the word.* **7** news: *I have just got word of the accident.*
verb **8** to choose words to express: *Simone worded her speech very carefully.*
Other words: **express, phrase**
Word building: **wording** *noun*: *He used polite wording in his letter.*

word processor

noun a computer program used for writing documents, letters, and so on

wordy

adjective using too many words: *a wordy explanation*

Word building: **wordily** *adverb*   **wordiness** *noun*

work

noun **1** effort made by the body or mind to do something: *It will take hours of work to finish this job.*
Other words: **exertion, industry, labour, toil**
2 something that needs to be done by effort: *I've brought some work home from school.*
Other words: **chores, duties, jobs, projects, tasks**
3 something made by effort: *a work of art | a musical work*
Other words: **creation**
4 a job by which you earn money: *His work is cleaning.*
Other words: **occupation, profession, trade**
verb **5** to do work: *The builders worked hard to get the house finished before the rain started.*
Other words: **labour, toil**
6 to have a job by which you earn money: *I worked in a bookshop during the holidays.* **7** to act or operate properly: *This remote control isn't working.*
Other words: **function, go**
8 to use or manage: *Do you know how to work this new program?*
Other words: **drive, operate, run**
phrase **9 work out, a** to solve, find out or calculate by thinking: *to work out an answer | to work out a sum* **b** to turn out: *I hope our plan works out all right.* **c** to train or practise a sport or exercise: *I work out every morning.* **10 work up, a** to excite the feelings of: *She worked herself up into a rage.* **b** to make increase: *I've worked up an appetite with all this running.* **c** to move gradually towards: *I'm working up to telling you what I got in the exam.*

workable

adjective able to be put into operation: *a workable machine | a workable plan*

worker

noun **1** someone or something that works **2** someone who has a particular job: *an office worker* **3** someone who is employed in a factory or does work with their hands: *The workers here get on well with the bosses.*

workers compensation

noun a scheme which provides workers with money or other benefits when they become sick or are hurt through their work

work-out

noun **1** a performance, especially of a sporting activity, done as a trial or test in preparation for a contest, and so on **2** a period of physical exercise: *a work-out at the gym*

workplace

noun a place of employment

workshop

noun a place where mechnical work is done, such as work on cars, appliances, and so on, smaller than a factory

world

noun **1** the earth and everyone who lives on it
Other words: **globe**
2 a particular area of life or interest: *the animal world | the world of sport*
Other words: **area, domain, field, realm, sphere, territory**

world-class

adjective among the best in the world: *a world-class athlete*

worldly

adjective **1** interested only in the things that concern us in our life on earth, rather than in any other life after death **2** used to the ways of the world

Word building: Other forms are **worldlier, worldliest. | worldliness** *noun*

World Wide Web

noun **the,** a system of storing information on the internet so that people all around the world can find it

Word use: This word is often shortened to **the web** or **WWW.**

worm   (*rhymes with* firm)

noun **1** a long thin animal with a soft body and no legs that moves by slithering along **2** someone whom you do not respect

Word building: **worm** *verb*

worn

adjective **1** shabby or damaged by wear or use **2** very tired

Word use: This is a form of the verb **wear**.

worn/warn Don't confuse **worn** with **warn**. To **warn** is to tell someone of possible danger.

worry   (*rhymes with* hurry)

verb **1** to feel anxious or upset: *Our parents worry if we stay out late.* **2** to bother or annoy: *Don't worry me now, I'm busy.* **3** to grab with the teeth and shake: *The cat is worrying a mouse.*

Word building: Other forms are **I worried, I have worried, I am worrying.**

worse

adjective bad to a greater degree: *My cold is worse than it was yesterday.*

Word use: This is a form of the adjective **bad**.
Word building: **worsen** *verb* to make or become worse   **worse** *adverb*

worship

noun **1** great love, honour and respect: *hero worship* **2** the showing of deep honour and respect for a god or a sacred person in a ceremony or prayer

Word building: **worship** *verb* (**worshipped, worshipping**)

worst

adjective bad to the greatest degree: *the worst winter for years*

Word use: This is a form of the adjective **bad**.
Word building: **worst** *adverb*

worth

adjective **1** equal in value to: *It isn't worth $10.* **2** good enough for: *a place worth visiting*
noun **3** value or importance: *a painting of great worth* **4** quantity or amount: *$50 worth of petrol*

Word building: **worthless** *adjective*

worthwhile

adjective useful or good enough to spend time on: *a worthwhile hobby*

worthy   (*say* <u>wer</u>-dhee)

adjective **1** deserving respect or admiration: *a worthy effort*
phrase **2 worthy of**, good enough for: *a meal worthy of a king*

Word building: Other adjective forms are **worthier, worthiest.** | **worthily** *adverb* **worthiness** *noun*

would   (*say* wood)

verb See **will**[1]

would/wood Don't confuse **would** with **wood**, which is the hard substance that makes up most of the trunk and branches of a tree.

would-be

adjective wishing or planning to be: *a would-be actor*

wound   (*rhymes with* crooned)

noun an injury such as a cut, burn or bruise

Word building: **wound** *verb* to hurt

wrangle   (*say* <u>rang</u>-guhl)

verb to argue or quarrel noisily

Word building: **wrangle** *noun*

wrap

verb **1** to fold paper or other covering around a parcel, and so on **2** to fold material around someone or something: *She wrapped the baby in a warm blanket.* Other words: **cocoon, envelop, muffle, swathe**
3 to fold so as to cover: *Wrap the scarf around your neck.*

Word building: Other forms are **I wrapped, I have wrapped, I am wrapping.** | **wrapper** *noun* covering

wrap/rap Don't confuse **wrap** with **rap**. To **rap** something is to strike it with a quick light blow.

wrath   (*say* roth)

noun Old-fashioned anger or revenge

wreak   (*sounds like* reek)

verb to carry out or inflict: *The storm wreaked havoc on the garden.*

wreak/reek Don't confuse **wreak** with **reek**. To **reek** is to give off a terrible smell.

wreath   (*say* reeth)

noun flowers and leaves tied together to make a ring

wreathe   (*rhymes with* seethe)

verb to surround: *Mist wreathed the valley.*

wreck

verb **1** to ruin or destroy
noun **2** something, especially a ship, that has been wrecked
Other words: **remains, ruin, wreckage**
Word building: **wreckage** *noun* the broken parts of a wreck   **wrecker** *noun*

wren

noun a very small bird with a long upright tail

wrench

verb **1** to twist roughly: *to wrench the door open | to wrench your ankle*
noun **2** a sudden sharp twist **3** a type of spanner
Word building: The plural form of the noun is **wrenches**.

wrest

verb to pull or grab roughly: *to wrest the gun from the robber's grasp*

wrestle

verb **1** to struggle with someone and try to throw them to the ground
Other words: **fight, grapple, scuffle, tussle**
2 to struggle or make a great effort: *to wrestle with a difficult problem*
Other words: **battle, fight**
Word building: **wrestler** *noun*   **wrestling** *noun*

wretch

noun someone who is very miserable and unfortunate
Word building: The plural is **wretches**.

wretched   *(say* rech-uhd*)*

adjective **1** poor, miserable and pitiful: *a wretched slum* **2** worthless or irritating: *The wretched door won't open.*
Word building: **wretchedly** *adverb* **wretchedness** *noun*

wriggle

verb **1** to twist and turn like a snake or worm
Other words: **squirm, wiggle, writhe**
phrase **2** get a wriggle on, to hurry up
Word building: **wriggly** *adjective*

wring

verb to twist and squeeze: *to wring water out of the floor mop | to wring your hands in grief*
Word building: Other forms are **I wrung, I have wrung, I am wringing.** | **wringer** *noun*

wring/ring Don't confuse **wring** with **ring**. You wear a **ring** on your finger. Bells **ring** when they give out a clear musical sound. When you **ring** someone, you telephone them.

wrinkle

noun a crease on something that is usually smooth
Other words: **crinkle, fold, furrow, ridge**
Word building: **wrinkle** *verb*

wrist

noun the joint where your hand meets your arm

write

verb **1** to form letters or words with a pen, pencil or similar thing: *to write on the blackboard* **2** to compose or create using words: *to write a poem* **3** to write a letter and send it: *I wrote to my sister last week.*
phrase **4 write down,** to set down in writing: *He wrote down everything he did on his holiday.*
Other words: **chronicle, document, record, recount**
Word building: Other verb forms are **I wrote, I have written, I am writing.** | **writer** *noun* **writing** *noun*

write/right/rite Don't confuse **write** with **right**, or **rite**.
Something is **right** if it is fair or good.
A **rite** is a ceremony, often a religious one.

write-off

noun Informal a car that has been so badly smashed that it can't be repaired

writhe

verb to twist and squirm, as if in pain or embarrassment

wrong

adjective **1** bad or evil: *It is wrong to tell lies.* **2** not correct: *the wrong answer*
Word building: **wrong** *verb* to hurt or treat unfairly   **wrongly** *adverb*

wrong-foot

verb in sport, to trick an opponent into moving the wrong way or losing their balance: *Louis Peade wrong-footed the keeper to score with a clean shot.*

wry   *(sounds like* rye*)*

adjective **1** showing displeasure or disgust: *She made a wry face as she tasted the soup.* **2** crooked or twisted: *a wry neck*
Word building: Other forms are **wrier, wriest.** | **wryly** *adverb*

Xx

X-ray

noun **1** a ray that can pass through something solid **2** a photograph of the inside of someone's body, used by doctors to help diagnose disease

Word building: **X-ray** *verb* to make such a photograph

xylophone (*say* zuy-luh-fohn)

noun a musical instrument made of a row of wooden bars of different lengths which you hit with small wooden hammers

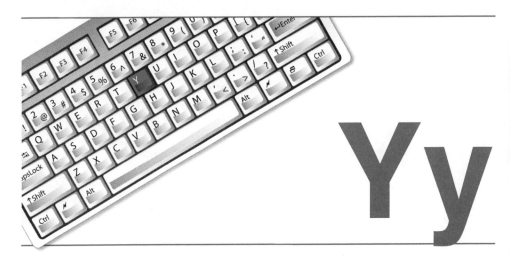

Yy

yabby

noun a small Australian crayfish which lives in fresh water

Word building: The plural is **yabbies**.
Word history: from an Aboriginal language of Victoria called Wembawemba. See the map of Australian Aboriginal languages at the end of this book.

yacht (*rhymes with* cot)

noun a sailing boat used for sport or pleasure

Word building: **yachting** *noun*

yak¹

noun a long-haired wild ox found in the highlands of the Xizang Autonomous Region (Tibet)

yak²

verb Informal to talk on and on without saying anything very important

Word building: Other forms are **I yakked, I have yakked, I am yakking.** | **yak** *noun*

yakka

noun Informal work

yam

noun a potato-like vegetable which grows in warmer parts of the world

Yamatji (*say* yam-uh-jee)

noun an Aboriginal person from mid-western Western Australia

Word building: **Yamatji** *adjective*: *Yamatji traditions.*
Word history: from the Watjari language of mid-western Western Australia

yank

verb to pull or tug suddenly

Word building: **yank** *noun*

Yank

noun Informal an American

yap

verb to bark with short high sounds

Word building: Other forms are **I yapped, I have yapped, I am yapping.** | **yap** *noun* **yapping** *noun*

yard¹

noun **1** a unit of length in the imperial system equal to about 91 centimetres **2** a pole attached to a sailing ship's mast that a sail hangs from

yard²

noun **1** the fenced ground around a house or other building **2** a fenced or walled area in which any work or business is carried on: *a shipyard*

yarmulke (*say* yah-mool-kuh)

noun a skullcap worn by some Jewish men and boys, especially on religious occasions

Word use: Another spelling is **yarmulka**.

yarn

noun **1** nylon, cotton or wool thread used for knitting and weaving **2** a long story, especially one about unlikely happenings *verb* **3** to tell such stories

yawn

verb **1** to take a long deep breath through your mouth, especially when you are bored or tired **2** to be wide open like a mouth: *The cave yawned before them.*

Word building: **yawn** *noun*

year

noun **1** the period of twelve months from 1 January to 31 December **2** any period of twelve months: *I saw Tom a year ago.*

Word building: **yearly** *adjective*

yearn   (*rhymes with* burn)

verb to want very much: *She yearns to go back to her home town.*

Word building: **yearning** *noun*

yeast

noun a substance which causes the dough to rise when you make bread

yell

verb to call out loudly or shout: *He yelled with pain.* | *She yelled her answer.*

Word building: **yell** *noun*

yellow

adjective of the colour of an egg yolk, lemon, and so on

Word building: **yellow** *noun*   **yellow** *verb* to make or become yellow

yellow box

noun a large spreading type of gum tree which grows in eastern Australia

yellowcake

noun uranium in the form in which it is dug out of the ground

yellow card

noun in sport, a yellow card shown by a referee to a player to tell them they have been cautioned

yellow fever

noun an infectious disease found in warm countries, caused by mosquito bites and sometimes resulting in death

yelp

verb to give a quick sharp cry: *The dog yelped when I hit it.*

Word building: **yelp** *noun*

yen

noun a strong desire or longing

yes

interjection a word used to say that a statement is correct, express agreement, or to emphasise that you know a statement is true: *Yes, what you have said is right.* | *Yes, you may go.* | *Yes, I know you want me to come but I haven't the time.*

yesterday

noun the day before today

Word building: **yesterday** *adverb*: *I did it yesterday.*

yet

adverb **1** at the present time: *Don't leave yet.* **2** up to a particular time: *He had not yet arrived.*

yeti   (*say* <u>yet</u>-ee)

noun a humanlike creature supposed to live in the mountains of Tibet (Xizang AR)

Word use: This is sometimes called the **abominable snowman.**
Word building: The plural is **yetis.**

yield

verb **1** to produce: *This type of wheat yields a good crop.* **2** to give in or surrender: *Don't yield to his argument.* | *The country yielded to the invader.*

Word building: **yield** *noun*: *an orchard's yield of fruit*

yobbo

noun a young male who looks slovenly, has no manners and is often noisy

yodel

verb to sing with rapid changes between your normal voice and a very high voice, as Swiss mountaineers do

Word building: Other forms are **I yodelled, I have yodelled, I am yodelling.** | **yodel** *noun*

yoga   (*say* <u>yoh</u>-guh)

noun a set of exercises which involve holding unusual body positions and deep breathing, in order to reach a calm, peaceful state of mind

Word history: from a Sanskrit word meaning 'union'

yoghurt   (*say* <u>yoh</u>-guht)

noun a food made by the controlled curdling of milk

Word use: Another spelling is **yogurt.**

yogi   (*say* <u>yoh</u>-gee)

noun someone who is an expert in yoga

Word building: The plural is **yogis.**

yoke

noun **1** a device consisting of a wooden crosspiece with curved ends fitting over the necks of two oxen pulling a load **2** a shaped piece in a garment, fitted about the neck, shoulders or hips, from which the rest of the garment hangs

Word building: **yoke** verb

yolk   (rhymes with coke)

noun the yellow part of an egg

yolk/yoke Don't confuse **yolk** with **yoke**. A **yoke** is a wooden cross-piece with curved ends, used for pulling or carrying loads.

Yolngu   (say yol-ngooh)

noun an Aboriginal person from some north-eastern parts of the Northern Territory

Word building: **Yolngu** adjective: Yolngu paintings

Yom Kippur   (say yom kip-uh, yom kip-oo-uh)

noun an annual Jewish fast day kept on the tenth day of the month of Tishri

Word use: Another name is **the Day of Atonement**.
Word history: from the Hebrew name for this day

yonder

adjective Old-fashioned being in that place or over there: yonder farm on the hill

Word building: **yonder** adverb: He went yonder.

you

pronoun the pronoun you use when you are talking to one person or to a group of people: Are you sure you know which way to go?

Word use: Other forms are **your** (your hat), **yours** (That book is yours), **you** (I gave it to you), **yourself** (Did you hurt yourself?), **yourselves** (How did you all hurt yourselves?).

you/ewe Don't confuse **you** with **ewe**, which is a female sheep.

you'd

a short form of **you had** or **you would**

you'll

a short form of **you will** or **you shall**

young

adjective **1** being in the early stage of life, growth or existence: a young animal | a young nation
Other words: **immature**
noun **2** offspring: Calves are the young of cows. **3** young children: the high spirits of the young
Other words: **youngsters, youth**

youngster

noun a child or young person

your

pronoun the form of **you** used before a noun to show that something belongs to or is done by you: your work

Word building: **yours** pronoun: These are yours. | Yours are very good.

your/you're Don't confuse **your** with **you're**. **You're** is short for **you are**.

you're   (rhymes with saw)

a short form of **you are**

youth

noun **1** a young person **2** young people **3** the time when you are young: I spent my youth on a farm.

Word building: **youth** adjective: a youth concert **youthful** adjective: youthful high spirits

you've

a short form of **you have**

yoyo

noun a toy made of two round, flat-sided pieces of wood or plastic with a length of string wound between them by which you can make it spin up and down

Word building: The plural is **yoyos**.

yucky

adjective Informal unpleasant

Word use: Another spelling is **yukky**.

yum cha

noun a Chinese meal in which you choose small individual serves of many different dishes displayed on trolleys

yummy

adjective Informal having a very good taste

zany

adjective funny in a silly or crazy way: *She has a zany sense of humour.*

Word building: Other forms are **zanier**, **zaniest**.

zeal

noun eagerness or enthusiasm: *zeal for the conservation movement*

Word building: **zealot** *noun* **zealous** *adjective*

zebra

noun a wild, horselike, African animal with a black-and-white striped body

Word use: The male is a **stallion**, the female is a **mare** and the young is a **colt**.

Zen

noun a form of Buddhism that is popular in Japan, which believes that you should meditate if you want to understand the universe

Word history: from a Sanskrit word meaning 'religious meditation'

zero

noun **1** the figure or symbol '0' **2** nothing
Other words: **nil**, **nought**

Word building: The plural is **zeros** or **zeroes**.

zest

noun keen enjoyment: *She does her work with zest.*

Word building: **zestful** *adjective*

zigzag

noun a line with sharp turns first to one side and then to the other

Word building: **zigzag** *verb* (**zigzagged**, **zigzagging**)

zinc

noun a bluish-white metal, used in making galvanised iron and some alloys

zip

noun **1** a fastener consisting of two rows of interlocking metal or plastic teeth and a sliding piece which joins or separates them
verb **2** to put (computer data) into a form that uses less storage
phrase **3 zip up**, to fasten with a zip: *Zip up your jacket before you go outside — it's cold.*

Word use: Other words for definition 1 are **zipper** and **zip-fastener**.
Word building: Other verb forms are **I zipped**, **I have zipped**, **I am zipping**.

zip file

noun a computer file that is compressed into a smaller size so it is easier to store and move

zit

noun *Informal* a pimple

zither

noun a musical string instrument that you pluck

zodiac (*say* <u>zoh</u>-dee-ak)

noun a part of the sky forming an imaginary belt through which the sun, moon and planets appear to travel, and which contains twelve constellations which are named and used in astrology

zombie

noun **1** a dead body brought back to life by supernatural means **2** someone who looks like a zombie and seems to have no mind

Word history: from a West African word meaning 'good-luck charm'

zone

noun an area marked off and used for a special purpose: *a military zone*

Word building: **zone** *verb*   **zoning** *noun*

zoo

noun a large area of land with enclosures where you can see wild animals

zoology   (*say* zoh-<u>ol</u>-uh-jee)

noun the science or study of animal life

zoom

verb **1** to move quickly with a humming sound: *Tom zoomed by on his skateboard.* **2** to go up suddenly: *The aeroplane zoomed into the clouds.*

Word building: **zoom** *noun*

zucchini   (*say* zuh-<u>kee</u>-nee, zooh-<u>kee</u>-nee)

noun a small vegetable marrow, usually picked when very young

Word use: Another name for this is a **courgette**.
Word building: The plural is **zucchinis**.

Appendixes

Overused words

The following is a list of words that are often overused in the writing of students. Alternative words that may capture a more precise meaning are shown below.

Overused word	Alternative words
bad	badly behaved, disobedient, mischievous, naughty | damaging, frightful, harmful, nasty | decayed, foul, off, rotten, spoiled, tainted
beautiful	exquisite, gorgeous, lovely
big	colossal, enormous, giant, huge, immense, massive | eminent, pre-eminent, prestigious
cry	bawl, blubber, sob, wail, weep, whimper | call, scream, shriek, yell
dirty	filthy, grimy, grotty, grubby, soiled
excellent	brilliant, exceptional, fantastic, marvellous, outstanding, sensational, superb, terrific
fair	just, impartial, reasonable | decent, honest, proper, right, truthful | clear, fine, sunny | blond, pale
fast	quick, rapid, speedy, swift
fight	brawl, fray, scuffle, tussle | argument, quarrel, row, squabble | assault, attack, oppose
full	brimming, bulging, bursting, overflowing, packed | entire, exhaustive, total
good	fair, fine, great, satisfactory | precious, valuable | abundant, adequate, plentiful, profuse | able, adept, capable, proficient, talented | merit, perfection, value, virtue, worth
great	enormous, huge, immense | exceptional, extraordinary, remarkable | eminent, famous, grand, outstanding, pre-eminent, prominent | cool, fantastic, sensational, terrific
happy	cheerful, ecstatic, joyful, thrilled | blessed, chance, fluky
hard	rigid, stiff, tough | awkward, complex, complicated, tricky | exhausting, taxing, tiring | energetically, forcefully, intently, strongly (*hard up*: broke, penniless, poor)
hate	abhor, despise, detest, loathe
help	assist, relieve, support | aid, assistance, support

Overused word	Alternative words
hide	camouflage, conceal, cover up, disguise
horrible	awful, nasty, shocking
laugh	cackle, chortle, chuckle, giggle, guffaw, snigger (*laugh off*: discount, dismiss, disregard)
like	appreciate, cherish, enjoy | desire, fancy, prefer
little	microscopic, minute, tiny | minimal, minor, slight
love	adoration, devotion, fondness | adore, care for, cherish
mad	crazy, demented, deranged | annoyed, cross, furious | impulsive, passionate
mean	miserly, selfish, ungenerous | cruel, malicious, spiteful, unkind
nice	enjoyable, splendid, terrific, wonderful | agreeable, considerate, courteous, helpful, polite, thoughtful | exceptional, first-class, marvellous, sensational, skilful, terrific, top | delectable, luscious, scrumptious, yummy
old	aged, elderly, mature, senior | ancient, antique, early, prehistoric | ragged, shabby, worn | former, past, previous
rude	cheeky, fresh, impertinent, impudent, insolent | crude, raw, simple
safe	immune, protected, secure, sheltered | careful, cautious, wary
save	defend, deliver, free | budget, conserve, economise
shy	diffident, reserved, self-contained | fearful, jumpy, nervous, timid, timorous
silly	idiotic, inane, nonsensical, ridiculous, senseless
slow	languid, leisurely, sluggish, unhurried | behind, belated, late
strange	abnormal, bizarre, extraordinary, peculiar, remarkable, unusual | foreign, unfamiliar, unknown
trick	hoax, practical joke, prank, ruse | craft, gimmick, skill, spectacle | delusion, false impression, figment, illusion | idiosyncrasy, peculiarity, tendency, trait | bluff, con, delude, doublecross, fool, hoodwink
wonderful	fabulous, magnificent, marvellous, sensational, superb
work	exertion, diligence, drudgery, grind, industry, labour | chores, duties, errands, jobs, projects, tasks | accomplishment, achievement, creation, feat, masterpiece, product | business, career, employment, occupation, position, profession, trade | labour, slog, toil | be employed, be engaged, be on duty, serve | function, go, play, run | drive, operate

Helpful hints for the spelling of tricky words

If you can't easily find the word you're looking up, it might be that the word begins with a letter or letters that you say in a different way to normal, or the word's first letter may be completely silent. Here is a table to help you track down those tricky words.

The first sound of the word	The possible first letters of the word	Example
f	ph	**ph**otograph
g	gh	**gh**ost
g	gu	**gu**ide
h	wh	**wh**ole
j	g	**g**em
k	ch	**ch**aracter
k	qu	**qu**ay
kw	qu	**qu**ite
n	gn	**gn**ome
n	kn	**kn**ee
r	rh	**rh**yme
r	wr	**wr**ite
s	c	**c**ereal
s	sc	**sc**ience
sh	s	**s**ugar
sk	sch	**sch**ool
w	wh	**wh**ite
z	x	**x**ylophone

Prepositions

A preposition is a word placed before a noun to show its relation to other words in the sentence. Here are some common prepositions with illustrations to show their meaning.

above my head

beneath the trees

inside the box

across the river

beside the chair

on the table

along the path

between the posts

off the ladder

at the corner

by the window

over the wall

behind the door

down the hole

through the window

below the bridge

in the cupboard

up the hill

Verb tenses

	Past tense	Present tense	Future tense
Simple	I swam*	I swim	I will swim
Continuous	I was swimming	I am swimming*	I will be swimming
Perfect	I had swum	I have swum*	I will have swum
Perfect Continuous	I had been swimming	I have been swimming	I will have been swimming

*Note: The main forms, or *principal parts*, of irregular verbs are shown in the **Word building** sections of the dictionary entries in the order: simple past tense, perfect present tense, continuous present tense. It looks like this:

Word building: Other verb forms are **I swam, I have swum, I am swimming**

Personal pronouns

Number	Person	Subject	Object	Possessive adjective	Possessive pronoun	Reflexive
Singular	First	I	me	my	mine	myself
	Second	you	you	your	yours	yourself
	Third	she	her	her	hers	herself
		he	him	his	his	himself
		it	it	its	its	itself
Plural	First	we	us	our	ours	ourselves
	Second	you	you	your	yours	yourselves
	Third	they	them	their	theirs	themselves

Note: *First person* refers to the person speaking.
Second person refers to the person spoken to.
Third person refers to the person spoken about.

Subjective case shows that the pronoun is the subject of a verb.
Objective case shows that the pronoun is the object of a verb.
Possessive case shows ownership of the thing named by the noun that follows.

Irregular verbs

Infinitive	Past tense	Past participle
be	was (sing.); were (pl.)	been
bear	bore	borne
beat	beat	beaten
become	became	become
begin	began	begun
bite	bit	bitten
bleed	bled	bled
blow	blew	blown
break	broke	broken
bring	brought	brought
build	built	built
buy	bought	bought
catch	caught	caught
choose	chose	chosen
come	came	come
cut	cut	cut
dig	dug	dug
do	did	done
draw	drew	drawn
drink	drank	drunk
drive	drove	driven
eat	ate	eaten
fall	fell	fallen
feel	felt	felt
fight	fought	fought
find	found	found
fly	flew	flown
forget	forgot	forgotten
get	got	got
give	gave	given
go	went	gone
grow	grew	grown
hang	hung, hanged	hung, hanged
hear	heard	heard
hide	hid	hidden
hit	hit	hit
hold	held	held
hurt	hurt	hurt
keep	kept	kept
know	knew	known
lay	laid	laid
lead	led	led
learn	learned, learnt	learned, learnt
leave	left	left
lend	lent	lent

Infinitive	Past tense	Past participle
lie	lay	lain
lose	lost	lost
make	made	made
mean	meant	meant
meet	met	met
mistake	mistook	mistaken
pay	paid	paid
put	put	put
read	read	read
ride	rode	ridden
ring	rang	rung
rise	rose	risen
run	ran	run
say	said	said
see	saw	seen
sell	sold	sold
send	sent	sent
set	set	set
shine	shone	shone
show	showed	shown
shut	shut	shut
sing	sang	sung
sink	sank	sunk
sit	sat	sat
sleep	slept	slept
smell	smelt, smelled	smelt, smelled
speak	spoke	spoken
spend	spent	spent
spin	spun	spun
spit	spat	spat
stand	stood	stood
steal	stole	stolen
strike	struck	struck
swear	swore	sworn
swim	swam	swum
take	took	taken
teach	taught	taught
tear	tore	torn
tell	told	told
think	thought	thought
throw	threw	thrown
tread	trod	trodden
wake	woke	woken
wear	wore	worn
win	won	won
wind	wound	wound
write	wrote	written

Contractions

Contractions are words made by shortening other words. Most common contractions are formed when two words are shortened and joined together. Often, one of the words is a pronoun, the word 'not', or an auxiliary verb. Here are some examples.

aren't	are not	it's	it has	wasn't	was not
can't	cannot	I've	I have	we'd	we had
couldn't	could not	let's	let us	we'd	we would
could've	could have	mayn't	may not	we'll	we will
daren't	dare not	mustn't	must not	we're	we are
didn't	did not	needn't	need not	weren't	were not
doesn't	does not	shan't	shall not	we've	we have
don't	do not	she'd	she had	what's	what is
hadn't	had not	she'd	she would	what's	what has
hasn't	has not	she'll	she will	who'd	who had
haven't	have not	she's	she is	who'd	who would
he'd	he had	she's	she has	who'll	who will
he'd	he would	shouldn't	should not	who's	who is
he'll	he will	should've	should have	who's	who has
here's	here is	there'd	there had	who've	who have
he's	he is	there'd	there would	won't	will not
he's	he has	there'll	there will	wouldn't	would not
I'd	I had	there's	there is	would've	would have
I'd	I would	there's	there has	you'd	you had
I'll	I will	they'd	they had	you'd	you would
I'm	I am	they'd	they would	you'll	you will
isn't	is not	they'll	they will	you're	you are
it'll	it will	they're	they are	you've	you have
it's	it is	they've	they have		

Types of writing and speaking

Discussion

Writing or speaking which gives more than one opinion on something
Example: debate, conversation about homework expectations

Explanation

Writing or speaking which tells how or why something happens
Example: explaining why ice melts, explaining how a computer works

Exposition

Writing or speaking which gives only one opinion on something, the purpose being to persuade
Example: advertisement, newspaper editorial, election speech

Information report

Writing or speaking which gives facts on something
Example: project on endangered animals, information brochure on sport

Procedure

Writing or speaking which tells how to do or make something
Example: recipe, instructions for making a kite, rules for playing a game

Recount

Writing or speaking which explains exactly how things happened
Example: news item, diary entry, excursion report

Drama

Writing or speaking which is meant to be acted out
Example: play, reader's theatre, mime

Narrative

Writing or speaking which tells a story
Example: fairytale, Dreaming story, novel

Poetry

Writing or speaking which expresses feelings and thoughts on people and things that happen, especially your own thoughts and feelings
Example: ballad, limerick, nursery rhyme

Abbreviations

AC	Companion of the Order of Australia
ACT	Australian Capital Territory
AD	in the year of our Lord (Latin *Anno Domini*)
a.m.	before noon (Latin *ante meridiem*)
AM	Member of the Order of Australia
anon.	anonymous
ANZAC	Australian and New Zealand Army Corps
AO	Officer of the Order of Australia
ASAP	as soon as possible
Av., Ave	Avenue
b.	born; (*Cricket*) bowled; breadth
BC	Before Christ
BCE	Before the Common Era
c.	cent; century; (before dates) about (Latin *circa*)
C	Cape; Celsius; Centigrade; century
C/–, c/o	care of
CBD	Central Business District
CCTV	closed-circuit television
CE	Common Era
ch., chap.	chapter
Co.	company
COD	cash on delivery
cont., contd	continued
Cres.	Crescent
DIY	do-it-yourself
DOB	date of birth
Dr	Doctor
Dr.	Drive (in street names)
E, e.	east; eastern
e.g.	for example (Latin *exempli gratia*)
ETA	estimated time of arrival
etc.	and so on (Latin *et cetera*)
ETD	estimated time of departure
F	Fahrenheit
FAQ	frequently asked question
fig.	figure
figs	figures
fol.	following
Fr	Father
FYI	for your information
GM	genetically-modified
Govt, govt	government
GP	general practitioner
h.	height; hour
h.c.f.	highest common factor
hcp	handicap
HMAS	Her (or His) Majesty's Australian Ship
HQ	headquarters
hr	hour
Hts	Heights
ID	identification
i.e.	that is (Latin *id est*)
Is., is., isl.	Island
ISBN	International Standard Book Number
ISP	internet service provider
IT	information technology
jnr, jr	junior
JP	Justice of the Peace
K	thousand; kilobyte
Kb, kb	kilobit
KB, Kb, kb	kilobyte
k.p.h.	kilometres per hour

l.	left; length	Qld	Queensland
L	learner (driver)		
l.b.w.	(*Cricket*) leg before wicket	r.	right; (*Cricket*) runs
l.c.d.	lowest common denominator	Rd	Road
LCD	liquid crystal display	RSVP	please reply (French *répondez*
l.c.m.	lowest common multiple		*s'il vous plaît*)
LPG	liquefied petroleum gas		
		s.	second(s); south; southern
m.	male; married; mass; million;	S	south; southern
	minute; month	SA	South Australia
max.	maximum	s.a.e., SAE	stamped addressed envelope;
Mb	megabit		self-addressed envelope
MB	megabyte	SE	south-east; south-eastern
MHR	Member of the House of	sec.	second; secondary
	Representatives	sect.	section
min.	minute; minimum	sen., snr, sr	senior
misc.	miscellaneous	SMS	short messaging service
MP	Member of Parliament	Soc.	Society
Mt	Mount; Mountain	SPF	sun protection factor
		Sr	Senior; Sister
n.	born (Latin *natus*); north;	St	Street; State; Saint; Strait
	northern	Sth	south
N	north; northern	Sthn	southern
n/a, n.a.	not applicable; not available	SW	south-west; south-western
NB	note well (Latin *nota bene*)		
NE	north-east; north-eastern	Tas.	Tasmania
no., No.	number	temp.	temporary; temperature
nos, Nos	numbers		
NSW	New South Wales	ULP	unleaded petrol
NT	Northern Territory	UV	ultraviolet
NW	north-west; north-western		
		v, vs.	versus
OAM	Medal of the Order of	Vic.	Victoria
	Australia	vol.	volume
p.	page	w.	week; weight; west; western;
P	provisional (driver's licence)		wide; width; with
p.a.	yearly (Latin *per annum*)	W	west; western
para.	paragraph	WA	Western Australia
p.c.	per cent	wk	week
PE	physical education	wt	weight
Pl.	Place (in street names)	www	World Wide Web
p.m.	afternoon (Latin *post*		
	meridiem)	y., yr	year
PO	Post Office		
PTO, p.t.o.	please turn over		

Numbers

Cardinal numbers

1	one
2	two
3	three
4	four
5	five
6	six
7	seven
8	eight
9	nine
10	ten
20	twenty
50	fifty
100	hundred
1000	thousand

Ordinal numbers

1st	first
2nd	second
3rd	third
4th	fourth
5th	fifth
6th	sixth
7th	seventh
8th	eighth
9th	ninth
10th	tenth
20th	twentieth
50th	fiftieth
100th	hundredth
1000th	thousandth

Roman numerals

Number	Roman numeral	Number	Roman numeral
1	I	43	XLIII
2	II	50	L
3	III	54	LIV
4	IV	60	LX
5	V	65	LXV
6	VI	70	LXX
7	VII	76	LXXVI
8	VIII	80	LXXX
9	IX	87	LXXXVII
10	X	90	XC
11	XI	98	XCVIII
12	XII	100	C
13	XIII	101	CI
14	XIV	115	CXV
15	XV	150	CL
16	XVI	200	CC
17	XVII	300	CCC
18	XVIII	400	CD
19	XIX	500	D
20	XX	600	DC
21	XXI	700	DCC
30	XXX	800	DCCC
32	XXXII	900	CM
40	XL	1000	M

Map showing the Aboriginal languages referred to in this dictionary

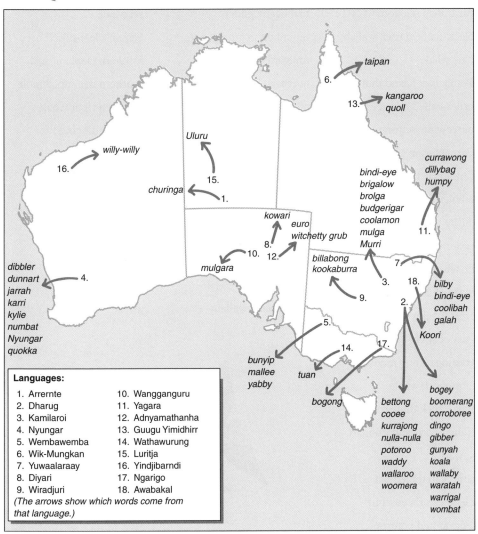

taipan

6.

13.

kangaroo
quoll

willy-willy

Uluru

16.

15.

churinga

1.

currawong
bindi-eye   dillybag
brigalow   humpy
brolga
budgerigar
coolamon
kowari   mulga   11.
euro   Murri
witchetty grub
8.
10.   12.
mulgara

billabong
kookaburra   7.

3.   18.   bilby
              bindi-eye
9.   2.   coolibah
              galah
              Koori

dibbler
dunnart   4.
jarrah
karri
kylie
numbat
Nyungar
quokka

5.

14.   17.

bunyip
mallee   tuan
yabby

bogong

bogey
boomerang
bettong   corroboree
cooee   dingo
kurrajong gibber
nulla-nulla gunyah
potoroo   koala
waddy   wallaby
wallaroo   waratah
woomera   warrigal
              wombat

Languages:

1. Arrernte
2. Dharug
3. Kamilaroi
4. Nyungar
5. Wembawemba
6. Wik-Mungkan
7. Yuwaalaraay
8. Diyari
9. Wiradjuri
10. Wangganguru
11. Yagara
12. Adnyamathanha
13. Guugu Yimidhirr
14. Wathawurung
15. Luritja
16. Yindjibarndi
17. Ngarigo
18. Awabakal

(The arrows show which words come from that language.)

Some of our endangered and vulnerable mammals

Australian sea lion

black-flanked rock wallaby

blue whale

Boullanger Island dunnart

brush-tailed rabbit-rat

burrowing bettong

Carpentarian antechinus

Christmas Island shrew

dibbler

dusky hopping mouse

eastern barred bandicoot

fin whale

fluffy glider

greater bilby

greater stick-nest rat

Hastings River mouse

humpback whale

Julia Creek dunnart

Kangaroo Island dunnart

kowari

large-eared pied bat

Leadbeater's possum

long-footed potoroo

mahogany glider

mountain pygmy possum

mulgara

northern bettong

northern hairy-nosed wombat

northern hopping mouse

northern quoll

numbat

Pilbara leaf-nosed bat

plains rat

quokka

red-tailed phascogale

rufous hare-wallaby

sei whale

Semon's leaf-nosed bat

southern elephant seal

southern marsupial mole

southern right whale

spectacled flying fox

spot-tailed quoll

subantarctic fur seal

Tasmanian devil

tiger quoll

western quoll

western ringtail possum

woylie

Source: Department of the Environment, Water, Heritage and the Arts, 2010

Australia's emblems

Australia

Floral: golden wattle

Australian Capital Territory

Faunal: no official emblem
Floral: royal bluebell
Faunal (bird): gang-gang cockatoo

New South Wales

Faunal: platypus
Floral: waratah
Faunal (bird): kookaburra

Northern Territory

Faunal: red kangaroo
Floral: Sturt's desert rose
Faunal (bird): wedge-tailed eagle

Queensland

Faunal: koala
Floral: Cooktown orchid
Faunal (bird): brolga

South Australia

Faunal: hairy-nosed wombat
Floral: Sturt's desert pea
Faunal (bird): piping shrike (unofficial)

Tasmania

Faunal: Tasmanian devil (unofficial)
Floral: Tasmanian blue gum
Faunal (bird): yellow wattlebird (unofficial)

Victoria

Faunal: Leadbeater's possum
Floral: common heath
Faunal (bird): helmeted honeyeater

Western Australia

Faunal: numbat
Floral: red and green kangaroo-paw
Faunal (bird): black swan

Prime Ministers of Australia

1901–03	Edmund Barton	Protectionist
1903–04	Alfred Deakin	Liberal
1904	John Christian Watson	Labor Party
1904–05	George Houston Reid	Free Trader
1905–08	Alfred Deakin	Liberal
1908–09	Andrew Fisher	Labor Party
1909–10	Alfred Deakin	Liberal
1910–13	Andrew Fisher	Labor Party
1913–14	Joseph Cook	Free Trader/Liberal
1914–15	Andrew Fisher	Labor Party
1915–23	William Morris Hughes	Labor/Nationalist Party
1923–29	Stanley Melbourne Bruce	Nationalist Party
1929–32	James Henry Scullin	Labor Party
1932–39	Joseph Aloysius Lyons	United Australia Party
1939	Earle Christmas Grafton Page (caretaker)	Country Party
1939–41	Robert Gordon Menzies	United Australia Party
1941	Arthur William Fadden	Country Party
1941–45	John Joseph Curtin	Labor Party
1945	Francis Michael Forde (caretaker)	Labor Party
1945–49	Joseph Benedict Chifley	Labor Party
1949–66	Robert Gordon Menzies	Liberal Party
1966-67	Harold Edward Holt	Liberal Party
1967–68	John McEwen (caretaker)	Country Party
1968–71	John Grey Gorton	Liberal Party
1971–72	William McMahon	Liberal Party
1972–75	Edward Gough Whitlam	Labor Party
1975–83	John Malcolm Fraser	Liberal Party
1983–91	Robert James Lee Hawke	Labor Party
1991–96	Paul John Keating	Labor Party
1996–2007	John Winston Howard	Liberal Party
2007–2010	Kevin Michael Rudd	Labor Party
2010–	Julia Eileen Gillard	Labor Party

Countries — people, languages, capital cities, currencies

Country	People	Official / main language(s)	Capital	Main unit of currency
Afghanistan	Afghan, Afghani	Pashto, Dari (Persian)	Kabul	afghani
Albania	Albanian	Albanian	Tirana	lek
Algeria	Algerian, Algerine	Arabic	Algiers	Algerian dinar
Andorra	Andorran	Catalan, French, Spanish	Andorra la Vella	euro
Angola	Angolan	Portuguese	Luanda	kwanza
Antigua and Barbuda	Antiguan	English	St John's	East Caribbean dollar
Argentina	Argentine, Argentinian	Spanish	Buenos Aires	peso
Armenia	Armenian	Armenian	Yerevan	dram
Australia	Australian	English	Canberra	Australian dollar
Austria	Austrian	German	Vienna	euro
Azerbaijan	Azerbaijani	Azerbaijani	Baku	manat
Bahamas, the	Bahamian	English	Nassau	Bahamian dollar
Bahrain	Bahraini	Arabic	Manama	Bahrain dinar
Bangladesh	Bangladeshi	Bengali	Dhaka	Bangladesh taka
Barbados	Barbadian	English	Bridgetown	Barbados dollar
Belarus	Belarusian	Belarusian	Minsk	rubel
Belgium	Belgian	Dutch, French, German	Brussels	euro
Belize	Belizean	English, Spanish, Carib, Maya	Belmopan	Belize dollar
Benin	Beninese	French	Porto-Novo	CFA franc
Bermuda	Bermudan	English	Hamilton	Bermuda dollar
Bhutan	Bhutanese	Dzongkha	Thimphu	ngultrum, Indian rupee
Bolivia	Bolivian	Spanish, Quechua, Aymará	Sucre (judicial), La Paz (legislative)	boliviano
Bosnia and Herzegovina	Bosnian	Bosnian	Sarajevo	marka
Botswana	Botswanan	Tswana, English	Gaborone	pula

Country	People	Official / main language(s)	Capital	Main unit of currency
Brazil	Brazilian	Portuguese	Brasília	real
Brunei	Bruneian	Malay, English	Bandar Seri Begawan	Brunei dollar
Bulgaria	Bulgarian	Bulgarian	Sofia	lev
Burkina Faso	–	French, Mossi	Ouagadougou	CFA franc
Burma (Myanmar)	Burmese	Burmese	Rangoon (Yangon)	kyat
Burundi	Burundian	French, Kirundi	Bujumbura	Burundi franc
Cambodia	Cambodian	Khmer, French	Phnom Penh	riel
Cameroon	Cameroonian	French, English	Yaoundé	CFA franc
Canada	Canadian	English, French	Ottawa	Canadian dollar
Cape Verde Islands	Cape Verdean	Portuguese	Praia	escudo
Central African Republic	–	French, Sango	Bangui	CFA franc
Chad	Chadian	French, Arabic	N'Djamena	CFA franc
Chile	Chilean	Spanish	Santiago	peso
China	Chinese	Chinese (Mandarin)	Beijing	yuan
Colombia	Colombian	Spanish	Bogotá	peso
Comoros	Comorian, Comoran	French, Arabic, Comorian	Moroni	Comorian franc
Congo, Democratic Republic of	Congolese	French, English	Kinshasa	Congolese franc
Congo, Republic of	Congolese	French	Brazzaville	CFA franc
Costa Rica	Costa Rican	Spanish	San José	Costa Rican colón
Côte d'Ivoire (Ivory Coast)	Ivorian	French	Abidjan, Yamoussoukro	CFA franc
Croatia	Croat, Croatian	Croatian	Zagreb	kuna
Cuba	Cuban	Spanish	Havana	Cuban peso
Cyprus	Cypriot	Greek, Turkish	Nicosia	Cyprus pound
Czech Republic	Czech	Czech	Prague	koruna
Denmark	Dane	Danish	Copenhagen	Danish krone
Djibouti	Djibouti	Arabic, French	Djibouti	Djibouti franc
Dominica	Dominican	English	Roseau	East Caribbean dollar

Country	People	Official / main language(s)	Capital	Main unit of currency
Dominican Republic	Dominican	Spanish	Santo Domingo	Dominican peso
East Timor	East Timorese	Tetum, Portuguese	Dili	US dollar
Ecuador	Ecuadorian	Spanish, Quechua	Quito	US dollar
Egypt	Egyptian	Arabic	Cairo	Egyptian pound
El Salvador	Salvadoran	Spanish	San Salvador	colón
Equatorial Guinea	Guinean	Spanish	Malabo	CFA franc
Eritrea	Eritrean	Tigrinya	Asmara	nakfa
Estonia	Estonian	Estonian	Tallinn	kroon
Ethiopia	Ethiopian	Amharic	Addis Ababa	birr
Fiji	Fijian	English, Fijian, Hindi	Suva	Fiji dollar
Finland	Finn, Finlander, Finnish	Finnish, Swedish	Helsinki	euro
France	French	French	Paris	euro
Gabon	Gabonese	French, Fang	Libreville	CFA franc
Gambia, The	Gambian	English	Banjul	dalasi
Georgia	Georgian	Georgian	Tbilisi	Georgian lari
Germany	German	German	Berlin	euro
Ghana	Ghanian	English	Accra	cedi
Greece	Greek	Greek	Athens	euro
Grenada	Grenadian	English	St George's	East Caribbean dollar
Guatemala	Guatemalan	Spanish	Guatemala City	quetzal
Guinea	Guinean	French	Conakry	Guinean franc
Guinea-Bissau	Guinean	Portuguese	Bissau	CFA franc
Guyana	Guyanan	English	Georgetown	Guyana dollar
Haiti	Haitian	French, Haitian Creole	Port-au-Prince	gourde
Honduras	Honduran	Spanish, English	Tegucigalpa	Honduran lempira
Hungary	Hungarian	Hungarian	Budapest	forint
Iceland	Icelandic	Icelandic	Reykjavik	krona
India	Indian	Hindi, English	New Delhi	Indian rupee
Indonesia	Indonesian	Bahasa Indonesia	Jakarta	Indonesian rupiah

Country	People	Official / main language(s)	Capital	Main unit of currency
Iran	Iranian	Farsi (Persian)	Teheran	rial
Iraq	Iraqi	Arabic, Kurdish	Baghdad	Iraqi dinar
Ireland, Republic of	Irish	Irish (Gaelic), English	Dublin	euro
Israel	Israeli	Hebrew, Arabic	Jerusalem	new shekel
Italy	Italian	Italian	Rome	euro
Jamaica	Jamaican	English	Kingston	Jamaica dollar
Japan	Japanese	Japanese	Tokyo	yen
Jordan	Jordanian	Arabic	Amman	Jordan dinar
Kazakhstan	Kazakh	Kazakh	Astana	tenge
Kenya	Kenyan	Swahili, English	Nairobi	Kenya shilling
Kiribati	–	I-Kiribati, English	Bairiki	Australian dollar
Korea, North	North Korean	Korean	Pyongyang	won
Korea, South	South Korean	Korean	Seoul	won
Kosovo	Kosovan	Albanian, Serbian	Priština	euro
Kuwait	Kuwaiti	Arabic	Kuwait City	Kuwaiti dinar
Kyrgyzstan	Kyrgyz	Kyrgyz, Russian	Biškek	som
Laos	Laotian	Lao	Vientiane	kip
Latvia	Latvian	Latvian	Riga	lats
Lebanon	Lebanese	Arabic	Beirut	Lebanese pound
Lesotho	–	English, Sesotho	Maseru	loti
Liberia	Liberian	English	Monrovia	Liberian dollar
Libya	Libyan	Arabic	Tripoli	Libyan dinar
Liechtenstein	Liechtensteiner	German (Alemannic)	Vaduz	Swiss franc
Lithuania	Lithuanian	Lithuanian	Vilnius	litas
Luxembourg	Luxembourger	French, German	Luxembourg	euro
Macedonia	Macedonian	Macedonian	Skopje	denar
Madagascar	Madagascan	Malagasy, French	Antananarivo	ariary
Malawi	Malawian	English, Chichewa	Lilongwe	Malawi kwacha
Malaysia	Malaysian	Malay, English	Kuala Lumpur	ringgit
Maldives	Maldivian	Divehi	Malé	Maldivian rufiyaa
Mali	Malian	French	Bamako	CFA franc
Malta	Maltese	Maltese, English	Valletta	Maltese lira
Marshall Islands	Marshallese	Marshallese, English	Majuro	US dollar
Mauritania	Mauritanian	French, Arabic	Nouakchott	ouguiya

Country	People	Official / main language(s)	Capital	Main unit of currency
Mauritius	Mauritian	English, French Creole	Port Louis	Mauritian rupee
Mexico	Mexican	Spanish	Mexico City	Mexican peso
Micronesia, Federated States of	Micronesian	English	Palikir	US dollar
Moldova	Moldovan	Romanian	Chişinău	Moldovan leu
Monaco	Monacan, Monegasque	French	Monaco-Ville	euro
Mongolia	Mongolian	Khalkha Mongolian	Ulaanbaatar	tugrik
Montenegro	Montenegrin	Montenegro Serbian	Cetinje, Podgorica (administrative centre)	euro
Morocco	Moroccan	Arabic	Rabat	Moroccan dirham
Mozambique	–	Portuguese	Maputo	metical
Myanmar, see Burma				
Namibia	Namibian	English	Windhoek	Namibian dollar
Nauru	Nauruan	Nauruan, English	Nauru	Australian dollar
Nepal	Nepalese, Nepali	Nepali	Katmandu	Nepalese rupee
Netherlands, the	Dutch	Dutch	Amsterdam	euro
New Zealand	New Zealander	English, Maori	Wellington	NZ dollar
Nicaragua	Nicaraguan	Spanish	Managua	córdoba oro
Niger	Nigerien	French	Niamey	CFA franc
Nigeria	Nigerian	English	Abuja	Nigerian naira
Norway	Norwegian	Norwegian	Oslo	Norwegian krone
Oman	Omani	Arabic	Muscat	rial Omani
Pakistan	Pakistani	Urdu	Islamabad	Pakistan rupee
Palau	Palauan	Palauan, English	Koror	US dollar
Panama	Panamanian	Spanish	Panama City	balboa
Papua New Guinea	Papua New Guinean	Neo-Melanesian, Pidgin, Motu, English	Port Moresby	Papua New Guinea kina
Paraguay	Paraguayan	Spanish, Guaraní	Asunción	guaraní
Peru	Peruvian	Spanish, Quechua, Aymara	Lima	nuevo sol
Philippines, the	Filipino	Pilipino, English	Manila	Philippine peso
Poland	Pole, Polish	Polish	Warsaw	zloty

Country	People	Official / main language(s)	Capital	Main unit of currency
Portugal	Portuguese	Portuguese	Lisbon	euro
Qatar	Qatari	Arabic	Doha	Qatar riyal
Romania	Romanian	Romanian	Bucharest	Romanian leu
Russia	Russian	Russian	Moscow	rouble
Rwanda	Rwandan	French, Rwanda	Kigali	Rwanda franc
Samoa	Samoan	Samoan, English	Apia	tala
San Marino	San Marinese	Italian	San Marino	euro
São Tomé and Príncipe	–	Portuguese	São Tomé	dobra
Saudi Arabia	Saudi Arabian, Saudi	Arabic	Riyadh	Saudi riyal
Senegal	Senegalese	French	Dakar	CFA franc
Serbia	Serb, Serbian	Serbian	Belgrade	Serbian dinar
Seychelles	–	English, French, Creole	Victoria	Seychelles rupee
Sierra Leone	Sierra Leonean	English	Freetown	leone
Singapore	Singaporean	Malay, Chinese, English, Tamil	Singapore	Singapore dollar
Slovakia	Slovak, Slovakian	Slovak	Bratislava	Slovak koruna
Slovenia	Slovene, Slovenian	Slovene	Ljubljana	Slovene tolar
Solomon Islands	Solomon Islander	English, Neo-Melanesian, Pidgin	Honiara	Solomon Islands dollar
Somalia	Somali, Somalian	Somali, Arabic, English, Italian	Mogadishu	Somali shilling
South Africa	South African	English, Afrikaans, and 9 other official African languages	Pretoria, Cape Town, and Bloemfontein	rand
Spain	Spaniard, Spanish	Spanish	Madrid	euro
Sri Lanka	Sri Lankan, Sinhalese	Sinhalese, Tamil, English	Colombo, and Sri Jayawardenapura Kotte	Sri Lanka rupee
St Kitts and Nevis	–	English	Basseterre	East Caribbean dollar
St Lucia	St Lucian	English	Castries	East Caribbean dollar
St Vincent and the Grenadines	–	English	Kingstown	East Caribbean dollar

Country	People	Official / main language(s)	Capital	Main unit of currency
Sudan	Sudanese	Arabic	Khartoum	Sudanese dinar
Suriname	Surinamese	Dutch, English	Paramaribo	Suriname guilder
Swaziland	Swazi	English, Swazi	Mbabane, Lobamba	lilangeni
Sweden	Swede, Swedish	Swedish	Stockholm	Swedish krona
Switzerland	Swiss	German, French, Italian	Bern	Swiss franc
Syria	Syrian	Arabic	Damascus	Syrian pound
Tajikistan	Tajik	Tajik	Dushanbe	somoni
Tanzania	Tanzanian	Swahili, English	Dodoma	Tanzania shilling
Thailand	Thai	Thai	Bangkok	Thai baht
Togo	Togolese	French	Lomé	CFA franc
Tonga	Tongan	Tongan, English	Nuku'alofa	pa'anga
Trinidad and Tobago	Trinidadian	English	Port of Spain	Trinidad and Tobago dollar
Tunisia	Tunisian	Arabic, French	Tunis	dinar
Turkey	Turk, Turkish	Turkish	Ankara	Turkish lira
Turkmenistan	Turkmen	Turkmen	Ashgabat	manat
Tuvalu	Tuvaluan	Tuvaluan, English	Vaiaku (on Funafuti atoll)	Australian dollar, Tuvaluan dollar
Uganda	Ugandan	Swahili, English	Kampala	Uganda shilling
Ukraine	Ukrainian	Ukrainian	Kiev	hryvnia
United Arab Emirates	–	Arabic	Abu Dhabi	UAE dirham
United Kingdom	Briton, British	English	London	pound sterling
United States of America	American	English	Washington	US dollar
Uruguay	Uruguayan	Spanish	Montevideo	peso uruguayo
Uzbekistan	Uzbek	Uzbek	Tashkent	sum
Vanuatu	Vanuatuan	Bislama, French, English	Vila	vatu
Venezuela	Venezuelan	Spanish	Caracas	bolívar
Vietnam	Vietnamese	Vietnamese	Hanoi	dông
Yemen	Yemeni	Arabic	Sana'a	Yemeni rial
Zambia	Zambian	English	Lusaka	Zambian kwacha
Zimbabwe	Zimbabwean	English, and Bantu languages	Harare	Zimbabwe dollar

A guide to the Macquarie Primary Dictionary

headword

clown

noun someone in a circus, often dressed up with a white face, a red nose and silly clothes, who makes people laugh

Other words: **buffoon, jester**

Word building: **clown** *verb* to act the fool **clowning** *noun* **clownish** *adjective*

Other words — choices to replace overused words

coastguard

noun someone whose job is to patrol the coast of a country, helping ships in danger and looking out for smugglers or illegal fishing boats

cockatoo

part of speech

noun a crested parrot

cockeyed   (*say* <u>kok</u>-uyd)

adjective **1** crooked: *Your tie is cockeyed.*
2 foolish or absurd: *a cockeyed plan*
3 having a squinting eye

phrase or sentence to show how a word is used

cocky[1]

adjective Informal too confident or smart: *The new guys on the job are always cocky, until they find out how hard it is.*

Word building: Other forms are **cockier, cockiest.** | **cockily** *adverb* **cockiness** *noun*

words that are spelt the same but have different histories

Word building — other members of the headword's family

cocky[2]

noun **1** a cockatoo **2** a farmer, especially of a small farm

Word building: The plural is **cockies.**

cold-blooded

adjective **1** without feelings of pity: *a cold-blooded murder* **2** having a blood temperature which changes as the temperature of the surrounding air or water changes: *Reptiles and fish are cold-blooded animals.*

Word use: The opposite of definition 2 is **warm-blooded.**

Word building: **cold-bloodedly** *adverb* **cold-bloodedness** *noun*

Word use — telling you something about the word